D0843140

Lévi-Strauss

Lévi-Strauss

A Biography

Emmanuelle Loyer

Translated by
Ninon Vinsonneau and Jonathan Magidoff

polity

First published in French as *Lévi-Strauss* © Flammarion, Paris, 2015

This English edition © Polity Press, 2018

This work received the French Voices Award for excellence in publication and translation. French Voices is a program created and funded by the French Embassy in the United States and FACE (French American Cultural Exchange).

This book is supported by the Institut français (Royaume-Uni) as part of the Burgess Programme.

INSTITUT FRANÇAIS
ROYAUME-UNI

Polity Press
65 Bridge Street
Cambridge CB2 1UR, UK

Polity Press
101 Station Landing
Suite 300
Medford, MA 02155, USA

ISBN-13: 978-1-5095-1198-3

A catalogue record for this book is available from the British Library.

Typeset in 10 on 11pt Times NRMT Pro by Servis Filmsetting Ltd, Stockport, Cheshire
Printed and bound in the UK by Clays Ltd, Elcograf S.p.A.

The publisher has used its best endeavours to ensure that the URLs for external websites referred to in this book are correct and active at the time of going to press. However, the publisher has no responsibility for the websites and can make no guarantee that a site will remain live or that the content is or will remain appropriate.

Every effort has been made to trace all copyright holders, but if any have been inadvertently overlooked the publisher will be pleased to include any necessary credits in any subsequent reprint or edition.

For further information on Polity, visit our website: politybooks.com

To the girls, and to their father and stepfather

Contents

Part IV
The World (1971–2009)

Acknowledgements

After these past several years, which I have now come to see as an extended conversation, it is with great pleasure that I express my sincerest thanks to Monique Lévi-Strauss, without whom, as the saying goes, this book would not exist. I found her to be endowed with that most important of anthropological skills: the ability to see her own career and that of her husband from a distance, and to consider them as objects of knowledge. In addition to a friendly (and gustatory) welcome, she gave me complete freedom of investigation and interpretation. She alone knows the extent of the debt I owe to her.

Matthieu Lévi-Strauss followed the course of my research with some initial perplexity, then genuine interest, providing me with a few lessons along the way in photographic technique and Burgundy zoology, for which I am grateful. From more of a distance, Laurent Lévi-Strauss kindly accorded me his confidence. As for Catherine Lévi-Strauss, she gradually revealed herself to be an attentive interlocutor and reader.

In the course of this research, I have been a frequent visitor to the Manuscripts Department at the Bibliothèque nationale de France, where the Lévi-Strauss Archive is held, as well as to the Laboratory of Social Anthropology, which has kept its own institutional archives and those of some of its researchers. Catherine Faivre d'Arcier initiated me into the mysteries of the former, Marion Abelès and then Sophic Assal into those of the latter. I would like to warmly thank all three of them here. I am also grateful to Grégory Cingal at the Jacques Doucet Library and Frédéric Cépède at the Office interuniversitaire de recherche socialiste.

In addition to the Paris-based archives, I went in search of documents, information and testimonials, following leads out into the Lévi-Straussian world. In Brazil, I am indebted to the many people who provided me with invaluable assistance, always in a kind and generous manner (and often in flawless French): Fernanda Peixoto, Afranio-Raul Garcia, Heloïsa Maria Bertol Domingues, Luis Donisete Benzi Grupioni and Manuela Carneiro da Cunha, as well as Mariza Corrêta, Helena Monteiro Welper and Antonio Carlos da Souza Lima. I am especially grateful to Luisa Valentini and Emmanuel Diatkine for 'translating' the city of São Paulo for me and teaching me to fully appreciate it. From Paris, my French friends Olivier

Compagnon, Anaïs Fléchet and Benoît de l'Estoile indulged me by acting as intermediaries. The Brazilian chapters thus owe much to them.

For the New York chapters, I would like once again to thank Pierre-Yves Saunier and the Rockefeller Archives Center, and especially the extremely efficacious Michele Hiltzik.

In Japan, Michaël Ferrier and Soizic Maubec played host to this French researcher who found herself utterly lost in translation. Yasu Watanabe, Jinzo Kawada and Atsuhico Yoshida generously recounted tales of their Japanese Lévi-Strauss.

In Paris, as well, many people agreed to take part in the sometimes melancholy exercise of remembrance and to recall the figure of Lévi-Strauss, the one they had personally known: his former colleagues at the LAS and elsewhere – George Balandier, Nicole Belmont, Carmen Bernand, Philippe Descola, Maurice Godelier, Françoise Héritier, Jean Jamin, Marie Mauzé, Jean Monod, Michel Perrin, Anne-Christine Taylor, Emmanuel Terray, Nathan Wachtel, Françoise Zonabend; contemporaries, friends and acquaintances who, in whatever institutional context or circumstances, had rubbed shoulders with or come to know Claude Lévi-Strauss: Anita Albus, Catherine Clément, Sylvie Dreyfus-Asséo, Pierre Nora, Élisabeth Roudinesco, Germain Viatte, as well as Alain Badiou (about Dina Dreyfus) and Inès de La Fressange. Jean-Jacques Lebel agreed to lend me one of his New York photographs and Frédéric Jude his 'photomontage' of the Laboratory team – a fitting expression of the small world of the LAS.

While I indulged rather rarely in academic discussion during the researching and writing of this book, I am nonetheless grateful to the many colleagues and friends who shared their insights. These include Jean-François Bert, Anne Collinot, Alice Conklin, Jean-Marc Dreyfus, Christine Laurière, Patrice Maniglier, Jean-Claude Monod, Wiktor Stoczkowski and Jean-Claude Yon. Others went as far as to read all or part of a manuscript that grew ever thicker with time: Antoine de Baecque, Vincent Debaene, Daniel Fabre, Thomas Hirsch, Maurice Olender, Yann Potin, Paul-André Rosental and Jean-Louis Tissier. I am keenly aware of how much this book owes to the time and energy they devoted to it. In the same way, I am grateful to my mother Denise Loyer and my father Jean-Claude Loyer, a seasoned professional indexer. I would also like to pay tribute to the support and discussion group of the Center for History at Sciences Po Paris and to the institution as a whole for granting me a sabbatical semester in the autumn of 2013, at a moment when I greatly needed it, thus allowing me to concentrate my energies on finishing this book. Finally, this learned assembly had a Palermo outpost – even though Lévi-Strauss himself never visited Sicily – in the form of the meticulous and inspired editing of Juliette Blamont, with the assistance of Crisitina Fatta del Bosco.

However important people have been, places have mattered just as much. And I promised myself I would conclude these acknowledgements with a nod to the great periodicals room, the so-called 'oval room', of the Richelieu branch of the Bibliothèque nationale in Paris, in which, sheltered from the world, I spent many a happy moment writing this biography, daydreaming about the glorious cities whose names are inscribed in mosaics under the rotunda – London, Babylon, Vienna, Thebes, Rome, Carthage, Jerusalem, Paris, Byzantium, Washington, Florence, Athens, Nineveh, Berlin and Alexandria. Like an offering to a history that is greater than us, these hours spent at the library pulled me out of my quotidian and rendered me oblivious to the passage of time.

Introduction: The Worlds of Claude Lévi-Strauss

I would have liked, once in my lifetime, to communicate fully with an animal. It is an unattainable goal. It is almost painful for me to know that I will never be able to find out what the matter and structure of the universe is made of. This would have meant being able to talk to a bird. But this is the line that cannot be crossed. Crossing this line would be a great joy for me. If you could bring me a good fairy who would grant me one wish, this is the one I would choose.

Claude Lévi-Strauss, Interview with F. Raddatz[1]

Around the world

For a long time, Claude Lévi-Strauss would spend his afternoons in his study at home on the fifth floor of 2 rue des Marronniers in the 16th arrondissement of Paris. This magisterial space – with its encyclopedic library, its carefully chosen objects, minerals, 'curiosities' and works of art – recomposed the world in miniature and ordered form.

Let us enter the sanctuary. A large rectangular room with a rounded wall on the window side, surrounded by shelves filled with books, bound journals, encyclopedias and dictionaries. The desk itself – of dark wood in the Spanish style acquired in New York – stood aslant, at the far end; Lévi-Strauss would sit at it to write, or to read or edit, in an armchair on casters so that he could move easily between a cylinder desk filled with stationery and a small steel table on which was perched a typewriter (with German keyboard). From the radio would flow an indispensable stream of classical music. Settled at his desk, sometimes leaning back with his feet up, Lévi-Strauss faced an enormous representation of Tara, the green asexual divinity from Nepal – an image of serenity and calm, purchased at Paris's Drouot auction house in the 1950s. A Thai crocodile, a giant carved tree root from China, and Japanese prints and sword guards rounded out the presence of the Far East. A few rare ethnographic objects, including the cedar-wood *haida* mace for bludgeoning fish that figures in one of the aesthetic meditations in *The Savage Mind*, further intensified the other-worldly atmosphere. On the desk were a few stones, and among them a cube of lapis lazuli and a dagger. No plants. Somewhere between a cabinet of curiosities and an artist's studio, the room was an ode to beauty, a visual and aural environment where, in the muffled afternoon quiet, all the elements could find harmony, coming together in the utopia of an enclosed space containing a world in microcosm: the library. Indeed, following Xavier de Maistre in *A Journey Around My Room*, Lévi-Strauss could travel the world without leaving the confines of his office, contemplating this paper edifice: on the wall to his left, Africa, Oceania and Asia; directly opposite, periodicals and index card files; to his right, South America; behind him, in the corner, North America, with the remainder of that wall devoted to encyclopedias and dictionaries – all within reach of a single turn on his rolling armchair. 'My library was a marvel', he would later say.[2] Indeed, the entire world was represented within its walls, and each book was placed where the population with which it dealt would have been situated on a map. This geographical classification (by continent) thus achieved a kind of anamorphosis of map and library – two homologous representations attesting to the fullness and richness of the world.

The sophisticated ordering of this circumnavigating library should not distract us from its essential components: the 12,000 books and, above all, the complete series of international journals, notably *Man* and *American Anthropologist*, as well as thousands of offprints, supplied the material necessary for scholarly endeavour. There could be no knowledge without the capillaries through which this data circulated, regularly indexed on cards. Like all scholars of his generation, Lévi-Strauss was an avid user of the index card, which had become, by the early twentieth century, an indispensable tool for all comparative study. He owned a piece of furniture designed to store these cards, which held summaries of all the books he had read at the New York Public Library during the war years – i.e., several thousand works. 'For a period, in the 1940s–1950s, I could say that nothing published in the field of anthropology escaped my attention.'[3] Lévi-Strauss's library encompassed the entire world and the full range of knowledge, constituting an archive for a kind of scholarly practice in which the impulse to exhaustiveness was still very much the order of the day. At the beginning of the 1960s, several uncaged parrots would fly about this den of erudition, having just arrived from Amazonia thanks to a complicated series of ploys contrived, at the limits of legality, by Isac Chiva, Lévi-Strauss's assistant at the Laboratory of Social Anthropology at the Collège de France. Chiva was well aware of his colleague and friend's love of animals, and that he had lived with some monkeys brought back from Brazil. Chiva knew that, if left to his own devices, Lévi-Strauss would have allowed dogs, cats and all manner of creature to find shelter in his study, transforming the office into a menagerie. Indeed, something of the sort did come to pass: the parrots would regularly make off with the anthropologist's glasses and soil the floor and furniture. Lévi-Strauss ultimately had to give up the birds, as well as his dream of a human existence at one with the animal world. He would manage, however, to revive this chimera by immersing himself in a world that suited him perfectly: that of Amerindian myth, in which animals and humans partook of the same universe.

The mystery of Lévi-Strauss

The Renaissance *studiolo* that served as Claude Lévi-Strauss's office is both revealing and surprising: it does not 'square' with the avant-garde persona of this pioneer of structuralism – that high-flying theory, often associated with the modernist context of the 1950s–1960s. Structuralism aimed to map the operations of symbolic thought through a new technique of comparison. It was not, as is often thought, a quest for invariants across the societies studied, but rather a method for identifying their differences, understood as variations, with an emphasis on the relations that allow for the passage from one to another. The theory, which was originally developed in the field of linguistics and then spread not only to anthropology but also to other fields (literary criticism, psychoanalysis, history, etc.), arose in connection with the triumph of science, as well as that of the anthropological discipline that Lévi-Strauss helped bring into the mainstream of social science in France during the second half of the twentieth century. So goes the standard story of the adventure of structuralism conjured up by his name, a story some of whose fundamental episodes, we discover to our surprise, took place in the study of a . . . Renaissance man.

Who, then, was Claude Lévi-Strauss? A child of the twentieth century, he was born in Brussels in 1908 and died in Paris more than a hundred years later, in 2009. He grew up in a Jewish family that had earlier enjoyed the classic French experience of upward mobility, from Alsace to Paris. In this bourgeois world, deeply rooted in the nineteenth century, Lévi-Strauss blossomed as a beloved only child, on whom rested all the hopes of a somewhat down-at-heel family. His father was an artist, as were two of his uncles. Those who did not dedicate themselves to the arts went into business. A large, warm and close-knit extended family, perfectly coherent in its secular and patriotic Judaism, peopled the childhood of the young Claude. A star pupil, he pursued his studies in the literary *classes préparatoires* at Paris's prestigious Lycée Condorcet, and yet decided against sitting the entrance exam to the highly selective École normale supérieure, in the first of what would become characteristic existential turns. He became something of a student dilettante, pursuing a double degree in law and philosophy, which led him to sit the competitive *agrégation* exam in 1931 in order to qualify as a professor. In these years, he was, above all, a committed socialist who, under the auspices of Karl Marx and the SFIO (the French section of the Workers' International), was keen to change the world. However, unlike many of his comrades, such as his cousin's husband Paul Nizan, he never became a communist. Rather than change the world, in 1935, he chose to leave the one in which he had grown up. An offer to teach in Brazil presented an opportunity to study Amerindians – who, from the perspective of Paris, were thought to be living in the suburbs of São Paulo. This personal and intellectual turn – he abandoned the old world of philosophy for the young world of anthropology – was of course decisive, and marked the beginning of a second period in his life, set in the new worlds of Brazil and, later, during the Second World War, the United States.

These biographical elements distinguish Lévi-Strauss's path through the twentieth century. Yet what weight are we to give to the two detours he took in the first half of his life? The first was his decision to distance himself from his family's Judaism. In the history of the social sciences, Lévi-Strauss is hardly the only intellectual to have broken with the synagogue, yet how much of a link can we establish in his case between the reconstitution of his identity as a non-Jewish Jew and the innovative character of his analytical and theoretical formulations?[4] The second reorientation was the one that took him away from the Old World of Europe, pitching it against the new worlds of Brazil and the United States and creating a triangulation of Europe/South America/North America from which the structuralist approach truly sprang. The genesis of this consummate French intellectual, hailed upon his death as a national monument, passed through long periods of expatriation, whether voluntary or forced. Indeed, between the years of 1935 and 1947, Lévi-Strauss was almost entirely absent from France, exploring the brush of the Brazilian Sertão from 1935 to 1939, then in exile in New York from 1941 to 1947, establishing himself first as a social scientist, then as liberated France's first cultural attaché on Fifth Avenue. This intellectual trajectory was unique among French scholars at the time, who were for the most part characterized by a rather stay-at-home bent, reinforced by their conviction that they were at the centre of the world. It is unquestionable that this mix of old and new worlds, classical French philosophy, Brazilian ethnographic experience and exposure to American anthropology – itself steeped in German traditions – contributed to the development of a powerful and powerfully original intellectual figure.[5]

The return to the Old World in 1947 marked the beginning of the period of his life dedicated to the writing of his major works, which are saturated through and through with this transatlantic life experience. Indeed, several decades of intense toil followed, during which Lévi-Strauss, now settled in Paris, experienced multiple setbacks before being enthroned at the Collège de France in 1959. A few years earlier, in 1955, in a fit of literary effusion over the course of just a few weeks, he wrote 400 feverish and intense pages recounting his Brazilian odyssey. *Tristes Tropiques* would become a classic of twentieth-century thought and quickly make its author famous the world over. It was in the 1960s, however, that Claude Lévi-Strauss, having become a public figure of the French intelligentsia, put structural anthropology at the centre of the intellectual and political debates of the times, then in the throes of Marxist revisionism and the endgame of decolonization. The austere savant, his persona shrouded in secrecy and silence, with a touch of cultivated dandyism, orchestrated a veritable structuralist moment among the younger generations, who felt they had found in it their America. At his side, Roland Barthes, Michel Foucault, Louis Althusser and Jacques Lacan were all gathered together at this 'structuralist banquet',[6] which saw the prestige of the human and social sciences reach its apex. The philosophy embodied by Jean-Paul Sartre found itself significantly challenged by this thought, which sought to relativize it, as Lévi-Strauss himself does in a few memorable pages at the end of *The Savage Mind*. His polemical zeal provided a stark contrast to the image that was to gradually take over: the image of a contemplative savant and aesthete, averse to political interventions of whatever stripe and taking great delight in his calculated provocations. Politically unclassifiable, he was seen by left-wing students after 1968 as an incorrigible reactionary. And, as if to prove them right, he became a member of the Académie Française in 1973.

He was then sixty-five years old and would go on to live for another thirty-six years. Such longevity accounts for the striking metamorphoses in the reception of his work. Whereas structuralism fell into a state of purgatory lasting several decades, Lévi-Strauss himself escaped any such intellectual discredit. In the 1980s, he became a sort of Zen monk in the world of French letters, which was then mourning the passing of its luminaries – Raymond Aron, Roland Barthes, Jean-Paul Sartre and Michel Foucault all died between 1980 and 1985. Little by little, the old and then very elderly man became a figure of national glory, albeit at some remove and increasingly affirming a distance from the century in which he lived. Yet, strangely, it was this very distance that enabled him to cast a most incisive and subversive gaze on our dispirited modernity. The more Lévi-Strauss aged, the more contemporary he seemed to become.

Beads of the necklace

The present biographical endeavour is intimately connected with the recent opening of Claude Lévi-Strauss's personal archives – the 261 boxes deposited at the Manuscripts Department of the National Library of France that constitute the core source material for this book, its treasure trove. Other archives were also consulted: the archives of the Laboratory of Social Anthropology at the Collège de France; in Brazil, the numerous traces left by the French university in São Paulo and by the ethnographic expeditions carried out in Mato Grosso; and, finally, in New York and Washington, DC, all the archives relating to French exiles during the Second World War. Building on this considerable mass of new material, much of which is available for the first time, this biography attempts to distinguish itself from the autobiographical thread of *Tristes Tropiques* by inserting this celebrated narrative into a history – one that would serve to renew its status, significance and impact. The biographical genre has had, for quite some time, a lot to answer for. It was Pierre Bourdieu who delivered the most direct critique of 'biographical reason', with its illusion of coherence, its tendency to rationalize the life course, to unearth 'callings' and give 'meaning' to life, quickly turning any existence into a Bildungsroman.[7] These pitfalls are undeniably real. And yet, drawing on new 'ego-documents' – i.e., correspondence, notebooks, memoirs, files, diaries, lesson plans, manuscript drafts, drawings, photographs, etc. – with the potential to recreate the various contexts that have framed the life of an individual, biographical studies remain, and have even prevailed as, a productive mode of understanding in intellectual history in the broad sense.

It makes for quite a challenge to imagine Lévi-Strauss as a young man: a kind of gravitas that is said to be the prerogative of old age prematurely congealed around his persona. Very early on, he already seemed old. The freshness of his letters to his parents are all we have today to help us conjure up the newly minted professor teaching philosophy to the young women of Mont-de-Marsan, a town in the southwest of France, where he held his first position. Indeed, from the first half of Lévi-Strauss's life no contemporary witness remains, except Antonio Candido de Mello e Souza in Brazil, now a major figure of the Brazilian intelligentsia, who still remembers the young bearded professor disembarking with his wife in São Paulo to teach sociology in 1935. Lévi-Strauss himself, when I interviewed him about his New York years for a previous book project in the early 2000s, told me that he was probably the only surviving participant in that extraordinary world of French exiles in the United States during the war years.[8] Not unlike many of the Amerindians he had met – the last witnesses of a vanished world, the memory of which they were the sole bearers – Lévi-Strauss became, in his way, the last man of the pre-1940 world. Thankfully, however, many of those who took part in the adventure of French anthropology from the 1960s onward are still with us. I met with them as much as time would allow. Not being an anthropologist myself, I was able to approach them free of any professional ego. And conversely, the brotherhood of anthropologists welcomed me with the benevolence that is often reserved for those who do not belong to the order. In the course of these interviews, I was given a sense of the extraordinary professional aura that the very name of Lévi-Strauss still evokes, an aura which is not fully matched by his broader intellectual celebrity. In a thousand details, the work of memory brought my interlocutors back to the singular stature of the man and the long shadow he cast across the entire discipline.

And yet the very subject of the present biography, Claude Lévi-Strauss himself, often insisted on how little individual identity he accorded to himself, and how little importance he ascribed, in the end, to the 'individual' of Western modernity – that object of all that hope and concern in philosophy, destined, according to the anthropologist and certain of his contemporaries, not the least Michel Foucault, to vanish into dust, to exit the stage. 'Move along now, there's nothing (left) to see!' The individual, here, will thus be less of an entity in itself than an occasion for sizing things up at a micro-historical level; no longer an essentialized substrate, but rather a scale at which to operate. Like the photographer in Antonioni's film *Blow-Up*, who discovers the premise of another story upon enlarging a series of snapshots, I have attempted, by adjusting my focal length on the figure of Lévi-Strauss, to uncover another point of view on the intellectual and artistic history of the twentieth century, for which the anthropologist constitutes an ideal vantage point.[9] In this, I hope not to have betrayed him. I have tried to produce a kind of *Japanese biography*, in the manner of the 'centripetal' philosophy of the subject that Lévi-Strauss thought he had identified in Japan: '[I]t is as if the Japanese person constructed his "I" by beginning from the outside. The Japanese "I" thus appears to be not an original given but a result towards which one moves with no certainty of reaching it.'[10]

Placed within a familial and disciplinary genealogy, the present biographical study is intended to be anything but the preordained temple of a demiurge. In the end, there is an undeniably magisterial body of work. Lévi-Strauss – the subject – appears in it, but only at the end of the line, as the sum total of experiences, travels and readings, in multiple contexts, eminently connected to the history of the century. It is indeed striking to note the extent to which this great figure of 'detachment' from the intellectual life of a period so marked by political commitment was tossed about by the currents of history, notably during the Second World War when anti-Semitism in the form of the Vichy regime forced him, along with many others, into exile.

Lévi-Strauss himself made a contribution to the defence of the biographical genre in anthropology. Beginning in the 1940s, many 'native biographies' were published in the United States, for the most part coauthored by anthropologists and their principal native informants, often partially 'civilized' Amerindians. The anthropologist Leo Simmons had thus commissioned the Hopi Indian Don Talayesva to write the story of his life, torn between two worlds and profoundly shaken by a spiritual crisis that brought him back to his native village to act as the 'meticulous guardian of ancient customs and rites'.[11] In the preface he contributed to this volume, Lévi-Strauss rather enthusiastically celebrated the change of scale: 'From the very start, Talayesva's narrative achieves, with incomparable ease and grace, what the anthropologist dreams his whole life of attaining but never fully manages: the restitution of a culture "from within", as experienced by the child and then the adult. A bit as if, as archaeologists of the present, we unearthed, one by one, the beads of a necklace; and then we were suddenly given a glimpse of them, threaded in their original order and supplely placed around the young neck they were intended to adorn.'[12] The metaphor of the beaded necklace captures the truly erotic excitement aroused by the promise of achieving the 'anthropologist's dream' that motivated Lévi-Strauss:[13] to reconcile the description of a social system with the ways it is refracted and internalized by each of its members, to subsume scientific objectivity into indigenous subjectivities – and to do so without allowing either to prevail. Biography would thus be the very site where the articulations between constraint and liberty, social determination and participant decision, between the emergence of an undeniably 'brilliant' thought and the collective foundation that gave birth to it, are most likely to appear in all their delicate and interwoven texture, not unlike that of the Indian basketry that Lévi-Strauss enjoyed sketching in his field notebooks.

Ethnographic knowledge and the anthropological discipline: the Other as object

Lévi-Strauss's biography tells the story of an individual as well as that of a scientific discipline, one of immense ambition, since it purports to embrace no less than mankind as a whole. Its name varies depending on national traditions; in France, Lévi-Strauss helped the term 'anthropology' to prevail, but that of 'ethnology' remains in common usage.

The ethnologists and anthropologists of the twentieth century were heirs to a vast domain of ethnographic curiosity, which had manifested itself in various scenes since the Renaissance – from the exploration of exotic lands abroad to the investigation of lower classes at home, and even the missionary animus of religious orders to convert pagans into Christians. Ever since voyages of exploration became possible, all manner of ethnographic impulses have fuelled scholarly enterprises with the Other as object. If it is generally understood that anthropology began to develop as a science in the second half of the nineteenth century, with the work of Lewis H. Morgan and Edward Tylor in the Anglophone world and Émile Durkheim and Marcel Mauss in France, it remained closely tied to the rarefied realm of curiosities, the unusual and astonishing objects that destabilized and called into question established knowledge.[14] Hence the celebrated cabinets of curiosities that whetted the appetite for knowledge of all European savants in the classical age.

To say that Claude Lévi-Strauss's study was reminiscent of a cabinet of curiosities is to acknowledge the fact that, in him as well as in the anthropological practice he came to represent, several orders of scientific time coexisted: not only curiosity, but also the drive for exactitude, the imperative for measurement, the properly ethnographic collection of 'facts', the regional synthesis of the anthropological field and, finally, at the ultimate level of generalization, the rules governing kinship and myth akin to the laws of Newtonian physics. This is what Lévi-Strauss called anthropology, appropriating the English-language term.[15]

Rather than the 'exemplary life' of a theoretician who imported hard science into the social world, I believe, on the contrary, that one should see in Lévi-Strauss a site of multiple and sometimes contradictory tensions between different modes of scientific practice, and in his biography a kind of open-air archaeology of the discipline, through its most illustrious representative. Indeed, in part, Lévi-Strauss practised the investigative method pioneered by Herodotus, adopting a distant and external gaze on others; he showed how structural anthropology rested on contrasting description and the study of differential gaps. Yet his anthropology was also steeped in affect, dreams and nightmares, bringing it closer to another knowledge project, which Daniel Fabre has identified as the 'paradigm of the last witness'.[16] This idea (fantasy?) was often expressed by Lévi-Strauss during his Brazilian voyage: that the anthropologist is face to face with the 'last' of the Indians, a potential informant of an entire world, but also the final product of an apocalyptic history. *Tristes Tropiques* gave expression to the tragedy of this history, and also, so to speak, accepted responsibility for it.

On the one hand, there is the research centre that Lévi-Strauss established in 1960 as the new locus of scientific production in anthropology: the Laboratory of Social Anthropology at the Collège de France. On the other, there is his home study, the humanist's lair, where the anthropologist conversed across the centuries with Montesquieu, Rousseau and Chateaubriand, with the anthropology of the Enlightenment, and even, reaching further back through another two centuries of discovery, with the explorer Jean de Léry, one of the first Europeans to discover the Brazilian coast, whose freshness of gaze was matched only by that of Montaigne, his companion in the last decades of his life. The undeniable modernity of Claude Lévi-Strauss's intellectual project has been emphasized often enough for us to feel comfortable, here, restoring the unabashed archaism of his approach, since he claimed to embrace everything; in him, the various strata of knowledge of classical Western modernity all jostled together.

The structure of a life and body of work

Lévi-Strauss cultivated a lifelong friendship with the linguist Roman Jakobson. The day after the latter's death, in October 1982, the anthropologist wrote: 'What do we mean, in fact, when we speak of a "great man"? Certainly not merely an original or engaging person. And still less the author of a considerable body of work that we have difficulty relating to the personality of its creator. What strikes one, most of all, when approaching Roman Jakobson is the intense kinship between the man and his work.'[17] Lévi-Strauss continued: 'The vitality, abundant generosity, and demonstrative power, finally the sparkling eloquence bursting forth in the man as much as in the work.' This 'intense kinship' between the man and his work can also be claimed for Lévi-Strauss himself, and even further reinforced and confirmed in his case by a homology with the very object of his work, or rather its anthropological foundation, namely, the Amerindians who, thanks to the work of the anthropologist, have become part of the narrative of the twentieth century, with their labrets, their mild manners and their ultimate denouement, as a kind of figure of repentance and hope. At the end of his journey, Lévi-Strauss described the profound inspiration he drew from the mythological material he had worked on in his four-volume *Mythologiques*, sketching what constituted a motif in the Levi-Straussian tapestry: a dualism, but one whose two elements were opposed in a perpetual seesaw movement, which, according to the Amerindians, set the universe in motion.

This unstable binary also characterized his intellectual drive and innermost personality, poised between, on the one hand, a careful attention to detail, rigorous empirical research and the botanist's keen eye, and, on the other, a powerful theoretical drive, feverish tendency to generalization and a penchant for bold hypotheses; between his Buddhist-inspired wisdom, his detachment from the world, his revelatory contemplation of nature and his sense of the joy of self-abnegation, and his worldly interventions, his socialist youth, his institution-building and his professional responsibilities; between the desire for intimate community and the rejection of it; between uncompromising abstraction and a quivering, raw sensibility; between the longing for a meaningful order and the metaphysical intuition of meaninglessness; between the quest for universality and the logic of difference; between science and art. This last opposition has generated much commentary, especially when Claude Lévi-Strauss became a member of the Académie Française in 1973, based on a body of scholarly work whose literary quality was seen as an asset by some and a liability by others. In a recent book, Patrick Wilcken offers a somewhat simplistic portrait of Lévi-Strauss as an *artiste manqué*, who redirected into scholarly work a creative sensibility left untapped since his decision as a teenager not to pursue an artistic career for a perceived lack of talent.[18] This characterization fails to see the active power of the unstable dualism or to grasp the fact that Lévi-Strauss, in this tension between art and science, strove for a kind of belletristic reconciliation, in which scholarly excellence was indistinguishable from the artistry through which it was presented. After all, did Buffon not enter the Académie Française with a *Discourse on Style*?[19]

To talk to a bird

At once a man of the nineteenth century, in his personal affect and family roots, and a vexed contemporary of the long twentieth century, Lévi-Strauss delighted in romping through sixteenth-century travel chronicles, recovering the fresh gaze of the Renaissance – which, for the most part, embraced the disruptions provoked by the discovery of the primitive. He also took part in and passionately engaged with the scientific advances of his time. Claude Lévi-Strauss did not hesitate, however, to point out atavistic paths – even privately suggesting a 'return to the Neolithic'. In his approach to science, in the twists and turns of his life, but also in his philosophy of history – insofar as he had one – and in his political and ideological positions, Claude Lévi-Strauss composed a singular score, made up of elements of both *sur*-modernity – just as his friend André Breton sought a *sur*-reality – and archaism, rejecting the rupture of modernity in its various binary oppositions (rationality vs. obscurantism, science vs. myth, evolution vs. cyclical time, progress vs. stability, etc.). The course of his life, like that of this biography, advances through time, but rather in the form of a spiral, proliferating recoveries of scraps of the past – 'there is so little chronology in our life'[20] – where the very remote in time might well appear closer than the very recent past. And his work, also, 'has a face turned towards anthropology's past, which it crowns, and another looking into and anticipating its future'.[21]

In this respect, the man who refounded anthropology would seem to be making a return today in our distraught and disturbed twenty-first century, in the grips of technological revolutions we do not control. Claude Lévi-Strauss is a *world-man*, through the restless wanderings that characterized the first half of his life, and a *time-man*, through his very long and varied life, especially through what he called his 'quixotism', by which he meant the 'obsessive desire to find the past behind the present'.[22] The multiple times that coexisted in him, as much as the wide range of places he covered, are the core of his striking philosophical and existential 'decentredness': nobody before him went quite as far in profoundly challenging our historical trajectory and its impasses. If the anthropologist offered no recipe or programme, he did exhort us to appreciate and protect our cultural, natural and social diversity, as a precious value that signals the contingency of our own system. As early as 1976, he demonstrated remarkable political imagination when he suggested, on the model of exotic societies that had managed to integrate the nonhuman, that we replace our conception of the 'rights of man' with the 'rights of the living'[23] – the human as a living being and no longer as a moral being, together with animals, plants, minerals and things rather than to their exclusion. Lévi-Strauss's thought offers us a truly reconciled humanism, commensurate with our anthropocene.

To talk to a bird, then. The thinker whose thought is often reduced to the inviolable opposition between nature and culture sought, throughout the course of his development, to *try out* – in his life as well as in his work – the lesson of inclusion offered by Amerindian myths, which were, in the eyes both of the anthropologist and of the native Americans themselves, stories from a time when humans and animals understood each other . . .

Part I

Yesterday's Worlds (. . .–1935)

1

The Name of the Father

But so long as a great name is not extinct it keeps in the full light of day those men and women who bear it; and there can be no doubt that, to a certain extent, the interest which the illustriousness of these families gave them in my eyes lay in the fact that one can, starting from to-day, follow their ascending course, step by step, to a point far beyond the fourteenth century, recover the diaries and correspondence of all the forebears of M. de Charlus, of the Prince d'Agrigente, of the Princesse de Parme, in a past in which an impenetrable night would cloak the origins of a middle-class family, and in which we make out, in the luminous backward projection of a name, the origin and persistence of certain nervous characteristics, certain vices, the disorders of one or another Guermantes.

Marcel Proust[1]

Yesterday's world: that combination of narratives, memories, images, smells, dreams, aversions, fears, postures of body and mind, and ways of being and thinking that are inherited, along with our name, on the day of our birth. A kind of backcountry, whether luminous or obscure, a ground that might be nurturing or barren, made of family legends sifted through social memory and national history, from which we may later feel the urge to extricate ourselves, but which, in the meantime, makes up the stuff of intimacy itself.

Indeed, the story of Claude Lévi-Strauss, born in Brussels on 28 November 1908, does not begin there. Just as he expressed feelings of nostalgia for times he had not known, he was, like all of us, replete with a history that he had not himself lived, but that he nonetheless incorporated. A history that was passed on to him in the form of a compound name, designed to articulate a social and individual destiny – a yesterday's world of Alsatian Jewish inflection, illuminated by the success of one family member in particular: Isaac Strauss, Claude's great-grandfather, whose name Claude's father appropriated, adding it to his own, Lévi, to produce this cypher of a name. A Jewish name, an old-line French Jewish name to be precise, which carried within it a strong sense of the lineage's artistic calling. An unstable name as well, recently compounded, whose patronymic fragility maps the vicissitudes of modern French Jewry. A name that had to be claimed, both literally and figuratively. Tracing a few of its historical twists will serve to delineate the powerful logic of this name, through the ups and downs of life, its legends and its silences.

A halo around the name

'With a name like yours!'

It was September 1940, following the French defeat and military demobilization at Montpellier. Claude Lévi-Strauss, then a teacher of philosophy, had been appointed to the prestigious Lycée Henri IV in Paris to begin teaching in the autumn of that year. Confined to the Free Zone in southern France, he went to Vichy to request authorization to return to the capital to take up his post: 'The Ministry's headquarters had been established in a municipal school, and the office in charge of secondary education was being housed in a classroom. The official in charge looked at me, dumbfounded: "With a name like yours", he said to me, "you want to go to Paris? You're not serious, are you?" It was only at that moment that I began to understand.'[2] The moment of realization, as was often the case with Lévi-Strauss, was simultaneously a moment of indecision and a decisive turning point – a biographical turning point (as for thousands of French Jews), but also an intellectual turning point, one that shook him out of a kind of historical naivety and into an awareness of the stigma that his name now bore. A dangerous name under the new conditions of occupied France. A name that, like all names, was classified and indexed, but that also, in a context of police identification, betrayed its bearer. There is a historical irony in the fact that his new perception of his name, revealed to him by the civil servant's astonishment, occurred in Vichy – the town of former family glory, where in 1861, his great-grandfather, Isaac Strauss, had hosted Emperor Napoleon III himself in the Strauss family villa, but now also the town that served as the administrative capital of the Vichy government.

    Less than a year later, Claude Lévi-Strauss left France to go into exile in the United States. In New York, he was welcomed by the new institution where he was to teach for the next few years, but which nonetheless strongly encouraged him to change his name to 'Claude L. Strauss'. Why? 'The students would find it funny',[3] was the answer he was given, because of the brand of jeans! Such were the misfortunes of the name, the fragile traces of historical and biographical adventures, sometimes tragic, sometimes ridiculous, but never without significance. The name – its connotations, its homonymic potential – could lead one to the concentration camps of a Europe at war or, less tragically, to misunderstandings that strained the self-esteem of a budding young intellectual. 'Lévi-Strauss, the pants or the books?' became a recurring refrain during his time in postwar America.[4]

    It seems plausible to imagine that this experience of onomastic stigmatization and mutilation was what made Claude Lévi-Strauss particularly sensitive to the issue, or rather to the *problem*, of names. In chapter 6 of *The Savage Mind*, he explores the attribution of proper names as the highest level of individuation. Contrary to certain anthropologists who considered them to be insignificant, a mere residue of intelligibility, the Lévi-Strauss theory posited that proper names were meaningful. Whether intended as a clear mark of identification – confirming an individual's belonging to such and such a social group, clan or caste – or freely created by the one who names, in both cases to name is always to classify (either others or oneself) and is thus always meaningful.[5] Consider the name one chooses for one's dog, for example: 'I may regard myself as free to name my dog according to my tastes. But if I select "Médor" I shall be classed as commonplace; if I select "Monsieur" or "Lucien", as eccentric or provocative; and if I select "Pelléas", as an aesthete.'[6] Thus, in the contemporary field of anthropology, Lévi-Strauss built a theory in which the dynamic of classification is operative down to the most elementary level, that of the individual who bears a name that is his own.

'Claude Lévi, aka Lévi-Strauss'

The anthropological stakes of a name thus always involve the assignation of a place in the world's taxonomic structure. The logic of naming may also give rise to affirmative reappropriations, for instance through name changes, which the civil register in post-revolutionary France made possible, if always with extremely tight constraints. In France, 'to officially change names is no easy task'.[7] It requires patience and strong motivation. The law of Germinal 11, year XI (1803) created the possibility for a special dispensation from the principle of the immutable character of names, but the final decision was up to an 'administrative court and constitutes a pure privilege that the court is always at liberty to refuse at its discretion'.[8] Furthermore, the procedure was a protracted one: adult individuals applying for a name change must first publish (at their own expense) a notice in the *Journal officiel* summarizing their application, then file a request with the ministry of justice detailing their motives for giving up their original name and adopting a new one, submitting a sworn affidavit, the birth certificates of their ancestors, and proof of their own identity and nationality. It was this lengthy process that Claude Lévi-Strauss chose to undertake, as attested by his personal archives.

The whole affair is rather intriguing and little known.[9] In the 1950s, the French administration refused to officially recognize the name 'Claude Lévi-Strauss', as the anthropologist was already commonly known, but which had in fact never been made official, with the addition of the name 'Strauss' to that of 'Lévi', his father's official name. The permissiveness of earlier years regarding surnames was no longer the case, and the compound name, which was considered a pseudonym in the eyes of officialdom, was no longer accepted. Many administrative headaches ensued, exacerbated by the birth of a second son, Matthieu, in 1957. Thus, on 24 October 1960, at the behest of his wife Monique, and with the help of a lawyer, Suzanne Blum, 'Gustave Claude Lévi, aka Lévi-Strauss, professor at the Collège de France' officially deposited his request with the Keeper of the Seals – in his own name and in that of his children, Laurent Jacquemin, born in New York on 16 March 1947 (and registered at the French consulate under the name of Lévi-Strauss), and Matthieu Raymond, born in Paris on 25 August 1957 (and registered under the name of Lévi) – to add to his given surname that of 'Strauss'.

Three arguments were put forward: first of all, his father, born in Paris in 1881, had consistently gone by the name of Lévi-Strauss, as shown in the many portraits signed in his own hand, which had become the property of Tristan Bernard, Victor Marguerite and Louis Jouvet, among others, as well as official papers attesting to his membership in professional organizations (such as the Fédération des artistes). Second, 'in adopting the name Lévi-Strauss, my father wished to preserve in our family the name of his maternal grandfather Isaac Strauss, born in Strasbourg on 2 June 1806', a conductor and famous composer of waltzes. Finally, as the Collège de France professor explained, with supporting evidence, his entire administrative and academic career to date had been pursued under the name of Lévi-Strauss: 'I would add that all of my literary and academic works – i.e., five books (including *Tristes Tropiques*, which has been translated into nine languages) and 150 articles – have been published under the name of Lévi-Strauss, which I believe I can say, in all modesty, has not been detrimental to the standing of French scholarship and thought throughout the world [. . .]. Finally, the reception that the scholarly community has seen fit to give to my work, published under a name with which certain theories and discoveries are henceforth linked, has conferred on this name a public existence independent of the person who bears it. The name of Lévi-Strauss has become an integral part of the discipline to which I have dedicated my life and, even if I were to be obligated to do so, I can no longer rid myself of it.' Warned that the jurisprudence of the highest administrative court, the Conseil d'État, was not favourable to the adoption of compound and foreign-sounding names, Lévi-Strauss sought to forestall any such objections by adding a final paragraph to his letter: 'The foreign-sounding name of Strauss might furnish a second argument detrimental to my request. I would therefore like to state that this name was adopted by my great-great-grandfather Loeb Israël, born in Strasbourg on 22 January 1754, who took the name Léon Strauss before the end of the eighteenth century, registering his two sons Maurice and Isaac, born in 1801 and 1806, under the name of Strauss. A name borne for nearly two centuries by a family with deep Alsatian roots would seem to belong to the national onomastic heritage.'[10] The request was submitted in 1960 and a favourable decision of the Conseil d'État was published in the *Journal officiel* dated 24 August 1961. All official papers were modified accordingly.

These administrative hassles would have amounted to mere farce if they did not resonate so profoundly with the history of French Jewish families in the aftermath of the war. In the postwar decade, some of these families seized on the relatively favourable legal context to exercise their right to change their surnames. It should be noted that most of the Jews who did so were immigrants from Central and Eastern Europe who had arrived in France in the interwar period, with Slavic or otherwise foreign-sounding names, and were seeking both to erase the trauma of war and to anticipate any potential return to harsher times. It was rare for an old-line French Jewish family to undertake the onerous process. In the case of Lévi-Strauss, the move can be accounted for by the somewhat trivial motivations already mentioned (repeated bureaucratic humiliations), which surely did play a part, but also the turmoil provoked by his having been prohibited from officially bearing a name that was an integral part of his sense of self. More profoundly, it gives us insight into the decisive role that his family history, and particularly the distinguished figure of Isaac Strauss, played in the dynamic of identity formation at work in Claude Lévi, 'aka Lévi-Strauss'. What was at stake here was neither to conceal nor affirm his Judaism, per se, but rather to lay claim to a prestigious lineage of French Judaism. He was already over fifty years old at the time and a professor at the Collège de France. Furthermore, the firm tone of his final lines, his manifest irritation and the simmering pride he felt in his body of work, to which he was continuing to add, suggest that this procedure was experienced as a kind of denial of nationality (he was indeed asked to provide proof of his French nationality).

In this curious affair of name change, his sense of identity and filiation were unsettled at a time when Claude Lévi-Strauss had already 'made a name for himself', casting wider still the luminous halo of that of his paternal great-grandfather, Isaac Strauss. The name that, as he stated, was no longer his to change anchored him in the illustrious history of emancipation and cultural integration of Alsatian Jews, who had become exemplary French citizens over the course of the nineteenth century.

A genealogy

The family archives kept by Claude Lévi-Strauss – with its birth certificates, marriage contracts, correspondence, genealogical trees, wills, passports, letters – reveal a teeming world of late eighteenth-century Alsace, with people inhabiting places like Brumath, Ingwiller, Bischeim in the Lower Rhine region, and Rixheim and Dürmenach in the Upper Rhine – i.e., outside the cities, from which Jews were in any case excluded. They feature rabbis and merchants trading in various goods, hawkers, second-hand garment dealers, not to mention corn and cattle traders, almost exclusively Jewish. Isaac Strauss's mother, née Judith Hirschman, was the daughter of Rabbi Raphaël, a grand Rebbe famous throughout eighteenth-century Alsace. The small world of Alsatian Jewry (a population of around 20,000 in 1784) lived by the Jewish calendar, spoke Yiddish and, until the French Revolution, followed the precepts of rabbinical law. They were in theory barred from owning real property, though they sometimes acquired it through unpaid loans with land collateral. This would explain how Élie Moch, an ancestor on the maternal side (but also the paternal side), the great-grandfather of Claude Lévi-Strauss's mother, should come to record receiving rent from tenant farmers. Everything changed with the emancipation of Jews, granted in 1791. From that moment, the community underwent a rapid transformation that brought it 'from being the western-most outpost of the Ashkenazi Jewish world to a modern Judaism that was defined in national terms'.[11]

Within a generation or two, many Alsatian Jews had relocated to Paris, via Strasbourg, where they were assimilated into all the canons of urban bourgeois life, even while conserving certain aspects of their original identity. Claude Lévi-Strauss's family experienced this manifold social mobility, which entailed dramatic transformations in living standards and mental horizons. His genealogical tree is representative of a broad swathe of the history of French Jewry, in its geography (from Alsace to Paris, via Bayonne), its historical contingencies (emancipation, the Empire and the creation of the Grand Sanhedrin, the war of 1870), its economic and social successes, its experience of expanded possibilities – the gradient of Jewish identity in their emancipatory, and hence beloved, French home-land. Yet there was always one name, among the Mochs, Lévys, Lévis and Hausers, that shone most brightly in the eyes of the young man and his entire family: that of his great-grandfather, Isaac Strauss. Long forgot-ten by the world, his legacy was revived by his famous descendant. When Claude Lévi-Strauss began to invoke him in interviews given in the 1980s, it was the whole glittering world of his childhood that was brought back to him – a world of music and amusements, deeply anchored in the bourgeois nineteenth century, which as an old man he recognized as profoundly his own, even if he had never actually met his great-grandfather.

Isaac Strauss: 'The Paris Strauss'

Who was this man, dubbed the 'Béranger of dance music'?[12] Isaac Strauss was born in Strasbourg in 1806. His father, Loeb Israël, changed the name of Isaac and that of his brothers Maurice (Moshe) and Léon (Isaïe), pre-empting the imperial decree of 20 July 1808 that required Jews to stabilize their names by declaring them at the civil register of their municipality. They were forbidden to use Old Testament surnames or to differentiate themselves in any way: 'Isaie' thus became 'Isaac', 'Loeb' 'Léon', 'Lazare' 'Gustave', 'Moshe' 'Maurice', etc. Although part of Isaac's childhood was spent in Bisscheim, the early talent he demonstrated on the violin brought him to Paris in 1828 to the Royal Conservatory of Music, where he was in Pierre Baillot's class, before the latter was recruited, through a competitive exam, as the first violin in the Théâtre-Italien orchestra then conducted by Rossini: 'My grandmother [Isaac Strauss's daughter] liked to tell the story that, kissed on the forehead at the age of seven, I think, by Rossini, she had sworn never to wash to preserve the traces of the divine lips.'[13] Isaac's inexorable ascension was made possible by two important developments: the invention of dance music (and especially waltz music), and the emergence of a cultivated high society that congregated at spa towns, beginning in the 1830s. Indeed, following the turbulence of the periods of revolution and empire, the dances of the Ancien Régime came to be seen as hopelessly outdated. There was not much dancing at all under Louis XVIII and Charles X. And so it was Louis Philippe, the bourgeois king, who revived the tradition of royal festivities. Isaac Strauss was the right man at the right time, contributing to the invention of the waltz, to which were added polkas, mazurkas, Scottish reels, marches, quadrilles, redowas and gallops – dances that had European courts as well as the bourgeois salons of capital cities spinning and twirling, not to mention the aristocratic clientele of spas who, even if they claimed only to be following doctor's orders, were in fact mostly seeking out the ardent amusements of society life. Isaac Strauss thus brightened up the listless lives of the convalescents of Plombières and Aix la Chapelle. However, it was first and foremost in Vichy that his career took off. When he arrived there in 1843, the spa resort was somewhat deserted. A few years later, it had regained its status as 'the place to be' – a miracle of music and sound management engineered by the equally practical-minded and enthusiastic Isaac Strauss. In December 1847, at the request of Louis Philippe himself, he succeeded the famous Philippe Musard (1792–1859) as the conductor of court balls, but 'he would never make the royal family dance. The sounds of the orchestra were drowned out by the roar of revolution.'[14] However, the various regime changes did not affect Louis Philippe's original choice, and neither as president of the republic nor as emperor did Napoleon III ever consider invalidating the decision. Indeed, for the following two decades, Isaac Strauss kept everybody dancing, from the youth of the capital to the aristocracies old and new of the French Empire and all European society.

He was, then, a kind of imperial impresario. A debonair symbol of triumphant Parisian society and its hurly-burly of festive energy, he was known, renowned and idolized by all and sundry – a staple of the theatre scene, a regular patron of Drouot auctions and a man who, according to his contemporaries, was possessed of impeccable urbane manners and knew no enemies. 'A small man with keen and clever eyes sparkling from behind his opera glass, his nose sitting somewhat flat above his jeering mouth',[15] the Alsatian accent never completely suppressed, Isaac Strauss was the favourite butt of many gossip writers and caricaturists, including Gavarni and Cham. His white necktie was described by chroniclers as a sign of the times, like 'Voltaire's cane, Balzac's opera glass, Girardin's streak of hair, and Thiers's eyeglasses. Indeed, the grandfather's tie even became the stuff of song, sung to the well-known tune of "Casquette au père Bugeaud": "Have you seen / The necktie / The necktie / Have you seen / papa Strauss's necktie?"'[16] Isaac Strauss was the composer of more than four hundred pieces of music, including the famous quadrille in Offenbach's *Orpheus in the Underworld*, and Berlioz celebrated him in his *Mémoires* as the creator of a 'wealth of capricious, pungent waltzes, with a novel rhythm and a gracefully original irreverence'.[17] However, he was just as much an arranger, who took up fashionable themes and reworked them for the tastes of the day. His celebrity was further enhanced by, and fully participated in, the new phenomenon of 'star' conductors. Indeed, he was one himself, along with the likes of Louis-Antoine Jullien and Musard, whom the public went to see as much as to hear. Their spirited

Caricature of Isaac Strauss, lithograph by Paul Hadol (1835–1875),
published by Bertauts (circa 1854).

baton strokes (Strauss would break at least two batons at every concert),
and their feverish direction seemed a perfect fit for the atmosphere of bac-
chanal that characterized many of the opera balls at the time of the Paris
carnival – the masks covering women's faces giving licence to considerable
audacity . . . As director of the opera balls, an Ancien Régime institution
that persisted until the Third Republic, Isaac Strauss was in a position
to considerably raise the profile of the fashionable tunes of the day. In
addition, the publication by Heugel of many of his piano scores earned
significant royalties for him and his heirs, and for a period of copyright
that the law of 1866 had only just recently extended to fifty years after
the author's death. Less the great artist celebrated in family legend, Isaac
Strauss was an extremely successful figure in the music world of his time,
whose business and trend-setting prowess far exceeded any claim to artistic
accomplishment.[18]
   He made his fortune thanks to a combination of musical talent, natural
flair, business acumen and close ties with the imperial family, to whom he
dedicated a series of pieces: 'Eugénie Polka' (dedicated to the Empress),
the 'Imperial March', etc. His entire life appears to have been consecrated

to imperial glorification, even though his great-granddaughter Henriette Nizan revealed that he was a Freemason, initiated into the fraternal order by his musical master, Baillot. Deeply attached to the Declaration of the Rights of Man and its philosophical ideal of tolerance, fraternity and equality, he nonetheless composed his core convictions out of the twists and turns of imperial politics. Henriette Nizan kept 'his apron' as a token of his commitment to Freemasonry, a somewhat curious heirloom 'next to the wonderful ball gown bequeathed by my foremother'.[19] These two garments together form a mysterious diptych of the Strauss legacy, as ambivalent as light opera itself, which, according to the genre's ethnologist Siegfried Kracauer, simultaneously represented the revenge of the social outsider against the high operatic form and provided a chirpy din adorning the wall of silence around the imperial dictatorship. The very lightness of light opera had the virtue of doing away with all pretence, with its 'mixture of gaiety and satire, revolutionary disintegration and backward looking tenderness'.[20] In the end, Isaac Strauss was knighted Chevalier de la Légion d'honneur in January 1870, at which point he resigned from his position as director of court balls, thus in effect voluntarily retiring six months before the imperial debacle, basking in the glory of his 'musical sceptre' – a perfect sense of timing in a life of considerable accomplishment.

When he died in August 1888, a score of articles celebrated his legacy, but in the form of brief notices and society columns – not the extended tributes one would expect at the passing of a great artist. At the funeral, the rabbi 'paid homage to the philanthropist who was one of the founders of the Alsace-Lorraine Society as well as many other charitable societies'.[21] His connection, both biographical and artistic, with the imperial era was such that he appears to have passed away with it. The Third Republic, which had little taste for exuberant dancing and the caustic showmanship of light opera, preferred to highlight his other life as an art collector (best described as a passion for curios) and his period of retirement as the patriarch of his mansion at 44 rue de la Chaussée d'Antin – later demolished to allow for the opening of a new street, rue Réaumur, in 1895 – surrounded by his five adoring daughters and large extended family.

Forgotten by the wider world – the fact that he shared a name with the 'Vienna Strausses', whose European fame far eclipsed his own, did not help matters – Isaac Strauss remained an object of worship within his family. The ancestor cult was started by his daughters, several of whom lived long lives, and especially Claude Lévi-Strauss's grandmother, Léa, who died in 1933 and provided a living link with this glorious ancestor, whose legacy shone all the brighter given that only 'scraps', 'fragments' and memories remained of its former material and symbolic glory: 'I have a few pieces: the bracelet Napoleon III gave to my great-grandmother as a token of thanks for her hospitality at the Strauss Villa in Vichy. The Strauss Villa, where the emperor stayed, is still standing. It has become a bar or a restaurant, I'm no longer sure which, but it has kept the name.'[22] The episode of the emperor's visit to the Strauss home in Vichy remained, in family lore, the crowning moment of their proximity to the throne, as attested by the bracelet made of a garter and

Postcard celebrating the visit of Napoleon III to the Strauss Villa in Vichy, 1861.

a diamond brooch 'of great distinction', as Mrs. Strauss pointed out in a letter dated 30 July 1861. There had been another artefact from the archives of a world doubly engulfed, for the object too was lost: the ring that young Queen Isabella of Spain had given Isaac Strauss in thanks for the 'Double Marriage' waltz he performed on the day of her nuptials in 1846 in Madrid. The great-granddaughter of Isaac Strauss, Henriette Nizan, remembered it thus: 'A ruby trimmed with diamonds. A ring whose own story is full of symbolic meaning: a hundred years later, I, the other Henriette in the family [Isaac's wife was also named Henriette], was to throw it away by mistake and burn it in the woodstove of the hotel where I was staying while fleeing the Germans.'[23]

Family memorial

Continuing our ascent up Claude Lévi-Strauss's family tree, we would do well to pause at the branch of his grandparents.[24] On the maternal side, Sarah Lévy, née Moch, and Rabbi Émile Lévy settled in Verdun – after having chosen France in 1871 like many of their coreligionists – where their five daughters were born (Hélène, Aline, Lucie, Louise and Emma, Claude's future mother). The Franco-Prussian War of 1870 was an intense moment in the lives of these patriotic Jews, as recorded in Sarah's *album amicorum*, together with scraps of verse, tokens of friendship and other mementos. This very Germanic form of personal writing ended symbolically with a poem by Sarah, evoking the defeat of 1870 and the unravelling of her world: 'Rumbles of cannon fire resounding / As the sun completed its course / We saw a rush of warring troops / All covered in blood, smoke and ash / Screaming at denizens to run for their lives / All was lost.'

On the paternal side, the distinguished Strauss family was joined in matrimony – through its daughter Léa (1842–1932), Claude's future grandmother – to Gustave Lévi (1836–90), one of the five children of Flore Lévi, née Moch, and Isaac Lévi, whose social ascension, from Ingwiller in Alsace (where their son Gustave was born), is revealed in a household inventory made in 1892, following the death of Flore, Claude's future great-grandmother. This inventory conjures up a traditional bourgeois interior, embellished with a few indulgences in the Japanese vogue of the last third of the century: a walnut writing desk, an alabaster clock, blue and white porcelain from Japan, a mahogany work table, an oil lamp, a bronze candelabra, a padded armchair, a canopy bed and silverware. The family's rise to bourgeois status can also be seen in the identity card issued by the National Guard of the Seine to Gustave, Claude's grandfather, which is undated and simply states his address – 10 rue de la Victoire – and profession – stockbroker. Several passports attest to his travels. His participation in local political life and the stock exchange defined the new Parisian horizon of his grandparents, a world of employees, brokers and garment merchants, where family connections played a key role when it came to securing a job, borrowing money or making social connections. Endogamous marriages were also economic exchanges. Gustave Lévi's bad deals on the stock market and his premature death account for Léa's downward mobility, becoming a young widow and mother of five – André (1866–1928), Pierre (1873–1912), Jean (1877–1933), Hélène (1867–?) and the youngest, Raymond (1881–1953), Claude's future father.

In fact, 'it would be more accurate to talk of one family rather than two'.[25] First of all, Claude's parents were second cousins, related through several common ancestors, specifically Élie Moch and Esther Dreyfus. But, even more to the point, the world of Jewish families from Alsace who settled in Paris, often in the same neighbourhood, was extremely close-knit. Beyond the 2nd arrondissement of Paris (a place of work and leisure, with its many theatres and cafés), it was in the 16th that most of the residences were concentrated. Thus, Claude's maternal grandmother, Sarah Moch-Lévy, lived a few blocks from her daughter, and Claude's mother, Emma: the former lived on rue Narcisse Diaz, while the latter moved to rue Nicolas Poussin after her marriage in 1907. Claude Lévi-Strauss's close kin consisted of a wide range of relatives – numerous uncles and aunts, a flock of cousins as well as great-aunts (more numerous than great-uncles, whose life expectancy was shorter) – all knitted together by an intense family life, governed by a coherent set of rituals, habits, mutual aid and sometimes surrogate parenting.

Henriette Nizan's *Memoirs*, as well as the Lévi-Strauss family archive, give a powerful sense of the importance of this world, which would later be echoed in the works of the anthropologist himself. It is, for example, striking to find in the correspondence between Claude's paternal great-uncle Alfred Lévi and great-aunt Palmyre (Gustave's siblings) – discussing the latter's only child, René Kahn, a scattered young man 'straying from the straight and narrow' – the same role as that played by Claude's maternal uncle, described by the anthropologist a century later in an article

Genealogy of Claude Lévi-Strauss

The Moch and Lévy branch

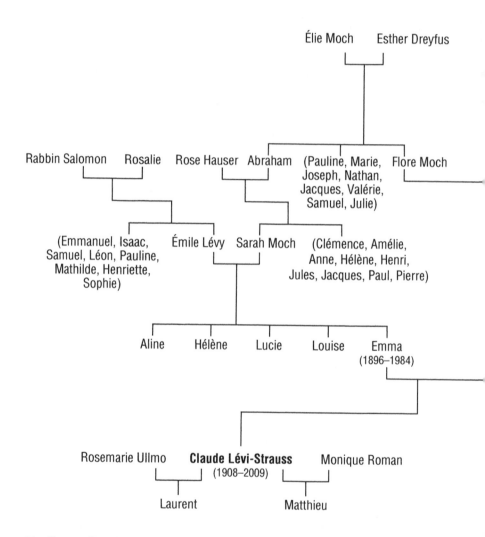

Family tree: "It would be more accurate to speak of one family rather than two." On both the maternal and paternal sides, the family has common roots in late-eighteenth-century Alsatian Judaism.

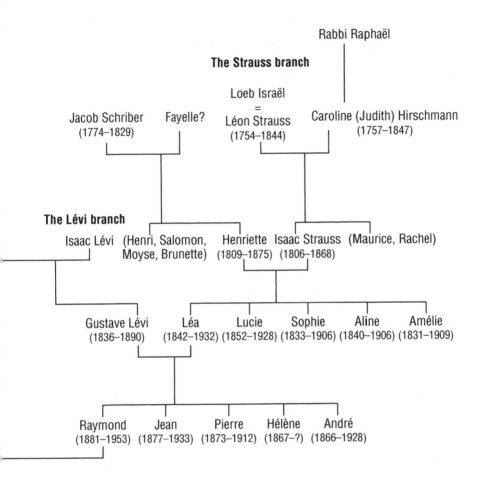

published in *La Repubblica* about Count Spencer's speech upon the death of his sister Diana.[26] He saw in this family dynamic the resurgence of an ancient structural function, that of go-between in case of conflict between parent and child, a substitute paternal authority but one that was not authoritarian, a kind of 'paternal mother'. Alfred's words reflected this same position, since, in the absence of the father, he offers his services as an intermediary, yet favours 'gentle remonstrance' and 'the power of persuasion' over 'more forceful means'.[27] Indeed, it is tempting to speculate that Claude Lévi-Strauss's reflections on the organization of kinship systems, presented in all their subtlety, was based in part on the rather refined model available to him through his own experience: the ancestral world preserved in family memory, a world of rural Alsatian Jews of the late eighteenth century, from which he hailed on both sides, who practised a kind of marriage between 'distant cousins' that was quite effective at inserting the individual properly into the social group. Not only were his parents second cousins but – he would later discover, to little surprise[28] – his third wife, Monique Roman (descendant of a branch of the Guggenheim family through her mother), also came from this same insular world. This offered a retrospective understanding that the kind of structures studied in exotic primitive societies could be found in the nineteenth-century rural societies of Europe, and indeed in his own genealogy. It is thus not so hard to believe that this heritage, appropriated through familial memory, might have constituted fertile ground, all the more so as its effects were unconscious.

The familial memory in question was largely managed by women, whose extraordinary longevity ensured its live transmission across generations. The women presided over epistolary exchanges, a vital family link when parents were still based in Strasbourg and sons in Paris. Flore Lévi, the paternal great-grandmother, showered her son Alfred with advice and prayers, spiritual recommendations, and trivial requests (an entire letter on slippers!) – an affectionate and lively mix that would later characterize the equally copious correspondence between Claude Lévi-Strauss and his own parents. Both of Claude's grandmothers were nearly 100 when they died – Léa Lévi (née Strauss) in 1932 and Sarah Lévy (née Moch) in 1955. Emma, Claude's mother, passed away in 1984, also at the age of nearly 100, surpassed only by her son, who lived to be 101, the only instance of male longevity in a family in which men more often left this world as much as thirty years before their wives. Léa Strauss was the guardian of the family record, collecting obituaries in a leather-bound notebook. It contains a wealth of information, including specifics regarding the dates of births and deaths, and various biographical articles. Claude Lévi-Strauss himself later contributed to the album. In his fine handwriting, he expanded the genealogical tree to include himself and his children, Laurent and Matthieu – like mountaineers connected by a rope. This double-entry ledger is representative of the common practices of obituary and genealogy, here naturally recycled into the anthropology of kinship – a true family memorial, as was common in nineteenth-century French bourgeois families, perpetuating the memory of the dead, who become united in the beyond as part of a clan whose construction rests on conserving their traces beyond disappearance and oblivion.[29]

The 'hitches' in Franco-Judaism

The Lévi-Strauss family epitomized the historical arch of French upward mobility, precocious and proceeding from an integrating universalism that encouraged the relegation of all forms of religious particularity to the private sphere. With the establishment of the Third Republic, Jews became Israelite citizens destined for assimilation into what had become a secular society. In the end, the republican state and the Jewish consistory shared the same vision of the ideal Jew: culturally assimilated, economically integrated, discreet in the practice of religion and patriotic.[30] But Pierre Birnbaum is right to challenge this somewhat overly teleological account. Franco-Judaism was a complex reality that has often been caricatured, or at least simplified: 'As opposed to what we are told in most analyses of Franco-Judaism and even of the *Bildung*, Jewish culture is not about to be definitively eradicated from the societies most affected by emancipation and the Enlightenment.'[31] This composite identity can be seen in innumerable little ways, in social forms, family structures and networks of association.

In interviews, Claude Lévi-Strauss had little to say about the professed lack of faith of his parents and relations. But a lack of faith is by no means incompatible with the maintenance of an acrobatic double identity. The latter is graphically rendered in letters of the 1860s from Flore Lévi to her sons.[32] They almost all start with a few pages written by the mother in French, at which point the father continues in Yiddish written in Hebrew script. This gendered division in content, language and script offers a clear illustration of what it meant to live between two worlds. Similarly, the dates of holidays, deaths and births – all of the ordinary logistics of family life – were noted using the Christian calendar, and then usually translated into the Jewish calendar – the mark of a double relationship with time. In the same vein, Claude Lévi-Strauss's parents, despite being unbelievers, were married in a synagogue prior to their civil wedding. Here again, traditional wedding practices were preserved in these highly assimilated families, all the more so given that Emma's father was a rabbi. Finally, the Jewish charity practised by Isaac Strauss was yet another classic mode in which a form of Jewish identity was preserved amongst very assimilated French Jews.

Claude Lévi-Strauss's maternal grandfather, Rabbi Émile Lévy (1848–1933), gave explicit expression to the dilemmas of a modernized Judaism in republican times, as well as of an anti-Semitism brought to the surface and rendered hysterical by the Dreyfus affair. He was the son of Salomon Lévy, himself a rabbi in Brumath – i.e., from that Lower Rhine region famous for producing rabbis. After completing his secondary education in Strasbourg, he entered the Paris Israelite Seminary in 1866, from which he graduated with a thesis on the ancient Jewish monarchy. In 1871, he adopted French nationality and, in 1876, he was appointed to the Verdun rabbinate, where he was to remain until 1892, becoming a respected and beloved figure in the community. In that year, after many unsuccessful applications, he was appointed to the important Bayonne rabbinate, a major hub of French Judaism, before ending his career in 1908 as rabbi of the Versailles Cultural Association and receiving a pension of 1,500 francs according to the law separating church and state. He became vice-president of the French Rabbinical Association and was awarded the Légion d'honneur in 1930. In addition, he was one of the founders of the Jewish scout movement and collaborated on the official Bible of the French rabbinate, which he wanted to see published in an abridged version for children.[33] Grandfather Lévy thus followed the quasi-prefectural career path of a dignitary of French consistory Judaism. Along with his colleagues, he had to navigate the issue of Jewish identity in a secularized society which had granted civil equality to Jews. Many of his Bayonne sermons dealt with the double peril of the loss of religious practices and of the now impossible and dangerous asser-tion of identity in a France on the road to secularization: 'On the one hand, it is religious indifference that lulls us into a slumber of well-being. The liberties that have been granted to us by our generous homeland have led us to forget what our ancestors suffered, and for what reason they suf-fered. On the other hand, our enemies are only too pleased with this indif-ference – which, I have observed, is only superficial – and we far too often hear our origins belittled, our rights denied, our mission contested.' Late nineteenth-century anti-Semitism rather strengthened the patriotic senti-ment of French Jews and their identification with the fate of the French Republic. It was one possible way to maintain a Jewish identity, whose messianic character was then channelled into love of the Republic. It also served to deny anti-Semites any opportunity, by never expressing this iden-tity other than as a shared belief in the civic nation. This high road also led to high levels of political legitimacy for French Jews.

Yet this acrobatic synthesis was always somewhat precarious. When Claude Lévi-Strauss was asked about how they reconciled an irreligious family atmosphere with the upholding of Judaic traditions, he said the situation was certainly not 'without its hitches'.[34] He then evoked a 'touch of madness' on the paternal side of the family. It would 'appear in sometimes tragic, sometimes comic form. One of my father's broth-ers, who was obsessed with biblical exegesis and whose head was not set too firmly on his shoulders, committed suicide. I was three at the time. A long time before my birth, another one of my father's brothers was ordained as a priest to spite his parents after a disagreement. For a time, the family counted among its members a Father Lévi . . .'[35] Lévi-Strauss's personal archive still bears traces of the tragic existence of the uncle who chose suicide: incoherent writings scribbled in 1912, in which he invoked God and his family (and notably his mother, an 'admirable woman'), and expressed a longing to die with his eyes open.[36] He took his own life in that same year. Claude Lévi-Strauss did not explore the texture of this 'touch of madness' any further, but it is quite clear in both cases – biblical exegesis and priesthood – that it took the form of an existential rift between 'national belonging and denominational loyalty'[37] and that the attendant suffering could sometimes be sufficiently acute for death to appear as the only solution. It also resonated with the malfunctioning, at the world-historical scale, of the well-oiled machine of Franco-Jewish assimilation, first with the Dreyfus affair and then the Vichy regime.

Art as legacy

Isaac's inclination: from religion to collection

Claude Lévi-Strauss's personal archive would suggest that he both over-estimated the extent to which Jewish identity was no longer operative in his family background and underestimated the psychological and spiritual tensions arising from the hybrid position of this assimilated Franco-Judaism. This may partly explain why he never delved very deeply into one of the distinctive features of the life of his ancestor Isaac Strauss: his taste for collecting. Lévi-Strauss depicted him as a kind of 'Cousin Pons, passionately fond of antiques, which he dealt in', adding that he owned a significant collection of 'Jewish antiques'.[38] In fact, what Claude Lévi-Strauss called Jewish antiques were Jewish ritual objects displayed at the 1878 Universal Exhibition in the galleries of the brand new Palais du Trocadero, which – in a troubling coincidence – hosted the Ethnology Museum, itself also recently established. Auctioned off for financial reasons after Isaac's death, the collection was acquired by Baroness Rothschild, who donated it to the Cluny Museum in Paris, over the vehement protest of Édouard Drumont.[39] The young Lévi-Strauss remembers being taken as a child into a room, which bore his name, dedicated to his grandfather's objects. The Strauss-Rothschild collection, as it was called, was devoted to objects pertaining to religious ceremonies and festivals – Shabbat, Hanukah and Purim – as well as to circumcision and marriage rituals: prayer books, reading desks, a silver spice box, kiddush cups, candleholders, bronze triangular lamps, Hanukah lamps, wedding rings and eighteenth-century ketubahs (marriage contracts).[40] The paucity of objects dating from before the sixteenth century attested to the persecution of Jews in Medieval Europe.

Isaac Strauss's passion for collecting was consistent with the relatively common practice among well-off Jewish families, and even more so among very wealthy ones, such as the Rothschilds or Ephrussis. Why this impulse to collect? As Edmund de Waal – a genealogist and distant relative of the Éphrussi family with a passion for the collection of netsuke ceramics assembled by his ancestor Charles Éphrussi – has explained, these families owned quite a few sumptuous mansions, around Parc Monceau in Paris and on the Ringstrasse in Vienna, which were in need of furnishings. Collecting was a form of social snobbery, a way of crowning their economic success by transforming it into artistic capital – an essential metamorphosis for these *nouveaux riches*, whose wealth was anything but ancestral.[41] In the 1870s, when a retired Isaac Strauss was completing his collection, Jewish elites, led by bankers and merchants, had a taste for the masterpieces of Renaissance Italy and for Japanese art, which reached a fever pitch during the Meiji period. If Isaac Strauss also collected works in keeping with the fashion of the times – paintings by Georges de La Tour, Van Loo and Boucher – the heart of his collection, his treasures, was unquestionably these Jewish religious objects, which distinguished his collection from others.

Daniel Fabre has pointed out the significance and impact of Isaac Strauss's legacy, in all its richness: 'He quite simply invented Jewish art. First, against the prejudice that Jews could not have an art since their religious law proscribed all images of beings created by Yahweh, a prohibition that their diasporic condition was supposed to have further reinforced. But also against his own Jewish community, which never laid claim to an art, in the modern sense of the term.'[42] By entitling his collection 'Hebraic religious art objects', as they were called in the 1878 Exhibition Catalogue, Strauss made 'the decision to transform them into works of art. He renames them with a word that simultaneously downgrades and transposes them', and by doing so, 'radically displaces their value and meaning': liturgical, religious objects turned works of art.[43] The same metamorphosis had also occurred for Christian objects, of course. More broadly, the twentieth century was to see this logic through to its conclusion.[44] However, Isaac Strauss was the first to have intuitively sensed the possibility of refounding Jewish identity through a translation from the sacred to the beautiful – i.e., into art. For Daniel Fabre, there is no doubt that this gesture of refounding expressed a 'desire to slow the disintegration of traditional religious life', as well as to maintain a form of singular identity that could no longer be expressed through religious life or even the outward maintenance of rituals. This is exactly what Claude Lévi-Strauss said in a tense interview with Victor Malka in 1984. When the interviewer rather aggressively presented him with the words of a former secondary school classmate – 'Lévi-Strauss knows how much he owes to the fact of being Jewish' – the latter replied: 'It's true. I know exactly how much. However non-religious my parents were, they had this tendency that seems characteristic of many Jewish families: a kind of cult, or religion, of culture. The Jewish people is defined as the people of the book and it is true that I grew up in a family of the book. I was, in this respect, from my earliest childhood, encouraged to read, to cultivate myself, and to develop a curiosity for all things. Unquestionably, culture was paramount in my milieu. *This is what was sacred.*'[45]

Taking this further, the conversion to aesthetics was also at the centre of fin de siècle Vienna and its enigmatic creative efflorescence. Many of its Jewish artists and intellectuals embraced this new ideal in response to their sense of being torn between various principles of belonging. They partook of a Germanness that was not coterminous with the Austro-Hungarian Empire (it overflowed into Germany). The German-speaking Viennese of Jewish descent were formed by the German intellectual and artistic world, while remaining minorities within their own empire. They had to deal, in addition, with the virulent anti-Semitism of Vienna's mayor, Karl Lüger, and of social Christianity. Neither fully German nor fully Austrian, they were no longer *shtetl* Jews; and their assimilation, still incomplete, did not provide them with any stable identity. According to Michaël Pollak, it was indeed this turn to artistic excellence and an investment in the artistic vocation that allowed them to fashion for themselves a more comfortable relationship to the world, a kind of *Kakanian* artistic patriotism, that was to burn brightest in the early 1900s.[46]

In Paris, Isaac Strauss's approach to collecting inaugurated this kind of identity transformation. And it was among his own descendants that it was to have its first effects.

What's in a name?

Not only was Isaac's collection dispersed after his death, but the Strauss name itself was destined for extinction, since his five children were all girls: Amélie, Henriette (Nizan's grandmother), Sophie, Aline, Léa (Claude Lévi-Strauss's grandmother) and Lucie. Four of them married, becoming Cahen, Schlesinger, Alphen and Lévi, respectively, while the fifth remained unmarried.

Then, something interesting happened, which Henriette Nizan recounts with considerable flair: out of the five sons-in-law in the family, two decided – in a move that at first appears to be motivated by simple snobbery – to add to their respective names that of the ancestor Strauss.[47] Now that aristocratic names were no longer an option, it had become common practice to adopt hyphenated names as a republican form of distinction. Yet the motivation here was clearly different. The sons-in-law who engaged in this patronymic montage were Robert Alphen-Strauss, Henriette Nizan's father, and Raymond Lévi-Strauss, the two members of the family with artistic callings. One was a musician, the other a painter, and both – as Claude Lévi-Strauss was to explain in his own official application for a change of name – sought not just to honour the legacy of their ancestor, but more importantly to insert themselves into the artistic lineage initiated by their father-in-law: 'The symbolic production of Isaac as ancestor to the artists of the family, an enormous family in which there were the most diverse callings, was a far-reaching operation.'[48] For Robert Alphen-Strauss, the double name remained only a stage name, whereas, in the case of Raymond Lévi-Strauss, it was transmitted to his wife and only son, Claude.

A few minor annotations confirm that, late in his life, Claude Lévi-Strauss perpetuated this new form of affiliation by systematically adding handwritten information to the family archive that all tended in the same direction. Beyond the gossip – Amélie, for example, is supposed to have been the mistress of Minister Rouher and 'the family generally considered that Aline was his daughter' – his notes highlight the more artistically inclined within the vast and nebulous family network. Aline Strauss married Maurice Schlesinger, a music publisher in Frankfurt. Her great-grand-nephew wondered, 'could he be related to Elisa Schlesinger, Flaubert's great love (the Madame Arnoux of *Sentimental Education*)?' And this scrupulously recorded, brief remark: 'Learned from my mother in September 1974 that Henry Caro-Delvaille [a maternal uncle, and himself an artist] was Isadora Duncan's lover.' Or these mentions, added to a complicated genealogical tree on the Moch side, concerning two unspecified relatives: 'a dancer at the Paris Opera' and 'an actress in Sarah Bernhardt's troupe, died on tour in the United States'. Or else: 'Edouard Jonas, grandson of Sophie [Strauss], a major antique dealer on the Place Vendôme.'[49]

Over time, Isaac Strauss's glory was eclipsed by the more lasting fame of the Vienna Strausses, and even that of the head of court balls before him, Musard, and finally by the collective character of operatic creation, which made the attribution of musical copyright a delicate matter (for example, some of the operettas attributed to Offenbach are in fact Strauss's). But the importance of Isaac Strauss's tutelary genius among his descendants was still palpable, some fifty years later, in the fastidious care taken by Raymond, Claude's father, in defending his grandfather's legacy when it was besmirched on a radio programme devoted to the balls of the Empire. In a letter addressed to the producers of the programme, Raymond wrote, after the customary niceties: 'During one of your programs I recognized the *London Galop*, the *Grand Galop de l'Opéra* and the *Nouvelle Sylphide*, but who else, other than a descendant of Strauss himself could have identified them, together with the polka-mazurka you played without attribution? And what is one to make of your crediting the quadrilles drawn from *Barbe Bleue* and the *Fortunio*'s song to Musard?' On 2 July 1953, a new letter thanking them for another programme on Strauss and Vichy struck an altogether different note, reversing the reproaches of the first: 'Thanks to you, the dream, nourished for so long, of rekindling the memory of my grandfather Strauss in Vichy has become reality.'[50]

Late into the twentieth century, grandfather Strauss remained the family totem, until his great-grandson Claude arrived to sweep away the polkas of the Second Empire and reinvigorate the lineage with new glory, albeit of a very different kind.

2

Revelations (1908–1924)

From a very early age, you were socialized into the richness of the world.
Roger Caillois, 'Speech delivered at the induction of Claude
Lévi-Strauss into the Académie française'[1]

Recovering the invisible threads of childhood can be a complicated affair. To be sure, there is a readily available narrative, one largely spun by Claude Lévi-Strauss himself through a series of interviews he gave in the 1980s, in which he made some 'understated and highly circumspect revelations'.[2] The *Libres Mémoires* of his cousin Henriette Nizan, several portraits and a few objects with related archives complete his depiction of a glowing childhood, during which he was drawn to the arts and invigorated by discovery of the world.

For the child, the world was his apartment, his neighbourhood, his city, Paris. Each of these concentric circles held its 'treasures', stuffed into pockets and exhibited in the evening as the day's loot, eyes filled with wonder. Discoveries of all kinds – art, music, literature, curios, urban landscapes, natural wonders – became so many revelations. The systematic recourse to religious language builds on the metamorphosis started by Isaac Strauss; indeed, herein lies the sacred!

In comparison with the scintillating wonders of home life, the world of school paled: no memorable teachers, no mentors – or at least not yet. All through secondary school, the young mind in the young body, imbued with a sense of independence, insisted on a kind of autodidacticism. A bourgeois and yet somewhat Bohemian education, a touch of downward mobility and very real financial difficulties during these decisive childhood and teenage years gave an original stamp to the young man whose long, serious face was regularly lit up by a most innocent smile.

Landscapes of childhood

Offenbach, Matzo Kugel, painting

This is the story of a young Parisian, but one born in Brussels, on 28 November 1908, rue Van Campenhout. A snapshot annotated in

Levi-Strauss's own handwriting depicts a third-floor corner apartment, with 'a studio, lemon tree, kitchen and bedroom'.[3] On the street, a brewery and a military barracks facing the Square Marguerite, in the northeastern part of the city. Claude Lévi-Strauss has also kept a sketch, drawn by his father, of the city viewed from the window of the room in which he was born: an image that served as a 'memory-object'[4] for him. Was Lévi-Strauss Belgian, then? He was not. The place of his birth was a feature of chance, of work that his father, a painter, was commissioned to complete by a network of Brussels-based friends. The young couple and newborn child remained in Brussels for several more months before returning to Paris. And yet, this anomalous birthplace does inaugurate a kind of Belgian thread that will run through Lévi-Strauss's life, especially through his political education. His third wife, Monique, though born in Paris, is Belgian. This touch of *Belgitude* stokes the French imagination – an ironic, humorous counterpoint to an arrogant Paris-centrism. A brief lapse in affiliation, a minor initial infidelity.

'Gustave Claude Lévi-Strauss', as he was called on his birth announcement, was soon to return to live among his own in the French capital. Following tradition, he was given the name of his grandfather, Gustave Lévi, who had died long before his birth, in 1890. The parents moved into 26 rue Poussin in the southern 16th arrondissement, near Porte d'Auteuil. The neighbourhood was still quite picturesque, wedged between the Bois de Boulogne and the Seine, full of artists' studios and small antique shops, and had a country feel to it. Indeed, Lévi-Strauss even remembered a farm at the corner of rue Poussin and rue La Fontaine.[5] On the outskirts of the

Postcard, Brussels, rue Van Campenhout, with Claude Lévi-Strauss's
handwriting indicating the apartment where he was born.

city, the streets that nurtured the boy's early childhood offered much to satisfy both the urban imagination and the taste for nature. Many a find could be had. Local life combined a kind of casual Bohemianism and a mixed bourgeois and working-class population.

The apartment in which Lévi-Strauss spent his entire youth, until leaving the parental home in 1931, was located on the fifth floor of a building that had been constructed in the late nineteenth century and was rather opulent, with neo-gothic flourishes and a steel and glass front door. But once inside the Lévi-Strauss apartment, the atmosphere radically changed. An artist's studio cum apartment, filled with traces of the father's activity – tubes of paint, canvases, easels – the four rooms were crammed full of books and furniture inherited from more glamorous days. There was also a small photo lab, where Raymond tried his hand at developing snapshots. Photography, which gradually became his arch nemesis, since he was primarily a portrait painter, was to be the object of numerous forays and of sometimes stormy discussions, as well as experiments between father and son, both 'crazy about' this still fairly new technology. From the start, the young boy was in constant contact with art materials and instruments: 'I was raised in studios . . . not an academic background at all. I already had brushes and paints in my hands when I was taught to read and write.'[6] One can conjure up this childhood full of creativity, between the 'artistic bric-à-brac'[7] of the father and the gustatory landscape of the mother, some of the highlights of which have been preserved in the archives: 'Ginger pudding, pumpkin and tomato soup, mushroom pie, birnen kugel, cabinet pudding, Alsatian kugel, gefilte fish, turnip chops, Alsatian horseradish sauce, matzo kugel, scharff chicken, apple tarte, beef tongue, veal cutlets in mushroom sauce.'[8]

His mother, Emma, born in 1886, was a slight woman, good-looking – mention is made of large black eyes – and full of energy. She became a mother at quite a young age (barely twenty-two when Claude was born) and was very proud of her son, happy to regularly summon all her culinary acumen to nourish him. The youngest of a clan of five daughters, she received no higher education – unlike her eldest sister, Aline, who attended the École normale supérieure and obtained an *agrégation* in philosophy – but was not without her talents. She had perfect pitch and could sing any tune, especially Offenbach, which the family knew by heart.[9] Descended from an Alsatian family and raised in Bayonne, both regions bastions of French cuisine, Emma Lévi-Strauss reprised the story of her kinfolk in the meals she cooked, which struck strong Alsatian-Jewish notes. Very early on, this astounding cook, who declined to follow the traditional codes of bourgeois cuisine, initiated her son into the guilty pleasures of the palate, which he was to maintain throughout his life, with the competence and seriousness of a true gourmet.

Many of the father's paintings are of a very young Claude, astride a rocking horse or in a pensive posture, a curly-haired little boy with a fine and somewhat feminine air, like many little boys at the time whose hair was often left to grow long. Another painting, another memory-object – this one by the uncle, Henry Caro-Delvaille – called *Ma femme et ses soeurs*, was purchased by the French state in 1904 and donated to the Musée du Luxembourg in Paris. It depicts the five Lévy sisters, five young women idealized by the artist, busying themselves in various ways. One is breastfeeding a baby, the others playing chess, in a bourgeois setting. Hailing from Bayonne, Henry Caro-Delvaille married the eldest of the Lévy sisters, Aline, and it was at their home that Emma met Raymond Lévi-Strauss, a painter with connections to Caro-Delvaille.[10] A third sister was to marry yet another artist, Gabriel Roby. However, the most famous of his two artist uncles was undoubtedly Henry Caro-Delvaille (1876–1926), who gained 'considerable fame for his female figures executed with poise and vibrancy'.[11] After the First World War, he pursued a career in the United States, but success eluded him. Gabriel Roby, for his part, left little in the way of a legacy. Of fragile health and short-lived, he 'had an even more difficult life than my father', his nephew would later recall.[12]

As for Raymond Lévi-Strauss, Claude's father, catalogues reveal he took part in Paris Salons from 1905 until 1921, with 'genre and portrait paintings'.[13] As he often reiterated, the young Lévi-Strauss grew up in an artistic milieu, surrounded by artists who were neither outcasts nor avant-garde, neither celebrated nor unknown. A pupil of Léon Bonnat, the official portraitist of Third Republic dignitaries, Caro-Delvaille and, less successfully, his brothers-in-law, worked at the margins of academic painting. Though lacking in official commissions, and thus forced onto an art market now organized more around galleries than salons, the three men upheld the academic values of the conscientious artisan, of work well done, technique, mastery, hard work, patience; in other words, the exact opposite of the avant-garde ethos, which valued fleeting inspiration, the freedom to capture the moment, the ephemeral, genius, etc. Masters of techniques whose value was quickly depreciating due to the rise of the new art, they recorded, with greater or lesser alacrity, the residual froth of an earlier time, one that coexisted for another few years with triumphant pictorial modernity. Lévi-Strauss's father – although he became friends with Daniel Kahnweiler, a friend of Picasso, a major promoter of abstraction and later a dealer in modern art, whom he met at the stock exchange when both were still working there – admired above all Maurice Quentin de La Tour. As his son concluded, 'he was not geared for his times'.[14]

When he was not on rue Poussin, or gallivanting around the neighbourhood visiting the studio of some artist friend or other, young Claude was caught up in the intense rhythm of a busy family life, marked by visits, strolls and weekly lunches at his grandmother's, Léa Lévi née Strauss, on rue Vignon, in an ambience that still preserved the bourgeois opulence inherited from Isaac. Léa's culinary offerings were more traditional than Emma's, and staff served at the large Sunday table. The young Claude would get bored there, take up a volume of Labiche's complete works, shut himself away in a corner and 'laugh all by [him]self'.[15] In this large family, proliferating on all sides, Claude Lévi-Strauss was a child whose singleness was striking by contrast. An only child (as his mother seems to have been too fragile to attempt a second), a pampered child, solitary and at the same time surrounded by family, he developed habits befitting his circumstances. Above all, he was an avid reader, especially of an abridged version of *Don Quixote*, which he knew by heart and would happily recite to great effect.[16] The *wunderkind* was also a sensitive child, with a penchant for telling and above all writing stories. Thus, his earliest known oeuvre, dating from when he was eight and a half, 'The Coal and the Matches', is a dialogue between a sack of coal and a box of matches, in which they recount how they came to cross paths in a kitchen. The coal was extracted from its 'good Belgian soil' by miners, the matches sliced thin from a beautiful fir tree and 'plunged in sulphur and phosphorus'. 'They died in peace. The coal, like Napoleon I, was burnt to ashes after its death, and the matches were thrown into the bin.' And on the back of the page: 'If you want more stories, just ask me.'[17] Besides his loyalty to Belgium, the charm of his prose lay in the precision of its vocabulary, its poetic style somewhat reminiscent of Francis Ponge, the attention to objects and plants that are given life, the material imagination and the abruptly tragic ending.

The bourgeois world of Lévi-Strauss's childhood, where courtesy calls and visiting cards were still in order, seemed difficult to recall for the older man evoking his childhood, as so much of it belonged to the bygone era of the nineteenth century, barely surviving the First World War. Hence the sometimes spectral quality of these figures, who shrouded the beginnings of a very long life.

The war in Versailles: patriotism and Judaism

The onset of war brought this small theatre of quiet childhood to an abrupt close. The father, of fragile constitution, became an ambulance driver. Fearing an attack on Paris, Emma and her son, together with the four Lévy sisters and their children, joined Rabbi Lévy in Versailles. Thus, Claude Lévi-Strauss spent the four years of war, from ages six to ten, at his grandfather's house. He went to school at Lycée Hoche, and grew up in a sprawling household of single women. The separation of families, and especially the prolonged absence of fathers, was of course a common experience of war.

War triggered a great upsurge of patriotism, even more so among French Jews, who often experienced it as a form of compensation, a repayment in blood for their emancipation. Their human, financial and ideological participation was also, in their eyes, a demonstration of loyalty, which had been called into question only a few years earlier by the Dreyfus affair. It was both a badge of their deserved integration and a promise of its full realization. One finds evidence of this unfailing patriotic support in the Lévi-Strauss family, with the added fervour specific to Alsatian Jews, who came, after all, from the 'lost provinces'. Claude's paternal grandmother, Léa Lévi, took out a second mortgage of 2,000 gold francs for the national defence in 1916; by 16 December 1915, she had already contributed 1,500.[18]

Up to 40,000 French Jews fought for France (out of a total community numbering some 190,000 in 1914), of whom 7,500 perished on the battlefield – a sizeable contribution to the national war effort.[19] The Lévi-Strauss family did not lose many of its own, at least not among Claude's close relatives, except for a 'first cousin much my elder, a brilliant École normale alumnus'. And, Lévi-Strauss added, not without a touch of pride: 'Maurice Barrès quoted and commented on his letters in *Les Diverses Familles spirituelles de la France.*'[20] Here again, the experience was widespread, but not insignificant: the loss of brilliant elders among siblings or in families ratcheted up a notch the hopes and expectations laid on younger ones, who experienced this new position as either a crushing burden or stimulating challenge.

For, in their own way, children had quite an intense experience of the war. Historians of wartime culture have long made this clear.[21] School, family, separation, mourning, patriotic fervour – everything around them reflected the war. They were, in a sense, its target, with their future as the official stakes of the civilizational struggle under way. They were readying for it and, in the meantime, between the palpable vacancy and anxiety, they lived their fatherless child lives 'punctuated by the boom and rumble of Big Bertha, whose shots were heard throughout the countryside'.[22] Claude Lévi-Strauss was indeed one of these children of 1914: 'Carried away myself by the enthusiasm, I went to give several gold coins that I had – the savings of an eight-year old child – so as to be part of the effort to support the French army. Giant posters called on our sense of solidarity, and since in my family, we were very patriotic . . . Our Alsatian origins and all. And the armistice, the scenes of jubilation and the great relief that followed. The sense of exhilaration lasted for days.'[23] Lévi-Strauss remembered the victory parade, which he watched from a building on avenue de l'Opéra, as a 'major event in [his] young existence'.[24] Several poems that have been preserved, including one addressed to his grandmother, accompanied by a drawing of a soldier carrying an *'honneur et patrie'* flag, provide further confirmation of this generational alignment.[25]

In addition, the Versailles years prompted one of Claude Lévi-Strauss's rare allusions to his 'Jewishness', long before the biographical interviews of the 1980s, in an 'upsurge' of childhood memories recorded in his 1955 classic work *Tristes Tropiques*. It comes up without much warning, while the author is pondering the relationship between the living and the dead among Bororo Indians, which is characterized by a profound religiosity encompassing all of social life and a surprising combination of mundane and sacred gestures, which reminds him of the 'casual religiosity of Buddhist temples'.[26] The Judaism of his childhood then surfaces as part of a purely oppositional logic: 'This casual attitude to the supernatural was all the more surprising for me in that my only contact with religion dated back to childhood when, already a nonbeliever, I lived during the First World War with my grandfather, who was Rabbi of Versailles. The house was attached to the synagogue by a long inner passage, along which it was difficult to venture without a feeling of anguish, and which in itself formed an impassable frontier between the profane world and that other which was lacking precisely in the human warmth that was a necessary precondition to its being experienced as sacred. Except when services were in progress, the synagogue remained empty and its temporary occupation was never sustained or fervent enough to remedy the state of desolation which seemed natural to it and in which the services were only an incongruous interruption. Worship within the family circle was no less arid. Apart from my grandfather's silent prayer at the beginning of each meal, we children had no means of knowing that we were living under the aegis of a superior order, but for the fact that a scroll of printed paper fixed to the dining-room wall proclaimed the motto: "Chew your food well for the good of your digestion".'[27]

To the warmth of the Bororo sense of the sacred, he opposed the cold and desiccated character of Judaism and, in fact, according to Lévi-Strauss, of all monotheisms. Proselytizing universalism excludes what more serene religions can allow. The transcendental and dreaded form of the sacred is far removed from this soothing intimacy with the spirit-world.[28] The entire description, including the comical epilogue on proper chewing, is intended to illustrate an artificial relationship to a religion that has been reduced to meaningless gestures and rituals, maintained only because one is Jewish. Claude Lévi-Strauss was circumcised and bar mitzvahed, but liked to recall that 'when we were refugees in Versailles, our mothers would prepare ham sandwiches for us, which we would devour in the park, hiding behind statues to avoid upsetting my grandfather'.[29] But it is difficult to assert an 'identity without content'.[30] However, despite the lack of properly religious content, this identity was constantly given substance by the experience of schoolyard violence: 'I was called a "dirty Jew" as early as primary school . . . And in high school as well. "How would you react?" I would punch.'[31] Similarly, a kind of elementary Zionism seemed to be a part of this not-so-bare-bones Judaism: 'In high school, I had Jewish friends and we considered that we were fulfilling an essential duty by sending money to plant a tree, our tree, in Israel.'[32]

The Dreyfus affair was not so distant. It had legally ended only a few years earlier, in 1906, with the rehabilitation of the innocent party. In the child's imagination, it had persisted in multiple ways, especially as an edifying story, which was dramatically tight and had a happy ending. It was through this saga, during one of the long wartime summers that they spent together on the Normandy coast, that Claude's cousin, Henriette Nizan, two years his elder, first drew him into theatrical production: 'I cast the roles, I chose the *mise en scène*, I constructed the props, we rehearsed over and over the story of the beautiful soldier [. . .]. As is often the case in fairytales, the final scene is radiant: Dreyfus, with a smile on his face, surrounded by soldiers standing at attention, receives a decoration, while the Republic, hovering in the sky, adorns his head with a *képi*.'[33] Indeed, during wartime the children turned everything into theatre, under the dynamic leadership of Henriette, who was close to her cousin whom she found very 'cute'. 'He had inherited his mother's good looks', resembling 'a kitten'. They would spend hours astride long sticks singing: 'We are the Polish lancers, we are . . . .' But in addition to historical drama, they also put on romantic plays like *Carmen*. 'Claude was Escamillo. I was Carmen. For our costumes, we took off all the ribbons from our mothers' blouses, and Claude fabricated a "suit of light" for himself that looked like a bull-fighter's outfit, or at least so it seemed to us, which was made entirely of dozens of small pink ribbons.'[34]

The richness of the world

'Of all the events that mark my childhood, none have left me with a more vivid memory than the first time I met Pierre Dreyfus. In the autumn of 1918, I entered Janson-de-Sailly Lycée. Paying a visit to the head teacher (as was done at the time), my parents were concerned about my solitary disposition and appealed to him for help. One day, after class, one of my classmates – dark-haired, skinny and rather small – whom I knew only by sight, came up to me and uttered the most astonishing phrase: "The teacher told me to come play with you." I recall being seized by an inner fury: they dared to assail my independence . . . And yet, from that day onward, for decades, Pierre and I were inseparable.'[35]

Claude Lévi-Strauss, aged ten, a solitary boy who appeared aloof, proud and fiercely independent, had a few select friends and tastes as defined as they were diverse, opening up to the wider world as soon as he left the school premises. Indeed, by contrast with the drab world of Janson, his education at home was free and full of creativity. It required excellence at school, to be sure, but promised a great deal in return. And the father initiated much of it, by inclination and by calling.

An education in the arts

A grandfather who was a composer and conductor, a father and two uncles who were painters – a biographical configuration to which Lévi-Strauss often attributed his own taste for the arts: 'My entire early childhood and adolescence were spent in this overheated atmosphere, in a relationship of intimacy with painting and music.'[36]

Painting was the father's domain. 'The image I have of him is that of a highly cultivated man with an insatiable curiosity, whose interests were not limited to the field of painting. He was also passionate about music and literature.'[37] Raymond Lévi-Strauss was a man of gentle nature. An authoritarian father he was most definitely not, even if his son did recall a few pranks (cheating at school) that incurred paternal ire and were met with harsh punishment. Confident in the instruction dispensed to Claude, and infused with great moral rigour, he was, in short, a consummate man of the Third Republic who, on Sundays, when school grades had been good, took his son to the Louvre as a reward. One can just picture the father and child strolling through the great repository of Western art, the father honing the son's eye for beauty, for fine execution, as well as for a form of pictorial honesty, pointing out the more technical challenges that revealed his own skill, acquired through his studies at the Beaux-Arts. This aesthetic education was not just an initiation into the history of art. On the contrary, what is striking was its very concrete relationship to artistic practice. For each intellectual discovery, the young Lévi-Strauss simultaneously tried his hand at creation. Before producing cubist-inspired drawings, informed by his later enthusiasm for Picasso, he learned to recreate the shapes of objects and of bodies with the greatest possible accuracy. Hence the little bunny rabbit that appears to be waking up, rubbing its nose and shaking its mischievous snout – one of his drawings that has remained, evidence of a classical studio training. The anatomy of the animal in motion is impressive for its accuracy and freshness. One cannot really tell if the young artist in short pants had talent. 'He was learning the ropes', as Roger Caillois would say.[38] Later, unquestionable graphic skill would be revealed in his travel notebooks, in the sketches, the patterns of Kadiweu facial and body paint, the precise representations of labrets, penis sheaths, maces, knives and feather diadems that are interspersed throughout *Tristes Tropiques*. For these drawings were all by Lévi-Strauss himself. An anthropologist requires many skills.

As for music, it played perhaps an even more important role in the life and work of Lévi-Strauss. Each week, his father took him to the concerts organized by Pasdeloup, an amateur orchestra and veritable institution that made it possible for large audiences of modest means to hear live music. The Lévi-Strausses also regularly went to hear the Colonne Orchestra at the Théâtre du Châtelet. Young Claude remembered being taken there at a very young age, being seated 'in these fifth loges that indeed no longer exist since we couldn't see anything from them – but happily, we could hear! – and being initiated to the entire Wagner repertoire'.[39] Note the resourcefulness of the father, determined to give his son a taste for the joys of music, and especially of opera, despite his limited means. Wagner was the object of a family cult, if not in the same way as Offenbach, with as much intensity. The son embraced this passion, to which, notwithstanding a few infidelities, he would remain attached throughout his life. 'Wagner played a capital role in my intellectual development and in my taste for myths, even if I only became aware of this fact well after my childhood. [. . .] Let's say that I was brooding on Wagner for several decades.'[40] Here again, from very early on, he was seized by the urge to take part. The young boy dreamed of being a composer, mimicked the sweeping and commanding gestures of the conductor, and took violin lessons with a violist from the Opera. Opera was for him a true passion, since it combined all the arts. It was a model of total art, of which Wagner was the most uncompromising example in the excited mind of the young Claude, prone to bursts of enthusiasm and diverse inclinations.

Indeed, music and painting did not reign exclusively over the adolescent dabbler: he also wrote a play, drafted a libretto and took photographs. One of his pictures illustrates the artistic proclivities of the young photographer as he discovers the spectral virtues of the new medium: it is a dramatization – complete with paper mask, bowler hat and candelabra – developing a postsymbolist variation on the theme of the Danse Macabre.[41]

'A thousand curiosities'[42]

Thus, a whole range of intellectual and artistic pursuits offered themselves up to the voracious young boy as he emerged from early childhood, ready for any and all form of experimentation: writing, musical composition, painting, photography, as well as, again, theatre. 'The parents of a friend of ours lived in Villa Scheffer, a mansion in which the receiving rooms formed a kind of small theatre. We put on several plays there. [. . .] We did Labiche, Courteline, Musset and, not lacking in audacity, we were rehearsing *Mangeront-ils?* by Victor Hugo – my colleague Jean Bernard was part of the troupe and remembers it – when Pierre's father died. This bereavement brought our rehearsals to an end. We stopped doing comedy entirely.'[43]

Besides its density and multiplicity, what might set this childhood apart from one with a classical bourgeois education, which of course revolved around these sorts of activities, was the passion with which certain of the interests were pursued, undertaken with the scrupulous rigour and obsessive energy of a zealot. For example, the cult of rare objects, of 'exotic curios': 'I have a most intimate relationship with them. I have collected them since childhood. My first, a Japanese stamp, which I still possess, was given to me by my father. I remember having placed it in a box, to decorate the bottom, and then every time I received a bit of money I would go to a store on rue des Petits-Champs called 'À la Pagode' to buy miniature furniture, Japanese or otherwise, to recreate a Japanese house in my box. This habit of collecting has never left me.'[44] The impulse to collect, the quest for the object, the aesthetic of the 'find' – whether it be a pebble on the beach, a rock fragment during a stroll, or an ancient coin – in which chance always plays a part, entails wandering the world, with all one's senses constantly at the ready.

The capital city of Lévi-Strauss's early years offered the perfect setting for this bubbling sensibility and its overflowing curiosity. The young Claude would traverse Paris, scouring book stalls along the banks of the Seine with his friend Pierre Dreyfus, nosing around; or, thanks to buses, zipping across the city, in long tracking shots that 'kaleidoscoped' his vision. 'When I was at the *lycée*, a time when all buses had an open platform at the back, I would huddle in a corner, first the right then the left, in order to see simultaneously passing before my eyes one side of the street and the reflection of the other side in the windows. When the bus came close to the sidewalk, a normal street became an alleyway in which the two sides threatened to merge in a harrowing way. And when it pulled away, the same street opened up like an avenue of unexpected width. But this urban phantasmagoria that I conjured up in this way was only stirring up and transforming another one, quite real.'[45] At the same time, in the early 1920s, another teenager with a keen mind, who also devoted his prodigious sensory and intellectual energies to discovering the beauty of his city, indulged in similar visual experimentation. The young Vladimir Nabokov, who had found refuge in Berlin, took great delight in the splashing iridescence of rain-pummelled asphalt, and shared with

Lévi-Strauss a passion for urban culture that made of the city an unparalleled spectacle, a treasure to be discovered, a mystery deciphered, triggering these hallucinatory visions that intensified reality more than they masked it.[46]

But the gaze was also turned in other directions. Nature's spectacle was just as vital for the adolescent Lévi-Strauss, quick to mount 'expeditions' of which today's teenagers could only dream. No need to venture very far; in the suburbs of Paris the landscape was already transformed, and on the outskirts of Paris one was transported to an entirely other place. 'Making the most of several days' vacation, I once set out with two friends to follow the Seine from Rouen to Le Havre on foot, carrying a heavy tarp as a tent. Waking up on our first morning, we discovered that an initial turn in the path had led us back to our point of departure. Discouraged, we gave up the plan. There were other trips, sometimes by bicycle, that were more successful: a Loire Valley château, the Belgian Ardennes and Luxembourg, from the Normandy coast to Vieux-Moulin [near Compiègne] through Bray.'[47] These early experiences of landscape, this first lesson in geography (the turn in the path), were followed by many others, including mishaps that sometimes lent the adventures of the young Lévi-Strauss a farcical quality: 'Around the age of fourteen, I discovered the quarries at Cormeille-en-Parisis. I fell into a pool of gypsum water and found myself up to my neck in plaster.'[48]

An heir without inheritance

Yet this childhood full of wonder was not entirely idyllic; indeed, Lévi-Strauss never concealed the recurring material difficulties and financial turbulence that often darkened the skies over rue Poussin.

Downward mobility and academic excellence

After 1918, everything looked the same as before and yet nothing quite was. To be sure, the family returned to the same building and apartment, now equipped with a telephone in the concierge's apartment (running down the five flights of stairs at full speed and merrily or pensively climbing back up, once the call was over, became a daily routine).[49] This device of technological modernity intruded into the old world as a sign of changing times. Another more troublesome one was inflation, which prevailed after the war; the monetary response to the public debt inherited from the war triggered, all over Europe and especially in France (though not as much as in Germany), an upheaval in prewar economic and social hierarchies. Established fortunes collapsed, young go-getters struck it rich. As Stefan Zweig described it so well in *The World of Yesterday*, the stable world and abiding realities, the temporality of the long nineteenth century, were being swallowed up.[50] This devaluation also affected the world of aesthetics, with the triumph of belle-époque modernity, which relegated the artistic tastes and works of the likes of Raymond Lévi-Strauss to a purgatory of the old-fashioned.

As far as the family was concerned, the course of downward mobility had already started a while back, and life had never been very easy, materially speaking. Raymond Lévi-Strauss, when he made his professional choice to give up work at the stock exchange, effected a kind of *coup de force*, which made sense in terms of the family genealogy, but was to leave him in a permanent state of economic precariousness. On the financial front, the post-1918 period intensified a previously existing state of financial dependence: the Lévi-Strauss couple lived in part on Isaac's royalties and the help of a rich brother of Raymond's – 'Uncle Jean' the stockbroker – who covered part of the family's needs, until he himself went bankrupt following the 1929 crash.[51] Portrait commissions for Raymond dwindled considerably after the war, to almost nothing. Hence the ambivalent status of this childhood, bourgeois in the cultural stimulation and lifestyle it provided (not leaving Paris for the holidays was out of the question), still in touch with the vestiges of former affluence, and yet constantly disturbed by the difficulties of making ends meet. Every penny counted with the Lévi-Strausses. Anxiety about paying the rent – a classic working-class concern – constantly hovered over this child of the 16th arrondissement. Whether or not to have domestic staff was another clear indicator of social status, and there never were any on rue Poussin. Which also explains why, when describing his mother, Claude characterized her as first and foremost 'a dutiful woman, who for a long time demonstrated extraordinary courage and self-sacrifice, performing all the domestic duties'.[52] For many years in the early 1920s, before acquiring an old silk farm in the Cévennes thanks to Uncle Jean's subsidies, the Lévi-Strausses would spend their holidays with Belgian friends, the Cahens, in a villa the latter rented. In exchange, Emma Lévi-Strauss would take care of the household chores and meals.[53] It is easy to imagine the effect of this kind of social fiction, one that dramatized the stark tension between the family's objective condition (being in charge of organizing meals) and a bourgeois subject position (being the host) derived from the past, and from values and friendships.

The father's professional failure must have been all the more painful as it was a vocational choice, and Denis Bertholet is right to see in Raymond a kind of 'anti-Isaac Strauss, a figure of decline'.[54] Furthermore, the other artist in the family, the violinist and conductor Robert Alphen-Strauss (father of Rirette [Henriette] Nizan), returned from the war missing several fingers that had been torn off by a grenade, preventing him from ever resuming his musical career. He went back to the world of business, from whence he came, and muddled along until retirement. The war thus sealed the fate of the artistic calling announced by the hyphenated name.

Are the children of a downwardly mobile bourgeoisie more likely to produce intellectual excellence and innovation? Does a desire to make up for the fallen father figure favour the development of a particularly effective form of compensatory commitment? Indeed, similar trajectories characterize two other major French intellectual figures of the century, who were to one degree or another comrades of Lévi-Strauss. First, Raymond Aron, with whom Lévi-Strauss has himself pointed out the 'many parallels in [their] lives: Versailles, Lycée Hoche, Condorcet and "family misfortunes"'.[55] While not related, both families emerged out of assimilated Judaism, were patriotic and enjoyed a certain degree of material comfort. In both cases, the father starkly rejected business in favour of an intellectual (Aron's father became an academic lawyer) or artistic calling, a choice enabled in part by the high regard in the Jewish tradition for pursuits of the mind. And for both fathers the choice resulted in failure. The young Aron was thus possessed by a desire to compensate for his father's humiliation: 'I would cancel his disappointments with my successes', as he would later write.[56] The loss of the family's money on the stock exchange in 1929 and the sale of their Versailles home further confirmed the son's relegation to the world of the salaried professorship, having lost all reserves of wealth and learning to live solely on his pay cheque. From his affluent childhood, Aron had nonetheless retained, he says, a kind of 'casual attitude' to money, which was never the case for Lévi-Strauss. The Beauvoir family also followed the same path of downward mobility, hit first by the First World War and then further by the 1929 crash. Here again, the disruption was dramatic, even if the emotional shock and pain at the father's decline was experienced differently due to the fact that the offspring were both girls. 'If he liked intelligent women, my father had no taste for blue stockings. When he declared to us "you girls will not marry, you will have to work", there was bitterness in his voice. I thought he felt sorry for us, but in fact, in our hard-working future, he saw his own loss of status. It was against his unjust fate of having two *déclassé* daughters that he was fulminating.'[57] In the end, though, regardless of the differences (economic or gender) in their initial situations, a kind of invisible hand of social redress guided all three family stories to miraculous recovery. The economic and financial capital that had vanished over one generation, or two in the case of the Lévi-Strausses, was transformed into intellectual (already present, to some extent) and, above all, academic capital.

Indeed, the Lévi-Strauss family took academic performance very seriously: 'This tragic atmosphere around my grades that reigned at home weighed heavily on me.'[58] A classic finding of intellectual sociology – the drive for academic achievement among Jewish families as one of the surest paths to upward mobility – was powerfully illustrated here. Financial insecurity only fed the logic of hyper-investment in elite education.[59] These heirs without inheritance, or rather heirs to 'an inheritance of being, not having',[60] readily assumed the role of star pupil. Indeed, Claude Lévi-Strauss did so effortlessly, despite his lack of enthusiasm for the classical educational system of the 1920s – i.e., the Jesuit tradition – martial in orientation and closed off to the world. As Raymond Aron remembered Lycée Hoche in Versailles: 'Its style had retained traces of the Napoleonic era. The pupils would enter the schoolyard in order; in class, they had to remain still and pay close attention for several hours in a row. I remember a German language teacher who, one day, gave the whole class a good grade because all the students had behaved impeccably as he

walked in – their arms folded on their desks.'[61] The same ambience characterized Janson-de-Sailly, where Lévi-Strauss attended middle school in
1918 and continued until obtaining the *baccalauréat* in June 1925, at the
age of sixteen. His boundless curiosity was given more opportunities to
soar outside school than inside, at least until philosophy classes started,
ushering in a period of intense interest in the discipline. This academic
excellence, which came quite easily to him, was one possible way of
compensating for social decline. There were others, more to do with the
resourcefulness of father and son, more in line with their taste for objects
and their tactile sensibility, which conferred on artisanal work a basic
dignity that was all the more fundamental with the Lévi-Strausses for its
resonance with long-established biographical practice.

Bricolage: a worldview

This biographical practice was also a social experience. When, in 1988,
Didier Éribon interviewed the octogenarian anthropologist and asked
him if he had had the childhood of a member of the Parisian bourgeoisie,
the latter gave a measured answer: on the one hand, a rich intellectual
life; on the other, financial concerns. And bricolage – these improvised
artisanal projects – served precisely as a kind of safety valve for family
anxiety, while also precluding any straightforward identification with
a classic bourgeois childhood. 'I remember the anxieties when there
weren't any commissions. Then my father, who was a great improviser
[*bricoleur*], would come up with all sorts of little projects. For a time, the
whole house became involved in printing fabrics. We carved linoleum
blocks and smeared them with glue. We used to print designs on velvet on
which we sprinkled metallic powders of various colours. [. . .] There was
another time when my father made small Chinese-style tables of imitation
lacquer. He also made lamps with cheap Japanese prints glued onto glass.
Anything that would help pay the bills.'[62]
   The son nevertheless derived considerable creative pleasure from these
survival strategies: he invented his own models, played at being a great
fashion designer during the fabric period and helped lacquer tables. The
entire apartment was filled with quirky objects of one kind or another,
according to the trend of the moment, each invested with the hope of
exchange for hard cash. This was the childlike stage set of a bourgeois
family turned Bohemian, more out of necessity than inclination.
   This spirit of bricolage, which became part of Lévi-Strauss's early
existence, also constitutes one of the sustained motifs of his own life
as well as that of structuralism. Indeed, it would become a reflexive
metaphor in many fields of contemporary thought. But we get ahead of
ourselves. Returning to the lacquer and velvet, the refined taste and artisanal know-how, the appreciation of materials, textures, objects and techniques, in which the young boy was immersed in the family home with a
mixture of enjoyment (creating new things out of scattered elements) and
anxiety (resources were limited), bricolage may well have constituted, for

Lévi-Strauss, the very locus of thought: 'My father was a great *bricoleur* and I was a great *bricoleur*. [. . .] The taste for bricolage was not simply a pastime, a hobby, it was about accessing something absolutely fundamental in the act of creation. [Bricolage] is about having a problem to solve. One has certain random elements available that bear no relation to the problem at hand. And then there is an effort of thought: how am I going to manage to resolve my particular problem with these elements that come from elsewhere. This seems to me to be essential in the functioning of human thought.'[63]

The son's taste for modernism

Between school and family life, concerns about the future and creative marvels, the child came of age. By the mid-1920s, as he was completing his schooling with distinction, he had become enthralled by the modernist agitation that was spreading through the world capital of the avant-garde. In June of 1923, at the age of fifteen, he attended one of the first productions of Stravinsky's *Les Noces* at the Théâtre de la Gaîté. Deeply moved, he returned for the next performance. That single evening, he later recalled, rendered all his past musical convictions obsolete.[64] Attending the symbolist opera *Pelléas et Mélisande* by Debussy, which dated from 1902, was another memorable musical experience – the new genre of interior drama, the enigmatic prose, the apparent simplicity of the orchestration. 'When Pelléas and Mélisande finally confess their love for each other [. . .] without accompaniment – the orchestra responds with a simple textbook progression moving from a tonic chord to its dominant seventh, except that in Debussy's spectral scoring it sounds like the dawn of creation.'[65] After the Wagner of his childhood, Debussy and Stravinsky, whom he 'venerated as a god',[66] were the conquests of his young adulthood. Always one to back up his words with deeds, Lévi-Strauss even recalled having made, in a surge of enthusiasm, 'large decorations for the room of one of [his] comrades that were entirely inspired by Stravinsky's *Noces*'.[67] But he also listened to black American music on the family gramophone. Thus, about a book by Claude McKay, one of the leading lights of the Harlem Renaissance, he spoke in 1931 of those 'negro voices of which the first recording of "Spirituals" ten years ago was a revelation for us'.[68] In the field of painting, it was Picasso he worshipped each week: 'When I was sixteen or seventeen, Picasso was for me a god, whom I placed on a pedestal next to Stravinsky. A week would not go by without my visiting the great galleries of paintings. And when I saw the latest Picasso on display I had the impression of experiencing a metaphysical revelation.'[69] Cubism was also the subject of a first article that he was invited to write at the time by an art critic friend of his father's, Louis Vauxcelles, entitled 'The Influence of Cubism in Daily Life', whose reception by its commissioner we do not know.

In these confessions about his passions as a young man, one is struck by the religious metaphor that recurs spontaneously, as if self-evident, to convey the force of the aesthetic experience: the serious-looking adolescent, strapped into his school uniform, is eager for disruptions, intellectual electroshocks and sensory jolts. From that standpoint, he was in harmony with the sensibility of his times: the new art, according to Walter Benjamin, yet another seismographer of modern culture, seeks out perceptual shocks rather than the sweet pleasures of enjoyment.[70] Yet what made the son's pulse quicken – artistic modernism – was also driving the father into bankruptcy. In the 1920s, the latter's pictorial practice was made completely irrelevant by the legitimation of the prewar modernist avant-garde. Debussy, Stravinsky, Picasso and, soon, surrealism, which the younger Lévi-Strauss followed avidly – this was no longer Raymond's world, and rather early in life (he was forty) the father was made to feel aesthetically obsolete.

Even as he inherited a sense of the sanctity of art and books, year after year the son gradually asserted himself against the father and his milieu. But his rebellion was gentle,[71] an offering to an insatiable curiosity for a world that had already been shattered in the trenches of the Somme, and that presented to Lévi-Strauss's generation a face covered in scars.

3

Revolutions (1924–1931): Politics vs. Philosophy

> The revolutionary, excitedly leaning over the boat's prow, suddenly discovers at each bend in the river entirely new perspectives, whose radical originality seems utterly disconnected from previous ones. The reality he perceives and constructs in front of him presents itself with the absolute novelty and total fullness that belong to mystery and dogma.
>
> Claude Lévi-Strauss, *L'Étudiant socialiste* (1930)[1]

Aesthetic raptures were followed by revelations of another kind – namely, intellectual and political. Moving from happy acceptance to rejection of the established world order, Lévi-Strauss appears to have followed the classic trajectory of youthful rebellion, as well as, more specifically, that of his entire generation, damaged and outraged by the mass slaughter of the First World War.

Between 1924 and 1931, his school and university years were ones of fierce militancy, in a sharp break with the conservatism of his milieu. It is difficult to imagine the great anthropologist as a socialist activist stirring up crowds of students in Parisian brasseries, and yet . . . Even if relatively well documented, this socialist period was systematically suppressed by Claude Lévi-Strauss himself, who either kept it entirely concealed or established a watertight seal around his activist and scholarly commitments, reducing them to a kind of 'youthful folly'. But everything points to the fact that, on the contrary, revolutionary socialism was for him a great revelation.

An archival scrap captures the duality of these years well: a white sheet of paper on which the young philosophy student scribbled some notes; on the other side, we discover a letterhead from the Assemblée nationale, where Lévi-Strauss was for a time assistant to the deputy Georges Monnet.[2] Between the ages of seventeen and twenty-three, he appears to have divided his time between his philosophy studies, which were both dense and superficial, remote from worldly concerns, and a political passion that emerged as the flip side of academic routine. If politics and philosophy were intertwined in the student's life, if they nourished each other through his reading, they remained starkly different undertakings: whereas politics runs along at full speed, academic philosophy is a tamer of passions. How was he to reconcile the two? By thinking politics. The young philosophy student, weaned on Marx and Kant, toyed with the idea . . . and it is probably not unreasonable to imagine that he could have become, several years on, with the rise of the Front populaire, an excellent chief of staff to a minister of education, or some such, and later a great thinker of the socialist left. This was, indeed, a most plausible scenario.

Converting to left politics and to philosophy

In 1924, Claude Lévi-Strauss was introduced to the study of philosophy, which was part of the curriculum in the last year of *lycée* for students choosing to study the humanities. For the best among them, the hope was to be accepted to *classes préparatoires*, once they had obtained their *baccalauréat*. These philosophy classes, as Raymond Aron has suggested, offered a critical perspective that, whatever the professor's political orientation, 'usually fostered the sentiments of the left'. It might even pave the way, in his opinion, for a 'conversion to left politics'.[3] The phrase is all the more suited to Claude Lévi-Strauss, given that the intensity of his relationship to the world, as we have seen, was often expressed in religious terms.

Marx, Belgium and a philosophy course (1924–1925)

Lévi-Strauss has often described his first meeting with Arthur Wauters, a friend of the Cahens, the Belgian family with which his parents spent many summer vacations. It took place during the summer of 1924, or perhaps 1925, since Lévi-Strauss has given different accounts of his age at the time. The abruptness, speed and wholeheartedness with which he threw himself into this watershed moment marked a clear rupture with his life up to that point, suggestive indeed of a true 'conversion'.

Arthur Wauters (1890–1960), an activist nearly twenty years his senior, became a kind of political 'elder brother', who initiated the young Lévi-Strauss into Belgian-style socialism. When they met, the former was already a rising star within the Belgian Workers' Party. Later, he became a professor of political economy at the Free University of Brussels, and then pursued a successful career in politics as chief of staff at the ministry headed by his biological brother Joseph Wauters, minister of labour and welfare. He was the political editor of the socialist newspaper *Le Peuple* from 1929 to 1937, at which point he was himself appointed minister of public health in the Van Zeeland socialist government. In 1940, while in power, he did not experience the vagaries of other social democratic politicians, since he joined the Belgian government in exile in London, and ended his career as Belgian ambassador to Moscow. It is easy to imagine the passionate discussions that ensued, in the idleness of summer, between the energetic teenager keen to understand the world and the still youthful 'aspiring theorist' who found a worthy audience: 'I was sixteen or seventeen years old. I think it was the year of my philosophy course. [. . .] So I asked this activist to explain to me how it all worked. [. . .] He immediately threw himself into my education, giving me numerous lectures, and above all having me read Marx, Jaurès, and many others.'[4] This intensive ideological initiation was almost immediately combined with a practical one: he 'brought me to Belgium as an invited guest of the Labour Party and, for two weeks, an older activist took me around from worker organizations [Maisons du peuple] to cooperatives . . . .'[5] Lévi-Strauss has even said elsewhere that he became a kind of 'ward of the Belgian Workers' Party',[6] further consolidating his link with that country and its political model, in which socialist ideals were implemented through the party's affiliation with numerous economic and syndicalist organs.

Indeed, the discovery of socialist ideas had the effect on him of being integrated into a new family, since his own was not at all politicized. As he recalled, it was 'a good bourgeois family that had seen better days, conservative in outlook. Except possibly at the time of the Dreyfus affair. My father and his brother used to tell a story about going to a pro-Dreyfus demonstration where Jaurès was speaking. At the end they went up to thank him, and he said ambiguously: "I hope that you will remember this." Which meant, "You come over to our side but then immediately back off." That was the exact truth.'[7] The son made up for the passivity and legitimism of the father with all the more energy, since his political commitment was aligned with his intellectual appetite.

In October 1924, Claude Lévi-Strauss began that special moment of his formal education – namely, the philosophy course – intended as the consummation of the *lycée* curriculum, endowing students with a form of critical thinking deemed essential by the founders of republican pedagogy. Unique to France, this secondary school training in philosophy was the heart of powerful intellectual and existential expectations – a moment of grace, of revelation, of sentimental identification with one's professor, etc. What appealed to young Aron, for instance, about his philosophy class, which was taught by an otherwise uninspiring professor, was the work, however laborious, of open-ended thought – the idea that what mattered was to ask the right questions, rather than to find answers. Surprisingly, nothing of the kind happened with Lévi-Strauss. From an academic point of view, even though he was listed on the honour roll, his grades were satisfactory but not exceptional: 'Very clear progress; thinking is getting more precise and solid; on the right track.'[8] Even though his philosophy teacher, Gustave Rodrigues, was an activist in the SFIO (French Section of the Workers' International), and the future president of the League of Human Rights, thereby seeming to bring together the two poles of philosophy and politics, the portrait given of him by his student thirty years later was cruel: 'On the philosophical level all he had to offer was a mixture of Bergsonism and neo-Kantianism which I found extremely disappointing. He expounded his dry dogmatic views with great fervour and gesticulated passionately throughout his lessons. I have never known so much naive conviction allied with such intellectual poverty.' He added dryly: 'He committed suicide in 1940, when the Germans entered Paris',[9] offering a glimpse into the despair of a man whose moral commitment would appear to jar with the dismissive treatment given him by his most accomplished student.

In any case, if politics and philosophy were inextricably linked by then, it was practical politics and the discovery of theoretical works that prevailed over the thin Bergsonian socialism provided by his philosophy teacher. For his conversion to socialism went hand in hand with the close reading of doctrinal works, which had a profound impact on the philosophical reflections of the young Lévi-Strauss. In all his interviews, he has consistently emphasized his discovery of Marx, but always pointed to 'many other' thinkers as well. Arthur Wauters had just published *L'Évolution du marxisme depuis la mort de Marx* (1924) when he met Claude Lévi-Strauss, and one is left to wonder whether, rather than to Marx himself, the young acolyte was not initiated into critical versions and theoretical revisions of Marx, which played a more important role in Belgian socialism than in its rather less doctrinally driven French counterpart. Still, Lévi-Strauss, if we are to take him at his word, read Marx rather than Bergson. And through Marx an entire philosophical tradition was revealed to him, as is often the case with major works that carry within them, in addition to their own genius, the major themes of their traditions: 'I was all the more delighted by Marx in that the reading of the works of the great thinker brought me into contact for the first time with the line of philosophical development running from Kant to Hegel; a whole new world was opened up to me.'[10]

Preparing for the École normale supérieure exam but not taking it (1925–1926)

In the autumn of 1925, our young Kantian-Marxist began the intensive two-year preparation course for the École normale supérieure at Lycée Condorcet, the most prestigious school of Paris's Right Bank and the historical challenger to the Latin Quarter's Louis le Grand and Henri IV, which produced the lion's share of successful candidates to the École normale supérieure. At Condorcet – as opposed to its Left Bank rivals, where first-year (*hypokhâgne*) and second-year (*khâgne*) students were separated – all students were combined in a single class, including those arriving fresh from *lycée* graduation and those having already completed their first year. The world of *khâgne* preparatory school was an intimidating one. Aron confessed to having entered with 'the timidity and ambitions of a provincial arriving in the capital'.[11] For the sociologist Pierre Bourdieu, himself a product of this training, '*khâgne* was the site where French-style intellectual ambition in its most elevated, that is to say, philosophical, form was exhibited'.[12] How did Claude Lévi-Strauss feel amidst this academic aristocracy, preparing for the highly competitive entrance exam to the elite École normale supérieure on rue d'Ulm?

His classmates were impressed by a certain aplomb, a gravitas, but also a sense of humour and unusual talents. In the words of Jean Maugüe, with whom Lévi-Strauss would cross paths again in Brazil: 'His slender silhouette that appeared to have come out of some Egyptian bas-relief seemed plagued by an incurable ennui. But his severe and prudent face was sometimes illuminated by the most unexpected, childlike smile. His reputation in *khâgne* was based on the figures he would draw in chalk on the blackboard, which conjured up in our minds the strange towns of German cinema, such as *The Cabinet of Dr. Caligari.*[13] Stéphane Clouet has unearthed Lévi-Strauss's grade reports, which attest to his solid performance, with perhaps a few weaknesses that were not crippling:[14] 'great subtlety' in philosophy, writes his professor, André Cresson; 'steady progress' in English (Mr Travers). Despite high grades, he is described as 'young' and 'still young and somewhat scattered', in French (Mr Parigot) and Latin (Mr Pécher), respectively. The comments of his history teacher, Mr Cahen, are more striking, for they appear to capture the sensibility of the young Lévi-Strauss, with all the benevolent insight of a spiritual adviser: 'Student of value, will mature. Knows a lot. A fine and penetrating mind. But these qualities are often marred by a most ordinary, almost sectarian rigour, the assertion of radical and dismissive theories, and sometimes his thinking settles for a rather banal, unspecific and unoriginal style.' This same history teacher, who offered such a severe assessment of the style of the future author of *Tristes Tropiques*, provided the impetus for the writing of the very first text Lévi-Strauss ever published, an essay on Gracchus Babeuf that was to become an opuscule, appearing in 1926 with L'Églantine, the Belgian publishing house of his new socialist friends. The text is an oddity in the vast literature around Babeuf, one of the pioneering and heroic figures of the communist saga. 'It is unquestionably Babeuf's work that marked the first appearance of socialism in history',[15] writes Lévi-Strauss. At the time, the figure of Babeuf was the exclusive reserve of ideological Robespierrism; the young socialist appropriated it with remarkable fervour, pointing out the doctrinal dimension and utopian relevance of the champion of agrarian reform and pure communism. If his sights were probably already set elsewhere, on his political activism, and if he appeared in any case not terribly enthusiastic about the education he was receiving, Lévi-Strauss was on the whole a good student in *khâgne*.

Why, then, did he decide against taking the noble path to the École normale before even once trying the entrance examination? His decision to abandon this course is difficult to decipher, especially given the material circumstances of his parents, which should have acted as a further incentive to try for the École normale. For, once admitted, students at the École normale, or *normaliens* as they were called, were considered civil servants and received a salary. The socio-demographic profile of these students in the interwar period was not that of the French haute bourgeoisie, and a good portion of this academic elite was motivated by material considerations.[16] Claude Lévi-Strauss did invoke difficulties in mathematics (at which he said he was 'hopeless') as well as in ancient Greek. He also appeared to not fully adhere to the spirit of *khâgne*, the intensive preparatory course, with its total devotion to philosophy. Indeed, his eclectic and not terribly bookish proclivities may even have foreclosed any affinity with the worldview of the aspiring *normalien*. His philosophy teacher, aware of his being different, even advised him to try something else: 'When I decided to leave the course, he said to me "Philosophy is not

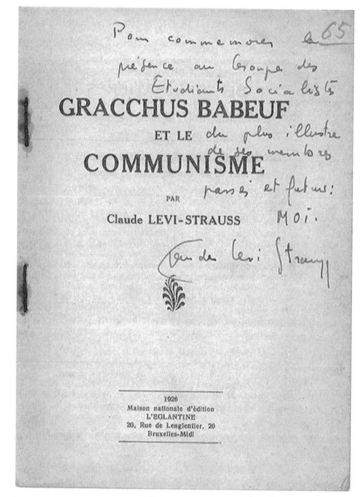

The cover of the book published by L'Églantine, with an inscription to
Maurice Deixonne, a friend from the Socialist Students group, in the ironic style
of young *khâgne* students of the time.

for you, but something close to it." And he suggested law. In the end, it
would be anthropology, but he had the right idea.'[17] This decision, which
was a proper exit in the sense of the term given by the sociologist Albert
Hirschman[18] – quitting, leaving, no longer being there – can also probably
be explained in terms of psychological, and even moral, factors: the brutal
sense of imposture combined with that of 'not being at [the same] level',[19]
low self-esteem (which did not preclude manifest pride), a refusal to play
the game and a sense of unease with organized competition. If the latter
stimulated the young Aron, it may well have discouraged Lévi-Strauss.
The decision to exit was not anomalous in his career, which contained

other examples, as a possible solution for escaping situations of stalemate or impossible choice.

Meanwhile, this decision had major consequences: the young student who was to enrol at the Sorbonne the following year for a double degree in philosophy and law would have free time to engage in political activities that *khâgne* would have foreclosed. Instead, lacking the salary that the *normalien* would have enjoyed, he had to work multiple small jobs, serving to broaden his social experience but never managing to keep at bay an ever-present anxiety about money. Finally, by moving away from the rue d'Ulm, Claude Lévi-Strauss was distancing himself from the 'young prodigies' of the French intelligentsia: Sartre, Aron, Nizan, Merleau-Ponty and many others. For this generation, the École normale was a necessary rite of passage. Just before he died, Pierre Bourdieu – who belonged to the following generation – looked back on his years at the École normale and drew an ambivalent picture of the French intellectual world, with all its grandeur and flaws, which he saw as resulting from its pedagogical model: a scholastic sequestration of a monastic kind (the rue d'Ulm cloisters), a knee-jerk faith in intellectual power, a sense of universal authority, an esprit de corps, as well as a profound ignorance of the social world which can lead to irresponsible ideological radicalism. All this was profoundly foreign to Claude Lévi-Strauss. This disparity may even account for later quarrels, especially with Sartre and his wholesale enthusiasm for the committed intellectual, which Lévi-Strauss's sensibility could not embrace. But we should not overstate this opposition: even if Claude Lévi-Strauss was not a *normalien*, he would pass the *agrégation*, qualifying him to be a professor of philosophy, and become secretary of a group of socialist students from the various Écoles normales, even while not being a student at any of them, making him a kind of 'phantom *normalien*'!

Apprentice philosopher and militant socialist

The zombie student[20]

One remembers the famous full-throated attack on philosophy delivered in *Tristes Tropiques*: Lévi-Strauss's dismantling of rhetoric – thesis, antithesis, synthesis – as the pillar of all essay composition and philosophical reflection; his critique of a mode of reasoning that had been reduced to 'an art of punning' and 'speculative acrobatics'. He dismissed this kind of mental gymnastics as artificial, facile, systematic, vain, futile and dangerous, for it made a parody of what it actually meant to think. 'I was confident that, with ten minutes' notice, I could knock together an hour's lecture with a sound dialectical framework, on the respective superiority of buses or trams.'[21] Whether deriding the rhetorical exercises or criticizing the desiccating effects of a discipline that proceeded 'in a vacuum', in a 'state of intense perspiration', Claude Lévi-Strauss recalled gasping for breath, feeling estranged, foreign, totally out of touch with the discipline as a student. Does the violence of his diatribe attest to that of his experience, or was it intended to serve as the opening salvo in the anthropological offensive he was mounting in the 1950s and 1960s to depose the reigning discipline, the 'crowning discipline',[22] of French education? Probably both.

Was Claude Lévi-Strauss really the 'zombie student' he claimed to be? From 1926 to 1930, he easily passed through the various stages of his studies, obtaining degrees. But this impeccable academic record does not preclude a form of imposture on the part of the good student who adapts, chameleon-like, to the criteria of academic excellence, while still feeling rather alienated from it. He did confess, in a 1971 interview, to having been a 'passionate Spinozist', adding that he was 'intransigent as to the idea and place of philosophy'.[23] Before revolting against it, Lévi-Strauss may indeed have been very invested in the philosophical project, with which he maintained an ambivalent relationship throughout his life.

In fact, his sense that academic philosophy was somewhat vacuous and lacking in substance was common to that entire generation of students, whose most groundbreaking representatives were each to draw their own lessons. In his *Memoirs*, Aron also condemned the kind of empty thinking machine that philosophical education had become – steering clear of any contact with the political and social world, like a frightened virgin. But it was Paul Nizan who delivered the definitive indictment in *The Watchdogs* (1932). While he agreed with Nizan's diagnosis and analysis, with 'a Marxist critique of institutional philosophy', Claude Lévi-Strauss did not identify with his energetic lampooning, however prone to it on occasion he might have been himself: 'I respected the masters he so vigorously attacked. For we had the same teachers, a few years apart. I respected Brunschvicg, Laporte, Robin, etc.'[24] The Sorbonne was then presided over by a few mandarins, Brunschvicg first and the most powerful among them, as well as Albert Rivaud, Jean Laporte, Louis Bréhier, Léon Robin in Greek philosophy, Paul Fauconnet and Célestin Bouglé (two disciples of Durkheim) in sociology, Abel Rey in the history of science, etc. All, recalled Claude Lévi-Strauss, had been his professors: in the autumn of 1929, Brunschvicg gave a course on Kant's *Critique of Practical Reason*, Rivaud on Descartes's *Principles* and Maine de Biran.[25] Students would then prepare, under their masters' supervision, for degrees in logic, psychology (a discipline that was very present but in non-empirical form), moral philosophy, sociology and general philosophy, which was often nothing but a history of philosophy, if not a history of philosophical progress. As the sociologist Jean-Louis Fabiani has shown, philosophy was and remains a discipline informed by 'the all-encompassing curriculum',[26] because it is taught as part of the last year of secondary school, and because of the close connections between secondary and university education in France. The *baccalauréat* curriculum thus determined many of the debates in the discipline. And this curriculum was characterized first and foremost by a very conservative approach. Indeed, between 1880 and 1914, it did not change much at all, and 'its fixed character has encouraged a reiteration of the same forms and worked against the inclusion of the human sciences in secondary education'.[27] On the philosophical land-scape of the time, the range of possibilities was limited to three options, which Lévi-Strauss delineated perfectly: 'either a philosophy that focused on abstractions, or one that focused on the self and intimate experience, or else one that claimed to reason based on a vast human experience, but which in fact mutilated it.'[28] In other words, either a metaphysics anchored in an idealist tradition, represented by Brunschvicg's neo-Kantianism; or the fashionable Bergsonian philosophy taught at the Collège de France by Henri Bergson himself, a celebrated philosopher well beyond the sphere of academia (whom Lévi-Strauss would later come to give his due); or else Durkheimian sociology as taught by his disciples, which Lévi-Strauss found to be too rigidly framed by a sectarian doctrine and categories that limited ('mutilated') any impulse towards the real world. Dissatisfaction thus prevailed. On at least one occasion, however, he caught a glimpse of a way out of the rarefied atmosphere of neo-Kantianism: the weekly psychopathology sessions organized by Georges Dumas at Sainte-Anne. Many a philosophy student was thus introduced to the spectacle of madness. Nizan, Sartre, Aron: all attended the sessions at different times. Lévi-Strauss, notwithstanding his ironic comments on the practitioner's tendency to mystify and the overly docile patients, was deeply struck by his confrontation with a mentally ill woman. 'No contact with savage Indian tribes has ever daunted me more than the morning I spent with an old lady swathed in woollies, who compared herself to a rotten herring encased in a block of ice: she appeared intact, she said, but was threatened with disintegration, if her protective envelope should happen to melt.'[29] Madness appeared as an elsewhere of philosophy, measured according to another outside: exoticism, a mental exoticism confronting the alterity of civilization.

As for law, which Lévi-Strauss was studying at the same time, his assess-ment was no less scathing. Law schools did not require students to attend lectures, and one could easily pass exams by mechanically memorizing text-books, a task to which a juridical acrobat could devote a mere two weeks during the year. This offered considerable benefits in terms of time, but was intellectually depressing, or even, for Lévi-Strauss, slightly disconcerting. In *Tristes Tropiques*, his analysis of the double law/philosophy programme that he followed for three years, from 1926 until 1929, suggests a kind of schizophrenia. Law, he says, appealed to sons of the propertied classes, to boisterous youth released from childhood, preparing themselves for a professional future in society. The humanities and the sciences, however, appealed to more introverted types, inclined to withdraw into their studies: 'The student choosing them does not bid farewell to the world of child-hood: on the contrary he is trying rather to remain within it.' The callings of teaching and research are thus 'either a refuge or a mission'.[30]

To resolve this antinomy, with which he lived until finally opting for philosophy in 1929, Claude Lévi-Strauss added a third discipline: politics, a form of extreme engagement with social life that broke with the logic of withdrawal, but into which the knowledge and reflection gleaned from the study and reading of philosophy could be channelled.

Politics: school of the present

Between the ages of eighteen and twenty-two, the apprentice philosopher's life was punctuated by short and intense periods of exam preparation – his tribute to the academic institutions – while the rest of his time was devoted to socialist politics and activism in all its ideological, organizational and material dimensions. This was real life! And everything was to be rebuilt.

The founding of the French Communist Party (or rather of the French Section of the Communist International) in December 1920, at the Congrès de Tours, had indeed drawn much young revolutionary energy away from its old socialist home. In an attempt to revive the socialist student movement, Marcel Déat – a *normalien* then directing the rue d'Ulm library and soon to become the secretary of the Centre de documentation sociale headed by Célestin Bouglé – and two younger *normaliens*, Georges Lefranc and Jean Le Bail, had created the Inter-*khâgnes* Socialist Group in 1924, which five years later became the Socialist Students Group of the five Écoles normales. Recruited by Lefranc, Lévi-Strauss – a fresh 'convert' still in *khâgne* – joined enthusiastically. What was the group about? Conferences, debates, reports, the usual stuff of student militancy, but with a strong determination to combat doctrinal sclerosis from within the socialist camp. Heterodox views were given voice, in a search for new models that would both make sense of the agitated postwar world and effectively compete with the enchanted halo of the bright beacon to the east. Revolutionaries, yes; Bolshevists, no. The entire socialist youth movement resided in that space. Lévi-Strauss was quickly integrated into the group and acted as mediator in relation to the Belgian model, into which he had already been initiated. On 22 April 1926, he gave a conference presentation on the Belgian Workers' Party, an economics-based party made up of cooperatives, unions and mutualist insurance schemes that were fully integrated into the socialist movement, in sharp contrast to the French model, as defined by the Charter of Amiens.[31]

Alongside the Socialist Students Group (GES), the second prong of the socialist youth offensive was the journal that was its offshoot, *L'Étudiant socialiste*. Founded in 1926, the Belgian student journal sponsored by Henri de Man and the Belgian Workers' Party gladly opened its pages to French writers, including GES members Georges and Émilie Lefranc, Jean Le Bail, Maurice Deixonne, Pierre Boivin and Claude Léwy – not to be confused with Claude Lévi-Strauss, who himself published seventeen reports between 1928 and 1933. All born between 1905 and 1910, these young activists – 'upstanding, serious, perhaps too serious for their age'[32] – founded the third prong to win back young minds: the Fédération nationale des étudiants socialistes (FNES), launched in 1927 to federate student groups throughout France and to lend the figure of the intellectual the central place it deserved within a party that was keen to distinguish itself from the excessive working-class ideology of French bolshevism. In 1927, the FNES numbered roughly eighty Paris-based members, and Claude Lévi-Strauss, who that year had become the GES secretary, was appointed secretary of the FNES in 1928. In the summer of 1928, his home address at 26 rue Poussin even served for a time as the FNES's official address. His political militancy was then running at full throttle.

It is worth trying to picture him, consumed by politics, ensconced in the smoky backrooms of Left Bank cafés – meetings were often held at the Normal Bar, on rue Claude Bernard, or at the Brasserie Modèle on boulevard Saint-Marcel. He would have been engaged in feverish discussions on the latest political tactics (relations between the socialist students and the SFIO 'Brahmins' or their communist peers), on doctrinal questions (Marxism and its necessary revisions) and more properly political issues that had arisen after the Cartel des Gauches (whether or not to participate in government), or sincere revolts against the world order that had emerged from the war, expressed with a fervent pacifism and messianic undertones. The room would often be split between a 'silent right', an 'implacable and clamorous left' and the 'massive and loquacious *normalien* centre'.[33] They frequently called each other by obscure pejoratives: 'Millerand reformist', 'thinly veiled participationist', etc. In a corner, some might be forging tactical alliances for the next Congress of the 'Fed', while others would be preparing the next pamphlet to be distributed in the Latin Quarter, territory the control of which had become a matter of intense rivalry with right-wing law students. The 1920s were marked by a return to the combative, pugilistic spirit of the 1900s, when the royalist youth movement the Camelots du Roi ruled over the boulevard Saint-Michel. Indeed, control of this section of Paris has long been a key political stake for student militancy, from the 'Agathon generation' to that of 1968. Hence the 'ritualized violence' that Lévi-Strauss would later recall, the many brawls in which physical strength was deemed a touchstone for political conviction, especially against the provocations of the leagues and the muscular communist barricades.

Claude Lévi-Strauss did not refrain from engaging in his share of fisticuffs, which was an essential part of activist life, or from signing petitions. He became a member of the SFIO in February of 1927, in the XVIth section of the Seine Federation, based on the address of his family home; payment stubs attest to his renewing his membership until 1935.[34] He also recalled signing and circulating manifestos in favour of Sacco and Vanzetti, whom he considered to be victims of 'a repeat of the Dreyfus affair', and his name was on the list of those who protested, in August of 1927, against the law of 7 March 1927 on conditions for mobilization and mental preparation in case of conflict. He demonstrated a real talent for organizing, mobilizing energies and leading men, especially at the third FNES Congress, held in Paris in 1929: 'Lévi-Strauss oversaw everything and, through a judicious grouping of deputies, quickly created an atmosphere of collegiality among Congress participants who were otherwise prone to snubbing each other.'[35] The extent of the activist skills he developed in such a short time is quite striking. Lévi-Strauss was a political virtuoso, having achieved a mastery, at the tender age of twenty-one, of the practices and customs, vocabulary, material conditions and personal dimension of political activism. Intellectual precociousness coupled with political precociousness.

In a pioneering work, Wiktor Stoczkowski has critically examined Lévi-Strauss's consistently asserted claim of the primacy of Marxism in his theoretical formation. Stoczkowski pointed out that the socialist milieu in which the young man's ideas developed was, in fact, dominated by the ideas of Henri de Man and the planned economy movement, for which *L'Étudiant socialiste* was an echo chamber. Henri de Man (1885–1953), a now largely forgotten Belgian intellectual figure, was one of the brightest thinkers of Marxist revisionism. He developed a programme for economic rationalization, economic planning and a form of federalism. His European consciousness, his concern for the emergence of new elites, his emphasis on the fundamental moral bankruptcy of Western civilization and his rejection of the dogma of class struggle all made him one of the most aggressive critics of orthodox Marxism at the time, earning him the glorious headline in *L'Humanité*, on 5 February 1928: 'De Man, the man who killed Karl Marx!'[36] Very clearly, in France as in the rest of Europe, there was a generation gap between the socialist party establishment, which faithfully invoked Marxism, and young militants enthusiastic about the revisionism of the likes of De Man. Claude Lévi-Strauss was undeniably part of the latter group when he excoriated 'the withering old doctrine' and invoked the need for socialism to develop theoretical principles that corresponded to the struggles of the postwar years. It was thus rather unsurprising that Lévi-Strauss, as the FNES general secretary, invited De Man, who was passing through Paris in January 1928, to present his theses to the socialist students. The conference took place on 23 January and did not include a single prominent figure of the SFIO, Blum having excused himself. Commenting on the power relations within French socialism, Claude Lévi-Strauss wrote a thankful and admiring letter to De Man: 'Thanks to you, socialist doctrines are finally awakening from their long slumber.' The tone became more personal when he explained what the discovery of De Man's book published in 1927, *Beyond Marxism*, had meant to him: 'a true revelation', he wrote, adding that it helped him 'get out of a deadlock from which he had thought there was no escape'.[37]

Claude Lévi-Strauss's later amnesia concerning his militant past – which he systematically downplayed – makes more sense in light of the tortuous course De Man followed during the Second World War. Unlike Wauters, De Man did not go into exile, adopting a collaborationist position reminiscent of French Pétainism. It did not take De Man long to recognize his mistake, however, and as early as November 1941 he left Belgium, first living as a recluse in a cabin in La Clusaz, in Savoie, until 1944, then going into definitive exile in Switzerland until his death in 1953. After the war, he was sentenced in absentia to twenty years' imprisonment by a Belgian military court. In the collective memory, the pariah came to eclipse the dazzling young socialist thinker of the 1920s and 1930s. It thus became understandably uncomfortable for Lévi-Strauss to claim this highly controversial figure as mentor.[38] Worse still, in 1983, the Israeli historian Zeev Sternhell made De Man's planned economy movement into not just an element of collaboration, but one of the core intellectual laboratories of fascism as it developed in France.[39] Indeed, Sternhell considered Henri De Man's 1940 decision as perfectly congruous with his earlier politics – a highly debatable point that has indeed given rise to much discussion among historians, but which must nonetheless have shaken Claude Lévi-Strauss, all the more so as one of his close friends, Marcel Déat, had taken the same path. Yet it bears repeating that twenty years after the publication of Sternhell's book, despite having been broadly commended for its insightful exploration of a number of intellectual traditions that had been neglected and for bringing to light a French fascism forged in the French anti-Enlightenment tradition, many historians continue to reject his teleological framework – a framework that examines ideologies and movements from what they became and then traces them backward in time, as though all 1930s heterodox socialists were bound to become 1940s collaborationists. In addition, the excessively broad definition of fascism and an overemphasis on the history of ideas are among the other criticisms that serve to qualify Sternhell's essential thesis. Be this as it may, in the 1980s, a period of revisionist memorialization already obsessed with the dark years, it had become difficult to invoke De Man in any other way than to apologize for 'being so mistaken'.[40] Hence Lévi-Strauss's understandable discretion on the matter.

But in contrast to this retrospective disillusionment, for young socialist students, and for Lévi-Strauss in particular, politics in the formative years of the early 1930s constituted a kind of 'parallel university'[41] that was energizing, demanding, and directly connected to political, economic and social realities. A world where there was ample room to breathe and where ideas anchored in contemporary realities were brewing. Rather than rhetorical flourish, politics taught them the art of concision, of brevity 'free of long-winded speech'.[42] In short, it was a school of life, rich in earthly nourishment, of which academic knowledge unfortunately offered precious little.

A student in search of odd jobs

His financial circumstances being what they were, and political activism providing no support in this regard, Claude Lévi-Strauss took up several odd jobs in addition to his already quite busy double life. His work experience further expanded his range of activities and social milieus, enriched his skills and confirmed the young man's undeniable social talent.

Thanks to an activist acquaintance, he was for several months responsible for reading the daily ILO bulletins on Radio Tour Eiffel, which broadcast from the basement of the Grand Palais Museum. This was the first, but not last, time he was to work as a radio newsreader, after having been so enthralled by radio technology as a child. Later, in 1931, he worked as the press agent for Victor Margueritte, who had just published *La Patrie humaine*, a pacifist pamphlet that the young man had to deliver to the hundred or so Parisian personalities for whom 'le Maître' had inscribed a copy. This served as inspiration for a paragraph in *Tristes Tropiques* on

Margueritte's aristocratic literary lineage, which included a whole range of figures (Balzac, the Goncourt brothers, Zola, Hugo) and fascinated Lévi-Strauss, giving him the impression of having casually stepped into the nineteenth century.[43]

In contrast to this temporality of the previous century, another work experience anchored him firmly in contemporary politics: from 1928 to 1930, the young socialist militant served as parliamentary assistant to Georges Monnet, born in 1898, who had become the socialist MP for Soissons in 1928. A large-scale farmer and journalist specializing in rural issues, a champion of the agricultural world, Georges Monnet was thus an outsider to socialism, with an unorthodox background. He started his parliamentary career under the SFIO banner, but something did not smell quite right. The young militant Lévi-Strauss stood at his side in a somewhat ambiguous position, since he was, as he himself later put it, 'the party's eye' on him, evidence of a doctrinal orthodoxy of which he himself was hardly representative. This might indeed have been the reason why the two men, who were only ten years apart in age, got along so well. Claude Lévi-Strauss even attended family gatherings (Georges Monnet was the uncle of the historian François Furet, who had just been born in 1927). Thus, Lévi-Strauss temporarily left the smoke-filled brasseries to join the corridors of the Chamber of Deputies, whose functions, rituals, spaces and rhetoric he quickly mastered. In his office at the National Assembly, the young assistant worked alongside André Chamson, a novelist he admired[44] and secretary of the Radical Party, but he also developed ties with Marcel Déat, the secretary of the Socialist Group, who became a friend as much as a mentor. Active on rural issues as well as on defence of human rights and cultural policy, Monnet gave Claude Lévi-Strauss responsibility for preparing his dossiers more or less in full. Here again, the latter proved very effective: 'I had written the entire presentation of the arguments behind the Wheat Office proposal; it was filed under Monnet's name; and I remember – at the risk of sounding immodest – that Poincaré had congratulated Monnet on the excellence of this particular presentation.'[45] The Wheat Office, an organ that was to create a state monopoly on the purchase and sale of wheat, was an old idea Jaurès had proposed in 1894. We can reasonably surmise that this project for a planned economy would have suited the admirer of De Man and may have given him further incentive to employ his full talent for rigour and clarity, complementing his legal skills nicely. In the end, the bill was rejected by the Chamber, but the Front populaire government raised it again and eventually created the new agency on 15 August 1936.

Beyond party politics, and in addition to his political activism, Claude Lévi-Strauss engaged in political reflection through the prism of philosophical reason. When, as a parliamentary assistant and now also a philosophy graduate, he chose to focus on Marx for his postgraduate studies, with a thesis on 'The theoretical postulates of historical materialism',[46] it was a way of reconciling the two sides. The topic was a heterodox one in the field of academic philosophy in France, which was not much inclined to German philosophy. Célestin Bouglé accepted it, but imposed a question for the orals dealing with Saint-Simonianism, which was more to his taste and to that of his colleagues. Célestin Bouglé was one of Durkheim's disciples, a popularizer who devoted himself to teaching rather than theoretical innovation, which was the brief of Marcel Mauss. Of socialist inclination, like the latter, Bouglé was one of the key pillars of studies of socialism in the interwar period: the editor of Proudhon's *Complete Works*, as well as an anthology of Saint-Simon, and author of a short overview published in 1933, entitled *Socialisme français: Du 'socialisme utopique' à la démocratie industrielle*.[47] The director of the Centre de documentation sociale, and future director of the École normale supérieure, he was a major figure, and a patron of budding young sociologists as well as *normaliens*. Even though Claude Lévi-Strauss was neither, Bouglé agreed to supervise the work of this young philosopher with a political temperament and considerable practical experience outside academia. 'An aberrant case',[48] since he had come to Marx and socialist doctrines from activism rather than philosophy, Lévi-Strauss's career path caught the attention of the affable Bouglé, who a few years later referred him to Georges Dumas, then looking for young academics willing to go to Brazil.

A socialist party thinker

The agrégation, *an endurance sport*

The bustling energy of previous years was followed in 1930–31 by a period dedicated exclusively to preparing for the *agrégation* in philosophy. In the end, philosophy had won out over law, which 'bored [him] to tears'.[49] Claude Lévi-Strauss put his political activities on hold and entered the monastery, so to speak, since preparation for this competitive examination was expected to be all-consuming. And yet Lévi-Strauss did not use a religious metaphor to describe his impressions of this experience, but rather one from the world of sport. Like all those who have succeeded at the examination, he retained rather fond memories, recalling its 'marathon dimension, in the face of an enormous curriculum'. As opposed to the entrance exam to the École normale supérieure, however, this competition did not seem daunting: 'It was like a major sports performance. I threw myself into it with gusto, and at no point did I feel that the undertaking required super-human capacities. It was high-level sport, but in a healthy and joyful atmosphere.'[50] Almost a kind of intellectual therapy, to which he brought the remarkable physical resilience and bodily endurance he would later demonstrate in other domains (especially ethnographic ones). Claude Lévi-Strauss, despite his thin and slender build – he was 1.79 metres tall – his elegant face and intellectual air, was a robust fellow. And the school of politics had tested his mettle.

In those days, students completed the practical side of *agrégation* even before passing the written exam. This is how Claude Lévi-Strauss ended up in the classes of Gustave Rodrigues, with whom he had studied a few years earlier at Janson-de-Sailly, alongside Simone de Beauvoir and Maurice Merleau-Ponty.[51] They took turns giving a lecture. Simone de Beauvoir described this period in her *Memoirs* and wrote of Lévi-Strauss, her exact contemporary (both were born in 1908): '[His] impassivity rather intimidated me, but he used to turn it to good advantage. I thought it very funny when, in his detached voice, and with a deadpan expression on his face, he expounded to our audience on the folly of the passions.' As for Lévi-Strauss, he also remembered Simone de Beauvoir at that time: 'Very young, with a fresh, bright complexion, like a little peasant girl. She had a crisp but sweet side to her, like a rosy apple.'[52] A charming vignette that heralded the intellectual jousting to come.

The big day of the exam arrived. Lévi-Strauss's personal archive has preserved a slight trace of it in the form of a draft of his essay on moral philosophy, the exact topic of which has been lost.[53] The draft is, however, revealing: the young candidate, so critical of the superficial rhetoric of philosophical reasoning, had become a master of it. Not a single phrase of the introduction is crossed out. It is very solidly constructed, with a classic foundation in Kant, presented in three parts: acts, intention, character. The dialectical argument is impeccably developed: 'We proceed from the exterior to the interior, and from the interior we find heteronomy', since indeed, temperament is determined by society, 'which has made us who we are'. Into this robust and somewhat formal argument, the applicant innovated by injecting elements from other disciplines, mainly law, but also history (Christianity and the Reformation) as well as sociology. He thus practised in his *agrégation* essay, at some risk, what he had called for in a highly favourable review he wrote at around that time of Armand Cuvillier's *Manuel de philosophie*: 'To highlight, as the starting point of all thinking and an essential element of all solutions, these new disciplines where experience and thought combine to lead to a liberating deepening of consciousness: psychology and sociology.'[54] And finally, in the conclusion to the essay, an incisive and personal note reveals the young man's strong sense of moral commitment: 'Being moral is to be displeased with oneself – to transform oneself – and not just to accept an ideal, but to achieve it in oneself as a martyr.'

For the oral exam, he drew an applied psychology question that should have appealed to him but which in fact disconcerted him. Like an athlete losing steam, he turned to drugs: 'A doctor, a friend of the family, gave me a vial of some drug – morphine? cocaine? – which, he claimed, would give me a lift if I drank it before the lecture. To prepare for this supreme trial, they shut you up in the Sorbonne library for seven hours. I hastened to swallow the contents of the vial in a glass of water and became so sick that I had to spend the seven hours of preparation time stretched out on two chairs. Seven hours of seasickness! [. . .] I appeared before the jury looking like death, without having been able to prepare a thing, and improvised a lecture that was considered brilliant, in which I believe I spoke of nothing but Spinoza. Perhaps the drug had done its job, after all.' The end result was that he came in third place and was the youngest in his class, at the age of twenty-two, to have passed. First place went to Ferdinand Alquié. Between sports metaphor and impish anecdote, the narrative of his *agrégation* exam cannot be taken entirely seriously. It ends with the purchase of a treatise on astrology for the announcement of the results, a final thumbing of the nose on the part of a young man who remained stubbornly resist-ant to philosophical rationality. Reality lay elsewhere. And it held surprises that three-part outlines could never fully anticipate. As the freshly minted *agrégé* arrived to give his parents the good news, he came upon his Uncle Jean, the family benefactor, who had come to announce the news that he was financially ruined. This was 1931, and the global crisis had taken two years to hit the French economy and financial markets. The upshot of the *agrégation* story was thus: 'I found out almost simultaneously that I had a profession and that my parents' material needs would thereafter be a con-stant worry for me.'[55]

'Transforming man into something worthy of being liberated': *Révolution constructive*

In the course of heated discussions between Claude Lévi-Strauss and his classmate Maurice Deixonne, in which the latter insisted that 'the goal of socialism is to transform man', Lévi-Strauss replied, 'it is also to transform him into something worthy of being liberated'.[56] Were these merely the lofty pronouncements of young philosophy *agrégés*? Certainly. But these statements also resonated with the need for a reform of the self that was an essential component of their socialist politics.

For the revisionist, socialist doctrine had a moral dimension, a spiritual idiosyncrasy that was alien to the Marxist tradition. De Man, in *Au-delà du marxisme*, saw the quest for equality as the revival of a Christian ideal. Similarly, Lévi-Strauss, a great admirer of the book, also identified a kind of continuity between Christian revolution and socialism, which he saw in the work of his Protestant comrade André Philip. He recognized that 'shifting economic interests are less and less a sufficient foundation for the socialist convictions of the proletariat'.[57] Justifications of a higher order were necessary. And so Wiktor Stoczkowski has spoken, in all earnestness, of a 'socialist eschatology',[58] tinged with messianic hopes and a pained and radical awareness of the failure of Western civilization, which encour-aged these passionate young intellectuals to adopt a religiously inflected language. But insofar as they were under Christian influence, it was a Christianity of the catacombs: a new world must rise from the rubble, a new humanism, a new man. Indeed, in the pages of *L'Étudiant socialiste*, Claude Lévi-Strauss regularly reviewed a sister publication, *L'Espoir du monde*, the Christian socialist organ. While himself an atheist, or at least an agnostic, he endorsed this messianic vision: 'Our task today is that of the prophet and martyr: to achieve within ourselves – and not just in our thoughts, but in our lives – a new order.'[59] Following the experience of the GES and FNES, the hard core of activists, students who had often become professors, decided to form a group that would remain within the SFIO, in the same way as the Fabians stood within the Labour Party in the UK. The idea, initiated by the Lefranc couple, was to write a collective book that would 'sound the alarm, a manifesto to raise urgent political

issues'.[60] Officially founded on 1 March 1931, the 'Révolution constructive' group was part of a generational movement, which operated on the
left but also on the right, to impose moral reform on a civilization deemed
in decay, fed on debased values, in a society where young activists saw
only confusion, competition, exploitation, crises, moral decline, etc. One
historian has dubbed this group the '1930s nonconformists', since they all
insisted, as did the young Lévi-Strauss, on the need for inner renewal first
and foremost.[61] In this new configuration, Claude Lévi-Strauss played a
role that was both central – his intellectual authority was clear and sought
after – and marginal, due to his gradual withdrawal. When tasks were distributed among the various members, he offered to take on a key part of
the book – no less than 'a sketch of a metaphysics at the service of revolution'.[62] The title of this chapter in the history of revolutionary socialism
that was never written gives a sense of both the intellectual ambition and
the 'demanding and exalted conception of the work of revolution'[63] on the
part of the man who formulated, without fulfilling, its programme.

'We, revolutionaries . . .'

In 1931, fresh from the *agrégation*, the twenty-two-year-old Claude Lévi-
Strauss was in many ways a young revolutionary intellectual of his time,
but one who already stood out through his various deviations from revolutionary *doxa*.

First of all, he was a socialist who rejected the ambiguity that prevailed in his party between a classically Marxist revolutionary rhetoric
and a reformist practice that played the parliamentary game. He and his
Révolution constructive comrades, children of the First World War, were
ardent pacifists, immune to the idea of violence as the midwife of history.
With a clear focus on action, on 'reconstruction', they aspired to a revolution without pathos, a 'tearless revolution'[64] that would rest on the creation, within capitalist society, of cooperative institutions: 'If, day after day,
we endeavoured to build socialist-minded institutions, they would gradually grow by virtue of their superiority, like chrysalises within a capitalist
cocoon, and the latter would eventually fall away, a dead and desiccated
envelope.'[65] These kinds of metaphors from the natural world were already
used at the time to describe the desired break with capitalism. But here we
are closer to the entomologist Jean-Henri Fabre than to Lenin . . .

As we have seen, these young activists also shared moral concerns that
they felt were pressing, and even, in Lévi-Strauss's case, fundamental. This
stood in stark contrast to the philosophical levity of other revolutionary
socialist movements, which remained quite removed from calls for religious
and ethical engagement. In the years 1930–31, an intense debate raged in
these circles concerning the regulation of brothels, which gave rise to an
exchange between Maurice Deixonne, who had just published an article
entitled 'Brothels' in *L'Étudiant socialiste*, and Claude Lévi-Strauss. The
latter was shocked by his friend's pragmatic approach, which led to a
support for the conservation of brothels on the proviso that regulations

guaranteeing hygienic conditions for prostitutes were put in place. 'What I found most disturbing is the way you seem to implicitly support the regulation of prostitution, and hence a form of regulated prostitution. There is a problem here that is somewhat reminiscent, in its position, to that of national defence: an absolute contradiction between an abstract solution and the concrete situation and current conditions, as well as such an incredibly revolting opposition between the two that it can only lead, for us, to a total and comprehensive rejection of the latter. And don't you think that this problem for socialists and socialist students is mostly a psychological one? The point is not so much whether, in and of itself, prostitution is a necessary evil, is avoidable, etc., but whether each of us, individually, can accept it. Thus, raised as a practical moral issue, I think the problem can only entail one response, on whose radical character I am sure we agree.'[66] A solid Kantian framework, with a typical combination of logical rigour and moral indignation, expressed with great clarity and a touch of intransigence. In a critical review, Lévi-Strauss took his point further: 'We revolutionaries are currently devoid of a system of moral values',[67] which seemed to him particularly damaging for the socialist cause. This was indeed one of the fields of thought in which he felt capable of building anew – he, the radical nonbeliever preoccupied by the demands of salvation. But there were other fronts on which his nonconformism and his own voice were expressed even more clearly: aesthetics and nature.

He had, for example, no qualms about defending in the socialist press the 'anarchist and revolutionary' novel *Voyage au bout de la nuit*, which was published in 1933 by an unknown Louis-Ferdinand Céline, even though it had already been praised to the skies by his political opponent Léon Daudet.[68] He immediately seized on it as the 'most important work published in the past ten years', even if he did push it in the direction of his own literary masters, Conrad and Pierre Mac Orlan. Still, the young critic rejected the binary opposition of the day: the classical aesthetic of Action française vs. the dogmatic and rather meagre vision of Marxist aesthetics. Claude Lévi-Strauss, then very far from the classical taste he was to display later in life, emphasized the value of avant-garde productions of all kinds, always with lavish enthusiasm. He admired Meyerhold, the 'most prodigious theatrical genius to have surfaced in centuries',[69] discovered Vladimir Mayakovski, the 'champion of the Russian revolution',[70] and read the surrealists, especially Aragon's *Le Paysan de Paris*. In Céline, as well as Nizan, Paul Morand and D.H. Lawrence, he appreciated the new forms that were in tune with the literary present. He had no trouble combining a revolutionary temperament with an avant-gardist impulse. On the contrary, in this period he exemplified the great utopia of the century: the alliance between political and artistic revolution, and their essentially complementary character. 'Social revolution, like artistic revolution, must be revolution full stop.'[71] It is worth recalling that at this same time, the communists were lionizing socialist realism, an aesthetic doctrine elaborated by Zhdanov that would reign over their thinking about art until the 1950s. But even in the socialist party, despite the presence of distinguished intellectuals like Léon Blum, a former critic, not everyone shared a faith in the spiritual and regenerative power of art, on which Lévi-Strauss insisted: 'Socialism, to be complete, must insert itself in the mind as much as in the realm of political economy ... A rich and novel aesthetic model is as full of revolutionary content as any union demand.'[72] As in the early days of the Russian Revolution, the true artist, for Lévi-Strauss, was on the side of revolutionaries and socialist struggle. It was for this reason, in his view, that it had become urgent to recognize the artist's place, status and function alongside other revolutionary agents. Indeed, his writings offer a preliminary sketch of an ambitious socialist aesthetics.

More surprising still was the very personal connection that, in Lévi-Strauss's view, bound 'the sense of nature and the revolutionary spirit'. On several occasions, but nowhere as explicitly as in the review he wrote of Paul Nizan's *Aden Arabie*, he explored this deserted corner, neglected by all socialist doctrines: the learned and dreamy contemplation of a cosmos that was larger than man, an experience every bit as redemptive as a sense of beauty and the fight for a better world, and at any rate their indispensable complement. *Aden Arabie* was published in 1931. It became an immediate literary sensation and a minor generational manifesto. Lévi-Strauss, while not a close friend, knew Nizan, who had married his cousin Henriette Alphen. He understood Nizan's revulsion for a corrupt civilization and shared his weariness, but he was critical of the celebrated pamphlet on two points. First, he poked fun at Nizan's 'laborious detours' – following a very '*normalien*' path, according to Lévi-Strauss – before arriving at the obvious: 'Capitalism is the culprit.' Many, including the socialist activists taunted by Nizan, had already 'figured that out, and in more commendable ways. While the latter paraded his melancholy through the exclusive neighbourhoods of exotic cities, they dedicated their evenings to the humbler artisanal tasks of revolution: patient recruiting of members, bundling of newspapers, writing of countless letters to bring together isolated souls . . . .'[73] A self-serving position that called for more modesty in the young rebel *normalien*. His second point had to do with that sense of nature so vehemently rejected by Nizan, and later by Sartre, for whom human presence alone expressed and redeemed a landscape. Nothing could be more alien to Lévi-Strauss, who was already deeply imbued with the idea that a 'philosophy of man could not entirely stand for a philosophy of the world'.[74] Indeed, he continued, 'to be saved',[75] the 'struggle for the revolution is not sufficient':[76] 'Contact with nature represents the only eternal human experience, the only one that we can be sure is true experience – the only absolute value today that we can call on to gain the assurance necessary to call into existence the absolute values of future organization.'[77] A very Lévi-Straussian voice could already be heard in this young philosopher and socialist activist.

In the autumn of 1931, Claude Lévi-Strauss, still somewhat dazed by the *agrégation* effort, continued to waver between philosophy, law and sociology. He half-heartedly began developing strategies for penetrating the academic networks of the law faculty. He confessed to his friend Maurice Deixonne – a comrade at Révolution constructive and a young philosophy *agrégé* like himself – of being tempted to respond favourably to an offer from Roger Picard to work for a 'politically unaffiliated' law review. 'The collaborators and readers are specialists: law professors, economists, etc. – i.e. "boring". Since I may one day orient myself towards the philosophy of law, I wouldn't mind being somewhat – though as little as possible – in contact with this world.'[78] The philosophy of law would allow him to go straight into academia and become a politically engaged academic, a common enough role in the Third Republic, for radicals and socialists alike.

Yet Claude Lévi-Strauss did not yearn for the academic sinecure. At *Révolution constructive*, the aspiration was not just to engage in politics but to think politics. Thus, one of Lévi-Strauss's close friends at the time, Pierre Boivin – a *normalien*, philosophy *agrégé* and former student of Célestin Bouglé, a clear and ironic mind, reliable friend and invaluable socialist activist – joined the staff of the education minister, Jean Zay, in 1936. This represented a possible path for Lévi-Strauss, notwithstanding his greater inclination to more theoretical work. As has already been mentioned, for the prospective book project, he had committed to undertaking an 'outline of a metaphysics at the service of revolution'. He did not shy away from placing ambitious intellectual demands on himself, writing to Maurice Deixonne that the book's objective was to invent 'a method that will allow us to develop the content of future civilization'.[79] This demiurgical impulse clearly aligns him with two of his models: what de Man represented for the Belgian Workers' Party, and perhaps what Marcel Déat was for the SFIO. He imagined himself at this time becoming 'the philosopher of the socialist party', and despite his break with this initial ambition, he could as an old man still appreciate what had stirred him in his youth: 'The socialist party was a very lively group where you could feel at ease. The idea of building a bridge between the great philosophical tradition – by that I mean Descartes, Leibniz and Kant – and political thought as represented by Marx was a very seductive one. Even today I understand how I could have dreamed of it.'[80] Becoming the theoretical architect of a new socialist Marxism would also have been a way to reconcile his two sides, his contradictory aspirations, clearly visible in his admiration for his two models: between the power of the mind and the desire to act, between the revolutionary audacity of a project for change and the rejection of pipe dreams, between vast ideological panoramas and lived experience, between the sweeping flow of the revolutionary river and the always radically new perspectives unfolding at each of its bends.[81]

4

Redemption: Anthropology (1931–1935)

> By whom or by what had I been impelled to disrupt the normal course of my existence? Was it a trick on my part, a clever diversion, which would allow me to resume my career with additional advantages for which I would be given credit? Or did my decision express a deep-seated incompatibility with my social setting so that, whatever happened, I would inevitably live in a state of ever greater estrangement from it?
>
> Claude Lévi-Strauss, *Tristes Tropiques*[1]

Between 1931 and early 1935, Claude Lévi-Strauss grew up quickly, becoming a soldier, a young professor, even a husband. These years of rapid ascent into adulthood followed the pattern of a *Bildungsroman*, passing through a diversity of worlds: military barracks, a small town, not to mention a newlyweds' household – Balzacian settings attesting to a very French youth and an entry into the socio-professional world that was as rapid as it was successful.

But suddenly, after a phone call from Célestin Bouglé in the autumn of 1934, Claude Lévi-Strauss was to set off on a different path. The young philosophy professor was presented with an offer to go to Brazil to give courses in anthropology at the newly founded University of São Paulo. An offer he accepted.

In mathematics, bifurcation theory models a situation in which a small change in a physical parameter produces a major change in the organization of the system. Claude Lévi-Strauss's conversion to anthropology belongs to this kind of 'bifurcation': it is a 'biographical accident' akin to an illness or a religious conversion, which eschews social scientific explanation and warrants attention for having resulted in nothing less than a transformation of the international intellectual landscape of the twentieth century. How are we to make sense of this abrupt and unpredictable departure, which remains, in the end, an enigma? In *Tristes Tropiques*, Lévi-Strauss used two metaphors to describe his leap into the unknown in 1935: anthropology was described as an 'exit' as well as a 'lifeline'. Somewhere between defection and redemption, choosing anthropology – as an interlude or as a calling – did not necessarily involve a radical break from the world that had made him. It is comparable to other breaks and commitments of the bright young minds of his generation. Anthropology was one possible way to reconcile life and writing, scholarly work and adventure, the sensory and rational worlds. It was also a way of withdrawing from a world into which one had too quickly integrated, in the hope of perhaps making a glorious return – not unlike teenagers in indigenous societies who leave their tribes to undergo trials that will later serve, if they emerge victorious, as sources of their own authority.

Growing up

In 1931, the young philosophy *agrégé* was posted to a barracks in Strasbourg as a private soldier. In 1932, he got married and took up his first teaching post at Mont-de-Marsan, in southwest France, followed a year later by an appointment to a *lycée* in Laon, while his wife, now also a philosophy *agrégé*, taught at Amiens. Military conscription, marriage, first job, financial independence – societies' milestones from late adolescence to adulthood were here condensed into the space of a few months. Yet this wholehearted embrace of adult responsibility did not preclude the main-tenance of strong ties to the family home. These ties were manifest in an intense correspondence, which now gives us a fresh glimpse into the life of the young soldier, professor and caring husband.[2]

'Private Lévi, 158th Infantry Regiment, Signal Corps, Stirn Barracks, Strasbourg': scenes from military life

Lévi-Strauss, future keen observer of the rites and myths of tribal societies, experienced one of the great rites of passage of Western democratic socie-ties of his time: compulsory military service. It was also one of the found-ing myths of the French Republic: the social and geographical intermixing effected by this year of civic and military training as a process of national distillation. The young private arrived at Strasbourg's Stirn Barracks in October 1931. He was appointed to the 158th Infantry Regiment, signal corps – that is, radio, telegraph, telephone and optical signals. A few months into barracks life, he managed, through political connections, to obtain a 'cushy' post in the press corps of the war ministry, allowing him to return to Paris in the spring of 1932.

But in the meantime, he performed his duty with energy and curiosity. The deprivations and discomforts of military life weighed on him, but he met them with humour and detachment, and delighted in recounting these experiences to his parents in great detail. Upon arrival at the barracks, he had to take a spelling test, write an essay ('narrate your life, etc.'), and complete four 'very difficult' mathematical exercises, 'which [he] barely managed to do'. He was uncomfortable with the lack of privacy in the communal bathrooms, and managed to locate, with a detailed map and directions, the only toilet that did provide a degree of isolation. He was also very concerned with the food and remarked on its poor quality, but reunions with the Alsatian branch of the family sustained him, even if it meant enduring the tedium of interminable Sunday lunches. Between his captain's presentations (with slide projections) on venereal diseases – 'in such a low tone that I couldn't make out a word' – the afternoon movie (documentaries on tanks) and the learning of Morse code, the time flew by. He soon obtained his matriculation number: 9835. Around him there was 'nobody from the 16th arrondissement or [his] social class', but pleasant enough fellows: three seminarians, a Jew of Russian extraction, and a sound engineer from Paramount with whom he had long technical discussions. There was another Jewish soldier, with 'a sound but naive political mind – I began his education!' (S12). Lévi-Strauss passed his time in an atmosphere of pleasant camaraderie, despite the social and intellectual differences. He deployed his tactical and oratorial skills in dealing with the captain, speaking as the voice of reason to obtain as many advantages as possible for everyone – gaining a degree of popularity, which gave him satisfaction – even while cultivating a certain aloofness. He rented a room in town, on rue Charles-Appell, which afforded him a modicum of peace and quiet during his rare hours of leave.

This time would be devoted to reading newspapers – *Le Populaire*, edited by Léon Blum, who 'represented for [him] something akin to God' (S36) – and detective novels or going to movies – to see the German version of *The Threepenny Opera*, which he praised highly, being richer than the French version, or to see René Clair's *Le Million* again, or to discover Raimu and Fresnay in *Marius*. He raved about how comfortable the Paramount movie theatre was, transporting him from Strasbourg all the way to the boulevards of Paris. Besides American classics, he also liked Soviet films, even while being fully aware, as a socialist, of their aestheticizing reappropriation in France, for 'it must be said that when we admire the beauty of the images or the directing, we are committing a genuine and serious mistake. These are not works of art but didactic films produced to edify and rally illiterate peasants' (S51). While cinema for Private Lévi was an important pastime, photography was the subject of a series of technical recommendations and theoretical reflections, continuing a discussion started several years earlier with his father. It was the medium of the times, of modernity and of his father's ruin, as well as that of a possible artistic rebirth if one understood its language: 'What would be disastrous is if the focus were sharp all over. In German photographs, what is commendable is precisely the fact that only one point, a quarter of a millimetre at the most, is in focus. This gives emphasis, and leaves other parts of the object to be treated more broadly, in the same way as a painting would. A uniform focus would yield only a poor documentary' (S27). 'It seems to me that photography's mission is to introduce aspects of things that the eye is not able to see; therein lies the secret of Man Ray's photography' (S32). Then came the practice. Lévi-Strauss's father sent him snapshots of flowers that the son criticized, sometimes harshly. They engaged in endless technical discussions and went on at length about the relative virtues of the Korette f/4.5 and the SOM Berthiot f/4.5. Lévi-Strauss wanted to have a camera, and even a movie camera, because 'military life is extremely photogenic, especially during marches'.

Marches in the Alsatian countryside were not a problem for Lévi-Strauss, even laden with kit, helmet and rifle. They even on occasion afforded moments of wonder, where physical effort only intensified his ability to capture the landscape in moving snapshots: 'We completed a beautiful tour, eastward towards the forest, then back along the Rhine River, magnificent under a lead sky, backlit by the sun; and finally across the Strasbourg Bridge where multi-coloured barges as big as ocean liners filled me with amazement' (S18). But military life was not all hikes in the countryside. Most of the time it was filled with various jobs, inspections, installation of antenna lines and, for the rest, 'it's like *lycée*: the workings of a telephone, sketches of various models, conventional communication signs, etc. etc. Yes, *lycée*, except that I have never horsed around so much in my life' (S36). Exercises for learning sound decoding, radio handling, plane communications: 'They communicate with us via radio, and we respond with enormous signboards that are several meters high, with multiple technical meanings – it is its own language that we work with on a daily basis' (S36). Note the clear interest in this linguistic gymnastics of coding and decoding, even if it was increasingly described with a certain irony, to highlight its pointlessness. Lévi-Strauss was becoming impatient and weary of sewing buttons. The curious experience of military life began to lose its charm as its novelty wore off. Indeed, he found the combination of idleness and activity increasingly difficult to put up with: 'You almost wish for war to justify our presence here!' The recreational dimension of military life – the training field as playing field – that he had initially enjoyed began to appear all the more puerile as he became critical of the ultimate effectiveness of the whole operation. A ground-to-air liaison demonstration was to be held for the benefit of the officers, in which Lévi-Strauss and his comrades were charged with deciphering messages from the pilots. The operation was a success, but also a tad pathetic. It all resembled 'baby games'. As for the non-commissioned officers, they were not up to the task: 'When you realize that all these bland and childish characters might well have been commanding real men in a real war!' (S50). The fiction of preparation for war tarnished the pacifist and anti-Versailles activist's experience of barracks life. At a certain point, he grew weary of playing war, all the more so since it was fundamentally outside his intellectual framework. He did not want any part of it and did not want to see it. 'The peaceful face of France: our training ground in Cronenbourg, two kilometres from Strasbourg, is peppered with metal and wood shelters that we mistook for tool sheds or the like. Today, one of them had its door open and we were stunned to discover inside an enormous cannon, mounted on pivots in reinforced cement with rails, etc. – all of it brand new and ready for action' (S27). He was stunned by this vision of the cannon, like a sudden return of the real or a subliminal image of the future.

Who was this young man, of whom we get a glimpse through the interlude of military service? A long and slender adolescent made broader by physical exercise, topped by an intellectual face that had swapped cigarettes for a pipe, whose 'giant bowl' he made a point of mentioning, as well as the fact that he 'carefully rubbed his nose with it . . .'. A leader of men who treasured moments of solitude, a man who enjoyed creature comforts as well as life in the outdoors, he humbly accepted the constraints of the soldier's life and, as far as we know, never tried to be declared unfit for military service. He was keen for new experiences and embraced military service as a change of social scenery every bit as much of a departure from his habitual landscape as was the Alsatian countryside. Yet, after a while, he became quite simply bored stiff. A powerful motif in his life, and the flipside of his avid curiosity, Lévi-Strauss's boredom could take on monumental proportions, from which only intellectual life could deliver him. The young soldier leaving his parents for the first time maintained a quite distinctive relationship with them, one that reversed the traditional affective polarities. He would advise his father regarding his professional activities and recommended that he retrain for the cinema. This paternal concern also led him to constantly reassure his parents, even if, from time to time, he also rebelled against the tyranny of parental correspondence (and concern). Indeed, whenever his letters stopped for a few days, the anxiety level rose. In the end, on a nearly daily basis, his parents would receive reading recommendations, advice on films to see, reflections and anecdotes in an uninterrupted flow of information, pronouncements and affection, all offered with the greatest of authority and a tender affinity.

Dina: the physiology of marriage, summer 1932

All of a sudden, in the summer of 1932, a wife entered the picture. Nothing previously, not a single reference is made to her in all the abundant family correspondence. And then the announcement of marriage, which Lévi-Strauss made 'informally official' to his parents. Dina Dreyfus broke into Lévi-Strauss's life like an apparition. Little is known about this woman, around whom there is an air of mystery. Where did they meet? Lévi-Strauss has provided no account of romantic intrigue. We are thus reduced to speculation: perhaps it was at the Sorbonne, where she also studied philosophy, or maybe it was socialist activism that brought them together; perhaps they met in the spring of 1932, when the young soldier was back in Paris, perhaps earlier. They shared an ardent commitment to socialism – Dina Dreyfus came from an Italian Jewish family and had directly experienced the upsurge of nascent fascist violence, when, in 1922, while living near Porta Pia above a communist party committee room, she witnessed the sacking of the socialist offices by a group of Blackshirts. The March on Rome, viewed through a child's eyes, was the founding trauma of her political commitment, as she would later explain.[3] We can thus surmise that her parents were Italian exiles in Paris, Jewish and leftist.

We have black and white pictures of her in Brazil, where, in a camp-site setting, we see a curly haired shepherdess, a somewhat androgynous lady adventurer with an air of youthful cheerfulness. Indeed, the young woman – as would the more mature woman later on – radiated a fantastic charm, enhanced by her elegant clothes, venetian blond hair and delicate perfume; with her pale eyes and rolling Italian accent, she possessed to the fullest what Madame De Staël called 'the tact of circumstances'.[4] Indeed, she seems to have made a deep impression on everyone she met, not least her students, now the only ones who can bear witness to what she had become by the 1950s and 1960s, namely, a *grande dame* of the institution of French philosophy.[5] But before all that, even though she never mentioned it, she had been Claude Lévi-Strauss's young bride, officially wed in mid-September 1932 – at the age of twenty – on the eve of their departure for Mont-de-Marsan, which was thus both the location of his first job and their honeymoon destination.

In fact, the summer of 1932 was not only a time of wedding preparations, which were in any case reduced to a bare minimum; it was also a moment of strategic planning and cartographic intelligence. 'Mont-de-Marsan would be possible, but only with a car [. . .], Alès would suit me, if the post was available. Guéret is too isolated in terms of communication with the outside world. Digne also. Saint-Omer is right next to Calais, but it's unpleasant country.' Other possible postings were considered: Foix, Rochefort, Aurillac . . . and Laon, but that was a double position intended for his friend Kaan and his wife. There was much agitation, comparison (Boivin was appointed to Béziers), inquiry and contacting general inspectors as long as positions remained unfilled. In the end, it would be Mont-de-Marsan: 'I am beginning to reconcile myself with the idea of Mont-de-Marsan, since there is no avoiding starting out in the middle of nowhere' (P10).

Banquets in the Landes: scenes from provincial life

A provincial *lycée* it would be then. The Lycée Victor Duruy, to be precise, with its pink brick and stone: 'I saw my classroom which overlooks the park; it isn't large and I will hold forth on a small platform which is precisely the size of the black table that sits upon it, and on which I will no doubt look utterly ridiculous' (M3). This was an obligatory step in the career of any young professor (once military service had been completed). After years immersed in highly intellectual studies and sophisticated training, newly minted professors were shipped off to provincial towns and regional administrative seats, charged with the forming of minds through philosophy classes. These periods were usually parenthetical. Some had a knack for turning them into moments of happiness and curiosity forged in exposure to other worlds, as did Simone de Beauvoir in Marseille with her marathon excursions into the Moorish hinterland. Who can say what effect this posting of brilliant minds to provincial hinterlands has had on the intellectual life of France?

Mont-de-Marsan is the administrative seat of the Landes region in southwest France, roughly midway between Bordeaux and the Spanish border, a charming little town traversed by the Midouze River. Upon arrival, the young couple was enthralled by the place: the pine forest on the edge of town (which also had poplar, chestnut and bay trees), the marvellous mushrooms, the extraordinary turnout at the biannual fair, the goose market with its long lines of web-footed birds, the shellfish and oysters from Arcachon that were hawked on the streets. While looking for a home, the newlyweds temporarily settled in a hotel and bought 'indescribable brown gaiters' for Dina, which made her look 'like a Persian princess' (M20). Once they had found an apartment, duly indicated on a postcard sent to his parents, the young couple began setting up their new life, which was regularly chronicled by the son, now husband, in letters to which Dina often added in her own hand, always very affectionately, 'your new daughter'.

That year in Mont-de-Marsan was for Lévi-Strauss a learning experience of multiple dimensions: giving his first classes, organizing his material life, cooking, getting accustomed to provincial living and life as a couple. The joyful tone of the letters from that year in the Landes suggests marital harmony and common discovery of things that became dear to both of them: the skies of the Landes region ('of a subtle and distinctive hue that I have rarely seen elsewhere, fine and delicate as well as sumptuous'), the bicycle rides (Dina learned to master the machine), the gourmet feasts provided by this bountiful region, and the local politics in which they both became intensely engaged.

Food is a recurring, almost obsessive, theme in the correspondence: precise and detailed descriptions of weekly menus, food prices and grocery budgets are provided, recipes shared between son and mother with further information requested – what about the 'prune-date-cream dessert, chocolate truffles, and Jewish meatballs'? (M7) – and stories of gastronomic expeditions (such as the one to Villeneuve-de-Marsan where they ate 'artichoke hearts in mushroom sauce and seared fatty goose livers all pink inside – exquisite'). Lévi-Strauss duly informed his parents that he had visited their friends in Bayonne, the Mathieus. He found them somewhat unbearable, but his boredom was offset by his enthusiasm for the lunch (just like in Strasbourg): 'Wonderful, stunning: anchovy filled olives, white pudding with apples cooked in the fireplace, wood pigeon that I will never forget for as long as I live, salad, cakes, fruit, coffee, Armagnac, walnut brandy, blackcurrant liqueur, and what have you, as well as a Spanish wine that scratches the throat.' Dina's comment: 'Claude was flush with colour and facial expressions, a lovely sight. He was a big hit with Thérèse, who had only ever seen him serious and severe as he usually is, but I now understand what a little Moscatel can do' (M19). Meanwhile, Lévi-Strauss went and bought a bottle of bootleg Moscatel, which he brought back carefully concealed in the sleeve of his raincoat.

Another character that featured in this abundant correspondence – one of a more clearly masculine bent – was the car. Besides the appeal of technological beauty that the automobile still held at that time, it was the exhilaration of speed that made it an object of desire, not to mention the necessity of having such a machine when posted to isolated places. But the purchase of one became vital when Lévi-Strauss entered local politics. Here again, a steady flow of information from father to son appears in the letters – pertaining to carburettors, engines, brakes, bodywork: 'Pierre's cousin doesn't like the monosix; very fragile engine, he says. The Peugeot 5 horsepower isn't bad' (M45). We should mention in passing that Pierre Dreyfus, a major actor in this car purchase, was to become head of the Renault Company in 1955 . . . 'Very pretty 5hp convertibles'; the new Ford 6hp is 'smashing' but too expensive for his budget, which only allowed for a more banal 5hp Citroën. In January 1933, Dina and Claude Lévi-Strauss returned from Paris in their new car. It was driven by others, but that did not stop its owner from raving about it: 'Apparently the lowered cylinder head works wonders; it allows you to maintain 75!' (M60). In the Bronze Age of the automobile, it was still quite an adventure . . . An adventure that Lévi-Strauss often recounted, connecting his passion for automobiles with the major development of that year in the Landes: his foray into local socialist politics. Having decided to run for local office, he bought a car to attend the dozens of scheduled meetings. And on the very first day, together with Pierre Dreyfus and Dina, Claude, at the wheel even though he had no licence, drove the car into a ditch. He came out of it with a full hour of amnesia, an injury to the forehead and a joint effusion in the left knee; Pierre Dreyfus vomited blood and lost sensation in half of his face; Dina was unscathed. The local press reported that they had been seriously injured and Radio Toulouse announced that they were nearly dead, to the alarm of their socialist comrades in the region (M70). The car was not insured and the loss of control was probably due to overinflated tyres. This accident figured prominently in the retrospective accounts Lévi-Strauss generally gave, in which he always suggested that it had brought his involvement in socialist politics to an end.[6] However, on the contrary, this incident did not seem to deter the young socialist from continuing his campaign: 'This race is all the more enjoyable that I am ineligible on two counts, being under twenty-five years of age, and having resided less than six months in the area. [. . .] My opponent is Milliès-Lacroix, the senator-mayor of Dax, fifty-five years old, and a reactionary. It should be a lot of fun' (M40). Neither eligible, nor elected, neither a licence, nor a car! Indeed, the car accident earned him a short satirical pamphlet, which he kept in his archives, entitled 'The Conference in Saint-Martin': 'You seek to direct the ship of state / And you can't even drive your car / Alas! You have brought yourself to a sorry state / while on your way to pontificate / You have also done damage to your face / and we are sorry to see you in this place / But, professor, we are worried that you strive / to steer us all before you learn to drive.'[7] The car accident neither extinguished his passion for automobiles nor tempered his political drive. A few weeks later, on 13 March, he was taking his driving test and . . . failing it (as would Dina later, like so many intellectuals who were more adept at dialectical reasoning than downshifting). He was furious about it: 'Brutal examiner, an aristocratic name. He brought me into a maze of small streets and abrupt turns, with slopes in every direction. I thought I was being very sensible and prudent remaining in second gear. But he didn't like it' (M63). This calamity further complicated his political career, which he nonetheless seemed to have no intention of giving up.

Indeed, local politics united his passions of the moment – the automobile and gastronomy – and so Lévi-Strauss decided to throw himself into it fully, following a suggestion by Broca, a friend from Montfort-en-Chalosse, that he create a new branch of the SFIO. 'I am looking forward to this new round of political activism, since I was beginning to find the Landes federation a bit dull! And then, of course, there is the comrades' foie gras!' (M30). Levi-Strauss's move was part of an offensive to reconquer that region of tenant farmers and large landowners, where socialists could assert arguments of class struggle eschewed by the centre-right Radical Party. This new assertiveness adopted by Lévi-Strauss in confronting the Radicals of southwest France would lead, a few years down the line, to major socialist gains in the Landes, boosted by the rise of the Front populaire. He spoke in front of the twenty-odd members of the new branch: 'I gave a presentation on socialism for one hour and fifteen, one hour and thirty minutes. [. . .] Some of these areas have not seen a socialist propagandist since Jules Guesde twenty years ago.' Broca showed him around his small goose factory, which also produced corks. Lévi-Strauss was dazzled and felt as though he were back in the days of apprenticeships and the guilds. He was all the more delighted with his gastro-political expedition as he had grown tired of the 'political inertia in Mont-de-Marsan', where the grassroots activists were 'paralysed by a municipal policy of cooperation with the Radicals; and since the Radicals are the only ones to fight against here . . .' (M26).

The young man, his wife by his side, went into full swing. He was now in on every action, travelling up and down the region, whipping up, if not crowds, at least group members. He would engage in propaganda exercises, dropping by the printer's after class. 'I am now practically the entire organization, since I am director of all propaganda. Sparks will fly!' (M59). This relation to politics – both earnest and playful – was no doubt not peculiar to Lévi-Strauss. Recall Paul Nizan in Bourg-en-Bresse, and all the young philosophy professors who became missionaries of the left in the provinces, and who, in the state of relative boredom in which they found themselves, were only too happy to engage in socialist or communist proselytizing to their flock. This model, typical of the interwar period, of philosophy professor/local activist is taken up with characteristic energy by Lévi-Strauss, always very determined and enthusiastic, confident in his ability to 'shake up' his world. In the context of the crisis of 1933, civil servants were threatened with a reduction in salary. A petition signed by the professors was handed to the director of the Duruy Lycée: 'Its tone was pathetically soft; I intervened and had them unanimously approve a statement of complete solidarity with the civil service unions. I was for my part favourable to a half-hour strike, but I did not propose it, since I knew no one would support me' (M60).

With his rhetorical skill and considerable experience in political activism, Lévi-Strauss quickly became a person of significance in the local community. In February of 1933, he was invited to speak at the opening of the new public school in Saint-Martin-de-Seignanx, representing the Federation, with the prefect, the regional school inspector and the local deputy (from the Radical Party) also in attendance: 'It was not a joking matter.' This really was the 'professors' republic' described by Albert Thibaudet, and venomously lampooned by Lévi-Strauss in *L'Étudiant socialiste*.[8] The local press spoke of the 'magisterial speech by Claude Lévi-Strauss on the institution of the public school – secular, free and compulsory'. In fact, barred from making jokes, Lévi-Strauss mounted a strong critique of the empty shell of radical secularism and offered a more developed vision of secularism as 'labour humanism', even while extolling the emancipatory virtues of republican education.[9] The young socialist, expected to not hold back, was asked to speak at the banquet that followed. Lévi-Strauss provided a kind of ethnographic account of this moment in the culture of left politics *à la française*: 'A beautiful glass-clad school, airy and spacious. Speeches by the mayor, the regional director of primary education, a school teacher, the Radical deputy Lassalle, and the deputy prefect; the kids sang the 9th Symphony. I was quite relieved not to have been made part of this demonstration of national togetherness. Following the school inauguration, pre-dinner drinks at the town hall, then off to the banquet dinner for 90, very proletarian guests (farmers, low-level civil servants, industrial workers) in a large wooden room all decorated with pine branches. And what a banquet! We started at 20 minutes before 2pm and at 6pm it was still going strong! I have never seen anything like it, nor eaten and drank so well. For starters, soup and assorted charcuterie; then a 1.5-metre-long salmon (no exaggeration!) that was brought out whole, cold and lined with mayonnaise; then beef fillet with mushrooms and Armagnac, cheese-filled artichokes, astonishing truffled turkeys, and salad; finally, monumental cakes garnished with ribbons, fruit, sparkling wine, coffee and Armagnac. The whole thing was well basted with red and white Saint-Émilion of the highest quality. It was unbelievable, more refined and delicious than in exclusive restaurants. I was therefore a bit impaired by the time they summoned me to address the inebriated assembly. I gave a speech on socialism and secularism that the deputy prefect did not much appreciate, but which was interrupted by applause. I was told it was good. I spoke for about 45 minutes, after which time Lassalle took over and said he completely agreed with me; but he was drunk and didn't pull it off very well. Then the deputy prefect spoke again, congratulated me (discreetly) and addressed Dina; finally, journalists from *La France* and *La Dépêche*. The excitement had reached a fever pitch. Lassalle did everything he could to win over this new and dangerous militant. A proper old man in grey tails came over to me to say, with considerable emotion, that a long time ago he had heard a speaker of my age and political affiliation who was the only one who compared with me – Pierre Laval – and that I would go far in life, and that he would remind me of his prophecy in seven or eight years' time' (M54).

Notwithstanding its folkloric character, which he deliberately emphasized to amuse his parents, the experience of local politics marked him indelibly. He would later tell Georges Charbonnier in an interview that there was 'a difference, not just of degree but of kind, between managing a municipal council and managing a parliament'.[10] In the former, decisions were made based on the ideology of the ruling party, to be sure, but also and primarily based on interpersonal relationships. For Lévi-Strauss, this

was the only level of authentic politics, the only possible scale for a concrete grasp of the issues. In other words, in a modern world that multiplies
levels of inauthenticity, with abstract decisions in which nobody fully
grasps anything, the notion of an 'authentic level' referred to that of local
politics, of which Lévi-Strauss, while never highlighting the intense biographical connection, was clearly a connoisseur. He continued, engaging
uncharacteristically in an act of political imagination, and at a time, 1961,
when he was carefully cultivating his image as an apolitical scholar: if the
anthropologist were to become a political reformer, 'he would probably
recommend a comprehensive decentralization, so that the largest number
of social and economic activities could be exercised at these authentic
levels, where the groups comprise men who have concrete experience of
one another'.[11]

But back to Mont-de-Marsan, in 1932–33. What about his teaching?
And his students? A few scattered elements reveal a contented professor
happily preparing his lectures and delivering them to the young men of the
lycée – five of whom were majoring in philosophy, ten in basic mathematics – and the young women at the secondary school, while 'pacing nonstop
from one end of the classroom to the other, so much so that by the evening
[he was] all washed-up' (M7). He suspected that his students did not
fully grasp the value of the raw material he was providing them, but they
'listen[ed] and seem[ed] interested'. 'My explanations of Baudelaire especially, though totally improvised and quite far-fetched, bl[e]w their minds.'
For the young mentor taught both philosophy and literature courses,
which allowed him to include authors from his own personal pantheon in
the curriculum – Baudelaire, and also Ibsen. He took particular pride in
his lecture on the Norwegian playwright, which commenced with 'an overview of the intellectual state of Europe between 1830 and 1910: painting,
the move to impressionism; music, Wagner; poetry, symbolism; literature,
Zola. [. . .] Then an overview of the Scandinavian intellectual fervour.' In
philosophy, he noted having given 'good exam questions on induction and
habit'. The students were expected to acquire a veneer of scientific knowledge. Alas, the man who would later attempt to raise the social sciences to
the level of the hard sciences was quite out of his depth, as he confessed in
the same light and humorous tone that echoes throughout his correspondence: 'I have once again tried to grasp Einstein's theory, which I planned to
explain to my students. I hope they will be more easily satisfied. O well, I'll
have to bluff my way through it . . .' (M31).

His former students offered their remembrances of him in 1984, sketching a bemused portrait of their professor, then barely older than the dozen
or so schoolboys he was teaching: 'He liked to pace constantly during his
lectures, in search of inspiration that never failed him. His keen and intense
black eyes would seize us all at a glance, and his effortlessly rolling gait
enabled him to pivot with rare poise, and with a disconcerting suddenness.
This outward agitation served only to anticipate, so to speak, the direction
of his thought, the search for the most appropriate term, never surrendering to the easy temptation of esoteric jargon. His professionalism was
impressive, and we were grateful for it: he never skipped over anything on

the curriculum, our papers were carefully and even benevolently graded. To my knowledge, not a single one of us was ever punished for anything, or even admonished. He was rather keen to encourage us, and sometimes even complimented us.'[12] None of the curriculum was glossed over, and there was no intrusion of socialist convictions in his teaching, which remained utterly politically neutral. Yet the young bourgeois of Mont-de-Marsan knew of their professor's political activism, which only further enhanced his prestige in their eyes, with its whiff of scandal . . .'[13]

An important ritual for all young professors was the performance review. In anticipation of the local inspector's surprise visit, Lévi-Strauss prepared 'dazzling courses'. In the end, Mr Roustan showed up for a 'very metaphysical' lecture (M82) by his young colleague, who was interrupted after only half an hour and congratulated in front of his students. The two men subsequently reconvened in the headmaster's office to discuss more serious matters: the posts that were to become available for the following year. Indeed, not unlike with his military service, Lévi-Strauss had exhausted the exotic charms of the provinces. Dina Lévi-Strauss was herself sitting the *agrégation* exam that year, for which, in addition to all his other activities, her husband helped her prepare. She successfully passed in July, at the age of twenty-one. After much equivocation, he was 'promoted' to Laon, in northeast France, while his wife was posted to Amiens.

To Laon . . . and back

This marked the beginning of a new life – the schizophrenic existence familiar to today's long-distance commuters, albeit perhaps on a different scale. Each in their respective *lycée* and city, Dina and Claude Lévi-Strauss scheduled all their courses for the first few days of the week, sleeping in hotels, and reconvened at the end of the week back in Paris at the family home on rue Poussin. As far as Claude was concerned, that year and a half in Laon – from October 1933 to Christmas 1934, when he was released from his teaching duties by the ministry of education – was crucial, since it marked the beginning of his evolution towards anthropology.

He continued his political activities, but in Paris more than in Laon, where he never lingered long, 'even though the town, in its rough and austere way, was not without charm. The stocky, squat cathedral there is an arresting sight.'[14] According to his predecessors and successors, Laon was a kind of provincial garrison, sought after by young professors who were looking to commute from the capital. Louis Farrigoule, aka Jules Romains, who was posted there from 1911 to 1914, described its advantages: 'The post in Laon . . . was very much sought after for its proximity to Paris – 1 hour and 44 minutes on the express – and for the light workload. One class of five or six students, no preparation for competitive exams, and a very easy schedule with classes conveniently grouped together, which allowed me to live in Paris and spend two nights a week in Laon.'[15] In 1936, a year and a half after Lévi-Strauss's departure, Jean-Paul Sartre was appointed to Laon. He also subscribed to the early week schedule, arriving Sunday night and leaving on the Wednesday five o'clock train. In his letters to Simone de Beauvoir, he repeatedly referred to what he called his 'Laon perspective': 'the slow and leisurely life (the provincial life of yesteryear); you do have to learn to be a bit bored, and feel time pass slowly'.[16] His colleagues all conspired to force Sartre to deliver the official speech on the occasion of the school's 50th anniversary (it was opened in 1887): 'Boivin, a former Laon professor and now Minister Zay's chief of staff, presided over the minister's visit, and probably prevailed upon him to come, in order to show off to his friends', Sartre explained mockingly to de Beauvoir. Laon, Boivin, Sartre, the Front populaire – a glimpse into what Lévi-Strauss's future, very much involved in these various circles (philosophy professors, socialists), might have been, but never was. He had already begun his bifurcation from this path.

The professor that succeeded him in January 1935, Valentin Feldman, was a brilliant philosopher, a Russian-Jewish immigrant who would later meet a tragic end: involved in the Resistance, he was arrested and shot at Mont Valérien on 27 July 1942. He was a very warm teacher who would develop fraternal relationships with his students, very different from Lévi-Strauss, who was rigorous, benevolent and caring, but remained intellectually neutral and never had the least intention of getting involved in his students' lives outside the classroom. Lévi-Strauss was neither a confidant, nor a mentor; neither a Feldman, nor a Sartre. Within the world of philosophy teaching, a new model had been steadily developing since the early twentieth century, in which the professor, no longer simply reproducing the philosophical thoughts of others, took on the function of intellectual production: their teaching became their oeuvre, which required a charismatic and often subversive voice that made one more than a professor – a mentor, a tutor, a confessor.[17] This was the style of Alain, revised and adapted by Sartre. However, this posture was not an option for Lévi-Strauss, whose profoundly idiosyncratic character resisted it. Even his political activities, which were much more intense than Sartre's at the time, were not known to his students in Laon, and in any case did not inflect the content of his courses in the least. Yet Lévi-Strauss did, at least retrospectively, embrace the paradigm of the 'vocation' that was part and parcel of this new model, applying it to anthropology and turning his back on philosophy.

Bifurcating

An outsider to anthropology

What was the state of French anthropology at the time? It was a field of knowledge that had gradually gained institutional recognition and that combined, in a particularly exciting way, both an absolute faith in science and the artistic sensibility of avant-garde movements fascinated by exotic worlds. All this informed by the humanist discourse of the political left, the colonial reformism of the Front populaire, and the enthusiastic support of high society. To paraphrase Lautréamont, we could say it lay at the intersection of the former surrealist Georges Bataille and the ethnographer Alfred Métraux, around a pre-Columbian object, whose exhibition was financed by the Viscount of Noailles, president of the Société des amis du Musée d'Ethnographie du Trocadéro, and which would end up ten years later, duly labelled, in that repository of the people's science, the Musée de l'Homme.

This French specificity – the 'enduring contiguity' between ethnography and avant-garde movements – has been frequently pointed out.[18] Nothing of the kind emerged elsewhere. In France, very strong ties of friendship and intellectual influence developed between some of the (often dissident) surrealists like Bataille, Leiris, Desnos, Queneau and Limbour and the world of ethnography. They all came together around a journal, *Documents* (fifteen issues were published), which in 1930 and 1931 became the hub of their new vision of the world. According to James Clifford, this collaboration rested on a common attitude that was fundamentally 'ethnographic', in that it challenged established certainties. The First World War had left this generation with a strong sense of the utter bankruptcy of Western civilization and, alongside it, of the paradigms on which it rested: reality, normality, superiority. This profound breach in the order of established beliefs allowed for the emergence of the strange in the familiar urban landscape – the surrealist quest – as well as for the shattering of the obvious by exotic alternatives that became powerful inspirations for the arts as well as for scholarship. This shared *Weltanschauung* can be seen in the complete abandonment of all hierarchical distinction between high and low culture in *Documents*. The journal adopted a surrealist approach, which confronted and juxtaposed images and texts ranging from Western high art to elements of urban culture, from regional crafts to photography, from exotic objects to Hollywood films, from Eskimo masks to Picasso paintings. The eponymous 'documents' were intended to evacuate the notion of art in favour of a new reception of objects in their contexts, as seen by both artists and anthropologists.[19] The lifelong friendship between Georges Bataille and the anthropologist Alfred Métraux, as well as Michel Leiris's move from anthropology to literature, are but a few examples of the web of personal, social and cultural relationships that characterized French anthropology in the 1930s.

Yet anthropology was also a field of knowledge that aspired to become a new discipline of the social sciences – which would require institutions and scholars. Interwar anthropology was established around a winning quartet of researchers – Marcel Mauss, Paul Rivet, Lucien Lévy-Bruhl and Georges Henri Rivière – as well as an ambitious project that inspired and transformed the discipline: the creation of the Musée de l'Homme to replace the 'jumble of exotica'[20] that was the former Trocadéro Museum. It thus indeed makes sense to conceive of this episode as 'a tale of two museums'.[21]

Marcel Mauss – an erudite scholar, charismatic professor, socialist, Bohemian and Dreyfusard, a man of 'inspired confusion'[22] (he was known for his silences) – had earned the status of founder of the discipline. His lectures at the Institut d'ethnologie – the first pillar of the new discipline, established in 1925 – were attended by a mixed audience of students and colonial amateur scholars, who provided considerable data for the nascent field. Mauss was also Durkheim's nephew. He trained the first generation of anthropologists who would do field work, but he himself never did. Above all, he supplied the theoretical foundations and scholarly ambition that could raise the discipline to a level alongside sociology in the pantheon of the new social sciences. Paul Rivet was, for his part, a former military doctor who had converted to anthropology while working in Colombia.[23] By then a renowned specialist of the Americas, Rivet was a subtle politician, a member of the Socialist Party and a founding member of the Comité de vigilance des intellectuels antifascistes (1934), deeply committed to his scholarly humanist mission in the murky context of the rise of authoritarian and fascist regimes in 1930s Europe. If he never had the intellectual prestige of Mauss, he played a decisive role in the process of institutionalization, from 1928 onward, in coordinating the transformation of the Musée d'Ethnographie du Trocadéro, and then, from 1937, as the director of the new Musée de l'Homme, the paradigmatic centre of anthropological knowledge production in France. Thanks to his many political ties, Rivet was successful at making anthropology part of the political agenda of the humanist and reformist left. Lucien Lévy-Bruhl, now forgotten, was a star at the time, an influential intellectual and renowned ambassador of French social sciences, internationally acclaimed on the basis, as is often the case, of a simplified and ossified version of his theories of the 'primitive mind'. Like Rivet a committed socialist, Lévy-Bruhl supplied anthropology with a network of political and social contacts that none of the other protagonists could rival. Indeed, Rivet often went to him for whatever funding or support he needed.[24]

Georges Henri Rivière was a radically different character – temperamental, multifaceted, charming, in sharp contrast with the monolithic convictions of the military doctor. And yet it was the latter who sensed that the flighty young man – who played the organ at fashionable parties, had a taste for jazz and collaborated with Joséphine Baker – would make a great ethnographic museologist; he hired him in 1928 to help 'prefigure' the Musée de l'Homme while waiting for it to be built, since its construction was tied to the Universal Exhibition of 1937.[25] The old 'Troca' (which dated from the Universal Exhibition of 1878), with its intricate style, gave way to the sharp lines and 1930s functionalism of the Palais de Chaillot, which was to house the Musée de l'Homme, itself part of the Muséum national d'Histoire naturelle. We will return later to this institutional creation, whose impact on Lévi-Strauss's career was all too marked. For now, the building of the discipline proceeded through the acquisition of a more scientific character, in sharp contrast with the largely extra-scientific and socialite atmosphere that characterized the exhibitions and public of the Trocadéro Museum.

With the coming to maturity of a new generation – Alfred Métraux, Marcel Griaule, Michel Leiris, André Schaeffner, Germaine Dieterlen, Denise Paulme, Louis Dumont, Jacques Soustelle[26] – anthropology first developed as a science of fieldwork, as opposed to armchair erudition.

Visiting exotic peoples, which comprised this sacrosanct 'fieldwork', was proof of scientific seriousness. It permitted the nascent discipline to distinguish itself from its counterfeit form, circulated by the many explorers of the time whose narratives were highly fashionable.[27] Even if the practice was new, the imperative to do fieldwork became central. Rather than an extended stay with a local population, it took the form of reconnaissance work, data gathering and, especially, the collection of objects.[28] As Vincent Debaene has reminded us, the methodology was characterized by a degree of amateurism, since the discipline had no manual, as opposed to in Britain where a solid ethnographic tradition had already produced many such works. Of course, Mauss had produced 'Instructions d'ethnographie descriptive à l'usage des voyageurs, administrateurs, missionnaires' in 1926,[29] but by and large anthropologists learned on the job. Hence the prominence of particular expeditions, including first and foremost the Dakar-Djibouti mission (1931), headed by Marcel Griaule.[30] Now canonical sites of institutional memory for French anthropology, these expeditions promoted the work of collecting at the heart of ethnographic knowledge. The museum and fieldwork thus became the two pillars – institutional and intellectual – on which the young science relied to distinguish itself from cabinets of curiosities and explorers. However, in the process, it became complicit in what is now a compromised set of forces: the colonial project.

Indeed, the largely colonial origins of the Musée de l'Homme had long been occluded by a dubious opposition between the Colonial Exhibition of 1931, associated with exotic trinkets, and the Musée de l'Homme (1938), considered to have been the epitome of scholarly humanism and democratic science. In fact, as Benoît de l'Estoile has convincingly demonstrated, both were expressions, albeit distinct ones, of a 'taste for others'. In 1930s France, both affirmed the positive value of human diversity in the name of a colonial reformism that brought together the major figures of French anthropology, some colonial administrators and most socialists. From this perspective, the young socialist activist Lévi-Strauss was perfectly aligned with Rivet's convictions when, in a 1929 article on 'socialism and colonization', he acknowledged the colonial legacy while purporting to change its direction: 'Confronted with the fact [of colonial empire], socialism, which is as much an organizational force, cannot adopt a negative attitude. Far from refusing funding for the colonies, we must be the first to demand it, and to insist that it be devoted in large part to the improvement of the indigenous condition.'[31] Rivet certainly did not turn down colonial funding from the Admiralty to use for financing his big museological project and expeditions, including the Dakar-Djibouti mission, for which an appropriations bill was unanimously passed in March 1931. The aim was to better understand the empire in order to better manage it, as the Front populaire colonial doctrine would have it. Rivet thus had no qualms admitting that the Musée de l'Homme, whose collections came essentially from the empire, was 'first and foremost a colonial museum'.[32] If anthropology had been associated with anticolonialism (that of the avant-garde movements with which it also had ties), 'it would be hard to imagine why it had been financed by public authorities'.[33] Indeed, it was mobilized to legitimize empire, not just within France but also internationally (especially in the US and the USSR), and Rivet would resign from the Comité de vigilance des intellectuels antifascistes (CVIA) in opposition to the explicit anticolonialism of the association he had cofounded. In other words, anthropology was not so much a science in the service of colonialism as itself one of the outcomes of this moment of reformist colonialism whose efforts it supported, finding in it a means of advancing its scientific interests.

In the world just described, Claude Lévi-Strauss hardly takes part at all. He does not belong to the group of students around Mauss, even if he did contact him in the autumn of 1931, after passing the *agrégation*: 'I obtained the *agrégation* in philosophy last July. I am very keen to pursue ethnographic studies and would be very happy if I could ask you for advice. I am leaving for military service around 20 October. If you would agree to meet me before then, I would be very grateful.'[34] The two young professors did indeed rub elbows with the world of anthropology – it seems Dina Dreyfus performed some work for the ethnographic museum, perhaps as part of her philosophy studies[35] – but in the end, these tentative forays revealed by the archives ultimately demonstrate just how much Lévi-Strauss was, as he always said, an outsider to anthropology at the time.[36] We can identify two early points of contact, but they were both tinged with imposture or pseudonym. First, in 1930, when Lévi-Strauss was still Georges Monnet's assistant, he wrote an article on 'Picasso and Cubism',[37] which was published in *Documents*, but under the deputy's name. Then, in 1931, his father was commissioned to decorate the Madagascar Pavilion of the Colonial Expo. Lévi-Strauss senior painted giant canvas panels in the hall of the ethnographic museum, with his son occasionally posing for him between two Malagasy women and various colonial administrators, and helping with the finishing touches. It is striking that Lévi-Strauss's first visit to the museum that Rivet and Rivière were busy reinventing should have been as colonial backdrop!

Not being a member of the church, he heard the call to depart as a divine injunction. More precisely, fifteen years later, by then an established anthropologist, he reconstructed that decisive moment in his life as a *deus ex machina* in a classical tragedy. This excerpt, a famous one, opens the fifth chapter of the second part of *Tristes Tropiques*: 'My career was decided one day in the autumn of 1934, at nine o'clock in the morning, by a telephone call from Célestin Bouglé, who was then head of the École normale supérieure. For a few years past, he had shown himself to be well disposed towards me, but in a rather remote and reserved way: first because I was not a *normalien*, and then, more especially, because even if I had been, I did not belong to his "stable", whose interests he jealously furthered. No doubt, he had been unable to find any better candidate, since he asked me bluntly: "Do you still want to study anthropology?" – "Most certainly." "Then apply for a post as a teacher of sociology at the University of Sao Paulo. The suburbs are full of Indians, whom you can study at the weekends. But you must give Georges Dumas a firm answer before midday."'[38]

The telephone call is dramatically narrated in *Tristes Tropiques* as a kind of *coup de théâtre*. The apparent eccentricity of the proposition, the bluntness of the request, the pressing character of the decision, the ignorant flippancy of Célestin Bouglé (Indians had long since left the suburbs of São Paulo . . .) – all these details contributed to making this rupture as radical and unexpected as a lightning bolt from the sky: exit Europe, enter Brazil! In fact, although Célestin Bouglé was certainly no intimate, he knew Lévi-Strauss well, having supervised his first research project in philosophy. And prior to this departure for the Americas, which is retroactively presented as entirely impromptu, Lévi-Strauss and his wife had requested his support for a Rockefeller Foundation grant 'to study anthropology in the United States'. Bouglé had then vouched for the young couple's seriousness with Tracy B. Kittredge, one of the foundation's envoys: 'I came to know these two youngsters when they were preparing for the *agrégation* in philosophy, which they both successfully obtained. I consider them both to be intelligent and hardworking. The young man, Claude Lévi-Strauss, submitted a very remarkable thesis on Marxism.'[39] But Lévi-Strauss's profile did not fit with the foundation's politics, as his American interlocutor explained to Bouglé: 'It seems to me unlikely that we will consider their application in the near future. I have the impression that they are only just beginning their anthropological studies. In general, we prefer candidates more advanced in their careers who have already demonstrated their individual ability in the specific field of the social sciences that they have chosen to pursue.'[40] First contact with their North American future and a first failure, at which point they could consider the Brazil option.

'Vocation' vs. 'impure motivations': why become an anthropologist?

Why does one become an anthropologist? Somewhere between a 'combination of circumstances'[41] and 'impure motivations',[42] Claude Lévi-Strauss defined the 'vocation' of anthropology as a kind of choice in which one is chosen rather than chooses: 'Like mathematics or music, anthropology is one of the few genuine vocations. One can discover it in oneself, even though one may have been taught nothing about it.'[43] In addition to this necessity, a number of other motivations were invoked: early predispositions (a taste for exotic curios), the professional opportunities offered by a young discipline ('things were moving'[44]), the inspirational role of a few anthropological works, including, in 1933, Robert Lowie's book *Primitive Society*, which gave him a glimpse into a possible reconciliation between his professional training and his taste for adventure. The role model here was Jacques Soustelle,[45] or, in a different way, Paul Nizan, who told him he had been drawn to anthropology.[46] To these manifold reasons, Lévi-Strauss later added his epistemological temperament, which he found analogous to the anthropological quest itself – what he called his 'Neolithic intelligence'.[47] In short, there were quite a few factors to explain both anthropology and departure. This decision – which proved fundamental to both the path of Lévi-Strauss's career and the evolution of the science of anthropology – was due to a multiplicity of factors of different kinds, underpinned by powerful socio-professional, intellectual and existential logics that were less specific to Lévi-Strauss than he thought.

It is indeed curious that such a professionally and socially successful young man, with strong family and marital ties, a young professor with a position, even one put off by the repetitiveness of teaching, very active politically at a time when his party was about to regain power (from the spring of 1934 with the Front populaire alliance), would seek and eventually accept a posting that would tear him away from all of this solid potential. Lévi-Strauss later reflected on the unease with one's own society that generally lay at the root of all decisions to study another. But he himself, as he was about to make this big leap, did not seem like someone in the least at odds with his surroundings.

Leaving for Brazil and choosing anthropology did not necessarily arise out of a sudden desire to break with his political and philosophical commitments, contrary to the clear-cut rupture described in *Tristes Tropiques*. The young militant had voiced some reservations about his political associates at Révolution constructive: he found his comrades sometimes overly critical of Blum, whom he strongly admired. In addition, in November 1933, the SFIO, following a stormy congress in July, underwent its 'neo-socialist' split, resulting from ideological differences and Marcel Déat's and Adrien Marquet's desire for independence. Thirty thousand members left to join the ranks of the new Parti socialiste de France, together with many deputies and senators and six federations.[48] Lévi-Strauss, although a close friend of Déat, did not cross that line, but he probably felt torn between two allegiances, an unstable position that perhaps made it tempting to escape onto a third path. Yet, there was nothing to demonstrate that anthropology was experienced as a substitute or a rupture; quite the opposite: it could just as well have served as a tool of political and philosophical revival. In many articles in *L'Étudiant socialiste*, Lévi-Strauss argued that Marxism, indeed all philosophical thought, must be 'plunged back into reality', fed by knowledge produced by 'fertile disciplines, such as anthropology, which did not exist in Marx's times, and from which today's Marxism stood to benefit'.[49] Thus the young philosopher and activist originally had a very political use of anthropology in mind, since, in his view, revolutionary socialism and the anthropological project both rested on a shared critique of Western civilization. In *Tristes Tropiques*, his move to the social sciences was described in terms of a 'disgust' for philosophy, which prompted him to turn to anthropology as 'a means of escape'.[50] However, in subsequent interviews he considerably qualified this narrative: 'I wouldn't say it was a rupture with philosophy. Because in the end, we're always doing philosophy. But another kind of philosophy that, rather than proceeding from introspection or the human condition conceived at the scale of our time and our society, strives to take as its starting point a reflection on all human experience, however remote from our own.'[51] Even at the level of party politics, Claude Lévi-Strauss had not given up on the idea of a political career when he left for Brazil: 'I left for Brazil just as the unhoped-for was happening. I can still picture myself in São

SFIO membership card, 16th arrondissement section. Lévi-Strauss joined in 1927 and paid his dues for the last time in 1935.

Paulo, feverishly listening on short wave radio to the result of the elections, hearing about the establishment of a Front populaire government and the appointment of Georges Monnet as minister. I was convinced that he was going to call me, that I would also take part in the event, and was ready to get on the next ship back. But nothing came.'[52] This short and cruel tale – which can only be truly appreciated by those who have themselves waited in vain for a call that never came – suggests that Lévi-Strauss, far from choosing anthropology out of a 'disappointment' with politics, was still quite invested in politics. A tale of two phone calls, then: the one of October 1934 enabling him to leave; and the one of May 1936, eagerly anticipated, that never came, requiring him to stay.

Among his professed reasons for going to Brazil, Claude Lévi-Strauss often mentioned, with a touch of guilty conscience, professional opportunities: 'The reasons that drove me to become an anthropologist were, I confess, "impure" ones. I was far from thrilled with the prospects opened up by the philosophy *agrégation* and I sought a way out. For sure, I had fun teaching that first year, but quite quickly . . . At the time, it was known among philosophy teachers that anthropology was a "way out", and it was Paul Nizan, whom I knew because he had married one of my cousins, who once talked to me about it. I loved camping, hikes in the mountains, life in the open air, and so I left.'[53] Lévi-Strauss had often blamed his inability to ever teach the same course or make the same presentation twice on some sort of congenital defect. This was indeed a serious liability for a professorial career, especially in secondary education. Anthropology thus offered a means of escaping the routine of secondary school teaching and moving directly to university teaching, whereas the *agrégés* of his generation spent at least a decade teaching in *lycées* in the provinces and then in Paris. To fully grasp the context for these 'impure' motivations, we should not forget that Lévi-Strauss was not a *normalien*, and thus a university position would be all the harder to obtain. There is no question that the choice of a new social science involved a degree of strategizing about the institutional advantages to be derived from pursuing a research field 'of least resistance'.[54] It is one of the reasons why there were so many Jewish intellectuals among the founders of the social sciences, in France as well as in Germany and the United States. Durkheim, Mauss, Lévy-Bruhl: so many newcomers who would have had a more difficult time breaking into the traditional fields. Viktor Karady has demonstrated how innovative scientific fields can be seen as offering 'paths to success off the beaten track'.[55] This was exactly Lévi-Strauss's partially conscious perspective in the early 1930s, which he subsequently made explicit: 'The social advancement of Jews in the nineteenth century coincided with the constitution of the social sciences as full-fledged disciplines. They represented a kind of "niche" – in the ecological sense of the term – which was partly vacant, in which newcomers could make a name for themselves without having to face too much competition.'[56]

'Motives of passion?' 'Yes, even passion'

The idea of a 'way out' remains, in the end, a bit of an enigma. Indeed, it was clearly a way out of secondary school teaching, but anthropology, in that it involved a geographical break, with the obligation to carry out fieldwork in remote places, amounted to a much more radical 'way out', which also appealed to other philosophers of his generation.

Nizan had set off from the École normale supérieure and submitted himself to the throes of a Rimbaldian journey. Once back from the Arabian Peninsula, he threw himself into communist activism. Others shared Lévi-Strauss's and Nizan's dissatisfaction with philosophy teaching. A yearning for new horizons, a desire to see the world: these were the expressions of a common anxiety that ran across the intellectual spectrum in the 1930s. It reflected a rejection of dry abstractions, as well as, more fundamentally, the melancholy of young intellectuals confronting a world that made no sense to them. In the end, they all aspired to a more authentic understanding of things and beings. Sartre, Nizan, Lévi-Strauss – each chose one of the three 'ways out' that were available at the time. Sartre went for phenomenology; Lévi-Strauss for anthropology; and Nizan for revolutionary politics. These were the three hard drugs available to young intellectuals in the 1930s – they could speed up the pace of life, give it greater meaning and substance, and take you to the heart of things.

Of these options, anthropology was not the least seductive. Not only was the discipline being revitalized and transformed by exciting characters, institutions and perspectives; it also broke with the tradition of letters, gave trivial objects a new dignity, and adopted an ambitious motto: 'To take all of man as a subject.'[57] In addition, it did away with the traditional division of labour between the armchair savant and the data-collecting field observer. Anthropologists now conducted their own fieldwork and were encouraged to define for themselves the materials on which they focused their analyses. Reconciling the intellectual and the explorer, fireside reflection and life outdoors, book learning and sensory experience, anthropology held out the possibility of doing away with the rigid categories that had been constitutive of Western thought and knowledge since Descartes. Around its cradle, the competing fairies of experience and knowledge hovered. To be both an intellectual and a man of action! It is easy to see how a passionate young man, little inclined to further exploration of a rhetorical mode whose depths he had already plumbed, should be tempted by anthropology as offering the promise of self-fulfilment. An 'escape' for Lévi-Strauss, an 'opportunity for redemption' for Michel Leiris – the religious overtones were commensurate with the magnitude of the expectations.[58]

Much later – talking about the writer Montherlant, whose eulogy he had to write as his inaugural speech at the Académie française – the newly minted academician drew a surprising parallel: 'The kind of experience for which many in my generation turned to anthropology, in Montherlant's generation was provided by war and then sports.'[59] In *Tristes Tropiques*, Lévi-Strauss draws attention to the 'beyond' that all societies (primitive and industrialized) generate in order to test their members who 'exit', thus allowing them to return, swathed in glory and having gained a legitimacy that could not be acquired in any other way.[60] In our societies, exploration, sporting exploits and the experience of war are among these situations of excess that demand from those who confront them that they exceed themselves and expose themselves to danger, which appeals to feverish young minds. Montherlant, Lévi-Strauss continued, considered sport as 'an intermediary activity between the great physical lyricism of war and the bureaucracy of peace [. . .], war was akin to an anthropological experiment carried to extremes. First, because of the exceptional trials to which it subjected the entire being; and then, because of the mixing of human beings it effected, at a time when French society remained less homogeneous than it thought it was, and when this mixing provoked a disorientation that would subsequently become hard to come by.' Each generation invented its own beyond: for Montherlant's, it was war; for Lévi-Strauss's, anthropology superseded that adventure whose imagination it appropriated while refusing its violence.[61]

To conclude on this 'choice' of anthropology, which satisfied a number of more or less conscious expectations, both personal and generational, suffice it to say that the choice of a particular science does not necessarily follow a very scientific logic. In 1961, Lévi-Strauss explained to Georges Charbonnier, who was asking him about how he arrived at anthropology, that the disciplinary choices of 'hard' scientists can have deep motivations, 'whose origins sometimes reach very far back into [their] personal histories' and to 'profoundly predetermined attitudes', even among mathematicians. 'Motivations of passion?' suggested the interviewer. 'Yes, even motivations of passion.'[62]

5

The Enigma of the World

Like a city-dweller transported to the mountains . . .
Claude Lévi-Strauss, *Tristes Tropiques*[1]

What, then, was Claude Lévi-Strauss's mental framework and cosmogony on the eve of his grand departure? This is not to attempt a sketch of his philosophical system – he did not have one – but to speculate as to his epistemological temperament, itself strongly tied to the experiences and discoveries of his childhood and adolescence.

His approach to the world as an enigma to be deciphered, his predisposition for contemplative exaltation, developed very early on in life, were fully operational in 1935. They constituted the foundations of an original personality that combined, not without tension, an exacting aspiration to rationality with an 'intimate mental rapture' – the springboard for long meandering reveries. This would not change. Like a city-dweller transported to the mountains, Claude Lévi-Strauss became exhilarated by the prospect of gaining an understanding of the chaos of the world and of putting it in order. A vital enough task to merit the dedication of . . . a life.

Epistemologies

His gaze was honed by a constellation of curiosities cultivated in childhood – a taste for collecting, taxonomic knowledge (minerals, animals), art, meandering in the multidimensional urban landscape, the discovery of nature. From the beaches of Brittany and Normandy to the rocky crags of the Cévennes, Lévi-Strauss gradually developed the premises of his intellectual identity. Emerging from childhood – after 'much scribbling about what one is and what one is not'[2] – he became convinced that, within this artistically inclined family, he would not himself be engaging in the act of creation but rather in its study.[3] Neither artist, nor musician (to his eternal regret), the young man felt that it was in the realm of knowledge that he would prove most able, investing the act of understanding with a demiurgic and sacred dimension to which he had no access via the noble path of creation.

The mystery of creation and the status of knowledge

He would often say that knowledge had no use, it must be an end in itself. 'To seek understanding – this is the only way to alleviate the tedium of life. It is the highest, perhaps our only justification.'[4] To find diversion, to achieve justification, to save oneself. If, as we shall see, knowledge entailed breaking through surface appearances and accessing the mysteries of deep explanation, it is no wonder that discovery of the real should have been expressed in terms of revelation. From this rational endeavour, much could be expected: both great joy and existential ground, placing knowledge at the heart of the process of secularization. Knowledge was redemptive, since it was the secular version of a religious quest through which one reconnected with the absolute.

There is no doubt that the young Lévi-Strauss, while remaining deaf to the call of religion, and even 'very intolerant on the subject', carried within him a very strong 'sense of mystery'.[5] But his thirst for intelligibility matched the expectations he placed on the act of knowing. Hence the passage in *Tristes Tropiques*, which has generated much commentary, in which he describes his kind of intelligence as 'neolithic': 'Like native brush fires, it sometimes sets unexplored areas alight; it may fertilize them and snatch a few crops from them, and then it moves on, leaving scorched earth in its wake.'[6] Why such a prodigious appetite? Because he had an aversion to repetition – which he realized in the course of his second year of teaching at the Lycée Laon – but more fundamentally because he suffered from a strange incapacity to apply his mind to the same subject twice: 'This handicap proved to be still more embarrassing when I found myself having to act as an oral examiner: as the questions cropped up at random, according to the accidents of the draw, I was no longer sure what answers the candidates were supposed to give. The dimmest of them seemed to say all there was to be said. It was as if the subjects were melting away before my eyes, through the mere fact that I had once applied my mind to them.'[7] On the one hand, the inexhaustible riches of the real, to which his sensory antennae gained him privileged and blessed access; on the other, the danger of a dissolution of the real when, for example, old philosophical refrains reduced its glow to a handful of hackneyed tropes. Depression then lay in wait: the world would give out. The choice of anthropology thus found its justification in the guarantee of infinite empirical material (all the cultures of the world) and in the aspiration to 'establish a new link between the universe and [himself]'.[8] One can imagine the young man's ardent desire to embrace the world, his readiness to do whatever it took to finally seize it fully, for it to not slip through his fingers, like the character of Cinna in the play he was to write a few years later, as he was briefly adrift between Brazilian expeditions: 'I said to myself that no human mind, not even Plato's, is capable of imagining the infinite diversity of all the flowers and leaves that exist in the world, and that I would get to know them; I would collect the sensations that are caused by fear, cold, hunger and fatigue, and that all of you who live in snug houses next to well-stocked barns cannot even imagine. I have eaten lizards, snakes and grasshoppers; and I approached these foods, the mere thought of which is enough to turn your stomach, with the emotion of one about to be initiated and the conviction that I was going to establish a new link between the universe and myself.'[9]

Understanding the world by eating it, or at least by using all of one's five senses. This very intimate conviction of the impossibility of separating the intelligible and sensory worlds, and of the value of the latter, is perhaps one of the main legacies of an 'opulent' childhood, which nourished this radical democracy of the five senses that remained characteristic of the life, and later of the work, of Lévi-Strauss: 'It annoys me to not understand the things that cannot be understood, to feel torn between two orders of knowledge, the sensory and the intelligible. Ever since childhood, I have felt a personal, an autobiographical need to try to build bridges between the one and the other.'[10]

Three mistresses plus one . . .

The possibility of reconciling the sensory and the intelligible does not exhaust all there is to say about Lévi-Strauss's intellectual character. Beyond this bridge, knowledge always entailed for him a leap into the void, a rupture, a fracture between appearances – reality as it is commonly given to us – and the real – the base, the bedrock of reality, a real that is more real than reality. This distinctive disposition was rooted in particularly rich biographical soil, and appears to have been planted very early on: 'In the end, the invariant in my personal history is that I was always fascinated by what appeared most incomprehensible, most arbitrary, and by trying to find, *behind it all*, a rationality.'[11] Lévi-Strauss would later express this impulse in philosophical terms, explaining it, in short, as the transposition 'to the human and social sciences [of] the philosophical distinction made by Locke and Descartes between secondary qualities and primary qualities (secondary qualities are deceptive; primary qualities correspond to reality).'[12]

In *Tristes Tropiques*, Lévi-Strauss offered three images of what was, in his view, entailed in the process of knowledge – psychoanalysis, Marxism and landscape, his 'three mistresses', as he called them. Each was connected to a very early encounter and presented as a short epistemological tale that reconciled his intellectual character and his life, shaping the epistemological structure of his worldview to enable the elaboration of an ambitious knowledge project.

Psychoanalysis first: it was as a *lycée* student that Lévi-Strauss first discovered Freud's writings, a mere ten years after they were first published, thanks to one of his classmates, whose father, Marcel Nathan, was part of the cohort of pioneering Freud disciples who, in Belle Époque Europe, formed a small gentlemen's club (with the exception of Marie Bonaparte, to whom Nathan was close). At the time, psychoanalysis was poorly received by the French medical establishment, in thrall as it was to the psychology of Pierre Janet. It was, rather, through art and literature that this new science of the psyche came to the fore in 1920s France. Even if – with the translation of several of Freud's books, and the publication of harsh critiques (notably by Charles Blondel) – psychoanalysis had become something of a 'craze', the sweeping curiosity and omnivorous intelligence of the young Lévi-Strauss is nonetheless quite striking here. Like anthropology, psychoanalysis had ties with the avant-garde artistic movements (especially surrealism), where it inspired considerable artistic production, in both the fine arts and literature, not to mention cinema (Doctor Mabuse). For the student of philosophy, Freud's texts made the entire structure of courses in psychology and the philosophy of the subject obsolete, with their binary oscillations between rational and irrational, intellectual and emotional, logical and pre-logical. The idea that the most significant elements could be extracted from the most irrational behaviour was a major intellectual shift, that Lévi-Strauss welcomed all the more since it confirmed his own natural inclinations – true reality never presents itself as such.

Marxism also required a shift to another level of reality, in the hope of understanding it more fully: 'Marx established that social science is no more founded on the basis of events than physics is founded on sense data: the object is to construct a model and to study its properties and its different reactions in laboratory conditions in order later to apply the observations to the interpretation of empirical happenings, which may be far removed from what had been forecast.'[13] This kind of modelling provided access to another order of reality. From then on, science for Lévi-Strauss would always take the form of a laboratory experiment, a cognitive *reductio* that was then to be put to an empirical test.

But the essential image of knowledge, for Lévi-Strauss, was offered by his third and most paradigmatic mistress, as illustrated by the vibrancy of the pages devoted to it in *Tristes Tropiques*: geology, a discipline he discovered as a teenager, on his own, so to speak, hiking the fragrant mountains of the Cévennes. In the late 1920s, his parents, though far from comfortably off, had bought a former silk farm where, for several years, the family went camping. Located near Valleraugue in the hamlet of Camcabra, the farm was in very remote country, and would provide refuge for the parents during the war. Later, in the 1950s, before the post-1968 influx, the region was modernized, roads were built, which, for Lévi-Strauss, marked the end of a land whose emptiness of any human presence and spectacular countryside had been indelibly imprinted on his mental landscape. He would go on long hikes, with map and tent, ascend Mount Aigoual at night (one of the trials to which he subjected each of his wives[14]), take dreamy strolls through geological temporality, and trace the lines between the layers of the Causses, the limestone plateaus in Languedoc. For Lévi-Strauss, the gradual unfolding of the disorder of a landscape into the order of a *longue durée* history was the very model of knowledge – a quest, through the rubble, brush and fissures, for a 'master' or 'noble' meaning, which suddenly illuminated the imperfections of perceptible reality in a sort of rapture of understanding. 'When the miracle occurs, as it sometimes does; when, on one side and the other of the hidden crack, there are suddenly to be found cheek-by-jowl two green plants of different species, each of which has chosen the most favourable soil; and when at the same time, two ammonites with unevenly intricate involutions can be glimpsed in the rock, thus testifying in their own way to a gap of several tens of thousands of years, suddenly space and time become one: the living diversity of the moment juxtaposes and perpetuates the ages. Thought and emotion move into a new dimension where every drop of sweat, every muscular movement, every gasp of breath becomes symbolic of a past history, the development of which is reproduced in my body, at the same time as my thought embraces its significance. I feel myself steeped in a denser form of intelligibility, within which centuries and distances answer each other and speak at last with one and the same voice.'[15]

Lévi-Strauss describes this 'epistemological moment' with the same fiery intensity as Marcel Proust discovering the mechanisms of unsolicited remembrance. In both cases, the powers of sensibility and rational intelligence combine to yield exponentially greater results. The profound experience of joy – one of the foundations of existence – lies in the collision of spaces and times and, finally, the fusion of subject and object (in this case, the landscape) culminates in a mystical form of communion whose 'miracle' is but a threshold. The difference lay in the physical effort required by Lévi-Strauss's approach – in which supreme knowledge is fundamentally achieved through movement (sweating, muscle flexion, panting) – whereas, for Proust, it is more a matter of chains of circumstance and the availability of the senses at any given moment.

The mountains definitely provided the ideal setting for Lévi-Strauss's process of intellection. This would later change, when he traded his uncompromising love of the rocky Cévennes for the world of the forest, which offered the same reward for less exertion. If the forest was the scene of his mature years, the mountains – and especially 'pasture mountains' between 1,400 and 2,200 metres high – was that of his youth. As opposed to the sea, whose charm was more 'diluted', the mountains provided a 'concentrated world', an 'upright' landscape that generated a condensation of meaning through the ascent of peaks and descent of valleys: 'The physical effort I spent in exploring it was something I conceded to it and by which its being was brought home to me. The mountain landscape, at once obstreperous and provocative, always concealing one half of itself from me but only to renew the other half through the complementary vista accompanying ascent or descent, joined with me in a kind of dance that I had the feeling of being able to lead all the more freely the better I had succeeded in understanding the great truths which inspired it.'[16]

This breathless miracle of knowledge was profoundly connected to childhood experience and possessed the same magical virtues. Indeed, as in the surrealist world, Lévi-Strauss's epistemological temperament entailed a capacity to imagine various layers of reality, all interconnected and hierarchized, since the final one, which subsumes all the others and gives them their meaning, is the real itself, endowed with a comprehensive and superior signification. It was of course not this kind of 'super-rationality' that the surrealists had in mind when they called for a 'letting go of everything' to enable its emergence. Yet in both cases, a process of unveiling is at work that makes visible, beyond surface appearances, a deeper reality, concealed and powerful.

There was another aspect of Lévi-Strauss's biography that fell within the paradigm of unveiling and the *Weltanschauung* of the young man as he was about to set sail for Brazil: his passion for detective novels, as he often discusses in his letters, with a preference for the Anglo-American style over the French. He was particularly fond of the American novelist S.S. Van Dine (aka Willard H. Wright) and his private investigator Philo Vance, an art connoisseur cum detective, and a bit of a dandy. From 1926 on, Lévi-Strauss read these novels as they were published and expressed informed opinions; of the last, he wrote that it was 'the best because it reverses the established conventions of the genre'.[17]

This enthusiasm for crime fiction – a genre born in the late nineteenth century and holding a dominant position in Western literature throughout the twentieth century, imposing a particular narrative form (especially on novels and films) – was characteristic of Lévi-Strauss's generation. Luc Boltanski has recently shown the relationship between contemporary forms of crime fiction, spy novels and the social sciences. All three rely on the construction of mysteries, have investigation as their primary instrument, and unveiling as their founding trope. Detective fiction and sociology both challenge surface appearances – based on irregularities, contradictions, absurdities or simple arbitrariness – to provide them with deeper meaning: 'A surface reality, apparent but probably illusory even though it has an official status, is countered by a deep, hidden, threatening [in the case of spy novel plots] reality, which is unofficial but much more real.'[18] The super-reality revealed by the criminal investigation, the conspiracy (of freemasonry, of international terrorism, of religious sects) that it exposes, corresponds to the attempt by the social sciences to describe the social world as a totality that obeys laws specific to it.

The ardent reading of crime fiction probably contributed to the development of an epistemology of mystery that is particularly striking in Lévi-Strauss, who frequently borrowed from the rhetoric of crime fiction to describe his anthropological project: 'On the one hand, a seemingly inexhaustible repertoire of mysteries, of coded messages to decipher; and, on the other, however difficult to achieve, certain principles of intelligibility that account for apparent absurdities.'[19] On several occasions, anthropologists congratulated him on his 'truly detective flair', which he used to untangle the transformation of myths and phenomena of circulation between distinct cultural areas. A method, in the words of Brazilian anthropologist Manuela Carneiro da Cunha, that was 'congruent with the detective fiction genre that Lévi-Strauss adopted in his last two *Mythologiques*'.[20]

Temporal settings

If the profound desire for knowledge was instilled very early on, and permanently, in Lévi-Strauss, its manifestations in time were decidedly more varied. It is always difficult to grasp, at any given moment, all the temporal horizons a person contains within them. Let us nonetheless offer a cross-section of the temporal strata that shaped Lévi-Strauss's scholarly mind as well as his fanciful temperament.

'Quixotism'

'For me quixotism is essentially an obsessive desire to find the past behind the present. If perchance someone someday were to care to understand my personality, I offer him that key.'[21] The past *behind* the present or the 'figure in the carpet'.[22] As if, here again, reality's core was to be found beyond the feeble lure of the present, but this time via a movement backward in time. Lévi-Strauss's own father was a kind of Don Quixote figure, 'ill-fitted' to his present, as his son would point out. The entire family lived in the afterglow of a fortune amassed in the previous century that had considerably dwindled over the years. It is no wonder the child saw this past in a light that made it more real than the depreciated present.

But by 1935, the young professor was fully engaged with his own times: he was on a professional career track; politics occupied his time and kept him attuned to the social, ideological and cultural dynamics of the day. He embraced the revolts, refusals and enthusiasms: revolution, the artistic avant-garde, Freud, Picasso, Stravinsky, pacifism, the desire for new horizons. As we have seen, he liked Céline and Nizan. Not so easy, in these circumstances, to pin on the young man setting out in 1935 (he was then twenty-six) the kind of 'biographical pessimism' – i.e., the idea that he would have much preferred to live in another century, the nineteenth – that he would effuse in his mature years. On the contrary, the young technophile, rhapsodizing about photography, cinema and the automobile, seemed indeed very much a creature of the twentieth century. Brazil was to change everything. However, in another sense, he may well have already been, and would always remain, a man of the nineteenth century – in his intense faith in the capacity of the human mind to understand and master the world. If the 'long nineteenth century', as well as the Alsace of the eighteenth century, were very much present in his mind, they did not yet function to devalue the present, since indeed everything suggests that, on the contrary, he was firmly rooted in his times, even if in a critical way. The past was vivid enough for Claude Lévi-Strauss, a young man who carried within himself epochs in which he did not live, for him to conceive of a movement in space as a movement backward in time, akin to the geological tracing he practised as a child. Indeed, just before crossing the Atlantic Ocean, in an attempt to gather information on Brazil and its inhabitants, he immersed himself in the narrative written by Jean de Léry in the last third of the sixteenth century – a preliminary mental operation before leaving Europe, a way of positioning himself on the threshold of encounter between two worlds.

A love of beginnings: the sixteenth century of Jean de Léry

At the end of 1934, having agreed to leave for Brazil the following February, Claude Lévi-Strauss undertook some research and reading at the library of the Musée de l'Homme (which was still the Musée du Trocadéro at the time). He came across Jean de Léry, and was enchanted. The time machine functioned thanks to the 'freshness of the gaze'[23] of the explorer from Geneva. Indeed, Léry left Geneva in 1556 to support Admiral Villegaignon, who had settled in Guanabara Bay (Rio de Janeiro) and was holed up in Fort-Coligny wracked by agonizing spiritual dilemmas. A Catholic, Villegaignon wanted to convert to Protestantism and asked Calvin to send him a dozen men who might help him overcome his crisis. Stuck between the Portuguese, who had settled in the north and were keen to consolidate their position along the Brazilian coast, and the Tupi Indians, initially living in relative harmony with the European settlers, the small contingent at Fort-Coligny was seized by a collective madness. Over the years, some inhabitants would take up indigenous wives and live as the local tribes. This is what happened to Jean de Léry, forced by an increasingly deranged Villegaignon to take refuge among the Tupi. And it was this sojourn that gave birth to the story – peppered with both spectacular and farcical episodes – that Lévi-Strauss found to be the stuff of high drama: 'What a marvellous film it would make!'[24] But he took particular delight in the kind of 'idyllic relationship which sprang up between [Léry and the Indians]', which 'inspired that masterpiece of anthropological literature, *Le Voyage faict en la terre du Brésil.*'[25]

Why a 'masterpiece'? Because it had the 'power to grasp the truth in beings and things while ignoring or rejecting conventions'. Nothing and nobody seemed to 'spoil his eye'.[26] As opposed to his arch rival André Thevet, author of *Singularités de la France antarctique*, Léry artfully managed to break free of the language of discovery, already well in place only fifty years into European exploration of the Brazilian coast. The sixteenth century aroused a sympathetic response from Lévi-Strauss, who was quick to see in it the beginnings he cherished: the century of contact that had not yet become routine, where something of the original wonderment remained. In the inaugural encounter between two worlds, both parties assessed and examined each other with guileless curiosity and equal dignity. This ability to observe the Other, to be shaken by it and to narrate it in ways that differ strongly from the canonical tales of Western modernity arriving in barbaric lands, this is what Claude Lévi-Strauss found in Jean de Léry, and more generally in the century of Montaigne and Rabelais: 'There is among the likes of Rabelais and Montaigne a wonderfully fresh gaze that would later disappear.'[27]

Claude Lévi-Strauss landed on American shores armed with this literary guide. Léry was his breviary. Everything brought him back to the sixteenth-century European and his Tupi: a shard of glass, a landscape, the melancholy sight of a coastline. As if in a state of temporal levitation, the anthropologist that he had not yet become engaged in a kind of dreaming. Like the child hiking in the mountains, the young man engrossed in his crime novel, the schoolboy perched on the bus platform, this European arriving in Rio with Léry in his pocket knew that the quest for another reality was the surest path to the truth, which, for him, always felt like a new dawn. 'Reading him helps me escape my century, reconnecting with what I would call "sur-reality", which is not that of the surrealists, but a reality more real than the one I have witnessed. Léry has seen things that are priceless, because it was the first time they were being seen, and it was four hundred years ago.'[28]

Part II

New Worlds (1935–1947)

6

France in São Paulo

Brazil was the great moment of our lives.
Fernand Braudel, 'Discours de réception à l'Académie française',
30 May 1985

On 4 February 1935, Claude Lévi-Strauss left for Brazil, where he remained for exactly four years.

He experienced his crossing, and in part also his sojourn, as a revisiting of the inaugural transatlantic voyages – of Columbus, the Portuguese Cabral, who landed at Salvador de Baja, as well as the other sixteenth-century explorers, with Jean de Léry foremost in his mind (and in his pocket, always ready to hand). The longstanding French presence in Brazil was still quite palpable in the 1930s and produced a kind of intimacy, enhanced by the creation of the University of São Paulo [USP], where Lévi-Strauss had come to work and teach in French, the second language of educated Brazilians.

The beginning of his career as an anthropologist was intertwined with an ambitious experiment in knowledge transfer between Europe and Latin America. The creation of the University of São Paulo in 1934 – where French professors (as well as, to a lesser extent, Italian and German ones) were to be sent to teach – was a project both thrilling and fragile, caught up as it was in a series of political, institutional and social dynamics that weighed on the future of the young, newly minted sociology professor.

Lévi-Strauss acknowledged owing a 'very profound debt' to Brazil[1] – where he was to return only once later in life, in 1985 – not just because, through its indigenous peoples, the country supplied him with the subject of his future dissertation, but because the physiognomy of its utterly New World landscape provided him with an extraordinary vantage point. Everything seemed to develop there at experimental speed, making the place a veritable laboratory of the human sciences. Indeed, Brazil was soon to become the Eldorado of French social science. If Georges Dumas's 'Operation Brazil' had originally been intended to graft French science and humanities onto Brazilian roots, it also served to bring Latin America into French historiography, geography and anthropology.

Indeed, by 1949 – i.e., fifteen years later – in a special issue of the journal *Annales* on South America, Lucien Febvre was urging young academics to go and see for themselves: 'Go there. See with your own eyes. [. . .] Do not read too much. Look around as much as you can.' It was 'a whole and still unexplored field of human life and experience [. . .] irreducible to simplistic formulae.'[2] The euphoric discoveries of Lévi-Strauss and the small São Paulo gang – comprising Fernand Braudel, Pierre Monbeig and Roger Bastide – only anticipated this programme, their eyes wide open to contemporary Brazilian reality, before turning, at least in the case of Lévi-Strauss, to the more or less preserved islets of the indigenous world.[3]

Heading to the Americas

On board the Mendoza

The dismal atmosphere surrounding Lévi-Strauss's departure – made vividly clear in the frosty description he gave of the farewell dinner organized by the Comité France-Amérique, at which Georges Dumas, the father of 'Operation Brazil', proffered final advice ('The main thing is to be well dressed!'[4]) – gave way to a sense of eagerness to leave. Finally, on 4 February 1935, Claude and Dina Lévi-Strauss, together with their two colleagues Jean Maugüe and Pierre Hourcade, boarded the *Mendoza* in Marseille. They set sail on a lovely Mediterranean winter's day, filled with 'the almost unbearable pleasure that one gets, when thirsty, from gulping down some iced, fizzy liquid'.[5]

The *Mendoza* was a multipurpose ship – half-cargo, half-cruise liner – belonging to the fleet of the Société générale des transports maritimes à vapeur, a company of which Lévi-Strauss would remain a loyal customer for all his transatlantic journeys. Picking up a few passengers along the way, the *Mendoza* made a long nineteen-day voyage, with numerous stopovers along the Spanish and African coasts, during which the boat would load and unload cargo. The first part of the journey thus consisted of a pleasant coastal cruise, which allowed them to tour the cities where they came to port. The first was Barcelona, where they arrived in the morning after having left Marseille just the night before. Lévi-Strauss rode all over town in a taxi, exhilarated by the city's broad avenues, the beauty of the place, the abundant vegetation (double lines of orange trees), and by Gaudí, whose name he appeared not to know: 'But the most incredible thing is the architecture, which is quite literally insane', he wrote to his parents[6] – the colourful mosaics, the flower-shaped church towers, the wrought-iron houses, 'puffed up "wonders" to live in'. The astonished delight is that of a young man who had never stepped foot outside France.[7] 'All this is so mad that it doesn't even look like architecture anymore: more like explosions of good mood.'[8] The travellers returned back down the *rambla* to the port. Later, it was Tarragona and its terraced colours: blue sea, heaps of bright yellow sulphur, barrels of red oil, and piles of oranges and black coal made for 'a marvellous tableau'. His youthful enthusiasm would often overwhelm entire letters. There were nine passengers on board, but on deck he felt as if he were all alone. His travel companions were quite agreeable,

Jean Maugüe in particular, a young philosophy professor who was escaping a teaching post in Montluçon, in central France – a brilliant and anti-conformist mind, who was to take part in Lévi-Strauss's Brazilian saga, and later narrate it in a very honest and endearing memoir, *Les Dents agacées*. But for the moment, 'one takes life as it comes'. Yet Lévi-Strauss, as a man with dependants, did not forget his parents, and was already encouraging them to join him in Brazil, for economic reasons, as if, in his mind, the city of São Paulo held the promise of an Eldorado for Europeans fallen on hard times and in the throes of economic crisis.

Past Dakar, the *Mendoza* took to the high seas for a twelve-day crossing to Rio de Janeiro. From then on, everything became new discoveries and delights, in a kind of ecstatic monotony. The nighttime throbbing of the engine brought on a 'serene happiness'.[9] Strangely, the Atlantic crossing, which deprived one of all bearings, was the opposite of a voyage. The sentiment of stillness was such that the boat became the scene of a kind of slide show, which offered its spectators a 'revolving stage of the world'.[10] Lévi-Strauss, in a 'state of grace',[11] focused on his intimate encounter with the undisturbed elements. In Maugüe's recollection, he appears 'walking around, almost always alone, on the ship's deck, his eyes wide open to be sure, but his entire being closed off, as if afraid to lose what he had just observed'.[12]

What was it, then, that so engrossed him, all senses on high alert? Perhaps the meandering clouds, or the 'supernatural cataclysms' of the rising and setting of the sun, to which he famously devoted several pages in *Tristes Tropiques* – pages he had in fact written on the spot, and that he saw fit, fifteen years later, to insert into the text. This somewhat conventional Proustian pastiche is, of course, a writerly exercise, but in its attempt to seize the concrete world and its sumptuous riches it is also putting language's capacity to capture and convey the real to the test. As if, on his way to discovering the 'wonders' of the New World, Lévi-Strauss had striven to train his eye and his pen to unveil its extraordinary, excessive and ineffable character.

The other memorable episode, midway through the journey, was 'the Doldrums', which opens chapter 8 of *Tristes Tropiques* – this area of calm where the winds of the two hemispheres converge and cancel each other out, producing a disturbing stillness, identified (and dreaded) by sailors as the equatorial line. The air is still. The sky more liquid than the sea, which itself has become greyer. One's sensory bearings are inverted, an invitation to change focal points at this ultimate stage, this 'last mystical barrier' that marks the definitive transition to the Americas. This watershed moment – somewhat feverishly experienced over a 'sleepless night spent on deck, watching and waiting for America'[13] – was also the starting point of a reverie on the myth of the Golden Age, the sixteenth century, and the first explorers, the imperial encounter and the 'harrowing test' to which the experience, knowledge and beliefs of the West was put, faced with discovery of another world.[14] Lévi-Strauss could still dream of his journey as though Europe and America were two planets, radically independent of one another.

The scent of the New World

Arrival in the New World was heralded by many signs – the presence of shrill-voiced tropicbirds and petrels, an escort of silver flying fish – but one first became 'conscious of it as a scent': a melange of tropical peppers and fermented tobacco leaves, a smell at once continental and ripe with vegetal decay, striking a 'powerful [olfactory] chord' that over the years would summon up for him the very name 'Brazil'. Finally, after smell it was the sense of sight that was solicited: an immense cordillera appeared along the shore, the *Serra do Mar*, along which the boat would pass from north to south, from Rio to the port of Santos. Its enormity, density and incommensurability immediately conveyed the scale of the New World, and the need to adjust one's perspective.

Rio was a disappointment. It offended his sense of proportion – a place not up to its reputation. The Corcovado and Sugar Loaf Mountain appeared to him as 'stumps sticking up here and there in a toothless mouth'.[15] He wandered about the city, much celebrated for its beauty, which reminded him of Nice or Biarritz under Napoleon III, in a mixture of familiarity and disorientation, rather more historical than geographical. A first note of disillusionment: 'The tropics are less exotic than out of date.'[16] Yet he noticed real differences: the distinction between public and private space was far more gradual than in our European cities. In Rio, the streets were extensions of the house, in a kind of osmosis between inside and outside. In yet another inversion that must have pleased him, due to the constraints of the city's site, Rio's social hierarchies were mapped onto the topography in opposite ways to those of southern European towns. Indeed, while the bourgeoisie in Marseille and Naples settled at the higher elevations, which were cooler and offered vistas on the sea, in Rio, the favelas were perched on the arid and sun-scorched hillsides and the well-to-do collected in the valleys that encircled the bay 'like fingers bent in a tight, ill-fitting glove'.[17]

This view gave way to an awed descent into the 'dreamlike' Tropics, along the Brazilian coast to Santos. There, a ribbon of fine sandy beaches stretched for thousands of kilometres, interspersed with small deserted islets and coves, with the dark green of the coastal cordillera looming above. Every so often, a sleepy little port would emerge, whose eighteenth-century palazzos bore witness to its former glory, that of the gold mining economy of Minas Gerais: Ubatuba and Parati were the principal ports from which gold was shipped to Europe. This journey through space, and hence inextricably also through time, finally came to an end in Santos, and in the present. The gold of the day in that part of Brazil was the black gold of coffee, and the port of Santos was the main export hub for a commodity that had constituted the wealth of the state of São Paulo since the late nineteenth century.

In Santos, the small French contingent was greeted by Julio Mesquita Filho – publisher of the newspaper *Estado de São Paulo* and a major figure of the local bourgeoisie, as well as one of the masterminds behind the creation of the University of São Paulo. The city of São Paulo, located

100 kilometres inland from Santos, was reached via a bumpy road, the *Caminho da Mar*, which started out by winding 800 metres up the coastal chain. For Lévi-Strauss, this was a first 'tropical shock' – from the coastal forest, preserved on the virgin slopes, wafted a new exuberance of vegetation. But once at the summit, the scenery changed: to the west, the immense ochre landscape of the great plateau of central Brazil, descending in tiers to the Amazon basin, like a 'tableland sloping downwards away from the sea, a springboard crinkly with undergrowth and surrounded by a damp circle of jungle and marsh'.[18] Note here the taste for metaphorical descriptions of geography in the style of Vidal de La Blache, with whom Lévi-Strauss would in some sense cross paths in Brazil, in the form of his disciple and son-in-law Emmanuel de Martonne. This barren plateau, which was to become a familiar Brazilian landscape for Lévi-Strauss – that of his life in São Paulo, as well as of his expeditions in Mato Grosso – first appeared to him in the inhospitable guise of crevices, ridges and ravines: 'A fine Breton drizzle started to fall.'[19]

The landscape that stretched from Santos to São Paulo, on the other side of the cordillera, could aptly be described as 'scarred'. With its deforested patches – farmed and then abandoned, in the violent and ephemeral impact of pioneers advancing in stages – one can read the entire cycle of the coffee economy and, alongside it, the cycles of Brazilian prosperity, where successive economic 'booms' (of gold, sugar, coffee, cocoa, rubber, etc.) have followed one another in an accelerated modernization process as chaotic as the landscape it has left behind. Indeed, the Brazil of the 1930s in which Lévi-Strauss disembarked was still emerging from its colonial period. The republic that put an end to the empire of Pedro II was founded in 1889 and slavery abolished in 1888, barely fifty years earlier. This first republic, which remained unchanged until 1930, rested on the power of the São Paulo coffee oligarchies and on the broad autonomy of the states, which competed with one another while being united in a federation. The coffee boom of the 1880s had transformed the western plateau of the state of São Paulo, covering it with *fazendas* – immense monocrop plantations farmed by half-enslaved populations and managed by overseers on behalf of large absentee *fazendeiros* families. In the same period, Brazil experienced a large influx of immigrants (more than three million) who settled in the south of the country and worked on the coffee plantations and in nascent São Paulo industries. In addition to Italian immigrants, a German population specializing in agricultural colonization had settled in the frontier areas of the southern states of Paraná, Rio Grande do Sul and Santa Catarina; there were also the Japanese, who had been coming to Santos since 1908 to work on coffee *fazendas*, and who then became small farmers of rice and vegetables. These communities that had taken root were indeed visible, and still very closed, when Lévi-Strauss and his colleagues landed in that already multicultural corner of Latin America, where one could move, as in New York, from 'little Italy' (in the Bexiga district) to 'little Tokyo' across very clear ethnic lines in the urban topography of São Paulo. While Rio and São Paulo were developing distinct urban identities – Rio as the town of leisure, the political capital, as opposed to São Paulo, the great city of industry – rural life, on the other hand, remained very traditional, plodding along at a colonial pace in the shadow of hinterland villages. Yet social, economic and urban transformations presented perils for the oligarchic order of the '*fazendeiros* republic': rural rebellions, communist agitation (the saga of the Coluna Prestes uprising of 1927), the tenentism of junior army officers who periodically revolted. In 1930, the new head of the state, Getúlio Vargas, ushered in a political settlement that brought the urban middle classes increasingly under the protection of the federal state. Vargas played a mediating role between local elites and army 'lieutenants', while supporting the rise of radical political movements, which set the political tone for the decade of the 1930s as highly conflictual, even before the coup of 1937 instituting the *Estado Novo*, which buttressed and hardened the new political dispensation. The young French minds arriving in São Paulo at the end of February 1935 were probably hardly aware of any of this. However, they would learn quickly, especially since the political and economic situation was directly tied to their coming to South America and was to have a determining impact on the projects and life of Claude Lévi-Strauss, more so even than on those of his friends.

The São Paulo mirage

Upon arrival in São Paulo, the group of French professors was received by the *interventor*, the governor general of the state of São Paulo, Armando Sales de Oliveira. They were put up at the Terminus, the city's luxury hotel, and hailed in the local press, which published photos and articles welcoming them – in short, they were very much *personae gratae*.

Carnival had just begun: 'That same evening we set out to explore the city. In a working-class neighbourhood, there was booming music coming out of a low house with green windows and we could see people dancing. We went closer. A black man guarding the door told us we could go in but only to dance, not to watch. We danced in earnest, but I'm afraid without any skill, bothering the young black women who, with complete indifference, accepted our invitations.'[20] Their wool suits were ill adapted to the hot São Paulo summer, causing them all to sweat profusely . . .

On the following day, one of their colleagues, Paul Arbousse-Bastide, a cousin of Georges Dumas who had arrived the year before to assume the chair in sociology and whom they saw as their senior, took them on a tour of the city. Lévi-Strauss often pointed out the value of these brief excursions through foreign cities – the condensed impressions and meaningful surprises offered up to the unspoilt gaze of the traveller in a hurry. These glimpses offered intuitions that longer stays only made hazier. What did he see of São Paulo on that day? The city was raucous, many-sided and seemed as if it were unfinished, as attested to by the photos he took with his Leica camera, which are collected in *Saudades de São Paulo*: buildings under construction, urban chaos, signs, and yet also a provincial atmosphere, very few cars, herds of cows peacefully trundling alongside crammed streetcars; a collision of times and spaces, part Chicago, part

Paris, part Lisbon; black people in white fitted suits, others in rags; palm trees under the Viaduto do Cha; no urban plan and yet large avenues (São João, under construction) that tracked the hilly contours of the landscape; the initial site of São Paulo, when it was just a Jesuit mission – a rock spur at the intersection of two rivers that flow into the Rio Tietê. From its missionary origins, the town had become the commercial and financial centre of the new coffee trade, whose business was all transacted in the 'Triangle' at the heart of the modern city. Then, from the moment of what Pierre Monbeig has called its 'second founding', São Paulo experienced vertiginous growth, going from 48,000 inhabitants in 1886 to 1.12 million by 1935.[21] Fully three-fourths of the population of São Paulo at the time was born outside Brazil. Half of the city was Italian and there were also significant German and Japanese communities, but only a few thousand French inhabitants. The exponential increase in wealth could be seen in the urban elements that gave the Brazilian city a European appearance: the streetcars and boulevards, the Praça da República with its gardens and municipal theatre. Then there was the established wealth of the *fazendeiros* who, through marital alliances and intense social networks, formed the town's high society, settling in the hills of Pacaembu and in the colonial mansions of Higienópolis, surrounded by gardens and palm trees. These were the people and places that had participated in the heyday of the Belle Époque. The São Paulo of the 1930s still retained slightly worn traces of it, but the new wealth – based on manufacturing rather than real estate, and generated by descendants of immigrants – had set its sights on Avenida Paulista, to distinguish itself. This avenue, which splits the city in two, became the eclectic scene for the many architectural styles imported by this new elite, shamelessly flaunting their success. 'The Matarazzos built an enormous Roman house, whose design was all geometric simplicity but made entirely of white marble. The Japhets, although of Jewish descent, had created a profusion of Muslim ornamental art around a caricature of a mosque. The Zenz family followed the British style, while Thiollier, a writer not without a certain talent, lived in a classic bourgeois house of the kind found in Rueil or Vésinet.'[22] The whole ensemble was dominated by the Martinelli, a skyscraper under construction whose pink silhouette further affirmed the Paulist capital's aspiration to become a tropical New York. It was thus in São Paulo, and not New York, that Claude Lévi-Strauss saw his first skyscraper, a singular and incongruous introduction to the New World city, via the copy rather than the original.

For São Paulo was a New World city, and Lévi-Strauss very quickly came to enjoy it as such: 'I never thought that São Paulo was ugly: it was a "wild" town, as are all American towns [. . .].'[23] By 'wild' he meant having a short evolutionary cycle, passing 'from freshness to decay without ever being simply old', caught up in the frantic pace of industrious cities.[24] Indeed, the city's inhabitants would boast that, in 1935, a house was built every hour. This was one of the reasons that accounted for the change in address of Lévi-Strauss's house, which was number 212 Cincinato Braga Street, and then became 315 – although he lived in the same house throughout his stay in Brazil!

That house in which the Lévi-Strausses settled, soon to be joined by Claude's parents, appears in some of the pictures in *Saudades de São Paulo*. Surrounded by foliage, it exudes a colonial charm and is impressive for its size and wrought iron gate (if slightly rusted), indicating a new level of comfort, further heightened by the Ford parked out front. The latter purchase provided an indication of how far they had come. Going from a Citroën 'Trèfle' to a Ford was to experience the kind of upward mobility these young professors were counting on, even while not quite knowing exactly what to expect: 'We were all obscure professors from provincial high schools, whose drive to break out and interest in research had caught the attention of Georges Dumas. After having lived very modest lifestyles, we settled into vast private villas with gardens, where our spouses were attended by servants (the first at our place was a very beautiful mulatto woman, whom we eventually had to let go because she would borrow my wife's dresses while we were away and wear them to dance in carnival clubs; she was followed by two charming Portuguese sisters whose combined ages was barely forty, and whom we had to employ together because they refused to be separated). [. . .] We were not at all used to this luxury, one example of which was the tailor, who would take our measurements and make his patterns at our house. The low cost of food and services gave us a feeling of having climbed several steps up the social ladder.'[25] As *Tristes Tropiques* explains, travelling entailed a shift in social as well as geographical space: one is displaced from one's social class – or placed into another. The Brazil trip made him richer; a few years later, the trip that was to bring him to New York would make him momentarily poorer. These social ups and downs were to characterize a good part of his life, before he settled into the comfortably bourgeois existence and 'living standard' to which he had always aspired but only achieved at the end of the 1950s. In the meantime, Brazil was a land of plenty. Fernand Braudel, who arrived a few weeks after Lévi-Strauss, would commute to the university in a rented car complete with Italian chauffeur!

The young professors settled in nicely. Not only were the material conditions very favourable, but Lévi-Strauss appreciated the charms of the city, the diversity of its vistas, the 'new sights' it offered to his keen walker's gaze. His neighbourhood – on the fringes of the wealthy area of *Jardim Paulista*, where most of his colleagues had chosen to live – delighted him. Close to Avenida Paulista, it overlooked a mixed neighbourhood that sloped down to the city centre, with an Italian and black population towards the bottom, near the slaughterhouses: 'Parallel to Avenida Paulista, a bit lower down, Cincinato Braga Street was still situated high enough that from it, close by, a vast panorama unfolded of the chaotic neighbourhood below. I would often stroll through this area, fascinated by the contrast between the very modern buildings, the still quite provincial avenues, the nearly rustic hillsides and the part of the city that still retained the look of a village.'[26] That urban landscape of *Bela Vista* (or *Bexiga*) is preserved today in a photograph, as well as in a painting by Raymond Lévi-Strauss, whose towering silhouette stands out in several snapshots.[27] Father and son shared a keen interest in the urban phenomenon. They were *flâneurs*, snoopers, collectors, sharing the same aesthetic relationship to the city, including its less contemplative forms. São Paulo was certainly not as easy to appreciate as Paris – not then and not now – but like all metropolises it recycled its products and fashions, which could be cleverly taken advantage of through skilled bargain hunting: 'At that time, one could stroll around São Paulo. Not like in Paris or London, in front of the antique shops. If I remember correctly, São Paulo had only one, which I believe was called Corte Leal. Instead of the pre-Columbian ceramics and indigenous artefacts we were hoping for, the shop window contained only a Kabyle porcelain, and a broken one at that. For the house of Cincinato Braga Street, I bought four or five pieces of Brazilian furniture from the end of the previous century made of solid Brazilian rosewood, like the ones you could still see in the *fazendas* but which were out of fashion in the city. But really, one should not expect objects of contemplation and reflection other than the city itself: an immense disorder, which combined, in visible confusion, churches and public buildings from the colonial period, tenements and structures from the nineteenth century, as well as others of more contemporary vintage . . . .'[28] Deciphering the urban text of São Paulo – a project to which Lévi-Strauss intended to devote himself, as the professor of sociology at the city's very young university that he now was.

The (small) world of French academia in Brazil

Within the academic world of Brazil, the University of São Paulo – established by decree on 25 January 1934 – stands as a kind of founding myth, both exemplary and cumbersome. A symbol of São Paulo's modernizing ambitions, it also marked the apex of sacrosanct Franco-Brazilian amity. From the start, the USP was charged with projects and 'missions', from both the French and Brazilian sides, making it a creation that was both necessary and fragile, and in any case never a place of academic freedom as conceived in Europe.

Why the USP?

For France, the founding of the University of São Paulo was clearly part of a policy of 'promoting cultural influence' abroad, to use the parlance of the ministry of foreign affairs, at a time when France, aware of its decline, was keen to invest in soft power and effectively combat the authoritarian propaganda of fascist Italy and Nazi Germany.[29] Created in January 1920, the Service des oeuvres françaises à l'étranger (SOFE) was the organizational centre of this intellectual paradiplomacy, which was run throughout the 1930s by the same man, Jean Marx, himself a former academic and professor at the École pratique des hautes études. During the interwar period, there was a clear shift in the focus of French cultural diplomacy from the Near East to the Americas and Central Europe. In 1933, more than 300 French professors were deployed to some 200 institutions of higher learning abroad. For the ministry of foreign affairs, this strategy of making intellectual inroads into Brazil was all the more apt since there was a tradition of French cultural influence in the country (in inverse proportion to its economic presence), there was no shortage of eager candidates given the tight academic job market in France and, finally, France could count on a first-rate 'Mister Latin America' in Georges Dumas.

Indeed, it was 'a sort of love at first sight' between the Protestant from the Cévennes with charcoal eyes and Brazilian high society. Dumas was known and admired by all, celebrated on each of the seventeen trips he made to Brazil between 1920 and 1938, leaving behind a trail of new institutions: the Franco-Brazilian Institute of High Culture in Rio in 1922, the Franco-Brazilian Lycée of São Paulo in 1923, the first mission to the University of São Paulo, as well as others to the University of the Federal District and those in Rio, Porto Alegre, etc. An academic, psychologist and alumnus of the École normale, Georges Dumas enlisted both his centrist political network and his troop of young *normaliens* in need of some fresh air (notably through his friendship with Célestin Bouglé), while maintaining good relations with the enlightened bourgeoisie of São Paulo, all in the name of secular and rationalist France – the France of Auguste Comte and the French Revolution. It probably stands to reason that this 'conquistador' of French social science in Brazil was himself a specialist of Comte.[30] To complete the portrait, we should add that the man was also endowed with a winning personality and uncanny powers of persuasion, as his students would realize, making him, together with his close friend Jean Marx, the consummate dealmaker in Latin America (with the help of Paul Rivet).

From the Brazilian side, the creation of the USP had much to do with the general sense of crisis on the part of the oligarchy, symbolized by Vargas's rise to the presidency in 1930 and by the eviction of São Paulo elites from centres of federal power. In 1932, an attempted coup by the oligarchs had failed. The creation of the USP was one of several attempts on the part of the old São Paulo families, which had been militarily and politically vanquished, to regain the initiative on the intellectual and ideological front, by acquiring new tools and promoting European standards of excellence for the youth of São Paulo, who were encouraged to 'catch up'.[31] This was how a school of sociology and politics (under American influence), a municipal Department of Culture and a 'faculty of philosophy, science and letters' (on an explicitly French model) could come into being almost all at once as the University of São Paulo. These institutions were marked by a desire for revenge that was less social (the landed haute bourgeoisie vs. the petite bourgeoisie allied to the army) than antifederal (the state of São Paulo vs. the federal state). Although not stated in so many words, this was how the French consul, Mr Pingaud, saw it and his report specifies the exact terms of the USP gambit: 'The University of São Paulo is designed to become a tool of Paulista intellectual imperialism in Brazil.'[32]

Like the French after the defeat of 1870, the Paulistas after 1932 read Renan's *Réforme intellectuelle et morale* and prepared for intellectual reconquest.[33] Among the supporters of this ambitious project, the

Mesquita family played a significant role, especially Julio de Mesquita Filho, a newspaper man and the owner of the great daily *O Estado de São Paulo* (circulation 50,000). He was described as a 'debonair lion' by Jean Maugüe, who admired his 'grey-green *Bandeirante* eyes' and his devotion to the French mission, 'which he considered his own'.[34] With the governor general of the state, Armando Seles de Oliveira, as an ally and brother-in-law, the Mesquita clan became the sponsors of several cultural projects (magazines, publishing houses, institutes) under the intellectual banner of the USP, while the Constitutionalist Party served as its political arm. In 1937, during the presidential campaign, the USP was pressed into the service of electoral propaganda. This made it vulnerable when, in October, Vargas's coup ushered in the *Estado Novo*, calling its future into question. But it was ultimately to survive, and serves as one of Brazil's most prestigious universities to the present day.

Cultural ambassadors or representatives of ascendant social science?

The young professors arriving in 1935 quickly became aware of the fact that they were in a kind of 'false position', on both the social and intellectual level: the rationale for the creation of the institution did not necessarily correspond to the ambitions surrounding their own expatriation.[35]

In addition, we should point out that there was a dramatic change in faculty recruitment strategy. The first mission, in 1934, consisted of senior professors, established in their fields and for the most part Catholic: Robert Garric in literature, Pierre Deffontaines in geography, Étienne Borne in philosophy, Émile Coornaert in history, Michel Berveiller in classics, and Paul Arbousse-Bastide, who was somewhat younger, in sociology.[36] Six professors whose political convictions were in line with those of the liberal and Catholic milieu of the São Paulo oligarchy, and who acquitted themselves in their extracurricular activities among São Paulo's high society with aplomb. In 1935, a change of profile betrayed a clear rupture in the diplomatic rationale governing the recruitment of faculty. No longer 'established talents', but now a few hand-picked young *agrégés*, keen to escape their stint in secondary education teaching and to collect material for their future dissertations in Brazil, which would allow them to apply directly for university positions once back in France. Their professional, intellectual and social profiles were radically different.

In 1935, besides Claude Lévi-Strauss, there was Fernand Braudel to teach history, Pierre Monbeig for geography, Jean Maugüe for philosophy and Pierre Hourcade for literature, with Paul Arbousse-Bastide remaining in his post. In another change, these new professors signed up for three years, rather than one as had previously been the case. Among these young *agrégés* that Dumas plucked out of provincial secondary schools, Braudel was the most advanced in his doctoral dissertation work, which was already well under way. Indeed, he travelled with a load of records and microfilms from the Seville archive, fodder for his dissertation on the sixteenth-century Mediterranean world, which commanded Claude Lévi-Strauss's total respect. To store this considerable material, Braudel rented a second hotel room upon arrival. The others, Lévi-Strauss and Monbeig foremost among them, had in mind to take advantage of the kind of intellectual virginity of Latin America to become specialists of a new science, whose value was as great as its scarcity, and which Maugüe sarcastically called the 'fabulous metal' (he himself being far less certain about his academic future).[37] Roger Bastide, who was to replace Lévi-Strauss for the 1938 year, left France with a thesis project on medieval mysticism, but the trans-Atlantic experience made him change his mind. The future great anthropologist of black Brazil, and foremost expert on Bahia's *candomblé*, shared Arbousse-Bastide's last name but was no relation. As a result of their considerable difference in height, the students quickly nicknamed them 'big Bastide' and 'little Bastide' ('o Bastidão' and 'o Bastidinho').[38]

Our young French academics were thus more or less openly discontented on three counts, which must have taken a bit of a toll on Claude Lévi-Strauss's otherwise very rich years in Brazil. First, their situation and function did not match the idea they had of their teaching and their reasons for coming to Brazil. Disembarking as 'ambassadors' of France, and hailed as such by the local press, Paulista society and local ladies in hats, they were expected to attend numerous events and give talks outside the university context. Claude Lévi-Strauss, for instance, gave a speech in the spring of 1935 entitled 'The Crisis of Progress', a text that has unfortunately not survived but on whose theme he was later to expand.[39] Yet neither Lévi-Strauss nor Braudel nor Monbeig had intended to become semi-professional diplomats or to speak in the name of France. On the contrary, they were working to build new scientific disciplines and promote new methodologies, according to a logic that was resolutely international rather than national.[40] The generation gap also involved a change of posture, from one of ambassador of French culture to one of universal scholar. As far as Claude Lévi-Strauss was concerned, coming to Brazil clearly entailed a commitment to the latter, whereas the institutional logic in which he found himself involved the former. A first rift, to which another would be added.

If Lévi-Strauss and his colleagues refused to take on the role of French ambassadors, they were no more eager to be seen as intellectual comrades-in-arms of the São Paulo oligarchy. However, Vargas and his clique held no particular appeal. The socialist in Lévi-Strauss felt uncomfortable in the 'slightly snobbish' Mesquita milieu, in relation to which he and his colleagues found themselves 'in the position of clients, in the Roman sense of the term'.[41] The young professors – themselves *nouveaux riches* with their recently tripled salaries,[42] their large villas, servants and cars – addressed a student body of modest backgrounds, who simultaneously admired them and saw them as 'servants of the ruling class'.[43] They were indeed encouraged to 'live the same kind of life as [their] new masters, that is, become habitués of the Automobile Club, casinos and racecourses'.[44] Unlike Jean Maugüe, who was drawn into them by a sentimental attraction, Claude Lévi-Strauss never frequented the salons of São Paulo, or rather only just enough to make some ironic observations on the Brazilian rules of the 'great game of civilization'. When in the late 1950s, the Paulistas read *Tristes Tropicos*, they did not much appreciate the vegetal metaphor and botanical register he used to describe them: 'Sheltering in this stony fauna, the elites of São Paulo, like its favourite orchids, constituted a more languid and exotic flora than it was aware of itself.'[45] The depiction that follows did not help matters: indeed, it describes the 'sociological minuet' by which roles were assigned – social roles (the haute bourgeoisie), political roles (the revolutionary, the anarchist, the legitimist), cultural roles (the avant-garde artist) – among a sparse population, where each category was to be represented by a single individual. These acerbic observations of Brazilian high society – however apt, as some in Brazil did point out, *mezza voce* – must also be seen in their context, that of the sociological imbroglio in which the French professors found themselves. French and Brazilian officialdom notwithstanding, if these young academics saw Brazil as a professional springboard for themselves, they also saw the training they provided to their young students as leaven for the rise of a new Brazil against the old – including against the aristocratic patrons of their own university. This historical irony would become clear in the space of the two decades between Lévi-Strauss's Brazilian experience and the writing of *Tristes Tropiques*.

In addition, for Lévi-Strauss, who was charged with teaching sociology at USP, all this was further compounded by the intellectual malaise he felt in the face of the definition and practice of that discipline in the country that had adopted Auguste Comte as its leading light. In Brazil, whose national flag since 1889 features the positivist motto '*Ordem e Progresso*', the positivist tradition – and Durkheimian sociology in its wake, for 'educated Brazilians had gone from Comte to Durkheim'[46] – supplied a 'philosophical basis for that moderate liberalism, which is the usual ideological weapon used by oligarchies to combat personal power'.[47] Lévi-Strauss arrived in Brazil in a 'state of open revolt against Durkheim and against any attempt to use sociology for metaphysical purposes'.[48] This momentary anti-Durkheimism, shared by other philosophers of his generation, can be explained in the case of Lévi-Strauss by the way in which Durkheim was 'passed on' to him. There was a 'gulf' separating the proponents of a 'living' Durkheimism – Mauss at the Collège de France, Granet at Langues orientales, Simiand at École pratique des hautes études (all of whom, with the exception of Halbwachs, who taught at university, worked at research institutes) – and the other disciples (Bouglé, Fauconnet, Davy). These latter tended to favour the centrist political party and republican power; they were established university academics at the Sorbonne who taught a philosophy that mixed law with a strict moralism that the young minds of the 1930s found intolerable.[49] And it was through them rather than the former group that Lévi-Strauss had been introduced to Durkheim. Hence his 'inconstant' attitude to the great sociologist, to whom he would return once he had discovered the true legacy.[50] Hence also the paradoxical compatibility between the young man and Marcel Mauss, Durkheim's nephew and first disciple, to whom Lévi-Strauss astutely wrote: Brazilians

CONFERENCIAS PUBLICAS PROMOVIDAS PELA FACULDADE DE PHILOSOPHIA

O prof. Claude Levi-Strauss realizou hontem a primeira dissertação da série que vae levar a effeito, sobre "A crise do progresso"

Ao alto, o prof. Claude Levi-Strauss, quando proferia a sua conferencia — Em baixo, aspecto da assistencia

Em proseguimento ao cyclo de conferencias promovido pela Universidade de São Paulo e que está a cargo dos professores da Faculdade de Philosophia, Sciencias e Letras, falou hontem, no salão João Mendes Junior, da Faculdade de Direito, o prof. Claude Levi-Strauss, cathedratico de Sociologia daquelle instituto de alta cultura.

Levando a effeito a primeira prelecção, da série, que, sobre "A crise do progresso", vae alli realizar, dissertou o conferencista sobre "Progresso e retrocesso".

Inicialmente, diz que o progresso como resultante de trabalhos e realizações do homem, é, por isso mesmo, a essencia do espirito humano.

Salienta, depois, que o bem e o mal, já occorridos, não podem ser considerados desta ou daquella forma, ou seja como um bem ou como um mal. Porque tudo quanto occorreu constitue eta-

pas da civilização, phases do progresso.

Rebateu a seguir o conceito segundo o qual a concepção do progresso pode ser comparada á evolução do homem. Este, frisou o conferencista, tem uma trajectoria que pode, mais ou menos, ser predeterminada, pela propria idade.

O progresso, no entanto, tem fluxos e refluxos, retrocessos e avanços, periodos de fastigio e épocas de decadencia, ou melhor — marchas e contramarchas.

Essas contramarchas, no entanto, nunca vão até o ponto de partida. E, sempre, antecedem um avanço maior, que vae alem do ponto em que se verificou o retrocesso.

Depois de se referir ás diversas phases do progresso humano, até a segunda metade do seculo XIX, quando teve inicio o desenvolvimento das industrias e da machina, observou que, após a conflagração européa, entrou a humanidade num periodo de du-

vidas e incertezas. Não se pode prognosticar, ao certo, se, doravante, o progresso será maior na Sciencia, ou na Arte.

Não pode haver duvida, comtudo, de que, em virtude desse phenomeno, estamos numa época de retrocesso.

E' evidente a ansiedade que empolgou, totalmente, os povos. Ha incertezas e hesitações, entre a humanidade.

Tudo está a indicar, no entanto, que, passada esta phase de agitações, entrará a humanidade num periodo de progresso ainda maior, que determinará uma evolução que attingirá, por certo, limites hoje imprevisiveis.

A CONFERENCIA DE SEGUNDA-FEIRA

A proxima conferencia será feita pelo prof. Pierre Hourcade, na segunda-feira vindoura, ás 21 horas, no mesmo local. O seu thema será: "Baudelaire e Verlaine, precursores do movimento poetico contemporaneo."

Article announcing Claude Lévi-Strauss's public lecture, 'La Crise du progress', in front of a select São Paulo audience, published in *Estado de S. Paulo* (9 August 1935).

see sociology 'as a kind of supporting technique for municipal and parliamentary administration'.[51] The turn to the new social sciences was for him, at the time, a means of breaking down metaphysical and ideological walls so as to grasp the complexity of a real that escapes all systematization. Which was why, once in Brazil, he was in no hurry to preach this domesticated form of sociology, especially as he was in the process of discovering the empirical tradition of Anglo-American anthropology. This intellectual disagreement rapidly turned into open disciplinary and institutional conflict with his colleague Paul Arbousse-Bastide, holder of the other chair in sociology.

The rise and fall of the French mission

When the chair in sociology was split into two, which the São Paulo patrons were very keen to do, Paul Arbousse-Bastide, who was already in post, wrote: 'I have unfortunately no sociologist to recommend for the second chair in sociology. It would of course have to be someone young (but not overly so) who has demonstrated some interest in sociological research and is likely to lock onto Brazil as a field of investigation.'[52] Through the auspices of Célestin Bouglé and Georges Dumas, as we have seen, the post was offered to Claude Lévi-Strauss. But once in Brazil, the young professor had no desire to teach sociology, since he had come to do anthropology. From the start of the academic year, in the spring of 1935, this disciplinary conflict became compounded into a power struggle. Unbending on the question of academic freedom, Lévi-Strauss bridled under the authority of Arbousse-Bastide, who held the vague title of 'head of mission', without being entitled to explicitly exercise it, and who also prided himself on directing the sociology department, which remained largely virtual at the time. In short, Lévi-Strauss categorically refused to have the content of his courses determined for him, and went a step further in submitting a fifteen-page counter-proposal, comprising both scientific and pedagogical aspects, whose title, 'Cultural Sociology and Its Teaching', made clear his programmatic ambitions.[53] In this short text, he accused sociologists of having remained in a speculative register and of considering sociology as a 'philosophy of the social sciences'. For, he continued, being 'in no position to put questions to the test of the real, the speculative approach continues to serve as an easy refuge'. He was challenging the very scientific status of sociology, which he felt was still in its infancy. The only two social science disciplines to have borne positive results, in his view, were archaeology and anthropology. He did take a few rhetorical precautions and spared the Durkheimian tradition, even including a few quotes from the master: 'Ethnography has often spurred the most fertile revolutions in the various branches of sociology', a phrase extracted from *Elementary Forms of the Religious Life*. Lévi-Strauss's rebellion, in which he went so far as to request a chair in cultural anthropology outside the sociology department, was met with disapproval by the Brazilian authorities as well as by the French ministry of foreign affairs, which was embarrassed by the situation.

Georges Dumas was furious: 'I am being harassed by the faculty in São Paulo [. . .]. Lévy-Strauss [*sic*] would like to have a chair of anthropology created for him and to teach anthropology in his classes. Arbousse-Bastide wants him to teach sociology, since he was hired to do so. Hence a conflict [. . .]. My own view is that Lévy-Strauss is somewhat of a brash upstart, and we should have done without his services, but bear in mind he was the only one we could find.'[54]

In July 1936, the 'Lévi-Strauss case' was even brought before the president of the USP, Antonio de Almeida Prado, in the presence of the two parties involved, as well as François Perroux, who had arrived in 1936, and was in charge of political economy.[55] It nearly came to disciplinary sanctions. The situation was all the more delicate in that the mission was split between the faithful supporters of Arbousse-Bastide and those who backed Lévi-Strauss – namely, Maugüe, Monbeig and, especially, Braudel, who threw his entire weight behind his young colleague, as Lévi-Strauss would recall fifty years later when he was initiated as a new member of the Académie française. This alliance had nothing random about it; all these young professors shared a vision of social science as grounded in fieldwork and, as much as possible, free of all dogma (positivist, Durkheimian, metaphysical, etc.), concerned with method more than content. And they were fully prepared to ignore the demands of the local Brazilian elites who had hired them. All this transpired in a kind of terminological haze surrounding the emerging field of social science in which Lévi-Strauss was caught – between ethnography, cultural sociology, primitive sociology, ethnology and anthropology. The feud was taken up a notch with the election of the Front populaire in France, which was as much a source of concern for the São Paulo oligarchy as it was a delight for Claude Lévi-Strauss. In this increasingly stormy political atmosphere, it is possible that Lévi-Strauss – whose leftist inclinations were no secret to anyone, given his connections with Paul Rivet and the Musée de l'Homme – was the victim of a small-scale witch hunt. Whatever the case may be, the situation degenerated further over the course of 1937 and culminated with the non-renewal of his contract in December of that year, at the end of his three-year teaching commitment.

All this looked a little like parochial Gallic rivalries, especially from the perspective of the other foreign faculty. The new faculty of 'philosophy, science and literature' comprised, in addition to its eight French members, six Italians, including the poet Ungaretti, the mathematician Luigi Fantappiè and an anti-fascist physicist, Occalini, as well as three German Jews who had fled Nazism, and one Briton. Like the New School for Social Research, which Lévi-Strauss would later frequent in New York, the USP was thus a fully international institution, if on a smaller scale. Yet each mission, and notably the French one, seemed plagued by a caricature of its national traits. Several of the French professors commented on the keen competition between them as they strove to demonstrate their academic excellence and capture audience share, whose vicissitudes they each monitored closely. 'All of us thought our careers were riding on our success or failure in Brazil, so we all attempted to surround ourselves with an exclusive court, more significant than that of our neighbour. It was very French, very academic, but there in the tropics, it was a little ridiculous and not very healthy.'[56] A courtier model, with diva attitudes, which the large lecture format only encouraged: 'We would leave our lecture halls like virtuosi leaving their concert halls.'[57] Jean Maugüe seems to have particularly excelled at this little game, striking his students with his panache and dramatically nonconformist views.[58]

The teaching load of USP professors consisted of six fifty-five-minute lectures per week, for a heterogeneous audience of roughly half socialites (especially the first year) and half students. From its second year, the newly established university shook up and reconfigured all the mechanisms of upward mobility, contributing to its appeal for 'young people anxious to obtain the posts that would be available to those who acquired the diplomas we awarded; there were also lawyers, engineers and established politicians who feared that they might soon have to compete against people with university degrees, if they did not have the wisdom to graduate themselves.'[59] In 1936, 209 students were enrolled, among whom 33 were in the first year of social science, and only two in the second year.

Open-air laboratory or sociological paradise

Even if the French expatriates liked to go to the Odeon Theatre to see films starring Gabin and Jouvet,[60] and cultivated the national passions, it was also true that their sensory antennae were all keenly tuned in to the Brazilian scene. Monbeig and Lévi-Strauss, as well as Braudel, immediately saw the 'unique experimental field offered by the New World'.[61] Just starting out in their careers, hailing from different disciplines and backgrounds, they all aspired to doing serious field research that could serve as a new basis for a living human science. A philosopher by training, Lévi-Strauss was completely taken by the Brazilian scene – its forms of urban development, its scale, the violence of its transformations – which he observed with his marked appreciation for the emergent and the disappearing. The friendship he developed with Pierre Monbeig expressed this geographical inclination, which characterized his Brazilian period, with regard to his teaching but also, and even more profoundly, his personal cosmogony.

Teaching against the grain

As a sociology professor at the University of São Paulo, and despite the difficulties he faced, Claude Lévi-Strauss developed a teaching and research programme that was coherent in terms of both content and pedagogical method, entirely concentrated on close observation and the primacy of the empirical over any speculative temptation. In so doing, he was blithely breaking from positivist-Durkheimian orthodoxy – which might also explain why Arbousse-Bastide saw red.

Against a sociology that he labelled 'metaphysical', he defended the idea that knowledge of primitive peoples – i.e., anthropology – was a necessary component of any good training in sociology. Thus, in 1935, he gave a course entitled 'Elementary Forms of Social Life'.[62] The required bibliography consisted of four classic texts: Durkheim's *Elementary Forms of Religious Life*, Robert Lowie's *Primitive Society*, Van Gennep's *L'État actuel des problèmes totémiques* and Westermarck's *History of Human Marriage*.[63] And he did not stop there. The range of his interests and courses ran from 'primitive sociology to urban anthropology, via linguistics, ethnolinguistics and physical anthropology', as attested by the course descriptions listed in the university catalogue.[64]

Lévi-Strauss was against academic cloistering and sent his students out into the city to conduct research: 'By way of fieldwork, I proposed that they work on the street where they live, the market, the intersection. They only had to observe the succession in space of the types of housing, the economic and social characteristics of the inhabitants, their professional activities, etc.'[65] São Paulo was undergoing rapid change, presenting an extraordinary opportunity for the budding social scientist to observe at first hand the kind of mass processes that had unfolded over centuries in Europe. It was not just his vagabond sensibility that was fascinated by São Paulo but also his scientific disposition; and the two came together here, as he explained to Célestin Bouglé: 'São Paulo is considered an ugly city, but I find it extraordinarily appealing, in all its disorder and incoherence. It is the "urban phenomenon" in pure form, and it is possible, while roaming its neighbourhoods, to find all the stages of city dwelling, from mud huts to the most North American of skyscrapers. From a sociological point of view, it offers a magnificent experience. The study of the city, the analysis of its growth and arrested development, the spatial configuration of its professions and nationalities form the very basis of my teaching.'[66] The inspiration and attraction of the city merged with the old interest of the French school of sociology for what it had called 'social morphology', the social organization of societies.

The young professor favoured direct observation and fieldwork; his teaching practices were based on document collection and interpretation, and an introduction to scientific methods. One of his former students turned drama critic, Décio de Almeida Prado, remembered this rather un-French practical pedagogy: 'One of the first projects he assigned was to do a social analysis of the city of São Paulo in the 1820s, as it appeared in documents from the time that he had identified for us. In his course on the laws of kinship in primitive societies, rather than rambling on, he gave his students a series of individualized family trees. He specified the social rules of the group and asked us who would marry whom.'[67] This was a long way from amphitheatre lectures and prima donna posturing. Besides, Professor Lévi-Strauss did not seek to dazzle with his brilliance, but to make his students think. He did not give lectures, but courses, an important distinction made by Brazilian anthropologist and former student Egon Schaden: 'His presentations were not lively, but the ideas were always clear. What was most admirable was the way he had us work and read through student presentations, seminars and discussion. He wasn't a famous professor, but many people attended his classes.'[68] This account is further supported by Almeida Prado: 'With Lévi-Strauss, words were a transparent channel that gave us a glimpse of the process of argumentation. If we learned one thing it was how to reason. Even in the development of his longest arguments we would not get lost and always followed the logical thread, since it was so well structured.' This pedagogical register, which we will see again at other places where Lévi-Strauss will teach, further confirms the trend towards an approach to teaching that favoured research over the transmission of established knowledge.

Building on his teaching and his request for a chair in anthropology, Claude Lévi-Strauss – always ambitious (and combative) – came up with a project for creating an Institute of Cultural and Physical Anthropology, which he outlined in an article published in *O Estado de São Paulo* on 17 October 1935, 'Em prol de um Instituto de Antropologia Física e Cultural'. The idea was to direct and centralize Brazilian anthropological research – while there was still time, for Lévi-Strauss felt it was a moment of anthropological emergency – within the framework of the university, on the model of major research institutes abroad. He proposed to conduct comparative surveys across the Americas and to train expert researchers. Towards these ends, he suggested creating a 'great American anthropological archive' and a great Atlas, 'in which maps of the American continent would show the geographical distribution [of cultural traits] and variations in density'.[69] The startling programmatic energy of the young professor, who conceived of research and the infrastructure of knowledge together (archives, atlases, surveys, institutional structures), was already manifest. In the autumn of 1935 in São Paulo, a scholarly vision was being sketched out, one that was to be partially fulfilled twenty-five years later with the creation of the Laboratoire d'anthropologie sociale. From the start, scientific practice and its material foundations were considered as inseparable.

Fieldwork before fieldwork

The city was not Lévi-Strauss's only hunting ground. His passion for empirical discovery regularly brought the small group of French scholars and their wives to the outskirts of São Paulo where, like modern day explorers (whose attire appears to have been inspired by those of earlier times), they would subject everything to their inquisitive gaze: 'This country and this society, made up entirely of contrasts, was the object of passionate curiosity for us. The members of the French mission – the historian Fernand Braudel, the geographer Pierre Monbeig, the philosopher Jean Maugüe and myself, along with our wives (Maugüe was the only bachelor) – formed a tight-knit group. We never missed an opportunity to run around São Paulo in search of new discoveries – by the seaside or in the ravines traversed by frail footbridges, or else in the coffee plantations north of the city – to satisfy our penchant for archaeological research.'[70] Two photographs serve to perfectly illustrate these recollections: in one,

Dina Lévi-Strauss, always at the head of the small gang, is intrepidly crossing a (rather frail-looking) bridge made out of vines; in the other, she is holding up a fragment of pottery – sure sign of a former indigenous presence on the coffee plantation[71] – to show it to Braudel (wearing a suit and tie, but with high leather boots that give him the look of an English horseman) and Jean Maugüe (with a cigarette dangling from the corner of his lips, as always). Monbeig, Braudel, Lévi-Strauss – the École des hautes études en sciences sociales in miniature out on a jaunt, and the dream of interdisciplinarity come alive in the field . . .

More than just on these Sunday excursions, interdisciplinarity charac- terized the friendship between Claude Lévi-Strauss and Pierre Monbeig, the pioneering geographer who pushed into the western hinterland of São Paulo and the north of Paraná, and who thirty years later would work on the 'integration' of Amazonia into Brazil. Over the course of his long stay in São Paulo, from 1935 to 1948, Monbeig had time to take the full measure of American phenomena, and to adjust to local scale, distances and tempos, before producing his masterwork on the 'nomadic landscapes' of frontier peripheries. Lévi-Strauss, for lack of anthropological expedi- tions (rendered impossible by the disappearance of Indians from the outskirts of São Paulo . . .), accompanied his friend and colleague – on foot and horseback, sometimes by truck – into the forest clearings and shifting settlements of pioneer society, a patchwork of European ethnici- ties: 'It is after a long night of travelling that the forest truly becomes an element of the landscape. It is broken up by large plantations and small fields of cotton, rice and corn. The look of the towns starts to change as well. There are wooden houses, towns made of planks that seem too large for their small stations. And more and more one sees clearings with trees strewn about on the ground, some still standing with their charred trunks looming over newly planted crops.'[72] In Monbeig's work, the metaphor of the battlefield regularly recurs to describe deforested areas. Lévi-Strauss thought of Brazil first and foremost as a 'burning perfume'.[73] Trundling along together, they 'smelled, observed and listened to the spaces they were crossing'.[74]

The proto-cities that had sprouted up along the railway routes (Londrina, the most established of them, Nova-Dantzig, Rôlandia, Arapongas, etc.) were a particular source of fascination for Lévi-Strauss. They offered him a live glimpse into the birth of a city, their unconscious orienta- tion along the points of the compass, the gradual differentiation of their functions, the intersection of organic evolution and aesthetic creation. It is 'the supremely human achievement',[75] perceived in its simplest, most elementary form, and further illuminated by the heuristic quality of all beginnings. 'In these rectangular spaces arbitrarily cleared in the heart of the forest, the streets too run at right angles and are, in the first instance, all alike; they are simply geometrical lines, with no intrinsic quality of their own. However, some are central and others peripheral; some parallel, and others perpendicular, to the railway line or the road. The former follow the direction of trade, the latter cut across it and, as it were, interrupt it. The businesses and commerce choose the first, which are necessarily much frequented; and, for the opposite reason, private houses and certain public services prefer the second or are forced back on to them. The combination of the two contrasts – between central and peripheral, on the one hand, and parallel and perpendicular, on the other – gives rise to four different modes of urban life which mould the character of the future inhabitants, encouraging some and discouraging others, prompting success or causing failure.'[76] It was a very geographically minded Lévi-Strauss speaking here, one who tended to express his thoughts in spatial terms, adopting a lexicon that could be readily translated into diagrammatic form. Between this sketch that he never drew and another, and more famous, one that he did draw a few months later, laying out the social structures of a Bororo village, the tropism for geography is striking.[77] From this perspective, the towns on the pioneer periphery effected a kind of transition between an old childhood inclination to observe the surface of the earth and the discovery of indigenous societies, crystallizing the contribution of the discipline of geography to a tradition that was still young but already well under way in France in the form of the human geography of Vidal de La Blache and his disciples. One of whom, Emmanuel de Martonne, happened to pass through Brazil in September 1937.

His visit prompted an excursion by a group of professors and students to Itatiaia, one of the highest summits in Brazil, about 300 kilometres northeast of São Paulo, in the Mantiqueira Mountains. Several photos in *Saudades do Brasil* recall this memorable lesson in geographical pedagogy – the effort it took to reach the nearly 2,800-metre-high rock massif, first by car, on barely passable tracks, then on horseback, and ultimately on foot. A curiously framed photograph immortalizes Emmanuel de Martonne's boots on the path leading to the summit – a sort of homage to the legwork of geographical field expeditions. At the top, it was a moment of revelation: 'Martonne improvised a presentation which – for me, with my literary background – appeared as a remarkable textual commentary. I understood that a landscape, viewed and analysed by a master, could provide fascinating reading, as capable of cultivating the sensibilities as a play by Racine.'[78] We should also mention that, for Martonne too, Brazil marked an important epistemological moment. It prompted him to revisit the question of sugarloaf mountains – i.e., the influence of the climate on erosion phenomena – to arrive at a new concept in his geographical thought, a zonal geomorphology that the decentred nature of the European peninsula alone enabled him to work out.[79]

Two earlier excursions had combined the charm of new discovery with access to Indian realities. Let us begin with the second one, chronologically speaking, which occurred in the summer of 1936, during the university winter vacation. Claude Lévi-Strauss invited Jean Maugüe and René Courtin, who had just arrived to take over the chair in law and political economy from François Perroux, to accompany him on a trip to the farthest reaches of the state of Goyaz, straight north across the Brazilian plateau, in the hope of encountering Indians on the banks of the Araguaia, a tributary of the Amazon. Their itinerary took them through Campinas, Uberlândia, Goiânia – the self-proclaimed new city,

Claude Lévi-Strauss (left), Jean Maugüe (centre) and René Courtin (right) posing
in front of the Ford that was to take them to the outer reaches of the state of
Goyaz, 1,500 kilometres north of São Paulo (summer 1936).

still under construction – and Goiás – the former diamond capital, now
rather sleepy in its colonial finery. Courtin, a future co-founder of the
newspaper *Le Monde*, had agreed to go as far as his new Ford would take
them, ready to sacrifice it on the altar of adventure. He was 'fascinated by
Claude Lévi-Strauss. The idea that indigenous populations could obey,
in their matrimonial rules for example, the most intricate mathematical
relationships, amazed him to no end. As if Lévi-Strauss was introducing
him to a world that was both modern and Kabbalistic. When he raised the
matter with Braudel, the latter, who was very strong in mathematics, did
not fail to offer ironic comment on the scientific pretentions of ethnographers who, he said, were often incapable of solving the easiest algebraic
equations.'[80] The three of them thus set off together. Lévi-Strauss carried
'over his shoulder a very beautiful camera, and [covered] his head with the
strangest of headgear, a canvas compromise between a Sherlock Holmes
and a Phrygian cap. As for Courtin, he was attired as if for a hunt in
the Cévennes, with flannel trousers and a wool jacket, carrying his long
shotgun for protection.'[81] Fifteen hundred kilometres later, the expedition
led them, through the thousands of landscapes and facets of that great
country in transition, to the designated spot. The next morning, after
sleeping in bags on the ground, they saw the silhouettes of two members
of the Karaja tribe, who led them to their village, where Lévi-Strauss
immediately started on his anthropological work, asking questions, trying
to make himself understood, taking notes. A young girl crafted two small
dolls representing an outsized penis, dolls on which Lévi-Strauss was to

write one of his first anthropological treatises. Their return to civilization was met with a mixture of melancholy and joy: 'From the back of the car, I observed Lévi-Strauss who was seated next to Courtin. However serious his expression, it betrayed the same jubilation we all shared about our imminent return to the metropolis, its comforts and first and foremost its bathrooms!'[82]

Yet, one year earlier, in the summer of 1935, the maiden anthropological voyage had already taken place. Together with other professors, during an excursion into Paraná which he himself described as 'academic tourism', then going on alone, with a civil servant from the Service for the Protection of Indians (SPI), he had penetrated deep into the great humid forest of evergreens of the coastal cordillera. He travelled for about ten days on horseback through the San Jeronimo reservation, which was home to the Kaingan people, a tribe that was probably related to the Gê and had been pushed southward by the Tupi-Gurani. Protected by the dense forest of southern Brazil, they were nonetheless driven out by the pioneer wave of German, Polish and Ukrainian immigrants, before being given safe haven on a reservation by the SPI, who in 1935 paid scant attention to these populations of people who had had brief contact with modern civilization and then inevitably slipped back into traditional lifestyles. Hence the anti-climax that cut short the expectations of an encounter with the great Other: 'To my great disappointment, the Tibagy Indians were neither completely "true Indians", nor, what was more important, "savages".'[83] Claude Lévi-Strauss was stunned to discover the surreal hotchpotch produced by the shock of civilizations, which brought together admirable pestles in polished stone and bits of old sewing machines. We are not far from the poet Lautréamont. The discourse that infuses this passage from *Tristes Tropiques* – the first Lévi-Straussian characterization of the West as a force of devastation – might not be contemporary with that inaugural encounter between the self-taught anthropologist and his object of study, which left him bitterly perplexed, but it is quite certain that, right from the start, he felt he had arrived too late. Not that there were no important anthropological lessons to be learned from the farcical syncretism, but it was too late for the dream of Jean de Léry. In the latter case, the scene was an epic one, whereas here first contact with the Indians played out in a rather 'tragicomic' vein. This passage ends on a sensory note, as if contact had been established in the end thanks to the possibility of sharing a tasty treat, in the form of a fat, cream-coloured larva – the *koro* – out of which 'spurted a whitish, fatty substance which I managed to taste after some hesitation; it had the consistency and delicacy of butter, and the flavour of coconut milk'.[84]

7

In the Heart of Brazil

I felt I was reliving the adventures of the first sixteenth-century explorers.
Claude Lévi-Strauss, *Conversations*[1]

At the beginning of their stay in São Paulo, the Lévi-Strausses of course social-ized regularly with the other French professors and, for a while, also some of the major local families, revolving around the figure of Julio Mesquita and the newspaper *O Estado de São Paulo*, who were, ultimately, their employers. Between the avenue São João, where the newspaper's offices were located, and the USP's School of Medicine, where the new faculty of literature, science and philosophy was housed, in the centre of the city, their world remained very European. Gradually, however, over the course of 1935, and even more so in 1936, the couple appear to have distanced themselves from both these milieus and to have developed a much deeper Brazilian centre of gravity.

This shift came largely from Dina Lévi-Strauss. For professional and institutional reasons, she got in touch with the main contact of their São Paulo years: Mário de Andrade. His luminous personality, and the very wide range of common interests on which their friendship could develop, drew the Lévi-Strausses into the heart of Brazil and, above all, its folklore, people and music.

Surrounded by his coterie of modernist friends, revolving around the newly created São Paulo municipal Department of Culture, Mário de Andrade was not only an ideal mentor for the young couple, but also the man who would help launch their first expedition. Between November 1935 and March 1936, the Lévi-Strausses underwent their first baptism by fire, experienced in the Conradian mode characteristic of the anthropologist's sensibility and yearning for adventure. At the end of the expedition they finally encountered their first 'true' Indians, which had the effect of desta-bilizing the European image of the 'noble savage' or the more American 'redskin'. Claude Lévi-Strauss lived these few weeks in 'a state of intense intellectual excitement'. From this first experience of fieldwork we have not only the retrospective meditations of *Tristes Tropiques*, laced with intense bitterness, but also many recently unearthed documents from the Brazilian period. Back in São Paulo, in March 1936, the intricate interlacing designs of the Kadiweu and the magnificent Bororo funereal rites appear to have definitively won him over to anthropology.

Dina, Mário, São Paulo, 1935–1938

'A minor cultural miracle'

As Antonio Candido has said, it was a veritable 'minor cultural miracle'[2] that saw the simultaneous creation of the University of São Paulo (1934) and the municipal Department of Culture (1935) at the very moment the Lévi-Strausses arrived in Brazil. Both served as institutional partners for the young couple, and, if the former brought them there, it was the latter that enabled them to remain.

Among its missions, the Department of Culture was charged with 'conducting research in support of public policy in the fields of culture and historical and artistic heritage conservation'.[3] Its activities in the fields of historical documentation, education, libraries and literary and cultural promotion mirrored the city's development and were part of an attempt to construct a unified culture. In some of its initiatives – mobile libraries, holiday camps, etc. – the Department of Culture was reminiscent of the Front populaire in France. In its convergence of avant-garde art and national culture construction, São Paulo was not so very different from Paris, where anthropologists and poets were trying to revive folk art and traditions as the crucible of a left-wing nation. Of course, São Paulo had a different political configuration: as we have seen, the local oligarchy patronized a number of scholarly and cultural institutions in an attempt to demonstrate that it was the 'working arm of a slumbering nation',[4] and thus to recapture its former political clout. Among these institutions, the Department of Culture was the fruit of an unlikely alliance between this increasingly marginal liberal elite and 1920s artistic modernism, based on a rediscovery of Brazilian roots that formed the backdrop of the cultural revival of the 1930s.

Indeed, this modernist movement – symbolically born in 1922 with Modern Art Week at the São Paulo Municipal Theatre – developed further thanks to the publication, in 1928, of Oswald de Andrade's *Cannibalist Manifesto (Manifesto Antrópofago)*.[5] In the radical mode of avant-garde movements, this text called for the rejection of Western rationality in favour of a 'liberating primitivism'. More to the point, it offered a vision of Brazilian culture as a process of 'cannibalization' of the disparate cultures that had gone into the making of Brazilian history.[6] This defence of diversity and hybridization – here strongly tinged with surrealist primitivism – echoed the various contemporary attempts to probe, identify and invent Brazilian reality in all its richness. Gilberto Freyre's *Casa-Grande e Senzala* was published in 1933, which Roger Bastide was to translate as *Maîtres et esclaves* in 1952 (with a preface by Lucien Febvre). An English translation had already appeared under the title *The Masters and the Slaves* in 1946. In this work, Freyre – an aristocrat from Recife who had studied with Franz Boas at Columbia University in New York – laid out a narrative of the formation of Brazilian society emphasizing the myriad effects of sexual relations between white patriarchs and their slaves in the plantation system.[7] The author demonstrated considerable courage in giving the sexual dimension central place, as well as in emphasizing the sense of shame felt by Brazilians as a mixed race people. If the book marked a significant turning point, it was, in the words of Afrânio Garcia, because of its 'promotion of interracial mixing as a national character-istic, in strong contrast to the long series of Brazilian publications since 1870 that had associated it with the degeneration of the population'.[8] Jorge Amado's novels about Bahia, Tarsila do Amaral's paintings and Heitor Villa-Lobos's musical compositions, all inspired by regional cul-tures, lend this moment of Brazilian culture a founding quality, a proud affirmation of national origins. But in the second half of the 1930s, this cultural nationalism became highly combustible and laden with ambigui-ties, since, from 1937 onwards, Vargas's *Estado Novo* systematically pro-moted samba schools and recuperated the ideology of the mestizo nation for its own authoritarian ends.

When the Department of Culture was created, Mário de Andrade (1893–1945) was offered the directorship, which came as a surprise to no one. Mário, as he is still referred to in São Paulo, where he is remembered as a prominent figure,[9] was one of the leaders of the modernist movement – a novelist, poet, literary critic, historian of music and professor at the con-servatory. His novel *Macunaíma* (1928) established his reputation, but did not earn him star status. He was neither a rentier nor a member of the São Paulo oligarchy, and he had never been outside Brazil, unlike the scions of well-to-do families who would round out their education in Europe. Mário de Andrade was a kind of poor cousin, self-taught and unmarried, a closeted homosexual who surrounded himself with women and lived with his mother and his sister, as charismatic as he was physically unattractive. He had dark skin and a volatile temperament.[10] He was the prime mover behind the improbable convergence, within the Department of Culture, of innovative artists and intellectuals, patrons prepared to sponsor them financially, and the phenomenon of reappropriation of indigenous culture as the leaven of a new 'Brazilianness'. Indeed, in addition to being a pro-lific and eclectic writer, he was a pioneer in the study of ethnomusicology, which he developed within the Department of Culture by creating an archive of sound recordings (especially from the northeast region), at the same time as John Lomax in the United States was recording the surviving songs of ex-slaves and prisoners and preserving the black musical heritage of the American Old South. This extraordinary character was at the centre of a group of São Paulo intellectuals, notably including Sérgio Milliet and Paulo Duarte, who were to form the Lévi-Strausses' circle as they gradually moved away from the French expat ghetto. Dina was the primary media-tor between these two worlds and, as such, she played an important part in this story.

The Anthropology and Folklore Society

'In the somewhat pretentious milieu of the *Estado de São Paulo*, which had close ties to political power (Julio de Mesquita Filho was, if I remember correctly, the brother-in-law of the state governor, Armando de Sales Oliveira), my colleagues and I found ourselves in the position of clients, in the ancient Roman sense of the term. Like others, I felt infinitely more at ease in the municipal Department of Culture. Mário de Andrade – a great poet, highly original mind and ardent lover of folklore and popular traditions – had gathered around him a group of highly cultured young historians, scholars and writers, including Sérgio Milliet, Rubens Borba de Moraes and, above all, Paulo Duarte, with whom I formed a strong friendship that continued to New York and Paris.'[11] Lévi-Strauss was not one to invoke friendship lightly. Indeed, he had few friends in the end, and to those who knew him after his return to Europe in the late 1940s even appeared not to have any at all.[12] Yet decades later, whenever he had occasion to talk about Mário de Andrade or Paulo Duarte his face would light up.[13] There was an undoubted surge of affection, in recollection of the unexpected brotherly ties that had developed with these slightly older men (they were between thirty and forty years old at the time) who were so profoundly Brazilian, which is to say also very European: 'I was close friends with Mário and Oswald de Andrade. They would always come to the house, and we would go out together. I could easily communicate with these Brazilian modernists on an equal footing because I was familiar with French intellectual and literary movements.'[14] To be sure, there were deep affinities between these men: an artistic sensibility combined with a yearning for anthropological knowledge, curiosity for the productions of the artistic avant-garde, with which Lévi-Strauss was still in sync, and an interest in folk culture and the discovery of Brazilian reality.

Over the three-year existence of the Department of Culture, from 1935 to 1938, the couple saw a lot of Mário de Andrade, their primary initiator into Brazilian folklore. They spent time together, enjoyed each other's company and went on excursions to villages around São Paulo, particularly attentive to the rich folklore on display during traditional festivals; they read each other's works and wrote to each other. So it was that, on receiving one of Mário de Andrade's books on ethnomusicology, Claude Lévi-Strauss wrote back, still under its charm (distilled slowly, as he had difficulty reading Portuguese at the time): 'What a trove of admirable things you have collected! On a makeshift instrument with a single string only, I spent a whole evening deciphering these tunes of such extraordinary melodic richness, charm and poetry. You have given me access to a new dimension of Brazil, and for that I am profoundly grateful.'[15]

This deep friendship drew the Lévi-Strausses into the network of the Department of Culture and led to their participation in the creation of an Anthropology and Folklore Society, which eventually saw the light of day in 1937. On the one side, the institution headed by Mário de Andrade was created to produce knowledge about the city, its development, and its social, cultural and physical transformations, as well as to train specialists with ethnographic research skills. On the other, the interests of the Lévi-Strausses were twofold but with converging effects. When she left for Brazil, Dina Lévi-Strauss seemed to have reached a tacit agreement with Georges Dumas that she would obtain a position, if not at the USP, at least at the Franco-Brazilian *lycée* of São Paulo. Yet, once settled in the country, she found herself jobless and with no income of her own. The issue was made less acute by the material comfort provided by her husband, but this modern couple, who had earned identical credentials, was far from satisfied with this situation. On several occasions, Claude Lévi-Strauss expressed his concerns over his wife's career – she was no less an *agrégé* than he – to Jean Marx and the local authorities. Keen to be more than just her husband's wife, especially since the responsibility of running the household was largely taken care of by Claude's mother, who had arrived together with her husband in 1935, with the help of the domestic staff. Dina thus had time to spare. As for Claude, his difficulties at the university and his ongoing conflict with Paul Arbousse-Bastide prevented him from realizing his project to create an Institute for Anthropology within the USP. However, the project was to find a home within the Department of Culture, with the benefit of solving several problems at once: Mário saw the institute as confirmation of the ethnographic mission of his institution; for Dina it was a professional opportunity; and Claude secured an institutional home for his research project. Indeed, it was the department that financed the couple's first expedition, undertaken in November 1935. Thus, the municipality and its Department of Culture gradually became the intellectual and institutional locus of the Lévi-Strausses' activities, and especially of Dina's.

Beginning in April 1936, she gave lectures on anthropology twice a week to about fifty students and municipal civil servants. The large number of interested students forced her to repeat the class, which was 'essentially practice oriented', as she put it to Jean Marx, focused on learning fieldwork methods.[16] With a few of her better trained students, she launched a collective survey in physical anthropology on 'Mongolian spots in the city of São Paulo',[17] a topic that was part of contemporary questionnaires in French anthropology. The following year, the department acquired a complete set of anthropometric tools and Dina Lévi-Strauss wrote a first set of instructions (for the most part in physical anthropology) for her students.[18] We should note here the importance of physical anthropology in Dina's intellectual and pedagogical preoccupations, and probably also those of her husband. Although the latter only rarely mentioned it, both tried to conduct anthropometric measurements during their expeditions, with great difficulty and almost no results.[19] Yet, in accordance with the prevalent notions of race at the time, and above all the prestige of physical anthropology, these methods were part of the Levi-Straussian repertoire in the 1930s.

The course taught by Dina, with increasing success, provided the impetus for the creation of the Anthropology and Folklore Society (SEF). Its impending birth was announced in São Paulo newspapers as part of a 'homage' paid by her students to 'Madame Lévy-Strauss' [*sic*]. There was a photo accompanying the enthusiastic article, featuring a radiant 'Gina Lévy-Strauss' [*sic*] at the centre, surrounded by students – Maria Stella Guimares, Mario Wagner Viera da Cunha, Cecilia de Castro e Silva, Raphaël Grisi, Annita Castello, Marcondes Cabral, Serafica Marcondes

Pereira, etc. – all gathered around a table covered with food, the figure of Claude Lévi-Strauss only just discernible in the background.[20] The caption read: 'Founded by Mário de Andrade, an anthropology club which will be the first of its kind in Brazil.' That 'club' – whose somewhat snobbish connotation Dina regretted – turned into a learned 'society' whose statutes (read over and amended by the legal apprentice Claude Lévi-Strauss)[21] were registered in 1937: Mário was its president, Dina its first secretary, and Mario Wagner the treasurer.

As its historian, Luisa Valentini,[22] has indicated, the SEF modelled itself on the Société des américanistes and the Royal Anthropological Society. Its aim was to professionalize research, standardize the collection of information, establish archives and systematize sources. Dina Lévi-Strauss was very much involved in the daily operation of the SEF. She was responsible for designing training and research programmes, which she did with a mixture of authority and humour that reflected the friendly relationship she had formed with Mário de Andrade.

Over the course of its existence, the SEF became a major intellectual hub in São Paulo. In a more open and vibrant atmosphere than at the university, one could think out loud and put into practice ideas about folklore, ethnography, science and art, in line with the subtle mixture of shared interests of its founders. They held conferences there: in May 1937, Dina Lévi-Strauss posed the question 'What is folklore?'; and her husband presented some of his recent work, including 'The material civilization of Caduveo Indians' and 'Some Karaja dolls'. A bulletin was created, in which the presentation on Karaja dolls, for example, was published. The *Revista do Arquivo municipal* was another organ that printed several of Claude Lévi-Strauss's writings: an article from his younger years on the impact of Cubism on the gaze of its contemporaries, called 'O Cubismo e vida cotidana', as well as his first genuinely anthropological article, which was also published in the *Journal de la Société des américanistes*,[23] 'Contribuição para o estudo da organização social Bororo'.[24] Use of the most advanced scholarly methods and teaching equipment was encouraged and practised, especially audiovisual technologies. Dina was thus equipped with a film camera when she went together with Mário de Andrade to a small colonial town on the outskirts of São Paulo to attend the 'festival of the Holy Spirit', a major, and powerfully syncretic, moment in Brazilian Catholicism: a procession of black kings whose Christianization is symbolized by men dressed in white, followed by the ride of the 'Cavalhada' and the 'Congada' ceremony, which re-enact the crowning. It was the subject of one of the films shot by Dina Lévi-Strauss unearthed at the São Paulo *cinémathèque*.[25] Her interest in São Paulo folklore justified her attendance at the International Congress of Folklore, which was held in Paris in June 1937, as a representative of the São Paulo SEF.

Cherished by her students and Mário de Andrade alike, Dina impressed everyone she met in São Paulo. One of her close friends, Mario Wagner, described the contrasting personalities of the couple – the one, warmhearted, effusive and affectionate; the other, reserved, serious, sometimes haughty. 'Mário had a soft spot for her, as we all did, because she was a beautiful girl of about our age. Lévi-Strauss was jealous of this situation – and he had reason to be. I often went to their house on Cincinato Braga because many SEF-related meetings were held there. Dina and I would talk endlessly. Lévi-Strauss regularly came by to see us but he never entered the room where we were. But he would pace up and down next door, as if to say: "I am here, and I would like the conversation to come to an end now!"'[26] The elective affinities between Mário de Andrade and Dina Lévi-Strauss, which gave birth to the SEF, as well as Dina's involvement and the role she played within it, explain why the Department of Culture was the repository for part of the collections brought back from the Lévi-Strausses' two ethnographic expeditions in Brazil. The Brazilian historiography has therefore tended to emphasize, perhaps overly, Dina's role. Nevertheless, it is certainly the case that, through her activities in São Paulo and the close ties she cultivated with the municipality and its personnel, she literally made the planning and execution of these expeditions possible.[27]

Ethnographic initiation (November 1935 to March 1936)

Starting hypotheses and conditions

As Lévi-Strauss explained to Marcel Mauss on the eve of his departure – 10 November 1935 – the timing was not ideal for an expedition to Mato Grosso, since it was the rainy season. But this was also the only period he had off from his academic duties, which entailed teaching full time. It was for this reason that he chose to visit Indians 'in relatively accessible regions'.[28] The plan was to go first into the swamps of Pantanal, the territory of the Caduveo, 'who are quite deculturated but have preserved an admirable tradition of ceramics, of which we are indeed hoping to find ancient specimens in an area that the National Museum has commissioned us to explore and study'.[29] Then on to visit the Bororo in Rio Vermelho, further north. Note the emphasis on the archaeologic dimension in the attempt to reconstruct American prehistory, which was indeed the broader epistemological framework for this expedition.

From the start, the expedition attracted quite a bit of attention, thanks to several articles published in the Brazilian press, as well as, on the other side of the Atlantic, a note published by Paul Rivet in the *Journal de la Société des américanistes* informing the academic community of this 'Mission to Brazil' co-sponsored by the French ministry of education. However, according to Luis Donisete Benzi Grupioni, 'Lévi-Strauss's first expedition into central Brazil was no different from others of the period. These were all based on a series of hypotheses derived from the theoretical concerns of the time, and were designed to build collections.'[30] What were these hypotheses? In an interview he gave to *O Jornal*, Lévi-Strauss explained that an old article published in the *Journal de la Société des américanistes* had caught his attention. The article posited a link between the

Um casal de scientistas francezes em visita ás tribus remanescentes de uma grande nação indigena

As ligações dos guayanús com as tribus industriaes que produziram a ceramica do Marajó — Curiosas observações do sr. e sra. Levy-Strauss, que acabam de regressar de Matto Grosso

Quando o professor e a senhora Levy-Strauss, aquelle professor de Sociologia da Universidade de São Paulo, e esta ex-assistente do prof. Dumas, no museu de Ethnographia do Trocadéro de Paris, resolveram aventurar-se em busca de contacto pessoal com os nossos indios do interior de Matto Grosso, em novembro ultimo, mal sabiam que dessa viagem resultaria, ape-

exiguidade de tempo da visita, resultando que o material recolhido, principalmente para seus estudos de anthropologia, foi pequeno, visto que sem uma real intimidade os indios se recusam ás verificações necessarias.

— "Rivet — diz-nos o prof. Levy Strauss — esteve cinco annos com os indios da America Hespanhola. Nós estivemos semanas. Colhemos apenas algu-

dios, bem como difficultaram a obtenção de chapas photographicas, temendo perigos de morte e enfeitiçamento. Quanto á parte propriamente ethnographica, os resultados alcançados são mais preciosos nas observações sobre a constituição tribal, organização da familia etc. etc. Uma publicação inserta no "Journal des Americanistes", anterior á guerra de 14, chamou nossa attenção.

No medalhão, o casal LEVY-STRAUSS. Em baixo, aspecto das malócas dos indios kaduveos

sar de sua rapidez, uma curiosa serie de contribuições para o estudo de nossos aborigenes.

Os estudiosos professores francezes, que acabam de regressar de Matto Grosso, fizeram essa excursão em missão scientifica do Estado de São Paulo, do Museu Nacional e do governo francez. Chegados agora a esta capital, o distincto casal de scientistas gentilmente concedeu ao DIARIO DE S. PAULO as impressões que tiveram dessa viagem.

A EXIGUIDADE DE TEMPO

Os dois scientistas francezes queixaram-se, primeiramente, da

mas medidas anthopometricas, mesmo assim em indios do sexo masculino, pois as mulheres se conservam em timida reserva.

Medidas sobre esqueleto e ossos, foi impossivel obtel-as, tanto entre os kaduveos como entre os borôros do Rio Vermelho, que visitamos posteriormente. Os borôros, após grandes commemorações funebres, enfeitam os ossos limpos e os atiram ao rio".

A CERAMICA DO VALLE DO AMAZONAS

— A classificação pelo sangue — prosegue o prof. Levy Staruss — tambem não foi conseguida, pois a isso se recusaram os in-

Nella se affirmava haver ligação entre as pinturas corporaes dos kaduveos e a ceramica do valle do Amazonas (Marajó e Santarem). Ora, os kaduveos são os ultimos guayacuru's, não pertencem aos povos de lingua gê, não são nem tupys nem tapuias, recendo ligar-se pela origem a tribus andinas. Esses indios acham-se localizados em Matto Grosso. Que curiosa ligação poderiam ter tido no passado, com as tribus industriaes que produziram a magnifica ceramica do valle do Amazonas? Consideramos uma das coisas mais essenciaes da nossa excursão, ter podido recolher precioso material destinado a elucidar essa questão. Já estamos procedendo a estudos sobre centenas de senhos corporaes, reproduzidos em papel pelos proprios kaveos.

SANTOS

(Da succursal do DIARIO DE S. PAULO) — R. Visc. de S. Leopoldo, 5 — Phone, 3-692

ACTOS DO INSPECTOR DA ALFANDEGA

esportivo, Militão Menna (reeleito); 2.º director esportivo, Araray Peniche;

INDIOS ESCULPTORES

body painting of the Caduveo and the decorative motifs on ceramics from
the Santarém and Marajó basin, with which archaeologists were quite
familiar. 'What kind of curious connection could there have been in the
past between the Caduveo [last descendants of the Guaycuru] and these
industrialized tribes, who have produced the magnificent ceramics of the
Amazon basin?' This line of inquiry was entirely in keeping with a 'classic'
set of questions regarding the geography of populations and civilizations:
the idea was to determine the exchanges that took place in the course of the
peopling of America, focusing on the lower regions of the Amazon, which
were far less documented than the west of the continent, home to the great
Andean civilizations whose striking achievements had drawn more attention from researchers. As he was about to set off, the young anthropologist
made a strange confession to Mauss: 'Of course, we would much prefer to
work on the Andean plateaux.' Never again would Lévi-Strauss express
a desire to focus on the Andes, as though the experience to come had
definitively swept away his doubts. For his part, the master encouraged
him to persevere both in his theoretical formulation and his geographical
orientation: 'Beware of focusing overly on the Andes, and conversely, you
are right to focus where you are. For everything I know about the prehistoric archaeology of Brazil, and especially the lower Amazon, points to the
existence of a great civilization there. Its highly developed terra cotta art is
more akin to Central America than to Peruvian America.'[31] Thus the goal,
especially with regard to the Caduveo, was to contribute to the mapping
of an ancient and great civilization that stretched from Central America to
the lower Americas, using precise archaeologic findings and anthropometric measurements.

Mauss added the following line at the end of his missive: 'Of course,
this letter is also addressed to your wife. I confuse the two of you, even in
my mind.'[32] This postscript can be interpreted in various ways, but it also
serves as a reminder of the phenomenon, once 'fieldwork' had become
essential, of 'ethnographic couples' forming a working and scholarly
unit, with no equivalent in any other discipline. Because it was still poorly
developed institutionally, anthropology attracted a significant number of
women – for example, in the 1930s, Denise Paulme, Germaine Tillion and
Deborah Lifschitz – and sometimes as part of a couple, thus providing a
solution to family problems raised by long absences. The ethnographic
couple also allowed for an effective division of labour, since female ethnographers could sometimes gain access to indigenous women more easily
than their male counterparts. Can a marriage stand the test of fieldwork?
Does it emerge stronger or compromised? Questions that did not seem to
cross the minds of the young couple as they were setting off, but which
would boomerang back at them a few years later.

Caduveo arabesques

A small group of three, lightly equipped (a few trunks and a tent), left
São Paulo at the end of November 1935: Claude and Dina Lévi-Strauss

were accompanied by René Silz, the unknown member of this team that would become famous. Silz was an agronomist, and former school friend of Claude's, who had come from France for the expedition. The notebooks of this first fieldwork have been lost. We must therefore rely on the retrospective narrative that Lévi-Strauss provides in *Tristes Tropiques* and some notes of Dina's that survive in the archives.[33]

The journey began by train to Porto Esperança, the last stop on the Noroeste line. After crossing the Paraná River to the town of Três-Lagoas, a three-day train ride led them into Mato Grosso, whose monotonous landscape was to become the insufferable yet necessary landscape of the time spent in the Brazilian interior: 'Flat or slightly undulated plateaux, sweeping vistas and scrub-type vegetation, with an occasional herd of zebus which scatter as the train goes past'.[34] From Porto Esperança, secondary lines ran, like flimsy footbridges, over the Pantanal swamp, the largest wetlands area in the world, which covers the entire central basin of southern Brazil, on the border with Bolivia and Paraguay. It was there, in that dream landscape, that the Caduveo lived, shielded by the mountains of Serra da Bodoquena, on a reservation assigned to them in the early twentieth century by the Brazilian state. 'Herds of zebus take refuge on the tops of hillocks which look like floating arches, while in the flooded swamps, flocks of large birds, such as flamingos, egrets and herons, form dense white-and-pink islands . . . .'[35] The aspiring anthropologists set up camp in 'Fazenda Francesca', a plantation run by Frenchmen about one hundred kilometres south of Porto Esperança. Dina, who had fallen ill and had had to turn back, joined them there. Lévi-Strauss describes the sleepy plantation that survived in almost complete autarky, unfailingly abiding certain rituals: for example, twice a day, at eleven in the morning and seven in the evening, the ritual of the *chimarrão* – the 'imbibing of maté through a pipe' – 'at once a social rite and a private vice'.[36] From there, a three-day ride on horseback was necessary to reach the Caduveo, who numbered around two hundred individuals distributed over three settlements. Nalike, the main one, consisted of five shabby huts. The travellers arrived there at the end of December, under an exceptionally severe tropical storm.

From the very outset, they were struck by the contrast between the wretched living conditions and 'degradation' of those Indians, who lived like poor peasants, and the survival of a brilliant material civilization, moving in the way it 'tenaciously preserved certain features of the past'.[37] It seemed to Lévi-Strauss that in the very dexterity of their daily work, weaving and basketry as well as the crafting of ropes and thread games, the Caduveo of the present established a direct and profound connection with the aristocratic and warlike tribe that they had still been in the nineteenth century, taking part in the Paraguayan War (1864–70) and displaying the proud figures of their horsemen. This comment reveals Lévi-Strauss's 'quixotism', which had him always looking for the gilding of the past under the mud of the present. But in that mud shone first and foremost beautifully crafted objects that he eagerly collected, thereby demonstrating his keen interest in the creation of collections, the veritable touchstone of all ethnographic work. He brought back trunks full of sculpted wooden

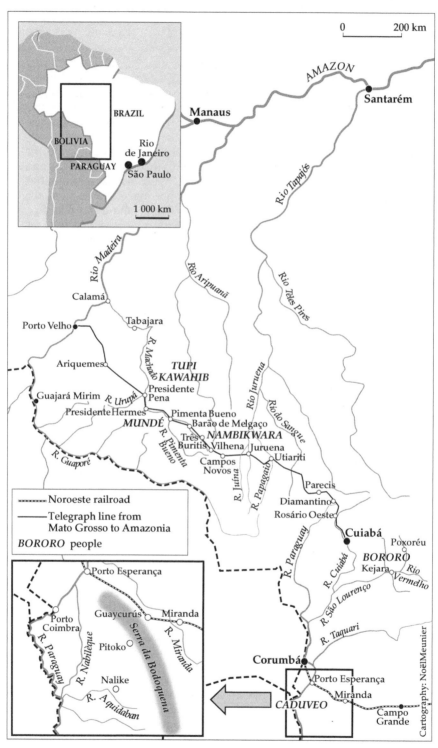

The itineraries of the two expeditions in the Mato Grosso.
The first (November 1935–January 1936) brought Claude and Dina Lévi-Strauss to the
Caduveo and then to the Bororo; the second (May 1938–January 1939) to the
Nambikwara, along the Rondon line.

statuettes (whose function remained a mystery), jewels, fans, hammocks and finely decorated ceramics. As for the string games that were to fill the notebooks of the next expedition, they constituted one of the themes in studies of the Americas at the time.

But the essential aspect for him lay in an extraordinary trait of Caduveo culture, which really fascinated Lévi-Strauss: the body painting drawn by the women, both young and old, in an expert hand, using *jenipapo* juice as ink.[38] Their bodies and faces, as shown in the photographs and drawings made by Lévi-Strauss, were covered with a fine lace of asymmetrical arabesques that reminded him of the motifs of Spanish baroque wrought iron. Throughout his two-week stay with the Caduveos, Lévi-Strauss was captivated by these arabesques. He tried to reproduce them and encouraged the women to draw the motifs on sheets of paper he was to take back with him: about four hundred drawings vertiginously delineating the infinite variety of false symmetries and inverted patterns, which remained nonetheless enigmatic. In the two extant films shot by Claude and Dina Lévi-Strauss during their time with the Caduveos, we see the women's coquetry as they indulge in the art of self-adornment, their confident hands tracing expert lines over the irregular contours of their faces.[39] From the start, Lévi-Strauss's painterly eye understood the high quality of this subtle art that had been miraculously preserved. Indeed, among the sources that had motivated Lévi-Strauss's choice of the Caduveos as a first fieldwork experience was the narrative of an Italian amateur painter, Guido Boggiani, who in the late nineteenth century had 'left tempting and suggestive indications' about them.[40] Lévi-Strauss was to return throughout his life to these compositions of unfailing abstraction, to these refined and systematic interlacings, as if to an enigma that begged for resolution, producing various interpretations as sophisticated as the original material. Starting from a diffusionist approach, he was to move, thanks to Caduveo arabesques, towards entirely different theoretical paradigms, probing the dualism of the paintings, their asymmetry and the social function of indigenous art – developments that are present in *Tristes Tropiques* but that had not yet been elaborated in 1936. It was to take Lévi-Strauss years of reflection to 'read' these mysterious patterns, which fuelled his entire scholarly life. Although they were unquestionably one of the sources of the structuralist intuition, they cannot mask the fact that, in 1936, Lévi-Strauss was not a structuralist.

Towards the end of his stay, on 15 January 1936, he wrote to Mário de Andrade about Nalike: 'Out here, women still paint their faces with designs of prodigious refinement, and they make very beautiful and sober pottery, of which I am bringing back quite a few examples. And interesting testimonials remain regarding the legends and social organization of the past. The material conditions are of course harsh: in Pantanal, the heat is often scorching – which did not keep us from sometimes shivering with cold at night in Nalike! – and the mosquitoes are exactly as we expected. But there are so many interesting and admirable things here that the rest becomes rather irrelevant. We are soon off for São Lourenço and the Bororo.'[41]

Caduveo motifs drawn by Lévi-Strauss in his notebooks, copying the
sophisticated arabesques and false symmetries that the women would paint on
their bodies and especially faces.

The Bororo opera

If the visit to the Caduveos led to the surprise discovery of this astonishing graphic art, the encounter with the Bororo also promised to yield
aesthetic returns of considerable value, but of a different kind. Whereas
the Caduveos were draughtsmen and painters, the Bororo liked to work
with fragile materials, feathers and flowers, wreaths of which adorned
their prolific rituals. This Lévi-Strauss could anticipate, since, unlike the
Caduveos, Bororo society had been regularly visited since the nineteenth
century. They were famous in the archives of South American ethnography
and represented a kind of 'prime cut'[42] for anthropologists, with whom
they provided a very complicated social organization, a high level of aesthetic production, a complex religious system comprising a rich pantheon
and astonishing rituals. Every day was a festival with the Bororo, and for
their visitors too, who became intoxicated by these endless ceremonies. In
short, the Bororo were an anthropologist's dream, and Lévi-Strauss had
high hopes as the small trekking party made its way, first by truck, then
canoe via the Paraguay River, from Corumba to the São Lourenço River
and its tributary, the Vermelho. On its banks, to their great relief, since
there had been talk of a recent devastating outbreak of yellow fever, the
Lévi-Strausses caught a glimpse of 'two nude forms moving on the bank:
our first Bororo'.[43]

Despite their regular contact with Salesian missionaries, the Bororo at first appeared to Lévi-Strauss to exist in a world sufficiently isolated to still be untainted. Indeed, the Salesian priests, who were a few years later to produce the imposing *Encyclopédia Bororo*, had, rather, been converted by the Bororo more than the other way around, to the extent that the Indians seemed in the eyes of our three Europeans to display few signs of acculturation, conforming instead to the way Western philosophy had long imagined noble savages: tall, naked, sturdy bodies, imbued with religious faith, devoting most of their time to adorning themselves and dancing, punctuated with great bursts of laughter. Proud and strapping feathered fellows were thus transformed into little chicks.[44] Lévi-Strauss was 'overcome by the wealth and ingenuity of that exceptional culture'.[45] Like at the Wagner operas he attended as a child, he was delighted by the overall spectacle offered up by this 'multicoloured skein'.[46]

From that very first night, Lévi-Strauss's educated ear delighted in the Bororo chants. It was 'wonderful to listen to: sometimes unleashing or stopping the voices with a short sharp crack; sometimes filling in the silences with the rattling of their instruments in long drawn-out crescendos or diminuendos; and sometimes directing the dancers with alternations of silence and noise, so varied in their duration, intensity and quality that no conductor of a large European orchestra could have surpassed them in indicating his intentions.'[47] He was to hear this concert of virile voices – only men sang – regularly during his three-week stay. Indeed, each night these proud war chiefs, smeared with red pigment made of pounded *urucu* seeds, would engage in various religious ceremonies; one of them, the *Marid'do* dance, was a funeral rite which Claude and Dina filmed. The film shows the making of the *Marid'do*, a wicker disc of 1.5 metres in diameter that is worn by the dancer as a diadem, the preparation of the dance tune, the invocations, offerings and dances that, here again, are performed only by the men, with the women seated, watching.[48] Dina Lévi-Strauss would often use the film in her classes.

Rituals (especially funeral rites), cosmology, matrimonial rules, myths – all classic objects of anthropology, and those on which Lévi-Strauss was to work throughout his entire life – were explored over the course of this brief but intense stay during which, thanks to the help of his interpreter and primary informant – 'a wonderful guide to Bororo sociology'[49] – he collected significant amounts of material. The presence of an interpreter was of course essential for the anthropologist, since the Bororo did not speak a word of Portuguese. But beyond the routines of fieldwork, a kind of illumination gathered together the various empirical findings into a theoretical intuition, as yet imperfectly formulated. It had to do with the geographical layout of the huts in the Bororo village of Kejara, which housed about 140 people. Kejara was a circular village whose diameter, which ran parallel to the river, theoretically split the space into two moieties and the population into two groups, the Cera and the Tugaré. At the centre was the men's house, where the bachelors slept and the men spent their time during the day; around it, the huts were laid out in a circle. Based on this schema, a complex geometry, as subtle as the Caduveo arabesques, governed alliances and movements: an individual always belonged to the same moiety as his mother, and could only marry a member of the other moiety. 'At the time of his marriage, a male native crosses the imaginary line separating the moieties and goes to live on the opposite side.'[50] This geography of social life was further complicated by hereditary subgroups and the onset of professional specialization. As in the pioneer towns, Lévi-Strauss engaged in an open-air reading of the spatialization of social and cultural forms, deciphering the 'ballet in which two village moieties strive to live and breathe each through and for the other', constructing an unstable balance between social hierarchy (the Bororo are not all equal) and reciprocity.[51] Here again, the empirical work of 1936, which eludes us for lack of archives, was overlaid with hypotheses developed in the years that followed and the abundant literature to which the dual structure of Bororo villages has given rise. At the time, it appears that the Lévi-Strausses' research was limited to gaining a more accurate sense of the extent of the territory of the Gê people, which constituted one of the sites and issues in the contemporary anthropology of the Americas, through the work of Curt Nimuendaju. Later, Lévi-Strauss invested the Bororo with a theoretical authority – they were 'great structuralist theoreticians', as he was to write – which converged with his own, still unconscious, structuralist thinking,[52] to crystallize into the scientific project of the same name. A retrospective fantasy construction, which nonetheless demonstrates the very special part the Keraja peoples played in Claude Lévi-Strauss's self-construction.

Back from the field

An expedition under inspection

In 2005, Claude Lévi-Strauss was surprised to discover objects he had not seen for seventy years, 'when, back from fieldwork, [he] unwrap[ped] them in the offices of the Department of Culture of the city of São Paulo, to be divided up between Brazil and France'.[53] As part of the 'Year of Brazil' festivities in France, an exhibition had just miraculously brought together the objects collected in 1935–36, offering them up for public appreciation, as well as to the reminiscences of the aged anthropologist.

These pieces, submerged in Lévi-Strauss's Brazilian past, essentially represented the ethnographic booty of his first expedition. They had remained in São Paulo, moving from one institution to another for over fifty years and were practically lost, before resurfacing thanks to Luis Donisete Benzi Grupioni, the exhibition's curator and a historian of ethnographic expeditions. Why this policy of sharing the loot, which did not at all apply in other research fields? It was only two years prior to the first expedition, in 1933, that decree number 22698 established the authority of the 'Inspection Council on Artistic and Scientific Expeditions' in Brazil.[54] For over three decades, until 1968, this *Conselho* supervised and inspected both foreigners and Brazilian nationals who undertook expeditions, paying particular attention to the preservation of cultural and artistic objects, but also botanical, mineralogical and animal specimens, upon the scholars' return. As Luis Donisete explains, it 'was the product of a period in Brazil's history when the national character was to express itself in the formulation of nationalist ideas, appropriation of the territory, and unification of state management, a process that emphasized the conservation of indigenous artefacts as constitutive of the historical and cultural heritage of the Brazilian nation.'[55] It might also have been a distant offspring of the Malraux scandal, which had created quite a stir a few years earlier: the young writer-adventurer had pilfered some Khmer statuettes from the Angkor Wat site in Cambodia. Although the council imposed a set of tedious administrative processes, with which Lévi-Strauss locked horns upon return from his second expedition, it sought to prevent all forms of colonial exploitation by dictating the conditions of genuine Franco-Brazilian cooperation. In that respect, it guaranteed the legitimacy and stability of collections which, when they originated elsewhere (Africa for instance), are today challenged, precisely because of the dubious conditions under which they were constituted.[56] These bureaucratic hurdles, annoying to anthropologists at the time, offer the added advantage of having generated documentation, and hence historical sources, which can now be consulted at the Museum of Astronomy and Related Sciences (MAST) in Rio.

The first expedition to the Caduveo and the Bororo was subject to a simple licensing agreement that was easily obtained from the council, and that allowed the Lévi-Strausses to conduct their research and circulate freely within the country. The sponsorship of the National Museum in Rio facilitated the process further. Upon their return, an inventory was drawn up, listing 161 Bororo, 164 Caduveo, 2 Terena and 1 Kaingang objects – i.e., 328 pieces that remained in Brazil, though not at the National Museum as originally planned, but rather at the Department of Culture where Dina and Mário de Andrade had decided to establish an Ethnographic Museum. The split between São Paulo and Rio was, as Lévi-Strauss told Heloisa Alberto Torres, director of the National Museum, a 'purely Brazilian negotiation' in which he had no business taking part. He did, however, try very hard to convince his interlocutor that the objects he had brought back, including the ceramics in which he took a particular interest, were quite inferior to those she already possessed in Rio.[57]

In *Tristes Tropiques*, Lévi-Strauss comments ironically on the suspicion that hovered over him, 'in case [he] should attempt, with sinister intent, to make a fast getaway with bows, arrows and feathered head-dresses, exceeding the share allotted to France'.[58] And yet this is precisely what happened. Indeed, the French share filed at the Musée de l'Homme in Paris comprised 602 objects (341 Bororo, 230 Caduveo, 31 Guarani/Kaingang) – in other words, considerably more than half of the total . . . To be fair, in addition to the ethnographic objects themselves, the Lévi-Strausses did leave their 8 millimetre films at the disposal of the Brazilians, which significantly evens the balance.

The anointment of an ethnographer

When the Lévi-Strausses returned to Paris, in the winter of 1936–37, the French portion of the collection was exhibited, with the couple present, in the Wildenstein Gallery, at the corner of rue du Faubourg-Saint-Honoré and the rue de La Boétie, from 21 January to 3 February 1937, under the title 'The Indians of Mato Grosso (Mission Claude and Dina Lévi-Strauss)'. The support of the Musée de l'Homme, as was clear in Paul Rivet's introduction to the catalogue, would have made it one of the first exhibitions to take place at the new museum, but delays in the construction of the palais de Chaillot ruined that plan. In the end, the potentially emblematic status of the exhibition gave way to a perhaps more significant location; indeed, the setting of the art gallery is a reminder of the important role played by aesthetic sensibilities and artistic milieus in the anthropological project at the time – at the very moment that the opening of the Musée de l'Homme was about to reconfigure the entire field.

Reminiscing about this pivotal moment, Lévi-Strauss insisted spontaneously on the beauty of the objects collected: 'It was a solid ethnographic collection – I can say that now that I have some basis for comparison. Among the Caduveo we had found decorated pottery and hides painted with motifs found nowhere else in America. The Bororo objects comprised mostly ornaments made of feathers and animal teeth and claws, since the Bororo richly ornament even their hunting weapons and their utensils. There were some spectacular pieces.'[59] This initial and principal outcome of the expedition – the exhibition – was an artistic, social and scientific success, and one that followed a certain anthropological recipe that sought to reproduce the *spectacular* dimension of primitive societies. The Bororo feathered headdresses were truly 'visual objects', to rival the most beautiful Dogon masks.

Creating a collection, in this case comprising more than 600 objects to enrich the meagre holdings of the Musée de l'Homme on prehistoric America, was indeed one of the core objectives of all expeditions at the time: collecting exotic objects considered doomed to disappear. This sense of needing to intervene before it was too late, which Lévi-Strauss felt deeply, was widely shared within the profession and gave rise to a discourse that constituted a sort of urgent anthropology. Thus, in the exhibition catalogue, Lévi-Strauss concluded: 'We have very little time left to collect what still survives and will soon disappear.' This sense of urgency stemmed from the steady appropriation of native lands and their integration into the modern nation-state (a process temporarily slowed down by the global slump in rubber and commodities prices), as well as the sharp demographic drop induced by the very effective birth control practised by indigenous populations. This mission to safeguard (objects, rituals, myths) might have been motivated by humanist concerns, but it was riddled with ambiguities. Lévi-Strauss did not react as Michel Leiris did to the Dakar-Djibouti mission[60] – seeing it as a full-fledged extortion, enabled by conditions of colonial domination. Yet, he had qualms: 'One felt ashamed to deprive people who have so little of a small tool the loss

MUSÉUM NATIONAL D'HISTOIRE NATURELLE
MUSÉE DE L'HOMME

UN INDIEN BORORO

INDIENS DU
MATTO-GROSSO
(Mission Claude et Dina Lévi-Strauss)
Novembre 1935 Mars 1936
GUIDE-CATALOGUE DE L'EXPOSITION
ORGANISÉE A LA GALERIE DE LA
"GAZETTE DES BEAUX-ARTS" ET DE "BEAUX-ARTS"
21 Janvier - 3 Février 1937

Cover of the 'Catalogue Guide' to the exhibition that was held at the Galérie des Beaux-Arts (Wildenstein Gallery), 21 January–3 February 1937, featuring a Bororo Indian. The exhibition was a resounding success and established the Lévi-Strausses' reputation.

of which would be irreparable . . . .'[61] The explicit scientific goal of collecting sometimes ran up against the impossibility of exchange. For this reason, the otherwise impatient Lévi-Strauss would ungrudgingly engage in long back-and-forth negotiations: 'I might ask an Indian woman if she would sell me one of her pots, and she would say yes. Unfortunately, it did not belong to her. To whom did it belong? – Silence. – To her husband? No. – To her brother? No, not to her brother either. – To her son? Not to her son. – It belonged to her granddaughter. The granddaughter inevitably owned all the objects we wanted to buy. We looked at her, she was three or four years old and was squatting near the fire, totally engrossed in the ring I had slipped onto her finger a short while before. And so we had to embark on lengthy negotiations with the young lady, in which her parents did not take part. She was unmoved by the offer of a ring and five hundred reis, but let herself be persuaded by a brooch and four hundred reis.'[62]

The other upshot of the expedition was the production of knowledge. In connection with the exhibition, Lévi-Strauss gave several conferences and seminars in Paris, which established the young scholar in the world of Parisian sociology. On 9 January, he gave a presentation and screened a film on the Indians of Mato Grosso in the grand amphitheatre of the Muséum national d'Histoire naturelle. On 11 January, for a considerably more select audience, he was invited by Célestin Bouglé to 'come and give a talk on your anthropological research for the benefit of our young colleagues – four or five philosophers only, who want to train in sociology outside their curriculum at the Sorbonne'. They convened at the Centre de documentation sociale, of which Bouglé was the director. But prior to the event, the mandarin invited him to 'tea with various sociologist colleagues'.[63] If it was Bouglé who introduced him into scholarly circles, it was Mauss whom he kept abreast of the expedition's findings. Lévi-Strauss reported to the 'master' a few points he considered certain: 'The existence, in social and economic life, of reciprocal and obligatory services from clan to clan, of the kind that has brought you to extend the potlatch area: the subdivision of clans into classes and an analogous system, at least in its essentials, to the Australian systems; finally, the coexistence of an economic hierarchy with a class hierarchy.'[64] Without any further comment on these conclusions, let us simply point out that the young scholar was still very much adopting the position of disciple. He was contributing to the drawing of the potlatch map initiated by Mauss's research. One of the objectives of fieldwork was to confirm the hypotheses put forward by the master, which is what Lévi-Strauss was doing here, even while raising a few highly political issues to which he would return (hierarchy and reciprocity, power relations and systems of domination in indigenous societies).

More importantly, Claude Lévi-Strauss's first scholarly publication in the field – 'Contributions sur l'organisation sociale des Indiens Bororo', published a few months later in the *Journal de la Société des américanistes*,[65] a highly respected academic review – was well received by the small world of French anthropologists, among whom his serious work and attendance at sociologist get-togethers had earned him a place. Lévy-Bruhl, the most renowned of these anthropologists at the time, tipped his hat to the young Lévi-Strauss, congratulating him on the speed and efficacy of his fieldwork: 'And this was your first fieldwork experience! You were born to be an anthropologist, and you have a promising academic career ahead of you.'[66]

More surprising was the reception accorded him by the great German ethnographer Curt Unckel. The latter had spent years in central Brazil by himself, and eventually adopted the Indian name that the Guarani of São Paulo had given him in 1906 – Nimuendaju. This name was already established as a scholarly reference in the discipline, and evoked a solitary mode of investigation, encyclopedic erudition, and the art of living in harmony with one's object of study. In 1936, Nimuendaju (who died in 1945 in an Indian village) was legendary in the field. And he was, furthermore, the leading specialist of Brazil's indigenous peoples, many of whose languages he mastered. Naturally, the young Lévi-Strauss, full of admiration and deference, sent him his article. On 10 November 1936, Nimuendaju responded, thanking him and engaging directly in a discussion of the division into exogamic moieties, addressing his young colleague as an equal. He also encouraged him to engage in a longer period of fieldwork as soon as the opportunity arose. And, on the very next day, he wrote to his colleague in São Paulo, Herbert Baldus, also a professor at USP, elaborating on the effect this article by an unknown anthropologist had had on him: 'Who is this Claude Lévi-Strauss? [. . .] I have read an article of his in the *Estado* [*de São Paulo*], 'Entre os selvagens civilizados', whose position on the indigenous question I found very interesting. Then his 'Contribution à l'étude de l'organisation sociale des Bororo' in the [*Journal de la Société des américanistes*], in which he [. . .] presents very valuable material, and which came to me as if I had commissioned it myself . . . What can be expected of him in the future?'[67] A few months later, on 17 January 1937, he continued: 'What is remarkable is that this man [. . .] who has only recently taken up anthropology, has so completely immersed himself in it in such a short time that he has managed to capture the sociological situation of the Bororo with great accuracy. When I think of how I struggled for six years on the sociology of the Canela, the concise nature of his presentation merits attention.'[68] Nimuendaju did not fail to inform his American colleague and correspondent Robert Lowie that a new star was born. Through Lowie, the entire rich network of American anthropology was opened up to Lévi-Strauss. This connection at that point represented only the promise of scholarly recognition, but it would prove crucial a few years down the line. When the time came for exile, the name of Lévi-Strauss would not be unknown in American anthropological circles, and the gates of the United States would open all the faster.

Meanwhile, let us consider this very significant epistolary anointment. Without ever having met him, Nimuendaju immediately seized on the kind of researcher that Lévi-Strauss was: quick to make sense of complex situations, able to build models based on fragmentary material. The intellectual panorama did not in any way interfere with the close-up. Nimuendaju hailed the eagle eye of his junior colleague, his attention to empirical detail and the precision of his commentary, based on brief flashes rather than extended immersion – the 'vista' of Claude Lévi-Strauss . . .

8

Massimo Lévi with the Nambikwara

An anthropological expedition into central Brazil begins at the Carrefour Réaumur-Sébastopol.

Claude Lévi-Strauss, *Tristes Tropiques*[1]

If preparing for his long expedition in 1937 was like staging a play, what went on behind the scenes was both hazardous and strenuous. Going to the outermost regions of central Brazil to visit various Indian tribes was a complicated undertaking. There was an accumulation of financial, administrative and political complications over the course of that year, with no shortage of unexpected challenges and hard-fought battles, in which Lévi-Strauss ultimately prevailed thanks to a combination of obstinacy and naivety. At the moment of departure, the institutional infrastructure that was to support the expedition collapsed, in the person of Mário de Andrade, who had suddenly become persona non grata with the new authorities. The expedition thus found itself orphaned, only to then become cosseted by an overbearing, almost abusive, mother, Heloisa Alberto Torres, who headed the National Museum of Rio de Janeiro. Lévi-Strauss was finally able to depart at the beginning of May 1938, to return on 12 January 1939.

It is now possible to tell the story of this famous expedition to the Nambikwara based on new material, offering alternative voices to the long requiem of *Tristes Tropiques*, which was published in 1955 nearly twenty years after the fact, and which engaged in a complex retrospective reinterpretation of the Brazilian fieldwork. Later still, in the two volumes of *Saudades*, published in 1994 and 1996, Lévi-Strauss's attitude was more congenial. At the time, the young anthropologist – with his explorer's hat squarely on his head, and his notebooks and Leica in hand – had learned his trade in a state of stupefaction and suffering, both physical and mental. Those who accompanied him on that journey – Brazilian ethnographer Luiz de Castro Faria and biologist Jehan Albert Vellard – have each produced their own versions of this long scientific odyssey known as the 'Serra do Norte Mission'.

This revisiting of the Brazilian expedition also presents an occasion to reassess the place of fieldwork in Claude Lévi-Strauss's scholarly life and work – of which it constituted an important cornerstone, if not always very visible. In its own ambivalences, and in the critical reception it has received, both then and now, this 'fieldwork' represents, as Eduardo Viveiros de Castro has aptly put it, a kind of 'missed rendez-vous' between Lévi-Strauss and Brazil.[2]

Archives of an expedition: the Serra do Norte Mission

Preparations

Back in Brazil for his third and last year of teaching, from March to November 1937, Lévi-Strauss was given to understand that his contract would not be renewed. The conflicts with Paul Arbousse-Bastide, as well as the new political context at the end of 1937, were altogether unfavourable. The atmosphere steadily deteriorated through the course of the year. In Rio, '*Integralistas*' were in the streets, displaying Nazi symbols (including the Swastika), and anti-Semitic propaganda became increasingly prominent. On the left, communist protests, strikes and demonstrations had followed one after another since 1935. In a letter dated 25 September 1937, Lévi-Strauss confided to Marcel Mauss: 'As for Brazil, the country is going through a period of considerable agitation, awaiting the results of a presidential election, which, for all we know, may well be rendered moot by a coup d'état. The faculty of philosophy has already nearly gone under in the fight. There is no doubt that its immediate future depends on the outcome of the struggle.'[3] Two months later, the struggle did indeed culminate in a coup and the establishment of the *Estado Novo*, an authoritarian regime presided over by Getúlio Vargas until 1945. The USP, which had been founded under the auspices of his political opponent, was right in the line of fire of the new regime. In São Paulo, Claude Lévi-Strauss – a Frenchman, a Jew and a socialist – would seem to have had a bit of a scuffle, for both professional and political reasons, with the USP oligarchy. According to Roger Bastide, who succeeded him in 1938, the decision not to renew his contract came from Julio Mesquita Filho himself: 'Claude Lévi-Strauss was apparently removed from the faculty through the direct intervention of Mesquita Filho, who considered Lévi-Strauss to be a "dangerous" element, connected to the French Front populaire, and a "communist".'[4] Claude Lévi-Strauss would later remember receiving a visit from Julio Mesquita, who went to see him at the Collège de France after his election, 'as a gesture – which [he] appreciated – to convey [to him] that he had recognized his mistake'.[5]

In this complicated political and institutional context, Lévi-Strauss was thus forced to leave the University of São Paulo, and to focus entirely on preparations for his second expedition, which he conceived on a much more ambitious scale than the first. The success of the exhibition on 'The Indians of Mato Grosso' in Paris, as well as the recognition of his colleagues, had encouraged him to pursue a future doctorate, and thus to gather material for it. To Mauss, he said he had tried to 'push as far as the resources of local libraries would allow, in the bibliographical preparation work for

[his] dissertation. The general frameworks are in place. What fieldwork will enable me to add remains to be seen.'[6] Lévi-Strauss was a highly organized doctoral student, who advanced on several fronts at once: he formulated a conceptual matrix and a set of research questions – i.e., an intellectual framework for his adventure. He also began looking around to put together a more substantial team than on the first mission. On Rivet's and Métraux's advice, he contacted Dr Vellard, a medical doctor and the director of the Biological Institute of Pernambuco, as well as Curt Nimuendaju. The latter declined, claiming that he was already engaged in a long-term study of the sociology of Gê populations on the eastern plateau, which would keep him busy for at least a year. In fact, Nimuendaju disliked Vellard and, more importantly, he was accustomed to working alone and reluctant to take part in a group expedition of the kind Lévi-Strauss was organizing. This is where the matter stood when Lévi-Strauss returned to France in 1937.

This Parisian interlude was fleetingly mentioned in *Tristes Tropiques*, in a few pages that barely interrupt the flow of his ever-deeper descent into the heart of Brazil, and into humanity as a whole. Yet, the seventh part of the book – on the 'Nambikwara' – opened with a disconcerting paradox: 'An anthropological expedition into central Brazil begins at the Carrefour Réaumur-Sébastopol.'[7] Lévi-Strauss then proceeded to describe a strategic moment in the run-up to the expedition: the purchase of the trinkets that would be needed to barter with the Indians, with whose exacting taste he was now familiar: 'In an area of Paris which was as unknown to me as the Amazon, I found myself engaging in strange practices under the watchful eye of Czech importers. Knowing nothing of their trade, I lacked the technical terms with which to specify my needs, and could only apply native criteria. I set about choosing the smallest of the embroidery beads known in French as *rocaille*, which were piled up in the trays in heavy hanks. I tried to bite through them to test their toughness; I sucked them in order to make sure that they were made of tinted glass and that the colour would not run at the first contact with river water; I varied the amounts purchased in accordance with the basic Indian colour scheme: first black and white in equal quantities; next red; then a much smaller quantity of yellow; and, for form's sake, a few blue and green which would no doubt be spurned.'[8] Imagine the baffled looks on these shopkeepers' faces (many of whom were Central European Jews who worked in the nearby garment district of the Sentier) on seeing the tall gentleman with a serious face biting and sucking on their beads! As Vincent Debaene has remarked, this passage stages an eerie inversion of the ethnographic experience: 'The ethnographer is an Indian among the Czechoslovaks of Paris.'[9] Adopting native aesthetic criteria, he became all the more estranged from his own world when he found himself in a working-class neighbourhood, far from the more upscale districts of western Paris with which he was familiar.

These few months in Paris also served to build up institutional logistical support and to clarify his professional status with the ministry of education. A ministerial decision from 5 June 1937, signed by Jean Zay, put Claude Lévi-Strauss in charge of a scientific mission into the 'Serra des Paressi' (the exact name was to change several times) and encouraged all possible support to that end. He was thus seconded from the ministry of education, and the Service des œuvres continued to pay the French share of his salary (3,000 francs), as well as 1,500 francs each month to his wife (in payment for her services to the city of São Paulo). After some wavering due to the non-renewal of his contract at USP, Lévi-Strauss and his wife were eventually guaranteed a monthly income roughly equivalent to what they had earned over the previous few years. Institutionally speaking, Paul Rivet, the director of the Musée de l'Homme, whose modern building now stood proudly atop the Chaillot hill in Paris, provided major and unflagging support. He agreed to officially endow the new Lévi-Strauss mission with the authority of the Musée de l'Homme, and he closely monitored the complicated developments unfolding, as we shall see, on the Brazilian side, actively exerting all his influence. With the ministry of foreign affairs, he insisted on the 'disinterested character of these purely scientific missions, quite popular with the South American peoples, as they tend to feel ignored and dismissed by European nations. Demonstrating by our actions that France is interested in studying their country is the surest way to win over their hearts. Thirty-eight years of experience has convinced me that this is the best form of propaganda, for it flatters and respects the ardent and testy patriotism of these peoples.'[10]

Finally, next to Jean Marx and Paul Rivet, the third figure to play a decisive role – and who would go on to play an even greater one in Lévi-Strauss's life several years later – was Henri Laugier, a well-known scholar, physiologist and patron of the arts, who, through his wife's contacts (and wealth), knew every one of the most famous avant-garde French artists. He was, like Rivet, one of those left-wing intellectuals who were naturally inclined to believe in the emancipatory and democratic virtues of science. In 1936, he was at the helm of the newly created Research Service, and later became head of the National Centre of Scientific Research (CNRS), which was founded in the same spirit in 1939. Thus, thanks to Laugier, as well as to Lévi-Strauss's Front populaire network, the mission was in part funded by the precursor to the CNRS.

SPI, anthropology, nation, exploration

As was the case with the first expedition, the choice of region and tribes to visit was the subject of much consideration, due to both material and intellectual concerns. Hypotheses were integrated into a general set of research questions, with sometimes rather wild ambitions thrown into the lot. Indeed, Amerindian research at the time was still quite wanting in material sources, which gave rise to all manner of intellectual frameworks for the big project of the day: 'understanding America' – i.e., understanding its peopling, the distribution of its population, and its exchanges and migrations, over the course of a history that was still thought to be relatively short – a few thousand years.[11] It also involved positing the unity of an American people, across South and even North America, despite civilizational differences between the rich worlds of the Andes and the populations Lévi-Strauss was preparing to visit on the western confines of the Brazilian plateau.

He gradually came to envision an itinerant expedition, which was standard practice at the time, that would loop around the western and most remote part of Mato Grosso, following a northwesterly diagonal from Cuiabá towards the Bolivian border and the Rio Madeira basin. This 'sort of cross-section through Brazilian anthropology, and geography'[12] was designed to bring him into contact with not one but several tribes of the Gê, Tupi and Arawak languages – i.e., a wide range of societies and variants, which would enable a mapping of the Brazilian indigenous population.[13] Proclaiming himself 'more anxious to understand America than to study human nature by basing my research on one particular instance',[14] Lévi-Strauss preferred the tracking shot to the zoom. In the end, he was mostly to encounter the Nambikwara people.

He had high expectations of these people, all the more so because so little was known about them. The sixteenth-century explorers mostly dealt with the Tupi-Guarani who lived near the coast and had only recently arrived on this ring of Brazilian shoreline. Northwest of Tupi territory, the Carib and the Arawak also formed the original populations of the Caribbean islands, which make the connection with Central and North America. Westward, in the hinterland, lived the mostly unknown Gê peoples, who had been studied by Nimuendaju and whom Lévi-Strauss, after his experience with the Bororo, held to be 'the survivors of a remarkably homogeneous culture, with a single language diversified into different dialects all belonging to the same family, and with a comparatively low standard of living contrasting with a highly developed social organization

The 'Picadia', a path through the *sertão*, which formed the one and only point of orientation for over 700 kilometres: the Rondon line.

The *sertão* in the dry season (Mato Grosso) – a wild and desolate bush landscape.

and complex religious thought. Should they not be recognized as Brazil's first inhabitants [. . .]?'[15] Here again, Lévi-Strauss managed to weave his own quivering enthusiasm for beginnings into the scholarly questions of the times: in his quest for the 'most westerly representatives of the Gê group', he was also hoping to find a kind of 'lost world' – to borrow the title of the Arthur Conan Doyle novel and of chapter 24 of *Tristes Tropiques* – an 'ur-culture' that his intellectual temperament endowed with both heuristic and aesthetic virtues. It was about getting back to the very founding moment of things and beings – to origins.

But two additional factors led Lévi-Strauss to this choice of target populations. On the one hand, there were a few sources, but not too many, which represented a good research strategy. These sources all dated from the 1910s, and were all connected to Marechal Rondon, a towering figure of early twentieth-century Brazil, who was still alive when Lévi-Strauss visited. They included the reports of the Rondon Commission, Theodore Roosevelt's *Through the Brazilian Wilderness* (1917), a Conradian account of a four-month expedition with Rondon in 1914 and, finally, *Rondonia* (1917), a book written by the anthropologist Edgar Roquette-Pinto, who had travelled through the region with Rondon in 1912 before becoming head of the National Museum in Rio de Janeiro.[16]

Cândido Rondon (1865–1957) was a military engineer imbued with positivist faith, of which republican Brazil produced many.[17] Founder of the Service for the Protection of Indians (SPI), in 1910, he had in mind to integrate indigenous populations into Brazilian society using peaceful means and technological improvement, through the establishment of colonization centres. This indigenous people's policy was generous in that it offered an alternative to the settler extermination project, but it was also designed to facilitate the Brazilian policy of the 'conquest of the west'. As a frontiersman, Rondon was particularly attentive to the indigenous communities living near the Bolivian border, like the Nambikwara. His aim was to complete the project of modern Brazil, while resettling the Indian communities and turning them into neo-Brazilian rural workers. From the perspective of the positivist military officers who had created the SPI, Indians were to be encouraged in their progress on the path of civilization through the exercise of a kind of 'tutelary power', as historian Antonio Carlos de Souza Lima has called it. They were thus assigned public lands, of which they enjoyed only usufruct and not ownership. The Civil Code of 1917, revised in 1928, had designated them as minors, whose interactions with 'nationals' and foreign anthropologists had therefore to pass through the SPI. Before the SPI lost its lustre – inevitable given that it never had financial and administrative resources commensurate with its objectives – it enjoyed a decade-long run, marked by Marechal Rondon's major accomplishment and overriding ambition: the bold construction of a 700-kilometre-long telegraph line between Cuiabá and the Bolivian border. Between 1914 and 1922, through bush and jungle, crossing rivers great and small, thousands of telegraph poles were erected by indigenous workers under Rondon's supervision, thereby achieving, in a kind of technological epiphany, his life's goal. In the process, he also delineated a region, which has borne his name ever since: Rondônia.

The irony of history would have it that this telegraph line, constructed at great cost to indigenous peoples, who were torn from their traditional life, was made almost immediately obsolete by the invention of the shortwave radio in the early 1920s. All that this positivist epic had produced was a thin dusty scar, the *picada*, across the *sertão*, which was in the 1930s the only way into this still remote region, and which provided rest stops at regular intervals along the entire line, in the form of telegraph offices – small shacks housing an individual or family. This small staff of *caboclos* and Pareci Indians represented a source of high-quality information on the tribes settled in the vicinity. It was yet another reason why Lévi-Strauss chose to take the Rondon line to explore that part of central Brazil. Indeed, this line was, in itself, a distillation of the anthropologist's own paradoxes: it served to integrate Indians into modern society, to conquer territory and to suture the Brazilian population to the land, but it was seen by Lévi-Strauss as a means to penetrate into hostile lands and gain access to worlds he hoped were still unexplored, untouched and isolated.

The web of Brazilian tutelage: Dona Heloisa and the National Museum

For the first expedition, the Oversight Committee (*Conselho de Fiscalização*), created in 1933, had readily granted a licence for its participants to circulate freely on Brazilian lands. It was, therefore, with some confidence that Claude Lévi-Strauss, in full compliance with regulations, submitted another request to the same committee for his second project: 'This expedition proposes to reach the region where the source of the Rio Juruena and Gy-Paraná is located, and to spend about one year there, among the indigenous populations, and to undertake observations and collect material relevant to the fields of anthropology and the natural sciences.'[18] The scientific team was to be composed of five people: 'an anthropologist' (Mrs Lévi-Strauss), 'an ethnographer' (Mr Lévi-Strauss), a naturalist and medical doctor (Dr Vellard, from the Biology Institute of Pernambouc), a linguist (named as Curt Nimuendaju, whom Lévi-Strauss, as of 10 April 1937, still hoped to include on his team) and, finally, an 'equipment manager and cartographer' (René Silz, an agricultural engineer who had participated in the first expedition).

The request was submitted to Heloisa Alberto Torres, who represented the National Museum on the Oversight Committee, and on 28 May 1937, received a positive response in principle, but with three conditions: the presence on the team of a delegate from the National Museum; the requirement that any material collected be exported via Rio de Janeiro (and not Santos); and only with the agreement of the Indian Protection Services (SPI). In a letter dated 11 June 1937, Claude Lévi-Strauss duly noted these conditions and offered every assurance that they would be scrupulously respected.[19] The matter seemed more or less settled and official completion of the process was pending. But the situation became more complicated when the head of the SPI, Colonel Vincente Teixera Vasconcellos, in a letter dated 24 September 1937, announced his institution's refusal to grant the required authorization on the grounds that the expedition might potentially disturb the peaceful relations and still fragile balance with the Indians that had been achieved in the region, thanks to the considerable efforts of the SPI. A ten-page memorandum followed, reviewing the various applicable regulations and recalling the mission of the SPI, which was to safeguard the Indians from the damaging actions of 'civilized persons', scientists and missionaries alike. The whole thing was delivered in a very categorical and paternalistic tone. Lévi-Strauss returned to France in the autumn of 1937 and seems not to have been immediately aware of the negotiations reverberating through the various agencies of Brazilian custodianship. It was a trifecta of the Oversight Committee, the National Museum and the SPI – three institutions that were intimately connected in their history and overlapping social networks, at whose centre stood the charismatic personality of Heloisa Alberto Torres.

In pictures – alongside young anthropologists about to depart, often in the gardens adjoining the National Museum in Rio – she exudes a tutelary benevolence, a mature woman of broad stature and bourgeois bearing, wearing a pearl necklace and with her hair in a bun, looking straight into the camera. Dona Heloisa was a woman of strong will and considerable power.[20] The Museum's director from 1938 to 1955, she was the daughter of the famous jurist Alberto Torres, one of the great figures of the Brazilian Republic, and was thus, from a very young age, a member of the Rio de Janeiro political and intellectual elite. She was an anthropologist by training and had worked with Roquette-Pinto, her predecessor at the Museum. She was formed in that positivist world (Rondon, Roquette-Pinto) which considered science as a way of conceiving society. The first woman to direct the Museum, she took over just as Vargas was install-ing his dictatorial government, which her political dexterity and social acumen helped her to navigate. Dona Heloisa never married, becoming the Museum's queen and a kind of matriarch of Brazilian anthropology. For twenty-odd years she was a pivotal figure, 'a director rather than an actor in the anthropological script',[21] linked via an epistolary pact with the many anthropologists doing fieldwork, often in total isolation and sometimes beset by fits of melancholia, whom she helped revive and reconnect to the world via the umbilical cord of her correspondence. She gathered, spread, selected and organized information according to strategies based on the interests of science as well as those of her country. Foreign anthropolo-gists all had to go through Dona Heloisa, whether they liked it or not. And Lévi-Strauss was no exception. Relations between them were not simple, not the least because Heloisa Torres was not entirely lacking in that banal form of anti-Semitic sentiment so endemic in Brazil at the time.

As director of the Museum, she sat on the Oversight Committee and was very close to the SPI – two institutions that were full participants in the expert management of the difficult process of Brazilian nation build-ing. The Museum was the first research institution created in Brazil, as early as 1818, and was originally dedicated to the study of natural history. Under the republic, however, it became the primary institution for anthro-pological thinking, regularly called upon by republican elites to provide opinions on the most pressing issue in Brazil at the time: how to create a united people out of its diverse and mixed population (indigenous Indians, freed blacks, European immigrants). It was thus not a site of pure scien-tific endeavour but, rather, an institution that produced science in support of national policy, with the SPI working as the indigenist branch of this institutional matrix.[22]

On the Brazilian side the expedition was deadlocked; but was Claude Lévi-Strauss aware of this fact? He wrote to Heloisa Alberto Torres from Paris, on 12 February 1938, to make a proposition that would transform the status of the expedition – and rid him of a participant he found troublesome: 'I have just been informed via cable that the city of São Paulo has accepted an offer I made several months ago, in the name of French authorities, for them to take part in the expedition which would now become, from an entirely French enterprise (this was, as you will remember, the structure which you were kind enough to have the Fiscal Commission authorize), a Franco-Brazilian undertaking. [. . .] I do not know what practical consequences would, in your opinion, ensue from the setting up of a collaboration which I believe to be very precious. As far as I am concerned, I think that since the expedition will take on a Franco-Brazilian character and include Brazilian members representing the city and University of São Paulo, the National Museum and SPI might want to delegate their oversight responsibility to them. What do you think of all this?'[23] She wrote her thoughts, in a tempestuous hand, on the back of the very letter of the man who thought he could see her off: 'The National Museum was quite keen to send a representative for scientific work. Since the expedition is taking a new turn, which satisfies legislative requirements, the Museum has no choice but to accept the proposition to withdraw its delegate. However, Mr Strauss, in previous letters, seemed perfectly aware that it was not only the oversight aspect that was of interest to the museum.'[24] Indeed, Dona Heloisa relied on these kinds of collaborations to train the next generation of Brazilian anthropologists to do fieldwork. In these circumstances, withdrawing its delegate meant that the Museum also withdrew its support with respect to the SPI, which meant that the expedition was now doubly deadlocked. Heloisa had a much finer grasp of the institutional imbroglio than did Lévi-Strauss, who was probably not fully aware of the reach of the bureaucratic apparatus that loomed over the destiny of his project. He did, however, realize, if somewhat too late, that he had made a faux pas. An alternative strategy was immediately put in place thanks to his São Paulo friends, first among them Mário de Andrade who, once again, saved the day. On 22 March 1938, the latter informed the Oversight Committee (as well as Heloisa) that the expedition led by Lévi-Strauss had become a project 'entirely' under the direction of the Department of Culture. He requested the granting of a licence and the appointment of an oversight member. From that moment on, things gradually fell into place over the course of the month of April. Which is to say that, until the very last minute, the expedition was in question – the source of much anxiety for Lévi-Strauss who, returning from France at the end of March 1938, wrote a panicked note from the boat, which had stopped over in Rio, to Mário de Andrade who was there: 'Dear Sir, I learned through Monbeig that you were here – and unfortunately I will miss you. The *Florida* sets sail at 4 o'clock. Is there any way we can meet? Monbeig has spoken to me of major difficulties confronting the expedition. I don't understand any of it. Please be assured of my friendship.'[25] The rescue operation was all the more acrobatic given that Mário de Andrade as well as Paul Duarte were, at that moment, out of political favour due to Vargas's coup. The Department of Culture was itself in survival mode.

The first outcome of these bureaucratic skirmishes was the transformation of a French expedition into a Brazilian one, passing through a Franco-Brazilian stage. It is easy to see why Lévi-Strauss would have been keen to proliferate his Brazilian administrative sponsors, even though he did not always measure the rivalries involved, for example between the National Museum and the São Paulo institutions. This 'denationalization' followed by a 'renationalization' highlights the acute political stakes involved in Brazilian anthropological projects at the time. In a second outcome, the scientific team for the expedition changed from its original iteration. The Lévi-Strausses, as well as Dr Vellard, were still on board, but Nimuendaju had declined for reasons we have already mentioned, and René Silz had disappeared. Luiz de Castro Faria, a young researcher at the Museum, was added to the team and designated as 'supervisor' with the following instructions: 'Remain at the head of the expedition,

The port of Corumbá: leaving for Cuiabá aboard a steamer on Rio Paraguay.

constantly monitor the conditions of encounter and relations with the indigenous peoples and regulate all measures taken by the researchers, including ordering the immediate return of the expedition if necessary.'[26] In addition, Castro Faria was charged with regularly cabling Heloisa and the Museum about the progress and activities of the expedition. While Lévi-Strauss retained intellectual and financial leadership – it was in his name that the French allowance from the Research Service, as well as the 60 *contos* (60 million *reais*) from the São Paulo municipal authorities, was paid – Castro Faria had strategic leadership, since he had the power (and duty) to abort the expedition, and change its itinerary, if he deemed it necessary. Given the situation, it is understandable that Claude Lévi-Strauss would have been reluctant to depart. He would have much preferred to be the only ethnographer on the team, for reasons that any doctoral student would immediately grasp. He intended to collect material for his doctoral work, over which he would have liked to have exclusive ownership. He said as much to Heloisa Alberto Torres in a letter dated 10 April 1937: 'My wife tells me that you would welcome my suggestions regarding the scientific orientation of the Brazilian scholar who is to accompany us on the expedition. You are, of course, the best judge. Though an ethnographer might not have much opportunity to do his own work, since the scientific findings of the mission, in this field, are meant to serve as the basis for my doctoral thesis.'[27] He goes on to suggest a biotypologist. In the event, neither Lévi-Strauss nor Castro Faria were to use the data collected during the mission for their doctoral work. Lévi-Strauss's thesis was to encompass a broader scope and it was indeed only in *Tristes*

Cuiabá: the 'capital' of Mato Grosso, and starting point of the 'Serra do Norte' expedition (June 1938).

Tropiques, some fifteen years later, that the Brazilian fieldwork was to resurface in all its glory, though with other resonances. Nonetheless, in 1938, Castro de Faria was both a potential rival and, as Lévi-Strauss ironically called him, 'Rio's eyes'.[28] This made for a highly uncomfortable position in the fragile equilibrium of the small team, which finally shook itself into motion at the beginning of May 1938.

The Rondon line

Cuiabá

The São Paulo press covered the final preparations before the major expedition took off – the radio set, the typewriter with German keyboard, the camera, the hunting rifles (after a licence to bear arms was obtained), ammunition, toys, trinkets, etc. Equipment weighing 1,470 kilos left from São Paulo together with Luiz de Castro Faria, travelled by train to Corumbá and then took the steamer up the Rio Paraguay all the way to Cuiabá. The Lévi-Strausses had already taken this same route when they went to visit the Bororo. The rest of the party accompanied the Lévi-Strausses, who flew directly to Cuiabá, the logistical staging area for all ethnographic treks into central Brazil. Everybody arrived at the same time, on 9 May 1938, with the exception of de Vellard, who joined them on 23 May after an increasingly irritating delay. There was an eighteenth-century baroque church sitting atop the town, which had the feel of a sleepy colonial administrative seat. It would come to life for the celebration of the fiftieth anniversary of the abolition of slavery later that year, but, for the time being, and throughout that month, there was nothing but the routine of meticulous preparation for an expedition: visits to local authorities, gathering of information on the Indians, selection of mules to carry the men and purchase of oxen to carry the equipment and perhaps serve as food. Hence the need to hire mule drivers and herdsmen. This was soon done, with the help of the head herdsman, Fulgencio, who hired reliable men. In the end, about fifteen mules and thirty-odd oxen, purchased with care and precision, turned the scholarly enterprise into a brightly coloured caravan. To be clear, the 'visitors' were often to outnumber the visited Indians. A lorry was planned to accompany them as far as the road remained passable – that is, until the outpost at Utiarity.

Over the blank days that passed, Dina Lévi-Strauss kept track in her diaries of the weariness she experienced. Unearthed in the personal archive of her ex-husband, they cover the weeks she spent with him until the end of July 1938:[29] 'radio test, more or less successful in the end, discussions on how to waterproof crates, search through the town for woodworkers willing to do the work as soon as possible . . . Order for food placed yesterday, not final . . . Tidying up, sewing, discussions and conversations. Getting in touch with Vellard especially important. Selection of animals, trial runs with the mules. The least little thing entails massive difficulties.' A tiring routine that consisted in doing the accounts over and over, packing the crates over and over, harnessing the oxen and making sure nothing was forgotten: 'The "cangalhas" and the "broacas", the swim trunks and the matchboxes, the 3,000 kilos of food (rice, *feyao*, sugar, salt, coffee, maté, cornflour, cassava flour, starch, "bollachas", pepper and condiments, lard, noodles) not to mention the boxes from São Paulo – soap and bathroom tissue, the missing ammunition, corn for the animals', plus the hammocks and the piles of medicine, which would prove useless when it came to the point . . .

It is incorrect to say that nowhere in *Tristes Tropiques* is this logistical underbelly of the expedition exposed.[30] It is, but always in an ironic and even farcical mode (the oxen episode and the fits of bovine temper), as incidental to the affair, even though it was essential. Indeed, the significant infrastructure required for the Lévi-Strauss expedition, its substantial financing – even though Lévi-Strauss had to request an extra advance from Paul Rivet due to the general increase in prices in Cuiabá – its considerable material and human resources (about twenty people in all) all recalled the great scientific expeditions of the nineteenth century, like the one to Egypt in the wake of Napoleon, or those undertaken by Humboldt. These operated in the borderland between ethnography, biology and natural science, bringing together experts from various fields to gather material that was to form the collections of the great museums. This kind of 'extensive' investigation favoured the brief visit over the kind of in-depth knowledge gleaned from long immersion, which characterized the 'intensive' form of fieldwork. In the 1930s in France, the prevailing model remained that of the scientific expeditions of the previous century, as exemplified by the famous Dakar-Djibouti mission led by Marcel Griaule, which traversed Africa from west to east, with considerable media attention and public funding, like a parade of savants foraging here and there for rare flowers to be analysed once back at the museum. British anthropology, by contrast, established itself on radically different fieldwork protocols. Bronisław Malinowski spent years in Melanesia, alone on the Trobriand Islands, before writing *Argonauts of the Western Pacific* (1922).

Curiously, the Malinowskian immersion model was represented at the time by a young American anthropologist, Buell Quain, whom Luiz de Castro Faria had just met on the Rio Paraguay. While they were both staying in Cuiabá, he was to form a brief friendship with Claude Lévi-Strauss. Hailing from Columbia University in New York, he was a student of Ruth Benedict, who sent him to Heloisa Alberto Torres; he was about to spend several months alone in the region of Xingu with the Trumai Indians. There were other American anthropologists doing fieldwork in Brazil at the same time: Charles Wagley, a student of Franz Boas, was living with the Tapirape Indians, and William Lipkind with the Karaja Indians of Rio Araguaia, where Lévi-Strauss had gone in the summer of 1937. Dina Lévi-Strauss found that Buell Quain had a 'strange' air about him. Quain himself thought he had contracted syphilis from a woman in Rio and had entered a 'necrotic delirium'. He was to experience a tragic fate: a few years later, he committed suicide in Rio. An endearing passing shadow who, in the heat of Cuiabá in May 1938, must have been quite taken aback by the flurry of activity for the sake of a scientific enterprise that probably did not conform to his Anglo-American conception of anthropology.[31]

The Lévi-Strauss expedition sought information on the condition and location of the Indians, for in that respect as well, everything was uncertain. A questionnaire was sent to the employees of the various telegraph offices on the Rondon line – Parecis, Ponte de Pedra, Capanema, Utiarity, Juruena, Nambikwara, Vilhena: '1) Are there Indians in the area? Who are these Indians? 2) Are they friendly or hostile? 3) Do they bring articles for barter? Do they expect gifts? 4) Do they come frequently? 5) Do they speak Portuguese? 6) Are they dressed like civilized people? 7) Where are their villages? 8) Do they invite civilized people to come visit their villages?'[32] The responses were somewhat less than encouraging. Whenever Indians were indicated as being in the area, the telegraph workers, decisive intermediaries for the genesis of the mission, warned against the potential danger they might present. Everyone still had fresh in their mind the recent series of massacres and retaliations, the latest of which was the murder of Protestant missionaries in 1930 in Juruena. In the face of persisting uncertainty, the tension mounted. The real risk involved in this kind of expedition into unknown territories suddenly appeared, as the flipside of adventure. Dina Lévi-Strauss worried: 'The adventure appears increasingly risky. Our "Nambiquara" really do have the worst reputation. Ferocious. Stories of terrible massacres. I am not prepared to die and I wish to return from this adventure. Otherwise, it will no longer be an adventure.'[33] In addition to the big question mark that hovered over the location of Indians and, above all, their likely disposition, the itinerary was not definitively set because of the many potential obstacles that could put an immediate end to the whole enterprise: 'We are now heading into the dry season with the rains said to resume as early as September, and to become quite strong by October. We might get stuck in the rain well before we reach our return path. And then we would have to wait until the following year. Yet it is impossible to plan for this eventuality, in terms of food or medicine, or anything else. There are so many unpredictable aspects to this journey that this one doesn't even worry me.'[34]

Indeed, Dina was increasingly slipping into a kind of depressive torpor as their stay in Cuiabá was prolonged inordinately. Her body was covered in red spots. She dreamt of a giant eye circled in a blazing red light, like 'the eye of Lucifer', which one cannot resist connecting to the purulent eye infection that would require her evacuation a few weeks later. Worried about what was to come, as well as what she had left behind, on the eve of the big departure she fell prey to a sentimental crisis that she expressed in novelistic terms, describing herself as a character called Ines who had 'lost peace in her heart', depicting Mário de Andrade as Emmanuel, 'a pederast, youthful believer turned revolutionary; a period of struggle and attempts – at poetry, literature, music. Will he become a great writer, a great pioneer, or nothing at all?'[35] Dina was very preoccupied with what was going on back in São Paulo: 'In a newspaper dated the 11th, I find out that the Department of Culture is in the hands of a new director. I don't know him. What could have happened to Mário? What will become of the department?'[36] The switching back and forth between the genres of fiction and diary shows how readily that generation of young intellectuals resorted to literature, and more specifically to the novel form, to try to make sense of their relationship to the world when the latter was in a state of turmoil. In the end, everything fell into place: 'I have only one desire now: to set off, to succeed, to return. I have no regrets. I can't imagine what my life would be like, either in São Paulo or in Paris, without this adventure. Only, I would like to be five years younger. [. . .] I am ready for complete detachment and am on the lookout for a sign; I don't know yet of what nature: departure, work, a new and unsettling experience that is not of the sentimental kind.'[37]

Utiarity: the ethnographic encounter

When the Lévi-Strausses, together with Castro Faria, set off on their truck at dawn on 6 June the expedition had in fact already lost its primary institutional support and sponsor in Brazil, the Department of Culture. It was thus a practically orphaned expedition that got under way that morning, on the Rosario Road heading northward.

The porters and most of the herd had already been on the road for a week when the lorry caught up with them, barely fifty kilometres from Cuiabá. Lévi-Strauss was furious: 'I lost my temper for the first, and not the last, time. But further disappointments would have to be endured before I realized that the sense of time did not exist in the world I was now entering.'[38] Their first stop-over was in Rosario Oeste, 'a village of about a thousand inhabitants, mostly black, stunted and goitrous'.[39] The first foothills of the Serra Tombador were coming into sight. The road was poor and full of potholes. At the top of the Serra, at a place called Caixa Furada, the chain-wheel of the driveshaft broke. The lorry was immobilized in the bush for a few days, the time it took the drivers to notify the next village of the incident and order the missing part to be sent from Rio. 'A forced immersion in *sertão*' was the result, which Lévi-Strauss took rather philosophically, as he explained to Mário de Andrade: 'This forced – and untimely – immersion in *sertão* gave us an opportunity to hunt, and to try out what would be the best of our daily fare from now on: *arara* [macaw bird] soup, *cuzido do tatu* [leg of armadillo], roast *veado* and *caetetu* [halfway between a wild boar and a hedgehog], the whole thing washed down with buriti wine – the perfect menu for an explorers club, wouldn't you say?'[40] A few pictures taken by Castro Faria serve to illustrate that brief interlude, during which they would be lulled to sleep in the evening with stories, 'tales of hunting and vengeance, *Macunaíma*-style attacks' [*Macunaíma* was a novel by Mário de Andrade], told by their drivers.[41] The lorry was stuck in the middle of the trail, blocking the way. Dina took notes. Claude, a pith helmet on his head, gazed at her, his thoughts elsewhere. On 14 June, they were in Parecis. The landscape, from then on, was a sandy plateau interspersed with low shrubs, deeply carved by small rivers running north to feed into the confluents of the Rio Tapajoz and Rio Madeira, part of the Amazonian basin. The entire region was called Serra de Parecis or Serra do Norte. Galleries of trees lined the river beds that the lorry painstakingly crossed – it had to be unloaded and reloaded each time. Ridges of very hard sandstone provided for magnificent waterfalls, like that of the Rio Sacre, or the great falls of Utiarity on the Rio Papagaio, where they arrived on 16 June after having travelled more than 500 kilometres. 'Already on the far bank we could see two naked figures: they were Nambikwara.'[42]

Once the moment of wonderment (shared and noted by Castro Faria) had passed, the three anthropologists set to work. There were about twenty Nambikwara Indians, drawn by the noise of the arrival of white men and the prospect of gifts. They were in fairly frequent contact with the guards of the Utiarity telegraph and the Jesuits of Juruena. One of these Jesuits was present at the first encounter and volunteered his services: his knowledge of the Nambikwara and a rudimentary command of their language. For this was immediate problem number one: unlike the previously visited tribes, this group did not have any Portuguese-speaking member, native informant or intermediary of any kind. This led at first to some apprehension and even discouragement: 'Unfortunately, it looks like the work will be extremely difficult: no interpreter possible, total ignorance of Portuguese, and a language whose phonetics seem to me, for the time being, completely inaccessible', wrote Lévi-Strauss to Mário de Andrade on the day after he arrived, coupling his remarks with more encouraging notes concerning the Nambikwara chants 'composed in an almost European style, with very "square" melodic structures but in 4/4, 4/5 time, reminiscent of popular songs transcribed by a modern man.'[43] As for Dina, she observed the women's bodies, naked like the men's, 'their breasts rather small but very forward and prematurely sagging like "goat udders"'. She attended the preparation of cassava pancakes, observed the techniques for spinning and manufacturing pendant earrings: 'Every day, after breakfast, I go and sit among the Indians, and remain there almost all day, observing. It is the only thing to do for the moment, in the impossible situation we are in, without interpreters, to work in a methodical way.' A few days later: 'We work a lot but without much in the way of results since it is difficult to pose questions without understanding the language and even more so to understand the replies.' Castro Faria observed the Indians bending their bows, and took many photographs. On 19 June, they played their phonograph for the amusement of the Indians and gave them sheets of drawing paper, but the Nambikwara did not make anything of them . . . That same day, Vellard joined them on the second lorry, while the oxen and mules that would take over from the now useless lorries were only to arrive two weeks later, on 9 July. From a physician's perspective, Vellard made note of the eye infections linked to a minuscule bee (*Melipona ducki*) nicknamed 'eye-licker' that landed on the eyes and spread the infection.[44] Naked and sleeping directly on the ground, the Nambikwara covered themselves in ashes for the night. Was this the cause of the many skin infections noted by Vellard? A major specialist in indigenous *materia medica*, he painstakingly sought to obtain detailed information on the curare mixture used by the Nambikwara, who were famous for their aptitude with poison. On 30 June, Vellard tested his curare on a dog, which died of asphyxia. A successful operation . . .

The ordinary eye infection recorded at the beginning of their stay became an epidemic of purulent ophthalmia a few weeks later, which affected the Indians first, then some of the mule drivers and then Dina Lévi-Strauss, who first tried to treat it with available medicines, but ultimately had to abandon the expedition on 22 July. Her husband accompanied her to Cuiabá, where she was evacuated to São Paulo and then Paris, her condition requiring constant treatment. She was leaving Mato Grosso and Brazil for good, as well as anthropology and her husband – but that is another story. Meanwhile, Castro Faria went to Juruena with the group of Nambikwara from Utiarity, where they were joined by Lévi-Strauss and Vellard, back from Cuiabá, on 1 August. There, they observed native bartering practices, while Castro Faria, in turn, contracted the eye infection, which was treated by Vellard. Claude Lévi-Strauss, the only 'survivor' of this ophthalmic devastation, returned to Campos Novos, where he spent two weeks alone with two bands of Nambikwara, who were initially ill-disposed towards him but eventually agreed to remain with him, providing the opportunity for a new crop of observations. Finally, a fortnight in Vilhena (from 4 to 18 September), in the company of other groups, rounded out the Nambikwara cycle, a period of fieldwork lasting nearly three months.

At first, Claude Lévi-Strauss was rather taken aback by the poverty he witnessed. The lack of aesthetic appeal of Nambikwara culture had something pathetic and painful about it. His first impressions were 'disconcerting', as he explained to Marcel Mauss: 'These people wandering across the sandy bush in search of snakes, lizards and bats immediately calls to mind Australia, but they insist they have, next to their formless villages, well-kept gardens. All at once, a wretched material culture, probably unrivalled in this sense in all of South America, and a collective life that appears very flexible, in contrast with their vigorous individual prohibitions.'[45] One gets the sense that he found little to latch on to at first, either in aesthetic, ritual or sociological terms: no beautiful pottery, no astonishing artisanship; no penis sheaths, no breathtaking headdresses; no complex rituals, no sophisticated social laws or kinship rules. As opposed to the Caduveo and the Bororo, the Nambikwara relentlessly drew the anthropologist back to the destitution of their condition. Still, Lévi-Strauss was 'intrigued', as he indicated to Mauss at the end of his letter. He thus set to work. His notebooks are filled with linguistic notes and glossaries, attesting to his determination to master as much as possible this language that presented an obstacle to communication. Gradually, living among these men and women, he was won over, a process of growing attachment whose stages are difficult to capture, but which can perhaps make sense if seen through the three powerful frames that expressed, then and throughout his life, the shock of the Nambikwara fieldwork: the infancy of humanity, fantasies of encounter, and 'human tenderness'.

As opposed to the Bororo and Caduveo groups – which he describes as 'learned societies' – 'with the Nambikwara the observer is taken back to what one might easily, but wrongly, consider to be the infancy of the human species'.[46] Claude Lévi-Strauss turns a negative into a positive: a material culture and society reduced to its simplest expression into the starting point for a search for the most elementary forms, the very essence of social life. A scientific approach he was to endorse throughout his life, dismissing questions about our societies, which are too complex to hope to understand much of anything. Elementary societies – the Nambikwara offering a stripped-down version – were the models. They gain in heuristic value what they lack in exotic aura. For Lévi-Strauss, this is one of the advantages of studying the Amerindians of the lower territories, in contrast with African studies, for instance: 'The source material that I and my colleagues found in South America was of a very different kind from that collected by our Africanist colleagues, who found relatively large-scale societies, which were characterized by complex social organizations and already had state forms and legal and police systems. Whereas the small communities that we found in South America brought us into contact with a radically different sociological experience. First, one had to travel quite far in search of them, and then overcome the language barrier. We found ourselves in the position of astronomers, confronted by bodies that are very far away, of which one perceives only certain characteristics, the most essential. And then in these very small societies, specific mechanisms [. . .], alliances, matrimonial rules and others, stand out very clearly.'[47]

In their elementary manner, the Nambikwara fully satisfied his fantasy of the inaugural ethnographic encounter, regularly rekindled by the reading of his personal bible, Jean de Léry. As opposed to the Bororo, the Nambikwara had only rarely been visited by Europeans. According to the testimony provided by Tito, a ten-year-old child who was part of the Utiarity group in 1938, and with whom documentary filmmaker Marcelo Fortaleza Flores reconnects, Claude Lévi-Strauss, whom he called 'Massimo Lévi', was only the second white man his parents had ever seen, after Marshal Rondon twenty years earlier.[48] Among Lévi-Strauss's scholarly fantasies, seeing what no 'civilized' person had seen and feeling oneself in the position of the first Renaissance Europeans were recurring themes. This powerful intellectual motivation was clearly also at work in a later encounter with the Mundé. The latter 'had never before been mentioned in any anthropological study',[49] and the promise of a virgin gaze therefore excited the anthropologist, even though he was perfectly aware of the 'circle from which there is no escape',[50] which he had so aptly described. The lack of an intermediary, the sign of a well-preserved group, also guaranteed the impossibility of understanding it: 'I had wanted to reach the extreme limits of the savage; it might be thought that my wish had been granted, now that I found myself among these charming Indians whom no other white man had ever seen before and might never see again. After an enchanting trip up-river, I had certainly found my savages. Alas! They were only too savage. [. . .] They were as close to me as a reflection in a mirror; I could touch them but I could not understand them.'[51]

In the end, as he passed days and nights in their company, Lévi-Strauss appears to have been won over by the Nambikwara's kindness, carefreeness, openness and desire to cooperate – the very people who had been described to him as ferocious and bloodthirsty. He was particularly careful, as a good ethnographer and disciple of Mauss, to capture the erotic atmosphere that permeated all aspects of Nambikwara life, the public and audacious love games, the bathing of the children, the puerile ambiance that characterized the young women's circle, the general concern for animals, the gentleness of parents towards their children, whom they never punished, the generally happy note of social life that emerges, in a nocturnal register, in the following passage from his notebooks at the time, and which he quoted verbatim in *Tristes Tropiques*: 'On the dark savannah, the camp fires sparkle. Near their warmth, which offers the only protection against the growing chill of the night; behind the frail screens of palm fronds and branches, hurriedly set up on the side from which rain and wind are expected; next to the basket filled with the pathetic possessions which constitute the community's earthly wealth; lying on the bare ground which stretches away in all directions and is haunted by other equally hostile and apprehensive bands, husbands and wives, closely intertwined, are aware of being each other's support and comfort, and the only help against day-to-day difficulties and that brooding melancholy which settles from time to time on the souls of the Nambikwara. The visitor camping with the Indians in the bush for the first time is filled with anguish and pity at the sight of human beings so totally bereft; some relentless cataclysm seems to have crushed them against the ground in a hostile land, leaving them naked and shivering by their flickering fires. He gropes his way through the scrub, taking care not to knock against the hands, arms or chests that he glimpses as warm reflections in the glow of the flames. But the wretchedness is shot through with whisperings and chuckles. The couples embrace as if seeking to recapture a lost unity, and their caresses continue uninterrupted as he goes by. He can sense in all of them an immense kindness, a profoundly carefree attitude, a naive and charming animal satisfaction and – binding these various feelings together – something which might be called the most truthful and moving expression of human love.'[52]

The ethnographer at work

Lévi-Strauss's fieldwork notebooks give us a very detailed sense of what this ethnographic experience with the Nambikwara, midway through the expedition, was like. These little notebooks – some bound, others loose pages – are the fragile trace of the work he carried out. They are literally the archive of the ethnographer, the black box of his subsequent interpretation, as well as a memoir of the strange experience of cohabitation.[53]

As Lévi-Strauss himself often conceded, his notebooks were 'appallingly kept',[54] casually mixing together logbook and information, filling tens of pages with vocabulary lists, linguistic cards (sometimes separate), phonetic and musical transcriptions (indicating the importance of sheet music, evidence both of his interest in ethnomusicology and his musical training), many sketches, diagrams (village maps, sketches of hands and bodies in string games, drawings of monkeys, *zog zog*, *cuxiu*, *guariba*, *barrigudo*), as well as plants, roof gables, faces with tattoos outlined, diagrams of weaves holding bamboo together, bits of bibliography and reading notes – he was reading the 1935 edition of Roquette-Pinto's *Rondônia* – dozens of kinship diagrams and double-entry tables, some anthropometric data. Texts that entail very distinct writing styles coexist side by side: ethnographic descriptions of childbirth ('the squatting woman holding a vertical piece of wood by the sides in both hands; the umbilical cord is cropped short and cauterized with embers, then with a plaster of warm ash'; the manner of 'doing one's business (*tarnikititta*)' ('one digs a hole in the sand with one's hands, squats over it, performs the task, then wipes up with a fragment of bamboo, holding it by one end and following the anus with the other, from front to back and top to bottom'); considerations of a more sociological nature related to the *seringueros* rubber harvesters (schedules, yields, number of trees felled, variations in the kilo price of rubber); demographic observations recording the ineluctable disappearance of the Indian population; fieldwork haikus

('Cuiabá-Rosario. A brown cow and a great burst of green cane coming out of its mouth / The sharp smell of burnt savannah / After Brotas volcanic rocks'); weather events, big and small ('The thunder roars, the sky darkens and we can see vertical columns of rain covering half the horizon. Will it come?'; 'With the sunrise, the day is set in place. Rays of light, fleeting clouds; shifts, returns, errors and modifications. All this, in the end, to make up the physiognomy of the day to come'). But these notebooks also contain 'notes towards a novel that was never written' involving a man, Plato, and a woman, Odile, trapped in the dead-end of 1920s Paris, who manipulate each other against a South American backdrop. This hodge-podge of Conradian ambiance and the themes of Nizan's *La Conspiration* provides a kind of release, jumbling together the previous few years of his life (politics, socialism, fascism), the expedition under way, historical fears (war), political action (in the form of conspiracy and arms dealing), sensuality and debauchery – the many permutations of Lévi-Strauss's daydreams during his hours of solitude. These notebooks – dominated in the end by kinship diagrams, linguistic notes and images – are multi-dimensional objects, beautiful in and of themselves, multicoloured and baroque, an artist's notebooks as much as scholarly records, giving full expression to Claude Lévi-Strauss's scientific imagination. They provide the material for an ethnography of the ethnographer in the field.

They also show that this expedition was true ethnographic fieldwork and not just a philosophical excursion, as has sometimes been insinuated about the work of an anthropologist who is said to be more speculative than empirical, as if the one precluded the other. If exhaustiveness was not on the agenda, what was however striking was Lévi-Strauss's quick and observing mind, the meticulous precision of his technical terms and forms, his attention to the real in all its extravagance, the material and symbolic aspects, the atmosphere, the dreams, all tracked with the intuition of an entomologist. This fieldwork is documented by numerous images, photographs taken by both Claude Lévi-Strauss (with his Leica and his 6 × 6 Voigtlander Superb camera) as well as by Luiz de Castro Faria (with his Contaflex). Much has been said about the startling contrast between these two collections of photographs: the one, by Lévi-Strauss, with its artistic sensibility, focused on the Indian population, capturing in close-up the often painful beauty of their simple presence in the world, later immortalized in *Tristes Tropiques*; the other, by Castro Faria, recording the backgrounds, the interactions between Indians and researchers, the team as a whole and the transportation logistics. Castro Faria's pictures are more revealing, insofar as they document ethnographic practices as much as 'ethnographic objects'. What do they reveal? 'We realize that some of the scenes that, in the *Tristes Tropiques* photographs, appear to be taking place in the middle of the savannah, in reality occurred just a few yards from a telegraph office.'[55] We have already pointed out the crucial role of intermediaries in these kinds of travelling expeditions – in this case, missionaries, telegraph employees and acculturated Indians. Their presence in the first part of the expedition guaranteed its relative success. Their absence in the second part accounted, if not for its failure, at least for the impasse

Lévi-Strauss experienced, for example with the Munde that he could not understand and later with the Tupi Kawahib, with whom his stay was cut short by an accident. The true ethnographic work of Claude Lévi-Strauss in Brazil was carried out within a rather narrow zone of contact between the Indians and the various 'others' whom they encountered. As Benoît de l'Estoile has pointed out, the Mato Grosso expedition did not benefit from the protection of colonial power, as opposed to those under way in Africa at the time; worse, it had to contend with a Brazilian state that was touchy and pedantic in relation to its precarious heritage project. Conditions were thus extremely difficult.

Fieldwork was experienced as a trial by fire, not just an initiation ritual that all aspiring ethnographers had to undergo, but as the price to pay for being uprooted from their worlds. And the ledger entries came in four major forms: disease, depression, boredom and danger. Dina noted upon arriving in Utiarity that Claude Lévi-Strauss's groin was covered in 'oozing eczema'. A sure sign, among others, of the hardships of field-work, and the way in which, if only in this respect, it was analogous to war. When the epidemic of purulent ophthalmia erupted, all members of the expedition contracted it, one after the other, except Lévi-Strauss, probably thanks to his glasses. It was a carnage. Dina, badly affected, was half blind by the time she left the battlefield. The physical care provided was rudimentary, as was the food, which, despite careful preparation, was sometimes lacking and represented, as Vellard noted, an ever-present obsession. A gruelling deficit of food and sleep, then. But the worst of the trial lay in the downtime of fieldwork, the delays, the slow pace, the barriers, which involved different relationships to time on either side of the encounter. Claude Lévi-Strauss's impatience on several occasions was more than just a character trait; it was the bitter flipside of adventure. 'So much time wasted!' ran the ethnographer's constant complaint. What to do when there is nothing to do? 'The anthropologist lingers about, marking time and champing at the bit; he rereads his old notes, copies them out, and tries to interpret them; alternatively, he may set himself some minute and pointless task, a sort of caricature of his true function, such as measuring the distance between hearths or making an inven-tory of the individual branches used in the building of deserted shelters. Above all, he asks himself questions. Why has he come here? With what hopes and what objectives? What exactly is the nature of anthropological research?'[56] This is when depression hits, as it did Lévi-Strauss during his solitary stint at Campos Novos, from 15 to 30 August 1938. The forced idleness brought back to mind all that he had left behind, and the comparison was, as always, unfavourable: 'It was now nearly five years since I had left France and interrupted my university career. Meanwhile, the more prudent of my former colleagues were beginning to climb the academic ladder: those with political leanings, such as I once had, were already members of parliament and would soon be ministers. And here I was, trekking across desert wastes, in pursuit of a few pathetic human remnants.'[57] An unfavourable and, in fact, false comparison, since Lévi-Strauss, as we have seen, had in fact not 'interrupted' any university career. Indeed, going to Brazil was what had enabled him to move directly to teaching at the university level, and his fieldwork was to open a clear path to a doctoral thesis, and hence to rapid advancement within the French higher education system, at a time when other colleagues of his were stagnating at provincial secondary schools. But the sense of dereliction was so strong at that precise moment that it swept everything else away. It was also at that moment, a moment of rage and distress, that Lévi-Strauss wrote a play, *L'Apothéose d'Auguste*, as the mirror image of his current existence.[58] Yet that suspended moment was not entirely negative, since it also afforded an opportunity to contemplate the ethnographic experience in all its plenitude and the perspectival shift that it effected. In this respect, it is also a dangerous moment of truth, from which some – one is reminded here of Buell Quain, among others – did not recover. The profession has had no shortage of suicides.

The apparent moral danger of fieldwork, especially in its solitary moments, existed side by side with a more immediate danger, even in situations where the indigenous population was favourably disposed towards the ethnographer, as was the case with the Nambikwara. Lévi-Strauss recounts an episode that illustrates the ever-present potential for disruption of the peaceful atmosphere, and above all the rapidity, unpredictability and in the end the inevitability of such disruptions, which could suddenly jeopardize the very life of the ethnographer turned intruder. Having brought with him in his trunks a few large multicoloured balloons of the kind that are released into the air in São Paulo for the festival of Midsummer's Day, one night he had the idea of showing the Nambikwara how they worked: 'The first balloon caught fire on the ground, and this caused great hilarity, as if the natives had some idea of what ought to have happened. The second, however, succeeded only too well: it rose quickly into the air, reached such a height that its flame merged with the stars, drifted about above us for a long time and then disappeared. But the initial mirth had given way to other emotions.'[59] The merry atmosphere gave way to one of clear hostility on the part of the men, while the women seemed terrified. This little incident could have ended very badly. Clearly, fieldwork was not simply about the gathering of data, but also involved behaving, experimenting and play-acting so as to provoke reactions that would hopefully prove instructive, while not always being able to anticipate the possible side-effects. Claude Lévi-Strauss thus initiated a traditional gathering of all the various Nambikwara groups, organized for his benefit by the chief of the Utiarity band. He was hoping to witness trade and negotiation practices within the larger community. It was in that context that he found himself, after a two-day journey from Juruena, in the presence of around seventy-five Nambikwara.[60] Prior to that meeting, he had observed that when he provided them with paper and pencils, the Nambikwara would trace serpentine lines mimicking his writing gesture. That night, when the time came to distribute gifts, the chief took out from his sack a piece of paper with 'wavy lines' he had himself traced on it, and pretended to read from it before handing each his due. The anthropologist was dumbfounded in the face of this unexpected performance, which inspired powerful speculations on the properly political functions of writing – an instrument of domination primarily, and only secondarily an artificial mnemonic device or instrument of knowledge – and an iconoclastic conclusion: 'My hypothesis, if correct, would oblige us to recognize the fact that the primary function of written communication is to facilitate slavery.'[61]

In wrapping up this review of the constraints and strategies involved in fieldwork, making it a rite of passage that the ethnographer imposed on himself, we should mention an aspect that was no less problematic for being more joyful, and that indeed represented a veritable taboo in the profession. Lévi-Strauss described the erotic atmosphere that pervaded the Nambikwara community, whose members, both male and female, lived entirely naked; he described the playful love games that seemed to him to be 'less of a physical nature than ludic and sentimental' – he 'never once noticed even the beginnings of an erection' – and reflected in anthropological terms about the social border between modesty and immodesty, and the shift in norms these societies invite. Yet he clearly also expressed his own unease: 'It was difficult, for instance, to remain indifferent to the sight of one or more little girls sprawling stark naked in the sand and laughing mockingly as they wriggled at my feet. When I went bathing in the river, I was often embarrassed by a concerted attack on the part of half-a-dozen or so females – young or old – whose only goal was to appropriate my soap, of which they were extremely fond.'[62] The ethnographer's body was thus challenged in ways other than by disease, hunger and thirst. How far was his initiation to go? Were sexual relations between anthropologists and natives strictly proscribed? Curt Nimuendaju had children with an indigenous woman – but he was an exception. In *Phantom Africa*, Michel Leiris tells how he fell in love with Emawayisch, the daughter of the possessed woman whom he was studying in Ethiopia.[63] In the case of Lévi-Strauss, however, this passage in *Tristes Tropiques* only goes to show how comfortable he was acknowledging the issues he had to confront, and which he did not even attempt to resolve. In a reversal of the anthropological relationship, the anthropologist was in his turn exploited and turned into a playmate by the young Nambikwara women. The issues were ones of appropriate distance and reciprocity, both of which challenged European erotic and moral codes. In a different way from Lévi-Strauss, Vellard was also disturbed by these constant assaults, and his reaction appears to have irritated the anthropologist. Confiding in his notebooks, Lévi-Strauss elaborates on the disastrous effects of a Christian upbringing on the development of harmonious sensual relations within couples.[64] In these notes, he appears rather savvy about matters of love, and a free spirit, in sharp contrast with the Protestant manners he exhibited.

The end of the journey: towards the Amazonian world

Once past Vilhena, the second phase of the expedition began, more uncertain still than the first, with its partially undefined itinerary, imperilled by the coming of the rainy season. The onset of the rains made turning back unthinkable. After Pimenta Bueno, the expedition was reduced to three scientists – Lévi-Strauss, now paired with Lucinda, the boot-clinging monkey that the Nambikwara had given him, Castro Faria and Vellard – and advanced mostly via waterways. The herd of donkeys and oxen – those that had survived – turned around and went back to Utiarity, guided by Fulgencio. The landscape was gradually changing: Amazonia loomed larger with each day of their northward trek. Already at Três Buritis, the cabins were built on stilts. Food supplies – rice, pineapple, corn, manioc – became easier to come by than on the plateau, while the new fauna and flora along the rivers supplied abundant game: peccary, deer, tapirs, macaws, parrots, etc.[65] They arrived in Pimenta Bueno on 1 October after having travelled for a good part of September. Lévi-Strauss was eager to meet with indigenous populations to 'establish how far the Nambikwara extend[ed] on that side, and if possible to study the Tupi of the Gy region. We haven't even been able to determine yet whether that group still exists.'[66]

This proved possible thanks to six Tupi Indians who worked for the telegraph line. During the last part of the expedition, Lévi-Strauss was to come into contact with two different groups. Each time, his hopes were dashed. The first group was reached after a five-day journey up the Rio Pimenta Bueno, punctuated by the sound of splashing paddles. They had to take care to avoid contact with the branches on the riverbanks while paddling, for fear of ant bites. The travellers stayed six days, from 9 to 15 October, with the Munde people, who had never before seen white people. The Munde removed all their body hair, used embers to burn the hair on the front of their heads into horizontal fringes, and broadly speaking took great care of their bodies. They spoke an unknown language, making communication over such a short span of time, in the absence of an interpreter, next to impossible. This encounter was thus a dead end. They returned to Pimenta Bueno. Vellard, suffering from a bout of malaria, went on ahead to Urupa; Lévi-Strauss and Castro Faria, together with five other men, went down the Rio Machado, arriving on 27 October in the territory of the Tupi, who welcomed them with great kindness. Although they were in the process of leaving their village, they returned to it at the request of the anthropological mission. The next day, one of their men, Emydio, accidentally fired his gun and wounded his hand, severing several of his fingers. Castro Faria accompanied him to Urupa, where Vellard could tend to the injury, while Lévi-Strauss remained with the Tupi for a few more days. The group comprised around twenty individuals, bound together by a polygamous system and elaborate rituals – a mysterious community, whose last secrets Lévi-Strauss was trying to extract. He noted that, in contrast to the Nambikwara, these people abhorred tobacco. The stay culminated with a two-night performance by the group's spirit-possessed chief of a sort of operetta, 'The Farce of the Japim Bird', in which he played the various characters. Lévi-Strauss faithfully recorded the entire episode in his notebooks: 'At the end of the second session, Taperahi [the chief], while still singing, suddenly got out of his hammock and started to stagger wildly about, demanding

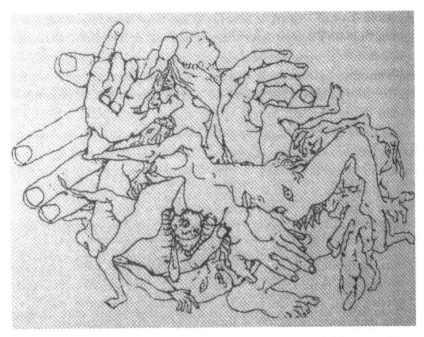

Drawing by Claude Lévi-Strauss after Emydio's accident, which is narrated in *Tristes Tropiques*: 'We [. . .] spent breakfast time watching Vellard extract a few splinters from Emydio's hand, reshaping it as he worked. The spectacle, which had something nauseating and yet fascinating about it, was associated in my mind with a vision of the forest, full of shapes and threats. Taking my left hand as a model, I began to draw landscapes made up of hands emerging from bodies as twisted and tangled as creepers.' (*TT*, p. 361).

cahouin;[67] he had been "seized by the spirit"; suddenly he snatched up a knife and ran at Kunhatsin, his chief wife, who only just managed to escape from him by running off into the forest, while the other men forcibly held him back and obliged him to return to his hammock, where he immediately fell asleep.'[68] Lévi-Strauss's ethnographic study thus ended on a tragicomic note, with this homicidal finale that closed the mission properly speaking.[69]

Everyone reconvened in Urupa, on the Rio Machado, where they waited for the motor ferry (whose schedule eluded them). They moped around, fished and explored the surroundings for two weeks, time enough to become acquainted with the pathetic world of the *seringueros* (rubber farmers), who were all more or less ruined by the crash in world prices. They were all exhausted, and malaria was lurking. Vellard had a dust up with Castro Faria, culminating in a final sparring match, in which all the tensions that had accumulated over the months spent together erupted, only to be forgotten by the time the boat finally showed up, on 27 November.[70] They went down the river without incident, encumbered only by the low water level after the dry season. The landscape was very beautiful, dotted with countless small islands. Castro Faria, who had been calling Lévi-Strauss 'Professor Lévi' throughout the voyage, finally dared switch to 'Claude'.[71] From time to time, they spotted a few natives working on plantations. At every stage of the expedition, Lévi-Strauss remarked on how few of them were left, whereas they had still been numerous twenty years earlier. Hence the feeling, shared by his companions, of meeting the last survivors, which lent the journey's end a twilight quality. The last Indians, but also the last inhabitants of an Amazonian world in full decline – the heroic figures and pioneers of yesteryear had given way to 'touching characters',[72] 'strongly marked by eccentricity and desperation',[73] and a poverty that was not unlike that of the indigenous populations themselves.

In Calama, where the Machado River flows into the Madeira, they left their canoe for a small steamboat, the *Cannamary*, whose level of comfort earned it the new name *The Vatican*. A few days later, on 7 December, they reached Porto Velho, with its population of about 4,000 and its English flavour, due to the railroad built by the British which had indeed turned the Amazonian port into an English dominion, complete with cottages and high tea. On 11 December, Vellard and Lévi-Strauss took an Amazonian Company boat that brought them to the Brazilian border, where they were to take a plane to Cuiabá. As for Castro Faria, he returned to Rio by boat via the Amazonian ring, Manaus and Belém. Back in Cuiabá, nine months after his first landing there, Lévi-Strauss was back in Nambikwara country, where he met up with the lorry transporting the ethnographic collections to São Paulo, to be divvied up between France and Brazil. Having left in May 1938, Lévi-Strauss was back in São Paulo on 12 January 1939.

'A philosopher among the Indians?'

Let us pause for a moment to consider this Brazilian fieldwork that had just been completed. It would later become the object of regular disparagement, not least from the anthropologist himself, who was perhaps overly inclined to present himself as an 'armchair' scholar. In 2001, the publication of *Another Look*, Luiz Castro de Faria's diary of the second expedition, reignited this recurring polemic, which represents one of the expressions of the ambivalent reception of Lévi-Strauss's work in Brazil.

Castro Faria takes 'another look'

As early as 1988, Castro Faria confided in Mathieu Lindon, who was interviewing him for the newspaper *Libération*, which had decided to revisit Claude Lévi-Strauss's Brazilian fieldwork on the occasion of his eightieth birthday: 'This expedition was the price that Claude Lévi-Strauss paid to be recognized as a true anthropologist. But he wasn't "cut out for it", as they say. He had difficulties communicating and disliked being so far from civilization and its comforts. He was introspective and quiet. He had no real relationship with either Vellard or myself. It was absolute individualism, each had their own notes. Vellard didn't know the first thing about what Lévi-Strauss had recorded, and vice versa. For a Brazilian, it was a somewhat different experience. In fact, the expedition consisted in travelling rather than working on one site: it took months and months to prepare for very brief contact with indigenous peoples [. . .]. For Lévi-Strauss, such uncomfortable living conditions were difficult to put up with. Loading and unloading everything all the time was too much for him. He was really "a philosopher among the Indians".'[74] Castro Faria speculated that 'it would have been very different if Dina had remained with us', since she 'was a "true" anthropologist, as opposed to her husband, who was never quite at ease doing fieldwork'.[75] Sidelining Claude in favour of Dina has remained to this day a widespread attitude among the Brazilians who discuss the status of fieldwork in Lévi-Strauss's work. In addition, it seems that Castro Faria was very impressed by Dina, who was warm and friendly towards him, in stark contrast to Claude's cold shoulder. Yet, Dina Lévi-Strauss's interest in anthropology did not outlive her return to France and separation from her husband. She would say later, in a filmed interview, that it had never been a vocation for her and that she was only following her husband;[76] she remembered fieldwork being physically taxing and having difficulty putting up with its rigours, succumbing rather quickly in the end, during the second expedition. The rest of her career would seem to confirm this assessment: after 1945, Dina, as Dina Dreyfus again, became a *khâgne* professor, then an inspector general for state education in philosophy, dedicating herself to the development of bold new pedagogical tools, such as a series of television broadcasts for schools in the 1960s, in which the 'masters' engaged in dialogue or discussion, often being interviewed by a young Alain Badiou. All the luminaries of French philosophy participated: Georges Canguilhem, Raymond Aron, Michel Foucault, Jean Hyppolite, Paul Ricœur, not to mention Pierre Bourdieu, Jean-Claude Passeron, Jean-Pierre Vernant and Michel Serres. Over the years, Dina Dreyfus became a major figure in academic philosophy, not because of her intellectual work, but rather because of her pedagogical passion and the 'luminous and almost violent force with which she invested philosophical engagement'.[77]

In 2001, with the publication of his diary, Castro Faria reiterated his opinion: 'The Serra Norte expedition was a complete failure.'[78] In fact, his diary – which includes other documents, telegrams he sent to Heloisa Alberto Torres, and especially his photographs – offers much more interesting testimony than this categorical and highly debatable statement would suggest. In providing a detailed chronology of the expedition, as well as its geographical itinerary and descriptions of its logistics, and refocusing attention on the participants, a rich and complex context is brought to light. In particular, it reveals how two men can share an experience based on radically different premises: while Lévi-Strauss approached Indian worlds with Jean de Léry in mind, Castro Faria was seeking the ethnographic discovery of his own country; he was reading Roquette-Pinto and the great writer Euclides da Cunha, and thinking in terms of a logic of modern nation-building through the uncovering of Brazil's heartland (*sertão*). In sharp contrast to this national and historical use of anthropology, Lévi-Strauss was on a redemptive quest for primitive societies on the verge of vanishing, some of whose languages and objects he hoped to preserve.[79]

Recovering the lost fieldwork

Contrary to the earlier view, some French and Brazilian anthropologists have attempted to rethink the question of fieldwork in Lévi-Strauss's work. Indeed, even though it was in some sense quite short – only six months in total, from July to December 1938 – and even though it did not supply, as Lévi-Strauss was hoping, adequate material for his doctoral dissertation (but for his minor thesis only), the Brazilian fieldwork was decisive in many respects – even if this would not come into focus until the publication of *Tristes Tropiques* in 1955.

In fact, Lévi-Strauss was more of a fieldwork anthropologist than he himself claimed. We have already discussed his strong empirical orientation, his acute sense of detail as well as of the big picture, his careful attentiveness to his surroundings, the powerful call of the real that the whole Brazil experience came to represent for him. None other than Nimuendaju, the archetypal figure of empirical erudition, saw him as such.[80] But he was an empiricist according to the traditions of the time and his own inclinations. The kind of expedition he organized – the big research enterprise, complete with oxen, mules and the whole imagery of exploration that this conjured up – was then very much the order of the day, but also, at the very moment they were setting off, on the verge of becoming obsolete as a scientific model and being replaced by that of Malinowskian immersion. This shift has been the source of a major misunderstanding: Lévi-Strauss is reproached for not having spent months, alone, among the Indians, and for having devoted only a few weeks, if not days, to each encounter. He would later declare that he was extremely pleased with this somewhat retro aspect of 'nineteenth-century science', whereas one might have imagined him as more of a solitary, long-distance seafarer. Although Castro Faria saw him as a 'philosopher among the Indians', always lost in thought, his work during the Brazilian years was not driven by particularly earth-shattering theoretical insights. The questions he raised were in keeping with a more classic research agenda of the times, dealing with the modes and stages of human settlement on the continent, based on enigmas that he found particularly stimulating – such as the contrast he observed with both the Bororo and the Caduveo between a rudimentary material culture and an elaborate social and ritual organization, the famous 'Gê anomaly' on which Nimuendaju was also working. The article he wrote in 1936 'does not anticipate in any way the bold speculations which, in the 1950s, came to characterize Lévi-Strauss's reflection on the populations of Central

Brazil'.[81] Between these two moments, structuralism had completely reconfigured his thinking. Neither did the young anthropologist question the working methods and 'mysticism of the object' inherited from Mauss. Moreover, as we have seen, he focused his energies on collecting objects rather than on the study of immaterial facts, for which Castro Faria implicitly reproached him. Indeed, Lévi-Strauss remained within the epistemological framework defined by the Musée de l'Homme: 'As I was preparing for my fieldwork excursions in Brazil, the Musée de l'Homme was in the making and Mauss had instilled a kind of "mysticism of the object". Not without reason, he thought that the least little object, if read correctly, reflected in microcosm the entire material and moral economy of a society. Overawed by these instructions, I spent time in the field collecting, studying and describing objects and their techniques of fabrication that I now wish I had devoted to beliefs and institutions.'[82]

No need, then, as Eduardo Viveiros de Castro has judiciously pointed out, to oppose the 'good' Nimuendaju (or the good Castro Faria), the empirical anthropologist who developed close ties with the natives, to the 'bad' Lévi-Strauss, the theoretician and poor fieldworker who remained aloof from concrete experience, and always had an eye on academic glory.[83]

The brevity of his encounters at each stage was the price he paid to discover a greater diversity in the groups he visited. This was another advantage to this kind of fieldwork. With the Nambikwara, as he was later to say, 'fieldwork [was] carried to its negative extreme. I had to try and make something of very little material.'[84] This was in sharp contrast to the anthropological profusion provided by the Bororo. Hence the very broad 'spectrum'[85] not just of indigenous practices, but also of anthropological postures, protocols and paradigms, which 'had to constantly adapt its perspective, and the questions it raised, to the specific and irreplaceable reality it encountered'.[86] It also provided an epistemological advantage, in that it allowed for a better understanding of the fieldwork carried out by others.[87]

In the end, although the area of specialization of Lévi-Strauss's fieldwork – the anthropology of the South American lowlands – did not provide the material for a dissertation based exclusively on this body of work, leading to specialized regional expertise, it did impact his intellectual development in another way, both more convoluted and more essential. According to Anne-Christine Taylor, the experience of fieldwork 'Indianized the scientific imagination'[88] of Lévi-Strauss by supplying the intellectual and sensory 'foundations' for the structuralism to come, through the characteristics detected by Lévi-Strauss in the populations he studied: the openness to the other, the primacy of relation over substance, the value attached to affinity, etc. In other words, if Lévi-Strauss was not a structuralist in Brazil, he would not have become one without the Brazilian Amerindians. And had it taken place in Africa, his fieldwork would not have enabled him to develop the theoretical hypotheses for which he would become famous a few years later. This makes for quite a reassessment of the place of fieldwork in the life and work of Claude Lévi-Strauss.

Spring 1939: an 'ascent through layers of time'[89]

The return to 'civilization' in São Paulo and then Europe was experienced by Lévi-Strauss as a return to the present. And the present, in that spring of 1939, was one of looming war and a sense of dark years to come, heralded by a few police incidents that marked his painful departure, a series of separations and a melancholy atmosphere. Back in São Paulo, alone in his hotel room at the Esplanade, where he resided until he set sail on 8 March, Claude Lévi-Strauss must have thought of his long hallucinatory travels as an extended parenthesis, as he contemplated reintegration into a world that had gone off the rails. Had it all been a dream? No, the trunks and the collected ethnographic material attested to the fact that something had indeed taken place.

'Three trunks, six cases and a canvas parcel'

Once again, the anthropologist had to deal with the process of sharing the collected material, involving a further bout of misunderstandings, mishaps and delays.[90] Two days after his arrival in the capital city, on 14 January, he wrote to Heloisa Alberto Torres to thank her for having regularly informed his wife of news of the expedition as it arrived by telegram from Castro Faria. He expressed regret about not having been able to take along 'the museum's recording machines. In a few hours, beautiful material could have been gathered . . . .' But, on the whole, he was 'delighted' by his trip and was coming back with 'a beautiful scientific collection', a detailed inventory of which he would send her presently.[91] Despite the affable tone, suspicion was rampant, especially on the part of the Oversight Committee, whose representative sent a message to the customs inspector in Santos on 23 January: 'Given the fact that there is material of considerable value, I call your attention to this matter and request that you display all the necessary vigilance so that our share of the material, by right, does not leave the national territory via the port and can be added to national heritage collections.'[92] Soon thereafter, Lévi-Strauss offered to divide the collection into two roughly equal shares: 760 items for Brazil, 745 for France, the 15 additional pieces in the Brazilian share comprising unique pieces that therefore had to remain in the country. The 1,505 items were listed in a 'Registro', a double-entry Franco-Brazilian ledger, based on the locations where they were collected.[93] On the Brazilian side, the objects were destined for the collections of the National Museum, next to the Roquette-Pinto Collections, but they never actually made it. As we have seen, they remained in São Paulo, first at the Department of Culture, then at various institutions, before disappearing altogether for over fifty years. On the French side, the export licence was granted on 2 March, but a problem arose concerning Vellard's collections, since the latter, less rigorous than Lévi-Strauss, had failed to provide a detailed inventory, which resulted in his being deprived of his zoological items. The ethnographic collections gathered by Lévi-Strauss were destined for the Musée de l'Homme – and comprised in all 'three trunks, six cases and a canvas parcel', as Lévi-Strauss wrote to Heloisa Alberto Torres on 1 March 1939, bidding her adieu and asking her to 'give Castro Faria [his] friendly regards'. A final imbroglio about the port of departure of the collections, in fact Santos rather than Rio, resulted in further 'cold sweats', until, on 8 March 1939, they finally departed, stopping over in Rio, where Lévi-Strauss was hoping once again to meet with Mário de Andrade, now marginalized and practically exiled in the Carioca capital, slowly succumbing to alcoholism and depression.

'Will everything get back to normal?'

Meanwhile, Dina, undergoing treatment for her eyes, was gradually recovering back in Paris, riveted by the news from Brazil. Left to her own devices and in a state of existential drift, she corresponded regularly with her Brazilian friend Mário, whom she tried to console before confiding her own disillusionments: 'You can easily imagine my despair at having had to abandon my husband and the mission. If this proves nothing more than a trial, I will accept it as such. I am also a little depressed, but this too will probably pass. Will everything get back to normal?' She was appointed professor of philosophy at the women's *lycée* in Besançon – starting on 1 October 1938 – but it seems her health did not permit her to take up that post. At the time, she lived in Paris, at 26 rue des Plantes, and led, as she described it to Mário, an 'idle and useless life', reconnecting with 'all sorts of sentiments and sensations from [her] "youth"'. She was then twenty-seven years old. Time became a blur: 'Did I leave Brazil two months ago or ten years ago?' She felt old and 'bitterly detached', 'even without taking the sentimental side into account'. Long letters followed. They reflected her anxious temperament, subject to all manner of questioning, as well as her passionate side, longing to live life to the full: 'The whole universe appears to me as a system of keys. There are good ones and better ones. Bad ones and worse ones. Religion is probably one of the best, in the form of a somewhat revised and corrected Revelation. Sound political and social thinking is another good, excellent key. Unfortunately, it has become somewhat rusty lately, and has trouble turning in the lock. Ethnography is a key as well. A good one, though somewhat thin. Or rather, it only opens a small lock, and even that takes quite a lot of effort.' She smoked, listened to records, read a lot, went out often, indulged herself in coquettishness and socialized regularly. Strangely, in this vortex, she resembled nothing so much as an existentialist type, of the Simone de Beauvoir variety.[94]

An atmosphere of disaster hovered over the deferred departure of Claude Lévi-Strauss from Brazil, a Brazil which he was later to say, like Braudel, represented 'the decisive experience' of his life, but with which he entertained ambivalent relations to the end. A month before his departure, in February 1939, he had met Alfred Métraux, who was on his way to Argentina. He saw him for the first time in Santos, where he had gone down to wait for him on the quay. For an entire day, they walked around the port, observing the loading and unloading of cargo, before heading to the deserted beaches on the shore, 'which were, for us, still haunted by the shadows of these Indians with whom Jean de Léry and Hans Staden had lived, and of whom Métraux was the definitive historian'.[95] What did they talk about? In his journal, Métraux gives us an inkling, as well as his first impressions of his future friend: 'Lévi-Strauss arrives. He looks just like a Jew out of some Egyptian painting: same nose and beard trimmed in Semitic style. I find him cold and stuffy, very French academic. He leads me along the beaches. [. . .] Lévi-Strauss is sick of Brazil. Vargas is a ruthless dictator whose only goal is to remain in power. His dictatorship relies mostly on the police. [. . .] Lévi-Strauss sees no hope for South America. He is almost inclined to see in this failure a kind of cosmic curse. He is intent on leaving Brazil, where all work appears impossible. [. . .] Random walks through the streets of Santos. At a café, scrawny prostitutes with bad teeth. Dance hall upstairs with jazz orchestra. In dingy cafés, carnival tunes blaring from radio sets, rhythmical and up-tempo. People sitting at the doors of their houses, gazing into the dark, empty street.'[96]

The intense melancholy, almost crepuscular, tone of the scene, the incidents with the police, recalled in *Tristes Tropiques* – such as the one in Bahia, where Lévi-Strauss had stopped over, and where he was accosted for taking a photograph of a street kid in rags – Vargas's toxic dictatorship, the meeting with Métraux: the final moments before departure were punctuated by signs of things to come, a West Indian version of Vichy repression, war, and exile.

9

Crisis (1939–1941)

To ward off misfortune, pretend it does not exist . . .
                    Claude Lévi-Strauss, *Le Figaro*, 22–23 July 1989

Setting sail from Santos on 7 March 1939,[1] Claude Lévi-Strauss arrived in Paris at the end of the month, two weeks after the Nazis had invaded Bohemia and Moravia, and exactly one year after the annexation of Austria into a German-speaking Reich that had become a threat in the heart of Europe. The still young anthropologist, at thirty years of age – though more mature from years of adventure, his still serious face now framed by a 'dubious beard'[2] – returned to Paris with his ethnographic objects and his monkey, Lucinda, in tow. As far as he was concerned, it was a time for unpacking his collections. But there would be no exhibition: 'While I was classifying and analysing the collection, the war broke out. This was also the time that my first wife, Dina, and I separated.'[3]

The two years that elapsed between his returning home in 1939 and his going into exile in 1941 were, strictly speaking, years of crisis. A 'crisis' is the period in the development of an illness characterized by sudden and decisive change – resulting in either recovery or death. For Lévi-Strauss, if not for the wider world, it led to recovery. He returned, in a state of stunned amazement, to a world on the brink of collapse – mobilization, war, defeat, the political revolution of Vichy that brought an end to seventy years of republican France, revocation, repression, separation from Dina and, finally, an almost miraculous exile, which would open up new horizons. Lévi-Strauss lived through this dark and tumultuous period – unthinkable even to those who experienced it – like a 'zombie',[4] neither understanding nor anticipating any of it. Hence the mad quality of those two years, during which the turn of events and the course of life had become utterly unpredictable. Lévi-Strauss would later contrast his voluntary expatriation of 1934 to the forced one of 1941. Yet, oddly enough, the second was probably more felicitous and unquestionably as productive as the first. A second paradox: history, which Claude Lévi-Strauss as a thinker was so keen to keep at a distance, exerted a much stronger hold on the course of his life than on that of other intellectuals who proclaimed themselves to be 'engaged' with world historical events.

Returning to Paris, to the present and to history

The smell of creosote

From an administrative standpoint, Lévi-Strauss remained on leave from teaching until the beginning of the 1939 academic year. According to a letter he sent to Marcel Mauss, he was then to begin as a substitute teacher at the Versailles women's *lycée*, while his wife would be sent to teach at the *lycée* in Troyes.[5] The war, of course, swept all these plans aside. But, in the meantime, he had several months in which to carry out the standard post-expedition work: unpacking, cataloguing and labelling the 650 objects brought back from his second expedition, which were perhaps less spectacular than those of the first, but just as significant and numerous. No feather diadems to match those of the Bororo, but many more modest artefacts: basketwork, labrets, belts, small ceramics, etc.

He spent his days at the Musée de l'Homme, engrossed in the laborious and painstaking task of indexing and referencing each object, to prepare them for display as part of a future exhibit and then for incorporation into the museum's Latin American collections, alongside those of his mentor and PhD supervisor, Paul Rivet. This long work of preparation was considered as preliminary to the scholarly publication to follow, which would provide detailed descriptions of the fieldwork and offer hypotheses, themselves the cornerstones of the young anthropologist's regional expertise and scientific legitimacy. Indulging in a bit of counterfactual history, had war not erupted, Lévi-Strauss would have published his doctoral research on the Indians of the Brazilian Central Plateau, a region that was still little known, and he would have become the foremost expert on that area. He would have contributed to the research agenda of the field of anthropology of the Americas, and would perhaps even have founded a school of thought, rehabilitating the study of Latin America within French anthropology, in which Africanist anthropology, for reasons of colonial proximity, was much more developed. But war did break out. One of its minuscule effects was to put an end to this anthropological work, to which Lévi-Strauss would never return, severed from his collections, forced to break from the epistemology of the object into which Mauss had initiated his entire generation.

During these months, in a kind of suspended animation, between April and July 1939, Lévi-Strauss spent hours in close contact with his objects. As he unwrapped them, the smell of creosote filled the air and magically transported him back to his Brazilian odyssey. This oily liquid, a mixture of phenol and cresol, served as a preservative and was copiously sprayed on the notebooks, photos and various objects to protect them from vermin. Its pungent smell made it a powerful vehicle for the past.[6] That odour – in which, fifty years later, Lévi-Strauss would still recognize the smell of adventure – operated as a kind of buffer between himself and his present. Over the course of that long Parisian maceration period of spring 1939, creosote would serve to perpetuate the Brazilian experience more than to bring it to a close. Lévi-Strauss was there and yet he was not there – 'I was elsewhere',[7] as he himself said. An absent presence who, every evening, after long hours of cataloguing, would emerge from the Musée de l'Homme, now housed in its majestic quarters, and breathe in the air along the banks of the Seine. What exactly did he smell?

The world of 1939 had difficulty reaching his nostrils. And yet it was right there, in front of his eyes, that the 1937 World Exhibition, sponsored by the Front populaire, had hosted the famous confrontation between Nazi and Soviet pavilions. The monumental, aggressively neoclassical architecture, the competition over building heights and their colossal character summed up, in the eyes of contemporaries, the ideological bipolarization of the interwar period and the mad rivalry between the two totalitarian powers. But years in the heart of indigenous Brazil had turned Lévi-Strauss into a man who had, temporarily at least, ceased to be a contemporary of his contemporaries, but was, rather, a kind of revenant. He explicitly addressed this fuzzy relationship to the present in a fascinating interview he gave in July 1989, on the occasion of the fiftieth anniversary of the summer of 1939: 'I heard about the Munich agreement in Amazonia, from an old newspaper I found lying on the floor of the hut of a rubber prospector.'[8] In response to the interviewer, who expressed astonishment at such obliviousness and irresponsibility, Lévi-Strauss remained unfazed and insisted on the various possible ways of being, or not being, in touch with one's present. Indeed, we are not all contemporaries of the same present. The very large gap that separated him from this period of acute crisis was to influence the subsequent course of the anthropologist's life in an essential way: from then on, he was to be ahead of or behind his present, but rarely in synch with it, marking a sharp contrast with his politically engaged youth. It was thus that, in 1939, he saw nothing coming, as he readily admitted – neither the war, nor the anti-Semitic hysteria, which he still explained to Métraux in rather crude Marxist terms.[9] He did not anticipate anything, or understand anything. Like so many others. The arrival of some new recruits at the Musée de l'Homme, all German and Russian Jewish exiles, such as Boris Vildé and Anatole Lewitsky, did nothing to alert him either.[10] An autistic defence mechanism, no doubt, but a posture of decentring as well: 'I was much more preoccupied with Indians than with the state of the world.'[11] To account for his lack of perspicacity, Lévi-Strauss often invoked, by way of explanation, a kind of genetic deficiency: a lack of imagination. This lack of historical imagination, which momentarily spared him the anguish of the worst to come, appears as the flipside of the enchanted respect for the richness of the real he had cultivated since childhood. Indeed, no need for imagination when the real, in all its grandeur, provides material for the wildest speculation.

Literary temptations and romantic breakup

This lack of imagination, which was, according to Lévi-Strauss himself, part and parcel of his psyche, may not have been only historical, but also literary, and even existential. Indeed, during the sequence of events that preceded the war, he tried his hand at novel writing but gave up, for lack of inventiveness in the description and the action of the characters. Yet, this aborted novel is not without interest. First, because it gave its title, *Tristes Tropiques*, to a quite different work that was to make its author famous some fifteen years later. From this stunted effort, nothing remained but the title and the literary inclination. Both *Tristes Tropiques*, from this perspective, illustrate, each in their own way, the duel between literature and anthropology. The literary yearning is palpable in Lévi-Strauss's 1954 work of indeterminate genre, this famous 'second book', as Vincent Debaene[12] has described it, giving voice to the more subjective underside of the objective discourse expected of a scholarly oeuvre. In 1939, the unabashedly subjective novel writing served as compensation for the scientific work in which he was engaged, day after day, at the Musée de l'Homme, and it probably constituted a form of escape from the serious-ness of scholarship. This attempt – quickly abandoned, according to its author – might have been a sign of the young scholar's anxiety, as well as dissatisfaction, with a commitment to scientific knowledge alone. But it did not lead anywhere.

The novel was of course not far removed from what the young anthro-pologist had just experienced: 'He took a deep breath. Everything was set now. As he was about to board the ship, whose overheated smell of paint, linoleum and food had turned his stomach, he fleetingly thought – once again – of returning to Vayras. And the mass of clouds unfurling in the sky framed, like a new and mournful fantasy, a backdrop of unimpressive mountains swollen with monotonous vegetation, a foreground of rocky slopes and, in the coarse shade of chestnut trees, large, dark shacks, held together without mortar, their walls mere piles of rocks lifted from the bottom of nearby streams.'[13] The novel, like Lévi-Strauss's life, featured the Old and the New Worlds, departures from Europe and new founda-tions, Oceania and the Cévennes region – as described in the lines just quoted, home to the main character, Paul Thalamas, a young Protestant who sports a 'dubious beard'. The novel opens with him leaning on the rail of an ocean liner bound for South America. The book was loosely based on a story that had made the news: a traveller went to Oceania and, with the help of a phonograph, fooled the natives into thinking he was a god.[14] In the novel, this initial plot was transformed into 'a story of refugees fleeing German occupation and trying to recreate another civilization in the Pacific'.[15] The traveller as hoaxer, but also as utopian – the fantasy of new beginnings so tied up with the New World. Everything was tied together in this novel, which, in its incomplete state, also expressed the budding anthropologist's need to describe his fieldwork experience through other lenses, as well as to exorcize the historical fears to which he claimed to be utterly oblivious. In the narrative, the historic disaster – the war – is conceived as a failure of the Old World and an opportunity for the New, in ways that strikingly anticipate his own exile to come.

Unlike Nabokov at Harvard, who classified his butterflies with one hand while writing novels with the other, Claude Lévi-Strauss catalogued his objects but had trouble finding a separate outlet for his interior life, which was then in an anguished state due to the breakup with his wife Dina. Claude's return had brought an end to their nine months apart, a painful experience for Dina, as we know from the letters she exchanged with Mário de Andrade. Racked with anxiety and guilt over having deserted the ethnographic mission, and receiving little news, Dina suffered from a mental anguish that was further compounded by her physical ill-health and the shock of the partial blindness she had experienced and believed would be permanent. Whatever the cause, the fact remains that their reunion was lukewarm – especially, it would appear, on his part. Wavering between strategies for reviving their love life and surrendering to indifference, the couple did not manage to rescue their relationship: 'Everything you said to [...], and that you partly repeated to me, if not exactly a revelation, made me realize how deep the abyss between us was. I didn't know that you had long ceased to love me, that indeed you had trouble putting up with me, and that I no longer meant anything to you. Still now, whereas it has been repeated to me twice in a single day, I can hardly believe it and feel as if in a dream. If I had known, I would have left much earlier, since there was no rekindling your love. I didn't know that you felt our marriage had been a mistake and that I had been such a disappointment. You should have told me earlier. I have asked you so often. It would have been less difficult . . . If there had been anything in your words that gave me hope, I would have given it another try. I would have tried to make you less unhappy. But I cannot bear living without being loved; and I am afraid that, without love, any attempt is doomed to fail.'[16]

Then came the dramatic event, and the classic solution to impossible choice: Dina attempted suicide, at home, on the rue des Plantes, and was saved, at the very last moment, by her mother-in-law, Claude's mother, who lived in the same building and had realized what was happening, coming to her rescue.[17] This denouement brought the couple's relationship to a definitive end, even though they were to meet again over the following months, in Paris and later in the Cévennes, and remained officially married until 1945. Indeed, the onset of war, mobilization and exile precluded any possibility of divorce. In several letters of 1940 and 1941, Lévi-Strauss still talked of his 'wife', and Dina of her 'husband'. Yet, from the spring of 1939, they had gone their separate ways and Lévi-Strauss started up an affair with Rose-Marie Ullmo, his friend Pierre Dreyfus's sister-in-law, who would become his second wife after the war. As for the more profound causes of this asymmetric disaffection, one can only speculate. Asked to comment on it at the end of his life, the old man simply said: 'She lived in her head. I never knew what she was thinking.'[18] Seven years of marriage consummated and torn to pieces on the altar of anthropology and the spatiotemporal discrepancies of romantic experience.

The war

Farce (the phoney war)

Like millions of other Frenchmen, Claude Lévi-Strauss was called to serve his country. He was thirty-one. Having previously done his military service in the logistics and signal corps, he was first appointed to the telegram censorship service of the postal ministry. For a few weeks, he was supposed to 'bring all telegrams that [he] deemed suspicious to the attention of a superior, who would immediately imagine that he was onto the biggest possible case, on which his own promotion depended. It was utter farce.'[19] This episode set the tone. Regarding his experience of 'phoney war', and then of war itself, all we can rely on are a few letters and subsequent accounts, but the both poignant and farcical register Lévi-Strauss struck echoed that of other testimonies of the times, especially of his contemporary Louis Poirier (aka Julien Gracq) in his recently published *Manuscrits de guerre*.[20] Both registered their impressions in a literary genre that André Breton, at the very same time and with an acute sense of historical timing, was about to endow with a new respectability: black humour.[21]

Lévi-Strauss requested training as a liaison agent for the British expeditionary corps, a position that the historian Marc Bloch also held: 'First they sent me to school somewhere in the Somme, and then I took some tests. My English was rudimentary, but I passed all the same. They sent me to the Luxembourg border behind the Maginot line, where the British soldiers hadn't yet arrived but were expected. I was there with three or four agents to meet them when they came. There was nothing to do. I used to take walks in the country to pass the time.'[22]

That episode ended on a note very reminiscent of Julien Gracq's *The Opposing Shore*: waiting for the allies, then waiting for the enemy. One comes, the other does not. Or rather, when the German offensive started, a Scottish regiment did arrive, but with its own liaison officers, making the presence of Lévi-Strauss and his comrades redundant, even counterproductive.[23] A bad decision across the board. Selected for the wrong reasons (his English was almost nonexistent) and sent where he would be of no use (no English troops), he was in the end transferred without ever seeing combat. Always irrelevant, he nonetheless had a close call: the evacuation 'probably saved our lives, for the regiment was decimated a few days later'.[24]

How did he experience these months of waiting in the Ardenne? 'It came almost right after Brazil. The anthropological experience continued under another guise. I mean I had become used to bizarre, strange, singular situations, and I found myself as a soldier in bizarre, strange and singular situations. It was a smooth transition.'[25] The analogy was not so much based on the aspect of physical hardship – Brazilian fieldwork was apparently much harsher than the war for Lévi-Strauss – as on a common experience of estrangement. Since anthropology in the field was like war, then war could become a sort of anthropological practice.

At the end of this period of idleness, expectancy and bewildering absurdity, a very significant episode took place: the lesson of the dandelion.[26] Just before the German offensive, Lévi-Strauss, a lone walker in wartime, combed the countryside, giving himself over, like Rousseau on St Peter's Island, to erudite reveries. 'In the prairies of Northern France, there were dandelions aquiver. Lévi-Strauss looked closely at the flowers: How was he to penetrate their mystery? The shape of it might be described as perfect, but did this make them any more intelligible? The only way forward was to see dandelions in relation to other flowers, to compare them, contrast them, in order to assign a rank to the dandelion within this long series of similarities and differences that compose the vegetal order.'[27] What should we make of this little fable? This staging of the birth of the structuralist method suggests the powerful force of a poetic bolt of lightning. If structuralism can be considered an intellectual offspring of war, it is probably in another sense, which we will develop a bit later. But this episode of naturalist rapture in the midst of an experience of self-detachment is highly plausible. The phoney war, and even the war itself, paradoxically served as opportunities to live with and in nature. Indeed, Julien Gracq's Lieutenant Poirier experienced similar epiphanies in the flax fields of western Flanders, in the thick of combat at Dunkirk, where he was eventually taken prisoner. But nothing of the sort happened to Lévi-Strauss who, having had no occasion to find himself in any combat zones, would not even bring to mind Fabrice at Waterloo.

Phantasmagoria (May–June 1940)

Indeed, private Lévi-Strauss was to live through what came to be called the 'Battle of France' almost without hearing a shot. After the Ardenne and the arrival of the Scots, he eventually rejoined his unit in a village of the Sarthe region (near Évron), after several detours. From there, they embarked by train to Bordeaux. Here again, confusion reigned. 'The train zigzagged through France', wavering between the two possible options available to the officers of his regiment, as well as the French army as a whole: either to comply with orders and proceed to Bordeaux to surrender, in accordance with the clauses of the Armistice signed on 22 June 1940; or to disobey orders and cross over to the Southern zone to be demobilized. In the end, the latter prevailed and the train stopped at Béziers. The soldiers were billeted on the Larzac Plateau and then wound up in Montpellier. In answer to the question 'So, you never saw active combat?' Lévi-Strauss was to answer: 'No. Except when strafing broke some tiles over my head, I was never exposed to the fighting.'[28] The level of combat faced by French soldiers during the Battle of France has recently been reassessed, establishing that the first weeks were pretty deadly and that some regiments did engage in real fighting. Yet, even those who did see combat have said it felt unreal, a sentiment that also coloured Lévi-Strauss's experience of the war: disorganization, erratic leadership, contradictory orders, pointless peregrinations across France, soldiers and civilians mingling together in the panic of escape, everyone looking for someone. Julien Gracq spoke of the 'phantasmagoria' of war.[29] A few months later, in *Strange Defeat*, Marc Bloch was to deliver an implacable diagnosis of this staggering defeat. But at the time, a kind of disorientated apathy prevailed. On 2 June, Lévi-Strauss informed Mauss that he had 'rushed around Paris' and now found himself idle: 'There are quite a few of us here that they don't know what to do with for the moment, you know why. We are kept busy, in the meantime, with all the inconveniences of garrison routine: marches, patrols, watches, roll calls, etc. I have no idea how long this might go on.'[30] It was as if the war had not yet begun . . . Later, Lévi-Strauss was to convey this sense of the inconsistency of reality in a different way: 'The war didn't seem real. We felt as if we were putting on a play, a remake of 1914. Our heart wasn't in it.'[31] Julien Gracq, who did see bullets fly and fired a few himself, used the exact same terms and spontaneously offered the same metaphor of illusion: 'Everything is fake, we all feel it. It is all simulacrum – everyone acts "as if". Going through the motions, issuing the proper orders befitting the tradition of "heroic defence". [. . .] Nothing authentic will come out of this war, nothing but the acute grotesquery of aping, down to the most minute detail, 1870 and 1914. In the vague hope, perhaps, of a magical conjuring.'[32] This sense of unreality that almost always accompanies forebodings of impending disaster also contributed to the trauma of defeat and the state of incredulity in the face of these few weeks of madness. For the French population of 1940, a brutal debacle of this kind was simply unimaginable. Raised in patriotic fervour, secure in the belief that their military might was the greatest in Europe, reassured by the Maginot Line – they shared a kind of faith in the invincibility of their country. This included those, like Lévi-Strauss, who were socialists and pacifists. In light of such widely held views, the reality of catastrophic defeat left everyone utterly dumbfounded, paving the way for the political revolution of Vichy. The latter began a few days later, on 10 July 1940, when the Front populaire parliament dissolved itself and voted the four constitutional acts that founded the new regime. It is difficult to say how Lévi-Strauss felt about the ritual hara-kiri performed by his socialist and centrist comrades and elders.[33]

In his chapter 'One of the vanquished gives evidence', Marc Bloch further confirmed the sentiments of Lévi-Strauss and Gracq. The defeat, he says, was fundamentally a defeat of the mind, a defeat of strategy. The French chiefs of staff replayed the war of 1914, whereas the German generals waged a present-day war, governed by the idea of speed. 'So true is this, that it was as though the two opposed forces belonged, each of them, to an entirely different period of human history.' Bloch concluded, in terms that Lévi-Strauss would not have disavowed: 'We interpreted war in terms of assegai vs. rifle made familiar to us by long years of colonial expansion. But this time it was we who were cast for the role of the savage!'[34]

To bring this odyssey to an end as it began, we rejoin Lévi-Strauss in Montpellier in July 1940: 'I took off from the barracks and went to the rector's office at the university to offer my services in case they needed an examiner in philosophy for the baccalaureat examinations that were about to begin. The timing was perfect, and I was demobilized a few days early.'[35] Which just goes to show that, in France, everything might collapse, but the baccalaureat exam must go on!

Taking shelter

In the South

The third round of these two years of crisis took place in the South. A historical and geographical South, but above all the South of the dividing line that, until November 1942, split France in two. The compass point had now taken on a vital political meaning: to the north lay the occupied zone under direct Nazi rule; to the south, Vichy France, which seemed to ensure security and relative protection, especially in the foothills of the Cévennes where Lévi-Strauss took shelter with his parents, who had moved into the family house in Camcabra, near Le Vigan. From that moment, for several months in his case and several years in theirs, this small cottage purchased about ten years earlier became a kind of secure hub, where they met, crossed paths, received mail, exchanged news. The Cévennes – a shaly, gneissic region whose fortress-like geography had withstood the onslaught of Louis XIV – returned to service, offering its long legacy of resistance, cemented centuries earlier by Protestant refusal, to the new pariahs. On the long hikes he had taken with André Chamson,[36] his neighbour from Valleraugue, the two boys must surely have invoked the history of nonconformism that radiated from the soil of that land.

Yet at that point (summer 1940) the new pariahs had not yet all come to understand their new status. As we have seen, Claude Lévi-Strauss often mentioned the strange steps he had taken in September 1940. Posted to the prestigious Lycée Henri IV in Paris, he worried that the new academic year was about to start: 'And so, guess what I did? I went to Vichy to obtain an authorization to return to Paris to take up my post! The Ministry of Education was housed in a school, one of whose classrooms served as the office of the Division of Secondary Education. The official in charge looked at me, dumbfounded: "With a name like yours, to Paris? You can't be serious!" It was only then that I began to understand.'[37] But he had still not yet fully understood. He returned to the Cévennes, where he was informed of his new assignment, to the Perpignan Lycée. There, he received further indication: his new colleagues shunned him and avoided all conversation on the subject of racial laws, about which there was beginning to be much talk. 'Only the physical education teacher was bent on showing me his sympathies – probably he was a future member of the Resistance.'[38] In 1988, during his interview with Lévi-Strauss on the subject, Didier Éribon found it hard to believe: 'So people were unaware of the gravity of the situation for the Jews?'[39] An infinitely complex historical issue, that has been the subject of constant debate ever since. What did people know, and who knew what when? Lévi-Strauss has commented on his attitude of denial and the pretence of normality which appear so unbelievable to us today: 'I think that one way of averting danger or protecting oneself from it is to hold on to one's habits. So long as one manages to keep living as one used to, danger does not exist. And in the end, this is probably why I requested to return to Paris – my tendency to be a homebody.'[40] With all the written and oral testimonies we have today, nothing could be more understandable than this apparently very nonsensical attitude. French citizens of 1940 who happened to have been born Jewish had grown up worshipping the French Republic, and many of them could not envision the possibility of state anti-Semitism. Of course, they had already seen the repression of foreign Jews, some of whom had become French citizens and then been stripped of their nationality by the law of 22 July 1940. And yet they felt socially, ideologically and economically distant from their coreligionists hailing from Eastern Europe. Indeed, even after the anti-Jewish decrees of October 1940, and even after the stigmatization entailed in the obligation to wear a yellow star, most of them retained enough trust in the French state to accept the command to register with the French police. Hélène Berr's *Journal* powerfully conveys both how little sense this young, upper-class Parisian woman had of her Jewish identity, and how the gradual tightening of the noose precipitated a painful awareness that she made every effort to resist.[41] Anything not to understand what was happening . . . And when the truth is revealed to her in flashes, the young woman persists in refusing to leave Paris. In the fragmentary descriptions of her daily survival, the reader is made to fully grasp the difference between 'knowing' and 'understanding'. In the final days of the *Journal*, she has 'understood' but does not consider leaving. She wants to remain at the centre of history. In her upper-class Jewish milieu, exile was strongly frowned upon, as an act of cowardice and confirmation of the prejudice against the wandering Jew.

Lévi-Strauss thus opted for the pretence of normalcy. After Perpignan, he returned to Montpellier, where he taught philosophy to students specializing in the hard sciences who could not care less about the subject. And such was the last philosophy course of Claude Lévi-Strauss's teaching career: a professor who had renounced his discipline pretended to be teaching students, who themselves only pretended to be listening. A total charade of a class, the fragile refuge for a charade of a daily existence, all of which would soon come to an end anyway, with the publication of the Statute on Jews of 3 October 1940 and the letter of dismissal that followed. Over the course of this short period of time, while he was still teaching in Montpellier, Lévi-Strauss read an important book that was to nourish his thinking on French anthropology and inspire him while also frustrating him: Marcel Granet's *Catégories matrimoniales et relations de proximité dans la Chine ancienne* (1939). This book brought questions of kinship to his attention. Excited by the analysis, he admired the way Granet had taken apart complicated kinship systems, as well as the intellectual ambition of the project as a whole: 'I discovered an objective way of thinking applied to social facts. And at the same time, I was annoyed, because Granet in his attempt to account for very complex systems got carried away and imagined solutions that were even more elaborate. In my opinion, simplicity should lie behind complexity.'[42] A scholarly conviction asserted in a historical context that belied any such clear-cut project – a scathing rebuttal of the aspirations of the intellectual life.

For henceforth, nothing would be either simple or normal. Once back in his Cévennes bastion, over the autumn and winter of 1940, Lévi-Strauss had to solve an equation with several unknowns. What to do? Should he stay or go? If he were to go, what direction should he take? Several options presented themselves, options which, in the shifting flux of their respective uncertainties, ran the gamut of the possible for the new pariahs of 1940. First, a letter from Georges Dumas reached him in December: the man who had sent him to Brazil offered to help him obtain an exemption under article 8 of the law of 3 October 1940. This article lifted the professional restrictions for Jews who had rendered 'exceptional service' to the French nation. This meant accepting Vichy and its depredations, while benefiting from a special dispensation that would allow Lévi-Strauss to continue teaching and making a living. Quite clearly, however, in view of the twenty or so distinguished academics who did receive this status from the Conseil d'État between 1941 and 1943 – including the historian Marc Bloch, physician Robert Debré and physicist René Wurmser[43] – the young anthropologist would not have made the grade. At that point, refusal and domestic exile presented themselves as more convincing and appealing options than the idea of leaving: 'I was still terribly romantic . . . My parents owned a cottage in the Cévennes to which they had moved at the beginning of the war, and I imagined that if necessary I would hole up in that region that I knew well, hide in the mountains and subsist on hunting and gathering, as I had in the Brazilian hinterland. I had a very poetic vision of things.'[44] This was a resistance plan of sorts, albeit an innocent one, closer to a local Robinson Crusoe adventure. Yet this fantasy did capture the allure of adventure that so many young men were keen to experience when they opted to go underground rather than submit to compulsory work service. The alternative to refuge in the Cévennes was to go into exile. Like the Huguenots of the seventeenth century, the choice was between a clandestine life of faith in the 'Desert' or expatriation to Protestant countries. Sometimes, one option prevailed over the other, in a precarious give-and-take in which all choices became momentarily impossible – 'the two sides of the scale are more or less even and are left that way for a long while'.[45] In the end, the decision to leave or not – the former strongly illegitimate in the minds of French citizens, and even more so for Jewish families – was based on a system of representations that made room for assessing chances and risks based on partial information, political persuasion and a historical imagination of what the future might hold in store.

During the winter months of 1940, two exit strategies began to take shape. The first, more immediately within reach, consisted in returning to Brazil. His familiarity with the country and its authorities, and his friends who remained, were considerable assets, even if the political situation was objectively unfavourable. At that time, when visas had become rare and precious, Lévi-Strauss would probably have agreed to it. He recounted in *Tristes Tropiques* how that option had abruptly closed on the cramped ground floor of the Brazilian embassy in Vichy: 'The ambassador, Luis de Souza-Dantas, with whom I was well acquainted and who would have behaved no differently had I been a stranger, picked up his seal and was about to stamp the passport when one of his counsellors interrupted him with icy politeness and pointed out that new regulations had been introduced depriving him of the power to do so. For a few seconds, his arm remained poised in mid-air. With an anxious, almost beseeching, glance, the ambassador tried to persuade his subordinate to look the other way so that the stamp could be brought down, thus allowing me at least to leave France, if not to enter Brazil. But all in vain; the counsellor continued to stare at the hand, which eventually dropped on to the table alongside the document. I was not to have my visa; my passport was handed back to me with a gesture of profound regret.'[46] The abortive motion of the ambassador's stamp presents a powerful image of the dramatic twists of history in situations of acute crisis.

Once again, exile was not a foregone conclusion. It represented one option among several on the shifting horizon of possible solutions that was gradually narrowing. Marc Bloch was on the verge of departure, visa and invitation to teach in the United States in hand; but, at the last minute, he chose to stay, because two of his children, subject to obligations of military service, could no longer accompany him.[47] Plans were so fragile and complex that a mere flick of the finger could enable escape – a chance encounter, a benevolent official, etc. – or conversely block it – as, in this case, the Brazilian ambassador's loss of political favour.

Yet, leave he did. Lévi-Strauss described how happy the Vichy officials were to let him go, which may come as a surprise. Indeed, Vichy policies were always in flux, but until 1942 the emigration of Jews and other undesirables was the preferred policy in high places. Between the winter of 1940 and May 1941, this conjuncture opened a window of opportunity – for several months it became possible to take the West Indian route to America, which is precisely what Lévi-Strauss was to do. At the same time, the administrative disarray of the Vichy administration was often an obstacle to securing the necessary papers in time, and especially exit visas. Hence the perilous chronology of the various visa expiration dates (exit visa, third country transit visa, entry visa), since in Vichy, as in Washington DC, both intentional and unintentional bureaucratic obstruction was not uncommon.

In a few weeks, despite all manner of difficulties, the American option prevailed. The letter inviting him to teach at the New School for Social Research, which he received from Alvin Johnson in the Cévennes, probably in January or February 1941, functioned in the same way as the phone call from Célestin Bouglé in October 1934 – as an accelerator of history and a conduit to the New World. Upstream from this letter, which is missing from Claude Lévi-Strauss's personal archive, one can trace, like the tip of an iceberg, a whole series of initial contacts, academic recommendations, as well as more official procedures – all to the credit of the mobilization of American society and philanthropy in coming to the aid of Europeans under the Nazi yoke.

On the American side: the rescue calculus

Beginning in 1933, the Rockefeller Foundation had put in place a programme to rescue German-speaking scholars who had been removed from their posts by the Nazis. About 250 positions were created for them, and the professors were dispatched to various American universities. As part of this programme, the Foundation acted as a sponsor for universities and academic institutes that might hire these academics in danger, providing grants to fund the first two years. One institution became particularly active in this process: the New School for Social Research. An unusual institution, created in 1918 and with leanings to the political left, the New York-based New School offered adult education through evening courses and saw itself as an alternative to standard academic teaching. From 1933, around sixty professors in exile joined the New School's faculty. They radically altered its course offering, and turned it into an exciting and cosmopolitan intellectual hub, focused on the new social sciences. When, in the summer of 1940, the Emergency Program for European Scholars was reactivated on a similar basis with like objectives, but now enlarged to include France and other European countries that had fallen under Nazi control, the New School and its dynamic director Alvin Johnson resumed their positions as direct interlocutors with the Foundation's advisers, serving as a kind of 'triage station'[48] within the organization, giving the new European arrivals some time, generally two years, to find positions on the American job market.

Claude Lévi-Strauss was to benefit from this programme, which was simultaneously generous, pragmatic and self-interested. In the minds of its promoters, the operation was almost botanical in nature: its purpose was to graft the best branches of the European intellectual tradition onto the still rustic bough of America. Since there were only a hundred or so grants available, the selection process was necessarily intense, and it was conducted according to precise criteria, which Lévi-Strauss's career and profile reflected.

Applicants were assessed based on a careful examination of their curriculum vitae, but the letters of recommendation addressed to Alvin Johnson proved more decisive. There were five letters in support of Claude Lévi-Strauss's application.[49] The first, dated 20 September 1940, was from Robert Lowie, a professor at Berkeley, explaining in a few sentences how very favourably impressed he had been by Lévi-Strauss's 'excellent article on the Bororo Indians', which he had read a few years earlier, thanks to Alfred Métraux. The second letter – written by Métraux himself, then at Yale, on 2 October 1940 – was longer and advanced arguments that were all the more effective that they were tailored to the foundation's criteria: the first point in favour of the young Lévi-Strauss lay in his contribution to knowledge of South America, which was bound to become a strategic field in the social sciences in wartime America. Métraux was well aware of the Rockefeller Foundation's interest in the South American continent, given the para-diplomatic role it played in the Roosevelt administration's 'Good Neighbour Policy'. In addition, Nelson Rockefeller had just been appointed coordinator of Inter-American Affairs, one of the most dynamic war agencies. Very clearly, this Latin American orientation (both scholarly and political) worked in Lévi-Strauss's favour. The next major argument was that the applicant was a young and promising scholar – as Métraux delicately put it: 'He is a coming man.' The foundation clearly preferred this kind of profile, which seemed a better investment than the old Sorbonne type ... The age factor was not determinant, but it did work against professors who were believed to have their best work behind them. The third argument was Lévi-Strauss's command of English, which Métraux deduced from the young Frenchman's clear familiarity with the American anthropological literature. In fact, as we know, his English was extremely rudimentary at the time. This emphasis on language skills in the assessment goes to show that the Americans were keen to recruit intellectuals who would be able to teach. Finally, the danger to which applicants were exposed played a key, though far from decisive, role – it was a necessary but not sufficient element. From the start, Métraux had been one of Lévi-Strauss's most enthusiastic supporters. Already in 1937, upon receiving his article on the Bororo, the senior scholar had told Lévi-Strauss how 'refreshing' and 'stimulating' he had found the study.[50] In 1940, he gave this judgement concrete and decisive effect.

The third letter, dated 10 October 1940, came from Professor John P. Gillin, a colleague of Métraux's at Yale's Institute of Human Relations. It deployed a national research strategy argument, and emphasized the fact that Claude Lévi-Strauss specialized in regions that were little known: 'The contribution of his knowledge and skills to the research centre on South American anthropology would be of great importance to American science.' This letter stressed the current interest of North American anthropology in South America, an area of specialization which was not well represented among American scholars, and highlighted the emergence of a Yale team engaged in research on the unity of the American world, which would be strengthened by the participation of Lévi-Strauss. The felicitous timing of his application was described, retrospectively, by the man himself in terms of a 'combination of circumstances. American anthropologists were beginning to think that they had looked at all Indians of North America and it was time to find something else. They looked south. My work came at the right time.'[51]

The fourth recommendation came from Georges Devereux, a Franco-American anthropologist who hailed from Jewish Romania via Paris, where he had trained with Mauss and Rivet. In the early 1930s, he had done his doctoral studies in anthropology at Berkeley, with Lowie and Kroeber, before doing extended fieldwork among the Mohave Indians. He was thus a young anthropologist (born, like Lévi-Strauss, in 1908), and the future founder of ethnopsychiatry, who added his favourable opinion to that of the others.[52] In addition to the criteria already invoked, he stressed his colleague's character as 'well-bred and most likeable', which was how his São Paulo friends had described the Lévi-Strauss couple. This small point was to reassure the Americans about Lévi-Strauss's future participation, should he be selected, in the social life of American academia, which was more demanding (and more all-engrossing) than in France. Roman Jakobson arrived in New York at the same time as Lévi-Strauss, benefiting from the same programme. But the linguist, widely recognized as brilliant, was almost refused because of his strong and irascible character, which made it difficult to imagine 'how he would fit in as a member of the permanent faculty at a university'.[53] In order to have any chance of being selected, then, one had to be not only brilliant, productive, English-speaking and young, but also good company and able to satisfy the demands of campus life. In this respect, Lévi-Strauss did not fully meet the requirements. Although infallibly courteous, he was also fiercely independent and protective of his personal life. It is unlikely that he would have had tea with his colleagues or listened to student complaints about their love life . . . On 6 November 1940, a final recommendation arrived from Julian H. Steward, of the Smithsonian Institute, Bureau of Ethnology, Washington DC, which further elaborated on the importance, at that stage, of recruiting anthropologists specializing in South America. And, indeed, barely arrived in the US, Lévi-Strauss would be contacted by this bureau, which was then coordinating a major collective work, *The Handbook of South American Indians*, edited, between 1940 and 1947, by the same Julian H. Steward.

At that point, Alvin Johnson considered that he had enough information on the Lévi-Strauss case. As he concluded in a letter dated 13 November 1940: 'He is undoubtedly a very good man and working in a field which requires more personnel.' He thus gave his support to inviting the young French anthropologist. It remained, however, to convince Rockefeller Foundation advisers, who were clearly a bit perplexed by Lévi-Strauss's meagre scientific production, quite apart from the fact that he had not published – or even written – his dissertation. Pressed to make difficult decisions, the Rockefeller Foundation expressed concern at the 'lack of documentary evidence of his scientific capacity'. It was at that moment that Paulo Duarte's letter of 2 January 1941 – addressed to Tracy B. Kittredge, head of the social sciences division at the Rockefeller Foundation – arrived. This letter of support did not raise any new points, but lent considerable political weight. As we will recall, Paulo Duarte was a friend of Mário de Andrade and the São Paulo group and a former member of the Brazilian diplomatic corps in Europe. Having remained close to Lévi-Strauss, he offered the powerful argument that the historical circumstances of the French defeat had prevented the candidate from completing his scholarly work, as he otherwise would have, and emphasized how eagerly awaited was the publication of his fieldwork study. A true friend, Duarte went to great lengths, repeatedly taking the time to meet with Alvin Johnson and foundation representatives. After a period of hesitation, Kittredge finally gave his positive recommendation and the foundation committed to providing a $5,000 grant over a two-year period.

A sum of $1,000 was set aside for travel costs, and an annual salary of $2,000 was transferred to the New School, which was to directly remunerate their new faculty member. In fact, Alvin Johnson had already sent an invitation, before the foundation's official support was granted. Aware of the urgency of the situation and the fact that Lévi-Strauss had been provided with private funds by his aunt, Aline Caro-Delvaille, long settled in the United States, Alvin Johnson must have sent his letter of invitation in January 1941. This slight muddle reflected the different rhythms of the two institutions: on the one hand, the New School, attuned to personal drama and quick to respond with an invitation that amounted to an employment contract; and, on the other, the Rockefeller Foundation, attentive to the requirements of American academia and following a procedure involving multiple checks, was necessarily much slower.

Money was the crux of the issue, but a visa was still needed from the state department at a time when the latter's policy was restrictive, supported by a very isolationist public opinion and a Congress that was not keen to welcome refugees from Old Europe. Roosevelt and the war did not fundamentally change matters. The vigorous mobilization of certain segments of American civil society contrasted sharply with the slow pace of consular bureaucracy and the openly xenophobic tendencies of some state department officials. There were, therefore, never any guarantees. Generally speaking, the process was simpler for academic refugees with an invitation to teach, needing an off-quota visa, but administrative red tape could trip anyone up; with a political past that was a bit too 'red' and financial prospects that were a bit too uncertain, the visa would be denied. Yet Alvin Johnson stayed on top of it and Claude Lévi-Strauss finally obtained his visa without mishap. Nobody appears to have been aware of his socialist militant youth.

The rescue calculus thus included complex negotiations between the Rockefeller Foundation, the New School and the state department, in which scientific legitimacy and financial means played a part, as well as having an acceptable sociopolitical profile and an assessment of the risk of persecution. In France, it all depended on a highly variable Vichy policy towards those whom the regime considered to be undesirables. It was a fine sieve that only allowed a happy few to escape from southern France, primarily through the port of Marseille, where pariahs from all over Europe had gathered. Lévi-Strauss was among them. Equipped with his affidavit and visas, he still needed to find a ship.

Exile

'The deportation of convicts' [54]

Hanging around the Marseille docks in February 1941, he found a ship that was due to set sail for Martinique. In addition, it was one of the liners of the Compagnie des transports maritimes, of which he had been a faithful client during his Brazil years. Recognized by a company employee who

The *Capitaine Paul Lemerle*, the ship on which Claude Lévi-Strauss
embarked in March 1941.

'still saw [him] as a minor ambassador of French culture',[55] he managed
to get a ticket on the *Capitaine Paul Lemerle*, which pulled up anchor on
24 March 1941, setting a course for the West Indies. Unlike his comrades
in misfortune, Lévi-Strauss did not have to avail himself of the services of
Varian Fry and his Emergency Rescue Committee – a major actor on the
exile network.[56] With his invitation and his own maritime connections, he
was repeatedly given special privileges, due to his rich transatlantic history
with the Compagnie des transports maritimes. This proved to be quite
useful, for the crossing on this occasion was certainly no vacation, and a
very far cry from earlier voyages: 'I did not begin to understand the situation until the day we went on board between two rows of helmeted *gardes
mobiles* with sten guns in their hands, who cordoned off the quayside,
preventing all contact between the passengers and their relatives or friends
who had come to say goodbye, and interrupting leave-taking with jostling
and insults. Far from being a solitary adventure, it was more like the
deportation of convicts. What amazed me even more than the way we were
treated was the number of passengers. About 350 people were crammed
onto a small steamer which – as I was immediately to discover – boasted
only two cabins with, in all, seven bunks.'[57] Lévi-Strauss was given a bed
in one of the two cabins on the *Capitaine Paul Lemerle*, an extraordinary
honour. Since, in addition to its human cargo, the boat carried clandestine
freight, it stopped many times along the Mediterranean and African coasts.

With the heat intensifying as they approached the tropics, remaining
in the hold below became increasingly impossible, and the boat soon

transformed into a floating menagerie, with all human activities being transferred on deck: laundry, cooking, as well as the more crucial matter of 'sanitary arrangements', which were quite difficult to perform in the two huts whose resinous pine planks became saturated with urine – a veritable ordeal for the more delicately constituted. This overloaded human cargo ship, drifting across the Atlantic, conjured up several images: of the slave trade, as well as of immigrants to New York at the turn of the twentieth century. But in Lévi-Strauss's biography, the journey was presented as a parody of the ethnographic voyage: this time it was the future refugees, 'fodder for the concentration camps',[58] who were the tribes at risk of extinction. Comfort gave way to hardship, small numbers to masses, luxury to poverty, and the pull of the Other to push from one's own country. Through whichever prism one sees it, this ghost-ship crossing appeared as the flipside of the epic of exploration, and as a metonym for mass exile during the war years. More than this, when writing *Tristes Tropiques* fifteen years later, the 1941 voyage had become for Lévi-Strauss, in retrospect, the ultimate and chaotic herald of a new era, the symbol of a saturated modernity, a hostile world that he no longer recognized as his own.

Among the human cargo on this ragged galley, however, there were quite a few distinguished passengers – artists, intellectuals, union leaders, politicians, journalists, doctors, lawyers: an entire elite of learned professions who had been forced out of Hitler's Europe, either because they were Jewish or because their political opposition had made them targets. Thus, there was a steady parade of silhouettes on deck whose prestigious names – Anna Seghers, Victor Serge, André Breton, to name but a few – jarred with their appearance, made haggard by their circumstances (not to mention the high seas). Victor Serge, a former companion of Lenin, thus appeared to the wide-eyed former militant socialist as 'a prim and elderly spinster'[59] whose stiff manners did not quite match his idea of a revolutionary. As for André Breton, 'very much out of place *dans cette galère*, he strode up and down the few empty spaces left on deck; wrapped in his thick nap overcoat, he looked like a blue bear'.[60] Lévi-Strauss recounted his first meeting with André Breton. During a stop-over in Casablanca, he overheard him state his name to the passport control official and decided to introduce himself, as a disciple would to a master. The difference in status between the thirty-two-year-old anthropologist and this leading surrealist was evident in the sense of intimidation the former felt in the presence of the figure of such considerable renown, whose dignified manner and 'regal aloofness'[61] – so anachronistic and out-of-place under current circumstances – he very much appreciated. The young man, star-struck yet also curious, sent the 'master' a note which started off a long series of exchanges on the question of the relationship between the work of art and the document – a crucial issue for both surrealists and anthropologists, already much debated in the early 1930s in the pages of the journal *Documents.*[62] One is perhaps surprised by these extended considerations on the nature of art undertaken in the middle of nowhere – they conjure up images of the two men, unshakeable in their gravitas but also incorrigible in their frivolity, immersed in their pure love of discussion, like a luxury they could no longer afford but indulged in nonetheless. Yet the scene is as plausible as it is outlandish. The same goes for Lévi-Strauss's flirtations with young female German refugees, to which he readily confessed, whereas he was usually rather reserved on such matters. These dalliances were symptoms of the historical collisions that set the emotional compass spinning, in a tremendous urge to live, at last, in the moment. It was neither the right place nor the right time to begin a romance; yet precisely because so glib in those circumstances, erotic and/or sentimental love had become necessary. Lévi-Strauss was, in fact, chasing two young German women as the boat arrived, one month after having left Marseille, in the bay of Fort-de-France, Martinique.

Vichy in the tropics

In Martinique, the refugees were treated as prisoners, placed under house arrest or penned up in camps outside Fort-de-France, in Balata, Pointe-Rouge and Lazaret. Claude Lévi-Strauss has described with sardonic humour the ship's arrival in Fort-de-France, in a Martinique where the officials felt confusedly guilty for the defeat in which they had taken no part. Zealous supporters of Pétain, the officers received this collection of anti-France rabble – Jews, foreigners, surrealists and anarchists – as a 'cargo of scapegoats, on whom these gentlemen could relieve their feelings'.[63] André Breton remembered the insulting commentary each of them received upon landing: 'In Pointe-Rouge (one of the camps on the island), to a young and most distinguished scholar, who was to pursue his research in New York [i.e. Claude Lévi-Strauss], they said: "No, you are not French, you are a Jew, and the Jews who call themselves French are worse than the foreign Jews" [. . .] To me: "A writer. Supposedly invited to give conferences and publish art books. A fat lot of good that'll do the Americans now, won't it! French? He can disembark, but under close surveillance".'[64]

In *Tristes Tropiques*, as in *Martinique: Snake Charmer* (a collection of Breton texts interspersed with drawings by André Masson, published in 1947), one feels the clash of discordant sentiments. For the Martinique that Lévi-Strauss was then discovering was first and foremost a harsh colonial order, rekindled by the transplantation of the Vichy revolution to the tropics.[65] Removed from the theatre of war and yet at the same time highly strategic, and surrounded by British and American ships, Martinique and Guadeloupe were then in the throes of severe repression and aggressive propaganda. Breton mocked the 'pathetic praise lavished in pidgin French on the latest measures by "good papa Pétain"'.[66] The refugees, French and non-French alike, felt the force of arbitrary colonial power and were subjected to abuse and humiliation: their nationality was denied, and the Jews among them were forced to assume that exclusive identity, which they had hitherto believed they could treat with a degree of indifference.

Denigrated and humiliated, the refugees were also ordered not to make contact with the 'coloured element. They are big children. Whatever you might say to them, they would misinterpret.'[67] The French police in tropical kit demonstrated a farcical zeal, presenting a spectacle of sham authority, both meticulous and impotent, devoured by mosquitoes. Lévi-Strauss observed a kind of siege excitement – 'soldiers suffering from a collective form of mental derangement, which would have repaid anthropological study'[68] – which he attributed to insularity and the excessive drinking of punch. This French police conjured up what Breton imagined to be characteristics of the German police. Albeit still at the metaphorical stage, the comparison between Nazism and colonialism – which would be fully developed later – was thus already present in the popular beliefs that Lévi-Strauss describes but does not comment on: some Martinique inhabitants 'explained that Hitler was none other than Jesus Christ who had come back to earth to punish the white race for having failed to follow his teachings during the previous two thousand years'.[69]

But Martinique was more than just this little island hell; it was also the site of the reunion of Lévi-Strauss (and the surrealists) with the New World. Free to move about – here again, a privilege he owed to his previous patronage of the transatlantic line – he was 'rediscovering with delight a host of vegetable species that were familiar to [him] since [his] stay in Amazonia'.[70] He kept himself busy with an inventory of the archaeological collections gathered by a religious order in Fort-de-France, and, losing himself somewhere on the Mont Pelé, enjoyed 'unforgettable walks across the island, which seemed so much more classically exotic than the South American mainland. It was like a deep arborized agate set in a ring of black, silver-flecked beaches, and in the valleys, which were brimming with a milk-white mist, one could only just sense the presence – more perceptible to the ear, through the sound of dripping moisture, than to the eye – of the huge, soft, feathery fronds of the tree-ferns, rising above the living fossils of their trunks.'[71]

From Fort-de-France, Lévi-Strauss was admitted as an immigrant into San Juan, Puerto Rico. *Tristes Tropiques* relates yet another episode with the police there, which closes a series of West Indian vignettes, itself part of the Brazilian memories, and all designed to convey a sense of that new government of men by administrations whose hysteria was equal to their ineffectiveness. The American police was no less ignorant than the French: the anthropological documents that Lévi-Strauss was carrying with him – fieldwork notes, bibliographical index cards (some in German!), vocabulary lists of native languages – were examined with the utmost suspicion by American customs officers, who were quick to interpret them as coded messages. Lévi-Strauss was thus placed under house arrest, until an FBI expert allayed their suspicions, and only after Jacques Soustelle – his former colleague at the Musée de l'Homme, and now an important envoy of Free France in South America – had interceded on his behalf. Lévi-Strauss left that American enclave, giving his impression of North America a permanent Spanish inflection, and arrived in New York on 28 May 1941 – nearly two months after leaving Marseille.

At that time, Dina was in Camcabra, the Cévennes home of Claude's parents, where she was writing a final letter to Mário de Andrade. Dismissed by the ministry of education for being Jewish, she managed to eke out a meagre living doing private philosophy tutoring in Montpellier.

She described the rationing, the wooden clogs (that she hated), the long lines to buy cigarettes. Having retained her love of beautiful fabrics and fancy dresses, she relied on a wealth of imagination to get by on that front. 'Brazil and easy living seem so far away! Many other things also seem far and forever gone: the lust for life (which as you know was never solidly anchored in me) and faith in the future of human beings.'[72] Dina talks of the all-pervading lie, the moral faults discovered in others and oneself, as if the war was shedding a cruel and revealing light: 'You know my husband has left Europe. He has arrived in New York after a journey of sixty-five days! He is now out of reach, if not out of trouble, and he might still need the help of his Brazilian friends.'[73] This kind thought shows that Claude and Dina Lévi-Strauss had parted if not on good terms, at least in agreement, amidst the dramatic circumstances that turned their separation into the end of a marriage, but also the end of a world. Why did not Dina follow her husband? Did the latter propose that she accompany him and take advantage of his invitation? Everything suggests he did. As early as 8 May 1940, although the spouses had separated several months prior, in a letter to Marcel Mauss concerning a possible American grant Lévi-Strauss is adamant that his departure should not interrupt his wife's professional career and suggests a similar arrangement to the one they had in Brazil, suggesting that she be detached from the ministry and paid by the Service des oeuvres.[74] On 21 July 1941, Lévi-Strauss wrote to Dr Rivet from New York: 'I must inform you that my wife and I have been separated since the outbreak of the war. [. . .] Before I left France, we would meet frequently, since the ministry had appointed us both to Montpellier, where she resided. She declined to take advantage of my departure to come along and try her luck in the United States.'[75] Dina herself had written to Mauss a few months earlier: 'I don't think I can apply for the US position. You know why. You know in what mental state I find myself. If I agreed today, I am not sure I would be able to honour the commitment a month or two from now. The very effort of making a decision is more than I can bear at the moment. [. . .] I might be letting go a unique opportunity. But I doubt I can still feel regret. [. . .] Turning this down is fulfilling – as much as I am able at the moment – an intellectual obligation.'[76]

Why did Dina Lévi-Strauss stay, when, from autumn 1940, everything seemed to suggest that the situation was only going to get worse? While we cannot know for certain, she probably did not want to follow a husband who was no longer really hers. A legitimate sense of pride on the part of an independent woman, who was also professionally qualified. Staying was also a way of saying she could go on living, and above all survive, without him. As her letters to Mário de Andrade show, she was still an enthusiastic young woman, with admittedly dark moods at times, but with a desire to live, and an intellectual character that would not let anyone else dictate what she was to do. Subconsciously, she might also have yearned to fully experience history, however tragic, as one of its actors. She remained close to Lévi-Strauss's parents, who were hiding in the Cévennes, and then in the Gard region, under the vigilant watch of Pierre Dreyfus's family.

The final sentence of her last letter to Mário de Andrade read: 'My self has ceased to appear to me as a privileged and intangible core, and I am fast dissolving, like the Ines in my novel that will probably never get written: "One day, Ines disappeared. She was never found again – she had changed into a river."'[77] This fantasy of dissolution is arresting in many respects, as an omen of her future underground life, as well as of her exit from this story, since she definitively left Claude Lévi-Strauss's life, which, once again, turned towards new horizons.[78]

10

A Frenchman in New York City: Exile and Intellectual Invention (1941–1944)

> I felt myself going back in time no less when I went to work every morning in the American room of the New York Public Library. There, under its neo-classical arcades and between walls panelled with old oak, I sat near an Indian in a feather headdress and a beaded buckskin jacket – who was taking notes with a Parker pen.
>
> Claude Lévi-Strauss, 'New York in 1941'[1]

As opposed to his Brazilian stay, the six years Claude Lévi-Strauss spent in New York City, between 1941 and 1947, are hardly mentioned in the self-analysis that is *Tristes Tropiques*. They surface as a trace in a paragraph on the mineral beauty of New York City, which is itself part of a broader commentary on urban America. Luckily, there are many other documents available, in addition to the few texts that were written subsequently, including the highly original 'New York in 1941'. For in New York, just as in Brazil, the way exile was perceived and experienced in the moment may differ from later recollections.

Exile is a fundamentally ambivalent experience. In 1941, Lévi-Strauss and his comrades had escaped the worst, but at the cost of being uprooted from their world and plunged into the unknown. As Patrick Waldberg, a friend of the surrealists, was later to say: they 'wore the alarm and terror of the year 1940 on their faces'.[2] Befuddled, bewildered and bony, they landed in a frightening city. Oddly, and for reasons that were not entirely specific to him, Lévi-Strauss was to feel right at home there. He always said so. These years were in every respect very intense ones, and they instilled in him a strong attraction for anything American. A young and promising academic, he had no problem circulating freely between the various strata of the city, and between the various European exile milieus and American society. He successfully and productively combined his thirst for discovery, his inclination for hard work, and a frivolous Bohemian daily life, which was for the first time free of family responsibilities. At thirty-two years old, Lévi-Strauss was among the youngest of the exiles. From an early age, the young man had had considerable family obligations, providing for his parents financially.[3] Later, back in Europe and approaching his forties, he was to look older than his years. A young man among the old, he would later become an elder who was not as old as he looked, and then, due to his longevity, always the eldest. Lévi-Strauss's existence ran counter to the traditional ages of life: in New York, ten years late, he led the life of a twenty-year-old bachelor, and in the emotional maelstrom of exile had one affair after the other – with a penchant for pretty, young Russians with a French education.[4]

For the biographer, the main challenge of the New York moment is of course to revisit the intellectual – as well as social, political, institutional and historical – genealogy of structuralism, which was officially born out of what would become *The Elementary Structures of Kinship*. A theoretical frame of reference that was conceived in New York and not Paris, in the 1940s and not the 1960s, structuralism has recently been the subject of new research that has challenged the whole idea of autonomous scientific creation, emphasizing its material, social, ideological and epistemological contexts.[5] A new historiography, inspired by the fields of science studies and sociology of ideas, has allowed for an approach that is both less idealist and richer in scholarly invention.[6]

In this chapter, structuralism – a method and a worldview, a paradigm in the strong sense of the term – confronts the experience of exile in all its diversity. It will not, therefore, confine itself to the traditional account, according to which Lévi-Strauss invented structuralism in New York because it was there that he met the linguist Roman Jakobson and had access to the wealth of resources of American libraries. The story is both more complex and more interesting. Let us retrace it at the archival level.

In the mugginess of a New York summer (1941)

Claude Lévi-Strauss arrived on 28 May 1941, but the haze of heat and humidity that enveloped the city on that day deprived him of the anticipated spectacle of arriving at the island of Manhattan. This spectacle had already acquired an iconic status in the Western imagination, but it remained a mental shock. Through the haze, the young anthropologist only felt he was 'in front of a marvellous model, whose actual dimensions were impossible to grasp'.[7] The welcome committee was there: his aunt Aline Caro-Delvaille,[8] who had gone to great lengths to have her nephew admitted on American soil; Aline's daughter Thérèse, who was half American; the Duartes (Paulo and Juanita) and Rirette Nizan, his cousin, who had managed to leave France with her children but had no news from her husband Paul, of whose death she was officially informed only a few years later.[9]

These events are known to us today thanks to the fifty-odd letters sent by Claude Lévi-Strauss to his parents, between 25 April 1941 and 13 September 1942.[10] A letter was sent once a week without fail, and together they represent a first-hand document of the beginning of Lévi-Strauss's New York adventure, offering a different perspective from that of the few texts he subsequently wrote about this period. The tone of these letters has a certain freshness: the young man was quickly won over by the city, which clearly titillated the city dweller in him. He demonstrated a great capacity to adapt to his American environment, which he immediately perceived as a favourable one. So much so that the letters offer a happy, light-hearted and even carefree chronicle, even if they also express worries about his close friends and relatives, his parents, Dina, the Dreyfuses, as well as the Cahens, the Belgian friends of his parents who had also fled to Camcabra. We should also keep in mind that, expecting censorship, he sometimes encrypted his messages, especially those dealing with international relations and general politics, and that, generally speaking, he was always mindful of the need to reassure his parents regarding his own situation. His letters thus 'read like word games',[11] and are rife with tensions, between happiness and heartache, between discovery and nostalgia, between work and politics, expressing the urge both to retreat into work and to participate in the social scene – in short, the very condition of exile in which Claude Lévi-Strauss was now to remain for the next few years.

Prof. Claude L. Strauss, 51 W11th Street, Greenwich Village

On 8 June 1941, Lévi-Strauss informed his parents that they could henceforth write to him at the following address: '51 W11th Street [. . .] in the name of Prof. Claude L. Strauss, The New School, having renamed myself because Lévi-Strauss is the name of a popular raincoat manufacturer [*sic*]'. A new address, a new professional identity, and a new name. The cumbersome homonymy with the blue-jeans giant (whom the French anthropologist did not appear to know) helped the newcomer to immediately dispense with the traditional hurdle that many a migrant must negotiate: the impossibly obscure sound of their names to American ears. He made no comment at the time but he later claimed to have found the imposition of a new name amusing. It is quite clear, however, that the truncation represented a symbolic echo of a 'damaged' identity, as Theodor W. Adorno, another New York refugee, was to call life in exile.[12]

With his salary of $180 per month – which he was gradually to supplement with odd jobs – and his guaranteed position, the young professor was certainly not wealthy, but neither did he experience any dramatic downward mobility. He found life quite affordable, especially the cost of food (always an important concern for him): one could be well and abundantly fed for a dollar a day. Like others, he was struck by the sumptuous abundance and practice of meals: lunch counters, delis, with no set times for eating and a self-service culture that he found very much to his taste. Always very detailed on the subject, he often provided descriptions of his meals, clearly designed as much to reassure his parents as to initiate them into the charms of American life. His typical fare consisted in 'a thick slice of roast beef, pork or lamb, or a hamburger steak (ground meat) with mashed potatoes and spinach, or some other vegetables, with butter, and according to taste, small buns, rye bread or English

False identity papers of Claude's father, aka 'Raymond Luce-Saunier', who spent
the war years in hiding in the Cévennes, while his son was living in the
United States under the name of Claude L. Strauss.

bread. I rarely have dessert, but when I do, it is most often a fruit pie –
blueberry, apple or pineapple – with occasionally a scoop of ice-cream
on top.'[13] As if seized by a pang of remorse, at the end of another such
description he added: 'I get sick with anger and sadness when I think of
Europe.'[14]

The major concern of his first week was finding a place to live. The ease
with which he secured one, and the surprise of discovering such havens in
the heart of New York, left him very favourably impressed by the city and
even inspired comparisons with the Paris of the Romantics. He was later
to write: 'The French surrealists and their friends settled in Greenwich
Village, where, just a few subway stops from Times Square, one could still
lodge – just as in Paris in Balzac's time – in a small two- or three-storey
house with a tiny garden at the back. A few days after my arrival, when
visiting Yves Tanguy, I discovered and immediately rented, on the street

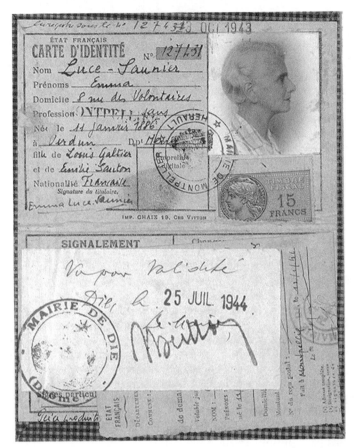

False identity papers of Claude's mother, aka 'Emma Luce-Saunier'. Both kept their first names and the initials of their true family name (Lévi-Strauss).

where he lived, a studio whose window faced a neglected garden. You reached it by way of a long basement corridor leading to a private stairway in the rear of a red-brick house.'[15] The configuration of the place, which made for a calm and secret existence, away from the gaze of passers-by at the other end of the underground passage, very much suited the new tenant. The 'quirky' apartment, 'in the elegant part of Greenwich Village, between 5th and 6th Avenues (the equivalent, let's say, of the part of boulevard Raspail that is towards the rue de Grenelle and rue du Bac)', immediately appealed to him, not to mention the modest rent – $50 per month, including the services of a cleaning lady, a 'beautiful negress' – and the automatic telephone in the hallway that recorded all messages received in his absence between 8 a.m. and 10 p.m.

But what appealed to him above all was that his studio was in fact an artist's studio, of which there were many in the neighbourhood: a large single room with wide windows that joined a glass skylight. He was thus able to live in an artist's studio in a neighbourhood, the Village, which, since even before 1914, had been the heart of New York's cultural and night life, with its many jazz bars, and which was the very epitome of the artist's quarter – hence the more or less accurate parallels that Lévi-Strauss, like many other refugees, made with the Paris he had left behind and according to which Greenwich Village was 'the local Montparnasse, halfway between Point du Jour and Porte d'Orléans'. For a while, he toyed with the idea of moving into the more academic Columbia University neighbourhood, on the Upper West Side of Manhattan, but the Bohemian ambiance and the cheap rents of the Village convinced him otherwise, all the more so given that his new residence was right next to the New School, located at the corner of 12th Street and 5th Avenue.

New York, first impressions

Being a foreigner only further sharpened, as if this were necessary, his critical urban gaze. In his first few weeks, Lévi-Strauss went all over Manhattan, on 'fantastic night walks'.[16] As in São Paulo, he marvelled at the contrast between the geometric, rational and orthogonal grid and the urban chaos. New York is a 'giant mess'. 'Whereas I expected everything to be uniform and standardized, I found it offers much more room for whimsy than in Europe.'[17] Some of the apartments he saw, and some of the shop windows, were 'incredibly bizarre'.[18] He quickly picked up on the exotic niches he would spot from the bus in the great multicultural chaos of the city: 'oriental bazars crammed with cotton fabrics and Hindu, Mexican and Indonesian woollens' that recalled 'our Moroccan bazars, only more refined. Everything you can find here could just as well come from European antique shops.'[19]

He would describe the architecture of a skyscraper, or of the entire Rockefeller Center, where his aunt Aline worked; he found Grand Central Station 'a surprise', since there were no trains to be seen – the platforms all being underground. He was struck by 'the dignified manner and courtesy of the common people. At no point does one feel social difference.' The street, itself, was 'a sumptuous spectacle undergoing constant renewal'.[20] Abuzz with excitement, he followed his surrealist friends into small bars 'full of sailors and prostitutes, all straight out of Mac Orlan', to listen to black music. He spent a Saturday night at the great Harlem dance club, the Savoy. The scene recalled a similar episode he had witnessed upon his arrival six years earlier in São Paulo, with carnival in full swing, but this time with the energy of African American New York, which was revealed to him in one evening: 'There was a huge black crowd dancing beautifully to the wonderful orchestra music, but with none of the African character of the Brazilian carnival – American style, but still totally possessed. Starting at about 2 o'clock in the morning, it became truly extraordinary, with the dance contest. The contestants were kids of fifteen to eighteen years old, Harlem rabble, and the girls had fashioned themselves incredible costumes, somewhere between a gymnast and a ballerina, and their dance moves were the most prodigious I have ever seen of this genre. An unbridled and acrobatic improvised dance, in which the boys grab hold of their partners (or the other way around), throw them up into the air, invent a thousand somersaults, all the while keeping the tempo and never losing the beat.'[21] In his appreciation of dance, as in other respects, New York was weighed against São Paulo, revealing an already polished sensibility that could draw comparisons within America. Indeed, from the start, his US experience constituted a third term between the Old and New Worlds, which required a 'form of triangulation'[22] that made any straightforward comparison moot.

In the end, Lévi-Strauss avoided two reductionist perspectives that are characteristic of exile narratives about New York: one consisted in a curmudgeonly tit-for-tat comparison with Europe, generally detrimental to the host country, which became seen as a model of inhumanity, materialism and uniformity, according to a firmly established and articulate French anti-Americanism;[23] the other, less cranky in tone, attempted to find equivalents in order to fold the unknown back into the known. Gustave Cohen, a former medieval literature professor at the Sorbonne and a future colleague of Lévi-Strauss at the New School and the École libre des hautes études, thus saw the skyscrapers as 'modern Cathedrals'.[24] As for the Swiss Denis de Rougemont, New York was an 'Alpine'[25] city of remarkable summits – the Empire State, the Chrysler, Rockefeller Center – and of deep, wind-swept valleys. It was rarer to find those who could appreciate the inordinate scale proper to New York, which gave it a specifically American allure, and which required allowing one's eyes to adjust. Lévi-Strauss, from the start, was one of these few who, in his very first letter from New York, quickly described his arrival and added: 'It is incredibly disproportionate.'[26] He saw that understanding the 'Big Apple' demanded that one grasp the full extent of this change of scales: 'Those who maintain that New York is ugly are simply the victims of an illusion of the senses. Not having yet learnt to move into a different register, they persist in judging New York as a city, and criticize the avenues, parks and monuments. And no doubt, objectively, New York is a city, but a European sensibility perceives it according to a quite different scale, the scale of European landscapes; whereas American landscapes transport us into a far vaster system for which we have no equivalent. The beauty of New York has to do not with its being a city, but with the fact, obvious as soon as we abandon our preconceptions, that it transposes the city to the level of an artificial landscape in which the principles of urbanism cease to operate, the only significant values being the rich velvety quality of the light, the sharpness of distant outlines, the awe-inspiring precipices between the skyscrapers and the sombre valleys, dotted with multicoloured cars looking like flowers.'[27]

This conception of New York as exceeding the scale of a city was later to be conceptualized through the term 'megalopolis', itself coined by a French exile to the United States, Jean Gottmann, who remained for a time after the war. Being a foreigner was no doubt necessary to operate this switch in visual 'registers' that Claude Lévi-Strauss invited his readers to make, and to appreciate the unprecedented quality of these urban formations on the East Coast of the United States. This approach to the city as both somehow falling short of – Rougemont felt like a 'contemporary of prehistory' there – and exceeding Western urban modernity invited geological references and encouraged Baudelairean reveries on Manhattan as an 'immense landscape of mineral and water'.

The anthropologist as New York artist

In addition to his long strolls and general initiation into New York life, Claude Lévi-Strauss deliberately and resolutely engaged in a triple offensive in the summer of 1941: producing his first major anthropological work, acquiring a mastery of the English language and making vigorous forays into the American academic world.

In writing *The Family and Social Life of the Nambikwara*, Lévi-Strauss intended to address two pressing concerns. First, he recognized that he had to publish quickly in English to make a name for himself in the American academic market – hence also the crucial decision to translate his own work, enabling him both to build up his bibliography (still rather limited in English-language publications) and to acquire a better proficiency in the language, of which he only had rudimentary command. Second, this work was in a sense overdue. Thus, over the month of July, he wrote two hundred pages based on his fieldwork notes, following the classic model for producing a monograph. This text, originally conceived as a passport into American academia, was in fact to serve as his minor thesis and was published in French in 1948, though never in English. Too long for an article, too short for a doctoral dissertation, the format he opted for was not the most strategic. However, what mattered most to Lévi-Strauss at that time was to provide an account, at long last, of the anthropological expedition that he had undertaken several years earlier. As he was to impatiently exclaim on a night of hard work: 'I am exasperated by these Indians with whom I have gone through so much, that I have been dragging around with me for so long, and that I have discussed at such length.'[28] Considering that he had written only one article on the Bororo at that time, it is quite clear that his impatience had more to do with a sense of belatedness in the accomplishment of his work, after two wasted years since leaving Brazil.

Much like his friend André Masson, the 'modern monk'[29] he visited at home in Connecticut, Lévi-Strauss locked himself up in his studio and engaged in a kind of head-on confrontation with kinship systems, the subject matter of the magnum opus to come. His apartment then became a true studio: 'There is already a large map of the two Americas on my wall, and on the bookshelves, the collection of books I have begun to acquire from the booksellers that dominate an entire neighbourhood.[30] [. . .] But for the time being, my work consists mostly in the study of these kinship systems, and it is a slow process, which involves preparing enormous sheets of paper, on which I construct complex collages and draw up endless series of grids before I can even begin to put my material in order. When this is finished, I intend to paper the walls with it!'[31] As a kind of Jackson Pollock of anthropology, Lévi-Strauss threw himself into the long and arduous work of disentangling kinship systems. The economy of knowledge, its material dimensions (paper, scissors and glue) and the very nature of the space in which it took place (an artist's studio) brought scientific production close to the artistic process.

Lévi-Strauss bought himself a clarinet. He played occasionally. He listened to 'wonderful concerts of recorded music' on short-wave radio, as well as to news of the surprise attack by the Nazis on Russia. He wrote, on 22 June 1941: 'What an unbelievable series of events this war is!' The scholarly aesthete would have liked to recover his 'Indian paperweight-pipe in sculpted black stone': 'There are just no refined objects for me to lay eyes or hands on, and I miss that terribly.'[32] Over the course of weeks and months, he reconstituted a working atmosphere that suited his taste and satisfied his need to surround himself with beauty in order to give birth to truth. On the coffee table, next to the ashtray – for Lévi-Strauss smoked black Puerto Rican tobacco he would buy in East Harlem – were two statues, 'one in light wood of a squatting golden-eyed warrior ready to pounce, spear in hand. The other was a small totem with two elongated triangles at the top that represented the spread wings of a bird',[33] which came from British Columbia.

Even while engrossed in his artisanal science, Lévi-Strauss was aware of the difficulties he faced in adequately treating the mass of documents and somewhat confusedly sought solutions in related disciplines. Thus, before calling on mathematician André Weil, he reached out to his Belgian colleague Barzin to 'treat the indigenous kinship systems through means of mathematical logic, of which he is a specialist'.[34] In vain. The mathematical solution was much slower than his own empirical processes and the elucidation of one kinship network would take months. A slight let-down for Lévi-Strauss, but a keen interest was aroused in Barzin: 'This flirtation with the savages has got him all excited as if he was doing crossword puzzles or solving a murder mystery.'[35] Similarly, a certain Mr Herzog, a (Hungarian) linguistics professor at Columbia came to give him his 'first lesson in "phonemics", the latest thing in American linguistic science'. After six hours of work, Lévi-Strauss felt 'somewhat enlightened and completely overwhelmed'.[36] These anecdotal episodes of the picaresque epic of modern knowledge reveal first and foremost a favourable situation (with colleagues in the other disciplines within arm's reach), which would later make possible more fruitful connections. When he subsequently revealed that, at the same time, at the same address, and in the same building, the mathematician and engineer Claude E. Shannon was engrossed in encoding information and beginning to formulate his mathematical theory of communication,[37] Lévi-Strauss has us marvelling.[38] Shannon, the father of cybernetics, was an imaginative, playful and nonconformist mind that inspired Jakobson's structure of the six functions of language. Here, in the middle of war, under the Greenwich Village foliage, a scientific paradigm of deciphering was presenting itself, in the form of a coincidence in street addresses.

Refugee or emigrant?

The decision he made early on to translate his article himself was a timely one, and ultimately very significant. Lévi-Strauss forced himself to maintain a high level of productivity – it was a 'real ordeal'[39] – but the linguistic skills he acquired in that painful birthing process proved an excellent long-term investment. Fortunately, he could count on his aunt Aline (an occasional translator), who edited his work, as well as on the help of a 'wonderful publication' – the inexpensive edition of Roget's Thesaurus that he had just acquired.[40] This immersion in the American idiom was solitary and in writing; for the oral dimension, having few opportunities to engage in serious discussion, he indulged in an 'orgy of cinema'. At the start of the new academic year, he was expected to give a course in English at the New School on the sociology of South America. Here again, he jumped in with both feet, and decided to address his students in English and without notes, for fear of being paralysed by his papers in front of his seminar students (ten in all), who were a rather cosmopolitan bunch and little concerned with the purity of the language, which in any case Americans on the whole did not fetishize. In the end, Lévi-Strauss and his students 'mumbled together'[41] on a 'rather cordial basis'.[42] One's relationship to the English language expressed a choice on the meaning and status of one's exile. It might be understood as a temporary refuge, leaving one's national identity unchanged and, in the French case, entailing quite a strong sense of intellectual superiority. This was the case for André Breton, locked up in his fortress and refusing to learn any English, for fear of 'polluting' his French. This type of exile was a kind of migration for support, where the host country served as a simple 'support space' while one waited for better days to come;[43] but exile could conversely involve a longer-term stay and more substantial hybridizations, with lasting transformative effects on the migrant's social, cultural, professional as well as national identity.

A majority of German exiles during the Second World War adopted the emigration approach to exile, which led, for most of them, to American naturalization. French exiles, however, tended not to lose sight of their homeland and cultivated a close-knit community that was rather lacking in curiosity about American reality. Like the counterrevolutionary nobility a few centuries earlier, many French exiles returned after the war having learnt nothing and forgotten nothing, to use Talleyrand's phrase. As we can see, the young Lévi-Strauss somewhat differentiated himself from this national pattern. He matured quickly under 'the sun of exile'[44] and threw himself into American academia with all the enthusiasm of a young man in a hurry, and not without success.

That summer of American acculturation and English immersion through writing was extremely taxing, even producing a sense of physical exhaustion, but on the whole quite productive. Indeed, by the end of summer, he was able to send his 200-page English manuscript to Robert Lowie for editing. The latter read through it and made a few comments: more concrete description needed to be inserted in passages that remained overly theoretical even for the average anthropologist, etc. Lévi-Strauss thought of transforming it to conform to the standards of an American doctoral dissertation. This raised the tricky issue of degree equivalence: 'The French in America generally consider that the *agrégation* is far superior to an American doctoral degree and should not be belittled by those aspiring to the lesser title.'[45] But in Lévi-Strauss's opinion, it seemed on the contrary that 'if one is considering a career in the United States, it would make more sense politically to align oneself with one's future colleagues'.[46] The other key figure in these early months was Alfred Métraux, of whose part in the favourable response he had received from the Rockefeller Foundation Lévi-Strauss was very well aware. In the summer of 1941, Métraux, until then a professor at Yale University, left this position for the Smithsonian Institute in Washington, in order to supervise, under Julian Steward, the vast collaborative project of summarizing the accumulated knowledge on South American Indian societies – the *Handbook of South American Indians* – which, as Lévi-Strauss explained to his parents, was likely to be 'the highest authority in matters of South American anthropology for the half-century to come'.[47] Lévi-Strauss therefore deemed it of the utmost importance that he should take part. Indeed, we should recall, his being invited to the United States had been in part conditioned on such participation. The area assigned to Lévi-Strauss in the overall organization of the work was 'bound to the north by the border of the state of Amazonas, to the west and southwest by the course of the Guapore River, to the east by Xingu, and to the south by a line that bordered southern Cuiabá – in short, almost all of Mato Grosso'.[48] This placed an enormous amount of work on the horizon, but was a project that would establish him squarely within the world of international anthropology, and earn him 'little money but much recognition'.[49] Several months later, on 27 November, he returned from three days in Washington, DC, whose aspect as a 'very rich and somewhat outdated spa town' left him completely cold, but whose Library of Congress blew his mind. Métraux had been given an office there. 'It really does resemble an intellectual hive', with everyone toiling away in their little cell, identical to all the others; the Smithsonian building stood like 'an ulcer in the middle of the palaces' on the Mall, with the charm of old America covered over by new constructions, especially those built to house the recently created war agencies. There he met with Julian Steward, whose very American academic style he found charming: 'tall, a short-cropped moustache and very child-like in his humour'.[50] Rather naively, Lévi-Strauss envisioned his participation in the *Handbook* as an automatic entrée to scholarly recognition: 'I am now assured of making history through a book that will probably remain authoritative for a century.' To his mind, his visit to the Smithsonian sealed his admission 'as a full member of the venerable temple of official American science'.[51] In addition, he was invited to publish part of his manuscript in the prestigious journal *American Anthropologist*, which again seemed to signal his successful and rapid penetration into the American academic world, thanks in no small part to Métraux's fraternal assistance.

Over the course of these early months, and with the laborious and almost monastic summer behind him, Claude L. Strauss threw himself into an active and rather selective social life. A tad opportunistic in his choice of companions, he built a social network that straddled multiple milieus: the world of American anthropology, of course – in which he already aspired to becoming a French beachhead, as demonstrated in his asking his parents to please tell Mauss (95, bd. Jourdan) that he 'was working a lot and that everyone here, especially Boas and Lowie, think of him and ask if there is anything they can do';[52] but also the Latin Americans – with whom he remained even more in contact after being offered the opportunity to direct a Latin American Center, which did indeed see light of day, that he thought would immediately establish him as an expert consultant in Washington where, he said, cultural areas were in fashion. 'My elder colleagues treat me every day with increasing and quite risible esteem. [. . .] But all this (writing letters to places all over South America for the future institute) which is for now very vain and useless, may one day become quite important, and help me create contacts and show myself to advantage.' An ambitious young academic with a touch of lucid fatalism. Beyond New York society life – to which he sometimes yielded at dinners organized by Mima Porter, a rich friend of his aunt Aline, who introduced him for instance to the famous journalist and intellectual Walter Lippmann – he kept to the margins of some of the French exile literary milieus around Henry Bernstein: 'All these people live in too much luxury for me to approach them. New York is such a big city that the different social milieus create as many independent cities that are piled up together but never mix. I would add that for a thousand different reasons I keep my distance from overly agitated worlds, not knowing how far they would go to enlist me, should I take part in them, and all is not sweetness and light in that respect, far from it.'[53] Wary of the New York Gaullists, he had lunch with Pierre Cot, former aviation minister of the Front populaire government, whom he called 'Pierre de Maille'[54] to trick the censors, and with whom he shared socialist affinities. On the French academic front, he maintained the same cautious distance, especially when the possibility of a Franco-Belgian school within the New School began to be discussed. Lévi-Strauss, when consulted on the matter, initially tried to resist the idea, but eventually conceded, immediately regretting the decision and awaiting 'the first opportunity to honourably withdraw'. What mattered to him was the New School itself. In addition, the Americans did not look highly on the creation of such an institution. 'I don't like the direction this affair is taking, far too closely tied to André L.[55] for my taste, and the past week has been so rife with intrigue, secret deals and casuistry that I am utterly sick of it. I made considerable effort to entirely withdraw from it and swore I would never get involved in any public activity of any kind again! Besides, I have more and better things to do than to make phone calls, prepare regulatory statutes and lick the boots of pathetic old men who are worried sick at the idea they might no longer have any undergraduate degrees to deliver. [. . .] The honours of parliamentary life that I used to enjoy so much no longer have any appeal at all, and I do not long for anything but to continue, uninterrupted and hassle-free, the regular pace of work that I have kept up over the past three months, and that could go on for another year given the amount of material I have to sort through and publish.'[56]

At first rather American-oriented and not very French-identified, which distinguished him from other exiles, Lévi-Strauss's position was to evolve over the years. But, from the very first months, he revealed his 'tremendous capacity to circulate across different, and even remote, social worlds'.[57] As Laurent Jeanpierre has pointed out, his retrospective description of New York demonstrated his acute sense of the opportunities for developing (or avoiding) contacts afforded by the condition of exile in the great metropolis. 'Like the urban fabric, the social and cultural fabric was riddled with holes.'[58] The open weave of the city held promises of discovery, caves of Ali Baba, but also offered possibilities for intermediation between sectors and segments that were unaware of one another. The psychological effects of this social mobility and this 'multifaceted'[59] identity were quite apparent to his aunt Aline, who found her nephew 'much more human, more benevolent, more tolerant, more amiable'.[60] Deadpan in his humour, Claude Lévi-Strauss knew how to be a pleasant guest. During a day outing in the country organized by the New School (and financed by its wealthy patrons), he readily entertained his hosts by 'telling stories of savages' and playing the explorer. In French circles, he commented on the national and international situation with a touch of dark humour: 'I have carefully repeated and circulated Tristan Bernard's witticism that brings a smile to everyone's face [. . .]: we are blocking the accounts and counting the Blochs.'[61] As good a way as any to attenuate the anxiety and guilt, the dark side of happy exile in New York.

Bohemian life in New York

Surrealist comradeship

By the end of spring 1941, New York City, already teeming with hundreds of European artists, was hosting an almost entirely reconstituted surrealist community, whose arrival, contrary to legend, did not arouse the intense attention that it has in retrospect. 'It is difficult to picture the atmosphere in New York in the early 1940s, with its motley crew of art refugees, among whom Dalí was the leading figure, closely followed by Pavel Tchelitchev and Eugène Berman, the set and costume designers of the Russian Ballet; Lyonel Feininger, a German American of the Bauhaus who had recently returned from Germany; George Grosz, whose formerly ferocious expressionism was toned down to satisfy an American scene always on the move. [. . .] In this crowd, the arrival of international stars – Chagall, Léger, Mondrian – and the surrealists – in order of arrival, Matta, Tanguy, Max Ernst, Breton and Masson – went unnoticed at first.'[62] Robert Lebel, an art historian and expert on old canvases, who became a close friend of the surrealists in New York, has described the awkward recycling of masters, politely sent on their way, referring even to their 'quasi-anonymity'.

With the exception of Max Ernst, who had just married Peggy Guggenheim, and Tanguy, whose wife Kay Sage was wealthy, the others could barely make ends meet. Over time, the capacity for integration of the painters and sculptors, who were better at making the most of their expatriation and selling their art, was clearly distinguished from that of the poets who, like Breton, or Péret in Mexico, were to remain in dire financial straits. A survival reflex as much as condition for creation, the typical sociability of the surrealists in the interwar years is all the more easily mapped given that they nearly all lived in the Village: Tanguy and Breton on 11th Street, Roberto Matta on 9th Street, Marcel Duchamp nearby, etc. Yet, New York did not really have a café scene, and so the members of the group – reconstituted thanks to Breton's energy, although Masson and Tanguy moved to the country, where the others would visit them on weekends – would meet at one another's apartments.

The young anthropologist was part of this French underground scene of somewhat fading 'stars'. In addition to Breton, Max Ernst, with whom he immediately struck up a friendship and remained close later, Duchamp, the watchful elder, and Tanguy, whose art he admired but whose character he deemed 'not easy', Lévi-Strauss the neo-New Yorker was also to meet an 'extraordinary figure', at his house on the west side of the Hudson: André Masson. And then, not far away, there also lived 'a curious man and even more curious artist. [. . .] He makes extraordinary sound creations that are articulated and made of wire and sheet metal. They are very complicated structures, some of which look like weeping willows, others like clusters of wisteria or orchids hanging from the ceiling, but always purely geometrical, and the whole thing turns and twirls with the least breeze . . .'[63] – this was Alexander Calder. Besides the core figures of the surrealist constellation, Lévi-Strauss was also introduced to its satellites: Robert Lebel, his wife Nina, Georges Duthuit, an art critic and Matisse's son-in-law, the sculptress Isabelle Waldberg and her husband Patrick Waldberg, a flamboyant character whom Lévi-Strauss described to his parents thus: 'He lives as a rentier on an allowance that he receives from who knows where for who knows what reason, an inheritance probably, which is parsimoniously dispensed by a bank since he is quite the "hothead". [. . .] He is a rather crazy, disorganized fellow, who had already led the craziest of lives, sometimes sleeping out on benches, sometimes leading the high life, but always very endearing.'[64] Waldberg, whose art historian's eye and familiarity with the Musée de l'Homme in the 1930s endeared him to Lévi-Strauss, never disappointed the latter's admiring curiosity. In addition to his multiple lives, Lévi-Strauss was to join the Office of Strategic Services in 1943, thus adding secret agent to his long list of professions. Waldberg, very close to the young scholar whom he saw increasingly taking part in the group's activities, also gives us a lovely portrait of Lévi-Strauss at the time: 'He appeared to me to be endowed with what I would call physical dignity: a slender and svelte body, an elongated face with chiselled features, an intense and scrutinizing gaze, sometimes dreamy and melancholy, and sometimes on the contrary staring fixedly, as if in a state of high alert, a rather constantly grave expression on his face, sometimes giving way to the most Nerval-like of smiles – all this made me think of some Spanish Grandee, an inquisitor of science, who would gladly trade the study of points of honour for that of the *"point supreme"*.[65]

Lévi-Strauss and the surrealists (Breton especially) shared the same elegant manners, which gave their conversations an air of ceremony and urbanity that already felt obsolete at the time, an aristocratic feel and a touch of dandyism, obvious in the case of Breton, but also present in Lévi-Strauss.[66] The latter was quickly made part of the games and activities imported from the surrealists of interwar Paris: charades, tarot card readings, exquisite corpse games, as well as 'truth games, whose point was to reveal everything while never falling into obscenity or vulgarity. All things considered, it sometimes reminded me of "Les Précieuses" and the salons of the Hôtel de Rambouillet.'[67]

They wandered around the city together, sampling exotic restaurants. The ritual surrealist trips to the flea markets were replaced by scouting for primitive objects. Claude Lévi-Strauss often recounted how Max Ernst discovered a little German antique dealer on Third Avenue who sold him Amerindian artefacts: 'Max Ernst told us about the dealer. We had very little money, so whichever one of us had a few dollars would purchase the coveted object. When Ernst was broke, he would let the others know. Since our antique dealer had found an outlet, more and more objects became available. In fact, [. . .] they came from a major museum that was getting rid of them because they were considered duplicates of works in their collection. As if there could be duplicates! When the dealer understood that he had a market, he became the intermediary between us and the museum.' The final stage of the process had the entire surrealist group visiting the storage facility of the Museum of the American Indian in the Bronx and directly selecting objects, which would then appear in the shop on Third Avenue a few days later. This kind of windfall defined New York for these exiles, and exemplified the 'fundamental harmony'[68] between Breton and Lévi-Strauss, which still fires our imagination today, with its renewal of the alliance between art and science.[69] This surprising friendship was forged in the convivial atmosphere of a lackadaisical existence, given vitality by the 'climate of intellectual ferment'[70] that characterized the group. Indeed, both men had one foot in the nineteenth century and worked on the same material – the irrational and myth – but each in their own way. These exchanges between surrealism and anthropology were nothing new, but in the New York of the war years Lévi-Strauss recognized his indebtedness: he owed to the surrealists – and in particular to the infallible flair of Breton, a kind of pedigree bloodhound of Beauty – an affirmation of his aesthetic judgement of anthropological objects, the cultivation of his eye, and the audacity of jarring compositions that produced explosions of meaning: 'The surrealists taught me not to shy away from the abrupt and unexpected juxtapositions that Max Ernst liked to use in his collages.'[71] This aesthetic of collage was incorporated into the intellectual raw material of a nascent structuralism, which rejected theories of cultural diffusion in favour of découpage and juxtaposition.

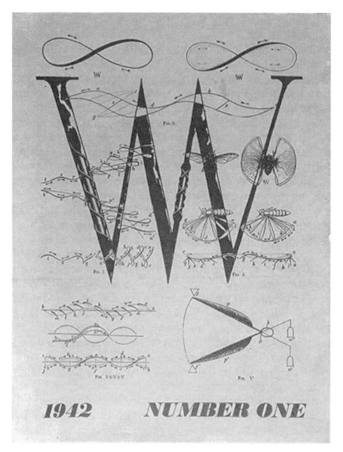

Cover of the first issue of the surrealist journal *VVV*, published in New York
during the war, in which Claude Lévi-Strauss wrote an article entitled
'Indian Cosmetics'.

The attempt to recreate the Bohemian life was only partially successful
for Breton, the guardian of the surrealist temple, who could not manage
to maintain the homogeneity of the group, despite the launching of a surrealist journal in New York, whose first issue was published in June 1942.
The editorial provided an explanation for the title's acronym: 'VVV, i.e.
V + V + V. We say Triple V, i.e. not only V as in our vow – and vigour – to
return to a habitable and thinkable world, Victory over the forces of regression and death that are currently unleashed on earth, but also V beyond
this initial Victory, for this world cannot and must not continue to be the
same, V over what contributes to perpetuating the enslavement of man by
man, and beyond that VV, that double Victory, V again, over anything that
opposes the emancipation of the mind, of which man's liberation is the
first and necessary condition.' The issue featured an article by Lévi-Strauss,
entitled 'Indian Cosmetics', in which he revisited Caduveo drawings. It is

framed by an Aimé Césaire poem and a series of surrealist images. In this context, the article gave in to the mystery of these arabesques and simply offered up the face paintings to the reader, providing no new analysis. It was only two years later that, in another text on the same topic, entitled 'Split representation in the art of Asia and America',[72] he took up and expanded on the motif of split representation. Based on a vast body of work from the Caduveo as well as Pacific Northwest tribes, ancient China and the New Zealand Maori, Lévi-Strauss tackled the riddle of analogies that did not match any known population contact to propose an interpretation that was critical of the cultural diffusion model and based on a first 'structural analysis of forms'.[73] Henceforth, and as opposed to his earlier intuitions of 1936, the Caduveo drawings no longer appeared related to Spanish influence, which arrived too late. From a sociological standpoint, split representations referred to the spatial representation of invisible hierarchies; from a psychological standpoint, 'the split representation is a function of a sociological theory of the split personality'[74] (biological vs. social, profane vs. sacred, etc.). This stylistic invariant over a geographical area that was so vast as to preclude any contact hypothesis became clear to

Cover of a book by André Breton, published in New York in 1946, with a photomontage by Marcel Duchamp.

him after his discovery of Kwakiutl transformation masks and Tsimshian wood decorations, this art of the Pacific Northwest that he discovered with delight in that Third Avenue antique shop as well as in the rooms of the Museum of Natural History arranged by Franz Boas.

Through the looking glass: the 'hidden passages' of New York

'There is in New York a magic place where all the dreams of childhood hold a rendezvous, where century-old tree trunks sing or speak, where indefinable objects lie in wait for the visitor with an anxious stare. [. . .] This region, to which disused but singularly effective museographic methods grant the supplementary prestige of the *clair-obscur* of caves and of the crumbling heap of lost treasure, can be visited daily from ten to five o'clock at the American Museum of Natural History, New York. It is the vast gallery on the ground floor devoted to Indians of the northwest coast which extends from Alaska to British Columbia.'[75] The encounter with the art of the Pacific Northwest coast, at the time considered to be of a lesser calibre, was one of the highlights of the New York experience. But it was not the only one: in a text written under strong surrealist influence, 'New York in 1941', Lévi-Strauss recalls the 'thousand and one Ali Baba caves'[76] offered by the city that now hosted the artistic heritage of the world to those who knew to go, like Alice, 'to the other side of the looking glass',[77] into its wonderland – entire warehouses full of Mochica, Nazca and Chimu earthenware; gold boxes inlaid with rubies and emeralds, relics of Russian emigration following the October Revolution; an entire series of original Utamaro prints, with which a young man fallen on hard times was prepared to part; very valuable Peruvian antiques sold off by a German baron; etc.

New York, far from the cliché of a city of absolute modernity, was a complex place that pitched together different spaces and times. If it did prefigure European cities of the 1970s in many ways, with its ubiquitous advertising and its taste for kitsch, it also conjured up the France of the July Monarchy, so masterfully described by Balzac in the first pages of *The Girl with the Golden Eyes*. In a visionary analysis, these pages, which Breton revered, compared the spheres of Parisian society with the circles of Hell, powerfully depicting the ever-changing power plays and the brutality of social mobility, both upward and downward, through real estate speculation in particular, generated by this phase of French capitalism.[78] It was an organic vision of a Paris in perpetual movement, determined by forces of assimilation and rejection that, according to Lévi-Strauss, the New York of 1941 recalled. Like the ebb and flow of the tide, the recycling, reclassification, collapse and rebirth of various social segments generated a certain amount of dross, stored away in the nooks and crannies of the big city and left there to be rediscovered once they had lost most of their value. A contrapuntal game the surrealists were fond of playing together with the anthropologist, already a regular visitor to auction houses: one had to monitor the depressions in the curve of taste to be able to seize the avatars of Beauty. Here was the aesthete-anthropologist turned 'ragpicker'[79] of the society of his time.

One could move through time but also geographical space by going from one block to the next. Lévi-Strauss discovered the multicultural reality of the American metropolis, here again heralding the situation in Europe post-1945, but then still completely novel to the Parisian eye. Paradoxically, New York enabled him to experience anthropology through all the senses. This is where he discovered Chinese opera, which he regularly attended, later bringing Albert Camus. Under the first arch of the Brooklyn Bridge, from the middle of the afternoon until midnight every day, a troop from China upheld traditions and performed pieces from the classical repertoire. Lévi-Strauss also regularly patronized New York's exotic, and especially Chinese, restaurants, with increasing expertise. A young friend of his at the time recalled that he would often take her out to Chinese restaurants and 'order dishes that were not listed on the menu'.[80] He even cooked a few dishes for her of his own invention, from a Peking duck and spices purchased in Chinatown – the young woman was duly impressed. Around the world in eighty meals: 'One day we would head to Harlem for barley meal fried chicken; another time we'd try Panamanian turtle eggs, moose stew, Syrian kefirs, softshell crab, oyster soup, Mexican palm tree worms, or octopus with the silky gaze.'[81] In New York, Lévi-Strauss found himself in North America, but also in China and Europe, in the past and the future – probably least of all in the present. This machine for moving backwards and forwards in time, in striking crisscrossing movements, was also an effective eraser of the present moment. This might well have been one of its most venomous charms.

New York was thus the city where anything could happen. Caught between a mass culture that was poised to take over and folk cultures – Chinese opera, Yiddish theatre, early Americana – for which the cosmopolitan metropolis had improbably played a preservationist role, New York appeared as a 'surrealist' city even though, paradoxically, it did not provide any inspiration for Breton, who did not devote a single line to it. According to Vincent Debaene, it was also a very structuralist city, in that its urban stratigraphy, and the collision of multiple times and spaces that it contained, made it a 'laboratory for a theory of symbolic forms based on variations in perceptions and the analysis of their interrelations'.[82] This is to give New York and Lévi-Strauss's experience of the city – which was, by his own admission, intense – all the importance that was its due.[83] The New York matrix also joined surrealist aesthetics and structuralist epistemology in another way: its breaches, its fleeting correspondences, its 'hidden passages', abolished the dictatorial rule of time. Through dreams, chance and games, on the one hand, and through emotional and cerebral fullness, on the other, one could escape the constraints of a history that 'obstructed one after the other all the open cracks in the wall of Necessity'.[84] As opposed to New York City, rich in sweet escapes, occupied France – locked down, cordoned off, reduced to a pure logic of repression – offered no way through the looking glass.

Academics and politics

On 14 February 1942, the École libre des hautes études (ELHE) was officially launched in New York, with three thousand people attending its inaugural ceremony. Despite its short lifespan – tied to the period of war – the institution has two lasting claims to fame: first, it lent its intellectual prestige to the cause of Free France;[85] and, second, it was within its walls at 66 5th Avenue that the historic birth of structuralism took place, thanks to the fabled encounter between Claude Lévi-Strauss and Roman Jakobson, who both taught there.

The École libre des hautes études: Gaullism and academic politics

The decision to open the École libre was made within New York Gaullist circles, independently of the Rockefeller Foundation, and its project to create a 'francophone academic International' was to include most of the French-speaking academic refugees. The goal of this politically engaged scholarly initiative was both to demonstrate the survival of French culture and to embody it in this university-in-exile of sorts, in the heart of New York City. It is therefore quite easy to see how the project would not immediately appeal to the young socialist anthropologist. Yet he was to take part, and to become increasingly active. Indeed, in 1944, as the institution faced a crisis, he agreed to become its general secretary, a position he had earlier declined in favour of Alexandre Koyré. Part university, part Collège de France, this distinctive institution – located at the crossroads between intellectual life and high politics, between the national and the international – remained throughout its existence fraught with tensions related to its exile status. Was it to be a permanent institution, or a creature of the war? A site of academic production, or a tool of political representation? An international research centre, or the valiant if somewhat tattered standard-bearer of a France that refused to give up the fight? What exactly was the École libre des hautes études?

According to the decree passed by Free France that marked its official birth on 7 February 1942, it was indeed a degree-granting university, and it quickly found a place within the local network of institutions of higher learning – boasting 326 students, 40 courses and 19 professors by February 1942. The student body reached 851 by the first semester of 1943, by which time 95 permanent or part-time faculty members had given a total of 548 courses. The overall organization into three faculties (letters, sciences and law) was directly inspired by the French university system. The École counted several prestigious members among its teaching staff, whose open lectures attracted, if not crowds, at least part of the cultivated broader public. The Thomist philosopher Jacques Maritain, as well as Gustave Cohen, were known to fill lecture halls of more than a hundred seats. The high profile of physicists like Jean and Francis Perrin, the mathematician Jacques Hadamard and legal scholars Bonnet and Mirkine-Guetzevitch guaranteed an audience, and brought the École a certain intellectual profile

Brochure for the École libre des hautes études (ELHE),
featuring a few of its faculty members.

on the New York scene. The younger and less renowned members of the
faculty, like Claude Lévi-Strauss, had a more restricted following. The
sculptress Isabelle Waldberg regularly attended his anthropology lectures,
along with Robert and Nina Lebel: 'Aside from us, there would be two
other students at the most, but the course was taught as if addressing a
large audience.'[86] In 1942, five students enrolled to study under Claude
Lévi-Strauss.[87]

The ELHE was also an institution for research and knowledge production. In addition to free public lectures, it held closed seminars, coordinated by the research centres and institutes that formed its academic core.
Three 'research centres' and four 'institutes' were created, including the
dynamic Center for the Dramatic and Cinematographic Arts, headed by
Jean-Benoît Lévy; the Law Institute, directed by the indefatigable Boris
Mirkine-Guetzevitch; and the Sociology Institute, a kind of extension of
the Centre de documentation sociale that Célestin Bouglé had founded
in 1920, financed by the Rockefeller Foundation, which, via Georges

Gurvitch, provided transatlantic support for sociological research. Georges Gurvitch – a participant in the Russian Revolution of February 1917, and former chair in sociology at the University of Strasbourg – was to become one of the leaders of French sociology after the war, making the most of his American experience. Claude Lévi-Strauss was of course a member of the Sociology Institute (which counted thirty-two French and American scholars, including Kingsley Davis, Florian Znaniecki, Pitrim Sorokin, as well as Alfred Métraux and the geographer Jean Gottmann), but, more importantly, he served as general secretary of the Latin American Center, which he developed through the creation of several local sections, forming a network of institutions affiliated to New York: a Haitian section with ethnologist Jacques Roumain; a Brazilian section with André Ombredane and his former São Paulo colleagues, Roger Bastide, Paul Arbousse-Bastide and Pierre Monbeig; an Argentine section, with Roger Caillois, who represented the Institut français d'études supérieures of Buenos Aires, and Robert Weibel-Richard; and a Mexican section, added later, under the leadership of Alfonso Reyes, with the participation, most notably, of Octavio Paz. This centre was of particular strategic interest to the Americans, who were engaged in the 'Good Neighbor Policy',[88] as well as to the French, since many Latin American students in New York were potential recruits for their courses given in French, which had remained a traditional second language for cultural elites in South America. Lévi-Strauss published several articles in the French press in New York, managing a deft balancing act between France, the US and South America. 'One might say [. . .] that the links that once strongly bound Buenos Aires, Rio de Janeiro and Paris are loosening every day in favour of new links, tied to Washington DC and New York. These news links do indeed exist, and they are getting stronger every day. I would say that, from a French standpoint, we should not be troubled by this. On the contrary, we should, we must, help strengthen them in every possible way. Since even from the great pan-American endeavour, France shall not be absent.'[89]

In the daily operation of the ELHE, two pedagogical models complemented rather than competed against one another: the lecture and the seminar. One was more French, the other more familiar to the American pedagogical tradition. One was more likely to perpetuate the continuity of French cultural 'enlightenment' and play the political role of intellectual representation – the École as the cutting edge of the French cause in the United States; the other, the result of more arcane, modest and borderless work, was resolutely oriented towards intellectual innovation. During the 1942/43 academic year, in the philosophy and sociology section that also included Georges Gurvitch, Alexandre Koyré and Raymond de Saussure, Lévi-Strauss gave two public lecture courses – in the first semester, on Thursdays between 8 and 9 a.m., 'Races and racism' (five lectures) and, in the second semester, 'Towards a new conception of man' (five lectures) – and two closed seminars – first and second semester, on Thursdays from 9 to 10, 'General anthropology' (fifteen sessions per semester).[90] This represented two distinct yet interconnected conceptions of what intellectual resistance entailed: perpetuating a tradition that, in France, was being trampled, and critiquing a cultural and political heritage in need of reconstruction.

For the ELHE had developed 'a very strong moral connection' with Free France, as René Cassin, education commissioner of the London-based French government-in-exile, himself recognized. From that perspective, the ambiguity of the adjective *libre* that had been bestowed on the École enabled it to appeal both to the supporters of academic freedom, always suspicious of state intervention, and to confirmed Gaullists. True, Free France partly financed the institution through a yearly subsidy, to which the Belgian government-in-exile contributed $10,000. It is therefore unsurprising that Jacques Maritain, otherwise rather lukewarm in his support of General de Gaulle, should have written to the latter, thanking him for sending his condolences on the death of ELHE professor Henri Focillon, whom Maritain was now replacing: 'Rest assured that the École will remain unshaken in its determination to unite all intellectual forces behind the resistance, in a common effort to combat oppression.'[91] While failing to become the French university-in-exile that René Cassin had called for, the ELHE was, at least in part, an instrument of Gaullist mobilization in the United States – thanks to the publicly engaged figures who taught there and the many debates and conferences that were held there, which were covered in both the French-speaking and mainstream press in New York, as well as the intellectual work it produced. Through ELHE research institutes and publications, some of its jurists, sociologists and economists had in mind to become the experts in all matters pertaining to the reconstruction of postwar France, Claude Lévi-Strauss among them.

Crystallization: the interdisciplinary ethos, Lévi-Strauss and Jakobson

It was thus precisely at that moment and in that place that Lévi-Strauss was first introduced to Roman Jakobson. The immediate intuition of structuralism that resulted from their meeting was subsequently described by Lévi-Strauss as an epiphany: 'At the time I was a kind of naive structuralist, a structuralist without knowing it. Jakobson revealed to me the existence of a body of doctrine that had already been formed within a discipline, linguistics, with which I was unacquainted. For me it was a revelation.'[92] In 1976, re-reading the lectures Jakobson had given in New York half a century earlier, Lévi-Strauss 're-experienced the excitement [he] felt so long ago'.[93] Lévi-Strauss was introduced to Jakobson by Alexandre Koyré, because the anthropologist was looking for technical help to 'grapple, in complete darkness, with some unknown languages of central Brazil'.[94] He emerged from the meeting having 'discovered structural linguistics, thanks to which [he was going] to be able to crystallize all the reveries inspired by the contemplation of wild flowers somewhere near the Luxembourg border into a body of coherent ideas [. . .]'.[95]

This cross-disciplinary fertilization is also the fruit of Lévi-Strauss's unfailing friendship for a man who was twelve years his senior, and who became a kind of irrepressible older brother, a mentor and intellectual model who elicited an immediate admiration that was never disappointed. Jakobson was an anti-fascist Russian Jew who had been based in Prague, where he was part of the Prague Linguistic Circle. He had experienced a veritable odyssey across war-torn Europe – via Copenhagen, Norway and Sweden – before reaching American shores. Jakobson's structuralism was deeply rooted in the revolutionary Moscow of the early 1920s, a cultural blender in which Russian formalism, the futurists, cubist art and folklore research had mixed to create a cocktail of lifestyles, urban spaces and intellectual endeavours comparable to that of 1940s New York, with its combination of academics and surrealist artists, large public libraries and primitive art collections, research seminars and Bohemian life.[96] The presence of Jakobson by his side throughout the war years altered his national model of the intellectual. Lévi-Strauss admired his vital physical energy – the man, unlike his younger associate, had a penchant for drinking and discussion until the wee hours of the morning – which was also manifest in his staggering multilingualism – he spoke seven or eight languages fluently – his wide-ranging curiosity, and his imposing body of written work across so many different languages and countries as to boggle the mind. He was an orator and a writer, a true intellectual athlete whose transnational biography lay at the intersections of distinct intellectual traditions. Jakobson was a world in himself. He was the very embodiment of a certain intellectual model that combined expansive erudition with the most rigorous theoretical ambition, a cosmopolitan frame of reference and a set of questions of universal scope. Lévi-Strauss saw this 'great man' regularly between 1942 and 1945 – from the autumn semester of 1942, each attended the other's classes. Not only did Jakobson share his linguistic insights with Lévi-Strauss, but he also introduced him to other important figures: Franz Boas, to whom we shall return later, as well as members of the psychoanalytic scene, including above all Raymond de Saussure, also an ELHE professor, to whom Jakobson had revealed the true importance of his father's linguistic legacy, as well as the émigré psychoanalysts Kris, Loewenstein and Spitz.[97] It was thus, week after week, before the sparse audience of ELHE seminars, that one of the major bodies of twentieth century thought was constructed, following the scientific conversion that led Claude Lévi-Strauss to think of a kinship system as a language, and to appreciate each of its elements as a phoneme devoid of intrinsic significance, whose meaning was revealed only by its relative position in relation to other constitutive elements. The attention to invariants and importance accorded to unconscious phenomena appear to have been research tropes imported from linguistics and psychoanalysis.

Lévi-Strauss later claimed that had it not been for Jakobson's friendly insistence, he would not have had the necessary commitment or conviction to put the subject matter of his courses into writing. Thus, what was to become his doctoral dissertation, 'The Elementary Structures of Kinship', was due in very large part to that intellectual, institutional, amicable and pedagogical environment of the École libre des hautes études, which was marked by an intense interdisciplinarity. Exile had indeed rendered such an approach necessary: pooling knowledge and resources was a means of ensuring intellectual survival. Indeed, they had common libraries, attended one another's classes and shared the same rooms. The interdisciplinary orientation in the French social sciences was also strongly promoted by the Rockefeller Foundation, and practised by the institution that hosted the ELHE, the New School for Social Research. This was the specific institutional configuration that gave birth to structuralism, a configuration that was itself homologous with the sort of intellectual innovation in which structuralism engaged – i.e., the importation of a linguistic model into anthropology. For this was, indeed, Lévi-Strauss's innovation.[98] This precise move in this precise place – through the circulation and de-compartmentalization of disciplines that it enabled and promoted, the ELHE provided the conditions for 'revelation'. It made available to the anthropologist an established body of work whose theoretical rigour could also be applied to issues of kinship, whose coherence he had otherwise failed to untangle. Recent work in the history of science has focused on the mechanisms of scientific innovation, and highlighted the dialectical relationship between innovation and institutions. Prone to decontextual-izing the history of structuralism, and faithful to his own personal break-through, Claude Lévi-Strauss always highlighted his magical friendship with Jakobson, rather than the specific *locus* that enabled such a meeting of the minds in the first place.

A political anthropologist

The other surprise to emerge, shedding a somewhat different light on Lévi-Strauss's image as a disengaged scholar withdrawn from politics, was the intensity of his involvement in the political debates both within and around the ELHE. He almost always depicted the fall of France in 1940 as a shock to his pacifist convictions and socialist faith of the 1930s. The curtain thus fell on his political life and he would remain from then on a curious and attentive spectator, but forever above the fray: 'To have been so vastly mistaken has inspired within me a definitive mistrust of my political judgements.'[99] In fact, the character that was taking shape in New York only very cursorily corresponded to this description. In his acts, his exper-tise, and his contributions to political anthropology, Lévi-Strauss emerges as someone who very likely 'hoped for a rearticulation of the dynamic between politics and sociology, but one vastly different from that of the socialism of his youth'.[100]

Within the ELHE, Lévi-Strauss appeared as a Gaullist, close to Alexandre Koyré and also the archaeologist Henry Seyrig, one of the London envoys to America alongside Jacques Soustelle. As such, he was in favour of reg-istering the school with the American authorities as a Free French institu-tion, even if this entailed compromising its intellectual integrity. This was one position in a debate among the faculty that pitched two opposing atti-tudes against each other about what the future of the school should look like after the war: 'Those who considered themselves wholly French had only one idea, to return to France and take up their profession. In their eyes, after the war, the École would have no reason to exist and would be disbanded. Other colleagues, recently naturalized or foreigners who had found refuge in France before the war, were unsure of the fate awaiting them. They wondered what was going to happen in France and preferred to wait and see; they wished to maintain the École, which kept up their ties with France while permitting them to remain within the shelter of the United States.'[101] It was as a member of the first camp that Lévi-Strauss succeeded Koyré as the École's general secretary, and he was to act accordingly over the few months he spent in Paris in the winter of 1944. Upon his return to New York, however, he incurred the wrath of some of his colleagues and resigned his post, only to come up with altogether different propositions once appointed cultural attaché for Free France, in December 1945.

We should also point out that Lévi-Strauss was one of the 'voices' of the French-language programmes broadcast by Voice of America, a key tool of the Office of War Information, which broadcast some 350 programmes a week throughout the world, and especially in Nazi-occupied France. The French section was directed by Pierre Lazareff, former 1930s press magnate and the future editor of the daily newspaper *France-Soir*, and included personalities from a wide range of backgrounds. Lévi-Strauss – unlike Denis de Rougemont, Julien Green or philosopher and union leader Paul Vignaux – did not contribute a regular column. He only served, as in the days of Radio Tour Eiffel, as a newsreader, as part of a team that included André Breton and Georges Duthuit, becoming the official French voice-over reader for FDR speeches, since his voice was supposed to better resist frequency jamming. Voice of America, a giant Tower of Babel in the middle of Manhattan, on 47th Street, was abuzz in the twenty-seven different tongues (including Swahili!) in which its programmes were broadcast, employing many members of the exile community. Working there was a way of participating in the American war effort as well as making ends meet. To take part in the war of the radio waves and the 'Résistance at a distance'[102] was one of the only forms of resistance available to them.

Lévi-Strauss was a Gaullist: he had signed an oath of loyalty to the Free French Forces and had been officially assigned to the French scientific mission in the United States. In addition, he was friends with many Gaullist or affiliated figures, starting with Henri Seyrig, with whom he had forged a deep connection. Yet he was no orthodox Gaullist, as is clear from two documents, which also reveal his unabashed political skill. The first is a memo dated July 1942 and addressed to Jacques Maritain, president of the ELHE, in which he offered his own diagnosis of the causes of France's defeat and suggested a few possible ways forward for France.

These forceful pages, which remain unpublished, stand out for their revolutionary tone and content:[103] they levelled an accusation against the colonial past of French and British democracies, pointing out the contradictions between their war aims and their colonial interests, and arguing that the world war was in fact an international civil war. Lévi-Strauss began with a radical rebuttal of the Gaullist argument regarding the illegitimacy of the armistice, and the provisional, rather than definitive, nature of the

French defeat, arguing that France had indeed been vanquished in 1940: 'On 17 June 1940, France might still have fought battles, but it had lost the war. [. . .] In the same way that the sadly famous motto "we shall prevail because we are mightier" failed to bring us, through the magical force of incantation, the strength we lacked or the victory we could not secure, just the same, the sterile proclamation that France has not been defeated will not, through the power of sheer repetition, change this painful, and contrary, reality.' A sharp rejection of the Gaullist credo.

In his view, the war turned on two axes, one of which indeed pitted democracy against totalitarianism, but a second of which, within the former camp, opposed the revolutionary movement to the established order, 'the supporters of a new humanism to the self-interested upholders of traditional values'. In this conflict, democracies were at a great disadvantage because they found themselves in contradiction with some of their own war aims: 'The historical development of totalitarian movements can be summed up here in a dramatic representation – condensed in time to less than two decades and, in space, to the European scene – of the spectacle Europe itself had been presenting on the world stage for the past century and a half. Europe sought to reduce the world to the status of supplier of raw materials and consumer of manufactured goods. Fascists similarly purport to assign an agricultural function to Europe, with Germany alone having the exclusive industrial role that Europe as a whole had tried to secure for itself.' Fighting in the name of social principles they do not themselves apply, it was through struggle that democracies could give rise to the new society that is the only force capable of winning the war: 'The independence of nations, the emancipation of the people, the equality of the races, promised as victory's rewards are in fact the preliminary conditions for victory. [. . .] It shall not be the triumph of democracies, but the triumph of a new society, which these democracies can and even must (since it is also their only chance) anticipate and embody in their very being. Military victory does not mark the beginning of the transformation of the world but its end point.' France should be the herald of this reordering. As the author ironically pointed out, rather than reproducing the military effort of the Allies 'at a ridiculously small scale', it was in providing intellectual support for this social transformation that France could and must play a major role in the war effort.

Lévi-Strauss demonstrated the same acute foresight for the new social and postcolonial order in the review he wrote of Julien Benda's *La Grande Épreuve des démocraties*, which was published in New York in 1942. While the review remained highly critical, it insisted on the grandeur of writing a resounding defence and illustration of liberal democracy in the context of its eclipse. 'The most radiant image liberal democracy can offer of its own twilight must surely be that of an old man suffering, like his compatriots, from cold and hunger, and meditating in a small hotel room in Carcassonne.'[104] Lévi-Strauss argued that nineteenth-century liberal democracy had not succeeded in integrating the masses into its system, making it a doomed model, and called for 'the advent of a democracy that is, at last, valid and viable'.[105]

A third document revealed both Claude Lévi-Strauss's political position and his vision for postwar France. He had been invited as a political expert to take part in the 23rd meeting of the Peace Aims Group of the Council on Foreign Relations, on 8 February 1943 in New York, in the presence of various state department officials. Two young Frenchmen represented the new generation; on the political left was Claude Lévi-Strauss, a member of the SFIO until 1935, and on the union left was Paul Vignaux, who had founded the Syndicat général de l'enseignement national (SGEN) in 1937. Lévi-Strauss delivered a series of reflections on the near and long-term future of France and Europe, which he prefaced with the insistence that it was no use trying to imagine the future of European society on a prewar basis. In this document, Lévi-Strauss outlined a clean break with the past at all levels – economic, political, colonial, mental. According to the record of the meeting, Lévi-Strauss 'expressed his opinion that Europe after the war would be a *tabula rasa* owing to the prodigious breakdown in institutions. The new system would not be so difficult to establish since the old would have been destroyed. The social revolution would spread all over Europe and whether or not it came from Russia depended upon the capacity of the Western European workers to build their own system first.'[106] First, with regard to the near future, both Frenchmen disapproved of the possible imposition of a provisional government by the Allies, which would, in their view, be counterproductive. Lévi-Strauss preferred provisional administration to be ensured by a body comprising general and departmental councils, within which natural leaders would necessarily emerge in the revolutionary context of post-liberation France. De Gaulle's name was not uttered once. Throughout this interview, Lévi-Strauss demonstrated a detailed knowledge of local politics. He thought France's weakness lay in the overly centralized power inherited from the Napoleonic era, when it was probably necessary in the cause of building the nation. But for some time already, the excessive concentration of power in Paris had been the source of much damage. He paid homage to local administrators and municipal council members, arguing that the best members of the Socialist Party had been the mayors of towns, large and small. While in favour of a thorough decentralization of power, Lévi-Strauss remained attached to the parliamentary system of the Third Republic, albeit with less power for the Senate, which had buried all the interwar reforms. Regarding the colonial empire, he thought independence should be granted to all colonies that were 'ready for it', such as Indochina and, with more reservations, Madagascar. As for the countries of the Maghreb – in Algeria, Tunisia, Morocco alike – all Muslim 'subjects' should be given full citizenship and their status thus aligned with that of Jews in Algeria: 'Everyone should enjoy citizenship rights regardless of their religious practices' (such as polygamy among Muslim Arabs). Based on this policy of cultural pluralism and generous citizenship, Lévi-Strauss believed that the Arab world would opt to remain within France rather than demand independence.

The final theme he broached recalled the socialist programme of *Révolution constructive*: the fight against nationalism, which was likely to

resurface in France after its liberation (especially in reaction to its humiliation), and the available means for countering it, outside the traditional
solution of international powers – useless, according to Lévi-Strauss, as
demonstrated by the pathetic history of the League of Nations. 'The disintegration of national sovereignty must start from within through a process
of federalism, on the one hand, and the creation of economic bodies, on
the other, that will undermine the differences between national groups', for
instance, workers' associations or business groups.

Beyond this exercise in Pythian prophesy – which did not hold up well in
light of the history of post-liberation France – Lévi-Strauss's politics were
only given expression in scholarly works of anthropology dealing with
explicitly political issues such as power, authority, war, the relationship to
foreigners and relations between social groups. Three articles published
during these New York years, traces of which were to resurface in *Tristes
Tropiques*, were never reprinted in subsequent collections – thus giving one
the impression of unearthing a veritable political anthropology, alongside
the more frequently cited aesthetic works and the doctoral dissertation
dealing with kinship questions then under way.[107]

In his essay entitled 'The social and psychological aspect of chieftainship in a primitive tribe: the Nambikwara of northwestern Mato Grosso',
which was first submitted for publication in English in 1943 and then
in French in 1947, Lévi-Strauss demonstrated how examining primitive societies could shed new light on contemporary societies. Exploring
chieftainship among the Nambikwara, he developed a theory of the state
and even made an anthropological case for the welfare state. Studying the
exchange of concessions between the group and its chief showed that 'the
interpretation of the state, conceived as a security system, recently revived
by discussions about a national insurance policy (such as the Beveridge
plan and others), is not a modern development. It is a return to the basic
nature of social and political organization.'[108] In that very same article,
Lévi-Strauss wondered about the origin and function of power, assigning
a fundamental role to the notion of reciprocity, and making consent the
cornerstone of legitimacy for power of any kind. Thus, far from endorsing
the psychoanalytic theories that made the chief a kind of symbolic father
and the state the outcome of a patriarchal model, anthropology provided
support for the theories developed by Rousseau and the Enlightenment
philosophers, for whom 'contract' and 'consent' were not the results of
secondary processes as their opponents claimed, Hume foremost among
them. For Lévi-Strauss, these were 'culture's raw materials, and it is impossible to conceive a political or social organization in which they would not
already be present'.[109] This conclusion echoed the work of Marcel Mauss
in his famous essay *The Gift* – an intellectual link that Lévi-Strauss would
make explicit a few years later. Just as the chief's power rests on his capacity for exchange, war is fundamentally an exchange, albeit an exchange of
violence.

In another essay of the period, the anthropologist argued that war
and trade were two related activities that could not be considered separately. Sometimes there was war, but the usual result of conflict between

Nambikwara bands was the exchange of gifts. Thus, while Lévi-Strauss was writing in times of global and total war, 'a radically different vision of war emerged from the reading of ancient works: not only negative, but also positive; not necessarily the sign of disequilibrium in group relations and crisis, but on the contrary the normal means for ensuring the functioning of institutions. Certainly, war pitted various tribes against one another, both psychologically and physically. And yet, at the same time, it established between them the tie of reciprocal exchange of services, perhaps involuntary but nonetheless inevitable, that is essential to the maintenance of culture.'[110] In all these political anthropological texts, Lévi-Strauss is an anti-Hobbesian. Was it the optimism of despair? In the midst of world war, he demonstrated 'the logical priority of social relations of reciprocity over war and power relations'.[111]

According to Laurent Jeanpierre, this downplaying of war and emphasis on exchange in the scholarly work of Claude Lévi-Strauss was also a function of the psychology of exile. Half here and half there, he spontaneously adopted a mediating position between two national cultures, aware of the depredations and suffering experienced by the homeland, yet without really *knowing* them. Between awareness and knowledge, especially of the destruction of European Jewry, lay the distance traversed by historical imagination, which the anthropologist claimed to lack. It is thus impossible to recognize and process what was happening for the first time, if not in the form of foreclosed images resurfacing ten years later in *Tristes Tropiques*, then through a 'mental tracking shot' of Bosch-like descriptions of overpopulated Asia and dislocated bodies left adrift.[112]

Being there, and not being there. Lévi-Strauss was already quite familiar with this split relationship to the present. As he wandered the Brazilian *sertão* in search of rudimentary forms of life, Chopin had come to mind; back in France mobilizing for war, his mind had remained in Brazil. Thus, the exile condition, which has sometimes been described as a 'double absence'[113] (from both the home country and the host country), had affinities with his subjective state. He flitted around New York, making his own honey from the pollen of American flowers, both wild and hothouse (libraries, universities). However, his New York bubble was anything but self-contained. Arriving, as all exiles do, with his 'litany of grief',[114] constantly anxious about the fate of his kinfolk, he was subject to the heartache as much as to the dazzle of exile. And when the moment of the Allied landing came, on 6 June 1944, France and the present caught up with him: 'I remember that day. I was in my studio in Greenwich Village, getting up in the morning. I had turned on my little radio to listen to the news. What I was hearing was so strange that at first it was unintelligible. Little by little I understood and I burst into sobs.'[115]

Should he return? Should he stay? The question was on the minds of all French exiles in New York. As Denis de Rougemont put it: 'Should one return? I am told that Mauriac wrote: "Should one leave?" (thinking of young French people, answering no, they should not). That Bernanos exclaimed: "Leave, the earth is vast!" That others protested that this debate was anti-patriotic, or anti-Communist, I can't remember which. All this I was told in letters I received from Paris, adding that I had better return, for fear of not grasping the European reality in general, and the French one in particular. I could content myself with replying: It is rather you who should come out, for fear of not grasping the reality of the world. After all, the French number forty million out of some three billion inhabitants of the planet.'[116] The question of returning to the homeland raised the much larger issue of national identity.[117] For Lévi-Strauss, though eager to return and rather indifferent to the siren songs of America, these two alternatives were quickly overtaken by a third position: he returned to Paris for a few months in the winter of 1944 to settle the question of the fate of the ELHE, and then returned to New York as a cultural attaché appointed by the provisional government of the French Republic. In other words, Lévi-Strauss circulated. He was the very figure of mediation, transatlantic mediation in this case, which he constantly worked to promote throughout his exile years and beyond.

Indeed, as he confessed to the coordinator of the Social Science Division at the Rockefeller Foundation, Roger F. Evans, his New York years – in contrast to other figures in exile (especially Breton) – had proved particularly productive. He emerged from them a different person, forever changed in his scholarly habitus, in his way of conceiving of problems in broad perspective and his theoretical and bibliographical scope, not to mention his look, the way he dressed – he was to hold on to his New York shirts for a long time – which lent his courtly demeanour, perceived as very French, a touch of American efficiency, democratic spirit and simplicity. Claude L. Strauss, the American . . . In any case, he felt deeply indebted to America and institutions like the Rockefeller Foundation: 'Over the past few months, while in France, I came to realize the full value of the assistance we received. We were able to enjoy the physical and mental security of which those who remained in Europe were deprived. And, what is more, these last four years, instead of having been lost in the all-consuming task of merely keeping alive and in flight, were made profitable and fruitful and were enriched through our contacts with American scholars, with American academic life and American libraries.'[118]

In 1945, Lévi-Strauss, with several published articles under his belt and his first major work well under way, stood as the finest example of the 'cross-fertilization' the Rockefeller Foundation had sought to promote. It was for this reason that he set out to repay his inestimable debt to the United States in the form of a renewed and rethought 'Franco-American cultural cooperation',[119] of which he intended to become the painstaking architect as the cultural attaché to the French embassy, from his perch in a mansion on 5th Avenue.

11

Structuralism:
The American Years

> I have acquired a lot, intellectually speaking, over the past three years, and
> it will probably take me a lifetime to complete the project I have devised for
> myself. All I wish for is a life that allows me to do so.
>   Letter from Claude Lévi-Strauss to his parents, 15 November 1944

It was the repayment of a double debt that provided the rationale for
Claude Lévi-Strauss's decision to spend two additional years in New York,
from 1945 to the autumn of 1947. On the one hand, his debt to the United
States, the country that had provided him with shelter during the war and
enabled him to become what he had become; and, on the other, his debt
to his own country, rescued and renewed by Free France and the team of
scholars, including many former exiles, who now presided over its new
cultural diplomacy. Thanks to the idealistic musketeers Henri Laugier,
Henri Seyrig and Louis Joxe, Claude Lévi-Strauss, the new cultural
attaché at the French embassy in New York, found himself in a position
to reshape Franco-American cultural exchange, giving it a greater degree
of reciprocity.

As a part-time cultural attaché, he led a somewhat schizophrenic life,
split between, on the one hand, social events and relentless organizational
efforts – since everything needed to be created from scratch to set up the
new cultural service – and, on the other, intense thinking and writing,
entailing a radically different kind of effort, required for the completion
of the manuscript of his main thesis. Even while insisting on the revolutionary nature of this work in epistemological terms, we must also take
into account the debt it owed to its precursors, placing *The Elementary
Structures of Kinship* in a specific intellectual context.[1] This major work,
completed in March 1947, was a long time in the making, unfolding
gradually in a slow but inexorable departure from the paradigms of 1930s
anthropology. The fruit of isolation, on the one hand, and of new connections (with American cultural anthropology), on the other, Lévi-Strauss's
structural anthropology maintained a complex and paradoxical relationship with the times in which it was born – times of turmoil and tragedy.

After 1945, it was possible, with a little help, to dream of another world
in which art and science would act as the levers of a new practical interna-
tionalism. This may have been what was brewing during the brief interlude

that came to be called 'the postwar', in Paris and New York, around the UN and then, later, UNESCO. Its creators were those scholars, enamoured of art, who formed Lévi-Strauss's professional and social entourage, 'Renaissance men'[2] all, eager to rebuild a new order of international relations.[3] Creating international research laboratories, organizing small and large exhibitions between countries, enabling scholarly exchanges, seeking academic excellence and shared innovation – all efforts to wrest universalism from the forces of destruction. The anthropologist took part in these initiatives, both up close and from afar, including by bringing back from his American years a book that contained all the knowledge of the world, or at least a book designed to reshape the science of anthropology and provide it with new foundations, which would serve as guarantees of modernity as well as safeguards against the kind of dangerous turns taken in the past. A new life was thus beginning for Lévi-Strauss, in New York still, but now on the Upper East Side. He traded his Bohemian life in the Village for family life with his new partner and soon his first child.

France's liberation, from afar

Anguish, joy and trembling: the torment of silence from Europe

For Lévi-Strauss as for many exiles, the emotion of D-Day and the subsequent liberation of Paris was experienced from afar, and with some feelings of guilt, made even sharper by the persistence of silence from friends and family. In October 1944, he had still received no news. He knew that the small town of Le Vigan (in the Cévennes), and so Valleraugue – where his parents were hiding (or at least where he assumed they were hiding) – had been liberated on 1 September. He had heard that his friend René Courtin – whose family home in the Drôme had sheltered the Lévi-Strausses, under the alias Luce-Saunier[4] – had been appointed to an important position.[5] This bode well. He tried to reassure himself, engaged in arguments and monologues, maintaining a one-way conversation, but admitted defeat in the face of the 'thousand question marks'[6] that tormented him: 'What had happened? Did you leave Camcabra? Why?' Re-establishing contact with close relatives was a long and difficult process, easier in areas liberated by the American army, which brought the mail to the United States. By 11 October he had still received nothing: 'I am thinking of you constantly.' The advance of the armies sounded the knell of his exile. In any case, he dreamt of France (of which he confessed knowing little of its current state) and felt again like a foreigner in New York. On 15 November 1944, with letters coming to the US via Portugal, he remained without word and became 'worried sick', learning of 'so many disappearances, so many tragic misfortunes', in a kind of loss of historical innocence that further aggravated his fears.

It was only on 30 November that he finally received a telegram from his parents, ending the ordeal of uncertainty. Yet still nothing from Pierre Dreyfus or his sister-in-law Rose-Marie Ullmo; nothing from Marcel

Mauss either, to whom he wrote a long letter of reunion on 2 October, in which he appears to have been unaware of the illness that had already been plaguing 'his old master' for several years.[7] This letter, brought in person by Dr Rivet, described the feelings of exile: 'No use conveying the emotions we have all felt over the last few months: a mixture of joy and anguish, hope and torment, which was but a pale reflection of what you must have felt yourselves, on the other side of the ocean.'[8] Attesting to the affection and admiration his American colleagues felt for both Mauss himself and his work, Lévi-Strauss also attempted to convey how he had tried to measure up to the disaster he had escaped: his assiduous, redemptive, productive work, labouring to bring back some intellectual spoils of war. This letter gives the impression that he felt he had a lot to make up for, having been living in the United States among the 'happy few' in a world at war: 'During these three years, I have sought to justify myself in my own eyes by working tirelessly, driven by a desire to be of use and to contribute to the rebirth, as soon as possible, of thought and science in Europe. I have thus worked hard, and I believe with some success [. . .] I have completed a book on the family and social life of the Nambikwara; and started work on another, of more considerable scope and ambition, which is well under way.' The latter project, he announced, was one-third written and intended to serve as his thesis 'in an area somewhat different from yours, a continuation of your thought'. He then explained that he had attempted to draw a 'typology of kinship systems and a systematization of marriage rules'. In taking up this classic subject of anthropology – kinship and alliance – Lévi-Strauss assessed the added value provided by his work in two ways: the abundance of documentation and bibliographical references covered ('while still not exhaustive'), and the originality of the method, which offered an organizing theory for a substantial quantity of empirical material. Both were fundamentally connected to his condition of exile: on the one hand, American libraries and, on the other, distance from the 1930s model of French anthropological knowledge, based on the museum, the cultural artefact and the 'master's advice'. Lévi-Strauss did not of course formulate it this way. Announcing his impending visit to Paris, he expressed 'happiness at the prospect of seeing [Mauss] again to ask for his advice, which [he] had missed so much while [his] book was taking shape'. And yet, in the genesis of this book, *The Elementary Structures of Kinship*, which was to become his thesis, it was perhaps his detachment from established European frameworks, his new institutional (the New School) and social (surrealist) environments, as well as his contact with other disciplinary paradigms (structural phonology) and previously unknown material (the documentary resources on North American Indians) that created the conditions of possibility for the epistemological rupture that was to take the name of structuralism. In his conclusion, Lévi-Strauss apologized for writing 'such a self-centred' letter and reiterated his wishes for their upcoming reunion in Paris, where he was to return to settle issues regarding the future of the École libre des hautes études, of which he had become the general secretary in June 1944, taking over from Alexandre Koyré.

Paris, winter of 1944–1945

Not many exiles enjoyed the privilege of returning to France so early. But Lévi-Strauss's presence in Paris was deemed useful. And so he received authorization, in the midst of war, for passage with an American naval convoy that brought him to England in December 1944, and then on to France and Paris via Dieppe 'in an American truck'[9] – a three-week journey in all.

Roosevelt's recognition of the Provisional Government of the French Republic, on 23 October 1944, paved the way for new Franco-American relations in which exiles who had lived in the United States played an important role. Henri Bonnet, a former refugee and professor at the ELHE, was appointed French ambassador to Washington. In addition, Henri Laugier, a former exile in Canada, put all his prodigious energies into the transformation of the Service des oeuvres françaises à l'étranger (SOFE) into the Direction générale des relations culturelles extérieures (DGRC), a new and modern section of the French foreign ministry with administrative and budgetary autonomy, approved by the order of 13 April 1945.[10] The experience of exile had broadened his horizons and, for Laugier, the time had passed when France could rely only on its writers, artists and scientists to spread its influence. Like Lévi-Strauss, Laugier had been instructed in the American way of the world and conceived of issues at the international level, well aware of his country's reduced status within the hierarchy of powers. Thus, cultural diplomacy held a singularly important place, on a par with the historic role that General de Gaulle had assigned to French thought in exile. It was in this context that de Gaulle had paid tribute to the ELHE, on 30 October 1943, in a speech delivered in Algiers to mark the sixtieth anniversary of the Alliance Française.[11] In the new France of 1944, still engaged in combat, the question of cultural diplomacy, and within it the role of the ELHE, was one of considerable importance.

The life of the École became engulfed in conflictual debates from the moment, in spring 1944, the US Department of Justice imposed an obligation on it to comply with the Foreign Agents Registration Act, given that many members of its faculty were involved in the political activities of Free France. This American legal requirement brought to the fore the tensions that were inherent to the nature of this institution of higher learning, which was both an institution for the production of knowledge, potentially able to integrate into the American academic system after the war, and, at the same time, as we have seen, a partisan political institution, born of and for war, with the aim of galvanizing energies around General de Gaulle.

Claude Lévi-Strauss was among those who considered the moral and political value of the ELHE to be greater than its scientific and academic value, and that such a hybrid political-academic form could not persist as such in the context of peacetime. It was for this reason that he found himself in Paris to decide on the future of the École. Between those who would have liked to remain in a gradually Americanizing institution and those who, convinced that its time had passed and its mission had been achieved, advocated its closing, Lévi-Strauss promoted a third way. He recommended the integration of the École, with a reduced faculty (mostly through the return of some professors to France) and altered expectations, into something larger – the Centre d'action culturelle en Amérique, aka the French European-American Foundation – which would guide and preside over the intellectual and cultural exchanges between France, Europe and the United States. This project to achieve a resolution of the ELHE issue by stepping up its level of ambition was presented by Lévi-Strauss to his Rockefeller Foundation interlocutors, whose support, not the least financial,[12] he hoped to secure. He proposed an entity organized into four departments: human relations (social sciences, civil society representatives, associations, municipal authorities, etc.); man and his environment (geographers, geologists, applied sciences); community life (expression of ideas, circulation of ideas, cinema, radio, press, publishing, etc.); and, finally, the École libre, reconceived now as a Center for Franco-American Higher Education that would offer 'not just to students but also to the cultivated broader public, as well as qualified experts, a kind of "sampling" of high quality French teaching, without curricular or exam requirements'.[13]

Claude Lévi-Strauss remained in Paris for several months, until May 1945. As he often did, he downplayed his role and the importance of his presence in an offbeat and mischievous account. His recollections of that winter were of time spent in 'a small office at the directory of cultural relations, which had moved into a hotel – an old furnished hotel – on rue Lord Byron near the Champs-Élysées'.[14] There, he was responsible for helping people who wished to visit the United States. Among them was Merleau-Ponty, who taught him what existentialism was – 'an attempt to re-establish great philosophy in the tradition of Descartes and Kant'[15] – and 'Jeanne Micheau, who was a famous singer at the time. She walked into my office, heavily perfumed, leading two enormous dogs on leashes.'[16] He thus depicted himself as an underling in some back office of an impecunious French administration. In fact, he was fully a part of the rebuilding process under way that saw the arrival of newcomers to rethink, rationalize and rebalance France's cultural influence abroad. From January 1945, Henri Laugier, head of the new department, appointed fourteen cultural attachés and advisors, among whom many former professors at the New York École libre. In the United States, Henri Seyrig had been in his post since September 1943. An archaeologist of some renown, specializing in Syrian antiquity, endowed with an artistic sensibility and a discreet yet unfailing patriotism, he was an uncommon personality, a man of the same moral fibre as Laugier, friends with many artists as well as with men of science and of action.[17] Keen to resume his activities in Lebanon, where he was to found the Institut français d'archéologie du Proche-Orient in Beirut (which he directed until 1967), Seyrig resigned his post and left Lévi-Strauss, with whom he had developed ties of close friendship, to succeed him in December 1945. The two men appeared together in a photograph published in the American press in 1945, at the opening of an exhibit on Le Corbusier in New York, in which their bond of mutual esteem and camaraderie is visible.[18] On the École libre question, as we have seen, Lévi-Strauss already acted as cultural advisor, calling on his contacts within American foundations, a dynamic and inventive entrepreneur of academic policy at the national and international levels. When he returned to the United States in May 1945, he had not yet been officially appointed, and was only unofficially in charge.

These few months in Paris were important for Lévi-Strauss in more ways than one. He saw members of his family again – his grandmother, 'extraordinarily ebullient and lucid',[19] aunts, friends, as well as Dina, who, much to his relief, was ready for divorce. Why divorce? The return to Paris also provided an opportunity for a reunion with Rose-Marie Ullmo, with whom he had had an affair before the war. As he was to later explain to his parents, he could not imagine life without her: 'Over the four years of war, despite a few very charming interludes, I came to realize that I care about Rose-Marie much more than I thought. I was waiting for my return to France to confirm these impressions and I was not disappointed in the least, quite the opposite. And it is now very difficult for me to imagine living without her. She is probably a surprising choice in the eyes of others, but that's how it is. I have never for a moment tired of her company and I have come to learn how much one can count on her qualities of courage, good humour, tenderness and generosity. She is always gay, easily happy, instinctively helpful and patient, and the fact that she is not an intellectual, but rather full of innocence and childishness, is a very great relief to me. Finally, at my age, when one has learned to distrust one's sentiments, that our affair and mutual attachment could withstand absence and so much more, is to my mind a sure sign that I am not making another mistake.'[20]

Why was she such a surprising choice? First, Lévi-Strauss's parents knew Rose-Marie very well, as she was Pierre Dreyfus's sister-in-law and came, as they did, from Alsatian Jewish lineage and from the same expanded Parisian kinship networks that formed a coherent, if not quite autarchic, world in itself. In choosing Rose-Marie Ullmo, Claude Lévi-Strauss, away from France for ten years, was coming home. Rose-Marie's father, Édouard Ullmo, had left Alsace after 1870, and, rather than moving to the French capital, opted to try his luck in El Salvador, with his cousin, Pierre Dreyfus's father. They established a trading firm and founded the Salvadoran Missions Bank. Their fortunes made, they returned to Paris. Rose-Marie grew up in the carefree and rather opulent world of the grande bourgeoisie, in one of these Jewish families very much structured around rituals, customs, mutual assistance and sometimes also substitute parenting. Claude Lévi-Strauss, a childhood friend of Pierre Dreyfus, was part of her familiar scene. They had all grown up together. The year 1940 sounded the knell for this happy period of their lives. As far as Rose-Marie was concerned, who was then married to Jean-Pierre Kahn and the mother of two children, war and the wandering existence that it ushered in was preceded by upheaval of a more intimate kind: her husband had left her for one of her sisters. A double trauma. Her happy temper was nonetheless not completely vanquished by these ordeals. When, in the spring of 1944, she was reunited with Lévi-Strauss – after several years underground with Pierre Dreyfus and his wife Laurette, Rose-Marie's sister, while her father was hiding in a hotel in Monte Carlo, which he was indeed never to leave – she was still the attractive, joyful and somewhat childlike and light-hearted woman that Lévi-Strauss described and that her friends had known. She liked to go out, to have fun, and was intent on making up for the lost time of the dark years. She was certainly no intellectual and the logic of his choice was clear: she was the anti-Dina Dreyfus. This was, perhaps, why his close friends wondered about the appropriateness of his choice.[21]

In the poorly heated and ill-provisioned Paris of the end of the war, Claude Lévi-Strauss, based on 'accounts heard here and there',[22] shuddered *in retrospect* at the thought of what had been endured. These months were for him a major moment for taking stock of the three years of oppression and depravity, a period of mental catch-up with the dangers experienced, by his parents especially. He went to check on the apartment at 22 rue Lavoisier, into which the latter had moved at the beginning of the war. He found a woman living in it, who had no intention of leaving, even after finding out that its legitimate tenants were still alive. While the Lévi-Strausses were still in Camcabra, he decided to bring legal action for eviction, as many dispossessed Jews did at the time. Here again, the war and its residual violence hit him with delayed effect. His parents were left with nothing. Their apartment had been emptied. It was for this reason that he asked them to draw up a list of their furniture, in support of the application for reparations. This inventory offers a glimpse into a bourgeois interior comprising accumulated family inheritance interspersed with *chinoiseries* (a lacquered tray): there was porcelain from Saxony, a stereoscope, a Pathé Gramophone with a collection of records, 160 hard-bound and soft-bound books, among which were many first editions, two modern paintings by Caro-Delvaille, two ancient cashmere shawls from India, a Sèvres china vase, a suspended Menorah in chiselled copper, around thirty canvases and pastels by Raymond Lévi-Strauss and a stamp collection. Of all this, nothing remained. The lost world of childhood. It was only in 1961 that Emma Lévi-Strauss, by then a widow, received 20,140 francs in compensation for German war spoliation, thanks to legal action taken by the Fonds social juif unifié against the Federal Republic of Germany.[23]

These few months in Paris, of great emotional and historic intensity, contrasted sharply with the life to which Lévi-Strauss now aspired. Indeed, the New York years, lived in relative isolation from the war, were probably a turning point, not only because of the crystallization of his ideas that occurred during this period, but also because it was at this time that the anthropologist assumed the scholarly life, in which he recognized a higher calling, as well as the promise of satisfaction that neither philosophy nor politics had provided: 'I have acquired a lot, intellectually speaking, over the past three years, and it will probably take me a lifetime to complete the project I have devised for myself. All I wish for is a life that allows me to do so. This is fully satisfying for me and you will probably find I have gained a certain balance that I don't think I had before.'[24] This sure sense of an anthropological calling and of the work to be done came neither immediately nor from the scramble in the brush of the Brazilian *sertão*, but rather were slowly distilled in the Americana reading room of the New York Public Library, where he went daily for years.

Refounding anthropology

In what exactly did this project, to which he claimed to want to devote his life, consist? In the genesis of *The Elementary Structures of Kinship* a new scientific paradigm was taking shape, hardened in its theoretical ambition, but whose political stakes were no less significant. Anthropological structuralism was the intellectual product of transatlantic exile whose universalism expressed one of the great hopes of the postwar period. But it was first of all the fruit of a successful grafting onto American anthropology.

The encounter with American anthropology

From 1941 to 1944, rain or shine, Lévi-Strauss went every morning to the New York Public Library, a ritual that at first served as an immersion in the immense American literature on North American Indians, as well as all the anthropological writings, great collections, explorer and missionary accounts. Rather than in the large NYPL reading room, he worked in the now defunct Americana section, a room of lesser proportions, containing a dozen or so tables. It was a kind of nineteenth-century scholar's cabinet, simultaneously enclosed and open to the four winds. Lévi-Strauss preferred it to the academic libraries of Columbia University and NYU favoured by his colleagues. Open to all, this old-world setting, full of charm, held a trove of treasures for its regular readers: the promise of documentary deposits to satisfy the appetite of the anthropologist, as well as – on open access shelves, methodically ordered – all the major works of that still young science that had not yet abandoned the ideal of exhaustiveness. Protected from the outside world behind ramparts of books, transported from the present to other encounters, Lévi-Strauss read, or rather devoured, books. Exactly a century earlier, another exile, Karl Marx, had similarly buried himself in the reading room of a public library, the British Library in London.[25] What exiles owe to libraries and what contemporary theory owes to exiles immersed in reading is well illustrated by the examples of Marx and Lévi-Strauss, not to mention Walter Benjamin and a host of others.

The library, then, took over from the expedition, to which Lévi-Strauss would never, in practice, return. It competed with the museum as a site of ethnographic knowledge acquisition (the rules governing such and such society) and held the keys to anthropological knowledge proper (the laws governing the human race as a whole). It was in the midst of war and American exile – such a consonance would not have occurred had he ended up elsewhere – that Lévi-Strauss became aware of the extent of the available anthropological material and, henceforth, of the task before him: 'clarifying', 'making sense of', 'ordering', 'sorting out' – all metaphors for describing the operation of science. As he would later say: 'If the war hadn't broken out, I would probably have done another fieldwork. Fate led me to the United States, where due to a lack of means and the international situation I was not in a position to launch any kind of expedition, but where, on the other hand, I was entirely free to work on theoretical issues. In this respect, I can say, the possibilities were limitless. I also became aware that in the previous twenty or thirty years a considerable quantity of material had been accumulated; but it was in such disarray that one didn't know where to begin or how to utilize it. It seemed urgent to sort out what this mass of documents had brought us.'[26]

The encounter with American anthropology did not only take place in the enchanted spheres of libraries. It was also a matter of personal contacts and, more generally, for Lévi-Strauss, of a singularly successful penetration of the American academic world. He rubbed shoulders with all the major figures of anthropology, and he did so very quickly and deliberately. For example, Ruth Benedict and Ralph Linton, both professors at Columbia, 'used to invite [him] to dinner to criticize the other. It was the talk of Columbia; they hated one another.'[27] Alfred Kroeber and Robert Lowie, whose decisive role in Lévi-Strauss's life we have already pointed out, both taught in California, but Lévi-Strauss would meet with them without fail on their frequent visits to New York. Not to mention Margaret Mead. Each of these figures supervised doctoral students who, in turn, produced texts that fuelled the machine of American scholarship, the scale of which could not be remotely compared to what was going on in France at the time. In the United States, the discipline was already solidly established and highly diverse, with numerous branches, institutions and journals. Like Georges Gurvitch in sociology, Lévi-Strauss was a productive cog in this machine, publishing articles in *American Anthropologist, Social Research* and *Transactions of the New York Academy of Science*.[28] As we have seen, he was also one of the contributors to the *Handbook of South American Indians* directed by Julian H. Steward and Alfred Métraux, the South American counterpart to the *Handbook of American Indians* that Franz Boas had completed between 1907 and 1910. He developed a strong friendship with Alfred Métraux (1902–63), a Swiss anthropologist, his elder by a few years, who had been settled in the United States since the late 1930s, and whom he had met in Santos in 1939, on the eve of his departure from Brazil. Like Lévi-Strauss, and for a longer time even, Métraux had been involved with the surrealists, especially his childhood friend Georges Bataille. An unstable and troubled personality, he was a great fieldworker, a specialist of many different regions, from Oceania (Easter island) to the Andes, the Argentinian Chaco and, later, Haitian syncretism, via his enthralled study of voodoo. Part of his biographical arch paralleled that of Lévi-Strauss: exile in America, the universal horizon of international institutions (UNESCO), three spouses. Yet the younger of the two gradually achieved ascendancy over the elder, developing a theoretical ambition that the latter lacked, even though his encyclopaedic knowledge was often called upon by Lévi-Strauss. They were inseparable until Métraux's death by suicide in 1963. Lévi-Strauss came to see his friend's entire private life as but a 'long preparation for suicide'.[29] This puzzling formulation becomes clearer when reading Métraux's diaries and expedition notebooks, which express in the highest degree the syndrome of the anthropologist: forever a stranger in the societies he visits and a staunch critic of his own, with no hope of any respite or reconciliation.[30] Between reports on his travels and social life in New York and Paris, anxiety, loneliness and depression always hovered on the horizon.

A radically different personality dominated the world of American anthropology, a tutelary figure who cast a giant shadow: Franz Boas. 'He was one of these nineteenth-century titans, the likes of which are no more to be found'.[31] A titan in the scope of his ethnographic studies, his scholarly curiosity and the orientation he gave to his work, both protean and yet structured around the notion of 'culture' and the rejection of all evolutionism. Physical anthropology, linguistics, ethnography, archaeology, mythology, folklore: 'nothing was foreign to him. His work covers the entirety of the anthropological domain. All of American anthropology issued from him.'[32]

Boas (1858–1942) was a German Ashkenazi Jew who had emigrated to the United States but retained throughout his life a strong German accent and loyalty, much bruised, to his homeland. He began fieldwork in the 1880s among the Inuits on the island of Baffin, before turning to British Columbia, of which he became a distinguished specialist. Lévi-Strauss admired Boas's prodigious empirical work, immense erudition and optimistic encyclopaedic approach, which appeared to him the best American anthropology had to offer. He also appreciated the democratic scientist in him, the enemy of Nazi anthropology who, in 1940, published a rigorous argument against the racist theories informing German power – *Race, Language and Culture.* In his view, 'culture' formed a totality that organized all social facts in a given society and was opposed to the biological notion of race. He produced a thoroughgoing critique of race in his study of immigrant populations, whose bodily transformations he observed and measured.[33] This kind of anthropology led to a strict cultural relativism that Boas would often illustrate through the story of one of his Kwakiutl informants whom he had brought to New York and who responded in a very singular fashion to the artefacts of the city; enthralled by the freak shows that regularly came to Times Square, featuring dwarves and bearded ladies, he remained utterly indifferent to the skyscrapers, subway and fumes that shrouded the city.[34] Lévi-Strauss once visited him with Jakobson at his home in Grantwood, across the Hudson from New York City. 'In his dining room was a superb carved and painted chest made by the Kwakiutl Indians, the subject of a large part of his work. I admired the piece and said unthinkingly that living with Indians capable of creating such masterpieces must have been a unique experience. He answered drily: "They are Indians like any others." I imagine that his cultural relativism didn't permit him to establish a hierarchy of values among peoples.'[35] Finally, the third element that struck Lévi-Strauss in Boas's work was the importance he gave to the linguistic dimension. Boas spoke several Indian languages and was the first to point out, as early as 1911, the unconscious character of linguistic phenomena, which justified the privileged position they held in the study of social facts.

Claude Lévi-Strauss, a self-taught anthropologist without any official mentor, multiplied acts of filiation: with Mauss, as we have seen, as well as with Boas, as expressed in the highly symbolic and dramatic scene of his death in 1942 at the Columbia Faculty Club: 'It was during the winter, which was incredibly cold. Boas arrived wearing an old fur hat that must have dated from his expeditions among the Eskimos sixty years earlier. His daughter Mrs Yampolski and several of his colleagues from Columbia were there, all former students: Ruth Benedict, Ralph Linton and a few others. Boas was very jovial. In the middle of a conversation, he shoved himself violently away from the table and fell backwards. I was seated next to him and bent down to lift him up. Rivet, who had started his career as a military doctor, tried in vain to revive him. Boas was dead.'[36] By contrast with the feuding siblings (Benedict and Linton) and first-born son (Kroeber), Lévi-Strauss metaphorically positioned himself as the legitimate heir. This filial posture would later find expression in his attempt to find a home for the master's library, which, in compliance with Boas's wishes, he tried to have acquired by the Musée de l'Homme and brought to Paris.[37] Heir to Mauss and to Boas, straddling two traditions and continents, he saw it as his mission to extract the best from each and to distil a new essence.

The structuralist afterthought: the logic of discovery

The micro-history of a writing event – the sudden and, to our knowledge, first appearance of the word 'structure' in Lévi-Strauss's thinking, in a letter addressed to Paul Rivet – allows us to 'track closely the logic of discovery'[38] and the epistemological revolution, to witness it almost live, in the form of an afterthought, a crossing-out, a hesitation or regret. It plunges us into the classic question of the history of science: what accounts for the shift to a new paradigm?

On 10 February 1943, Claude Lévi-Strauss informed Paul Rivet, his prospective thesis supervisor, that, 'in a sudden flash of inspiration', he had begun to write a book on the 'prohibition of incest': 'it is a very technical work because it is based on an analysis of kinship systems; I am afraid it might be somewhat difficult to publish. Nevertheless, I believe it offers rather new perspectives on a classic issue, which it raises in new terms.'[39] A classic issue, new perspectives, new terms: indeed, this is exactly how one might define this undertaking of his. Kinship systems were a classic object of anthropology, which, from Lewis Morgan to Radcliffe-Brown and Marcel Granet, to name but a few, had led to the accumulation of much data on the rules of marriage and filiation, though not to any synthetic theory to shed light on this fascinating profusion of practices that nonetheless seemed to obey quasi-universal rules. The subject was thus far from new and the books devoted to it formed a small library in themselves. Yet the anthropology of kinship was to become, together with the

LATIN AMERICAN CENTER

66 WEST 12TH STREET, NEW YORK CITY   Telephone, ALgonquin 4-1239

CENTRE D'ETUDES ET D'INFORMATIONS   *OFFICE DIRECTEUR*
POUR LES RELATIONS AVEC
L'AMÉRIQUE CENTRALE ET L'AMÉRIQUE DU SUD

GILBERT CHINARD   HENRI FOCILLON
JACQUES MARITAIN   ALFRED MÉTRAUX
BORIS MIRKINE-GUETZÉVITCH   FRANCIS PERRIN
CLAUDE LÉVI-STRAUSS, *Secrétaire Général*

Le 6 Décembre 1943.

Professeur Paul Rivet
46 San Luis Potosi
México, D.F.

Mon cher Maître,

Ce n'est pas sans de cruelles hésitations que je vous
ai adressé avant-hier le télégramme que vous avez sans doute reçu.
L'offre de partir au Mexique, que j'ai toujours rêvé de connaître, un
séjour d'une année dans une région si passionnante, avec de si confor-
tables moyens de travail, la perspective de reprendre enfin le travail
sur le terrain - tout cela m'a follement tenté et je n'ai pas besoin
de vous dire combien je vous suis reconnaissant d'avoir pensé en
premier lieu à moi. Mais il faut être raisonnable: et je crois qu'il
ne serait pas complètement raisonnable de ma part de partir vers de
nouvelles aventures avant d'avoir mené à sa fin l'énorme besogne que
je me suis assignée. J'ai en effet, durant ces derniers mois, changé
très profondément mon programme de travail. La sociologie Nambikuara
est déjà rédigée depuis près de deux ans et, comme je vous l'ai dit,
j'ai l'intention d'en faire une thèse complémentaire. Par ailleurs,
je projette de réserver la publication de tous mes documents
linguistiques pour le lendemain de la soutenance. Reste donc la thèse
principale. Vous vous souvenez peut-être qu'à l'origine elle devait
être consacrée à la sociologie du Matto Grosso. Mais depuis lors le
petit livre que j'avais commencé d'écrire sur l'inceste s'est
transformé en un ouvrage de dimensions considérables qui me semble
beaucoup plus approprié à une thèse, comme aussi aux besoins intellectuels de la France au lendemain de la victoire. Je me suis attaché
en effet durant toute l'année passée à rassembler tout ce qui avait
été fait sur l'organisation de la famille en Angleterre et aux Etats
Unis (en Australie aussi) pendant les dix dernières années. Je
présente ces résultats dans un ouvrage systématique qui n'est pas une
compilation, puisque je m'attache à dépasser les positions actuelles
et à définir ce qui pourrait être - si je ne suis pas trop
ambitieux - la position de l'école française de demain. D'un autre
côté, je n'ai voulu refaire ni Westermarck ni Durkheim, comme bien vous
pouvez penser. J'ai essayé d'élaborer une méthode positive pour
l'étude des faits sociaux, que je caractériserais sommairement en
disant qu'elle est un effort pour traiter les systèmes de parenté
comme des ~~peuteuse~~, et pour transformer leur étude de la même façon,
et en s'inspirant des mêmes principes, que l'a fait la phonologie pour

/structures

The structuralist afterthought: letter from Claude Lévi-Strauss to Paul Rivet, 6 December 1943.

lesser known corpus on political anthropology and aesthetics, the primary material for the structuralist hypothesis, precisely because Lévi-Strauss knew he could draw on a mass of documents and information collected from around the world, a scale that matched the ambitions of his thought and of the theoretical model he was about to develop.

On 6 December 1943, Lévi-Strauss wrote to his 'dear master' – who had left France in 1941 for Colombia and then Mexico – to explain the profound changes to his project. His minor thesis was now going to focus on the social organization of the Nambikwara; and, as for his principal thesis, everything had changed: 'You may remember that originally it was to be devoted to the sociology of Mato Grosso. But since then, the short book I had begun to write on incest has transformed into a work of considerable proportions which seems to me more appropriate for a thesis, as well as for the intellectual needs of France in the aftermath of victory. [. . .] I have tried to elaborate a positive method for the study of social facts, which I would roughly characterize as an effort to treat kinship systems as ~~sectors~~ [structures], and to transform their study in the same way, taking inspiration from the same principles, as phonology did for linguistics. In other words, I am trying to present a "systematic analysis of kinship forms".'[40]

Where did the term 'structure' come from?[41] The notion was present in certain aspects of Saussure's work. The *Course in General Linguistics* (1916), while not using the term, considered language as a system to be studied as a form and not a substance. The term had been used explicitly by some of the thinkers of gestalt psychology since the 1920s. But its chief source was, of course, the work of the Prague Circle, whose structural phonology dated from 1928, with the paper by Roman Jakobson, S. Karcewski and Nicolas Troubetzkoy:[42] the different sounds of a language form a structure once they signify only through their reciprocal relationships of opposition and distinction. In the 1940s, the notion of 'structure' was thus 'in the air' even though it remained anchored in the discipline of linguistics.[43]

Lévi-Strauss justified the importation of the lexicon and model of structural phonology – discovered thanks to one of its principal promoters, Jakobson – into kinship anthropology, in an article published later, in which he explained the profound homology between phonemes (in linguistics) and kinship terms (in anthropology): 'Like phonemes, kinship terms are elements of meaning; like phonemes, they acquire meaning only if they are integrated into systems. "Kinship systems", like "phonetic systems", are built by the mind at the level of unconscious thought. Finally, the recurrence of kinship patterns, marriage rules, similar prescribed attitudes between certain types of relatives, and so forth, in scattered regions of the globe and in fundamentally different societies, leads us to believe that, in the case of kinship as well as linguistics, the observable phenomena result from the action of laws which are general but implicit. The problem can therefore be formulated as follows: although they belong to *another order of reality*, kinship phenomena are *of the same type* as linguistic phenomena.'[44] Hence the idea of employing a method that was 'analogous in its form (if not its content)' to that used in phonology. The kinship system was thus a language that needed to be deciphered in order to make sense of the unconscious laws governing marriage, birth and filiation, the intimate and affective core of social life.[45]

Retrospectively, much can be made of this crossing-out, at once banal and revolutionary, that substituted 'structures' for 'sectors', and thus set the terms for the birth of structuralism. It announced a project for greater theoretical rigour in anthropology, in search of true scientific legitimacy, or, as Lévi-Strauss put it, of a unifying principle that would simplify and explain the terribly confusing array of kinship configurations.[46] This systematizing ambition was noted by Alfred Métraux, who confided in his journal that he had visited with Lévi-Strauss and discussed the state of anthropology: 'He wants a return to philosophy, to a conception of the whole.'[47] Structuralism – beyond even kinship anthropology, on which it was to leave a lasting mark as an arcane subdiscipline characterized by an impressive, if not intimidating, mathematical and graphic formalization, i.e., the kinship diagram – was thus a more sweeping attempt to refound the social sciences on the basis of greater scientific and technical rigour and effectiveness, bringing them closer to the standards of the hard sciences.

Structuralism and wartime exile: the political stakes of refounding anthropology

This 'treatise on logic' that Lévi-Strauss announced arrived in a context of intense politicization at the end of the war. Rivet was one of the figures of Free France and was preparing to move to Algiers. In the letters that followed this structuralist *aggiornamento*, Lévi-Strauss expressed a sense that he was building something solid and novel, and not just for himself, but for France: 'I have the feeling, no doubt illusory (but the mistakes that are made in the course of working can be forgiven), that I am in the process of constructing a "great book". If I can bring it back to liberated France, it will provide a new foundation for young anthropologists and sociologists to put them on a par with their foreign colleagues. They will not only find everything that has been done in recent years in other countries, but perhaps even more besides.'[48] Was this the megalomania of a young researcher in the grip of the hubris of scientific creation? In these repeated declarations of faith, one should read the expression of an ambitious and inventive scholarship, 'unabashedly asserting its theoretical orientation' and evincing an 'ambitious philosophical inclination',[49] defining France's fundamentally scientific and intellectual calling for a nation now deprived of other attributes of power. Lévi-Strauss harboured no illusions on this front and his wartime Gaullism stopped short of the patriotic howls of wounded national pride.

Structuralism can thus be seen as a kind of intellectual war tribute, brought back by the exiled scholar in his trunk, with a view to raising the bibliographical, documentary and cognitive level of his country, to catch up after the wasted years of war. But the militant scientism that characterized the first generation structuralism of *The Elementary Structures of Kinship* – with its mathematical formalization, diagrams and logical rigour – was also part of an effort to establish the scientific legitimacy of a discipline that had formerly been pressed into the service of colonialism and fascism, both of which were obsessed with physical anthropology. Indeed, throughout the interwar period, the race paradigm was so intimately connected to the study of humanity, to the interpretive grid of human diversity, that it was difficult to break free of it, even for leftist anthropologists like Rivet and Boas.[50] In the late 1930s, Rivet had launched the journal *Races et Racisme* as a forum for the progressive popularization of ideas, emphasizing the instability of physical types, the long history of intermixing and the incoherence of the category of race. Boas's work was included. Yet, 'by combatting racism with the same weapons as its supporters, they did not challenge the terms of the debate, they situated their thinking within the same interpretative frameworks and did not offer a radically different conception that would move beyond the concept of race.'[51] This is precisely what structuralism did: it did not oppose 'culture' to 'race'; it changed the coordinates of reflection by opposing 'structure' to 'content', reconnecting with the universal by delimiting practices that could be observed everywhere – the incest prohibition – which were neither 'foundations' nor 'origins', but universal rules that conditioned human interplay across its infinite variations. The same Lévi-Strauss who, with one hand, constructed a treatise of logic, revived with the other the political stakes of anthropology, which the breakout of war had only made more pressing.

Thus, his course syllabus for the first semester of the 1943/44 academic year – devoted to 'the place of primitive peoples in the postwar world' – explored six issues: '1. The definition of so-called primitive cultures and the current distribution of so-called primitive or backward populations. 2. The economic, social and cultural rights of so-called primitive peoples. The notion of natural law in light of modern sociology. 3. Is the continuation of the colonial regime necessary to modern civilization? The various political dimensions of colonialism and the nuances of colonial economic exploitation. 4. The state of so-called primitive and backward societies under multilayered economic regimes. Countries under colonial regimes and countries under noncolonial regimes. 5. The issues of cultural contact under colonial rule and noncolonial rule. Disappearance and collaboration. The forms of assimilation. Cooperation and antagonism. 6. The philosophical and sociological problem of the coexistence of fundamentally diverse cultures. Cultural universalization or regionalism.'[52] One is struck here by the powerful challenge to colonialism, or, at any rate, the need to question its legitimacy. Nowhere did anyone at the time venture as far on this issue, neither among the partisans of Free France nor among the Resistance. As in other domains of political thought, the New York intellectual scene represented a kind of vanguard of critical reflection on the colonial system, connected to the question of survival and protection, which had suddenly become dreadfully topical.[53]

For structuralism was also a product of this time, marked by a reversal in the significance of westward travel, as has already been noted. Lévi-Strauss, boarding the *Capitaine Paul-Lemerle* in 1941, did not do so as an anthropologist setting off to study a disappearing people; it was, rather, he and his kin who were, this time around, the tribe under threat of extinction. Similarly, in Martinique, the white exiles were treated according to the rules of the colonial order which, in the same historical reversal, were now applied to them. This is what made friendship possible between André Breton and Aimé Césaire, equalized by their common condition as pariahs.[54] It was this context of disaster that Jacques Derrida emphasized when he recounted the birth of structuralism: 'Structure is perceived through the incidence of menace, at the moment when imminent danger concentrates our vision on the keystone of an institution, the stone which encapsulates both the possibility and the fragility of its existence. [. . .] It is during the epochs of historical dislocation, when we are expelled from the *site*, that this structuralist passion, which is simultaneously a frenzy of experimentation and a proliferation of schematizations, develops.'[55] The 'historic' dislocation here refers to the European civil war and the systematic destruction of a part of humanity and the flower of its culture.

Lévi-Strauss had an intimate sense of its significance when he learned of the dismantling of the Réseau du Musée de l'Homme, a branch of the French Resistance, and of the execution of Boris Vildé and Anatole Lewitsky on 12 February 1942 at Mont Valérien.[56] The dreadful news reached New York a few months later, in July 1942, and Lévi-Strauss immediately turned to Rivet, to whom he sent, in everyone's name, a consoling telegram. The old master, wallowing in Colombian isolation and infinite historical guilt, gave no sign of life.[57] Finally, on 17 August 1942, a 'distraught' Lévi-Strauss attempted to infuse some strength and courage into Rivet by fending off remorse and projecting him into the future: 'Among those who always got it right, you are one of the only ones, and I am tempted to say the only one, whom we still have with us. For in what state shall we find those who are in jail, or in concentration camps? There is thus an essential reason for which you must cease torturing yourself, dear master, with this terrible moral crisis you evoke: you do not belong to yourself, you belong to us, you belong to the France of tomorrow. And even if this were not the case, do you not know how much we would reproach you for your heroic attitude, which exposed you to the greatest dangers, the very same dangers to which our comrades have succumbed, and which would not in the least have increased their chances of survival? [. . .] And far from a cause for remorse – for how could it be? – it seems to me, on the contrary, that this thought should bring you, in your immense grief, a sense of calm resignation in the face of these cataclysmic events, against which one is irreducibly powerless. But I am wrong to speak of resignation here, which only applies to myself. For our friends will be, as you know, avenged.' Lévi-Strauss then added the text he had written to accompany the exhibition on the French Resistance that had been held in New York: 'In Paris there was a great scientific institution devoted, in its very essence, to the fight against racism and its lies: the Musée de l'Homme. Its director, Professor Paul Rivet, a Paris municipal council-lor, is the first French intellectual to devote himself, heart and soul, to the anti-fascist struggle. Its deputy director, Jacques Soustelle, joined the Free French forces from the very beginning. Their collaborators dedi-cated themselves to a single task: revealing, in their infinite diversity, the countless creations of the human genius. The Germans had their revenge. After holding them in confinement for months, they eventually massacred Dr Rivet's colleagues – who, following his example, had kept the museum open in occupied Paris, in defiance: Boris Vildé, Anatole Lewitsky, Pierre Walter, Jules Andrieu, René Sénéchal, Léon-Maurice Nordmann and Georges Ithier.[58] The millions of humble human beings who have been made known and dear to us through their work will punish the true barbarians.'[59]

It was indeed this precise moment, this tragic historicity, that para-doxically constituted the condition of possibility for anthropological structuralism: 'In fact one can assume that ethnology could have been born as a science only at the moment when a decentring had come about: at the moment when European culture – and, in consequence, the history of metaphysics and of its concepts – had been *dislocated*, driven from its locus, and forced to stop considering itself as the culture of reference. This moment is not first and foremost a moment of philosophical or scientific discourse. It is also a moment which is political, economic, technical and so forth.'[60] Structuralism was thus also a form of scholarly combat, the counterpart to a dreamy melancholia in the face of primitive worlds on the verge of vanishing, which 'structures' contributed to reintegrating into a humanity that was at once one and diverse.[61] The evolution of the disci-pline, the discovery of new horizons and, ultimately, exiled Western knowl-edge, chased out of Europe by Nazism, all combined to give meaning to this new and genuinely transatlantic intellectual product: structural anthropology.

By the end of 1943, the research was already well under way: 1,500 articles and books had been selected, 1,200 were already analysed. Lévi-Strauss had planned another three months of reading, and one year for the writing. But his research suffered from the complications that had beset the École libre des hautes études, which kept him busy throughout 1944. This is one of the reasons for Lévi-Strauss's return to New York as a cultural attaché in May 1945. He had in mind to carry out his diplomatic mission and his scholarly work at the same time.

Between science and administration

A new life

The summer and autumn of 1945 dragged on in somewhat morose uncer-tainty. On the professional front, Lévi-Strauss performed the functions of a cultural attaché, but did not enjoy any of the trappings of office. His principal task consisted in refitting (for $60,000) the splendid mansion on 5th Avenue that France had acquired just before the war and was finally assigned to the cultural services in 1945, with the Consulate being relocated elsewhere, after a decision that reflected Laugier's ambitious international cultural policy.[62] Lévi-Strauss enlisted the services of Jacques Carlu, the architect who had designed the Palais de Chaillot and taken up exile in New York, taking some pleasure in his role as designer and interior decorator. His thesis manuscript – 'I have completed the bulk of it'[63] – and the 5th Avenue building were the two objects of his attention, as reflected in the architectural metaphor that runs throughout his correspondence at the time. There were indeed a great many French architects in New York, where they had flocked to study the new techniques and materials used in the United States. At around that time, an exhibition on Le Corbusier was held in New York, which Lévi-Strauss visited, together with Seyrig. In a published photograph, we see him meditating, cigarette in hand, over the models on display, perhaps imagining himself the Le Corbusier of social science . . .[64]

In fact, this new position that impinged on his recently avowed scholarly calling was the upshot of a professional calculation, as he explained to his parents: 'I hesitated and thought it out. As you know, my greatest desire was to return to France after so many years in exile; but the opportunities were not all that attractive to me. Rivet is an unreliable protector, and I would probably have had to spend quite a few years at some provincial university before I made it to Paris. The New York position is an important one and represents, on the contrary, a significant promotion. In two or three years, if I do well, I will be able to easily trade it for a nice chair in Paris.' Between the advantages of a good deal and the disadvantages of prolonged separation from his home, there was also the issue of time and of his manuscript that remained unfinished: 'So in the end I said yes, somewhat melancholy at the idea of prolonging my stay in the United States and of temporarily, or at least partially, abandoning science for administration.'[65] In his mind, this was an opportunity he could not pass up, a boon which, in a very different way from the phone call from Georges Dumas in October 1934, was also a boost.

On 1 January 1946, he wrote on letterhead of the French embassy, as 'cultural attaché'. He was officially on the job. He moved into the disarray of the mansion where he was to reside, the renovation work being rather chaotically completed in the spring of 1946 – 'each team of tradesmen demolishes what the previous one has just done'.[66] But, at last, he enjoyed a prestigious address on the Upper East Side: 934 5th Avenue, opposite Central Park: 'Imagine more or less the Avenue de Villiers if it were located where the Boulevard de Suchet is, on the Bois [de Boulogne] side, very elegant, very snobbish, very beautiful and very boring.'[67]

A new address, a new line of work, and a new wife, an essential attribute of his new function but also the consequence of a serious and solid attachment. The desire to take a wife – and a French wife – was also a function of his having grown tired of his Don Juan lifestyle: 'My next letter will most likely be from a married man. Honestly, I am really looking forward to it. A recent affair, with a member of the oldest and highest

European aristocracy, bored me stiff and really put me off bachelor-hood.'[68] Following complicated untanglings with their respective partners, Rose-Marie Ullmo, who had only just arrived in New York, and Claude Lévi-Strauss were married on 16 April – in 'mercifully American style', added the newlywed: 'The ceremony must have taken all of 5 minutes!'[69] There was nonetheless a big reception, a month later, which gave a sense of the degree of upward social mobility in the anthropologist's life: petits fours, maids, and roughly a hundred people in attendance at the personal apartments of the cultural attaché. There were French VIPs of various stripes, the French ambassador to the UN, Consul General Alexandre Parodi, artists, including Chagall, Jacques Lipschitz, American academics and writers, a black American dancer, Jean Cassou – and all until two o'clock in the morning.[70]

These apartments had been entirely furnished (at low cost) by Lévi-Strauss, who rhapsodized about the richness of New York public auctions, which featured objects from all over Europe of uncertain origin and value. As a result, 'they are sold sometimes for an exorbitant price, sometimes for next to nothing – the price variations are incomprehensible'.[71] This random pricing allowed him to acquire 'very beautiful Italian Renaissance furniture, always in the sombre and homespun style that characterizes our furnishings': a large table, chairs, a chest, a utensil rack, all large-sized, from the mansions of rich Americans who had experienced a reversal of fortune and disposed of their cumbersome furniture; and a desk, most probably of colonial Spanish design, with syncretic patterns carved on its legs. In addition, Calder had given them one of his very fine and graceful 'mobiles' that 'hangs from the ceiling of the apartment and harmonizes well with both the primitive objects and the Renaissance furniture'.[72] This very particular interior provided the setting for a life that revolved around three poles: modern art (Calder), primitive objects and solid wood furniture. It combined an immemorial past – the times of colonial encounters and Renaissance humanism (sixteenth century) – with a fragile contemporary present. The temporalities that Lévi-Strauss's mind variously occupied, in a fine calibration of solid anchorage and ethereal and labile lightness. A precarious balance, like the kinship structures that he studied in his doctoral opus, between withdrawal into oneself and absolute reciprocity, between contradictory constraints that the man desperately tried to alleviate – the unstable equilibrium of a Calder mobile, which was the very form of Lévi-Straussian structuralism.

'Two lives in one'

The couple settled in at 934 5th Avenue. Rose-Marie Ullmo had not come to New York alone. She had two children, aged eight and ten, whom Lévi-Strauss was glad to take in, all the more so that they were 'sweet and calm', the apartment was large and, above all, his office was isolated, one floor below. However, he had no intention of assuming financial responsibility for them and asked his father-in-law to 'do what is necessary for their needs to be met on an entirely independent basis',[73] which did not seem to be an issue, given his in-laws' significant financial resources. If Lévi-Strauss now made a very good living, his budget had to cover the monthly payments he made to his parents. He repeatedly insisted that they accept his support and renounce seeking any remunerative activity: 'Under no circumstances can I allow you to ask for a job from Rivet or any of my other friends. I do not want them to think that I hold an important post in New York and will not even take care of you.'[74]

The first months were a race against the clock: 'I am terribly busy, between the notes, reports and telegrams that need to be sent to Paris on questions of scholarships, faculty and student exchanges, conference series, books to be sent, French exhibitions in America and vice versa, and the people parading through my office all afternoon with business of this kind. I am hoping to find a more efficient and productive way to organize my service than is the case at the moment, but I lack personnel and I am not yet sure of the budgetary constraints (probably tighter as a result of the devaluation) for 1946. In addition, there are important visitors who take up more of my precious time: Sartre and Le Corbusier are coming now, soon it will be Camus, etc.' On one side, he worked when he could on articles[75] and on his manuscript; on the other, he undertook the myriad tasks incumbent on his official function, sometimes enjoyable but also often frustrating – things did not move fast enough, he did not have enough typists, an essential asset for a bureaucrat – and frequently quite dull. The socializing, which was an essential component of his job, bored him and wore him out. 'The lunches and dinners, one after the other, are on the whole deadly boring. Meeting with great men is decidedly disappointing, even when it is Jean-Paul Sartre or Stravinsky, whom I found to be like a fussy and timorous old Russian lady.'[76] Stravinsky, one of the gods of his youth . . .

The new cultural attaché was a dynamic manager who took pride in proving himself to be up to the task with which he was the first to be charged (in peacetime, at least). Hence, notwithstanding the constant and probably sincere complaints he voiced over how little time he had, it is quite clear that he also enjoyed the temporary whirlwind of his existence. His artistic streak was called upon, for instance when he attended a John Cage concert, or a production of *Tristan*, or prepared the exhibition of a French artist who had invented a new stained-glass technique. His days were full up with encounters, sometimes discoveries, and also disappointments: 'I will shortly be meeting with an international antique dealer who would like to sell an entire museum he bought in Alaska to the Musée de l'Homme; then, I will attend the rehearsals of a *ballet nègre* for which I am trying to organize a French tour. And there are also concert, exhibition and conference issues that need to be settled, and who knows what else . . . I often miss the leisure and calm of my former life, but then, one must live a little.'[77] It was almost as if, unconsciously, he needed to accumulate enough experience and excitement to last him for the rest of his days, and expand still further his range of activities before his final embrace of the scholarly life.

However, he gradually managed to organize his schedule so as not to have to work all day for the cultural services, and to make time for his own projects. Every morning, he would go down to his office, where he would remain from 9 a.m. to 1:30 p.m. then come back up for lunch; he would then work on his thesis in his personal office, from 2 p.m. to 5:30 p.m.; and finally, after 5:30, he would go through the phone calls with his secretary and sign letters. This packing of 'two lives into one' worked, but it was 'of course a delicate balance'.[78] Yet Lévi-Strauss was to stick to this rhythm for a good part of his life, which would remain divided between pure research and writing, on the one hand, and administration (of science), on the other. At that time, the balance could well have definitively tilted towards administration. Indeed, in the spring of 1946, Henri Laugier was appointed deputy secretary general of the UN and tried to bring his young protégé along. In the end, it did not work out and, deep down, Lévi-Strauss felt a sense of relief. It would have been difficult not to follow Laugier, and the anthropologist would then probably have pursued a career as a high-level international civil servant, a bit like Stéphane Hessel whose wife, Vitia, was a close friend of Claude Lévi-Strauss in New York.

The twin births of the spring of 1947

By early March 1947, two weighty, freshly typed manuscripts lay on the desk of the cultural attaché – 300 to 350 pages each, comprising 1,200 footnotes and 80 figures – bearing the title 'The Elementary Structures of Kinship, Volume 1: Restricted Exchange; and Volume 2: Generalized Exchange'. To Rivet, he wrote: 'I was hoping to announce two pieces of good news at once, but Rose-Marie refuses to produce her baby, who has been expected any day for a week now. And since I have beaten her to the finish line by several lengths, I will not wait any longer to announce to you that, as of two weeks ago, my book is completely finished.'[79] Not unlike that expected baby playing hard to get, the completion of *Elementary Structures* had been repeatedly deferred over the previous two years, as if at each step the book's own power had generated new developments, new verifications, new corrections. At long last, there it was, preceding by a few days the birth of his son Laurent, on 16 March 1947. The description of the birth was limited by the abrupt expulsion of the father from the hospital room: he saw nothing, heard nothing, and was shown his baby thirty seconds before he was asked to make himself scarce again: 'As for the baby, this morning I found him really hideous; by 4 o'clock, a little less so, but still rather ugly. He weighed 4.1 kg at birth, and bears a striking resemblance to me, indeed shockingly so – for he looks like I do now, and not at all like I must have (I surmise) at his age.'[80] Two weeks later, he was correcting the second volume of his thesis while casting ironic glances at his offspring: 'I hope that, as the months go by, he shall acquire a soul, which he is still utterly lacking.'[81] On 15 April 1947, Laurent was circumcised, like his father. Little by little, Lévi-Strauss struck a more playful note, if with a still somewhat mocking tone showing through the tenderness: 'I find myself more at ease with him than I expected, a little as if he were a new type of monkey, probably less interesting than the real ones, but who, one already senses, will become something more. Our relationship mostly revolves around my making noises that interest him intensely and that he tries, indeed in vain, to reproduce through mimicry as I make them.'[82] Structural linguistics had particularly focused on the acquisition of language, an immense mystery and challenge for science.[83] Lévi-Strauss no doubt listened very attentively to the first babbles of his son, whom he coddled, bottle-fed and changed into new diapers, as he used to do for Lucinda, the monkey he brought back from Brazil. For his initiation into fatherhood, he was inspired by two models with which he had direct experience and which converged around a tremendous gentleness: on the one hand, his own father, a serious man yet little inclined to authority; on the other, the Nambikwara fathers, whose relationship of great physical tenderness with their children he had highlighted. Between the two – in addition to the role of somewhat distant but playful stepfather that he had already assumed with Rose-Marie's children – he found his way as a father.[84]

A new French cultural policy in the United States

The reshuffling and reorganization of France's cultural policy abroad was made possible, as we have seen, by the role given to intellectual elites within Free France. Henri Laugier and, from 1946, his successor Louis Joxe, were to translate this policy into action by breaking with interwar practices oriented towards high society and by promoting professionalization and democratization, engaging in activities that now included scientific and professional missions, academic exchanges and the hosting of scholarship students. Conditions during this period were highly favourable: between the end of the war and the announcement of the Marshall Plan (June 1947), science and the arts appeared as the principal levers for re-establishing dialogue between nations. The scholarship programme of Senator Fulbright (1946) contributed, while serving its own domestic ends, to the implementation of these new cultural policies of France in the United States.

Though a 'part-time' cultural attaché, Claude Lévi-Strauss dedicated great energy and effort to increasing the effectiveness and implementing reforms to rationalize and harmonize a public policy to whose general philosophy, now quite significantly transformed, he fully adhered. He was certainly no pen-pusher. In the various traces of his mandate that were left behind, the great administrator he might have been – if a tad impatient perhaps – shines through. The policies on French conference speakers, for instance, illustrates the kind of activities that Lévi-Strauss tried to promote. In this field, he argued, the point was to move away from the Alliance française's old practice of sending a great writer to preach the gospel to a group of French-speaking American old ladies. Seyrig had already pointed out the slight 'decrepitude' of the Alliances françaises, which were unfriendly to the new men sent by Free France, since most of their personnel in the United States were still Pétain supporters.[85] Yet the Alliances françaises, due to their longstanding presence, dense networks and libraries (including provincial ones), were still a force to be reckoned with. The cultural services thus considered creating a single service responsible for organizing all French conferences in the United States: 'I added that the Alliances françaises could no longer provide the same services as in the past; that cultural relations were no longer the prerogative of small groups of idle amateurs; that it was necessary to open up to new circles, especially academic circles.'[86] Lévi-Strauss proposed that the Alliances françaises, the France Forever committees,[87] university French departments and campus Maisons françaises should all merge into a single entity, so as to economize their resources and maximize their impact. On several occasions, he insisted on a choice of conference speaker, whom he preferred to be rather young, resilient, not overly eager for acclaim and, above all, English-speaking. Always concerned about efficiency, he recommended that maximal use be made of every speaker, whose travel expenses were paid for by France, emphasizing the benefits of penetrating not just the already conquered territory of the East Coast, but also into the small towns of the West and Midwest as well. He registered several successes: the conference of Albert Camus and Vercors, which had drawn a full house, under the auspices of the Franco-American Academic Committee. To his mind, beyond the existentialist craze he had impassively witnessed, this success 'proves us right in our conviction that traditional methods are outdated and that our conferences must be highly publicized and organized according to a broad, academic strategy, like the one we inaugurated yesterday'.[88] At times resigned, he would simply report the facts. For example, Mrs Guilbert's talk – entitled 'Paris, its artists, its GIs and I' – had drawn crowds. Lévi-Strauss's commentary: 'Mrs Guilbert's talent is of a decidedly low level. I am forced to admit that she is nonetheless quite effective, and that this dimension of the American situation should not be overlooked when we try to reach out to women's clubs and provincial associations.'[89]

Following the same logic of rationalization, Claude Lévi-Strauss considered creating a Centre du livre français in the United States, that would coordinate and centralize the sale of French books, making the most of American distribution networks. He recommended specific techniques – targeted mailing lists (to universities, French professors, scholarly societies) – to reach a particular readership that had almost no access, since the sale of French books was then next to nonexistent, due to prohibitive prices and a shortage of paper.[90] For sure, the cultural services maintained their traditional missions – for example, organizing major art exhibitions and tours for the Comédie française in the US – but the spirit and mode of implementation were transformed. In exchange for the Comédie française, Lévi-Strauss suggested bringing the Martha Graham dance company to Paris. He was indeed very attuned to the emergence of a new art of choreography, which appeared to him to 'represent in the United States today a particularly fertile and original form of artistic activity'.[91]

Lévi-Strauss enjoyed recounting ironic memories of his work as head of the cultural services: 'I had a few ideas but all failed miserably. First, I set out to organize an exhibition of early American art in Paris. But the state department was very reluctant, thinking it would give a poor image of the United States. Then, I tried to acquire a collection of native art from the Pacific Northwest, whose owner wanted to trade it for a few paintings by Matisse and Picasso. But this time, the French authorities, and especially the director of museums, Georges Salles, were opposed.'[92] Even in these failed attempts, one sees the revolution in thought manifest in his projects: to trade great works of French modern art for native artwork that was barely recognized as such. Just as the institutional resources of the new cultural policy were being increased (a network of cultural attaché posts across the entire world), and it was still fumbling for a way to distinguish itself from its previous, essentially linguistic, approach (the Alliances françaises, French language instruction as a symbol of the country's cultural might), it was breaking far more radically with the traditional policy of extending influence through prestige events.

Those involved in postwar French cultural diplomacy had grasped, and Lévi-Strauss chief among them, that what had crumbled during the war was not only France's prestige abroad, but more fundamentally its identity as a great nation in terms of culture, the land of arts and letters, and that the universalist approach now had to give way to one of reciprocity. The many missions that fell under the cultural attaché's mandate after the war (academics, doctors, architects, entrepreneurs, etc.) embraced an ideal of professional cross-over, but one in which the French now had much to learn, and not the other way around. Another intervention, small but significant, expressed this desire to enrol France in the international sphere of knowledge and culture, without any special prerogatives: Lévi-Strauss requested that the James Hyde Prize, awarded to works on the history of Franco-American relations or of nineteenth-century France, be opened to foreign authors, which had not been the case.

In the same spirit, he strenuously combatted the pompous rhetoric that often attended the presentation of French art, and more generally the self-satisfied tone, which he found simultaneously ridiculous, obsolete and counterproductive. 'A healthy policy of cultural relations, in my view, consists in earning the praise and admiration of our foreign friends, but also in leaving it up to them. By buffeting them with declarations that often sound excessive, we create a clash and produce exactly the opposite effect from the one we are trying to achieve. [. . .] It is not by proclaiming that painting is a specifically French art form, or that contemporary French literature is the greatest in the world that we convince the public of these verities.'[93] The anthropologist Lévi-Strauss was indeed the right person to challenge the 'civilizing mission'[94] that had been the French Republic's official doctrine in the colonies, and more generally in its relationships with other countries, especially in South America. The 1940 debacle had in any case put an end to this messianic ambition from a previous age.

Yet, the postwar marked the rise of a new generation to international literary stardom. As if nothing had happened, the French literati were being celebrated anew. But this time, it was Sartre, Simone de Beauvoir, Camus, Vercors, Malraux and no longer Georges Duhamel, Maurois and Gide. It is somewhat rich to see Claude Lévi-Strauss, the New York cultural attaché, welcoming without batting an eye the new celebrities from the world of French letters, more or less his age, who had emerged suddenly from an occupied France about which he knew nothing. New York was thus the scene of many significant encounters, symbolic vignettes of twentieth-century intellectual and artistic life. If the meeting in New York between Breton (who resided there) and Sartre, in January 1945, suggested a passing of the baton from an ageing surrealism to an existentialism on the rise, the more official one between Lévi-Strauss, then unknown, and Sartre, about to reach peak fame, prefigured the future fading of existentialism in favour of structuralism, which was to dominate the 1960s.

In the meantime, and for the rest of 1947, Lévi-Strauss was left to champ at the bit. He was now driven by a keen desire to return to France. He pressed Louis Joxe to find him a successor as soon as possible, but the search took several months.[95] He also tried to lay the groundwork for his return to France, gradually realizing that his original calculation had been a bit of a gambit – it proved far more difficult than anticipated to 'negotiate' a chair in Paris. Lévi-Strauss was coming back from about ten years abroad. He was still unknown, and the postwar academic world had been largely reshaped in his absence and, furthermore, on an ideological foundation that was largely foreign to him. Even though he held a *maîtrise de conférences*,[96] which allowed him to defend his thesis at the Sorbonne, he was far from having arrived. Yet, however complicated, the return to France had now become a vital necessity: 'On several occasions I had to decide whether to return to France or to remain in the United States, but such choices have had no bearing on the feelings of profound gratitude I have towards that country. The help I received there probably saved my life, and for several years I found there an intellectual climate and the opportunity for work that to a large extent have made me who I am. Only, I knew in my bones that I belonged to the Old World, irrevocably.'[97]

Part III

The Old World (1947–1971)

12

The Ghosts of Marcel Mauss

At the back of the room, I notice our great master and mentor Marcel Mauss. His Semitic features, alert and intelligent, wear an inscrutable smile, timeless like that of the Buddha.[1]

Agnès Humbert, Résistance, 1946

This chapter of Lévi-Strauss's life is haunted by ghosts, skeletons in the closet, shamans and the unconscious, both individual and collective. In autumn 1947, the anthropologist, now almost forty, returned as a prodigal son to a Europe still covered in scars from the war. He was also returning to a French anthropology that had not rid itself of the memories of Nazi occupation, locked in silence and a malaise that lasted well into the second half of the century. His American social scientist outlook, his name, his background, all put him at odds with the French academic scene, in which he still hoped to play a role befitting the work 'in the grand style'[2] he was bringing back in his trunks.

What was French social science in 1947? Prestigious institutions – in the field of anthropology, the Musée de l'Homme, the Musée des arts et traditions populaires – and a few new research centres within the fledgling Centre national de la recherche scientifique (CNRS). But for lack of any real anchorage in the universities, it was mostly represented by a few respected masters and intellectual traditions vaguely identified with disciplines still in the making. The war had disrupted these configurations and these men (there were few, if any, women in positions of power in the world of science at the time): some left, others remained and a few even thrived. All found themselves after the liberation of France in a milieu undergoing a process of recomposition, 'in the shadows of the untold history of the dark years'.[3] The play in which they were all acting would sometimes take a Shakespearian turn.

Marcel Mauss, a brilliant and generous mentor, both original and intense, had been laid low by Nazi occupation and anti-Semitism, and had lost his mind. Between 1945 and 1950 (when he finally died), in a state of presence/absence, he became a kind of King Lear figure, holed up in silence and innocence. For his part, Paul Rivet, the deposed king returned from exile, was unable to install an heir apparent. The collapse of these two pillars allowed the lesser barons, who had carved out their fiefdoms during the war, to rule. Historian Lucien Febvre, the only heir of the Annales School after the assassination of Marc Bloch, operated from a neighbouring kingdom, with clear expansionist ambitions, supported in that endeavour by a dynamic elder son, Fernand Braudel. Finally, Georges Gurvitch, the suzerain of sociology, played the part of the irascible and powerful uncle ruling over the Sorbonne,[4] anointed by his American exile, which had, however, not fundamentally changed him.[5] In this still undecided contest – who was to play the lead role? – Claude Lévi-Strauss entered late, in the autumn of 1947, back from long travels to the far reaches of the world. After a twelve-year absence from his kingdom, the exiled son had returned.

As far as he was concerned, it was his thesis defence – the ultimate academic rite, performed on 5 June 1948 – that would give him the opportunity to present his *Elementary Structures of Kinship*, which was subsequently published in 1949. It was also the time for a few consequential articles which – by establishing his intellectual, programmatic and epistemological filiation with Marcel Mauss, whom he had chosen as mentor – marked a sharp turn in the French social sciences. These few years were thus fertile and productive, and at the same time haunted by professional as well as personal failure, coloured by the state of doddering obliviousness to the world into which Mauss had fallen and was to remain until his death in 1950. For Claude Lévi-Strauss, the fact that Mauss had lost his lucidity was a 'very harsh blow'.[6] During a visit to the master, as he was to later recount, the latter confused him with Jacques Soustelle.[7] An inaugural non-recognition that was symbolic of other disillusionments to come. One must remember that the much honoured and decorated Lévi-Strauss experienced many setbacks in the struggle for peer recognition, which is the stuff of any academic career.

Kinship according to Lévi-Strauss

The ritual of the Sorbonne doctoral defence

When the candidate appeared at the Sorbonne, on 5 June 1948, to defend his doctoral thesis, he was thirty-nine years old. This was the ultimate academic rite of passage, which in French academia was highly codified. As his major thesis, he presented a weighty volume entitled *The Elementary Structures of Kinship*, a world tour of the rules and systems developed by primitive societies to organize their relationships of filiation and above all their alliances; his minor thesis, 'The Family and Social Life of the Nambikwara', was, properly speaking, an anthropological monograph, the direct outgrowth of his fieldwork in Brazil ten years earlier.[8]

The major work was a break with the traditional logic of a thesis in anthropology, which was supposed to make of the anthropologist returning from fieldwork a specialist in their regional area, with the doctoral work comprising a considered reflection on fieldwork notes. The text of *Structures* did not conform to the classical presentation of French anthropology, nor to the scholarly protocols governing the evaluation of the work on which it was based. Hence the initial difficulty of selecting members of the jury, which should be composed of competent authorities on the various parts of the world covered in the work. In the end, Lévi-Strauss defended in front of a committee comprising Marcel Griaule, a renowned Africanist, the jurist Jean Escarra, a specialist of Chinese law, Albert Bayet, a sociologist of religion and moral questions, Émile Benveniste, a linguist linked to Jakobson with expertise on the Indian subcontinent, whose name Lévi-Strauss himself had suggested to the man who had agreed to preside over this motley group, Georges Davy, the last of the living Durkheimians, a sociologist of archaic forms of contract, who was dean of the Sorbonne and known for his 'cantankerous disposition'.[9]

As we have seen, Lévi-Strauss had originally chosen Paul Rivet as his supervisor, but this choice became impossible as the director of the Musée de l'Homme was nearing retirement. He had also thought of Mauss, but in that case it was ill health that stood in the way. Davy thus represented a pragmatic solution, which did not reflect any intellectual affinity. Quite the opposite; Lévi-Strauss remained at odds with a large part of the Durkheimian legacy, of which Davy was an eminent representative. He would later explain to the British anthropologist Rodney Needham, who had asked him about the use in *Elementary Structures* of inapt Durkheimian expressions, such as 'mechanical solidarity' and 'organic solidarity': 'As a matter of fact, I can still remember why I purposefully introduced, in three or four instances, these Durkheimian terms in my book. It was, basically, so that my doctoral committee would see something vaguely familiar in my terminology and not find my book too foreign.'[10] This purely rhetorical and calculated use of Durkheim may come as a surprise. Did Lévi-Strauss feel so removed that he had to provide proof of a common language? In any case, he went on to explain that 'generalized exchange' had nothing to do with 'organic solidarity' in the Durkheimian sense. In its very title, *The Elementary Structures of Kinship* both echoed and challenged a classic of Durkheim's sociology, *The Elementary Forms of Religious Life* (1912) – and expressed the same theoretical ambition, the same propensity to grasp the social through the 'elementary', and the same voracious erudition. And yet, Lévi-Strauss, like a convict being led to the gallows, expected little understanding from his jury (with the exception of Benveniste, 'probably the only one who understands what I have attempted to do'[11]), as if he was only too well aware of having produced a kind of unidentified scholarly object.

The defence did not prove him entirely wrong. In the absence of the official thesis report, which could not be found, we have had to rely here on a letter from Mariel Jean-Brunhes Delamarre.[12] A geographer and anthropologist of rural life with connections to Musée de l'Homme circles, and the daughter of geographer Jean Brunhes, she was very attuned to academic gossip, as exemplified by the nimble tone of the long and spirited message she sent to the anthropologist André-Georges Haudricourt, an open-minded Marxist then posted to Hanoi who was well versed in linguistics and its applications to anthropology. According to the letter, the discussion on the minor thesis went well, even though Griaule 'called for a more in-depth analysis of some of the indigenous concepts (the notion of person, the role of tradition)'. It was when they turned to the major thesis that the going got rougher. Attacks were quickly levelled after Lévi-Strauss provided a clear presentation of his method and the close relationship between kinship systems and language:

> Davy (president of the major thesis committee) – after the opening ritual compliments – attacked L.-S. on several counts. A monumental work, the work of a philosopher – but why systematize so furiously – some assertions were not self-evident but postulated – like Descartes you begin with self-evident truth, but unlike Descartes, your self-evident truth is neither clear nor self-evident – marriage appears to you as a phenomenon of exchange and reciprocity because it is designed to meet needs that you consider correspond to native psychobiological dispositions, for example the need for a rule as such. On what basis do you support this conviction regarding the initial element of *homo socius*? In addition, your method is rather curious – you first establish a number of facts – and it is only after one enormous volume devoted to this that you launch into three monograph studies, as if to say: 'Very well! Now, let us check and see if I can indeed find such a system in the facts.' You are a highly specialized algebraic mathematician – your self-evident truths suggest a logic, a truly prodigious kinship directive – women are at the heart of the exchange – but they are like objects – they are traded back and forth – this is, according to you, what presides over the rules of marriage – and even enables you to establish algebraic formulae that indicate the various positions of women within social structures – But you are entirely oblivious to the class perspective, on the one hand, and to the mystical element concealed within the exchange (in marriage, the feminine mystique, and the child's), on the other – In your view, this is all just a system of combined signs, etc.

Benveniste took over and said he felt, on the contrary, 'familiar with [his] manner of working'. Then Escarra: 'In your Chinese example, you rely on rules, on a code, on prohibitions – but one should be careful because this system defined by the aristocracy was only observed by its members. Every time we speak of matrimonial rules, it is specified that these rituals are reserved to the nobility. Looking at this code, one is made to believe that all of China gets married following these decreed rules – whereas it is clear that the people never obeyed a single one of them – and this is the vast majority.' The attacks on his empty logic and mathematical formalism gave way to the contrary yet complementary reproaches of a lack of empirical control. After 'it is all artificial' came 'it is all false'. It is indeed striking to see formulated here, at this threshold moment of Lévi-Strauss's intellectual production, the two major critiques that were to remain as constant as his own arguments.

Since the discussion had been going on for over five hours, Bayet only added a few words. Final verdict: high honours. This letter suggests that neither its author nor the jury fully grasped the novelty or even the basic argument of what Lévi-Strauss was developing. The persistent opacity of the thesis did not dissipate with its publication. In the meantime, following the defence, Benveniste sent him in writing a few detailed corrections, mistakes in the transcription of Sanskrit, and concluded with a jab at the arrogance of the impetuous young man: 'One more word. The position you adopt unquestionably gives you the right to pass judgement on your predecessors. Yet, is it really fair to say: "Malinowski, with his characteristic agility"? Is this really all that characterizes Malinowski's work?'[13] Three letters and ten days later, Lévi-Strauss maintaining (and justifying) his critical view of Malinowski throughout, the master was won over by the disciple: 'One must be resigned, I see now, to retaining from Malinowski only the observational data. It is a sign after all that anthropology has become more rigorous. As your impressive work shows.'[14]

'The rules of the game'

Reading it today, this 'impressive work' has retained its exorbitant character: even while belonging to the perfectly identifiable field of kinship anthropology, it remains an unclassifiable world-encompassing book, a monster of a book. As Lévi-Strauss put it later: 'Around 1942–43, when I began to study kinship, I could base my work on a century of systematic studies of kinship systems. I had access to materials that had been described and analysed in a relatively homogeneous technical language – today we would say, "normalized" – and this made it possible to go on to the next stage, comparison.'[15] Lévi-Strauss had drawn on two entire bodies of literature, one French (until the mid-1930s) and the other American, particularly abundant and new to the French reader. The freshness of the material was part of the novelty promised in the introduction, which haughtily dismissed any new 'grinding out of examples already exhausted by the past discussions of Frazer, Briffault, Crawley and Westermarck'.[16] Also striking was the unprecedented tone, both experimental and interdisciplinary. The author admitted his shortcomings and occasionally wobbly hypotheses, but that was a side issue: what mattered were the audacity of his interpretation and the progress of the discussion. On Lewis Morgan, one of his predecessors, to whom the book was dedicated, Lévi-Strauss concluded that '[his work] was especially great at a time when scientific precision and exact observation did not seem to him to be incompatible with a frankly theoretical mode of thought and a bold philosophical taste'.[17] Lévi-Strauss's book was certainly not a work of philosophy, even if its argument raised and revolved around a few big questions: a hypothesis on culture, a contribution to the theory of incest, a reflection on the intellectual basis of dualism and reciprocity, an analysis of the structural implications of the various types of marriages, with theoretical thrusts and bursts of generality that Anglo-American critics would later describe as 'typically French'. It was a profoundly anthropological work, delving into a thick and dense corpus of material – the author prided himself on having indexed 7,000 articles and books – to demonstrate the value and acute sophistication of the solutions developed by savage societies to manage and survive socially. Hence the hubris of its logical quest as much as its 'ordering' of the real.

According to Lévi-Strauss, the incest prohibition had no natural foundation, even though it could be empirically observed in almost all societies. It was thus a rule emanating from the sphere of 'culture', but whose universal character belonged to the natural order. 'Where does nature end and culture begin?'[18] Lévi-Strauss's answer to this riddle, with which the traditions of philosophy (Rousseau) and psychoanalysis have long struggled, followed a characteristic logic of reversal: the prohibition of incest, negatively formulated, turned into an invitation to reciprocity. By 'projecting' women and girls outside the blood clan, and by assigning them spouses from other groups, the incest prohibition created the first artificial bonds, which were social in essence, between these groups. 'Considered from the most general viewpoint, the incest prohibition expresses the transition from the natural fact of consanguinity to the cultural fact of alliance.'[19] It was therefore 'the fundamental step because of which, by which, but above all in which, the transition from nature to culture is accomplished'.[20] It thus became *the* rule, the supreme law of the gift. Structural interpretation identified the prohibition of incest, in kinship language, as a 'zero phoneme', that had no meaning in and of itself (neither a natural nor a moral foundation) yet that imposed positive prescriptions (ties with other clans). It was therefore the main operator at work in the constitution of these rules and ties. Why did these rules of exogamy and prohibition apply so strictly to traditional societies? The rigour with which they were enforced matched the level of 'incestuous desire'[21] in these societies: it is because there is an incestuous desire (nature) that there is a rule (response from society), and not because of any spontaneous horror in the face of incest.

The difficulty arose from the fact that this universal theory was based on particular regional cultures – for the most part societies located in Asia and South-East Asia, but also Melanesia and Africa – and that there were exceptions, such as Arab societies, to whom this reasoning was more difficult to apply. To reconcile the quest for a universal law with the infinite diversity of marriage rules, Lévi-Strauss undertook an exercise in modelling, which tended to reduce the profusion of kinship data to a few simple principles, a few nomenclatures that formed a system and could together provide a veritable 'grammar' of kinship, a systematic chart in which all options could be logically deduced, for they were not infinite. Such a grammar, such a system of systems, could only make sense, once viewed as a comprehensive whole. In concrete terms, this entailed a strategy of reduction through the establishment of typologies. First, the distinction between the 'elementary structures of kinship' that prescribed a specific kind of spouse, as opposed to 'complex structures', in which marriage was left to individual free choice, as in our contemporary societies. This formed a gradient: the first type was never entirely prescriptive, and the other never entirely free (as we know, spouses are chosen from one's milieu, with a comparable cultural and educational level, etc.). The decision to focus exclusively on 'elementary' structures proceeded here again from a research strategy and temperament which, in Lévi-Strauss, favoured 'small islands of organization'[22] within the 'vast empirical stew'.[23] With regard to elementary structures, the author's classificatory zeal revealed three possible solutions, which in part mapped Granet's typology: dualism, restricted exchange and generalized exchange. The basic idea was that 'a man must obtain a woman from another man who gives him a daughter or a sister'.[24] In so doing, men, both takers and givers of women, opened 'cycles of reciprocity' that were more or less long: from one generation to the next in the first case (back and forth), over a few generations in the second, over *n* generations in the third – labelled 'differed exchange' for that reason by Granet. It entailed a fair amount of trust, for the received woman eventually compensates, in the form of a gift, for the woman who was given up, but with a lag. On the contrary, in dualist societies, the reciprocity is exemplary. But if dualist societies provided perfect illustrations of the reciprocity principle, they constituted a particular case of restricted exchange, itself a restricted version of generalized exchange. In all these exchanges – in which the woman is the privileged intercessor, the object and not the agent – marriage is always located between two limit cases, ranging from absolute reciprocity (in generalized exchange) to absolute withdrawal into oneself (in incest).

Constantly increasing its focal length, *Elementary Structures* was intended to provide the basis for a general theory of exchange in which the social was considered as a vast system of communication. Whatever the material used – kinship, later myth, rites, cooking – the aim was to discover 'the rules of the game'. This game revealed in its very principle the universality of exchange and reciprocity in the societies being studied: exchange of women first of all, exchange of words, exchange of goods. These three major categories comprise the signs that circulate within a social semantics that combines the codes specific to each. 'The ingredients of this theory have long been familiar. It is in their fusion, and in the elevation of reciprocity and exchange to the status of almost Newtonian laws of social motion, that Levi-Strauss's innovation lies.'[25] Taking up and expanding the intuition developed by Mauss in *The Gift*, harnessing Marcel Granet's typology of matrimonial exchanges, Lévi-Strauss broke new ground by throwing structural linguistics into the mix. He admittedly referred to Mauss much more than to Granet. And clearly, 'forgetting' Granet allowed him to conceive of and present structural anthropology as more of a rupture than a continuity – especially with regard to the influence of the Durkheimians, of whom Granet was one of the most original representatives – emphasizing its new alliances (phonology) rather than its old cousins.[26]

This world of laws and obligations – of prescriptions and proscriptions, of interconnected and infinitely declined rules – is properly speaking the kinship regime our contemporary societies have left behind, under the influence of feminism, individualism, new reproductive technologies, etc.[27] The matrimonial bond is now considered as the very expression of sentiment, of intimate emotion, and of a highly individual romantic choice. Hence the barely audible quality of the voice of the kinship anthropologist, with his patterns, kinship diagrams and mathematical formulas. Yet this did not exclude flights of meditative fancy, such as the one that ends the book, a phantasmagoria of the golden age, an age in which, according to the Andaman myth of future life, women are no longer exchanged: 'i.e. removing to an equally unattainable past or future the joys, eternally denied to social man, of a world in which one might *keep to oneself*'.[28] A little endogamous fantasy (keeping to oneself) to close this grand treatise on exogamy . . .

The solitary monument of Elementary Structures

In this fabric of exchanges, in which the essence of the social is revealed, women are thus precious objects. Like words, and like goods, they are signs: it is because value is attached to them that they are worthy of being exchanged, and not the other way around. Later, this description of women as 'signs' would be distasteful to feminists. Lévi-Strauss defended himself in his way, simultaneously serious and flippant: 'It's a futile argument. One could just as well say that women exchange men; all you have to do is replace the plus sign with the minus sign and vice versa – the structure of the system would not change. If I put it another way, it is only because that is what nearly all human societies think and say.'[29] It so happened that it is men who, in the vast majority of cases, exchange women and not the other way around. Yet, as Didier Éribon has pointed out, it is striking that one of the first female readers of *The Elementary Structures of Kinship*, Simone de Beauvoir, was not in the least disturbed by this.

Indeed, the glowing review by Simone de Beauvoir, published in *Les Temps modernes* soon after the book came out in June 1949, introduced this work of considerable theoretical scope and erudition to a wider intellectual circle. Georges Bataille's review in the journal *Critique* extended this further.[30] Lévi-Strauss's thesis was thus first read by the 'progressive' intelligentsia of the Parisian Left Bank – a milieu to which he was not entirely foreign. There were links. In this case, it was Michel Leiris, whom Lévi-Strauss had recently met and immediately befriended – 'I didn't know his work and read it with delight'[31] – who told Simone de Beauvoir about this monumental work, as she had just finished writing *The Second Sex*. Keen to bring her own anthropological reading up to date, she went to Lévi-Strauss's house to read the proofs of *Elementary Structures*. She found in it an empirical description of male–female relations that covered the full range of matches and a reflection on the seam between nature and culture, a central issue in her own work. Her reading revealed a fine understanding of Lévi-Strauss's work, even though she entirely overlooks several essential methodological aspects – nothing for instance on structural linguistics – and indulges in a few philosophical manoeuvres that seem rather far-fetched today. 'His own thought belongs obviously to the grand humanist current that considers human existence as bearing within itself its own reason.' Pointing out echoes with Marx and even Husserl, she also finds herself 'singularly struck by the correspondences of certain descriptions with the thesis of existentialism'.[32]

A clear case of intellectual hijacking? Frédéric Keck is probably right to see in the text a possible 'compatibility between the philosophy of existence and the structural method applied to human phenomena'.[33] Fifteen years later, the controversies that were to oppose Sartre and Lévi-Strauss and simultaneously made them into antithetical paradigms would shut down that possibility. In the meantime, we should note the concurrent publication of these two books in 1949: *The Second Sex* and *The Elementary Structures of Kinship*. Two dense books, both of which emerged out of long bibliographical sifting and also well equipped on the conceptual front, resting on solid theoretical frameworks. Both authors, as we know, had passed the *agrégation* in philosophy. The immediate celebrity of the one contrasted with the initial obscurity of the other. In addition to refounding, reinvigorating and reorienting the feminist movement, *The Second Sex* lent itself more readily to summarization in pithy formulas and theses: 'One is not born, but rather becomes, a woman.' Nothing of the kind in *Elementary Structures*, which was intended as a scholarly work and published by an academic publisher: Presses Universitaires de France (PUF).

The publishing fortunes of *The Elementary Structures of Kinship* highlight what this work subsequently became: a monument, not always read, a kind of frightening totem of the discipline, which did not circulate widely and slowly went out of print, before being given new life with the second printing in 1967. The initial print run specified in the contract signed on 16 February 1948 was 2,000 copies. PUF only agreed to publish it thanks to a subsidy from a national research council, the CNRS. Ten years later, in 1958, when the book finally sold out, the publisher refused to reprint a work deemed 'unfortunately too weighty'[34] and offered that its author recover the copyright – which he did. The book was only translated into English twenty years later, as a result of its growing fame, after several unsuccessful attempts that resulted in a marked cooling of relations between the anthropologist and PUF.[35] The strictly academic and scholarly reception of the book was not at all unfavourable, as attested by several reviews (by Roger Bastide, in addition to those by Simone de Beauvoir and Bataille) and the Paul-Pelliot Junior prize, with the 50,000 francs that went with it, awarded at a luncheon held at the Rôtisserie Périgourdine, on Place Saint-Michel – photographs of the event were published in *Combat* on 11 November 1949.[36] This recently created prize, awarded by historians and members of the Académie française, gave Lévi-Strauss a modicum of acclaim on par with the measured praise that his book had received. This was a far cry, however, from the intellectual event that commentators would retrospectively make of it. Yet some discerned its potential long-term impact: 'I would like to convey', Benveniste wrote to him, 'at least in a quick note, how much I enjoyed re-reading your two works, now objectified in published form – your incredibly evocative descriptions of the Nambikwara, in which extremely rigorous analysis does not come at the expense of human sympathy, and above all your book on kinship. I do not know how it will be received by qualified anthropologists, but I believe that sooner or later the method of structural analysis will prevail here as elsewhere and that you will be credited with having opened up new avenues. Your work will stimulate the most fertile discussions, from which not only this issue, but many others besides, will emerge transformed.'[37]

A benevolent prophet of the scientific legacy of Lévi-Strauss's work, Émile Benveniste understood that the book was going to incubate for a decade or so and gradually acquire a 'foundational' status, including for the critiques it periodically elicited. The first among them dated from 1950, when the philosopher Claude Lefort attacked the book in *Les Temps modernes* for its abstraction and the excessive reduction of the real to models and categories.[38] Lévi-Strauss responded a year later: 'The term "social structure" has nothing to do with empirical reality but with models which are built up after it.'[39] *Elementary Structures* had even acquired a kind of aura, due to the book's unavailability for years. Emmanuel Terray has described having asked Alain Badiou to borrow his copy of the first edition in 1957, since it was difficult to procure one: 'I copied one hundred pages from it by hand, which I still have. And when I finished copying the pages, given the effort it had taken, Alain could not but give me the book. That is how I have the first edition. For me, at the time, and I still hold this opinion, the progress this book represented was comparable, in its field, to Marx's *Capital* or to Freud's *Interpretation of Dreams*.'[40] Besides the shock waves it emitted, much of the awe inspired by the book rested on an unquestionably fetishistic dimension, which became clear in the Anglo-American reception of the French edition of the book: '[The copies] in libraries either fell apart (the work was miserably manufactured) or were stolen, and the few remaining copies were treasured by their owners the way bootleg copies of Henry Miller used to be.'[41] Between going out of print in 1958 and the new edition in 1967, *Elementary Structures* thus stood, at the height of the structuralist craze, as a lofty and solitary monument, sublime in its quasi-underground status.

The outsider

Let us rewind ten years, to the autumn of 1947. Claude Lévi-Strauss, freshly arrived from the United States, had not taken part in the great reshuffling that occurred at the moment of liberation. During his first visit to Paris in the winter of 1944, he had sensed that the return would be a battle and had shared his impressions with Jakobson, who wanted to return to Europe at the time, prior to giving up on the idea: 'Everyone has managed very well without us, and the posts are all either taken or claimed by small cogs solidly lodged in the machinery.'[42] If the exile's position did have its advantages – having an American experience and network – it also had the disadvantage of confining one to an in-between world and to delaying reintegration. This outsider position within the French academic world probably accounted for some of the professional failures to come.

The thesis defence opened doors at the Sorbonne for Lévi-Strauss. But, in actual fact, it was never really an option. However, while the anthropologist was still only a *maître de recherches* at the CNRS (from the end of 1947 until March 1949), two institutions offered possible future opportunities:

one, the Musée de l'Homme, whose direction had been left vacant by Rivet's retirement, was already quite familiar; the other was the Collège de France. During these two years, from 1948 until 1950, Lévi-Strauss failed to obtain a position at either, ending up in early 1951 at the École pratique des hautes études – not within the dynamic 'Sixth Section' of history and social sciences, with which he had already formed strong intellectual ties, but within the more low-profile 'Fifth Section' of religious studies.

A view on the Musée de l'Homme

Who was going to succeed Paul Rivet, 71 years of age and planning to retire soon, as head of the Musée de l'Homme? Lévi-Strauss was a potential candidate, as assistant director of the museum, along with Jacques Soustelle, Rivet's beloved disciple, who loomed larger still because of the leading political role that his early and steadfast commitment to General de Gaulle had ensured him.

From his new apartment at 13 avenue d'Eylau, in a posh building a stone's throw from the place du Trocadéro, Lévi-Strauss could cast tender glances at the object of his desire, as he suggested to his friend Roman Jakobson: 'I have a very beautiful apartment, wonderfully located, with a view over the place du Trocadéro, the Palais de Chaillot and the Eiffel Tower, 200 metres from the Musée de l'Homme and its library; only it has no bathroom and the heating doesn't work. All this will get fixed in due time.'[43] In the heart of a particularly cold Parisian winter, when provisions were still rationed, material hardship did not really matter when compared with the promise of satisfaction on this front. Yet Lévi-Strauss did not have his head in the clouds. He knew (if only in part) what to expect: 'In the meantime, I have been granted the use (for three months) of the director's office at the Musée de l'Homme, which is heated and will remain empty until someone is selected to succeed Rivet, who is himself in Mexico, and who will retire to his apartment upon his return. Do not draw any conclusions from this: the successor's selection is proceeding in the confusion of unimaginable intrigues. But I am neither in line for it, nor considered as a potential candidate, ignored as I am by the all-powerful museum trustees. In all likelihood, Millot will be appointed, as was already expected. The privilege of using the sumptuous office for the interim period was granted to me precisely because I am not in the running.'[44]

This tumultuous succession drew on a long institutional history. The old conservative physical anthropology inherited from Paul Broca still held sway within an active network of learned societies and journals, which had been revived under the Vichy regime. At the opposite end of the spectrum, a cultural anthropology had been on the rise since the beginning of the century, fuelled by the Durkheimian offensive which, thanks to Mauss, Rivet and Lévy-Bruhl, had found a foothold on the margins of the university – in the Institut d'ethnologie and the École pratique des hautes études – and was solidly anchored at the Musée de l'Homme. Yet the latter institution remained under the administrative supervision of the Muséum national d'Histoire naturelle, with the director's position being tied to a professorship at the museum.[45] Its directors laid great store in the biological foundations and anthropometric measurements that had been the matrix of a racialism bolstered by the war, and only partially called into question in its aftermath, and which in addition enabled the building of disciplinary bridges with prehistory, paleo-botany, etc. Rivet, himself a military doctor, was a somatic physician who had converted late to linguistic anthropology. To have no medical training was thus an almost insurmountable obstacle to being appointed director of the Musée de l'Homme.[46]

And yet the situation was evolving: 'Rivet (this is strictly between us)', Lévi-Strauss confided to Jakobson, 'has engaged in a major campaign to hand over his position to me; but it is too late. He might have succeeded, had he started a year ago. Now, he has discredited himself by partaking in previous unlikely schemes, that have all foundered. I must therefore put more effort into not being a candidate than I would have had to in order to be selected [. . .]. Now, there is nothing to be done: it will be either Vallois or Soustelle.'[47] In the end, although it took two years, on 27 January 1950, Lévi-Strauss announced to Jakobson that 'Vallois won out easily over Soustelle', putting the Musée de l'Homme into the hands of the 'most narrow-minded physical anthropology'.[48] A few days later, news reached the United States, and Lévi-Strauss received an offer from Alfred Kroeber at Berkeley to come back to work in the US, the first of several propositions from the other side of the Atlantic that were to arrive with the same regularity as professional failures in France in those years.

Dr Henri Victor Vallois was none other than the author of the *Anthropologie de la population française* in three volumes, an applied ethno-racist study in line with Vichy policies – at a time when, within the powerful Alexis Carrel Foundation, racial categories served the purposes of either population control (moderate version) or full-fledged eugenics (radical version). As Daniel Fabre has pointed out, anthropological knowledge had been directly drawn upon by the Vichy regime, just as it had been by the Nazis.[49] It is therefore rather telling that Henri Vallois was appointed to replace Rivet, whose exile had been triggered by the first wave of arrests that dismantled the Musée de l'Homme Resistance network in 1943.[50] In the aftermath of that operation, abuses of anthropology and collusions between the discipline and the Vichy regime were such that the latter authorized the creation in 1942 of the first chair in anthropology at the Sorbonne. Georges Montandon, the dark angel of French anthropology, and a representative of the worst anti-Semitic leanings of a certain kind of physical anthropology, came close to being elected to that chair, which eventually went to the Africanist Marcel Griaule. The appointment of Vallois to the helm of the Musée de l'Homme thus signalled the return of that shameful heritage, as much as Rivet's failure to impose his successor.[51]

As a Jew coming from abroad, and from that America detested by both the far right and the communists, Lévi-Strauss did not experience any of this, or only from a distance. This postwar settling of scores had proceeded by means of institutional purges that were anything but discreet – Georges-Henri Rivière and Marcel Griaule, for instance, had to briefly leave their posts, prior to being reintegrated – and they shrouded this moment in its own kind of violence, a violence that was manifest in the turmoil of Marcel Mauss, and in the indictment that lay in the contrast between the integrity of his body and the evacuation of his mind. It continues to haunt the field of French anthropology, as a sense of remorse. And catharsis would be long in coming. Vallois was appointed in 1950, the year Mauss died.

At that time, Lévi-Strauss was preparing to wrap up his post as assistant director,[52] after more than two years of daily trips to the Palais de Chaillot's comfortable director's office, which had ultimately escaped him. Hired by the CNRS as a researcher and as a professor at the Institut d'ethnologie, he spent most of his time at the Musée de l'Homme, very near his home. But there was officially another assistant director, André Leroi-Gourhan, in charge of prehistory, who rarely came to Paris, since his teaching duties kept him in Lyon. 'The two assistant directors get along, but at a distance.'[53] The cautious coexistence they initiated then has since become legendary among French social scientists. If their fields of study were close – the vast and remote regions of peoples without writing, remote in prehistoric times for Leroi-Gourhan, and in exotic spaces for Lévi-Strauss – their theoretical horizons were radically opposed: the former began from material culture (especially techniques and tools) and took *homo faber* as the centre and starting point of social organization; the latter worked from representations and the symbolic activity specific to man and then moved to objects (techniques, productions, kinship relations, myths, rites). All the ingredients were thus present for them to develop an aggressive jealousy, which they were both intelligent enough to transform, over the years, into a reasonable alliance. As Leroi-Gourhan would later recall, not without humour: 'Now we support one another in friendship after having endured each other's company in suspicion.'[54]

Double setback at the Collège de France

During these same years, and more or less in parallel, Lévi-Strauss was applying for a chair at the prestigious Collège de France – a temple of knowledge, 'a fearsome place, off limits, where as a student I didn't allow myself to enter'.[55] The idea of bringing him into the Collège came from one of his mentors, the physiologist Henri Laugier. The latter contacted his colleague Henri Piéron, the 'famous psychologist, communist',[56] and friend and partner of Henri Wallon, both professors at the Collège. To seek a position at that celebrated institution at the age of forty was not especially uncommon. It was thus with confidence and serenity that the ball was set rolling, as soon as he arrived in France: 'I thought that everything was arranged by mysterious powers, that all I needed to do was let myself be carried along.'[57] He was prone to such bursts of naivety in his letters to Piéron, which were full of deference and optimism.[58] Then came disillusionment, followed a second time in 1950. Twice rebuffed, the candidate gave this interpretation: 'I had lived outside of France for the past thirteen years and was in no position to understand that I was going to be the stakes in a battle between clans within the Collège, between liberals and conservatives.'[59] He added that it was at this same time (in February 1949) that Georges Dumézil was elected. In April 1950, it was Braudel's turn. Both these men, together with Benveniste, the modern historian Marcel Bataillon and geographer Pierre Gourou, became his staunchest allies, but to no avail. Lévi-Strauss, stunned by this double setback, 'was convinced that [he] would never have a real career'.[60] As he told Jakobson, who had complained about his silence: 'The failure at the Collège was very hard to take, all the more so that I consider it as definitive, having resolved never to apply again anywhere and to anybody. But this decision has forced me to reflect quite a bit and I have had to change my perspective on quite a few things, myself included.'[61] The way this double misfortune actually unfolded and was received was somewhat more complicated than the sketch offered by Lévi-Strauss. The failure was, each time, of a different nature, having more to do with the profile of the post than with any particular candidate. In 1949, it was strictly disciplinary – sociology was defeated by art history. In 1950, it was more about the individual candidate, and Lévi-Strauss was defeated by the historian Louis Chevalier; but neither his competitor nor the line of argument deployed corresponded to a quarrel between Ancients and Moderns, or, paradoxically, vice versa.[62]

The whole affair began when Henri Wallon, who held the chair in childhood psychology, retired. That chair was a 'foundation chair', endowed by the City of Paris and the *département* of the Seine, and was subject to an agreement with the Assembly of Collège de France professors, which was very protective of prerogatives regarding appointments to the chair. When the time came to replace Wallon, there were two opposing camps: one, led by literature specialists Jean Pommier and Edmond Faral and by sociologist-geographer André Siegfried, wanted to create a chair in 'the psychology of art' (with René Huyghe in mind); the other, around Piéron, would have liked to re-establish the chair in 'comparative sociology', in line with the one Marcel Mauss had held, which had disappeared with Maurice Halbwachs (and for which Lévi-Strauss was the candidate). The campaign led by Piéron, which was probably inadequate, and the strenuous mobilization on the part of the opposing camp account for the very honourable defeat of Lévi-Strauss, since at the Assembly of 27 November 1949, the 'psychology of art' option received twenty-one votes (the absolute majority was twenty) and 'comparative sociology' sixteen votes. Still, it came as a surprise. In theory, it should have all ended there.

But the special status of this chair created a second act to the drama, and a second application: in March 1950, the Municipal Council rejected the chair in psychology of art, which likely did not reflect the concerns of the council members who had recommended its creation. An imbroglio ensued, which led to the following compromise: the chair in art was to be maintained, so long as a new chair in sociology was created.[63] On 26 November 1950, the professors thus met once again to elect a second new colleague. For Lévi-Strauss, this time it was Benveniste who ran the show.

After praising the French school of sociology and the richness of the Anglo-American school of anthropology, he advocated for Lévi-Strauss, who promised both to perpetuate the tradition and to bring innovation. Described as having been 'trained in the crucible of fieldwork', his long American experience constituted, according to Benveniste, a clear comparative advantage – an argument that cut both ways . . . Henri Piéron only added a few words about the chair's title – 'comparative sociology' – with the comparison being between primitive and contemporary societies. This was a true science, he added, perhaps for the benefit of his hard-science colleagues, for it was now based on fieldwork!

For the opposite side, Roger Dion proposed a chair to be entitled 'history and social structure of Paris and the Paris region'. Dion's speech struck an ambitious chord, similar to that of Benveniste. Invoking a filiation with Halbwachs and urban sociology, the chair would be dedicated to identifying the laws governing the development of society based on vast empirical studies. And Paris offered a plethora of untapped archival material and quantitative data. The growth of the capital city was a grand and underexplored subject of historical and urban sociological inquiry. Dion thus managed to present a subject of historical, geographical and sociological interest that could bring together the various disciplines of the Collège, emphasizing the modern character of its research tools, especially statistics, and potential partnerships with INED, the national demographics institute. This new institution, created in 1945 'on the ruins of the Fondation Carrel', was the heir to a demographic knowledge marked by an implicitly (or explicitly) racist psychology that had been mobilized by the Vichy regime under the pretence of a rhetoric of modernization.[64] Louis Chevalier was of this school.[65] This was thus not the 'Ancients' camp in the strict sense, as the intervention of biologist Jean Roche further demonstrated. The latter identified statistical tools as a driver of future scientific progress, already under way in his own field. As he concluded: 'Our mission is not to contribute to the development of sciences whose foundations have already been laid [sociology and anthropology] as much as to promote that of new disciplines [urban statistics].' Taken together, these two speeches gave the impression that it was Lévi-Strauss who represented the perpetuation, however brilliant, of a tradition, whereas Chevalier was boldly clearing a path through a jungle of unexplored mysteries. André Siegfried's letter, which was read aloud during the session, delivered the final blow: 'I believe [. . .] that sociology should be represented among the disciplines taught at the Collège de France, but not so much in the form of the sociology of primitive peoples or anthropology – however interesting research in that field may be – but rather in the scientific observation of current social phenomena. [. . .] The Collège must not ignore these [demographic] questions that comprise a science in the making, an avant-garde science, which is precisely in keeping with the spirit of our institution. It so happens that a whole team of researchers, statisticians and scholars is today passionately investigating these issues in France.'[66] The results of the vote: twenty-two chose the history of Paris and thirteen comparative sociology, with two abstentions.

The verdict came as a bombshell for Lévi-Strauss, who had not seen it coming. Was it the result of latent anti-Semitism, as he himself suggested in veiled terms? An anti-Semitism tinged with anti-Americanism, as suggested in the letter that Jean Pommier (who had abstained) sent to his old friend Henri Laugier, following the second defeat: 'One of Lévi-Strauss's coreligionists at the foreign ministry let it be known that if we did not take him, America would offer him a position worthy of his talent. So he'll be alright. You told me he was of my calibre. This is no understatement. One of his coreligionists at the Collège de France read to us yesterday the opinion of some foreign scholar, who compared Lévi-Strauss's book on kinship to *On the Origin of Species.* It was not a Pommier that the majority passed on, then, it was a Darwin. What possessed them?'[67] It was well known that a similar kind of hostility animated Edmond Faral, the Collège administrator from 1937 to 1955. This conservative Latin scholar, who was fiercely opposed to linguistics and who would foam at the mouth at the mere mention of Jakobson's name, was thus an irreconcilable enemy of Lévi-Strauss.[68] He had secured a favourable position by strategically allying himself with men who also stood for 'science in the making' and could boast a historiographical project that was useful for the conduct of public affairs and promoted a dialogue between research and expertise on the burning demographic questions of the early days of the Fourth Republic.

After two years of campaigning for positions at the Musée and the Collège, which were unfortunately intertwined, it was a total rout. In the aftermath of his latest setbacks, Lévi-Strauss wrote to Piéron to thank him nonetheless for having interceded in his favour: 'The blow was too brutal and harsh for me to bring myself to talk about it these past few days. But it would be ungrateful of me to defer writing to you any longer. In my utter sadness, which I have no doubt you also share, I remain grateful to you for conceiving of this wonderful project, for trying to see it through over the past few years and, finally, for defending me last Sunday with a warmth and conviction noted by all those who have written or called since. I know that Mr Benveniste and yourself have done everything you possibly could. Now that it is time to put to rest this vain and enticing endeavour, I wanted to thank you again with all my heart.' All he could do now was to 'try, if possible, to erase even the memory of this experience'.[69]

Catch-up session: the Vth Section

Between the two rounds of elections to the Collège de France, over the winter of 1949–50, the institution that was about to reject him nonetheless invited him to give a series of lectures sponsored by the Loubat Foundation for American Antiquities. This kind of invitation usually signalled the recognition that led to a future appointment. For Lévi-Strauss, it marked his first forays into American mythology, as he told his faithful correspondent and friend Jakobson: 'For I am deep into mythology as well! I am currently giving the lectures of the Loubat Foundation for American Antiquities

COLLÈGE DE FRANCE

FONDATION LOUBAT

ANTIQUITÉS AMÉRICAINES

M. CLAUDE LÉVI-STRAUSS

fera au Collège de France une série de six conférences sur le sujet suivant :

L'EXPRESSION MYTHIQUE DE LA STRUCTURE SOCIALE CHEZ LES POPULATIONS INDIGÈNES DE L'AMÉRIQUE

Ces conférences auront lieu les Jeudis, à quatre heures 1/2, dans la salle 5, à partir du 5 janvier 1950.

L'Administrateur du Collège de France,

Edmond FARAL.

IMPRIMERIE NATIONALE. — J. M. 99805. O.

Poster for the Loubat Lectures, given by Claude Lévi-Strauss
at the Collège de France in the winter of 1949–50.

at the Collège de France, and I have chosen to focus on the theme of the wolverine in North America, of which I am trying to provide a structural analysis. This entails studying the connections between: 1) the traits of the figure (gluttony, clownishness, obscenity, scatology, cannibalism, beggary, etc.); 2) the sociological level at which it is expressed in each culture (collective behaviour, individual vocation, ritual personification, folkloric theme, mythical theme, etc.); 3) the relation between the "territory" defined by these two axes and the rest of the social structure. This has yielded rather striking results, which were totally unexpected and caught me off-guard; for I am almost brought back to Engels, the *Origins of the Family*, etc. [. . .] The Arthurian cycle is part of this affair, for I am almost sure that the character of Percival developed from a figure analogous to that of the wolverine found in American rituals.'[70] At one of these lectures, attended by a scholarly audience with a few artistic figures sprinkled in, 'Max Ernst came to hear me. I happened to describe a Hopi divinity while expressing my regret that I was unable to obtain a slide to illustrate my point. The following week, Max Ernst brought me a drawing big enough to show for a lecture. I still have it.'[71]

In the years 1948–50, Lévi-Strauss was on the lookout for a position anywhere he could find one. The doors of the university, the Musée de l'Homme and the Collège de France had all gradually closed for him. Only those of the École pratique des hautes études (EPHE) remained ajar. Since his return to Paris, he had cultivated a strong intellectual relationship with the modernist core of the EPHE. The creation of the VIth Section of the EPHE in the autumn of 1947 was one of the great institutional developments of the day, transforming the face of the social sciences in France. It was the result of an aggressive push by American philanthropy at the outset of the Cold War, which had met with partners eager to benefit from its support and 'entrepreneurs' determined to promote their own intellectual projects. This accurately encapsulates the history of the birth and development of what was to become the École des hautes études en sciences sociales (EHESS) in 1975.[72]

The project was a success, despite a double constraint that left those involved in its creation with little room to manoeuvre. On the one hand, the literature and law faculties did not look kindly on the creation of a social science hub outside the university. The institution of the university, which had always excluded some of these disciplines, was systematically hostile to those who tried to escape its reach, hence a law that governed the creation of social science institutions external to the universities, beginning with the École pratique des hautes études, founded in 1868. On the other hand, the objectives of the financial backers – i.e., until the late 1950s, primarily the Rockefeller Foundation – weighed on these new institutions. What were these objectives? On the political front, the American backers originally proved broadly liberal, while they themselves were subject to heavy pressure from the US state department. This pressure was to grow over the course of the 1950s. Yet the Rockefeller Foundation remained intent on positioning itself 'somewhere between hysterical McCarthyism and support for Joseph Stalin . . . .'[73] In the end, the institution of the VIth Section – under the direction of Lucien Febvre and then, from 1956, Fernand Braudel – managed to collect disdained disciplines and fields of knowledge (anthropology, sociology, demographics), to promote a genuine scholarly agenda (emphasizing methodological issues), and to recruit researchers whose profiles did not fit into the standard academic mould. Thanks to financial resources that, while not sufficient in themselves, were nonetheless decisive, since they automatically triggered additional funding from the French ministry of education, the new institution quickly established itself, through individual scholars, sites, journals, collective studies and publications that lent it a prestige rivalling that of the universities. In reality, funding from the Rockefeller Foundation never amounted to more than a quarter of the VIth Section's budget. Yet in the highly polarized academic world of this Cold War period, the social scientists of the VIth Section were seen as lackeys of American imperialism. As described by Jean Gottmann, a French geographer who spent the war years in exile in the United States, had close ties to the Foundation, and returned to Parisian academia from the wilds of North America in 1948, the members of the VIth Section were considered 'representatives of the American millions attempting to conquer French thought'.[74]

Standing opposite the Marxist core that dominated the Sorbonne and reflected the intellectual aura of the Communist Party, the VIth Section thus represented a clearly 'American' pole, even though most of those affiliated with it were also clearly on the (non-Communist) left, as Lévi-Strauss himself still was. The latter took part in the birth of an institution that he was to support throughout his entire life. It was Lucien Febvre who, from the vast ocean of his readings, had noted with interest the article published by Lévi-Strauss in 1943 in the New York journal *Renaissance* entitled 'Split Representation in the Art of Asia and America'.[75] Febvre tied the author of that article to the destiny of that new born institution. As early as November 1948, Lévi-Strauss was invited to join the VIth Section as a collaborator, without any further official status to sanction the arrangement. A somewhat heterodox administration was part and parcel of the innovative character of the institution. He participated in the inaugural season of the VIth Section, with a course on the 'Religious Life of Primitive Peoples'. The following year, in 1949–50, he taught a course entitled 'The Place and Future of Primitive Populations in the World'.[76] Within this new institution, historians had taken control of operations. Innovative, building on two decades of productive work at the Annales, they were at the same time members of an old and established academic discipline, which was not the case for either sociology or anthropology.

Lévi-Strauss, though close to the historians of the VIth Section, was in the end to obtain a post within the Vth Section, containing the field of 'religious studies'. Maurice Leenhardt, who held the chair in 'Religions of non-civilized peoples', which Mauss had held from 1901 to 1940, was due to retire. At the end of 1950, following his second failure at the Collège de France, Lévi-Strauss was thus finally appointed to the Leenhardt chair. Yet here again, nothing went smoothly. In the end though, the combined support of Keyré and Dumézil, together with friendly pressure from Braudel and Febvre, overcame Leenhardt's open hostility.

The lean and austere figure of the missionary Leenhardt, who went off to evangelize the Kanaks in Grande Terre (New Caledonia), was long forgotten. Yet his role – within a lateral and fertile branch of French anthropology, outside the grand national tradition running from Mauss to Lévi-Strauss – has been recently reappraised.[77] Indeed, one could hardly imagine more opposite temperaments: Leenhardt is often seen as a great fieldwork anthropologist, who remained in the field for more than twenty years, between 1902 and 1926. His seductive appeal, in his lectures, came from the way he 'incorporated' indigenous religious phenomenology – one could hear Kanak thinking![78] – in a way that radically broke with the rationalist tradition. Together with his wife and many children, he was beloved and revered in New Caledonia, where still to this day he is presented as an ancestor and defender of the Kanak movement. But this pastor, who converted to anthropology, was also a typical figure of the complex colonial world that rested on alliances between administrators, missionaries and scholars. Maurice Leenhardt thus remains 'at the intersection of colonial reformism and the scientific study of indigenous societies'.[79] He led a brilliant second career as an anthropologist, becoming Mauss's successor after the war, as well as the president of the Société des océanistes and director of the overseas department at the Musée de l'Homme. Claude Lévi-Strauss's profile was the very opposite of that of the colonial scholar.

His election to the Vth Section at the beginning of 1951 enabled Lévi-Strauss to leave the CNRS and his assistant-director position at the Musée de l'Homme. He was now a director of studies at the EPHE and continued to teach within the VIth Section without any official status, following a practice that had become common at the institution. Yet this situation revealed the limits of his new position: indeed, Claude Lévi-Strauss had not been appointed to the VIth Section, which was the beating heart of scientific modernity at the EPHE. Lévi-Strauss's qualified success was clear to his contemporaries: 'Claude Lévi-Strauss belongs in the VIth Section. I, for one, would only accept a position in the VIth Section, for the IVth and Vth are full of poor devils who haven't the faintest idea what science is.'[80] André-Georges Haudricourt's sweeping judgement had the merit of clarity – even though the 'poor devils' in question included such prominent figures as Koyré, Dumézil and Louis Massignon, the great scholar of the Arab world, and even though the chair held by Lévi-Strauss had been Marcel Mauss's, who passed away just a few months before his appointment, further reinforcing a spectral filiation with a man who had never really been a close friend.

This last-ditch appointment also had other consequences. It is generally held to have marked an inflection point, a 'rerouting' of Lévi-Strauss's preoccupations away from kinship and towards mythology, informed by the title of his new chair and the subjects of his lectures. As he himself recognized in a letter to Jakobson: 'I also had to start teaching at Hautes études, which has got me looking into questions of religious anthropology that I have hardly studied up to now. I am focusing on the various kinds of relations between the dead and the living; here again, there are systems. As regards kinship, I find myself utterly blocked, and in a way that I had not at all expected, by issues whose difficulty I had not anticipated. I have realized that to move from elementary to complex structures we must consider intermediary systems that pertain to both, i.e., that operate simultaneously on a structural basis and a statistical basis (one can either choose one's partner according to the rules or at random, insofar as this kind of choice does not infringe the rules). And I cannot seem to theorize these systems, because each of them admits a number of solutions that is too great to study intuitively. For several weeks now, a mathematician has volunteered to help me during his spare time, but we are having trouble finding a common language.'[81]

If Lévi-Strauss's work is often thought to be monolithic, characterized by its continuities (most notably methodological and systematic), it could also be considered, as here, from the perspective of its ruptures and bifurcations. The first, that of the doctoral thesis, in which he broke with the academic model of the anthropological thesis; and the second, his giving up kinship anthropology and all the plans to think through complex structures, which were never taken up, and his pouring himself into the field of myth, as if they were in a communicating vessel, with the Loubat Lectures serving as connecting tube.

Fathers and sons of French social science

Lévi-Strauss and the historians

A friend and ally of the historians of the VIth Section, Claude Lévi-Strauss also increasingly positioned himself as their challenger. There is no doubt that he readily identified with the scholarly ethos of the small group. He was thus invited to take the reins of a journal intended to bring together anthropologists, linguists and geographers: *L'Homme*. He was to be its co-director with Pierre Gourou and Émile Benveniste. Lévi-Strauss devoted quite a lot of his time to the project over the following years, as is made clear by his abundant correspondence on the subject with Benveniste and the long negotiations with various potential publishers (Hermann, Plon). He was also asked by Lucien Febvre to personally monitor the 'Tensions' project conducted by UNESCO in partnership with the VIth Section. He was thus fully taking part in the life of the institution, based on common thinking and a common commitment to interdisciplinarity. He regularly made suggestions to Braudel: for example, why not hold a monthly meeting with representatives of the various disciplines? A common faith in collective work brought them together: 'The complexity of the social sciences has become such that progress can only be expected from collective work.'[82] Lévi-Strauss's primary asset, in the eyes of his historian colleagues, was his familiarity with the world of American foundations, which he knew very well (including some of its members personally). This would prove useful on numerous occasions.[83] Braudel and Lévi-Strauss spoke the same language and knew how to develop links with other institutions such as INSEE and UNESCO, one of the great sources of funding for the social sciences in the 1950s. Both men were comfortable with administrative arcana and could also manage the financial issues and basic accounting involved in research, especially collective research and fieldwork.

In 1949, the *Revue de Métaphysique et de Morale* published an article entitled 'History and Anthropology', which Claude Lévi-Strauss had written in 1948 on Raymond Aron's request. If the article begins with a long defence of the need for a historical approach in anthropological work and a sharp critique of Malinowskian functionalism – Lévi-Strauss admitted to being shocked by the attitude of Malinowski and his disciples, who did not prepare for their fieldwork by reading on the history of the societies they were going to study in order to keep their 'vision unsullied'[84] – it was mostly, and rightly, remembered for its central statement: 'We propose to show that the fundamental difference between the two disciplines is not one of subject, of goal, or of method. They share the same subject, which is social life; the same goal, which is a better understanding of man; and, in fact, the same method, in which only the proportion of research techniques varies. They differ, principally, in their choice of complementary perspectives: history organizes its data in relation to conscious expressions of social life, while anthropology proceeds by examining its unconscious foundations.'[85] A bold position if ever there was one, but one that Lévi-Strauss justified by paraphrasing Marx: 'Men make their own history, but they do not know they are making it.' To history, the conscious realm; and to anthropology, the unconscious![86] Oddly, Lévi-Strauss was pursuing this line of thought at the very moment he began reading Lucien Febvre, while the kind of historiography described in the article was precisely the one that the historians of the Annales school wanted to move beyond. Later, he was to explain to Didier Éribon that he had in mind the 'extreme cases' – i.e., precisely the most traditional kind of history, defined by reigns, treaties, alliances and wars – which Braudel and his group rejected. The entire aim of the article, he went on, 'was to show that a destructive and outworn opposition should give way to the work that anthropologists and historians can henceforth carry out side by side in close collaboration'.[87]

This call for a dialogue between the various disciplines, as it was retrospectively interpreted, sounded in 1949 rather like an offensive on the part of the young discipline of anthropology. Talking about that period, Lévi-Strauss added that, if he was reading Febvre, he was also 'enjoying' a series of books by Albert Franklin on private life in France from the thirteenth to the eighteenth century. These works of pure erudition, concocted by the curator of the Mazarine Library, constituted, for Lévi-Strauss, in addition to pleasurable reading, the best that history had to offer: a reservoir of details and anecdotes that lent themselves to profound social meaning thanks to a rigorous interpretative approach. This was indeed what historical anthropology would become, several decades later. In any case, this brazen and restive article of 1949 marked the first in a series of lively exchanges between Claude Lévi-Strauss, history and historians. Encompassing common causes – the VIth Section, the social sciences and interdisciplinarity – competitions and 'misunderstandings' (as exemplified here in the ambiguous use of the notion of 'extreme cases'), these discussions also engaged, albeit *mezza voce*, with Claude Lévi-Strauss's own relationship to history, somewhere between a sense of absolute contingency and the temptation to bypass it.

The return to Mauss

At the intellectual level, the reintegration of Claude Lévi-Strauss into the field of French socio-anthropology seems to have transpired through a 'return to Mauss', as revealed in two important and related texts: one, not well known, entitled 'French Sociology', published in English in 1945 (and in French in 1947), which was dedicated to Mauss; the other, the famous 'Introduction' to the first edition of the master's selected works (1950), which was entirely devoted to him. Both purported to take stock of and to narrate the history of the social sciences in France, and to provide a serious discussion of prospects and expectations, all in a critical and synthetic style that signalled their author's own position. This 'return to Mauss' inaugurated an abiding phenomenon in contemporary theoretical creation, which was to experience other 'returns' (to Freud for Lacan, to Marx for Althusser, etc.). Each time, the critical reassessment of the founding figure was part of an attempt to clear the way for a second founding moment, a process that often entailed a periodization of the author's life and work – i.e., the 'young Marx' or the 'old Mauss'. The case of Mauss was also distinct in that – while beloved by his disciples, friends and colleagues – his renown in his field did not compare with that of Freud or Marx in theirs. The major figures of the discipline at the time were Durkheim and, especially, Lévy-Bruhl, the most celebrated interwar sociologist-philosopher, and the best known of the founding triumvirate of French anthropology.[88]

This return to Mauss was thus as much an exhumation as it was an affirmation on Lévi-Strauss's part, all the more so given that most of the master's writings had gone out of print.[89] Yet the question of Mauss's legacy was an essential one in the 'profound theoretical, practical and methodological restructuring under way, especially with regard to the sometimes violent confrontation between the anthropologists who were followers of the Marxist tradition, attached to the materiality of societies, and those who focused primarily on the analysis of representations and symbolic systems'.[90] In the then ongoing debate over the definition of the discipline, its requirements, its methods and practices, the two Lévi-Strauss texts made muscular interventions. They marked an essential moment in his life – at the dawn of his French academic career, they announced the arrival of and linked his name to a vast intellectual project to rebuild the social sciences under the sign of Mauss.

The text entitled 'French Sociology', dedicated to Mauss, was commissioned by Georges Gurvitch, while they were both still exiled in New York. It was part of a collective work of international scope edited by Gurvitch, *Twentieth Century Sociology*, destined to become a landmark.[91] Logically, Lévi-Strauss attempted to define the traits that he deemed characteristic of the discipline in France: the gap, from the very beginning, between an ambitious theoretical posture and a lack of concrete data – a historical trait that was constantly emphasized and criticized by American anthropology; the fact that in France – as opposed to the US and Britain – there was no clear distinction between anthropology and sociology, as the example of Durkheim himself, and later Mauss, showed, even though the latter's work had marked a clear orientation towards the study of primitive societies; and, finally, the relentlessly critical stance of philosophy and the social sciences in France, impervious to an 'integrative' use of knowledge. The methods and attitude of French sociology had enabled it both to fertilize other disciplines and, more surprisingly, to work in collaboration with artists: 'In the years immediately preceding the Second World War, the "Collège de Sociologie" directed by Roger Caillois, became a meeting place for sociologists, on the one hand, and surrealist painters and poets, on the other. The experience was a success. This close connection between sociology and every tendency or current having Man, and the study of Man, at its centre, is one of the more significant traits of the French school.'[92]

In this article, Claude Lévi-Strauss appears very much in command, engaging in a combative discussion of Durkheim's *Elementary Forms of Religious Life*, criticizing his notion of the 'elementary', which, in his view, confused the logical (elementary = simple) and the chronological (elementary = original). He also challenged the Durkheimian approach to the symbolic dimension, which treated the symbol as nothing but the translation of an 'outwardness', whereas, according to Lévi-Strauss, it is 'an inherent property of social facts'. The idea, which would be more forcefully taken up in the 'Introduction' to Mauss's works, was already being expressed here: 'Sociology cannot explain the genesis of symbolic thought, it has just to take it for granted in man.'[93] From the very beginning, everything is meaningful in social life. But it does not follow from the fact that everything is meaningful that this meaning is clear to men. Against Durkheim's 'progressivism', Lévi-Strauss proposed the idea of an unconscious logic of history, which should indeed be the terrain of investigation for the social sciences, since it is at this intermediary level of unconscious thought that 'the apparent opposition between the individual and society disappears'.[94] But in the history of French sociology as seen by Lévi-Strauss, uncle Durkheim (who 'always remained a teacher of the old school, his conclusions toilsomely reached and dogmatically asserted'[95]) was followed by his brilliant nephew Mauss, also a philosopher by training, but much more gifted and relying on 'newer, better and richer material'. Thanks to 'his fabulous memory, his untiring intellectual curiosity', he was able 'to build up a worldwide – and, if one may say so, a time-wide – erudition: "Mauss knows everything." [. . .] Not only does he know everything, but a bold imagination, a genius-like feeling for social reality urged him to make a highly original use of his unlimited knowledge.'[96] In his conversations, and in his teaching, 'unthought-of comparisons' flourished. While he often seemed 'obscure by the constant use of antitheses, short-cuts and apparent paradoxes', these would, 'later on, prove to be the result of a deeper insight, gratifying his listener, suddenly, with fulgurating intuitions, providing the substance for months of fruitful thinking'.[97] The panegyric to Mauss continued: 'In such cases, one feels that one has reached the bottom of the social phenomenon, and has, as he says somewhere, "hit the bed-rock".'[98] It is quite clear that the newly appointed professor was going above and beyond the call of duty in completing his appointed task – that is, providing an overview of the discipline in its characteristics, issues and prospects. Along the way, he took the opportunity to position himself within the history he was recounting, moving beyond the antimonies identified in Durkheim and fleshing out the programme outlined by Mauss.[99] He reasserted what had indeed become the main asset of French sociology, after having been its principal liability for so long: the boldness of its theoretical advances.[100]

In his group portrait of the discipline in 1945, Lévi-Strauss devoted two laudatory pages to the man who commissioned the article, Georges Gurvitch, in which he attempted to assess a body of work that revolved around the Durkheimian system, drawing on two sources of inspiration: Bergson's thought and phenomenology, on the one hand, and the reality of social mobilization and the trade-union movement, on the other. Indeed, as he explained, this exiled Russian Jew – steeped in Marx, and intimate with Proudhon and utopian socialism, who had taken part in the Russian Revolution – was an original theorist whose work was nourished by large quantities of legal material in the sociology of law, of property and of work. He thus painted an appealing portrait of Gurvitch as a man with authentic historical and political experience, as well as a thinker whose 'ontological pluralism' was based on his vision of multiple social forms. It is quite easy to understand why Gurvitch was pleased with such a description of his philosophy and methodology, and even moved by the kind appraisal: 'I went to a great deal of trouble to understand him, and he said that there had never been anything better written about him.'[101] This ego flattery might go some way to explaining what has otherwise remained a bit of an enigma in sociological scholarship: why Gurvitch, a few years later, would have entrusted Lévi-Strauss with the task of writing the introduction to the collection of Mauss's works for a series he directed at the Presses Universitaires de France,[102] whereas Lévi-Strauss was neither a close friend nor a disciple of Mauss, and had indeed met him a total of three times. Other names suggested themselves: Georges Davy, Maurice Leenhardt, Gabriel Le Bras, or even Georges Dumézil. Did Georges Gurvitch – himself a heterodox Durkheimian who, by the late 1940s, had become one of the leading figures of French sociology, directing the Centre d'études sociologiques,[103] editing the journal *Les Cahiers Internationaux de Sociologie* and a book series, and who was soon to be appointed professor at the Sorbonne – prefer to call on someone outside that inner circle? Yet another mystery hovers over this edition and its critical apparatus, having to do with the selection of the Mauss texts to be included – a delicate operation given the singular nature of his work, characterized by its dispersion, its collective authorship, the diversity of its subjects and variety of its forms (notes, articles, discussions, reviews). In his 'Introduction' to the (almost) complete works of Mauss undertaken by the Éditions de Minuit from 1968, historian Viktor Karady wrote that the selection of the texts, 'no doubt the result of laborious compromise'[104] between the preface writer and the editor, was nonetheless largely the work of Lévi-Strauss. The collection mostly comprised Mauss's later writings,[105] liberated from Durkheimian influence, and appeared to him to reflect more of a Lévi-Straussian than a Gurvitchian selection.[106] Yet Lévi-Strauss was to correct Karady on this point: 'In fact I did not play any part in the preparation of that book, of which I became aware only when the publisher sent me the printed proofs, together with a request for an introduction that I had three weeks to write.'[107] There is no reason to doubt his claim, which he reiterated on several occasions, even though it indeed jars with a book that has since been received, in the history of the social sciences, as an 'invitation to structuralism'.[108]

An invitation to structuralism

The 'Introduction' offers an enthusiastic reading of Mauss, of his thought 'riddled with insights',[109] of his keenness to break new ground, such as techniques of the body and the archaeology of bodily attitudes. According to Lévi-Strauss, reading Mauss was an overwhelming experience: 'Few have managed to read *The Gift* without feeling the whole gamut of emotions that Malebranche described so well when recalling his first reading of Descartes: the pounding heart, the throbbing head, the mind flooded with the imperious, though not yet definable, certainty of being present at a decisive event in the evolution of science.'[110]

For better or worse, Lévi-Strauss's appreciative reading was also an active reappropriation on his part, riddled with formulations that bore the mark of his interests, references and intellectual positions at the time. In the footnotes, two figures appear, Michel Leiris and Jacques Lacan, whom he had recently met. The discussions of psychology and anthropology, of madness and shamanism, echo Lévi-Straussian themes of these years. The explanation of the 'total social fact', one of the key concepts of the Maussian legacy, leads to a conclusion according to which 'for the first time, the social [. . .] becomes a system, among whose parts connections, equivalences and interdependent aspects can be discovered'.[111] Commenting, after Mauss, on the rigorous rules governing the exchange of gifts in Polynesian weddings, Lévi-Strauss remarks on one of its variants and concludes: '[It] could have been inferred, had it not been a matter of observation.'[112]

This 'Introduction' is indeed shot through with a spirit of turbulent excess. Lévi-Strauss identified in Mauss the early signs of a structural method, pointing out the contemporaneity of *The Gift* and the *Principles of Phonology* – even while admitting that Mauss had no knowledge of it.[113] He then noted that the 'way of posing the problem' was correct, as shown by the most recent research on kinship anthropology (his own . . .). Finally, he predicted that this linguistics/anthropology connection would lead to a 'vast science of communication'. All living interpretation is predatory: it extends, it critiques, it surpasses. This is exactly what Lévi-Strauss did – extracting, much to Gurvitch's astonishment, a pre-structuralist Mauss. Let us consider a further stage in the appropriation. Claude Lévi-Strauss proclaimed himself the chosen disciple, whose duty it was 'not to let the most fruitful aspect of his thinking be lost or vitiated'.[114] For 'Mauss halt[ed] at the edge of these immense possibilities, like Moses conducting his people all the way to a promised land whose splendour he would never behold.'[115] Very rarely did Lévi-Strauss resort to biblical metaphors, but it was only appropriate here to describe the reconstructed genealogy of structuralism as the new Tables of the Law! If Lévi-Strauss felt entitled to indulge in what Georges Gurvitch rather sarcastically called, in the 'Foreword' to the first edition, a 'very personal interpretation of [Mauss's] work' – some would call it a veritable appropriation of his legacy – it was indeed because he had already set foot in the land of Canaan: *The Elementary Structures of Kinship* was intended to take up the 'aggressive agenda' defined for anthropology, realizing and surpassing the promise and intuitions of the master.

Indeed, if Mauss's great discovery – namely, the centrality of the reciprocity principle in social life – was taken up, it was also critiqued in a new analysis of 'mana' (the Polynesian term, also used in Melanesia, to designate the unknown before it is named, a 'thing' or 'stuff' full of mystery and sacredness), which concluded the introduction. As Lévi-Strauss confided to Jakobson: 'I am defending a new theory of "mana", which is highly inspired by phonology. I turn "mana" into a symbolic zero value, having no symbolic signification of its own, but whose role is to mark the fact that, on such and such occasion, or for such and such specific object in a category, there is more signification in play than in the usual relation between the signifier and the signified. In short, something akin to your "zero phoneme", which I cite in the text.'[116] Lévi-Strauss found in the field of linguistics – 'phoneme zero', 'floating signifier' – equivalents for the symbols in their pure state that the ethnographer located in indigenous life. Both 'hau' in magic and 'mana' in exchange pertain to symbolic activities that are defined by their relational dimension, regardless of the content of what is exchanged: relations between men (exchange of gifts), relations between men and gods (magic). The 'relational aspect of symbolic thinking'[117] makes it like a language endowed with meaning, which signifies from the very start, long before knowledge, a signified, which is attached to it.[118] It is thus because the objects of anthropologists are signs (most notably mana, hau, kinship, etc.) that the 'Introduction' to Mauss's work reconfigured the anthropological project as a general semiology.

This pivotal text is also important in that it marked the beginning of a dialogue, via Mauss, with Merleau-Ponty and philosophy. The anthropology it conjured up was intended to be a self-reflexive knowledge that thought its own practices and methods. Here again, the aim was to reach 'the bedrock'. In the end, it was through an astronomical metaphor that Lévi-Strauss summed up this triple redefinition – theoretical, epistemological and programmatic – of what he had begun to call 'anthropology',[119] quoting Mauss and completing the loop of his exemplary creation-filiation: 'We must, before all else, compile as large as possible a catalogue of categories; we must begin with all those which we can know that mankind has used. Then it will be seen that in the firmament of reason there have been, and still are, many moons that are dead, or pale, or obscure.'[120]

Anthropology and psychoanalysis: '. . . the farthest reaches of the universe and the innermost secrets of our minds . . .'[121]

Lévi-Strauss had long been acquainted with psychoanalysis, having read Freud, as we have seen, very early on. Its theoretical impact was decisive, in that the young man learned that even the apparently wildest and most fanciful phenomena could be subjected to rational analysis.[122] Later, his immersion in the surrealist milieu and his acquaintance with Raymond de Saussure in New York made him aware of the practical and theoretical issues in psychoanalysis, of its aesthetic relays and its existential bent. It is nonetheless right to identify a 'psychoanalytic moment' in the late 1940s, when Lévi-Strauss, who had just met Jacques Lacan, simultaneously published three articles (in 1949) dealing with the notion of the unconscious. It was thus as an anthropologist that he engaged in dialogue with psychoanalysis, and as an anthropologist that he identified the unconscious as the 'bedrock', the truth of ancient and exotic societies accessible to the social sciences, without ever letting go of the avowed scepticism he felt towards the therapeutic cure itself and its effects.[123]

The first article, which we have already discussed, dealt with the separation between history – seen as the study of a society's conscious expression – and anthropology – concerned with its unconscious expression.[124] The second, 'The Sorcerer and His Magic' – first published in *Les Temps modernes*, and later in the book *Structural Anthropology* – recounts several shaman stories. One of them, Quesalid, was one of Franz Boas's Kwakiutl informants on Vancouver Island. Having become, almost in spite of himself, a renowned shaman, he remained very lucid about the degree of showmanship involved in his operations, as well as surprised by his capacity to relieve pain.[125] He discovered the power of performance and the 'effectiveness of symbols' based on a 'consensus'[126] phenomenon at the heart of the shared belief between sorcerer, patient and a particular community.

The third text – also published in 1949 and dedicated to Raymond de Saussure, entitled 'The Effectiveness of Symbols'[127] – follows a shaman through his ritual incantation when dealing with a difficult childbirth. The scene had been described by a Swedish ethnographer and collected in a village in Panama. The shaman accompanied the baby on its way from the uterus to the vagina, all the way to delivery, and helped to chase away the *Muu* evil spirit that had seized the foetus and refused to let go of it. Throughout the article, the shamanic work is contrasted with a psychoanalytic cure. In the latter case, the patient who re-experiences, through transference with the psychoanalyst, painful events in his past, is ultimately free of them; in the former, it is the shaman who undergoes abreaction, speaking in the name of the patient, whereas the psychoanalyst remains silent. In both cases, the unconscious is a logically structured world that can be brought to light. Lévi-Strauss shows the identity between the processes at work. The effectiveness of the shamanic practices demonstrates the strength of primitive societies, which also possess effective knowledge. A touch of Lévi-Straussian irony is apparent in the double reversal: the shaman who, in his 'abnormal' behaviour, could be compared to a 'patient' beset by psychopathological trouble, is here confronted by his symmetrical figure – i.e., the psychoanalyst in our society. Note that in both cases the cured patient becomes potentially capable of administering a cure (the psychoanalyst must have undergone analysis himself; the shaman must have experienced rites for exorcizing nefarious spirits). Finally, Lévi-Strauss strives to depict psychoanalysis as a contemporary mythology of our societies, especially as seen from America, which works as an efficient system of collective interpretation. Published in *Les Temps modernes*, a journal in which Lévi-Strauss appears, in retrospect, to have published quite often during the postwar years, the text on the shaman can also be read as a discreetly ironic commentary on the guru-intellectual, the shaman of modern times, in a journal directed by one of them.

The two 'return to Mauss' texts analysed above express the same exigency: the very essence of sociological knowledge cannot be content with

what men, even savage ones, say or think they are doing. It would otherwise dissolve 'into a verbose phenomenology'.[128] The explanation never
resides at the conscious level, that of the speech of the actors involved,
but rather in the confines of unconscious mental structures, the promised
land of twentieth-century social science, to pursue the biblical metaphor.
It is also at that intermediary level of symbolic thought – neither too high
(metaphysical), nor too low (historical records) – that the intelligence of
a social science that posits a coherence and purpose to human behaviour,
albeit one not immediately accessible to the actors themselves, can come
into its own. This unconscious stratum thus offered both object and access,
a programme and a kingdom. From that perspective, a clear convergence
bound the anthropological and psychoanalytic projects together: 'It is the
same type of operation which in psychoanalysis allows us to win back our
most estranged self, and in anthropological inquiry gives us access to the
most foreign other as to another self.'[129] Both disciplines mediate 'in the
one instance between a subjective and an objective self (psychoanalysis),
and in the other instance between an objective self and a subjective other
(anthropology)'.[130] They both also seek to expand human reason, into
dark and obscure zones, 'to the farthest reaches of the universe and the
innermost secrets of our minds'.[131]

Lévi-Strauss first met Jacques Lacan in 1949, at a dinner organized
by Alexandre Koyré. This meeting was both essential and asymmetrical. Essential for Claude Lévi-Strauss who, through Lacan, was to meet
Monique Roman, who would become his third wife a few years later.
The Lacans and Lévi-Strausses went on to develop a friendship that was
further reinforced by the good relationship between their spouses, Sylvia
Bataille and Monique Roman, and in which art played an important role.
Lacan's gentlemanly manners and natural charm did the rest: 'We used
to go with the Merleau-Pontys for lunch at Guitrancourt, where Lacan
had a country house. Once, my wife and I wanted to find a hideaway in
the country, and Lacan had just bought a new car he wanted to take on
the road. The four of us took off together. It was a lot of fun. You should
have seen Lacan descending on a shabby provincial hotel, in his most
regal manner ordering that his bath be run that very instant! We hardly
ever talked about psychoanalysis or philosophy, instead it was usually
art and literature. His knowledge was vast. He used to buy paintings and
works of art, and this was the subject of our conversations.'[132] If Lévi-
Strauss did not owe his knowledge of psychoanalysis to Lacan, it was to
The Elementary Structures of Kinship that Lacan attributed the shock of
discovering structural linguistics and the personal use he could make of it,
which Élisabeth Roudinesco has called an 'orthodox sublation of Freud's
doctrine': 'Lacan's encounter with the thought of Lévi-Strauss meant he
had at last found a theoretical solution to the problem of how to make a
complete overhaul of Freudian doctrine. In the process, the unconscious
was to a large extent freed of the biological cast that Freud had lent it, in
a direct line from Darwinism. Instead it was seen as a language-related
structure.'[133] This language structure was fully revealed in a few fundamental texts of 1953, especially the 'Rome Discourse' of 27 September, which

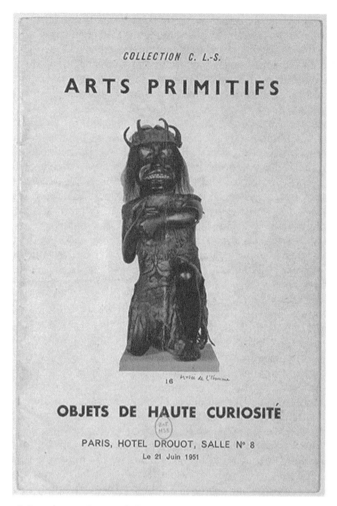

COLLECTION C. L.-S.

ARTS PRIMITIFS

16

OBJETS DE HAUTE CURIOSITÉ

PARIS, HOTEL DROUOT, SALLE N° 8

Le 21 Juin 1951

Cover of the sales catalogue of the Drouot auction house for the Lévi-Strauss collection (exotic and Hebraic objects), 21 June 1951.

inaugurated the Lacanian reform movement in psychoanalysis. In his seminars over the following years, Lacan's thought burgeoned through a return to Freud's texts, reinterpreting them through the prism of structural linguistics and Lévi-Straussian anthropology. For Lacan, then, meeting Lévi-Strauss was a bedrock, on which rested an abiding admiration. For Lévi-Strauss, it was a sentimental attachment, strengthened by a sense of seduction, a shared sociability and common tastes, but no intellectual influence.[134] Their friendship would last a decade, when it was undermined and ultimately destroyed under the weight of misunderstandings and budding celebrity. But in the late 1940s, it embodied the special and still very open dialogue that Lévi-Strauss entertained with psychoanalysis.

On 21 June 1951, a large collection of objects labelled 'of high curiosity' was auctioned at the Hôtel Drouot auction house in Paris. Several series of objects of diverse provenance were thus paraded in front of potential buyers: from British Columbia tribes (Haida, Tshimshian, Tlingit, Kwakiutl) a totem pole, a helmet crest, a shaman statue, articulated masks and large masks with hand-operated sides; from Pueblo (Hopi) tribes, polychrome wood statuettes; Kachina dolls, a New Guinea mask, as well as vases and ceramic objects from ancient Mexico and Peru; a parchment manuscript – the Book of Esther, dating from the eighteenth century – and 'three Hebraic books bound in ancient gold-leafed leather, of which two were part of the Bible published by Estienne (sixteenth century) and the third in Spanish, entitled *Orden del Selihoth*, printed in Amsterdam in the seventeenth century'. The choice piece was unquestionably the one that figured on the cover of the catalogue: 'A shaman statue in patina wood. One leg kneeling, two arms folded across the chest, head slightly turned to the left. The two-piece garment is made of leather decorated with polychrome facial patterns and edged with cut fringe; the leather head dress is adorned with a diadem of bear claws. The eyes are inlaid with copper, the teeth made of dog teeth, and the eyebrows and moustache out of fur. Tsimshian.' It sold for 75,000 francs, out of a total of 1,534,000 francs, which did not represent an extraordinary sum.[135] It was thus that the Lévi-Strauss collection was put into circulation, bought up by the Musée de l'Homme, the Leyde Museum, as well as a few individual buyers (the auctioneer himself, as well as André Malraux, who had started work at the time on *The Voices of Silence*, and Jacques Lacan, who had considerably greater means than his friend).

Lévi-Strauss and his wife Rose-Marie had just separated, and he found himself wanting for everything – money, an apartment, and material for his work. On 11 June 1951, he wrote to Jakobson: 'These days, I find myself in utter chaos: homeless, cut off from my work and forced, for lack of money, to take on mercenary jobs for UNESCO. But I am hoping to solve the most urgent problem by the summer, that of housing.' No easy task in postwar Paris . . . We do not know much about this second separation: Rose-Marie Ullmo was a cheerful, rich, carefree woman, yet one who was also marked by the war and traumatized by the experience of being left by her first husband for her sister. When the relationship deteriorated, she didn't know how to react to a husband who, for his part, had become more and more closed off – 'I live in a grave',[136] he then confided to Monique Roman. In company, he had become increasingly silent, and Rose-Marie increasingly talkative. Above all, she did not seem to understand (or accept) the importance of work for her husband, of the magnitude of the task that lay ahead. The less than successful return to France, in professional terms, probably did not help. When Lévi-Strauss did speak of this new breakup, he did so following an account of his professional failures, as if it had been the crowning touch: 'After this double disaster, I was convinced that I would never have a real career. I broke with my past, rebuilt my private life, and wrote *Tristes Tropiques* . . .'[137]

Lévi-Strauss thrived on ruptures, both in his private life and his work. His renunciation of an academic career, of the grand bourgeois lifestyle enabled by Rose-Marie's wealth and of writing exclusively in a scientific mode all opened up new horizons. Yet, one has the strange impression that, in the early 1950s, everything was in place for what was to emerge only a decade later. Lévi-Strauss asked Braudel to change the title of his course for the VIth Section. He wanted to move from 'Primitive Civilizations' to 'Structural Anthropology' which 'corresponds perfectly to the research I have been doing as a director of studies and offers the additional advantage of introducing into the French nomenclature a term whose currency has become widespread abroad over the past twenty years'.[138] The institutional development of the discipline under this new semantic rubric, peer recognition and the freedom to pursue his own work were still to come. If we imagine that, in the late 1940s, Lévi-Strauss could have been appointed to the Collège de France and founded his research centre (as outlined in his application), as well as the great anthropological journal *L'Homme*, whose title and coeditors had already been chosen, then what happened next seems like a long hiatus, a ten-year pause, to which he would allude in his inaugural lecture of 1960.

13

Manhood

In actual fact, there are no peoples still in their childhood; all are adult, even those who have not kept a diary of their childhood and adolescence.
Claude Lévi-Strauss, Race and History¹

'Not only did my doctorate open doors to university teaching, it also made me feel like I had become an adult.'[2] Even though he became financially independent, and responsible for his parents' livelihood, very early on in his life, the long path of an academic career and the circumvolutions of history and exile had delayed Lévi-Strauss's entry into manhood. His father died in 1953.

The setbacks he suffered upon his return from America served to bring that period to a close. Having hit rock bottom both professionally and emotionally, Lévi-Strauss was given what his friend André Breton termed 'extraordinary succour':[3] first of all, a new companion; then, a fresh perspective on his career in France, together with a new orientation to international horizons.

Indeed, this was the moment when the structuralist paradigm – hitherto largely confined to France, albeit with international ambitions – asserted itself on a larger stage, following several theoretical incursions by Lévi-Strauss to the United States in 1952, 1953 and 1954. Thinking on a different scale had both scientific and political consequences, and, above all, impacted the articulation between the two. At that time, Lévi-Strauss had developed ties with the fledgling institution of UNESCO, the UN agency for education and culture. For, indeed, the desire to think big brought the anthropological ethos momentarily into line with a programme for reflecting on the postwar world, on the roots of evil, the challenges of demographic change, and the problem of 'underdevelopment', with the struggle for decolonization fully under way. It was in this context that, in 1952, Lévi-Strauss published a brochure entitled *Race and History*, as part of a UNESCO series, which reinterpreted the history of humanity from an anthropological perspective. Seen through this lens, 'the West no longer appears as an end but as an accident',[4] as noted by Roger Caillois, a brilliant critic of this text, who, unwittingly, helped in making it better known to a wider public.

Vita nova

In the early 1950s, Lévi-Strauss's aspiration for a *vita nova* was based on a 'new deal' of the cards in both his sentimental and professional life. The use of the phrase, 'new deal', which came from the language of game theory, was typical of Lévi-Strauss: it combined a sense of both a lack of room to manoeuvre, and the persistence of possibilities, however limited in number. It also captured the element of chance and good luck.

A new deal

Luck to be sure, but also a powerful determinism, a shared set of friends and tastes, brought him to Monique Roman, who was to become his third wife in 1954 and to share the next (and last) fifty years of his life. Was Lévi-Strauss a ladies' man? 'One day', reported Gilles Lapouge, 'he confided in me that he was polygamous, but that, so as to comply with French law, rather than collecting all his wives at the same time, he decided to string them out over the years, "like the beads of a necklace".'[5]

Let us pause a moment to consider the third and final bead of that necklace:[6] Monique Roman was born in 1926 in Paris (but conceived in Shanghai!) to Ruth Emma Rie, an American woman of Jewish descent from a cultivated Viennese background, a polyglot out of proclivity and necessity.[7] The exoticism on her father's side was of a more discreet variety, Jules Roman being of Belgian origin. While Claude Lévi-Strauss was a Frenchman born in Brussels, Monique Roman was a Belgian born in Paris. A Franco-Belgian symmetry, which gave rise to administrative misunderstandings down the line. Her father came from a more modest background than did her mother, but having become an engineer, he could provide his family with a degree of economic prosperity that afforded Monique and her young brother a comfortable childhood in the 16th arrondissement of Paris. The large apartment on rue des Marronniers in which she grew up was the very one that the Lévi-Strausses were to move into a few decades later.

But the paternal 'success story' came to an incongruous and tragic end: disregarding the horrified warnings of his family and blindly pursuing his drive to prosper and to enhance his children's facility with foreign languages, he had no qualms about going to work, in 1939, in Nazi Germany, where he was hired as a consulting engineer, importing a metal-casing technique originally developed in America. He was Belgian and his wife American. He was imprisoned on 10 May 1940. During the war, trapped in their German nightmare, both parents eked out a living, penniless and under surveillance; their health declined while the kids remained enrolled in school and managed to survive the war years and Nazi-ruled Germany. This incredible story became the subject of a book by Monique Lévi-Strauss, written over fifty years later, entitled *Une Enfance dans la gueule du loup.*[8]

After a banal bourgeois childhood in Paris, the wild episode of war bent the arc of Monique Roman's biography to a logic of survival. At the end of these German years, followed by a short stay in a camp for repatriated persons, the young woman returned to Paris; she was already mature, capable of 'getting by' in a hostile environment and not caving in to despair. In 1946 and 1947, she was in the United States, where part of her mother's family lived, and graduated from Simmons College in Boston. At that time, Lévi-Strauss was still in New York. Not yet acquainted, both returned to Paris at the same time, in 1947. At age twenty, she had the looks of a young American starlet, tall for a woman of her generation, slender and willowy, and her typically American carefree and outspoken manner only added to her charm. Her steely temperament was matched by an intense intellectual and artistic curiosity. On arriving back in Paris, she met the Jolas family through Clara Malraux – a close friend of her mother's – who took her in as a daughter alongside their own, Betsy, a future music composer, and Tina, who became an anthropologist, but who is remembered in the annals of French poetry as the wife of André du Bouchet and the indefatigable lover of René Char.[9] Eugene Jolas was a writer and literary critique of American descent, who had settled in Paris but had recently spent the war years in the United States. In the large apartment on Avenue Kléber where they settled after the war, Maria and Eugene Jolas, who had been friends of James Joyce in the 1930s, entertained everyone who mattered in European modern art. Their daughters shared their tastes with the enthusiasm characteristic of young people in their twenties. For two years, Monique lived with them, and this turbulent world of intellectuals and artists was not very far – either socially or geographically – from that of Claude Lévi-Strauss upon his return to Paris. She was well acquainted with the Massons, with whom she spent holidays, as well as the Leirises, the Merleau-Pontys and, indeed, Lacan, through whom, as we have seen, she was to meet her future husband. She was a regular at Royaumont, attended a few lectures at the Collège de France and frequented that part of the 16th arrondissement – she lived on rue Magdebourg – around the Palais de Chaillot and Musée de l'Homme. The future couple met at the intersection of these itineraries and multiple common threads, under the double auspices of foreign languages and libraries.

Indeed, in addition to her attractive physique and unfailing good spirits, Monique Roman had a secret weapon: her linguistic abilities. She was fully trilingual in French, English and German, and fluent in Italian, which made her a sought-after collaborator within the French world of monoglot intellectuals. Lacan had hired her as a translator. It was also for translations of German anthropological works that Lévi-Strauss had engaged the services of the young woman who, between 1949 and 1950, went to work every day at the Musée de l'Homme, in the vast directorial office, the temporary use of which the assistant director, perched on an ejection seat, had been given. His interest in the substance of language, and the value he placed on linguistic abilities, distinguished Claude Lévi-Strauss from the average French intellectual, who continued to labour under the belief that his language still radiated with all its eighteenth-century intensity. Lévi-Strauss read, wrote and spoke English quite well (albeit with a confirmed

'Frenchy' accent), had a solid understanding of Portuguese and could read Spanish. While having nothing of the linguistic genius of a Jakobson, he saw to it that he was not provincialized by an incapacity to access anthropological literature in other languages. Here again, it was his early sense of a change in scale that led him to respond to one of his students who regretted she could not delve further into her topic because of her ignorance of the German language: 'But surely, Miss, the German language can be learned!'[10] This positive and determined attitude to foreign languages echoed the practice and breathtaking erudition of Marcel Mauss, whose footnotes reveal the scope and linguistic diversity of his bibliographical sources.

But he came to work closely with Monique Roman on another matter: She helped him order the books for his library. Lévi-Strauss had returned from the United States with a professional library of some 12,000 volumes. That library was his private lair, and the chief resource (together with his index cards) for the work already completed and to come. It accompanied him, in all its bulk, to his various residences. At times manageable, when it was well ordered; at others, unruly and impracticable, when it was not. When manageable, it gave him the certainty of impeccable erudition and up-to-date information, ready to hand, thanks to the particular role of journals and the many offprints. When unruly, it was dead weight. And, sure enough, since returning from New York, Lévi-Strauss had complained about not having had the time and energy to organize his library. He called upon Monique to help him in this vast undertaking, which provided a perfect setting for their budding love affair . . . The task proved in part pointless, since Claude soon moved out of the apartment on avenue d'Eylau and into Monique's small studio apartment nearby, prior to acquiring an apartment in to which the new couple moved in the autumn of 1951. They were married three years later, as soon as his divorce from Rose-Marie Ullmo became official.

Their new abode, at 11 rue Saint-Lazare, was acquired thanks in part to the proceeds of the sale of the exotica, with which Lévi-Strauss parted 'painfully but without much hemming and hawing'.[11] It was a large, five-room apartment overlooking two very quiet courtyards, that featured all the trappings of a former opulence: mouldings on the ceilings, but no central heating; a makeshift bathroom, but a stylish tile stove. On the street below, farmers would still come to ply their produce. Lévi-Strauss loved his new neighbourhood, full of surprises and quirky shops, still redolent of its seedy past and surrealist urban feel. Breton lived nearby, on rue Fontaine. The Drouot auction house was a stone's throw away, and at that time Lévi-Strauss dropped by there almost daily. Weekends were devoted to the flea market. Their lifestyle, as well as their neighbourhood, had changed, becoming more Bohemian than bourgeois, marking a contrast with their former, more affluent, lives. They gradually adopted an improvised, alternative mode of existence, which owed much to the ingenuity and cooking talents of the mistress of the house. They maintained an open house for their friends: Henri Seyrig on his visits from Beirut, Jakobson in transit through Paris, not to mention Alfred Métraux, a regular boarder with a legendary predilection for pot-au-feu, Georges Henri Rivière, who ran the Musée des arts et traditions populaires and felt a deferential fondness for Lévi-Strauss, his junior, the Leirises, Pierre Gourou, the anthropologist Henri Lehmann, the Schaeffners, etc. Lévi-Strauss warmly welcomed all those with whom he could engage in real conversation, 'but no small talk'.[12]

It was precisely this lifestyle that he weighed against the serious and tempting propositions he received from the United States at that time, in 1952 and 1953, and that he ultimately turned down: 'I was happy with my Bohemian life. I preferred going to the flea market every Saturday to living in Cambridge, Massachusetts.'[13]

Portrait of an unknown man

The welcoming host of rue Saint-Lazare did not fully correspond with the portrait of the new professor that his students at the Sorbonne and the Musée de l'Homme would later draw. Françoise Héritier met him in the first half of the 1950s: his face was still quite full, his hair had whitened and become sparser – a nascent baldness that suited the intellectual well. He looked older than he was and, according to his future disciple, was endowed with a very remarkable kind of beauty, with his 'elephant eyes', the heavy eyelids and sagacious gaze of a mammal that the Africanist anthropologist would later learn to appreciate. Not unlike that kind of 'shy' tree found in Africa, whose trunk and foliage peel away, he would often stand with his torso leaning backward, suggesting an emotional distance that might have been unintentional, but that was conveyed by his very posture.[14]

Some students had vaguely heard of Lévi-Strauss, but in truth only a few. However, he gradually managed to build a reputation for himself. Michel Tournier, in an homage, recalled the apprentice-philosophers who, like himself, would regularly attend lectures at the Musée de l'Homme in order to obtain a credential in anthropology. These 'lunar beings' would thus be put into contact with the real, the concrete: they were made to handle crania, and acquire a modicum of knowledge in natural history. All this would provoke in him a somewhat baroque sense of wonder, at a world of objects and people whom he found as poetic as they were strange. 'But everything would change on Tuesdays, the day Claude Lévi-Strauss gave his lectures on anthropology. First of all, the elegance of an Oxford-educated Assyrian prince made for a sharp contrast with the "rough and ready" look of his peers. But above all, with him, it was a new language that had to be learned. It was now out of the question that we should confuse "crossed cousins" and "parallel cousins", patrilineal and patrilocal filiations, bilateral marriage and dualist organization, disharmonic regimes and generalized exchanges. About this or that tribe in central Brazil, the black board would soon be covered with algebraic looking signs that illustrated its social organization. Just like bodies have their chemical formulas, each society was assigned its specific formula, unlike any other. But there was something else. We would suddenly find out that Lévi-Strauss had trundled along and camped out with these Indians fifteen years earlier. There were only a hundred of them left then, and they had probably entirely disappeared since. It is there that I first heard of ethnocide. We were thus faced with this paradox: at the very moment it was taking shape as an exact science, anthropology was acquiring a tragic dimension.'[15] Distinction, distance, shyness, aloofness – Métraux, for his part, found him to have a 'Capitolian'[16] air – whatever words were chosen, the character was imposing. Nobody dared use the familiar form of address ('*tu*') with him – not his juniors, nor his seniors, nor his anthropologist contemporaries, with whom he did not seem to share a common experience. This was, of course, largely untrue, but one must keep in mind that he had received his intellectual training far from Paris. And then, all of a sudden, there he was, both exotic and accomplished: 'We didn't see him grow up', as Françoise Héritier would later put it. 'He just appeared, fully armed, like Athena donning her helmet.'[17]

Forging the Mythologiques

Besides the lectures he gave at the Institut d'ethnologie of the Musée de l'Homme, Lévi-Strauss's main teaching activity consisted in a seminar he held once a week at the Vth Section of the École pratique des hautes études, stairway E of the Sorbonne. That course, which became a joint seminar of both the Vth and VIth Sections, was later relocated for lack of space from the Sorbonne to the rue de Varenne. For about ten years, every Wednesday from 2 to 4 p.m., roughly fifteen people attended, following an inalterable ritual: the first hour was devoted to Lévi-Strauss's lecture proper; the second turned it into a seminar, with visiting guests – from abroad or from other disciplines. Jakobson, of course, and Benveniste were invited to present on the results of their research, as well as, among others, a young ethologist and baboon specialist, and other anthropologists, often freshly returned from fieldwork, like Georges Balandier, Louis Dumont, Georges Condominas and Isac Chiva – whose research in the Sologne region Lévi-Strauss had 'sponsored', in the terminology of the time. The audience consisted of his friends, including Jacques Lacan, the physicist Pierre Auger and Alfred Métraux, as well as a handful of wide-eyed students, ready to convert to a discipline they were in the process of discovering – including Françoise Héritier and Michel Izard. In the late 1950s, the latter two would in turn present on their respective fieldwork. At this still rather modest level, the seminar became a place that mattered, and that offered a particular kind of 'intellectual enchantment',[18] for it invited its participants to think both meticulously and on a large scale, in a fiery mix of attention to detail and serious empiricism, on the one hand, and theoretical boldness and interdisciplinary perspectives, on the other. The seminar soon dropped its quaint title – 'Religions of Primitive Peoples' –, which had come to seem quite reactionary, in favour of a label that reflected more adequately the political horizon of its ambitious form of knowledge. 'One day I was talking about the customs of an African population, and a black member of the audience whom I did not know got up and said, "I belong to this society and don't agree with your interpretation." Two or three other incidents of the sort led me to change the name of the chair to "Religions of Non-Literate Peoples".'[19] The new course title, made official by ministerial decree on 9 February 1954, was more appropriate, even though it still defined the societies it studied in terms of a lack. But this lack was a fact, not a value judgement, and literacy was indeed not particularly valued in Lévi-Strauss's work. The primacy of oral culture was simply an observation, not a regret, which called for numerous commentaries on its anthropological implications.

It was at this seminar that Lévi-Strauss's ideas on mythology took shape, the very ideas that were to fill the second great cycle of his work, in the 1960s, comprising the four volumes of *Mythologiques*.[20] The course abstract allows us to get a picture of his 'thought process unfolding',[21] as it was penetrating, with all its analytical power and propensity for risk, the vast realm of myths. These seminars constituted a forge in that the approach was always experimental: the method was to look very closely at 'how it works', to test hypotheses on a body of ethnographic material that also needed to be collected.

In 1951–52, Lévi-Strauss chose to devote his course, 'The Visitation of Souls', to a comprehensive mapping of the possible relations between the living and the dead: the grateful dead, who allowed for a kind of *modus vivendi* between the departed and those who had survived them; or the reign of a kind of frantic speculation in which the living engage, at the cost of their peace, and at the expense of the dead, who make them pay for it. This presented an opportunity for Lévi-Strauss to return to his Brazilian years, since the rich Bororo funereal rituals provided an example combining both attitudes, complementary and opposed. As the course progressed, the existence of dual, ternary and even quinary configurations was revealed, through the reduction of symbols and recurring objects. The whole point of the game was then to find a correlation between these cosmological systems and their social structures: 'The representation found in these societies of the relation between the living and the dead is no more than the projection, on the screen of religious thought, of real relations between the living.'[22]

From 1952 to 1954, Lévi-Strauss and his students focused on the mythology of Pueblo Indians, examining the various versions of their creation myths, first among western and central Pueblo Indians (Hopi, Zuni and Acoma), then among eastern Pueblos (Keres, Tiwa and Tewa), while holding out the possibility of making larger comparisons based on the initial conclusions. Over the course of these three years, assisted by a promising young philosopher, Lucien Sebag, and archaeologist Jean-Claude Gardin, he laid out the principles of his method, confirming its productive and innovative character along the way. The point was to resist surrendering to the delights of the mythological picturesque, or giving in to a sweeping comparativism, or imagining an anthropological content of myth. It required patience to refrain from precipitously assigning meaning and to retrace the 'mythical logic' in all its 'character of necessity and universality'.[23] What were the general principles? All mythical discourse was to be treated 'as a kind of metalanguage, of which the constitutive units were *theses* or *sequences*',[24] similar to phonemes – insignificant in and of themselves, yet taking on meaning when articulated in relation to one another. Furthermore, myths were to consist of all their variants, with no one prevailing over others due to its earlier or richer character. There was no original myth, but rather an infinite reproduction mechanism that gave myth a 'layered structure'.[25] Like a Tinguely machine, in which each element is in a relationship of interdependence with all others, everything was connected in the production of myth. This new approach also prompted a rethinking of an older issue in anthropological theory, that of the relationship between myth and ritual, which was at the centre of the 1954/55 course. Here again, the conclusions overturned some of the assumptions of the discipline, which tended to consider myth as the foundation of ritual. According to Lévi-Strauss, there was neither antecedence nor duplication, but a complementarity in the way a single psycho-sociological system signified: that difference translated into the opposition between the 'metalanguage' of myth and the 'paralanguage' of ritual. The formulations of the course abstracts, which were later published, aptly expressed the experimental dimension of the approach: 'we wondered about . . .', 'it appeared to us that . . .', 'we shall test the myth against . . .'. But the conviction that underlay this vast investigation was that social life and mythological life represented homologous structures and that both emerged out of the same laws – laws that could then be discovered through their reciprocal echoes. As Lévi-Strauss wrote to Georges Balandier: 'It is thus possible, I think, to escape the Durkheimian dilemma: religion may be an illusion and yet offer a means to access reality "at an angle".'[26]

Following the first year of the seminar, Lévi-Strauss presented a codicil to the understanding acquired 'at an angle' in an article published in *Les Temps modernes*, entitled 'Santa Claus Burned as a Heretic'.[27] In it, he tried his hand at the anthropological description of a news story from his own society, a genre he was to not take up again for forty years. The event had taken place in Dijon on 24 December 1951: in front of the children in the youth clubs, a Santa Claus figure was hanged in effigy in front of the Cathedral, on the recommendation of Catholic authorities, supported by the Protestant church, who were keen to express their disapproval regarding what they considered as the pagan recuperation of the Nativity celebration, via the growing success of Santa Claus. This phenomenon was confirmed by the anthropologist's analysis, following long synchronic (comparison with Kachina dolls) and diachronic (the Saturnalia of the Roman world, the medieval Abbé de Liesse) explanations to understand the relatively modern appearance of Santa Claus in Europe (nineteenth century) as not only the successful importation of an American practice but, more profoundly, as a new way of managing relations between the living and the dead. It was more than just an initiation ritual, though it was also that, since the gifts we give our children are in fact gifts to the afterworld, of which they are only intermediators. The honourable prelates of Dijon had been spot-on: belief in Santa Claus fuelled a hotbed of paganism. 'It remains to be seen whether moderns as well can defend their right to be pagan.'[28]

The measure of the world

In addition to his teaching, Lévi-Strauss was active in other domains and at other levels – notably, in the United States in the early 1950s. If the institutional and intellectual obstacles he encountered in France played a part, Lévi-Strauss reoriented his efforts to the international level because he had a strong theoretical point to make. Indeed, it reflected a moment of faith on his part in the ability of science to serve as a universal mechanism for knowledge. The human and social sciences and the natural and physical sciences were all engaged in a dialogue, which he helped to organize, both intellectually and practically, within the framework of the UNESCO International Social Science Council, of which he became general secretary in 1953. The change in scale was a product of the experience of war and exile, as well as his grasp of issues that took the full measure of the world of the second half of the twentieth century – a united, interconnected world, experiencing demographic growth that, in the eyes of Lévi-Strauss (and of many others), had become the very image of a catastrophe in the making. The promotion of demographic knowledge, and of the population question as a major social and political issue, was part of his UNESCO mandate, though it was also most likely catalysed by a trip he made to Pakistan in 1950, at the request of that very institution.

Big science

Several international meetings, especially in 1952, served as the stage for these scientific forays, which were conceived as such, as if being a foreigner allowed for greater freedom to propose ideas and voice critiques – to think big and strike forcefully. Comparing the ethnographer Rivers to a Galileo of anthropological science, which then found its Newton in Mauss, there is little doubt that Lévi-Strauss fancied himself the Einstein of international social science.[29]

This was clear, for example, at the July 1952 Conference of Anthropologists and Linguists, held in Bloomington, Indiana, for which Lévi-Strauss was chosen to give the closing address – in itself an honour and source of gratification. The tone he struck was one of synthesis: Lévi-Strauss took a broad view, juggling the various perspectives, cleverly outlining the different issues, while also hierarchizing them. The professor from France indulged in a staging, a dramatization, of a scenario of the unification of the sciences. According to him, linguistics had been the only human science rigorous enough to rival the exact sciences, the only one to have managed to open the narrow door to sacred knowledge: 'For

centuries the humanities and the social sciences have resigned themselves
to contemplating the world of the natural and exact sciences as a kind of
paradise which they will never enter. And then, all of a sudden, there is a
small door which is being opened between the two fields, and it is linguistics which has done it.'[30] Until literary critics, psychoanalysts and philosophers had finally followed suit and rushed through this narrow door over
the following decade, the anthropologists and linguists had been on 'an
unhappy merry-go-round',[31] wasting time running after each other, the
one demanding more concrete data on societies, the other calling for more
modelling. The whole point of his conclusion was to reveal the possible
correlations between language and culture, and to distinguish between different levels of approach: between a given language and culture or, more
generally, between language and the symbolic activity of representation.[32]
The essential question at the core of Lévi-Strauss's agenda was the following: What 'common ground' can be found for the different disciplines?
The entire speech sprung from the correlations and permutations between
linguistic terms and social structures, kinship relations, marriage rules and
myth, as in a vast echo chamber, to conclude, as often, on a note of mounting generality with dramatic overtones and great fervour. The aim was to
found 'a science both very ancient and very new, an anthropology conceived in a broader way – that is, a knowledge of man that incorporates all
the different approaches that can be used and that will provide a clue to the
way according to which our uninvited guest, the human mind, works'.[33]

A month earlier, in New York, Lévi-Strauss had taken part in a vast
conference organized by the Wenner-Gren Foundation, bringing together
roughly eighty scholars, including all the leading lights of Anglo-American
anthropology – Margaret Mead, Alfred Kroeber, Robert Lowie, Julian
Steward, etc. Here again, he led the charge for the unification of science
through well-adapted research strategies, among which the structuralist
proposal was the most productive. After all, did not anthropology, in the
various cultural fields with which it dealt (clothing, arts, myths), obey
a similar principle of differentiation as natural history, with its branch-
ing out into various species? Lévi-Strauss proliferated metaphors. The
anthropologist was a kind of botanist: he picked a few random samples
and placed them in his herbarium. Yet primitive societies were more fragile
than field flowers – hence the gap between the ethnographic data, which
was unevenly distributed across the various societies and remained very
fragmentary in any case, and a theoretical framework that was 'far more
advanced',[34] a gap which characterized that particular moment in anthropology. This was an anomaly in the history of science, in which the opposite situation is far more common. As well as a botanist, the anthropologist
was also a 'ragpicker', rummaging through the trash cans of history and
feeding on the refuse of other disciplines – i.e., on the minutiae of concrete
life. The latter remark, and especially the use of the term 'trash', caused a
bit of a stir at the conference, whose collective spine bristled. His colleagues
did not appreciate the comparison. 'Margaret Mead came to me and said,
"There are words that never should be uttered." That day marked the
beginning of our friendship, which lasted until her death.'[35] Lévi-Strauss

spoke as the theorist of structuralism, whose American genealogy he retraced (among many others, over the years), emphasizing the centrality of Kroeber, the paradoxical position of Boas, Lowie's decisive role, etc. In order to clarify the notion of 'model', which was likely to trigger sterile polemics, he insisted on the nature of intellectual construction, of what he called a 'structure', which is in no way empirically observable.[36]

These two interventions, followed and preceded by others, which revealingly all took place on American soil, were thus intensely programmatic and epistemological. Lévi-Strauss had set out to work out the definition and clarification of what he considered the discursive foundation of a true international interdisciplinary approach. Whether turning to linguistics or to the natural sciences, he saw connections everywhere: with genetics, game theory, cybernetics – no stones were left unturned, convinced as he was that this was a moment of 'massive theoretical convergence'[37] under the banner of structuralism, which was to subsume all scientific energies. On 11 June 1951, he wrote to Jakobson: 'My dream over these last two years has been to create a centre for structural research in France where we would apply a fundamental method to all [unreadable] the sciences of man, in whatever order, where they seem likely to be immediately compatible. I have very specific projects for the study of style (in fine arts and music) and comparative mythology. And I also have three or four young scholars who are well trained and ready to work with me.'[38] And later, on 9 January 1952: 'I am thinking more and more about creating a research centre for structural analysis where we would undertake the simultaneous study of kinship, mythology and linguistics.'[39] When Jakobson urged Lévi-Strauss to join him at Harvard, Lévi-Strauss replied that he would rather develop the 'European branch' of a future structuralist centre, based in Paris.

What do these dreams of research institutions tell us? First, that the structuralist offensive was carried out on the international stage, even though Claude Lévi-Strauss himself would be its leading figure in Europe – a means for him to escape the French environment, which remained a hostile one, while still making alliances with American scholars. We should also point out that the structuralist research centre of which he dreamt was not what would later become the Laboratory of Social Anthropology, which never exerted any 'structuralist discipline' on its members. But for the time being, the theory-driven Lévi-Strauss was keen to develop links with all disciplines, and especially across all vernaculars, in order to unify the social sciences as much as possible. Mathematics was one that he had already drawn upon in the *Elementary Structures* to formalize kinship relations. At the time, he was also taking part in an international project developed by MIT, financed by the Ford Foundation and inspired by Jakobson, who wanted to publish a book directed by his friend Claude, as part of the series he edited: *Mathematical Trends in the Social Sciences*. A seminar was organized in Paris reflecting the ambition of the project. It included among its participants the mathematicians Georges Guilbaut and Lionel Penrose, the psychologist Jean Piaget, the sociologist Paul-Henry Chombart de Lauwe, the physicist Pierre Auger, and Lacan (who was responsible for a chapter on 'Aphasia and Communication'). The seminar met every Wednesday at 6:30, beginning in March 1953: 'Even Benveniste has agreed to come!' But the project was aborted and the book never published, even though the group's activities did result in the publication of 'The Mathematics of Man',[40] in the *International Social Science Bulletin*, one of the journals published by UNESCO.

This scientific hubris fired up an intense correspondence with Jakobson. Settled at Harvard in 1949, the Russian linguist longed to form a 'dream team' composed of himself and his 'brother' Claude, Talcott Parsons, the great sociologist who had developed a semantic approach to social issues, as well as Clyde Kluckhohn, the head of the Department of Social Relations. It was in that context, made even more favourable by the growing renown of Lévi-Strauss on the American academic scene, that, in the autumn of 1953, he received, through the offices of Parsons himself, an offer of a full professorship with tenure at Harvard – i.e., at the very top of the American academic hierarchy. This offer was only the latest and most flattering of a long series, based on his considerable interaction with American colleagues. The growing gap between the tepid recognition he received in France and his growing international reputation kept the American option open.[41] As Margaret Mead is reported (by Jakobson) to have said: 'People do not understand you and hinder you from having a position which you merit. [. . .] In any case remember that my position now is strong enough to support vehemently your career here if desired by you.'[42] At Berkeley, Kurt Lewin and Alfred Kroeber had already voiced the same sentiments as early as 1950.

In those years, Lévi-Strauss became a fellow of the Royal Anthropological Institute of Great Britain and Ireland (1948, honorary fellow in 1955), a corresponding member of the American Museum of Natural History (1952), and a member of the Royal Netherlands Academy (1956). As Parsons said in his offer letter, foreign scholars were aware of the 'great distinction and originality' of his contribution to anthropological studies, and of the 'breadth and catholicity' of his interests.[43] These words acknowledged his scholarly stature. Yet Lévi-Strauss declined the Harvard offer.

Why did he refuse, thus reiterating his choice to remain in France, despite the professional setbacks he had just experienced? For Lévi-Strauss, as for other French intellectuals, the United States might have been the source of preliminary recognition, but his life course remained unwaveringly wedded to France, despite continuing to have international ambitions. Indeed, he travelled far less from then on, with a few specific and significant exceptions (Japan and British Columbia). Furthermore, campus life did not particularly appeal to him. The narrow social horizon, the conformism of students and the prosaic comforts of small American cities were not in the least tempting. This Parisian promenader would have been bored to death in Cambridge [MA] or Cornell. He might have considered the British universities, Oxford and Cambridge, which, as he confided to Jakobson, seemed to 'offer a wonderful combination of what we like from both sides [of the Atlantic]'.[44] But in any case, his son Laurent, his parents – his sick father needed care until his death in January 1953[45] – and his new life all anchored him in Paris. Political factors were a further disincentive: the hysterical McCarthyism of 1952–53 provided a powerful discouragement. He opened up to Kluckhohn, who replied: 'It is quite true that there are forces in American politics that you will find quite abhorrent.' But, he added, there are 'strong counter-currents',[46] especially at Harvard, a university that was more 'liberal' than 'mainstream' American public life. Little interested in finding himself doubly confined in a microcosm from which universal science was supposed to spring, Lévi-Strauss also reacted as a man of the left, hostile to the unfriendly America represented by the senator from Wisconsin. It was thus not from an American campus, not even from the Harvard campus, that he set out to take the measure of the world, but from UNESCO, an agency of the United Nations, to which he had been connected in many ways since its creation in 1945.

The International Social Science Council:
the demographic argument

Wiktor Stoczkowski was the first to point out how surprisingly little the commentators on Lévi-Strauss's work had made of his long association with UNESCO. The new institution (founded in 1945) was located near the Musée de l'Homme; prior to its move in 1958 into the new building constructed for it on the Place de Fontenoy, it was housed in the Hotel Majestic on avenue Kléber. In the early 1950s, that part of the 16th arrondissement boasted a bevy of social scientists of international stature – anthropologists freshly returned from fieldwork, demographers, economists – a well-travelled and cosmopolitan little group organized around social science and exile networks, and determined to work for the future of the world. Lévi-Strauss participated in that polyglot enclave in the heart of the Parisian capital, through his friendships – with Otto Klineberg, the head of the social science department at UNESCO in the late 1940s, and especially with Alfred Métraux, in charge of the division for the study of race problems – as well as through his convictions. He fully shared the ideal of a Scientific International that would come to replace those that had been annihilated by the war. From this perspective, as Stoczkowski has pointed out, the anthropologist of the 1950s remained true to the young socialist of the 1930s.[47]

Lévi-Strauss was among the group of scholars who had written the first UNESCO declaration on race, as early as 1949, which was followed by a second. That same year, he supervised one of the eight studies produced by UNESCO on the causes of tension between social groups. This study was conducted in the French commune of Nesle-Normandeuse, which had been selected, both for its small scale and for its mixed rural and industrial character, by psychologist René Blancart and anthropologist Lucien Bernot – a student of Lévi-Strauss whom he later sent to the hills of Chittagong, in East Pakistan.[48] The 'Nouville' project (the pseudonym for the village) anticipated the better financed studies that were to be launched in the 1960s, in which interdisciplinary ambition and anthropological methods, hitherto reserved for exotic worlds, were brought to bear on

European rural life.[49] If the psychological dimension was of little interest to Lévi-Strauss, who considered it a 'constraint' imposed by UNESCO, he was 'fascinated', for practical and theoretical reasons, by the ethnographic aspect of the study, applied for the first time close to home. 'Would the project hit obstacles that would prove fatal to its success? Would it enrich our understanding of a world so close to us, about which we thought we knew all there was to know? Could ethnographic methods be transposed, without significant alteration, from small, so-called primitive or archaic societies to a French village steeped in history?'[50]

Not surprisingly, Lévi-Strauss was part of the committee of experts that met in 1951 to set up, under the aegis of UNESCO, the International Social Science Council, headed by Donald Young. It came as no surprise either that he should become its general secretary in 1953. His American contacts, his connections with foundations, his interest in scientific projects with theoretical and systematic ambitions – everything pointed to it, not to mention the material advantages which, at that moment in his life, could not be ignored. This position provided him with supplemental income – 80,000 old French francs per month (i.e., around £1,500) – and perks that included a secretary and subscriptions to the leading international scholarly journals.[51]

This new post was also a position of power, which confirmed Lévi-Strauss's status as a rising figure in the eyes of those with whom he spoke the language of modern science, namely Braudel and the VIth Section. Indeed, he included them in his activities, among them this international project, headed by Georges Balandier: 'The object of this research is the study of a sample of 200–300 works and articles dealing with the rapid social transformations that have taken place in the so-called "underdeveloped" countries, following the introduction of modern industrial and agricultural techniques.' What were their conclusions? And what were the 'logical assumptions and methodological principles' that drove these studies? 'The ultimate aim was to encourage the various disciplines involved (historians, geographers, economists, sociologists, psychologists, jurists, anthropologists, etc.) to work on models at the same level of abstraction.'[52] This work of bibliographical synthesis was intended as a practical contribution, yet it never lost sight of the remarkable reflexive dimension: What were the assumptions? What do we mean when we talk about 'underdevelopment'? etc.

We do not have to take Claude Lévi-Strauss at his word when he described his eight years, from 1953 until 1961, at the helm of ISSC: 'I tried to give the impression that an organization without goal or function had a reason for existing.'[53] His often disparaging remarks about his parallel administrative activities do not do justice to the reality of his daily involvement. Quite the contrary, according to Wiktor Stoczkowski, 'the archives of the International Social Science Council reveal that Lévi-Strauss's tenure was characterized by rich and intense activity, which clearly reflected a very personal commitment, especially in the early years'.[54] Reassessing the importance of his UNESCO work also sheds light on the genesis of what some consider to be Lévi-Strauss's obsession with demographics. It is indeed quite clear that, far from being an 'idiosyncratic eccentricity',[55] the neo-Malthusian thematic was a widely shared preoccupation throughout the early twentieth century, promoted within various international organizations, from the International Labour Organization in the 1920s[56] to UNESCO in the 1950s, as one of the major challenges of the twentieth century. This growing anxiety regarding population growth did not preclude another, and opposite, concern, especially in France, regarding demographic stagnation and decline – both combining in an anxious expectation of an upcoming geopolitical tipping point through a revised version of the 'yellow peril'. For it was Asia that had, for some time, constituted the epicentre of this alarmist rhetoric. And it was from Asia that the first great postwar shock came: the traumatizing publication of Indian census figures. In 1951, a newly independent India had reached 312 million inhabitants.[57]

As the ISSC general secretary, Lévi-Strauss was charged with defining social science research programmes and strategies. Very early on, he singled out the demographic issue and made proposals of 'a highly provocative and unorthodox character'.[58] In a ten-page memo presented on 21 February 1953 to the members of the executive committee, he emphasized the increasing urgency of gathering data on the 'demographic structure of human societies'.[59] He then proceeded to outline three main ways of approaching these phenomena. First, an interdisciplinary study of overpopulation, taking into account subjective dimensions, such as the different levels of awareness and tolerance of demographic density in various societies. Second, an analysis of the change in political scale resulting from the development of multinational states, such as the USSR and the US, but also India and China, as well as reflections on the optimal size of national groups in the modern world: was the super-state the most appropriate form? Third, a reflection on the social and cultural impact of UNESCO literacy campaigns: did their impact on traditional societies correspond to initial objectives? Wiktor Stoczkowski has emphasized the extent to which these questions ran 'against the grain'[60] of UNESCO's principal articles of faith. By then, Lévi-Strauss already considered the primary cause of totalitarian and genocidal regimes to be, at its core, demographic in nature, whereas UNESCO, in its very founding principle, had determined that the root of evil was ignorance and illiteracy. Whereas UNESCO promoted the supranational credo, Lévi-Strauss remained sceptical and sensitive to the risk that ties of interaction would be destroyed by the dilution of what he termed the 'levels of authenticity' of social life. Finally, in daring to subject the literacy policies to critical review, he was taking on one of UNESCO's hobbyhorses, indeed very nearly its raison d'être.

If the demographic problem became so central in the early years of ISSC, through various international symposiums and conferences, this was because it echoed one of the major concerns of its general secretary, who had taken it upon himself to become one of its active promoters as *the* number one issue, both in terms of research and policy. The rise of the demographic question, and the often tragic tone in which Lévi-Strauss addressed it, and would continue to do throughout his life, coincided with a trip he made to Pakistan on behalf of UNESCO in 1950, and which appears to have been decisive. That journey to the densely peopled tropics made a lasting impression on him, grafting images of overpopulation onto statistics of demographic 'growth', creating the effect of a claustrophobic nightmare.

Pakistan as proof positive

Commissioned by Alfred Métraux to conduct a study of the state of social science research and teaching, Claude Lévi-Strauss travelled around Pakistan from 3 August to 23 October 1950. 'The task was not terribly taxing given the near nonexistence of social science in Pakistan at this time.'[61] This assessment was further developed in three notebooks[62] filled with his travel notes, which reveal subtle alterations he made in the pages devoted to that experience in chapters 14, 15 and 16 of *Tristes Tropiques*, which precede the account of his Brazilian expeditions, as well as in the famous (and infamous) moment of the conclusion that lays out an opposition between Islam and Buddhism. For the purposes of his study, Lévi-Strauss conducted many interviews, mostly with officials (appointed to the new ministries) and academics, always straddling the blurry line between the political and academic worlds. The situation was not favourable. It had not escaped him that UNESCO and he himself were perceived in Pakistan as lackeys of the United States. He often despaired, struck by the absurdity of his mission. The two most pressing problems were, quite clearly, land reform and capital investment: 'What is the point of talking about anything else?'[63] Over the course of the few months he spent there, he moved constantly across the two halves of that new hemiplegic country, from west to east (Karachi–Delhi–Dacca) and then east to west (Dacca–Lahore–Peshawar), except for the ten days, from 28 August until 8 September, that he spent in the hills of Chittagong on the Burma border, a Hindu enclave within Muslim Pakistan. A moment of epiphany on what was an otherwise oppressive trip, that long week he spent with the Kuki and the Mogh was his first opportunity to discover early Buddhist temples. Lévi-Strauss felt he could breathe again. After brief, impromptu fieldwork, he indulged in a few comparative observations on these Tibeto-Burman societies. 'The point was not to capture the totality', says Vincent Debaene, 'so much as to grasp the differences relevant to specific theoretical points.'[64] The Kuki dwelled in well-kept villages built on stilts on hilltops, whereas the Mogh, who had arrived later, lived in cruder villages located in the depths of a damp valley. Yet their religious life was far more sophisticated than that of the Kuki. Lévi-Strauss also seized this opportunity to further explore and qualify some of the conclusions he had drawn in *Elementary Structures* regarding the Kuki system.[65] This manner of comparing differences – the core of the structuralist approach – was the intellectual template for the travelling Lévi-Strauss, who spontaneously applied it, according to the constant play of oppositions and mirror effects, to make sense of his trip to the East and give substance to the shock of his Asia experience.[66]

Indeed, the 'crowded tropics' of the East were in diametrical opposition to the 'empty tropics' of America, in the rear-view mirror of his memory, and prompted his demographic reflections, which constituted one of the great objects of his political gaze. In the same way, the opposition between Muslim and Buddhist civilizations was not only a function of his sympathetic view of the Buddha and his own sensibilities. This structural opposition also imposed itself as an interpretive framework because of the recent history of partition in 1947, of which he makes so little in *Tristes Tropiques* that he has been rightfully reproached for his de-historicizing tendencies. In actual fact, he was fully aware of the painful history of the independence of the Indian subcontinent, the massive population displacements to which it had given rise, and the massacres and famines engendered by the civil war. Arriving in Karachi, which had been 99 per cent Hindu, he noted that all the professors had left with their libraries and papers. His notebooks show that, for each new phenomenon or sensation, he wavered as to which factor to attribute them, Islam or 'Asia'. Between this ambivalent hesitation revealed in the notebooks and the very aggressively critical views on Islam he offers in *Tristes Tropiques*, there has been a clear evolution, an erasure of the initial equivocation. This hardening can be seen in several instances. In the watery warmth of the Bengali countryside, Lévi-Strauss suddenly paused to describe the barracks of the jute workers; several years later, repeating the description word for word, he added a paragraph comparing this phenomenon with the force-feeding of geese he had observed in the Landes region of France in his youth.[67] Similarly, when he visited the revered temple to the Kali goddess in Calcutta, he compared the rest house where the pilgrims are hosted to a slaughterhouse; but the reference to the concentration camps dates from 1955, not 1950.[68]

In Pakistan, Lévi-Strauss remained keenly observant and attentive to detail, which he carefully recorded in his notebooks: 'At the Metropolis Hotel [in Karachi], people speak Urdu and English, but the Messieurs–Dames restroom sign is in French.' 'I am told that in Urdu, the word for "yesterday" and "tomorrow" is the same.'[69] He smoked the local tobacco and wanted to taste all the street food. He noted the very prominent display of contraceptives ('vaginal jelly') in pharmacies. He described in detail the composition and names of male and female garments, but did not dare photograph them. However, while he maintained an anthropological gaze, his frequently violent reactions were those of a Westerner allergic to the demographic density of the East. For, in his view, this density amounted to a constant denial of the very possibility of human relations, i.e., of the possibility of behaving obligingly, of believing in the good faith of others. In the countless beggars, from whom he averted his gaze, he could only see in the other the 'nothingness' of his own humanity. He found human relationships of this sort – based on a profoundly unequal society comprising despots and beggars – strictly speaking intolerable. As Vincent Debaene has pointed out, these critical moments strangely elicited a Sartrean language of 'nothingness' and 'reification', as if this were the only appropriate vocabulary in a situation 'so perfectly, so totally unbearable'.[70] And a true insult to the epistemology of UNESCO, whose 'Tensions' programme was revealed to be nothing but a pathetic joke: 'It has been ages since anything that could be seen as tense has broken or been blown to smithereens.'[71]

At the midpoint of Lévi-Strauss's life, Pakistan thus acted as a catalyst for his moral concern about the fate of our world – for if America stood as an image of our past, Asia heralded the future of the West, anticipating the increasing overpopulation of the planet. Yet Lévi-Strauss regularly highlighted another danger, that of authoritarian rule (i.e., state rule) by religion in that newly founded state. He saw this aggravation of religion – in its Puritan, bigoted, provincial form (reminding him of Lourdes and Lisieux, in Catholic France) – as the prerogative of newly installed elites, who were apathetic, passive, tyrannical and irresponsible. The government could not care less about the social sciences. 'Islam is enough!', as a sociologist colleague of his explained. Lévi-Strauss concluded: 'Their own version of "Work, Family, Country" is "Unity, Faith, Discipline".'[72] Some of his colleagues – in Dacca, for instance, where the ties with British universities were still strong – went so far as to say that British rule had been far less constraining on academics. Lévi-Strauss thus had a very negative experience of the emergence of new decolonized states, an experience that explains his subsequent wariness and served to crystallize, around religious sectarianism and buffoonish authoritarianism, everything that might feed his pessimistic vision. And indeed, after the enchantment of the plane trip, and the aerial view so conducive to happy reveries about the surface of the earth, he returned to France filled with an anxiety that was to continue to drive his critical and sometimes toxic vision of modernity.

The Occident as accident

For Lévi-Strauss, becoming an anthropologist, as he was later to say, meant 'thinking and writing at a different scale. First geographically, considering that our society is but one among others. And then, across a much greater temporal scale.'[73] This was precisely the perspective that informed the short text of about fifty pages published in 1952 as part of a UNESCO series, entitled *Race and History.*

Race and History

More than any of his other works, *Race and History* was tied to the context in which it was produced, even if it was able to free itself from it: a commissioned work, undertaken in part to put food on the table,[74] *Race and History* became, over the years, a classic of antiracist literature.[75]

If a racialized conception of society, as we have already noted in previous chapters, still had considerable currency after 1945, including with anthropologists, the antiracist discourse, while perhaps a minority position, now carried a certain political legitimacy that had been painfully affirmed by the world conflict. The idea that wars stemmed first and foremost 'from the minds of men'[76] was at the core of what Wiktor Stoczowski has called the new 'international doxa', expressed at the UN conference in London that gave birth to UNESCO, and of the educational agenda of the new institution. A campaign against racism was thus launched in 1949. One of the essential components of the plan was to gather a learned assembly of scientists, charge them with defining the notion of race and thereby anchor antiracism in science and reason, turning racism into a kind of quaint obscurantism. The learned assembly met in Paris from 12 to 14 December 1949. Lévi-Strauss, as assistant director of the Musée de l'Homme, was part of the group. Their work, the aim of which was to collectively draft an acceptable text, gave rise to the UNESCO 'Statement on Race Problems',[77] which was made public in June 1950. A long series of critiques coming from renowned scientists soon undermined its authority, which rested on an overly performative discourse: racism was essentially cultural, there were more similarities than differences between men, physical appearance was insignificant, etc. 'The UNESCO statement on race proclaimed everything that one wanted science to demonstrate, but it certainly did not present the scientific knowledge on the question.'[78] Hence the convening, at the request of UNESCO's director general, of a new expert committee and the drafting of a new statement, approved on 26 May 1952, which did not fundamentally differ from the first, but adopted a more measured tone.

It was in this context of laborious genesis that Alfred Métraux – appointed in April 1950 to head the Division for the Study of Race Problems of the UNESCO Department of Social Sciences – commissioned a series of brochures dealing with the various aspects of the race question, from a pedagogical and strictly scientific perspective. The French anthropologist (and writer) Michel Leiris, the American zoologist Leslie C. Dunn, the Mexican anthropologist Juan Comas, the American sociologist Arnold M. Rose, and Otto Klineberg (director of the department) were solicited, together with Lévi-Strauss, who was reading the proofs of his own contribution at the time the second UNESCO statement came out, in May 1952. It is rather striking that these books have all now more or less become obsolete, except for Lévi-Strauss's, which retains its force still today. Why? Probably for quasi-psychological reasons: just as, in 1940, he ridiculed the famous mantra 'We shall win because we are strongest'; just as the Gaullist credo, according to which France had not lost the war, left him cold; here he declined to attack racism on biological grounds, only for it to resurface in cultural terms – as indeed it has. Averse to the rhetoric of exhortation, the anthropologist proceeded to write a brisk fifty-page essay that tackled the issue of human diversity head-on.

From the very beginning, he shifted the emphasis away from that of the original commission: 'It would be a waste of time to devote so much talent and effort to demonstrating that, in the present state of scientific knowledge, there is no justification for asserting that any one race is intellectually superior or inferior to another, if we were, in the end, indirectly to countenance the concept of race by seeming to show that the great ethnic groups constituting human kind as a whole have, as such, made their own peculiar contributions to the common heritage.'[79] Any articulation between a given race, or even a given society, and a psychological trait was antiscientific. The link between the signifier (being black, yellow or pygmy) and the signified (laziness, carefreeness, etc.) had to be severed. And yet human diversity did exist! How can we reconcile this observation with that of the unequal accomplishments of societies, while still rejecting any racial and cultural hierarchy? The demonstration mostly relied on the debunking of what Lévi-Strauss called 'faux-evolutionism' – i.e., a kind of Darwinism in the cultural and social domain, which, since the eighteenth century (Vico, Condorcet) and through the nineteenth century (Comte), had developed a simplistic representation of the progress of humanity as a tall ladder that all peoples would climb rung by rung, albeit at different speeds. According to this conception, primitive societies were vestiges of what Western society had been, since we were all destined to climb the same ladder. As often in this work, the arguments rested on metaphors. Instead of the ladder metaphor, Lévi-Strauss offered that of a knight moving across a chess board. In his view, then, human development should not be understood as following a single, homogeneous (and of course also ethnocentric) path, but rather as a 'progress' – and the suddenly playful expression is reminiscent of Montaigne – 'in a series of leaps and bounds, or as the biologists would say, mutations'.[80] On the one hand, the hard destiny of unilinear progress; on the other, human societies dispersing 'by leaps and skips' in various directions, some emphasizing aesthetic production, others the integration of the young, still others the production of mechanical energy, etc. Insofar as progress existed – and how could this be denied? – it should therefore be rethought according to a new typology. And here again, the next step in this reasoning began with a metaphor. Like a gambler whose luck depends on several dice (this also works with roulette) and who, when he throws them, gets several different scores, it does sometimes happen that 'the scores add up to a lucky combination'.[81] Similarly, according to Lévi-Strauss, societies had progressed based on the more or less cumulative character of their respective histories; some moments had been conducive to accumulation – this was the case with the Neolithic revolution and the industrial revolution, and, in both instances, the accumulation had been such that it impacted the entire world, and its actual point of origin soon became moot. This gambling metaphor thus allowed him to introduce notions of probability and strategy, as civilizations were not just subject to random luck, but also conceived plans, made calculations and sometimes even 'play as a syndicate' to maximize their results. This was undoubtedly, in Lévi-Strauss's view, the main reason for the tremendous successes of the West, when for example, in the early Renaissance and for a large part of the sixteenth century, Europe attained optimum diversity, having become the site of encounter and fusion of all kinds of influences (Greek, Roman, German, English, as well as Arab and Chinese). It was able to create the conditions for letting all these cultures bloom, while, by comparison, the American world, which in some ways was no less developed (if we think of the Inca Empire), was more homogeneous, less differentiated and also less cumulative. The European 'coalition' proved more productive than the American 'coalition' – another way of narrating, and accounting for, the great defeat of pre-Columbian America. This notion of 'coalition' had the added advantage of aligning this text with the UNESCO doctrine that endeavoured to rebuild the postwar world on the basis of cooperation between its different actors.

Yet another point of convergence: the promotion of interbreeding as a condition of cumulative history, founded on exchanges, migrations and even sometimes wars, which allowed for the circulation of men, goods and ideas. Yet *Race and History*, in its conclusion, takes a less comfortable turn when it identifies a true antinomy of progress: diversity, the essential asset of cumulative history, also acts, 'as the game goes on',[82] as its greatest obstacle, for it leads to an inevitable uniformization. Differences diminish, the potential for difference decreases. This was where we now stood, according to Lévi-Strauss (and still more so today, six decades later, in the early twenty-first century). But already in 1952, he noted for the very first time the existence of a global civilization, for the so-called 'underdeveloped' countries did not want to remain as they were; they wanted, rather, to 'develop'. International organizations like UNESCO constituted the very stages on which these poignant dramas played out. Whereas the West sought to preserve cultural identities, even while promoting 'progress', these societies – soon to be new states – no longer had the option of opting out of the great global game of development. When Lévi-Strauss explained, *in fine*, that the way to recreate the potential of differentiation is to diversify the social body through the appearance of classes (as with the appearance of the proletariat in the days of the industrial revolution) or to aggregate outside elements (through colonization), he was describing, as solutions for keeping the game going, the two historical phenomena that were most intimately connected to Western predominance: capitalism and imperialism. It was at this price that – to the present day, i.e., 1952 – 'the state of disequilibrium which is necessary for the biological and cultural survival of mankind'[83] had been maintained. It is hard to miss the bitter irony here, since of the two antagonistic forces of diversification and unification, it was the latter that was to have the last word in the end. Yet Lévi-Strauss concluded on the 'sacred duty of mankind to bear these two contradictory facts in mind'.[84] Yet, and this amounted to an *ex ante* critique of some of the future tendencies of UNESCO, the point was not to cherish a few local traditions and folklorize a few strange mores, but indeed to preserve the structural conditions necessary for the very existence of diversity, rather than its historical content. The finale – 'we must hearken for the stirrings of new life . . .' – was no optimistic wager, but a moral imperative, always present in Lévi-Strauss, the idea that, faced with the unavoidable forces of entropy, 'there are men – some men – who can slow its progress, however temporarily'.[85] Like the lookout in Julien Gracq's *Rivage des Syrtes* (1951), the critical intellectual could survey the coming end. And this may have been the only heroic position remaining: that of sentry.

On 9 January 1952, Lévi-Strauss told Jakobson that he had written, for UNESCO, 'a short introduction to the philosophy of history conceived in a structuralist and Neumanian spirit'.[86] This formulation – revealing

316
The Old World (1947–1971)

of both the text's modesty ('an introduction') and ambition ('philosophy of history') – invites us to consider an essential, albeit seldom raised, question: what is the connection between structuralism's theoretical and epistemological apparatus and the conception of progress 'by leaps and bounds', i.e., cultural relativism? Was the author of *The Elementary Structures of Kinship* and of the 'Introduction to the Works of Marcel Mauss' the same as that of *Race and History*, or was the latter an independent voice, with its own distinct politics? First of all, we find the same constellation of metaphors across the three texts, all revolving around games. The conditions for cumulativeness in history are formalized thanks to game theory, which plays a central role, as we have seen, in the structuralist construct. Similarly, and more importantly, human civilizations are seen as complex entities, in which the whole matters more than its parts, in which relations and exchanges are more decisive than entities, in which the principle of differentiation is the driving force of all invention: 'We have sought to show that the true contribution of a culture consists not in the list of inventions which it has personally produced, but in its difference from others.'[87] Theory and politics thus converged, erecting themselves at a universal scale to capture societies in their diversity and common humanity, as complex and incommensurable ensembles in a state of fragile disequilibrium, like a Calder mobile whose balance it was incumbent on men to maintain.

Controversies and attacks

In the end, the short book created a scandal. That it should have triggered a few hostile attacks was not in itself surprising: while not a militant text in any way, *Race and History* was a profoundly political text which – in the space of a few pages, and in a new vein (that of the scientific argument) – reconfigured an entire worldview, one that was firmly held by a majority of Lévi-Strauss's contemporaries. A double transgression.

Roger Caillois was the first attacker, and the most virulent. After an appropriate delay – following the customary timeframe of intellectual jousts in journals – he published 'Illusions à rebours', an article in two instalments, in the *NRF* issues of December 1954 and January 1955. Caillois has been somewhat forgotten by posterity, but the *normalien*, *agrégé*, with ties to interwar surrealist circles, was friends with Bataille and a distinguished member of the Collège de sociologie – described by Lévi-Strauss himself as a successful institution in his overview of the field. Caillois's training, his intellectual temperament and his career, were quite reminiscent of Lévi-Strauss's own. Like the latter, he had spent the war years in exile, albeit in Argentina. A similar experience of expatriation, followed by a similar return to France and a common participation in the UNESCO project. They also shared a passion for mythology, and a connection to Dumézil. In short, he was a kind of twin brother, who subsequently turned into a 'nemesis'.[88] As Lévi-Strauss himself conceded: 'Caillois was a man of great culture, curious about those unexpected connections that occur, as he used to say, "on the diagonal". He had taken Marcel Mauss's courses and been inspired by them. We ought to have gotten along.'[89] Although the balance of authority between the two men has since been reversed, Caillois occupied positions of power in the first half of the 1950s that made him, more so than the anthropologist, an intellectual to be reckoned with: he was a member of the editorial board at Gallimard, and directed its 'La Croix du Sud' series on Latin American literature; as a 'director' at UNESCO, he held a more senior position than Lévi-Strauss. On avenue Kléber, this internecine struggle between two officials of the institution became a matter of some embarrassment.[90] It had been several years since Caillois had dropped his old obsession with the irrational, the sacred and the primitive, in an acrimonious return to his old quarrel with surrealism.

'Illusions à rebours' was a brilliant piece, yet also amateurish and naive, and a profound conformism today shows clearly through the impassioned diatribe. It belonged to a genre that had developed in the interwar period, which might be labelled 'defence of the West'. Indeed, Caillois argued, Lévi-Strauss – and Paul Valéry, Dada, Spengler, etc., before him – felt a deep rancour for their own civilization. He accused the scholar of prejudice – 'rejection preceded study' – and all anthropologists (he had a gripe with Leiris as well) of hypocrisy, bad faith and, ultimately, ingratitude. Indeed, Caillois's main argument in defence of Western superiority (which was religious and moral) was that the West had single-handedly invented science, including anthropological science. What credit did cultural relativism give to rationalism and the scientific mind? Aside from this legitimate question, Caillois's attack was *ad hominem*, ferocious, imbued with a kind of knowledge that seemed quaint but nonetheless cut to the quick. Lévi-Strauss responded with uncharacteristically polemical punch, and a fierce energy, resulting in a logical, rhetorical and scientific knockout of Caillois, in thirty-three dense pages. The article – entitled 'Diogène couché',[91] published in *Les Temps modernes* in the spring of 1955, an anomaly in Lévi-Strauss's writings, in that it has never been republished – revealed formidable talents that he clearly refrained from exercising in intellectual discussions thereafter.[92] We shall return to this point later.

'Diogenes proved the existence of movement by walking; Mr Roger Caillois went to sleep so as not to see it.'[93] Thus began Lévi-Strauss's scathing reply, which characterized his detractor's argument as a 'hybrid exercise that begins with dinner table buffoonery, moves on to the homilies of a preacher and concludes with the lamentations of a penitent'.[94] Citing precise examples, he rebutted his misleading reductions and truncated quotes pasted together. But what aggravated him supremely was the accusation of ingratitude, levelled at anthropologists who were critical of their own civilization. At this rate, he declared, all of science would be politically muted. 'America has its McCarthy. We have our McCaillois.'[95] This cutting jibe, which met with much success among the chattering classes, was followed by a long excursus on the divided condition of the ethnographer, caught between subjectivity and objectivity. This was, after all, at the core of the chapters of *Tristes Tropiques* he had just written, in the winter of 1954. It was in the text of March 1955 that the metaphor of the anthropologist as a Lazarus figure appeared for the first time – the 'victim of a sort of chronic uprooting', who is 'psychologically mutilated' and 'comes back from the dead', in short one who is 'resurrected'.[96] The differences between Lévi-Strauss and Caillois can be captured in two game metaphors: whereas the former put forward the image of a game of dice or roulette, which by definition remained open-ended, the latter conceived of humanity's evolution as a puzzle, soon to be completed, with the West supplying its final pieces.[97] Lévi-Strauss recapped the various steps in his argument, in which he endeavoured to 'deal seriously with a serious subject', as a result of which Caillois was hoist with his own petard: the words Callois had used to describe Lévi-Strauss – 'indecisive surrealist, amateur anthropologist, muddled agitator'[98] – were turned into a self-portrait of the former member of *La Révolution surréaliste*, and his hateful outburst into an attempt to evade his own responsibilities, resulting in an outbreak of intellectual acne. 'And may he go elsewhere in search of his imagos.'[99]

This 'gut reaction' was published in *Les Temps modernes*, incidentally featuring a reference to Sartre.[100] Was this controversy then part of the ongoing literary feud between the old guard of the former *NRF*, Paulhan and Gide's journal, which had resumed publishing after its anti-Semitic wartime slip, and *Les Temps modernes*, the journal founded by Sartre under the banner of existentialism and left-wing politically engaged writing? In other words, was this joust a 'classic battle between conservatives and progressives in the French culture wars of the 1950s?'[101] Clearly it was not. Indeed, the cultural relativist idea, according to which each culture had its own value, was a truly 'new idea' in the face of what remained the more commonly circulated notions of evolutionism and Western superiority – if not racial superiority, at least of the cultural, technical and even moral superiority of the West. The various positions involved here do not readily align with the political and ideological left vs. right, conservative vs. progressive split. Despite Caillois's vehement tone, and the personal importance he might have tried to lend his position, at the time it was essentially banal and commonsensical. If anything, progressive evolutionism was quite an important part of the DNA of the Republican left, that of the 'civilizing mission' of the 1880s. More generally, this perception of the times (the optimism of progress, the intense investment in the future) that Lévi-Strauss had debunked in his critique of unilinear teleological progress was, strictly speaking, Western post-revolutionary modernity itself. Certainly, this modernity presented itself in various forms, from the temporality of urban elites to that of rural peoples, from the races that were relegated to the margins of history to those promised rapid civilizational catch-up. The constant throughout was a mad faith in the future.[102] Communism itself was an offshoot of this Western modernity, whose vision it very much shared, as further confirmed by the very negative review of *Race and History* published by Maxime Rodinson in the intellectual journal of the French communists, *La Nouvelle Critique*.

Enrolling others in addition to the two main protagonists, the controversy spread and turned into a full-fledged 'affair'.[103] Aimé Césaire added a significant appendix to the second, revised and expanded edition of *Discourse on Colonialism*, published in 1955. A great friend of Michel Leiris, his voice resonated with a singular power, alongside that of Lévi-Strauss, yet independently of him, since the two had never met – the voice of a black intellectual composing one of the first works in a 'postcolonial' key. He pointed out how Europe's violent colonizing project had rebounded on Europe itself, leading its practices and representations into 'savagery'. Over time, this fully integrated violence had paved the way for Nazism – an intuition already developed by Lévi-Strauss in a 1942 memo.[104] Césaire undertook a critique of 'colonial knowledge', first among which was ethnography. This discipline, according to Césaire, had not been uniformly steeped in the miasma of degenerate science; at least it had extracted itself from it thanks to the likes of Leiris and Lévi-Strauss. This was precisely what Caillois held against them: 'The great betrayal of Western anthropology, which with a deplorable deterioration of any sense of responsibility has done everything it could to cast doubt on the comprehensive superiority of Western civilization over exotic civilizations.' Equally combative, Césaire also indulged in angry derision. He demolished Caillois's position, which he described as crude and philistine, while also emphasizing how significant his ideas were in 1954–55: 'Significant of what? Of the state of mind of thousands upon thousands of Europeans or, to be very precise, of the state of mind of the Western petty bourgeoisie. Significant of what? Of this: that at the very time when it most often mouths the word, the West has never been further from being able to live a true humanism – a humanism made to the measure of the world.'[105]

The Caillois–Lévi-Strauss controversy, wrote Métraux, 'has been the big event in Parisian literary circles'.[106] Before *Tristes Tropiques*, and as a kind of preamble, it threw Lévi-Strauss into the intellectual limelight, and, for the time being at least, on the side of Sartre and *Les Temps modernes*, which orchestrated the fight. Indeed, the Lévi-Strausses were invited to attend the premiere of *Nékrassov*, as Lévi-Strauss ironically pointed out to Dolorès Vanetti, Sartre's great love in New York, who had remained a close friend of his (and of Lévi-Strauss's): '"Diogène couché" alone has earned me favours that no other publication had merited, which is a bit pathetic.'[107]

This emergence from obscurity via a public debate did not make up for a lack of academic recognition in France, by contrast with his growing acclaim (including of a controversial nature) abroad. With one foot in UNESCO, and the other in the US, where he took part in symposiums and seminars, his energetic publication of theoretical and programmatic articles made Lévi-Strauss a familiar figure among scholars the world over. If in Parisian existentialist circles recognition came from political engagement, at UNESCO it rested on commitment to an antiracist credo of human brotherhood that would rid the minds of men of all evil. Some, like Michel Leiris, who partook of both worlds, moved easily from one to the other, intellectually, socially and geographically. Leiris was thus a habitué of bus number 63, nicknamed 'the ocean liner', that brought him from his home (on quai des Grands-Augustins) and its Latin Quarter social life to the Musée de l'Homme, where he worked and rubbed shoulders with a very different set. But for the likes of Alfred Métraux, the Latin Quarter was so exotic that it transported him to South America: 'Eerie Saint-Germain at night. A long avenue reminiscent of Argentina.'[108] Lévi-Strauss leaned more to the side of Trocadéro than Saint-Germain, but he remained, in the end, equally foreign to both of these intellectual universes.

14

The Confessions of
Claude Lévi-Strauss

Every anthropological career finds its principle in 'confessions', written or untold.

Claude Lévi-Strauss, 'Jean-Jacques Rousseau,
Founder of the Sciences of Man', 1962

Setting out to explore *Tristes Tropiques* – one of the most prominent episodes in the life of Lévi-Strauss, written in rage and received as a 'bombshell'[1] in the mid-1950s – it is tempting to see it as, above all, a great 'Book of Disquiet'.[2] Its peculiar combination of disenchantment, derisiveness and wisdom and its steady moral resonance coupled with introspective urgency are as disturbing as they are seductive. Indeed, the seduction comes precisely from the book's capacity to disturb. As opposed to Fernando Pessoa, who published his book under one of his many pseudonyms, *Tristes Tropiques* had an author – Claude Lévi-Strauss, a forty-six-year-old anthropologist, on sabbatical from himself for a few months, an academic outcast in his own country, in a state of irresolution. A midlife crisis that unleashed a challenge to the world, to the self, and to thought in general, after which nothing would ever be quite the same again – neither for himself, nor for his readers, and they would be many. Ten years after the end of the war, the book turned anthropology into 'a passage and a passion';[3] and it brought the anthropologist-turned-writer considerable celebrity.

Midlife, mid-oeuvre – *Tristes Tropiques* is a pivotal book, which reorganized time both around and within itself. A narrative of return, a work of Proustian proportions, it imposed its own relationship to time, its love of beginnings and anxieties about the future, for which the congested present served only as a slippery slope. The intimacy with its times that all 'bestsellers' evince, even retrospectively, stood in sharp contrast here with the clear biographical and political disengagement with his present that Claude Lévi-Strauss effected: 'A man lives two existences. Until the age of forty-five he absorbs the elements surrounding him. Then, all of a sudden, it's over; he doesn't absorb anything more. Thereafter he lives the duplicate of his first existence, and tries to tally the succeeding days with the rhythms and the odours of his earlier active life.'[4] Would this prediction by Pierre Mac Orlan, a favourite of Lévi-Strauss's in his younger years and one of the explicit inspirations for *Tristes Tropiques*, apply to its author? In any case, the modernist theoretician and energetic reformer of the human sciences proved to be classical in style and now also conservative in aesthetic taste, even while professing a well-known admiration for exotic cultures. It is also this paradoxical relationship to his own historical time that made his intellectual journey through the century quite unique.

Tristes Tropiques, time travel

Getting it off his chest

At the origins of *Tristes Tropiques* was the North Pole, in the person of Jean Malaurie. In the early 1950s, Jean Malaurie was an ambitious young man who cut a fine figure as a great explorer: he had been on two of the French polar expeditions to Greenland (in 1948 and 1949), led by Paul-Émile Victor, after which he settled among the Inuit, drawing the first genealogy of 300 individuals over several generations. His training as a geomorphologist led him to participate in mapping explorations, while his taste for adventure brought him, by dog sleigh, all the way to Thule, where he discovered an American military base that had been secretly built without consulting the native populations. This became the subject of a first book, *The Last Kings of Thule*, which inaugurated the 'Terre humaine' series.

Indeed, in 1954, the young man made a proposition to the Plon publishing house to create a new series of 'philosophical travel writings'. The moment was propitious in more ways than one. First, on the publishing front, the cultivated readership seemed ready to take the leap into the human sciences, whose rigour was tempered by an existential dimension otherwise missing from philosophical arguments. The very same publisher had indeed already launched two other series prior to 'Terre humaine, Civilisations et sociétés. Collection d'études et de témoignages'. The first, 'Recherches en sciences humaines', headed by Éric de Dampierre, was created as early as 1952; and the second, headed by historian Philippe Ariès, was launched one year later dedicated to new forms of historiography on 'contemporary and ancient civilizations'. Gallimard quickly jumped into the nonfiction fray, with 'Bibliothèque de philosophie' and 'Bibliothèque de psychanalyse', also launched prior to the big human sciences breakout of the 1960s. But the mood of the times was also favourable to Malaurie and his collection in another way: colonial empires were disintegrating quickly, either gradually transitioning to independence while maintaining ties with the metropole (British version), or brutally collapsing and descending into futile colonial wars (French version). In 1954, the trauma of Diên Biên Phu was thus experienced live by the entire French community. The colonial paradigm was no more, even if it took time – a long time – for the full effect of this collapse to manifest itself. The gradual decolonization of territories and minds inevitably altered the status of 'travel narratives', which had, for almost a century, accompanied the exploration and then colonization of these 'dark continents', these 'middle' and 'far' Orients of 'monsoon' Asia. Place names all over the globe still bear traces of this.[5] Colonization and appropriation, both material and symbolic, gave way to a form of anthropological and sociological understanding. The narrative of the 'civilizing mission' in confrontation with 'savagery' would give way to a scientific discourse on the diversity of populations, the need for their preservation, and the recognition of those recently liberated as legitimate interlocutors. Together with the status of anthropology, the ultimate aim of travel changed: for a long time, the Europeans had travelled vicariously, through highly codified accounts full of vivid images, which were enough to give them a thrill of excitement.[6] Now obsolete, the narrative could no longer serve as a proxy for travel. Technical developments, especially in the field of aviation, and the new wealth brought by the postwar boom made mass mobility possible, at least in theory. However, leaving one's home country remained costly. 'Held back by barriers that are no longer technical but economic, one's desire is enhanced', writes Lévi-Strauss. 'Being forced to remain in one's country ceases to be a physical necessity and becomes a social injustice, and the right to travel takes on a moral valence.'[7] Club Med would provide its own response to this new 'right', which did not figure in the Universal Declaration. In the meantime, though, this series of autobiographical and reflexive works – politically engaged yet also drawing on a vast body of anthropological, geographic and historical knowledge – had everything going for it, and all the necessary qualities for success. The winning combination of 'amateurs and academics',[8] which was the original feature of the 'Terre humaine' series, was perfectly attuned to its times. As well as to Lévi-Strauss.

It was through the geographer Pierre Gourou, a professor at the Collège de France, as well as a friend and supporter,[9] that Claude Lévi-Strauss met Jean Malaurie.[10] The latter had been struck by the photographs illustrating Lévi-Strauss's minor thesis, *The Social and Family Life of the Nambikwara* – a book he had otherwise found 'boring'.[11] But never mind! Photographs were indeed an essential part of the collection and its spirit. Contacted for his talents as a photographer rather than an anthropologist, Lévi-Strauss accepted this proposition which, in the spring of 1954, came along at just the right time.[12] Lévi-Strauss did not so much want to take a break, or even 'an intermission',[13] as he would himself later describe the book – these terms belong to the post facto reconstruction of his career, with its highlights and its 'trifles'. *Tristes Tropiques* was anything but a trifle: a kind of scriptural eruption bursting forth from an astounding mix of guilt, fury and nihilism. The deeper psychological state that presided over the book's writing was indeed the impulse to burn his bridges and take a leap into the void. Convinced that he had no future at the university, Lévi-Strauss could afford to 'write what came to [him]'.[14] As he confessed to Merleau-Ponty, who around 1954 was already entertaining the idea of a third application by Lévi-Strauss to the Collège de France: 'I'm writing a book [*Tristes Tropiques*], and when you and the professors at the Collège read it, you won't be trying to get me elected there any longer.'[15] This sense of transgression and liberation was coupled with 'guilt' for not working on the second volume of the complex structures of kinship, which he still thought he could write: 'I believed I was committing a sin against science.'[16] A minor work that took precedence over the oeuvre (and in so doing, allowed for its later realization), *Tristes Tropiques* served many other functions within its author's own personal economy, beginning with his de-identification with an exclusively scholarly self, perceived as a kind of mutilation: 'I was exasperated', he said, 'at the thought of having been assigned a tag in the academic records, like a soulless machine, that turned men into formulae.'[17] And then the achievement of a long-frustrated literary aspiration: 'Without fully realizing it, I was giving myself over to an unfulfilled desire to write a literary work.'[18] Lévi-Strauss turned this aspiration, which had occasionally given rise to attempts, into one of the subjects of his book, deliberately weaving in passages that expressed his literary yearnings – the purple prose of the sunset – and references to his unfinished novel (a few pages long) and play (*L'Apothéose d'Auguste*, in three acts).[19]

From these secret rendezvous with literature only the title remained – *Tristes Tropiques*, the one he had originally chosen for his novel.[20] Yet this way of experiencing literary writing as infringing on the sacred duty of science does not explain everything. It all happened as if Lévi-Strauss, at that moment in his life, had something 'to get off his chest', both subjectively and objectively: 'I had many things to get off my chest . . . In the end, I churned out [*Tristes Tropiques*] in four months' time, and in a permanent state of intense exasperation, putting into it everything that came into my mind, throwing caution to the wind.'[21] Between his unavowed desires and the professional and intellectual impasse in which he found himself (with regard to the complex structures of kinship), the sense of crisis met a more general consternation: 'At the time, I was dominated by a sense of powerlessness in the face of a world in which the variables had become too numerous to be mastered by thought.'[22] For once in his life, Claude Lévi-Strauss thus chose to *let himself go*; he unleashed his pen.[23] Later, this would no longer be necessary. Out of the blue, he revealed everything – what he believed in and dreamed about.[24]

Taking up the intimate and political crises of its author, *Tristes Tropiques* is a broad transgressive synthesis whose desperate, fiery writing – experienced as a catharsis – was to allow him to partially resolve them.

'Offering up recollections'[25]

On 31 January 1955, Lévi-Strauss wrote to his friend Dolorès Vanetti: 'I am furiously at work on my book, which has to be finished by March to be published in September; we never go out anymore, nor see anyone. [. . .] And thus no flea market, no auctions at Drouot.'[26] Begun at the end of October, the manuscript was submitted at the end of March. In five months, nearly five hundred pages were produced in a kind of trance that revealed the psychological adrenaline rush and rage it triggered. The manuscript bore traces of this exercise in speed-writing, but also of the small family business on rue Saint-Lazare, made up of Lévi-Strauss and his wife Monique,[27] who worked flat out to deliver the goods in time. 'There is, strictly speaking, no

(I)

Je hais les voyages et les explorateurs. Et voici ~~pourtant~~ que je m'apprête

à raconter mes expéditions. Mais que de temps pour m'y résoudre! Quinze ans

ont passé depuis que j'ai quitté pour la dernière fois le Brésil et, pendant

toutes ces années, j'ai souvent formé le dessein d'entreprendre ce livre;

chaque fois aussi, une sorte de honte et de dégôut m'en ont ~~prananan~~ empêché.

Eh quoi? Faut-il maintenant narrer par le menu tant de détails insipides,

d'événements insignifiants? L'aventure n'a pas de place ~~légitime~~ dans la

profession d'ethnographe; elle en est seulement une servitude, elle pèse sur

le travail efficace du poids des semaines ou des mois perdus ~~àxattsindraxis

texxxinx~~ en chemin, des heures oisives pendant que l'informateur se dérobe,

de la faim, de la fatigue, parfois de la maladie; et toujours, de ces mille

corvées qui rongent les jours en pure perte et ~~qui expliquent que~~ la vie
          réduisent

~~dangereuse~~
coeur   *à une* ~~fastidieuse~~ *parodie*
~~d'aventure~~ au sein de la forêt vierge ~~ne ressemble à rien tant qu'aux plus~~

~~creuses périodes~~ du service militaire... Qu'il faille ~~payer par~~ tant d'efforts

et de vaines dépenses pour atteindre l'objet de nos études ne confère aucun
          il faudrait plutôt considérer comme
prix à ce qui ~~est seulement~~ l'aspect négatif de notre métier. Les vérités

que nous allons chercher si loin n'ont de valeur que dépouillées de cette

gangue. On peut, certes, consacrer six mois de voyage, de privations et d'é-

coeurante lassitude à la collecte (qui ne prendra elle-même que quelques jours,

parfois même quelques heures) d'un mythe inédit, d'une règle de mariage nou-
                              cette scorie de la mémoire
velle, d 'une liste complète de noms claniques, mais ~~soulever la plume pour~~

~~noter~~ "~~à~~ 5h.30 du matin nous entrions en rade de Recife tandis que piail-

laient les mouettes et qu'une flotille de marchands de fruits exotiques se

pressait le long de la coque", ~~est-ce que~~ ~~cela même~~ ~~mérite même l'effort~~
été
~~de le transcrire?~~   ~~mérite~~ ~~~~ / *l'effort de soulever*

la plume pour le fixer?   ~~un tel~~
                    souvenir vaut-il même

first draft for *Tristes Tropiques*: Lévi-Strauss typed the manuscript directly on a small portable typewriter with a German keyboard that he had bought from a second-hand shop in São Paulo and had used ever since his stay in Brazil. The original typed manuscript was very dense: comprising 465 pages of uninterrupted small print, it does not even feature breaks between the chapters. Its first reader was Lévi-Strauss's wife, who received the manuscript in instalments of thirty pages each, while he kept on writing. Monique Lévi-Strauss did not directly annotate the text, she returned it to him with separate sheets of papers that listed her notes and comments, for the most part concerning form – pointing out repetitions, contradictions and the occasional obscure formulation. Lévi-Strauss took inspiration from it and then proceeded to manually make the many corrections in pencil directly onto the original manuscript.'[28] Two remarks about this husband and wife writing team. First, the usual gender hierarchy that presided over such work was somewhat altered – the wife was not a typist at the service of her husband. Indeed, the male writer typed his text himself and his female partner played an editing role, reading and reworking it. In addition – and in this respect Monique Lévi-Strauss played more of the traditional woman's role – she constantly reassured him as to the importance of the work to which he was in the process of giving birth. An enthusiastic as well as a careful reader, she thus played a crucial part during the writing phase, marked by periods

'Typewriter on which *Tristes Tropiques* was written. It has a German keyboard, but I was unaware of the existence of other keyboards when I bought it second hand in São Paulo, as I was under the impression one had to have a typewriter in the field, unsuspecting as I was that the living conditions would be such with the Nambikwara that the most elementary conditions for using it would be lacking. This was my one and only typewriter for the following twenty years. After which time, I always had to use German keyboards, customized for the requirements of the French language.'

of despondency (further accentuated by fatigue) and especially of doubt regarding the value and timeliness of the work in progress.[29]

But the manuscript shows signs of other techniques as well. The speed at which it was completed was also due to its use of cutting and pasting of hitherto little used or unused material. These fragments pasted together with adhesive tape, these bits and pieces of text borrowed from some course notes or other (on Rousseau for example), as well as entire chapters that were taken wholesale from his minor thesis on the Nambikwara, reveal *Tristes Tropiques* to be a work of *montage*, in the Jean-Luc Godard sense of the term. Various excerpts of his Brazil and Pakistan expedition notebooks were lifted and included verbatim. See, for instance, the description inspired by the aerial view of the Arabian Desert that he flew over soon after his stopover in Cairo, on his way to Karachi: 'First castles emerge from the opalescent sand. Then, hard and dry, as if trampled by some monstrous beast, which has done its best to press it flat with furious stampings. The sand gradually merges into the mist, itself a kind of celestial sand [. . .] How delicately coloured are the sands. The desert takes on the tints of flesh: peach-blossom, mother-of-pearl, the iridescence of raw fish.'[30] In the documents on which he drew for the drafting,[31] we also find notes for courses he taught at the New School for Social Research during his New York years, such as the rant about *seringueros* and the ups and downs of the rubber economy in Amazonia; as well as old newspaper clippings from his Brazilian years, which he integrated, such as the article on Tibagy Indians.[32] Within this patchwork, the task of producing the manuscript consisted almost entirely of transitions and conclusions, all of which reflected his 'extreme attention to language – "that divinity of which we must make a cult"'.[33]

The object and motive of *Tristes Tropiques* become clearer: 'To revive memories which go back nearly twenty years is like looking at a faded photograph. But at least they may be of some documentary interest: I offer my recollections, such as they are, for the municipal archives.'[34] On the one hand, the recycling of 'recollections', the reserve of experience and of writing awaiting meaning; on the other, the time that had elapsed between the Brazilian fieldwork and its restitution, more than fifteen years later. And the gamble that memory is not only the capacity to forget and recall, but, more profoundly, the power to decant, to understand and make sense of: 'What has happened is that time has passed. [. . .] Events without any apparent connection, and originating from incongruous periods and places, slide one over the other and suddenly crystallize into a sort of edifice which seems to have been conceived by an architect wiser than my personal history. "Every man", wrote Chateaubriand, "carries within him a world which is composed of all that he has seen and loved, and to which he constantly returns, even when he is travelling through, and seems to be living in, some different world." Henceforth, it will be possible to bridge the gap between the two worlds. Time, in an unexpected way, has extended its isthmus between life and myself; twenty years of forgetfulness were required before I could establish communion with my earlier experience, which I had sought the world over without understanding its significance or appreciating its essence.'[35] This memory plate tectonics was also apparent in the biographical complicity that Lévi-Strauss felt with one of his favourite authors, Jean de Léry. The latter had left for Brazil at the age of twenty-two; Lévi-Strauss was twenty-six. He waited eighteen years to write his *Voyage*; Lévi-Strauss about fifteen to write *Tristes Tropiques*. What happened in the interim? 'For Léry, the French Wars of Religion, the disturbances in Lyon, la Charité-sur-Loire, the siege of Sancerre – which he experienced first-hand and on which he wrote a book. And for myself: the Second World War and the flight from persecution.'[36]

This is what makes *Tristes Tropiques* a profoundly Proustian narrative: a series of disappointments – reality does not measure up to the hopes of a noble mind and heart – a retrospective telling, a quest for connections and for overcoming contradictions through the passage of time, in the epiphany of the remembrance of things past.[37] True understanding can only come through remembrance. Then, anything becomes possible – adventure makes sense, and so does love, and the writer's and anthropologist's calling can happen. This writing of memories poured forth, heedless of temporal and spatial architecture, but faithful to the scale of the self, which gave him a freedom of composition that has been noted by all readers. Michel Leiris saw in Lévi-Strauss's rejection of chronological time an 'experiment in taking control of the flow of time', in the manner of 'Proustian illumination'.[38] The 'mental tracking shots' and the overall free-flowing style also recalled Virginia Woolf's 'stream of consciousness'. The main plot recounts the narrator's training, the choice or calling of anthropology, the São Paulo years and the two expeditions into Mato Grosso to meet the Caduveo, the Bororo and the Nambikwara, and then more briefly the Tupi and the Munde. The description of these societies, 'done as if on a chalkboard',[39] makes up the core of the book, whose demonstrations were post-fieldwork. The Nambikwara occupy a special place: it is the book's moment of happiness, a kind of verdant paradise of childhood love, an idyllic note that is soon followed by the descent of scholarly ambition into exhaustion, in the face of the elementary forms of the Munde. The (structural) truth appears here as a series of demystifications leading to a reflection on meaning and its opposite (meaninglessness), hence the Buddhist note of the book's ending. Knowledge meets non-knowledge. In what can also be seen as a *Bildungsroman*, there is room for the North American exile experience, Pakistan and considerations on the 'crowded Tropics', fieldwork depressions and a theatre piece; as well as the inevitable evolution of humanity towards a 'set menu', the sin of greedy Western modernity devouring the entire world and coughing up its waste. Finally, the vanity of the quest for meaning that closes the book – with its thunderous and devastating opening, 'I hate travelling and explorers' – on a note of tender and contemplative suspense: the gaze of a cat.

Oneself and others: a 'memorial to research'[40]

Yet *Tristes Tropiques* is also a work of anthropology. It is in line with and yet subverts a tradition identified by Vincent Debaene as the 'second book', the literary complement to the scientific study, the scholarly monographs and erudite articles, published prior to it. This second book – but it may also be that chronologically, it comes first – attempts to conjure up the fieldwork as well as the atmosphere of the societies visited, using literary means that are better suited to making sense of what does not make sense, of capturing the strangeness, and of fully conveying the poetic dimension of the fieldwork experience. It is thus always more than an ethnographic account. For Leiris, in *Phantom Africa*, the aim was to resurrect a 'paradoxical life';[41] for Métraux, in *Ethnology of Easter Island*, it was to find the 'grandeur'[42] enshrouding the mysterious statues.

Tristes Tropiques has often been described as the disappointed narrative of a failed fieldwork, of an experience of otherness that eluded the anthropologist, before being restored to him much later, through its recomposition by the passage of time and the move to writing. Indeed, with its dull and weary moments, its erratic wanderings, its ridiculous episodes (when Lévi-Strauss gets lost in *sertão*), its tragic crises (Emydio's hand injury) and its dramatic events (the widespread eye infection), the book is no glorification of adventure, no exaltation of anthropology. For this is mostly where the disillusion lies. Patient and scrupulous study, far from bringing insight into the Other, is rather presented as something of a dead-end: the sought-after otherness is either adulterated – the natives are no longer what they used to be – or else their radical otherness, as for instance that of the Munde, makes them unattainable because of 'the absence of a Friday'. 'The voyage shows that reality cannot simply be grasped in experience.'[43] Indeed, it is precisely the deception of travelling that is at the core of *L'Apothéose d'Auguste*, the cathartic play Lévi-Strauss drafted in Campos Novos, at a moment of profound discouragement. A variation on the play by Corneille, which Lévi-Strauss knew backwards, as he did much of Racine's works as well, it features a traveller, Cinna, who returns home after criss-crossing the world, crowned in glory yet not fooled by the actual experience. The anthropologist exorcised his own obsessions through Cinna: the 'deceptiveness' of travel and the lessons drawn from it,[44] the feeling that 'the means at one's disposal as an observer and a writer never measure up to what one sees and tries to describe'.[45]

A few years prior to the momentous publication of Malinowski's *Diary*[46] – a deeply sobering vision of fieldwork by one of its confirmed practitioners – *Tristes Tropiques* was thus, after Michel Leiris's *Phantom Africa*, and every bit as critically, one of the first narratives to shine a light on the backstage of anthropology. The book describes the behind-the-scenes, and not just the ethnographic content, of an expedition, even if the narrator's companions are all reduced to silhouettes. It was its introspective urgency that made it 'postmodern before its time',[47] lending it an innovative and paradoxical quality, even while it would later be critiqued by the postmodernist anthropologist Clifford Geertz.[48] But it also pioneered a model of critical and reflexive ethnography, echoes of which can clearly be felt in Philippe Descola's *The Spears of Twilight*, a work on the Jivaro published in the same series some forty years later.[49]

What possible way out was there from the impasse of fieldwork and the mystification of exoticism? 'Perhaps, then, this was what travelling was, an exploration of the deserts of my mind rather than of those surrounding me',[50] wonders the narrator, obsessed by a Chopin melody (étude no. 3, opus 10) of which he was not even particularly fond. It is finally at the end of the adventure of writing that one discovers the true value of the first unfinished journey. 'The geographic voyage [. . .] becomes a veritable archeology of the self.'[51] Through the book's architecture – its 'unbridled associationism', its changes in scale, its whimsical comparisons, its collisions of time and space – Lévi-Strauss attempted to convey an 'inner geography' that would not be so much the expression of his self as the means of converting and apprehending the 'logic of sensation' he was to explore a few years later.[52] Like Roquentin in Sartre's *Nausea* (1938), the narrator swaps the debased adventure of travel literature for the 'adventure of the ordinary', where the banality and triviality of things (a work of basketry, a gesture) are embraced and their meaning revealed by the true adventure that can only be intellectual. In *Nausea*, Roquentin the historian, back from his travels, no longer believes in the historian's enterprise, nor in the accumulation of knowledge; conversely, the familiar town of which he is a denizen suddenly appears foreign, absurd, even dull to him. Frédéric Keck has shed new light on the project of *Tristes Tropiques* by comparing it with *Nausea*. In both cases, 'there is no adventure', as the jacket blurb for *Nausea* proclaimed.[53] Both books, he concludes, resulted from a similar crisis of philosophy and meaning, resolved in a manner that was, if not identical, at least parallel: through rendering visible phenomena intelligible, thanks to phenomenological consciousness, on the one hand, and to a musical model for grasping logical relations, on the other. In both cases, an Odyssey of the gaze.[54]

It was through the reintegration of the observing subject that anthropological science could achieve the only form of objectivity within its reach. Lévi-Strauss had just written as much in an overview of the place of anthropology in the social sciences (1954): the young science of anthropology 'is not distinguished from other humanistic and social sciences by any subject of study peculiar to it alone. [. . .] It proceeds from a particular conception of the world or from an original way of approaching problems.'[55] He was later to drive this point home: *Tristes Tropiques* 'shows not only what is in front of the camera but also what is behind the camera. And so, it is not an objective view of my ethnographic experience, it is a view of myself living these experiences.'[56] This exercise in decentring – seeing oneself observing, seeing oneself as an other – is one of the reasons for the intellectual fascination exerted by *Tristes Tropiques* for generations. The avowed and revered model for Lévi-Strauss here was the one he considered as 'the founder of the human sciences': Jean-Jacques Rousseau.

Just as one recognizes Chopin melodies in Serge Gainsbourg songs, so reading Lévi-Strauss often feels like rereading Rousseau, sometimes without knowing for sure (since he is not always explicitly cited). This was not plagiarism, but rather a profound integration. Steeped in Rousseau, who was himself deeply immersed in the ethnographic literature of his time, Lévi-Strauss pays emphatic tribute to his 'master' and 'brother', the Savoyard vicar, in *Tristes Tropiques* itself, and then a few years later in Geneva, on the occasion of the 250th anniversary of the philosopher's birth. The celebration prompted him to reflect on the deep affinities between anthropology and Jean-Jacques's philosophical project. For, according to Lévi-Strauss, what made Rousseau an anthropologist at heart was precisely the paradox of his life and work: 'That Rousseau could have, simultaneously, advocated the study of the most remote men, while mostly given himself to the study of that particular man who seems the closest – himself.'[57] This contradiction was familiar to the anthropologist who, at one point or another, identified with Rousseau, in his sense of alienation from himself when confronted by the hardship of fieldwork, to the physical and moral trials that it entails. Rousseau's furious misanthropy is an ethnographic experience: 'But I, detached from them [my contemporaries] and from everything, what am I? That is what remains to me to seek.'[58] What anthropologist had not asked himself this question? What am I and what am I doing and looking for among the savages? For Lévi-Strauss, this was the key point of all ethnographic endeavour worthy of the name. Self-decentring, or what he called retracting from the 'evidences of the self', is the only foundation, in reason, of access to the other. It is in feeling foreign to oneself, experiencing oneself in the third person, that the anthropologist can understand the other as an 'I'. The same operation, albeit symmetrical, was enabled by psychoanalysis;[59] hence the recurring comparison of fieldwork with the analytical cure. Another pillar of Rousseau's thought, pity, heralded a more directly political outlet for ethnographic knowledge, which, with Jean-Jacques, was more revolutionary than reactionary.[60] Lévi-Strauss liked everything about Rousseau – the anthropologist, 'the Indian revolutionary prophet', as he called him, the happy botanist, the musician, the delicate and sensitive man, the tormented soul, the nature lover, the political thinker and, above all, the one who had discovered, 'in identification, the real principle of the human sciences and the only possible basis for ethics. It is because he also restored for us its ardour, burning for the last two centuries and forever in this crucible, a crucible uniting beings whom the interests of politicians and philosophers are everywhere else bent on rendering incompatible: me and the other, my society and other societies, nature and culture, the emotional and the rational, humanity and life.'[61]

Public reception: 'a moment in Western consciousness'

The book came out in October 1955. For the readers of *Les Temps modernes*, who had followed the polemic with Caillois a few months earlier ('Diogène couché' had been published in March 1955), *Tristes Tropiques*, a few advanced pages of which had been published over the summer,[62] was Claude Lévi-Strauss's final word. The context of its public reception contributed to a dramatization and politicization of its interpretation. It was also a sign, surprising today, of the renewed alliance between Lévi-Strauss and Sartre, whom we know was 'dazzled'[63] by *Tristes Tropiques*, despite its rhetorical jabs at existentialism, quipped as 'shop-girl metaphysics'.[64]

The historical, philosophical and political expectations raised by the book made its publication into an event. It was widely reviewed in the French press.[65] The book received attention from the national, as well as regional, Swiss and Belgian press, various journals, including a long front-page article in the *Times Literary Supplement*, when the book had not yet even been translated into English, relegating Simone de Beauvoir's *The Mandarins* and Camus's *The Fall* to inside pages.[66] Yet it took two months for the critics to react – perhaps a sign that they actually read the book! – and Lévi-Strauss, still in the throes of a failure complex, wrote to Dolorès Vanetti, on 28 November 1955, that he was 'too depressed by the general indifference to the publication of *Tristes Tropiques:* three or four vaguely positive reviews in the daily press, and then nothing. For two months now, all they talk about is the Femina, the Goncourt and other prizes.' He continued on a more exciting topic: 'In the ancient cookbooks of the New York Public Library you will find absolutely sensational aphrodisiac recipes to be adapted as canned foods . . .'[67] His wife Monique recalled that disappointed references to the mediocre sales of *Elementary Structures* peppered her husband's conversations at the time: 'You will see, 800 copies . . .'[68]

While Lévi-Strauss was worrying himself sick and dreaming of artificial pleasures, the great pens of the French press and intelligentsia were busy writing: Georges Bataille, François-Régis Bastide, René Etiemble, Roger Grenier, Maurice Blanchot, Michel Leiris, Jean Lacroix, Jean Cazeneuve, Gaëtan Picon and Claude Roy would all praise the book and comment on the incisive alliteration of its title. One of these commentators played a special role, being the first (or nearly) to express himself and to allay what its impatient author had mistaken for indifference. Raymond Aron's article, published in *Le Figaro littéraire* on 24 December 1955, offered a properly political perspective on the book. Nearly all the commentary explicitly referred to the disasters, from war to Auschwitz and Hiroshima, which were also disasters of science. The title of Blanchot's review, 'L'homme au point zéro' ('Man at zero point'),[69] was a reference to the return from the camps.[70] This resurgence, ten years later, of the shock of the camps, which cast a black shroud over Western civilization, was all the more striking since the concentration camps appear only obliquely in *Tristes Tropiques*, as images of the historical unconscious. In much the same way as *Hiroshima mon amour* (1959) – in which Alain Resnais registered this anxiety, reverberating after a fifteen-year lapse of time, in fictional form – *Tristes Tropiques* was read as the symptom of a critique of the West of itself, ten years after the end of the war.[71]

Raymond Aron was thus the first to emphasize this radical departure from the progressivist narrative that had been laid out by Auguste Comte and Durkheim, and which was foundering in Lévi-Strauss's time, for the 'road that leads to a sovereign and triumphant European civilization' had lost its relevance from the moment 'the arrival point was compromised at the very least by the crematoriums of Auschwitz'.[72] Yet Aron pursued his analysis of a Lévi-Straussian politics forged 'in the crucible of *The Persian*

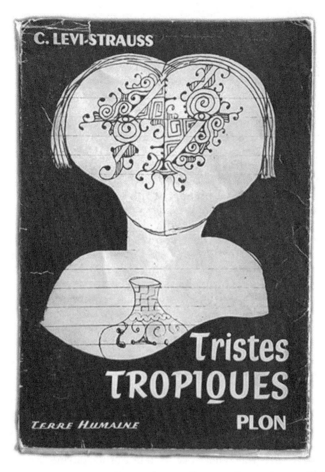

Black and white cover of the first edition of *Tristes Tropiques*. In 1956, a red banner was added: 'All the Goncourt authors warmly recommended it.'

Letters', which is to say, since Montesquieu, through the eyes of others. By so doing, he validated the idea, present in other reviews, according to which major contemporary problems called for new thinking about man, emanating from the new (or old but renewed) sciences of man. These sciences would be better able to grasp the complexities of the present than a philosophy dismissed for its 'provincial' dimension, since it emanated from Western civilization. According to Aron, Lévi-Strauss sought 'in so-called primitive societies [. . .] a theoretical model of human society thanks to which we will manage to disentangle the ordinary and artificial in the current nature of man'. On the matter of technical progress, the end of which he does not call for, even though he is fully aware of its costs, Lévi-Strauss 'harbours no illusion about the advent of a community reconciled with itself'. From this point of view, he was more on the side of Rousseau than Marx. Aron recognized the extent to which Lévi-Strauss's relativism, already expressed in *Race and History*, was unacceptable to many: 'No society is entirely good or entirely bad and the ratio of advantages and disadvantages in each is about the same – a conclusion which is bound to offend Marxists more than conservatives.' Finally, Aron shared Lévi-Strauss's pessimism, who also concluded that the world was beginning 'to become too small for those who live in it'.

In the book's famous peroration, Lévi-Strauss gave new energy to the metaphor of entropy already used by some thinkers of Western decline (such as Valéry), by connecting it to the origins of the nascent information science developed by Robert Wiener: excessively numerous exchanges, as he had already explained in *Race and History*, level the world and unavoidably contribute to its growing inertia 'which one day, will be final'.[73] Hence the Leiris pun on anthropology, which Lévi-Strauss suggested might be more aptly called 'entropology', a discipline 'concerned with the study of the highest manifestations of this process of disintegration',[74] a science of entropy. The particular pathos of *Tristes Tropiques* hit home, prompting sublime laments denouncing the West's appropriation, transformation and paving over of gorgeous Polynesian island coastlines, and of the way conservation had turned worlds into squalid suburbs in what was not yet called – the word had just been coined by Alfred Sauvy in 1955 – the Third World. It formulated, in an anachronistic and sumptuous language, a present time that did not know itself to be sick, but had its suspicions. And yet this cry – which can easily be seen as resonating from its historical, ideological and intellectual context – was nonetheless quite unique and at times rather scandalous. The Lévi-Straussian interpretation of the Shoah represents a good case in point: in line with his experience of the Western and Eastern tropics, of exile and the West Indies, he saw it as an example of the regularly recurring phenomenon of the expulsion of humanity by a part of itself, 'when people begin to feel cramped'. 'When looked at in this light, the events which have occurred in Europe during the past twenty years, at the culmination of a century during which the population figures have doubled, can no longer appear as being simply the result of an aberration on the part of one nation, one doctrine, or one group of men. I see them rather as a premonitory sign of our moving into a finite world, such as Southern Asia had to face a thousand or two thousand years ahead of us, and I cannot see us avoiding the experience unless some major decisions are taken.'[75] It was this pessimism buttressed by fatalism that made some bristle. Georges Balandier, who was a very close friend of Lévi-Strauss's at the time, recoiled at the political consequences to which such a position seemed to lead. For him, as well as in his view for Lévi-Strauss himself, the anthropologist was a 'kind of revolutionary, but his protest led him to opt for flight outside his familiar territory',[76] with a strong penchant for turning back to the past rather than projecting into the future. Yet, as opposed to Lévi-Strauss who derived great joy from the 'indefinable grandeur of man's beginning',[77] Balandier credited these societies with a capacity to evolve, to change, to take part in history, as much as a desire to persist and to remain the same. Lévi-Strauss's friend Michel Leiris, for his part, found the end of the book somewhat too prone to disenchanted musings and chose to latch onto the optimistic patches that were better suited to his political mood at the time: 'Nothing is settled; everything can still be altered. What was done, but turned out wrong, can be done again.'[78] This praise of beginnings that, at the end of *Tristes Tropiques*, seemed to be the only way out, was illustrated by the elegant photographs of the book, which offered a melancholic counterpoint to Lévi-Strauss's historical pessimism, and signalled the profound function of anthropology as a science of the last days. These carefully composed photographs of Indians have made the book and its author famous. The original cover of 1955, which was not the photograph of the young Nambikwara with his lip and nose ornaments, featured a Caduveo pattern on a black background, selected by Lévi-Strauss, whom we imagine, writing his letter to Malaurie, as a seventeenth-century Dutch painter, brush in hand: 'I would pay particular attention, first to the high proportion of white that I have suggested (and which reduces, I think, the mournful aspect that I dread), and second, to the "frothy lace" effect that I have attempted to emphasize in the young person's neckline.'[79]

The great divide between art and science

The other major theme that runs through the book's critical reception pertains to what we might call a new 'great divide'. Was Lévi-Strauss a scholar? A writer? Could one be both at once? One and not the other? If *Tristes Tropiques* could be categorized as a 'philosophical journey', it nonetheless threatened the progressive division of knowledge, which the entire oeuvre, in its way, called into question.

Blurring genres

'*Tristes Tropiques* is neither monograph, nor travel narrative, nor autobiography. It is all of them at once, and much more. The book does not fit into any predefined genre, least of all the boring genre.'[80] Hailed by the press as an unclassifiable object, even though it was often placed in the tradition of philosophical voyage running from Montaigne to Montesquieu, its hybrid and undecided character, between science and literature, was striking. From that point of view, it offered a 'privileged lens'[81] through which to consider the reconfiguration of the relationship between literature and the human sciences, born in the nineteenth century of a double gesture involving a rejection of rhetoric and an alignment with scientific 'rigour' which had long constituted the ideal horizon.[82] It was unsettling, for, although the work of a scholar, of a professional anthropologist, it was written in the language of a literary writer, or what is considered as such. The press lavished praise on its prose style, invoking big names. With Montaigne's fresh gaze and under Rousseau's fraternal gaze, it was Chateaubriand, his twin brother, who had come back as an anthropologist: 'Lévi-Strauss is a Chateaubriand who has seen the river Meschacebe.'[83] Michelet, Claudel, as well as Bossuet's funeral orations were all referenced. This is what Vincent Debaene has aptly nicknamed the 'dialogue of the luminaries', which, thanks to its grat classical style, transformed *Tristes Tropiques* into literature and lent it political force. This analysis was shared by Pierre Nora: 'Recourse to the great style of the classics wrested *Tristes Tropiques* from the arbitrariness of individual experience and gave the learned man of letters the tone and stature of a Knight Commander. Through the grace of words, it was the West, from the heights of its tradition, that appeared to be speaking through his voice.'[84]

This tension expressed itself in a variety of ways, which map the various ways of conceiving the historical division between fields of knowledge, as it developed in France, from the belletrists of the classical age, which encompassed all fields, to the more contemporary focus on the sole work of writing, which characterizes the modern conception of literature, from Flaubert to Roland Barthes. The critical reception of *Tristes Tropiques* heightened these differences: it was seen as either reviving the ancient belles-lettres tradition, or marking a new offensive for literature with the ambition to federate all thought, or else as the ultimate and definitive expropriation of literature. In the first case, Lévi-Strauss was compared to a moment in science when scholars were endowed with the gift of speech: 'Ah! The wonderful nineteenth century, when the reporting counted as much as the experience, when the account was equal to the journey, and the expression commensurate with the discovery; or when, very simply, from Ampère to Pasteur, from Renan to Taine, the scholar knew how to present his truth in a beautiful language shared by all.'[85] In the second case, we find an article by Gaëtan Picon, which labelled Lévi-Strauss a 'writer in action', for his prose style of course, but above all for his 'constant connection to the very movements of life': 'first and foremost, it is this link between the quest and the experience, this emotional echo that weaves together the search for truth and the search for oneself, which elevates this scholarly work to the rank of literature'.[86] But this idea was most fully developed in Georges Bataille's review, 'Un livre humain, un grand livre',[87] published in the journal *Critique*, in which he argued that literature had to reclaim the human in all its dimensions. If everything that engages the human was literature, then 'literature', according to Bataille, 'appears as the future of the human sciences'.[88] And *Tristes Tropiques* stood as resounding proof. The third option was exemplified by Jean-Claude Carrière who, while not pronouncing on the author's status as a writer, noted that *Tristes Tropiques* was 'an indictment of the modern novel, which was so narrowly specialized that it was incapable of breaking down barriers between the literary public and the majority of readers'.[89]

Adopting the inverse position, Maurice Blanchot considered Claude Lévi-Strauss to be decidedly on the side of science, since literature, in his view, was not only a matter of belletristic style. Siding with him, though only implicitly, was Roland Barthes, whose total silence Vincent Debaene has tried to interpret. Indeed, Barthes did not write a single line about the book and hardly ever referred to *Tristes Tropiques*. This puzzling silence – Barthes and Lévi-Strauss were soon often to be associated as part of the structuralist cabal – also shows that Barthes and Lévi-Strauss, despite their dates of birth, 'were not contemporaries'.[90] Whereas Barthes was producing *Writing Degree Zero* (1953) and taking part in the Nouveau Roman scene, Lévi-Strauss felt no affinities with contemporary literature, whose 'unbearable boringness'[91] he was to indict ten years later. And, in a way, the 'Terre humaine' series, as a whole, had retrospectively taken sides in this debate, with Jean Malaurie (like Lévi-Strauss) making no secret of his contempt for modern literature, as well as for modern science (represented by Lévi-Strauss), both of which he found equally 'desiccated' and 'dehumanized'. Against this overly scientific anthropology, which was to develop notably through the structuralist project, throughout the 1950s, as well as against a literature he considered overly cerebral, Malaurie celebrated his series as a form of resistance and an expression of free speech, whether it came from those he called the 'epic scholars' or from the natives themselves, speaking in their own name. Indeed, one of the major strengths of the series was that it encompassed anthropological works and autobiographical narratives by indigenous people, such as *Sun Chief*, for which Lévi-Strauss wrote the preface one year after *Tristes Tropiques*.[92]

Despite its highly classical prose, *Tristes Tropiques* was introduced by the journalist Sonia Orwell to the English-speaking world as one of three works that mattered on the French literary scene of 1956, alongside Michel Leiris's *Fourbis* [*Scraps*] and Marguerite Duras's *The Square*.[93] Similarly, the book was sometimes referenced together with a beautiful work by the Cuban writer Alejo Carpentier, *The Lost Steps*, to which it was tied by mysterious links, as if the novelist had sought to stage the vast movement backward in time that *Tristes Tropiques* had, in its own way, embodied. In any case, the quarrel over the book's genre was reignited by a final controversy. Three days before the Goncourt Prize jury's lunch meeting, during which it was to select the prizewinner, its members confided their dilemma to the press: they would have liked to give it to *Tristes Tropiques*, but this was impossible due to the fact that Claude Lévi-Strauss's book had been classified as an essay and not a novel, and was thus 'outside their jurisdiction'.[94] And then came the final jolt: Lévi-Strauss declined to accept the Plume d'or, the explorers' prize of the Salle Pleyel, which had been awarded by a jury made up of several explorers, including Paul-Emile Victor, Maurice Herzog, Frison-Roche and Max-Pol Fouchet. The prize came with 250,000 francs. Reached by telephone, the anthropologist declared that 'several votes were not to his taste'. This sensational rejection immediately enhanced his literary status, since it associated him with a novelist who had also turned down a prize (the Goncourt attributed to *The Opposing Shore*). A 'new Julien Gracq' was born!

A quarrel over magical art

A significant episode, which took place somewhere between the end of the writing of *Tristes Tropiques* and its publication in the summer of 1955, sheds new light on these reflections by bringing into play definitions of art

The Old World (1947–1971)

and science – and above all of the line separating them and their respective legitimacy – with regard to the acceptance of the term 'magic'. André Breton had received a commission for a book on 'magical art', which was to be published as part of a four-volume series devoted to religious art, classical art, baroque art and art for art's sake. For Breton, 'magical art' was a relevant and unjustly disregarded category in art history. He included in it many forms (from ancient as well as more recent civilizations): 'primitive' art, Western popular art, Romantic art, art of the insane, modern art, as well as Uccello, Arcimboldo, Leonardo da Vinci, Dürer and everything that in his view constituted an authentic 'art of creation' (as opposed to an 'art of imitation'), which emitted particular enigmatic radiations that immediately identified it as such. Yet, because 'inspiration failed him', according to Lévi-Strauss,[95] or out of a desire to be informed about 'anything that might contribute to authorized opinion', according to Breton himself,[96] the latter sent a questionnaire on magical art to around sixty of his friends and acquaintances. 'In the presence of an object falling into the category of *magical art*, what methods guide your approach and further examination?' 'Can objects of a magical kind enter your personal life?' A third exercise entailed ranking specific works as to whether they qualified as magical art or not: (1) an Egyptian drawing; (2) a Gallic coin; (3) a Haida pictograph (from British Columbia); (4) patterns from the Marquesas Islands; (5) the Philosophical Mercury; (6) a moon figure in an eighteenth-century deck of Tarot cards; (7) a vase by Paolo Uccello; (8) a painting by Hans Baldung, *The Bewitched Groom*; (9) Munch's *Scream*; (10) a painting by De Chirico, *Il Ritornante*; (11) a Kandinsky frontispiece. Lévi-Strauss initially ignored the request. Contacted again by Breton, he asked his seven-year-old son Laurent to respond in his stead, thinking that a child's reaction might be of interest to the surrealist, all the more so because his son had 'ranked the pictures without hesitation'.[97] Breton was mortified by what he interpreted as a 'reprimand' with 'all the outward signs of contempt'. 'Allow me to believe that your objections would not have suffered from being formulated in a less unfriendly and less systematically destructive manner. Since I have, in your view, emptied these notions of "art" and "magic" of all value, why don't you restore their specificity, which would apparently be child's play for you?' He ended his message with a very curt: 'I am sorry to have been a source of irritation and derision.'[98]

What are we to make of this quarrel? With regard to aesthetics, the two men had much in common. They were flea-market companions, and Lévi-Strauss admired Breton's 'infallible eye' and especially his concept of the 'find' as the encounter between a certain sensibility and an object that was destined for it. It was thus less his conception of art, or even of magical art, that was at issue, than competing views of the use of the term 'magic'. Lévi-Strauss's non-response was a gesture of demarcation of the boundaries of science: 'The term "magic" had a precise meaning for me; it was part of the anthropological lexicon. I didn't like to see it used any which way.'[99] In the end, in Breton's eyes, the term 'magic', in its confused and catchall meaning that so irritated Lévi-Strauss, was above all a lever for recasting all of (especially Western) art history in terms of a new hierarchy of value. The anthropologist acknowledged the impulse, but only two years later, after receiving a copy of *L'Art magique*, inscribed to . . . his son! In a letter of reconciliation, he confessed to enjoying its very beautiful pages on Gustave Moreau, De Chirico and Henri Rousseau, 'but, let's be honest, I can't always follow your lead concerning prehistoric, primitive or even savage art – a term, incidentally, that I have also proclaimed I prefer over the other. As for the term "magic", the sad cause of our falling-out, it is quite clear that you give it a very different definition from ours. But it is, after all, a label like any other, and I will only retain from this reading that it greatly contributes to exploring the new dimension that surrealism has managed to identify in the plastic arts, by linking up works that are apparently very remote from one another, and yet all possess a very profound *"je ne sais quoi"* in common. It is this *"je ne sais quoi"* that you have called "magic", a choice in which anthropologists cannot follow you, since in their language the term has been given a narrow technical meaning. And I concede an additional defeat, since I have yet to come up with a better name for it.'[100]

Double twist: the magical formula of myth

Just as *Tristes Tropiques*'s elegiac complaint was striking its powerful chord, and as Lévi-Strauss's 'solemn eloquence' and 'draping rhetoric'[101] were resonating with the broader public, *The Journal of American Folklore* published an article by the anthropologist that followed the reverse course: from literature to mathematics. That dense and brilliant text, brazenly theoretical, laid the foundation for the four volumes of the *Mythologiques* to come. In 'The Structural Study of Myth',[102] Lévi-Strauss offered a double methodological proposition: first, the syntactic unit of myth is a 'mytheme' which, like the phoneme and morpheme, only signifies in relation to other units; second, myths must be read like orchestral sheet music, both horizontally and vertically, i.e., both diachronically and synchronically, by analysing all versions of the myth regardless of origin or importance. A demonstration was carried out through the example of the Oedipus myth (which presented the advantage of being widely known), including its Freudian interpretation, which Lévi-Strauss took to be the ultimate version of the myth. For the point was always to obtain significant correlations with 'the final outcome being the structural law of the myth'.[103] For the Oedipal myth, a double opposition between two series of two terms emerged from the analysis, which led to a contradictory structure of the myth, between a belief in human autochthony (man born from the earth) and recognition of the fact that each comes from the union of a man and a woman. The myth serves therefore to mediate and mitigate this observation, which is both incontestable and yet never ceases to amaze – that one is born from two. It is a 'kind of logical tool' that ensures connections between the various vegetal, animal and human domains, as well as between the living and the dead, between the apparently irreconcilable registers of indigenous cosmology. Following an extended discussion of Pueblo mythology, its 'ash-boy' and 'tricksters', we arrive at the idea that, in the group comprising all the variants of the myth, the extreme versions are symmetries inverted according to the logic of a double twist, in the same way as the image coming out of a photographic device is inverted and reversed. The vertiginously erudite presentation ends abruptly with a rather casual proposal: 'Although it is not possible at the present stage to come closer than an approximate formulation which will certainly need to be made more accurate in the future, it seems that every myth (considered as the collection of all its variants) corresponds to a formula of the following type: fx(a): fy(b) = fx(b): fa-1(y)'.[104]

This cabbalistic, almost magical formula, which would appear to reveal the location of hidden treasure on some mysterious island, is characterized by an 'uncertain status', and is perhaps, according to Denis Bertholet, more of a 'moral object' than a 'scientific one'.[105] Although an entire tradition in Brazilian anthropology (around Manuela Carneiro da Cunha) has recently given the formula a new relevance, some anthropologists have made scholarly use of it (most notably Pierre Maranda)[106] and several mathematicians have declared it valid, let us just say that its aim was also to *signify* the possible mathematical formalization of the analysis of myth, and thereby to establish its rigorous logic, in the same manner as modern science. This famous 'canonical formula', this sort of mantra of modern anthropology, is discreetly mentioned in the second volume of the *Mythologiques*. Lévi-Strauss himself would return to it later, in *The Jealous Potter* and *The Story of Lynx* (1985 and 1991). The idea might have come to him during the seminar of 1952/54 given with mathematician Georges Guilband on the mathematics of the human sciences.[107] Yet it was not without a certain irony that its author introduced it, describing himself as a 'street peddler' trying to explain 'as succinctly as possible, how the mechanical toy which he is trying to sell to onlookers worked'.[108]

Just as, according to Gaëtan Picon, the language of *Tristes Tropiques* elevated the scholar's work to the level of literature, so establishing the imprimatur of mathematical science for the analysis of myth was undeniably, for Lévi-Strauss, 'to raise' it to the highest and most indisputable status of thought.

A paradox

With Lévi-Strauss, we are thus dealing with one of the leading edges of the theoretical avant-garde, with the explicit goal of modernizing the human and social sciences on the model of the hard sciences. At the same time, the man had a professed taste for traditional aesthetics, from figurative painting to tonal music, and the prose of *Tristes Tropiques* struck contemporaries for its classicism and anachronistic feel, as compared to the literature of its time.[109] The critiques he levelled against modern art were the very same as those addressed to him and his anthropological work (abstraction, dry formalism, empty signifiers, etc.).

This contradictory relationship that Lévi-Strauss had with time was all the more puzzling given that structuralism, as an intellectual construct, would seem to be entirely compatible with the project of modernist art in general, and of that of the 1950s in particular. Some authors have highlighted its affinities with the musical compositions of Stockhausen, Xenakis, Boulez and Messiaen, all of whom were in Paris at the time, creating works whose titles – 'Perspectives, Structures, Syntaxes, Configurations, Quantities, etc.' – amply demonstrated their common affiliation with a certain cultural mood.[110] They shared a similar emphasis on repetition, series and mathematical rigour, as well as austerity. In painting, abstraction emptied representation of content and separated the signified from the signifier, just as structuralism initially did. Unlike Lévi-Strauss, Jakobson established a genealogy for structuralism in which the original impulse came from modern art, more precisely in early twentieth-century Russian literary futurism and Cubist art: 'Perhaps the strongest impulse towards a shift in the approach to language and linguistics, however, was – for me, at least – the turbulent artistic movements of the early twentieth century. [. . .] Those of us who were concerned with language learned to apply the principle of relativity in linguistic operations; we were consistently drawn in this direction by the spectacular development of modern physics and by the pictorial theory and practice of cubism, where everything "is based on relationships".'[111]

This happy complicity with the artistic avant-garde of the time contrasted with the distance from it that Lévi-Strauss professed in his radio interviews with Georges Charbonnier, broadcast in 1958. He expressed himself freely on his tastes, as well as, for the first time, on what he saw as the 'dead end' of modern art. He liked the genre paintings of Joseph Vernet, port landscapes which, viewing them at the Musée de la Marine, allowed him to re-experience the eighteenth-century relationship between land and sea. However, his dispute with modern art – beginning with impressionism in painting and Flaubert in literature (although he knew Baudelaire by heart) – should primarily be understood in its stark contrast to all that characterized primitive art: an art in profound harmony with a group that understood its meaning and to which it fully belonged; an art that signified far more than it represented; an art that related to objects more than it tried to innovate forms, since tradition imposed itself naturally. This suggested an implicit understanding of modern art as a 'cul-de-sac': an art that represented but did not signify, whose 'languages' could be played with (in the 'manner' of this or that artist) as so many empty signifiers which, sociologically speaking, could not communicate with any group. In Lévi-Strauss's view, the determined experimentation with new forms did not constitute fertile ground, but rather a harbinger of crisis. In short, abstract painting was 'nothing more than a system of signs, but "outside language"', since this sign system was the creation of an individual who was, indeed, liable to frequently change systems.[112] Hence the exhaustion of a modern art that was a prisoner of itself. He went so far as to consider the possibility of the extinction of all artistic activity – it had been born, had lived, and could die. In his view, this 'academicism of meaning' was casting a pall over all modern art.[113]

What are we to make of these views which, today as then, appear rather heretical and in stark contrast with one of the most ardently held consensus views of our contemporary society, with its voracious appetite for 'culture'? From a strictly biographical perspective, we should recall that this position, which was to solidify over the years, had not always been his. Indeed, there was the young man of the 1920s, enthused by Stravinsky and 'worshipping' Picasso. We should also recall that his modernist tastes at the time had been shaped in opposition to his father. It is as if the death of Raymond Lévi-Strauss, in 1953, had set the son back on the path to traditional concepts – and to the modest craft for which the paternal figure stood, in both art and literature. As if he had been won over by his ancestral worlds, now a man of the nineteenth century as much as of the twentieth. We must also keep in mind the exception of surrealism, which, despite his quarrel with Breton, represented a shared experience he never disavowed. Here again, the New York years played a role, but more than anything it was an aesthetic affinity, which, for Lévi-Strauss, enabled the extraction of surrealism from modern art, whose 'demiurgical' dimension the surrealists and Lévi-Strauss both completely opposed. It was also during the New York years that he truly discovered primitive art, which served to relativize modern art.

This triple polarity was, from then on, defining: primitive culture (vs. Western culture), classical art (vs. contemporary art), and modern science. It formed the identity of a multifaceted aesthetics that signalled, in the mid-1950s, a more generalized and deliberate disengagement from his times – not so much with regard to information, citizenship and socio-professional accomplishments as in the affirmation of his own temporality: the love of beginnings, and a sort of growing aesthetic aversion to his present. We must not forget the radical nature of *Tristes Tropiques*'s denunciation of Western modernity: '[Lévi-Strauss] makes Franz Fanon sound positively genial.'[114] In this context, it should come as no surprise that art, one of the main points of entry into any society, should be subject to this kind of flamboyant rejection: a time of decadence could only give rise to a corrupt art. Lévi-Strauss ceased very early on to be a man of his times, but in a profoundly original way, which makes his work 'available', of 'enduring "irrelevance"',[115] both rooted in its time and yet inaccessible to it.

This combination of being both 'in tune' and 'out of sync' came to define *Tristes Tropiques* almost immediately: an 'enigmatic classic'.[116] Claude Roy has pointed out how the staging of accumulated experience ('Having travelled the world . . .') conveyed a sense of wisdom and gave the book a conclusive dimension, in contrast with the speed and nonchalance with which it was written, with its suggestion of having been pasted and scraped together. This is precisely the metamorphosis entailed in the reception of *Tristes Tropiques*: we know that the book spurred an oeuvre yet to come, whereas the reviews all left the impression that it was concluding one. In actual fact, it was neither an inauguration nor a closure. The book glowed with countless sparks that were all present in previous texts – *The Elementary Structures of Kinship*, the *Introduction to Marcel Mauss*, *Race and History* – as well as those still to come, especially the *Mythologiques* cycle. *Tristes Tropiques* was by no means a mere 'distraction' from science, nor was it a rest stop on a predetermined path from one mountaintop to another – the one, *The Elementary Structures*, only partially attained and the other, *Mythologiques*, masterfully ascended. To consider Lévi-Strauss's work as offering a clarification and reformulation of the major problems in anthropology – kinship, totemism, mythology – according to a single paradigm bringing to light a single human operation, would be to suggest that the structuralist programme remained stable throughout the period from 1947 to 1971, whereas we know full well that it did not. From this perspective, *Tristes Tropiques* stands apart. As Clifford Geertz has suggested,[117] we should rather examine the rest of his work in light of the pivotal text of *Tristes Tropiques*, taken as a centre around which all of his past and future books turn, each spinning a thread in this ever-changing fabric, a weaving together of several works in one: the political thread, the anthropological strand proper, the moral and philosophical thread and, finally, the symbolist thread, in search of patterns and a throw of the dice that might abolish chance.

Oddly, although the term 'structuralism' is practically absent from the text, *Tristes Tropiques*, in its very success and singular character, represents a possible poetic expression of structuralism through the kind of thought it deploys: surges of meaning through sensory short circuits, contemplative stasis, effects of conjunction and disjunction, a repertoire of oppositions/inversions, arabesque patterns of symmetry, and the enchantments of art and achievements of science, conceived as distinct but not radically separate.[118] A post facto structuralist manifesto, this crisis book produced its own myth: that of the anthropologist in search of his Grail, which accounts for the massive impact of the book in the years that followed its publication.

An advertisement for the academic discipline, it exerted a veritable power of *conversion* over many young men and women, who keenly identified with the intellectual and aesthetic quest, as well as with the torments of its author, who had dared to put himself at risk. Many read it in a trance, as one of those books that changes lives, as Walter Benjamin had so wonderfully described them: 'It started with Aragon's *Paysan de Paris*. Evenings, lying in bed, I could never read more than two to three pages of it because my heart started to pound so hard that I had to put the book down.'[119] Everyone, from Pierre Clastres, to Luc de Heusch, Jean Pouillon, Emmanuel Terray, Michel Izard, Olivier Herrenschmidt and so many others since, has attested to the existential shock, and subsequent professional shift, triggered by their reading of *Tristes Tropiques*. If not all its readers became anthropologists, the book did – over the years and through many editions – win over an exceptionally broad public to the human sciences, triggering a reconfiguration of the publishing landscape in these disciplines in the 1960s.

This conquest of the broader public can be traced in the various uses to which the book was put, including some rather curious ones: an excerpt was submitted for discussion by student interns at Radio France for the overseas territories in July 1956;[120] pages of it were soon included in school curricula, and in anthologies of twentieth-century classics; in May 1956, excerpts were even read aloud at the International House of the Cité

Universitaire in Paris, where the Buddhist festival of Vesak was celebrated to commemorate the 25,000th anniversary of the Buddha's death, in the presence of Thailand's ambassador![121] Among its many glorious achievements, we should thus add that *Tristes Tropiques* marked a turning point in the reception of Buddhism in France and the West.

The first English translation, by John Russel, with the translated title *A World on the Wane*, was published in 1961, based on an abridged version of the text.[122] But before the English language edition, there were Brazilian (1958), German (1959, *Traurige Tropen*, published by Suhrkamp), Italian (1959, Mondadori), and Israeli (1960) translations. Its rise to international notoriety was steady, prompting new translations of his older works, which in turn occasioned new articles about Claude Lévi-Strauss, following the virtuous circle of celebrity. For the anthropologist had now become a public figure. In the summer of 1956, he was featured in a full-page portrait in *Elle* magazine, with the flattering caption: 'The most brilliant man in France.'[123] He was interviewed and consulted; his austere face became familiar. This 'literary' coronation irritated certain of his colleagues, especially Paul Rivet with whom Lévi-Strauss, as he later explained, suddenly found himself persona non grata, pending a belated reconciliation. But Émile Benveniste reacted very positively: 'One is encouraged to imagine, beyond what one reads, the possible destiny of a work that tackles so many issues.' Lévi-Strauss must have been comforted by these comments – he had received absolution, on the scientific front – even though they ended on a teasing note in a postscript: 'I am afflicted with a reading eye that cannot let anything go. I hope that for the next edition of your book, a gracious Nambikwara will agree to the singular form of "lice" (p. 298 end) and that you will transfer the cumbersome appendage of your "straying away from" (p. 384) to "without my noticing" (p. 315). Is it to pave the way for a future translation that you use an Anglicism on p. 337? Forgive me for these trivial comments.'[124]

In July 1956, *Les Temps modernes* published a long, lucid and in-depth article, which was the first systematic study of what its author, Jean Pouillon, had no qualms calling 'Lévi-Strauss's *oeuvre*'. It took stock of all his writings, and not just the latest book, as well as reviews of his work (Claude Lefort, the Marxists in the person of Maxime Rodinson, etc.). This extended analysis, both generous and careful, of a new paradigm was, in and of itself, a sign of intellectual recognition. And for it to be published in the journal of Sartre and Simone de Beauvoir, which had made and unmade reputations in France since the end of the Second World War, only lent it greater prestige. From this perspective, the success of *Tristes Tropiques* solidly established structuralism as a competitor to existentialism, emancipating it from the earlier intellectual movement, in which Lévi-Strauss had, as we have seen, taken part. Repeatedly published in *Les Temps modernes*, and defended by the journal, including in his polemic against Caillois, it was also on this terrain – not yet enemy territory – that he was recognized as a legitimate interlocutor of the waning Sartrism of the late 1950s.

In 1957–8, Lévi-Strauss seemed to be emerging from the crisis that had hovered over the genesis of his opus. His private life was again changing.

After Laurent, his first-born son to whom *Tristes Tropiques* was dedicated, his second son Matthieu was born in 1957, of the union with his third wife Monique. Soon thereafter, they moved from rue Saint-Lazare into a vast family apartment belonging to Monique's parents on rue des Marronniers – in the very upscale 16th arrondissement, which Lévi-Strauss did not like. Having exorcized his literary temptations, he summed up the *Tristes Tropiques* episode with characteristic self-deprecation: 'I tried to write a creative book and did not manage to. The anthropologists accuse me of having produced an amateurish work, and the public of having written a book of erudition. But all this leaves me indifferent. As soon as I finish a book, it is dead to me. Let us just say that I engage in a ritual of enchantment, generating an image of my thought.'[125]

15

Structuralist Crystallization (1958–1962)

Ideas form a complete system within us, comparable to one of the natural kingdoms, a sort of bloom whose iconography will be traced by a man of genius who will pass perhaps as mad.

Honoré de Balzac, *Louis Lambert*, 1832[1]

'Crystallization' is a recurring, but not unambiguous, metaphor in Lévi-Strauss's prose. It evokes the sudden change of state of a saturated solution or, on the contrary, the slow process, described by Stendhal, by which a mineral deposit comes to coat a tree branch.[2] This double meaning captures the life of the anthropologist perfectly. Indeed, suddenly, over the course of a couple of years, everything came together. And if up until then he had experienced numerous career setbacks, from the end of the 1950s this structural maladjustment came to an end, making the decade-long *différance* seem worthwhile.

In 1959, Claude Lévi-Strauss was finally elected to the Collège de France. This appointment made possible the realization of two projects he had had in mind since the late 1940s: a research centre and a major French anthropology journal. In addition, he published three books in four years: a structuralist manifesto (*Structural Anthropology*), a short critical work (*Totemism*) and a thick and dense anthropological study proper, which was to redraw the intellectual map of the times (*The Savage Mind*). These institutional and publishing successes served to 'crystallize' certain aspects of Lévi-Strauss's thought: his way of posing questions, his worldview and his model of understanding – in short, the structuralist paradigm itself, henceforth a serious competitor in the theoretical marketplace.

This happy turn in Lévi-Strauss's life was closely connected to the institution of the Collège de France. The academic recognition and the material means it provided profoundly and lastingly transformed the anthropologist's daily life, and that of anthropology with it. The connection also operated at another level: Georges Dumézil, one of Lévi-Strauss's most faithful supporters at the Collège, commissioned him to write a book on totemism for a series he was editing, which ended up as two books. The turn to magical thought was thus beginning to bear fruit. And the publication of *The Savage Mind* only further confirmed the fascination exerted by Lévi-Strauss's intellectual style, with its combination of rigour, theoretical-political audacity, and existential resonance: 'It is by design that I am using the term "savage"', he said about the title of his latest book. 'It expresses an emotional and critical charge, and I believe that one should not drain the emotion out of these issues.'[3] This intoxicating cocktail, this breath of fresh air, anticipated the more general appeal of the young social sciences in France at the time, in defiance of the dominion of philosophy and theoretical humanism. The Collège de France – which Roland Barthes and Michel Foucault were to join a few years later, followed by Pierre Bourdieu – became a new centre of French intellectual life. From then on, it was on the Place Marcelin-Berthelot, and no longer at the Café de Flore, that innovative, and hardly dispassionate, ways of exploring the big questions were being developed.

Place Marcelin-Berthelot

It is a part of Paris that – studiously discrete, midway up the Montagne Sainte-Geneviève – has stood since the sixteenth century as a kind of scholarly paradise. Its professors are free of the constraints of curriculum and professional assessment. When Claude Lévi-Strauss finally arrived at the Place Marcelin-Berthelot, the prestigious institution was set to attract a broader public, beyond its usual varied and rather sparse audiences of the late 1950s.

'Crossing my Rubicon'

On 26 October 1958, Lévi-Strauss wrote to Fernand Braudel to keep him informed of 'new developments which, this time – though they still filled [him] with dread – appear favourable to [his] crossing [his] Rubicon . . .'[4] Intent on applying for the third time to the Collège de France, he engaged in the usual formalities: sending the bibliography of his works, paying courtesy calls, etc. On that occasion, he discovered that *The Elementary Structures of Kinship*, his doctoral thesis, was out of print, and apologized to Braudel: 'A cursory survey has revealed that there is not a single copy left in Paris. I have launched searches in the provinces and second-hand bookshops.'[5]

Since his double failure of 1949–50, the situation had of course changed: his own, first and foremost, with the success of *Tristes Tropiques*, which had transformed the ambitious young scholar into an intellectual to be reckoned with on the public scene. His serious countenance had become familiar to a public that now spread well beyond traditional academic circles. The contrast between his growing celebrity and rather modest professional position – as a lecturer at an institution whose considerable promise would eventually be realized, but whose profile remained marginal at the time – had become striking. The VIth Section of EPHE then comprised only a few dozen researchers and, while maintaining a high level of scholarly activity, was up against the colossus of the Sorbonne, with its myriad of courses, students, traditions and academic accomplishments. Indeed, while fully aware of the formidable obstacles he would face, Lévi-Strauss had not ruled out joining its ranks.

As early as 1955, the philosopher Maurice Merleau-Ponty, with whom Lévi-Strauss had developed a close friendship, offered to help him with any of the various opportunities that were opening up: 'You know that I strongly resented the attitude of certain academics towards you. I would like to say once and for all that I will always support you in any attempt to give your research the influence it deserves. Thus, whether at the Sorbonne, by the end of this year, or at the Collège, if I can do anything in this respect, consider me always ready to do so.'[6] When Marcel Griaule, who had held the chair in anthropology at the Sorbonne, died in 1956, an opportunity arose . . . but the position went to Roger Bastide. The opposition was just too strong, especially from Georges Gurvitch, and too extreme for the doors of his alma mater not to close for him forever. But at the Collège de France, by contrast, the disappearance and creation of various chairs over the course of the decade had transformed the scientific and political landscape. Braudel had been appointed in 1950, Merleau-Ponty in 1952. This new generation joined forces with Gourou, Benveniste and Dumézil, all of whom unconditionally supported Lévi-Strauss, whereas the 'Faral camp' was now in the minority. And since 1955, Hispanicist Marcel Bataillon, who was favourable to Lévi-Strauss, had become the Collège administrator.

Despite these favourable conditions, it still took the full force of Merleau-Ponty's fellowship, 'as forthright as it was belated',[7] and all his patient determination, to prevail upon Lévi-Strauss to reconsider his decision to renounce his 'career' and never again apply for any position.[8] The Rubicon was as broad as the earlier double setback had been humiliating. Strictly speaking contemporaries (both were born in 1908, though Lévi-Strauss looked older . . .), the two *agrégés* in philosophy had first met in 1930 during a training for young teachers at Lycée Janson-de-Sailly (together with Simone de Beauvoir), then again briefly in 1945, and finally became regular companions in the early 1950s as part of the circle of friends that included the Lacans, Leirises and Jakobsons. The members of that small group were also connected through their respective wives – Sylvia Bataille-Lacan, Suzanne Merleau-Ponty, Louise Leiris and Monique Roman – who already knew 'Merleau' independently. Merleau-Ponty embodied the project of phenomenology that dominated French philosophy after the war. But, as opposed to Sartre, he showed an increasingly keen interest in the human sciences, psychology and anthropology, from which he hoped to gather material for the development of a 'new way of conceiving of Being'.[9] His break from Sartre (over communism) and his close ties with Lévi-Strauss in the early 1950s firmly established his status as an intellectual 'fellow traveller'[10] of the social sciences. As François Dosse has suggested, Merleau-Ponty was one of the rare 'bridge' figures between existential philosophy and the social sciences.[11] It was thus as part of this agenda that he conducted a masterful lobbying campaign at the Collège de France, winning over to his side men such as Gaston Bachelard and Martial Guéroule (chair in the history of philosophical systems), who were aware of the potential marginalization of philosophy and ready to give Lévi-Strauss's structuralist project a chance. Merleau-Ponty presented this project to his colleagues as a great and venerable adventure, running from Mauss to Lévi-Strauss, and continuing under their very eyes.

For it was Merleau-Ponty who, on 30 November 1958, presented a report in support of the creation of a chair in social anthropology before the faculty assembly.[12] He did not leave anything to chance, elaborating his argument in terms of an expansive intellectual, moral and philosophical project that contrasted with the hastily put together reports in support of more immediately consensual candidates. First, he highlighted the continuity of a chair in social anthropology, its exotic title notwithstanding, with the tradition of the French school of sociology from Durkheim, Halbwachs and especially Mauss, himself a former professor of that very institution, and whose filiation with the candidate was illustrated by the 'Introduction' to his work that Lévi-Strauss had written eight years earlier. Merleau-Ponty recalled the perennial questions of the nature of social facts, the relationship of man to others, the relations between subject and object, to which neither Durkheim's systematic ambition nor Mauss's intuitive genius had offered fully satisfactory answers: 'The French school lacked this access to the other which nonetheless defines sociology. How can we understand the other without sacrificing him to our logic, or it to him?'[13] According to the philosopher, the interest of structural anthropology lay precisely in its capacity 'to substitute relationships of complementarity for antinomies wherever it can': 'social facts are neither things nor ideas, they are structures'.[14] The point of structure (whose meaning, he pointed out in 1958, had been debased by excessive use) was that it overcame the contradiction between an objectifying thought (that of the anthropologist) and native thought: The point is 'neither to prove that the primitive is wrong nor to side with him against us'. On the contrary, the project was designed to accommodate 'the point of view of the native, the point of view of the civilized man, and the mistaken views each has of the other'.[15] This profound presentation of the structuralist system of thought concluded with the false conundrum intrinsic to this kind of oratorical exercise (which consisted in promoting the creation of a chair regardless of the person who was to occupy it): 'That this overview of social anthropology is also the abstract description of someone in particular, that there is a specific scholar to pursue this research and teaching among us, should you so decide, is all the more clear that this report is based on reflections on a body of work that radiates a serious, personal and sensitive intelligence.'[16] On 30 November, two days after his fiftieth birthday, Lévi-Strauss was thus informed of the 'present' that had just been given him and announced the news to Jakobson on 26 December: 'The Collège de France has created a chair in social anthropology.'[17] No other proposal was presented to compete with that of Merleau-Ponty and Marial Guéroult, who spoke second. And indeed, no other candidate was to apply for the position, so entirely identified was it with Lévi-Strauss – even though, as custom required, a second-tier candidate, Jean Guiart, put himself forward for form.[18] All this more closely resembled a consecration than a hard-won battle.

Nonetheless, Lévi-Strauss, feeling anxious and superstitious, insisted on abiding by all the protocols and carefully preparing for the second stage of the process. Indeed, after the position's profile had been defined, it still remained to appoint someone to it. He asked to visit his former vanquisher, Louis Chevalier.[19] 'No intrigue in sight', according to Dumézil. Indeed, in 1958–9, the situation was radically different from what it had been ten years earlier. It all went very smoothly, as though Lévi-Strauss's candidacy were a foregone conclusion. The geographer Roger Dion, a former supporter of his competitor, spared him a new visit, considering himself sufficiently informed to 'recommend, with full knowledge of the case, that [his] colleagues approve [his] application to the chair of social morphology [*sic*], for which no one else in France seemed more qualified'.[20] In the end, on 15 March 1959, Merleau-Ponty again went on the offensive. This time, the mask was off: 'In suggesting that we submit for ministerial approval M. Claude Lévi-Strauss as our first-choice candidate, I am fully aware of recommending to your attention an intellectual endeavour of considerable greatness.'[21] Lévi-Strauss was elected to the position with thirty-six of forty-four votes.[22] This was the end of a long 'purgatory',[23] the cost to himself of which he would never forget, and whose happy ending he would recall every time his gaze came to rest on the photograph of Merleau-Ponty, which remained on his desk for the rest of his life. His debt of gratitude took on even greater magnitude with the philosopher's sudden death of a heart attack on 3 May 1961, a year after Lévi-Strauss joined the Collège.

The title chosen for the new chair – 'social anthropology' – was in many respects an oddity in France. It echoed the fundamental decision, made by Lévi-Strauss on his return to France, to use the then unused term of 'anthropology', instead of the standard 'ethnology'. Chiselled into marble in the Collège's official records, the terminology marked a major semantic shift for the entire discipline. As Jean Jamin has pointed out, the use of this term immediately placed the discipline within an international semantic field. It was also a way to reconnect with the theoretical ambition of nineteenth-century anthropology as the study of nature and the human species within the framework of evolution, even though Lévi-Strauss, as we have seen, fundamentally diverged from the evolutionary approach.[24] Through the strategic use of that term, he brought together several intellectual traditions: that of the French Durkheimian sociology of the relations between the individual and society, as well as that of American cultural anthropology (itself strongly influenced by the German tradition, via Boas) centring on the dialectic of nature and culture. Lévi-Strauss's reconstruction of anthropology was thus openly heralded as a synthesis, drawn from his life and research experience, endowed with philosophical gravitas, thanks to the Kantian resonance of the multivalent term. Pierre Bourdieu, then a young philosopher about to defect to sociology, has attested to the success of this manoeuvre and to the 'extraordinary prestige that the discipline of anthropology had just acquired, among philosophers themselves, thanks to the work of Claude Lévi-Strauss, who had also contributed to this *ennobling* by substituting for the traditional French designation of the discipline [*ethnologie*] the English label anthropology, thus combining the prestigious connotations of the German sense – Foucault was then translating Kant's *Anthropology* – with the modernity of the Anglo-American meaning'.[25]

'The field of anthropology'

On acceding to the Collège de France, Lévi-Strauss found himself not only in the lair of scientific innovation, but also, and not without a certain pleasure, within a world of traditions, protocols and rituals. The first among them entailed his delivering an 'inaugural lecture' – i.e., an introduction to the courses to come – which took place on 5 January 1960 at 2:15 in the afternoon, before an impressive and varied audience drawn from cutting-edge science and intellectual high society.

The texture of his voice is missing, but reading it today, this inaugural lecture, published as a brochure by the Collège de France, sounds like a rather typical text by the author, with its sudden theoretical thrusts, unexpected references, and fervent tone punctuated by dreamy and melancholic lulls – calms after a storm. It was, as often the case, a double or triple-barrelled text, with stratified meanings, among which, first and foremost, his election placed anthropology at the centre of contemporary knowledge.[26]

In the scope of its questioning, the breadth and sweep of its 'field', its synthetic and all-encompassing capacity,[27] anthropology was defined as a science of the twentieth century, in dialogue with other disciplines, yet offering a particular perspective, constantly honed by the artistic sense of its times. This offered an occasion for Lévi-Strauss to pay public tribute to surrealism: 'We owe to it having discovered or rediscovered at the heart of our studies some lyricism and some integrity.'[28] Within the walls of the Collège de France, Lévi-Strauss, buttoned down in a severe suit, allowed himself all manner of audacities, presenting his discipline in a revolutionary fashion, as a combination of radical objectivity and radical subjectivity, as Michel Leiris had already suggested in *Phantom Africa*,[29] based on a specific empirical methodology – fieldwork, a confrontation of oneself with oneself – together with an ambitious speculative methodology: 'The anthropologist practises integral observation, observation beyond which there is nothing except – and it is indeed a risk – the complete absorption of the observer by the object of his observation.'[30] Thus, from the field to the lab and from the lab to the field, back and forth between the inductive and the deductive methods, between the individuality of a being and the definition of a system, these successive forays through the looking glass, inherent to the anthropologist's calling, authorized a definition of anthropology as 'the only science to use the most intimate kind of subjectivity as a means of objective demonstration'.[31] A seductive programme.

In one sense, Lévi-Strauss launched into a vertiginous theoretical demonstration, comparing, through logical reversals, myths of an Oedipal nature – myths of enigma, made of questions to which we suppose there are no answers – and myths of the Graal-Buddha variety – myths of answers without questions. Is the one a transformation of the other? In this journey to the heart of structuralist mechanics, in the company of Oedipus, Buddha and the Algonquin owl, the conclusion hit like a ton of bricks: Parsifal is an inversion of Oedipus. A vast play of construction and interpretation brought the solution to the incest enigma (Oedipus) together, whereas the answer without a question was semantically linked to chastity (Parsifal). In another sense, the initiate sent his theoretical armada back to port: 'Against the theoretician, the observer should always have the last word, and against the observer, the native.'[32] He concluded his lecture from the native's point of view, giving the Indians who had taught him the most the final word: 'To them I have incurred a debt which I can never repay even if, in the place in which you have put me, I could justify the tenderness I feel for them, and the gratitude I owe them, by continuing to be as I was among them, and as, among you, I would never want to cease from being: their pupil and their witness.'[33] To be a witness – the speaker intended to be one in the strong sense of the term, with a funereal and crepuscular inflection characteristic of Lévi-Straussian anthropology. If, at roughly the same moment, Siegfried Kracauer was defining history as the science 'of the last things before the last',[34] for Lévi-Strauss, anthropology was indeed the science of the last men.[35]

In the audience, everyone had a sense of being present at a historic moment. That lecture was a milestone in the construction of the discipline, but also in the alternative definition of a 'science in the making', one that rejected a naive objectivism that could not serve as support for the young human sciences. Integrating subjectivity as well as the native's perspective in a single gesture of overcoming antinomies, structural anthropology inaugurated its second act, characterized by the introduction of the notion of 'transformation', and the establishment of a disciplinary dynamic that the election of its 'pontiff'[36] to the Collège de France could only promote. It was for this reason that Lévi-Strauss tried, in his way, to reflexively engage with all the stages of the discipline. The long playful digression on the number eight, which served as a preamble to the lecture, was certainly a homage to superstitious thought, but also an offbeat way of claiming a genealogy: 1858, the year Franz Boas and Émile Durkheim were born; 1938, the year George Frazer gave his inaugural lecture for the very first chair of social anthropology in the world, at the University of Liverpool, twenty years prior to the decision by the professors of the Collège de France to create one in Paris. And Claude Lévi-Strauss was born in 1908, a subliminal date that does not appear in the lecture, but that Merleau-Ponty easily deciphered, embarrassed by their contemporaneity, which he found to be a burden![37]

In the eyes of 'Lévi-Strauss the American', laying claim to a history was first a way to reconnect with French sociology, not only by declaring that 'by creating a chair in social anthropology, it is Mauss's chair you want to restore',[38] but also by renewing ties with a figure of whom he had been an 'inconstant disciple': Durkheim. It was all very well for Lévi-Strauss to deplore the latter's disappearance, or even 'loss', in France, and to keep quiet about his own anti-Durkheimian rebellion of the Brazilian years.[39] Just as the newest member of the Collège de France was emphatically praising him, Durkheim was at the centre of a power struggle within French social science. A celebration of the hundredth anniversary of his birth was due to be held at the Sorbonne a few months later, on 30 June 1960, under the supervision of Georges Gurvitch, who had vetoed Lévi-Strauss's participation. Deprived of a voice, the latter took advantage of the influence of the inaugural lecture to hail the 'demiurge', architect of a 'powerful logical framework' and 'prodigious edifice', which was however still haunted by a few 'metaphysical ghosts' that his nephew Marcel Mauss had managed to opportunely exorcize.[40]

This exclusion put into relief the violence of the intellectual, symbolic and personal conflict between Lévi-Strauss and Gurvitch, as well as, implicitly, the rivalry between their respective institutions. During the 1960s, it was common knowledge that Lévi-Strauss's name was not to be uttered at the Sorbonne. To one of his English correspondents, Lévi-Strauss said of Gurvitch: 'He positively hates me'. Gurvitch had already distanced himself from the introduction to the work of Marcel Mauss that Lévi-Strauss had written in 1950.[41] In 1955, he launched a frontal attack in an article, 'Le concept de structure sociale',[42] in which he critiqued the static, overly reductive and abstract tendencies of structuralism in its Lévi-Straussian version. The latter reacted in 1956 in a bitter article – his last of this kind, it seems – which opened with the scathing line: 'Georges Gurvitch, whom I must admit I understand less and less each time I happen to read his work . . . .'[43] Lévi-Strauss proceeded to tackle a series of issues concerning structure and to respond to various critiques, but above all, he protested what he considered his adversary's bad faith: 'By what authority does Gurvitch appoint himself our mentor? And what in fact does he know of concrete societies? The crux of his philosophy would appear to be high regard for the concrete (involving praise of its richness, complexity, fluidity, inexpressible character and creative spontaneity), and yet this philosopher is imbued with such pious reverence that he has never dared to undertake a description or analysis of any concrete society.'[44] Against a sociologist who had, in his view, remained largely a philosopher, lacking any fieldwork experience of any kind, Lévi-Strauss spoke in the name of anthropologists and their experience of 'living reality' while delivering a lecture in structuralism: 'But actually our ultimate purpose is not so much to discover the unique characteristics of the societies that we study, as it is to discover in what way these societies differ from one another. As in linguistics, it is the discontinuities which constitute the true subject matter of anthropology.'[45] Even according to his close friends, Gurvitch was an anxious, fickle and megalomaniacal character. Renowned for his dogmatism, he was convinced that he was the great mind of contemporary sociology. Even if he exercised an autocratic power over the Sorbonne and retained a small loyal following of left-wing sociologists, close to Marxism and averse to the reign of structuralism – Jean Duvignaud, Lucien Goldmann, Henri Lefebvre, Roger Establet and Georges Balandier – his last years were painful ones. Indeed, in 1957, Raymond Aron was elected to the second chair in sociology at the Sorbonne and quickly developed a curriculum that attracted students. And across the rue Saint-Jacques, at the Collège de France, Lévi-Strauss posed an even more formidable threat.[46]

The Collège de France often rewarded complicated career paths, at the margins of or outside the university, of which Lévi-Strauss's provided a perfect illustration. First sent abroad and then at the École pratique des hautes études, he had been doubly excluded from the national *cursus honorum*. In this respect, Lévi-Strauss was very representative of what Pierre Bourdieu called, in *Homo Academicus*,[47] the 'consecrated heretics', who, in the 1960s, engaged in 'quarrels' with the Sorbonne, based on a set of teaching experiences, attitudes and scholarly ethics distinct from those practised at the university. In other words, the new masters of the Collège de France, Lévi-Strauss, as well as Benveniste and Dumézil, and later Michel Foucault and Roland Barthes, remained to some extent marginal figures. There was, at least, a real risk of this. Bourdieu's oxymoron underscores the fact that the institution on the Place Marcelin-Berthelot could also become a golden prison. Indeed, Collège de France professors did not have doctoral students and could not supervise doctoral research. They had no academic power and no research teams. With his background as an academic entrepreneur in São Paulo and at the New School, as well as his recent experience as a scientific expert at UNESCO, Lévi-Strauss was very well aware of the importance of the institutional framework and of the importance of logistics. It was a very good thing to get into the Collège de France, as long as one could get out . . . This is precisely what he did by insisting on the creation of a research centre connected to his chair, the Laboratory of Social Anthropology (LAS), and by founding a journal of international scope, *L'Homme*, intended to stand as the world-class French journal in the field, on a par with *Man* in Britain and *American Anthropologist* in the United States. The research centre and journal were the long arms of the new position, which emerged all the more quickly in that they had been already fully conceived, at least in the mind of their creator, since his first application to the Collège de France in 1949. The names for both had already been determined, as well as the personnel (the journal was to be headed by a triumvirate made up of Lévi-Strauss himself, Pierre Gourou and Émile Benveniste) and their respective roles.

But the Collège, in its infinite wisdom, must have thought it necessary to postpone these well-laid plans until we reached a year with an eight – that is to say, 1958. One last key to the biographical subtext of the 'inaugural lecture' was the fact that Lévi-Strauss liked to remind his new colleagues that 'this lecture, which they were now applauding, could have been given ten years earlier'.[48]

Crystallization of the paradigm

Over the course of the next few years, between 1958 and 1962, Lévi-Strauss published three books: *Structural Anthropology* (1958), *Totemism* (1962), and *The Savage Mind* (1962). A manifesto with a strong programmatic and epistemological proposition, a short theoretical-critical work and, finally, a full-fledged anthropological treatise which, in the early 1960s, established structuralism as a new paradigm, in method and action, before the deep-water diving of the *Mythologiques*.

A structural manifesto

The project of publishing a collection of articles was not new. It dated from the early 1950s, when Lévi-Strauss had floated the idea to Gallimard. The unfortunate outcome is now renowned as one of the famous publishing house's biggest blunders, together with its refusal of the first volume of Marcel Proust's *Remembrance of Things Past*. Received by Brice Parain, subsequently labelled as one of the 'opponents of anthropology',[49] his proposal was turned down on the basis that – and the expression stuck – his thought 'hadn't matured'.[50] A publishing setback, which only added to the other setbacks of that period and fuelled a lasting grudge against Gallimard.[51] But in 1957, following the success of *Tristes Tropiques*, Lévi-Strauss could take a more optimistic view. The collection of articles seemed all the more legitimate since the itinerant career of its author, between New and Old worlds, had made many of his articles, for the most part published in the United States, inaccessible to a French readership. Seventeen articles were collected and organized into thematic sections corresponding to the anthropologist's research interests between 1945 and 1956. They included, in a section entitled 'Language and Kinship', the seminal texts on the grafting of phonological analysis and kinship structures; then, texts focusing on Brazilian material and a section called 'Social Organization', including a particularly controversial article in Brazilian anthropology, 'Do Dual Organizations Exist?' (1956). A third section, 'Magic and Religion', comprised his reflections on religious anthropology and shamanism, notably 'The Sorcerer and His Magic' (1949); then came a section on 'Art', some articles of which dated from the New York years ('Split Representation in the Art of Asia and America', 1945). A final section was added at the very last moment, which responded to the various academic critiques of the concept of 'structure', stirring up a methodological hornet's nest.

The decision to include the response to Gurvitch, simply entitled 'Postscript to Chapter XV', gave the whole book a polemical tone, further confirmed by the title, which 'snapped like a flag':[52] *Structural Anthropology* defined the field of battle for the anthropological discipline and its structuralist leadership. In it, Lévi-Strauss defined and clarified terms, established genealogies, and identified enemies: 'Marxist progressivism' (of Maxime Rodinson in *Nouvelle Critique*),[53] and Gurvitch's philosophizing sociology. In both cases, he defended his position by going on the attack: on the one hand, he claimed to be more faithful to Marxism than its official standard-bearers,[54] and rejected the self-righteousness of the communist argument, as if his challenge to the concept of progress would leave the working class with no hope. On the other, as we have already seen,

he refused, in the name of a fieldwork epistemology and the patient empirical inquiry that had become central to the anthropological project, to cede
to Gurvitch a monopoly on the concrete.

A third enemy, of a very different kind, had arisen in 1957: Jean-
François Revel, an ambitious young philosopher with connections in
journalistic circles, who had just come out with a pamphlet – *Pourquoi les
philosophes?* – a chapter of which targeted Lévi-Strauss's structuralism.[55]
Once again, Lévi-Strauss sent the author home to reread his Marx and
Engels, and more generally pointed him in the direction of anthropology libraries, before offering a critique of his kind of philosophical essay
writing: 'If one of my colleagues were to come to me and say that my
theoretical analysis of Murngin or Gilyak kinship systems was inconsist-
ent with his observations, or that while I was in the field I misinterpreted
chieftainship among the Nambikwara, the place of art in Caduveo society,
[. . .] I should listen to him with deference and attention. But Revel, who
could not care less about patrilineal descent, bilateral marriage, dual
organization, or dysharmonic systems, attacks me [. . .] for "flattening out
social reality". For him everything is flat that cannot be instantaneously
expressed in a language which he may perhaps use correctly in reference
to Western civilization, but to which its inventors explicitly denied any
other application. Now it is my turn to ask: Indeed, what is the use of
philosophers?'[56]

Beyond its narrowly polemical dimension – emphasized here because of
its subsequent disappearance from the work of Lévi-Strauss, who did not
find himself suddenly without enemies but no longer felt the urgent need
to confront them – *Structural Anthropology* was a combative book, an
aspect not lost on Jakobson, as shown by his musings, immediately upon
reading it, about 'the present and forthcoming struggle for anthropology
and linguistics'.[57] The book was published by Plon, with initial contact
having been made by Éric de Dampierre, who directed its series dedicated
to research in the social sciences. Yet, after *Tristes Tropiques*, Gaston
Gallimard was hoping to lure Lévi-Strauss to his team. As René Étiemble
wrote to him on 8 May 1956: 'Are you aware that Gaston Gallimard is
very eager to meet you, shower you with admiration, entrust you with any
series you should like to direct?'[58] The two men did meet, but Lévi-Strauss
obstinately refused to have any commercial dealings with Gallimard. This
offers another key to his divergent intellectual path. The entire French literary elite was published by this prestigious house; and soon, with the arrival
of Pierre Nora, the human sciences were to follow suit. But Lévi-Strauss,
for his part, had chosen Plon, and irrevocably so. Although less prestigious
on the intellectual scene, Plon was to remain his exclusive publisher, but
only under certain conditions, which he had made clear early on: 'You
know better than anyone that my book was originally intended for another
publisher, who had conceived the idea, and that at your insistence, always
courteous of course, I gladly agreed to save it for you, but this reverses the
author–publisher relationship.'[59] This angry letter, sent to the Plon literary
editor in mid-summer, was quite clear: Lévi-Strauss would not put up with
any casual attitude towards manuscripts, nor any delays or silence. He also

demanded that he be given free rein to alter his work until the very last moment, which he did, obsessively. The contract, signed on 23 September 1957, gave him free rein to negotiate the English translation rights himself, and granted Plon no exclusivity over subsequent books. In addition, he insisted that *Structural Anthropology* not be published as part of any series. In other words, and this was the key to his loyalty to Plon, he intended to deal with his publisher as an equal. Indeed, over the years, it became easier and easier for him to lay down the law. Such complete autonomy would most probably not have been possible at Gallimard. He thus made the conscious choice to be the master of his own domain, with a more modest publisher, rather than one of the many invited guests to the venerable halls on rue Sébastien-Bottin.

Twin books

With the publication of *Structural Anthropology*, structuralism had its manifesto. Many a student procured a copy, and the first print run quickly sold out. By spring 1961, 4,500 copies had been sold and the translation rights into English negotiated with Basic Books, which published a first edition in 1963 (in a translation by Claire Jacobson). The term 'structures' became ubiquitous in the human sciences. It came to shape the questions, the ways of framing issues as well as solving them, the methods and approaches, all resting on a certain vision of the world, which, at the turn of the decade, was being increasingly adopted by all, including its critics. Two interdisciplinary meetings, both of which took place in 1959, attested to this phenomenon.[60] The first was a conference organized by Roger Bastide at the Sorbonne, which brought together a wide array of researchers, from the embryologist Étienne Wolff to the linguist Émile Benveniste, from the psychiatrist and psychoanalyst Daniel Lagache to the sociologists Henri Lefebvre and Raymond Aron, from the historian Pierre Vilar to Lévi-Strauss himself, all convened to reflect on the 'meaning and use of the term structure'[61] and, in so doing, to highlight the almost universal fecundity of the concept in the natural as well as social sciences. The second meeting took place at Cerisy, home of the famous 'Cerisy Conferences', ten days of intensive debates held in the congenial atmosphere of the famous chateau. This meeting was even more emblematic of the omnipresent nature of the structuralist concept, in relation to which everyone now positioned themselves. Indeed, the conference was led by Lucien Goldmann, Maurice de Gandillac and Jean Piager, who were not structuralists, and tried to define a path towards a genetic structuralism, more open to history and diachrony, to the conciliation of dynamics and permanence. This was one of the more common critical perspectives at the time, elaborated most notably by Goldmann who had recently published *The Hidden God* (1955). The conference also included a contribution by Jean-Pierre Vernant on the myth of races in Hesiod's poems.[62]

This crystallization of the structuralist paradigm continued with the double publication, in 1962, of twin books, conceived as a unit and written quickly, which formed a kind of dyad between the two Lévi-Straussian landmarks of kinship, on the one hand, and mythology, on the other, while also serving as a 'prelude'[63] to the latter. The moment was retrospectively narrated as 'a kind of pause'[64] in his research that would allow him 'a break between two bursts of effort'.[65] In this view of his work, the scholar tended to downplay the role of pure contingency – i.e., in this case, of Georges Dumézil's intervention.

Indeed, originally, his colleague had commissioned him to write a book for a series he directed at PUF called 'Myths and Religions'. The series comprised short introductory essays on controversial issues designed for a broad reading public, and free of any critical apparatus. Vernant had produced a volume on *The Origins of Greek Thought* (1962); three years earlier, Dumézil had contributed *The Gods of the Ancient Northmen*. André Leroi-Gourhan was also to take part. The series editor suggested that Lévi-Strauss write an overview on totemism, a field the anthropologist had never tackled but that appealed to his intellectual turn of mind. The complexity of the material (observers could not make sense of the intellectual sophistication of totemic systems, failing to determine their use and function), the centrality of the theme in anthropological literature and the challenge of grasping the deeper meaning – the elements of an enigma that was bound to arouse Lévi-Strauss's curiosity. In addition, Lévi-Strauss felt a debt to Dumézil, who had contributed to his election to the Collège de France. He could not turn down the offer. In 1960/61, his Collège lectures thus served for the first time to jumpstart a future book, a method that Lévi-Strauss was to follow for the next twenty years. In accordance with the mission of his home institution, his teaching was indeed experienced and practised as a 'testing ground'[66] for his ongoing reflections, words uttered from the lectern soon turning into published works. This form of forced writing, for which the lecture served as intermediary stage, proved highly productive, as attested by the speed with which the next two books were produced: *Totemism* was written in the spring of 1961 and completed by July, while the writing of *The Savage Mind* (which still lacked a title) started in July and was finished by November 1961. Lévi-Strauss wrote to Jakobson on 17 November: 'I have finished the second book.'

Is this 'second book' the brother or the son of the first? It seems that, as the lecture series unfolded, the argument became increasingly laden with material, so much so that it was going to be impossible to fit it all into the short format of the PUF series. The second book thus gradually acquired an independence and a style of its own. After the theoretical ground clearing and overview provided by the first book, the pyrotechnic display of new ideas followed, the patient and passionate exploration of classificatory logics, the scholarly encounter with owls, beavers, salmon, otters, squirrels, weasels, wolverines and cravings of pregnant women . . . 'A small scholarly and pedagogical book thus gave birth to a big fat one, simultaneously philosophical and literary, on the relationships between the mind, nature and history.'[67] Lévi-Strauss had anticipated this double pregnancy and spoke openly to Dumézil about it, who in turn talked to the PUF: 'The PUF reacted as expected to the shock of receiving the two volumes.'[68] Actually, according to Dumézil, the publisher was ready to accept both volumes, provided they be given a somewhat arresting title, which would highlight the intimate connection between them, such as 'Totemism' and 'Beyond Totemism'. 'I sincerely hope you can find the magic words',[69] Dumézil insisted. As we now know, the magic formula was to be 'The Savage Mind'. But the second book had by then become entirely disconnected from the first. It was ultimately published by a non-academic publisher, Plon, and intended for a broader public, one that had already had an opportunity to savour the distinctive quality of the chiselled prose describing scientific practices, the philosophical forays suffused with anxiety, which had become characteristic of a very personal, and now recognizable, voice – a unique voice.

The end of an illusion

From Durkheim to Van Gennep, from Frazer to Malinowski, entire generations of anthropologists had been enthralled by the diversity and richness of totemic rituals, especially those of the aborigines of Southern Australia, meticulously chronicled by Spencer and Gillen.[70] Were totems symbols of the animals and plants that were necessary to the group's survival (such as the ones providing their food, for instance)? Were they more complex representations, born of an ignorance regarding mechanisms of reproduction and imagining a genesis between men and animals? Or did they function, rather, as pure identification objects for this or that clan or set of siblings? But then, what was the deeper logic that informed them? Between 1870 and 1910, many hypotheses were formulated regarding totemism, a true touchstone of the anthropologist's calling, triggering a striking 'theoretical rush', before declining in the interwar period. It was thus paradoxically an obsolete question that Lévi-Strauss was taking up in 1960. If he restored its deep chronology, and restored its forgotten centrality within the discipline, it was nonetheless in the end only to bury it once and for all!

Indeed, the main thesis of *Totemism* leads to the complete dissolution of the very notion, which is held to be a 'mirage'. Lévi-Strauss wondered at length about the reasons for the sustained fascination held by this institution which, at the end of the day, he considered to be an illusion. 'Totemism is like hysteria.'[71] The very first sentence of the book compares the two concepts, both of which emerged in the nineteenth century to serve a similar purpose: to circumscribe Western rationality by opposing it to everything that it was not – primitive religion and neurosis. In *Totem and Taboo*, Freud had posited an equivalence between the beliefs of primitive peoples and neurosis. Lévi-Strauss's book disturbed and unsettled its readers by highlighting the optical effects of anthropological illusion. In an interview given for the release of the book, the author drove the point home: 'Up until now, I had avoided this hornet's nest. But at some point, the anthropological house had to be put in order, it had to rid itself of the notion of totemism.'[72] And indeed, since that book, the concept of totemism has been rendered permanently illegitimate in anthropological debates, replaced by a new interest in logics of classification. Indeed, it was Lévi-Strauss who made this conceptual leap: he went from totemism as an institution to totemism as a logic, as an intellectual activity, following the intuitions of Boas, Radcliffe-Brown and, above all, Marcel Mauss and Durkheim in their essay 'On Some Primitive Forms of Classification' (1903).[73] The solution found by Lévi-Strauss to the totemic enigma was the following: the totem was neither utilitarian nor analogical, neither a religious institution nor a psychological order; it was an instrument for associating, by homology, two series of relations, one pertaining to nature (the natural species) and the other to culture (social groups, clans, siblings, castes, etc.). The point was, so to speak, to borrow from the combinatorics of natural life (the differences between cat/lion/lynx, etc. or the oppositions between eagle and wolverine, for instance) to grasp social life in all its diversity, conflict and unity. It was thus not the characteristics of such and such animal that explained why a clan chose it as its totem (according to a symbolic logic), but rather relations of analogy, difference and opposition that formed a totemic code equivalent to a social code, in all its unity and diversity. Primitive peoples would thus find, in the immense repertoire of the natural world with which they were intimately familiar, natural species chosen not because they were 'good for eating' but because they were 'good for thinking'.

The tight logical argumentation expected of Lévi-Strauss did not preclude a few facetious comparisons, which have also become part of the anthropologist's trademark, between Bergson's philosophy and that of an old Dakota Sioux, both characterized by the 'same desire to apprehend in a total fashion the two aspects of reality which the philosopher terms continuous and discontinuous'.[74] This effort to unite the two perspectives, which turned Bergson into 'an armchair philosopher who in certain respects thinks like a savage',[75] Lévi-Strauss termed 'totemism from within'. And anyone could experience it within themselves. This is indeed how Dumézil, who had commissioned the book, interpreted its deeper message, as he wrote to Lévi-Strauss as soon as he had finished reading it: 'In the abstract as well as in concrete examples, it is loaded with humanity. The mind holds its place of honour: seeping out of one and the same brain, it erects quite similar worlds. May the young, thanks to you, refrain from drawing easy boundaries, and may they see within themselves the Australian – or the Viking.'[76]

Odds and ends: *The Savage Mind*

The 'second book' took off, at full speed, from what the first had established: it was determined to explore 'the flipside of totemism'. As in a tapestry, the overly smooth surface of (dismissed) anthropological theories quickly gave way to an explosion of colour, whose contours remained blurry.

The opening section takes the reader on a world tour (Philippines, southern California, northern Rhodesia, etc.) of the ethno-botanical and ethno-zoological lexicons of primitive populations, and dazzles with the stunningly precise terms, the incredible attention to detail and the carefully parsed distinctions that characterize these encyclopaedic forms of knowledge, whose rigour and richness rival that of Western science. For this is the essential and revolutionary thesis of the book, delivered, with supporting evidence, in a whirlwind of ethnographic references: the fifteen species of bats identified by the Negrito of the Philippines; the hundreds of vegetal species listed in the Navajo lexicon (North America); the medical knowledge of Siberian peoples, who use spiders and white worms to treat sterility, squashed cockroaches for hernias, macerated red worms for rheumatism, etc.; the seven therapeutic virtues of bear flesh, as well as the dozen virtues of bear brains, and the five virtues of bear blood, identified by Bouriate populations (Siberian peoples); the coming of spring deciphered through the careful examination of the developmental state of the bison foetus by the Blackfoot Indians. This colourful preamble highlighted both the extraordinary erudition and the rigorous classification of knowledge, informed not by utilitarian but by strictly intellectual motivations: 'so that some initial order can be introduced into the universe'.[77] The first chapter – entitled 'The Science of the Concrete' – is, like the rest of the book, simply breathtaking. Captured by the ethnographic lens, several essential notions of Lévi-Straussian reasoning are introduced, notably bricolage and transformation. It also features – between analyses of the ruffled collar of Elizabeth of Austria in a portrait by Clouet, and of a Haida mace – a veritable theory of art, conceived in the gap between these two objects, and located 'halfway between scientific knowledge and mythical or magical thought'.[78] What is this frilly collar doing here? From the profound aesthetic emotion stirred by the 'thread by thread' reproduction of a lace collar, Lévi-Strauss launches into an analysis of the scale model, of the integration of the event within the structure and of the parts within the whole, drawing on his aesthetic sensibility to reflect on the desire for a total understanding of the universe that appears to him as the defining characteristic of what he calls the 'savage mind'.[79]

The study of plants, animals, constellations, rocks, just like the impulse to group them, distinguish them and identify them, characterizes a thought process of which totemism is but one illustration within the general problem of classification. This giant combinatorics borrowed from the book of Nature allows human societies to play the 'great differentiation game', which, thanks to elements such as the totem, as well as the notion of species, allows for the establishment of differences even while preserving unity. Lévi-Strauss then introduces the notion of 'bricolage' to describe some of the processes of the savage mind, the formation of new arrangements from 'odds and ends under the constraint of improvisation'.[80] The point is to reuse scattered and small-scale materials to confront a malfunction and fix it like any other enigma by rearticulating it into a whole: 'In the speculative order, mythic thinking operates the way bricolage does on a practical level.'[81] The bricolage motif was, as we have seen, deeply rooted in Lévi-Strauss's life.[82] Held up as a true familial value (of bits and pieces), it was practised by Lévi-Strauss's father, by Lévi-Strauss himself and by his son Matthieu, who inherited a taste for it. Not only did the anthropologist confess to being a big do-it-yourselfer, but he also asserted the talent on an intellectual level, when, in a surrealist fashion, he described his work as a deal of his note cards in the same way as playing cards, allowing the mind and the objects to meet without the intervention of a subject. In its attempt to import and graft models of intelligibility borrowed from linguistics, structuralism itself could be likened to the inventive work of bricolage.[83]

A further dimension made for a more dynamic and less staid structural analysis: moving from one society to another, switching locations, transformed the meaning of mythical elements. This notion of transformation, already present in an earlier article, was developed in *The Savage Mind*, and further systematized in the volumes of the *Mythologiques*. It gave the theory more flexibility, by not collapsing structure and system, and allowed Lévi-Strauss to move from one signifying system to another via invariant relationships, through what he called a 'transformation'.[84] Indeed, all structures involved transformations, whose study provided the sole means of revealing the identical properties of different systems. At which point Lévi-Strauss liked to quote Goethe: 'All forms are similar, and none is like the others. So that their chorus points the way to a hidden law.'[85] We can imagine these signifying codes as moving in their kaleidoscopic fashion, turning the 'savage mind' into an infinite play of mirrors, decomposing and recomposing the prism of relationships between nature and culture.[86]

The very title of the book resonated with a plurality of meanings, or at least connotations, channelled by the work's distinctive poetics, whose scholarly character opened onto the title's magnificent pun, a formidable challenge for any attempt at translation: the fine shades of the *Viola tricolor* (the wild pansy, or *pensée sauvage* in French) richly playing on the act of thinking (*pensée*, in French) – a brilliant cover, inviting its readers into the botanizing world and mood of its author. It is to be understood, in its universal simplicity, as an echo of the great works that had shaped the discipline: Tylor's *Primitive Culture*, Lowie's *Primitive Society*, which had converted Lévi-Strauss to anthropology, as well as, and above all, in contradistinction to Lévy-Bruhl's *Primitive Mentality*. Finally, it was to serve as a rebuttal to the notion of a 'pre-logical' principle governing societies dominated by affect. Adopting the opposite view, Lévi-Strauss continually stressed that 'the savage mind is logical in the same sense and the same fashion as ours'.[87] At the height of decolonization, the substitution of the term 'savage' for 'primitive' had an 'incongruous'[88] feel to it. It was of course a sign of Lévi-Strauss's fierce rejection of the evolutionist model, but the 'savage' also carried with it the sweet smell of eighteenth-century travel literature, the Pauls and Virginias of our Western imagination. Lévi-Strauss owned the term, explaining: 'I use the term savage intentionally. It carries an emotional and critical charge and I think we should not try to temper the passions.'[89] The savage mind, he insisted, was not to be mistaken for the mind of the savage, since its dynamic was universal. It characterized neither a kind of population, nor an age of humanity, but a stratum of the universal mind. The book's iconography, most often 'at a remove', without any explanatory relationship with the text, is left for the reader to ponder, carrying one off to more eccentric moods and odd tastes – as, for instance, with the 'physiognomic heads' of Charles Le Brun or the drawings by Grandville illustrating the continuities between the animal and human kingdoms – and perhaps causing the contemporary reader 'to recoil'.[90]

These bold audacities gave *The Savage Mind* a scandalous aura and made it a 'centrepiece of the structuralist programme'.[91] Its subversive potential emerges incrementally, in its ability to alter its readers' worldview. Indeed, for many, reading it was an earth-shattering experience. For this work of anthropology is also about us: it seeks to demonstrate that 'there is no gap between the way so-called primitive peoples think and the way we do'.[92] Superstitious forms of thought, strange beliefs, practices such as bricolage, art, poetry, folkways, etc. constitute a model of intelligibility that is operative in Western society and that coexists with, rather than contradicts, other ways of thinking. The first scandalous assertion was thus that the average Westerner is endowed with a savage mind. But the philosophical and epistemological reach of this Odyssey was wider still: Lévi-Strauss intended to move beyond the opposition, in place since Descartes's *Cogito*, between the realm of the sensible, of sensory perception (of the false, the fictional), and that of the intelligible (of the true, the real). In so doing, he was challenging the traditional history of science, based as it was on the foundational rupture between the sensible and the intelligible, between the 'secondary qualities' and the 'primary qualities'. This entailed considerable audacity on the part of a scholar who was as concerned with his scientific legitimacy as was Lévi-Strauss. As it turns out, this premise bears some resemblance to a very current view in the history of science, according to which scientific modernity, far from resting on a radical break with older forms of knowledge, relies rather on their recycling, reuse and adaptation, and on the gradual discounting of a body of traditional ideas and positions.[93] Lévi-Strauss only made matters worse with his conclusion that the two paths – the savage and the scientific mind – were bound to converge. Indeed, did recent discoveries – telecommunications, microscopes and calculators – not give new strength to the meanings (even if the interpretations were not right) that primitive populations had already ascribed to certain phenomena, whose importance they discerned?

To assert that contemporary science and the savage mind combine to constitute the entire process of human knowledge, in a long-awaited reconciliation of body and mind, was no small matter. And indeed, some of his readers, including close ones, did not find this iconoclastic vision to their taste. The great specialist of nuclear physics Pierre Auger, an old acquaintance he had made in the United States, was among them: 'Your book pulls off a hard-fought victory, and its strategy leaves little room for objection. Yet, as you might expect, its conclusion does not align with my own way of "situating", in relation to each other, the two paths of thought – the two sources of decision and behaviour, if I may call them so! You speak of "merging" and of "converging", which seems to imply they lead to, or at least overlap on, common ground; and this is something to which I cannot subscribe. If the domesticated path allows us, somewhere along the way, to catch a sudden glimpse – thanks to you – of a large stretch of the savage path, this glimpse is caught from above, which precludes the reverse from happening.'[94] He went on to express his fear that the book might be misinterpreted as a kind of defence and illustration of the irrational . . .

The reception of the book, which came out in May 1962, built on the cumulative effect of the almost simultaneous publication of *Totemism* (in March of that same year). The French press hailed it as an event, especially because of its ninth and final chapter, 'History and Dialectics', an explosive appendix that delivered an attack on Sartrean existentialism, and was interpreted by the public as announcing an impending intellectual takeover. Before delving into the specific stakes involved in that philosophical quarrel, we should take the measure of the immediate impact of *The Savage Mind*. While it was by no means easy reading, the book followed in the steps of *Tristes Tropiques* in reaching a previously unknown readership that went well beyond anthropological circles, thereby further confirming the influence of the structuralist programme, thereafter considered one of the major intellectual contributions of the century.[95] Claude Roy, in the left-leaning newspaper *Libération*, heralded a 'great civilized book' and compared its author to that of *Psychopathology of Everyday Life*: 'Freud brilliantly demonstrated that our unreason had its reasons, which consciousness could not ensure. Now Lévi-Strauss has demonstrated, in a profound and new way, that the apparent chaos of primitive myths and rituals obeys a deeper order and principles that had remained invisible until now.'[96] Claude Mauriac in *Le Figaro*, Robert Kanters in *Le Figaro littéraire*, as well as Jean-François Revel in *L'Express*, a former opponent who had walked the road to Canossa, paid tribute to the originality, virtuosity and sweep of the argument. In *Le Monde*, it was Jean Lacroix, a left-wing Christian philosophy professor in Lyon, and co-founder of the journal *Esprit* alongside Emmanuel Mounier, who reviewed the book (as well as all those that followed): 'His anthropological works [. . .] are also philosophical events',[97] for ever since Durkheim, he continued, philosophy and the social sciences have been deeply connected in France. Highlighting some of the central arguments in both works, Lacroix remarked: 'Whatever their differences in perspective and method, Lévi-Strauss's positions are in profound harmony with those of Foucault on madness and dreams.'[98] But the principal interest of Lacroix's article lay in his laying out (more than Lévi-Strauss himself) the philosophical implications of such an anthropological perspective. 'Some of Lévi-Strauss's phrases, albeit polemical in intention for the most part, smack so much of what is sometimes called "vulgar materialism" that one cannot help but worry.'[99] Lacroix was referring here to the passage in which Lévi-Strauss expressed the idea that this original logic of association, which characterized the savage mind, was 'a direct expression of the mind and, beyond the mind, probably of the brain'. These concerns notwithstanding, 'the greatness of Lévi-Strauss, the secret of his immense appeal abroad as well as in France, and of his sway over an entire generation of young minds across various disciplines, lies in his producing a rigorous and strictly scientific work, while also reflecting on this very work, scrutinizing its method, not just delineating its philosophy, but more profoundly letting this philosophy inform his research, in which it naturally finds expression. [. . .] So that in the end, without any acrimony or provocation, but as if on the same level as his research, Claude Lévi-Strauss might be producing the most rigorously atheistic philosophy of our time.'[100]

The time of structuralism

In the early 1960s, now established in the minds of a broad public, elucidated in great books, Lévi-Straussian structuralism fascinated and irritated many, and even worried some. It exerted a special kind of appeal, in a historical and sociological context favourable to its crystallization, while firmly positioning itself through major 'duels'[101] on the French intellectual scene. The structuralist paradigm – its method, worldview, questions and approaches – was now shared by other thinkers in new disciplines – Roland Barthes, Michel Foucault, Jacques Lacan – but Lévi-Strauss unquestionably embodied its very essence.

Fascinations: a substitute messianism?

How was it that, suddenly, in the space of a few years, the complex analysis of small isolated tribes in South America began to inspire readers and attract initiates? How did the cryptic language of systems, codes and rules come to displace the discourse on the subject and consciousness? As Bernard Pingaud would later comment, it was no longer a question of 'man mak[ing] meaning but of meaning com[ing] to man'.[102] Let's listen to what the converts had to say on the matter. But converts to what? We should draw a distinction here between the appeal of anthropology and of the new social sciences more generally, and the adoption of structuralist languages and frameworks. If all anthropologists were not structuralists – many were and remained Marxists – it was certainly the case that structuralism, under Lévi-Strauss's leadership, promoted the rise of anthropology.

Structuralist anthropology appealed through a combination of contradictory traits that were at once aesthetic, epistemological and political. For some, bogged down in narrow monographic research, a dose of Lévi-Strauss brought first and foremost a big breath of fresh mountain air. As the Africanist anthropologist Luc de Heusch wrote to him: 'Twenty years ago, I came back from fieldwork feeling disoriented. Reading *The Elementary Structures of Kinship* and *Tristes Tropiques* opened up new horizons where I could finally breathe, a stretch of land across which I could take great strides. In that place, I still feel better than anywhere else.'[103] Many experienced a similar intellectual intoxication with the broadened perspectives opened up by anthropology as defined by Lévi-Strauss. To which was added the elegance, too refined in the eyes of some, of structural analysis – the symmetrical dynamics, mirror effects and inversions that acquired, in the hand of the master, 'a degree of self-evidence that one felt a kind of jubilation tracking the relationships they delineated. At the same time, they were driven by the same political ideas as *Race and History*. It gave a sense of being among one's own, albeit at a distance, and at the same time in a kind of theoretical paradise.'[104] This was how Catherine Clément expressed herself as a young philosopher quickly won over by Lévi-Straussian anthropology, becoming a zealous exegete and informed propagandist.[105]

The new social sciences were riding high against philosophy, with their promise of theoretical pleasure, scientific rigour and political subversion. 'However different or opposed they might be,' according to Africanist Marc Augé, 'anthropologists of my generation, whether Marxists or former Marxists, had the feeling that in their concerns and in their work, they were participating in the larger issues of their time, both on a strictly intellectual level, by validating, adopting or invalidating Marxist theory, and on a practical level, by taking a stand on the conditions of economic development and on the defence of endangered societies. In this sense, we were all political – these varied and sometimes opposed forms of politics being remarkably, and in some sense paradoxically, part of an intellectual environment which claimed that the social sciences were sciences in the same way as the natural sciences, and that they could aspire to the same degree of objectivity.'[106] The possible substitution of the primitive, or rather the savage, man as a new figure of alienation replacing the proletarian, appeared between the lines in a moving letter that Régis Debray, an *agrégé* in philosophy who had joined the Latin-American resistance movements and had recently been freed from prison, wrote to Claude Lévi-Strauss on 25 December 1969, to thank him for intervening on his behalf with the Bolivian President: 'Along with a few other books (novels and tales mostly), *Tristes Tropiques* encouraged me to leave the beaten paths of the School and explore America. It was the early 1960s, and I did not encounter primitives there but revolution, an encounter that proved in the end as extraordinary and as earth-shattering as one with a forgotten people. Like all philosophy students, I learned to think with *Structural Anthropology*, as others had earlier done with the *Discourse on Method*. Like all teachers, at the end of the school year, I have tried to think out loud about *The Savage Mind*. The circumstances of my life, and my limited intellectual abilities, did not permit me to continue to follow your work on the world of American myth. Tens of thousands of young people could tell you the same story, and I have no more right to waste half an hour of your work time than any of your other readers, whether in France or abroad.'[107] Revolution or primitive peoples – this alternative already characterized, in part, the possible ways Claude Lévi-Strauss could grasp the reality of the world in his younger years. Yet, in the meantime, revolution had moved away from Europe; it now stood on the side of the forgotten peoples of History. Between the *maquis* of the Cuban revolutionaries and the fieldwork sites of anthropologists, a few bridges, however rickety, indicated that both could find themselves on the same side, that of a rejection of the world order.

At the same time, the fortunes of structuralism are often understood in the context of the general ideological retreat of the late 1950s, marked by the death of Stalinism, the 20th Congress of the Communist Party of the Soviet Union, and the arrival of Soviet tanks in Budapest, all of which shook the communist firmament and opened up alternative possibilities.

Indeed, this was the spirit of an incisive article written by François Furet, published in the journal *Preuves* in 1967, following up on intuitions developed by Raymond Aron ten years earlier.[108] At the conclusion of a dense analysis, the historian reduced the structuralist craze to a new 'opium' for French intellectuals, prone to ideological addictions, who had substituted Marxist cocaine with structuralist LSD . . .[109] Furet aptly described the French intellectual left as disappointed and demoralized by history – 'for so long a tyrannical mistress before she became an unfaithful one'[110] – which had ridden roughshod over all its hopes, including those raised by the newly independent countries, with Ben Bella and Boumédiène's Algeria serving, from 1965, as a sobering experience for even the most committed anticolonial partisan. These disillusionments were further compounded by the new situation of France, its territory now reduced to a hexagon and, notwithstanding Charles de Gaulle's strong assertions to the contrary, a sense of itself as no longer being one of the world's great powers. 'Having been expelled from history, the France in which they live consents the more willingly to expel history', Furet further contended.[111] After the ideological surfeit of Marxism came the call for the structuralist vacuum. And the postwar humanist injunction fell between the cracks: Intellectuals 'were no longer obliged to hope for anything', as Michel Foucault was later to put it.[112] Or, in a typically grandiose formulation by Furet: 'The analysts of man's "dissolution" have succeeded the prophets of his advent.'[113] Indeed, they were sometimes one and the same, those who had moved directly from Marxism to structuralism, according to a curious process of 'contamination' that Furet thought to be 'specifically French'.[114] Furet attempted to show that, ironically, the fascination exerted by Lévi-Strauss over many former Marxist intellectuals had little to do with any political or philosophical affinity, but rather with 'an inverse relationship into which nostalgia for Marx has been able to insert itself. Stated simply, the structural description of man as object has, in every respect, taken the place of the historical advent of the man-god.'[115] In the guise of oppositions (structure vs. process, the natural science model vs. the historical model), both were in fact governed by the same deterministic ambition, the same conception of truth to be unveiled beyond apparent or even conscious meaning, the same 'old totalizing dream'.[116] A false opposition, and a true substitution, accounting for the success of structuralism and for the defection of several young communist intellectuals, who left the party to join the ranks of anthropology under the structuralist banner, including Alfred Adler, Michel Cartry, Pierre Clastres and Lucien Sebag.

Confrontations 1: Sartre

Lucien Sebag, for his part, was one of the protagonists involved in the major intellectual confrontation of the early 1960s, between the Sartrian regnum, which had gone unopposed since the end of the war, on the one hand, and the structuralist position, orchestrated by its anthropologist challenger, on the other. Like Sartre and Lévi-Strauss, Lucien Sebag had obtained the *aggrégation* in philosophy, but like the anthropologist (and as opposed to the philosopher) he was not an alumnus of the École normale supérieure. A brilliant, elegant, handsome and taciturn character, the Sephardic Jew with a tragic destiny was a concentrate of all the contradictory aspirations of the 1960s.[117] Passionately in love with Lacan's daughter Judith, as well as a patient of her father's, he committed suicide in January 1965, at the age of thirty-one. A comet, then, shooting across the skies of Lévi-Straussian anthropology, prone to all manner of audacity and seemingly held in high esteem by the master. If he was in mourning for the Communist Party, he had not renounced the possibility of a dialogue between structural analysis – of which he was one of the early practitioners, engaged in the collective study of Pueblo myths – and Marxism.[118] Claude Lévi-Strauss tapped him, together with Jean Pouillon, another bridge figure, to lead his École pratique seminar focusing for an entire season on Sartre's 1960 book, *Critique of Dialectical Reason*. This response to the arguments of Merleau-Ponty, attempting to combine existentialism and Marxism into a coherent whole, was the philosopher's second (and last) great theoretical opus, after *Being and Nothingness* (1943). Sartre had sent a copy to Lévi-Strauss, with a friendly inscription: 'To Claude Lévi-Strauss, as a token of faithful friendship, a book whose main positions, as he will see, take inspiration from his own and, above all, from his way of posing them. With my deepest consideration.' Lévi-Strauss was indeed cited on several occasions in the *Critique*, always in a laudatory manner.[119]

We should underscore the original aspect of this intellectual debate at the time: a seminar as the context for a discussion, whose seriousness, Lévi-Strauss insisted, was a mark of the highest respect.[120] This was no longer hostile intellectual polemics. For the first time in French intellectual life, the seminar emerged as a forum for discussing new ideas. What exactly was said in the course of this seminar? Is the final chapter of *The Savage Mind* a faithful reflection of these discussions? To Jakobson, who expressed doubts about the appropriateness of concluding a great anthropological work with a polemic against Sartre, Lévi-Strauss replied sharply: 'The chapter on Sartre might appear strange and "out of tune", but before passing judgement on it, it must be put in the French context – the ideas defended by Sartre in his book rest on a doctrinal ground whose foundation is very broad. And I don't think this chapter is "sketchy", in that it sums up the work of a seminar held over several months; but, as a result, it does unfortunately make allusions. Finally, I would point out that it does not mention dialectics, or only negatively. The whole point of the chapter is to show that historical knowledge, far from being above, or outside, savage thought – a kind of privilege of white and civilized man – is, on the contrary, part and parcel of it.'[121]

The arguments about 'analytical reason' and 'dialectical reason', the obligatory passages on 'praxis' and 'structure', engaged the chapter in the debates of the time, far more so than the rest of the volume. It is rooted in the intellectual context of the early 1960s and is, as a result, 'perhaps the most difficult for today's reader to engage with'.[122] With typical concision, Lévi-Strauss summed up its main intention in his letter to Jakobson: to defend the 'analogical' savage mind against the dialectical Western mind. An attack on the subject, the 'trappings of personal identity' and the 'self-evidence of the ego', it was above all a vigorous assault on the primacy not so much of history as of the philosophy of history, and a protest against the diktat of historicity as the exclusive mode of intelligibility. Lévi-Strauss engaged in a kind of encompassing/subsumption of the subject and its relationship to time in order to demonstrate, in Sartre and others, the partial and limited character of overly universalizing generalizations, which only served to reveal their own ethnocentrism. Sartrian philosophy (and philosophy in general) only grasped one of the historical modes of man, while anthropology aspired to encompass them all. Lévi-Strauss had an easy time of it demonstrating the local character of the examples used by Sartre to advance his argument: bus queues, café waiters, labour strikes and boxing matches. As evidence of Sartre's provincialism accumulated, and Lévi-Strauss's victory became ever more certain, in a dazzling final turn of the tables, the latter deposed philosophy by transforming it into a mere archival record of Western modernity. No sooner had Sartre attempted to engage with anthropology and psychoanalysis as the 'auxiliary sciences' of philosophy than Lévi-Strauss lashed back in response: 'This philosophy (like all the others) affords a first-class ethnographic document, the study of which is essential to an understanding of the mythology of our time.'[123] It was held up by history which, 'in Sartre's system [. . .] plays exactly the role of a myth'.[124]

In retrospect, this sparring match had far-reaching impact. Frédéric Worms has identified it as the 'general tipping point' into a new philosophical moment in the history of the century:[125] after the moment of existence, came that of structure. Indeed, the controversy did not so much confront two solutions to the same problem as initiate a reformulation of the problem itself. It appeared to contrast a subjective approach, centred on freedom and the act of creation (roughly represented by Sartrian philosophy), and an objective approach, embodied by Lévi-Strauss and based on the human sciences, whose aim was 'not to constitute, but to dissolve man'[126] – to 'dissolve man' in the chemical sense of the term, i.e., not to disappear but to decompose into more fundamental elements that can lend additional intelligibility.[127] There was thus something else at stake here: what it meant to understand. The controversy therefore mapped the shift from one model of meaning to another – a meaning which, with Lévi-Strauss, depended neither on a subject nor interpretation, but was nonetheless a cultural fact, enclosed in a system of signs similar to the one discovered by structural linguistics: 'Language is human reason which has its reasons and of which man knows nothing.'[128]

Sartre did not respond. Neither immediately, nor later.[129] In that sense, the controversy was one-sided, even though Sartre entrusted Pierre Verstraeten with launching the attack in *Les Temps modernes*, in which he published an article entitled 'Claude Lévi-Strauss ou la tentation du néant', in July 1963.[130] Yet even still, Lévi-Strauss emerged victorious from the ring. By that point, nothing could shake the sense of a generational takeover, even though only three short years separated the two contemporaries. The press seized on the event: 'De *La Nausée* de Sartre à *La Pensée sauvage* de Claude Lévi-Strauss',[131] said the *Tribune de Genève*. Indeed, from an anthropological perspective on the intellectual world, the break was radical, involving style, image, models and places. From the smoked-filled cafés of the Left Bank to the laboratory of the Collège de France, from the omniscient intellectual to the austere scholar, from the chummy 'comrade', who had grown up in a world of books and within the cloister of the École normale, to the aesthete of the 16th arrondissement, explorer of new worlds. This intellectual shift was also a disciplinary shift. It was quite clear that the attack on Sartre's dominion was also a revolt against philosophy. In 1960, the prophet-intellectual appeared obsolete. The controversy with Sartre thus also revealed a structural change in the intellectual world: the terminology and research protocols of the social sciences were about to expose the still very German-inflected French philosophy as old-fashioned, and out of step with its times.

One year later, it was to yet another philosopher that Lévi-Strauss turned (rather than confronted), in another discussion which remained more confidential at the time, and marked a more pacific dialogue with philosophy.

Confrontations II: Ricœur

In November 1963, an issue of the venerable journal *Esprit* came out dedicated to structuralism, a method recognized as 'original and fertile'[132] by Christian philosophers, but that appeared to have developed into a 'vast and coherent system of the human mind',[133] which 'posed problems'.[134] Just as Lévi-Strauss had engaged with Sartre's arguments in a seminar, so a year of preparatory work preceded the publication of the issue, followed by a roundtable in which Lévi-Strauss was invited to participate. He adopted a modest and non-confrontational posture: 'It seems to me that a book is always like a prematurely born child. This one strikes me as a rather repulsive creature by comparison with the one I wish I had given birth to, and one I am not overly proud of subjecting to the gaze of others.'[135] The discussion, and more specifically the exchange with Paul Ricœur, revolved around three points: the validity of what Ricœur considered as the 'over-generalization' of structuralism, the question of a new model of meaning and, finally, the identification of Lévi-Strauss as a philosopher.

Ricœur's article, 'Structure and Hermeneutics', questioned the steady expansion of the field of knowledge covered by structural analysis, which laid claim to all fields of human knowledge, all the social sciences and perhaps even all sciences in general. 'Initially', he wrote, 'structuralism made no claim of defining the entire constitution of thought, even in its savage state, but rather of delineating a well-defined group of problems which have, one might say, an affinity for the structural treatment.'[136] Was structuralism not only applicable to certain structural material, such as Amazonian tribes? Lévi-Strauss did not hold the savage mind to be geographically limited to this or that territory and claimed, on the contrary, that it was a kind of 'common denominator'[137] between 'them' and 'us'. Paul Ricœur, steeped in biblical thought and the Judaic tradition, tried to distinguish patterns of thought for which the diachronic and hermeneutic dimensions seemed more effective than structural analysis alone.

This final point led to differences over the new model of meaning introduced by the structuralist programme, for which nothing made sense except in relation to, or by opposition with, something else. Whereas for Ricœur, a Christian and a scholar of hermeneutics, there was indeed a 'meaning of meaning', for Lévi-Strauss, meaning was never first, and searching for it just did not make any sense. The discussion ended with Ricœur expressing his concern: 'As you see it, there is no "message" [. . .]; you have despaired of meaning; but you save yourself with the thought that, if people have nothing to say, at least they say it so well that what they say can be subjected to structural analysis. You will find meaning but the meaning of a non-sense, the wonderful syntactic arrangement of a proposition that says nothing. I see you at the junction between agnosticism and a hyper-intelligence of syntaxes. Which makes you both fascinating and worrying.'[138]

But when Ricœur asserted that what he called the structuralist philosophy was an order devoid of a subject, a 'Kantianism without the transcendental subject', Lévi-Strauss fully agreed: he himself considered his research to be linked to Kantianism, in that it explored the conditions and constraints of the operations of the human mind. In any case, as he bluntly put it, he did not much care to categorize his philosophical perspective. In fact, he deliberately left it vague. *The Savage Mind* was not a philosophical work, but a moment 'where I take the liberty of looking at the surrounding landscape, but precisely at a landscape where I will not, cannot and shall not go: that philosophical landscape that I can see out there, but that remains out of focus because it is not part of my itinerary'.[139] A Romantic traveller in a Caspar David Friedrich painting, the anthropologist took other paths than the 'one way street'[140] of philosophy.

Deposing philosophy

A vulgar Kantian, a Marxist, an incorrigible materialist, or a pathological hyper-logician? What were the philosophical foundations of Lévi-Strauss's work? People around him seemed obsessed by the question; he would always dismiss it casually, in an offhanded way that spoke volumes. Two years later, in the 'Overture' to *The Raw and the Cooked*, he referred to the philosophical polemic of the ninth chapter of *The Savage Mind* as 'minor poaching', a slight deviation from a course that intended 'never to encroach on the only too closely guarded preserves of philosophy'.[141] Unfortunately for him, from the 1960s onward, he was often read in France as the philosopher he did not care to be. It was thus with slight irritation that he responded to the publication of a new issue dedicated to him of the *Cahiers pour l'analyse*, a new journal produced by a group of philosophers from the École normale supérieure, close to Lacan and Althusser.[142] 'Needless to say I was immensely flattered by the interest that you have shown in me in your recent publication. Yet, I cannot help but feel somewhat uncomfortable, for it is a bit of a philosophical lark, is it not, for you to scrutinize my texts with a care that would only be warranted for a Spinoza, Descartes or Kant? In all honesty, I do not hold what I write to be worthy of such consideration, especially with regard to *Tristes Tropiques*, in which I did not claim to pronounce the truth, but rather to scribble down the musings of an anthropologist in the field. I would be hard put to defend its coherence. [. . .] And to be completely frank with you, I am surprised that minds as astute as yours, if they must wonder about me, should not wonder why I make such a casual use of philosophy, rather than find it remarkable. Indeed, I have no respect for it, and I take the liberty of changing modes – idealist, materialist, realist, etc. – from one book to the next, and even from one sentence to the next, as would a versatile painter or musician. My goal is not to formulate a system, but rather, to use any available means, any concept that has fallen into the public domain of the philosophical tradition, if it can serve my profound intention to lead my contemporaries to grasp the unique flavour of an institution or belief. Philosophical considerations are but thrown together foundations on which I erect the most precious objects.'[143] The letter, the draft of which remains in the archive, was, as was often the case with him, written in one go on the back of the one he had received. He did not mince words: Lévi-Strauss embraced his 'predatory' approach to a body of texts, of which he made purely instrumental use, since he cared little for producing philosophical work of his own. The tone was iconoclastic, similar to that of Montaigne, in the avowed incoherence of this 'fickle'[144] philosophy. Lévi-Strauss professed a kind of 'temperamentalism' which the young philosophers of the École normale took as a provocation.

In fact, this somewhat haughty indifference concealed a ferocious and radical settling of scores with philosophy as the dominant discipline. The speech he delivered as his inaugural lecture and the conclusion to *The Savage Mind* leave no doubt as to the imperialism of the Lévi-Straussian project, which aimed to include philosophy as part of its anthropological overview of all forms of rationality, modern Western reason (philosophy) being but one province of this vast territory, and neither the largest nor the most fundamental. Would Merleau-Ponty, to whom *The Savage Mind* was dedicated, have approved of his friend at this stage? Probably not. Indeed, although Merleau-Ponty had introduced an entire generation of young philosophers to the importance and challenge of the social sciences (and thereby encouraged some to change careers), he was not prepared to compromise on the leadership role of philosophy – its mission as orchestra conductor. It was nonetheless clear that Lévi-Strauss did not need a philosopher to reflect on the meaning and methods of his knowledge project. Merleau-Ponty's sudden death in 1961 averted any direct conflict, leaving the book's dedication to immortalize an ambiguous alliance, sealed in a wholehearted and belated friendship born of eternal gratitude.

The complexity of Lévi-Strauss's relationship to philosophy probably also derived from the fact that it was not informed only by disciplinary concerns, but also by a more personal and idiosyncratic desire to settle scores with the *normaliens* (which he was not), with the figure of the prophet-intellectual (which he did not want to be), and finally with the whole of the philosophical guild, then represented by his ex-wife Dina Dreyfus, who resurfaced as the ever-present voice of conscience, chastising the traitor (to philosophy). In February 1963, she published a harsh ten-page article in *Mercure de France* entitled 'De la pensée prélogique à la pensée hyperlogique'.[145] While demonstrating an in-depth understanding of *The Savage Mind*, the article entirely rejected all its conclusions and equated Lévi-Strauss with Lévy-Bruhl. Dina Dreyfus found the parallel between the scientific mind and the savage mind unacceptable, for it contravened the hierarchy of truth and the hold over the real: 'Far from constituting a "science of the sensible and concrete", the formal creations of the classifications operated by the savage mind lose sight of the real.'[146] Further, she added: 'The obsessive neurotic spends his lifetime ordering his closets and drawers, inventorying their contents, inventing more and more specific and subtle systematic orders. Should we mistake this classifying frenzy for some sort of speculative power? The logical mind, when left to its own devices and not tempered by judgement, leads to a hyper-logic, whose consequences are no less absurd than that of the pre-logical "rule of participation", to which Lévy-Bruhl reduced all primitive thought. Lévy-Bruhl considered primitive peoples as big children, still caught up in affect. Lévi-Strauss reduces them to well-ordered machines.'[147] To the indictment of formalism was added an indictment of subjectivism: 'It is indeed sometimes hard to tell if the frenzy for classification of the savage mind emanates from the object described by the sociologist, or from the sociologist himself.' The article concluded with a charge against the social sciences, which took man as an object and entertained guilty 'dreams of total formalization'. Finally, the text locked onto its core target: 'In truth, the anthropologist aims to achieve nothing less than a new hierarchy of the sciences, crowned by anthropology which, though a newcomer, is to represent the universal tool of the human sciences, in the same way as mathematics in the natural sciences, and which might further claim, via notions of messages and information, i.e. of linguistics and cybernetics, the status of science of the sciences, encompassing philosophy itself.'[148] Hence Dina Dreyfus's surprise at the book's dedication to Merleau-Ponty. As far as we know, there was no response to the article . . .

This dedication, as we have seen, expressed Lévi-Strauss's gratitude, fondness and admiration, more than any philosophical affinity. Soon after Merleau-Ponty's death, Lévi-Strauss had confessed to Jakobson: 'I sense the intensity of the loss even more now that he must be replaced, for I felt very far from his philosophy, and yet to hold a chair entitled "Philosophy", I can't think of anyone else. Of him alone could we say: he thought. With him gone, all we are left with are historians and exegetes. The chair's title will probably need to be changed . . . .'[149] A week later, Lévi-Strauss informed Fernand Braudel of the results of the strange inquiry with which he had been entrusted: 'Not without difficulty, I have finally obtained – albeit indirectly – a few indications regarding Sartre's potential availability. It seems entirely out of the question that he should consider the project, in any shape or form. I deeply regret it, but I do not think it is worth insisting. He alone, in my opinion, could have done justice to a chair labelled "Philosophy". In any case, this leaves the field clear for other projects.'[150] And that was it: exit, philosophy![151]

'A Hero of our time'

The English translation of *The Savage Mind* was undertaken by Sybil Wolfram, an Oxford philosopher recommended by the British anthropologist Rodney Needham.[152] Over the course of several months, exchanges between Claude Lévi-Strauss and his translator became increasingly acrimonious. The former impugned the latter's capacity for understanding, the latter questioned the former's command of the English language. Their disagreements soon became public: 'The translation of *La Pensée sauvage* was becoming a matter of international concern.'[153] In the end, Sybil Wolfram abandoned ship. The draft was revised by a team of translators coordinated by Ernest Gellner, an anthropologist at the London School of Economics, whose name had been suggested by Julian Pitt-Rivers. The result is often considered rather appalling, in terms of its language. The choice of title condensed all the difficulties raised by its translation: *The Wild Pansy*? *Untamed Thinking*? Lévi-Strauss suggested *Mind in the Wild*. The book finally came out in 1966, after four years of back-and-forth, under the title *The Savage Mind*.

This laborious process may well have been an 'anthropologically interesting case of misunderstanding between cultural traditions'.[154] It put into play, and twisted up, the singular positions and relationships between philosophy and anthropology, both in France and in Britain. Paradoxically, Sybil Wolfram reproached Lévi-Strauss for his obscure language and proximity to 'continental philosophy', whose speculative vapours he had inhaled deeply. In Britain, anthropology had developed very early as part of the academic landscape, on a firmly empirical foundation. It was thus on that basis that Lévi-Strauss's work was fiercely discussed in the British academic world, which never entirely abandoned its suspicion of Lévi-Strauss's poetic style and philosophical tone. While by the mid-1960s, most of his work had been translated into English – *A World on the Wane* [*Tristes Tropiques*] in 1961, *Structural Anthropology* in 1963, *Totemism* in 1964, *The Savage Mind* in 1966 and *Elementary Structures of Kinship* in 1967 – its Anglo-American critical reception was coloured by the scholarly controversy broiling within the strongly internationalized discipline of anthropology, a discipline that was in the process of profound reconstruction. In sharp contrast with the French reception, the arguments were sometimes technical and required solid anthropological erudition.

The quarrels between anthropology insiders nonetheless made their way onto English colleges and American campuses. Lévi-Strauss was depicted in the mainstream press, sometimes rather ironically, as a pure French export, or as an 'ultracivilized Gallic mind on the ways of the "savages"', to quote a promotional brochure, which included a photograph of the anthropologist, in a Prince of Wales checked suit, peering at an open book with a vague air of surprise.[155] Marshall Sahlins, himself an anthropologist, introduced the man from the Collège de France in the following way: 'Claude Lévi-Strauss is a famous French anthropologist. More than that, he is an acclaimed savant, a man of letters and high style, of delicate perception and a penchant for Reason. In other words, Lévi-Strauss may be more French than anthropologist, perhaps even a French national resource – a *philosophe*.'[156] This very caustic article, published in *Scientific American*, compared the star presence of Lévi-Strauss at the Smithsonian's 300th anniversary, in September 1965, with the other 'French' star of the year: the *Mona Lisa*, on loan from France to the Metropolitan Museum of Art in New York. Mona Lisa was Italian, but like Lévi-Strauss she had an enigmatic smile.

A few years earlier, Lévi-Strauss had been introduced to the New York, and American, intelligentsia by a keen observer and sympathizer of the French intellectual scene: the novelist, essayist and radical feminist Susan Sontag, a disciple of Simone de Beauvoir, who had spent time in Left Bank circles during her Parisian years in the mid-1950s. In November 1963, in the *New York Review of Books*,[157] she introduced Lévi-Strauss with much ado as the latest grand intellectual to come out of a Paris that had no shortage of such figures. According to her, in stark contrast with Sartre, who was his total opposite, Lévi-Strauss was the product of a national tradition, that 'cult of *froideur, l'esprit géometrique*'.[158] In an intriguing yet erroneous connection, she associated him with the 'Nouveau Roman' and literary modernism with which, as we know, Lévi-Strauss had in fact little affinity. She dramatically narrated his rise, concluding on the moral and political commitment for which the anthropologist stood. 'Groaning among the shadows, struggling to distinguish the archaic from the pseudo-archaic, he acts out a heroic, diligent, and complex modern pessimism.'[159] At the same time, in the *Times Literary Supplement*, George Steiner traded '*froideur*' for '*hauteur*' in the Lévi-Straussian project, and turned him into a 'moralist' in the seventeenth-century sense of the term, which he had quite a hard time defining for his Anglophone public.[160]

Here was Lévi-Strauss in the early 1960s, become, after a long courtship, a 'hero of [his] time'. His difficult writing notwithstanding, young students were fascinated by the style of his thought as much as by what he promised. As Michel Foucault put it in *The Order of Things*: 'Structuralism is not a new method; it is the awakened and troubled consciousness of modern thought.'[161] The simmering worry, the 'anthropological doubt', which Lévi-Strauss had discussed in his inaugural lecture, promoted the discipline to the rank of those that merited a lifetime of study. If Michel Foucault, a philosopher by training, but one who settled into the human sciences project of the 1960s, never worried about defining his discipline, Lévi-Strauss was to devote a significant part of his life to channelling young (and not so young) energies and to organizing collective work. In this, he followed the example of Durkheim and his group of disciples at *L'Année sociologique*, that 'famed workshop where modern anthropology fashioned part of its tools'.[162]

16

The Manufacture of Science

Science is not the work of one man.
Letter from Claude Lévi-Strauss to Howard Gardner, 10 April 1970.

Every morning for twenty years, from 8 a.m. until noon, Claude Lévi-Strauss was to be found at the Laboratory of Social Anthropology he had founded together with Isac Chiva in 1960, following his appointment to the Collège de France. First located on avenue d'Iéna, then on Place Marcelin-Berthelot, in the Chalgrin Building, the LAS – the acronym rapidly prevailed – was the first social science research centre at the Collège de France. It hosted the journal *L'Homme* (1961) and became, in the 1960s and 1970s, the institutional home of French anthropology.

As it prospered, the LAS brought together anthropologists, linguists, historians, research assistants, archivist-librarians, visiting professors from abroad, secretaries, adjuncts, both men and quite a few women, young and not so young; and presiding over this small and restless world of increasingly professional social science was the tall silhouette of a man in his fifties, who was not only the intellectual leader of structuralism but the new founding father of French anthropology. In this chapter, we shall settle into the heart of a scientific knowledge factory – its symbolic and material centre, the laboratory, and its institutional practices, the discipline – in an attempt to conduct an ethnography of a scholarly site, comprising a specific tribe of researchers, with its own government, rituals, conflicts, values and beliefs.[1] In short, an anthropological study of anthropologists . . .

In his way of engaging in the fight for the recognition of the discipline, Lévi-Strauss kept his distance from the institution and the organization of men, allowing science to arise out of a cumulative process of combined and shared knowledge. This was the principle that governed the collective endeavours he led: journal, laboratory and seminar. All those who took part in them remembered that indefinable 'Lévi-Strauss touch' – a mixture of courtesy, irony, rigour and kindness that always stopped short of familiarity. There could well have been a conflict between Lévi-Strauss's solitary, artisanal and even artistic mode of scientific practice and the new scientific order whose rise he promoted – except for the solution he found to this apparent contradiction in the strict management of his time, of which he was already rather adept: mornings were devoted to others, at the laboratory; afternoons to himself, at home.

Rebirth of a discipline

Through his American experience, Claude Lévi-Strauss had become aware of the historicity and diversity of the grouping of issues and topics into what we call 'disciplines'. For what is a discipline[2] but an organization of knowledge that varies according to national academic traditions and research institutions, and that can be shaken by the sudden eruption of a cross-disciplinary paradigm (structuralism) calling for the formation of new scholarly ligatures? Modern science was built on such a system of disciplines and the gradual process of professionalization of its activities. Thus, nothing is chiselled into the marble of truth. Disciplines are born, and disciplines die.

In the 1960s, Lévi-Strauss's resolve converged with that of the French state of the newly constituted Fifth Republic, which professed an eagerness to modernize and a determination to base its policies on the new social sciences of sociology, economics and demography, underwriting a more rational decision-making process. This was a moment of faith in the ability of scientists to light the way for ambitious policies, a honeymoon period that also involved cold, hard cash.

Identification

When Lévi-Strauss, at the height of his intellectual notoriety, set himself the task of reforming French anthropology, he could draw on his long institutional and pedagogical reflection and panoptic perspective on the discipline, at an international level: an 'emerging science',[3] whose territory (regarding philosophy and sociology) and alliances (with linguistics, geography-history and psychology) he jealously guarded. A vast territory was thus claimed (knowledge of man in general), drawing on intellectual and logical tools and methodological and investigative principles. This intellectual 'licensing'[4] process was decisive, and Lévi-Strauss executed it masterfully. From then on, and despite a certain lingering semantic confusion, ethnology/anthropology had a place on the map of French knowledge, where it also had serious rivals.[5]

As early as 1954, in an article commissioned by UNESCO on 'The Place of Anthropology in the Social Sciences and the Problems Raised in Teaching It',[6] Lévi-Strauss had made it clear that anthropology, in his view, was not so much defined by any particular object – war axes, polygamy, cannibalism or, more generally, primitive societies – as by 'a particular conception of the world or an original way of approaching problems'.[7] Indeed, anthropologists might study phenomena in so-called 'civilized' societies and, conversely, the aforementioned artefacts might also be the objects of investigation by prehistorians. Beginning in the early twentieth century, the discipline had found its methodological Rosetta Stone in long, meticulous and arduous fieldwork with the population under study – the core of the anthropological knowledge project.

If empirical fieldwork had become essential, it was only a first stage, called 'ethnography', i.e., the collection of oral and written data and material objects, generally destined for exhibition in museums once classified. The second stage – 'ethnology' – marked a first step towards synthesis, by suggesting geographical, historical or systemic conclusions, and by isolating a particular custom or institution to attempt to make local sense of it. The third stage, that of anthropology proper, provided further synthesis and sought to draw conclusions that would be valid for all human societies. In France, he continued, 'the final stage of the synthesis was left to other disciplines – sociology (in the French sense of the term), human geography and, sometimes, even philosophy'.[8] Operation Lévi-Strauss – as laid out in his 1960 inaugural lecture at the Collège de France – was thus to repatriate that stage of the generalizing process to the home office of anthropology and to no longer leave it to others (and other disciplines) to draw conclusions in universal terms. The accomplished anthropologist should therefore first be near-sighted, in an intellectual sense, and then far-sighted – removing the ethnographer's glasses, taking in the view from above and, after retreating to the theoretical back office (the laboratory), producing universal models capable of accounting for the observed phenomena.

Over the course of the previous decade, Lévi-Strauss had continuously reformulated and honed (not without the occasional slip) the programmatic ambition, systematic definition and heuristic promise of anthropology, but its core definition was now clearly articulated, in sometimes polemical terms: The error of 'opponents of anthropology [. . .] stems from the fact that they regard the goal of our discipline as the acquisition of a complete knowledge of the societies we study. [. . .] Confidence diminishes even more when some of us are prone to replace with schemes and diagrams those facts which elude us. But actually our ultimate purpose is not so much to discover the unique characteristics of the societies that we study, as it is to discover in what way these societies differ from one another. As in linguistics, it is the *discontinuities* which constitute the true subject matter of anthropology.'[9]

Professionalization

For the benefit of certain colleagues newly returned from fieldwork, Lévi-Strauss would sometimes exclaim: 'Here, we do not train anthropologists, we discover them!'[10] Even though anthropology had its own objects, methods and questions, as a science that only belatedly joined the ranks of the disciplines, it had long enjoyed a more or less felicitous spirit of autodidacticism. Georges-Henri Rivière had thus completed his training in cabarets as much as in museums, and Alfred Métraux was educated at the École des chartes. French anthropologists prior to 1945 formed a heterogeneous group: 'From defrocked priests and clergymen to amateur philosophers and would-be writers, from errant administrators to reformed adventurers, they did not form a professional order, if any order at all, given the fact that the sense of a calling often mattered more than the training.'[11] Lévi-Strauss himself fit the description: trained in philosophy (like Jacques Soustelle), he had not attended any of the few institutions that actually taught anthropology. It was his Brazilian fieldwork that had made him an anthropologist.

Yet by 1960, moving from calling to training was very much on the agenda. What form of pedagogy seemed best adapted? In a global overview of the teaching of anthropology, Lévi-Strauss was rather hostile to the idea of creating an autonomous anthropology department, as was commonly the case in the Anglo-American world. While seemingly ideal, the format was difficult to import into places like France, with academic traditions that drew a sharp distinction between the arts and the sciences faculties (indeed, on which side of the great divide was anthropology to fall?), where certificates in anthropology could be obtained from arts, sciences and law faculties alike. Yet, he also added in 1954, 'an anthropologist, whatever his particular line, cannot dispense with a basic knowledge of physical anthropology'.[12] Withholding judgement, the anthropologist's preference was for a school or institute, keeping in mind the 'interfaculty approach'[13] of a discipline that thrived on straddling several. An 'irregular system'[14] had characterized the Institut d'ethnologie of the University of Paris since its creation (1925). And if a lesser degree of institutionalization had also resulted in a lesser status for anthropological studies, at least if was more in line with the spirit of a discipline requiring multiple forms of expertise.

It was thus from the Institut d'ethnologie that Lévi-Strauss spearheaded the institutional, pedagogical and political offensive to offer both a coherent training programme and a platform for the discipline. In a letter of 5 May 1957 that appeared to express his last wishes, a gravely ill Paul Rivet (who had made amends with his former doctoral student) bequeathed to Lévi-Strauss the family estate – the other two protagonists in the story, Mauss and Lévy-Bruhl, having by then already passed away: 'I entrust you with the Institut d'ethnologie: with you and my sister in charge, I can rest assured as to its future. If I were to pass away, I think you should bring Leroi-Gourhan on board, despite his flaws, because he is a Sorbonne professor, and the institute is intended to act as a liaison between the museum and the university.'[15] Which Lévi-Strauss did, upon Rivet's death in 1958.

From 1960, two directors presided over the fate of the institute, which then served as a kind of clearing house for the various anthropological studies available in Paris. There was no undergraduate university degree in anthropology before the 1970s. The various courses were awarded as supplemental certificates for other degrees (in sociology, philosophy, history, etc.). At the Sorbonne, the courses were taught by André Leroi-Gourhan and Roger Bastide. All the courses listed in the Institut d'ethnologie prospectus were divided into general and specialized courses, with the latter intended for doctoral students, since advanced studies had just been established in 1958.[16]

Within this somewhat anarchic landscape, with its guarded principalities, Lévi-Strauss promoted a reformist spirit which he made public in a short article denouncing the 'colonial rule' that weighed on the institute and advocating for its emancipation from the exclusive tutelage of the university, especially for doctoral studies. In addition, he proposed the creation of a faculty assembly (twenty-two members by 1958) as a solution to the dispersion of courses of study in anthropology and a means for establishing a modicum of coordination. The reform was adopted by the professors concerned and approved by the administration. The institute was thus governed, for the next ten years or so, by a faculty assembly that constituted a new platform for the promotion and definition of scientific practices in anthropology. On this occasion, Lévi-Strauss proved a zealous promoter of synergies and a driving force for the discipline. A co-director of the Institut d'ethnologie as well as a member of the CNRS committee on 'Anthropologie, ethnographie et préhistoire', he played a key role in the institutionalization of the discipline, both within the field and in relation to public authorities.

Regarding the latter, Lévi-Strauss sometimes erupted in anger against a public administration that he deemed, in these matters at least, arbitrary and punctilious, as for instance when it objected to institutions receiving funds from ministries to which they were not directly subject. This is, indeed, what happened with the Institut d'ethnologie, whose grant for funding its publications could not be approved, because it emanated from Stéphane Hessel at the ministry of education. Lévi-Strauss was furious.[17] He suggested the public finance office circumvent the problem by officially awarding the grant to the Marc Bloch Association, which, as he wrote to his friend Hessel, served as an 'unofficial banker' to the VIth Section and whose 'role was kept secret from the public for obvious reasons'.[18] Lévi-Strauss was not just a skilful negotiator with public authorities, he was also a scientific entrepreneur who had acquired considerable fundraising experience in the United States, and was not averse to an occasional bending of the rules when it was for a good cause. Like the Vatican, the EPHE thus had its unofficial bank . . . Yet, France being France, it was primarily from public authorities that the social sciences, and especially anthropology, could obtain funding in the early 1960s, all the more so given that the French state was about to launch a full-fledged research policy for the first time.

Socialization

After the war, French social science institutes had benefited from several individual and uncoordinated initiatives, while remaining, as far as research was concerned, very marginal in comparison to the university.[19] The 'penury' of the social sciences was a constant cause of complaint, even though UNESCO had been providing funding and commissioning studies. The Marxist left looked very unfavourably on these 'American' sciences of capitalist social engineering. French social scientists were thus isolated in dealing with a state that aspired to achieve urgent transformations after the war, but whose commitment was quickly overtaken by colonial and Cold War concerns. With the advent of Gaullism, the situation rapidly changed. True, these transformations of the early 1960s aligned with a long French tradition of state-supported, bureaucratic and centralized knowledge, promoted by the absolute monarchy going back to the seventeenth century.[20] This urge to promote knowledge was nonetheless reasserted with new vigour on the eve of the most prosperous period of the postwar Golden Age. It rested on an optimistic faith in the capacity of the new social sciences to make sense of social realities, and above all to assist rapid transformations that were both inescapable and desirable (or at least presented as such). 'Modernization' was the new fetish in these days of economic planning and accelerated social change. The opening of universities to the children of the lower middle classes triggered a flow of new students that called for the creation of new posts and new curricula.

Money was flowing in and new posts were being created, less at the university, still reluctant to accommodate the new disciplines, than at the CNRS and the EPHE, whose VIth Section comprised forty-eight senior members in 1956 and eighty by 1962. An undergraduate degree in sociology and another in economics were created. Funds were released to equip laboratories, which, aligning on the hard sciences, hired a broad range of staff members: research assistants, computer technicians, archivists and armies of adjunct lecturers now peopled the world of the human and social sciences. Career prospects were not an issue, since the French state and society were generating considerable demand for these new professionals who could help resolve, or at least shed light on, the fresh problems raised by industrial society: demographers, economists, sociologists, social psychologists and . . . anthropologists, even though the latter were not quite as necessary for the vast modernization offensive. In 1962, the Délégation générale à la recherche scientifique et technique (DGRST) was created, an inter-ministerial body whose funding structure was novel in that it was based on multiyear contracts, as was the case for the famous 'Actions concertées'. One of these projects became a celebrated symbol of the heyday of collective studies, and sometimes also of its nadir, crystallizing as it did all their euphoria as well as their disappointments: the study on Plozévet, a village in the Bigouden country of western Brittany. The site was selected because of its isolation, to enable the study of 'the French agricultural and rural world and its adaptation to modern living conditions'. The CNRS, in turn, launched the RCP (Recherches coopératives sur programme), which supported other major interdisciplinary studies in different French regions of Aubrac, Châtillonnais, Baronnies, Margeride and Corsica. These studies provided a panoramic view of the 'emptied France' of the 1960s and 1970s. The anthropologists took it as an observation post on a rural world that was understood to be in its death throes. For the sociologists and economists, it was the laboratory of an inexorable modernization process. These state-sponsored initiatives – whether emanating from universities, the CNRS or the DGRST – promoted scientific practices that were oriented to collective, and preferably interdisciplinary, work (combining, as was the case in Plozévet, the natural and social sciences).

How did anthropology, and more specifically its leading figure, position itself within this new world? On a strictly personal level, it is quite clear that Lévi-Strauss was appalled at the idea of entire brigades of researchers (around a hundred for Plozévet) occupying a village for several months or years. The immediate reaction of the confirmed soloist was of an aesthetic nature: '[The studies] sometimes yielded good results. I would not adopt them for myself. Anthropology is I think more of an artistic creation. It is a one-on-one between a man and a society. In addition, the purer forms of savage societies are such delicate objects that it would be very dangerous to alarm them, and potentially damage them, by deploying such a cumbersome research apparatus. However, in the case of more robust and solid societies, I see the point of such studies. But again, I am not inclined to them.'[21] Yet as coordinator and promoter of the discipline, Lévi-Strauss made a strategic contribution to this kind of initiative that brought in funding and new posts. He sent Africanist anthropologist Michel Izard to Plozévet, which enabled his laboratory to take part in the project.[22] Similarly, LAS researchers participated in the so-called Châtillonnais RCP study, launched in 1967.[23] Four anthropologists – Françoise Zonabend, Marie-Claude Pingaud, Yvonne Verdier and Tina Jolas, all members of the LAS – were sent to Minot, a municipality of 370 inhabitants located in the southeast of the Châtillonnais region. Initially, the project was to produce a monograph of a French village, in the style of what Lucien Bernot had done with Nouville.[24] The 'ladies of Minot'[25] who, upon arrival there, became the 'ladies of Paris' thus conducted studies of local kinship structures, matrimonial strategies and parental terminologies, to which they added, over the course of their stays in the field, studies on the adaptations and uses of the past, professional occupations, culinary practices, etc. In addition, ever alert to the 'importance of details',[26] they undertook a full-fledged anthropology of the contemporary peasantry. The model of inquiry differed from that of Plozévet, where haematologists crossed paths with demographers, botanists had discussions with anthropologists, and sociologists took a back seat to economists. In Minot, four anthropologists conducted a study over several years (from 1967 to 1975), at the rate of several days a month, and finally produced four individual books, each of which developed one of the various threads of what had been the collective fieldwork material, but was personal in its writing and analysis.[27] Four books, then, and not thousands of pages of dull and unpublishable studies. The anthropological analysis of familiar territory was as painfully received in Minot as in Plozévet by the populations concerned, who were hostile to the operation of socio-anthropological objectification, to which they had been subject without their consent, and who did not very much appreciate being characterized as the 'Indians of Burgundy' or Brittany.[28]

Lévi-Strauss, as we have seen, was a key figure in this disciplinary dynamic. He was very much in the know when it came to research policy and participated fully in its making. Yet, paradoxically, the question of the 'usefulness' of the human sciences remained an open one in his view. For the human sciences had been called upon 'to finally demonstrate their useful character in their turn (following the social sciences)'. From his perspective, though, this all-out mobilization was dangerous. The human sciences, he asserted in 1964, were 'in their prehistoric stage. Even supposing that they may, one day, be used for practical purposes, they have little or nothing to offer at present. The true way of enabling them to develop is to support them generously but, above all, to ask nothing of them.'[29] We must distinguish, then, between his strategic arguments (designed to obtain funding) and his personal convictions, which considerably tempered his expressed expectations for the human sciences, even while composing the specific notes they might play as part of the scholarly symphony.

In his view, the explanations provided by the human sciences were often vague and approximate, as well as prone to error, while their predictions were random. 'But, they may only understand a quarter to a half of what they have to consider, and may be able to predict in only one out of two or four cases, yet they are able, because of the intimate connection between these half-measures, to give to those who practise them something that comes between pure knowledge and practical efficiency – *discrimination*, or at any rate, a certain kind of discrimination which makes it possible, with slightly better understanding, to act a little less clumsily, although without ever being able to determine exactly what is owed to either of the two aspects. For discrimination is an ambiguous virtue, depending on both knowledge and action yet differing radically from either of these two taken alone.'[30] It was based on their respective degree of 'complicity' with the society they studied that Lévi-Strauss proposed to distinguish between the 'social sciences', operating at the heart of the societies they studied (economics, legal studies, political science, social psychology and certain branches of sociology), and the 'human sciences', which operated from outside all particular societies (prehistory, archaeology, history, anthropology, linguistics, philosophy, logics, psychology). Only the latter could afford to adopt the 'uncompromising attitude' required to operate as a truly fundamental science, prepared to challenge an entire set of hypotheses and representations of the world.[31]

Lévi-Strauss was thus a man of action who built institutions designed to engage (and more importantly to allow others to engage) in a kind of research unconcerned with any practical application. This was a far remove from the dream of social engineering, which expected expert technicians to provide ready solutions for immediate implementation. When, in 1968, left-wing students – among whom were quite a few sociologists – mounted a violent challenge to the human and social sciences for their complicity in official decision-making, Lévi-Strauss, who had always been resistant to any such instrumentalization, did not feel in the least targeted by the critique, for he had never adhered to any such belief.

A mythical laboratory: The Laboratory of Social Anthropology (LAS)

Why a laboratory for anthropology? This new institution marked the epistemological shift in the discipline initiated by Lévi-Strauss: the point was no longer to describe (materially and symbolically) a given society, but to pose certain questions based on it. The objective now was to build theoretical models and not to collect, and then exhibit, material artefacts. It was for this reason that, in the narrative of the discipline, the LAS founded by Lévi-Strauss in 1960 came to stand as a new symbolic centre, as the Musée de l'Homme had done for anthropology in the 1930s. Other new research institutes were being started up at that time, such as Raymond Aron's Centre européen de sociologie (CES). But, unlike the CES, which no longer exists, the LAS has endured. More than fifty years old, it has become a major institution, a kind of 'resource commons' of the discipline, where many contemporary anthropologists, both French and foreign, have received their training and pursued their research.[32]

Grand beginnings . . .

In the early days, a certain acrobatic skill was required, but this initial lack of resources has only served to enhance the grand narrative of its origins. The power of the founding myth, which in moments of doubt and difficulty is regularly recalled, is indeed one of the distinctive characteristics of the LAS. It all began in 1960, between index cards and bathroom pipes.

At the outset, Lévi-Strauss pulled off something of a 'coup' against his superiors (and especially Gaston Berger), managing to convince them, thanks to his position at UNESCO, of the need for Europe to have a copy of the *Human Relations Areas Files*, an ethnographic database produced at Yale University of which there were only twenty-five,[33] and to entrust him with the responsibility of managing this information resource. In 1961, it comprised about two million index cards, organized in 380 double metal filing cabinets, weighing 7.5 tons and taking up 18 cubic metres of space.[34] These files were indexed line by line based on preselected terms, thus allowing for very rapid access to basic documentary information about a range of established anthropological topics. To the dream of systematic erudition was added the appeal of a proto-computer, which then represented the kind of cutting edge information technology that could enhance the scientific legitimacy of the entire discipline. This 'information centre for comparative anthropology' was the foundation, justification and jet engine of the laboratory, originally conceived and organized around the *Files*. These cabinets of sliding drawers full of index cards separated by cardboard dividers still stand to this day at the heart of the LAS, in the building in which it has been located since 1982, as a perennial reminder of their founding importance.

According to Lévi-Strauss, they were 'a research tool that compares, for the human sciences, with what a telescope or an electron microscope might be in the field of the natural sciences. [These files] comprise the contents of 3,000 books and articles concerning 289 populations. There are only twenty-five copies of the files in existence, twenty-three of which are located in the United States, one in Japan and one (ours) in Europe. It is regularly expanded through a subscription service with its manufacturer:

thus, between June 1960 and February 1962, we have received 232,000 new files on forty-seven populations. The rate of expansion is thus 150,000 per year.'[35] Lévi-Strauss resorted here to a numbers game. He also often dropped the names of users of the *Files*, which included a number of prestigious figures. Raymond Aron had consulted them for his research on 'war in primitive societies', and Gabriel Le Bras on 'markers of prestige in oral cultures', as well as Jacques Lacan, who had tracked down all the 'gestures of agreement and refusal in the world'.[36] As for Pierre Bourdieu, the assistant director of the Centre de sociologie européenne, who was still hesitating between anthropology (his studies on Algeria and the Béarn region) and sociology (of cultural practices), he had issued a 'request for research on the origin myths of fire, technology and women in Indo-European and African civilizations', for his current project on 'the relationship between myth and ritual in Indo-European civilizations'.[37] The peremptory tone and immense scope of the request for information startled Lévi-Strauss, who was nonetheless pleased to be able to demonstrate such keen interest in the *Files* from outside the discipline.

Year after year, like some monstrous creature, the *Files* kept growing bigger and heavier, whereas the space allocated to them remained the same, known as 'Mr Guimet's bathroom'. The LAS of the early days was something of a Bohemian laboratory, an incongruous space, an economy of ingenuity, headed by the already famous Professor Lévi-Strauss. The discrepancy between the scholar's aura and the meagre resources of the young laboratory struck all its visitors, with the exception of Susan Sontag who described it as a 'richly endowed research centre'.[38] In fact, as its founder recalled, 'we were originally hosted in an annex of the Musée Guimet, on avenue d'Iéna: Émile Guimet's old private mansion.[39] With three or four colleagues, I occupied a room that had once been a bathroom. Pieces of pipe still stuck out of the walls, which were covered with ceramic tiles, and I had what was left of the bathtub drain under my feet. We barely had room to move. I met with visitors on the landing, where we were able to offer them two worn-out lawn chairs.'[40]

What else was there? Desks, closets, metal filing cabinets, slide and microfilm cabinets, a ladder, a coat rack, two secretary desks, ten armchairs, as well as data processing and scientific machines: a stencil duplicator, two photocopy machines (Arcor and Polymicro), a projector for still images, two microfilm readers, an electric calculator, a stereophonic record-player, a camera, three tape recorders, electric typewriters (Olivetti, 'extended carriage' Everest, Olympia, Royal, etc.), and a celestial globe.[41] In other words, reproduction, photographic and recording machines to be used in the fieldwork studies initiated by the laboratory, the results of which it collected in the form of reports, then dissertations and books. Thus, the LAS accumulated the whole material environment necessary for social science research, while awaiting better conditions.

At Lévi-Strauss's side, fewer than ten people shared the premises of the LAS: Isac Chiva, its assistant director; Françoise Flis (Zonabend), his collaborator on the journal *Études Rurales*; Nicole Belmont, in charge of the *Files*; Solange Pinton, research coordinator; Tina Jolas, archivist;

Jean Pouillon, managing editor of the journal *L'Homme*; Michel Izard, research coordinator; Lucien Sebag, technical advisor in charge of the 'Mythologies' project; and Robert Jaulin, the Africanist anthropologist. Others quickly joined, for, despite the meagre resources, many young scholars wanted to take part, including Anne Chapman, Arlette Frigout and Olivier Herrenschmidt. But between the library, the *Files*, the journal, the secretarial office and the director's office, the ninety square metres on avenue de Iéna were bursting at the seams, and the growing enterprise was in desperate need of space. Chiva regularly complained to Clemens Heller, the key figure for logistics at the VIth Section of the EPHE: 'As far as I am concerned, I have half a desk in a room that I share with M. Claude Lévi-Strauss, the laboratory's director, Jean Pouillon, the managing editor of *L'Homme*, and Mrs Françoise Flis, my collaborator. The people in charge of accounting, mail, library resources and archiving as well as the receptionist are all five of them crammed in a single room together with the other members of the laboratory's secretarial staff. The three typewriters are tapping away while the single phone line we have is ringing, which makes the level of noise and clutter unconducive to any sustained work.'[42] This provisional situation was to last for several more years, and it was only in 1965–66 that the LAS was given new premises and a new lease on life.

Three men in a bathroom

The contrast between the long search for the ideal research facility and the immediately successful selection of close collaborators was striking. By inviting Isac Chiva and Jean Pouillon to work by his side, Lévi-Strauss laid two very solid cornerstones of the edifice he was in the process of building. The longevity of these two 'teams of horses', 'associates', 'skiffs' – all valid metaphors for describing their collaborations over two decades – attests to the team leader's discerning gaze. Two very different men who, together with Lévi-Strauss himself, formed an impressive, unpredictable and inseparable trio, which lent the LAS, from the very start, a modern, efficient (despite the difficulties) and appealing air. The three men were serious yet also ready with a pun – a trinity of wit – and scrupulous in carrying out their responsibilities; yet they never took themselves too seriously, and left ample space for silence and autonomy, which characterized the atmosphere of the Lévi-Straussian ecosystem.

Isac Chiva was a survivor of the Iasi massacre of 22 June 1941, one of the first of the Second World War pogroms.[43] After the war, he decided to flee Romanian anti-Semitism and the lead weight of communist rule. He left on foot from Bucharest in November 1947 and crossed all of Europe, via Budapest and Vienna, arriving in Paris on 20 January 1948. He was twenty-two, and accompanied by his two friends Paul Celan and Serge Moscovici. The three of them decided together to stop speaking Romanian. A Yiddish speaker in his childhood, who had then adopted the Romanian language, Chiva's capacity for learning foreign languages was part of a kind of linguistic survival kit. In his new French life, he opted for an anthropology of the near, focusing his studies on the Sologne, then the Touraine regions, and later Corsica. Encouraged by Lévi-Strauss, he pioneered studies, in collaboration with the Centre pour l'énergie atomique (CEA), on the socioeconomic transformations triggered by the installation of nuclear power plants at the Bagnols-sur-Cèze and Marcoule sites, thus conducting an anthropology of high technology. At the Musée des arts et traditions populaires (ATP), where he was a research fellow, he worked of course with Georges-Henri Rivière, but also Marcel Maget, his doctoral supervisor, and Claude Lévi-Strauss, who became his 'sponsor' at the CNRS in the early 1950s. Chiva and Lévi-Strauss never spoke (or very little) of their common Jewishness; nor did Chiva elaborate much on his extraordinary odyssey as a young man. But when the time came, in 1955, to secure the support of Jacques Soustelle, then resident-general in Algeria, to assist Chiva in obtaining French nationality, Lévi-Strauss did so with all the vigour and diligence of which he was capable. In 1959, Chiva left the CNRS to join the VIth Section of EPHE, hired by Fernand Braudel to create the journal *Études rurales* and to coedit it alongside the medieval historian Georges Duby. At the same time, Lévi-Strauss asked him to join in the LAS adventure, which started a year later. He accepted both offers, with the idea of 'having the two machines converge'.[44]

From then on, Chiva deployed his numerous talents as ambassador and prime minister of the LAS. He put his many connections in the world of research as well as in government circles into the service of the young laboratory, acting as liaison when necessary and negotiating with the different actors, all the while demonstrating an exceptional talent for institutional arrangements, financial negotiations and management of 'human resources', as it was not yet called. Indeed, he served as a kind of 'go-between' for the laboratory researchers and anthropologists and, together with Lévi-Strauss himself, as their main interlocutor. If he sometimes garnered hostile reactions, Chiva knew how to defuse situations and often served as a kind of substitute father figure, including for Lévi-Strauss's own son Laurent, who joined the laboratory in the late 1960s. Chiva advised and helped him. He was very close to him and considered him as an adoptive son, in the same way as he did Celan's son. He was also close friends with Pierre Bourdieu, whose first article, 'Célibat et condition paysanne en Béarn', he published in *Études rurales* in 1962.

Sacrificed to a certain extent on the altar of scientific administration, Chiva's entire scholarly activity focused on European rural communities, a peasant world that had been entirely closed to the young Eastern European Jew that he was. Fascinated by an object that had rejected him, Chiva, at the end of his life, claimed he still felt 'profoundly alien'.[45] This Romanian Jewish survivor and the French Israelite from old bourgeois stock were in near total agreement, based on a debt of gratitude that Lévi-Strauss expressed on several occasions, especially during difficult periods for Chiva, due to physical or emotional problems: 'I have not said that the laboratory helped me directly in my own work', he wrote to him in 1976, 'but that I could never have managed to do it if you had not so greatly relieved me of the task of managing that institution. And this is so beyond question that you would not contest it yourself. I don't often say it, but I am profoundly grateful to you for this. However, I wish, even if the laboratory were to suffer as a result, that in the next few years you would decide to live for yourself a little, and under less impossible working conditions than those you have suffered until now.'[46] When Chiva reproached himself for not producing a substantial body of work, Lévi-Strauss would reassure him; when Chiva fell ill, Lévi-Strauss felt guilty. Still in 2003, Lévi-Strauss applied the efficient balm of writing, in a trembling hand: 'I would not allow myself to forget that prior to the past twenty years, there were another twenty during which – to use your expression – your presence by my side was in no way symbolic. For I would never have embarked on the adventure of the laboratory if I had not known that you were ready to come along with me.'[47]

Jean Pouillon was 'alien' in a different way. He came from elsewhere, professionally speaking, but also politically and ideologically. A philosophy student, in 1945 Pouillon became a parliamentary secretary, a privileged vantage point from which to analyse French politics and one that left him with a considerable amount of free time (not to mention an ample living). Time to write a book on the notion of time – whose structural perspective Lévi-Strauss was later to emphasize[48] – as well as to take part in the postwar literary and intellectual life. He was in Sartre's and Simone de Beauvoir's inner circle and one of the kingpins at *Les Temps modernes*. What is less known is that he cultivated close ties with the world of pataphysics, and a long standing involvement with Georges Perec.[49] In 1956, he published a long article in *Les Temps modernes* on the work of Claude Lévi-Strauss, which demonstrated an in-depth understanding of the structuralist project, expressed in concise and precise language. It was in 1958, at the age of forty-two, that he conducted his first anthropological fieldwork in the mountains of central Chad, where he tried his hand at making sense of the politico-religious organization of the Hadjerai peoples.

When, in 1960, Lévi-Strauss offered him the editorship of the journal *L'Homme*, which was to be launched the following year, Pouillon was known as one of the *'porteurs de valises'* ['the suitcase carriers'] who supplied aid to the armed struggle of the Algerian FLN; he was, in addition, one of the most active signatories of the 'Manifesto of the 121' advocating the desertion of French military personnel called up to fight in Algeria, and one of the first five to have been sentenced following his signing, alongside Maurice Blanchot, Dyonis Mascolo, Jean-Paul Sartre and Maurice Nadeau. It was at this precise moment that Lévi-Strauss chose to hire this controversial figure, whereas he himself remained silent and abstained from taking any part in the political life of intellectuals – and indeed declined to sign the Manifesto of the 121. What are we to make of this move? These two men chose each other, in a way, and the fact that Lévi-Strauss called upon Pouillon would seem about as improbable as Pouillon accepting his offer, above all under these circumstances, whose gravity and divisiveness, right in the middle of the Jeanson trial, must be kept in mind.[50]

In the 1960s, Pouillon divided his time between *Les Temps modernes* and *L'Homme*, between existentialism and structuralism, attempting an

Cover of the first issue of *L'Homme*, a journal published from 1961 by the Laboratoire d'anthropologie sociale and intended to enhance France's position in the international field of anthropological research.

impossible reconciliation before finally resolving to embrace his contradictions, which he called his 'divergent squint'.[51] He became the 'attentive, affable, discreet and firm'[52] editor of a journal that was originally to straddle three disciplines (anthropology, linguistics and geography) but whose anthropological component unsurprisingly outgrew the others, as was made clear by the hiring of André Leroi-Gourhan, Georges-Henri Rivière and André-Georges Haudricourt a few years later. By the mid-1960s, thanks to its imposing presence, the seriousness of its articles and the name of Lévi-Strauss, *L'Homme* had managed to successfully establish itself in the field of international social science journals. Linked with the structuralist paradigm but open to others, it was, like the LAS with which it was associated, the integrative platform for a booming discipline that was supported by a dynamic institution: the VIth Section of the EPHE.

For thirty-five years, Pouillon was 'the man at *L'Homme*'.[53] In the first issue, a discreet note called on interested researchers to address their correspondence to him. Having become a central figure in the structuralist world, he transformed what had been a reference to the individual work of Lévi-Strauss into a collective research project, attracting many researchers who found in the journal an attentive ear and a prestigious outlet for their work. This tall, bespectacled and slightly stooped man was brilliant, quick, with a strong sense of friendship and a penchant for collective intellectual experiments, in which he was still engaged ten years later, when he finally succumbed to pressure from his friend Jean-Bertrand Pontalis to take on new responsibilities at *La Nouvelle Revue de psychanalyse*, created in 1970. A journals man, he was a passer-on and a passer-by; as Michel Izard recalled, 'there is an inimitable Pouillon way of tackling an anthropological question as if *in passing*',[54] what Françoise Héritier recalled his 'anthropological punning'[55] and others his 'epistemological wit',[56] a rather idiosyncratic way of expressing his 'pleasure at not comprehending', at the oddity of anthropological situations where misunderstandings reigned: 'The pleasure of not understanding spurs one to try again and again, and does not preclude the occasional success, while still preserving, as vividly as possible, the memory of the initial puzzlement.'[57]

Pouillon and Chiva were, in the end, not very academic types. They carried inside themselves plural worlds that protected them from all forms of sectarianism and made room for dreams and play.[58] Like Lévi-Strauss himself, these men had kept alive the child's taste for discovery. They formed a small band forged in masculine camaraderie within a laboratory that comprised as many women researchers as men. It was this team that set out in conquest of scientific recognition, but first of new premises and new resources.

1966: a (double) fresh start

The early years at LAS were punctuated by a long series of complaints, calculations, vociferations and justifications, all revolving around the crucial question of physical premises. If Lévi-Strauss finally managed to have his laboratory relocated to the Collège de France, on Place Marcelin-Berthelot, this was due to his and Chiva's relentless importuning year after year, but also to the Collège's desire for reform and the new economic plan confirming the French state's commitment to investment in the sciences.

In 1961, Lévi-Strauss submitted a request to Marcel Bataillon, the Collège administrator at the time, for the 500 square metres of office space he considered necessary to decently accommodate the *Files*, an adjoining reading room, two offices for archivists, a photographic workshop, fifteen offices for researchers and a reading and conference room.[59] This in itself highlighted certain changes in scholarly practices: the human and social sciences, under Lévi-Strauss's leadership, now had research ambitions that required considerable archival and publishing infrastructure. The shift was in step with the Collège de France's realization that its own scholarly brand, though still prestigious, had become somewhat old-fashioned. Marcel Bataillon, and then his successor Étienne Wolff, were keen to initiate a transformation of the institution, promoted by the state, and to move away from the artisanal phase of research, mindful of not 'thinking too small'.[60] Funding from the French state's Fifth Plan (1966–70), amounting in these boom years to twenty-eight million new francs, was there for the taking. There was thus ample scope for Lévi-Strauss to have the faculty assembly vote for social anthropology to be granted the status of 'laboratory chair', which entitled it to far greater office space. We should point out, however, that in 1966, out of fifty-two chairs, thirty-eight had no laboratory.[61] In the human sciences, professors generally requested 150–200 square metres, as was the case for Benveniste, Braudel and Berque. However, Jean Filliozat (Indian languages and literatures) and René Labat (Assyriology) had requested 1,000 square metres, while François Perroux (analysis of economic and social facts) wanted 950. Lévi-Strauss requested 2,000 without batting an eye, and added in the margins for Chiva's attention: 'We must not settle for a centimetre less!'[62] The aggressive stance of the young discipline reaped what it had so doggedly and ambitiously sowed, and what it had carefully justified in terms of needs. The LAS began to move into its new home in 1965, but building work (financed by the VIth Section) continued until 1967, and even 1970, when the walls were given their final coat of paint.

In the beginning, the rooms were run-down and poorly lit, but the location – at the heart of the Latin Quarter, in a building that, much to Lévi-Strauss's delight, recalled an earlier moment of science – was incomparable. The sumptuous and old-fashioned decor fulfilled his scholarly dream of settling, with his modernist ambitions and scientific avant-gardism, into a Baudelairian cabinet of curiosities: 'I remember that during my visits as a candidate in 1959, I had gone to see the gentleman who held the chair in geology. His laboratory was on the top floor, in a wing of the building constructed at the end of the eighteenth century by Chalgrin. In addition to the professor's office and some attics, there were two large and majestic rooms where a few isolated individuals could be found working at big oak tables. Along the walls, with decorative pilaster at the corners, were mahogany cabinets, high enough to lean on, rather plain but admirably designed and proportioned. Under the Restoration these must have represented the *ne plus ultra* of what we today call office furniture. I learned that they contained the mineral collections of Louis XIII. [. . .] I was seized with a sudden desire. Nowhere else, I thought, would I rather spend my days than in these spacious, silent and secret rooms, which still retained the aura of a mid-nineteenth-century library or laboratory. That was how I saw the Collège de France that I aspired to enter: the workplace of Claude Bernard, Ernest Renan . . . .'[63] Once settled in, Lévi-Strauss had to agree to partition these spacious rooms, but, while the mineral collections went to Sceaux, he preserved the professor's original office intact, 'with its old-fashioned enclosed bookcases and woodwork painted to look like oak. That was a job for a real craftsman, which added to the cost.'[64] The new location had yet another consequence: it definitively distanced the LAS from the Musée de l'Homme (to which it had been geographically close), symbolically consecrating the autonomy of the laboratory as a new anthropological institution, integrated into the Collège de France, whose chair was considered inseparable from the work of the laboratory, and vice versa. The LAS on Place Marcelin-Berthelot marked the abandonment of the museum model.

From the start, it was a joint creation of the Collège de France and the École pratique des hautes études (Vth and VIth Sections), the two institutions at which Lévi-Strauss taught. Thanks to the alliance with Braudel, the overall arrangement was the following: the EPHE would finance most of the payroll, as well as operating and publishing costs, while the Collège would be responsible for the facilities and related costs, like small equipment, etc. By 1 January 1966, the LAS had obtained its affiliation with the CNRS – the longstanding friendship between Lévi-Strauss and geographer Pierre Monbeig (a São Paulo man), the CNRS assistant director, likely facilitated matters. The national institution would contribute considerably to funding, research work and the recruitment of scientific personnel. If the laboratory was a creature of the VIth Section, with which it shared a scientific project, its incorporation into the CNRS (Convention number 51), together with the move to the new offices, brought it into a kind of institutional adulthood, with greater financial resources, considerable space and the broader prestige of a teaching chair. The LAS had the honour of being the first social science laboratory of the Collège de France.

This triple affiliation (EPHE, Collège de France, CNRS) was an administrative oddity, a complicated arrangement, but a good provider of resources. The funding and staff grew: in 1962, the laboratory's budget was 174,292 new francs, out of which only 9,000 came from the Collège de France. By 1966, the Collège gave 108,891 new francs, while the CNRS provided 100,000 (55,000 for operating and equipment costs, 11,000 for temporary workers, 34,200 for travel expenses). The VIth Section continued to contribute to the financing of the laboratory, but the exact amount is unknown.[65] The LAS thus gradually became a substantial operation: by 1967, it boasted fifteen doctoral students, eighty journal subscriptions, and numerous temporary and permanent researchers in residence, from France and abroad, all the more easily accommodated now that the attic rooms had been transformed into additional offices. The seven permanent staff members in 1960 had become a team of fifty-nine by 1982, including thirty-three researchers.

For this rapid growth Lévi-Strauss and Chiva paid a high price – with the increased resources came greater administrative responsibilities. From 1966, the amount of paperwork intensified: activity and project reports, receipts, committee meetings, as well as budget forecasts, proposals, accounts, statements of medium-term projects and goals. The LAS administrative archive offers a glimpse into a regime of scientific production that anticipates the one of today. It is full of discussions of funding, equipment and staff. A laboratory is like a small business that must account for and show returns on its investments. In this case it was public money. Which is why Lévi-Strauss, very fastidious in this regard, was particularly attentive to the importance of 'making things known, of the need to publicly account for the multiple activities of a publicly funded scientific organization, in great detail and with the utmost attention to form'.[66] He himself drafted, or at least thoroughly reviewed, the annual activity reports. If they displayed the same elegant clarity of his prose style, they also showed the same concision, especially by comparison with the demands of today, since each report was no longer than twenty pages at most.

Alongside these new public accounting practices introduced by the CNRS, the LAS retained its initial fundraising culture, as strongly encouraged by the VIth Section and Braudel. Indeed, American philanthropy in France was more inclined to finance laboratories and research centres than public university structures, whose accounting practices and outcomes were more unpredictable.[67] Monique Lévi-Strauss was called upon to organize many a dinner at the couple's home, on rue des Marronniers, in honour of Ford and Rockefeller Foundation emissaries, men whom Lévi-Strauss already knew from his New York days, and whose interest in his activity he would foster through a combination of seriousness and sociability, greatly aided by his wife, who was both an excellent cook and a fluent English speaker. She gladly participated in these events, of whose strategic importance she was well aware.[68] Various foundations contributed to the development of the LAS over the years, but one in particular played a decisive and enduring role: the Wenner-Gren Foundation for Anthropological Research, a major institutional actor in the world of anthropological research. Lévi-Strauss cultivated a relationship with Paul Fejos, its director and driving force, and, upon the latter's death, with his wife Lita Binns Fejos.[69] In 1960, the foundation paid the annual $2,000 rent to the Vth Section of the EPHE for the LAS offices in the annex of the Musée Guimet. The grant was renewed every year until 1965; later, the foundation would also fund travel grants. All this was provided in exchange for Lévi-Strauss's services as a consultant, evaluating applications and providing diverse expertise.

More than fifty years after the laboratory's founding, we are in a position to measure the full magnitude of Lévi-Strauss's institutional acumen, in erecting this rather unlikely scaffolding: a laboratory straddling three institutions, tied up in a sometimes constraining tangle of administrative hierarchies, yet one that guaranteed the longevity of the whole. In its unabashed combination of public institutional culture and private financing, as well as its collective conception of science, 'this complex organization owed a great deal to his previous experience around the world, as a researcher, teacher and cultural diplomat'.[70] It stands as a monument to this period of his life, profoundly his.

Laboratory life

From 1960 until 1982, when he retired from the Collège de France, Claude Lévi-Strauss was intensely involved in the life of the LAS. His correspondence with Chiva attests to this new task of running the 'laboratory machine'. Whether from Paris or the countryside, from France or abroad, he exchanged an uninterrupted flow of letters with the laboratory whose development he oversaw, torn between satisfaction and impatience, amusement and annoyance. For laboratory life was no picnic. Between the departures on assignment, the personal dramas large and small, and daily logistics, he had to manage the political and sentimental energies of a very particular group of people. The LAS was a distinctive ecosystem, which differed from the other great social science laboratories created at the time, such as Georges Balandier's Centre d'études africaines (1957) and Raymond Aron's Centre européen de sociologie (1960).

A tribe of 'disappearing people'

Françoise Zonabend, who officially joined the LAS in 1964, mysteriously said: 'We were disappearing people.'[71] Anthropologists leave, and then return, changed. Indeed, fieldwork was the absent heart of the LAS, just as the *Files* were its symbolic centre.

As surprising as it may seem, Lévi-Strauss always hammered home to his students the absolute necessity of doing fieldwork. All remember him to be very open about everything except fieldwork, which was preferably to be conducted among peoples who were the most preserved from contact with civilization. Pierre Clastres, who arrived at the LAS in the early 1960s, prepared a doctoral dissertation under Lévi-Strauss's supervision entitled 'The Social Life of a Nomadic Tribe: The Guayaki Indians of Paraguay'. After Paraguay, he switched to Brazil, where he still hesitated as to which path to follow: 'Regarding your projects, I understand that you are renouncing the Bororo, but it seems necessary to me that you spend a few months with a still intact and active population. Otherwise, you will always be lacking the experience.'[72] A few months later, Lévi-Strauss further specified his recommendation: 'I remain convinced that your anthropological training shall remain incomplete so long as you have not spent several months with a tribe whose traditional lifestyle has for the most part been preserved. Otherwise, you run the risk of being constantly reproached for not having acquired, as part of your intellectual and mental training, an experience that I myself hold to be as fundamental as training analysis in psychoanalysis.'[73] In fact, from the early 1950s, he had always expressed how much he valued the fieldwork experience, which alone could give anthropological training its 'backbone'. Indeed, in his view, the anthropologist could only access the required level of interpersonal interpretation through an intense personal experience, an 'inner revolution that will really make him into a new man'.[74] Fieldwork was a 'crucial stage of his education prior to which he may possess discontinuous knowledge that will never form a whole'. After engaging in fieldwork 'his knowledge will acquire an organic unity'.[75] Lévi-Strauss pursued the psychoanalytic metaphor, defining the mission of the thesis director as providing '"supervised" fieldwork'.[76] His correspondence with researchers off doing fieldwork shows him acting as an elder, in close contact with his anthropologists in training, sharing in their inner transformation – which he would then re-experience from afar.

So, apprentice researchers would set off to far-flung corners of the world. This was no small part of the appeal of the job. But it was no small task either to arrange for the financing and organizing of these journeys, often complicated and sometimes even dangerous. Indeed, it constituted one of the main missions of the laboratory, aside from documentation, intellectual training and publications. As Lévi-Strauss reiterated time and again to administrative superiors and colleagues, the LAS was to be 'constantly regenerated by the contribution of "fresh" material from the fieldwork of researchers trained for that purpose'.[77] Hence the demand for funding, and the regular reports on projects already under way. Anne Chapman, for example, conducted fieldwork in Tierra del Fuego in 1963–64, where she met 'the last of the Ona Indians, aged 95, who still spoke her language, knew her customs, and the traditional chants which she [the anthropologist] recorded on tape, thus capturing the ultimate, and richest, testimony of a formerly much-vaunted culture, whose definitive disappearance would come with the death of the elderly Lola'.[78] At that time, roughly ten researchers were engaged in fieldwork or returning from it: Arian Deluz in Côte d'Ivoire, Lucien Sebag and Pierre Clastres in Paraguay, Bernard Saladin d'Anglure with the Inuits of Hudson's Bay, and Arlette Frigout with the Pueblo of Arizona; Robert Jaulin had just returned from Colombia (Bari Indians) and Maurice Godelier was on his way to New Guinea.

The comings and goings of the various members sometimes gave the laboratory the feel of a train terminal: on the platform, incidents were recounted, anecdotes shared, situations assessed. The two stationmasters, Chiva and Lévi-Strauss, managed logistics from Paris, which sometimes involved some quick thinking, between shortages of funds, emotional crises and accidents. They received film to develop, provided intellectual support for emerging hypotheses, raised morale when it was low – for example, when Pierre Clastres lost all his belongings in a fire in the cabin where they were being stored. This was not to be the last of his misfortunes. While in São Paulo, following in the master's footsteps, an administrative imbroglio left him penniless, with nothing but an expired passport. He waited for the CNRS to send him a money order. This took several months, which considerably annoyed Lévi-Strauss, who called for a veritable 'war council' to unblock the situation. Pouillon even turned to Sartre, who interceded on his behalf and asked some rich Brazilian friends of his to lend Clastres some money! At the other end of the world, following a landslide caused by abundant rains, Maurice Godelier's car turned over and he was sent to Port Moresby Hospital, where he was diagnosed with a severe fracture of the femur. Lévi-Strauss was worried sick, and despaired: 'We are really unlucky in our fieldwork!'[79]

Even so, Chiva and Lévi-Strauss were like a couple of doting nannies, watching over their little charges. The umbilical cord of correspondence was crucial: Clastres called Lévi-Strauss 'Monsieur', and the latter addressed him as 'my dear friend'. Clastres identified with the master in his disappointment with fieldwork that did not meet his expectations. Indeed, he reread *Tristes Tropiques* at that time: 'I can assure you that, compared with the Guayaki, the Nambikwara look like a highly developed society. And this is precisely what I am worried about: Guayaki culture (regarding economic, social, and religious life as well as art, chiefdom, myths, etc.) seems to me too poor to be primitive.'[80] Off in a very Lévi-Straussian universe, Clastres was having second thoughts and talked of submitting a dissertation proposal in political anthropology. Lévi-Strauss, open-minded, replied: 'Alright. Political anthropology is nearly virgin territory to which you can contribute much.'[81] A few years later, in 1971, doing fieldwork with Jacques Lizot in Venezuela, visiting the Yanomami Indians, he got stuck in Caracas, almost 'killed off' by a virulent case of malaria, but claimed to be happy with his work and asked Chiva to tell Lévi-Strauss, notably about the aspect that was of the most interest to him: 'political power and the relations between chiefdom and society', which was to become the subject of his doctoral work. In the end, several years down the line, Clastres heeded the advice of his doctoral supervisor, while still striking out on his own path, since he visited a quasi-intact tribe with whom he lived a 'memorable experience'. In Caracas, two years earlier, Jean Monod was hit in the arm by a stray projectile while taking part in a student demonstration, and put out of commission for two months. The tone of his letters to the two Parisian bosses was different based on which one he was addressing – warmer and more familiar with Chiva, more formal and ceremonious with Lévi-Strauss. Yet the two men discussed the letters they received from their wards together, lamenting or rejoicing over them, not without a shared sense of humour: 'The letter from Monod is a beautiful piece of literature; I am saving it for him, as it could find a place in his next book!'[82]

The overriding imperative to find funding for fieldwork led Lévi-Strauss and Chiva to seize any and all opportunities and make arrangements that were sometimes a bit perilous. In 1967–68, Jean Monod, who had originally been drawn to the LAS by its 'scope'[83] and the intellectual stimulation of Lévi-Strauss, and had been 'converted'[84] to studying the Americas, thus found himself embarking on a strange fieldwork assignment to Venezuela. He was to accompany the French contingent of an international team of physicians, whose main goal seems to have been genetic research. The French cohort was under the direction of the Comité à l'énergie atomique. A large company of about fifteen American researchers was deployed around the anthropologist Napoleon Chagnon – a specialist of the Yanomami, one of the largest isolated groups of humans living in the remote mountains of Venezuela, on the border with Brazil – and a geneticist specializing in atomic contamination. The two young ethnographers that Lévi-Strauss managed to get on board, Jean Monod and Jacques Lizot, felt quite out of place on this opaque project and strongly suspected they served as the 'anthropological alibi' for a radically different and somewhat dubious purpose (having to do with hypotheses related to nuclear war).[85]

The LAS was thus a multifaceted laboratory, whose life was also shaped by the rhythm of the seasons: the arrival of droves of foreign colleagues (in June) signalled the coming of summer. Lévi-Strauss was happy to meet with them – when he did not flee them . . . allowing himself periods of absence as he advanced in years. But the LAS was also rife with disappearances of an emotional and existential kind. Is the anthropological calling particularly prone to such vanishings? Indeed, the LAS was full of ghosts, suicides, nervous breakdowns and 'shady deaths'.[86] Métraux's shadow hovered over it. He took his own life in 1963. More tragic still, since the victim was younger and full of promise, Lucien Sebag committed suicide in 1965. He was a disciple of Lévi-Strauss, if ever there was one: 'With Sebag, he felt there was someone who fully understood him.'[87] To honour the dearly departed acolyte, and so that all would not be in vain, Lévi-Strauss made a very strange request of a young Argentine student who had come to seek his advice. He offered to Carmen Bernand (then Munoz, her maiden name) that she 'clean up' the fieldwork notebooks left behind by Sebag, and undertake a kind of posthumous doctoral ventriloquism, to which she agreed. The book, *Les Ayoré du Chaco septentrional: Études critiques à partir des notes de Lucien Sebag* (1977), gave the deceased young man one final opportunity to make his voice heard.[88]

Finally, on a more melodramatic, if ultimately no less tragic, note, the laboratory was also haunted by the memory of Arlette Frigout. A specialist of Pueblo and Hopi Indians,[89] she believed Lévi-Strauss (as well as de Gaulle) to be in love with her and showed up in his office one day armed with a revolver. The latter went pale but managed to keep his composure and get away from the woman, only falling apart once he arrived back at home. Frigout was asked to leave the LAS, and committed suicide a few years later.[90] Although her obsession with the master was clearly an individual case of emotional fragility, which had been revealed during her very difficult fieldwork experience,[91] it nonetheless shed light on the situation at a laboratory where the level of intellectual and affective energy caused quite a few sparks to fly.

The ladies of the lab

From the very outset, the LAS counted many women among its personnel, and not only in the usual secretarial and librarian posts, but also as anthropological researchers, the sign of a discipline that in institutional terms had yet to find full recognition. Their backgrounds were varied, with many roads leading to anthropology. Françoise Héritier, who joined as a 'research coordinator', had studied geography, while Nicole Belmont described herself as a 'young woman from a good family' who had been hired as a temp at the Musée des arts et traditions populaires. 'On loan' from Georges-Henri Rivière to his friend, she was responsible for Lévi-Strauss's personal research material, until the latter advised her to pursue doctoral work on 'babies born with the caul'.[92] Then there was Edna Lemay, Lévi-Strauss's secretary at the Conseil international des sciences sociales, who followed him to the LAS, before she switched to Fernand Braudel. Later on, Janine Kevonian and Evelyne Guedj took over as Lévi-Strauss's personal secretaries. All were strong personalities and very pretty women, as the various group photographs taken over the years show. Lévi-Strauss and Chiva's hiring techniques were highly idiosyncratic: they considered faces first, staring at them in total silence, before looking at applications.[93] Marion Abelès remembered being subjected to this ritual before applying as the new LAS librarian, upon Liliane Poëtte's departure.[94] A male gaze, but one that nonetheless remained irreproachably courteous at all times. Lévi-Strauss called women by their first names and men by their family names. They called him 'Monsieur', with a mixture of deference and reverence. After 1968, with Nicole-Claude Mathieu and a few others, the LAS developed a more staunchly feminist culture, which may have changed the relationships with the men at the lab, but did not have much effect on relationships with its director. In the meantime, in the 1960s, women wore skirts: 'It wouldn't have dawned on anyone to come to the laboratory wearing trousers. Women who work had to have style.'[95] This internalization of a certain way of being female at work only echoed what was going on outside the lab. Claude Lévi-Strauss never imposed any dress code of course, but he himself was always impeccably attired. By that time, he no longer wore a silk tie but a kind of bolo tie, a copper drawstring tassel that gave him a slightly original look. This sartorial care also expressed a kind of gentlemanly respect for the other that both Lévi-Strauss and Chiva cultivated.

The laboratory was not without its share of conflicts, from professional rivalries to proverbial hatreds and petty jibes. 'At the lab, the ladies seem to be at loggerheads again. X complains of constant barbed comments. The others are quite offended that, without telling anyone, she has brought in a temporary assistant, whereas others might have done the job. Everyone's a little to blame here, again. I try my best to smooth things over until it all gets sorted out with everyone going on vacation.'[96] In moments of tension, the reigning atmosphere was one of a 'seraglio',[97] where nothing was addressed openly. Yet several factors contradict the existence of the kind of hierarchical organization and professionalization of tasks that can sometimes lead to acrimony. First, the striking professional mobility that characterized pioneer institutions of this kind, at which status mattered less and the boundaries between 'support' and 'research' staff were porous. It was thus possible to begin as a librarian and end up as an anthropologist affiliated with the CNRS, a move that has become unthinkable today. In addition, this small tribe of men and women seemed to maintain very strong bonds of seduction and sociability. 'There were very attractive men and women there, who were all intelligent and sometimes very good-looking.'[98] Indeed, as in the rest of academia, the world of LAS anthropologists was characterized by a very strong practice of endogamy: many a couple was made, unmade, and remade. A veritable sentimental ballet, where professional activity always involved private life choices, especially with regard to fieldwork. Françoise Héritier first married Michel Izard, then Marc Augé, who also specialized in African anthropology but was closer to Balandier. Michel Izard, for his part, found a new partner in Marie Mauzé, an anthropologist and member of the LAS who specialized in the tribes of British Columbia. Isac Chiva married the Africanist Ariane Deluz. The LAS included other couples still: Pierre Maranda, a Canadian colleague and very close friend of Lévi-Strauss, and his wife the anthropologist Elli Köngäs, as well as Pierre and Hélène Clastres. Even after divorce, the former couple would often continue to work side by side at the laboratory. Moving in together was sometimes akin to the abduction of Helen. Robert Jaulin, an Africanist (*La Mort Sara*, 1967) then Americanist anthropologist and a sharp and brilliant mind, who introduced the concept of 'ethnocide' in the late 1960s and revised anthropological fieldwork in light of his turn to left-wing politics, set off for Colombia bringing Solange Pinton, the LAS librarian, with him on a very glamorous journey. They disappeared for several months with the Bari Indians, on the Venezuelan border. Another flamboyant personality was a friend of Monique Lévi-Strauss, hired to take care of the *Files*: Tina Jolas. She was an erudite, brilliant, bilingual woman who had translated works of British anthropology, notably the famous *Diary* of Malinowski.[99] But her main concern in life was love. Married to the poet André du Bouchet, she fell in love with René Char, with whom she engaged in a passionate, sacrificial and lasting liaison until his death.[100] She was one of the four fieldworkers in Minot: 'Every morning, she went to fetch her letter from Char.'[101]

A Lévi-Straussian institution

Surprisingly, there was no theoretical orthodoxy at the LAS. While Raymond Aron, the charismatic leader of French sociology in the 1960s, did not really have any paradigm to offer his students, Lévi-Strauss, the leading figure in anthropology, did have one at his disposal, for which his laboratory could have served as the operational base. But this was not the case. A question of temperament, probably: Lévi-Strauss was not inclined to playing the intellectual guru, and still less the life guru. The LAS, a 'community of loners', as Isac Chiva had defined it, was thus never the 'collective intellectual' of the Durkheimian school, nor the fusional group that worked as a great intentional family at the Centre de sociologie européenne, founded by Bourdieu in 1968,[102] where everyone embraced Bourdieu's sociological vision and principles. In contrast, Lévi-Strauss would sometimes say that 'there isn't a single structuralist at the LAS!'[103]

The LAS was thus not conceived as a theoretical engine room, but as a place where researchers, who were free to choose their objects of study as well as their methodologies, would receive the resources they needed to pursue their work. In other words, the instrument was collective, but intended for research that was conceived as individual. This ran somewhat counter to the logic promoted by the CNRS consisting of collective thinking in the pursuit of increasingly integrated research. From that perspective, in the mind of Lévi-Strauss, the LAS was probably more of a workshop than a laboratory. Nevertheless, the laboratory and seminar it hosted were sites of scholarly community, insofar as they provided forums for discussing and comparing experiences and findings from all over the world.

Indeed, in addition to theoretical pluralism, which sometimes led to 'harsh' debates,[104] the LAS was also characterized by a generalist orientation: even if all the regions of the globe were not represented (especially

East Asia, which was treated by other fields and institutions in the French orientalist tradition), the Americas, Africa and Oceania all had their anthropologists. In yet another decisive choice, the great divide between exotic and European societies was nonexistent there. The presence of Isac Chiva and the journal *Études rurales* attracted specialists of the European rural worlds, to which the post-1968 regionalist revival added new recruits, definitively taking the anthropology of the near beyond the field of folklore. At the laboratory, Françoise Zonabend, Marie-Claude Pingaud, Yvonne Verdier, Nicole Belmont and others were all Europeanists who also maintained lively exchanges with medieval and modern historians, who were themselves in the midst of an anthropological turn. Claude Lévi-Strauss took a keen interest in it and, even though he never practised it, considered this anthropology just as legitimate, for it used similar methods as the anthropology of the remote. At first, Africanists were not expected to join the LAS – Lévi-Strauss was an Americanist after all (as is often forgotten) – and, above all, other specialized laboratories already existed, notably that of Georges Balandier. In addition, Africanists – working on societies that had experienced colonialism and were in full, postcolonial historical transformation – initially felt less comfortable in the structuralist world that had developed out of other empirical contexts. Many were Marxists or affiliated with Marxism. However, from the mid-1960s onward, the aggregative logic of the LAS, supported by Lévi-Strauss, met with success. The laboratory became richer; and it was headed by an anthropologist of international renown who directed a journal which, like the laboratory on which it depended, did not impose any official party line. Brilliant young researchers had already chosen it as their home. It was thus not entirely surprising that senior researchers at the Vth and VIth Sections, especially Africanists, should join the LAS. This was the case of Claude Tardits, as well as Julian Pitt-Rivers and Hans Dietschy. Whereas Africanists traditionally outnumbered others within French anthropology, they did not dominate the LAS in the early years, but did become better represented later, in the 1980s.

Indeed, if the laboratory as well as the journal *L'Homme* affirmed a generalist orientation, one of the original missions of the LAS in Lévi-Strauss's mind nonetheless unsurprisingly remained the revival of the French field of American anthropology. 'As you may already know, our laboratory strives to give new life to French research on the Americas, which had fallen into deep slumber since the passing of Dr Rivet.'[105] For sure, Rivet's personality had helped catalyse the study of the Americas, but the specialization had already acquired a 'quaint' quality by the time of Lévi-Strauss's youth, which had probably also contributed to its appeal for the young anthropologist, steering him in that direction.[106] Yet, at the start of the 1960s, he intended to turn this liability (both empirical and intellectual) into an asset, exploring these still virgin lands and encouraging young researchers to do their fieldwork there. With the director general of the CNRS, he pleaded the case with customary flair: 'Study of the Americas is now going through a serious recruiting crisis in France and it seems to me that an effort needs to be made to rebuild research teams in a field where France has always been a leader.'[107] During the 1960s, Lévi-Strauss enabled (directly and indirectly) numerous anthropologists to go off to the Americas for fieldwork: Arlette Frigout (Arizona), Pierre Clastres and Lucien Sebag (Paraguay), Robert Jaulin (Colombia), Jacques Lizot (Colombia/Venezuela), Jean Monod (Venezuela), Simone Dreyfus-Gamelon (Brazilian Amazonia), Carmen Bernand and Marina Le Clézio (Mexico).

However, a curse seemed to plague French anthropology of the Americas. A series of deaths, departures and clashes literally decimated the generation that was to succeed Rivet and Métraux. After the latter's suicide in 1963, and that of Lucien Sebag in 1965, it was Pierre Clastres who died ten years later in a car accident. But he had already crashed out of the LAS, followed by Robert Jaulin and then Jean Monod, because of ideological differences that had crystallized just before or after 1968. Arlette Frigout was also, as we have seen, part of that shipwreck. It was thus the grandchildren of French anthropology of the Americas – a generation later, starting with Philippe Descola – who were to realize the Lévi-Straussian dream of reviving the field. But in the history of that subdiscipline, there was a paradoxical missing link: that of the LAS of the 1960s.

The LAS thus adopted a strategy of consolidating disciplinary forces rather than one of thematic coherence: it was neither a centre of specialized expertise nor the home of a theoretical cabal, but a pluralistic workshop designed to showcase a thriving discipline that combined the lure of adventure, the seduction of literature and the rigour of science. The latter dimension was strikingly apparent in the naive enthusiasm for computers, in which Lévi-Strauss held great store and with which he tried, rather precociously, to equip the laboratory. Indeed, some research questions, for instance in kinship anthropology, were amenable to computer processing, especially those related to matrimonial alliances, tackled in the 1960s and 1970s by Françoise Héritier-Izard. Lévi-Strauss was forced to renounce this project for lack of appropriate mathematical and computer tools. He was therefore very interested in the proposition made in 1967 by Francis Perrin, his colleague at the Collège de France. The latter had just acquired an SDS 9300 computer for the nuclear physics laboratory, and was offering to share it with other laboratories, including those in the social sciences. For several years already, Lévi-Strauss had been in touch with the Documentary Automation section of the Marseille CNRS and with other agencies in other cities, but 'we can't seem to make any progress because it all plays out like a game of chess by mail'.[108] In fact, as he explained to Perrin, his efforts ran up against the difficulty of finding people knowledgeable in both anthropology and computer science. Yet in 1967, Lévi-Strauss and Chiva believed they had finally found such a rare bird: Georges Kutukdjian, a young Lebanese man with scientific training who spoke five or six exotic languages. Alas, he did not prove entirely up to the task and was replaced a few years later by Marion Selz, who developed general programs for processing genealogical data.[109]

This ambitious agenda for computers strongly marked the culture of the LAS, even if all social science laboratories would soon begin to use high-performance tools.[110] The laboratory's move to the main buildings of the Collège de France and its resulting proximity to the hard sciences played a determining role. It had to be up to the scientific standards of nuclear physics.

This also sprung from a more idiosyncratic and little noted trait of Lévi-Strauss: his ardent technophilia.[111] He loved technology and the new objects it produced. He appreciated the potential comforts it could provide, but above all technology satisfied his intense childlike curiosity for 'inventions', and sometimes also his sense of Beauty. He thus had a fascination for 'calculators', as he called them, those large interconnected cabinets which, at the time, were still rather oversized and made quite a racket when processing data. 'The basement of the Maison des Sciences de l'Homme was for a while occupied by the Computer (with a capital C), which took up the entire space!'[112]

The art of the right distance[113]

From 1966 onward, the LAS developed in a prestigious institutional and physical space. The laboratory was directed by a man who governed through a certain moral authority, exerted in silence and with discretion, without always managing to conceal his lack of enthusiasm for the task: 'He was a man of duty. He satisfied all his teaching, research and administrative obligations, but he found being a lab director a chore!'[114]

Arriving at the laboratory every morning, Lévi-Strauss would spend the first hour in a debriefing session with Chiva on current matters. He would read and send off correspondence. And by noon he had left for his other life, at home on the other side of Paris: 'We would see him moving furtively through the corridors, as he was leaving or arriving, but he never tried either to make eye contact or to impose his presence on others. Walking as he did, slightly stooping forward, he had a . . . Groucho Marx look to him. . . .'[115] However, all his students and collaborators recall his extraordinary availability and accessibility – one had only to knock on his door. Yet he was also keen not to waste time – which meant that one had to state one's business in clear and concise terms, and avoid chitchat. His unfailingly courteous yet never familiar manner, in addition to the formal decor of his office, could quickly turn an audience into an intimidating trial: 'Lévi-Strauss had an office (that I later inherited) . . . a square, monumental office, whose original architecture has unfortunately not survived', explained Françoise Héritier. '[. . .] Part of the office served as a conference room, with two slightly worn out leather club chairs. The entrance was a double door, one of which was quilted . . . He would come to greet you in between those two doors and lead you to an armchair, and had a way of holding your hand . . . And then he would wait for you to speak. Of course, at that moment it could become very embarrassing; not that he had any intention of embarrassing the poor fellow who found himself there, but the layout of the place, and its size, was intimidating. He would courteously wait for us to bring up whatever it was we had come to see him about. [. . .]

The audience was never very long. But it was very precious. He always found, in his pithy way, the right words.'[116] More often than not, it would all end very well, but Lévi-Strauss never made an effort to keep the conversation going. Ensconced in the fabled armchair, his interlocutors, especially female ones, were often struck dumb by the master's silence and would struggle to string a few words together. Yet he was always very attentive to everything one said to him and demonstrated a rare capacity for listening.

Claude Lévi-Strauss was a rather stubborn doctoral supervisor, and quite anti-conformist in certain ways. He was no classic mandarin, whose prestige was indexed on the number of students they had, which on the contrary he limited as much as possible. He was also an open-minded supervisor, who did not assign topics or enforce methodological dogma. He trusted everyone to find their own intellectual way: 'The notion of a research supervisor does not make much sense, since the foremost quality of a researcher is to know how to direct oneself, leaving us to provide advice on this or that specific point which might be causing trouble.'[117] He was, however, very implicated in the material problems his students might face, and did not spare any effort in assisting at this practical level. When Carmen Munoz arrived in Paris from Argentina to follow his lectures, he immediately inquired as to her circumstances and, upon finding out that she was short of money, he called Alain Touraine who offered her teaching at the new university in Nanterre. Similarly, Jean Monod, who already had dependent children, was given an opportunity to coordinate a study on deviants that the editor of the magazine *Elle*, Hélène Gordon-Lazareff, was prepared to finance. Monod set to work and undertook a two-year study of 'greasers', producing an original work of urban anthropology. When it was being considered for publication, under the title *Les Barjots*, Lévi-Strauss advised Monod to demand the equivalent of a year's salary from publisher Christian Bourgois, in order to be able to write comfortably.[118] Thanks to his American contacts, he was often in a position to obtain grants from foreign foundations and universities for his students. With remarkable attentiveness, he was particularly on the lookout for independent minds and literary eccentrics, for whom he had a soft spot. Within the CNRS, he was on the frontlines in the battle for fellowships and post-docs, and wrote flamboyant letters of recommendation, as if, in the end, it was in this support role that he could be most useful.

Reluctant to supervise students, he was also loath to direct colleagues, already researchers in their own right, for whom the intellectual tutelage imposed by the French academic system struck him as particularly absurd. When he found himself on an assessment committee, as he did for example for the South Pacific anthropologist Jean Guiart, specialist of the New Hebrides, he played the academic institutional game, but pointed out its absurd character: 'After so many years that have seen us sitting side by side – and I hope I can say fraternally – at EPHE assemblies, I feel particularly shocked by the paradoxical situation that transforms such a satisfying relationship and places us today on opposite sides of the barricade, I as an examiner, and you as a candidate. If you agree, let us consider this shift from an anthropological perspective, and we can conclude that the oddity of kinship relations is not the exclusive prerogative of exotic societies, since the rules that prevail in the broad academic family are so designed as to overturn collateral relationships and turn them into caricatures of ascendant–descendant relationships, placing me in a position whose absurdity, please believe me, I can feel, and would impel me, if I could, to assume the role Swedish universities ritually assign to one member of a doctoral committee: that of the buffoon, whose burlesque interventions are designed to remind all participants – the committee itself, as well as the candidate – that human institutions must never be taken too seriously.'[119] This tongue-in-cheek academic, this 'committee buffoon', nonetheless produced a dozen pages of dense commentary, which showed the extreme care and scrupulousness with which he took his role . . . He imposed this same attention to quality and form on himself and his colleagues, in the writing of reports, letters and articles alike. He brooked no laxity in this regard. If he was reluctant to supervise, Lévi-Strauss read and commented in writing on everything that was submitted to him, and with a surprising promptness for those who knew how busy he was.

The laboratory's political model was for the most part that of an enlightened monarchy with a charismatic leader. 'There was a master and there were disciples, who did their best to be up to the task.'[120] Maurice Godelier conveyed here a sense of the mode of governance that prevailed, through admiration for and distance from the 'boss'. No need to legislate appropriate behaviour. Lévi-Strauss was adamant that researchers use the offices they were lucky enough to have obtained, and that he had fought to get for them. When a researcher left for fieldwork, his or her office was immediately reassigned. There were no keys to the third floor offices that were reserved for researchers. This maximum occupancy requirement also applied to himself: in the afternoons, his office was available for others to use.

On essential matters, decisions were made by Lévi-Strauss and Chiva. Crisis management was their exclusive prerogative. For example, Lévi-Strauss made the unilateral decision to part ways with Robert Jaulin, and later Clastres. Regarding everything else, however, a kind of informal direct democracy was the rule, since LAS members would gather in general assembly on a regular basis, with each member, including the housekeeper, having one vote . . .[121] The operation of the LAS was still rather light by today's standards, given that Lévi-Strauss, notwithstanding his devotion, only spent half his day there. He was indeed very keen to save time, and to rationalize as much as possible the daily bureaucratic operations, avoiding all formalities. This was also why he attempted to nip any potential conflicts in the bud, since they were likely to develop within such a small community, where, as in the rest of the intellectual world, egos were prone to clash. The distribution of funding (for travel and the occasional publication), deliberated in general assembly, did not generate protest, since Lévi-Strauss saw to it that the allocation of resources was done with complete impartiality. His moral authority, great and a bit terrifying, shielded him from challenges that, when they did arise, tended to be addressed to Isac Chiva.

Gruss aus Ingweiler.

Evang. Kirche.

Synagoge.

Kath. Kirche.

Colourized postcard of the family's original hometown – Ingweiler (Alsace)
– with its Catholic church, its Protestant church and its synagogue.

Musician and director of Opera balls, Isaac Strauss, Claude's great-grandfather, with his viola, his wife and his five daughters, as well as his brother, a.k.a. 'Uncle Schreiber'. Photograph taken in Vichy in 1858. He coordinated the concert programmes in this spa resort and was largely responsible for the town's renaissance.

Photographic portrait of Léa Straus one of the five Strauss daughters wife of Gustave Lévi and Claude's grandmother, who died in 1932, at the age of nearly a hundred.

Isaac Strauss,
the 'Béranger of dance music'.

Gustave Lévi, son of Flore Moch and Isaac Lévi, Raymond's father and Claude's grandfather. He mad some bad deals on the stock exchange and died pre-

Raymond Lévi-Strauss and his son Claude,
in a sailor's outfit, Paris, 1915.

Claude Lévi-Strauss,
the mischievous child.

Claude Lévi-Strauss,
the serious child.

Claude Lévi-Strauss riding his
mechanical horse, oil on canvas
painted in 1912 by his father,
who gave up business to devote
himself to his art.

Oil on canvas, by Raymond Lévi-Strauss depicting his son Claude in 1913.

Portrait of Claude Lévi-Strauss as young man – on rue Poussin, in the 1920s – sporting the glasses of a intellectual and the determined lo of a socialist activist...

Oil on canvas, by Raymond Lévi-Strauss depicting his wife Emma, Claude's mother, in 1913.

The house at Camcabra, in the Cévennes region (Valleraugue); ide's parents acquired this former silk farm in the late 1920s; turned every summer until 1964

Photograph of the 158th Infantry Unit in December 1931, where Claude Lévi-Strauss completed his cannon service, at the Stirn barracks in Strasbourg. He circled his friends in the squad. In the first row, 'the spyglass, the 37mm canon, the Stokes mortar, the telephone, the wireless telegraph and the optical apparatuses' (letter to his parents, 7 January 1932).

THE BRAZILIAN YEARS (1935-39)

Above: São João Avenue, photographed by Lévi-Strauss on a carnival day. In the background, the city's first American-style 'skyscraper', the Perdio Martinelli. São Paulo, the Chicago of Brazil, a New-World city whose wildness Lévi-Strauss very much appreciated.

Top-right: The Lévi-Strauss home, on Cincinato Braga Street, with their car parked in front. The couple of young professors, who had previously been teaching at provincial lycées in France, enjoyed a whole new standard of living. 'Travelling is moving in space as well as up or down the social ladder' – in this case, up.

Above: Raymond Lévi-Strauss in São Paulo, 1935.

Left: A musical and conjugal moment. Claude and Dina Lévi-Strauss in São Paulo. In Brazil, Dina married anthropology along with her husband. She was to break with both in 1939.

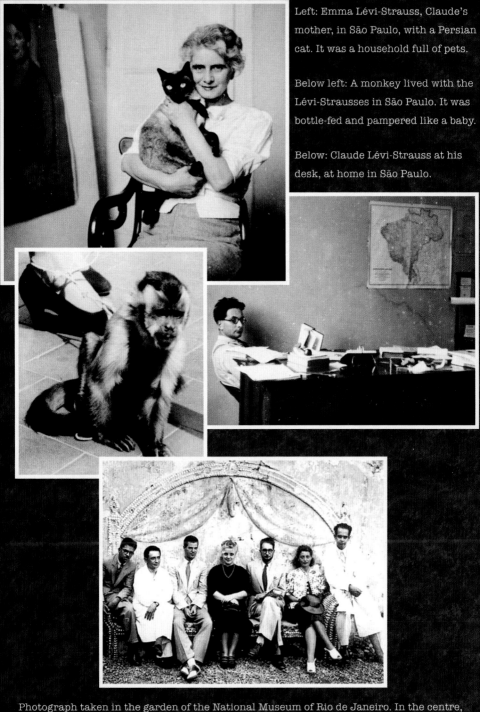

Left: Emma Lévi-Strauss, Claude's mother, in São Paulo, with a Persian cat. It was a household full of pets.

Below left: A monkey lived with the Lévi-Strausses in São Paulo. It was bottle-fed and pampered like a baby.

Below: Claude Lévi-Strauss at his desk, at home in São Paulo.

Photograph taken in the garden of the National Museum of Rio de Janeiro. In the centre, Dona Heloïsa Alberto Torres, the museum's director and queen of Brazilian anthropology. Lévi-Strauss, in his Sunday best, is sitting to her right. Luiz de Castro Faria is sitting at the far right. Between the two men, a young American anthropologist, Ruth Landes. To the left of Heloïsa, the anthropologists Charles Wagley, Raimundo Lopes and Edson Carneiro.

TWO RIDERS IN THE FOREST

First foray outside São Paulo. Lévi-Strauss, accompanied by Pierre Monbeig,
rode through the great temperate forest in northern Parana state,
a pioneer region which the geographer was studying.

The Rio Papagaio falls,
a clearwater river on whose
banks the anthropologist
met his first Nambikwara.

IN THE HEART OF THE TROPICS

ARCHIVES OF EXPLORATION

The second ethnographic expedition to central Brazil required considerable logistical support: mule-drivers, cows and a lorry that had to be loaded and unloaded at every river crossing; it was later abandoned for a pirogue, better suited to riding the rapids

First Expedition: The Caduveo and Bororo
(December 1935 – January 1936)

'A tangle of a thousand colours', the Bororo society struck the anthropologist for its rich ceremonies, especially funerals. Among these, the display and dance of the *Marid'do*, a basketwork disc that the dancer wears on his head like a diadem. This ceremony was filmed by Claude and Dina Lévi-Strauss.

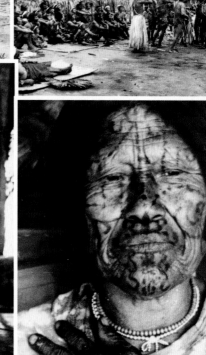

A young and an old Caduveo woman, their faces covered with a 'mesh of asymmetrical arabesques whose patterns follow a subtle geometrical logic', painted with a bamboo spatula dipped in jenipapo sap. This was one of the first puzzles to capture the anthropological attention of the young Lévi-Strauss.

A Nambikwara woman and her baby sleeping on the ground, naked.
A photograph by Claude Lévi-Strauss, published in *Tristes Tropiques*, that became
the ultimate expression of the deprivation of Amerindian populations
as well as of the 'human tenderness' the anthropologist celebrated in his book.

Basketry, the quintessential craft of oral cultures and a noble art to which Lévi-Strauss paid tribute in his final book, *Look, Listen, Read*. Nambikwara women carrying large panniers with the few possessions they took with them in their slash-and-burn migrations. These large baskets were functional objects which, according to the anthropologist, struck an unstable balance between nature and culture.

The anthropologist's camp at Utiarity,
on the Rio Papagaio, with the Nambikwara.

The anthropologist's
equipment: helmet,
leather boots, coveralls
and the precious Leica
camera slung over
his shoulder.

Lévi-Strauss (above) with his monkey Lucinda
on his shoulder and (right) photographing a
Nambikwara archer.

Extracts from Lévi-Strauss's expedition notebooks: drawing of the monkey Zog Zog, a sketch of the weaving pattern, an illustration of a string game, a colour lexicon, musical transcripts, an animal glossary and language cards. Together, these 'very poorly kept' notebooks constitute the essence of ethnographic fieldwork and the material that would fuel the anthropologist's reflections once back home.

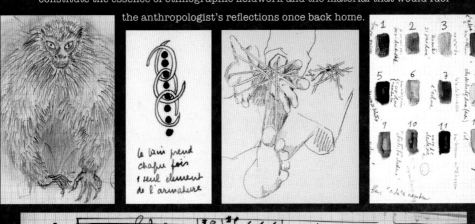

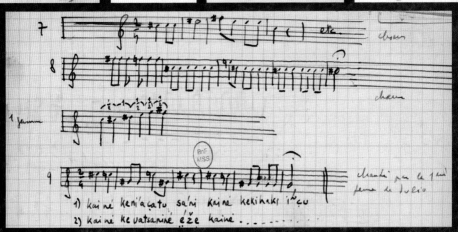

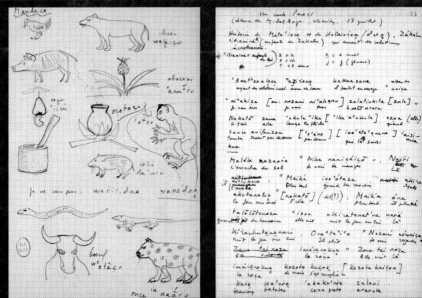

Bohemian life...

Dinner at the restaurant *Au bal Tabarin*, New York, 1943, where the exiled artists that
Lévi-Strauss had befriended and spent time with during the war years regularly gathered.
From left to right, standing: Bernard Reis, Irene and Esteban Frances, Mrs. Calas, Arshile Gorky,
Enrico Donati, Nico Calas; seated: Max Ernst, Nogouche Gorky, André Breton, Mrs. Kiesler, Mrs. Reis,
Elisa Breton, Patricia Matta, Frederick Kiesler, Nina Lebel, Matta, Marcel Duchamp.

The surrealist group met regularly at the home of the gallerist Pierre Matisse.
In addition to the regulars, there is Denis de Rougemont (in the back row,
second from the left), Aimé Césaire (far right) and his wife Suzanne (seated second from left),

Claude Lévi-Strauss's New York apartment at 51 W 11th Street, in Greenwich Village. The furnished apartment was a kind of large studio with a glass skylight. Lévi-Strauss had pinned his maps of North and South America above his bed and set up his index cards on a semi-circular table.

Claude Lévi-Strauss in conversation with William F. Russell (Columbia University),
Fiske Kimbal (director of the Philadelphia Museum of Fine Arts),
and Georges Wildenstein (director of the *Gazette des beaux-arts*), on his left.

Rose-Marie Ullmo, Claude Lévi-Strauss's second wife (in 1946)
and Laurent Jacquemin Lévi-Strauss, born in New York in March 1947

Claude Lévi-Strauss in a light-coloured suit,
as a newly minted cultural attaché in New York in 1946.

MASKS

From very early on, the masks of British Columbia were a source of fascination for
Lévi-Strauss, who first discovered them at the Museum of Natural History in New York
and then began collecting them, with his surrealist friends. He returned to them thirty years
later to provide a structural analysis of these masks in *The Way of the Masks*.

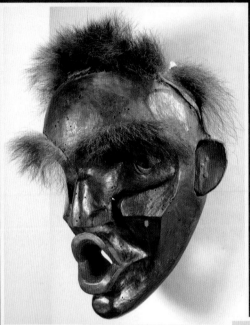

Above and top right: Dzonokwa (Kwakiutl)
masks of fierce ogresses. They feature red
hair, sunken eyes and wide open mouths.

Right: Swaihwe (Salish) mask: as opposed
to the preceding masks, this one is coloured
white, with bulging eyes and its tongue
sticking out.

These relationships of inversion were
combined with rich ethnographic and
mythological material to demonstrate
that the masks only make sense in
relation to one another.

Swaihwe (Cowichan) mask: this one also features the same bulging eyes, but a bird's bill has replaced the nose and mouth.

COLLÈGE DE FRANCE

The eminent professors of the Collège de France in 1966–67.

Claude Lévi-Strauss in conversation with Jean Malaurie in 1974, on the occasion of the twentieth anniversary of the 'Terre Humaine' series, in which the anthropologist had published *Tristes Tropiques* in 1955.

Right: Collège de France professors in 1976–77. Gender diversity was represented by the one and only female member, Jacqueline de Romilly, who can be seen sitting in the front row.

Lévi-Strauss represented the discipline of anthropology, alongside André Leroi-Gourhan, while Raymond Aron represented sociology. Historians were more numerous: Jean Delumeau, Georges Duby, Emmanuel Leroy-Ladurie, Jean-Pierre Vernant and Paul Veyne.

Above: Roman Jakobson giving a lecture at the Collège de France in 1972. In the front row, the established scholars – notably his 'brother Claude' and Georges Dumézil; sitting further back, the aspiring youngsters.

Below: Lévi-Strauss seated at his desk in a houndstooth suit, surrounded by his fetish objects (paperweight, inkwell, bookmark), in 1964.

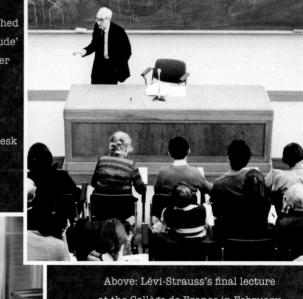

Above: Lévi-Strauss's final lecture at the Collège de France in February 1982. The professor spoke with his left hand in his pocket, while his right hand would point to a board that was often covered with diagrams.

THE LABORATORY OF SOCIAL ANTHROPOLOGY

'Anthropology of the family or the future of entropy': photomontage by Frédéric Jude for Claude Lévi-Strauss's eightieth birthday in 1988. It provides a snapshot of life at the laboratory, which included technicians and administrators, researchers and visiting colleagues from abroad. Surrealist in spirit, it reveals the convivial and playful atmosphere around this small circle of scholars.

POUR LA PATRIE LES SCIENCES ET LA GLOIRE

Left: Claude Lévi-Strauss, in his last office at the Collège de France in September 1988. On the wall, a print by the Canadian artist Bill Reid of a thunderbird and the photograph of Maurice Merleau-Ponty that remained by his side ever since the death of his friend in 1961.

Claude Lévi-Strauss in the Files, the enormous and regularly updated anthropological documentation filing system that made the LAS unique in Europe, and served as tangible evidence of its status as a high-tech scientific laboratory in its time.

Above right: The anthropologist crowned by the motto of the École Polytechnique: 'For country, science and glory'. In 1982, the laboratory moved into the former amphitheatre of the École Polytechnique, which had itself moved to Saclay on the outskirts of Paris.

Left: Claude Lévi-Strauss in his office at the Collège de France in 1970, his finger pointing to Amazonia on the map. Lévi-Strauss always lived and worked amongst maps, especially of America.

Lévi-Strauss surrounded by LAS members, upon delivering his final lecture at the Collège de France (1982). In front on the right (leaning on desk) was Nicole-Claude Mathieu; then, standing behind her, from left to right: Eva Kempinski, Evelyne Guedj, Marie-Claude Beauregard, Marion Abelès, Françoise Héritier, Michel Izard (behind Lévi-Strauss), Isac Chiva, Marie-Elisabeth Handman, Yasmina Hamzaoui, Nicole Belmont, Daniel Daho and Françoise Zonabend. In the back row, from the right: Marc Abelès, Gérard Lenclud, Jacqueline Duvernay, Patrice Bidou, Monique Lévi-Strauss, Jean-Marie Benoist, Marion Selz, Jean Pouillon, Claude Tardits, Sidney Mintz, Florence Decaudaveine and Maurice Godelier.

Left: The Académicien and his medals. He received the 'Grand Croix de la Légion d'Honneur' in 1991. The embroidered motifs were modelled on an ancient leaf pattern. 'It is, after all, one of the rare occasions when a man can dress up like a woman', according to Lévi-Strauss.

Right: A reception at the Académie Française, on June 27, 1974: Lévi-Strauss leaving the Institute with his wife, flanked by the Garde Républicaine.

Left: A reception at the Académie Française: Claude Lévi-Strauss flanked by his wife and mother.

THE ACADÉMICIEN

Session at the Académie Française, 1985.

Claude Lévi-Strauss's new tribe, 1985.

United States, Canada, Japan: Lévi-Straussian geographies

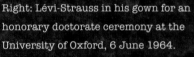

Above: Lévi-Strauss with students and journalists on board a ferryboat to Vancouver Island, in February 1973.

Left: Lévi-Strauss at the foot of a totem pole, in front of the Victoria Museum in Vancouver, February 1973.

Right: Lévi-Strauss in his gown for an honorary doctorate ceremony at the University of Oxford, 6 June 1964.

Island. This was their first trip to Japan, in November 1977. Five other trips
v, with the last in 1988. Japan became the 'other face of the moon' and comp
circle of Lévi-Strauss's zen old age and his childhood passion for 'japonaiser

Right: Monique Lévi-Strauss and Matthieu.

Below: Monique Roman, in Saint-Tropez, in the summer of 1947. She had just returned from two years in the United States.

Below: Laurent Lévi-Strauss, born in 1947, son of Claude Lévi-Strauss and Rose-Marie Ullmo, in Camcabra.

Left: Claude Lévi-Strauss at his desk, on rue des Marronniers, photographed by his young son Matthieu in the mid-1960s. The two of them shared a passion for photography. Later, Matthieu supervised the printing of a selection of photographs from Brazil for *Saudades do Brasil* (1994).

generations at Lignerolles (Burgundy): Grandpa Lévi-Strauss with his grand-daughter Julie seated by his side, Monique and their grandson Thomas at the desk just behind, and above them all a portrait of Léa Strauss, Claude's grandmother, with her grandson Claude on her lap, painted by Raymond Lévi-Strauss.

Below: The Lignerolles baskets: Claude and Monique Lévi-Strauss, with their daughter in-law Catherine and their grandchildren in the kitchen, having just returned from mushroom gathering.

Below: As a gentleman farmer in Lignerolles, wearing Clarks shoes and jeans. By his side, Monique, in long leather boots, and the caretaker's dog Fanny.

Above: Claude Lévi-Strauss in the country – in the background, the house he and his wife acquired in 1964, the Château de Lignerolles, in northern Burgundy.

Claude Lévi-Strauss in the 1950s, at his home at 11, rue Saint-Lazare, a working-class and Bohemian neighbourhood he rather liked.

The anthropologist in his office, on rue des Marronniers. Behind him, a massive green Tara, the asexual Indian goddess.

Above: Claude Lévi-Strauss's grave in the Lignerolles cemetery. The headstone is made of a local porous stone, commonly found in the surrounding woods.

Above, right: An animated Claude Lévi-Strauss, in 1985.

Right: Painting by Anita Albus (detail), *Eisvogelpaar* (Pair of

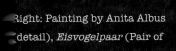

Above: Claude Lévi-Strauss, in ceremonial cape, on the River Seine. On the occasion of the exhibition 'Claude Lévi-Strauss's Americas', organized by the Musée de l'Homme in Paris in the autumn of 1989, the anthropologist rode on board a long red cedar pirogue (made by Canadian artist Bill Reid), which, with its dozen paddlers from British Columbia, made its way up the Seine from Rouen to Paris. At the end of their journey, they were greeted by the Paris mayor, Jacques Chirac.

Right: Claude Lévi-Strauss wearing an embroidered bead jacket (made by Plains Indians) that his old New York friend Dolorès Vanetti gave him as a gift for his eightieth birthday.

Generally speaking, before 1968, while almost 'everyone at the LAS was on the left',[122] little or nothing was said openly. Political disagreements and critical discussions were forestalled by both the intellectual charisma of the master and a kind of gentlemen's agreement, although these were not quite enough to ward off deeper turmoil, as with Jaulin, Clastres and Monod. 'Lévi-Strauss was not looking to stir up trouble. He was looking to maintain peace.'[123] In 1968, as we shall later see, after attending a meeting or two, he declined to engage in discussion with a movement he did not like and simply withdrew to his Aventine Hill – deserting the laboratory, even while keeping an eye on it – and returned home. This policy of defection on the part of a grand professor, one very rarely contested, was a discreet form of protest against the risk of squandering the hard-won resources provided by this long-desired institution, a human and social sciences laboratory that everyone recognized Lévi-Strauss did not need for his own work, but which had become, over the years, a spearhead of anthropological research in France and abroad.

The primacy of anthropology

Pierre Bourdieu remembered the special place occupied by the journal *L'Homme*, and more generally the discipline of anthropology in the 1960s: 'It exerted a great attraction on a number of new entrants (of whom I was one).'[124] Was it the appeal of the structuralist paradigm, as we have analysed it? Above all, by the mid-1960s, it was the outcome of the successful breakthrough of anthropology on the disciplinary front. As opposed to sociology, which remained relatively marginal at the time (Bourdieu talks of a 'pariah discipline'), anthropology, thanks to the struggle waged by Lévi-Strauss, had managed to make a place for itself as a full-fledged science.

The Lévi-Strauss seminar

In post-liberation years and into the 1950s, the café had been the symbolic locus of Sartre's intellectual authority – prompting ironic comments about his 'chair at the Deux Magots'. The intellectual giants of the 1960s and 1970s also operated from outside traditional academic institutions, but from yet another locus: Lévi-Strauss, Barthes, Foucault and especially Lacan all held their 'seminars'. The word originally had clerical connotations, but it had come to designate above all an alternative pedagogical model to that of the lecture, one practised at the margins of the academic system, around the EPHE and the Collège de France. Its purpose was not to diffuse an already stabilized knowledge, but rather to create a space in which knowledge could go in search of itself.

This is why the seminar was associated with marginal yet prestigious institutions like the EPHE, which had imported the format from Germany, and later the United States, where Lévi-Strauss had already practised it.

Thus, ever since 1950 and his election to the Vth Section of the EPHE, the anthropologist held his seminar, whose itinerant character – from the rue de Varenne to the Sorbonne – did not detract from its growing renown. At first a crucible for the discipline, by the 1960s it was a locus of intellectual power: sought after for the access it provided to the master, it was the place where everyone thought 'it all happened'. At that point, Lévi-Strauss sought to limit the flow of applications, in an attempt to preserve the protected environment of a small community of professionals. Starting in December 1968, he capped enrolment at forty and filtered newcomers, selecting them, as he explained to an unfortunate candidate, on the basis of their anthropological training, rejecting those who were 'attracted by certain dimensions of structuralism from a philosophical or literary angle. My seminar is principally intended for professional anthropologists, and it features presentations of a very technical nature based on the results of fieldwork that require, on the part of participants, an in-depth knowledge of the discipline.'[125]

What exactly went on at the seminar? Lévi-Strauss favoured fieldwork reports, having a voracious appetite for new material and a great concern for maintaining a high level of empirical precision and ethnographic erudition. The programme was characterized by a broad geographical range and wide diversity of subjects – from baboons to delinquents to Indians. The lack of any particular structuralist terminology in the presentation of data was also striking.[126] From 1969 to 1970, the sessions on ethnographic case studies were complemented by others devoted to discussions of theory: three seminars were held by Dan Sperber on a 'critique of the propositions of structuralist anthropology';[127] and Marshall Sahlins, an American anthropologist who was at the LAS in 1968/69, returned to the Maori text on which Mauss had based a large part of his theory of reciprocity, to show how the famous anthropologist had misunderstood its original point. In the pages of his notes that have been preserved, Lévi-Strauss wrote: 'This is completely wrong!' Sahlins's presentation continued thus: 'When Lévi-Strauss expanded "total services" into a grandiose system of matrimonial exchange – the "promised land" to which Mauss had led his people, but whose splendours he himself had never had a chance to contemplate – a significant number of British and American anthropologists immediately rejected the idea, unable to bring themselves to "treat women as if they were goods".' Lévi-Strauss's handwritten annotation reads: 'It is not women that are treated as if they were goods, but goods that are found to have something "womanly" about them.'[128] The seminar thus sometimes resonated with strong theoretical disputes. It also served as a site for the critical reading of texts: for example, it was within this framework, as we have seen, that Sartre's book, *A Critique of Dialectical Reason*, was analysed. In 1962, Lévi-Strauss also devoted a few sessions to the book by the British anthropologist Rodney Needham, *Structuralism and Sentiment*. In fact, as Françoise Héritier put it, Lévi-Strauss's seminar, like his work itself, attempted to grasp 'both ends' of the chain, both the ethnographic and the anthropological, empirical erudition and model building, the meticulous description of the most diverse social realities and the elucidation of the formal logic of collective life. Gradually, and without any structuralist discipline prevailing, something came together, which was properly speaking the collective work of the seminar, a way of tackling issues that made sense of the extraordinary diversity of themes and regions of the world. Just like a mayonnaise is always more than the sum of its ingredients, the work carried out within the seminar gave a certain tone to the research of each of its participants. Anthropology acquired its vocabulary, its register, its colour, its unity within difference.

Lévi-Strauss appreciated presentations that were rich in new material and based on precise and lively accounts of protracted study, such as Bernard Saladin d'Anglure's presentation on the Eskimo populations, of which he had developed a remarkable body of knowledge. At the end of a presentation, Lévi-Strauss would moderate the discussion with members of the audience. Interventions bounced back and forth, with the exchanges and comparisons drawn by the most audacious participants prolonging the discussion further, until the master of ceremonies took a few minutes to sum up the gist of the discussion in a few words, often described as 'luminous'. Everything had been said.[129] But sometimes boredom followed by impatience would be the order of the day. 'You have tortured us', he would sometimes say to the speaker to whom he had entrusted the seminar session. He had found the theme unworthy, or poorly prepared, and above all he felt it had been a waste of time. Over the course of the presentation, his entire body would manifest his boredom, in successive stages: 'First, he would discreetly smoke, then slowly and meticulously clean his glasses; then, in a final stage, lean back on his chair, his head thrown backwards with his glasses in his hand. Anyone noticing these signs felt sorry for the poor speaker.'[130] The verdict could be harsh, which is why he was feared. For his young colleagues, speaking 'at the seminar' was an honour, a necessity, and an ordeal. Françoise Zonabend presented her work on the village of Minot, crippled by anxiety and the imperative 'not to disappoint'.[131] After the seminar, she was summoned to the master's office: 'It will be very good, it will be better than Nouville', he said.[132] Michel Perrin talked about his study of death among the Guapiro Indians, in which he adopted a kind of structuralist approach. He successfully passed the test and Lévi-Strauss turned to him over the break and told him: 'You are welcome at the LAS. You must return to Venezuela.'[133] Once time was up, discussions would sometimes go on, maybe at a café, but without Lévi-Strauss. He never took part in these friendly gatherings with colleagues which others, like Barthes and Lacan, did regularly.

With Lacan, according to Élisabeth Roudinesco, seminars functioned as moments of 'collective catharsis' and the atmosphere, at least initially, 'resembled that of a Socratic symposium'.[134] With Barthes, the seminar form was infused with a kind of utopian pedagogy coupled with amorous projection – it dreamed of becoming the very body of a textual togetherness in denial of any form of authority.[135] Lévi-Strauss's seminar, by contrast, was a research laboratory and the 'somewhat anxiety-inducing'[136] locus from which the discipline built itself, moving from marginal to central among the related human and social sciences.

Remapping the disciplines

The imposition of a new and ascendant discipline at the centre of the disciplinary universe had an impact on the borders. The primacy of anthropology over history, the royal discipline of the human sciences in France, can be measured in its contamination of an entire swath of Annales historiography which, starting in the 1960s, took a sharp 'anthropological turn'.

As André Burguière has pointed out in his history of the Annales School, Braudel's seminal article on the '*longue durée*' was a tactical intervention which, in 1958, was a matter of 'safeguarding the rights of history against the onslaught of Lévi-Straussian structuralism'.[137] Separating the *longue durée* from the short time of events and the cyclical time of conjunctures, Braudel meant to 'show that the structures set forth by Claude Lévi-Strauss are not situated outside time any more than other aspects of reality'.[138] This general tendency towards the immobilization and freezing of time was nothing new; indeed, as early as 1947, Braudel had himself insisted on the immobility of spans of Mediterranean time. Yet, from the late 1950s, a true 'historical anthropology' was beginning to emerge.

Together with the work of Marcel Détienne, that of Jean-Pierre Vernant provided one of its finest examples. A Hellenist of a new kind, he developed a psycho-historical approach in his research on Ancient Greece, strongly influenced by Dumézil and Lévi-Strauss,[139] setting out to explore the 'mentalities of the Greeks', the symbolic systems through which they filtered and made sense of the world around them. In analysing the Hesiod poem *Works and Days*, he worked on it in the manner of Claude Lévi-Strauss, emphasizing its trifunctional structure, according to Dumézil's seminal thesis on Indo-European societies. The abundance of mythological material, together with a dearth of serial data, might explain the appeal of structural anthropology for specialists of Ancient Greek societies. In their analyses of myths, Jean-Pierre Vernant and Pierre Vidal-Naquet felt free to adopt a broad comparative and transcultural perspective (between Hellenic tales, Mesopotamian texts, China, India and pre-Columbian America), legitimized by their rallying to the banner of Lévi-Straussian structural anthropology.

The penetration of anthropology into the writing and conceptualization of history can also be detected in the work of Emmanuel Le Roy Ladurie. Following his dissertation on the peasants of Languedoc, and his inaugural lecture at the Collège de France entitled 'L'histoire immobile' (1973), he wrote a book that became a history bestseller in the 1970s – *Montaillou* (1975) – in which he applied the analytical grid of structural anthropology to peasant culture, as he would do again with urban culture a few years later, in *Carnival in Romans*, a 'structuralist reading of the carnivalesque scene'.[140] Georges Duby was yet another historian who – in *The Three Orders: Feudal Society Imagined* – incorporated the lessons of the Dumézil archetype to give a structural dimension to his analysis of social theory in medieval ideology. These studies paved the way for what François Dosse has called the 'historian's turn to structure', which ultimately led to joint publications in the 1980s. The finest example of this kind of cross-disciplinary collaboration was *A History of the Family*, coedited by two historians, André Burguière and Christiane Klapisch-Zuber, and two anthropologists, Martine Segalen and Françoise Zonabend, with a preface to the first volume on 'remote worlds' by Claude Lévi-Strauss and Georges Duby.[141] This sweeping collective overview of family institutions and practices from prehistory to the present stands as an exemplary illustration of the fertile dialogue in which the two disciplines ultimately engaged.

While Lévi-Strauss maintained friendly relations with the historians whom he helped bring over to the Collège de France (Le Roy Ladurie, Duby), he continued to hold the view that 'history can lead to anything, provided you get out of it'.[142] If it had a place in the quest for intelligibility, it would be a mistake to assume it was its final outcome. And indeed, beginning in the 1970s, the power relations were reversed: the force of the anthropological model made historians look like anthropologists of the past.[143]

A science engaged in international debate

In the 1960s, Lévi-Strauss's international influence grew, following the translation of his work into many languages. The critical reception of structuralism in the field of British and American anthropology, networks of scholarly correspondence, friendships, honours and polemics around Lévi-Strauss all placed French anthropology, and French researchers, on the international radar screen. This 'de-provincialization' was a key element in the discipline's attainment of its dominant position.

Lévi-Strauss knew, appreciated and hosted in Paris a good portion of the Anglo-American anthropological community, both senior and junior. The renowned professor Sir Evans-Pritchard was thoroughly charmed by the Lévi-Strauss couple. On 6 June 1964, he received them at Oxford with all the pomp and circumstance due the awarding of an honorary degree: lunch with the chancellor, meetings with students, dress code instructions ('a dark lounge suit but a white tie is not required'),[144] public portrayal delivered in Latin, etc. In return, Lévi-Strauss submitted a request that Edward Evans-Pritchard be awarded the *Légion d'honneur* (reserved for foreign nationals). This was finally granted in 1971. A sentimental soul, Evans-Pritchard wrote to Lévi-Strauss that upon hearing the news he had burst into tears! Lévi-Strauss was invited to give the Frazer Lectures at Oxford in 1970. For years, he had been regularly exchanging letters with Raymond Firth (a professor at the London School of Economics), as well as with Meyer Fortes (Cambridge) and Edmund Leach (Cambridge), who had become a big fan, even though he had called the *Elementary Structures of Kinship* a 'splendid failure'.[145] He added in one of his letters: 'Your devastating lucidity arouses my envious admiration.'[146] Finally, Rodney Needham wrote a book on Lévi-Strauss's work, *Structure and Sentiment* (1962), and supervised the translation of *Elementary Structures*, which was published in English in 1969.

Lévi-Strauss's eminent position within the scientific International was crowned in 1965 with the awarding of the Viking Fund medal, attributed through a vote of the entire anthropological community. In 1961, he had campaigned for it to go to Alfred Métraux, but to no avail. Five years later (following the irregular frequency of this prestigious prize), it was on him that the essential symbolic and material gratification was bestowed, making him, in Chicago where he went to receive it in April 1966, the world representative of anthropology.[147] His international status was also sealed during that decade by a series of *doctor honoris causa* from European and American universities – Brussels in 1962, Yale in 1964, Chicago in 1965 and Columbia in 1971 – which provided him with opportunities to reconnect with his American past, evoking the figures of Robert H. Lowie and Alfred Kroeber – who had died suddenly in Paris in 1960, just a few hours before he was to dine with Lévi-Strauss – as well as Franz Boas, the patriarch of Columbia, who had died in Lévi-Strauss's arms.

Meanwhile, and this did nothing to detract from his growing reputation, the fires of scholarly controversy, in which his Anglo-American colleagues played a leading role, burned bright. Lévi-Strauss's sparkling prose, 'the elephantine erudition of this Parisian savant',[148] and his generalizing tendencies often made them uncomfortable.[149] Leach for instance questioned the supporting examples in *Elementary Structures*, which in his view presented a limited basis for a general theory. He drew on his own knowledge of Kachin (Burma) populations to put pressure on the magnificent Lévi-Straussian edifice. Leach and Needham criticized the confused manner with which Lévi-Strauss made use of 'preferential marriage' and 'prescriptive marriage', engaging in the kind of necessarily technical discussion which, it must be said, did not take place in the same terms in France. But kinship anthropology was a classic and much explored topic in Anglo-American anthropology and Lévi-Strauss, as we have seen, based his analyses on material largely drawn from Australia and Asia, to which 'specialists' could easily present ethnographic counterexamples. The criticisms would be less virulent on the publication in English of the *Mythologiques* cycle, since this time Lévi-Strauss had relied more on his strictly Americanist area of expertise.

Under attack, Lévi-Strauss first responded in the Huxley Memorial Lecture he gave in 1965 before a learned assembly of British anthropologists, then took up the substance of this presentation in the 'Preface' to the French second edition of *Elementary Structures*, which came out in 1967. That text provoked some unease, since he was explicitly refuting Needham, the official translator of the book – hence the somewhat irritated tone of the latter who, when consulted, deemed the addition of a new preface 'unnecessary', and who severed ties once the translation was complete in 1969.[150]

He expounded on the differences he had with some of his colleagues, regarding for example his thesis on the superiority of alliance over filiation in the operation of kinship systems, as well as on the changes in his thinking that were directly linked to some of the critiques – he had, for example, revised the chapters on the Kachin system following Leach's remarks. He

Top: Claude Lévi-Strauss's seminar; middle and bottom:
moments of conviviality at the lab following Claude Lévi-Strauss's final lecture
at the Collège de France, in 1982.

also launched a new research project on specific systems, such as those of the 'Crow-Omaha' group, which he then relabelled 'semi-complex' systems, and which he considered to constitute a transition stage between elementary structures and complex structures, in which many alliances were forbidden but none was prescribed.[151] More fundamentally, he tried to clarify the controversy by turning it into a more epistemological reflection: even if ethnographic observation did not always confirm categories, 'it is none the less true that the empirical reality of so-called prescriptive systems only takes on its full meaning when related to a theoretical model worked out by the natives themselves prior to ethnologists'.[152] For Lévi-Strauss, reality was one thing but the norm was what mattered most: what men did was, in terms of anthropological heuristics, less important than what they thought they should do (even if they did it inconsistently or not at all).

Scholarly controversies, for Lévi-Strauss, often amounted to questions of vocabulary, especially as far as international debates were concerned, where potential confusion was further exacerbated by translation issues. In that respect, he displayed an extraordinary optimism regarding scientific language and its ability to communicate without much residue. This nonetheless required 'fixed terminology' and an international anthropological lexicon, a task whose urgency he repeatedly emphasized, and reasserted on that occasion. Conditions were deemed to be ripe for the universal language of science to break through at long last.[153]

In the mythology of the anthropological discipline, Lévi-Strauss does not figure, strictly speaking, as a founding father – he arrived too late in the century – but the LAS did mark a new beginning. Thanks to the determination of its director, funding and research positions were in abundance. Even if these came at considerable effort, it was a time of major public investment. The institutional offensive led by Lévi-Strauss had been a success, even more so than that of Durkheim and sociology at the beginning of the century, all things equal. Although at the margins of the university, anthropology now had its place among the human sciences in France, and even among the sciences full stop.[154]

The LAS was its nerve centre. From without, it appeared as an avant-garde laboratory, richly endowed in resources, output and promise, and distinguished by the aura of its director. From within, despite the unavoidable squabbles, there was a prevailing sense of belonging to a chosen community, further blessed with an atmosphere of sociability, enduring friendship, a way of living and working together, and an 'implicit yet weighty sense of the legacy of Jewish persecution'.[155] It was an honour to be a member of the LAS, and without exception participants wanted to prove themselves worthy of membership. The group photographs that marked each passing year,[156] the dedication of the second volume of Lévi-Strauss's *Structural Anthropology* (1973) 'to the members of the LAS', the television programme 'L'invité du dimanche', 20 June 1971, by Pierre Dumayet, filmed on the premises of the laboratory,[157] as well as all the parties and tributes, convey a sense of a convivial and tight-knit community gathered around a man who, as time went by, became a kind of guardian figure, in whose protective shadow the lab remained forever sheltered.

The leading position of anthropology and of the LAS came in part from the consolidation of the discipline, which paradoxically thrived on the promotion and practice (in the journal *L'Homme*, for example) of an interdisciplinary approach, a sign of modernity in the social sciences. It also thrived on the recognition and prestige garnered in the 1960s by Lévi-Strauss himself, who in the space of ten years produced four thick volumes on the anthropology of myth, an example of work conceived and thought outside the core interests of the discipline. This was the other side of Lévi-Strauss, not the administrator of collective research, but the more familiar figure of the great mind on a vertiginous and solitary journey across the ocean of Amerindian mythology.

17

The Scholarly Life

Count Buffon enjoyed sleeping. Yet he subjected himself to a rigorous discipline, for fear sleep would deprive the writing of *Natural History* of precious time. Joseph, his servant, was instructed to wake him up at dawn, using force if necessary. Every day, the scholar thanked his servant, and gave him a crown to compensate him for enduring his daily morning insults.

Anne Collinot, 'Entre vie et œuvre scientifique: le chaînon manquant'[1]

In her evocation of this self-imposed morning torture routine, historian of science Anne Collinot draws our attention to the biographical dyad – the life and the work – and to what she calls the 'missing link' between them: labour. How are we to integrate personal life into our anthropology of scholarly practice? How are we to avoid reducing the scientific persona to the accumulated output – the oeuvre in its highest form?[2]

Ever since the nineteenth century, a narrative has taken hold that opposes science (or art) and life: scholarly, artistic or poetic production supposedly entails leaving the realm of life behind, as if the scholarly or literary life transcended mere social existence. And yet scholars and artists are subject to the same imperatives as everyone else, from womb to tomb! If we refuse to bracket personal and family life, to take the space and time of labour out of the equation, certain questions are necessarily raised, which will be the centre of our attention in this chapter. What shape does the scholar give to his life? What is its temporal economy, with the choices regarding this precious resource being the most delicate of all? What value is assigned to scholarly pursuits: passion, vocation, initiation, revelation, edification, accumulation, revolution? What is the scholar's perspective on the promise of the scientific priesthood?

With respect to the Lévi-Strauss of the 1960s, one can indeed speak of a 'scientific priesthood'. That decade stands out for its combination of productivity and widespread recognition; he attained star status, which had a disturbing effect on his rigorous schedule. While he refused to play the role of structuralist champion that was foisted on him, he was forced to make certain accommodations with it, even while never ceasing to push back. Between 1964 and 1971, Lévi-Strauss wrote some two thousand pages of the *Mythologiques*, his paper opera in four acts: *The Raw and the Cooked* (1964), *From Honey to Ashes* (1966), *The Origin of Table Manners* (1968) and *The Naked Man* (1971) – a body of work which, in its hermeticism, its polysemy, its digressions, its plasticity, its uniformity of approach, constituted an oeuvre in the most traditional sense of the term. The fruit of twenty years of research and almost ten years of writing, he had produced his 'Tetralogy', his 'Remembrance of Things Past', his 'Human Comedy'. This intellectual marathon was an oddity, a unique and solitary achievement which, in its very approach, embraced the thought process that it was meant to elucidate: 'In short, the peculiarity of this book is that it has no subject.'[3]

City Lévi-Strauss, country Lévi-Strauss

Where do scholars work, and how do they inhabit their spaces? Several images immediately come to mind: Rembrandt's *Philosopher in Meditation*, Kant off on a walk (always the same one), Rousseau collecting plants, and the contemporary scholar, a sorcerer's apprentice in his laboratory. But there is no straight line from the alchemist's cabinet to the modern laboratory.[4] Lévi-Strauss is a good example in this respect. A scholar withdrawn in his library, a professor at the podium or puttering around his country home, he brought together several scientific regimes and participated in several temporalities. Going from the LAS to his own study on rue des Marronniers, in the 16th arrondissement of Paris, he did not so much cross Paris (from the centre to the west) as travel back in time: if the LAS – in its very name, 'laboratory' – embodied scientific modernity, Claude Lévi-Strauss's study, as we saw in the introduction, in which he spent a large part of his life and produced his works, was closer to a Renaissance *studiolo*. There, in an intimacy with oneself, the 'one-on-one with innumerable books'[5] would engender new ones.

The study

After Matthieu's birth in 1957, the Lévi-Strausses decided to move out of the rue Saint-Lazare apartment, and leave a neighbourhood Claude very much liked but which was ill-adapted to daily strolls with an infant, given the lack of any park or garden nearby. The opportunity arose, in 1958, to take over the apartment owned by Monique's parents, and in which Monique herself had grown up, at 2 rue des Marronniers, in the 16th arrondissement. It was a vast bourgeois apartment, on the fifth floor with an elevator, in a turn-of-the-century block of brick buildings that stood slightly back from the street, whose style conjured up hotels along the coast of Normandy. That end of the street exuded a tasteful opulence – a concierge lodge, a vast hallway, parking for the cars – that was distinct from both the luxury of nearby buildings and the quaint charm of some of the houses (Balzac's was a stone's throw away). A relative calm reigned, in the shadow of the giant construction site of the Maison de la Radio that was being built in those years.[6] In moving to the rue des Marronniers,

Claude Lévi-Strauss was obeying a classic rule he had observed in many of the tribes he studied: matrilocality. It was also, in a way, a return to his childhood roots, though residential life in this neighbourhood near Passy was a far cry from the plebeian and Bohemian atmosphere of the rue Poussin. Indeed, he did not care much for this neighbourhood, where he would nonetheless live for the rest of his life, and often complained about 'how dull the streets are'.[7]

One of the apartment's advantages was the vast room with western exposure, via a large double window, that opened off to the left of the entrance, which Lévi-Strauss turned into his study. Hermetically sealed from the rest of the apartment by a thick padded door and walls covered with books, it was more reminiscent of a psychoanalyst's office or Proust's bedroom, with its cork-lined partitions insulating the activity of writing. The only inviolable rule in the home, which his two sons – especially the younger one who lived with him, whereas the other would only visit – were never under any circumstance to break, was 'No noise!'[8] And casually coming into his study to recount their latest adventures, as Victor Hugo's daughter famously did, was unthinkable . . .[9] Like the Renaissance humanist that he was, the anthropologist needed to withdraw into a space of concentration, fully his own, where access to knowledge was reserved to those capable of abstracting from society. Upon entering his cabinet, Machiavelli would cast off his everyday attire: 'I give my entire self over to the Ancients.'[10] Let us now imagine Lévi-Strauss in his office, giving his entire self over to the savages . . .

This quasi-spiritual retreat was distilled by two intellectual stimulants conducive to setting to work and reflection: music and tobacco. Indeed, as is little known, Lévi-Strauss was an avid smoker until the mid-1960s – consuming two packs a day, if not three. The cotton curtains that adorned his window and the kilim rug in the entrance attested to this. But what singles him out from other intellectuals, most of whom were smokers, is that after giving up cigarettes, he took to snorting tobacco.[11] He offered a detailed account of his tobacco-related pleasures to his friend Dolorès Vanetti, who had just sent him a selection of tobaccos from different regions: 'I am quickly moving from one box to the next, for as incredible as it may sound, all these tobaccos have such radically different aromas they might as well be different fruits. My inclination for black tobacco probably causes me to favour the Copenhagen, which smells of seaports and sailboats with tarred rigging; but the peppermint flavoured Red Top is also quite interesting; and the Peach does indeed smell of peaches. So many delights of which our non-snorting contemporaries are entirely unaware!'[12] Lévi-Strauss's taste for music was, on the contrary, quite well known. It was not just essential to his wellbeing, it accompanied his work like a friendly screen that separated him from the world around him, and also acted as a stimulant. This is why he would fly into fits of rage against the chatter on musical radio stations, especially France Musique and Radio Classique. He did not listen to records: the idea of it ending and then having to change it discouraged him. He thus had to rely, for better or worse, on the radio. When asked to account for this habit, he compared his absent-minded music listening while working to the use of nude models by painters: 'Even the most blasé of painters, who is accustomed to working from live models, cannot fail to respond to a beautiful body with a certain erotic excitement. This mild state of tension stimulates and sharpens the artist's perception; he paints better. Consciously or unconsciously, the artist seeks this state of grace. My relationship to music is of the same order. I think better while listening to it.'[13]

As has already been said, Claude Lévi-Strauss's impressive scholarly library offered a world tour of knowledge. Next to the journals and the index card files,[14] within closer reach, were the many dictionaries: foreign language dictionaries – Harraps (English), Sachs-Villatt (German) – as well as French dictionaries – the Grand Robert, the Bailly, the Littré, the Bayle and the Trévoux, as well as old French and Latin dictionaries, to help make sense of ancient ethnographic accounts. Diderot and D'Alembert's *Encyclopédie* was also on board for the journey. He constantly referred to it: 'Look at my library. It contains thousands of books, with which I have lived for years. Often, I don't even need to look for the title . . . The spine, the look of the volume, are enough for me to know immediately which one it is.'[15] This intimate relationship to books was part of an ancient lettered tradition – quotes, references, verifications – whereby to write books one had to be surrounded by books.[16] When writing the *Mythologiques*, Lévi-Strauss lived under a mountain of books: tomes on botany and astronomy, the *Encyclopédie*, books on zoology by Brehm and by Pliny the Elder – ancient science (covering, roughly speaking, the whole of accumulated knowledge in the eighteenth century), in order to document the ethnographic context of the myths he was studying.[17] Lévi-Strauss, the representative of modern science, thus also partook of an ancient scholarly tradition that came straight from the world of *belles lettres*. The love of knowledge made no distinction then between science and literature. A contemporary Buffon, Lévi-Strauss was an erudite, meditative scholar, who worked and felt at home in his smoke-infused den, moving to and fro from his scriptorium to his bookshelves, day in and day out, electrified by the 'fine contacts and circuits produced between the tip of the quill and the vast charge of static electricity from the library'.[18]

The professor at the podium

When he was not at the LAS or in his study, Lévi-Strauss was lecturing. Beginning in January 1960, every Tuesday from 2:30 p.m. and Wednesdays from 10 a.m. (later, the second course was held as a seminar on Mondays), he was to be found in room 6 of the Collège de France. As he exclaimed to his friend Jakobson: 'Teaching is so hard! I am completely out of practice!'[19] Indeed, although it was not part of the French university system, the Collège de France functioned for all intents and purposes in the same way, which was traditionally based on lecture courses. Lévi-Strauss thus delivered his lectures *ex cathedra*, as opposed to his seminars, which were organized around student presentations. And he had not delivered lectures of that kind since his days in Mont-de-Marsan, where he taught philosophy and rhetoric to young men at the *lycée*.

The audience was of course different, as were the expectations. Ernest Renan used to say that the true Collège de France professor did not prepare his lectures – he himself made sure he did not. In fact, as we have seen, all the Collège de France required was that a new course be taught each year. This transformed the concept of the course by ridding it of its repetitive dimension, which came as a relief to some and a source of anxiety to others. The 'neolithic' mind of Lévi-Strauss was perfectly suited to this demand for creativity, so that his course 'preparations', which sometimes only amounted to a few notes but were always based on copious reading, constituted an intermediary stage towards a future manuscript, which was generally published one to three years later. Indeed, never was a Collège de France lecture more clearly the 'trial run' for an intellectual project – the writing of the *Mythologiques* – than during the ten years from 1960 to 1971, during which time the four volumes were published. As early as 1961–62, while finishing *Totemism* and *The Savage Mind*, he began research on cooking myths that would lead to *The Raw and the Cooked* (published in 1964); in 1962/63, he tackled the body of myth on which he would base *From Honey to Ashes* (published at the end of 1966); and in 1963/64 and then 1966/67, his lectures turned to the myths analysed in *The Origin of Table Manners* (published in June 1968). Finally, in 1965/66, then again for three years from 1967 to 1970, he collected the enormous body of material that he chose to present in a single final volume, *The Naked Man*, published in 1971.[20] The lecture, as practised by Lévi-Strauss, was thus no more an occasion for delivering established knowledge than was his seminar; it was a half-cooked affair, retaining all its capacity for experimentation. It was for this reason that he refused to be recorded, wary of chiselling into stone what he was putting forward as mere hypotheses. After each course, Jean Pouillon delivered a transcript of it in shorthand to him, which served as the basis for the manuscript to come. This approach to the course was not without risk, as it involved performing without a safety net.[21] Hence his visible nervousness before each course, and his level of anxiety throughout the time of the year that he taught at the Collège, from December to June.

In contrast with this anxious concentration, Lévi-Strauss's extraordinary virtuosity as an orator has been universally corroborated by all who attended his courses on Place Marcelin-Berthelot. The Collège's ceremonial protocol further added to the spectacular dimension of his lectures. The porter would announce the entrance of 'Monsieur le professeur' onto the stage. Since there are no recordings, we can only rely on audience testimonies. Two potentially contradictory features appear to have characterized Lévi-Strauss's oral presentations: on the one hand, an acrobatic rhetoric, with a global sweep pulling in vast quantities of data and analyses in long Proustian sentences, which had everyone wondering anxiously how they would end up. But he always seemed to land on his feet! And more often than not, the end of a long sequence signalled the completion of a line of reasoning and sometimes, with a perfect sense of timing, the end of the lecture. However, the enchantment of Lévi-Straussian arabesques, both oral and written, were also based on the free associations of a surrealist spirit, on a 'free jazz of the mind'[22] that played on ruptures and clashes as much as progressions. Yet, the vertiginous dimension of his sentences never detracted from the force of his presentation or the clarity of his demonstration. From that perspective as well, 'he spoke as he wrote'.[23] His left hand in his pocket, and sometimes a piece of chalk in the other, he would explain his argument in a clear and plain voice. No rumblings, no eruptions, no hyperbolic staging of his ego, no facile sleights-of-hand. If he unquestionably seduced the members of his audience, including the professional anthropologists among them, he did not mesmerize crowds in the manner of a guru, like Lacan. At least, only as a guru of clarity, to Lacan's guru of obscurity. Lévi-Strauss did not particularly enjoy writing, but his course forced him to do so; he did not like speaking either, at least not one-on-one, but the course required him to engage in a form of public speaking that was addressed to everyone and no one in particular, which suited him better.[24] We should not forget that, at the age of twenty, he had been a brilliant political speaker: from republican eloquence (the award ceremony speeches) to academic lectures, a successful transfer of skills that made him into a great professor.

From the Latin Quarter to Passy, this great professor was a true Parisian, enamoured of the grand metropolis. Yet he was never happier than when he withdrew to his country house, far from his courses, and far from the company of others.

Claude Lévi-Strauss's Thebaid

'The good times with houses are when you desire one; afterwards, the trouble begins!'[25] Claude Lévi-Strauss was trying to console Isac Chiva, amidst fallen roofs and leaky pipes in his new Normandy country home.

The country house the Lévi-Strausses eventually acquired in 1964 had long been an object of desire. Visited for the first time in 1954, it was deemed too bourgeois by Monique; dozens of visits and some ten years later, the house known as 'Château de Lignerolles' was up for sale again . . . 'This time it seemed perfect to me. It would appear I had grown more bourgeois in the meantime!'[26] Lévi-Strauss had had enough of the Cévennes region, encroached upon by noisy summer tourists and a steady flow of automobiles that, by the 1950s, disturbed the solitude so dear to the anthropologist.[27] He turned to Burgundy, and more specifically the Châtillonnais, which he had long identified, when he was in New York, as one of the least populated regions in France. Lévi-Strauss's motivations can be inferred from the somewhat embarrassed letter sent to him by the old Burgundian and former director of the École de la France d'Outre-Mer (ex-École coloniale) Robert Delavignette, who had scouted on the anthropologist's behalf a region he knew well: 'I am afraid, should I find something, that you will be disappointed, for you have an idealized conception of how wild the Châtillonnais region has remained. Those deserted villages and ruins of the plateau, from Tonnerois to the former Burgundy bailiwick of the Montagne, are far from quiet! The radio, the van, the farm tractor all create a constant whirring din!'[28]

Still, Lévi-Strauss set his sights on this forgotten corner, a border country (between the Côte-d'Or and Aube regions) comprising vast chalk plateaux and classic cuestas interspersed with wooded valleys. This was not the pleasant countryside of Touraine, nor the rich lands of Normandy, but a region of forests and former metal industry, lost in time, 'where one can feel the watershed under one's feet and the forests are so vast they say one can walk to the Swiss border without ever leaving the woods or crossing paths with a single soul'.[29] A geographically rough and almost Gracqian landscape, tempered by a sense of long historical time – 'the Châtillonnais trees emit Gallo-Roman smells'[30] – and its proximity to great, ancestral figures: sixty kilometres to the west, Montbard and Buffon, and, above all, fifty kilometres to the south, la Margelle, the birthplace of his dear Jean de Léry,[31] which in Lévi-Strauss's mind brought them closer together and confirmed his choice of Lignerolles.

Close to the Aube valley, at the northern end of the old Duchy of Burgundy, lies a vale and a village, Lignerolles, next to which stands the 'Château de Lignerolles', in fact a hunting lodge erected in the Second Empire period (from 1864 to 1868). Of relatively modest and elegant proportions, it is set in a twelve-hectare park, partly wooded, that is crossed by a river, the Aubette, which sometimes overflows its banks in winter. The soundscape is almost mountain-like: running water and leaves rustling in the wind. One enters the house through monumental front steps, which lead to a large salon, whose walls are covered in green fabric and whose wide windows at both ends frame a moving image of the surrounding foliage. There are a few comfortable old armchairs and paintings by Raymond Lévi-Strauss – a large portrait of Léa, the grandmother, with her two-year-old grandson Claude by her side, oval frames of ancestors, Élie Moch and Esther Lévy, as well as a smaller one of 'Dina my wife'[32] as an intellectual at work, preparing for the *agrégation* exam. An almost British cosiness, which also characterized Lévi-Strauss's study, in the ground floor corner, with a view of the grounds: a notary's desk from Chicago, a two-drawer rosewood cabinet brought back from Brazil; on bookshelves covering an entire wall, detective novels, especially by Erle Stanley Gardner, the idol of his youth, in English editions, as well as the complete works of Conrad (Canterbury edition), and a wide range of selected volumes – Montaigne, Pascal, Cardinal de Retz, Racine, Delacroix's *Journal*, Musset, Gobineau, Eugène Sue, Benda, etc. And at its core: books on flora and fauna, works of Burgundian erudition,[33] atlases, guidebooks, etc. With its pictures, paintings and furniture brought over from the New World, Lévi-Strauss's house in Lignerolles was a shrine to family traditions, an attempt to gather the vestiges of the past (his father's paintings, in particular) into a coherent world: that of his own life, which picked up the thread there, where family prosperity had left off, in the Second Empire.

Beginning in 1964, Lévi-Strauss would migrate for a few months to Lignerolles, for long and more or less studious summers stretching from July to September. He would return throughout the year for the school holidays, including at Christmas, the rigours of winter notwithstanding, until the very end of his life. Essential breaks from the claustrophobia of urban life, these stays in the country were not so much about productivity as moments of relaxation devoted to reading and reverie. 'I read and I do odd jobs [*bricoler*].'[34] Of course, he did overdue reading, of various manuscripts he had accumulated over the school year – 'but nothing, in the end, that I could not have done without'.[35] Still, he reread Fernand Braudel's *La Méditerranée* in its new luxury edition, which had been sent to him by its author: 'I am taking it with me to Lignerolles, already breathing in the great gusts of sea air that it will blow over the Burgundy forests, and certain to rediscover many enriching topics for contemplation, and to find many others that I was not mature enough to appreciate, eighteen years ago.'[36] It was also a good time for reading through proofs, and worse, through translations of his books, especially into English, which he carefully checked, assisted in this regard by his wife's fluent command of English, as well as German.[37] But this was not the essence of it: he lived in tune with the weather and the ups and downs of his passion for mushrooms. 'It is still scorching hot here, and totally dry. For mushrooms, it's a disaster.'[38] Or: 'I am envious of your sun; here, it only showed up for three days, around the 15th of August. But, on the upside, there are mushrooms a-plenty! Girolles, horns of plenty, even porcinis, and countless others, more or less mysterious. My time has been spent mushrooming, proofreading and index writing.'[39] From 1958, Lévi-Strauss was in contact with the Wassons, a couple of independent writers who had published a two-volume book entitled *Mushrooms, Russia and History* (New York, 1957), which he strongly promoted, even though its authors were amateurs and the book somewhat 'crazy'. As he wrote to Isac Chiva: 'They have nevertheless discovered and even founded ethno-mycology, and I would like to help them, not just because I am (according to their typology) a "mycophile", but because there is a wonderful field of research out there, and one in which young French researchers could make a place for themselves.'[40]

The daily strolls through the surrounding countryside provide the perfect pretext for geology lessons. He unabashedly indulged his passion for identifying mushrooms, birds and plants: 'He lived in his Bonnier',[41] recalled his wife – i.e., in Gaston Bonnier's *Flore complète portative de la France, de la Suisse et de la Belgique*, one of the masterworks in his library. Rare birds of the region caught his attention – short-toed snake eagles, kingfishers, black storks – and small wildcats that he attempted to save and even, for a while, to raise. Birds, toads, bats, all sorts of animals in distress that he saw along his route, were tenderly cared for and observed. This happy intimacy with animals, revealed in a later photograph of Lévi-Strauss playing with the caretakers' dog, Fanny, was an inheritance from childhood as well as a key to the reconciled humanism that Lévi-Strauss was one of the first to defend. Later, in the 1980s, Monique became a beekeeper: she had five hives producing 100 kilograms of honey per year. Lévi-Strauss encouraged this activity and could spend hours observing his wife, dressed in the very net suit he had worn in Amazonia, capturing swarms buzzing in the linden trees, with the help of a large bag attached to a pole. The challenge of the whole affair being to catch the swarm, and especially the queen, and then introduce the 50,000 bees into the sheet that led to the hive.

Always impeccably dressed in high leather boots and a light vest, Lévi-Strauss gallivanted through the countryside, walking in the woods, taking in the spectacle of nature. He did odd jobs, cut wood, unknotted the ivy from around his trees. But this Burgundian gentleman farmer had little contact with the small community of local squires, who were all passionate equestrians. A chatelain in spite of himself, Claude Lévi-Strauss remained in his village, where they called him 'the professor' and where he never refused offers from the mayor to participate in local ceremonial events.

In the woods of Lignerolles . . .

The powerful feeling for nature that Lignerolles rekindled in Claude Lévi-Strauss's life was indeed an essential driver, a kind of 'shock absorber' for his very active life in Paris. But it was also more than that. The capacity to dream and to breathe, the felicity of a rarefied human presence, gave him access to Being, against which the contemporary subject did not measure up well. Lévi-Strauss's mushrooms, like Nabokov's butterflies, allowed him to shift scholarly (they were both erudite) and imaginary gears to former times, those of his own childhood for sure, but also and more profoundly, of the childhood of humanity.

When Lévi-Strauss, finger to the wind, went sniffing for mushrooms under the bushes, he was reconnecting with Neolithic man, olfactory intuition and a model of knowledge based on clues.[42] He put himself in the position of a savage mind in these civilized forests on the eastern edges of Burgundy, closing the loop of a forest route that had begun in Amazonia. A route through the forest that was also a route through life, since his childhood was spent by the seaside and his youth on the craggy heaths of the Cévennes, with a strong penchant for highlands. Maturity offered him the surprises of a natural landscape better suited to old age: 'It is the forest, now, which attracts me. I find it has the same charms as the mountains, but in a more peaceful and welcoming form.'[43] In the race against the clock of modernity and the shrinking of non-urbanized vital space, the forest stood as an unexpected obstacle, a happy stasis that Lévi-Strauss enjoyed to the fullest in Lignerolles: 'A community of trees and plants keeps man at a distance and hurriedly covers up his tracks. The forest, being often difficult to penetrate, demands of anyone venturing into it the same concessions that the mountains, more peremptorily, require of the walker. Its horizon, being less extensive than that of the great mountain ranges, soon closes in on a limited world, creating an isolation as complete as that of the desert wastes. There, a population of grasses, flowers, fungi and insects pursues an undisturbed and independent existence, to which we can only be admitted if we show the proper degree of patience and humility. A few dozen square yards of forest are enough to abolish the external world; one universe gives way to another, which is less flattering to the eye but where hearing and smell, faculties closer to the soul than sight, come into their own. Blessings such as silence, coolness and peace, which we thought had vanished, reappear.'[44] Forests indeed had all the qualities to attract this Robinson Crusoe: not only did they keep man at bay and in perspective, but they delivered an independent world in miniature, a kind of natural phalanstery that had long been for him the foundation of a renewed and revolutionary humanism. Recalling the last few lines of his 1931 review of Paul Nizan's *Aden Arabie*: 'Contact with the natural world represents the only eternal human experience, the only one we can rest assured is a true experience – the only current absolute value on which we may call to gain the security that will enable us to bring to life the absolute values of our future organization.'[45]

Physiologies of knowledge: a disciplined life

To continue our study of Lévi-Strauss at work, we turn from his various spaces to the shape he gave to time – habits, sacrifices, values, and the way the scholar shared them with (or inflicted them on) those around him.

The scholar and his family

The scholarly life was also the life of a couple.[46] Lévi-Strauss was lucky to find in Monique Roman a loving wife, but also one who immediately understood the iron discipline that this workaholic's schedule would impose: priority had to be given to science and the body of work in the making . . . 'That was the deal!'[47] she said, as if it went without saying. And indeed the 'deal' was never questioned. Monique was her husband's indispensable first reader, perusing every word he wrote (including his letters). She also attended his lectures at the Collège (though not the seminars), but above all she cordoned him off from the world, sparing him from social events as well as family ones; she smoothed over any problems in their material existence and made sure her husband's mind was as unburdened as it could be. In marrying Claude, she was thus also marrying into a certain vision of an intellectual and scholarly future.

Did they form a traditional couple? Reciprocity, a central concept in the work of Lévi-Strauss, was also at the heart of this enduring relationship: 'Claude gave me a great deal of self-confidence. From the moment I met him, he always solicited my opinion, listened to me, and made me feel I had a good mind. We talked about everything and made decisions together after discussing our respective points of view. "Let's try", he would always say. This was a big thing for a woman, such consideration. It was like the small Japanese crinkled paper flower that blooms in water!'[48] Besides the intellectual authority that impressed his wife, his more idiosyncratic charms never ceased to endear her to the man who became, over the years, an intellectual superstar and an icon of the century. First, his radical independence of spirit: 'At home, like at the seminar, you never knew in advance what was going to come out of his mouth!'[49] Such unpredictability was a powerful antidote to the dullness of everyday existence, the daily routine that he would sometimes break with shy amorous gestures. A Parisian *flâneur*, he often wandered the streets of the city. He would come back with odds and ends gleaned at antique dealers and the Drouot auction house, which he casually laid at the feet of his wife, like small offerings. Alongside the scholar engrossed in study, the surrealist fellow traveller had survived in him, attentive to objective chance, 'marvels' (a word he often used), coincidences, and the capacity of objects to suddenly rise up. This great escape into dream added colour to their life as a couple, and later as a family of three.

After the birth of his first son Laurent, Lévi-Strauss did not particularly care to have another child. But that was also part of the 'deal'. Monique and Claude's son Matthieu, born in 1957, rekindled Lévi-Strauss's fascination for infants, language acquisition and the delights of the early years of life. Clearly, he was not the same father for both Laurent and Matthieu. On the academic front, for instance, he appears to have been more demanding of Laurent, with whom he was quite harsh, whereas he was more relaxed with Matthieu, if not downright lax, giving little importance to school results, writing his son's papers for him and indulging him when he suddenly felt ill on the eve of exams. The boys' temperaments were very different: one was plagued by the typical guilt of children of divorce and later had difficulties finding his way, weighed down by his father's name; the other blossomed into a Huckleberry Finn of the 16th arrondissement, venturing far and wide quite early in his adolescence, as his father had, going to Sicily, Norway by bike at the age of sixteen, backpacking across the Pyrenees, etc. At fifteen, he read *Tristes Tropiques*: 'Not bad at all!' he concluded before his flabbergasted parents.[50] Driven by early passions which later led him to choose studies in medicine and biology, he could effortlessly capture his father's attention. Moments in the life course also account for the classic difference between the two sons: Matthieu's childhood, in the 1960s, unfolded at a much more comfortable time for Lévi-Strauss than that of Laurent, who in any case lived with his mother and saw less of his father as a result. Yet with neither son was Lévi-Strauss in the least an authoritarian father figure: 'Why can't you leave him be!' he would often say to his wife. Mindful of table manners – the third volume of the *Mythologiques* is dedicated to his son Matthieu – but not in the least fussy or a stickler for politeness or cleanliness, Lévi-Strauss was not much of an 'educator' in that sense. The still vivid memories of the endlessly drawn-out Sunday lunches of his youth made him very tolerant of childish impatience. In the end, he was mostly protective of his own peace and quiet, and not averse to having his children take part in intellectual games. For instance, when he asked Laurent to respond to the questionnaire on magical art Breton had sent him. Similarly, he asked Matthieu to draw lists of synesthetic correspondences, which he then sent on to Jakobson. 'Very impressed by Matthieu's synesthetic data, very puzzling',[51] answered the American linguist.

Matthieu Lévi-Strauss remembers from when he was young that his father looked old to him – and indeed he was, forty-nine years old at the birth of his second son. He was also in poor health, prone to fainting spells, frequent digestive trouble and minor illnesses. Then, strangely, longevity took hold. In the 1960s, Lévi-Strauss's body was not yet marked by the fragile spirituality and ascetic patina it was to have later. Besides, he was in fact no ascetic, with regard to food or anything else. If he was not a big eater, he had an intense sense of gustatory pleasure that remained one of the major sources of delight in his life. His two previous wives had already noted this, but Monique was in a better position to provide in this respect, on a daily basis, and Lévi-Strauss would be overcome with 'gastronomic affection' when the food was to his taste. He was so grateful he would cry! Each meal was a brief ceremony to be experienced in silence (all the way to the cheese course) and during which he was not to be interrupted: 'You can ask him for anything, but after the cheese course', Monique would recommend to those who shared his meal, and especially her son and stepson.

In 1968, on his wife's advice, he went on a sugar-free diet, which quickly proved effective – the digestive problems disappeared. In addition, over the course of a few weeks, Lévi-Strauss lost about fifteen kilos. A bodily revolution in tune with the times . . . though everyone around him thought he was gravely ill. From then on, and for the forty years remaining to him, he maintained a characteristically slender figure, even skinny, which symbolically fit the Western (clerical) image of the body of a true intellectual – as if a fragile corporeal form was a sure sign of serious thought.

The thirteen gardens of Montbard

At Buffon's estate in Montbard, the house and study stood thirteen gardens apart – thirteen gardens that had to be traversed, twice daily, marking the passage from work to family life. The scholar's intensive work regime thus informed the way space and time were organized, the practice of professional and personal sociability, and ultimately a whole physiology of life devoted to intellectual labour. Depending on the period and the personality, there have been many ways 'to cross the thirteen gardens of Montbard'.[52]

Around the rue des Marronniers, the clerical regularity of the strict schedule divided the long days into sequences: getting up between 6 and 7 a.m., having breakfast, showering and shaving, then leaving for the LAS; when he stayed home, the early morning was devoted to letter writing – the post arrived at 9. At noon, Lévi-Strauss almost always lunched at home, and less and less often in town: the noisy and crowded Parisian restaurants were hostile territory for this confirmed claustrophobe. Besides, he always knew he could expect a good lunch at home . . . In the afternoon, when not teaching, he worked in his study. At around 5:30 p.m., he went down to buy his papers and tobacco and visit his mother, who lived nearby in a ground-floor apartment. If a specific light was on, it meant Dina Dreyfus was visiting her former mother-in-law – the two women remained very faithful to each other until the end – and Lévi-Strauss would continue on his way. If the light was off, he would drop by and chat with her for

ten minutes or so, and then close the shutters for the night. This family
code amused Matthieu, who sometimes accompanied his father. The visit
to Emma Lévi-Strauss was a daily obligation the son fulfilled for about
thirty years, until her death in 1984. In the evening, he would read two
newspapers and several magazines, dine, and go to bed early, at around 11
p.m. – thus bringing his busy, well-ordered and well-rounded day to a close.
Television appeared rather late in Lévi-Strauss's life, in 1974, when Marcel
Jullian, just appointed as director of Antenne 2, proposed that he become
one of the channel's administrators. In order to fulfil his new responsibilities, Lévi-Strauss requested that a television set be delivered to his home.

In the 1960s, Lévi-Strauss turned down a steady flow of invitations to
participate in conferences or to teach at American universities – the worst
being conferences dedicated to his own anthropological work, which he
did his best to discourage. He was particularly wary of American forms of
academic sociability: 'To be honest, the idea of gathering so many people
together in some Chicago hotel is rather frightening to me. But unless
the conference can be held on a pleasant campus, far away from the city
and surrounded by countryside, there is probably no alternative.'[53] He
declined an offer to teach for a semester at Harvard, for he 'disliked the
idea of being separated from his family for that long'.[54] Lévi-Strauss was
thus a homebody by inclination as much as duty. But if he often gave the
impression of shunning professional events and anthropological gatherings (which he no longer needed to attend as much as he had in the past),
he was, on the contrary, ready to respond to solicitations from strangers,
young men and women seeking his counsel for a presentation, bibliographical orientation, or personal issues. For example, a girl in her final year of
secondary school informed him that she had a presentation to do on him,
and more specifically on *Tristes Tropiques*, and asked if she could briefly
interview him. Her request was granted on the spot! The very next day, he
replied: 'I would be happy to meet with you. As I don't know when you
are free, and my availability is rather limited, would you be so kind as to
phone the laboratory to arrange for a time that suits us both?'[55] A student
at the École supérieure de commerce wrote to him in the name of his classmates, who could not make sense of a passage in *Tristes Tropiques*, which
was part of their curriculum. Indeed, by the 1960s, *Tristes Tropiques* had
already made its way into school and university curricula, turning Lévi-
Strauss into a contemporary classic. The anthropologist promptly replied:
'If I remember correctly, I think the idea that Europe was "lucky to be a
woman" referred to the emotional and tender component of the Christian
ethos, which might have been further developed by Buddhism had Islam
not intervened between the two and had it not provoked in response an
attitude of aggression and conquest in Europe, which found expression in
the crusades for example.'[56] In contrast, he would grudgingly respond –
but respond nonetheless – to requests that seemed informed by less worthy
considerations: 'I hate being called master (a title nobody in my entourage
would even think of giving me). If you want to see me, all you need to do
is call the laboratory and arrange a time. But let me tell you straight away:
you will be disappointed. I live in total isolation, do not see anyone, do

not go out and do not have any contact with what you call the "literary circles". I work ten hours a day, Saturdays and Sundays included. This is the kind of life I lead . . .'[57]

This paradoxical availability inflected a carefully managed relationship to time: the jealous care he took of it, and the resentment he felt towards those who wasted it, was the best way to secure time for his own work and pleasure. 'He had little patience for things that made him anxious or bored.'[58] Whether it was dull conferences, social dinners or traffic jams – which drove him insane – Lévi-Strauss was terribly impatient. Always very worried about being late, he would arrive early for appointments, so much so that those who accompanied him found it annoying. It systematically followed the same pattern: so as not to disturb the other party by showing up before the agreed time, he would do a lap around the block, champing at the bit . . .

This explains why, in the end, this very busy man appeared to his son in the 1960s to be very available – regularly visiting the Drouot auction house, spending all school holidays in the country, and still free to indulge in all manner of little projects around the house.[59]

Writing, speaking, keeping quiet

Lévi-Strauss is famous for his resounding silences. At home with his wife he spoke little but was endowed with 'an uncanny talent for listening'.[60] He was also very enthusiastic about the 'tabloid' stories his wife recounted to him, and very keen to hear about scenes of city life, the comical aspects of which could trigger fits of laughter to the point of tears. To provoke such reactions, the narratives had to be quick and incisive sketches, like the *New Yorker* cartoons he used to read in the US. As a host, he was always courteous but had little inclination to shine and even a tendency to withdraw into silence in the presence of chatty guests, except when they were intellectual friends whom he admired, such as Jakobson, who was known to stretch an evening into the wee hours – something almost no one else could achieve with Lévi-Strauss. From time to time, Monique would call Michel Leiris to the rescue, for a dinner through which her husband was likely to sit in complete silence: 'He did not say a word, which chilled everyone!' He made no effort to conceal his boredom or listen to the confessions of random guests. At home, his wife acted as an efficient barrier against the social demands that became increasingly intense as his renown grew. At the laboratory, it was his secretary who would do the screening. He hated the telephone, and kept all phone conversations to a bare minimum. Thirty seconds into a conversation, once the question motivating the call had been made clear, his interlocutors were left with no other option but to mumble their thanks and hang up. A stinging experience . . . but one that served to underscore the regime of endless talk in our societies, against which Lévi-Strauss took a stand by celebrating the economies of scarcity in savage societies: 'Among us, language is used in a rather reckless way – we talk all the time, and seize any pretext to express ourselves, ask questions, offer commentary. This way of abusing language is not at all universal. There are cultures – and I am inclined to say most of the cultures of the world – which are rather thrifty in relation to language. They don't believe that language should be used indiscriminately, but only in certain specific frames of reference and *sparingly*.'[61] Being fundamentally parsimonious in speech, Lévi-Strauss, once again, shed contemporary garb in favour of another mode of human living and speaking.

Extremely disinclined to unnecessary talk, whether in person or on the phone, he preferred to write letters, which generally took up the early part of his day. Scholarly life was one of correspondence. The medium of collective work and social and professional positioning, as well as controversy and the circulation of information, his correspondence reflected the fits and starts of an often lively field of knowledge, in which mood swings, bad faith and anxiety sometimes surfaced. Lévi-Strauss had failed to cite the specialist of India Louis Dumont in a bibliography. The latter expressed both his disappointment, albeit with considerable modesty, and, worse, his sense of having been symbolically murdered: 'It is difficult not to feel hurt by this silence, all the more so that unconsciously you have me figure among the dead objects.'[62] Lévi-Strauss's bibliographies set the standard for international scientific excellence – to not appear was to no longer exist. 'You are a public figure, almost an institution, and everyone pays the greatest attention to what you do, and do not do. If a French author who claims to be a structuralist is not mentioned by you anywhere, it is for him a black mark.'[63] In this context, it is easy to see why one of the chief objectives of Lévi-Strauss's letters was to defuse situations, to clear up what he often referred to as 'misunderstandings', to placate egos, to offer balm for wounds large and small inflicted on this milieu. Even while they were becoming theoretical opponents, if not downright enemies, Georges Balandier responded warmly to a letter he received from Lévi-Strauss in 1966: 'You cannot imagine how moved I am by your very cordial letter. I am flattered by the interest and favourable judgement you express for my "Kongo". Your appreciation is most important to me. It outweighs all others I have received.'[64] Lévi-Strauss always acknowledged receipt of the books he was sent, though he sometimes added that he would not have time to turn to them before the following summer, which he would do, sending another letter. His correspondents appreciated his commitment to form, as well as his promptness in responding. Lévi-Strauss was well aware of the fact that the academic and intellectual world in general was one of symbolic retribution, in which the yearning for recognition was insatiable. Even the most brilliant minds were sometimes beset by doubt. The anthropologist paid for the peace of mind he needed by providing reassurance whenever possible, in short messages, letters, tributes and book inscriptions. The anthropologist Georges Devereux – an old friend whom Lévi-Strauss helped to repatriate to France in the early 1960s by securing a post for him at the EPHE – thanked him for taking part in his retirement ceremony: 'Even if I had not been struck dumb by emotion, I could not have expressed how grateful I am to you – and not only for your warm and friendly speech.'[65]

'Why did I do all that work?'[66]

All creative lives perhaps entail renunciations. In *Cousin Bette*, Balzac explains that the Polish sculptor Wenceslas Steinbock could only attain the pinnacle of his art when dominated by an old maid; in the arms of his lover, he became nothing but a lustful and unproductive dreamer. This kind of work ethic is even more common in the world of science, where tenacity and endurance are held to be as important as passion, inspiration and talent. The team of sociologists working around Émile Durkheim all believed in such austere labour, with the exception of Marcel Mauss, whose Bohemian imagination rejected the rhythm of science, even while interpreting it sociologically. Mauss wrote to his friend and colleague Henri Hubert in the following terms: 'In fact, you and my uncle have retained the ideal promoted at École normale supérieure and the *lycée*. Your life, your entire life is oriented to matters of the intellect, and seeks either renunciation or the loftiest pleasures, there is no middle ground. You, my dear friend, have habits that were ingrained in you by a very violent school education. [. . .] But it is that same education that makes you so often unhappy and, as I have told Durkheim and mean to tell you, for no reason. Renunciation, my dear fellow, is of course necessary, and I have long been able to distinguish, indeed better than others, between what I must refuse to desire and what I must desire'.[67]

Claude Lévi-Strauss, as we have seen, was not a pure product of meritocratic excellence. The scholastic mould had not shaped him as much as it did others. Yet, it was precisely in terms of renunciation and sacrifice that he spoke of his life at the time of the *Mythologiques*: 'It was a time when I got up between five and six every morning, and I didn't know what it was to have a weekend. I really worked . . . .'[68] And: 'The series engaged my mind, my time, and my energy for over twenty years. [. . .] I was a monk.'[69] The need to learn, almost by heart, more than a thousand myths, not to mention all the variants, and to explore their ethnographic contexts, represented an enormous amount of material to absorb, and this took time: 'You have to let myths incubate for days, weeks, sometimes months, before something suddenly clicks . . . .'[70] Intellectual work, far from allowing the body to rest, was presented as a true physical feat. Scientific knowledge, he wrote in the 'Overture' to *The Raw and the Cooked*, 'advances haltingly and is stimulated by contention and doubt'.[71] This ascetic dimension was frequently expressed in terms of certain recurring metaphors in the letters he sent to decline invitations. Embarrassed to be refusing yet again to attend the conference organized by the Wenner-Gren Foundation in Burg-Wartenstein, he wrote: 'My colleagues must understand that I have engaged in an incredibly difficult task, which consists in holding together more than seven hundred myths. And I feel rather like a coach driver steering seven hundred horses, terrified that his reins might get tangled if his gaze were to wander.'[72] The coachman of a diabolical carriage or, more classically, the Conradian explorer of uncharted territory: 'The books in the Mythology series illustrate the unfolding, almost on a daily basis, of a work of discovery. I laboured in a virgin forest that, for me, was an unknown world. I was laboriously clearing a way through barely penetrable thickets and clumps.'[73] In both cases, though more dramatically in the first, the metaphors enhanced the physical violence of the effort at intellectual concentration entailed in the marathon project of the *Mythologiques*.

In 1971, having just emerged from the virgin forest, he confided to Raymond Aron about the inescapable existential trade-off one had to confront at the end of the journey, between the satisfactions derived from the work produced and its 'cost of production': 'If you grant that I have produced a body of work, and even supposing that it is a lasting one, I mostly measure – and believe me, with some melancholy – the disproportion between its intrinsic value and the price I have had to pay for it. What I admire in you, on the contrary, is precisely that you have managed to produce a universally recognized body of work, without having to sacrifice your social relations to it, whereas I felt incapable of handling both at once. It is that amazing vitality that has also allowed you to seize every issue, armed with an intelligence that is always informed and ready to react, whereas I close myself off from most, less out of a conscious decision to do so than a fragility that forces me to use my resources sparingly.'[74] Lévi-Strauss, a thinker of finite resources, applied the awareness that he made universal to his own self, that of a necessary economizing of means. By contrast, Raymond Aron appeared to him as a kind of inverted twin: Lévi-Strauss repeatedly highlighted Aron's intellectual agility, his impeccable thought process, the result of a brain that had been well trained at the École normale – qualities that he did not recognize in himself.

Were there compensations to this life of a galley slave? Honours and glory, perhaps? Arriving late in the game, they reassured but did not fulfil him. The satisfaction of having completed something, then? 'I can't say that I write in a happy frame of mind. It is more like anxiety, distaste even. Before beginning, I spend days staring at a blank page before coming up with the opening sentence.' 'And when the book is out?' 'It's dead, it's over, it has turned into a foreign body. The book passes through me. I'm the place where, for some months or years, things are elaborated or put into place, and then they become separate from me through some kind of excretion.'[75] It may have been shocking to some when Lévi-Strauss wrote that his intention was not 'to show how men think in myths, but how myths operate in men's minds without their being aware of the fact', and further still that one should proceed 'as if the thinking process were taking place in the myths themselves'.[76] This eventual demise of the subject was one of the major themes of the time, with the 'death of the author' being but a version of this death of the subject, on the structuralist agenda of Althusser, Foucault and Barthes. Lévi-Strauss put it simply – he did not identify with the books he had written: 'They are not my children.'[77]

Besides, scholarly books did not elicit the same illusion of eternity as literary works seemed to do. Science, as opposed to literature, could only lay claim to provisional truths. Their future expiration could even be seen as the guarantee of their current value. In that respect, Lévi-Strauss was as serene as Dumézil, who used to say: 'In twenty, thirty years, this will seem completely out-of-date.'[78] To one interlocutor, he gave full licence to criticize his work: 'Scholars are a little bit like snakes: they shed articles and books like old skins which, after they are written, become dead and barren matter. Others can then pick them up and shred them to pieces. You should feel free to demolish my paper, this is the way science progresses.'[79]

But why do all that work, then? 'When I work, I suffer moments of anxiety, but when I don't work I'm bored, and my conscience keeps pricking me. Working doesn't make me any happier, but at least it makes the time pass.'[80] Keeping boredom and guilt at bay, two central motifs in Lévi-Strauss's life, would already be quite an achievement. But in fact, just as we are not obliged to believe that renouncing social life was much of a sacrifice for Lévi-Strauss, so retreating into study, the monk's life, can also be seen as an entirely consensual self-immolation on the altar of science. In the end, work allowed him to indulge in many of the things he liked to do, at a lesser cost (to his conscience): listening to music, identifying plants, mushrooms, animals and constellations, odd jobs [*bricolage*], etc. Looking at the locations and concrete activities involved in his work, we realize that Lévi-Strauss successfully turned his tastes, hobbies and obsessions into the material for his work and thought (we have only to think of bricolage). As in a bourgeois kitchen, nothing went to waste – the secret of a successful life . . . For the better part of two decades, he lived part of his time in the intimacy of myths 'as if [he] were in a fairy tale'.[81] What are we to make of this? An escape from the here and now, this long conversation with myths might also have been a way to satisfy his taste for beauty and his urge to reconnect with childhood and play.

In Lévi-Strauss's den, throughout the 1960s, visitors would catch a glimpse of strange scraps of paper: these were the material for 3D constructions of the spiral-shaped structure of myth, whose logic of transformation he was attempting to illustrate. Like fragile witnesses to his alternative existence – both very serious and not so serious, for how could spending one's lifetime deciphering nonsensical stories ever be only serious? – which nonetheless culminated, after much effort, in four weighty tomes, one every two to three years from 1964 to 1971, and each eagerly awaited by all those, ever more numerous over the course of the 1960s, who had fallen under the spell of structural anthropology.

Claude Lévi-Strauss's 'Tetralogy'

Strangely, at the moment when Michel Foucault and Roland Barthes were demolishing the notion of the author and desacralizing texts by historicizing them,[82] Lévi-Strauss the author, who had made a dramatic entrance onto the literary scene with *Tristes Tropiques* in 1955, was confirming his central and singular presence in the thought of the time, progressively reinforced by each of the four volumes of his 'Tetralogy'. Did he have such a monumental achievement in mind from the start? His 'Mythologiques',[83] whose Virgilian tone has been little noted, seem to have been self-engendering, following a process which, according to their author himself, largely escaped him, and from which he himself miraculously escaped.

A great anonymous voice from the beginning of time[84]

What is a myth? Lévi-Strauss replied (with the Amerindian populations) that it is 'a story of the time before men and animals became distinct beings',[85] this separation being seen as the original flaw of the human condition. Mythology thus stages the anthropomorphic world of early times, in which ape-women coexisted with men in the shape of jaguars, in which vultures took off their feathered tunics to take human form, in which women slept with snakes and copulated with the moon, and in which Dame Grizzly and Dame Bear turned into young damsels. These metamorphoses attested to the instability of human and animal kingdoms and were further complemented by evil and sometimes cannibalistic spirits, sexual, adulterous and incestuous affairs, a whole Freudian world rife with scatological references, opposing the anus and the mouth, full of bodily secretions and expulsions: vomit, menstruation, ejaculation, defecation, phlegm, etc. Myths differed from other productions of oral tradition, such as tales and legends, but there were no absolute criteria for the distinction. In the end, what characterized myths was their aspiration to seek 'explanations that encompass the totality of phenomena',[86] rejecting the Cartesian division. On the contrary, myths tackle a wide range of issues that arise in various domains – cosmological, physical, social, juridical – and aim to account for all of them at once. Already in *The Savage Mind*, myths were defined as 'mental edifices which facilitate an understanding of the world'.[87] By providing accounts of origins – fire, celestial water, the sun and the moon, tobacco, death, etc. – they serve as *imagines mundi*, to explain 'why things, which were different at the beginning, became what they are, and why it could not be otherwise. Because if things changed in one realm, the entire order of the world would be overturned due to the homology among all realms.'[88]

Where did myths come from? Does a myth have an author? Just as a myth, in Lévi-Strauss's view, is always a sum of its variants, none of which is more authentic than any other, in the same way, he considered that even if there may have been an original author in some distant past, this question was better left aside: 'It's a lot like mushrooms – you never see them grow!'[89] The question of the genesis of myths was thus dismissed as the very epitome of a question without an answer, for myths are 'a message that properly speaking is coming from nowhere',[90] whose meaning only comes from their collective reception, and not from any possible individual about whom we can never know anything.

And yet much can be derived from a perceptive anthropology of myths: 'We have to resign ourselves to the fact that myths tell us nothing instructive about the order of the world, the nature of reality or the origin and destiny of mankind. We cannot expect them to flatter any metaphysical thirst, or to breathe new life into exhausted ideologies. On the other hand, they teach us a great deal about the societies from which they originate, they help to lay bare their inner workings and clarify the *raison d'être* of beliefs, customs and institutions, the organization of which was at first sight incomprehensible; lastly, and most importantly, they make it possible to discover certain operational modes of the human mind, which have remained so constant over the centuries, and are so widespread over immense geographical distances, that we can assume them to be fundamental.'[91] Dismissing all esoteric interpretations of myths – and thereby rejecting all (vile) contemporary political uses of mythology – Lévi-Strauss pointed to two main lessons from the study of mythic thought: the first ethnographic and local (to better understand a certain society or group of societies); the other, more universal in scope and related to the very operation of the human mind and to the early mechanisms it obeyed, paradoxically expressed in these nonsensical stories in the form of rebuses, full of absurd incidents.

Rosettes and spirals

As we have already noted, Lévi-Strauss did not enter the world of myth for the first time in the early 1960s: he already had behind him nearly a decade of seminars, marked by two essential texts – 'The Structural Study of Myth' (1955) and 'The Story of Asdiwal' (1958–59) – not to mention the experimental work carried out by Lucien Sebag and Jean-Claude Gardin on Pueblo mythology. The toolbox for the structural study of myth was already in place, and almost complete, when Lévi-Strauss decided he needed 'more room to manoeuvre'.[92] What were the main lessons drawn?

First, the idea that, in any given worldview, myths tap the resources offered by a series of dialectical oppositions and correlations between objects, beings and behaviours, in an attempt to make sense of an opaque reality. Behind the explicit meaning of the myth, revealed in its plot, is an implicit and concealed meaning, whose much deeper significance can only be reached through structural analysis. What did this entail concretely? First, the story had to be divided into sequences that mapped the armature of the myth, since the mythic substance was not to be found either in its style or in its narrative mode, but in its plot. To this armature, structural analysis added other categories: codes (sensory, astronomical, dietary, sexual, etc.), axes, mythemes, schemes, which, in the end, focused on the symmetries, asymmetries, inversions and homologies that provide access to the figurative and latent meaning of the myth. For a myth can never be reduced to its appearance. The notion of the mytheme, as we have seen, was borrowed from that of the 'phoneme' in structural linguistics: in both cases, meaning does not lie in any essence but in a relative position. A mytheme, such as the canoe journey in the third volume of *Mythologiques*, did not have any meaning in and of itself. In this example, the canoe trip that Moon and Sun take along a river, in the bow and stern of a fragile skiff, is a metaphor for the motif of the 'right distance', neither too close nor too far, at once together and separate, which serves to evoke all situations in which the excess of one term over the other threatens the balance of both: marriages that are too close (the risk of incest), too far (between women and snakes), being too close to the sun (the risk of getting burnt) or too far (the risk of putrefaction), etc. The pirogue metaphor provides logical terms for connecting space – concepts of disjunction (too far) and conjunction (too close) – and time, since this trip down the river takes a certain amount of time, which turns into space – the journey accomplished between the points of departure and arrival. Myths always serve as logical mediators, whose profound and layered structure can only be revealed by studying their many variants, in their repetitive and differential transformation. The point was not to omit any variant, and yet not to consider any one as more valid than any other, since it was in their differential repetition, in their spiral shape, that the profound structure of the myth could be perceived. At the end of the journey, various loops of different sizes were obtained, comprising groups of myths in a single ensemble of transformations, which themselves characterized major mythical cycles. In the end, these cycles could be reduced to a single myth. This is the paradoxical conclusion Lévi-Strauss reached at the end of his interplanetary journey through the hyperspace of myth.

This is also what allowed him to begin, almost arbitrarily, with the Bororo myth of the 'bird-nester', the M1, and to study its 'semantic contagion'[93] to closely related myths featuring matching elements, repeating patterns and links that contradicted one another, at various levels of analysis. He then followed a method his graphical mind referred to as 'radiating rosettes': 'The myth taken as the centre radiates variants around it, which form the pattern of rose curves that progressively enlarge and become more complicated. And no matter which variant at the edge you choose for a new centre, the same thing happens, producing new rose curves that partly overlap with the first and extend beyond them. And so forth, not indefinitely, but until these incurved constructions bring you back to the starting point. The result is that a once indistinct and confused field reveals a network of lines of force and is seen as being powerfully organized.'[94]

This organization was transformed into four large volumes that encompass 813 myths and 1,000 or so variants, all collected on American territory by ethnographers, travellers and missionaries, and then translated into a Western language. This raw material, little exploited by an anthropological discipline that had largely dismissed it, added up to an ensemble that excluded, as Lévi-Strauss would later suggest, an entire swath of American mythology: Navajo, Hopi and Pueblo myths, as well as the myths of the Inca, Aztec and Mayan empires. In short, all those that accompanied more complex and layered societies, those myths that Lévi-Strauss characterized as 'theological myths' (i.e., which may have been written by the more learned members of the group to further assert the domination of a ruler or a god) and that were therefore less relevant for structural analysis.[95] The underlying hypothesis was that a single population had spread throughout America, migrating across the Bering Straits between 50,000 and 15,000 BCE.[96] The unit of analysis was thus provided by history, which legitimized the comparisons, and highlighted the very object of anthropology: to make sense of diversity.

If 'the world of mythology is round',[97] as Lévi-Strauss was wont to say, the four volumes of the *Mythologiques* conformed to a spherical shape: the

2,000 pages follow a double arch, one geographical and the other logical, that opens in central Brazil, spreads out to all of South America and then moves on, in the third volume, to the Mesoamerican isthmus and finally to North America – whose myths were inflected by a more intense economic and social life, and presented Lévi-Strauss with inverted versions of the South American myths that had served as his starting point. After the antinomy of the raw and the cooked, at the core of cooking myths, came the opposition between honey, the less-than-raw, and tobacco, the more-than-cooked. Cooking thus gave way to its 'surroundings', and the logic of sensory qualities – raw/cooked, fresh/rotten, damp/burnt, etc. – to the logic of forms – empty/full, container/contained, etc. The third volume, *The Origins of Table Manners*, presented a veritable domestic morality, based on cooking and its surroundings, and offered a mythology of periodicity, opposing the continuous and the discontinuous, conjunctions and disjunctions. This progression towards greater abstraction continued in the fourth volume, *The Naked Man*, in which Lévi-Strauss abandoned the world of cooking and proceeded to that of cladding, both delving deeper and returning to more of the same, the 'naked' being the cultural equivalent of the 'raw'. Moreover, this double movement mimicked that of myth, in which each unit could be reflected in others, through a generalizing mechanism of reiteration that the scholar identified as taking the form of a spiral.[98] From the raw to the naked, his journey ended on a final chapter entitled 'One Myth Only': the several thousand myths under consideration would ultimately be 'variations on the same theme', that of the passage from nature to culture and the resulting rupture with the world of communication between all living beings that mythology celebrates, even as it confirmed its effacement.

The status of scholarship

Like all of Lévi-Strauss's books, the four volumes of the *Mythologiques* form a scholarly whole – 813 myths, for the most part American, are subjected to analysis, as well as about 1,000 variants. There were also 50 or so myths that originated in China, Japan and Polynesia, as well as a few from the ancient Greco-Roman world and several strays from the European and Christian peasant world of charivaris. About 350 tribes were mentioned, each with their respective institutions, rites, religious beliefs and social organizations. But this was not all: Lévi-Strauss made truly colossal efforts to inventory and identify the various animal and vegetal species, technologies and astronomical knowledge, as if he deemed it necessary for the anthropologist to emulate Amerindian knowledge if he or she was to correctly interpret their mythical representations. Dozens of diagrams, plates, bestiaries, detailed indexes, and a bibliography of several hundred titles complemented this monumental, exorbitant project – a veritable 'Human Comedy' of early times.

In this respect, the material in the *Mythologiques* marked an important moment in the cycle, since after *The Savage Mind* and the foundational

articles, Lévi-Strauss had to provide ethnographic 'evidence' in support
of the validity of the structural analysis of myths. The entire project
was thus thought out as a case study running to more than 2,000 pages.
Erudition unquestionably flattered Lévi-Strauss's scholarly inclinations
and allowed him to delve into the world of cabinets of curiosities. But
it also held further importance as an essential gear in the structural
machine, without which the 'analysis would be spinning its wheels'.[99] In
the three stages of structural analysis as defined by Maurice Godelier, the
establishment of the ethnographic context was an essential prerequisite,
without which the analysis would be crippled. Lévi-Strauss often said
so: the lack of sufficiently precise ethnographic data made it impossible to engage in the kind of serious formal analysis that might unearth
more profound semantic meanings. This is precisely what held him back
from including biblical myths. This was also what sharply separated him
from the literary structuralists, who interpreted tales and legends that
were, in his view, insufficiently documented. The issue of ethnographic
scholarship was thus central to his critique of Vladimir Propp's pioneering work. And so, ethnographic erudition was in the end what distinguished structuralism from a simple formalism, in which all content
was evacuated in favour of a pure formal logic. Instead, structuralism
was designed to be anchored in concrete data, which, although filtered
through interpretative models, still served to differentiate it from the
strictly tautological value of morphological studies that were not rooted
in any ethnographic context. This is an essential point regarding Lévi-
Strauss, who has been so often, and so strangely, accused of adopting
an overly theoretical approach. The fragile frame of his abstract schema
was nonetheless heavily laden with freight – a cargo ship rather than a
catamaran.

   Lévi-Straussian analysis also paid homage to a venerable ancient model
of scholarship in its formulation of a genuine epistemology of detail: 'the
tiniest details [. . .] acquire both meaning and function',[100] as he wrote in
The Naked Man. This was the moral imperative of structural analysis,
which Lévi-Strauss kept hammering home in his writings as well as in his
seminars. This 'weight of detail' belongs to a model of knowledge based on
clues, which Carlo Ginzburg has identified in early twentieth-century psychoanalysis, police investigations and the historiography of art. In these
three fields, interpretations could be put forward, invalidated and turned
around by a detail (a symptom, an iconographic fragment) that orients
research towards new paths. It is precisely within this framework that the
valorization of detail as well as of 'intuition' in structural analysis should
be understood.

   This reconnection with (and renewal of) ancient models of scholarship entailed a demanding and time-consuming investigative practice, to
which the files of scholarly correspondence attests. These files capture
the anthropologist in medias res, struggling with a thousand extremely
specific questions which he submitted to specialists all over the world.
For example, he enquired of Bernard Fontana, an anthropologist at the
University of Arizona, about a 1938 bibliographical reference on the

production of honey in pre-Columbian America, which identified two species of bees (the *Trigona* and *Melipona*). The aim was to confirm (or refute) the hypothesis that native populations collected honey before colonization, even if in Arizona the practice was apparently little more than a century old. Hence the hypothesis of an indigenous practice that had disappeared, and then reappeared with the introduction of other bees upon the arrival of the Europeans.[101] There are many letters attesting to his efforts to precisely identify the botanical and animal species that appear in Amerindian myths. Thus, Jacques Berlioz, a researcher at the Muséum national d'Histoire naturelle in Paris, replied to him on 13 February 1963: 'The bird that has been designated *Nomonyx dominicus* is a diving duck of the ruddy duck family (Anatidés-Oxyurinés). It is a fresh water bird, with a thick, short bill – blueish, with ruddy feathers that become white on the belly, its face all black – and a tail made of thick stiff feathers that the bird often holds cocked upward when swimming. Like all ducks of this group, it dives underwater to search for food (mostly vegetal) and is very widespread across intertropical America.'[102] At the museum, Lévi-Strauss also consulted Claudine Berthe-Friedberg, a specialist of ethnobotanics. This prompted erudite exchanges on the classification of Bombacaceae and Malvaceae (Kapok tree) species, as well as on the inverted cycles of reproduction of the cockspur coral tree, the 'ceibo'. A great friendship with the anthropologist Pierre Maranda was started up in 1966 under the favourable auspices of a correspondence on porcupines. Maranda was able to mobilize the resources of the Harvard Library and the Peabody Museum. Three years later, the discussion picked up again, this time on the smells released by certain kinds of ants, aptly called 'odorous ants'. Maranda launched an ethnographic and entomological investigation among his Vancouver colleagues. On 2 December 1969, he learned from Melville Jacobs, a professor in Seattle, of the existence of 'pissing ants', thus named because of the strong smell of urine they give off when crushed. Maranda fielded yet another request from the insatiable anthropologist: his colleague, Michael Kew, would soon write to him to 'provide semantic elements on the classification of the reproductive substances of salmon'.[103] Lévi-Strauss inquired of Jean-Claude Pecker, his astrophysicist colleague at the Collège de France, about the movement of constellations in South American skies. Pecker consulted the *Annuaire annuel du Bureau des longitudes* (Gauthier-Villars), the basis for all calculations carried out in works of celestial mechanics and spheroid trigonometry. On 31 January 1966, he replied: 'I have done some quick calculations on the rising, apex and setting of the Seven Sisters, Aries, Orion and the Southern Cross, in the Chaco Forest (25 degrees south) and at the equator (close to Guyana). [. . .] Indeed, the Seven Sisters–Orion movement and the Aries–Seven Sisters movement are comparable, but when we try to superimpose the two groups by sliding the Chaco sheet over the Equator sheet, the overlap does not work with regard to precipitation. The shift in symbolism from Guyana to Chaco that is identified on p. 78 of your manuscript is thus not explainable by the gap in the rainy season between these two regions.'[104]

It was at this fine-grained scale of research that the standard of scholarship of Lévi-Strauss's structuralism operated, not as a crutch for shaky hypotheses, but at the heart of the thought process, both scientific and mythic.

Myth and music

It is not often the case that a work on South American indigenous myth should be dedicated 'to music', or that its 'overture' should indulge in a long and passionate discussion of musical language, followed by a scathing indictment of contemporary musical forms. If Lévi-Strauss had demonstrated his intense musical sensibility in the beautiful passage on Chopin's opus no. 10 in *Tristes Tropiques*, *The Raw and the Cooked* shocked the musical avant-garde of the time with its radical positions against *musique concrète*, which he saw as 'floundering in meaninglessness',[105] and, more surprisingly, against serialism, whose refined syntax did not prevent it from going similarly astray.

As early as 1955, Lévi-Strauss was already suggesting that myths should be read like orchestral scores, but in the four volumes of *Mythologiques*, musical metaphors became ubiquitous: 'fugues', 'short symphonies', 'cantatas' and 'variations' were used to express the baroque form of the mode of reasoning (spirals and rosettes), organized into chapters of varying lengths, which the reader is never sure have fully come to an end: 'There is more', he regularly adds. At the end of each stage, a provisional conclusion is drawn, and then immediately quashed by a new issue that reopens the interrogation, as if the quest were indeed never-ending. Feats of scholarly gymnastics! 'This may seem like a roundabout procedure but it is in fact a shortcut', he claimed.[106] We follow the anthropologist in the same way that we allow ourselves to be carried along by a catchy tune. The legitimacy of the musical texture that is given to the work hangs on the 'isomorphism'[107] it claims between the system of myth and the system of music: both are art to the full, especially opera which, like myth, tries to solve all the issues at once according to the various codes (music, voice, dramatization, text) and offers, over a few hours, an experience that is 'as varied as the spectacle of the world'.[108] Lévi-Strauss, like Michel Leiris, was familiar with opera from childhood and was particularly fond of Wagner, though Leiris preferred Verdi.[109] The great Wagnerian opus was a direct inspiration for his own work, and if Lévi-Strauss said of Wagner, in the overture to *The Raw and the Cooked*, that he was the 'undeniable father of the structural analysis of myths',[110] he wrote in the 'Finale' to *The Naked Man* that he himself had also composed a tetralogy, not of sound but of sense.

According to Lévi-Strauss, these profound affinities came from the common characteristics of myth and music, of their 'both being languages which, in their different ways, transcend articulate expression, while at the same time – like articulate speech, but unlike painting – requiring a temporal dimension in which to unfold. But this relation to time is of a rather special nature: it is as if music and mythology needed time only in order to deny it. Both, indeed, are instruments for the obliteration of time.'[111] The analogy also works from a historical perspective: the grand musical form was born in the seventeenth century, just as the mythic form was disappearing from Europe, as if the one were taking over from the other.[112] In that respect, while Lévi-Strauss did not hide his view that this musical form of European modernity was now dead, his readers may still see (or rather hear) his 'Tetralogy' as the prolongation, and indeed the survival, of a proximity to the gods that both forms had managed to convey for centuries, and that anthropology now resumed.

Whatever its fate, Lévi-Strauss believed in this profound homology between myth and music, which many musicologists have since challenged, and sometimes rejected.[113] In any case, before being an appreciation, and expressing itself as an aesthetics, music functioned as a cognitive model for structural anthropology – at an even deeper level than mathematics for *The Elementary Structures of Kinship* and painting for *The Savage Mind*. As many commentators have pointed out, one of Lévi-Strauss's last articles was devoted to Rameau.[114] His oeuvre ended on a musical note, dubbed, as early as 1964, the 'supreme mystery of the science of man'[115] – a language both intelligible and untranslatable. Music never ceased to puzzle, amaze and inspire Lévi-Strauss who thought he had found, in the language of myths, a simpler form of its magic.

The Lévi-Straussian revolution

As opposed to what he had done in *The Elementary Structures of Kinship* and *Totemism*, Lévi-Strauss did not engage in any critical ground-clearing prior to developing his theses in *Mythologiques*. Yet the concept of 'myth' would seem to have called for similar treatment to that of 'totem': just as there was a 'totemic illusion', Lévi-Strauss demonstrated that there was a 'mythical illusion'. But Lévi-Strauss proceeded stealthily, up until the great 'Finale' of *The Naked Man*, in which he does deliver a few blows to his predecessors, yet stops short of naming or discussing them. By contrast with his usual mode, his offensive position did not require any clear identification of opponents. Kinship and totems were such classical objects of anthropology that he could not do without a review of the various theories before introducing his own. It was different with myth: if collecting material on myths had been of interest to both professional and amateur ethnographers, myth as an object of study had developed somewhat outside the field of anthropology, in philosophy, psychoanalysis, and in the new fields of philology and comparative mythology that had developed in the nineteenth century.

Compared to these older approaches, Lévi-Straussian analysis represented, in the words of Jean-Pierre Vernant, 'continuity, rupture, and a new departure'.[116] Today's young researchers, like Gildas Salmon, tend to accentuate the radical character of Lévi-Strauss's disruption, which was also intended to reclaim myth for the anthropological discipline.[117] Indeed, from Plato to Ricœur, philosophy had engaged with myths in much the same way as rational thought had with totems: both (myths and totems) negatively defined the limits of philosophical reason, of the 'logos' as opposed to the 'mythos'. The field of mythology was thus defined by its exclusion from philosophy.[118] Against such an instrumental approach, Lévi-Strauss made sure he kept the territory of myth within deliberately vague boundaries, including with regard to tales and legends, and rejected any definition that treated myth as a rational aberration. Alongside philosophy, philology also adopted a genetic approach, in its search for an original version, whose various avatars were but degraded versions of the primal truth. This only helps us to see clearly how Lévi-Strauss effected a reversal of perspective: in his view, as we have already said, the idea of an original version was a delusion empty of any heuristic value. The only productive approach involved examining the different variants, which served to highlight the operations of the human mind and its schemes of reconfiguration, making it possible to perceive, as when turning a kaleidoscope, the method in the transformations.[119] In the end, Lévi-Strauss did launch a more frontal attack on the comparative mythology that had developed as a specialized field of knowledge in the nineteenth century, though only in his later interviews with Didier Éribon. This represented an even more pressing challenge, given that, as Gildas Salmon has pointed out, one of Lévi-Strauss's major contributions was to have made possible a new comparative perspective, to have invented 'a new comparative practice'.[120]

Indeed, the study of mythology had unfolded in a comprehensive comparativism – dubbed a 'comparativist mania'[121] by Lévi-Strauss – that cast a very wide net and relied on vague resemblances to produce weighty concepts, such as Jung's collective unconscious, and a universal mythology loaded with prejudices projected onto it by its analyst: 'A comparative study of Indo-European, American and African myths is valid; a mythology with universal pretensions is not. [. . .] That everyone may find in myths what he or she is looking for simply proves that nothing of the sort is actually there.'[122] It was not in resemblances, which grew more superficial as the scope expanded, that meaning could be found, but rather in differences, and more specifically in the relationships between these differences. The primacy of intercultural difference inverted the hierarchical order that organized the production of knowledge in the social sciences: first, a monograph on a small subject, then a comparison with other societies and, finally, a synthesis. In fact, to enable comparison, the adequate scale had first to be found, and so the analysis had to begin with synthesis: 'As for the comparative method, it does not, as I have so often said, consist of first making comparisons and then generalizations. Contrary to accepted belief, it is generalization that is the basis for comparison.'[123] From this perspective, the *Mythologiques* series introduced a new comparative method that differed from the functional comparativism of *Elementary Structures*, as Émile Benveniste pointed out in a letter of 26 November 1964, after receiving the first volume: 'This book must be read either very quickly, straight through, which I could not do, or else somewhat distractedly in small increments, which I did, and while I cannot claim to have followed all your exegeses in detail, I am amazed by the ingenuity and rigour with which you set

out to discover – and then to interpret, through systematic connections –
the significant elements of the myths. [. . .] It is a very special and rich
work, in which so many calls and echoes are intertwined that, regardless of
the musical references that frame it, I was constantly reminded of a composition by Messiaen, rightly or wrongly, I don't know. In any case, you
have brought the study of myth to a whole new level, which also heralds
a transformation in your mode of analysis.'[124] The intertwined calls and
echoes, the musical form and the bonds they create affected intelligibility
differently, as if Benveniste had sensed that the *Mythologiques* represented
a new way of doing structuralism.

Within this renewed structuralism, as Gildas Salmon has shown, the
influence of psychoanalysis on myth analysis, through such notions as
condensation and displacement, became much stronger. Throughout his
life, though, Lévi-Strauss maintained his quarrel with psychoanalysis, even
as far as the very severe critiques he expressed in *The Jealous Potter* (1985).
The fact remains, however, that to find a way out of the apparent absurdity
of myth, Freudian psychoanalysis proved essential for the anthropologist.
Freud had developed a philological model for the interpretation of the
work of dreams, considered as altered texts whose true meaning needed
to be re-established. Dreams were thus considered as coded texts, riddles
involving a transformation from the deeper dream to the sometimes anecdotal and often irrational manifest content it offered upon waking. Between
the two versions, Freud identified various processes of distortion that Lévi-
Strauss adopted for his own purposes: images, symbolic representations,
condensation processes that brought together various associated ideas and
dream elements into a single nodal point, displacement through which
incidental elements become central (to circumvent censorship), etc. Just as
this work of reformulation is constitutive of dreams, so transformation is
constitutive of myths. According to Gildas Salmon, this similarity between
the work of myths and the work of dreams, the idea that all alteration is
meaningful, the decisive importance of detail, the urgent need to faithfully
collect all available narratives (of both dreams and myths): all are evidence
that psychoanalysis was one of the fountainheads of structural analysis. If
Richard Wagner was its 'undisputed' progenitor, Freud stood as a no less
productive, though more troublesome and thus less acknowledged by Lévi-
Strauss, father figure.

In tune with myths

By 1964, when *The Raw and the Cooked* came out, the French press was on
alert, and several long review articles, non-specialist yet in-depth, attest to
the existence of another, very French, myth – that of the 'cultivated general
public'. In *Le Monde*, Jean Lacroix presented the first volume as a 'treatise
on method, or rather the method itself being applied'.[125] Following a short
pedagogical introduction to structuralism, he recounted the first narrative
of the bird hunter that serves as a basis for some of the myths related to
cooking. Lacroix offers the following warning: 'The impatient reader will

vainly skip ahead to find out what the meaning of all these myths might be – and of all those he has just read about. But there isn't any. And this might be the source of some disappointment at first, for one clings to the idea of a riddle, whose key the author should provide.'[126] This provisional suspension of meaning, this deceptive quest of Lévi-Strauss might well elicit initial irritation. But it is designed to achieve greater meaning: 'Shall we insist on asking which signified are designated by these various signifiers that signify to one another? It must then be made clear that myths signify the mind that formulated them, by means of the world of which it is itself a part.'[127] In Lacroix's view, 'what makes Lévi-Strauss so great and so influential is that he is, so to speak, on the lookout: he does not extract the truth so much as lets it arise.'[128] He then concludes his review on the 'admirable lesson in submissiveness, receptiveness and humbleness that characterize the scholar'.[129] Claude Mauriac, the renowned critic at *Le Figaro*, presented a somewhat haughty Lévi-Strauss in his own words, responding to the accusation of overinterpretation: 'What does this matter? For if the final aim of anthropology is to contribute to a better knowledge of objectified thought and its mechanisms, it is in the last resort immaterial whether in this book the thought processes of the South American Indians take shape through the medium of my thought, or whether mine take place through the medium of theirs.'[130] The journal *Combat* devoted an entire page to the book and gave it over to Brian de Martinoir, a Cambridge professor of anthropology, who duly noted the 'major event in the history of ideas in the twentieth century: the birth of a new discipline, or rather of a new scientific attitude that is in the process of thoroughly transforming the concepts and methods of the human sciences'.[131] The professor also noted Lévi-Strauss's participation in 'Parisian literary life', struck as the reviewer was by the apparent incongruity of a highly specialized and technical work, an arduous and complex book, being discussed in the intellectual salons of the capital city, its journals and even its daily press.

As if to prove him right, the literary supplement of *Le Figaro* published an interview with Lévi-Strauss by Thérèse de Saint-Phalle: 'I am trying to lay the groundwork for a philosophy of man that would be in dialogue with contemporary scientific thought. I do not believe (and this is a tendency among young philosophers that seems to me highly dangerous) that philosophy should rebel against science.'[132] He had the confidence to hope that 'one day we shall achieve a unified theory of myth comparable to the one Einstein developed for the universe'.[133] But Lévi-Strauss was not averse to launching a few barbs of his own: 'A myth is as rigorous an object as a crystal. To endow it with moral meaning is silly.'[134] As for Jungian archetypes, he found the idea of a 'master key to dreams' outrageous. By 1968, *The Raw and the Cooked* had been published in English and, by 1971, in German, as *Das Rohe und das Gekochte*. In 1978, a pottery workshop called 'The Raw and the Cooked' was opened on the rue Lacépède in Paris . . . Lévi-Strauss was an export brand that also generated a few spin-offs.

With the publication of *From Honey to Ashes* in 1966, the file of press clippings expanded further. To round out our overview of the Lévi-Strauss events of the time, we should add to the list the special issue of *Les Temps modernes* devoted to the 'Problems of Structuralism', in November of that year. The critical reception of the second volume was characterized by the addition of very long in-depth interviews alongside the usual critical reviews, as for instance the one with Jean-François Revel in *L'Express*, which expressed a perplexity that was not uncommon: 'Faced with all these oppositions and harmonies, divisions and complementarities, incompatibilities and convergences, through which Mr Lévi-Strauss builds the incredibly complex and subtle structural systems of these societies, one is torn between a sense of necessity and a sense of gratuitousness. Are these rigorous deductions or arbitrary combinations?'[135] Jean Lacroix performed the ritual exercise in *Le Monde* that accompanied every Lévi-Strauss publication, providing a thorough examination of his work from a philosophical perspective, full of moral and political goodwill, and identifying with Lévi-Straussian humanism and the acute 'moral sense' that distinguished him from other structuralist thinkers.[136] Another long interview, running over several pages, was published in *Les Lettres françaises*. It may come as something of a surprise that this crown jewel of the communist intellectual press would so heartily embrace a thinker who never pledged any allegiance, and who even, with every passing year, posed an ever clearer intellectual challenge to Marxist thought. In fact, the 1960s were marked by an open-mindedness on the part of the French communist intelligentsia.[137] Edited by Aragon, the weekly cleverly positioned itself at the centre of the intellectual and artistic debates of its time, hence its paradoxical openness to the New Wave in cinema and the Nouveau Roman in literature.[138] Raymond Bellour began by asking Lévi-Strauss about his sources – often very long myths collected by native informants and translated with their help by generations of ethnographers – and about his working methods: 'I had to summarize without losing anything. I had to learn this kind of gymnastics – a very difficult intellectual exercise, but a very useful one, for it is through work of this kind that one manages to distinguish what is essential from what is not. The parts of the book that are based on compilation required more sustained effort on my part than those where I speak in my own name.'[139] Despite its strenuous nature, the work of deciphering also brought considerable pleasure: 'I read myths with jubilation. When I think of the great forerunners like Frazer and Lévy-Bruhl, who considered this intimate contact with the matter of myths as the most thankless part of the job, it seems to me that anthropology has radically changed. I think this is in part due to surrealism.'[140] He admits his thinking had evolved, especially regarding the crucial opposition between nature and culture. More inclined to considering it as an objective divide in *The Elementary Structures of Kinship*, he now saw it – under the combined influence of animal psychology, genetics in biology and game theory in physics – as 'an antinomy of the human mind'.[141] His relationship to philosophy, on the other hand, remained just as acrimonious, and Lévi-Strauss was always ready to respond to attacks levelled by the intellectual left: 'To demand that what may be true for us be true for all, and at all times, seems indefensible to me and indeed to partake of a form of obscurantism. It is a theologian's attitude, of which the history of philosophy offers many examples. [. . .] Some are clearly driven by the desire to maintain philosophy's control over kinds of research that are trying to become positivist. [. . .] This is ultimately the source of the misunderstanding that has put me at odds with certain philosophers: since I reject their approach with regard to my field, they figure that I will attempt to impose mine on theirs, for they cannot conceive that one might change perspectives based on the levels of reality under consideration.'[142] *Le Nouvel Observateur*, a weekly competitor of *Les Lettres françaises* that represented a 'modern', anti-Stalinist and anti-imperial left, also devoted full coverage to Lévi-Strauss, replete with photos, a sidebar entitled 'What is Structuralism?', selected quotes and a short biographical paragraph 'How Does One Become an Anthropologist?' The flattering introduction read: 'At the age of fifty-eight, Claude Lévi-Strauss, a professor of anthropology at the Collège de France, is one of the men who exerts the greatest sway over the next generation of intellectuals.'[143] Guy Dumur, otherwise a famous theatre critic, interviewed the anthropologist on his relationship to contemporary thought, pointing out the paradox of the modernist use of structuralism and Lévi-Strauss's defence of the past. Lévi-Strauss's politics was indeed also a politics of memory. Nostalgic for times when there was a clearer balance between the various cultures, on the one hand, and between man and nature, on the other, he did not fight 'to perpetuate this diversity [. . .] but to perpetuate its memory'.[144] How so? 'To put it bluntly, for the past several hundred or even thousand years, so-called "primitive" thought has been the doormat of philosophical thought. We considered what was in the minds of "barbarians" (for the Greeks and the Chinese), or "savages" (more recently, for us) to be of interest only insofar as it helped us to understand the progress of consciousness in Western civilization. I do the exact opposite. [. . .] Philosophical reflection only serves for me as a tool for making my contemporaries understand something else in a language that is accessible to them.'[145] Philosophy as a standard of wealth and a means to contemplate the beauty of the savage mind . . . This kind of exploitation of philosophy became a permanent feature of Lévi-Strauss's discourse. An article by philosopher François Châtelet in *La Quinzaine littéraire*, as well as an interview with Gilles Lapouge in *Le Figaro littéraire*, rounds out this non-exhaustive overview of the press coverage of Lévi-Strauss. The second volume, *From Honey to Ashes*, translated by John and Doreen Weightman, was published in New York in 1973 by Harper and Row, like the previous volume.[146]

The Origins of Table Manners was first published in June 1968. The date of its publication, in the middle of that spring's political upheaval, accounted for the less flamboyant critical reception of a work that was particularly important to Lévi-Strauss. Besides yet another enthralled discussion by Raymond Bellour in *Les Lettres françaises*, and the obligatory review by Jean Lacroix in *Le Monde*, it was his close friend Jean Pouillon in *La Quinzaine littéraire* who clarified the 'lesson in comportment' delivered by Lévi-Strauss in his third opus. As with structuralism itself, he explained, myths are properly speaking 'mediations', which both separate and unite, thereby maintaining the right distance. 'It is thus in every sense of the term a lesson in comportment that Indian myths deliver to us, a lesson that – to use two of the epigraphs that Lévi-Strauss has selected with the utmost care – should rescue us from "our utterly mistaken attitude to women, and our relations with them" (Tolstoy), and remind us that "no society can exist without exchange, no exchange without a common standard, and no common standard without equality" (Rousseau).'[147]

A zen anthropology?

The Naked Man, the fourth and final volume of *Mythologiques*, was reviewed somewhat differently, since it allowed, with a little perspective, for an assessment of the project in its entirety. In addition, the book ended with a 'Finale' that was as sombre as the 'Overture': at once melancholy, sentimental, polemical and violent, it even offered, *mezzo voce*, a few personal confessions. To read the press response, one had the sense, beyond the sheer scholarly virtuosity and theoretical innovativeness, of a work leavened with material that was 'human, all too human' and given an original musical form. All this conferred a sense of closure and a definitive quality to the work – an intimidating work, to be sure, but also one rich in a 'wisdom' that, lacking any other meaning, was valuable as such.

Le Nouvel Observateur called on Michel Izard, an Africanist anthropologist at the LAS, as if the final volume, more arduous and voluminous, required a kind of introduction or even translation. The publication of *The Naked Man* thus made it possible 'to take the measure of a project that has now reached its completion'.[148] Twenty years of study and eight years of writing went into what came to be called, following Lévi-Strauss, his 'Tetralogy'. In the end, a lesson emerged: the perpetual self-generation of myths and the existence of 'meta-myths' obeyed a pure logic of inversion, parallels and opposites that was immanent to the immense quantity of material stirred up by Lévi-Strauss. Despite changes and inflections, notably the outlining of an ethics and even an economics from the third volume onward, the second part of *The Naked Man*, focusing on Oregon myths, seemed to close the loop, as the anthropologist reconnected with all the themes tackled in the preceding volumes, only in inverted form. Cladding thus echoed cooking, and the naked the raw, providing a roundup, at least formally, of a body of material that was, in itself, infinite.

The 'Finale' intrigued and disconcerted its readers. The fifty-odd pages struck a Buddhist note that was beginning to define Lévi-Strauss's approach and character: on the one hand, his rejection of the position of the author, as well as its corollary, that of the subject; and, on the other, a complex signifying process that ultimately led to 'nothing' – the 'nothing' that closed the book.[149] Thus, at the very moment he had become the grand author of a monumental and celebrated work, Lévi-Strauss rejected the title with the utmost vehemence. This was, first and foremost, his way of expressing not merely modesty but also a methodological principle: the anthropologist had to withdraw and abstract himself from his own fundamentals. This initial asceticism was key to successful anthropology. But even more fundamentally, his immersion in myths had enabled him, he said, to experience the inconsistency of the ego in a powerful way. As opposed to all of Western philosophy, which had turned the subject into a 'spoiled child', he experienced himself as 'the insubstantial place where anonymous thought can develop'.[150] Far from being the author of his books, then, he was but an additional operator, a sound box, in the great transformation mechanisms of the mythic text: 'If there is a point at which the Self can reappear, it is only after the completion of the work which excluded it throughout (since, contrary to what might be supposed, it was not so much the case that the Self was the author as that the work, during the process of composition, became the creator of an executant who lived only by and through it); then, it can and must take a comprehensive view of the whole.'[151]

The other element that would serve to buttress this 'zen anthropology'[152] was the understanding of the signifying process as illustrated by Lévi-Strauss himself, and the outcome he assigned to it. For what did 'signifying' signify? The anthropologist broached this question in a letter he wrote to Octavio Paz after receiving a copy of the book the Mexican ambassador (then posted in India) had written about him: 'None of those to whom I have asked this question could provide me with an answer that was not tautological or based on a vicious circle, and it is a good subject for meditation that all the words mean something except that one.' Why was that? 'Because to signify', continued Lévi-Strauss, 'is to transpose one code into another, and "meaning" resides in the apprehension of a homology between the origin code and the destination code; but since the destination code can serve as the origin code to a third code, this can go on ad infinitum, and the question of meaning becomes itself meaningless.'[153] There is no meaning external to man, unless one is to believe in God – this was the answer he had already given to Paul Ricœur and hermeneutics. 'If the project must make sense . . . .'[154] he would often write to his correspondents regarding the *Mythologiques*. His entire approach wavered between an explicit quest for a comprehensive meaning and the possibility of an absence of meaning that would sometimes surface, like a dizzy spell, sweeping away all scholarly confidence. In fact, this comprehensive meaning, whose exact definition he left to others, found provisional expression in an antinomy that subsumed all others: that between being and non-being, i.e., the foretold disappearance of the subject, of man, which he sketched out as a fate that was both unavoidable and almost a relief – a dawn-like dusk, once the chimeras of Western philosophy were dead and buried.

For the 'I' that was rejected by the scholar, immersed as he was in the 'we' of myth, was taken up by the polemicist, for a few vitriolic pages at least. A true 'scalp dance', as Michel Izard put it, it was a response that seemed rather more like a riposte, and not terribly zen. Besides the methodological objections, concerning the status of the myths he used, and of their summarized versions, and also the remarks on the 'synoptic charts' and on the ethnocentric hubris that led him to apply a Western mathematical grid (canonical formula) to a human reality outside that culture,[155] it was yet again for philosophers that he reserved his most intense rage. He railed against their 'obscurantism', their humanist theology, their latent mysticism, their intellectual laziness, their sense of 'grievance'[156] at the dialogue he had established with myths, 'which has no need of them and to which they have nothing to contribute'.[157] Existentialism – 'a self-admiring enterprise that allows contemporary man, rather gullibly, to commune with himself in ecstatic contemplation of his own being'[158] – had turned into 'an ideological café du commerce' mired in 'problems of local interest, beyond which they cannot see because of the fog created by their clouds of dialectical smoke'.[159] This impassioned diatribe resonated widely in the press, as demonstrated by this headline in *Le Figaro*: 'Philosophers, stay away from myths.'[160] The article reproduced a few relevant pages of the 'Finale', alongside a photograph of a stern-faced Lévi-Strauss that lent gravitas to the otherwise sacrilegious discourse.

As opposed to the 'platitudes and commonplaces of the philosophers',[161] he did take some critical comments into account, especially those coming from linguists. For example, to what extent did working with translations, rather than original-language sources, create a bias? Other criticisms, from anthropologists, would follow, but these came later, and continue to this day. These have concerned several issues:[162] the link between myths and rites, Lévi-Strauss having often (though not always) held rites – which he considered 'the bastardization of thought, brought about by the constraints of life'[163] – in low regard; the question of the historical variants of myths, and of his ability to adjust his own grid accordingly; the kind of bonds that tied myths to the societies that produced and recounted them. On the latter question, Lévi-Strauss only ever mentioned a form of 'adherence'[164] between the myth and the techno-economic infrastructure, while of course refraining from turning it into a 'reflection' of the social organization. Finally, Maurice Godelier has remarked that Lévi-Strauss never considered the question of what credence to accord these myths, which he seems to have always taken for granted.

These critiques and controversies, not to mention the polemical, even polemicist, dimension of the 'Finale', attested to a tumultuous critical reception which, while overwhelmingly laudatory in the mainstream press, was not and would never be unanimous, either with regard to the *Mythologiques* or to his work as a whole. The critical appropriation of Lévi-Strauss, as well as the more or less acerbic discussions to which it gave rise, had generated a grand total of 1,384 books and articles by 1977![165] Lévi-Strauss the author was very ambivalent about what attitude to adopt vis-à-vis his critics: 'When [the comment] is hostile, I'm irritated, because I tell myself that I ought to clear up the factual errors, dispel the misunderstandings. However, I resent the author of such remarks less than the temptation he inspires in me to drop my work to respond. And then, after being stirred up for a moment, I calm down, knowing that I wouldn't change his mind.'[166] This was a rather pacifist reconstruction of his approach to his work. In fact, Lévi-Strauss knew how to encourage the process of critical engagement as the only productive approach in the sciences. He was therefore not in the least averse to making his points in rather forceful ways. And yet, this combative attitude was gradually obscured by his near-universal consecration, compounded by his own self-representation as a wise and level-headed scholar – an image that began to circulate on television as his celebrity reached its apex in the early 1970s.

Structuralist stardom

From recognition to celebrity

Celebrity represents a rather vague horizon for thinkers, and one that is not necessarily prized.[167] There is a considerable distance from peer recognition to public recognition, and an even greater one to the quasi-iconic recognition of contemporary celebrity. From the 1960s onward, the growing influence of television on intellectual and social life (anticipating that of the Internet today) transformed 'famous people' into recognizable faces. Academic glory traditionally arrives through other channels: it is citation of the work, not the visual recognition of the scholar, that ensures intellectual prestige. Foucault, at the Collège de France, accepted microphones but not cameras. Lévi-Strauss, as we will recall, barred both. Yet, through photographs published in newspapers upon every new publication, and especially through the coverage on the radio and television, in which he agreed to participate, he quickly became one of the new group of commonly 'seen' intellectual faces, both in France and abroad.[168]

One standard, albeit more traditional, first step in the process of acquiring national celebrity status in France at the time was making it into the *Petit Larousse illustré* dictionary. Lévi-Strauss found his way into the 1965 edition, alongside his contemporary Simone de Beauvoir, as well as Pierre Boulez, Maurice Halwachs and his nemesis Georges Gurvitch, listed in between the Duke of Lévis-Mirepoix and Leviticus, the third book of the Torah. A photograph came later, in 1981. But the moment that best captured the tipping point from renown to celebrity took place in January 1968. On 11 January Lévi-Strauss was awarded the CNRS Gold Medal by Alain Peyrefitte, the French minister of education. This ceremony, the French equivalent of the *honoris causa* doctorates that had already been awarded him abroad, was certainly prestigious, and was being given for the first time in recognition of research work in the social sciences – but it was not much known outside the academic world. However, the press covered it: *Le Monde* published an article on 13 January 1968. On that same day, the less elite *France-Soir* pointed out that Lévi-Strauss, whose name 'unmistakably conjures up structuralism, has an ever-growing appeal among advanced *lycéens* and students at our universities and Grandes Écoles'. A few days later, on 21 January the guru-in-the-making was seen on television, in an episode of the programme 'Un certain regard' devoted entirely to him.[169] This was not the first time: he had already been invited in 1959, to Pierre Dumayet's 'Lectures pour tous', to discuss *Sun Chief*, an Amerindian autobiography published in the 'Terre humaine' series for which he had just written the preface.[170] In 1964, Lévi-Strauss appeared again on Dumayet's programme to talk about *The Raw and the Cooked*.

At the end of the programme, the journalist had quipped that the book was definitely 'not for everyone, not a *lecture pour tous*'. A good sport, the anthropologist replied: 'Alas, I am afraid you might be right!'[171] From the start, Lévi-Strauss had always been a good communicator. Both on the radio and on television, Lévi-Strauss established himself as a great pedagogue, capable of addressing broad audiences in understandable terms, whereas in writing he did not spare his readers any complexity. Always evincing a certain gravitas, he would hazard a few anti-humanist remarks and bold comparisons – 'man must be studied as if he were a mollusc' – a sure recipe for media success. To Jakobson, himself no stranger to the television studio, he confided: 'The other programme (the one on which you are alone) has been scheduled for March. I will probably see it earlier, but it is not ready yet. Mine aired last Sunday. As you can see, we are all over the Parisian scene [. . .]. Structuralism is becoming official doctrine – and this will soon be held against it . . .'[172] Prophetic words in January 1968. Meanwhile, in the late 1960s, before the first stones of May '68 were cast, the power of the small screen – nearly all French homes were equipped with a television set by then – made Lévi-Strauss a public figure. And as the years went by, he learned how to use this audiovisual tool, becoming a master, despite his repugnance at the sight of himself. With clarity, modesty, poise and broad-mindedness, he assumed the posture of the great scholar, well served in this by his intellectual bearing and a touch of dandyism. From then on, each of his televisual appearances served to further confirm his stature, and, to this day, watching these programmes conveys a sense of the more harmonious balance that then existed – and no longer does – in relations between intellectuals and the media, between the realms of the readable and the visible.

Along with celebrity came certain disadvantages of his new visibility: people now recognized him, and the famous man had fans. A young American woman, convinced she had travelled next to the great man on board the Milan–Paris train, thus wrote to him, in an approximate and charming French reminiscent of Jean Seberg's, to offer him her typing and translating services, while confessing she was utterly inexperienced in such matters. A true gentleman, Lévi-Strauss kindly replied that he had not left France that year and there must have been some mistake: 'But I found your letter very touching, and if you want to drop by the laboratory one of these days, we can discuss your projects, though given the current academic situation, I cannot promise anything.'[173] He also wrote a playful, tongue-in-cheek letter to *Playboy* magazine, which had just run an article on the recently published translation of *The Raw and the Cooked*: 'Your review of my book *The Raw and the Cooked*, in the September 1969 issue, pp. 30–32, misses my point. Far from underestimating the "relationships man develops with his environment and with others", I argue that the only way to fully understand them is to understand the frameworks in which man operates – language, kinship systems, myths and rituals. [. . .] In other words, we cannot study the behaviour of human beings, whoever they may be, prior to knowing about their anatomy. But that anatomy should be a prerequisite will come as no surprise to the *Playboy* reader.'[174]

This new celebrity, amplified by a genuine structuralist vogue – indeed, the coach of the French football team himself declared he had reorganized the team according to 'structuralist principles'![175] – boosted book sales. Rumour had it that simply adding the adjective 'structural' to a book's title guaranteed an increase in sales of 1,000 copies.[176] Indeed, the second half of the 1960s and the entire decade of the 1970s produced numerous best-sellers in the human and social sciences, whose readership had previously been limited to specialists. Carried along by the works of structuralists, publications in the new disciplines – primarily psychoanalysis, anthropology, linguistics and the new literary criticism – attained sales figures that would be the dream of any publisher today: Lacan's *Écrits*, 900 pages of hermetic prose published in 1966, sold 36,000 copies. More emblematic still: Michel Foucault's *The Order of Things*, published by Gallimard, sold 20,000 copies in 1966 alone. Of course, this publishing paradise called 'structuralism' also extended to Lévi-Straussian territory. If the new edition of *The Elementary Structures of Kinship* managed to sell a few thousand copies, it was *Tristes Tropiques* that became a classic, bolstered by new paperback editions: by the end of 1963, 36,818 copies had been sold. Lévi-Strauss had a strange reaction to this belated success, expressing a certain perplexity regarding the merits of the new methods for democratizing books and reading. He explained his position on the matter to Thierry de Clermont-Tonnerre, his contact at Plon: 'The figures for *Tristes Tropiques* in the 10/18 series that you communicated to me are honourable but by no means outstanding. I have therefore come to the conclusion, as I believed from the outset, that my books would be best served by a modest but regular printing, over several consecutive years, but that it is neither in the publisher's nor the author's interest to aim for a very large circulation in paperback format, which kills the original edition and does not really bring significant benefits. For my part, I am quite adamant I do not want to relive the experience again, and I would be grateful if you could make my decision known to Gallimard concerning the publication of *The Savage Mind* as part of their "Idées" series.'[177] Gallimard tried again to convince him in 1969 with new copyright arrangements, but was refused yet again.

Lévi-Strauss was not especially profit-minded, but he did insist on being scrupulously informed of his book sales, on receiving royalties corresponding to the percentages agreed upon (which paperback editions did not always do), and especially on following contracts to the letter. He refused any abridged editions of his works and took considerable care with the quality of iconographic reproductions. By 1965, the 50,000-copy print run of *Tristes Tropiques* in the 10/18 paperback series had sold out. Yet Lévi-Strauss stuck to his guns and persisted in his attitude, which had come to be perceived as elitist but which, in his view, reflected both a sense of the compensation due the completed work, since paperback editions were less favourable for authors, and above all the sense that, as opposed to novelists, he did not write for a general public. He thus refused to authorize any French paperback editions of *The Savage Mind* and *Totemism*, though he could not impose the same restrictions on foreign publishers.

With success come misunderstandings

'I never read the critics, for if they do not agree with me, it upsets me, and if they do, it is necessarily due to a misunderstanding!'[178] A central motif of the Lévi-Straussian worldview, often invoked, as in this case, in a joking manner, the misunderstanding inherent to success was captured in July 1967 in a cartoon by Maurice Henry published in *La Quinzaine littéraire* on 1 June 1967, entitled 'The structuralist banquet'. It depicts four middle-aged, bespectacled Western men, clad in simple loincloths and gathered for an improbable intellectual pow-wow; Michel Foucault holding forth, Jacques Lacan looking weary and conspiratorial, Claude Lévi-Strauss engrossed in the reading of a paper, and Roland Barthes list-lessly dreaming. Four icons of the 1960s, who embodied the excitement over the ever-widening circle of application of the notion of 'structure': Lévi-Strauss to kinship and myth, Barthes to literary narrative, Lacan to the unconscious, and Foucault to scientific episteme. Others might have been added to the lot: Althusser who expanded it to all of society, Christian Metz to cinema, Greimas to semantics, etc. Roland Barthes attempted to theorize the 'structuralist activity' (1963) while Jean-Marie Benoît, a philosopher close to Lévi-Strauss, sometimes described the 'structural revolution'[179] in a messianic tone quite unlike that of his mentor. In 1968, the sociologist Raymond Boudon wondered: 'What good is the notion of structure?'[180]

Confronted with this intellectual vogue, this abusive use of terms and this new media exposure, Lévi-Strauss had different reactions. First, he quickly distanced himself from the hero worship expressed in the many letters he received. More importantly, he attempted to delineate the con-tours of structuralism himself, through a game of exclusion and inclusion intended to rescue science from ideology – though it must be said that he never served as gatekeeper of the discipline, since, as we have seen, he always resisted any conflation of anthropology with the structuralist approach. Finally, he adopted a humble attitude, claiming that he sought

'The structuralist banquet': a caricature by Maurice Henry, published in *La Quinzaine littéraire* on 1 June 1967.

only provisional truths in particular fields and pointing out that structuralism had already changed several times. He replied to a philosophy teacher
who had asked him to clarify his approach and goals: 'I do not try to formulate proposals and hypotheses on the nature of the human mind. I strive
much more humbly to solve anthropological problems in very specifically
defined fields. [. . .] It goes without saying that structuralism will experience
the same fate as all other systems of interpretation. Consequently, I do not
grant much importance to the philosophical implications of my anthropological work. They offer a provisional and convenient opportunity to take
stock, and they will gradually change. Indeed, they have already changed
several times.'[181] Lévi-Strauss could not be considered an intellectual guru.
It was in refusing this status, which the French intellectual world offered
him, that he maintained a singular position.

In this strategy of differentiation, Lévi-Strauss played with the references
he accepted and those he rejected. As the years went by, we know, his intellectual affinities with Lacan became weaker; he paid tribute to Foucault's
prose and recognized that he had restored confidence in philosophy, while
expressing reservations regarding the relevance and historical accuracy of
his analyses;[182] and when the day came, against Dumézil's advice,[183] he did
not vote in support of Foucault's appointment to the Collège de France.
On the other hand, he was at times sarcastic and even cruel regarding
Roland Barthes and the so-called 'literary structuralism'.[184]

Lévi-Strauss made several forays into the field of literary analysis and
criticism. The most famous one is the article he coauthored with Jakobson
on Baudelaire's 'Cats' ['Les Chats'], published in 1962, a joint study they
presented to celebrate their twenty-year friendship. Originally, it was
Lévi-Strauss who tried his hand playfully at a morphological, syntactic
and phonetic analysis of Baudelaire's sonnet; then Jakobson took up the
challenge, and the two mulled it over together for a day in Paris. The text,
published simultaneously in France in *L'Homme* and in the United States
as part of Jakobson's book *Poetry of Grammar and Grammar of Poetry*,
confirmed the legitimacy of treating literary texts and of the promise held
by such a project. Yet, two years earlier, in 1960, Lévi-Strauss had produced another important text at the intersection of anthropology, semiology and narrative analysis: a thorough review of Vladimir Propp's 1928
book, *Morphology of the Folktale*, that was then still largely unknown in
France, and had only been translated into English in 1958, with a French
edition in 1965. Lévi-Strauss paid tribute to Propp's intuitions, which, in
many ways, had anticipated his own analysis of myths – the hypothesis
that there was, strictly speaking, only one folktale, as there was a single
myth, and that the others should be treated as a series of variants. Yet this
text was mostly for him a chance to differentiate structural analysis from
the formalism to which Propp was confined, according to Lévi-Strauss, in
the absence of any ethnographic context regarding the societies that had
produced these tales. Interpretation was thus condemned to spinning its
wheels, 'condemned to remain at such a level of abstraction that it neither
signifies anything any longer nor has any heuristic meaning'.[185] It was a
form without a content. 'For structuralism, this opposition does not exist.

There is not something abstract on one side and something concrete on the other. Form and content are of the same nature, susceptible to the same analysis.'[186] In the end, his dispute with Propp was characteristic of his dispute with all of literary semiology, in which Propp's work stood as seminal.

In the early 1960s, when Roland Barthes went to see Lévi-Strauss to discuss the possibility of the anthropologist supervising his doctoral work on the semiology of fashion, the latter turned him down, while recommending that he read Propp.[187] A few years later, in 1965, Lévi-Strauss responded to a study on the application of structuralism to literary criticism, and the same argument resurfaced, expressed with a level of ferocity he only allowed himself because it was intended for publication in an Italian journal: 'Visionary and incantatory, this criticism is perhaps structural insofar as it uses combinatorial analysis to support its reconstructions. But in so doing, it offers to structural analysis a raw material more than a contribution. As a specific manifestation of the mythology of our times, it lends itself well to analysis, but in the same way as one could, for example, structurally analyse the reading of tarot cards, tea-leaves, or palms: provided these were coherent ramblings.'[188] His reproach against this kind of structural analysis of literature was that it resulted in a tautological circle between the object analysed and the analysis, a kind of ventriloquist discourse. As with Sartre's *Critique of Dialectical Reason*, Lévi-Strauss reduced this prose to anthropological source material that documented the French intellectual world and its pathologies . . .

But he was embarrassed when these uncharitable comments made their way back to the French intellectual scene, just as a kind of quarrel between Ancients and Moderns was erupting, ignited by the publication of a book by Raymond Picard, a Sorbonne professor and specialist of Racine, entitled *New Criticism or New Fraud?* (1965), which was intended as an aggressive response to Roland Barthes's *Sur Racine* (1963). The clash between the structural *'nouvelle critique'* and established academic, historical and genetic criticism was rather pompously dubbed the 'Dreyfus affair of French letters' and offers a stunning vantage point from which to view the various positions. Unwittingly, Lévi-Strauss found himself 'dragged' into it as the leading figure of structuralism in France, and did more than distance himself from Barthes, who was very affected by this escalating polemic.[189]

The final stage of this fracas on the margins of structuralism was marked by the arrival at the LAS of Algirdas Julien Greimas, a researcher at the VIth Section of the EPHE, together with Christian Metz, with whom, from the 1966 academic year onward, he coordinated a new semio-linguistics section.[190] They were only guest professors, a point on which Lévi-Strauss insisted: they were given access to laboratory facilities but they retained full budgetary and scholarly autonomy. For four years, Greimas and the brilliant group around the journal *Communication* (1961) – Barthes, Umberto Eco, Violette Morin, Tzvetan Todorov, Gérard Genette, as well as the new recruit Julia Kristeva – fell within the intellectual and physical orbit of structural anthropology. In 1970, this collaboration came to an abrupt end: narrative structure and mythical structure decidedly did not speak the same language. At that point, Roland Barthes had just published *S/Z*, an analysis of Balzac's novella *Sarrasine*, a book Lévi-Strauss did not like. The book's structuralist rhetoric struck him as being too much of a caricature of itself: 'His comments seemed to me far too much like those of Professor Libellule in Muller and Reboux's *À la manière de Racine*.'[191] Offering caricature for caricature, in lieu of acknowledgements, Lévi-Strauss sent Barthes a 'folly', in the form of a pastiche of the latter's analysis, which the latter unfortunately took seriously.[192] This infinite regress of pastiche, and Barthes's naive reception of it, revealed first and foremost a degree of admiration and esteem on Barthes's part for Lévi-Strauss, whom the former always addressed in his letters in a tone of friendly deference. As far as Lévi-Strauss was concerned, the strategic refusal to legitimize and integrate 'literary structuralism' was rooted in the risk of empty formalism that it posed to 'genuine' structuralism, in which the anthropological, historical and linguistic content was never separate from form. For Lévi-Strauss, *S/Z* was precisely that: a content-less form. This is what made it so easy for him to imitate, a little as he had done in his youth when he developed a tripartite argument to demonstrate the superiority of buses over subways. Barthes represented the danger of a structuralist discourse whose inauthenticity seemed confirmed by his later work and his change of 'styles': 'I never felt close to him, and this feeling was confirmed by his later development. Late in life Barthes went completely against what he had done before, which, I'm convinced, was far from his true nature.'[193] By contrast with Lévi-Strauss, for whom structuralism was a lifelong affair, for Barthes it was only one of the languages he spoke among others (Marxist, Brechtian, Sartrian, Blanchotian, etc.), even if his biography reveals the deep roots of his structuralist moment – dualism, the figure of the void – and the paradoxical role it served as a springboard into writing. Indeed, Barthes himself later recognized that the 'euphoric dream of scientificity' that animated his structuralist writings was in the end not 'his truth'.[194] This did not prevent Lévi-Strauss from supporting his application to the Collège de France in 1976. Lévi-Strauss's relationship to literary structuralism was, thus, similar to that of an illegitimate child, which one does not recognize, but does not fully disown either.[195]

In the face of these 'counterfeits', these bastard offspring, Lévi-Strauss unwaveringly designated the members of his chosen family, the structuralist library of his choosing. To young enthusiasts, eager to pursue further reading, Lévi-Strauss, who seems to have intended it as a test of the soundness of their commitment, recommended first that they read Saussure's *Course in General Linguistics*, 'our Bible'. 'Then, if curiosity persists: Dumézil's *Archaic Roman Religion*, Jakobson's *Fundamentals of Language*, Benveniste's *Problems in General Linguistics*. And, finally, my own books . . . .'[196] Among French authors, he would most often name Dumézil, Benveniste and Vernant. Structuralist lore has recorded small quarrels emanating from Dumézil, who was reluctant to be annexed to the Lévi-Straussian galaxy, manifesting in the sudden use of 'Dear Sir' in lieu of the habitual 'Dear friend'. As he wrote to Lévi-Strauss: 'What somewhat upset me recently was something else. I do not like when your epigones either annex me or oppose us one to the other, referring to my "Mythologiques" as "Myth and Epic". I have a hard time accepting the fact that someone at Vincennes University chose to work on "The Structuralism of Lévi-Strauss and the Structuralism of Dumézil". Among those of your disciples who have applied your views to the Classical world, Détienne's *Orpheus* (my esteem for the author remaining undiminished!) irritates me like a weak student paper. All this is of little importance [. . .] for I believe you feel even worse than I do about the excesses of so many of these authors, young and not-so-young alike, who are too easily drawn to structuralism.'[197]

On that occasion, as on so many others, Lévi-Strauss rushed to write an appeasing letter to his elder colleague. The latter, in moments of reverie, would return to the meaning of collaborative scientific work, to the 'cross-fertilization' between two works and, from Princeton where he spent a few months in the autumn of 1968, having just retired, paid a resounding homage to his famous younger colleague: 'It is always difficult to say what X owes to Y, and Y to X, you to me, and me to you. I think that what matters most is the excitement, the sparks that certain readings ignite, and not others, no doubt because our inner workings run this way and not that. With each one of your books, hundreds of times, you have done me this service, restoring the unrest to my adventure, reopening crevices that had been perhaps too hastily filled and may well yet lead deeper. But I am too old, I no longer have the time. My only concern now is to clean up the cadaver for the autopsy.'[198]

'At this late hour in my career . . .'

'At this late hour in my career . . .'[199] – the 'Finale' of *The Naked Man* presented itself as a closing of the curtain on the life of its author. He was then sixty-three years old. Over the eight preceding years, he had written 2,000 dense pages, and he declared himself 'tired'. As he confided to the *New York Times Review of Books*: 'I'm written out.'[200] The enervation that comes with a relaxation of intellectual intensity, after two decades of engagement, was offset by a sense of accomplishment at having brought the project to completion. He had overcome the Saussure syndrome after all! 'I have been throughout my work obsessed by what happened to Saussure with the *Nibelungen* on which he worked for years, and to which he devoted decades and dozens of notebooks. It is quite apparent to anyone who reads them that, as his fascinating study advanced, he became so overwhelmed, drowning in his own material, that he no longer mastered its thread. This was the danger that hovered over me as I was composing the *Mythologiques*. I adopted as an absolute principle that I should never succumb to this and that I would see this project to completion at all costs, even that of subjecting the reader to a trial.'[201] Having won the race against the clock, and averted the risk of drowning, only added to his sense of achievement and allowed him to accept the approach of old age with greater serenity: 'There is a moment in the life of any man of science or aspiring to be one, when he gets the sense he has completed his work, said what he had to say.'[202] No need, then, to delay it further. If, over the following decades, Lévi-Strauss was to publish many more important books and texts, he always considered his later publications as a postscript to a completed corpus.

A year earlier, in 1970, he received for his sixtieth birthday (albeit two years late), one of the ritual signs of academic recognition and scholarly filiation: a Festschrift, in which his peers and disciples, colleagues and friends offered testimony of their comradeship with the master in texts of varying formats and content.[203] Max Ernst provided a drawing in the shape of a rebus. Patrick Waldberg wrote about their New York years. The table of contents offered a snapshot of Lévi-Strauss's life and networks: the entire anthropological universe was represented, alongside a few historians (but not Braudel) and linguists. The ceremony took place at the Collège de France, at the LAS, with the film director Yannick Bellon documenting the proceedings in view of a film that was never edited.[204] There were young men with long hair and orange tunics and serious old men with mischievous airs: Raymond Aron, Michel Leiris, Jean Pouillon and Lévi-Strauss himself, jokingly discussing a structuralist ballet production in which the kinship systems would be represented through choreography: a corps de ballet comprising eight subgroups with eight huts on stage, mathematicians giving instructions to the choreographer, a Mack Sennett or Buster Keaton spectacle, with a musical score by Stravinsky . . .

Indeed, Lévi-Strauss loved Chaplin, Keaton, the Marx Brothers and that whole line of great American comics, whose deadpan verged on genius. To this tradition of filmic comedy, he added the family (and in part generational) love of wordplay, the punning humour of the Second Empire and Offenbach. Later, he very much appreciated the rather particular irony of the American television series *The Sopranos*, which he watched religiously. Despite the gravitas that seemed an inherent part of his being, and in addition to the sense of irony that has often been recognized, Lévi-Strauss also enjoyed fits of laughter, which he considered, together with music, one of the possible means to attaining a state of beatitude. A curious passage in the 'Finale' does justice to Lévi-Straussian laughter – a comical incident, a witty remark, a funny riddle, which, in the shortcut that characterizes it, contrasts with the laborious course of life. He came close to placing laughter at the same level as music, that other mystery, that other lacrimal comfort.[205] Why do we laugh? It is the conjuncture of disparate 'operational fields'[206] that triggers laughter. It is regenerative, countering the state of anxiety and forcibly expunging the physiological obstructions that too often paralyse our existence. With his own existence now taking a new, final turn, Lévi-Strauss allowed himself the pleasure, between laughter and tears, of a total success, which he would not even have imagined possible twenty years earlier: 'Music brings to completion, in a relatively short space of time, something that life itself does not always manage to achieve [. . .]: the union of a project with its realization, and this, in the case of music, allows the fusion of the two categories of the sensory and the intelligible, thus simulating in an abbreviated form that bliss of total fulfilment which is only to be attained over a much longer period through professional social or amorous success, that has called into play all the resources of one's being; in the moment of triumph, tension is relaxed and one experiences a paradoxical sensation of collapse, a happy sensation, the opposite of that produced by failure, and which also provokes tears, but tears of joy.'[207]

18

The Politics of Discretion

So many hands for transforming the world and so few gazes for contemplating it!

Julien Gracq, *Lettrines*[1]

The indictment delivered in *Tristes Tropiques* resonated powerfully with many readers on the left and far left. By the 1960s, the radicalism of the austere Collège de France scholar's thought was drawing hordes of angry young people to him. And yet, the man was perceived as anything but a firebrand. The judgement he had admiringly passed a few years earlier on Don C. Talyesva, a Hopi chief who was anxious to preserve his tribe's traditions in Pueblo country that had long been Americanized, calling him an 'enlightened conservative', and a 'systematic and applied reactionary',[2] fit Lévi-Strauss himself perfectly. Like Lacan from this perspective, the contradiction was striking between his now 'Tocquevillian' temperament – distrustful of revolutionary rupture, protective of traditional institutions, etc. – and his ethos as a scholar, which often disrupted his explicit political position.[3] Lévi-Strauss, Lacan and Roland Barthes were all dismantling the historical dispensation of the twentieth century, in which the political avant-garde and the intellectual and artistic avant-garde were one and the same.

Perhaps we should not take Lévi-Strauss's own claims to have renounced his youthful socialism and definitively abandoned the political arena at face value. This chapter's argument develops this intuition: Lévi-Strauss was not so much withdrawn from politics as he was contributing to the reshaping of political space at another level. He was certainly no 'engaged' intellectual, and rejected the label. This decisive break from the great model of the time entailed, on his part, a new way of conceiving the articulation between politics and scholarship, a radical disruption that the advent of the new human sciences had ushered into the field of political thought a century earlier.[4] A kind of 'modesty' further separated him from the crusading and prophetic posture of a certain kind of intellectual – a reluctance to pursue all the implications and consequences of his theses, and a certain inclination for enigma and veiled references.[5] By contrast with the de facto aristocratic model, based on the representation of majority opinion by a self-proclaimed minority (intellectuals), Lévi-Strauss promoted a way of being a public intellectual that was much more democratic and confident in people's ability to pass judgements of their own. Often called upon, he took care never to speak in anybody's name.

An actively 'disengaged' intellectual, then, the anthropologist 'intervened' less through his signature at the end of manifestos than through the explosive attacks that his ethnographic studies allowed him to launch against a self-satisfied humanism that had become his main target. If *Race and History* had provided a radical critique of the notion of progress in history, *The Savage Mind* and then the *Mythologiques* cycle troubled our most intimate convictions and initiated the shift towards a concrete and restored form of humanism that ultimately came to define Lévi-Strauss's politics.

A contemplative sociologist

The philosopher Pierre Zaoui has recently rehabilitated the quaint virtue of discretion as a means of achieving happiness.[6] More importantly, he highlighted its paradoxically political, or rather micro-political, dimension. For discretion is alien to the grandiloquence of contemporary politics. The idea is not to save anyone – neither oneself, nor others, nor the world. This moral and political (not to mention psychological) posture captures the peculiar position Claude Lévi-Strauss occupied on the political spectrum of his time. He believed himself to be neither indispensable nor responsible for the fate of his contemporaries, but he turned out to be available to all that was going on, as well as unpredictable in the stands he took, and refused to take. Allergic to the prophetic stance of the engaged intellectual, he asserted his impersonal scholarly self, disconnected from any direct competence in terms of action – a citizen like any other, confronted with history.

Refusing the model of the engaged intellectual

Interviewing Lévi-Strauss in 1988 about structuralism's ebb in the early 1980s – after having dominated the intellectual scene of the 1960s–70s – and the related return of more traditional forms of philosophy, Didier Éribon was surprised that the anthropologist did not appear more troubled by it: DE: 'You must deplore this return.' CL-S: 'Why would I do that?' DE: 'Because you developed your work against the traditionalist philosophy'. CL-S: 'That's true, but I don't feel responsible for the salvation of my contemporaries.'[7] A scandalous dereliction that was characteristic of Lévi-Strauss's reflexive refusal to speak in anybody's name. It was of course a clear disavowal of the intellectual's role as it had been defined in the late nineteenth century, that of mediator of the ends of history, a champion of the just and the good and, later, of the chosen representative of the oppressed. All of that heroic history, much of it French, running from Voltaire to Sartre via Zola, was casually dismissed by Lévi-Strauss:

'I imagine that my intellectual authority, to the degree that I am recognized as having any, rests on the totality of my work, on a scrupulous attention to rigour and precision that, in limited areas, had granted me the right to be heard. If I insist on the right to pronounce on questions I'm unfamiliar with or am ill-informed about, I'm abusing public confidence.'[8] In fact, he felt reverence and admiration for the fights in which Voltaire and Victor Hugo had engaged at considerable risk, and for which they sometimes paid a high price – twenty years of exile in Guernsey for the latter. But he detested the more contemporary figure of the intellectual guru: 'It is a role that condemns you to misleading your following, unless you're a saint, and then some!'[9] In Lévi-Strauss's view, this was an intolerable form of imposture.

However, this formulation is in need of nuance. Indeed, most of the early supporters of Dreyfus were not know-it-all intellectuals, philosophers and novelists, prone to endless petitioning.[10] Like Mauss and Durkheim, many came from the social sciences, and their support for Dreyfus and socialism was experienced as existentially coherent: the critical distance with one's own society engendered by anthropology and sociology called for socialist hope and struggle for justice which, in this case, involved standing up in defence of an innocent man. Mauss studied the daily political news with a scholarly eye.[11] He felt no contradiction between his intellectual practice and his political activism. The model of the engaged intellectual thus had two historical forms: that of the Dreyfusard scholar; and, later, that of the Sartrian public intellectual. Lévi-Strauss rejected the latter and could no longer assume the former. He felt an increasing discontinuity between politics and knowledge, between the man of action and the man of science. And ignoring the disconnect between these two levels of human activity could only lead to an impasse: 'Sartre had genius, a word I would not apply to Aron. Sartre was a being unto himself, with enormous talent, capable of achieving fame in a wide variety of literary genres. That said, his case proves to a striking degree that a superior intellect may talk nonsense if it wishes to predict the course of history and, still worse, play a role in it. The intellect can only do as Aron did, to try to understand after the fact. The virtues of the people who make history are of a completely different type.'[12] If the role of intellectual authority was no longer an option, particularly now that 'the world has become too complex',[13] moved by a 'number of variables' that was 'immense',[14] then only two options were still available: the first, which Aron adopted, consisted in making politics one's object of study, and developing a dedicated expertise that allowed for valuable judgement. But this was a full-time job! The second option was more radical: agreeing to be a simple citizen, whose judgement had no more or less value than any other opinion: '[Their positions] will probably be no less emotional, nor more coherent, and unless the scholar has devoted to the study of each political issue as much care, time and skill as to those that earned him his scholarly reputation (but then when will he have had time to pursue science?), I do not believe the legitimacy of their political judgements can rest on their reputation as a scholar.'[15] This defection sharply contrasted with the dominant discourse of the time. Rejecting the posture of the engaged scholar (let us recall Frédéric Joliot-Curie, a major figure of the French Communist Party), he could only claim to be an involved scholar, perhaps a dismayed scholar, one caught up nonetheless in the world of which he was part, whether he liked it or not.

Sociologist and citizen

An involved scholar, then, Lévi-Strauss was first and foremost an informed citizen and an avid reader of the national press. He subscribed to two dailies, *Le Monde* and *Le Figaro*, and bought *France-Soir* every day, for as long as that paper was published; he also read several weeklies: *L'Express*, *L'Observateur* (later *Le Nouvel Observateur*) and *Le Figaro Magazine*. The drama of politics interested him and he followed it with a mixture of passion and distance.

In a way, his position was in line with the profoundly democratic posture promoted by the new social sciences in the early twentieth century: 'For what, indeed, did they have to say as critical sciences? They asserted that sociologically informed individuals were capable, through a superior capacity for reflection that political philosophy did not allow them, of thinking for themselves within the society to which they belonged, of acquiring a new understanding of how it worked, as well as new possibilities for action.'[16] In the relationships he formed with his contemporaries and in his obstinate refusal to play the role of intellectual authority figure, which he was so often invited to play, Lévi-Strauss affirmed a democratically mature society in which all well-informed members would be capable of forming their own independent opinion. Never did he dictate or decree a ready-made solution. When consulted, he sometimes provided elements for reflection, but always let his interlocutors draw their own conclusions. As Bruno Karsenti has shown, this revealed a faith in the emancipation of critical judgement that was intrinsically that of the social sciences.

As a citizen, Lévi-Strauss was difficult to situate on the French political spectrum: a socialist activist in his youth, in the 1960s he became a conventional Gaullist, after being a heterodox Gaullist during his New York years. He refused to sign most of the left-wing intellectual petitions that were sent to him, and chose a publishing house, Plon, that leaned somewhat to the right. But he kept many friends among the Surrealists and, above all, he was an anthropologist, which in the 1950s placed him on the left by default. Thus, in August 1967, Michel Leiris, who had just returned enthused from Cuba, did not find it incongruous to invite Lévi-Strauss to join him on a trip to the land of Fidel Castro, among 'people who are not bureaucrats of Progress as so many are, but who are truly revolutionizing the revolution!'[17]

In politics, as in many other respects, Lévi-Strauss was difficult to predict – fiercely independent in his judgements, which he pronounced only when expressly asked. To take an example: in 1953, a friend of André Breton asked him to sign a petition regarding the Finaly affair. This scandal, which was then all over the national and international news, and had been for several years, concerned the custody of two Jewish children born in Grenoble in 1941 and 1942, whose parents had been deported and killed during the war. Entrusted by them to a Catholic institution, the children had been placed with a tutor, a former Resistance fighter and ultra-Catholic who, because by then they had been baptized, refused to return them to their closest relatives (their two aunts) after the war. A long legal process and a veritable manhunt for the children, who were being hidden with the support of elements in the Catholic clergy, were only the final episodes of a painful, yet also revealing, saga, which ultimately came to an end in 1953, with the return of the children to their aunts. Prior to its resolution, however, the case had become a public 'affair', in which religious actors – the Jewish consistory and the archbishopric, as well as political forces – intervened. The entire left-leaning and anticlerical press, as well as the progressive Christian community, also became very involved as the scandal took on an international dimension, since the children were brought to Francoist Spain. What did Lévi-Strauss have to say? After explaining his refusal on principle to sign any petition, he was happy to discuss the matter, but only in private: 'The Finaly affair presents to the contemplative sociologist such as me the fascinating resurgence of many archaic attitudes and conceptions. Those of the Church that you condemn are among them, but they are not the only ones. I already feel somewhat put off by your formal neo-Jacobinism; and even more so by your proclaiming the absolute rights of the maternal family, which your text does not explicitly do, but nor does it repudiate this position. It has now been almost twenty years that I have been teaching the antinomy between nature and culture, and that a Chinese baby raised in France would be in every respect a Frenchman ... It should not follow, from the legitimate condemnation of those who allegedly kidnapped him, that we can undo the irrevocable. But once again, please treat all this as a purely private and friendly conversation.'[18]

Beyond the anticlerical sentiment, Lévi-Strauss thought as an anthropologist mindful of the child's life and development, in which, as he had observed in many societies, the adoptive family prevailed over the rights of the biological family. This response – at once 'hesitant', fully aware of the dilemma and the impossibility of arbitration, as well as provocative, paradoxical and utterly free of prejudice – was quite typical of the anthropologist. Albeit in the form of a private letter, he nonetheless expressed his views honestly, since he felt that in this specific case he could contribute elements for reflection, while not trying to pass judgement for others, and categorically refusing, as far as he was concerned, to support any petition. We will now turn to a few of the encounters this 'contemplative sociologist' citizen had with the historical moment in which he found himself.

Confronting history: the Algerian war, colonialism and underdevelopment

On 21 November 1955, Claude Lévi-Strauss wrote to a brilliant anthropologist who had not yet become the pariah of the discipline, but was once again caught up in politics: Jacques Soustelle. Then governor general of Algeria, he had expressed his dismay at finding the name of his colleague among the signatories of a letter supporting the creation of an Action Committee for Peace in Algeria, published in *L'Express* on 7 November 1955.[19] Lévi-Strauss replied by assuring Soustelle of his complete confidence in his ability to 'steer French politics in a healthier direction. Still, it is what it is, and there are limits at which even those who remain completely withdrawn from politics (like myself, who in ten years have signed only two documents, that of academics against the European Defence Community and the present one) feel morally obliged to take a stand. I would only add that if I had given any thought to the personal impact on you of the document in question, I would have very naively believed that it could only support your actions with the government, in a direction I have never doubted. Which only goes to show that when one has been withdrawn from "public affairs", one had better remain so.'[20] This *L'Express* petition was signed by a broad spectrum of intellectuals, ranging from Dyonis Mascolo to Robert Antelme, Edgar Morin, the former communists of the rue Saint-Benoît linked to Marguerite Duras, all the way to Frédéric Joliot, a bona fide communist, as well as François Mauriac, Roger Martin du Gard, a few academics – Georges Gurvitch, Georges Canguilhem, Jean Wahl, etc. – Abbé Pierre and Mgr Cazaux, the bishop of Luçon. Many of these names would reappear at the end of the many manifestos that punctuated the Algerian 'events', but not that of Lévi-Strauss, especially not – for which he was later much reproached – at the end of the famous Manifesto of the 121, the so-called 'Declaration on the right to civil disobedience in the Algerian War', that was made public on 6 September 1960. He thus reiterated his confidence to Soustelle.

Yet, when the latter sent him his book on Algeria, a year later, Lévi-Strauss felt rather uneasy and declined to review it. Their relationship became increasingly distant, as Soustelle drifted to the right-wing paramilitary OAS (Secret Army Organization), and then went into exile for a decade (to Italy and Tyrol), finally returning to France in October 1968 in a kind of limbo, having been neither tried nor amnestied. The State Security Court had decided not to prosecute him for his participation in the assassination attempt against de Gaulle in 1962. Throughout this period, Lévi-Strauss never severed links entirely; he corresponded occasionally and consistently defended Soustelle's right to resume his teaching within the EPHE's VIth Section. This was granted in 1969.

Returning to the 1955–56 period, Lévi-Strauss was then already fully aware of the foreshadowing of 'disaster' in Algeria, following the reckless, repugnant and benighted French policy: 'Fifty years of modest and patient research', he wrote in *L'Express* in 1956, 'undertaken by a sufficient number of anthropologists, could have led to outcomes in Vietnam and North Africa similar to those Britain has achieved in India thanks – at least in part – to the scholarly work it has pursued there for a century – and there might still be time for black Africa and Madagascar.'[21] Concerning Algeria, all that was left for the colonial power to do was pack up and leave, as the only way to avert war. This is clearly the gist of what Lévi-Strauss believed in the mid-1950s.

French anthropology had emerged from the war years without having completely freed itself of the memories of its previous right-wing inclinations, and thus all the more intensely asserting its commitments to the left, in solidarity with UNESCO-led antiracism. Each in their own way, anthropologists contributed to the reasoned argument for the eradication of prejudice that had weighed on anthropology and Western thought in general.[22] This was the sentiment that had governed the short texts published in the early 1950s, such as Lévi-Strauss's *Race and History* and Michel Leiris's *Race and Civilization*, to name but two of the books published in that series by UNESCO.[23] Yet, with regard to colonialism, the profession as a whole was more equivocal, conscious of the common destiny that the discipline shared with the colonial enterprise. For sure, Paul Rivet unambiguously denounced the abuses of colonialism, but he stopped short of embracing immediate independence.[24] The model, in this respect, was the kind of indirect rule practised by the British, which allowed for a gradual withdrawal from the colonial relationship, with topical support from anthropological knowledge. Yet, over the course of the 1950s, some anthropologists, notably Michel Leiris, broke with this model. At a 1950 conference entitled 'L'ethnographe devant le colonialisme' ['The Ethnographer in the Face of Colonialism'],[25] he recommended that anthropologists take on a new role: no longer that of mediators between the native populations and their colonial governors, but that of 'natural advocates' for colonized peoples. From then on, a new generation around Leiris and Georges Balandier reoriented anthropology towards a clearer relationship to history, required by their now explicit anticolonial stance.

Here again, Lévi-Strauss stood out from the rest of the discipline. With *Race and History*, he had broken with the logic of the 'civilizing mission' and the intellectual foundations of colonialism in a much more resounding manner than the signing of any petition ever could have. And yet, while not siding with the former colonizers, he distrusted the newly emerging independent states, which even more ardently embraced the notion of progress of which he had been critical, and were perhaps even more hostile to their own 'backward' populations. It was for this reason that, although he was perceived to be profoundly in line with decolonization struggles, he refrained throughout this period from lending any support or taking any public position: 'That is a misinterpretation. The societies I was defending or for which I was endeavouring to bear witness are even more threatened by the new dispensation than they were by colonization. The governments of countries that have won their independence since the Second World War have no sympathy for the "backward" cultures that still exist among them. [. . .] Colonialism was the major sin of the West. However, with respect to the vitality and the plurality of cultures, I don't see that we have made a great leap forward since its disappearance.'[26]

Seen from the perspective of today, his position, distinct as it was from that of his own camp, appears less paradoxical and has a contemporary feel. It resonates with some of the positions of what would become 'Postcolonial Studies' in the 1990s.[27] A critical examination of the colonial intellectual matrix and a calling into question of the categories that, within the process of independence itself, reproduced the Western model, including notions of 'progress', as well as the nation-state, secularism, economic development, etc. A few years later, in 1961, Lévi-Strauss provided, in the same spirit, a radical critique of 'underdevelopment', which had become a guiding paradigm for international institutions, the UN first among them: 'The societies which today we call "underdeveloped" are not such through their own doing, and one would be wrong to conceive of them as exterior to Western development or indifferent to it. In truth, they are the very societies whose direct or indirect destruction between the sixteenth and the nineteenth centuries have made possible the development of the Western world. [. . .] That same development and its greedy requirements have made these societies such as they are today.'[28] Following Marx's intuition, historians have shown how the eighteenth-century slave plantation economy (sugar cane) in the West Indies enabled the 'primitive' accumulation of capital necessary for the industrial revolution to take off in Europe.[29] Capitalism, colonialism and slavery are thus intrinsically linked through a violent and intensely interdependent history. Here again, Lévi-Strauss anticipated what is today called 'connected history',[30] re-establishing, in this provocative text presented at a UNESCO roundtable in 1961, the early connections that served to globalize the futures of remote societies and bring them into the Western system. Written for the UN International Social Science Council, this analysis was of course highly critical of many of the policies implemented under the auspices of UNESCO and the UN, which thereby received the stamp of good conscience: i.e., the industrialization of so-called 'underdeveloped' societies and the introduction of literacy into so-called 'backward' populations. Leaving his readers to draw their own conclusions, Lévi-Strauss offered this bitter pill in the hopes it might shake the certainty of people in positions of power, full of good intentions, which were themselves not entirely disconnected from a certain colonial logic.

Confronting history: Israel and French Jews, 1967

While reluctant to speak publicly, Lévi-Strauss was completely open in his private correspondence. One of the dramatic moments in contemporary world history, the Six-Day War (and its aftermath) revealed him to be more of a Gaullist than de Gaulle himself, and in disagreement with the interpretation Raymond Aron offered a year later, in *De Gaulle, Israel, and the Jews* (1968). As noted by Pierre Birnbaum, who was the first to highlight the importance of this exchange between the two men during the 1967 conflict, Aron confessed to having abandoned his traditional objective stance and experienced a 'burst of Jewishness'[31] over the few days during which the fate of Israel appeared in the balance, threatened by the bellicose attitude of the Arab states.[32] Ten years earlier, he had condemned the 1956 Israeli-Franco-British expedition to the Suez Canal, which had been nationalized by Nasser. And later, in 1982, he condemned the invasion of Lebanon by Israel and the massacres of Palestinians. As we know, a few months after the conflict, on 27 November 1967, at a press conference held at the Élysée Palace, de Gaulle delivered a speech on Zionist history that set the basis for a new Arab policy in the Middle East and – whether intentionally or not, we will never know – uttered a phrase that has gone down in the annals: with the Jewish state having tripled its territory through recent conquests, he spoke of the Jews, both the diasporic and in Israel, as 'an elite people, sure of itself and dominating'. Aron never forgave de Gaulle for this phrase, which he considered as an expression of a particularly French kind of anti-Semitism, now sanctioned in presidential discourse.

In response to Aron's book, which the author had just sent him, Lévi-Strauss confessed an admiration for its tone and high-mindedness, even while radically disagreeing with its argument: 'Indeed, from the very start, we have been witness to a systematic attempt to manipulate public opinion in this country. Recall *France-Soir*'s headline – "The Egyptians have attacked" – splashed across its front page. And it has continued well beyond the Six-Day War. That some French people, Jews and non-Jews alike, should hold a different view of the events from that of their government, and defend their opinion publicly, is completely legitimate. But that they should take advantage of their privileged positions in the press (where it is incumbent upon them to remain measured and intellectually rigorous) to spread propaganda, and thereby attempt to influence the state of affairs, smacks of conspiracy, and I would even say of treason. As a Jew, I was ashamed of it, as well as of the later impudence of some Jews in important positions, who openly dared to speak in the name of all . . . Such gross misconduct needed to be reined in and I suppose they had it coming. I regret that it took the form that it did, but I admit that, at least this once, the chosen epithets were alas deserved: for certain Jewish elements in France, taking advantage of their control over the print and audiovisual press and of their positions, and usurping the right to speak for others, did indeed sound "sure of themselves and dominating".'[33] Aron admitted to being taken aback by the forcefulness of this response, but he rejected the idea of any systematic ideological manipulation, if only because television and radio were both state-controlled. He arrived at the conclusion that perceptions of the matter were inescapably subjective, a point on which Lévi-Strauss could fully agree.

It would seem that recent history has vindicated Lévi-Strauss to some extent. All conspiracies aside, a new rhetoric and an effective press campaign – invoking the struggle of David against Goliath, and the genocidal danger hovering over Israel – did scare a large swath of the French population, both Jewish and non-Jewish, at precisely the moment when the Egyptian, Jordanian and Syrian armies were being routed by Israeli tanks, rockets and Mirage planes (sold to them by France). For the first time in France, the sense of a 'Jewish community' was being expressed, and it was indeed the beginning of a small-scale emigration to Israel, and of a long-term process of reconnection with Judaism for a generation of young French Jews in search of their roots.[34] A new kind of French Jewish identity was emerging, which struggled to reconcile several identities, in which Israel had its place. This brings us back to the disagreement between the two intellectuals: Aron – who was engrossed in critical self-reflection on his own silence in the face of the Jewish genocide, when he worked for Free France in London from 1940 to 1944 – was prepared to embrace this new way of being Jewish in France, whereas Lévi-Strauss, on the contrary, rejected it instinctively.

He knew himself to be Jewish, through his history, his experience of exclusion, and specific traits and attitudes that he readily accepted as specifically Jewish, such as an 'attuned sensitivity' for example. Yet, he did not compromise on his sense of being both French and Jewish: 'I feel totally, entirely and exclusively French, even if it matters to me to know that my roots are anchored in an ancient past full of culture and events.'[35] But that past escaped him, and especially the long period between ancient exile from the land of Palestine and arrival in Alsace, where he 'found his ancestors had settled' in the eighteenth century. 'What had happened in between?'[36] His ignorance of the historical sequence rendered any bond with Palestine totally abstract. Indeed, when after much hesitation he finally went to Israel in 1984, he never had the impression of 'actually touching [his] roots':[37] 'Israel has interested me enormously, less because I find it to be a nation of distant cousins (I don't have that kind of family feeling), than as the bridgehead held by the West in the East, the Ninth Crusade, as it were.'[38]

This final analogy was telling. It echoed a passage of another letter to Raymond Aron, in which the anthropologist confided in him about what it was that created an intimate obstacle to any sense of belonging to Israel: 'You are absolutely right: there is no objective historical truth beyond the various ways individuals and groups perceive situations and events. This is all the more true for me regarding the case at hand, for my perception of the Israel situation remains subordinate to another, to which I am even more sensitive: one that happened a few centuries ago on the other side of the world, when another persecuted and oppressed people went and settled in lands that had been occupied for centuries by weaker people, whom they proceeded to displace. I could not very well feel the destruction of the Red Skins as an open wound, and react in an opposite manner when it is Palestinian Arabs that are at issue, even though (as is the case) the brief contacts I have had with the Arab world have filled me with an ineradicable antipathy.'[39] Here again, Lévi-Strauss surprises: this time, arguing that Israeli settler colonialism was no different in its considerations (especially that of victims) from those of the Europeans (Protestants, Jews and other minorities) who had conquered the New World. He thus positioned himself at the heart of left-wing and far-left anti-Zionism, which was to emerge over the following years, with the figure of the Palestinian on its banner, now the symbol of a new form of exploitation.

Confronting history: 1968

His age notwithstanding – he was then sixty years old – Lévi-Strauss could have been an active participant in the events of May '68: his anthropological commitment and his cultural relativism, his unsparing and persistent critique of the West, opened up an intellectual space eminently compatible with the '68 upheaval. His writings formed a possible stepping stone for a radical contestation of the model of Western civilization, its modes of organization and soft repression. And indeed, some of the young militants of May were confirmed structuralists.[40] However, this was not the case, either intellectually – the 1968 movement is generally perceived to have buried a triumphant structuralism, an interpretation endorsed by Lévi-Strauss – or biographically. From this paradox sprung several others that, once again, made Lévi-Strauss impossible to situate on the ideological spectrum of the time and politically unidentifiable, despite a few cursory comments in the vein of the 'disoriented-mandarin-trying-to-save-the-old-Sorbonne'. Neither actor nor spectator, he simply absented himself.

Lévi-Strauss spent the beautiful month of May in the heart of the Latin Quarter, at his Collège de France laboratory, a stunned onlooker to the ongoing spectacle, one who had not purchased a ticket and quickly left the theatre, to take shelter at the other end of Paris – and another world – at home in the 16th arrondissement. At the beginning, he walked around the Sorbonne 'with an ethnographer's eye'.[41] The customs of the tribe of 'youth', a new category of French society in the 1960s, were no less compelling than any other – and certainly no less exotic. Some meetings followed. On 14 May, Dumézil thanked him for participating: 'I am very grateful to you for having agreed to take part in this roundtable, in this protest, as we now say, in the amphitheatres of what used to be the Sorbonne. I have no idea how to proceed. Jacques Le Goff will lead the discussion, and I hope you will speak in my stead!' Yet, far from wandering around dreamily, as Michel de Certeau did,[42] embracing the liberated discourse as a new incarnation of that of the mystics he had studied, and far from reading the new city covered in graffiti as a critique of the symbolic order, as Roland Barthes deciphered it,[43] Lévi-Strauss was quickly put off, and disappeared. 'Once the first moment of curiosity had worn off, once the strangeness had become tiresome, I found May 1968 repugnant.' 'Why?' 'Because I can't accept cutting down trees for barricades (trees are life, and life is to be respected), turning public places that benefit everyone and are the responsibility of all into trash heaps, or scrawling graffiti on university buildings or elsewhere. Nor can I accept bringing intellectual work and the management of institutions to a halt because of a war of words.'[44] The great palaver of '68 – what Michel de Certeau dubbed the 'capture of speech', emphasizing its emancipatory potential – was experienced by this man of few words as an explosion of empty talk and a springboard for narcissistic self-expression. What Edgar Morin called 'the breach',[45] an extraordinary disruption of the time and pace of a society, was here understood as total and sterile 'paralysis'.

Besides the fear of seeing his patient efforts to build a research centre in the human sciences reduced to nothing, it was not just his environmentalism and respect for public space that accounted for the sense of alarm he felt in response to the events of 1968. On the one hand, the anthropologist in him valued continuity over rupture. He had no fondness for sudden outbreaks, whose painful backlash he always anticipated. He was no longer the young socialist he had once been, and had long since given up on the revolutionary myth of the new dawn, which was oddly enough rehabilitated by the (often anti-communist) leftists of May '68. On the other hand, his very definition of science as an ordering of the world pitched him against the disorganized character of real life. May '68 must have seemed to him as the triumph of a rather pointless muddle, opening the floodgates to the kind of overindulgent chatter that was, in his view, characteristic of our society. Yet, as opposed to many of his colleagues, traumatized by their violent, public de-legitimization in the turbulent amphitheatres of May, Professor Lévi-Strauss experienced little contestation, either in the sedate assemblies of the Collège de France, and even less so at the LAS, which only lost a single member in the turmoil of 1968 – Anne Chapman – for having challenged the authority of Isac Chiva to make certain decisions. Nothing more.

Congenitally averse to the logorrhoea of general assemblies, Lévi-Strauss could not help but see 1968 as a symptom, an end rather than a beginning. Over the months that followed, he developed an original anthropological interpretation, which drew on neither the paranoid conspiracy theories nor the more sociological theme of civilizational crisis that circulated in right-wing circles. Lévi-Strauss did not identify a crisis of youth in the ongoing events, but rather a profound failure of our societies to integrate their youth; worse still, an abdication that had culminated in the constitution of youth as an autonomous category. In 1969, while the American press was hailing the handover of power from Sartre to Lévi-Strauss, the latter claimed on the contrary that recent events had brought young people back to more Sartrian positions. He offered part of his diagnosis to a *New York Times* journalist, while, it must be said, refraining from expressing himself on the issue in the French press (or only much later): 'We have found that we don't have any mechanism for integrating the new age groups, while those exotic societies that anthropologists study have always confronted the problem and most often have extraordinarily precise mechanisms.'[46] Whereas in Western societies, the assimilation of young people was a long and gradual affair, running from kindergarten through university, in exotic societies children enjoyed complete freedom until suddenly 'extremely brutal initiation rites radically separate the young man or girl from what has been his prior existence'.[47] According to Lévi-Strauss, the mass media promoted challenges to authority and the formation of youth subcultures, based on a full awareness of the resulting economic opportunity: youth consumption represented a very promising market. This impossibility of integration was thus a 'sign that the adult generations are no longer sure of their values',[48] nor at all certain that they wanted to pass them on: 'The moment they feel unable to hand anything down, or no longer know what to transmit and rely on the following generation, they are sick.'[49] Case closed. This vision of things sprang from an intimate and early sense of political, cultural and intellectual decadence: 'Even while at the *lycée* I used to say that my generation, myself included, could not bear comparison with that of Bergson, Proust and Durkheim at the same age. I don't believe that May 1968 destroyed the university but rather that May 1968 took place because the university was destroying itself.'[50] The typically Lévi-Straussian causal inversion aside, this melancholy appreciation is distinguished by an element of self-critique, which this scrupulous man always took care to include in his indictments of society. He was not the doctor; he was part of the sick body.

In the autumn of 1968, as the ministry of education was about to pass a sweeping reform, Claude Lévi-Strauss went into action to lead a campaign at the Collège de France to preserve the special status enjoyed by this 'cenacle of specialists' among French academic institutions. On 1 October 1968, he addressed a letter to all Collège de France professors, which began: 'Following our discussions of last spring, and in view of those to come, I feel the need to clarify my conception of the future of our institution – a conception that I may not be alone in holding.'[51] On the administrative front, he favoured regrouping the Collège around its own chairs, and divesting it of the management of CNRS-affiliated laboratories. This was indeed the main thrust of the letter. On the teaching front, he conceived of the Collège as a unique space of free exchange between enlightened minds 'specializing in the most diverse range of sciences – exact, natural and human – charged with maintaining and developing the creative value of such an association'.[52] Scientific innovation was, in his view, largely founded on this ancient and distinctive institutional model, that had to be protected from passing turbulence. Politically, he unquestionably wanted to spare the Collège de France from the new democratic regime of co-management, as much out of a fear of messy democratic rule as a distaste for time-consuming meetings. This position, which may legitimately be considered as conservative, was, however, qualified by the last paragraph, which partly protected him on his left flank: 'The author of these lines, himself the director of a laboratory of modest size that has long been managed through direct democratic rule, regardless of rank and position, is on the contrary convinced that it is by making each laboratory, institute and team the common responsibility of all participants that we can best justify that the Collège itself, as an autonomous body, is and should remain the common responsibility of its members.'[53]

What he objected to, in the higher education reform that was passed on 12 November 1968, was precisely its disregard for the various scales at which democratic decision-making might operate. On 20 November 1968, he wrote to Raymond Aron: 'Yet I find myself in a paradoxical situation, having for about four years implemented at my laboratory – of around thirty people – a form of direct democratic rule that disregards rank and status. And it works very well. But it seems to me no real democracy is possible outside of very small formations (Rousseau and Comte have already pointed this out), in which ideological excesses are tempered by relationships between individuals. For co-management to have any chance of succeeding, an admissions process is required so that the status of student becomes a cherished opportunity, rather than a right to be squandered; and it should then be organized at a basic level, i.e., at the level of small teaching and research teams, before perhaps being ultimately generalized. Instead, the university is being handed over to an inevitable coalition between the infantilism of the student masses and the reactionary conservatism of the assistants.'[54] Conclusion: let us embrace radical democracy within laboratories, and intellectual aristocracy within the Collège de France as a whole. To each scale, its political model.

The anthropologist and the city

Claude Lévi-Strauss's personal archive bears traces of a surreal exchange between the anthropologist and public planning authorities. Surreal, but also unthinkable today – style and flair on both sides, civil servants quoting Rousseau and Montaigne. The palpable respect for 'Monsieur le Professeur' probably attested to Lévi-Strauss's particular authority, as well as to a certain relationship between 'technocracy' and 'scholars' in 1960s France. In this instance, representatives of the former were attentive to, and eager to learn from, the latter.[55]

The anthropologist who specialized in the study from afar of small isolated and faltering societies was also intensely a man of his time and place. Even while refusing to insist on any practical application for the human sciences, he did not shy away from dialogue with decision-makers when called upon. This was 1963, and the heyday of French central planning, supported by a genuine belief in the possibility of forecasting (urban growth, for example) and in the need to humanize and rationalize the distribution of people, resources, flows and activities across urban space. The big question was how to integrate anthropological data into the Plan's forecasts. Was it possible? Was it even desirable? Clearly, Lévi-Strauss was deeply attuned to the efforts of the planning authorities, even if he may have had his doubts about the ultimate efficacy of any such actions. In any case, he considered it a sign of 'great intellectual maturity for a society'.[56] Indeed, 'societies without written language are entirely planned and intend to be planned'.[57] But as opposed to modern planners who, worried about rapid and uncontrolled change for their civilization, wondered about how to strike the right balance between the 'value of change' and the 'value of persistence', ancient societies aimed to shield themselves from change and the historical future altogether.

Lévi-Strauss jokingly compared advertising slogans of the time – 'Omo is here, filth is gone!' – to ritual forms of Vedic literature, attesting to the persistence of formulas for warding off diseases, enemies, fear, etc. But, fundamentally, his point was to make clear that any effort at planning, to be thorough, should take into account not only the most manifest economic data, but also unconscious mythological levels. For example, a recent government campaign had attempted to redirect consumption towards cheaper cuts of beef. The anthropologist pointed out the still active dimension of the mythological unconscious that opposed boiled and roasted meats, according to an identified system of mental oppositions: 'roasted is male, boiled is female. Roasted is camp, boiled is village. Roasted is fresh, boiled is rotten; boiled is family, roasted is society'.[58]

The point of it all was to honour the democratic obligation of the social sciences mentioned earlier, which dictated that the acquisition of a specific and not necessarily sharable knowledge (erudition, technical vocabulary, theoretical tools, etc.) should nonetheless be returned, *one way or another*, to the societies that had enabled its study and aspired to an understanding of its own motives.[59] In the case of anthropologists, and more specifically the specialist of exotic societies, such restitution, however deferred, however media-inflected (as was the case here), was still in order – difficult though it may be. Other examples show that Lévi-Strauss, while he refused to adopt the role of 'expert', considered it his duty to respond to such solicitations, when he thought he could make a scholarly and civic contribution to the debate. Thus, again in 1963, he responded to a questionnaire on 'Urban Civilization and Mental Health'.[60] His response betrayed some of his 'rustic bias': it was not urban life, but the proliferation of a suburban civilization that, through a 'segregation of man from the natural environment', constituted the real danger. This was why the *'maisons de la culture'*, a major project of the new ministry of cultural affairs, spurred by the fiery passion of André Malraux, did not, in his view, offer a universal solution: 'culture is not everything' and its 'maisons', should they fail to realize this, would become mere 'alibis', celebrating a profoundly inauthentic relationship to the arts and creation. This was an argument that was to carry great weight with the leftist critics of Malraux's cultural policy.[61] For them, 'culture' was a distraction from revolution; for Lévi-Strauss, it distracted from humble pleasures, from a sense of awe of, and a concrete relation to, history and nature, in which all human beings should be able to anchor themselves. Hence his final suggestion that 'small biological or archaeological stations' be set up on nature reserves, to usefully complement, in his view, the urban *maisons de la culture . . .*

Whether having to do with underdevelopment, planning or cultural policy, Lévi-Strauss's position was always the same, in line with his civic and democratic understanding of the role of the intellectual: he would contribute a few elements to the debate, assemble facts and ideas, but steered clear of interpretation and even more of political action. Everyone was left free to draw their own conclusions . . .

'All science is political'

While developing new relationships between the scholarly and the political, Lévi-Strauss did not claim to be engaging in political work, nor even politically identifiable work. The same can be said of Jakobson and Lacan. Still, over the course of the 1960s, their so-called structuralist theories came, on the contrary, to be seen as a marker of political radicalness. Frédérique

Matonti calls this phenomenon of the politicization of reception 'reclassification', through which social agents give a political meaning and dimension to theoretical objects initially intended to remain within the scholarly sphere.[62] External factors account for this paradox: the development of a large student readership in the human sciences; the density of the intellectual space of new journals (*Critique, Tel Quel, Lettres nouvelles, L'Arc*, etc.) that encouraged prophetic discourse; together with, as François Furet has famously pointed out, a destabilization of the political order, marked by de-Stalinization and the end of decolonization, and the resulting ideological vacuum that, according to the historian, paved the way for the conversion of Marxism into structuralism.[63]

This politicization was particularly pronounced in relation to Lévi-Strauss: the anthropological gaze was theorized as inherently revolutionary, the bearer of a renewed humanism; the structural epistemology developed in the *Mythologiques* converged – less explicitly, but in fact no less firmly – with a radical critique of humanism that had been formulated in the West since the sixteenth century. In other words, if Lévi-Straussian anthropology became politicized, it was also (even if not only) because anthropological structuralism clearly had a politics. As Lévi-Strauss himself had written in reference to Paul Rivet, well aware of the artificial character of these distinctions: 'All science is political . . .'[64]

Ethnographic revolution and generalized humanism

After the war, the connection between anthropological science and politics was mediated by the inescapable question of humanism; it was raised by, or rather imposed on, Sartre, Merleau-Ponty, Camus, etc. Foucault claimed to have avoided it for this very reason. As for Lévi-Strauss, he confronted it with the new critical tools of his discipline: 'Faced, as were those of my generation [. . .] with the postulate of humanism, but convinced by ethnographic experience of its limitations, I initially set out in search of the conditions of possibility of a renewed form of humanism.'[65]

Indeed, anthropology overflowed into other disciplinary fields, serving fundamentally as a 'technique of estrangement'.[66] Thus conceived, the anthropological posture of the decentred self satisfied the fundamental need of any culture aspiring to put itself into perspective with another culture, remote in either time or space. In a striking text of 1956, published in the weekly *Demain*, Lévi-Strauss equates this anthropological drive with the dynamic of humanism itself: 'Anthropology is neither a separate science, nor a new one. It is the most ancient, most general form of what we designate by the name of humanism.'[67] The 'three humanisms' announced in the title of the article matched three moments of comparative perspective achieved through active estrangement. First, the classical humanism of the Renaissance, developed through the rediscovery of texts of Greek and Latin Antiquity, of which clerics were the first and sole beneficiaries. Then, in the eighteenth and nineteenth centuries, the world grew bigger thanks to geographical exploration and new spaces – India, China,

Japan, etc. – were integrated to shed new light on the 'exotic' humanism of the Enlightenment. In Montesquieu and Voltaire, references to Persians or Hurons were used to forge a critical perspective on the habits and customs of one's own society, to be able to see them in new ways. Finally, this bourgeois humanism was followed in the twentieth century by a democratic humanism, through the increasing expansion of the geographies taken into consideration, as well as of the spheres of new perception. The return (in time and space) to the early societies studied by anthropology made available to all a corrosive new gaze on our world. This democratic humanism gave rise to a generalized humanism. This still optimistic thread was woven by Lévi-Strauss in 1956. The worm was in the apple; the constitution of humanity as a separate (from nature) and sovereign realm had already given rise to the worst abuses. Yet, hope for renewal was not entirely in vain.

In the tribute Lévi-Strauss paid to Rousseau in 1962, his tone had become more alarmist as to the state of the world: 'In this world, more cruel to man than perhaps it ever was, all the means of extermination, massacre and torture are raging. We never disavowed these atrocities, it is true, but we liked to think that they did not matter just because we reserved them for distant populations [. . .]. Now, brought together in a denser population which makes the universe smaller and shelters no portion of humanity from abject violence, we feel the anguish of living together weighing on each of us.'[68] The separation of man from his natural matrix, the promotion of the subject as the ultimate locus of truth: these were the historical foundations of a perverted humanism which, erecting boundaries between humanity and the rest of the living (animal and vegetal worlds), had initiated a 'vicious circle' – one that, 'the one boundary, constantly pushed back, would be used to separate men from other men'. Since humanity had been granted a privileged status, it should come as no surprise that it would be confiscated by a minority decreed more human than others, who were thus relegated to the purgatory of animal nature. There was no lack of historical examples, particularly in the twentieth century of mass massacres. But the starting point was not even the sixteenth century: anthropologist Emmanuel Terray has rightly pointed out the influence, in this process, of the major monotheistic religions, in which man is the privileged interlocutor of a single god.[69]

Little by little, Lévi-Strauss moved closer to a sceptical pessimism, under the combined effect of several factors: his increasing obsession with 'demographic catastrophe', which in his view reduced humanism to futility; as well as his awareness of the internal contradictions of that humanism, which emptied it of all meaning. In the end, only anthropology, 'that unrestricted and unbounded humanism',[70] could confront these contradictions. As Wiktor Stoczkowski has reminded us, Lévi-Strauss's socialism gradually faded in the 1950s. The Marxist vocabulary of inequality and class gave way to one centred around the category of the West, colonialist and imperialist – in other words, guilty. The destruction of indigenous tribes, their risk of extinction, were echoed in a politics of conservation, including that of the mere memory of a vanished diversity. Lévi-Strauss's originality in this reorientation consisted in expanding the moral imperative by concentric circles, to include not only the human species, but all the living world. This was what he meant by a 'generalized humanism': the identification with nature, an obliviousness to oneself, the capacity for pity – virtues that so surpassed the terms of traditional humanism that he was often perceived by his contemporaries as an 'anti-humanist'.

The centrality of man in the universe – the rotten core of historical humanism – was condemned by the morality of Amerindian myths – a morality of discretion, to return to this term, which is also the final word of *The Origins of Table Manners*: 'Since childhood, we have been accustomed to fear impurity as coming from without. When they assert, on the contrary that "hell is ourselves", savage peoples give us a lesson in humility which, it is to be hoped, we may still be capable of understanding. In the present century, when man is actively destroying countless living forms, after wiping out so many societies whose wealth and diversity had, from time immemorial, constituted the better part of his inheritance, it has probably never been more necessary to proclaim, as do the myths, that sound humanism does not begin with oneself, but puts the world before life, life before man, and respect for others before self-interest: and that no species, not even our own, can take the fact of having been on this earth for one or two million years – since, in any case, man's stay here will one day come to an end – as an excuse for appropriating the world as if it were a thing and behaving on it with neither decency nor discretion.'[71] This verdict, delivered with classical flourish, resonated powerfully at the time, and even more so today. Because 'deference towards the world' serves less than ever to guide our uses and practices, Lévi-Strauss's warning has devastating political force, perhaps explaining why the anthropologist appears more decisive than many a subversive philosophy. 'But above all', as Pierre Zaoui has put it, 'he is more radical, his lesson goes further.'[72]

The politics of structuralism

More than anthropology itself, structural anthropology involves a radical critique of humanism. Indeed, as we have seen, Lévi-Strauss constantly denounced the 'prison' that man had erected for himself, brick by brick, this carceral engagement with himself, as one of the 'greatest obstacles in the way of the progress of philosophical thought'.[73] Throughout the 1960s and beyond, Lévi-Strauss's increasingly untimely declarations were not only intended to pursue a polemic against an arrogant and mind-numbing form of humanism; they were also 'the correlatives of a radicalization of Lévi-Strauss's approach in his strictly scientific work'.[74] Indeed, according to the philosopher Patrice Maniglier, whereas *The Elementary Structures of Kinship* was still informed by a humanist anthropological project, based on the search for a universal cultural invariant – the prohibition of incest – and an opposition between nature and culture, which indeed elevated humanity to a separate order, this was no longer the ambition behind the *Mythologiques*: this 'anthropological project [. . .] was not guided by the question of humanity'.[75] This second structuralism was no longer obsessed with the passage from nature to culture, two categories which it no longer considered impermeably distinct. The arbitrariness of the starting point and the absence of any endpoint, the indefinite body of myths, and the analysis of variants all transformed the structural analysis of myths into an operator that stripped mythology of all content, of all simple signifiers. The infinite mirroring that it staged in the endless translation of one myth into another incorporated its ultimate consequence: that the anthropological book itself was a variant of myth.[76] 'This means that Lévi-Strauss's work does not reveal the essence of myth as such, nor the structures of mythical thought in general.'[77] In other words, the objective of anthropology was no longer to identify a universal invariant, a kind of hidden godhead that would define humanity. Quite the contrary, its object was the very thought process at work in myths, which can only be caught as a dynamic, an 'irradiation'[78] that animates the human mind but never circumscribes in any definitive way what is human and defines, by exclusion, what is not. A restored, generalized humanism could not accommodate a social science that objectivized the human. It was for this reason that structural anthropology, version 2.0, that of the *Mythologiques*, could serve as the locus for a renewed humanism. Science and politics here walked hand in hand. This interpretation, which sees in the structural analysis of myth a true political matrix for thinking the contemporary world, is a radical reading of structuralism, but one that the later works of Lévi-Strauss to which we shall return – especially the collection of articles entitled *We Are All Cannibals*, in which the anthropologist reflects on new forms of parenthood – would appear to confirm.

'Opting for the Neolithic'

Lévi-Strauss had a taste for history but little faith in it. In his view, it only partially contributed to intelligibility and nobody could predict its avatars, let alone its ends. In *The Savage Mind*, he drew on the example of the aristocratic revolt of the Fronde in seventeenth-century France, showing the complexity of the sociological forces at play and the uncertainties that it held in store. And yet, the various parties at the time fully committed themselves to their cause, to the death. Hence concrete man lived in history and 'wisdom consists for him in seeing himself live it, while at the same time knowing (but in a different register) that what he lives so completely and intensely is a myth, which will appear as such to men of a future century'.[79] The distinction between these different levels of perception was the catalyst for a political chastening which, slowly but surely, led Lévi-Strauss away from a certain pathos of modernity, palpable in *Tristes Tropiques*, to a free and unapologetic rejection of 'progress': 'In that which we call progress, 90 per cent of our effort goes to remedying the harm resulting from the advantages gained by the remaining 10 per cent.'[80]

Savage societies went to extraordinary lengths, surprising to a modern mind, to resist change. The remoteness of his gaze brought Lévi-Strauss to exit the order of historicity of his contemporaries: as opposed to them, he did not value change, but dreaded disappearance and aspired to conservation. The acceleration of the time and pace of society appeared to him as the great danger that attended the global integration of a single indivisible humanity, to its great misfortune. This way of presenting (and shifting around) the issues was properly political, even though (or rather, because) it subverted the categories of classical politics: 'progress', 'left', 'right', 'reaction', 'reform', 'revolution', etc. Lévi-Strauss was a reactionary insofar as he promoted a 'return to', but then he was an ultra-reactionary: for far from longing for a return to the *Ancien Régime*, he would have, if possible, returned to . . . the Neolithic. As he confessed to Raymond Aron, who must surely have been dumbfounded: 'Man's salvation would have consisted in rejecting this role of subject, or of agent [of change, of transformation], i.e. to opt for the Neolithic, if you will allow me this simplification.'[81] A Neolithic radicalism that required all the conviction of a simple, contemplative citizen, supremely free, to assert it with such candour in that post-'68 period. The old professor was here making trouble for the troublemakers. To new dawns, dreams of a new world and a free body, of emancipated class and, soon, gender relations, he offered his own political myth: a deference for the world, a respect for custom and a reciprocity of respect, the right distance, discretion, the ancient character of institutions, the value of permanence, identification with nature. Rather than shouting 'pleasure without bounds', he opted for the ecstasy of silent existence and the solitude of a walk in the forest.

Part IV

The World (1971–2009)

19

Immortal

The best way of being right in the future is, in certain periods, to know how to resign oneself to being out of fashion.

Ernest Renan, *What is a Nation?* (1882)[1]

The remaining years of Lévi-Strauss's life, of which there were many, were characterized by a dialectic of repetition and variation. He returned to his past to examine anew some of the questions still pending and calling for resolution. In *The Way of the Masks*, published in 1975, he revisited his New York years, when, with the surrealists, he had been astonished by the 'naive and ferocious'[2] expressions of British Columbia masks, of which he became an informed collector. Thirty years later, he developed a structural analysis of these objects, thus applying his method to a material object for the first time. The enigma of art became his Holy Grail.

Throughout his final years at the Collège de France, from 1976 to 1982, his attention was focused on a new ethnographic object: house societies. Yet this was also a return to a field he had long ago abandoned, in this case kinship anthropology, to consider an aspect that had remained opaque, a shoreline that had remained unexplored and largely unnoticed. This was 'less a project for the future than a sort of reordering of his own material'.[3] His several trips to Canada's west coast, between 1973 and 1975, were more of a reunion than a discovery – he communed more than studied. In the end, between the British Columbia masks, the trips to Vancouver and Ottawa, and his research on the 'house', anthropological structuralism of that decade was very much a Canadian affair.

In May 1973, this pattern of proliferating returns was interrupted by his election to the Académie française. The anthropologist thus became an 'immortal' at a time when structural anthropology was in a much more vulnerable position, challenged on all sides by a radical and sectorial critique that signalled the beginning of a new turn in the social sciences and in contemporary thought more broadly. Confronted with this ongoing paradigm change – social actors vs. structure, strategies vs. rules, plural and decentred narratives vs. the single Grand Narrative, agency vs. constraint – Lévi-Strauss responded with a rather astute sense of historical nose-thumbing, imperturbably persevering in his being, and in his belief in permanence, even that of the Académie française and its antiquated rituals. He thus embraced with panache the rather 'uncool' position that was being assigned to structural anthropology. A provocative free spirit, the iconoclastic anthropologist turned himself into a devil's advocate and joined the tribe of green frock coats, partly to poke fun at young leftists and partly to experience, for once in his life, the pleasure of dressing like a great Indian chief.

Structuralism cannibalized

In 1970, before being presented with the Festschrift in honour of his sixtieth birthday, which was being celebrated two years late, Lévi-Strauss offered this response to the kind speeches of Jean Pouillon and Pierre Maranda, the volume's editors, and to the members of the LAS who had all gathered with many other colleagues and friends: 'As in the life of societies, there are three stages to a scholarly life: the first is when you are still unknown, and you produce your best work – this is the most positivist stage; the second is when you begin to achieve a certain renown, often based on misunderstandings – this is the metaphysical stage; and finally the third, in which I feel rather firmly ensconced right now, is when you are ripped to pieces – the stage of cannibalism. I cling to the hope that there is a fourth stage – which owes nothing to Comte, Vico or Hegel – in which one stands equally remote from the three previous stages: no longer renowned, fallen into a general condition of quasi-indifference, in which you will remain forever mired. This volume, presented to me in the second stage, anticipates the third.'[4]

This short Comte-like fable might have been intended as a wink to the young (and not-so-young) initiates, both inside and outside the genial circle of the laboratory, ready to tear into a structuralism that had so insolently dominated the previous decade and was ready to be knocked off its theoretical pedestal in the next. Indeed, the process was already under way. In *What is Structuralism?* – a collection of essays, organized by discipline, published in 1968 – François Wahl, the editor who had conceived the collection, claimed he had no intention of orchestrating a critical backlash, but rather wanted to give expression – structuralist expression, of course – to the 'problems of the second generation'.[5] Yet what had originally brought them together was no longer intact. At the international level, disagreements of varying degrees had created rifts within the discipline, and generated different tribal groupings, vividly described by New York sociologist Daniel Bell, not without a touch of humour: 'relativist sociologists', who rejected the idea of a universal human nature; 'functionalists', who objected to the idea of an underlying structure in which the coherence of culture was rooted, rather than in the actual interdependencies of daily life; 'materialists and evolutionists', who looked down on the 'mentalistic' approach of structuralism; and 'cultural anthropologists' (Clifford Geertz), who found structural analysis lacking in the kind of thick description on which all anthropological fieldwork must be based.[6] The status of structuralism – as one theory among others or as a common approach to science – was at the centre of these debates.

At the national level, the wave of critique spread out across different projects, temporalities and arguments, in part (but to what degree?) propelled by the experience of 1968. From within anthropology, and sometimes even within the LAS (the Americanists Robert Jaulin, Pierre Clastres, Jean Monod and Jacques Lizot), emanated a radical critique of the anthropological discipline as complicit with colonization and what Jaulin called 'ethnocide'. A revival of the dispute with a Marxist-inspired anthropology sprang from new questions about history raised by some of the anthropologists close to Lévi-Strauss, including Maurice Godelier. Panning out to include all the social sciences, the structuralist paradigm was challenged and influenced by Pierre Bourdieu's critical sociology, whose emergence pointed to new orientations, as well as an unprecedented autonomy for sociology. Finally, on the philosophical-theoretical plane, properly speaking, we should point out yet again how so-called 'post-structuralism' (Derrida–Deleuze–Lyotard, as Barthes called it) operated in relation to structuralism as much through rupture as recovery. In the end, it was indeed a kind of ripping to pieces, which, in the press, took on the appearance of an epochal shift. This did not trigger any reaction from Lévi-Strauss other than the usual return to the silence of the laboratory. Out of fashion, but content to be so, the structuralist master retreated into the catacombs of scholarly work for another two or three decades.

Guilty anthropology

The very year Lévi-Strauss was fêted by colleagues and friends, Robert Jaulin's manifesto *La Paix blanche. Introduction à l'ethnocide* [White Peace: An Introduction to Ethnocide] was published. Jaulin, an anthropologist of Africa, had published a famous study entitled *La Mort Sara* (1967) [The Sara Death], in a much more structuralist vein, before becoming an Americanist and doing fieldwork with the Bari, an almost entirely isolated tribe on the border of Colombia and Venezuela. Mesmerized by his charisma, Jean Monod, Jacques Lizot, with whom he had stayed in Venezuela, and Pierre Clastres formed a group of brilliant young scholars (and not-so-young: Jaulin was forty-two years old in 1970, and Clastres thirty-six), who had emerged within Lévi-Strauss's circle and been radicalized in the late 1960s – although most of them had found themselves in the remote regions of native America when paving stones were being thrown on the boulevard Saint-Michel, and had therefore entirely missed out on May '68.

Considering anthropology to be an auxiliary science of colonial rule and, ultimately, an agent of destruction of native populations, these anthropologists mounted an extremely radical challenge not only to their own fieldwork practices, but to the very discipline itself, and to its scientific pretensions more generally. The strict separation made by Lévi-Strauss between science and politics was rejected as a fiction. According to Jaulin, scientific endeavour was overdetermined by politics, which indeed lay at the heart of the epistemological question insofar as anthropological description took place in an ethnocidal context.

If the first act of the rebellion was the publication of *La Paix blanche*, Act II played out in an issue of *Les Temps modernes* (June–July 1971), which echoed and amplified the international debate on 'anthropology and imperialism' initiated by the American journal *Current Anthropology.* The issue included a short story by Pierre Clastres, 'The Highpoint of the Cruise',[7] a kind of dark Conradian parody featuring a group of tourists who show up among the savages – their crass vulgarity overflows in all directions and the historical complicity is exposed between the anthropologist and the tourist, a 'well-intentioned whitey' caught in his own trap and given over to his prejudices. In that same issue, Olivier Mannoni offered a reflection on 'fieldwork': 'When Griaule unwittingly described the Abyssinians in a way that benefited Mussolini . . . .'[8] In the end, beyond the indictment of anthropology as a colonial science, it was objectivity itself, as a means of turning men into objects, that was designated a form of colonial violence. Rodolfo Stavenhagen then posed the question, 'how are we to decolonize the applied social sciences?'[9] In contrast with the rather moderate tone of the articles, Jean Monod's letter, which was appended to the journal issue, struck a decidedly different note, full of violent despair. His 'eulogy for an old lady'[10] was intended to shock: Monod celebrated the funerals of anthropology in a kind of (self-)destructive rage: 'A moving old lady, moribund, she thinks herself still irresistible, as in the good old days of her Triste Tropification.'[11] While Jaulin had attacked Lévi-Strauss's 'sleights-of-hand', Monod had it out for his pale imitators, whom he accused of 'bluff' and 'buffoonery'.

The author of this seething rant against the master and his cult of science was none other than a major admirer of Lévi-Strauss, and his assistant at the Collège de France. He had been awestruck by *From Honey to Ashes*, which he had read in the middle of the jungle, recognizing the empirical relevance of the intellectual acrobatics of structural analysis in what he was experiencing among the Piaroas. But as time went by, he turned away from Lévi-Strauss's anthropological 'wizardry'. Rather than collecting the last vestiges of a doomed culture, his goal was to help Amerindians survive.[12] Object of study or political subject? The figure of the Amerindian was at the core of this political critique of anthropology, having become an alternative figure of oppression to the Marxist proletarian. But neither left-wing anthropologists of Amerindians, nor Lévi-Strauss himself, identified with the evolutionist scenarios of Marxist anthropologists, most of whom were Africanists. In their common rejection of progress as the inexorable fate of all societies, they were on the same side of the barricade. And yet, somewhere between admiration and rejection, the murder of the father did indeed take place, thus abrogating the gentlemen's agreement that had long held between Lévi-Strauss and Monod.

By 1970, Jaulin had already left the laboratory to found the anthropology department of the new Jussieu University in Paris, which served for a few years as an alternative hub, hosting anthropologists as well as representatives of the American Indian Movement (AIM). The goal was to produce a decolonized anthropology, focusing less on accurate empirical description than on making knowledge available to the indigenous struggle. Courses offered at Jussieu did not resemble the erudite assemblies of the LAS: students engaged in practical as much as theoretical work. Under Jaulin's supervision, they learned to weave, build huts, make pottery, etc. In 1974, Jaulin provocatively announced his intention to apply to the Collège de France. Lévi-Strauss reproached him for 'needing a wall to bounce his ball against',[13] but followed up with a conciliatory letter, to which Jaulin responded in the same tone. In the face of attacks from his Americanist 'offspring', Lévi-Strauss kept quiet. It was only later that he was to conclude that one could of course opt to integrate into a tribe, as Jacques Lizot was to do, engaging in permanent 'fieldwork'; but the first time around, 'knowledge lies on the outside'.[14]

Jaulin and Monod had thus distanced themselves, as had Lizot in his own way. Clastres remained a bit longer, thanks to whom anthropology found a central place in post-1968 political debates, as pointed out by Yves Cohen, a historian and reader of anthropology who was himself involved in the leftist movement: 'Around 1968 precisely, anthropology, whose narrative was largely based on the study of chiefs and chiefdoms, came to develop another perspective that challenged the typical twentieth-century anthropological view of humanity as necessarily hierarchical. It did not deny that there had always been chiefs, but rather that there had always been hierarchies – relations of cascading authority organized around chiefs, on which everyone necessarily depended.'[15] As we have seen, Pierre Clastres was a disciple of Lévi-Strauss who, full of admiration and a desire to emulate the master, had done fieldwork in America, before taking a path less trodden by anthropological structuralism: that of political anthropology.[16]

In 1974, he published a collection of texts that became an important work, and that has more recently enjoyed something of a revival, for example in anti-globalization circles.[17] *Society Against the State* showed that, in archaic societies, power was not linked either to the chief's generosity, or to the 'consent' analysed by Lévi-Strauss, using the example of the Nambikwara chiefdom, itself part of a fundamental reciprocity that generated social life and its stability. On the contrary, Clastres identified the sphere of power as outside the group, as if Amerindians only saw it as a negative force that had to be controlled. He demonstrated that these Amerindian societies made significant efforts to prevent any hierarchies from forming, or in any case from being perpetuated. In the end, according to Clastres, the formation of the state, even in embryonic form, did not represent progress towards political modernity, but a failure of these effective mechanisms for 'discouraging' hierarchical formations. It is easy to see the appeal of his thesis in the context in which it was born. The subversion of 'infra-political' and 'political' categories, the brilliance of his demonstration based on serious fieldwork, the radiance granted to societies outside the purview of the Western leviathan – all this combined to make Pierre Clastres's reputation. After offering this distillation of the libertarian aspirations of the 1970s, the anthropologist died three years later in a car crash on the roads of the Cévennes. This untimely departure, whether accidental or not, was all the more tragic for the history of anthropology as it followed quickly on the sudden disappearance of several other promising young Americanists. Yet by this time, the rupture with Lévi-Strauss was already complete. Following an inopportune and overly excited letter he had sent to a colleague in the name of the laboratory – and on LAS letterhead – Clastres had been summoned by the boss, very strict regarding the respect of form, and summarily asked to leave. It was thus that a whole generation – won over to the anthropology of the Americas by Lévi-Strauss, but grown resentful of the master's overbearing position – unceremoniously cast off from the shores of structuralism on which they had landed a decade earlier.

Structural anthropology in the face of Marx

Although he had grown up reading Marx, and had a deep knowledge of his work, to which he regularly returned – he never set out to write without rereading a few pages of *The Eighteenth Brumaire* – Lévi-Strauss had a long standing quarrel with Marxist intellectuals. As early as *Tristes Tropiques*, Maxime Rodinson had reproached him for sapping the morale of proletarians both at home and abroad.[18] At stake was his fundamentally anti-evolutionist conception of history, which could not accommodate general laws, of a revolutionary nature or otherwise. In 1973, the work of an anthropologist couple, Raoul and Laura Makarius's *Structuralisme ou ethnologie. Pour une critique radicale de l'anthropologie de Lévi-Strauss*, criticized structuralism's anti-evolutionism, quoting Sartre, who saw in the anthropologist 'the last barrier that the bourgeoisie could find against Marx':[19] abstract diagrams, the rejection of the concrete, and formalism were in turn brandished as the trappings of a mechanistic theory, nostalgic for 'the sterile and defeatist theses developed by Lowie and his disciples'.[20] The ideological Cold War continued on into the 1970s, albeit as a somewhat quaint affair.

Alongside the orthodox literature, Marxism was alive in anthropology in a much more dynamic and developed form, mostly among Africanists. The figure of Georges Balandier and the researchers working around him had formed an alternative critical hub since the 1950s.

Balandier and Lévi-Strauss, formerly close friends – recall that it was in part thanks to the former that the latter joined the UNESCO International Social Science Council and obtained a post at the VIth Section of the EPHE – gradually grew apart over a 'disagreement'. A personal matter perhaps, but also a theoretical one: 'I was interested in the current situation in the African world, and the other so-called underdeveloped worlds', Balandier declared in 2010. 'From the 1950s, Lévi-Strauss's structuralism had become an anthropological approach that did not make much use of history. [. . .] In my view, structuralism was an analysis that would today belong in the field of cultural studies, i.e., an analysis of forms, relations, frameworks, languages, etc., hence one that was disconnected from circumstances, from peoples' actual conditions, from societies and cultures in their historical contexts. All this provoked a disagreement between us, and we gradually grew apart. First, against the structural approach, I initiated what I called a dynamic and critical anthropology, centred on change and not taking narratives at face value. Then, I developed *dynamist anthropology*, which I proposed in parallel with *structural anthropology*.'[21] An alternative or competing project, Balandier's anthropology was supposed to be solidly anchored in the future of societies. This was, according to him, as much a function of his own background as a dodger of the French Compulsory Work Service and young Resistance fighter, as it was of the African situation, which he discovered after the war, with the anticolonial struggle in full swing. It is quite clear that their different areas of concentration, and hence the different societies they studied, played no small role in the development of their differences, even if there was certainly more to it. In the early 1970s, a political and historical anthropology that focused attention on contradictions, troubles, conflicts and disorders gained favour among the new generation of researchers, and Balandier is today considered, especially in his early analysis of the 'colonial situation',[22] as one of the seminal figures of postcolonial studies. By the same token, he also enabled many young aspiring anthropologists, like Emmanuel Terray, to reconcile their anthropological careers with their Marxist politics.[23] Yet, his way of insisting on Lévi-Strauss's ahistorical approach, and the (voluntary or involuntary) misunderstandings that ensued, periodically resurfaced in the debates. This was the case in 1975, when Lévi-Strauss agreed to participate in a discussion, later published in *L'Homme*, with Maurice Godelier, an anthropologist of Oceania and a member of the LAS who was nonetheless something of a free spirit in the Lévi-Straussian firmament. In the field of economic anthropology, of which he was one of the experts, Godelier tried to find in Marxist thought resources to make structuralism more dynamic, and tried to develop, in his own words, 'a theory of structural transformations'.[24]

Throughout the discussion, moderated by Marc Augé, Lévi-Strauss appeared embarrassed, and even annoyed, by this 'friendly quarrel'[25] that Godelier and others picked with him about history, Marxism and the priority of causalities. Lévi-Strauss expressed himself with precision. History, in his view, was synonymous with irreducible contingency. He took an example: the mental equipment of Amerindians did not differ from that of the Greeks at the same time. Thus, Amerindians could also have moved from mythology to philosophy, and from philosophy to science. Yet, this did not happen. 'The only difference is that something occurred in the Eastern Mediterranean at a certain moment, but which we can in no way maintain was a necessary passage.'[26] The uniqueness of the event and the (political) refusal to consider Amerindians as lagging behind the Greek 'miracle' accounted for the utter impossibility of drawing a general rule out of historical evolution. Lévi-Strauss continued, using a recurrent expression of his: 'By this I mean that history cannot be short-circuited. After all, history exists and we must *bow* before it.'[27] On the one hand, Godelier and the more or less structural-Marxist anthropologists were keen to discover the laws that governed the transformation of structures leading societies from stage A to stage B; on the other, Lévi-Strauss conceded that the current generation would probably be in a position to factor in a greater number of variables and to correlate more and more data, especially, we might add, in fields that still remained two blind spots for structuralism: economic anthropology (relations of production) and political anthropology (relations of domination). The fact remained, added Lévi-Strauss, that if the birth of philosophy in ancient Greece could be explained after the fact by such and such political or legal development, it was impossible to find 'a law, i.e. we can't be certain that under the same conditions the same thing would happen elsewhere'.[28] It was, strictly speaking, this impossibility that Lévi-Strauss saw as history: a troublemaker, the ultimate limit to the drive for intelligibility, and the sign of its failure, perhaps even its vanity. Godelier was not wrong to see in this position a 'form of homage which turned against history'.[29]

'The logic of practice' vs. 'the savage mind'

It might seem odd that the Festschrift offered to Lévi-Strauss for his sixtieth birthday should include an article, already somewhat dated, by Pierre Bourdieu, 'The Kabyle House or the World Reversed', originally written in 1963.[30] Reading it today, one finds – the first surprise – that the author is an anthropologist. Indeed, as the title already suggests, this study of the house as a miniature world using spatial oppositions, inverted symmetries and correlations between the polarities of domestic space and the values assigned to them, is a reminder that in the history of the social sciences there was an early Bourdieu who was very much under Lévi-Straussian influence. Yet that article, as its author reminds us, was 'the last work [he] wrote as a blissful structuralist'.[31] If Pierre Bourdieu is not immediately associated in our minds with the universe of structural anthropology, despite the IOUs, it is because his 'coming out' came rather late, essentially in the introductory pages of *The Logic of Practice*, in which Bourdieu – recounting the how and the why of this enthusiastic moment of his life, that of the Algerian fieldwork – confesses he never intended to contribute to the 'philosophical glosses' which surrounded structuralism.[32] As with love stories, it was thus at the moment when they were drifting apart that Bourdieu felt inspired to describe, in the warmest of terms, the shock that Lévi-Strauss had been for him in his intellectual youth. Later, jibes and disagreements notwithstanding, his admiration for Lévi-Strauss as a person and for his intellectual ethos remained, as his correspondence clearly reveals.[33] This was not the case for Aron, another of Bourdieu's spiritual fathers, with whom he definitively severed ties in 1968.

From structuralism, Bourdieu took the idea of a 'relational mode of thought',[34] as opposed to a substantialist one. The power of reproductive structures, the binding character of rules in both unconscious and systematic ways, and a kind of panlogism – these are the dimensions of the structuralist project that Bourdieu assimilated.[35] The idea that science must reveal the profound and therefore hidden laws of social workings was also borrowed from Lévi-Straussian epistemology, and indeed shared by a whole generation of structuralists determined not to defer to 'experience'. *Distinction* (1979) has sometimes been described by Pierre Bourdieu himself as a transposition of the structuralist model onto complex societies: 'There was [in this book] a typically structuralist intention, which consisted in saying: meaning lies in differences, in differential intervals. Symbolically speaking, to exist is to differ – and this is Lévi-Strauss.'[36] Yet, he added, the material is entirely different from that of savage societies. Applied to highly differentiated societies, not only to symbols but also to practices and behaviours, to the social and economic fields, anthropological structuralism 'produces different results'.[37] With its graphs and diagrams, *Distinction* had a structuralist look to it, but one that was more sociological with its substantial statistical apparatus. Focusing on the very core of the realm of social disavowal – that of individual judgements of taste – as Lévi-Strauss had earlier done with choices of spouse, Bourdieu showed how individuals were subjected to their social fate.[38]

From 1975, with the creation of the journal *Les Actes de recherché en sciences sociales*, Bourdieu began to modify and differently inflect his initial structuralist project, violently attacking the Althusserians, while simultaneously developing a strategy to unify the human sciences around sociology. Just as Lévi-Strauss had attempted to do in the early 1960s, so Bourdieu was building an intellectual and institutional project in the mid-1970s that rested on a new paradigm – 'practical logic', and with it 'habitus', 'strategies' and 'field' – with a journal and a research centre to disseminate it into the academic and public sphere.

What was his critique of structuralism based on, at the time of the publication of *The Logic of Practice*? 'I wanted, so to speak, to reintroduce agents, which Lévi-Strauss and the structuralists, among others Althusser, tended to abolish, making them into simple epiphenoma of structure. And I mean agents, not subjects. Action is not the mere carrying out of a rule, or obedience to a rule. Social agents, in archaic societies as well as in ours, are not automata regulated like clocks, in accordance with laws which they do not understand. In the most complex games, matrimonial exchange for instance, or ritual practices, they put into action the incorporated principles of a generative habitus. [. . .] This "feel for the game", as we call it, is what enables an infinite number of "moves" to be made, adapted to the infinite number of possible situations which no rule, however complex, can foresee. And so, I replaced the rules of kinship with matrimonial strategies.'[39] This gives a sense of what separated Bourdieu's epistemology from structuralism, as well as what it retained from it, even unconsciously – the game metaphor being a recurring one in Lévi-Strauss. Just the same, what characterizes the habitus as a system of patterns that are both 'classificatory principles'[40] as well as 'organizing principles of action'[41] can be seen as echoing those of the savage mind, both practical and theoretical, both classificatory thought and effective action (for instance, Lévi-Strauss repeatedly pointed out the operational dimension of native medicine).[42]

Whatever the case may be, for Bourdieu, cutting loose from Lévi-Strauss at that time was a way to free himself from the overbearing, objectivist position, this 'perspective of God the Father',[43] which had become intolerable to him. Not unlike Jaulin and Monod, in a way, but refusing to abandon the necessary moment of objectification, Bourdieu tried to topple the epistemologically privileged observer by objectivizing him in turn.[44] One of the deeper causes, at least from a biographical perspective, of this drift towards practices, agents and strategies lies with his traumatic and repressed memories of fieldwork in Algeria during the war, causing him to retrospectively wonder about this 'so obviously misplaced *libido sciendi*'.[45] This very anxiety was not alien to Lévi-Strauss, who suffered from 'anthropological doubt'.[46] And this was also why – despite Lévi-Strauss's rather chilly riposte to Bourdieu, without mentioning him by name, in which he indicted the return of a 'fashionable spontaneism and subjectivism'[47] – the anthropologist did not see fit to vote against the sociologist's appointment to the Collège de France in 1982.

Leaving structuralism behind: Derrida and poststructuralism

Just as Bourdieu's ambivalent move away from anthropological structuralism signalled a change already under way in the social sciences – a greater attention to actors, a sense of the interplay between freedom and constraint, micro-history, the centrality of the body, etc. – the birth of what has been retrospectively labelled 'poststructuralism' fuelled a philosophical movement that resumed a close dialogue with the human sciences and radicalized the structuralist gesture, bending it to breaking point.[48]

It was in 1966 that Jacques Derrida duly noted the major act of 'decentring' carried out by Lévi-Strauss: 'The absence of the transcendental signified extends the domain and the play of signification indefinitely.'[49] The very architecture of the *Mythologiques* illustrated this new logic of meaning, as a constant back and forth between differences (variants of the myth). Derrida's philosophical project initially consisted in drawing all the metaphysical consequences entailed: 'The [structural theory of meaning] does not allow us, in effect, to postulate any foundation of meaning outside the movement of signs, beyond signs.'[50] Derrida and Deleuze, as well as Barthes in his way, were to develop theories of difference, desire, the fragment, the nomad, and writing, opposed to a structure now seen as logocentric, enclosed on itself, leaden and even totalitarian and patriarchal, at the very least haunted by a fantasy of original unity.

This 'deconstruction' of structuralism was, in fact, a contemporary phenomenon – the 'post' being more logical than chronological – since it was in 1967 that Derrida furbished its first weapons with the simultaneous publication of *Of Grammatology* and *Writing and Difference*. In a section of the former work, entitled 'Writing and Man's Exploitation by Man', Derrida undertook a critique of the famous chapter 28 of *Tristes Tropiques*, 'A Writing Lesson'.[51] In this chapter, Lévi-Strauss recounted how a Nambikwara chief had quickly instrumentalized the act of writing to reinforce his authority over the group, rediscovering, in fast-forward, what had been, according to Lévi-Strauss, the historical arch of writing in human societies – its intimate relationship with the dynamics of enslavement and exploitation among men. Derrida condemned the 'repression' of writing on the part of Lévi-Strauss, who had readily succumbed to the Rousseauian myth of an idealized savage speech contrasting with an alienated Western writing. Within Derrida's theoretical and historical narrative – a historicization of this eviction of the written in favour of the spoken (the *phone*) – he identified Lévi-Strauss as a representative of Western logocentrism. The philosopher thus explored the scientific preconceptions of this anthropology and 'tied it to an entire metaphysical tradition from which it claimed to break'.[52] In the anthropologist's 'declared Rousseauism',[53] he saw a perpetuation of the figure of the noble savage and the notion of a primordial society that was good and unitary, prior to the sin of writing. We should point out, in passing, that this 'deconstruction' through the phenomenon of writing paradoxically promoted it: it was to become a key epistemological question in the discipline of anthropology in the years to come. Indeed, the anthropologist wrote about societies that did not write. This statement, banal in itself, would now call for an interrogation of the operation of anthropological transcription and the stakes entailed.[54]

With *Writing and Difference*, Jacques Derrida introduced a new concept, that of '*différance*', whose heterodox spelling expressed the double signifying potential of the word in French – i.e., that of differing and that of deferring, of postponing. '*Différance*' became a key concept for deconstruction, a principle of subversion of all secret metaphysics, injecting a new dynamism into the structure and imposing on it a perpetual play of movement, endless and interminable, as Lévi-Strauss himself would say. Yet the anthropologist was the main target of this operation, intended to give structures a certain 'play', or 'shakiness', to endow them with greater historical depth: the single grand narrative gives way to plural, partial, off-kilter stories, turned out by individual and collective identities that were multifarious and mobile, labile and indeterminable. In the move from structure to difference, Michel Foucault, Jacques Derrida, Gilles Deleuze, Jean-François Lyotard and others (Barthes) broke with structuralism, while extending its internal tension:[55] they came out of it, in the double sense. This version of the story, in which structural anthropology was on the side of a 'hard', or even 'violent' structuralism, imposing its authoritarian system on interpretation, was imported wholesale into the United States, engendering misunderstandings largely due to gaps in translation. For at the time Derrida gave his famous conference on 'Structure, Sign and Play in the Discourse of the Human Sciences' at Johns Hopkins University in 1966, only a few books of Lévi-Strauss had been translated:[56] *Tristes Tropiques* (in abridged form), *Structural Anthropology* and *Totemism*. It is thus ironic that Lévi-Strauss's essential work of the 1960s – the *Mythologiques* project – 'passed' into American academia through the poststructuralist lens.

*Structural Anthropology 2 (1973): laying out
the structuralist corpse*

The collection of articles published in the second volume of *Structural
Anthropology* in the autumn of 1973 arrived in the midst of this contradictory dynamic: on the one hand, structuralism was being annotated,
expanded and ingested in massive quantities at new academic institutions
like the University of Vincennes, where students made it part of their
staple diet; on the other hand, and at the same time, it was being criticized
and torn to pieces within the world of the social sciences and philosophy
by its putative offspring, who were more or less violently breaking away
from its remote, implacable and often silent authority. This situation
was further compounded by the election of Claude Lévi-Strauss to the
Académie française in May 1973, which cast additional doubts, both theoretical and political, on the entire project of Lévi-Straussian structuralism.
Thus, at the very moment when the founder of structural anthropology
was becoming 'immortal', in the autumn of 1973, the press was in the
process of drafting its obituary.

In *Le Monde*, Christian Delacampagne pointed out this curious coincidence: 'One could argue that structuralism needed this official consecration. What is surprising, in any case, is that it obtained it at a time when it
was increasingly under challenge, and from all quarters. Yet Lévi-Strauss
appears oblivious to this, and seems less prepared than ever to open
up his fundamental principles for discussion.'[57] The journalist did not
seem impressed by the anthropologist's strategy of selective response:
engaging with critics when dialogue seemed possible, as with Luc de
Heusch and Maybury-Lewis, and refusing to respond to more frontal
'ideological' attacks. 'Yet the question looms large today: Is structural
anthropology a science or is it just the expression of a philosophical and
political position (structuralism) within a discipline that was, as a result,
doomed from the start?'[58] The article ended with a double affront: an
overview of the entire gamut of anti-structuralist critique available on the
marketplace of ideas at the time (Makarius, Derrida, Jean Monod, etc.)
and a glib and mean-spirited conclusion on the pleasures of penetrating
into the 'intimacy of a great man, listening to him by the fire, as is the case
in this volume, casually discussing Picasso, movies, Eastern souk-cities,
etc.'. Here was Lévi-Strauss, transformed into a sweet old man, with
a tendency to babble, soon for the retirement home and the writing of
memoirs . . . In *Le Nouvel Observateur*, Jean-Paul Enthoven continued in
a similar vein: with the second volume of *Structural Anthropology*, 'we no
longer have the impression of being present at the creation of the world,
as was the case with the grandiose fresco of the *Mythologiques*, but this
may be just as well'.[59] 'Having left Europe to discover a different world,
Lévi-Strauss is returning to it with disenchantment as his only baggage.
Clearly, something in his work is coming to an end, from the invitation to
travel that served as its opening to the reveries of a lonely anthropologist
that form a kind of conclusion. The end of the journey is perhaps the
end of an anthropology in which Claude Lévi-Strauss roamed in search

of a world that we have lost.'[60] Far from the sound and the fury of intellectual fads, Lévi-Strauss 'still inspires his readers with a kind of sacred
respect and awe that recall what Hannah Arendt said of "totalitarian
thought"'.[61]

Structural Anthropology 2 was thus reviewed with a note of disappointment. Indeed, as opposed to the first volume, which contained many articles previously unpublished in French, the second did not appear to offer
any surprises: the texts were all well known, since, in the meantime, Lévi-
Strauss himself had become well known, and after 1958, his work had been
widely disseminated. Yet it is striking that, if some reviewers did point to
the emergence of 'another Lévi-Strauss' – moralizing, misanthropic, disenchanted, who tread beyond the boundaries of science – his attempts at the
development of a new humanism were nowhere discussed.[62] Inaudible in
this context of critical ebb, they went entirely unnoticed. Similarly, it might
have been pointed out that even though Lévi-Strauss refrained from using
the term 'ethnocide', this did not prevent him from offering a critical reappraisal of his own discipline, as in his Collège de France inaugural lecture
(1958), which opened the volume. Meanwhile, in the eyes of several journalists, it was exile that seemed to characterize Lévi-Strauss's life: that of
native Brazilian lands, that of New York during the war, and now that of
the Académie française . . . In terms of exile, the latter compared favourably with Amazonia: indeed, like Amazonia, the Académie was a perennial
forest of evergreens![63]

Apotheosis

Handsome as an anthropologist at the Académie

When did thoughts of the Académie française first cross Lévi-Strauss's
mind? He had a tendency to attribute the idea to others, going so far as
to claim he had never thought of it himself.[64] It seems that the initiative
came from the d'Ormesson family, with the uncle Wladimir beginning
a process in the 1960s, which his nephew, Jean, would apparently see to
fruition in 1972, the year Maurice Druon, the Académie's permanent secretary, began sounding out members and promised Lévi-Strauss a smooth
application process. The latter did not want to take any chances, and would
only consider applying if he was certain of success. This was a recurring
trait of his, which he himself pointed out on that occasion: 'I am a nervous
nelly and [. . .] all competitive situations worry me sick.'[65] It should be
remembered that his professional career was rife with setbacks. After 1950,
whenever he became affiliated with an institution, it was upon invitation,
as was the case for the Collège de France in 1958 and the Académie française in 1973. There was no place in Lévi-Strauss's psychic economy for the
idea that competition stimulates creative energies and greater productivity.
He was thus visibly relieved when his only challenger, Charles Dédéyan,
a literature professor at the University of Paris, announced he was withdrawing his candidacy.

He submitted to all the formalities of academic ritual, sending his application letter to each of the members of the Académie: Marcel Achard, Marcel Arland, Roger Caillois, André Chamson, René Clair, Jean Delay, Maurice Druon, Pierre Emmanuel, André François-Poncet, Jean-Jacques Gautier, Pierre Gaxotte, Maurice Genevoix, Étienne Gilson, Julien Green, Jean Guitton, René Huyghe, Eugène Ionesco, Georges Izard, Joseph Kessel, Jean de Lacretelle, Louis Leprince-Ringuet, duc de Lévis-Mirepoix, Thierry Maulnier, Jean Mistler, Paul Morand, Wladimir d'Ormesson, Marcel Pagnol, Jean Rostand, Jacques Rueff, Henri Troyat and Étienne Wolff. Four 'immortals' were recently deceased: Jules Romains, Pierre-Henri Simon, Henry de Montherlant and Cardinal Daniélou. His campaign was handled by Maurice Druon: 'For the time being, as far as I can tell, your prospects appear excellent. *So far so good.*'[66] At the same time (in April 1973), Druon had agreed to take over from Jacques Duhamel at the ministry of cultural affairs, where he stirred up a hornets' nest with his inopportune statements, threatening the heads of theatres that were deemed subversive: 'Those who come to the door of this ministry, hat in one hand and Molotov cocktail in the other, will have to choose.'[67] It was thus a rigid Académie – entrenched in its defence of the literary and political order and wary of post-'68 social movements, in which the historical hatred between Gaullists and ex-Vichyists had dissolved into a staunch common conservatism – which the anthropologist was about to join.

In the end, on 24 May 1973, Lévi-Strauss was elected by a small margin to the seat formerly occupied by Henry de Montherlant: sixteen votes in favour out of twenty-seven present. Paul Morand, held up in Toulouse, could not vote. There was one blank vote and ten marked with a cross, 'a mark of disgrace, since it signals opposition to the candidate's character'[68] – a 'reaction that one might have thought to have been done away with since the dark days of Nazi occupation',[69] explained the *Le Figaro* journalist. Clearly, anti-Semitism had not disappeared – even with the most anti-Semitic of them, Paul Morand, not voting. In addition, some members objected to Lévi-Strauss being the only applicant. Others, including those who had voted for the 'writer', i.e., the author of *Tristes Tropiques*, had difficulty with the founder of structuralism, the theorist of a structural anthropology that the members found laughable. Meanwhile, they were all given *Structural Anthropology 2* as summer reading! Despite Druon's reassurances, the fact remains that the Académie française 'gave the student Claude Lévi-Strauss the worst marks of his career'.[70] He 'almost flunked'.[71] This hazing ritual on the part of the Académie, and the circumstances of his election (as well as his surprise at the violence of the use of the cross), might well explain the irreverent tone of his reception speech. He was admitted, tolerated, but not warmly welcomed. As for him, it was indeed the institution itself and not its members that he intended to join. For Lévi-Strauss, the mediocrity of some of the members, let alone their ideological convictions, did not detract from the symbolic power of the whole.[72]

If his wife and sons supported him, the prevailing sentiment among his friends, colleagues, and the younger generation at the LAS was one of consternation: 'They felt I was betraying them. They had a mythical idea of the Académie. They thought I was going to abandon them, move into another sphere.'[73] Indeed, some of the letters he received in that period expressed a certain reticence mixed with discomfort and above all incredulity. What the hell was Lévi-Strauss embarking on? A question that was posed, more or less explicitly, and quite delicately, by Michel Leiris, who refused to contribute to the purchase of the sword for the new Académie member: 'Gaston Palewski and Claude Tardits have put me in a situation which – since it involves you – I find very unpleasant: to register their non-participation, which gave my abstention a somewhat polemical dimension, whereas I wanted it to remain something implicit and tacitly agreed. Indeed, my neutrality has a slightly critical edge, but it boils down to this: I have too much admiration for you not to consider that your joining the Académie is too much of an honour for it!'[74] At *Nouvel Observateur*, Jean Daniel echoed the same sentiments: 'The Académie can expect to benefit greatly from your application and you not at all, for your joining the forty others could serve only to distinguish them while adding nothing to your glory.'[75] The impetuous Catherine Backès-Clément, then a member of the Communist Party, was more direct: 'Please understand me, it is not the institution that is the problem. No Marxist could claim that. It is the current context, together with the recent cultural orientation; it is those with whom you will necessarily rub shoulders, and who would seem, frankly, unworthy of you. I have spoken with you about threats to those of my generation; increasingly often, these come from statements by Académie members. One must weigh in on the other side, and of course to do so, be a member. But what is the real power of that place and of you, in that place? My question is not really reticent, it is full of our worries. And it is a real question: I recognize that I am not answering it, and that it will remain for the future to tell.'[76]

Why him? Why it?

By electing Lévi-Strauss, the Académie opted for change, and found an ingenious way to appoint a successor to Montherlant, the great writer and author of *La Reine morte* and *Les Jeunes Filles*. Although he has now fallen into relative obscurity, he represented at the time the very best of prewar French literature, an artist of style, whose twin figure Paul Morand, with his mix of great classical style and political infamy, happened to be seated next to Lévi-Strauss. For the Académie, in search of new breadth, it was also a way to open its doors to the human sciences, Lévi-Strauss being the first anthropologist to be admitted to their company, as he was to recall in the very first sentence of his reception speech. It is easy to see how, in this period of ebb, to phrase it as straightforwardly as Druon did with Lévi-Strauss,[77] the institution stood to gain from the arrival of this great intellectual who, always unpredictable, did not consider it ridiculous or inappropriate to quibble over the meaning and definition of words along-side thirty-nine other elder gentlemen. No other intellectual of his ilk would have even considered such a proposition as anything but a joke, especially in the early 1970s.

But for Lévi-Strauss, though he had never desired it, being invited to join the Académie gave him a pleasant feeling of *kairos*: 'I felt the moment had arrived.'[78] In his inaugural speech, he invoked the seductive appeal, quite natural to an anthropologist, of 'historical accretions'[79] – of institutions that, due to their long history, form the backbone of socie-ties. The temporal scale measured in centuries of the Académie française constituted an invariant in our modern and contemporary history. As he later told Braudel, who was himself elected in 1985, joining one of the few French institutions that spanned three centuries, he was responding to the 'call of the *longue durée*'.[80] It was also a civic gesture, at once solemn and derisory, which Lévi-Strauss had described through the narrative of one of his recent journeys to British Columbia, a few months earlier, during which he came to attend a nocturnal initiation ritual: 'Had it been necessary, that Indian night would have sufficed to make me understand and admire the fact that, despite the divisions in our society, forty people were willing to overlook what might otherwise separate them to form a community, whose members have vowed to remain faithful to a few very simple values: love of their language and respect for their culture and for the settled customs that the centuries have bestowed upon them. I come to you, Gentlemen, like the old Indians I have known, intent on bearing witness until the end for the culture that had made them, however bat-tered and, as some were prepared to say, doomed it may be.'[81] In love with rituals and lost causes, Lévi-Strauss peppered his speech with several other indications: as a member of the Académie, he was guaranteed an escape from the social death of retirement, thanks to *ante mortem* immor-tality (rather than *post mortem*, which was never guaranteed). A means of preparing for life after the Collège de France, which was to be perpetuated by a weekly meeting (the Thursday sessions) which we know Lévi-Strauss would faithfully attend until the end. On a more serious note, the anthro-pologist repeatedly spoke of his apparent lack of a sense of personal identity.[82] In the end, what the Académie provided was, on the horizontal plane, a 'principle of constancy'[83] and, on the vertical, an 'imperative of filiation'[84] – a double dissolution of the individual into the body of the Académie and into the genealogy of a seat (the twenty-ninth, in his case). Académiciens exist only at the juncture of these two axes – a place that, upon one's death, is immediately filled by another. This was both a way to develop institutionally and to free himself of the burden of existing individually. Finally, in the words of the anthropologist, this institution 'gathers a surface into a volume. It bridges distances, brings together spiritual families and individuals in unforeseen ways.'[85] No doubt he was also driven by a desire to break free, to escape to the polar opposite of the academic world, of anthropology, of the social sciences and of the intel-lectual left that had formed his natural social networks. Indeed, was he not also describing himself when he cited Montherlant's 'particular delight in sometimes playing against his own camp'?[86] This is precisely what Lévi-Strauss did by joining the Académie.

The final and most obvious reason was the love of language. Describing Montherlant's formal traditionalism, his 'strong language', his supreme command, Lévi-Strauss concluded: 'It is our duty to maintain language at such lofty heights.'[87] Much later, he tried to explain to a sarcastically inclined American journalist the meaning of this exotic assembly, which symbolized national literary prestige and had no other function than to exert a guardianship over French vocabulary and purity of the language: 'The dictionary is only the visible part of the Académie's function. But it also has a symbolic role. As an honorary confraternity, it attests to the attachment the French nation has for its language. You can see that affection for their language in many other ways as well, for instance all the fuss they make here about changing the spelling of a word. You rarely see that in other countries. Take the United States. Americans readily abuse their language by adopting terms like "thru traffic". I don't think Americans respect their language. For them it's just an instrument that they adapt to their needs, and use with total liberty.' 'Is that bad?' the journalist asked. 'Not necessarily. That's what gives savour to American English. There are new words all the time, an incredible creation of new words and expressions. But it's a completely different attitude from ours.'[88]

In the end, for all these reasons, both explicit and implicit, Lévi-Strauss rejoiced at the prospect of joining this company of old sphinxes, this sort of English gentlemen's club, whose homosociability recalled the activities in a Bororo 'men's house'.[89]

'Lévi-Strauss is going to restructure the Académie'[90]

The induction ceremony took place on 27 June 1974. Over the previous summer, Lévi-Strauss had read over all of Montherlant. 'No small task',[91] as he told Chiva. The member who would receive him into the Académie was none other than his former foe, Roger Caillois, who had sharply attacked *Race and History* in 1954.[92] 'I learned that he had supported me. I was touched by this. Once I was elected, I asked him to give the induction speech, telling him that the only way I could thank him was to give him the last word. He equivocated a bit, and then accepted.'[93] The staid academic ritual was slightly unsettled by the striking speech, of high literary quality, as Lévi-Strauss acknowledged to Caillois, who had shared it with him beforehand, as was customary: 'The style is superb, and I find it full of poetry, charm, and even joy, which is no small feat on such a tedious subject.'[94] A literary discourse that nonetheless included a scathing critique (partially redundant with the one he had made twenty years earlier) of the man whose praises he was supposed to sing. Hence the surprise and touch of scandal surrounding that out-of-the-ordinary event.

In the meantime, Claude Lévi-Strauss went to Moreau, the tailor on boulevard Malesherbes, to be fitted for his Académie uniform.[95] Filmed and interviewed by Jean-Claude Bringuier on that occasion, his passion for customs and rituals comes across very clearly. Rigour and meticulous attention to the ceremonial trappings were in order. 'Did we take it in enough under the arms?'[96] his wife wondered, doubtfully. The embroidered patterns were inspired by an ancient motif of upturned leaves. The cape weighed three kilos and, with the bicorn hat, the entire uniform came to at least four . . . Looking at himself in the mirror, with a faint smile on his lips: 'I think we dress more gaily. After all, this is one of the rare occasions in our society when a man can dress like a woman.'[97]

It was thus kitted out like a horse that he arrived, on 27 June 1974, for a ceremony attended by the usual Académie audience – generals, former politicians, writers and socialites – as well as members of the LAS, some of whom wore black armbands as a sign of mourning! Claude Lévi-Strauss's reception speech was first and foremost addressed to them, rather than to the members of the Académie: 'I was explaining to them'[98] how the Académie's initiation ritual was no different from those practised by the societies studied by anthropologists. 'Like the initiated who, wrapped from head to toe in a thick hood, attempts to walk again and to take his first steps into his new life, probing the ground with a pole bristling with spikes like a lightning rod, I stand before you here, also in special garb, armour as much as adornment, and fitted with a weapon, both intended to defend their wearer against the social or supernatural evils to which all those who change states are exposed. I find myself surrounded by two solicitous sponsors, akin to those the Amerindians, looking for modern equivalents of their own customs, now call "baby-sitters": those charged with the care of novices reduced to an infantile state. In the great ceremonial house in which I found myself then – rectangular rather than round – I heard the beating of drums of various sizes, intended to encourage the initiated to intone his chant now and then. Here today that chant is called a speech, but by giving it the form of an encomium, does your tradition not intend for me to be inspired by my illustrious predecessor, playing for me the role of guardian spirit?'[99]

This extended parallel between the green-clothed tribe and that of the savages, between his new existence in the Académie and the rebirth to themselves of initiated adolescents, between the sponsors of the new member and the 'baby-sitters', was both entirely expected coming from him and very amusing in its affectionate irreverence for the old men lavished with honours and somewhat overly confident in their talent. Lévi-Strauss, even while fully playing the game, sprinkled a few insolent remarks into his discomfiting preamble: 'The value of institutions is not based on that of the individuals that compose it at any given time.' This was good news for the Académie française, discredited as it was after the Vichy period by the clearly collaborationist position taken by many of its members.[100] As well as a lecture in sociology, this statement was also a warning to those currently assembled: Lévi-Strauss did not intend to join the ranks of its 1974 membership, but to play his part, as a pawn, in the history of an institution to whose perpetuation he would thus contribute.

The rest of the speech was a eulogy for Montherlant. Paying closer attention, one detects a kind of self-portrait in relief. Or perhaps Lévi-Strauss, seeking in the writer what he could not find in himself, had simply endowed him with such traits. In any case, Lévi-Strauss's Montherlant was the 'incomparable restorer' of a belletristic style that ran from Bossuet and Saint-Simon to Rousseau and Chateaubriand. He was proof that one could still write in a sublime language. The anthropologist was moved by the writer's disjointed temporalities, a characteristic they both shared. While Lévi-Strauss claimed to be a man of the nineteenth century, Montherlant also wanted to live outside his century, and in a double sense: 'He did not revive Antiquity, he revived the seventeenth century revival of Antiquity.' This 'dazzling act of recovery' fit well with Lévi-Strauss's quixotic side. He was also taken with Montherlant's unpredictability, his contradictions and alternations, what he called his 'diurnal obscurity', a fickle disposition that he did not see as the basis for his position of political 'accommodation' during World War II – about which he said not a word. Nor did he mention his homosexuality. Both Montherlant's ethics – his 'devotion to beings [. . .] and his contempt for men' – and his lofty morals – 'rejecting the idea that life has meaning is to impose on oneself the very harsh, but inescapable task of giving it one' – sounded very Lévi-Straussian indeed. The privilege he granted Montherlant's character, that of having always known how to 'govern himself', was also a personal ideal, one that had probably led him all the way to the Académie, where nobody had expected him to wind up – least of all the black armbands and the young generation of structuralist converts of the 1960s.

In conclusion, Lévi-Strauss quoted his predecessor's predecessor, one of the guardian angels of the twenty-ninth seat, Ernest Renan, whose tutelary spirit was particularly well suited to that phase of French intellectual life and to that of Lévi-Strauss himself: 'The best way of being right in the future is, in certain periods, to know how to resign oneself to being out of fashion.'[101] This haughty acceptance of a form of obsolescence was Lévi-Strauss's great strength during this critical decade. If his joining the Académie inevitably pushed him rightward on the intellectual and political spectrum, he did not experience the anticipated ostracism. As opposed to Raymond Aron who, over the same decade, lost his preeminent position over French sociology, Lévi-Strauss remained, even under attack, the leader of the discipline of anthropology, at both the national and international level. The ebb of structuralism found him solidly established at his Collège de France laboratory, surrounded by a team of anthropologists none of whom was a true disciple, even an unfaithful one. Having left the LAS intact, he failed to restructure the Académie française, as a journalist at the *Canard Enchaîné* had predicted he would do upon his election. His 'diurnal obscurity' was now matched by his two institutional sides – the Collège and the Académie, two institutions that may have sometimes crossed paths historically but that nonetheless represented distinct ambitions and itineraries in French culture, not to mention rivals in terms of seniority.

Structuralism was no longer in fashion – duly noted. Its putative leader provocatively joined the adversarial camp in the intellectual world of France. In so doing, a strange mutation occurred, as if, gradually, the spirited (though austere) structuralist theorist had given birth to a pensive and melancholy scholar, enthralled to customs and usages, an old zen master who would come to dominate the intellectual scene of the 1980s. It was indeed made quite clear in Roger Caillois's speech that it was the latter, and by no means the former, who was welcome in the Académie.

Between the Collège de France and the Académie française, Lévi-Strauss, long cloistered, made several forays into the wider world. He added a new privileged location to his affective geography: British Columbia, and Canada more generally. Between 1973 and 1975, several visits structured his discovery in the form of reunion with a country, a landscape, and a mythology over which he pored yet again – they are central to the final volume of the *Mythologiques* – but in a different way, this time for a book in which the anthropologist pondered the mystery of the masks, in all their indents and protrusions, of the Pacific coast of Canada. And through them, he explored for the first time the aesthetic dimension as one of the ambitions and objects of structural analysis.

The way of art

British Columbia is a coastal region wedged between the Pacific Ocean and a mountain range, beyond which the vast plateau of Columbia stretches all the way to the Rocky Mountains. It is an anciently inhabited land, to which many archaeological remains attest: a hundred or so small tribes (including, from north to south, the Tlingit, the Tsimshian, the Haida, the Kwakiutl,[102] the Bella Colla, the Nootka and the Salish) settled there, using a wide variety of languages, social organizations and cultures, and displaying an extraordinary vitality in the art of living, i.e., in aesthetic and religious production. As Boas and his disciples had found them in the early twentieth century, it was an anthropologist's dream! And indeed, British Columbia has since served as a laboratory of Americanist anthropology, before becoming one of the field's most canonical sites.

A mythic itinerary

'The peoples who have lived [on the Pacific Northwest Coast] for thousands of years, their social institutions and their art have played an essential part in my theoretical thinking, just as they have affected me profoundly aesthetically.'[103] These are the words of Lévi-Strauss in June 2000, weaving into a single sentence a whole series of questions that turned the Canadian moment into yet another locus of the anthropologist's life and work:[104] a theoretical question in structural anthropology that found material for a significant comparison with the Amazonian data. Together, these two bodies of material were to anchor the structural analysis of myth in an empirical reality that it had been early on accused of lacking. But this theoretical curiosity was inseparably combined with an artistic feeling, raising questions about the impact of the latter on the former in scientific invention, and bringing the aesthetic issue to the fore as the crux of this physical and mental journey. The art of British Columbia had been part of Lévi-Strauss's life from his New York years until his final book, *Look, Listen, Read* (1993), whose final section focuses on the figure of the Amerindian artist. As Marie Mauzé has rightly pointed out, Lévi-Strauss recycled a paragraph from a 1943 article that already dealt with the art of the northwest coast, thereby 'reinforcing the [biographical] loop effect'.[105]

In reality, his encounter with British Columbia occurred between 1973 and 1975, but it had taken place much earlier in the form of an emotional electroshock, in one of those 'revelations' that form the basis of abiding passions.

It all began in 1939 with a trapeze-shaped Haida pipe made of argillite that Lévi-Strauss, upon his return from Brazil, acquired from the André Le Véel Gallery. The mythological motifs decorating the object had caught his eye. He re-experienced this magnetic confrontation with the objects, forms and decorations of British Columbia again a few years later in New York, during a visit to the central hall (conceived by Boas) of the American Museum of Natural History. The way Lévi-Strauss then narrated it, which was republished in the opening chapter of *The Way of the Masks*, was as a kind of magic spell: '"There is in New York", I wrote in 1943, "a magic place where the dreams of childhood hold a rendezvous, where century-old tree trunks sing and speak, where indefinable objects watch out for the visitor, with the anxious stare of human faces, where animals of superhuman gentleness join their little paws like hands in prayer for the privilege of building the palace of the beaver for the chosen one, of guiding him to the realm of the seals, or of teaching him, with a mystic kiss, the language of the frog or the kingfisher".'[106] The text then describes an experience of physical confrontation with objects, masks in particular, provoking a sense of awe and dread that signals their intimate connection to the realm of the supernatural. 'Upsetting the peace of everyday life, the masks' primal message retains so much power that even today the prophylactic insulation of the showcases fails to muffle its communication.'[107] The Museum of Natural History and its northwest coast room remained, for Lévi-Strauss, a veritable primal scene, as opposed to Boas, who studied the same artefacts but without any particular spiritual connection: 'They are Indians like any others!' he had once said, reluctant to establish any hierarchy between the various indigenous cultures. In sharp contrast with this attitude, Lévi-Strauss had a true affinity for the aesthetics of these tribes, some of whose objects would remain lifelong companions: the Tsimshian dragonfly mask, one of the objects purchased in 1951 which is now at the Sessions Pavilion of the Louvre, a Tlingit war helm (bought from Max Ernst in New York when the latter, who had separated from Peggy Guggenheim, was short of funds), a Chilkat ceremonial blanket and a Haida mace that was displayed on the bookshelves of his library.[108]

It was, then, these 'living pillars' (i.e., totem poles), cannibal crows, salmon fishermen and the Dzonokwa ogress that Lévi-Strauss went to visit during his two stays in Vancouver, which were, strictly speaking, neither fieldwork nor academic events. In February 1973, the French anthropologist was invited by the Vancouver Institute of the University of British Columbia to host a week-long seminar. There is film footage of him handling masks and commenting on them in front of assembled students and colleagues.[109] In July 1974, he returned with his wife and son, setting aside ten days to tour around in a 'camper' sleeping three people, covering several hundred kilometres a day. Their itinerary led the Lévi-Strausses to the northern part of Vancouver Island, then to Alert Bay on the very small island of Cormorant (one of the sanctuaries of Kwakiutl culture), and then by ferryboat to Prince Rupert, before turning back southward through the Skeena and Fraser valleys – the ultimate goal of the expedition, the mythical setting of the story of Asdiwal, the young Tsimshian chief and salmon fisherman who was the main character of a series of four variants of a myth collected by Boas and studied by Lévi-Strauss. In his 1956 article on the myth, he had turned it into a lesson on the methodology of structural analysis. This accounts for the special status of that journey, experienced as a 'pilgrimage' following the mythical itineraries that he had mapped, identified and discussed earlier in life.[110] Indeed, this was the term he used to describe his journey to Isac Chiva: 'Our trek through British Columbia went wonderfully: enchanting spectacles and moving pilgrimages to the Kwakiutl, the Tsimshian (where I followed the Asdiwal itinerary), the Thompson and the Lilloet. I am returning inspired, enriched and quite exhausted as well for, even when you share the driving, 2,200 kilometres in a "camper" – i.e., a 3.5-ton truck with a passenger cabin that blocks the rear view – is trying on the nerves.'[111]

It was a true reunion of the soul with the extraordinary landscapes of the Skeena, Nass and Fraser valleys that overwhelmed the emotions of a traveller rashly labelled 'galactic'[112] by the local press, overly eager to enshrine the scholarly gentleman from Paris. In fact, this voyage through the looking glass (of myth) assured and renewed his 'almost carnal bond'[113] with the Amerindian societies who had not yet had their last word.

'We Kwakiutl': the Canadian turn

Indeed, there was something Lévi-Strauss had not anticipated when preparing for his trip to the northwest coast: the revelation of an art and a community of Canadian Indians endowed with unanticipated vitality. Lévi-Strauss thus came to conjugate British Columbia in the present tense.

Already in 1973, he had had the rare privilege of attending a guardian spirit dance among the Salish Musqueam living on the outskirts of Vancouver. These Amerindians, in daily contact with the city, far from embodying immaculate cultural integrity, had adopted Western clothing. Yet, Lévi-Strauss paid 'homage to a vibrant culture that was necessarily hybrid',[114] that had adopted elements of modernity but stayed the course of tradition. The following year, he met with Amerindian chiefs, one of whose daughters, Gloria, also an assistant curator at the Vancouver Museum of Anthropology, sent him a few tins of candlefish oil ('t'lina'), dried fish (to dip into it), berries, and a special kind of salmon (the 'Nimkish River sockeye'), which, she added, 'with typical arrogance, we Kwakiutl know to be the very best'. This statement in the first-person plural overturned some of the most established coordinates of Lévi-Strauss's mental system. He was astounded to discover that, as Catherine Clément later pointed out, 'as opposed to his sad tropical intuitions, the "savage" cultures, martyred by Western colonial expansion, were not all dead. Better still, they were coming back to life, giving powerful inspiration to a new contemporary art.'[115]

Lévi-Strauss thus wrote: 'It is in visiting not only the sites but also the Indian groups themselves that I discovered what was not at all news to locals: the prodigious renaissance of an art that, while I would not say it had ever entirely disappeared, had been – between roughly 1920 and 1960 – persecuted and oppressed by missionaries and by Canadian authorities who prohibited ceremonies and confiscated family heritage, consisting of masks, boxes, decorated copper pots, etc., which constituted the ancestral treasures of noble houses.'[116] The ban on potlatches was lifted in 1951 and the artistic rebirth of the Native Americans began in the 1960s. It was documented by anthropologist and art historian Bill Holm as early as 1965, in his seminal work *Northwestern Coast Indian Art*,[117] which endowed this two-dimensional art with its own vocabulary – the 'form line' – and a degree of respectability. The book became a kind of bible for Native American art. Among those he met, the most important for Lévi-Strauss was Bill Reid, one of the most prolific representatives of the blossoming of a contemporary autochthonous art.

Born Canadian of a Haida mother and a father of Scottish and German descent, Bill Reid (1920–88) died an 'Amerindian' thanks to the 1982 amendment that restored Amerindian status to children of mixed native and European ancestry.[118] His syncretic biography informed his art, which combined European techniques – gold- and silver-smithing and jewellery-making – with native inspiration in the patterns and sometimes the materials (the cedar wood of his coffers). Lévi-Strauss was dazzled by his many talents: 'We are indebted to Bill Reid, an incomparable artist, for having maintained and rekindled a flame nearly extinguished. That is not all: Bill Reid by his example and by his teaching has given rise to a prodigious artistic flowering, the results of which the Indian designers, sculptors and goldsmiths of British Columbia offer up today to our amazed eyes. [. . .] Gifted like his predecessors, known and unknown, Bill Reid covers the full range of forms of expression known to them: from monumental wooden sculptures to precious jewellery in gold and silver, as well as wall decorations, the spirit of which, on a lesser scale, his prints in red and black carry on.'[119] Many of Bill Reid's qualities appealed to Lévi-Strauss. His very existence as an artist signalled the dawn of a renaissance that seemed very promising to the anthropologist, both for the future of these communities and for contemporary art in general. Lévi-Strauss readily identified him as a major force of revival. Indeed, he would have liked for Bill Reid to have decorated his Académie sword. The timeframe being too short, he commissioned a bolo tie locket instead. The Canadian artist would often turn to works of anthropology to draw inspiration from ancient and vanished patterns to which he would give new life. This relay between anthropological documentation and artistic creation blatantly disproved the accusations of 'ethnocide' being levelled at the discipline at that very moment. Museum institutions and anthropologists played an important role in gaining recognition for Bill Reid, and more generally integrating Amerindian artists into the artistic scene, commissioning works from them, funding 'residencies', and more generally the co-creation with local communities of a common heritage derived from a history that, though often violent, was also shared. This was the historical and political role that Lévi-Strauss also sanctioned when, in November 1975, he accepted the invitation to inaugurate the new gallery of the National Museum of Man in Ottawa (today the Canadian Museum of History), devoted to objects of the Pacific Northwest Amerindian world, called the 'Children of the Raven', in reference to a Haida creation myth.

The unexpected element at this Canadian event was an unprecedented enthusiasm for an art which, in a way, carried everything else along, proof of a world that was in the end more liveable – as though Lévi-Strauss's melancholy tone had been (temporarily) suspended. The note of lament that characterized anthropology as rescue was here out of place. Anthropology could now be the science not of the 'first' men, nor of the 'last' men, but of the new first men. The encounter between the Western anthropologist and the Amerindian artist (or at least the artist who had reconstructed himself as such) brought Lévi-Strauss into a new field of possible action. He remained very attuned to what was emerging in Canada in the 1970s, a new model for the relationship between the modern state and native peoples, and became an unfailing supporter of the cause of the Kwakwaka'wakw First Nations until his death. In the course of Lévi-Strauss's life, the 'Canadian turn' replaced the Romantic aesthetic of the ruin with a more optimistic vision of a new dawn that might – who knows what the future brings? – turn into a bright new day.

The way of the masks

In 1975, like an offering to this land that had become so dear to him, Lévi-Strauss published an illustrated work entitled *The Way of the Masks*, which, as its title indicated, focused on several masks from British Columbia under whose spell he had been for more than thirty years. This work formed the first of what he later called his three 'minor *Mythologiques*': *The Jealous Potter* and *The Story of Lynx* were to follow, in 1985 and 1991 respectively. Available in the prestigious Pléiade edition of his collected work published in France in 2008, these three books are now credited with an importance and meaning that their originally modest character, both in terms of size and purpose, did not seem to warrant. What do these texts represent in the overall economy of his work? What status are we to grant them? Many readers and specialists agree that they should not be considered as simple introductions (even though they might also serve that purpose), and even less so as the dregs of his previous oeuvre. Their appeal now lies

in the new form that they invented and in the continuing efflorescence of
Lévi-Strauss's scholarly production. Frédéric Keck thinks of it in terms
of 'pentimento',[120] in the painterly sense. With Lévi-Strauss, nothing was
ever closed. As Eduardo Viveiros de Castro has pointed out, 'that is not
all'[121] is a recurring phrase in Lévi-Straussian prose. As though the interminable character of the study of myth had contaminated all his work.
Thus, 'the closing of the four volumes [of the *Mythologiques* series] did not
have the last word'.[122] After the operatic unfurling of the tetralogy, here
was a detective story, with an initial mystery, a few clues and a reassuring
resolution of the problem: Why did the organs of North American masks
sometimes feature as protuberances and sometimes as cavities? The author
conducted his investigation on a field with which he was familiar, delivering
a lesson in aesthetics that challenged the categories of Western art.

The material for the book grew out of a year of teaching at the Collège
de France in 1971/72. Lévi-Strauss focused on the homogeneity of a small
group of myths from British Columbia which he correlated with a few
masks, as well as with copper production and trade, a source of prestige
in Amerindian societies of the northwest. The idea for the book had been
suggested by a man of whom Lévi-Strauss thought highly, Gaëtan Picon.
This academic and prolific essayist was a close friend of André Malraux,
then minister of cultural affairs, on whom he had written a book. Picon
subsequently became Malraux's director general for arts and letters at the
ministry, from 1960 to 1966.[123] He was friends with many poets and artists,
whose work he published in the series he edited for the Swiss publishing
house Skira, 'Les sentiers de la creation'. The books in this series were
elegant volumes whose reproductions, typography and iconography were
handled with care. Lévi-Strauss did not hesitate at the prospect of contributing to this prestigious collection, which appealed to him in every way:
'path [*sentier*] made me think of way'.[124] And so *The Way of the Masks*
was born, at a moment of strong interest in primitive art – which was not
yet being called tribal art.

Yet *The Way of the Masks* was not just a coffee table book. Erudite
and rigorous as always, the anthropologist continued his demonstration
of the validity of structural analysis, applied for the first time to fine
art. Like myths, masks did not make sense when considered in isolation.
They acquired meaning only when related to a system of transformations
(with other masks), itself connected to the local ethnographic context.
Hence the question: why was this Salish Sxwaixwe mask, with its exag-
geratedly bulging eyes and protruding tongue, so distinctive, so singular in
comparison with other masks from the surrounding area? This question
was explored through a comparison with two other characteristic types
of masks: the Kwakiutl mask of *dzonokwa*, which appeared as the exact
counter-mask of the former, with its sunken eyes and concave mouth, its
black colour and hair decorations; and the Xwexwe mask, which took up
characteristics of the Sxwaixwe, but which came from the Kwakiutl, and
was therefore also aesthetically distinct from the *dzonokwa* mask. The book
related aesthetic forms to economies and myths, preserving a relative
autonomy for the formal logic, but relative only, since, for Lévi-Strauss, the

aesthetic sphere was always embedded in the society in which it developed. Yet this relationship did not obey, as with certain Marxist approaches, a logic of reflection, but rather one of twists, inversions and concealments. Just as the Dene myth of the Woman of Metals inverts the actual conditions of copper circulation, so 'a mask is not primarily what it represents but what it transforms, that is to say, what it chooses *not* to represent. Like a myth, a mask denies as much as it affirms.'[125] As it presents itself to us, *The Way of the Masks* reads as a 'discourse on the structural method'.[126] Yet the sophisticated theoretical apparatus applied by Lévi-Strauss does not detract from the object's artistic appeal. For while offering an explanation, structural analysis preserves and even enhances the opacity of artistic invention. In other words, art still signifies its surrounding world, but its signification never obeys a simple relationship of analogy or duplication. It moves stealthily.

Toward a general aesthetic

This beautiful book, originally published as a two-volume box set, unquestionably brought the anthropologist into contact with a new audience. His aesthetic pleasure was more clearly expressed and the structural analysis, while no less rigorous, seemed less dryly academic. As Georges Dumézil put it: 'This is a delightful feast.'[127] Patrick Waldberg, his friend from the New York years, highlighted the quality of the reproductions and the book's attention to detail: 'I lingered for a long time over the exquisite sea otter, captivated by its little eye.'[128] Michel Leiris was grateful to Lévi-Strauss for revealing 'objects of reverie steeped in a current of reflection that, far from curtailing the imagination, incites one to further dreaming'.[129] This revitalizing of intelligibility through the imagination, and vice versa, was also appreciated by others and formed part of the principal appeal of the book.

The considerable number of reviews attested to the enthusiastic reception of *The Way of the Masks* in the daily press in France, as well as in journals and weeklies.[130] The book also benefited from its publication during the Christmas season. If many of the reviewers noted the change in format of he who had become the 'Sherlock Holmes of ethnography',[131] they mostly insisted on the centrality of the aesthetic dimension in his latest work: to what extent did art provide a means of resolving some of the problems of structural analysis? And of posing fertile and little broached questions, such as that of the temporality of structures? Could *The Way of the Masks* even be considered as a new step towards the construction of an aesthetics that had been formulated for the very first time in 1959 in his radio interviews with Georges Charbonnier?[132] Art had always been a part of the anthropologist's work, from the face paintings of the Caduveo women to the feather art of the Bororo. But here, Lévi-Strauss's anthropological conclusions and some of his side comments appeared to address a Western aesthetics that we know the anthropologist considered to be, and already for some time, at an impasse. In *Le Quotidien de Paris*, the art critic Pierre Daix, a former communist, clearly stated: 'Taking a convoluted path, Claude Lévi-Strauss has just made a fundamental contribution to a modern aesthetics.'[133]

Indeed, the art of British Columbia was, like all tribal art, an art of signifying rather than representing. What Amerindians were interested in was the relationship to the supernatural, which could not be represented but could, however, be signified. For Lévi-Strauss, the greatness of that art was thus its figuration of what could not be figured (the supernatural) through signifying recompositions, through a dialectic between medium and motif, which turned a chest decorated with bear patterns into a true incarnation of that bear. This vital and dialectical relationship between the (graphic) decoration and the (material) structure produced meaning: the chest became a 'box-that-speaks'. It was a bear reincarnated as a house. Art signified ... It was this 'lesson in intelligibility'[134] that was

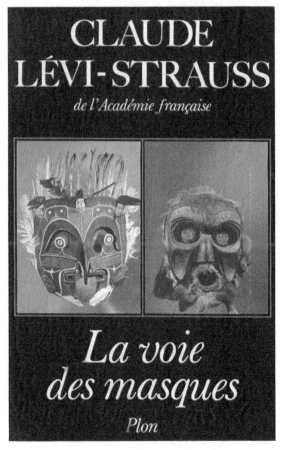

Cover of *The Way of the Masks*, republished by Plon in 1979.

emphasized. Lévi-Strauss was here making very different use of tribal art from that of the Western artists of the early twentieth century: they had engaged with these ancient forms as a source of new modern inspiration. What these objects, decorations and forms actually meant to the societies that had produced them was never a question for Picasso, Derain or Matisse. Lévi-Strauss looked for topical meaning, which structural analysis revealed to him, before reimporting this primal truth into artistic modernity: the demand for meaning, as well as the constraining force of tradition, ways of doing, tricks, solutions beginning to take shape. As opposed to the Romantic aesthetic of the inspired and solitary artist, Lévi-Strauss claimed: 'When [the artist] thinks he is expressing himself spontaneously, creating an original work, he is answering other past or present, actual or potential, creators. Whether one knows it or not, one never walks alone along the path of creativity.'[135] The subversive potential of such a statement was on a par with the Romantic credo, that had spread to all modern and contemporary art, of the 'genius' who creates *ex nihilo*.

Gaëtan Picon, the series editor, was, as we mentioned, a close friend of Malraux's. The latter's aesthetics, developed through several powerful volumes that left a major mark on their times – *The Imaginary Museum* (1947), *The Twilight of the Absolute* (1949), *The Voices of Silence* (1951) – no doubt served as a point of reference in what was beginning to emerge as structural aesthetics. Malraux and Lévi-Strauss were indeed both quick to highlight non-Western art and to compare it to Western masterpieces. The difference between them lay in their use of the idea of the Beautiful. With André Malraux, culture was experienced as aesthetic delight and emotional shock, which was opposed to scholarly knowledge. This conception had guided the development of the project of Maisons de la Culture, which Malraux had kept at a safe distance from the popular education programmes and even more so from the ministry of education.[136] With Lévi-Strauss, on the contrary, the one did not spoil the other; knowledge spurred and gave new impetus to the search for meaning inherent to aesthetic pleasure. Similarly, the two men had different conceptions of the act of creation and of the artist. For Malraux, inspiration and the creative subject ruled supreme. Lévi-Strauss was warier of the grandiloquence of the modern artist (since the eighteenth century); for him, the artist-artisan was created from a cultural, religious, mythical, material and economic substrate that he rearranged according to homologies or oppositions with his surrounding world. Aesthetic intensity came from the signifying force promised by such intimacy: art was of the world. It pulled out of it only to better return to it.

Four years later, *The Way of the Masks* was republished in a more portable format, which would serve as the basis for the English translation, with the addition of three appendices in the form of 'excursions' – confirming the impossibility of ever truly bringing the work to a close. Two of them marked new incursions into history, either as the result of a new object in common – the 'house society' that Lévi-Strauss identified in both Kwakiutl and medieval societies – or through an examination of the evolution of mythic structures over time, studying the more or less deformed iterations that developed over time. This elicited surprise and ironic comment: the great master of ahistorical structuralism was thus finally turning to Clio? For, by the mid-1970s, relations between historians and anthropologists were in fact quite cool . . .

Anthropology and history: I love you, me neither

The 1970s and 1980s marked a new stage in the life of Lévi-Strauss, who engaged in a kind of *pas de deux* with history. The first act dated back to 1949 and his article 'Anthropology and history'; the final act unfolded in 1983, with the Marc Bloch Lecture on 'History and anthropology'. The inversion of the two terms was the outcome of almost half a century of debate, part of the larger discussion between history and the social sciences.[137] This new moment of dialogue between Lévi-Strauss and the historians took place through reflections and research in which he engaged over the course of his last lectures at the Collège de France, between 1976 and 1982. After two decades completely immersed in myths, Lévi-Strauss returned to his work on kinship anthropology and social organizations.

The notion of the 'house'

At the beginning of the second excursion added to the revised 1979 edition of *The Way of the Masks*, Lévi-Strauss retraced the path that had led him to formulate his hypothesis on a new kind of social organization: the house. This path wound through the Kwakiutl, one of the British Columbia tribes that had already perplexed Boas, whose work provided Lévi-Strauss with his ethnographic material. He had sensed his elder colleague's 'hesitations' and 'regrets' over the failure of the classic anthropological vocabulary to describe a system that was partly patrilineal, partly matrilineal, predominantly but not always matrilocal (i.e., the couple lives with the wife's family), etc. This sensation of dealing with an anthropological UFO was further intensified by Mauss and Durkheim, who had produced interpretations that diverged from those of Boas, who had himself eventually settled for the indigenous term 'numayn' to describe what he saw.[138] Lévi-Strauss picked up the question at that stage, following a logic of writing with which he had now grown quite familiar: a mystery had arisen that called for resolution; of a limited nature, it proceeded from material that had been pushed to the side, to the margins of grander investigations.

Over the following years at the Collège de France, from 1976 to 1982, he went on a world tour of some forty societies that presented similar traits to those of the Kwakiutl and did not fall into any of the standard categories: neither 'lineage' nor 'tribe', 'clan' nor 'village'. The 1977/78 course explored Indonesia, then came Melanesia in 1978/79, Polynesia in 1979/80, Micronesia and Madagascar in 1980/81 and, finally, Africa during his last year of teaching at the Collège de France in 1981/82. Yet the epistemological shift necessary for designating and understanding this as yet unnamed reality did not occur through geographical comparison: 'Had anthropologists looked towards history – that of medieval Europe of course, but also that of Japan of the Heian and following periods, that of ancient Greece, and of many others as well – it might have been possible to recognize the house.'[139] It was in this use of the conditional that the possibility and the project of dialogue between anthropologists and historians lay.

What exactly did the notion of house refer to? In both noble and peasant houses of medieval Europe, in the Japanese aristocratic lineages of the Heian period (tenth to eleventh centuries), in the great Fiji chiefdoms and the ancient kingdom of Madagascar, the house was 'a legal entity possessing a domain, perpetuated by transmission of its name, wealth and titles through a real or fictitious descent line which is recognized as legitimate as long as the continuity can be expressed in the language of descent or alliance or, most often, both together.'[140] These house societies thus employed kinship in both its lineage form and its fictional form, i.e., alliance or even adoption: in the absence of a male heir, titles could be passed on through daughters or sisters, who then served roles Lévi-Strauss was delighted to find described in a medieval metaphoric expression as 'bridge and plank'.[141] Two lines of transmission (one for names, the other for titles) most often coexisted, as with the Kwakiutl. Hence the tensions and even conflicts that sometimes erupted in these societies, more flexible, but which placed side by side the generally antagonistic principles of exogamy and endogamy, filiation and residence. For Lévi-Strauss, the moment at which these new organizations developed coincided with the societies' opening up to history and, as Maurice Godelier critically explained, disguised all manner of sociopolitical manoeuvres as kinship.[142] Lévi-Strauss made his theory about this social structure even more explicit: it pertained to 'a structural state where political and economic interests tending to invade the social field did not yet have distinct languages at their disposal and, being obliged to express themselves in the only language available, which is that of kinship, inevitably subverted it'.[143] Then 'the old bloodlines' yielded to more daring matrimonial considerations and familial strategies. This was why in medieval Europe, the notion of house was widely used both at the top (noble houses, as in the 'House of Bourbon') and at the bottom (peasant houses, especially in the mountainous regions of southern France) of the social ladder, the two strata most hostile to change.[144]

This 'threshold' between cold and hot societies that 'house societies' represented, according to François Hartog, also indicated a terrain of possible collaboration between historians and anthropologists.[145] Kinship anthropology increasingly called on, and fed on, history. From the Kwakiutl to the court of Louis XIV, from the Occitan *'oustau'* to the 'Yurok' of California, history and anthropology shared many 'interference zones'.[146] It was thus with a certain solemnity that, in his last lecture at the Collège de France, Lévi-Strauss evoked this common ground of the two disciplines, emphasizing the ongoing inversion: it was no longer elementary societies that served to explain certain aspects of more complex societies, but the other way around. An ultimate subversion that the anthropologist deployed again, verbatim, in his Marc Bloch lecture one year later: 'The time has passed when one turned to anthropology almost automatically to interpret old or recent customs, the significance of which was unclear, as survivals or traces of a social state always exemplified by savage peoples. In the face of this discarded "primitivism", we can better understand how modes of social life and organizational forms well noted in our history can illuminate those of different societies, where they appear less distinct and seemingly scrambled, because poorly documented and observed over too-brief periods. Between so-called "complex" societies and those wrongly called "primitive" or "archaic" there is less distance than is usually supposed. To bridge that distance, it is equally appropriate to climb up from there to here as to descend from here to there.'[147]

'The mortal kiss of the fairy'

In 1988, a television broadcast coordinated by Didier Éribon conveyed a sense of this new harmonious relationship between the anthropologist and certain historians: five scholars, two of whom were historians, Jean-Pierre Vernant and Jacques Le Goff, were invited to describe the impact of structural anthropology on their scholarly practices, and Lévi-Strauss responded in turn with a commentary.[148] In an ambiance of intellectual affinity, Le Goff, recounting how he and Vidal-Naquet had submitted a text by Chrétien de Troyes, *Yvain, the Knight of the Lion*, to structural analysis, curiously confided: 'Reading Lévi-Strauss, I felt the mortal kiss of the fairy.' It was as though the historian had sensed the threat of dissolution of his own discipline coming from the powerful appeal of structural anthropology. But Lévi-Strauss added: 'We have now come to a point where we feel we are doing the same thing.' History and anthropology would thus pool the resources available to the social sciences in their respective disciplines: in space for anthropologists and in time for historians.

It was thus no longer a matter of one-sided contracts (1949) – the conscious realm for history and the unconscious for anthropology[149] – or spirited counter-offensives – Braudel's article on the '*longue durée*' (1958). As proclaimed in a 1971 special issue of *Annales*: 'The war between history and structuralism will not come to pass.'[150] Though, as François Hartog has wittily pointed out, this was all the more true as it had already happened![151] The boundaries between the disciplines had long been crossed: historical anthropology dealt with the unconscious bases of societies and attempted to grasp their 'mentalities'. Historians had also learned from Lévi-Strauss to let go of their spontaneous conception of linear time, marked by evolution and progress. They had integrated the diversity of social times and historicities and begun to make it an object of history. And so André Burguière was able to enthusiastically conclude this historic issue of *Annales* on a vision of perpetual peace: 'A little structuralism veers away from History; a lot of structuralism returns to it.'[152]

Indeed, throughout the 1970s, historiography grew increasingly anthropological: the 'new history', officially consecrated by Jacques Le Goff in 1978, was interested in diet, bodies, dwellings, family structures, technologies, beliefs, political cultures, etc. Bolstered by an increasingly obvious public success and the no less evident ebb of structuralism, the new historians openly drew on an anthropological framework that was rather eclectic and predatory. For the majority of them, it was the objects of anthropology rather than orthodox structural analysis that they adopted.[153] This inversion of disciplinary power, the fruit of a successful conversion of historians to the anthropological brief, did not in any way prevent Lévi-Strauss from sponsoring historians at the Collège de France and the Académie française.

He supported the election of Georges Duby to the Collège in 1970, Emmanuel Le Roy Ladurie in 1973 and Jean-Pierre Vernant in 1975, whom he took it upon himself to introduce to his colleagues. At the Académie française, where historians were traditionally better represented than anthropologists, he supported Fernand Braudel's election in 1984 and that of Georges Duby in 1987. With the latter, he formed a particularly close friendship and an appreciation of the historian's literary qualities, as well as his grace, originality and richness: 'This exceptional gift you have of bringing back to life and connecting us to a history that, without you, would have remained lost in the oblivion of time immemorial.'[154] His repeated praise of Duby's productiveness and multifaceted curiosity reflected what Lévi-Strauss considered to be the very essence of history: disciplined writing and the restoration of a lost world through empathy – all in all, a vision of history informed very much by Michelet. It was the writer he liked in Duby. His books never failed to elicit 'literary pleasure and sociological interest',[155] as he wrote to the historian directly.

As for Braudel, whom he had known for half a century, Lévi-Strauss admired his empirical talent, the 'trapper's instinct',[156] the tremendous capacity to assimilate sources, and the ability to combine, contrary to what is commonly thought, all histories, small, medium and large. 'You show that between all the conceptions of history, there is no need to choose',[157] he told Braudel as he was handing him his sword on 19 March 1985. The two old men buried the disciplinary hatchet: 'All human sciences become support for one another in turn.'[158] Between the Braudel of *The Identity of France* and the nearly eighty-year old Lévi-Strauss, attentive to the *longue durée* of rituals and institutions threatened by his own society, the common understanding ran deep. Since nothing was ever that simple between Lévi-Strauss and history, he could not help but end his speech on a final twist: 'In light of your famous distinctions, how are we to interpret this unquestionably historical event that is Fernand Braudel's entrance into the Académie française?'[159] A factual history, surely: the vacancy of chairs, Braudel's doubts; then a conjunctural history as well: a period of broader representation of history and the social sciences had begun at the Académie française; and finally, the long-term history of the Académie itself, a deep structural trait of French national identity, to which Braudel could not remain indifferent.

This new role that Lévi-Strauss took on – of rubbing historians up the wrong way, of taking responsibility for reminding them of the imponderable nature of the event – found perfect illustration in Jéhan, one of the characters in Jules Romains's *Men of Good Will*, which the anthropologist was fond of quoting: 'In reacting against the historians of yesteryear, who brought everything back to the marriages of kings, the vagaries of royal favourites, the rivalries between ministers, I wonder if we have not gone too far. [. . .] What matters certainly is the deeper movement of humanity, the future of the masses, civilization obeying the secular laws of development . . . This is all very well. [. . .] Our modern conception may be correct when history is viewed from Sirius and over a ten-century phase [. . .] but when it comes to finding out whether, at this particular moment, Tsar Nicholas does or does not advise the King of Serbia to invade Austria, that's another kettle of fish.'[160] The role of Lévi-Strauss in the drama that played out between anthropology and history premiered at a solemn event: the Marc Bloch lecture, created by the École des hautes études en sciences sociales (EHESS) to recognize the great minds in the social sciences, from both France and abroad. The scene unfolded on 2 June 1983. François Furet was then the president of the EHESS, which had moved into its building on boulevard Raspail in 1975. Lévi-Strauss's retirement was the occasion for solemn adieus from an institution of which the anthropologist had been an integral part since its founding in 1947, and which had often basked in his glory. The exercise was something of an acrobatic act, since the EHESS had since become the temple of the new history. Lévi-Strauss thus addressed an audience comprised mostly of historians, under the gaze of the allegories painted by Puvi de Chavanne that adorn the great Sorbonne amphitheatre. But this pomp did not deter him. While he conceded the ongoing convergence between structural anthropology and historical inquiry – they often 'got on well' – he ended on a provocative note: 'The time has come for anthropology to tackle turbulence, not in a spirit of contrition but, on the contrary, to extend and develop the exploration of levels of order, which it still holds to be its mission. To do so, anthropology turns again to history: not just to the so-called "new" history, to whose birth it may have contributed, but to the most traditional form of history, sometimes said to be out-of-date: buried in dynastic chronicles, genealogical treatises, memoirs and other written sources on the affairs of prominent families . . . [. . .] Indeed, between that history of events and the new history – the former recording in detail the doings of important persons, the latter focusing on slow demographic, economic and ideological transformations, rooted in deeper layers of society – the gap no longer seems so great once you compare the expert matrimonial matches conceived by Blanche de Castille to those that peasant families practised, all the way to the mid-nineteenth century.'[161] This conclusion surely did not fail to have its effect on the assembled historians, who bristled at the praise of dynastic history as a model for the new anthropology . . .

Yet the paradox lay in the fact that, by the early 1980s, the 'new history' was, indeed, in the process of changing its paradigm, returning to events, narratives and biographies – as Jacques Le Goff was soon to demonstrate, through his history of the life of Saint Louis IX of France. But above all, this was the historiographical moment of *Realms of Memory*, a collective work begun in the early 1980s that found a dialectical way out of the deadlock of the structural new history, reconnecting structure to event, historical invariants to specific institutions, dates and border areas, in a newly justified micro-historical approach. It is thus unsurprising that it should have been the great coordinator of this project, Pierre Nora, who wrote an amused chronicle of this half-century-long turbulent marriage between Claude Lévi-Strauss and the discipline of history. Nora wrote to Lévi-Strauss upon reading, in advance, the text of his lecture that he intended to publish: 'It is moving to thus complete the circle of the famous *Structural Anthropology* article [published in 1949] and ultimately short-circuit the history that was your contemporary. All in all, you made the leap from a critique of classical history to the heralding of a future one, recycling the [illegible] of "small history", moving with supreme elegance beyond the so-called 'new" history. Well done.'[162] The Académie française would soon figure in the second volume of *Realms of Memory: The Construction of the French Past, Traditions* – which Lévi-Strauss labelled a 'museum book' and in which he identified 'a brand new and original way of writing history'.[163] Lévi-Strauss would help Pierre Nora in joining him at the Académie française in 2001, taking the place of François Furet, who had died only a few months after his election in 1997 and been but a ghost member. On that front as well, things came full circle.

Claude Lévi-Strauss and women, from Marguerite Yourcenar to Françoise Héritier

In house systems, Lévi-Strauss had described women as 'power operators'.[164] The Fujiwara clan in Heian Japan had secured its stranglehold over public affairs through multiple strategic marriages, some far and others quite close. This interlacing of political calculation and the cause of women found an echo in two strictly contemporary events in Lévi-Strauss's life, one of which did much to establish the anthropologist's reputation as a reactionary misogynist. In 1980, Marguerite Yourcenar was the first woman to be elected to the Académie française and, the following year, Françoise Héritier was made the second female full professor at the Collège de France. Concerning the former, Lévi-Strauss sided with those who opposed the election of a female member; in the case of the latter, however, he presided over the Africanist's election and insisted on her over all potential male competitors. As opposed to what feminists have argued at the time and since, these diametric positions did not reflect a flexible form of chauvinism, but rather very different appreciations of the respective institutions. For Lévi-Strauss, the Collège de France had always been a temple of emergent science and so it was to choose its members based on their individual qualities as scientists. By contrast, although of more recent founding, the role of the Académie française, in the Lévi-Straussian cosmology, was to slow down the tempo of a 'hot' society – it owed its prestige and vigour to its scrupulous respect for tradition.

Marguerite Yourcenar's candidacy unleashed a storm at the Académie.[165] The writer was well known to, and appreciated by, the members of the Académie, as attested by the many prizes they had showered on her throughout the 1970s. The issue was her sex. In theory, nothing barred the institution from bringing women into its ranks. Each Académie was sovereign in the matter, and some members had already taken the first step. From the moment Jean d'Ormesson took the lead, campaigning loudly in the Parisian salons and newspapers, members found themselves divided into two camps, which did not track traditional ideological oppositions so much as generational antagonisms.[166] The 'moderns' (the most recently elected members), supported by a majority of the newspapers, *Le Figaro* included, wanted to move with the flow of history and bring their institution into line with the evolution of society which, since 1945, had seen a massive increase in women's education and their gradual rise to the heights of achievement and power. The social trend was working in their favour, after seven years of 'modernization' by the Giscard d'Estaing administration, which had promoted women to ministerial positions (Simone Veil, Françoise Giroud). Yet the language these 'moderns' used was not modern at all: they invoked Marguerite Yourcenar's abstract literary worth, without mention of her sex, going so far as to fantasize about the virile character of her writing. At the very least, she had absolutely no links with feminism and, if a further argument was necessary, Marguerite Yourcenar, having settled thousands of kilometres across the ocean from Paris on Mount Desert Island in Maine, was unlikely to be much of a presence! In the opposite camp, her detractors were more discreet, having become decidedly inaudible in those years of the late 1970s. The 'ancients', among them the 'young' Claude Lévi-Strauss, invoked respect for tradition and 'esprit de corps' to legitimate the maintenance of an all-male community. According to Alain Decaux, Claude Lévi-Strauss adduced the example of Amerindian tribes: 'Whenever the latter changed something fundamental in their organization, they would disappear. According to him, the same applied to the Académie française: we were a tribe and one threatened with extinction if we allowed a woman among us.'[167] On the one side, opportunistic 'feminists'; on the other, a Paris-based English gentlemen's club. In the end, the matter was decided by fiat: Valéry Giscard d'Estaing, running in the presidential election the following year, decided to get involved in this highly symbolic process and put all his weight behind Marguerite Yourcenar.[168]

Although Académie members had looked far and wide, all the way across the Atlantic, to find a woman to reinvigorate their traditions, it was very close to home that Claude Lévi-Strauss found his chosen successor to direct the LAS. In 1981, Françoise Héritier was seen as one of the few Lévi-Strauss disciples to have pursued his work in kinship anthropology into areas that, failing the necessary computer skills, he had himself abandoned. But it was not just the excellence of her anthropological work and the richness of her conclusions that had prevailed here.[169] She was above all considered to possess the requisite skills for directing a research team. Unlike other members, including Maurice Godelier and Michel Izard, Claude Lévi-Strauss deemed Françoise Héritier to be well equipped to carry out such a delicate task: that of succeeding him. His *auctoritas* enabled him to impose his hand-picked heiress, over the grumblings of those who were passed over. The fact that Françoise Héritier was a woman clearly appears to have mattered insofar as the laboratory was highly feminized and feminist. Françoise Héritier was a rigorous and demanding person, yet also warm, collegial and devoid of theoretical dogmatism – although herself a loyal structuralist. Since the LAS she was to direct was linked to a chair at the Collège de France, she had to be appointed professor at that institution, which was no easier task than being elected to the Académie française.[170] At the time, there was only one female full professor, the Hellenist Jacqueline de Romilly. On 29 November 1981, Lévi-Strauss submitted to a vote the creation of a new chair devoted to the 'comparative study of African societies', to which Françoise Héritier – whose work on semi-complex kinship structures he had just described and praised, without mentioning her by name, as was the custom – promptly applied. The anthropologist also wanted to honour the Africanist school and Africa itself, that both his *libido sciendi* and his life course had led him to neglect, and which he nonetheless insisted should be seen as 'a conservatory, a laboratory and an observatory': a conservatory of very rich metaphysical and cosmogonic systems; a laboratory of multiple forms of syncretism, as a territory of migration; and an observatory of developments in the contemporary world.[171] A 'cutting-edge Africanism' was thus taking over from structural anthropology – both the same and other. Françoise Héritier was soon to swap kinship anthropology for a symbolic anthropology of the body that she would develop over the two following decades.

The founder of a research institution, Lévi-Strauss meticulously planned for the future survival of his creation. And survive it did: Lévi-Strauss has since died, but the LAS lives on. In contrast to other demiurges, who leave scorched earth behind them – having considerable difficulty imagining that art, science or an institution could continue on without them – the famous anthropologist handed over the reins gracefully. At the end of the session that confirmed Françoise Héritier's appointment to the Collège de France, he gave her the key to the professors' toilet and whispered: 'Now, you must call me Claude'.[172]

20

Metamorphoses

Please be apart of the statue when the earthquake occurs.
                    Announcement to visitors at the Nezu Museum in Tokyo

Jacques Le Goff: 'What is your favourite colour?' Claude Lévi-Strauss: 'I would say green, and Le Goff knows why better than anyone – green was the colour of knights errant.'
                    'Océaniques' television programme, 31 October 1988

If an orientation to Canada had characterized Lévi-Strauss's life and anthropology following the publication of the final volume of the *Mythologiques*, in the 1980s it was Japan that figured prominently in his existence, if not in his work. Although he agreed at heart with Mme de Staël, for whom travelling was, 'no matter what people say, one of the saddest of life's pleasures',[1] he nonetheless went to Japan a total of five times between 1977 and 1988. On the cusp of old age – he was eighty years old on his last trip – Japan was for him a utopian space, re-enchanting the world. Like Italy for Stendhal, Japan injected a measure of hope and joy into Lévi-Strauss's later years. So much so that he came to be seen as the Buddhist monk of the French intelligentsia – slightly mischievous behind the serious facade.

Indeed, on this decimated intellectual landscape, which by the mid-1980s was bereft of its leading 'minds', Lévi-Strauss became a figure simultaneously omnipresent and alternative, a sort of thinker of the third kind, a daydreamer whose 'wake-up call' sounded the knell of political and intellectual modernity. His intense pace of publication made him a regular media presence from 1981, the year he was officially dubbed 'most influential French intellectual',[2] through to 1991, when the last of his 'minor mythologiques', *The Story of Lynx*, was published. Over this span, he produced no fewer than six books![3] Having cut down on his work load and retired from teaching in 1982, Lévi-Strauss was more available and eagerly took part in public debates, no longer as the leader of structuralism – which indeed he never meant to be – but as a distiller of what he called 'wisdom', the only promise the so-called human and social sciences could honestly be expected to keep. The young students in more or less open revolt against Lévi-Strauss the Académicien might well have asked him, as they had after 1968: 'From where are you speaking?' He would surely have responded: 'From afar'– the view from afar of the anthropologist, as well as that of the old man, looking back on his own society. Lévi-Strauss found himself in a paradoxical position: as the last of the Mohicans, he was called upon to perpetuate a venerable national institution – that of the prophetic intellectual, born of a historical and ideological ecosystem (in a nutshell, the grand narrative of Progress) that he condemned – whose very terms and existence he rejected.

This moment in the anthropologist's life was marked by yet another paradox: his ubiquitous media presence was not incompatible with a kind of self-dissolution, as if Lévi-Strauss had been gradually absorbed into the body of myths he had been analysing for so long. Indeed, vast and ever wider spirals, isomorphic with the mythological process itself, triggered dramatic metamorphoses: visits to Japan (from 1977 to 1986) rekindled the anthropologist's childhood passion for collecting; a trip to Israel (1985), and his Jewish heritage, which he reassessed and questioned anew; and the return to Brazil (1985), which prompted an ambiguous reunion with the country that had become so closely associated with his work. Similarly, *The Jealous Potter* rounded out half a century of intermittent dialogue with psychoanalysis, while *The Story of Lynx* revisited the inaugural moment of our modernity in the sixteenth century, when the Old and New Worlds met for the first time on the shores of South America. Lévi-Strauss as a child, Lévi-Strauss as Isaac Strauss's great-grandson, Lévi-Strauss as a bearded Brazilian, Lévi-Strauss as Jean de Léry, Lévi-Strauss as Montaigne.

Zen master of the French intelligentsia

In the early 1980s, Pierre Bourdieu incisively grasped the type of intellectual authority wielded by Claude Lévi-Strauss. Just as Sartre had combined the prestige of the writer and that of the professional philosopher, so the anthropologist combined the scientific legitimacy of his chair at the Collège de France with the literary credentials of the Académie française, while also making inroads into the world of art – via now well-established biographical episodes: his family heritage, his Bohemian life in New York, his friendship with Max Ernst.[4] He could both enjoy the honours lavished on an official intellectual – the Légion d'honneur, as Grand Officier in 1985 and Grand Croix in 2001 – and indulge the whims of his still youthful and rebellious mind, soon to be rediscovered by a new generation of leftist journalists, including, to name but two, Didier Éribon at the *Nouvel Observateur* and Antoine de Gaudemar at *Libération*.

In 1981, Lévi-Strauss was selected as the most influential francophone intellectual by a survey of 600 figures from the worlds of the arts and sciences, ahead of Raymond Aron and Michel Foucault.[5] Was it, as he himself was wont to say, because he was more of a consensus figure than his two famous colleagues? Was it a reward for his impressive longevity, which was to continue for almost another three decades, while the first half of the 1980s would see massive mortality among the major French intellectuals who marked the century? In the space of a few years, just as the left was finally coming to power, Jean-Paul Sartre (1980), Roland Barthes (1981), Raymond Aron (1983), and Michel Foucault (1984) all passed away, one after another, not to mention the symbolic disappearance of Louis Althusser. Several generations found themselves suddenly orphaned.

The figure of the 'master thinker', quaintly traditional and yet essential, that had played such a central role in the saga of French intellectual life, disappeared together with those who had embodied it. In 1980, in the first issue of a new journal, *Le Débat*, the editor, historian Pierre Nora, published an editorial that read simultaneously like an obituary and a programme: 'What can intellectuals do?'[6] he asked. The period had seen a proliferation of intellectual 'memorials',[7] and Nora was not alone in recording the – most probably final – passing of the figure of the importuning and omniscient intellectual, an abiding and committed participant in the century's struggles who – through a very French, post-revolutionary transfer of sacredness onto the world of arts and letters, as the historian would have it – was expected to set ultimate ends: 'The intellectual-oracle has had its day.'[8] Intellectual power was no longer sacerdotal, continued Nora; it had become more scholarly but also less charismatic, while remaining very aristocratic. Of this reconfiguration of the intellectual world of the early 1980s, Lévi-Strauss was both symptom and actor. As we have seen, he very early on rejected the role of the intellectual that was available to him and invented a subtly subversive alternative to this model. He came to embody that moment in the social sciences that shifted the sources of intellectual legitimacy – moving from Café de Flore to Collège de France, it subsumed both positive and theoretical knowledge of human society to guarantee the ongoing influence of intellectual discourse.

Strangely, whereas he was not in the least a militant campaigner, he did not consider keeping working-class hopes alive to be a categorical imperative, and he had neither the style nor the manner of prophetic engagement, Claude Lévi-Strauss was, despite himself, committed to this national historical figure of the 'grand intellectual', even while considerably altering it. If all-out interventionism remained alien to him, he did not refrain from expressing his views on the contemporary world, but always from an overtly remote position. His 'view from afar', the title of the collection of articles he published in 1983, was still explicitly that of an anthropologist, but also increasingly that of an old man, and then of a very old man, avowedly out of synch with his times.

An intellectual in orbit: the media construction of an intellectual eminence

Throughout these years, Claude Lévi-Strauss, though a discreet man with a reputation for secrecy, regularly received journalists, often at his home or at the Collège de France. Several famous television programmes bear witness to this fact: on 4 May 1984, an episode of *Apostrophe*, hosted

by Bernard Pivot at the height of his popularity, was devoted entirely to
him. Françoise Giroud, in *L'Express*, pointed out just how exceptional
this was: 'There are those, the vast majority, who come to see him, and
then there are those whom Bernard Pivot comes to see – the jewels in the
crown.'[9] On 14 October 1991, Bernard Rapp's programme, *Caractères*,
also ran a special on him, shot at the Musée de l'Homme, in the midst
of objects on which he commented and which in turn told his story: a
nineteenth-century statue of a shaman, the feather coat of a sixteenth-
century Tupinamba chief, the travel headgear of a Karaja. Numerous long
interviews with newspapers rounded out this intense media presence, often
occasioned by the publication of a new book.[10] And there were many over
the course of that decade: *The View from Afar* in 1983; *Anthropology and
Myth* (digests of his Collège de France lectures) in 1984; *The Jealous Potter*
in 1985; *Conversations with Claude Lévi-Strauss*, a collection of interviews
with Didier Éribon, in 1988; *Des Symboles et leurs doubles* (a selection of
his writings as a coffee table book) in 1991; and *The Story of Lynx*, also in
1991. Together with the exhibition devoted to him in 1989 by the Musée de
l'Homme, this accounted for the constant flow of media attention, not to
mention visits to consult the master on this or that issue, or simply, by the
end of the decade, just to check in with him and bask in his glow. There
was an oracular dimension to the ritual, but more in a nostalgic than a
prophetic mode. The man's charms were not lost on the visiting journalist. Lévi-Strauss was capable of turning an obligatory press event into an
unforgettable encounter (for the interviewer at least). A very courteous
host, he remained humble and even-tempered, chose his words carefully,
and cultivated his profile as a character from former times. He dazzled
his interlocutors with an explosive combination of pedagogy, humour
and an absolute freedom of expression coupled with a sure instinct for
provocation. Ultimately, he conveyed a kind of wisdom, which he had long
claimed was precisely the criterion by which the contribution of the social
sciences should be measured.

  Listening to Lévi-Strauss, both journalists and viewers appeared amazed
that they could understand him! The clarity of his words, the 'supreme simplicity of the performance',[11] as Pierre Nora wrote about his *Apostrophes*
appearance; it was Lévi-Strauss's language, as well as his felicity with
stories, that accounted for his appeal. Gilles Martin-Chauffier put it thus
in *Paris-Match*: 'The amazing thing is that it is all crystal clear. There is no
schema, no signified, no syntagmatic chains, nor any paradigmatic ensembles – none of the usual gibberish with Lévi-Strauss.'[12] His elimination of
the structuralist vocabulary came as a surprise, and a relief. The recourse to
a classical language, free of the jargon of the human sciences, did much
to burnish his aura. In the manner of zen masters, Lévi-Strauss peppered
his presentations with terse parables, the meanings of which he elegantly
left for his listeners to figure out. As the *Paris-Match* journalist put it: 'A
little Japanese fable here, an old Sioux legend there, a brief comment to
connect the two and that's all there is to it!'[13] His television interviews were
also punctuated with a few strong formulations that would be discussed
in the press the following day. As, for example, with his plea to Bernard

Pivot to give man credit for elaborating the complicated constructions he had studied in the field of kinship and myths: 'It cannot be that men spend their lives raving madly.' Or when he casually offered the following conclusion: 'We are becoming our own colonized people.'

Behind the guise of the severe scholar, the crow's feet at the corner of his eyes betrayed a tongue-in-cheek wit, which never failed to seduce. As, for instance, when, during an interview with *Le Figaro*, he compared humans and molluscs: 'To draw a rough comparison, for which I apologize in advance, think of molluscs: they are soft and rather repulsive creatures, who nonetheless secrete shells that are prodigious creations of great beauty, which are incarnations of mathematical laws in addition. Well, it seems to me that humanity is rather similar.'[14] He relished incongruities of this sort, and his astounded interlocutors were no less delighted: 'Our foremost celebrity mind is also keen to have fun.'[15] Discussing the unachieved dreams of childhood and his unrealized artistic aspirations, he joyfully concluded: 'Failures? We all are failures, more or less!'[16] He made connections between Freud and Labiche, unsettled the hierarchy of artistic dignity, and cultivated a very special register of 'gentle provocation' which only grew stronger with age. The young socialist confessed to having become an 'old, right-wing anarchist ... faithful to Marx'.[17] More daringly, he liked to quote Gobineau, a taboo figure held to be one of the early theoreticians of modern racism. Lévi-Strauss, on the contrary, admired him and said so without hesitation: 'What did Gobineau say? That we were heading toward total standardization, together with a kind of equally total stupidity.'[18] Drawing on his special authority and above all his relationship to time, Lévi-Strauss indulged in a highly provocative critique of the contemporary world, delivered with the tone of one who no longer belonged to it, or barely. This was the case when he discussed UNESCO antiracist dogma in 1971, then that of the French NGO SOS Racisme beginning in 1983, running the risk of being recuperated by the emerging extreme right. He was spoken of in the same breath as Jean-Marie Le Pen: 'I cannot say that I have any sympathy for a number of views held by Mr Le Pen, but I believe that, in letting the confusion I have highlighted reign, we have made his task much easier.'[19]

The form of wisdom dispensed by the anthropologist was also a tribute to his old age, visible on screen, since he became prone to an 'essential tremor'. As Françoise Giroud noted, he spoke 'with the simplicity of those whom age has freed of their share of drama'.[20] This intellectual turned national heritage monument thus enjoyed a form of celebrity that differed radically from that of the structuralist and anti-humanist guru of the 1960s. The words of this pessimistic old bonze seemed impervious to the passage of time and his spiritual vitality to the conformism of the 1980s.[21]

A modern at large

At that time, when asked about his relationship to Rousseau, Lévi-Strauss repeatedly claimed to identify as a kind of Janus-faced combination of

the antithetical Rousseau/Chateaubriand couple. In a long interview with
Jean-Marie Benoît at *Le Monde*, on the occasion of the publication in
1979 of a book on the anthropologist's work,[22] he stated: 'I would like
to make a confession. The kind of intimate relationship that I feel connects me to Rousseau, I also feel with Chateaubriand, who is Rousseau's
opposite, while still being the same thing. So that the figure with whom I
feel closest is neither Rousseau nor Chateaubriand, but a kind of chimera,
a Janus made up of the Rousseau-Chateaubriand dyad, which represents
the double aspect of the same man, even though they made diametrically
opposite choices.'[23]

This avowed contradiction regarding the fate of rationalized democracy promised by the revolutionary epiphany likened him to those that
Antoine Compagnon has identified as the 'anti-moderns' of French
literature:[24] 'moderns who were at odds with modern times'; 'moderns
who were reluctantly so, torn moderns, and even untimely moderns'.[25]
Following Albert Thibaudet, Antoine Compagnon has taken up and
explored a category that did not fully align with conservative or reactionary, who were all unabashedly disappointed by their times. The anti-
modern was the repository of a more complex relationship to the present.
The greatest exemplar, Baudelaire, articulated a poetic art of modern
life even while resisting it. It was Baudelaire who wrote to his friend, the
artist Édouard Manet, an enigmatic line that Lévi-Strauss was fond of
quoting: 'You are but the first to have entered the decrepitude of your
art.'[26] To situate Lévi-Strauss's aesthetic and biographical orientation, we
must not forget that the young man loved modern art and remained an
ardent technophile. Indeed, he lived a powerful intimacy with his present
that continued to fuel a still lively curiosity in his old age – as attested by
his obsessive reading of the press. Anthropology would not come to an
end with him, and he found it quite natural that anthropologists should
take an interest in, for example, the electronic calculator, since the discipline had always positioned itself at the cutting edge of what each epoch
assigned to humanity.[27]

All this did not preclude a growing sense of disconnection, but one
characterized by nostalgia and ambivalence rather than simple rejection. In his essay, Antoine Compagnon insightfully points out the strong
attraction to anti-modern writers: Baudelaire, Barbey d'Aurevilly, Léon
Bloy, Chateaubriand, Proust, Flaubert, Péguy, and so many others. If the
anti-modern genius penetrated literature in the nineteenth century, it is
much more difficult to locate in the scientific world that professes a methodological optimism in the capacity of science to accumulate knowledge.
We are already very familiar with Lévi-Strauss's critique of the narrative
of progress – i.e., the belief, anchored in Enlightenment humanism, in
an emancipatory evolutionism – articulated as early as 1952 in *Race and
History*. Already in 1935, the first public lecture delivered by the young
Professor Lévi-Strauss in São Paulo was entitled 'The Crisis of Progress',
echoing a whole post-First World War generation that had had a sense of
the crisis of historicity seared into its very flesh and was defined by the end
of the previous century's optimism.[28] Concerning science, Lévi-Strauss

had always given special status to scientific progress, which he considered beyond question. Yet, even scientific progress was not without its contradictions: 'There is progress, because it is in order to progress that we accept regression in other domains. And one form is unquestionable: scientific knowledge, which I hold to be absolute progress. The trade-off is that three quarters of scientific progress is devoted to neutralizing the negative effects of the remaining quarter.'[29]

Lévi-Strauss was being an anti-modern of the twentieth century when he casually established a highly polemical link between, on the one hand, the kind of humanism wrought by the Judaeo-Christian tradition, the Renaissance and the Enlightenment, which in his view had combined to turn man into lord and master, and, on the other, the contemporary catastrophe: 'My sense is that all the tragedies we have experienced – first colonialism, then fascism and finally the extermination camps – do not stand in opposition or contradiction with the so-called humanism as we have practised it for several centuries but, I would say, almost as its natural continuation.'[30] A precocious critic of what he termed a 'depraved humanism', Lévi-Strauss did not however subscribe to the wholesale liquidation of the modern project initiated by 1980s postmodernism, which was founded on a de-historicized reading of the Shoah and a dismissal of the grand narratives of the revolutionary project. Lévi-Strauss's critical project, which opposed the first universalism, preceded the advent of the second, and challenged them both with a universalism of the living world. His reflections on the unexceptional status of the Shoah in the history of mass destruction also sounded increasingly sacrilegious. From this point of view, the other universalism of the century, historically seemingly opposed to the liberal democratic universalism of the West, did not appear to him as an alternative to modernity: 'I think that the communist and totalitarian ideology was but a ruse of history to promote the speedy westernization of peoples who had remained outside of it until recent times.'[31] Who could disagree? Certainly no recent visitor to China . . . Strangely, as historian Christophe Charle has pointed out, until the end of the twentieth century it was the rare few in the West who escaped the power of this regime of historicity, combining an ideology of material progress and abundance and a belief in the 'absolute power of science, art and technology to change man, woman and life, a universal pedagogical ambition'.[32] Lévi-Strauss was one of this small phalanx.

Finally, the Académie member shared with the untimely anti-moderns a punctilious attention to language – an early casualty that heralded wider degradation – and an expansive recourse to tradition, as when he extolled the virtues of rituals, the vital need for intermediary bodies for the protection of the individual, the value of belief, habit and custom. Insofar as Lévi-Strauss was anti-modern, it was because he wrested tradition from the conformism of conservatives and, as Walter Benjamin recommended, 'ignite[d] the explosive materials that are latent in what has been'.[33] He was a traditionalist and anti-conservative nonconformist.

The view from afar

A third collection of articles came out in 1983, in the same format as those of 1958 and 1973, yet entitled *The View from Afar*, and not *Structural Anthropology 3*. The scopic title was complemented by a cover that evoked the zoological plates of another age: miniature medallions, painted by Anita Albus, a German artist whom Lévi-Strauss had met a few years earlier, and whose erudite and artisanal poetics and naturalist inspiration, drawing on the great Enlightenment botanists, he greatly appreciated. Structuralism no longer held sway. The title of the first volume's hint of 'manifesto', and the 'doubling down' aspect of the second, were no longer in order. From then on, it was this distance, this remoteness, that marked the intellectual identity and unclassifiable political vitality of its author. In the heyday of the leftist governments in power and Mitterrandian lyricism, the 'progressive' press saw him as a paradoxical conservative. Reviews were less than favourable, as illustrated by the half-hearted *Le Monde* article by Jacques Meunier, dismayed at the 'moralizing and conservative remarks',[34] the scathing review in *L'Humanité* – a 'speculative and obscurantist logomachy as pernicious as it is surreptitious'[35] – and the silence on the part of *Libération*. Indeed, in this collection of articles, which included his public and political 'interventions', Lévi-Strauss engaged with the left on two fronts: the old socialist and communist left's progressivism was first chastised in favour of a radical anti-evolutionism, a rejection of philosophies of history and progress, as well as for an increasingly perceptible ecological and anti-industrial streak. But in a more contemporary vein, he lashed out at the leftist conception of spontaneity, at post-1968 cultural vitalism, at the cult of 'creativity' taken up, amplified and recycled into the heritage of the old left by the new charismatic socialist minister of culture, Jack Lang. Whether in education or in creation, Lévi-Strauss rejected the idea of a spontaneously free and immediate creativity. By contrast, he praised the need for (pedagogical) mediations and for boundaries (distance), the inescapability and fecundity of constraints at all levels – educative, artistic and political. As opposed to the first two volumes, which had focused on questions of theory, the third was profoundly of its time, which he challenged in a highly critical and original way, outside any received ideological grid. The dogmas and values of the late twentieth century world were subject to ruthless questioning: Freedom? Creativity? Art? Tolerance? The Other?

The highlight of the volume was its opening chapter, 'Race and Culture', written in 1971 but discovered by most readers only twelve years later. As Lévi-Strauss explained in the preface, it was originally commissioned by UNESCO when he was asked to open the international year of antiracism with a major lecture, which, in the minds of its organizers, was to echo the text published as a pamphlet almost twenty years earlier by that same organization, *Race and History* (1952). Wary of the 'periodic displays of good intentions'[36] and the manifest inanity of the UNESCO antiracist rallying cry, the anthropologist opted for honesty. 'The result was a lively scandal.'[37] René Maheu, the then director general, attempted to defuse the bomb with a short speech that was designed not only to 'exorcise my blasphemies by anticipating them, but also – and above all – to upset the timetable'[38] by shortening the time available for the heretic's speech. The unpredictable Lévi-Strauss . . . This very dignified member of the scientific establishment had indeed not thought twice before launching an attack against the self-righteous hypocrisy of the UN.

The ethnologist's first sin at the conference was to 'put the fox' [of genetics] 'in the sheepfold' [of the social sciences][39] and to insist on the need for a new dialogue between the two. He thus brought the biological and the cultural together but reversed the dynamic of determination of the old physical anthropology: it was not race that dictated culture, but cultural factors that sometimes influenced the course of natural selection. Lévi-Strauss had always insisted that nothing should be taboo in science . . .

But the real issue lay in the final pages. The anthropologist flatly refuted the credo that had become firmly established at the heart of UNESCO: the idea that the circulation of knowledge and the development of exchanges between men helped them better understand and communicate with one another. On the contrary, he concluded, the increase in communication resulting from demographic growth could only lead to the disappearance of cultural diversity and a fraudulent form of intermixing. Even more shocking still, he exonerated hostility towards the other from its racist connotations and considered that 'all true creation implies a certain deafness to the appeal of other values, even going so far as to reject them if not denying them altogether'. Attached to 'old particularisms', the anthropologist saw this relative lack of communication as the price to pay for the survival of optimal diversity.

The text of 'Race and Culture' (1971) could well have been included in *Structural Anthropology 2* (1973). But Lévi-Strauss decided then not to add fuel to the fire and to leave it out. It was thus only published for the first time in 1983. Far from calming the waters, the belated publication only intensified the scandal. Indeed, the French left was then reeling from the election of the first National Front mayor, in the town of Dreux. Everyone was taken aback; his students were worried. 'The media remained silent. Here and there, there were whispers that the master had become more reactionary than ever, and even defended racist positions; people whispered, but nobody really talked openly about it.'[40] In Catherine Clément's view, these rumours were mistaken, and Lévi-Strauss was expressing the 'profoundly conservative, yet also profoundly innovative reflections' of an 'ecological moralist'.[41] Yet the Africanist Emmanuel Terray recalls having had his doubts.[42] This was also an effect of the delayed publication, heightened by the new political context, with an ascendant Far Right rooted in a particularist form of neo-racism. This new Lévi-Strauss was constantly being compared to 'Race and History', as if the two texts were in contradiction, the one praising the fecundity of hybridization and the other setting isolation as the minimum condition of great creation. In fact, exclaimed an acerbic Lévi-Strauss, who was clearly little disposed to retreat on this point, 'these are two sides of the same reality'.[43] The most pressing risk of our times, in his view, was the homogenization of the planet, 'but worse still, the doctrinal virtue that is attributed to it. Why should everyone love everyone else?'⁴⁴ Racism was not xenophobia and xenophobia was not insensitivity to the other. Lévi-Strauss responded to the general confusion on the use of the term 'racism' with a lexicological hygiene that he deemed urgent. Emmanuel Terray today maintains that '*Race and Culture* did not argue in favour of withdrawal into the self. We were mistaken at the time.'⁴⁵

His speech 'A Belated Word about the Creative Child', which he delivered on the occasion of the hundredth anniversary of the École alsacienne in Paris, also caught the attention of the media. The irony of the title was already a can of worms. As Catherine Clément has said: 'There was enough there to get the whole French left up in arms'.⁴⁶ Lévi-Strauss started by explaining that the very fact of raising the question was evidence of our own incapacity to create: 'For it is we ourselves, the frenzied consumers, who are becoming ever less capable of creating. Tortured by our deficiency, we anxiously await the coming of the creative man. And since we cannot glimpse him anywhere, in despair we turn to our children.'⁴⁷ He proceeded to deliver a scathing critique of the illusion of creating out of nothing, and rejected the notion of 'creativity' in the name of that 'hemming in' of freedom necessary for smooth development into adulthood, as well as for the survival of our societies: 'We see the products of a creative freedom that has been neither educated nor bridled, in the houses, villas and cottages – the one more hideous than the other – that people have constructed in the countryside.'⁴⁸ The constraint of school education, which cannot simply amount to not constraining the child's spontaneity, was nothing more than the constraint exerted by any reality on its participants. His demonstrative development on this sobering curtailment of creative freedom was a true structuralist tour de force. Lévi-Strauss went on to show that even Lautréamont's famously incongruous phrase – 'the chance encounter of a sewing machine and an umbrella on a dissecting table' – still obeyed a logic of combination and that the freedom to invent is never exercised except within a pre-established framework.⁴⁹

Following his defence and demonstration of the 'harsh necessities of training',⁵⁰ he closed his pedagogico-aesthetic tract on a political note with some 'Reflections on Liberty', which Lévi-Strauss decided to make public. These remarks were originally delivered in 1976 when he was invited by Edgar Faure to testify before the National Assembly's special committee on liberties. The stakes were significant since, in these few pages, Lévi-Strauss offered nothing less than a reformulation of the principles of political philosophy into a new declaration of rights, no longer based on the nature of man but on the logic of the living. Why? The anthropologist had no difficulty demonstrating the historical, relative and variable character of the idea of freedom according to different societies. In fact, freedom articulated in terms of human rights belonged to a Western and ethnocentric conception of human nature. It was thus in the name of a true universality – one that would include the men and women of so-called 'underdeveloped' countries, and those of the East and the Far East whose Buddhism had fashioned a worldview compatible with this perspective, as well as those of the primitive tribes that still survived – that he asserted a definition of man not as a moral being but as a living being, who had rights as a species, like any other animal and vegetable. These few pages were incredibly ambitious, for they sought to determine, in the words of philosopher Patrice Maniglier, the foundation of value: 'Value, Lévi-Strauss has essentially said, does not lie with the conformity of the thing to the ideal – thus, the value of man does not lie in his moral quality – but precisely with the fact that it is real, i.e., also singular and ephemeral, and as a result precious. It is insofar as something is irreplaceable that it is worthy of respect, infinitely precious in its very finitude.'[51]

This more concrete and more universal conception had the advantage of not placing man at the centre, and thus of re-establishing true chains of causality. So, 'as embarrassing as it may be to admit, before we even dream of protecting nature *for* man, we have to protect it *against* him. And when, in a recent statement, the minister of justice stated that "justice cannot remain indifferent to the assaults man endures from pollution", he too was turning the facts upside down. Man does not endure pollution: he causes it. The right of the environment, which everyone talks about, is the right of the environment in regard to man, and not the right of man in regard to the environment.'[52] Lévi-Strauss compared our conservationist fetishism regarding works of art (museums to house them, etc.) to our utter irresponsibility regarding the creations of nature, whose destruction entailed irremediable loss. Suffice it to say, his proposition was received as a pure provocation, at a time when a waning Marxism was yielding to a confused 'human rights ideology', which rested politically on a critique of Soviet totalitarianism.

If he had to go against the tide (or to be ahead of his time), he might as well go all the way. Although he almost systematically refused to sign petitions and take part in meetings, Lévi-Strauss wrote to the Brazilian secretary of the interior in February of 1981 to protest against the deforestation policies that were encroaching on the territory and life-world of the Nambikwara.[53] He also lent support to the 'Friends of foxes and other smelly animals'.[54] He was particularly attentive to heritage preservation and spared no effort to save the Ranelagh Theatre, to keep Vauban's plans-relief in Paris,[55] and to restore the barns of the Orthodox monastery of la Malvialle (in Puy-de-Dôme).[56] Finally, he happily agreed to be one of seventeen professors who would award the prizes to the 'finest artisans of France' ('meilleur ouvrier de France'), in the presence of the French president, at the Sorbonne on 24 February 1980. In the 'Clothing Accessories' category, Claude Lévi-Strauss chose to award the honour to Miss Marie-Paule Boyer.

In the 1980s, Lévi-Strauss had created a unique position for himself: a member of the Académie française, he also kept a tight rein on the field of anthropology; considered an anti-humanist in the 1960s, he was now seen as a profound moralist, his stature enhanced and even sanctified by old age, just as his work was about to become classic, even while it rubbed everyone up the wrong way. Pierre Bourdieu, who was not one for deference, confessed a discreet admiration, and wrote to him: 'I very much liked that you expressed your "weariness" with the "periodic displays of good intentions" in matters of racism and your refusal to take part in sanctimonious good causes; as well as in the "abuse of trust" involved in certain forms of commitment. This intransigence, which we could call ethical, is probably what most moved me . . . .'[57] The intellectual authority he had acquired had as much to do with age as with the man's temperament: he was sufficiently advanced in years to enjoy the benefits of old age, but not yet quite enough for his wisdom to have become emollient. As Pierre Lepape wrote in *Télérama*, everyone was stunned by his energy: 'When he donned the green gown, we thought he was retiring, and would simply concern himself with managing his intellectual capital. [. . .] This book refutes the pessimistic predictions: Lévi-Strauss is still a young man. Fighting the fight, with sharp teeth and boundless curiosity, excited by polemics, enthralled to paradox . . . One of the last masters.'[58]

Retirement

To retire: to withdraw from work, from a large part of one's life and one's social world. Yet a withdrawal (even a military one) is not necessarily a debacle. Lévi-Strauss's retirement felt like a smooth transition to a lighter life, characterized by a schedule that remained set, but free of its teaching and administrative duties. Although 1982 marked the end of precisely half a century of teaching, the Collège de France professor did not wish to deliver a final lecture or make his departure an overly solemn affair. In a way, the Marc Bloch lecture of 1983 served to bid his adieus. Between his two afternoons a week at the LAS, in which he continued to participate as a simple member, and the Thursday sessions at the Académie, Lévi-Strauss cultivated a mode of living that stood in stark contrast with the austerity of his prior scholarly existence. Freed from the anxiety of teaching, and still physically able, he was a rather spirited and light-hearted retiree, dividing his time between writing, albeit now at a more tranquil pace, and his various meetings, where he was always warmly welcomed. As Pierre Maranda put it, using an old Quebecois expression, at the age of seventy-four, Lévi-Strauss found himself 'light ankled' [*jarret léger*].[59] A dusk he managed to turn into a new dawn, without excessive expectations.

Totem of the discipline: 'For country, science and glory'

Every Tuesday and Friday afternoon, Claude Lévi-Strauss made his way punctually to the Laboratory of Social Anthropology, directed as of 1982 by Françoise Héritier-Augé. From 1985, this no longer brought him to the rue des Écoles but to the rue du Cardinal-Lemoine, where new office space had been assigned to the LAS, the site of its third incarnation.

Indeed, starting in the mid-1970s, the LAS, like most thriving institutions, began to experience growing pains: the increasing size of the *Files*, a dearth of office space, a lack of room for the ever more numerous students and researchers. This raised the question of the 'sustainability of the laboratory'[60] that Lévi-Strauss had, as his final mission, taken in hand, in dialogue with the administration of the Collège de France. The École polytechnique's move to the suburb of Palaiseau in 1976 freed a considerable amount of space atop the Montagne Sainte-Geneviève in central Paris: 'Then another miracle took place. In 1977, the president of France gave the Collège a part of the old buildings of the École polytechnique, which are located on the Montagne Sainte-Geneviève. The Collège decided to put several of its laboratories for the human sciences, ours included, together in this space. In this way, we doubled our floor space. It took seven years of effort to obtain the funds and complete the remodelling, but again I was able, before retiring in 1982, to oversee the outfitting of a place that had a distinguished history of its own and to take care that the cast-iron architecture and the decoration of the venerable Arago amphitheatre – which was to become our library and around which our offices would be distributed – were respected.'[61]

The amphitheatre, part of the heritage of nineteenth-century science, built between 1879 and 1883, had been designed to host the physics lectures of the École polytechnique. While its oak tables and mahogany closets evoked a kind of *Ancien Régime* of the natural sciences, the glass and metal architecture of the Arago amphitheatre conjured up the nineteenth century of train stations and universal exhibitions, that of scientific conquest, echoed in the École polytechnique's Comtian motto – 'For Country, Science and Glory' – that still adorns the walls of the LAS today. Taken with a touch of irony, the proud slogan might not actually be entirely unsuited to the LAS.

The amphitheatre's seating was removed, the floor raised to the level of the first gallery, and the mezzanine of the second tier turned into an office for the former director, with a view over the entire library. Small, but flooded with light from its glass roof, Lévi-Strauss's office, at the top of a twenty-seven-step spiral staircase, appeared to be floating in mid-air.[62] With its panoptic perspective, it offered a unique observation point for keeping track of the comings and goings of all and sundry. Like the God on his throne in baroque paintings, Claude Lévi-Strauss from his empyrean could meditate on country, science and glory ... While down below, the plebs – researchers and the new director herself – referred to him fondly as 'Cap Sur'[63] (for Captain Surveyor) and went about their business. Françoise Héritier still remembers the powerful presence of this shadow puppet in the sky: 'I really enjoyed seeing his profile silhouetted against the skylight.'[64]

The head of the lab gradually became a familiar but distant figure, who had let go of the *potestas* of old age to retain his *auctoritas*, based on solidarity and respect, attentive friendship and patient indulgence of the younger generations. Lévi-Strauss, faithful to the LAS until the end, became over the years a kind of tutelary figure, a guardian angel. With his celebrity growing over time, many a pilgrim, both known and unknown, came to pay their 'visit to Lévi-Strauss'. According to the librarian Marion Abélès, 'it was a constant procession' – a contemporary version of the nineteenth-century visit to the 'great writer'.[65] This ritual was practised by foreign colleagues in particular, who came to test the waters of French science and knowledge by calling on Lévi-Strauss. His presence, both spectral and stately, most certainly played a role in the laboratory's fate, but it was still too soon to tell in precisely what way.

Lévi-Strauss received visitors, and kept his hand in the work of the lab's various members, through short messages left in pigeonholes, attesting to his unfailing attention, or through a bibliographical reference, a critique or a compliment. He handed over the reins of the journal *L'Homme*, while continuing to contribute articles and reviews. On each year ending in '8', he was celebrated as a venerable ancestor: in 1988, his eightieth birthday was thus feted at the LAS in the company of all his young colleagues and friends: Marie-Hélène Handmann, one of the laboratory's members, booked a string quartet, and a cake topped with a wild pansy [*pensée sauvage*] was served to mark the event. Salmon and candle-fish oil imported directly from British Columbia complemented the culinary festivities. The photograph immortalizing the event includes, among the small group of attendees, the anthropologist's two sons – the younger Matthieu, thirty-one years old, and the elder Laurent, forty-one years old, who had been a frequent visitor at the lab in the early 1970s, as he was preparing his doctoral thesis in rural sociology.[66]

For a man of Lévi-Strauss's generation, one of the preconditions for certain activity was the assistance of a secretary. The obsessive quantity of his corrections made such outside support necessary. Upon retirement, as with all professors, he lost this perquisite of office. Mentioning this in passing to Bernard Pivot during the television programme devoted to him, all of France was moved to action! Lévi-Strauss's correspondence includes at least ten letters from unknown women generously volunteering their services (gratis) for the cause of science. Among them, one at least deserves to be quoted in full, for it provides a good illustration of the anthropologist's fame and aura: 'This afternoon, I was watching reruns of Bernard Pivot's programme *Apostrophes* and I was quite stunned to hear you say that you had no secretary, due mostly to a lack of funds. Like many television viewers, I imagine, I had the surreal idea of writing to you to offer my "services", on a volunteer basis of course. Surreal because I have no references to persuade you; I am neither a student of anthropology, nor an *agrégée* in philosophy, nor even one of your readers, for this very afternoon, when I tried to acquire a copy of *Tristes Tropiques*, I found my regular bookshop closed. Worse still: my profession is fashion modelling; but I am about to sign an exclusive contract that will leave me at liberty nine months of the year and "free from want". It thus seems only reasonable to devote my time to interesting pursuits, since I will have no material concerns. You will therefore readily understand that I have nothing to recommend me other than my driver's licence, my extreme kindness and my goodwill.'[67] The letter was signed 'Inès de La Fressange'. In the letter were enclosed some fashion headshots, no doubt intended to lend support and validity to the offer . . . Lévi-Strauss replied: 'Dear Madam, the echo of your fame has reached me, and I was very moved by your proposition. Yet my aim was to draw attention to the lack of resources for ageing scientists more than to my own personal case. If you came to work for me, I would spend my time staring at you and would not get anything done.'[68]

In the end, it was indeed a pretty and intelligent woman who took over Claude Lévi-Strauss's secretarial work. Like Inès de La Fressange, she was not a particularly gifted typist, but she was young, direct and very frank with the old man, to whom she recounted her cat stories, her mis-adventures and her tempestuous life. Eva Kempinski, according to all the testimonies of those who met her, developed a unique relationship with Claude Lévi-Strauss, unburdened as it was by professional ego, which often strained relationships among colleagues. From below, they could be seen joking around and sometimes even laughing out loud. From above, Marie Mauzé, who had the adjoining office across the mezzanine, would overhear them chatting away – a mischievous father, amused by his impish daughter, in whose whimsies he enjoyed sharing.

Quiet days at the Académie

Little is known about the Académie française. This institution, at once anachronistic and dynamic, is quite secretive – and intent on remaining so. Louis-Bernard Robitaille, a Canadian journalist who became its amused chronicler, found that once past the doors of the *cour d'honneur*, the two interior courts and deserted antichambers have a *Last Year at Marienbad* feel to them . . .[69] It was unquestionably the 'rarefied' dimension of the Académie that the claustrophobic Lévi-Strauss appreciated: lots of space, including to park cars in a grassy courtyard, a few minor privileges, and a stipend, which increased each year, amounting to 582 francs a month in 1977.[70] In an age that counted in millions, 'these forty people favoured the qualitative – if not necessarily quality – over the quantitative'.[71]

Every Thursday afternoon the weekly session was held, with the sitting director presiding. In the order of their election, the members would file into a salon reserved for the purpose and discuss the words being con-sidered for the dictionary; propositions regarding their definitions would follow. No outsider has ever attended these sessions, which are therefore imbued with a certain mystery. As opposed to more evanescent members, Claude Lévi-Strauss attended almost every week. He only departed from this routine in the last two years of his life, from October 2007. In this noble assembly, he served as a 'great man'. As one of the few intellectual pillars of the Académie, he was listened to 'with a kind of reverence'[72] every time he spoke, which was rare. His interventions generally had to do with the introduction of anthropological terms such as 'matrilineal', or with proper names.[73] Some of his colleagues balked. Alain Peyrefitte, for instance, wondered whether it was really necessary to impose overly complex words, and more generally proper names, rather than 'sticking as closely as possible to the objective, mercifully recently reformulated, of producing a "dictionary of proper usage", free of any encyclopaedic ambi-tion'.[74] Lévi-Strauss immediately sent him a full dossier on the 'Inuit(s)', which had been the cause of the dispute, and promptly won him over.

Similarly, the anthropologist took considerable care to short-circuit all reflexively ethnocentric definitions, as in the case of the adjective 'rancid', an unappreciated flavour in Western gustatory classification, but not in primitive culinary cultures.[75] To bring words and definitions that, without him, would not make it into the dictionary, or else not with sufficient dignity, reflecting the full plurality of their recorded meanings – these were the properly political stakes of Lévi-Strauss's presence in the Académie française. He performed this intellectual sandblasting without raising his voice – he was in proper company – but with a kind of intransigence based on the unanimous respect he commanded. As Bertrand Poirot-Delpech, a fellow Académie member, attested in 1991: 'My admiration for your work and your subtle use of words has now been compounded, these past five years, by my weekly Thursday appreciation of the ironic wisdom of your remarks, and their sharp precision in contrast to our approximations.'[76] In 1990 the first volume of the ninth edition of the *Dictionnaire* was published, work on which had casually begun in . . . 1935! The level of activity had considerably intensified with the appointment of Maurice Druon as permanent secretary.

Aside from the weekly routine of the dictionary sessions, the Académie also experienced more fevered moments: for example, Marguerite Yourcenar's election, as we have seen; or the spelling reform initiated by Maurice Druon, in 1991, that triggered a tempest in a pond of 'nenufars' [as opposed to 'nenuphars'] and was ultimately abandoned. In between, a new spike in temperature occurred when in 1984 Yvette Roudy, the new socialist minister of women's rights, set up a committee on the terminology of women's occupations, presided over by the 'écrivaine' Benoîte Groult.[77] The Académie française, aggrieved at having its prerogatives thus usurped, reacted to address the core issue. It is common knowledge – he has said so himself – that Lévi-Strauss 'wielded the pen' on that occasion.[78] The text of the Declaration, delivered in the session of 14 June 1984, relied on a linguistic rationale that completely disregarded the minister's proactive feminist policy: 'It is to be feared that the task assigned to this committee proceeds from a misconception of the notion of grammatical gender, and will only lead to propositions that conflict with the spirit of the language. [. . .] It is indeed necessary to recall that in French, as in other languages, there is no relationship of equivalence between *grammatical gender* and *natural gender*. The French language has two genders, traditionally called "masculine" and "feminine". These terms, inherited from ancient grammar, are in fact improper. The only acceptable way of defining grammatical gender in French, with regard to the way they actually function, consists in distinguishing between, respectively, *marked* and *unmarked* genders. The unmarked gender is thus the *extensive* gender, as in, for example: "all men are mortal", and "this town numbers twenty thousand inhabitants", who are indifferently men and women. The marked gender is the *intensive* gender, limited to animate beings establishing a segregation of the sexes. As a result, to reform our occupational vocabulary and place men and women on a completely equal footing, it is recommended that, in all cases that are not already established by usage, the words of the so-called "feminine" gender – in the French language, a primarily discriminatory gender – be avoided; and that, whenever the option remains open, we favour the unmarked gender for occupational denominations.'[79] QED. Paradoxically, the guardian of language purity declined to be prescriptive: 'The only master in the matter, usage, indeed did not err. When occupational terms were awkwardly fashioned, because they were thought lacking, their poor yield (due to the fact that the unmarked case already comprised in its use those of the marked case) quickly endowed them with a derogatory connotation: as in *cheffesse, doctoresse, poétesse*, etc.' The declaration ended by emphasizing how the so-called feminine gender only occasionally served to designate the female and recommending the utmost caution, for 'changes, deliberately brought about in one field, can have unforeseen consequences on another. [. . .] They run the risk of sowing confusion and chaos in the subtle balance born from usage, that appears better left for usage to alter.'[80] The latter recommendation was recognizably Lévi-Straussian in spirit: the world of language, like the natural and social worlds, was a subtle and ancient construction that man might attempt to change from time to time, but only with considerable sensitivity and without 'forcing' it. This position – received as yet another reactionary and chauvinist caprice on the part of the incorrigible members of the Académie, Lévi-Strauss chief among them – incurred the wrath of Philippe Saint-Robert, the commissioner general for the French language in the prime minister's office, who did not respond in substance but thought he detected a whiff of critique of the very existence of terminology commissions like his own. As for Benoîte Groult, she responded in the 17 July issue of *Le Monde*, indicting the 'verbal terrorism' and 'phallocratic demonstration'. One year earlier, in September 1983, Georges Dumézil, himself a member of the Académie, had explained in *Le Nouvel Observateur* that language was not 'a garden to be mowed and staked, but rather a forest'.[81] Lévi-Strauss fully shared this vision and often referred journalists to that article which, in his view, definitively settled the matter.

Apart from these occasional flare-ups, the Académie member led a rather quiet existence, though not entirely without controversy. Invested in the life of the institution, Lévi-Strauss was intent on bringing in certain figures and pursued this endeavour with the utmost efficacy: Dumézil in 1979, Braudel in 1984, Duby in 1987, and later Pierre Nora. More scandalously, he staunchly supported the pariah of French anthropology, Jacques Soustelle, who donned the green gown in 1983. Lévi-Strauss was the sitting director in 1987 when the candidacy of Maurice Duverger came up. The jurist submitted his application and a press campaign was launched against the candidacy, organized notably by André Glucksmann, who brought to light a 1941 article by the jurist that was quite accepting of anti-Semitic Vichy legislation. No trace remains of Lévi-Strauss's response, but Duverger was rejected. For the elect, the large pool of aspiring members entailed a time-consuming correspondence with those who submitted their applications with 'trembling audacity', which was the established expression. Lévi-Strauss was among those who did not 'receive' Académie visits, in compliance with the rules, but this still required a letter of explanation. And then there was the preparation of induction speeches, and the letters of thanks for books he received from fellow members, who were all very productive and highly sensitive to any attention from their famous colleague. Ultimately, in all this hustle and bustle, the peaceful routine of the ordinary Thursday sessions distilled a refreshing ennui, all the more so that Lévi-Strauss knew very well how to deal with this most terrible of enemies, i.e., by reviving the tradition of schoolboy pranks and impish wit. He found in the writer Jean Dutourd as mischievous a playmate as could be wished for. They slipped each other short epigrammatic quatrains that offer an alternative glimpse into the ordinary workings of the Académie. The dark intrigues: 'In this double election / I suspect a trick / To let into our congregation / What is otherwise called a dick.' And, as for the long drowsy afternoons: 'For Mister Claude my neighbour / Who seems so bored with his labour / A rhyme from the writer / Of *The Best Butter*.' To which the anthropologist replied: 'As *The Horrors of Love* author / You know they suffer with less ardour / Than those of us condemned to be / Members of the Académie.' In between the two messages, sketches of a small dog: 'a yappy little companion to be added to Mr Lévi-Strauss's menagerie'. The anthropologist responded with drawings of cats. Many a cat passed between the two old men, who would send each other 'feline' greetings. On the occasion of Lévi-Strauss being awarded the Grand Croix of the Legion of Honour in 1991: 'I have chiselled this poem / In Mr Claude's honour / Whose valiant shoulder / Will soon bear a great emblem.' Mr. Claude replied: 'Of these honours received / So far down the stream / It must be believed / That life is but a dream.' On 4 October 2001, things decidedly went on for too long: 'The dullness of this controversy / Makes me yearn for the old barroom philosophy / That used to bore us endlessly.' And in the same vein: 'It is too long that it goes on / Goodness what a snooze / Hélène[82] is no Madelon / She doesn't pour us booze.' Dozens more of such rhymes can be found in Lévi-Strauss's personal papers.

An intimate archive of Académie life, this modest doggerel attests in a way to his paradoxical attachment to an institution that generated considerable tedium. For tedium was part of the rite, the time that needed to be spent to penetrate the texture of its passing. A strange institution that was an important part of this final stretch of Lévi-Strauss's life, including him in the recaptured past of a belletrist modernity. Was the Académie not, as Druon said, 'the last monarchical institution of the Republic after having been the first democratic institution of the Monarchy?'[83] It placed him in a felicitous temporality, a most British chronology that did away with the revolutionary rupture. Indeed, Lévi-Strauss did not believe in *tabula rasa* at either the collective or the individual levels.

An art of living

In 1984, Emma Lévi-Strauss died, at the age of ninety-eight. Her son Claude thus became an orphan at the tender age of seventy-six. But is one any the less so for it? Maurice Druon sent him a beautiful condolence letter: 'Your mother was on the verge of achieving a century. This makes for an extraordinary situation for a son, for whom childhood remains intertwined with all the stages of a life largely completed. However prepared we may be for a disappearance that we know might happen any day, we become accustomed at the same time to the mother being immortal. And it thus comes, however predictable, as a surprise. The death of a parent indeed always comes as a surprise, no matter when or how. It is with this cruel surprise, with this tearing of the oldest memories, with this assault on the fibre of the moral being that I extend to you, in all friendship, my deepest sympathies.'[84] Emma was buried, next to her husband, in Montmartre Cemetery, but Claude declined to reserve a place for himself in the same vault. Responsible for his parents from a very young age, he decided that the ultimate separation would also entail a bodily separation. As for himself, he decided he would be buried in his countryside.[85] Emma was not just Claude's mother; she was an exceptionally endearing character, who continued throughout her life to see her two former daughters-in-law, both of whom remained faithful to her in turn. Hence the son's wish to give to each of them a piece of Emma's jewellery, in memoriam – a wish that was fulfilled via Monique, who thus met Dina Dreyfus and Rose-Marie Ullmo one last time.

A link had disappeared, moving everyone up the generational chain. Lévi-Strauss hoped for progeny – something he had not craved as fervently as a father – that might counterbalance the loss of an ancestor. In 1989, he observed that his two sons 'seem to have become confirmed bachelors, much to [his] regret'.[86] To Dolorès Vanetti, his old New York friend, who 'had continued to hold a place in [his] heart',[87] he confided other developments. Within the Lévi-Strauss couple, the time for reciprocity had come. While the husband's activity was slowing, the wife effected a regime change and threw herself into an increasingly demanding professional life. She had been involved for a few years already in historical research on nineteenth-century textiles, and especially the cashmere industry. She published the results in 1987, as *Cachemires: L'art et l'histoire des châles en France au XIXe siècle*.[88] 'Here, Monique, now an author (on cashmere shawls) and a series editor (of books on textiles),[89] is much busier than I am.'[90] A few years later, in 1989, Lévi-Strauss confirmed this role reversal between them, which was also linked to their difference in age – he was eighty-three and she sixty-three: 'At home, life is changing: Monique is terribly busy – an author, a speaker, an expert at major shawl auctions, a series editor at Adam Biro, who published her book.[91] As for me, I had promised myself I would not write anymore; and then I became so bored. I have therefore started a book on which I am making progress at a snail's pace – an effect of old age. It will be a kind of sister book to *The Jealous Potter*, also on North American mythology. If I live long enough, it should keep me busy for two or three years. Apart from this, I have almost entirely ceased to see anyone; I no longer lunch or dine out. I receive visits every once in a while, at home or at the laboratory, where I have kept an office and a secretary.'[92]

Exaggerating his confinement – he did see people and receive journalists – he explained his strategy to combat boredom through a slow process
of writing that accompanied the slow passage of time. The decelerated
pace of life characteristic of this moment was experienced by Lévi-Strauss
in a melancholy and fatalistic way, as he explained to Bernard Rapp on
television in 1991: 'I am writing increasingly slowly, with increasing difficulty and greater suffering. But doing nothing and living the life of a retiree
is just too boring. One is better off suffering and feeling as if the days are
not endless but on the contrary, go by very quickly, since one produced so
little.'[93] This form of salvation through work continued for another few
years. Midway down that slope where one feels every minute of every hour,
Lévi-Strauss was seized by the occasional burst of inspiration: between
1985 and 1991, three books attested to the continuing circulation of ideas
and forms, despite his advanced age.

Even in his dreamy semi-idleness, he remained very protective of his
time and space, and always very fastidious regarding punctuality, as the
journalist Jacques Chancel was to find out. Arriving late to their appointment, the journalist found no one there and, after apologizing, received
the following letter, on 16 October 1991: 'Your "four short minutes" is a
fine excuse! You requested to meet at 11:50, to discuss, or so I thought, the
tone of the taping that was due to begin at 12 o'clock sharp. You were not
there. At 12, I was told you were about to arrive; at 12:05, that I had to
continue to wait. And it was nearly 12:10 when I finally left your floor. You
have, I know, many obligations. But I also have mine (in addition to being
of a certain age which, it seems to me, deserves some consideration). [. . .]
But this doesn't matter; let's forget about it. We will have other opportunities to meet, and perhaps even have an exchange.'[94] In the meantime, the
anthropologist crossed the programme off his list, thereby teaching the
new masters of the media a lesson in etiquette. He was the one, somewhat
exceptionally, who held the cards in that new media-dominated world, by
then already well established.

The old man retained the same physique he had acquired in the late
1960s, whose fragility gave him a paradoxically youthful look and kept
him relatively healthy, despite collapsing on numerous occasions. Indeed,
this was a trait that was preserved in old age without being accentuated:
Lévi-Strauss, a highly claustrophobic and sensitive person, was prone to
fainting at the drop of a hat. He would frequently pass out at the sight of
blood or when he found himself in stiflingly hot environments. This was
particularly frequent on social occasions, at large dinner parties where the
crowd and a desire to escape the tedium would send his head spinning.
'One day, for instance, he fell from the table at a dinner party organized
by Alain Peyrefitte at the ministry of justice. Everyone was in a state of
panic. He was so pale they all thought he was dead. I refused to call the
paramedics, knowing full well that once in the car and on our way home,
he would feel much better!'[95] This somewhat dramatic way of taking his
leave remained with him, the sign of a body that failed him when his
scrupulous mind imposed tedious tasks on it. But on the whole, his body
still bore him valiantly, despite the shaky hands and the serious dental

problems – judging by the intense correspondence between him and his dentist, Jean-Claude Albaret.[96]

While proclaiming he was not much inclined to move, Lévi-Strauss travelled then more than he had over the previous decades. It was the time for last times – in 1989 he told Dolorès Vanetti he would like to visit the United States 'one more time'; he had returned to Brazil in 1985. But it was also a time for first times: Japan, whose discovery played a crucial role at that moment in his life, as well as Israel. Later, in the 1990s, the only trips he would take were down memory lane.

Mythical transformations (1): The making of a biography

As has already been pointed out, it was in the 1980s, through articles and television programmes, that a biographical narrative began to emerge, in part managed by Lévi-Strauss himself. A major instance of this was the book of interviews with Didier Éribon, unanimously hailed for the quality and interest of the exchanges the journalist had orchestrated. *Conversations with Claude Lévi-Strauss*, originally published in 1988, was received as the memoirs that the anthropologist, who read those of others avidly, never wrote himself. For many of its readers, it was an occasion to discover the personality of the man – the ironic modesty, endearing humour and nonconformist intelligence of the refined aesthete with a cheerful spirit and a reserved yet also impassioned character. A certain reinvention was accomplished in the public mind: it was no longer the structuralist but the 'fine mind' that people found moving and appealing.[97] From whence did this biographical upsurge come? Daniel Fabre identified in it a desire to speak up again and to clarify his origin narrative, following the Caillois episode at the Académie française which, as we will recall, had been a bit venomous.[98]

The biographical impulse was also the belated product of Lévi-Strauss's 'quixotism', which, as we have seen, he defined as 'an obsessive desire to find the past behind the present'.[99] To use a geological metaphor familiar to the Lévi-Straussian turn of mind, it was as if the sedimentation of the past allowed him, decades later, thanks to the opening of some fissure or perhaps a landslide, to exhume the deep layers of biographical structure: 'As one moves into old age, bits of the past rise to the surface, or, to put it another way, loops are closed. The *Mythologiques* series brought me back to Wagner, whose cult surrounded me when I was a child and who, when I was an adolescent, I thought I had outgrown. *The Jealous Potter* sent me back to the books of my childhood. If the time is given me, I'll undoubtedly once again find *Don Quixote*, which was my passion when I was ten.'[100]

Japan: finding the past

The posthumous publication of the collection of articles *The Other Face of the Moon*[101] documents Lévi-Strauss's Japanese period, between 1977 and 1988, during which he made five trips to the land of the rising sun. In the life of the anthropologist who, since the 1950s, had become something of a homebody, this strong penchant for Japan stands out. Yet it should be made clear that, as knowledgeable as he might have been about the past and present of Japanese society as well as its art, Japan was not a field of research for him – indeed, it was not even a field of study. His stereotypical views on Japanese alterity have been criticized by some and attributed to a form of Far Orientalism.[102] Even if these critiques are not entirely off base, they fail to take into account the specific uses he made of Japan at that point in his life. Indeed, the point was probably altogether a different one: Japan had the power to short-circuit biographical time, to bring him back to his childhood, but also to open him up to a possible vision of the future – Japan as the bearer of an original solution, straddling the ancient and the new, what he called the 'double standard'. Certainly, Lévi-Strauss's Japan was part delirium. It was because he felt a boundless attraction for this country, which he viewed through 'dazzled' and 'quasi-childlike' eyes.[103]

Five visits, then.[104] The first was the longest: for six weeks, between 17 October and 26 November 1977, Claude and Monique Lévi-Strauss were hosted by the Japan Foundation, a public institution, in grand style; they were provided with a chauffeur and translator, Mrs Watanabe Yasu, an invaluable luxury, for exploring the ins and outs of an inscrutable Japan. Their travel plans were carefully arranged and they had a full schedule. Nothing was left to chance, and especially not the gifts they brought for their hosts – small pieces of jewellery, scarves and various traditional European objects that were likely to please. For his part, Lévi-Strauss gave talks, which ultimately formed the series of 'Japanese writings' that have since been published. Papers written for specific occasions, and so in part 'forced' – this was the traveller's stock-in-trade – they deal with anthropology and industrial modernity as well as with Japan itself, in which Lévi-Strauss confessed he had a keen interest but no professional expertise.[105] He wrote to the Suntory Foundation, his host for the second visit, in March 1980, to explicitly say as much before accepting their invitation, which was too tempting to resist: 'If I bring very little to the discussion, at least I will learn a great deal'.[106]

This invitation contrasted quite sharply with those of other intellectuals who also made their way to Tokyo in the late 1970s. And they were quite a few! In the autumn of 1977, when Lévi-Strauss arrived, Paul Ricœur was there giving talks, as was Michel Foucault, who had given four interviews on television – a piece of information that was duly reported to the anthropologist . . . Indeed, quite a few structuralist intellectuals took part in the French intelligentsia's Japanese moment, a kind of flipside to the ideological tourism to the socialist lands of the glorious future. What were they going in search of? Perhaps, as Japan specialist Emmanuel Lozerand has suggested, like Barthes ten years earlier, they sought a place where meaning was suspended and the subject diluted.[107] In any case, as opposed to the others – Barthes, Foucault, etc. – the anthropologist was there on the invitation of the Japanese, rather than through the auspices of the cultural services of the French embassy, which only assisted him once he had arrived. As a result of the tastes he had so strongly affirmed over the course of his initial visit, he very quickly became seen as a true Japanophile. It was therefore not at all as a missionary of structuralism that he disembarked. By then, his work had already been translated into Japanese, thanks to several Japanese anthropologists, notably Junzo Kawada, who had published a new translation of *Tristes Tropiques* in 1977, twenty years after the first. If structuralism had come this far without him, he was happy to have it discussed without him as well! A reluctant speaker, who was keen to honour his commitment to his Japanese hosts, but nothing more, Lévi-Strauss showed up (almost) empty-handed, to learn from Japan.

Over the six weeks they spent in Japan in the autumn of 1977, the Lévi-Strausses travelled throughout Honshu, Japan's main island. Within the context of an LAS research project on the concept of work, Lévi-Strauss met with a wide range of artisans and craftsmen in diverse areas of the country: pastry chefs in Kyoto (at the 'Tsuruya-Yoshinobu' pastry shop), sake brewers ('Okura Shuzo'), swordsmiths in Nara, kimono weavers and dyers in Kanazawa ('Kaga-Yusen'), carpenters and woodturners in the 'Japanese Alps' of Gokayama and Takayama, fishermen and chefs specializing in the *kaiseki* cuisine of Kyoto, paper makers and folk musicians. One of the highlights of the trip, according to his translator, was his meeting with lacquer artisans in Wajima: the concentration of different trades and the multiplicity of tasks required to produce a lacquered bowl struck Lévi-Strauss who, perhaps remembering the family lacquering activities of his childhood, insisted on inviting the entire company to his farewell dinner. 'These artisans were quite grateful for the interest Lévi-Strauss showed in their activity. They knew he was a famous scholar . . . .'[108] He also met with artisans who had been awarded the honorific title of 'Living National Treasure', including a famous sixteenth-generation *raku* potter in the Kyoto region. This distinction, Watanabe Yasu recalled, had delighted Lévi-Strauss, for whom artisanal knowledge indeed deserved to be elevated to the highest degree of national pride. In one of his papers on Japan, he compared the extraordinary vitality of the artisanal traditions he had observed in Japan with their relative decline in France. In his view, this discrepancy was due less to the relative survival of traditional techniques than to the preservation of ancient family structures in Japan, and their extinction in France.[109]

He of course visited the zen temples of Kyoto, sampled the Chinese-style zen cuisine, and attended a tea ceremony – but there, his Western impatience got the better of him and he left in the middle! As for the evening in the company of geishas, he abstained . . . The translator became a friend of the couple, whom she would accompany again on a subsequent visit. Lévi-Strauss encouraged her to call him 'Claude' but she declined any such familiarity. With his agreement, she called him 'Sensei'. He rather liked the term, for it was the Japanese term of respect for 'professor', unaware as he was of the mandarin connotation of the title – the kind of misunderstanding that was rife in Japan for even the most well-disposed visitors and that contributed to its highly exotic charm. Between his passion for mushrooms – Lévi-Strauss went on a short hunt for *matze-take*, an autumnal mushroom, in the Kyoto region – and an invitation from the imperial couple to attend a garden party at the Akasaka Palace, his first visit to Japan was a wonder.

In March 1980, he returned on a more modest one-week visit to Osaka, invited by the Suntory Foundation,[110] the philanthropic arm of a corporation that had been manufacturing and distributing alcoholic beverages – whisky, beer and wine – since 1899. Though he was not much of a drinker, Lévi-Strauss accepted the invitation and took advantage of his trip to do a little '*namazu-e* shopping'. Indeed, Osaka and Kyoto hosted some of the best-stocked shops of nineteenth-century folk art – Japanese engravings of daily life and major events, such as earthquakes, that as a child, Claude Lévi-Strauss had gone in search of at 'La Pagode' on the rue des Petits-Champs in Paris, and that had come to constitute a small personal collection of treasures, amidst the Japan mania of the times.

The third visit, which took place from 9 to 21 May 1983, was initiated by the Japan Productivity Centre, a kind of think-tank for Japanese industrialists. In April 1986, on his fourth trip, Lévi-Strauss took part in the eighth edition of the Ishizaka lectures, public talks financed by the Ishizaka Foundation, another Japanese philanthropic institution. Each time, Lévi-Strauss's interventions were part of a programme of corporate brainstorming, in which social scientists were invited to share their thoughts on global transformations with an audience of business leaders.[111]

Photograph of Claude Lévi-Strauss (second from the left) on a panel, from the 'Japan Speaks, 1980' photo album.

Aside from these public talks, Lévi-Strauss arranged each time for an excursion of varying lengths into parts of the country that interested him. In 1983, on his third visit, accompanied by Professor Yoshida, he went to the Amami Islands, in southwestern Japan, between Kyushu and Okinawa. The whole Okinawa archipelago forms a semi-circle of roughly sixty islands stretching from southern Japan to Taiwan. For centuries, these lands constituted the autonomous Ryukyu kingdom, cultivating a strong and distinct identity that had been shaken by the establishment of American military bases during the Korean War. They had nonetheless remained a sanctuary for rituals and traditions of ancestor worship, and a favourite fieldwork site for Japanese anthropologists, whose work Lévi-Strauss observed. Atsuhiko Yoshida, an anthropologist who specialized in possession rituals and a former naval officer, recalled Lévi-Strauss as being very attentive and curious, always drawing comparisons, but not in the least interested in taking part: 'I don't want to ask questions. Just watch!' He was keen to observe a fishing village and how the Japanese anthropologists went about doing their fieldwork there, the kind of questions they asked. The visit was full of delightful surprises, even though it was also a challenge to sleep on tatamis and kneel for meals. For the Lévi-Strausses' Western bodies, especially Claude's elderly one, the experience was somewhat taxing . . . Conversely, the food, far from posing any challenge, was a constant source of pleasure. Lévi-Strauss always insisted on eating the traditional cuisine that was offered in the small taverns where they lodged.

In 1986, on his fourth trip, the anthropologist was offered a sizeable sum in exchange for giving three talks. He accepted the offer and decided to spend all of it during his stay. He spent nine days in Kyushu, together with his wife and his official translator, who had organized 'a long tour rather than a leisurely holiday'. Between 17 and 26 April, they visited Kagoshima, Kirishima, Udo, Miyazaki, Mount Aso (volcano and sanctuary), Kumamoto, Mount Unzen, Nagasaki and Fukuoka. On the island of Kyushu, the birthplace of Japanese mythology, was to be found the cave of Amaterasu, the sun goddess, and the Uto Sanctuary, linked to the story of the two hunter-fishermen brothers and the poison woman. 'Ah, this is Melusine!' the anthropologist exclaimed. According to Wanatabe Yasu, Lévi-Strauss moved through these places in a state of awe, seized by a comparative frenzy. Indeed, the alert anthropologist drew constant parallels, releasing his sweeping intelligence into the wild, and now at a global scale – the Japanese Orient figuring as the missing link between America and Europe.

It was also on this 1986 trip that he travelled up the Sumida River, accompanied notably by Africanist anthropologist Junzo Kawada. The journey up this river (on board a traditional craft) that runs through Tokyo prompted the taking of a few photographs: they feature Monique and Claude Lévi-Strauss, bundled up and surrounded by the youthful faces of their Japanese hosts. Everyone is smiling in these pictures, Lévi-Strauss included, despite the rather aggressive surrounding urban environment (tall buildings and an industrial port area), which did not quite match the peaceful images of ancient Edo that had stuck in his mind since childhood.

Despite the 'shock', he wrote, 'modern Tokyo did not strike me as ugly',[112] and the old fishermen's neighbourhood of *Tsuku dajima* struck in him a rare lyrical chord.[113]

What did Japan represent for the old man that Claude Lévi-Strauss had become? It was a time machine, but it also pointed the way to a more desirable future, a possible alternative model that he summed up with his notion of 'double standard'.[114] Between the past and the future, Japan held everything together and fulfilled Lévi-Strauss's yearning for continuity. He also made epistemological use of Japan: the 'other face of the moon' was a figure of thought for better understanding its visible face, just like the Japanese Orient was the other face of the Occident, in a confrontation that was however not simply binary, but triangular. Japan was at once a 'world turned upside-down', and a bridge between Europe and America.

As he put it: 'What I had gone to find in Japan was the image, probably illusory, of an exoticism that is, so to speak, less spatial than temporal.'[115] For this very reason, he hesitated for a long time before embarking on such a journey: this abrupt confrontation with reality threatened to shatter his child's vision of Japan inspired by prints. The 'green paradise of childhood loves', which Japan unquestionably was for Lévi-Strauss, expressed itself in his writing about rice with yakinori which, 'with that flavour of seaweed, is as evocative of Japan for me as the madeleine was for Proust!'[116]

If the confrontation with this imaginary Japan was indeed sometimes traumatic, for nature had also been severely abused in Japan, its modernity was not experienced as a catastrophe. Lévi-Strauss was unquestionably interested in ancient Japan, but he liked Tokyo, and became quite keen on the electronics district of Akihabara, identifying in this thriving industry the expression of ancestral qualities (meticulousness, precision, etc.) of Japanese craftsmanship. For the anthropologist, the 'double standard' provided a key to understanding Japan: it was a set of original solutions that made room for both the past and the future, bringing together a very vital world of belief with a sophisticated scientific and technological dimension: 'Japan, perhaps alone among nations, has until now been able to find a balance between fidelity to the past and the transformations brought about by science and technology.'[117] Here again, Lévi-Strauss was delighted with this ideal alternation between tradition and modernity, between the closed and the open, which allowed him to develop a new metaphor: Japan functioned 'as a filter or, if you like, as an alembic, which distilled a rarer and more subtle essence'.[118] In this panoramic view, Lévi-Strauss underplayed, and even ignored, what he called the 'ideological vertigo' that had taken hold of Japan in the first half of the twentieth century. He considered this slide into authoritarian rule as epiphenomenal and refused to confront it, as was made clear by the misunderstanding that arose in the course of his discussion with Professor Kawada. Lévi-Strauss was rhapsodizing about the moral discipline of the Japanese, their availability, the professionalism that characterized all their services, which he boldly linked to the directness of the Japanese 'yes': 'We say *oui*, you say *hai*. I have always felt [. . .] there is much more in *hai* than in *oui*. That *oui* is a sort of passive acquiescence, whereas *hai* is a leap toward the interlocutor . . .' Kawada: '[. . .] For our generation, which lived through the ultranationalist and militarist regime before 1945, the word *hai* thus evokes the spirit of unconditional obedience to a higher power [. . .]' CLS: 'But let's come back to the beauty of Japanese nature.'[119]

The theory of Japan as an 'inverted double' and a 'mirror' of the West was certainly nothing new. But Lévi-Strauss refined the cliché by bringing his intelligence and erudition to bear.[120] The theory of the subject, of language, the anthropology of the body, were all made to contribute in turn: the centripetal subject vs. the centrifugal subject, like the Japanese artisan who pulled the plane (or the needle) to himself, rather than away from himself, as did the Western craftsman.[121] This was the play of oppositions that any traveller might indulge in for fun.[122] A Frenchman in 2010, for example, finds it amusing that Japanese people are allowed to smoke in bars but forbidden to smoke on certain streets . . . But there was more to the 'other face of the moon' than just an 'upside-down world'. A heuristic tool in keeping with the structuralist ethos, which consisted less in identifying oppositions than in grasping differences within similarities. One of the most powerful appeals of Japan for Lévi-Strauss was that it stimulated his comparatist energies – even if this sometimes led him to flirt with universal mythology – and led him to detect in it the play of differentiation: 'I have the pleasure of discovering extreme states of a series of transformations',[123] he claimed. As, for instance, in the Japanese legend of the mute prince who recovered his capacity of speech: 'That narrative came as a shock to me. A short-circuit of memory made me recognize it as an episode from the life of Croesus as Herodotus recounts it.'[124] The dynamic was not just binary but triangular: Japanese mythology was not only compared to the corpus of stories from antiquity, but also from the Americas. Thus, the story of the white hare of Inaba, which marks the opening episode of the *Kojiki* (the most ancient Japanese chronicle of myths and legends, dating from the eighth century), was compared to South-American versions of a very similar mythical episode, with the figures of the evil stepfather and the ferryman featured in the two mythologies, which 'are both similar and different'.[125]

What should we make of this? 'It is as if a mythological system, perhaps native to continental Asia and whose traces would have to be discovered, had gone first to Japan, then to America.'[126] In the Lévi-Straussian imagination, Japan decidedly served as a bridge, a site of mediation, between his childhood and old age, between tradition and modernity, and between the Old and New Worlds.

Like a loved one, Japan appeared to the anthropologist to be endowed with innumerable seductive features that also formed objective homologies between specific traits of Japanese culture and his own personal idiosyncrasies. And, as always with him, it all began with the taste buds: 'When he was in Japan', according to Junzo Kawada, 'we had meals together on several occasions, and I was pleased to see how well he enjoyed the tastes of another culture. For example, *dojo nabe*, which is a stew of small monkfish cooked whole in a saucepan; or *koi no aria*, fillets of raw carp in very thin slices served on ice, that are eaten with a vinegary sauce and soy paste; or even *konowata*, the intestines of sea cucumbers that are eaten raw and salted, prized by the Japanese as a sake accompaniment, etc.'[127] Lévi-Strauss's culinary curiosity regarding Japanese cuisine knew no bounds – except for his strong revulsion to the idea of eating horse meat, 'the one and only chink in his culinary cultural relativism'.[128] As opposed to Chinese gastronomy, which was fattier and more synthetic, Japanese cuisine was based on 'divisionism',[129] characterizing, according to Lévi-Strauss, the most diverse sectors of Japanese culture. This effort 'to keep separate what ought to be so' was one of the keys to his taste for Japan. What he called its 'Cartesianism of feelings',[130] the extreme care devoted to classifying and distinguishing the various dimensions of reality – as, for example, the various vegetable and animal substances that went into the making of a meal in order to better savour each flavour and to establish fresh relations between the pure elements.

The Japanese system of writing appeared to partake of the same spirit. Indeed, in *The Jealous Potter*, the final meditation on the signifying process rested on the example of Japan:[131] on the one hand, two syllabaries (*katakana* and *hiragana*) determined sound very precisely, but not meaning, due to the numerous homonyms; on the other, ideograms derived from the Chinese (*kanji*) produced meaning but their phonetic expression could vary based on context. All Japanese readers therefore had to use both codes jointly. Meaning sprang from their mutual and gradual adjustment. As with the meaning of myths and dreams, Japanese signs thus did not immediately deliver a signified real. Different from the Western model of meaning production, this initial suspension followed by clarification profoundly agreed with Lévi-Strauss, who was taken by the fragility and availability of meaning, the respect for reality, and the aversion to metaphysics. From this perspective, Barthes in *The Empire of Signs* was on the same wavelength.[132]

Reading Lévi-Strauss's enthusiastic description of the Jōmon potters' art, one cannot help but think of his own scholarly and personal style. Their speedy and reliable execution, their masterful technique, the time they devoted to meditation and the 'properly Japanese gift for concision'[133] are indeed also his. When he admired the 'art of imperfection' of the zen artist Sengai, a contemporary of Hokusai, the precision, rigour, sobriety and elegance are all eminently Lévi-Straussian values. It is therefore unsurprising that Japanese art should have been, since childhood, a source of wonderment and revelation as well as a tool for thinking Western aesthetics anew. The taste for rough materials and imperfect bowls developed by the masters of tea ceremonies in sixteenth-century Japan, as well as the extreme sophistication of the lacquers and porcelains, appeared to him as the very pinnacle of beauty, of this very Japanese aesthetic tradition of *wabi-sabi*, characterized by refinement in simplicity. One must therefore imagine Lévi-Strauss as a master potter, a calligrapher or a zen master, definitively liberated from the dictatorship of meaning, on his way to discovering the notion of 'thusness', i.e., things as they are, beyond subject and object, good and evil, and any judgement whatsoever. With the zen master, as Françoise Héritier has very insightfully pointed out, he also shared a 'way of thinking, both elliptical and yet very precise',[134] a taste for anecdotes, oddities, puns, concrete examples and all this 'oblique pedagogy'[135] in which no question was to receive a definitive answer. His attention was particularly drawn to *kōan* – the zen tradition of dogged meditation on an absurd notion, such as 'the noise of one hand clapping' – and *haikus* – short poems that would often adorn ink-wash paintings. Meaning either breaks down or attenuates itself. Not that Lévi-Strauss practised *kōan* with his disciples – nor did he beat them either, as zen masters could do! – but his withdrawal into enigma, his verbal parsimony, his unshakeable affability, and the construction-set lightness of his theoretical edifices all pointed to a Lévi-Straussian zen-ness that only became stronger with age.

In the end, Japan was to remain the happy experience of a relative alterity that Japanized him in return. This world in miniature – as all islands are – propelled him into the future, since Japan, at that time, offered a condensation of values and attitudes to which he was very much attuned. It was the miniature of a world in which the anthropologist could continue to live.

Israel, Judaism: A return to origins?

'In 1985', Lévi-Strauss told his Japanese hosts, 'I visited Israel and the holy sites, and then about a year later in 1986, the places where the founding events of your most ancient mythology are supposed to have unfolded. My culture, my background, ought to have made me more sensitive to the first sites than to the second. Exactly the reverse occurred. Mount Kirishima, where Ninigi-no-Mikoto descended from heaven, and the Amanoiwato-jinja, opposite the cave where Ohirume, the goddess Amaterasu, was confined, elicited in me emotions more profound than the supposed location of the Temple of David, the cave of the Nativity, the Holy Sepulchre, or Lazarus's tomb.'[136] In true structuralist logic, the meaning of his visit to Israel can only be apprehended (here, negatively) in relation to the plenitude of his experience of Japan, and Kyushu in particular. In much the same way as in *Tristes Tropiques*, where the prosaic Judaism of his childhood was contrasted with the rich symbolic world of the Bororo, the biblical sacred did not resonate with him at all. First, as he himself pointed out, because of the lack of any continuity between the ancient Jewish Palestine of 2,000 years ago and the presence of his family in Alsace in the eighteenth century;[137] and, second, because – as opposed to the Japanese who, in his view, naturally inhabited a mythical atmosphere – Westerners had drawn a sharp distinction between what belonged to myth and what to history. Hence his lack of any concrete sense of belonging.[138] Whatever abstract interest he had in Israel and fascination for specific locations – especially for Massada, along the Dead Sea, and along the River Jordan – it simply did not strike a chord.

Yet it is undeniable that, over the course of the 1980s, Claude Lévi-Strauss did return, in another sense, to the Jewish question. In 1988, at the same time his interview with Didier Éribon provided a 'narrative of origins', he produced a curious article that was in many ways rather unexpected: 'Exode sur *Exode*', with its title's enigmatically erudite pun – '*exode*' is to be understood here as 'amusement', a rare seventeenth-century meaning, as well as 'exodus' – is a text that progresses stealthily, a 'fantasy'[139] that, while piquing the reader's curiosity, ultimately confirms all the great structuralist theories, albeit in a deliberately minor key. In it, Lévi-Strauss compares the Jewish ritual of circumcision as it is justified in the Bible to the Bororo imposition of a penis sheath: 'Instead of excising the prepuce, a natural part of the penis, the Bororo add a sheath to it, a fabricated object which as such becomes a cultural element. As a result, to impose a cultural penis sheath or to remove a natural penis sheath belong to the same project: to mark the penis with a cultural sign, either by addition or subtraction. The result is to expose the head of the penis in one case, to conceal it in the other. [. . .] The inverted practices of excising the prepuce and wearing a penis sheath are thus reduced to combinatorial variants whose unity only becomes apparent at a deeper level.'[140] And this is indeed what makes them comparable.

Daniel Fabre recalls Jean Pouillon's surprise upon receiving Lévi-Strauss's article, submitted for publication in *L'Homme*, of which he was then the editor.[141] Indeed, Lévi-Strauss had always claimed that for lack of ethnographic data, it was 'impossible to study the anthropology of ancient Judaism' – a claim the article partially contradicted. This text thus signalled another transformation: it appeared to repeat the opposition staged in *Tristes Tropiques*, but this time no longer denigrating ancient Judaism, since circumcision functioned as the symmetrical inverse of the penis sheath, in an identical move to mark the body for similar purposes. Finally, the text orchestrated the subliminal combination of two collections of objects that operated as the two boundaries within which Claude Lévi-Strauss's ambiguous and complex Judaism, refashioned by his own introspection, had evolved: on the one hand, his collection of Bororo objects – including many penis sheaths – that he had exhibited upon his return from his first Brazilian expedition in 1937; on the other, the collection of Jewish ritual objects inherited from his ancestor Isaac Strauss – among which ritual circumcision knives – which, as a result of a reorganization of the Cluny Museum collections, resurfaced in the life of the great-grandson in the early 1980s.

As we will recall, this sizeable pioneering collection of religious art objects had been purchased by Baroness de Rothschild, and then donated almost in its entirety to the Cluny Museum, whose west wing she inaugurated in 1890, later to be joined by a few other donors, such as Camondo – the whole collection retracing the history of the Jewish community in medieval and early modern France and Europe.[142] In 1980, Alain Erlande-Brandenburg, the chief curator of the Cluny Museum, asked Victor Klagsbald, a consultant at the Judaica department of the Israel Museum in Jerusalem, to draw up an inventory of the Cluny collection. In 1986, this collection, now inventoried, was added to the permanent collection of the new Museum of Judaic History and Art, housed in the Hotel de Saint-Aignan, on rue du Temple

mishkenot sha'ananim
newsletter
No. 2 Jerusalem, February 1985

News from Mishkenot

The distinguished Jewish-French anthropologist and philosopher, Claude Lévi-Strauss, made his first visit to Israel at the beginning of January and stayed in Jerusalem as a guest of Mishkenot Sha'ananim. The central part of his visit was devoted to an "Encounter" at Mishkenot devoted to the topic "Myth in Contemporary Western Societies". The encounter was chaired by Prof. Zvi Werblowsky and the panel consisted of Professors Nathan Rotenstreich, Shmuel Eisenstadt, Saul Friedlander and Dimitri Segal. The audience consisted of a large group of Israeli personalities including Prime Minister Shimon Peres. In addition to the encounter, Prof. Lévi-Strauss also agreed to an hour-long interview for Israel Television which was conducted by Prof. Saul Friedlander of Tel-Aviv University. The following are brief excerpts from Prof. Lévi-Strauss' remarks made in leading off the Mishkenot encounter:

"I've always been very careful to avoid using the word 'myth' in too general a meaning. If you ask an American-Indian, either in North or in South America, what is a myth, he will probably give you the same answer, that is, that myth relates to a time when men and animals were indistinct from each other, could assume each other's form and talk to each other. This is, if I may say so, a kind of super-interpretation of our myth of the Tower of Babel which exclusively concerns mankind and the separation between men, while in the mind of those people the problem is a much wider one; it relates to the tragic moment when living beings ceased to be members of the same community and dispersed and became strangers to each other. In the second place, I think we should be careful when we speak about myth in western contemporary society because our ways of dealing with a problem of a general nature are extremely different from the mythological approach. If, instead of an American-Indian, I myself try to express what is a

continued on page 2

Prof. Claude Lévi-Strauss with Prime Minister Shimon Peres at Mishkenot

Claude Lévi-Strauss in Jerusalem walking with Shimon Peres during his visit to Israel
from 30 December 1984 to 5 January 1985
(*Mishkenot Sha'ananim Newsletter*, no. 2, February 1985).

in Paris. According to Daniel Fabre, who was the first to point out this temporal coincidence, 'it all hinged on a sudden confrontation with objects'.[143] Beloved objects that he visited in his childhood and that surreptitiously returned at the same time as the very texture of the past.

On that occasion, Lévi-Strauss wrote a foreword to the catalogue: 'When I was born, twenty years after his death, Isaac Strauss had already become a family legend. Yet my father, who was born in 1881, could still remember his early childhood visits to the Chaussée d'Antin and that, on one of these, Ambroise Thomas[144] had been present and had sat him on his lap. But it was mostly through the stories of my paternal grandmother, the youngest of Isaac Strauss's five daughters (who were forbidden to knit and sew so as not to waste any time that might be devoted to music), that I have become somewhat familiar with this half-century, already imbued with a mythical aura, during which a modest Alsatian family hobnobbed with illustrious characters of great musical and literary talent, who played important roles in their contemporary history, both in France and abroad.'[145] Couched in a very Proustian poetical style, this highly personal essay conjured up a rich family mythology: the family deities (Rossini, who would kiss his grandmother hello, and Berlioz), the heroes (Isaac Strauss) and the nicknames they were given. Alongside the sacred history, the gossip column – in a tone that was very reminiscent of Labiche – alluding to the alleged affair between one of Strauss's daughters and a dignitary of the Second Empire. Like in Kyushu, where history and mythology mingled, his personal history was intimately related to this rich family mythology that he fully claimed as his own, giving him a sense of belonging and of happy continuity between that (Jewish) Alsatian family, its ups and downs, and the individual he had become.

Objects, and Isaac's objects in particular, were the visible incarnation of this natural suturing: 'At the homes of Strauss's two daughters, who were still alive in my day, and at those of their siblings' children, I had seen a few paintings, antique furniture and objects, remains of his collection that have almost all since disappeared, due to German spoliation. Together with a passion for music, I developed in these quaint apartments a sense of the history of art and a low taste for antique knick-knacks: my double inheritance from this ancestor who was at once a composer, a conductor and an avid collector in those bygone days when disdained treasures, rejected even by professionals, awaited the savvy eye of a Cousin Pons to be rehabilitated.'[146] In addition to the stories, it was above all these objects, which he curiously called 'antique knick-knacks', that opened up onto the past and the recognition of just how much his own identity owed to that world: 'The memory of Isaac Strauss enables me to weld back together the various links of the chain. Through those I have known and who knew him, whose own mother narrowly escaped the guillotine, they say, though I have no idea why, I feel I belong to other centuries, less through the dubious legacy of chromosomes that would account for common passions, than through the intimacy that had been cultivated since childhood with sensory objects of a musical, aesthetic or decorative kind, among which figured those now gathered together again in this exhibition, which I used to be brought to see in the room where they were permanently exhibited at the Cluny Museum, and where the name of Isaac Strauss, engraved on the door's frontispiece, filled me with a sense that not only through their original source, but also through their association with my entire family past, they were somehow part of me, or rather, that in more ways than one, I was part of them.'[147] This beautiful text was also very meaningful: indeed, if it prompted the recognition of a Jewish identity that was in no way connected to the Shoah, and even less to the foundation of Israel, but had everything to do with the world of Isaac Strauss, it is striking that the identity in question remained somewhat elliptical, since at no point were the 'antique knick-knacks' labelled with their rightful name of Hebraic antiques, nor was the term 'Jewish' used even once, either to describe his Alsatian family or to describe the objects that figured in the catalogue. It included, among many other pieces, a Chanukah lamp, a Megillah and its sheath, richly ornate wedding bands, a Torah ark, a Kether, etc. Striking silences in the Lévi-Straussian biographical reconstruction . . .

Brazil: the failed return

Another country, another debt. Lévi-Strauss always used that word to describe his relationship to Brazil which, according to Eduardo Viveiros de Castro, was characterized by a mutual ambivalence – an ambivalence that also tainted the relationship of Brazil to its indigenous peoples, who had become part of the universal thought of the twentieth century through the work of Claude Lévi-Strauss.[148] More profoundly, such ambivalence might have been the expression of the necessarily failed encounter between observer and the observed, which hovered like a giant shadow over the indeed highly postmodern monument of *Tristes Tropiques*. Claude Lévi-Strauss's return to Brazil, repeatedly planned and postponed (not only in 1941, in the tragic circumstances we have already recounted), finally took place in October 1985, the same year as his visit to Israel, and between two to Japan.

He went as part of the official delegation accompanying President François Mitterrand and some members of the French government. Having originally travelled on a cargo ship in the 1930s, he was returning aboard the Concorde. Manuela Carneiro da Cunha, a Brazilian anthropologist who taught at the University of São Paulo and a close friend of Lévi-Strauss, narrated a trip within the trip: 'The owners of *Estado do São Paulo*, the family that had founded the university, had organized a visit by Lévi-Strauss to the Bororo, whom he had met fifty years earlier. The trip comprised Claude Lévi-Strauss, his wife, Monique and no longer Dina, a journalist at *Estado* who did not speak a word of French, a photographer and myself. Our craft was a small twin-engine plane. We set out from Rondonopolis, in Mato Grosso. We arrived. Nobody knew where the village natives who were supposed to greet us were. The Bororo were an hour's drive away. We made it to the Indian post, a hundred yards from the village. The post chief was stunned. He told us a big celebration had indeed been prepared for us – but elsewhere. He made radio contact and Lévi-Strauss very politely returned along the path. Two hours later, we arrived back in Rondonopolis. We took another plane with a local guide. There did not seem to be much gas in the tank. We flew over an Indian village where nobody was expecting us. It turned out that the landing strip was not eight hundred but five hundred metres long. A storm was brewing. Not to be late to the banquet Mitterrand was throwing in honour of the Brazilian president in Brasilia, we turned around, not having met a single Indian. The storm hit and the gas gauge suddenly dropped. Everyone was petri-fied, but Lévi-Strauss remained placid. We then realized there was a second gas tank! We landed safely in Brasilia, where a crowd of journalists had gathered to interview Lévi-Strauss, who simply responded: 'I have nothing to say, and in any case, this is an *Estado* exclusive.'[149] Manuela Carneiro da Cunha added that, as far as Lévi-Strauss was concerned, seeing the land-scapes and skies of Mato Grosso from the air had been ample reward . . .[150] According to Edouardo Viveiros de Castro, this disappointing return to Brazil was the ultimate and final culmination in a series of failed attempts to reconnect with Brazil. And yet, this failed visit 'precisely enacted, if not in so many words, a version of the Bororo myth of the bird catcher':[151] the hero caught between heaven and earth and the terrible storm being essential elements in this myth that opened the *Mythologiques* cycle. This episode – also recalling Tintin's adventures in South America, including the brush with certain death – would thus be 'the greatest achievement, for it allowed him to truly experience the myth to which he had devoted a significant stretch of his long life, becoming the story. That is a rare opportunity.'[152]

Mythical transformations (2): The minor mythologiques

As we have already discussed with regard to *The Way of the Masks*, the three texts that Lévi-Strauss nicknamed his 'minor mythologiques' experimented with a new form that was deliberately more modest, couched in a lively narrative style, and targeting a wider readership even while sacrificing neither theoretical rigour nor the level of erudition, which was regularly described in the press as 'vertiginous'. The two works that followed – *The Jealous Potter* (1985) and *The Story of Lynx* (1991) – 'each marked a new intervention into the French intellectual field from the remote point of view of the Amerindian continent'.[153] Lévi-Strauss spoke from a faraway place that no longer existed (that of myth) in order to address his contemporaries in novel ways, including and especially to offer provocations. In *The Jealous Potter*, he wrapped up his long dialogue with psychoanalysis (begun in 1949), challenging some of its assumptions and 'shrinking' Freud's own head – before drawing his famous comparison between Sophocles and Labiche.

With *The Story of Lynx*, which became a classic work for an entire gen-eration of anthropologists of Amazonia, he disrupted the five hundredth anniversary of what he preferred to call the 'invasion'[154] – rather than the 'discovery' – of America by Europeans who, in 1992, were preparing to celebrate this epic event of modern times with much pomp. Lévi-Strauss dampened the enthusiasm and called for a recognition of the destruction of the peoples and cultures of the New World as an 'act of contrition and devotion'.[155] In *The Story of Lynx*, the scene of the inaugural encounter between the two worlds was reinterpreted through the lens of Montaigne, on the one hand, and Amerindian thought, on the other. Haunted by the spectre of Jean de Léry as he approached the shores of Guanabara Bay in 1936, Lévi-Strauss was obsessed with the image of the first confrontation between the Old and New Worlds. With his last book, he concluded this intellectual and existential journey with a final attempt to travel back in time – not only that of his own life and of the century, but that of Western modernity.

The Jealous Potter: *'Freud among the Jivaro'*[156]

The Jealous Potter had its origins in a Collège de France course, 'Sketches of an American Bestiary (1964/65)',[157] in which Lévi-Strauss examined a group of myths of the Jivaro tribes, who lived on the border of Bolivia and Guyana. These myths staged a series of oppositions between the cosmic power symbolized by the figure of the sloth and a 'chthonic people of dwarves with no anus'[158] – whose anal retention contrasted with the incontinence of the howler monkey, itself differentiated from the oral rapacity of the nighthawk. We recognize here many of the characters featured in *The Jealous Potter*, its specific scatological register and psychoanalytic lexicon, which is unsurprising since the book recycled the Collège de France course while connecting it to a new schema, now no longer the conquest of cooking fire but a splitting off or rather a 'harmonic resonance' of this thematic: the acquisition of pottery, i.e., the cooking of the earth that will contain the food to be cooked. Through the course of this excursion into pottery, the physiological cycle – absorption/ digestion/ejection – and the technical cycle – extraction of clay, modelling, cooking – are intertwined.

First of all, the anthropologist establishes the connection between pottery and the jealous temper in many Amerindian myths, which he combines with other connections as if he were putting together the pieces of a puzzle: the feminine character of pottery (whereas agriculture is a masculine practice), the nighthawk myths dealing with marital discord, as well as, according to an astronomical code, the discord between the stars. To the nighthawk-pottery-jealousy triangle is added a fourth element, that of the red ovenbird, whose myths result from an inverted transformation of the nighthawk myths. Hence the return, thirty years after its original formulation, to the canonical formula which, in this specific case, could be stated as follows: 'The "jealous" function of the nighthawk is to the "potter" function of the woman as the "jealous" function of the woman is to the "inverted nighthawk" function of the potter.'[159] The

552   The World (1971–2009)

book's publication marked the beginning of a series of projects and studies that reassess the relevance of the canonical formula, which had somewhat receded in the Lévi-Straussian oeuvre.[160]

Intermingling a large number of mythical themes – discord between the stars, meteor-excrement, the severed head and mutilated body – Claude Lévi-Strauss explored yet again one of the passages between nature and culture of which pottery was a profound expression. Jealousy, at the anthropological level, served to maintain a conjunction between two elements threatened by disjunction. He also reminds us, through a few amusing anecdotes, that the development of myths always relied on precise botanical, zoological and astronomical knowledge. Thus, the anal incontinence of the howler monkey is indeed based on fact, as he himself experienced with a monkey he had adopted as a pet during his Brazilian expedition: 'But if I or my companions tried to approach him, he would instantly produce an astonishing quantity of excrement, roll it into balls with his hands and pelt us with these projectiles.'[161]

'Anal incontinence', 'oral rapacity': *The Jealous Potter* uses some of the categories popularized by psychoanalysis, precisely because, according to Lévi-Strauss, myths had thought them through long before Sigmund Freud. Each of the books the anthropologist wrote offers a philosophical, metaphysical or simply contemplative digression, in the form of a critical reappraisal of the intellectual fetishes of our civilization. In *The Savage Mind*, it was Sartre and dialectical reason; in *The Naked Man*, Western humanism; in *The Way of the Masks*, modern aesthetics. Here, Lévi-Strauss launched a subtle, corrosive and radical attack, often in a humorous tone, on Freud and psychoanalysis. Pierre Nora was right to point out, in a letter to the author, its veiled violence: 'You have the courtesy of calling a dialogue with psychoanalysis what is in fact one of these settling of scores for which you have a knack. We had been waiting for it since the end of *The Elementary Structures of Kinship*; it is decisive.'[162]

What was this all about? As Lévi-Strauss reminds us, Freud had given *Totem and Taboo* the subtitle: 'Resemblances Between the Mental Lives of Savages and Neurotics'. In a sacrilegious move that he had already made in 1949 when he published his article on shamanism, Lévi-Strauss reversed the equation: '[. . .] I have set out to show instead that there are points on which the psychic life of savages and psychoanalysts coincide.'[163] In his view, psychoanalysis rediscovered with its own language elements of mental life that had already been captured by mythic thought. Better still: Lévi-Strauss understood *Totem and Taboo* as a variant of a Jivaro myth: 'All Freud did – all he ever did – was to produce a modern version' of the myth . . .[164] This should come as no surprise since Freud – and, Lévi-Strauss caustically added, this was precisely where his 'greatness' lay[165] – had a gift for 'think[ing] the way myths do'.[166] This iconoclastic link between psychoanalysis and mythic thought (in this case, Jivaro thought) was further established by one last ironic piece of linguistic evidence: 'How wise are the Americans in calling psychoanalysts "headshrinkers", thus spontaneously associating them with the Jivaro!'[167] It was thus quite inappropriate that psychoanalysis should take it upon itself to say what myths thought and said. Indeed, if myths delivered their meanings in a variety of codes (astronomical, botanical, zoological, psychosexual, etc.) and if their 'messages' lay in the convertibility of all codes into one another, psychoanalysis used a far less rich language that was limited solely to the psychosexual code that served as its ultimate signified.

This is his main objection to psychoanalysis, which, in addition, tends to reify this psychosexual and sexual content. In a 'short exercise in structural analysis' that juxtaposes word for word Sophocles' *Oedipus* and Labiche's *The Italian Straw Hat*, Lévi-Strauss set out to demonstrate that both texts responded to similar issues but formulated them in distinct codes. Beyond the intellectual lark, he defended the idea that 'the mould was more important than the content'.[168] It was this mould that myths unveiled and that psychoanalysis thought it necessary to fill with a one-dimensional content: sexual reality. The diatribe against psychoanalysis thus gave way to a reflection on the signifying process: what is signifying? It is always, as in myths, translating one code into another, in the way that the dictionary explains a word by another, establishing connections between terms, as practised in Japanese writing.

The entire press hailed Claude Lévi-Strauss's new 'divertimento',[169] with its light and facetious tone, its provocative puerility (shrinking Freud's head!), which turned arid structural analyses into a much more entertaining read. The book's reception was further heightened by the simultaneous publication, in October 1985, of an issue of *Magazine littéraire* entirely devoted to the anthropologist, under the supervision of Catherine Clément. Here again, reviews were numerous: a long interview that ran over two issues of *Le Nouvel Observateur*,[170] articles by Robert Maggiori in *Libération*, by Jacques Meunier in *Le Monde*, by Jean-Paul Morel in *Le Matin*, by Pierre Daix in *Le Quotidien de Paris*, by Jean-Maurice de Montremy in *La Croix*, etc. The book had much to recommend it: its pedagogical value was celebrated, as well as its narrative dimension, its sense of theoretical suspense and its omission of heavy scholarly analysis. 'Lévi-Strauss pulled down the scaffolding',[171] wrote Maggiori. This 'bit of structural analysis'[172] was an enjoyable read, unique of its kind on the French landscape. It was now 'no longer indexed to theoretical battles'[173] that would pre-empt its meaning. A 'hall of mirrors' or 'theoretical Rubik's Cube', *The Jealous Potter* was thus a 'structuralist banquet', as the Canadian anthropologist Pierre Maranda wrote, as well as a playful (scatological) and sometimes provocative short treatise. Alongside this enthusiasm, scholarly commentaries were rare: Emmanuel Desveaux and Charles-Henry Pradelles de Latour wrote two 'Abouts' in *L'Homme*.[174] It should be pointed out that the only sour note, in *Le Matin de Paris*, came from an anthropologist, Jean Bazin, who confessed his 'perplexity': 'One gets the sense that, letting his gaze wander about this collection of myths that has become so familiar to him, and indulging in free association perhaps more than in structural analysis, Lévi-Strauss might have acted more as a creator than as a positivist scholar.'[175] When the English version came out in 1988, the *New York Times Book Review* (on 22 May) published a review by Wendy Doniger O'Flaherty, a historian of religion: 'Mr Lévi-Strauss beheads not only Freud but the Jivaros. [. . .] In fact, he thinks and acts not like an actual Jivaroan myth-maker but like a character inside a Jivaro myth, a beheader of the father.'[176] Three years earlier, Pierre Enckel, in *L'Événement du jeudi*, had already diagnosed the 'mythical transformation' of the author of structural analysis: 'Not content with being an *académicien*, Claude Lévi-Strauss is on his, way to becoming a god – the anthropologist's ultimate avatar . . .'[177]

The Story of Lynx: *Under the mask of Montaigne*

Published by Plon in 1991, *The Story of Lynx* was the famous anthropologist's final book, and had been announced as such. Indeed, if not precisely the 'last book', it was the last anthropological work he published in his lifetime. The anthropological dimension proper was combined with a political manifesto, which itself opened onto a dreamy meditation that revealed, more than any other of his works, its author's 'worldview'. Hence the unrivalled public and critical interest (and sometimes controversy) triggered by this last opus, in which he appeared to be showing his hand.

Yet again, Lévi-Strauss narrated a complex story, a 'convoluted journey into the intricate myths of both Americas'.[178] It advances incrementally, through meteorological phenomena, thick fog and high winds, through the lynx of the title and its twin the coyote, through roots, the Dentalia Thieves, a child ravished by an owl, bodily wounds as adornments, salmon, bears, wolves, the moon and testicles . . . The plot is at times far-fetched, in the manner of Gaston Leroux's *The Mystery of the Yellow Room.*[179] Everything combines to suggest that Amerindian thought had as its founding principle a bipartite ideology. It is considered through the figure of impossible twinning.[180] Indeed, twins, so often present in all mythologies, are not on the side of identity in American myths – like Castor and Pollux, or Remus and Romulus, to take but a few European examples – but, on the contrary, on that of absolute difference – as are Lynx and Coyote. This Amerindian twinning expresses a dichotomous model based on 'a precarious balance, in a perpetual see-saw movement'[181] that sets the universal machine in motion and can be seen in social organization and art – one of the young Lévi-Strauss's first articles in New York, remember, already dealt with the split representation at work in many of the artistic productions of primitive societies (Caduveo, Maori, ancient China, etc.).[182] By the end of the excursion, the anthropologist has established that America was characterized by a dynamic bipartite logic, echoing his colleague and friend Georges Dumézil, whose claim to fame was to have revealed the tripartite ideology structuring the Indo-European world.

The book took on a strong political dimension, with the bipartite Amerindian ideology paving the way for a critical reappraisal of the original sixteenth-century encounter between the Old and New Worlds, and a better understanding of why it had been so catastrophic. Indeed, how can we account for the paralysis that took hold of the 20,000 armed Incas in the face of 165 Spaniards? This question had long presented a historiographical puzzle, prompting various explanatory theories. Again, Lévi-Strauss delivered his own just as the five hundredth anniversary celebrations of the so-called 'great discoveries' were set to begin. Since, according to his conception, all unity contains a duality, this 'philosophical clinamen' made room for the Other, 'in the form of a hollow space'.[183] This was why, Lévi-Strauss contended, the whites were in some sense already present in Amerindian thought before they even showed up on American shores. Hence their stupefaction, since the Aztecs saw Cortez and his conquistador companions as the very embodiments of Quetzalcoatl, the god whose return they had been awaiting. Moctezuma thus sent them ambassadors laden with offerings reserved for the gods. This openness to the Other which, in those historical circumstances, proved fatal to the Amerindian worlds, is nonetheless, if one reads Lévi-Strauss carefully, also a mark of the greatness of these civilizations (the high civilizations of the Andes are not here considered as distinct from the less complex Amazonian ones), by contrast with the Europeans who, discovering that they formed only half of the human species, hastened to suppress the other half like a bad dream . . .

Of this originary encounter of modernity, Lévi-Strauss surmised, it was Montaigne alone who had grasped its crucial character. As opposed to what one might think, the open minds of the Renaissance were not all equally shaken by the American jolt, since the latter was discussed in terms of, and in a way forestalled by, the rediscovery of the ancient world. Its contemporaries mostly wanted the 'savages' to confirm what the 'ancients' had said of them.[184] It was at this point that Lévi-Strauss pulled the philosopher out of his hat, making a belated yet decisive appearance, in both his life and his work.

Our mental image of the old Lévi-Strauss appears under the mask of Montaigne, who took the place long occupied by Rousseau. From Montaigne, beyond their common cultural relativism, he drew two lessons: practical wisdom and a scepticism regarding knowledge. In chapter 18 of *The Story of Lynx*, Lévi-Strauss returned to the text of the *Essays*, and especially to 'An Apology for Raymond Sebond', of which he defends a radical interpretation: Lévi-Strauss's Montaigne is a nihilist of knowledge[185] who refuses to give any power to the conquering reason of modernity. Lévi-Strauss therefore read this passage as part of a 'formidable project of refutation of knowledge',[186] and a 'ravaging critique that [. . .] reduces any rational mode of knowing to nothing'.[187]

Was it not Montaigne who had proclaimed that 'we have no communication with being'[188] – an insight Lévi-Strauss considered as his most fundamental contribution? The end of *The Story of Lynx* is enshrouded with this dwindling *libido sciendi*. The anthropologist has clearly left behind the triumphant scientism that he harboured in the 1960s, although even then it never clouded his critical reflexivity, to which *Tristes Tropiques* attests. Yet the mood has decidedly changed.[189] For what was he to do if all attempts at knowing were doomed to fail, if 'the more knowledge progresses, the more it understands why it is it cannot succeed?'[190] How was one to be a

serene Westerner? 'Our way of dealing with life can only be a kind of compromise between our thirst for knowledge, our laborious acquisition of
knowledge, and, on the other hand, the conviction that seen from afar, or
from a more profound perspective, these efforts lack any ultimate meaning.
We live in contradiction. We might as well get over it.'[191] Rereading
Montaigne thus encouraged him to engage in 'the lucid management of
this schizophrenia'.[192] Wisdom, here, comes down to 'living life as if it had
a meaning, this even though intellectual honesty assures us that this is not
so'.[193] Or, like Montaigne, in order to make life somewhat less unbearable,
learning to distinguish between 'conventional truths' and 'truths for intimate purposes'.[194]

It was indeed an implicit self-portrait Lévi-Strauss delivered when he
concluded: 'Though profoundly subversive, this relativism manifesting
itself by falling back takes a conservative coloration.'[195] This was also
how the numerous and mostly positive reviews interpreted his reflections on Montaigne: as Didier Éribon put it in *Le Nouvel Observateur*,
as 'the focal point crystallizing his own philosophy'.[196] The significant
press coverage was further stimulated by Lévi-Strauss's appearance,
on 14 October 1991, on the literary television programme hosted by
Bernard Rapp, as well as the publication of François Dosse's *History of
Structuralism*.[197] Assessing the historical impact of the movement that
had become identified with the anthropologist's name contributed to
its interment in the cemetery of ideas, and facilitated the process of his
emancipation from it, which was already under way in the media – as if
Lévi-Strauss no longer had anything to do with this outdated structuralism, now deemed too hard, too cold and too complicated. Adieu systems
and theories! Jean-Paul Aron had led the anti-structuralist charge in *Les
Modernes* in 1984. Yet, paradoxically – for he did not disavow any of his
earlier positions and indeed multiplied his declarations of faith in structuralism – Lévi-Strauss did not suffer from this sudden devaluation. Quite
the contrary: he was given credit for its legacy, while remaining unscathed
by its fall from grace.

Beyond Montaigne, the political importance of the book was under-
scored, as well as the anthropologist's new sensitivity to history (and to
the most painful history at that), which was proof that nothing was ever
forever settled for him. Roger-Pol Droit's bewildered review in *Le Monde*
gives a sense of the risks involved in each of the 'minor mythologiques':
'Building the edifice while destabilizing it, changing tactics and even strategies, playing a new game against oneself.'[198] This 'vital and subtly calibrated
transformation'[199] was proof that 'the anthropologist's structuralism had
never been more open'.[200] And, as Roger-Pol Droit majestically concluded:
'On the threshold of old age, the wise man has lost his wrinkles.'[201] In *Le
Monde des livres*, Marc Augé classified the book within the photography
category of the 'focus' section: 'The point for the anthropologist is to
adjust the focal distance and exposure time of the powerful, and perhaps
overly so, camera of structural analysis.'[202] Augé appreciated Lévi-Strauss's
self-imposed limitation of the cultural sphere – the Amerindian world –
and his refusal to indulge in any facile universal mythology.

However stirring that 'plea for the New World' may have been, it also irked some and provoked sharp dissent, this time clearly expressed. By contrast with the considerable praise, the Christian-inflected critique of Lévi-Straussian thought reminds us of its scandalous, indeed unacceptably provocative, trenchancy. As the review in *Famille chrétienne* put it: 'All this [the brio of the argument] should not be allowed to mask the most fundamental aspect of his thought which, while it claims to be driven by humanism, in fact, under the guise of human science, affirms relativism, negates human nature, rejects monotheism, and especially the Christian messianic message. One is left with a profound scepticism revealed most fully in the homage the book pays to Montaigne and confirmed by numerous nihilistic comments: "Human beings find sensory satisfaction living life as if it had a meaning, this even though intellectual honesty assures us that this is not so." Intellectual honesty perhaps, but the truth is that the human sciences cannot, by definition, replace philosophy or faith.'[203] Indeed, Lévi-Strauss had just granted an interview to *Le Figaro littéraire*, in which he calmly stated that 'nothing has been more dangerous for humanity than the monotheistic religions'.[204] Judaeo-Christianism in particular, he continued, had perhaps been necessary for rationalism and science to emerge, but this had come at a heavy cost: 'Intolerance, imperialism, the one true way', as the title of this *Figaro littéraire* interview highlighted . . .

On the far right, *Valeurs actuelles* published the only thoroughly negative review that rejected both the approach and the content of Lévi-Straussian anthropology, whose 'fussy jargon, difficult to read and understand', only made matters worse, and whose content comprised an 'accumulation of stories in which animals metamorphose in order to deceive humans, in which elements turn into living beings, women copulate with beasts, and the whole affair is made more complicated with mathematical-symbolic formulas and other psychoanalytic interpretations'.[205]

Finally, besides these two extreme enemies, part of the 'new philosophy' school of the 1980s, on a mission to critically reassess what it called '68 thought', was quite hostile to Lévi-Strauss's avowed anthropological relativism. Alain Finkielkraut, author of the 1987 philosophy bestseller *The Defeat of the Mind*, was on the front lines of this renewed combat by philosophy against the human sciences: a careful reader of Lévi-Strauss, he criticized anthropology for negating the superiority of the Western philosophical, scientific and artistic tradition, including in its fight against mass culture – a fight that Finkielkraut was quite certain was also Lévi-Strauss's, describing him as 'a romantic and desperate mind, whose very vocation originated in his sense of terror in the face of the standardization of the modern world'.[206] Finkielkraut could not abide the provocative assimilation of philosophy to a specific Greek particularism. He was light-years away from Lévi-Straussian thought. In the very manner in which he expressed his hostility, he revealed this thought's subversive power better than all the homages and apparently unanimous praise. Engaged in a head-on combat against the rise of mass culture, this champion of the free subject and the incommensurable value of high culture could only understand anthropology, whether in its structural version or otherwise, as an intimate enemy that introduced doubt and confusion by undermining the very terms of the confrontation: 'Because it does not believe in the primacy of artistic, literary and philosophical works over other so-called cultural practices, and because it does not make any room for the freedom of the individual, anthropology is unlikely to provide us with the means to stand up to this terrifying standardizing assault. [. . .] And thus, after pricking the conscience of Western civilization, cultural relativism ends up increasingly serving it as alibi',[207] continued Finkielkraut in an article entitled 'The Anxieties of an Anthropologist'.

The avatars of Claude Lévi-Strauss

In the autumn of 1989, two years prior to the publication of *The Story of Lynx*, Jean Guiart and Bernard Dupaigne organized an exhibition on Lévi-Strauss's various travels, from Mato Grosso to British Columbia:[208] 'Lévi-Strauss's Americas' was exhibited at the Musée de l'Homme, which, due to ongoing construction work, had failed to host his first exhibit in 1937, upon the young anthropologist's return from Brazil. This exhibit featured a Nambikwara encampment, Caduveo huts, Bororo funereal ornaments, penis sheaths, emblazoned objects, bows and arrows as well as masks, heraldic poles and animal statues. In the foyer of the Musée de l'Homme a beautiful fifty-foot long canoe dug out of a 700-year-old red cedar trunk – the 'Wave Eater' (*Lootas*) – crafted by Canadian artist Bill Reid. Eighteen Haida paddlers came from British Columbia and travelled up the Seine for six days, from Rouen to Paris, where Claude Lévi-Strauss, cloaked in a ritual red blanket, accompanied by his wife and Bill Reid, joined them for the last stage, which was broadcast on television, from the Palais de Chaillot to the Hôtel de Ville, where they were greeted by the mayor of Paris, Jacques Chirac.[209] Halfway, the canoe crossed the Pont des Arts bridge right in front of the Académie française, at which point Lévi-Strauss silently hailed the members of his other tribe. The scene is worth visualizing – and the press offered a partial account:[210] over the course of six days, the regular slapping of paddles, through the landscapes of Normandy and then Ile-de-France, French children lining the shores, their heads dressed in colourful feathers, shouting: 'The Indians are coming! The Indians are coming!' And then, finally, the incongruous arrival in the heart of a late twentieth-century Western city. The political power of this dramatization – in which Lévi-Strauss, immune to ridicule, graciously agreed to take part – rested on the slow descent into the past that it conjured up, symbolically inverting the terms of the 'discovery'. For, this time, it was the Indians who had come to meet the white man.

Had Lévi-Strauss gone native? As an anthropologist, he had studied the endlessly transformational logic of myths, and claimed to have written a new variant himself – his tetralogy. His life also seemed to have unfolded through a series of metamorphoses, as if it was itself playing out all possible variants: Lévi-Strauss the demiurge playing with the laws of humanity. On several occasions, he confessed he thought like a savage and, costumed in native gear, sitting among the paddlers, he was paying tribute to history; he had even turned into a mythical character, that of the bird-hunter or, perhaps, as Wendy Doniger astutely suggested, one from a Jivaro myth.

'Human life is but the exhaustion of a structure', wrote philosopher Patrice Maniglier.[211] In the 1980s, the avatars of Lévi-Strauss operated in full sight of the media and yet did not crystallize into any single majestic figure of the author. Lévi-Strauss appropriated the texture of myths, and enacted a myth of his own existence, in all its variants. Like his double, Don Quixote, his impossible twin: 'the sad-faced knight attempted to understand the world from books. He himself turned into a novel, i.e. into language', wrote Philippe Lançon in 1991.[212] With his emaciated face and fragile frame, the octogenarian Lévi-Strauss embodied a Don Quixote worn out by centuries of hard work. And at the same time, with his polemical energy, his unpredictable capacity to speak freely, and his keen interest in contemporary issues, he had returned to live in the present.[213]

21

Claude Lévi-Strauss,
Our Contemporary

Life is short; it is just a matter of a little patience.
Claude Lévi-Strauss, *The Story of Lynx*[1]

In 2005, Olivier Orban, Claude Lévi-Strauss's editor at Plon, sent him the draft of a new cover for *The Savage Mind*, which had been reprinted continuously since its original publication. Alas, in lieu of a *Viola tricolor* (the eponymous wild pansy), the proposed cover featured a common geranium! The very old man that the anthropologist had now become protested this 'gross blunder'[2] with all his force, as being detrimental to both science and art. The devil was in the details. In this case, what the mishap revealed was a (publishing) world in a hurry, in which Lévi-Strauss no longer cared to take part, even while he continued to observe the game and reflect on its rules.

The paradox of the first decade of the twenty-first century lay in that slight indecision that goes with very long lives: Had he died? Was he still alive? He was a national and international monument, an 'immortal' according to the Académie française, who was further immortalized in 2008 by the publication of his works in the prestigious 'Bibliothèque de la Pléiade' series, as well as an icon – a stamp featuring his face was issued in Belgium in the year 2000, alongside a series celebrating the seventy-nine individuals who had 'made' the previous century. All these insurance policies against mortality did not keep him from dying, in his one hundred and first year of existence, on 30 October 2009. But, in a way, the event of his death did not change anything to the ongoing rediscovery of his work, nor to the reassessment of his legacy, spared the fate of being embalmed or declared old hat. A rich issue of *Cahier de l'Herne* was published in 2004, a countless number of journals and intellectuals engaged in a reappraisal of structuralism, generating, both before and after his death, an impressive philosophical and anthropological literature.

Beginning in 2009, posthumous works were published: the 'Japanese' writings as well as a collection of essays, *We Are All Cannibals*, which extended and intensified this logic of recovery.[3] Translated into many languages – *Tristes Tropiques* came out in Turkish in 1999 and Arabic in 2001, *Race and History* in Lithuanian, Slovenian and Catalan in the 1990s – the works of Lévi-Strauss became classics, making a return in

The homepage of Google France on Claude Lévi-Strauss's 105th birthday,
28 November 2013.

our twenty-first century, disoriented by technological revolutions, economic crisis, political inertia and an overwhelming sense of emptiness.
He had been a very old man, a citizen of the world, who still spoke out at
times, to express in refined language, a language of yesteryear, incongruous and even subversive ideas – on cloning, artificial insemination, the
freedom to criticize religion, and to comment on the inanity of certain
contemporary art . . .

The enigma of Beauty

Lévi-Strauss often said it: far from being merely an object of scholarly
interest or even of some personal secret garden, art and the enigma of
beauty always played a crucial part in both his life and his thought. After
the publication of *The Way of the Masks* in 1976, he confided to Maurice
Olender in an interview emphasizing the importance of aesthetics in the
human sciences: 'In the end, it is aesthetic issues that appear to be key in
the human sciences, since – as strange as it may seem – when we have a
very strong aesthetic feeling – when we listen to music, or when we look at
a painting or a statue – we are incapable of accounting for that emotion.'[4]
This was already the theme of the last book he published during his lifetime, *Look, Listen, Read*: a final detour through his childhood residence on
rue Poussin, as well as an erudite introduction to the experience of beauty
in which theoretical passion combined with the anthropologist's ultrasen-
sitive faculties of hearing and sight to produce an aesthetics that broke
with the canons of the times – a 'savage aesthetics',[5] as Martin Rueff has

suggested, highlighting the extent to which this text was fully a part of the body of anthropological work. It was also in the name of his long familiarity with beauty in all its shapes and forms that Lévi-Strauss took part in the stormy debate that divided the community of French anthropologists in the mid-1990s: he was an unflagging supporter of the project to create a new art museum in Paris, a museum of so-called 'tribal art', later named the Musée du Quai Branly, which opened its doors in 2006.

The lost craft

We would do well to recall his childhood inclination for art, his regular visits to the Louvre with his father, as well as his passion for Wagnerian opera and then, as an adolescent of his times, the modernist shock when he discovered Debussy, Stravinsky, cubism and photography.[6] There was also his taste for the world and its objects – no matter how humble they might be in savage societies, they commanded respect. The cult of objects in Western societies was, for Lévi-Strauss, a surviving trace of the animist past.[7] A man of taste and an aesthete, the anthropologist was also an avid collector in New York, alongside André Breton and Max Ernst, in search of the 'wonder' of the day, of the 'precipitate of desire' as it appeared to the discerning eye, due to the singular imprint it left on

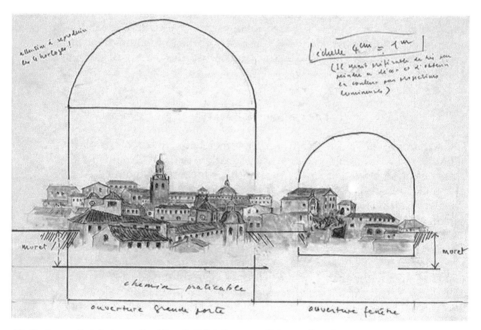

Preliminary sketch drawn by Claude Lévi-Strauss of the set for *L'Heure espagnole*, an opera by Maurice Ravel, produced in Grenoble by René Leibowitz in January 1970.

the retina. Engrossed in the world of myth, Lévi-Strauss worked like the painter Nicolas Poussin,[8] with three-dimensional models that expressed his perception of mythological variants. In the midst of completing his major works, in the late 1960s, he designed the sets for the opera *L'Heure espagnole* (music by Ravel) that was produced by René Leibowitz. This was a little-known episode in the life of Lévi-Strauss, the 'seeker of art'.[9]

Known as a conductor and musicologist, René Leibowitz was a disciple of Messiaen who performed the music of Schoenberg and the Viennese School. As he was dining one evening in 1969 at the Lévi-Strausses, with whom he was friends, he recounted the difficulties he was facing with the production of the opera, which had primarily to do with staging. A few days later, Lévi-Strauss sent him a diagram proposing a solution. At the time, the anthropologist was in the process of finishing *The Naked Man*, whose final pages offer a structural analysis of Ravel's *Boléro*, giving fresh dignity to this celebrated and mysterious piece. Leibowitz proposed that Lévi-Strauss go further and design the actual sets for his opera. *L'Heure espagnole* was performed at the Maison de la Culture in Grenoble in January 1970, with sets (and costumes) by Claude Lévi-Strauss – though the latter seems to have been disappointed with the workmanship. Everything was more beautiful in scale model. This was one of the precepts of Lévi-Straussian aesthetics. In any case, the experience gave the anthropologist a great deal of satisfaction and he said he was ready to change careers! He was again asked to work on a new opera composed by René Leibowitz, which was likely to be staged at the small Milan Scala by Luigi Rognoni, but the composer died that same year, in 1972, and Lévi-Strauss appears not to have pursued it any further.[10] The model for *L'Heure espagnole* was shown as part of an exhibition on Ravel at Lincoln Center in New York. An American journalist expressed his astonishment at discovering this new arrow in Lévi-Strauss's already ample professional quiver, always characterized by excellence . . . It was again displayed in public in 1975, alongside several watercolour sketches, as part of another Ravel exhibition held at the Bibliothèque nationale de France.

This passion for art gave rise to a way of thinking whose intellectual importance was made clear in *Look, Listen, Read*, but over the years it also prompted Lévi-Strauss to engage in polemics springing from his maverick aesthetic positions. In the 1980s and 1990s he was joined by a few art critics and curators, among them Jean Clair.[11]

Indeed, ever since the publication of his interviews with Georges Charbonnier in 1961, the public had been familiar with Lévi-Strauss's surprisingly anti-modern positions on art, which contrasted both with his own adolescent feelings and, even more so, with the alleged modernity of his scholarly research.[12] His positions were startling: one would have expected the structural anthropologist to have 'homologous' tastes for modern art, the Nouveau Roman in literature and serialism in music. Far from it! In 1966, he made sacrilegious comments about the idol of modernity (and of his own youth, in which he had been devoted to Picasso): 'This is a work which, rather than contributing an original message, gives itself over to a sort of breaking down of the code of painting, a second-hand interpretation, much more an admirable discourse on pictorial discourse than a discourse about the world.'[13] Even though he retained a personal admiration for Picasso, this captured the essence of his critique: in rejecting figuration, modern art had dissolved the object and recorded the inevitable loss of the world, itself prefiguring its own increasing disconnect from society, which ceased to understand its meaning. From then on, and Lévi-Strauss located this shift with the Impressionists in the late nineteenth century, modern art has been trapped in a dead-end discourse on itself. Hence the increasing obsolescence and futility of twentieth-century artistic modes and trends, the constant stream of movements, the frantic desire for novelty, the bombast of the avant-garde – which unfold under the impassive gaze of a public trained to wait in line for any great exhibition, moving seamlessly from one to another, immunized against the virus of art.[14]

All this had been said and written, but in the early 1980s, Lévi-Strauss had his aesthetic 'coming out' with the publication of an article entitled 'The Lost Craft' in the journal *Le Débat*.[15] He created a bit of an uproar, both because of the strong assertion of his figurative tastes – the Italian *Quattrocento*, the Flemish fifteenth century, Japanese art (up to the nineteenth century), and even certain artists deemed minor such as Joseph Vernet and his 'maritime' paintings – and his development of an anti-modern aesthetics resting on two principles: first, the primacy of nature and the object on the artist's subjective perception; second, art as knowledge, as a knowledge process.

From first principles, Lévi-Strauss concluded that one must 'submit to the intangible order of things'[16] and reject the extreme subjectivism encouraged by the doxa of modern art: 'The indulgence of man in his own perception runs counter to the deferential, if not humble, attitude before the infinite richness of the world.'[17] He therefore identified with a classical aesthetics that conceived of copies of nature as a second-order creation, the most ambitious creation to which man could possibly aspire. To recreate the 'physiognomy of things',[18] to reconstitute the real and thus reveal it to itself, to uncover its most profound laws – for this was the knowledge offered by art – the artist had to go through a long learning process which a pernicious illusion led him to believe could be replaced by the spontaneous creative gesture so dear to the Romantics: 'The subject was gradually rejected in favour of what is now called, in a revealingly understated way, the "work" of the artist; one would not be so bold as to speak of a "craft". Yet it is only if we persist in conceiving of art as a means of achieving knowledge – of a content that is outside the "work" of the artist – that an artisanal skill inherited from the old masters could regain its importance and maintain its place as an object of study and reflection.'[19]

Ultimately, Lévi-Strauss longed for a dilution of the boundary between the artisan and the artist, since this historical separation seemed to him to be part of the problem. 'Craft', 'artisan', 'process', 'formulas', 'manual exercise': the anthropologist did all he could to aggravate and irritate his contemporaries, artists and critics alike. His views on modern art and aesthetics triggered a storm of reactions, made all the more intense by the fact that the issue of *Le Débat* in which his article appeared also contained a reappraisal of nineteenth-century 'academic' art by Pierre Vaïsse and an article by Bruno Foucart on religious art. The issue as a whole – entitled 'Nineteenth-Century Art and Us' – could indeed be taken as a manifesto against the perversions of artistic modernity, announced in the introduction through a quote by one of its most brilliant representatives, of whom Lévi-Strauss was very fond: Baudelaire, who had hailed Manet as 'only the first in the decrepitude of [his] art'. The journal's editors introduced Lévi-Strauss's article as a 'brutal and provocative assessment whose significance made it seem to us worth sharing with our readers, among whom it will surely elicit thoughts and reactions'.[20]

Indeed, in the very next issue, one of the leading lights of contemporary art, Pierre Soulages, replied in an irate essay, 'The So-Called Lost Craft'.[21] Beyond the lampooning of ideologues who would claim to dictate art – a page-long text by Paulhan, 'When Artists Prove Philosophers Wrong',[22] was added to the response – better than artists themselves, Soulages's main objection to Lévi-Strauss's argument was that it infringed on the freedom of art and the painterly act. In a passionate yet conventional way, he paid tribute to spontaneity and creativity while indiscriminately mocking the 'sad craft', scholarly analyses, institutions and academies. The following issue featured other responses, from Pol Bury, Pierre Daix and Jacques Ellul, in a section now entitled 'Debating Modern Art'.[23] Lévi-Strauss was even likened to a Soviet Communist Party apparatchik! And there must have been some truth to it, since it was a former Stalinist who said so . . .[24]

This diatribe was in fact the first part of a text Lévi-Strauss had written a year earlier for the exhibition catalogue of Anita Albus, a young German painter he had met in 1978. Very isolated in the post-1968 artistic context, Albus was then working at the Bavarian State Library in Munich, rediscovering ancient techniques and producing paintings in miniature formats, most often botanical and zoological motifs. After reading some of Lévi-Strauss's work, notably his interviews with Georges Charbonnier, she sent him one of her books. Following an extremely laudatory response from the master, which seemed miraculous, in 1978 she decided to go to Paris to show him her originals. This encounter evolved into an admiring friendship: Lévi-Strauss found Albus's technique splendid, compared her to Dürer – including in her physical appearance, which reminded him of German Renaissance women – especially his watercolours, praised her 'unique gift for interiorizing nature',[25] 'as if through you we had become privy to a second creation, but one which reconstitutes under our dazzled eyes the supreme perfection of the first: that which must have been available in the Garden of Eden before the fall'.[26] He was moved by her 'exquisite kingfishers'[27] and her 'plump green caterpillar',[28] adoring in her art both the strict naturalism and the atmosphere of old lullabies, of 'miniature myths'.[29] Alongside this rhapsodizing were exchanges on Nicolas of Cusa, Van Eyck, Panofsky, Focillon, as well as on *mezzo tinto* and the techniques of ancient Japanese books, especially those of Utamaro. They regularly met in the country, where, a few years later, Anita Albus bought a house near Lignerolles. This is where she took the famous photograph of the anthropologist with a jackdaw bird on his shoulder. She described him as a profoundly silent man: 'We no longer have any notion of such silence.'[30] Meanwhile, Lévi-Strauss encouraged her to organize an exhibition and offered to write an introductory text, should such an exhibition take place, in which '[he] would expound [his] ideas on art in general, and on [hers] in particular'.[31] The exhibition did take place, in 1981 in Munich, and the catalogue opened with the promised essay, 'To a Young Painter'.[32]

An appreciation of the craft, the precious ancestral knowledge, the love of scale models and of *trompe-l'oeil*, their common passion for nature, the ghost of Dürer – their agreement was total, as if Anita Albus's art had come just in time to demonstrate a possible version of the Lévi-Straussian aesthetics. He spoke of her in terms of 'the almost miraculous rediscovery of a tradition with two aspects':[33] that of Flemish realism, on the one hand, and of Boschian allegory, on the other. He connected her art to everything he liked, the Flemish tradition of course, as well as medieval illuminations, and Utamaro. For the originality of Anita Albus's approach lay in drawing the conclusions of the state of affairs described by Lévi-Strauss in the first part of his text (the one published in *Le Débat*), 'return[ing] to the very origins' and 'taking things back to their beginnings',[34] and thus resuming the task. This reactionary project, in the original sense of the term, might have been conceivable at the artistic level, but not at the political or even technological levels. This was why Claude Lévi-Strauss's aesthetics took on a proselytizing, and even somewhat messianic tone, which was unusual for him. He was very keen to contribute to this new direction for the arts that he was calling for. And Anita Albus was, in his view, the best standard-bearer at that point in time.[35]

And yet, chronologically speaking, it was another artist who first caught his attention, and prompted him to write a short text on the occasion of her Paris exhibition in 1969. Sheila Hicks, famous in the United States and the world over, has long remained relatively unknown in France, as has textile art in general, which is not well represented in national collections. Claude Lévi-Strauss and his wife Monique, a renowned expert in this field, were admirers of Hicks's rich installations and of the reinventive power of her creations – building on centuries of ancestral knowledge that projected her imagination to ancient Peru, India and Persia. The combination of art and craft, the rigour of a unique know-how, the fragile bridge extended to remote civilizations, ours and those of others – what more to delight the eye of the Baudelairian dreamer? 'Her wall hangings, with their unfathomable shadows, have the lively and warm feel of fleeces. In their complex structures, they explore perspectives that could only be those of dream palaces; they offer the same smooth depth, radiance and mystery as a starlit sky. Nothing better than this art to provide both adornment and antidote to the functional and utilitarian architecture to which we are condemned.'[36] That was in 1969. Today, Sheila Hicks is being celebrated in France: her work is on exhibit in many places and is the subject of a major retrospective at the Centre Georges Pompidou in Paris in autumn 2018.

Look, Listen, Read: a savage aesthetics?

Look, Listen, Read – published in 1993 and announced as his final book by the author himself – immediately took on a testamentary aura. It followed in the polemical and theoretical wake of the decades-long intimate and demanding relationship that the anthropologist had to art, an art that was very dear to him. In one of the introductory essays in the Pléiade edition of Lévi-Strauss's collected works, Martin Rueff argues from the outset that the book's reception exemplified and perpetuated a 'misinterpretation'[37] regarding the importance of what he considers to be the central element of the structuralist edifice. It is this same sentiment that informs the reassessment of the 'minor Mythologiques' staged by a younger generation of scholars in this same Pléiade edition. It is indeed true that, in the summer of 1993, when the book was first published, the daily and weekly press rejoiced in this delightful 'caprice',[38] a re-engagement with a Western culture of which the anthropologist would not have been so fiercely critical if it had not also been so profoundly his own. The 'effervescent musings',[39] the 'rambling and clever digressions into the mysteries of creation',[40] the 'ballads of an explorer'[41] and the 'reflections of an ambling mind', these meditations on art explored the elegant environs of theory, the fancies of old age, the return of the prodigal son. What motivated such a caprice? 'I had had enough of mythology and I needed to cleanse my mind by looking at something radically different',[42] Claude Lévi-Strauss told Didier Éribon in *Le Nouvel Observateur*, adding that this enabled him to empty his drawers, since he had accumulated a lot of material on the subject over forty years.

The biographical dimension did not go unnoticed in the press. The book choreographed a resurgence of memories in two strata: childhood, of course; and, less known to the wider public, the surrealist friendships in New York, documented here through publication of the two texts Breton and Lévi-Strauss exchanged in March 1941, on the boat carrying them away from a France at war.[43] They discussed, as we will recall, the status and specificity of the art object, as well as the artist's intentionality, challenged by the automatic principle (automatic writing) that the surrealists had introduced in the early 1920s. A few reviewers, including Antoine de Gaudemar at *Libération*, broke with the cavalier and frivolous register (in part established by the author) and insisted on the both metaphysical and heuristic dimension of art for Lévi-Strauss.[44] Metaphysical first, 'for men and women differ, and even exist, only through their works';[45] they alone provide evidence that 'something actually happened during the course of time'.[46] And heuristic, for art did not only temper Claude Lévi-Strauss's fundamental pessimism by opposing 'something' to 'nothing', it also functioned for him, as we have seen, as a source of knowledge, a thought in the making, often anticipating the hypotheses of the human and natural sciences. Lévi-Strauss thus found in Delacroix's *Journal* formulations that anticipated Benoît Mandelbrot's fractal theory, which was only formalized in 1975.[47] While noting the extent to which this final book fleshed out the genealogy between structuralism and artists and aestheticians, recognized as structuralist precursors – Rameau, Poussin, Chabanon, etc.[48] – contemporary readers mostly insisted on the pleasures afforded by this celebration of old age, on the beauty of this 'French garden', offering, as if in passing, a few lessons in applied structuralism. All in all, Claude Lévi-Strauss was deemed to have aged very well . . .

Fifteen years after its publication, *Look, Listen, Read* was perceived in a radically different way – as a laboratory rather than an application of structuralism. It 'is not the book of an aesthete, however brilliant', Martin Rueff wrote in 2008; 'it is aesthetics that make it possible to confirm certain of the practices and hypotheses of structuralism, as well as to reconcile several understandings of symbolism and to solve a few of the major puzzles of structural anthropology.'[49] Rueff thus stages a reversal of the position of Lévi-Strauss's last book. It no longer holds a final, and in some sense marginal, position (as a magnificent sunset at the end of a tempestuous day), but a cardinal, and even inaugural, place: 'One would do well to make this last book the privileged point of entry into Lévi-Strauss's system',[50] Rueff continued, granting it a similar status to that of aesthetics in Kant's philosophy.

The title has a strange ring to it: three verbs, an angular quality, designed to capture not the authors and artists, but the aesthetic operation itself, which cannot be reduced to the creative process. A first chapter on the artist Nicolas Poussin, a second on the composer Rameau, and a third on the philosopher and art critic Denis Diderot – about whom Lévi-Strauss is not generous. Moving from a structural analysis of the works as variations (painting, music) to an analysis of the materials (sound and colour), Lévi-Strauss ends his quest for the intelligible structures of sensibility with a chapter on the traditional objects of primitive societies, in which form, material and meaning coalesce. The six parts of the book are shot through with connections and resonances, which create a kind of echo chamber. Thus, in its very structure, the book enacts one of its conclusions: what we find pleasurable is the perception of several orders of formal relationships. Lévi-Strauss had a knack for unearthing unknown figures, such as Chabanon and Louis Bertrand Castel, inventor of the ocular harpsichord in the late eighteenth century. He likes nothing more than to bring them together with optical neurologists to try to penetrate the mysteries of Rimbaud's poem 'Vowels' and to hear the sound of colours. In this deliberate chronological disorder, the Lévi-Straussian aesthetics flaunted its utter disregard for art history and even for any system of fine arts. To the distinctions drawn by the latter between noble and vulgar art, arts and crafts, he substituted what Martin Rueff has called a veritable 'savage aesthetics', whose revolutionary dimension lay in the fact that it does not mark the 'triumph of the sensing subject, for it is not subjective'.[51] It is an aesthetics without a subject for, according to Lévi-Strauss, subjectivity itself operates according to received constraints. It does not oppose 'natural beauty' to 'artistic beauty', since the latter only aspires to re-enact the operations of nature through different means.

In analysing the famous (at the time, in 1754) musical sequence in Rameau's opera *Castor et Pollux* – Fa, La, Mi – which connects the 'Que tout gémisse' chorus of the Spartans to the 'Tristes apprêts' lament of Télaïre's monologue, Lévi-Strauss was struck by the extraordinary polemic this tonal modulation triggered in the Enlightenment salons. Was it because the audiences of the time knew more about music than we do? Undoubtedly. Many were more than music aficionados; they were musicians themselves. The gap between the musical comprehension of audiences and the technical skill of musicians was much narrower than it is today, where the pleasure derived from music is of a lesser grade. Such a sentiment was already being expressed in the nineteenth century by Amaury-Duval, Ingres's favourite student, whom Lévi-Strauss quoted: 'Just as some appreciate an art form without prior study or even comparison, we loved all kinds of music indiscriminately, and went unashamedly from operetta to the andante of the *Symphony in A.*' The anthropologist added: 'It seems to me that the average opera lover or concert goer of today is not very different'.[52] In his view, art was quite obviously created by a small circle of people for a small circle of people. Small numbers were a condition for any true communication, which otherwise degenerated into a passive consumption. And the nature of our perception became degraded in corresponding measure.

Such praise for the small circle of initiates found its political and social echo in the anthropologist's view of the societies he studied – which were made up of groups of forty to two hundred people – as the optimal size for authentic social life and a democratic politics worthy of the name. This led him to adopt an objectively elitist position, making him very critical of all democratization policies, such as those being implemented by the French minister of culture, Jack Lang. In an interview he gave to *Paris-Match*, Lévi-Strauss was invited to react to the ministry's initiatives concerning rock music, cooking, comic books and fashion: 'I would be a poor anthropologist indeed if I ignored or disdained what is commonly referred to as "popular culture". However, I believe it retains its value only if, precisely, it remains popular, untamed or savage, if I may put it that way. I therefore find any intervention of public authorities in these domains to be misconceived.'[53] And yet, far from following the likes of Alain Finkielkraut, he rejected established cultural hierarchies – writing unforgettable pages on basketry – and offered an image of authentic art as it is experienced in primitive societies, where artists deemed untalented are readily put to death. A matter of life and death, art served as the mediator with the supernatural and a site 'out of this world',[54] a place which, according to Lévi-Strauss, we no longer even aspired to reach.

From one museum to another: the Musée de l'Homme to the Quai Branly

The transatlantic discussion of March 1941 between the young anthropologist and the 'Pope of Surrealism' – what is the difference between a document and a work of art? – resurfaced at the centre of the intense decade-long debate around the new museum project for a Musée des Arts Premiers, whose name was to change repeatedly over time. For this was not just another museum, nor merely one of President Chirac's major public works projects; this represented a thorough reorganization of the scientific field in anthropology. At every step, the team in charge of the project made sure to involve Lévi-Strauss in the technical and administrative operations that led up to the creation of the museum. Indeed, the intellectual imprimatur of such an authoritative figure was crucial in this particularly conflictual environment and context, involving large and highly sensitive issues regarding the use of artefacts that could be considered as despoiled objects, plundered from other civilizations by Westerners, who now refused to return them, and indeed presumed to exhibit them and narrate their significance.[55]

The project also reflected the changing status of museums in the formation of anthropological knowledge. Claude Lévi-Strauss belonged in part to the generation of the Musée de l'Homme, a museum of which he had even briefly been director alongside Paul Rivet. Yet in founding the LAS in the 1960s, he had also contributed to the shift of anthropological production from the museum to the academic research centre. He nonetheless remained throughout his life a fellow traveller and supporter of museums – of the Chaillot Museum of course, as well as of the American Museum of Natural History in New York, to which he paid enthusiastic tribute during his time there. Later, Lévi-Strauss became close to Georges-Henri Rivière – his son Matthieu's godfather – and participated with him in a process of museological rethinking that would inform the Musée des arts et traditions populaires, which opened in 1972 in a modern building located in the Bois de Boulogne, and whose cultural gallery was indeed largely inspired by the master of structural anthropology. Alongside Jean Cuisenier, who took over from Georges-Henri Rivière, he was often seen championing its exhibitions, explaining the institution's role and purpose on television. At that same time, in the 1970s, he visited the great Canadian museums and witnessed the first attempts at developing an approach to museology in collaboration with the indigenous communities themselves.

It was thus as a keen-eyed observer and lover of museums that he sided in favour of the new museum project. To understand this decisive commitment, which many anthropologists, colleagues and friends who were hostile to the plan took as a stab in the back,[56] we must break the 'charitable silence'[57] around the chronic crisis that had surrounded the Musée de l'Homme for a very long time. Indeed, the museum's glory days only lasted for a few years after its 1937 inauguration, magnified by the heroic struggle of some of its personnel against the Nazi occupation. But after 1950 and Lévi-Strauss's failed attempt to take over from Paul Rivet, the Musée de l'Homme had been reclaimed by physical anthropology and the tutelage of the Muséum national d'Histoire naturelle. It suffered from its disconnection from the university system, no longer able to award degrees, and teaching only supplemental courses for training in anthropology that was being done elsewhere. Finally, its 1971 administrative fragmentation into three laboratories had proved disastrous for its management, now in the hands of an openly 'conflictual triumvirate',[58] characterized by cheap shots, infighting and open hostilities between the directors. By the early 1990s, the Musée de l'Homme had become the sleeping beauty of the Palais de Chaillot. It had magnificent collections (most of which were stored out of sight of visitors), an illustrious history and a famous name, but it was now a shadow of its former self. Moreover, for lack of direction and resources, its research activity was practically nonexistent. With its somewhat dusty exhibits, it remained a site of historical interest and very dear to the older generation, who cherished it as the ancestral home of a now ragged French anthropology.[59]

What motivated Claude Lévi-Strauss in his support for the new museum project was both his conviction that the Musée de l'Homme would be impossible to renovate and his sense of the change in public perceptions of the Other. On 16 August 1996, he formally expressed his support in principle in a hand-written letter he sent from Lignerolles to the French president, Jacques Chirac: 'Please forgive this hand-written letter – the old typewriter I have in the country is decidedly no longer in working order. [. . .] The committee's summary proposal seems judicious. It takes into account the fact that the world has changed since the creation of the Musée de l'Homme. Ethnographic museums can no longer offer, as they could then, an authentic sense of life in societies far different from our own. With a few exceptions that will not last, these societies have indeed gradually been integrated into global political and economic dynamics. When I look back at the objects I collected on my fieldwork trips between 1935 and 1938 – and this applies also to all the others – I can see that their interest now lies chiefly in their documentary and, above all, aesthetic value. In their former capacity, they should belong to a laboratory or a research department; in their latter capacity, to a great museum of art and civilization, such as the one the Musées de France is now calling for. Indeed, by maintaining the physical anthropology and prehistory research centres in the same institution, the committee has preserved the spirit of the Musée de l'Homme, which was a milestone in the history of ideas, and one that the temporary exhibits thereby made possible will perpetuate and illustrate. [. . .] Finally, I am inclined to think that at a time when Europe is on everyone's mind, European anthropology would be better suited to the Musée des arts et traditions populaires.'[60]

The opening of a new museum had a domino effect on other institutions and their collections. Pending the opening of the Musée Branly, several of the more spectacular exotic art works were to be exhibited at the Sessions Pavilion of the Louvre, thus 'training the public's eye' to see them from an art history perspective. The collections of the Musée de l'Homme were to be combined with those of the Musée des arts Africains et Océaniens (MAO, the former Colonial Exposition Pavilion at Porte de Vincennes), while there was also talk of transferring those of the Musée des arts et traditions populaires. As for the two Musée de l'Homme research centres (other than anthropology), they were expected to remain and thrive within a renovated Palais de Chaillot. In 1997, Germain Viatte, in charge of steering the operation, invited Lévi-Strauss to join the scientific committee, comprising Claude-François Baudez, Georges Didi-Huberman, Jean Jamin, Jacques Le Goff, Michel Laclotte, Maurice Godelier, Pierre Rosenberg, Henry de Lumley (the director of the Musée national d'Histoire naturelle) and Jacques Kerchache, the project's developer, himself a tribal art dealer and personal friend of Jacques Chirac's. A few months later, Lévi-Strauss confessed to being somewhat disappointed by the status report Germain Viatte had sent him, finding that it had 'fallen short of the ideas that had inspired the initial project'. Resigned to the state of things, he added, however: 'As things stand, all we can hope for is an uneasy compromise. And if we settle for this, what was initially a great affair will have lost much of its interest.'[61] In 1999, Stéphane Martin, president of the public agency Museum of Arts and Civilizations, informed him of the progress of the construction work to prepare the rooms of the Louvre to exhibit non-Western art objects. On 15 April 2000, Lévi-Strauss was shown around the Sessions Pavilion for the first time, and he was not persuaded. He jotted down a few impressions for himself that he did not make public – impressions of a 'simulacrum': 'It is not – as is often claimed – the Louvre that has been adapted to host these objects. It is the objects, through the selection that was made and the way they are presented, that have been adapted to fit the Louvre. [. . .] We are offered a "Louvre style" exhibit, and the overall effect of this implicit reference, under such high ceilings and in such a monumental architecture, is that these objects that we thought we were glorifying ring hollow.'[62] In Lévi-Strauss's view, the Louvre annex, which officially opened in 2002, should not become permanent. Things picked up in the early 2000s, with the construction of the building on the Quai Branly designed by Jean Nouvel, and then the closure of the Musée de l'Homme and the Musée des Arts Africains et Océaniens, while their collections were being packed for the transfer. In 2005, the Musée des arts et traditions populaires closed and its collections were transferred to the new Marseille-based Musée des civilisations d'Europe et de Méditerranée (MuCEM), whose doors finally opened in 2013.

How did Lévi-Strauss feel about all this activity? Publicly, he simply reiterated his support in principle. In fact, as Jean Jamin confided, 'Lévi-Strauss consciously allowed them to exploit his name'[63] in support of a project that, in spite of it all, he considered to be a unique opportunity to revitalize anthropology – a financial, public and symbolic windfall. In addition, he did not feel the least ambivalence regarding the two main questions that hovered over the entire Quai Branly museum project. The first had to do with the perceived antagonism between the art object and the anthropological object, as the museum effected a kind of decontextualization and postmodern 'aestheticization' of the indigenous objects, which triggered the fury of anthropologists. The second revolved around postcolonial politics and the status of objects acquired in a colonial context.

Sociologists refer to the 'aestheticization' process as 'artification' – which refers to the metamorphosis experienced (or suffered) by objects from the moment they are exhibited in a museum. Philippe Descola has shown that the issue is broader and also concerns the 'cultures of the self' and not only the cultures of the Other. Indeed, most Louvre visitors also require explanations about the masterpieces of Western art, having lost, for instance, the codes necessary to understand a significant part of Christian art.[64] In this case as well, paintings and objects that originally belonged in churches, as part of their rituals and discourses, had undergone the same kind of transformation as a result of their transfer to a museum. In fact, as Descola has pointed out, there are now different ways, often coexisting in the same museum, to contextualize and restore the meaning of these otherwise silent objects – among which, strategies to present their scientific as well as their aesthetic dimensions, that should not be perceived as mutually exclusive. In this respect, the Musée du Quai Branly appears to have endorsed this diversification, and even provides, in Descola's view, a specifically French version of it, 'in its universalist and encyclopaedic conception of the cultures of the world, typical of the French tradition'.[65] Besides, as Lévi-Strauss showed in the final pages of *Look, Listen, Read*, primitive societies have also developed their own versions of the artist figure, their own strictly aesthetic functions and value judgements, though these may of course differ from the Western ones. This is the line of argument he adopted, reiterating it to his interviewers in 2006, one year before the museum's inauguration: 'Can we consider that an object retains its meaning once it is cut off from its ritual and community context? A mask that serves a ritual function is also a work of art. The aesthetic perspective does not trouble me in the least. The Louvre museum is first and foremost a museum of fine art – its perspective and role are aestheticizing. This has not prevented the development of art history and sociology, nor kept museum curators from producing very good scholarship. Arousing public interest and emotion through beautiful objects does not worry me at all. Aesthetics is one of the ways people discover the civilizations that produced them. And some will thus become historians, observers, and experts of these civilizations.'[66] The idea here is that the secularization of ancient ritual objects, turned into future works of art, is one of the possible means of reconnecting with what these objects bear witness to – an idea that harks back to his great-grandfather Isaac Strauss's effort to collect Judaic ritual objects.[67]

If the aesthetic recasting of these objects was not an issue for Lévi-Strauss, how did he feel about their colonial origins? In this regard, museum promoters insisted on their desire to break with the colonial style of 1930s French anthropology, i.e., that of the Musée de l'Homme. Yet, as Benoît de l'Estoile has rightly shown, there was in fact no rupture with this perspective: it was the Musée de l'Homme and MAO collections, most of which came from the French colonies, that constituted the permanent collection of the Musée Branly. The colonial link was all the more operative here for its being repressed, rather than exhibited, making impossible any shared history of the past of anthropological collecting between colonies and metropole. By contrast with several British museums, Branly did not opt for a postcolonial approach that explicitly owned up to its violent heritage – if only through its name.[68] Perhaps because it was only partly made up of Musée de l'Homme collections, perhaps also because the anthropologist Lévi-Strauss had brought his collections back to Paris from outside the French colonial context, the Quai Branly Museum had an easier time with this embarrassing continuity with the Chaillot museums. Similarly, the museum's much decried connections with the art market, prominently represented by Jacques Kerchache, could only appear shocking to those who denied the reality of a similar alliance between scholars and merchants in the days of the Trocadéro Musée d'Ethnographie, and then of the Musée de l'Homme.

Under these conditions, while there is little doubt that Lévi-Strauss, like his colleagues,[69] was annoyed by the pretentious phrases flickering in the darkened galleries of the Branly Museum, he did not protest against the extensive use that was made of his name – the great auditorium that hosted the lectures of the Université populaire, directed by Catherine Clément, was christened the 'Claude Lévi-Strauss Theatre'. This institution thus became, against all odds, a new Lévi-Straussian site, *par excellence*.

The anthropologist in the public sphere

Lévi-Strauss pointed out that, 'in a curious twist', the relationship between anthropologists and the peoples they study was now often reversed, with the latter calling upon the former to assist them in courts of law in order to claim ancestral rights to this or that territory or practice.[70] But in his home country as well, anthropologists could be of use. Throughout his life, Claude Lévi-Strauss wavered between the temptation of silence and a firm opposition to applied science, until he gradually came to represent, both in his restraint and in his speeches, another kind of relationship to the political. His strategy, in line with the 'view from afar' stance, was to actively play on the phase difference, the gap, at both the professional (that of the anthropologist) and the personal (that of Lévi-Strauss himself) levels, that separated him from the contemporary world in order to position himself at the core of the most trenchant and burning questions of the day.

This apparent paradox was at work in a body of 'intervention texts' that were posthumously published in French in 2013: the collection of articles that Lévi-Strauss had written for the great Italian daily *La Repubblica* between 1989 and 2000, collected under the title of one of the essays, *We Are All Cannibals*.[71] To which could be added the three talks he gave in Tokyo as part of the Ishizaka Lectures, 'Anthropology Confronts the Problems of the Modern World', published in 2011.[72] It is worth noting that all these texts, which 'confronted' the most pressing contemporary issues – artificial insemination, new forms of parenthood and filiation, epidemic diseases, relationships to animals, etc. – were first delivered or published outside France, as though expatriation allowed him to speak more freely. It was thus only ten or sometimes twenty years later that the wider French public, as well as many of the anthropologist's friends, discovered his bracing analyses. They revealed Claude Lévi-Strauss's remarkable precociousness and audacity, his 'openness to legal, social and other solutions', an attitude that, according to Maurice Godelier, 'certain of his disciples had not adopted at the time'.[73]

From the beyond, so to speak, and in a highly conflictual context (regarding the issues raised, for instance, by the Taubira Law of 17 May

2013 that legalized marriage between same-sex couples), Lévi-Strauss gave voice to a perspective that was both calming and radical, scandalously relativist in a way that nobody anymore dared to be.

Science, politics, expertise

On the occasion of Lady Diana's death in 1997, and the critical speech delivered by her brother Earl Spencer at the princess's funeral, Lévi-Strauss offered a short lesson in kinship anthropology that, in the context of the 1990s, went quite far: 'Contrary to what has long been believed, consanguinity is not the foundation of the family.'[74] Kinship was made of relations of consanguinity (brother/sister), but also of alliance (husband/wife) and filiation (parent/child). While pleading for an enlightened relativism regarding conceptions of the family, Lévi-Strauss was defining his own position as an anthropologist in the *polis*: this did not consist in making sense of 'vestiges' of the past but, rather, in isolating the archaic dimensions of the present, in this case the resuscitation of an ancient form of kinship. 'The faraway illuminates the near, but the near can also illuminate the faraway.'[75] This capturing of the *arche* of the present defined Claude Lévi-Strauss's way of being contemporary.

Indeed, anthropologists were the only ones who were not caught off guard by the new realities of artificial procreation enabled by biological science. Why was that? Because, answered Lévi-Strauss, the peoples studied by anthropologists very often distinguished between biological paternity and social paternity, and displayed considerable inventiveness in imagining kinship arrangements; finally, procreation and filiation were considered distinct relationships, and many of these societies did not seek any truth in procreation, as opposed to ours which is obsessed by it.[76]

His thoroughgoing relativism led him to take what might appear rather bold positions. He thus commented on the role of anthropologists in the trials against African immigrants who had had ritual excisions performed on their female children. He brushed off the argument according to which excision eliminates all female sexual pleasure, 'which our societies have made a new article in the declaration of human rights', by declaring that 'we would do better to admit that we know nothing about it . . . .'[77] Furthermore, female excision did not appear to him as substantially different from male circumcision. Both were attacks on the physical integrity of the child designed to mark his/her cultural difference and erase all trace of masculinity in the female body (clitoris) and of femininity in the male body (foreskin). If Western societies were disturbed by one ritual and not the other, it was only, according to Lévi-Strauss, because ambient Judaeo-Christian culture had suppressed any sense of shock from male circumcision. Indeed, 'there is no common measure by which to judge systems of beliefs or, a fortiori, to condemn one or another of them, unless we claim – but on what basis? – that only one (ours, of course) conveys universal values and must be imposed on all.'[78] The lack of a common measure by which to judge cultures did not, however, preclude ethical choices. If the anthropologist called upon to testify in court speaks in support of a relativist perspective that contributes to a better understanding of these customs, including those that might appear barbaric to us, it was perfectly legitimate for judges to take other considerations into account: 'An ethical choice, with the future of the host country's culture hanging in the balance, can be made only between two possibilities: either proclaim that anything that can be justified on the basis of custom is permitted everywhere; or send back to their own country those who – as is their right – intend to remain faithful to their practices even if, on whatever grounds, they gravely offend the sensitivities of their hosts.'[79]

Yet it is not up to the expert to make this choice: 'Social choices are not up to the expert as such, but – and he is one himself – to citizens.'[80] This fundamental assertion by Claude Lévi-Strauss serves as the opening line to a collective book, *Au-delà du Pacs*, that provides a critical analysis of the knowledge mobilized during the debates on the creation of non-marriage civil unions (*Pacte Civil de Solidarité*, or Pacs) open to same-sex couples in the 1990s, and more generally, of the challenges it posed to the now all-powerful figure of the expert that claimed to provide grounds based on reason and truth for choices that were in fact political and social. Lévi-Strauss always guarded against any such confusion of registers, including by keeping quiet. And yet, as the sociologist Éric Fassin has pointed out, Lévi-Strauss and *The Elementary Structures of Kinship* were invoked at the time by both Elisabeth Guigou, the socialist minister of justice, and Renaud Dutreil, a conservative MP opposed to the new bill.[81] The 'experts' who were consulted, such as sociologist Irène Théry, who wrote a report,[82] also made abundant use of a form of applied anthropology considered to provide our disoriented societies with a 'symbolic order', a kind of immemorial truth anchoring society in the family, and the family in sexual difference. In Éric Fassin's view, the reason anthropology had such an impact on these Pacs debates – which resurfaced, almost unchanged, ten years later – was that homophobia had remained a taboo in public discourse. The political risk in terms of damage to reputation was too high, hence strategies to work around the homophobic taboo. Failing any possible straightforward expression of hostility, same-sex parenting was rendered impossible, by making it unthinkable: 'No society allows for homosexual parenthood',[83] as the headline of a major Catholic newspaper read in 1998.

Neither guru nor expert, Claude Lévi-Strauss rejected all predetermined uses of the social sciences – even if this entailed the risk of a 'silence of science'.[84] In fact, the scholar did not stay silent, but nor did he respond on demand, especially when he felt this meant he was walking into a minefield, and that his explanations were sure to be misunderstood. He would thus choose the time and place – such as his articles for *La Repubblica*, or when he was awarded prizes and distinctions, which often served as occasions for profoundly political speeches. In the Netherlands in 1973, where he was awarded the Erasmus Prize before an assembly of crowned heads, he endeavoured to raise awareness among his audience regarding the dangers of deteriorating living environments, 'diminished' by overexploitation. Among many other distinctions, he was later awarded the Meister Eckhart Prize at the German embassy in 2003, and the 17th Catalonia International Prize of the Government of Catalonia in 2005. Each time, he spoke openly, resorting to a certain metaphorical violence but never adopting the apocalyptic tone that had become fashionable at the turn of the millennium. A kind of moral claustrophobia can be heard in his speeches, in which a vigorous pedagogical tone replaced the sumptuous lament that had characterized his mature years. The final incarnation of Lévi-Strauss was bracing rather than melancholic.

Cannibals all!

The fast-changing French society of the 1990s and 2000s was a propitious time for the intervention of anthropologists, not only because of the 'return' of ancient vestiges, but also because there were thresholds, and more than one might think, where ancient and hypertechnical societies met. 'The border appears less sharp than one would like to imagine',[85] explained Lévi-Strauss. In these circumstances, the title of the collection of articles from *La Repubblica* – *We Are All Cannibals* – expresses an essential characteristic of Lévi-Straussian politics: beyond the mere parallel between 'them' and 'us', it entailed a veritable recasting of our times as savage, not to decry their barbarity – which is what the traditional left would have done – but to draw inspiration from ancient and exotic societies that may have confronted the same issues and found solutions that provide precious 'food for thought'. Lévi-Strauss gave several examples taken from our very contemporary daily lives. He thus delivered a lesson in liberalism and prudence (especially for lawmakers, for whom he encouraged restraint), demystifying our modern fetishes (science, progress) and stripping away the veils of modernity (the barbarity of our meat industry and our agribusiness). This move to universalize the savage within us – rather than to exclude it as subhuman – advanced a project that in part intersected with that of Bruno Latour: to become again the nonmoderns that we have never ceased to be.[86] For Lévi-Strauss as well as for Latour, this watchword was designed to bridge the double great divide on which modernity is founded: between them and us, and between nature and society.

In 1993, the news was of a new disease called Creutzfeldt–Jacob, which had surfaced following the injection of patients with hormones extracted from human pituitary glands or from grafts of *dura mater*, a kind of membrane around the human brain. In 1996, 'mad cows' were making headlines. It was discovered that a disease afflicting cows in several European countries, of the same family as Creutzfeldt-Jacob, had been contracted through bone meal made from cattle and then fed to the livestock. Lévi-Strauss read both these artefacts in terms of an 'expanded cannibalism'.[87] In the one case, the medical injection was identified with practices of consumption of human products; in the other, cows had been turned into cannibals by man, and the horror the idea inspired only went to show the profound link between this expanded cannibalism and the eating of meat.

Beyond the intention to be provocative (which, of course, also played a role with Lévi-Strauss), his position followed from his original perspective on contemporary social events: 'Let us reverse the tendency',[88] he declared. The point was not to proscribe or denounce cannibalism, but quite the opposite: to highlight its commonplace character, to universalize it. First, because cannibalism was in the end an ethnocentric category that 'exists only in the eyes of the societies that proscribe it'.[89] For others, there was simply a wide range of practices – involving exocannibalism (eating one's enemies), or endocannibalism (eating a member of one's tribe or family) – and variants – consumption in small or large quantities, in fresh, putrefied or mummified states, of raw, cooked or charred flesh, etc. Cannibalism could be intended as food (out of taste), or as a political (punishment, vengeance), magical, ritual or therapeutic act. The latter function, continued Lévi-Strauss, came close to our own practice of organ transplants. The iconoclastic dimension of the celebrated scholar's analysis, which basically equated a custom perceived as barbaric with a practice founded on science, is obviously very much part of the point. 'The practice always entails intentionally introducing into the bodies of human beings parts or substances from other human bodies. The notion of cannibalism, thus exorcised, will now appear rather commonplace. Jean-Jacques Rousseau saw the origin of social life in the sentiment that impels us to identify with others. And after all, the most simple means to identify others with oneself is to eat them.'[90]

Expanded cannibalism allowed Lévi-Strauss to represent our carnivorous practices as barbaric madness and to evoke, with all the aversion of a highly sensitive fellow, the horror of butcher shop windows in which bloody cuts are displayed: 'A day may come when the idea that human beings in the past raised and slaughtered living things for food and complacently displayed slabs of their flesh in shop windows will inspire the same revulsion as what travellers in the sixteenth and seventeenth centuries felt about the cannibal meals of American, Oceanian or African indigenous peoples.'[91] Was Lévi-Strauss advocating that we all become vegetarians, then? It is unquestionable that, in his view, the meat-based diet was a luxury that neither animals nor men would soon be able to afford. Yet in his own daily life, the anthropologist did not renounce meat. A gourmand, he enjoyed it prepared in any fashion, though always in small quantities.[92] In fact, he did not advocate renouncing meat altogether. Adopting a prophetic turn, which was rare in his writings, he conjured up a future human race for whom eating meat would become a rarefied, costly and almost risky practice. 'Meat will appear on the menu only under extraordinary circumstances. It will be consumed with the same mix of pious reverence and anxiety that, according to ancient travellers, accompanied the cannibal meals of certain peoples. In both cases, it is a matter of communing with ancestors and of incorporating into ourselves – at our own risk and peril – the dangerous substance of living beings that were or have become enemies.'[93] So, eating the flesh of living beings, yes, but with all the respect that is their due – this was the ultimate lesson in wisdom to be drawn from mad cows.

The second major theme broached in the *La Repubblica* articles was the new forms of parenthood and filiation enabled by assisted reproduction technologies, which had proliferated extravagant scenarios in the face of which both law and morality found themselves at something of a loss. In a 1989 article entitled 'Il segreto delle donne', Lévi-Strauss raised the question: 'How should a court decide in a case where the surrogate mother delivers a disabled child, and the couple that employed her services rejects it?'[94] This dilemma did indeed arise in the summer of 2014, when the Australian parents who had financed a surrogacy refused to take a Down's Syndrome baby that the Thai surrogate mother had delivered.[95] The substance of this article was already developed in the second Japanese lecture, delivered in 1986, part of which explicitly addressed questions of assisted reproduction: artificial insemination, egg donation, the use of surrogate mothers paid and unpaid, the freezing of embryos, *in vitro* fertilization with sperm provided by the husband or by another man and with an egg from the wife or from another woman. 'Depending on the case, a child born of such procedures may have one father and one mother as usual, or one mother and two fathers, two mothers and one father, two mothers and two fathers, three mothers and one father, or even three mothers and two fathers, if the sperm donor is not the father and if three women participate: the one donating an egg, the one providing her uterus, and the one who will be the child's legal mother.'[96] There was nothing here to bemuse the anthropologist. He had much to say on each of these issues, since the societies he studied, though unacquainted with scientific reproductive technologies, had imagined 'metaphorical equivalents'[97] to solve the same problems, especially sterility.

For example, the Samo of Burkina Faso had invented the equivalent of insemination with donor sperm, as Françoise Héritier's work had shown: any girl who was to be married first had to have sexual relations with a lover who would impregnate her. She then brought to her new husband the child she had borne, who would be considered the firstborn of the marital union.

Among other African populations, a husband who had been abandoned by one or more of his wives retained a right of paternity over future children. 'He need only have the first postpartum sexual relations with his former wife after she has become a mother. That act determines who will be the legal father of the next child. A man married to an infertile woman may thus arrange for a fertile woman to name him the father, gratis or in exchange for payment.'[98] Other African examples included the Nuer of Sudan, who 'make an infertile woman the equivalent of a man; in her capacity as "paternal uncle", she therefore receives the livestock representing the "bride price" paid for the marriage of her nieces, and she uses it to purchase a wife who will provide her with children thanks to the remunerated services of a man, often a stranger. Among the Yoruba of Nigeria as well, rich women can acquire wives, whom they impel to pair off with men. When the children are born, the woman, the legal "husband", claims them, and the biological parents must pay her handsomely in order to keep them.'[99] In addition to these African models, regularly cited by anthropologists, Lévi-Strauss offered that of the Levirate, in force among the ancient Hebrews, which allowed and at times required that a younger brother sire a child in the name of his deceased brother. 'This is the equivalent of *post mortem* insemination.'[100]

In our societies, as the separation between biological reproduction and social filiation becomes increasingly clear, it is paradoxically the biological relationship that has taken increasing precedence in law, as shown by the 1972 French law allowing paternity suits to go forward, whereas, since the Napoleonic code, French law had considered the mother's husband to be the child's legal father. Should the conclusion then be that our societies ought to model themselves on these examples from tribal societies? Must all desires be considered legitimate? Far from dispensing positive solutions, at this stage Lévi-Strauss confined himself to illustrating the broad range of possible solutions. And even in our societies, sperm donation, if not the renting of uteruses, was not unknown before the advent of modern technologies, but, as Lévi-Strauss mischievously puts it, 'that type of service was rendered without a fuss and, as it were, "close to home"'.[101] Suffice it to say that, if he did not consider that 'anything' should be possible – since the possible social combinations were not unlimited – the anthropologist revealed himself to be quite open to all the 'arrangements' that other societies, before ours, had experimented with and found themselves none the worse for it. He thus concludes: 'The wise course, no doubt, is to trust that the internal logic of every society's institutions and system of values will create viable family structures and will eliminate those that produce contradictions. Only time will tell what will be accepted or rejected in the long run by the collective consciousness.'[102]

The eagerness of legislators and moralists to proscribe was dismissed as irrelevant. Lévi-Strauss thus distanced himself from the part of the discipline instrumentalized by those whom Jeanne Favret-Saada has called the 'conservative left'[103] during the Pacs debates, i.e., part of the elite, sociologists, experts, jurists, journalists and political advisers who produced a 'Lacanized' version of Lévi-Strauss's thought. The latter sought to demonstrate that the heterosexual symbolic order necessarily formed the foundation of all societies and that it would be inescapably destroyed by Pacs. Lévi-Strauss never adhered to that credo. As early as 1956, in an article entitled simply 'The Family',[104] he constantly warned against approaching with a 'dogmatic spirit' an object, the family, which, whenever one believed one had grasped it, slipped through one's fingers. We must understand, he added, that 'the conjugal family does not emerge from a universal necessity: a society can conceivably exist and be maintained without it'.[105] In the 1980s and 1990s, he remained just as much of a free spirit, but refrained from making his opinions public in France. The writings expressing this position – which he was, in vain, pressed to make public at the time – were only discovered in France after his death. The irony of the story is that this deferred intervention placed Lévi-Strauss's reflections right at the heart of a burning debate, since, on this question, history had been stuck in an eddy for more than twenty years.

These interventions on the part of the anthropologist in the (Italian) public sphere are strikingly fresh in their tone and casual heterodoxy. An iconoclasm that also shone through when Lévi-Strauss asked: why do primitive societies resist 'development'?[106] Because they choose unity over internal conflict; because they reject the spirit of competition and majority rule in favour of unanimity; and because they are loath to take the path of historical change – which does not mean they do not change. He wondered aloud in *La Repubblica* in October 1990: 'Is There Only One Type of Development?' He went on to inform his readers of recent revisions made to our knowledge of prehistory regarding the birth of agriculture. Far from allowing for more mouths to be fed, it seems that agriculture was the result of demographic pressures that precipitated the domestication of plants and animals. Before that, peoples who did not practise agriculture led comfortable lives – hunting and gathering provided for a well-balanced diet, so long as there was effective demographic control to allow for the reproduction of a coherent and viable set of small groups. Thus, agriculture might in fact have been neither desirable nor necessary. If it provided for more food over a given time and space, it also required much more work and toil. 'Seen from a different perspective, agriculture represented a regression', concludes Lévi-Strauss.[107]

Twenty years before Jared Diamond wondered, in 2012, 'what can we learn from traditional societies?',[108] Lévi-Strauss initiated the debate by challenging the assumptions of contemporary *homo economicus*. Economic anthropology has shown that not all human activities relate to production and that economic activity itself is not limited to rational calculation. Claude Lévi-Strauss calmly deflated the often implicit biases of modern economic science – which, he says, is no science at all, for, if it was, it would allow us to anticipate and intervene in market societies, which clearly it does not! Behind a 'screen of supposed rationality',[109] economic science is a fiction that might be valid in its own models but is in no position to claim universal authority: 'Anthropology reminds the economist, in case he should forget, that human beings are not motivated purely and simply to always produce more.'[110]

A structural politics?

This posthumous Lévi-Strauss that we are now discovering, sorting through some of the more impassioned issues of our modernity, demonstrates the 'demanding ethics of [anthropological] knowledge'[111] at the root of an authentic structuralist politics.

A political Lévi-Strauss? The assertion comes as a surprise given the decades of depoliticizing interpretations of both his thought and his life. From Claude Lefort to Pierre Clastres and Pierre Bourdieu, many have accused him of conceiving of social life, following in Marcel Mauss's footsteps, as a system of reciprocity and a grammar of signs, ignoring questions of domination and violence. Philosopher Patrice Maniglier, and an entire generation of scholars who have returned to the 1960s and the history of structuralism,[112] have recently pushed back against these conceptions, which they attribute, above all, to a misconception of what sign systems actually entail.[113] Long holding Lévi-Strauss to be a pessimist, which he was, critics have failed to see that the 'discovery of meaninglessness does not rule out engagement with the world'[114] or the search for meaning. As Lévi-Strauss reiterated at the end of *The Naked Man*, despite this awareness of his own finitude, 'man has to live and struggle, think, believe, and above all preserve his courage'.[115]

Just as an awareness of the vanity of meaning did not put an end to the quest for understanding, so an awareness of one's finite condition did not discourage action. On the contrary, both spawned a renewal of morality and politics founded on the beauty of the world and on its nullity, notions which are all over Lévi-Strauss's writings. Patrice Maniglier has rightly insisted on the importance of a text Lévi-Strauss wrote in 1976 as a contribution to the reflections of the Rights Committee of the French National Assembly.[116] The text offered a description of this renewal in broad strokes: in founding the value of all things – be they animal or vegetable, a human individual, a monument, a landscape, an object, etc. – on their 'irreplaceability', it argued that 'value does not lie in a thing's conformity to an ideal but in the thing itself, in its ability to develop its own irreducible singularity, in what Spinoza would have called its *"potentia"*.'[117]

This is precisely where structural politics and savage aesthetics meet: in the celebration of things themselves, outside the subject's use and perception of them, in the reconciliation of morals and aesthetics, and of man with nature. Lévi-Strauss thus invites us to find 'in the beauty of this world [. . .] and not in the ideas we entertain of it, the sole source of all claims to the subject's responsibility: the respect due to human beings is then but one illustration of the respect owed to all things mortal'.[118] This arrangement, or better still, this settlement with reality, and not just its condemnation or even critique, is one of the legacies of structural anthropology to help guide us out of the confusions of this early twenty-first century, exposed to ever more intense contradictions, impossible choices, and a profound inertia concealed behind a pathological acceleration of temporal and social rhythms.

Ageing, dying, rebirth

The shattered hologram

For Claude Lévi-Strauss, old age (ninety years old in 1998) and then very old age (one hundred years old in 2008) involved, as Montaigne had taught him, looking death in the face, preparing for it and, at the same time, not thinking too much about it, seeing it as an end but not an objective: 'I want death to find me planting my cabbages.'[119] Failing that, the anthropologist devoted his time to seasonal occupations, to putting his affairs in order, sorting through his papers and deciding, pressed by his wife Monique, which of the three thousand photographic negatives from his Brazilian expeditions to print. She felt that the photographs would have to be captioned and that only her husband was in a position to do so. Initially reluctant, he ultimately relented.[120] Monique Lévi-Strauss took charge of printing these negatives in the small darkroom that their son Matthieu had set up in the apartment when he still lived there. It should be noted that these negatives had in fact already been printed by American intelligence services at the beginning of the Second World War, since the United States was about to enter the conflict and sought to collect strategic photographic documentation. Indeed, back then, Lévi-Strauss considered these photographs so important that he took the negatives with him to New York in 1941, despite their weight and bulk. He later claimed that he was no longer interested in photography, yet he would not entrust the Brazilian negatives to anyone – which was why his wife and son were enrolled in the *Saudades* project.[121]

In the autumn of 1994, fifty-five years after Claude Lévi-Strauss's return from Brazil, *Saudades do Brasil* was first published by Plon.[122] A 'coffee table book' comprising roughly 200 photographs selected from among the 3,000 snapshots, it provided a photographic narrative of the 1930s expeditions that gave body and texture to the often-invoked Bororo, Caduveo and Nambikwara peoples, now immortalized in the annals of anthropological science. We also get glimpses of the urban construction site that was the city of São Paulo, as well as of several sleepy towns in the Brazilian hinterland. Although he had been fascinated by photography in his youth, Lévi-Strauss now confessed to harbouring mixed feelings about this art he considered to be quite minor. He was not even persuaded by its virtues as documentary: to the instant flash of photography, he claimed to prefer the sustained attention required for drawings and sketches. And yet, all the critics enthusiastically hailed this 'version of *Tristes Tropiques* in negative form'.[123] Between the two versions, the anthropologist moved from melancholy to nostalgia, made all the more poignant by the photographic image's power of Proustian resurrection. The young bearded man standing at the margins of the camp was 'the Lévi-Strauss of the Brazilian *sertão*', as Proust would have spoken of 'the Albertine of Balbec'. In the eyes of Emmanuel Desveaux, an Americanist anthropologist and disciple of Lévi-Strauss at the time, *Saudades* was thus also a salute from the old man to the budding anthropologist of the 1930s that he no longer was – a 'photographic epitaph'[124] that echoed the 'poetic epitaphs' of the Renaissance. In his way, he was preparing for the 'upcoming caesura, which he awaited with serenity'.[125] If this tombstone closed the Americanist cycle through a return to visual roots, the book also threw up a few fragile bridges fleetingly conjured up by the photographs: some feature Lévi-Strauss's father, who initiated his son into photography, silhouetted against the São Paulo house; and it was Matthieu, one of Lévi-Strauss's sons, who helped select and develop the 200 photographs in the book. Between father and son, a silver halide thread connected three generations of Lévi-Strausses via Brazil.

In 1994 and 1995, two children were born to Matthieu and Catherine Lévi-Strauss: Thomas and Julie. They arrived late in the life of their

Claude Lévi-Strauss's Leica, a fetish object from his Brazilian expeditions.

grandfather, who could nonetheless derive from them a desire to live that became, with each passing day, increasingly complicated. It is yet another photograph that provides an iconic record of this layered generational temporality: it features Lévi-Strauss in his armchair at Lignerolles, attentive to his two grandchildren, with his granddaughter on his lap and his grandson on Monique's, the whole scene itself crowned by a large painting (painted by his father) of him, as a child, in his grandmother's lap.

Death was awaited first with serenity, then with some impatience – in any case, without any qualms. Dust to dust. In the meantime, one had to live on, or at least survive. This deferment that characterizes all lives beyond a certain age was to be a long one for Lévi-Strauss. Between 1994, when *Saudades* was published, and his death in 2009, no fewer than fifteen years went by. Each of his rare public speeches, in the 2000s, further highlighted the incongruity, the imposture even, of this very long life: 'As years pile up, I feel each day that I am usurping the time that remains for me to live and that nothing justifies anymore the place I still occupy on this earth.'[126] After the 1990s, he made it to the year 2000: 'For more mundane reasons', he wrote to Isac Chiva, '(age first among them), I did not think I would reach the year 2000 either. I do not attach any particular significance to this, certain as I am to have lived in my early childhood still in the nineteenth century; the numbers are meaningless . . . .'[127] If he refused to be of the twenty-first century, he had indeed, after all, cultivated a certain distance from his present for a long time. And yet, he remained religiously attuned to the news, an omnivorous reader, who skimmed through the many books he was sent, and also enjoyed some, especially those of Michel Houellebecq. At the cinema, to which he seldom went, he had been following Éric Rohmer from the beginning. Lévi-Strauss had even been tempted to have him join the Académie française, but after testing the waters with a few of his colleagues, he understood it would be a fiasco, and renounced the idea.[128] Many of his former interests remained keen ones. Time was running short, and yet he had never had as much time on his hands: he indulged in the guilty pleasure of rereading books – *Julie, or the New Heloise* 'from cover to cover',[129] as well as faithful old Balzac, and the great memoir writers. People still came to see him, and he was solicited; he pleaded with them to 'have mercy on the old folks!'[130] The letters from the 2000s read like a long litany of invitations declined; ceremonies were an ordeal for him. As were some visits: French President Nicolas Sarkozy invited himself to Lévi-Strauss's house for a brief and compulsory visit, in honour of his hundredth birthday, which was also celebrated at the Musée du Quai Branly in November 2008.[131] In October 2007, he fell and broke his femur. From that moment on, he spent most of his time bound to his wheelchair and secluded in his apartment, with no desire to be seen in such a sorry state.

He would like to have been spared this new stage of decline. And yet it was precisely this process that he had beautifully described in January 1999, on the occasion of a celebration at the Collège de France of a special issue of the journal *Critique* edited by Marc Augé, dedicated to his work.[132] Speaking in front of his colleagues and friends, he delivered, without notes, yet another tribute to Montaigne: 'Montaigne says old age diminishes us each day and cuts into us in such a way that, when death does occur, it only takes away a quarter of a man or half a man. Montaigne died at the age of fifty-nine, and he probably had no notion of the extreme old age in which I find myself today. At this great age that I never imagined reaching, and which is one of the most curious surprises of my life, I feel like a shattered hologram. This hologram no longer exists in its entirety and yet, as in any hologram, each of the remaining parts has kept an image and a representation of the whole. I thus feel today there is a real me, who is but a quarter or half of a man, and a virtual me, who still keeps alive an idea of the whole. The virtual me develops a book project, begins organizing its chapters, and tells the real me: "It is your job to continue." And the real me, who cannot do it any longer, tells the virtual me: "It is your job, only you can see the totality." My life now unfolds in this very strange dialogue.'[133]

The dialogue ended on 30 October 2009. 'I am surviving myself',[134] he would say in dark jest. After surviving himself even longer than others, he finally passed on, lucid to the end – a month shy of his 101st birthday.

Funeral in the village

His death, on Friday 30 October, was a well-kept secret. His wife, Monique, requested strict confidentiality from the nurse who came every day and instructed her to say, if asked, that he had been hospitalized; the funeral home mortician and the civil servant at the city hall also agreed to take part in this conspiracy of silence, listing the deceased's name only on the following Monday, which meant it circulated on Tuesday 4 November, the day death notices were published in *Le Monde* and *Le Figaro*. The concierge was informed that an unmarked vehicle (rather than a hearse) would come and take the coffin away to the funeral parlour and then to Lignerolles. The press, then, was only informed on Tuesday, by which time he had already been buried that very morning. News spread rapidly, both in France and abroad.

In accordance with the wishes he had expressed in multiple documents, the anthropologist was thus buried in an informal fashion in the Lignerolles cemetery, with a strictly private ceremony.[135] As we have seen, great care was taken to avoid the inconveniences of fame, even if this meant angering those who, although perhaps intimate friends, were still not deemed intimate enough to attend the funeral, which remained restricted to family members. On Tuesday morning, Claude Lévi-Strauss's body was interred in the presence of his wife, his two sons and daughter-in-law, his two grandchildren, as well as the mayor of the village and his wife. The anthropologist had entertained the idea of being buried in some remote patch of brush in the valley of the Aubette River in Normandy, and had even been granted the required prefectural authorization, but, in the end, pressed by his wife who worried about the various difficulties this would have involved, he opted for the cemetery. Likewise, he did not want to be laid in a coffin and would have preferred to be buried in a simple shroud, but here again, his wife was opposed, for fear of complications. The burial was not preceded by any religious ceremony.

Claude Lévi-Strauss's grave is located at the top of the cemetery, on the forest side. The path on the left-hand side as you exit the Château's gardens circles around the outer wall and takes you around the village, past a bridge and a pretty, refurbished Burgundy wash-house on the right. The cemetery sits on high ground, sloping down to the edge of a forest. It is a small quadrangle encompassing around fifty graves, an enclosed village cemetery overlooking the valley and lulled by the gentle murmur of the river, disturbed only by the snap of gunfire during hunting season. For this is hunting country. At the bottom of the cemetery, the tombs of four Royal Air Force pilots are aligned in a row – on their way back from a bombing mission in Germany in 1944, their plane was shot down and crashed in Châtillonnais. They died young – the four's combined age does not reach that of Lévi-Strauss. Above, the anthropologist's grave displays a simplicity that befits him: no tombstone, just a slight bulge in the ground and some gravel, crowned by a 'holey rock' (the likes of which can be found all over the forests of that region), a karst formation that gives the tomb a troglodyte look. The grave becomes one with the earth and pleas for self-dissolution, of which only a social and institutional affiliation remains: 'Claude Lévi-Strauss, de l'Académie française (1908–2009).' As he had written in *Tristes Tropiques:* 'The self is not only hateful: there is no place for it between *us* and *nothing*.'[136]

As opposed to Guillaume le Maréchal, whose public, popular, ritualized death Georges Duby famously described in great detail, in a book Lévi-Strauss prized,[137] the anthropologist exited the stage on the sly. This deliberately private death stood in sharp contrast to the monument he had become. It allowed him to escape a state funeral at the Invalides military cemetery which, as a bearer of the Légion d'honneur's Grand Croix, he would certainly have been accorded; as well as to escape the ritual embalming ceremonies bestowed on great intellectuals – a figure with which he had never identified. He thus died as he had lived. Over the following days, the press obituaries of Lévi-Strauss gradually shaded into funeral orations for French culture. France celebrated the 'century of Lévi-Strauss'[138] and the 'man of eternity',[139] while tributes piled up around the world.

Just as the death of Philip II of Spain marked the end of a history (and of Braudel's dissertation) that continued on after him, for structural dynamics survived the death of the sovereign and continued to delineate the 'Mediterranean world' that is the subject of the book,[140] so the disappearance of Lévi-Strauss had no effect on the rediscovery of his work in the 2000s. The physical body of the anthropologist gave way to the material and symbolic body of his work, that was to find its final embodiment in two paper memorials: his personal archive, deposited with the Bibliothèque nationale de France since 2007, and the Pléiade edition of his collected works, published in 2008. This was in the 'spirit of the double funerals'[141] so familiar to the anthropology of religion, which the scholar had practised in his early days.

Paper memorial (1): archiving oneself

Confronted with his imminent demise, Lévi-Strauss did not want to leave it
to others to decide what he intended to bequeath to his friends, contemporaries and heirs. 'As for my papers, I can't make up my mind, and I struggle
against the temptation of destroying it all', he wrote to Isac Chiva.[142] Finally,
it was Jean-Noël Jeanneney, then director of the Bibliothèque nationale de
France, who approached him first and suggested that he deposit his papers
at the manuscript department of the Bibliothèque nationale, one of the bastions of French literary canonization. His personal papers, of both scholarly
and historical value, were of interest to a number of institutions: the French
National Archives, the Imec Institute (Institut mémoires de l'édition con-
temporaine) in the Ardenne Abbey, the archives of the Collège de France
and of the Académie française. What mattered most to Lévi-Strauss was
organizing his archival legacy and freeing his heirs of this administrative,
financial and existential 'burden'. He intended to sell enough of his archive
to cover the inheritance tax on the apartment of the rue des Marronniers
and on the house in Lignerolles, and to donate whatever was left. Which is
why, in 2007, the Lévi-Strauss Archives were transferred to the Bibliothèque
nationale in three instalments: the first as acquisition, the second as payment
for property transfer fees, and the third as donation. This combination of
donation and purchase was relatively common practice, and if it required
ministry of finance approval, it did not entail quite the same sums as were
recently spent on keeping the Guy Debord and Michel Foucault archives
in France. Between 2007 and 2015, philosophy and social science archives
had been drawn into the kind of speculative market dynamic that had long
prevailed in the domain of arts and letters.

Lévi-Strauss was fully aware of both the use and exchange value of
archival material. In a little noted passage in *The Savage Mind*, he analyses
the function of the *churinga*, objects the aborigines of central Australia
consider sacred. Made out of stone or wood, oval-shaped, with pointed
or rounded ends, they are often engraved with symbols that represent the
physical body of an ancestor. They are the materialization of the past in
the present. Conferred on the descendant believed to be the ancestor's
reincarnation, *churinga* are stored away in piles inside natural caves, and
periodically taken out to be polished and offered incantations. 'Their role
and the treatment accorded to them thus have striking analogies with the
documentary archives that we secrete in strongboxes or entrust to the
safe-keeping of solicitors, and which we inspect from time to time with
the care due to sacred things.'[143] Indeed archives (*arca* = chest, strong-
box) and *churinga* are characterized, according to Lévi-Strauss, by a
double character, both sacred and probative. Sacred because archives are
endowed with a 'diachronic significance to which they alone attest';[144] and
probative because archives adduce documentary evidence of what once
was. The *churinga* thus provide us with a distorted image of our own practices: the celebration of our myth of history, ever since Michelet invented
its usage by historians, even as he was making it the documentary and
affective guarantee of national life.[145]

The 'Lévi-Strauss' archival body also confers on history a certain physical existence: 261 boxes deposited with the Bibliothèque nationale de France attesting to the fact that the Lévi-Strauss adventure did indeed take place, and that the century of Lévi-Strauss, in all its diachronic magnitude, has now become part of the arcana of history. The manuscript culture of old France – with its wood panelled libraries, velvet upholstery and lecterns, its erudite scholarship, pious silence and the care with which yellowing papers are consulted – preserve the anthropologist in a scholarly atmosphere that he would have appreciated. He did not quite make it into the dematerialized era. The archives pulse with a still very recent life, felt in Lévi-Strauss's fine handwriting on certain documents, his annotations specifying such and such detail of family history, or the context in which such and such expedition notebook was kept (or lost). There is little doubt that these records were sorted, selected and made available for historiographical purposes, of which the present biography is but one example.

Its posthumous presence alongside the great writers in the manuscript department invites us to see his bequest to the Bibliothèque nationale as part of a process of 'literarization' of Lévi-Strauss's work, which was further advanced by the Pléiade edition of 2008. It even allows us to indulge the suspicion that Lévi-Strauss may have actively dreamt of joining Marcel Proust in the pantheon of French letters. In fact, there is no dedicated site for social science archives in France. Lévi-Strauss's scientific library is his only legacy to end up at the Musée du Quai Branly. Rather than his posterity as a great writer, the arrival of the Nambikwara and kinship structures within the manuscripts sanctuary of the BNF might therefore herald a new metamorphosis of literature itself, engaged in a new dialogue with the knowledge of its times.

Paper memorial (2): the Pléiade

On 22 September 2004, the distinguished publisher Antoine Gallimard wrote to Claude Lévi-Strauss that he would like to 'open up' the prestigious Bibliothèque de la Pléiade series and would be delighted, in this case, to 'devote a volume to a selection of [the anthropologist's] works, which have their rightful place in literature'.[146] This short missive brought an end to a historical quarrel of half a century between the anthropologist and the Gallimard publishing house. As we will recall, following a rejection from Brice Parain in the early 1950s, he had never published a single page – with the exception of his Académie française induction speeches (for Payrefitte and Dumézil). A few months later, Lévi-Strauss sent the literary director of the Pléiade series an outline that provided an overview of his entire work, while taking into account the editorial constraints of the series and its readership, as well as the need not to go more than 2,000 pages for a single volume: *Tristes Tropiques* (1955), the book that made him famous, then an ensemble comprising *Totemism* (1961) and *The Savage Mind* (1962), and finally the three 'minor mythologiques' – *The Way of the Masks* (1975), *The*

Jealous Potter (1986), *Story of Lynx* (1991) – that Lévi-Strauss considered as possible introductions to the structural analysis of myth; and, finally, closing out the volume, *Look, Listen, Read*, which placed art and aesthetics in cardinal – and ultimate – position. The selection thus did not include, to the indignation of some of his more zealous colleagues, the great summits of his scholarly work: *The Elementary Structures of Kinship* (1949) and the four volumes of the *Mythologiques* (1964–71), deemed, along with the methodological texts of the three collections of *Structural Anthropology*, too technical and erudite for a nonspecialist readership. Neither did Lévi-Strauss include the two texts he had written for UNESCO, *Race and History* (1951) and *Race and Culture* (1971), both having already been republished by Albin Michel as a single volume in 2001, with a substantial introduction by Michel Izard.[147] As it stands, rearranged and recomposed by its author based on former elements, the Pléiade volume represents Claude Lévi-Strauss's final book – and an invitation to take another path through his work.[148]

In fact, many did not wait for the Pléiade's centennial edition to embark on a re-examination of structural anthropology, which they found intact after two decades of hibernation, and to initiate what Brazilian anthropologist Edouardo Viveiros de Castro has aptly called the 'second spring of literature on Lévi-Strauss'.[149] Indeed, in the 2000s, a steady stream of reinterpretations expanded the Lévi-Straussian bibliography, transforming the cultural status of his work into that of a contemporary 'classic'. Many journals devoted entire issues to the anthropologist – a phenomenon last seen in the late 1960s: *Critique* (1999), *Les Archives de philosophie* (2003), *Les Temps modernes* (2004), *Esprit* (2004), and *Philosophie* (2008). An impressive issue of the *Cahiers de L'Herne* – popularized by the famous photo by Anita Albus on its cover, of Lévi-Strauss and the jackdaw – came out in 2004; and, in 2009, the *Cambridge Companion to Lévi-Strauss*, edited by Boris Wiseman, was published.[150] Death did nothing to stem the flow, which had reached such magnitudes that, in his introduction to an issue of the journal *Europe* in 2013, Bernard Mezzadri wondered whether it had not become a kind of funeral cult, a ritual to exorcize the now cumbersome presence of the illustrious deceased.[151]

The scope of the centennial celebration in 2008,[152] consecrated by the Pléiade volume, caused some to fear that this 'formidable paper memorial'[153] would have the effect of mummifying the body of work, depoliticizing it (by excluding *Race and History*) for the pure reading pleasure of lovers of literature. In a review published in *L'Homme*, Emmanuel Desveaux expanded on this double critique: he called attention to a potential fossilization and regretted the 'apparent literary-philosophical recuperation the founder of the Laboratory of Social Anthropology had himself submitted to'.[154] He wondered about the team that had been given the task of writing the critical apparatus – a literature specialist, Vincent Debaene, as editor, two philosophers, Frédéric Keck and Martin Rueff, and only one *bona fide* anthropologist, Marie Mauzé. A fact that Emmanuel Desveaux interpreted bitterly as a 'belittling of anthropology as a discipline',[155] which he saw as quite symptomatic: indeed, the reappraisal of

Lévi-Strauss's work in France in the 2000s did not come primarily from within the field of anthropology.

Being included in the prestigious Pléiade series during one's lifetime is a privilege reserved to only a handful of authors, including André Gide, Paul Claudel, Saint-John Perse, Marguerite Yourcenar and Julien Gracq, his (almost) strict contemporary, as well as of course Henry de Montherlant, to whose seat he was elected at the Académie française in 1973. Lévi-Strauss's name might stand out among these grandees of the French literary pantheon. However, the Pléiade series does not only include literary writers, in the way our conception of literature has progressively defined them: Rousseau, Diderot, Sartre and Camus also figure among its authors, as well as André Breton, the third tome of whose *Oeuvres*, on art, was published in 2008, at the same time as the Lévi-Strauss volume, marking the ultimate surrealist encounter of the century. Rather than seeing it as a consecration with embalming and adulterating effects ('de-disciplinarizing', so to speak), other anthropologists (although they did happen to be Brazilian) took a different view of the matter. Eduardo Viveiros de Castro hailed this supreme honour: 'We, anthropologists from all over the world, can take pride in and be grateful for the tribute that was thus rendered to our discipline in the person of its most illustrious practitioner. . . .'[156] The decision to opt for an anthology rather than the complete works seemed essential to Viveiros de Castro. Far from freezing and fixing the work in definitive form, it reflected on the contrary one of the characteristics of structural analysis: its perpetual incompleteness, the incapacity to close an argument constantly rekindled by the 'telling phrase' from Lévi-Strauss:[157] 'That is not all.' Just as the structural analysis of myths focuses on the particular state of a system in perpetual imbalance, the Pléiade volume presented the current state of transformation of the system of Lévi-Straussian thought. Viveiros de Castro also rejoiced over the very Amazonian selection of texts, and from the later period (most of them post-1975), which brought the Tupinamba once again into the Pléiade series – the first time was through Montaigne – and now through one who considered himself to be, across time, an interlocutor and even disciple of the sixteenth-century philosopher. Finally, Viveiros de Castro concluded, the series itself, which Jacques Schiffrin entitled 'Pléiade' in 1931, had a very Lévi-Straussian ring to it: 'We should recall that the eponymous constellation is, in Amerindian thought, an eminent sign of continuity.'[158] All told, the metamorphosis of the deceased into a leather-bound volume, becoming part of a series – between the continuum of the whole and the discontinuous fragments of each of its volumes – that carried with it the very French ambition of encompassing all of human knowledge and art, made sense. Like the Amerindian chests which, as Lévi-Strauss explained, *were* the body of the animal whose representation was sculpted into the wood, here he was now also incorporated into the material of this discrete, proper and desirable book-object.

Its initial print run was 15,000, but 30,000 copies were sold over the first five years. This unexpected success – considering the fact that these 2,000 pages do not make for easy reading – confirmed the renewed relevance of a body of work that constantly insisted on its resolutely untopical character. Lévi-Strauss had indeed become a classic, in the way Barthes defined the classics in terms of the seventeenth-century moralists: 'With these writers who are held to be serious – i.e., boring – there is also the art of a higher comedy, in which people, in an intelligent society, might indulge who find entertainment in being ceremonious.'[159] Interminable, like Amerindian mythology, complex, sometimes ambiguous, and accepting of its contradictions, the collection reveals itself, upon reading and rereading, to be open to the four winds, available for any and all possible appropriation.[160]

The Claude Lévi-Strauss to come

What is left of Lévi-Strauss? The question had been raised even before his actual death, for structuralism had all but disappeared from the international intellectual agenda. In a way, as we have seen, Lévi-Strauss had welcomed this decline with a certain relief. He had himself described the programmed obsolescence of his research as a normal stage in the process of the accumulation of knowledge. Yet he had the satisfaction of seeing his work not only celebrated, commemorated and extolled (and so in part embalmed) as a major body of thought, but also reappraised, and reread by new generations who drew out of it a particularly invigorating atmosphere and restored to structuralism as a whole a productiveness it seemed to have lost. It was this 'return' of Lévi-Strauss among some young philosophers and a segment of French, British and Brazilian anthropology that was the great surprise of the 1990s–2000s.[161]

A legacy without will and testament

Although they do not constitute a coherent school of disciples, Lévi-Strauss's heirs can be found all over the world. Yet the legacy of the French scholar remains a highly ambivalent one in British anthropology, where his reception had been very critical from the 1960s, perhaps because the theoretical dimension of his work always obscured its erudite foundations, which were constantly challenged. In short, as Maurice Bloch has put it, admiration was always mixed with a degree of 'difficulty' as to where to situate this unclassifiable work – a difficulty that resurfaces, at least, in the often ironic tone of the British anthropologist Patrick Wilcken's biographical treatment, *The Poet in the Laboratory*. At heart, Wilcken regards the work of Lévi-Strauss with a mixture of fondness and incredulity, somewhat as he might observe a sorcerer's apprentice inventing new formulas. Vincent Debaene has pointed out how, in the United States, four decades of poststructuralist, postmodern and postcolonial critique have demoted structuralism to the status of a 'fad' that has lost its value in the marketplace of ideas, though not without having developed a highly particular local version, which is still active in the American academic imagination, that is seen as synonymous with 'the authoritarian violence of a systematic science. [. . .] It has been perceived as the ultimate incarnation of logocentric Western science.'[162]

In France, Lévi-Strauss's legacy is a powerful one, but conflictual. Kinship anthropology, all but abandoned outside France, saw brilliant advances with the work of Françoise Héritier (transmission of substances, construction of sexual power relations) who took over from Lévi-Strauss at the Collège de France and as director of the LAS. On kinship or even on mythology, two highly technical fields, Lévi-Strauss's two major contributions – his dissertation and the four volumes of the *Mythologiques* – are still the subject of very heated debate: 'The jury is still out.'[163]

A weighty issue of *L'Homme* focusing on kinship issues included a particularly biting 'afterword' by Claude Lévi-Strauss, always ready to jump into the fray, even in 2000. He returned to the complexities of exchange as a matrix of kinship and alliance relations, asserting once again that he had always given precedence to alliance over filiation – as opposed to what others had had him say – and reminding us that a natural family can only exist if integrated into a pre-existing society. Finally, he returned to the vexing issue of the past fifty years: the exchange of women. 'How many times do I need to repeat that it is indifferent to the theory that men exchange women or the other way around? [. . .] I did not decree that men were the agents and women the subjects of the exchange. Ethnographic data simply taught me that, in the vast majority of societies, the men act or conceive of things in this way and that, as a result of its general character, such a disparity stands as a fundamental trait.'[164]

This polemical intensity also characterized some of his final texts, such as 'Retours en arrière'[165] (1998), in which he responded to a reading of his former polemic with Sartre that he considered dishonest; and 'Female Sexuality and the Origin of Society' (1995), a case against the American feminist theories whose extreme physiological bias he described as 'genital Robinson Crusoe tales'.[166] Finally, to those who accused him of underestimating the violence of social life, and of providing an irenic account of it in his theory of exchange (a constitutive condition and matrix of society), he replied with 'Apologue des amibes'[167] (2000). The single-celled amoebae generally live on their own but they may collect in societies of several thousand individuals should food (bacteria) be lacking. Lévi-Strauss then observes that the chemical substance given off by the amoebae that enables them to aggregate is the same as that secreted by the bacteria that the amoebae feed on. He then has no trouble extrapolating about a graduated vision from communication to sociability to devoration – the upper limit of society – that he had already defined in his discussion of cannibalism. Violence does figure in Lévi-Strauss, but always on a continuum, made of gradients and thresholds. It is not so much foundational as inextricably linked to all social life.

In France, even among those who declare themselves the heirs of anthropological structuralism, the legacy is therefore manifold, and sometimes polarized. For the rest of the discipline, which – like all disciplines – has diversified and become divided, the structuralist paradigm is no longer on the agenda – or only as part of a historical review of the discipline.

Around Alban Bensa, for instance, an 'anthropology of action', which gives a broader role to historical explanation and to the interactions between the various participants, conceives of itself as a social science of the contemporary world that is openly critical of the 'high conceptualization' of structural anthropology.[168] Many of those who work on the South Pacific – especially on New Caledonia – and on Africa identify with this broad historicization of anthropological knowledge, intended to reincorporate the political dimension that structural anthropology had seemingly bracketed.[169]

Lévi-Strauss's 'striking return' to philosophy

The surprising new lease on life given to Lévi-Straussian studies in the early twenty-first century did not come from anthropology. Paradoxically, and through a 'curious twist' – to use a formula that often recurs in Lévi-Strauss's prose – it came from philosophy, yet not from the *philosophia perennis* that the anthropologist had rejected in the 1930s, i.e., from a philosophy sure of its categories, speculating in complete autonomy, and ignorant of discoveries in the natural and social sciences. The movement came from a new generation of philosophers who had processed the lessons of the century and duly noted the end of the primacy of philosophy as a discipline. 'In light of the progress of modern science, the situation [of the philosophical discourse] can no longer remain the same',[170] concedes Bruno Karsenti, one of the artisans of this new dialogue between philosophy and the social sciences.

This dialogue took place in several issues of both generalist and specialized journals: *Archives de philosophie* (2003),[171] *Esprit* (2004)[172] and *Philosophie* (2008).[173] Marcel Hénaff, one of the key figures, with Claude Imbert, of this philosophical reappropriation of structuralism, had alerted Lévi-Strauss in 2003: 'There is a new generation of very gifted philosophers who are raising new questions about your work and are giving your thought all the conceptual attention it deserves.'[174] Jocelyn Benoist, Michaël Foessel, Frédéric Keck, Patrice Maniglier, Jean-Claude Monod and Gildas Salmon are among the figures who have explored the impact of structural anthropology on philosophy, while also offering new and more open interpretations of structuralism. Focusing on the issue of symbolism (notably on the exchange between Lévi-Strauss and Ricœur), they benefited from a favourable intellectual climate, highly critical of the philosophy of consciousness that had reigned supreme in the 1980s, and rode the anti-constructivist wave which, while not quite endorsing scientism, still reasserted the value of truth. The fact that structuralism had never given in to postmodern sirens, at the risk of being relegated to the intellectual backwaters, now became an asset in its reappraisal.[175]

These recent interpretations of Lévi-Strauss emphasize the dynamic character of structuralism, made clear in the *Mythologiques*. In *The Elementary Structures of Kinship*, Lévi-Strauss still posited incest prohibition as a universal, and a specifically human, trait that prompted the passage from nature to culture: his anthropology established a distinct humanity. By contrast, in the *Mythologiques*, he had distanced himself from the dichotomy of nature and culture. His analytical method, moving from one myth to the next through transformation, itself illustrated the book's purpose: to grasp the functioning of the mind as it was operating, rejecting any outside signified. The ultimate and radical point of the *Mythologiques* was that the anthropologist's own scholarly work was itself part and parcel of the transformation cycle, a variant and possible translation of the mythical structure.[176] Similarly, with regard to the functioning of social life, Lévi-Strauss turned Mauss's legacy upside down: asserting the symbolic origin of society (rather than the social origin of the symbolic function), Lévi-Strauss did not deem it necessary to grant precise meaning to any particular rule, contract or alliance, but rather took the view that society made sense in and of itself, establishing social relations through the reciprocity it required. Under these conditions, a norm could always be substituted by another, within a system of arbitrary signs: 'The subversive dimension of structuralism lies in its formalizing (i.e., in its emptying of all content, and hence of all legitimacy) the structures of domination. [. . .] If the structure determines the place of the chief, it also designates it as a place to be taken.'[177] In Jocelyn Benoist's words, the equivalence of the terms, their interchangeability and the contingent character of norms are at the root of 'structuralism's progressive destiny'.[178] The Lévi-Straussian structuralism that emerged in the 2000s out of these philosophical readings was thus opposed to the substantialist conceptions of the symbolic order – whether they placed at their centre the family, the heterosexual couple or God... The symbolic arrangements that govern the rules of kinship and domination are thus made and unmade, as in a turning kaleidoscope. Nothing allows us to think that one is better than another – if not the power of time, of *usage*. Which is, essentially, how Claude Lévi-Strauss had responded to many of the bioethical issues of our time, as we have seen, in a very open-minded way.

His 'return to philosophy' can thus be interpreted in several ways: on the one hand, Lévi-Strauss, who has always said he did not set out to produce a philosophy, even though he had no qualms about 'poaching' on its territory, partly renounced that polemical position and declared himself 'a philosopher in relief'[179] in his final years, an 'interpreter'[180] of the lessons to be drawn from the sciences, thereby supporting a very relativistic and modest conception of philosophy: 'From now on, science plays a much more effective metaphysical role than any philosophy: not only does it increase the scope of our knowledge, but, in this increase, it also helps us understand that our knowledge has limits.'[181] On the other hand, it is the philosophical discipline itself (or part of it) which – revolutionized, regionalized and relativized – returned to structural anthropology as a situated form of knowledge ready to recognize others. It was thus only thirty years after the *Mythologiques* that Lévi-Strauss drew one of the lessons from his great project and announced a third possible interpretation of this return to philosophy: 'Whether we like it or find it a cause for concern, philosophy now stands at the forefront of the anthropological stage. Not our philosophy, the one my generations had asked exotic peoples to help them get rid of; but in a striking twist, their own.'[182] For Brazilian anthropologist Eduardo Viveiros de Castro, structural anthropology was to have been and continued to be a war machine, which, after undermining the 'metaphysical foundations of Western colonialism', enabled the 'overthrow of the colonialist foundations of Western metaphysics'.[183] This meeting of Western philosophy and native metaphysics, through structural anthropology, could only have happened through the substantial renewal of Americanist, and primarily Amazonian, anthropology of Lévi-Straussian influence.

Going up the Amazon

Long considered a rather dusty byway of regional anthropology, marginal to the theoretical energies of the discipline, the anthropology of the Americas, especially of the Amazonian lowlands, also returned to the fore in the 1990s. Lévi-Strauss duly registered this fact in an issue of *L'Homme*, coedited by Anne-Christine Taylor and Philippe Descola, and entirely devoted to new ethnographic, archaeological and archival research that had substantially altered the Americanist field.[184] It was a genuine 'explosion perpetuated by the enthusiasm and zeal'[185] of researchers who not only renewed our understanding of Amazonian societies, but also had a powerful theoretical impact. The work of Viveiros de Castro and his students on Amerindian cosmology and that of Manuela Carneiro da Cunha on the Amazonian forest challenged the opposition between consanguinity and alliance, i.e., between nature and culture – the native Amazonian cultures being integrated into an animist framework that conferred onto animals and plants a spirituality and way of life comparable to those of humans.[186] Brazilian fieldwork has thus produced a new set of reflections, first around what Philippe Descola calls the anthropology of nature, which he formulated in *Beyond Nature and Culture*,[187] and then around the notion of 'perspectivism' developed by Viveiros de Castro and his Brazilian team.[188]

These anthropologists initially realized that structuralism proved very productive for processing Amazonian data. As Lévi-Strauss himself had already noted, structuralism worked well in Amazonia! As if its Amerindians had been natural structuralists . . . Which is why, as Anne-Christine Taylor was the first to point out, Lévi-Strauss's scholarly imagination had been so strongly 'Indianized':[189] his theory of the alliance, the weight granted to affinity over kinship in his social system – all this was very Amerindian indeed. Behind the universalistic rhetoric, structuralism was thus strongly connected to the particular region of its fieldwork. It should be said that Lévi-Strauss did not object to this kind of 'regionalization' of his thought, when Paul Ricœur appeared to be heading in that direction in their 1963 exchange.[190] Yet, this initial focus on its regional specificity was followed by a second reappraisal of structuralism from the perspective of the 'minor mythologiques', and especially *The Story of Lynx*, which takes on a crucial importance here. Indeed, uncovering the openness to alterity, the priority of the non-identical over the identical, and asymmetrical dualism, was to re-establish a relationist and dynamic understanding of structuralism, 'against the grain',[191] with, at its centre, the notion of transformation that ran counter to the ideological universals with which Lévi-Strauss had at times been associated in his past.

Within this renewed Amazonian framework, structuralist anthropologists and Amerindians think in the same manner and take part in a common dynamic. In other words, anthropology was 'in no way privileged over the forms of thought it studies'.[192] This was precisely what Lévi-Strauss meant when he concluded that his analyses could be understood as a variant of the myths he studied. To claim, as Eduardo Viveiros de Castro does, that anthropological knowledge is but 'a structural variant of indigenous *praxis*'[193] was of course quite revolutionary: 'It is explosive!'[194] And it was Lévi-Strauss who lit the fuse by going up the Amazon. Far from a violent form of knowledge of the exotic Other – reifying its object of observation, and reducing it to diagrams and figures – anthropology, in this new version of structuralism, appears as the translation into Western thought of the shock of Indian metaphysics. A return to philosophy, then, but to theirs, not ours – or to ours as a variant of theirs. Or the other way around, since it makes no difference.

Lévi-Strauss, our contemporary

In his introduction to Jan Kott's book, *Shakespeare Our Contemporary*, the director Peter Brook explains how a Polish man in the 1950s would be quite well placed to feel the Shakespearian historical dramas in his bones:[195] the conspiracies and the hatreds, the pre-dawn political assassinations, the fear, the terror . . . he knew it all well. By contrast, the English, who had now become peaceable Victorians, no longer had any relation to to the passions, violence and fury of the Elizabethan world. Chronological and geographical discrepancies sometimes produce this kind of *kairos* – the *here and now* of the contemporary. This is how, albeit in quite different terms, the philosopher Georgio Agamben has defined the meaning of 'contemporary':[196] a persistent untimeliness, a deliberate disjunction, a difficult relationship to one's present. The true contemporary, says Agamben, cannot fully adhere to his time, to its values and expectations. But there is more: 'The ones who can call themselves contemporary are only those who do not allow themselves to be blinded by the lights of the century, and so manage to get a glimpse of the shadows in those lights, of their intimate obscurity.'[197] Agamben sees in the darkness of the present a light that strives to reach us, but cannot. This is why it takes courage: 'It is like being on time for an appointment that one cannot but miss.' Finally, the third and last feature of the contemporary is that he 'perceives the indices and signatures of the archaic in the most modern and recent'.[198] Was this not precisely what characterized Lévi-Strauss's pessimistic and quixotic, untimely relationship to time, which had turned his life into an open book on the twentieth century and, of course, much more – on our Western modernity, immemorial time, the prehistoric and today?

His existential disagreement with the present found expression in anthropological structuralism as the relativist, relational and transformational space–time of mythology, which is not far from the expanding universe of astrophysics or quantum mechanics. The earth became one world in the second half of the twentieth century, through widespread urbanization and intensive interconnection.[199] The first decentred views of it were provided by satellite in 1957. Since then, 'moonrises' and 'earthsets' have taught us to consider the world as finite.

Claude Lévi-Strauss dreamt his whole life of a machine that could travel back in time and enlarge space, which his Proustian incubation led him to find in art and science, the only keys to real life. A few years before his death, in one of his final texts, the 'opening speech' he gave at UNESCO's sixtieth anniversary celebration, he startled us once again by professing a moderate optimism. He made the theory developed by the eighteenth-century philosopher Giambattista Vico his own:[200] the history of human societies endlessly repeats the same problems, but each period gets to the same point via different paths – these '*corsi*' and '*ricorsi*' which Lévi-Strauss had no qualms generalizing to all living things.[201] Such history in spirals suited him well since it reconciled several philosophies of time, both Western and non-Western, leaving room for a degree of diachrony, while also insisting on periodicity. The finitude and entropy of the world, its foreseeable standardization, could also sometimes loosen its embrace, as shown in the short historical parable presented by Claude Lévi-Strauss not without a certain relish. From the final quarter of the fourteenth century to the first half of the next, spurred by increasing exchange and the development of networks of traders and collectors, the whole of Europe became dominated by the international gothic style, whose features were clearly identifiable (a deformation of human bodies, an overabundance of finery and a morbid fascination). 'Far from spreading, that state of indistinctness was the setting from which sprang and diverged, while maintaining contact, the Flemish and Italian schools of painting, which were the most markedly diverse forms in Western art.'[202] Leaving it to Lévi-Strauss himself to conclude: 'People say: "It's either this or that", and it's always something else.'[203]

Notes

Introduction: The Worlds of Claude Lévi-Strauss

1 'Entre Marx et Rousseau', *Die Zeit*, 2 September 1983.
2 Claude Lévi-Strauss, 'Lévi-Strauss en 33 mots', remarks collected by Dominique-Antoine Grisoni, *Le Magazine littéraire*, 233, October 1985, p. 26.
3 Claude Lévi-Strauss, 'Il y a en moi un peintre et un bricoleur qui se relaient', *Le Monde*, 21 June 1974.
4 On this question, see the reflections of Viktor Karady, 'Les intellectuels juifs et les sciences sociales: Esquisse d'une problématique', in Johann Heilbronn, Rémi Lénoir, Gisèle Sapiro (eds.), *Pour une histoire des sciences sociales: Hommage à Pierre Bourdieu*, Paris, Fayard, 2004, p. 166; see also Pierre Birnbaum, *Géographie de l'espoir: L'exil, les lumières, la désassimilation*, Paris, Gallimard, 2004.
5 See Benoît de l'Estoile, 'Genèse d'un "intellectuel français"', *Slate*, 6 November 2009.
6 The caption to a caricature by Maurice Henry, published in *Quinzaine littéraire*, 1 June 1967, depicting Lévi-Strauss, Michel Foucault, Roland Barthes and Jacques Lacan as 'savages'.
7 Pierre Bourdieu, 'L'illusion biographique', *Actes de la recherche en sciences sociales*, 62–63, 1986, vol. 62, pp. 69–72.
8 Emmanuel Loyer, *Paris à New York: Intellectuels et artistes français en exil aux États-Unis, 1940–1947*, Paris, Grasset, 2005.
9 On the heuristic value of the change in scale effected by microanalysis, I would highlight, from a substantial bibliography, two texts by Jacques Revel: 'Introduction', in Revel (ed.), *Jeux d'échelle: La microanalyse à l'expérience*, Paris, Gallimard, 1996; and an interview with Revel, 'Un exercice de désorientation: *Blow-Up*', in Antoine de Baecque and Christian Delage (eds.), *De l'histoire au cinéma*, Paris, Complexe, 1998, pp. 103ff.
10 *ACPMW*, p. 25.
11 Claude Lévi-Strauss, 'Préface', in *Soleil Hopi: L'autobiographie d'un Indien Hopi by Don. C. Talayesva*, texts collected by Leo W. Simmons, Paris, Terre humaine, 1959, p. ix.
12 Lévi-Strauss, 'Préface', in *Soleil Hopi*, p. x.
13 See Daniel Fabre, Jean Jamin and Marcello Massenzio, 'Jeu et enjeu eth-nographiques de la biographie', *L'Homme*, 195–196, July–December 2010, pp. 7–8.
14 See Christian Licoppe, *La Formation de la pratique scientifique: Le discours de l'expérience en France et en Angleterre (1630–1820)*, Paris, La Découverte,

1996. More recently, Simon Schaffer, *La Fabrique des sciences modernes*, Paris, Le Seuil, 2014; and the work of Stéphane Van Damme, notably, *Descartes: Essai d'histoire culturelle d'une grandeur philosophique, XVII–XXe siècle*, Paris, Presses de Sciences Po, 2002, and *A toutes voiles vers la vérité: Une autre histoire de la philosophie au temps des Lumières*, Paris, Le Seuil, 2014.

15 See the seminar organized by Daniel Fabre, Christine Laurière and André Mary, 'Entreprises ethnographiques: missions, explorations et empires colo-niaux', EHESS, 2014–15, especially the first paper delivered by Daniel Fabre: 'Formes de l'enquête et paradigmes de la curiosité ethnographique'.

16 Daniel Fabre, 'D'une ethnologie romantique', in Daniel Fabre and Jean-Marie Privat (ed.), *Savoirs romantiques: Une naissance de l'ethnologie*, Nancy, Presses universitaires de Nancy, 'Ethnocritique', 2010. Daniel Fabre also dedicated a seminar to this subject – 'Le paradigme des derniers' – which was held at the EHESS from 2008 to 2011.

17 Homage written by Claude Lévi-Strauss after Jakobson's death, at the request of Kristina Jakobson, CLS Archives, NAF 28150, box 181, 'Correspondance reçue'.

18 See Patrick Wilcken, *Claude Lévi-Strauss: The Poet in the Laboratory*, London, Bloomsbury, 2010.

19 See Walter Lepenies, 'Introduction', in *Les Trois Cultures: Entre science et littérature, l'avènement de la sociologie* [1985], Paris, Éditions de la maison des sciences de l'homme, 1990, pp. 1–3.

20 Marcel Proust, cited in *LLR*, p. 5.

21 Eduardo Viveiros de Castro, *Cannibal Metaphysics*, Minneapolis, University of Minnesota Press, 2014, p. 46.

22 Didier Eribon, *Conversation with Claude Lévi-Strauss*, Chicago, The University of Chicago Press, 1991, p. 94.

23 Claude Lévi-Strauss, 'Reflections on liberty', in *TVFA*, pp. 279–288.

Chapter 1   The Name of the Father

1 Marcel Proust, *In Search of Lost Time*, vol. II, New York, Modern Library, 2000, p. 480.

2 Claude Lévi-Strauss, 'Autoportrait', remarks collected by Catherine Clément and Dominique-Antoine Grisoni, *Magazine littéraire*, 223, October 1985, p. 20.

3 Didier Eribon, *Conversations with Claude Lévi-Strauss*, Chicago, The University of Chicago Press, 1991, p. 30.

4 Eribon, *Conversations*.

5 On this point, see the illuminating notes provided by Frédéric Keck in the 'Notices' to the French Pléiade edition of *La Pensée sauvage*, pp. 1790–1791.

6 *SM*, p. 182. Médor is a commonplace French name for a dog, much like Fido or Rover in English.

7 Nicole Lapierre, *Changer de nom*, Paris, Stock, 1995, p. 95.

8 René Worms, cited in Lapierre, *Changer de nom*, p. 95.

9 The elements of his application are collected in the file 'Changement de nom', in Claude Lévi-Strauss's personal archives, deposited at the Manuscripts Division, CLS Archives, NAF 28150, box 210.

10 All quotations are extracts from Lévi-Strauss's letter of 24 October 1960, addressed to the Keeper of the Seals.

11 Paula E. Hyman, *The Emancipation of the Jews of Alsace: Acculturation and Tradition in the Nineteenth Century*, New Haven, Yale University Press, 1991,

p. 7. I would like to thank Jean-Marc Dreyfus for his suggestive remarks on Alsatian jewry.

12 This paragraph is based on material in the file 'Documents généalogiques: Isaac Strauss', CLS Archives, 28150, box 207.

13 Claude Lévi-Strauss cited in Henriette Nizan, *Libres Mémoires*, Paris, Robert Laffont, 1989, p. 8.

14 Elegy delivered by M. Amédée Boudin, *Panthéon de la Légion d'honneur*, Bureaux, 5 passage Chausson, 1870, p. 7.

15 'Isaac Strauss, chef d'orchestre et compositeur', *Journal de Vichy*, 19 June 1952.

16 See Nizan, *Libres Mémoires*, p. 8, and also the obituary in *Le Temps*, 16 August 1888.

17 Hector Berlioz, *Mémoires*, Paris, Michel Lévy, 1870, pp. 6, 7.

18 See Jean-Claude Yon, *Offenbach*, Paris, Gallimard, 2000; and the interview with Jean-Claude Yon, 21 March 2011.

19 Nizan, *Libres Mémoires*, p. 9.

20 Siegfried Kracauer, *Jacques Offenbach and the Paris of His Time*, Cambridge, MIT Press, 2002, p. 395.

21 *Le Temps*, 16 August 1888.

22 Eribon, *Conversations*, p. 4.

23 Nizan, *Libres Mémoires*, p. 10.

24 This paragraph is based on the family archives in the CLS Archives, NAF 28150, box 208.

25 Interview with Jean-José Marchand, ORTF, 1973; reprinted in Émilie Joulia, *Claude Lévi-Strauss: L'Homme derrière l'œuvre*, Paris, JC Lattès, 2008, p. 167.

26 Claude Lévi-Strauss, 'Le retour de l'oncle maternel', *La Repubblica*, 24 December 1997; reprinted in *Claude Lévi-Strauss*, éditions de l'Herne, 2004, pp. 32–35.

27 Undated letter, around 1890, CLS Archives, NAF 28150, box 206, 'Correspondances familiales', file 'Lettres de Flore Lévi'.

28 Interview with Monique Lévi-Strauss, 25 February 2011.

29 See Yann Potin (ed.), *Françoise Dolto: Archives de l'intime*, Paris, Gallimard, 2008.

30 Hyman, *The Emancipation of the Jews of Alsace*, p. 138.

31 Pierre Birnbaum, *Sur la Corde raide: parcours juifs entre exil et citoyenneté*, Paris, Flammarion, 2002, p. 51. See also Pierre Birnbaum (ed.), *Histoire politique des juifs de France: Entre universalisme et particularisme*, Paris, Presses de Sciences Po, 1990.

32 CLS Archives, NAF 28150, box 206, 'Correspondance familiale', file 'Lettres de Flore Lévi'.

33 Information contained in the entry on Rabbi Émile Lévy in Jean-Philippe Chaumont and Monique Lévy (eds.), *Dictionnaire biographique des rabbins et autres ministres du culte israélite*, Paris, Berg International, 2008, pp. 458–459.

34 Eribon, *Conversations*, p. 6.

35 Eribon, *Conversations*.

36 CLS Archives, NAF 28150, box 208, 'Généalogie familiale'.

37 As Denis Bertholet has astutely noted in his *Claude Lévi-Strauss*, Paris, Fayard, 2003, p. 13.

38 Eribon, *Conversations*, p. 4.

39 The champion of anti-Semitism and powerful patron of the newspaper *La Libre Parole* contested, with the virulence for which he was known, the legitimacy of depositing Jewish objects in a French national museum.

40 See the description of the collection in an article dedicated to it in the journal *Connaissance des arts*, February 1980.

41 See Edmund de Waal, *The Hare with Amber Eyes: A Hidden Inheritance*, London, Picador, 2010.

42 Daniel Fabre, 'D'Isaac Strauss à Claude Lévi-Strauss: le judaïsme comme culture', in Philippe Descola (ed.), *Claude Lévi-Strauss, un parcours dans le siècle*, Paris, Odile Jacob, 2012, p. 271.

43 Fabre, 'D'Isaac Strauss à Claude Lévi-Strauss', p. 272.

44 See Nathalie Heinich and Roberta Schapiro (eds.), *De l'Artification*, Paris, Éditions de l'EHESS, 2010.

45 Interview with Victor Malka conducted in 1984 for the book *Aujourd'hui être juif* (éditions du Cerf), extracts of which were reprinted in *Information juive: Le Journal des communautés*, 281, July–August 2008, p. 15. The italics are my own.

46 See Michaël Pollak, *Vienne 1900*, Paris, Gallimard-Julliard, 1984.

47 See Nizan, *Libres Mémoires*, p. 56.

48 Fabre, 'D'Isaac Strauss à Claude Lévi-Strauss', p. 276. This operation was undertaken at the same time by Raymond Lévi-Strauss's brother-in-law, the husband of Emma's older sister Aline, himself an artist: the painter Henry Caro-Delvaille, born Delvaille.

49 Citations are taken from the CLS Archives, NAF 28150, box 206, 'Correspondance familiale'.

50 CLS Archives, NAF 28150, box 206, 'Correspondance familiale'.

Chapter 2   Revelations (1908–1924)

1 Paris, Institut de France, 27 June 1974.

2 Daniel Fabre, 'D'Isaac Strauss à Claude Lévi-Strauss: le judaïsme comme culture', in Philippe Descola (ed.), *Claude Lévi-Strauss, un parcours dans le siècle*, Paris, Odile Jacob, 2012, p. 268.

3 CLS Archives, NAF 28150, box 210, 'Enfance'.

4 Claude Lévi-Strauss, 'Autoportrait', remarks collected by Catherine Clément and Dominique-Antoine Grisoni, *Magazine littéraire*, 223, October 1985, p. 18.

5 Didier Eribon, *Conversations with Claude Lévi-Strauss*, Chicago, The University of Chicago Press, 1991, p. 3.

6 Pierre-André Boutang and Annie Chevallay, 'Claude Lévi-Strauss par lui-même', DVD 1, Arte Éditions, 2008.

7 Patrick Wilcken, *Claude Lévi-Strauss: The Poet in the Laboratory*, London, Bloomsbury, 2010, p. 23.

8 CLS Archives, NAF 28150, box 208, 'Généalogie'.

9 Eribon, *Conversations*, p. 4.

10 When he proposed, Raymond is said to have asked Emma: 'Would you trade your "y" for my "i"?' Matthieu Lévi-Strauss, interview with the author, 9 March 2015.

11 Jean-Paul Morel, '26, rue Poussin', *Le Magazine littéraire*, 311, June 1993, p. 33.

12 Eribon, *Conversations*, p. 5.

13 Eribon, *Conversations*.

14 'Une approche de Claude Lévi-Strauss', interview with Jean-Claude Bringuier, in *Le Siècle de Lévi-Strauss*, Éditions Montparnasse, 1974, DVD 2.

15 Eribon, *Conversations*, p. 93.
16 Eribon, *Conversations*, p. 134: 'For the amusement of guests, we would ask them to open the book to a random page and read a phrase. I would then pick up the text without hesitation, since I knew my abridged edition by heart – I can still see the pink, slightly glazed paper of the cover.'
17 Text preserved in the personal archives of Claude Lévi-Strauss: CLS Archives, NAF 28150, box 210, 'Enfance'.
18 CLS Archives, NAF 28150, box 208, 'Généalogie'.
19 Philippe Landau, 'La patrie en danger: d'une guerre à l'autre', in Pierre Birnbaum (ed.), *Histoire politique des juifs de France: Entre universalisme et particularisme*, Paris, Presses de Sciences Po, 1990, p. 77.
20 Eribon, *Conversations*, p. 7.
21 See Stéphane Audoin-Rouzeau, *La Guerre des enfants, 1914–1918*, Paris, Armand Colin, 1993; Manon Pignot, *Allons enfants de la patrie: Génération Grande Guerre*, Paris, Seuil, 2012.
22 Lévi-Strauss, 'Autoportrait', p. 18.
23 Lévi-Strauss, 'Autoportrait'.
24 Letter from Claude Lévi-Strauss to Stéphane Clouet, 8 November 1983, in Stéphane Clouet, '"Révolution constructive", un groupe d'intellectuels socialistes des années 1930', doctoral thesis, 3 February 1989, University of Nancy II, p. 21.
25 CLS Archives, NAF 28150, box 210, 'Enfance'.
26 *TT*, p. 222.
27 *TT*, pp. 222–223.
28 See André Mary, 'In memoriam Lévi-Strauss (1908–2009)', *Archives de sciences sociales des religions*, October–December 2009: http://assr.revues.org/index21483.html, pp. 5ff.
29 Lévi-Strauss, 'Autoportrait', p. 19.
30 Denis Bertholet, *Claude Lévi-Strauss*, Paris, Fayard, 2003, p. 13.
31 Lévi-Strauss, 'Autoportrait', p. 19.
32 Lévi-Strauss, 'Autoportrait', p. 19.
33 Henriette Nizan, *Libres Mémoires*, Paris, Robert Laffont, 1989, p. 51.
34 Nizan, *Libres Mémoires*, pp. 55–56.
35 Claude Lévi-Strauss, 'Souvenirs d'enfance et d'adolescence', in *Pierre Dreyfus, 1907–1994*, Paris, Gallimard, 1995, p. 83.
36 'Le "regard éloigné" de Claude Lévi-Strauss', *Libération*, 2 June 1983, interview with Didier Éribon.
37 Lévi-Strauss, 'Autoportrait', p. 18.
38 Roger Caillois, 'Discours prononcé pour la réception de Claude Lévi-Strauss à l'Académie française', Paris, Institut de France, 1974.
39 Lévi-Strauss, 'Autoportrait', p. 18.
40 Eribon, *Conversations*, p. 176.
41 Photo in the CLS Archives, NAF 28150, box 210, 'Enfance'.
42 Caillois, 'Discours prononcé pour la réception de Claude Lévi-Strauss'.
43 Claude Lévi-Strauss, 'Témoignages et souvenirs', in *Pierre Dreyfus, 1907–1994*, p. 85.
44 Claude Lévi-Strauss, 'Lévi-Strauss en 33 mots', remarks collected by Dominique-Antoine Grisoni, *Le Magazine littéraire*, 233, October 1985, p. 27.
45 '*L'Express* va plus loin avec Claude Lévi-Strauss', *L'Express*, 15–21 March 1971, pp. 139–140.
46 Vladimir Nabokov, 'Details of a sunset' [1924], in *Details of a Sunset and Other Stories*, New York, McGraw-Hill, 1976.

47 Lévi-Strauss, 'Témoignages et souvenirs', p. 84.
48 'Des ratés? Nous le sommes tous plus ou moins', interview with Claude Lévi-Strauss by Martin Peltier, *Le Quotidien de Paris*, 6 May 1984.
49 Bertholet, *Claude Lévi-Strauss*, p. 15.
50 Stefan Zweig, *The World of Yesterday*, Lincoln, University of Nebraska Press, 1964. From the original German: *Die Welt von Gestern: Erinnerungen eines Europeärs*, 1942.
51 Interview with Monique Lévi-Strauss, 14 January 2011.
52 Lévi-Strauss, 'Autoportrait', p. 18.
53 Interview with Monique Lévi-Strauss, 25 February 2011.
54 Bertholet, *Claude Lévi-Strauss*, p. 16.
55 Letter from Claude Lévi-Strauss to Raymond Aron, 11 September 1983, Aron Archives. I am grateful to Dominique Schnapper for having given me access to this correspondence.
56 Raymond Aron, *Memoirs: Fifty Years of Political Reflection* [1983], Teaneck, NJ, Holmes & Meier, 1990, p. 28.
57 Simone de Beauvoir, *Memoirs of a Dutiful Daughter* [1958], New York, Harper Perennial Modern Classics, 2005, pp. 231–232.
58 Lévi-Strauss, 'Autoportrait', p. 18.
59 Viktor Karady, 'Les intellectuels juifs et les sciences sociales: Esquisse d'une problématique', in Johann Heilbronn, Rémi Lénoir, Gisèle Sapiro (eds.), *Pour une histoire des sciences sociales: Hommage à Pierre Bourdieu*, Paris, Fayard, 2004, p. 167.
60 Aron, *Memoirs*, p. 34.
61 Aron, *Memoirs*, p. 34.
62 Eribon, *Conversations*, p. 5.
63 'Claude Lévi-Strauss, le dernier géant de la pensée française', *Le Figaro*, 26 July 1993, p. 9.
64 *TT*, p. 377: 'I had been brought up to admire Wagner, and had discovered Debussy quite recently, but not before Stravinsky's *Noces*, of which I heard the second or third performance, had revealed a world which appeared more real and more substantial to me than the savannahs of central Brazil, and brought about the collapse of my previous musical convictions.'
65 Alex Ross, *The Rest is Noise: Listening to the Twentieth Century*, New York, Farrar, Straus and Giroux, 2007, pp. 98–99.
66 'Le "regard éloigné" de Claude Lévi-Strauss', interview with Didier Eribon.
67 Claude Lévi-Strauss, interview with Jean-José Marchand, ORTF, 1972, in Émilie Joulia, *Claude Lévi-Strauss: L'Homme derrière l'œuvre*, Paris, JC Lattès, 2008, p. 175.
68 Claude Lévi-Strauss, report on Claude McKay, 'Banjo', *L'Étudiant socialiste*, 2, November 1931, pp. 14, 15.
69 Lévi-Strauss, report on Claude McKay, 'Banjo', p. 29.
70 Walter Benjamin, 'The work of art in the age of its technological reproducibility' [1935], in *The Work of Art in the Age of Its Technological Reproducibility, and Other Writings on Media*, Cambridge, Belknap Press, 2008.
71 Claude Lévi-Strauss, interview with Jean-José Marchand, in Joulia, *Lévi-Strauss*, p. 173: 'Well, I was saying before that I had been raised in an extremely artistic milieu, as we say, but a very conservative one in relation to what was going on at the time. And so these were adolescent discoveries, a rebellion – even if the rebellion was never very violent – at any rate a reaction against [my father's] milieu.'

Chapter 3   Revolutions (1924–1931): Politics vs. Philosophy

1 *L'Étudiant socialiste*, 2, November 1930, p. 14.
2 CLS Archives, NAF 28150, box 211, 'Notes de philosophie, années de formation'.
3 Raymond Aron, *Memoirs: Fifty Years of Political Reflection* [1983], Teaneck, NJ, Holmes & Meier, 1990, p. 48.
4 Claude Lévi-Strauss, 'Autoportrait', remarks collected by Catherine Clément and Dominique-Antoine Grisoni, *Magazine littéraire*, 223, October 1985, pp. 18–19.
5 Letter from Claude Lévi-Strauss to Stéphane Clouet, 8 November 1983, in Stéphane Clouet, '"Révolution constructive", un groupe d'intellectuels socialistes des années 1930', doctoral thesis, 3 February 1989, University of Nancy II, p. 39.
6 Didier Eribon, *Conversations with Claude Lévi-Strauss*, Chicago, The University of Chicago Press, 1991, p. 8.
7 Eribon, *Conversations*, p. 9.
8 CLS Archives, NAF 28150, box 210, 'Enfance'.
9 *TT*, p. 51.
10 *TT*, p. 57.
11 Aron, *Memoirs*, p. 60.
12 Pierre Bourdieu, *Sketch for a Self-Analysis*, Chicago, The University of Chicago Press, 2008, p. 5.
13 Jean Maugüe, *Les Dents agacées*, Paris, Buchet-Chastel, 1982, p. 81.
14 For this entire paragraph, see Clouet, '"Révolution constructive"', pp. 38–39.
15 I am grateful to Maurice Olender for providing me with a copy of the pamphlet: 'Gracchus Babeuf et le communisme', *L'Églantine*, 6, 1926, p. 23.
16 Jean-François Sirinelli, *Génération intellectuelle: Khâgneux et normaliens dans l'entre-deux-guerres*, Paris, PUF, 1995; Christian Baudelot and Frédérique Matonti, 'Le recrutement social des normaliens, 1914–1992', in Jean-François Sirinelli (ed.), *École normale supérieure: Le livre du centenaire*, Paris, PUF, 1994.
17 Eribon, *Conversations*, p. 9.
18 Albert Otto Hirschman, *Exit, Voice, and Loyalty*, Cambridge, Harvard University Press, 1970. The author theorizes 'exit' as one possible response, alongside criticism and loyalty, to a crisis situation or feeling of discontent within a company or an institution. Expanded to wider domains, the model created by Hirschman has become a classic tool of the social sciences.
19 Eribon, *Conversations*, p. 17. Asked about his relations with Nizan, Claude Lévi-Strauss responded: 'Then, with him as with others, I had the feeling of not being quite at the same level.'
20 Eribon, *Conversations*, p. 10. Of his studies in philosophy at the Sorbonne he said: 'I went through it all rather like a zombie.'
21 *TT*, pp. 51–52. The rest of the paragraph is based on this same page.
22 Jean-Louis Fabiani, *Les Philosophes de la République*, Paris, Les Éditions de Minuit, 1988.
23 Claude Lévi-Strauss, 'The ultimate problem for the social sciences will be to bring thought and life together', *Le Magazine littéraire*, 58, November 1971, p. 23.
24 Eribon, *Conversations*, p. 17.
25 In his class notes, the following quote by Maine de Biran, underlined by Lévi-Strauss: 'With no effort, no knowledge!' CLS Archives, NAF 28150, box 211, 'Notes de philosophies, années de formation'.

26 Fabiani, *Les Philosophes de la République*, p. 15.
27 Fabiani, *Les Philosophes de la République*, p. 15.
28 Claude Lévi-Strauss, 'Le regard du philosophe', *Le Magazine littéraire*, October 1985, p. 59.
29 *TT*, p. 20.
30 For this entire paragraph, see *TT*, p. 52.
31 See Alexandre Pajon, *Lévi-Strauss politique: De la SFIO à l'Unesco*, Paris, Privat, 2011, p. 32. Report on the Lévi-Strauss presentation by Georges Lefranc. The 1906 Charter of Amiens had as one of its principal aims to establish a separation between the union movement and political parties.
32 Clouet, '"Révolution constructive"', p. 84.
33 *L'Étudiant socialiste*, February 1934, 5, p. 12, cited in Pajon, *Lévi-Strauss politique*, p. 38.
34 CLS Archives, NAF 28150, box 210, 'Activités politiques'.
35 Pierre Hanon, *L'Étudiant socialiste*, May 1929, cited in Pajon, *Lévi-Strauss politique*, p. 47.
36 Wiktor Stoczkowski, *Anthropologies rédemptrices: Le monde selon Lévi-Strauss*, Paris, Hermann, p. 123.
37 Letter from Claude Lévi-Strauss to Henri De Man, 17 October, IIVSG, Amsterdam, Hendrik De Man Papers, folder 253, cited in Stoczkowski, *Anthropologies rédemptrices*, p. 127.
38 Stoczkowski, *Anthropologies rédemptrices*, pp. 129ff.
39 This is one of the theses developed by Zeev Sternhell in *Neither Right Nor Left: Fascist Ideology in France*, Princeton, Princeton University Press, 1995.
40 Interview with Monique Lévi-Strauss, 25 February 2011.
41 Georges Lefranc, cited in Clouet, '"Révolution constructive"', p. 97.
42 Lefranc, cited in Clouet, '"Révolution constructive"', p. 97.
43 *TT*, p. 49.
44 See his laudatory review of Chamson's novel, 'Héritages', *L'Étudiant socialiste*, 9, June–July 1932.
45 Claude Lévi-Strauss, interview with Stéphane Clouet, 11 December 1985, in Clouet, '"Révolution constructive"', p. 138; Pajon, *Lévi-Strauss politique*, p. 49.
46 Dissertation transferred to the Lévi-Strauss personal archive, CLS Archives, NAF 28150, box 1.
47 See Claude Ravelet (ed.), *Trois Figures de l'école durkheimienne: Célestin Bouglé, Georges Davy, Paul Fauconnet*, Anamnèse, 3, Paris, L'Harmattan/Imec.
48 Lévi-Strauss letter to Stéphane Clouet, in Clouet, '"Révolution constructive"', p. 73.
49 Eribon, *Conversations*, p. 10.
50 Claude Lévi-Strauss, in Émilie Joulia, *Claude Lévi-Strauss: L'Homme derrière l'œuvre*, Paris, JC Lattès, 2008, p. 177.
51 Who were all to pass the *agrégation* in 1930.
52 Both quotes from Eribon, *Conversations*, p. 12.
53 CLS Archives, NAF 28150, box 211, 'Années de formation. Notes de philosophie'.
54 Claude Lévi-Strauss, *L'Étudiant socialiste*, 9, June–July 1931, p. 19.
55 Eribon, *Conversations*, p. 13.
56 Georges Lefranc, 'Retrospective', p. 17, cited in Clouet, '"Révolution constructive"', p. 176.
57 Claude Lévi-Strauss, report on a conference by André Philip, 'Socialisme et christianisme', *L'Étudiant socialiste*, 2, November 1930, p. 14.

58 Stoczkowski, *Anthropologies rédemptrices*, ch. 7.
59 Claude Lévi-Strauss, review of a pamphlet by Jean Guéhenno, 'Lettre à un ouvrier sur la culture et la revolution', *L'Étudiant socialiste*, 6, March 1931, p. 15; cited in Stoczkowski, *Anthropologies rédemptrices*, p. 167.
60 Clouet, '"Révolution constructive"', p. 162.
61 Jean-Louis Loubet del Bayle, *Les Non-Conformistes des années 1930*, Paris, Seuil, 1969.
62 Stoczkowski, *Anthropologies rédemptrices*, p. 165.
63 Stoczkowski, *Anthropologies rédemptrices*, p. 166.
64 Letter from Claude Lévi-Strauss to Stéphane Clouet, 5 February 1986, cited in Clouet, '"Révolution constructive"', p. 528.
65 Eribon, *Conversations*.
66 Letter from Claude Lévi-Strauss to Maurice Deixonne (n.d.), Deixonne Archive, OURS Archives.
67 Claude Lévi-Strauss, review of Jacques Viot's *Déposition de blanc*, in *L'Étudiant socialiste*, 7, April 1933, pp. 14–15.
68 Claude Lévi-Strauss, *L'Étudiant socialiste*, 4, January 1933, p. 13.
69 Claude Lévi-Strauss, *L'Étudiant socialiste*, 2, November 1930, p. 13.
70 Lévi-Strauss, *L'Étudiant socialiste*, 2, November 1930, p. 13.
71 Claude Lévi-Strauss, article on 'proletarian literature', his first in *L'Étudiant socialiste*, July–August 1928.
72 Claude Lévi-Strauss, *L'Étudiant socialiste*, November 1928, pp. 31–32.
73 Claude Lévi-Strauss, review of Paul Nizan's *Aden Arabie*, in *L'Étudiant socialiste*, 8, May 1931, p. 9.
74 Claude Lévi-Strauss, report on a conference given by M. Déat to the school-teachers of the Aube region, *L'Étudiant socialiste*, 2, November 1930, p. 14.
75 Lévi-Strauss, review of Nizan's *Aden Arabie*, p. 9.
76 Lévi-Strauss, review of Nizan's *Aden Arabie*, p. 9.
77 Lévi-Strauss, review of Nizan's *Aden Arabie*, p. 9.
78 Letter from Claude Lévi-Strauss to Maurice Deixonne, 3 September 1931, Deixonne Archive, OURS Archives.
79 Letter from Lévi-Strauss to Deixonne, 3 September 1931.
80 Eribon, *Conversations*, p. 15.
81 Claude Lévi-Strauss, report on a conference given by M. Déat to the school-teachers of the Aube region, p. 14, and review of Marcel Déat's book, *L'Étudiant socialiste*, February and March 1931.

Chapter 4   Redemption: Anthropology (1931–1935)

1 *TT*, p. 376.
2 This paragraph and those that follow are in large part based on the correspondence between Claude Lévi-Strauss and his parents, which Monique Lévi-Strauss has organized and allowed me to consult at her home, for which I am very grateful. Copies of the letters can also be found in the CLS Archives, NAF 28150, box 178. This correspondence, which runs over the course of the years 1931–33, comprises more than 200 letters, which are rarely dated. Generally, only the day of the week is mentioned. All the quotations are taken from the now published collection: Claude Lévi-Strauss, *'Chers tous deux': Lettres à ses parents (1931–1942)*, Paris, Seuil, 2015. The letters are organized according to the town from which they were sent: S for 'Strasbourg, military service'; M for

'Mont-de-Marsan'; P for 'Paris' (the number of the quoted letter is indicated in brackets).

3 Bertrant Saint-Sernin, 'Dina Dreyfus ou la Raison enseignante', *Les Temps modernes*, 516, 1989, p. 152.

4 Saint-Sernin, 'Dina Dreyfus', p. 148.

5 See the testimonials of Françoise Héritier, Catherine Clément and Sylvie Dreyfus-Asséo, who had her as a philosophy professor in *khâgne* at Lycée Fénelon or as a school inspector, as well as of Alain Badiou, a close friend of Dina Dreyfus who took part in the educational television shows she hosted during the 1960s.

6 Eribon, *Conversations*, p. 14.

7 CLS Archives, NAF 28150, box 210, 'Activités politiques' and 'La Conférence à Saint-Martin'.

8 Claude Lévi-Strauss, review of Albert Thibaudet, *Les Idées politiques de la France*, in *L'Étudiant socialiste*, 4, January 1933, p. 14.

9 'Socialisme et laïcité: Discours d'inauguration prononcé à Saint-Martin-de-Seignanx (Landes) à l'occasion de l'inauguration d'une école laïque', text of the speech delivered by Claude Lévi-Strauss, published in *L'Étudiant socialiste*, 7, April 1933, pp. 4–5.

10 Georges Charbonnier, *Entretiens avec Claude Lévi-Strauss* [1961], 'Le niveau d'authenticité', Paris, Les Belles Lettres, 2010, p. 53.

11 Charbonnier, *Entretiens avec Claude Lévi-Strauss*, p. 54.

12 Testimonial by Robert Lorans in the special issue 'Informations' devoted to alumni of Lycée Victor-Duruy in Mont-de-Marsan, Christmas 1984, LAS Archive, FLAS, press review.

13 Testimonial by Robert Lorans.

14 Eribon, *Conversations*, p. 14.

15 Jules Romains, cited in Christian Carette, 'Claude Lévi-Strauss et le Lycée de Laon, 1933–1934', *L'Ami du Laonnois*, 46, September 2010.

16 Jean-Paul Sartre, cited in Carette, 'Claude Lévi-Strauss et le Lycée de Laon'.

17 See Jean-Louis Fabiani, *Les Philosophes de la République*, Paris, Les Éditions de Minuit, 1988.

18 James Clifford, 'On ethnographic surrealism', *Comparative Studies in Society and History*, 23/4, October 1981, p. 545.

19 See Vincent Debaene, *Far Afield: French Anthropology between Science and Literature*, Chicago, The University of Chicago Press, 2014, pp. 71ff.

20 Clifford, 'On ethnographic surrealism', p. 554.

21 Clifford, 'On ethnographic surrealism', p. 553.

22 Expression used by André Leroi-Gourhan, cited in James Clifford, *The Predicament of Culture*, Cambridge, Harvard University Press, 2008, p. 124.

23 See the very thorough book devoted to him by Christine Laurière, *Paul Rivet: Le savant et le politique*, Paris, Éditions scientifiques du Muséum national d'Histoire naturelle, 'Archives', 2008.

24 Thomas Hirsch has re-examined Lévy-Bruhl's career and recovered his true place in the social sciences in France. See Hirsch, 'Un "Flammarion" pour l'anthropologie? Lévy-Bruhl, le terrain, l'ethnologie', *Genèses*, 90, January 2013; see also his doctoral thesis: 'Le temps social: conceptions sociologiques du temps et representations de l'histoire dans les sciences de l'homme en France, 1901–1945', under the supervision of F. Hartog, Paris, EHESS, 2014.

25 See Nina Gorgus, *Le Magicien des vitrines: Le muséologue Georges Henri Rivière*, Paris, Éditions de la MSH, 2003.

26 Maurice Leenhardt, already in the field in New Caledonia for over a decade, was precocious; his motivations for leaving (he was a missionary) and his belonging to a previous generation set him apart.

27 See Debaene, *Far Afield*, pp. 36ff.

28 See Benoît de l'Estoile, who has devoted a chapter to this issue, 'Collecter les cultures du monde: des ethnographes en expedition', in *Le Goût des autres: De l'exposition coloniale aux arts premiers*, Paris, Flammarion, 2007.

29 Which were meticulously transcribed by Denise Paulme in 1947 for the *Manuel d'ethnographie*.

30 Jean Jamin, 'Objets trouvés des paradis perdus (à propos de la mission Dakar-Djibouti)', in Jacques Hainard and Roland Kaer (eds.), *Collections Passion*, Neuchâtel, Musée d'Ethnographie, 1982.

31 Claude Lévi-Strauss, 'Le socialisme et la colonisation', *L'Étudiant socialiste*, 1, October 1929, pp. 7–8.

32 Paul Rivet in a letter to Daladier, 31 March 1938, cited in l'Estoile, *Le Goût des autres*, p. 73.

33 Rivet, cited in l'Estoile, *Le Goût des autres*, p. 74.

34 Letter of Claude Lévi-Strauss to Marcel Mauss, 4 October 1931, Marcel Mauss Archive, IMEC. I thank Alice Conklin for informing me about the existence of this letter.

35 'Rapport sur le travail fourni par les étudiants en 1932', sent by Georges Henri Rivière to Marcel Mauss, no. 1176, 3 June 1932, Mauss Archive, IMEC.

36 As he recalled in *TT*, p. 53: 'I knew nothing about anthropology, I had never attended any course and when Sir James Frazer paid his last visit to the Sorbonne to give a memorable lecture – in 1928, I think – it never occurred to me to attend, although I knew about it.'

37 Georges Monnet (Claude Lévi-Strauss), 'Picasso et le cubisme', *Documents*, 3, 1930, pp. 139–140.

38 *TT*, p. 47. Georges Dumas, a great psychologist of the interwar period, is mostly remembered for the part he played in French cultural missions to South America. The creation of numerous schools, universities and research centres was his life's work.

39 Letter from Célestin Bouglé to Tracy B. Kittredge, 26 October 1934, Archives Nationales, 61 AJ 94. I am grateful to Thomas Hirsch for bringing this exchange to my attention.

40 Letter from Tracy B. Kittredge to Célestin Bouglé, 7 November 1934, Bouglé Archives, ENS rue d'Ulm.

41 Eribon, *Conversations*, p. 16.

42 Claude Lévi-Strauss, 'Ce que je suis, I', *Le Nouvel Observateur*, 28 June 1980, p. 16.

43 *TT*, p. 43.

44 Eribon, *Conversations*, p. 16.

45 Jacques Soustelle (1912–90) became a *normalien* in 1929 and obtained the *agrégation* in 1932. Trained by and a disciple of Rivet, he left as soon as he passed the *agrégation* to study the Otomi Indians in Mexico. There he learned the nahuatl language and rudiments of the Mayan languages. In 1936, he published *Mexique: Terre indienne* and he defended his thesis in 1937, before becoming assistant director of the new Musée de l'Homme in 1938.

46 Eribon, *Conversations*, pp. 16–17.

47 *TT*, p. 53: 'I have a Neolithic kind of intelligence. Like native bush fires, it sometimes sets unexplored areas alight; it may fertilize them and snatch a few crops from them, and then it moves on, leaving scorched earth in its wake.'

48 Alexandre Pajon, *Lévi-Strauss politique: De la SFIO à l'Unesco*, Paris, Privat, 2011, pp. 152–153.
49 Claude Lévi-Strauss, 'Marcel Déat: perspectives socialistes', cited in Stoczkowski, *Anthropologies rédemptrices*, p. 164.
50 *TT*, p. 52.
51 'Le "regard éloigné" de Claude Lévi-Strauss', *Libération*, 2 June 1983, interview with Didier Éribon, p. 29.
52 Claude Lévi-Strauss, 'Autoportrait', remarks collected by Catherine Clément and Dominique-Antoine Grisoni, *Magazine littéraire*, 223, October 1985, p. 20.
53 Lévi-Strauss, 'Ce que je suis, I', p. 16.
54 Viktor Karady, 'Les intellectuels juifs et les sciences sociales: Esquisse d'une problématique', in Johann Heilbronn, Rémi Lénoir, Gisèle Sapiro (eds.), *Pour une histoire des sciences sociales: Hommage à Pierre Bourdieu*, Paris, Fayard, 2004, p. 166.
55 Karady, 'Les intellectuels juifs', p. 165.
56 Claude Lévi-Strauss, 'Ce que je suis, II', *Le Nouvel Observateur*, 5 July 1980, p. 18.
57 Expression used by Michel Leiris in 'La jeune ethnographie', cited in Debaene, *Far Afield*, p. 44.
58 For this entire paragraph, see Vincent Debaene, 'Ethnography's Prestige', in Debaene, *Far Afield*, pp. 44ff.
59 Émilie Joulia, 'Discours de reception, le jeudi 24 juin 1974 à Paris', in *Claude Lévi-Strauss: L'homme derrière l'œuvre*, Paris, JC Lattès, 2008, p. 106.
60 *TT*, 'The Quest for Power', p. 39.
61 Jean-François Bert, *L'Atelier de Marcel Mauss*, Paris, CNRS éditions, 2012, p. 126: 'According to one of his students in the early 1930s, A.G. Haudricourt, Marcel Mauss mentioned in his lectures one single experience of "fieldwork": his long military service as an interpreter during World War One.'
62 G. Charbonnier, *Entretiens avec Claude Lévi-Strauss*, pp. 18–19.

Chapter 5   The Enigma of the World

1 *TT*, p. 59.
2 Claude Lévi-Strauss, 'Des ratés? Nous le sommes tous plus ou moins', interview with Claude Lévi-Strauss by Martin Peltier, *Le Quotidien de Paris*, 6 May 1984.
3 Interview with Jean-Claude Bringuier, *Le Siècle de Lévi-Strauss*: 'I am not engaged in the act of creation. I devote myself entirely to the study of creation.'
4 'L'Express va plus loin avec Claude Lévi-Strauss', *L'Express*, 1027, 15–21 March 1971.
5 Didier Eribon, *Conversations with Claude Lévi-Strauss*, Chicago, The University of Chicago Press, 1991, p. 7: 'And besides, even if I remain deaf to religious answers, I am more and more penetrated by the feeling that the cosmos, and man's place in the universe, surpasses and always will surpass our understanding. It happens that I get along better with believers than with out-and-out rationalists. At least the first have a sense of mystery.'
6 *TT*, p. 53.
7 *TT*, p. 53.
8 *TT*, p. 380.

9   *TT*; see the delightful article by Nathan Wachtel, 'La quête de Cinna, Claude Lévi-Strauss', *Critique*, 620–621, January–February 1999, pp. 123–138.

10   Lévi-Strauss, 'Des ratés?'

11   Lévi-Strauss, 'Des ratés?'

12   *'L'Express* va plus loin avec Claude Lévi-Strauss', p. 111.

13   *TT*, p. 57.

14   Interview with Monique Lévi-Strauss, 29 October 2011.

15   *TT*, pp. 56–57.

16   *TT*, pp. 339–340.

17   Letter to his parents from Mont-de-Marsan, cited in Claude Lévi-Strauss, *'Chers tous deux': Lettres à ses parents (1931–1942)*, Paris, Seuil, 2015.

18   Luc Boltanski, *Mysteries and Conspiracies: Detective Stories, Spy Novels and the Making of Modern Societies*, Cambridge, Polity, 2014, p. xv.

19   *'L'Express* va plus loin avec Claude Lévi-Strauss', p. 141.

20   Manuela Carneiro da Cunha, 'Un diffusionisme structuraliste existe-t-il?' in Philippe Descola (ed.), *Claude Lévi-Strauss, un parcours dans le siècle*, Paris, Odile Jacob, 2012, p. 29.

21   Eribon, *Conversations*, p. 94.

22   Henry James, *The Figure in the Carpet*, 1896. The figure, like Poe's purloined letter, is lying in plain sight and yet remains invisible. Cf. Pascale Casanova, *La République mondiale des lettres*, Paris, Seuil, 1999, pp. 11ff.

23   'Sur Jean de Léry: Entretien avec Claude Lévi-Strauss', interview by Dominique-Antoine Grisoni, in the introduction to the new edition of Jean de Léry, *Histoire d'un voyage faict en la terre du Brésil*, Paris, Le Livre de Poche, 1994, p. 7.

24   *TT*, p. 83.

25   *TT*, p. 83.

26   'Sur Jean de Léry', p. 9.

27   'Sur Jean de Léry', p. 9.

28   'Sur Jean de Léry', p. 13.

Chapter 6   France in São Paulo

1   Claude Lévi-Strauss, *Loin du Brésil*, interview with Véronique Mortaigne, Paris, Chandeigne, 2005, p. 11: 'Brazil was the most important experience of my life – because of the distance and the contrast, but also because it determined my future career.'

2   Lucien Febvre, 'L'Amérique du Sud devant l'histoire', Introduction to 'Quarante-huit études, essais, comptes rendus et mises au point: À travers les Amériques latines', *Annales*, October–December 1948, republished as a special issue *Cahier des Annales*, 4, 1949, p. 208.

3   For this Brazilian chapter and those that follow, I would like to extend particular thanks to Fernanda Peixoto, a professor at USP, for the warm welcome she extended to me in Brazil; my intellectual debt to her work and that of her students (Luisa Valentini foremost among them) is reflected in the footnotes that follow.

4   *TT*, p. 21.

5   *TT*, p. 61.

6   Letter from Lévi-Strauss to his parents, 5 February 1935, written on board the *Mendoza*, from the private archives of Monique Lévi-Strauss.

7   Letter from Lévi-Strauss to his parents, 5 February 1935.

8 Letter from Lévi-Strauss to his parents, 5 February 1935.
9 *TT*, p. 61.
10 *TT*, p. 62.
11 *TT*.
12 Jean Maugüe, *Les Dents agacées*, Paris, Buchet-Chastel, 1982, p. 81.
13 *TT*, p. 77.
14 *TT*, p. 74. For a historical and comparative analysis of this trial, see Romain Bertrand, *L'Histoire à parts égales: Récits d'une rencontre Orient-Occident, XVI–XVIIe siècles*, Paris, Seuil, 2011.
15 *TT*, p. 79.
16 *TT*, p. 87.
17 *TT*.
18 *TT*, p. 92.
19 *TT*.
20 Claude Lévi-Strauss, *Saudades de São Paolo*, Instituto Moreira Salles, Companhia das Letras, 2009, p. 43. French translations by Luisa Valentini, whom I would like to thank for her extraordinary generosity during my stay in São Paolo.
21 Bartolomé Benassar and Richard Marin, *Histoire du Brésil, 1500–2000*, Paris, Fayard, 2000, p. 299.
22 Maugüe, *Les Dents agacées*, p. 87.
23 *TT*, p. 97.
24 *TT*, p. 95.
25 Lévi-Strauss, *Saudades de São Paolo*, p. 8.
26 Lévi-Strauss, *Saudades de São Paolo*, p. 49.
27 This painting is hanging in one of the reception halls of the Maison de l'Amérique Latine, on boulevard Saint Germain in Paris.
28 Lévi-Strauss, *Saudades de São Paolo*, p. 16.
29 On these questions, see the doctoral dissertation by Hugo Suppo, 'La Politique culturelle française au Brésil entre les années 1920–1950', IHEAL/University of Paris III, 1999.
30 Georges Dumas was the author of a book entitled *Psychologie des deux messies positivistes: Saint Simon et Auguste Comte*.
31 Sergio Micelli, *Les Intellectuels et le pouvoir au Brésil*, Paris, Éditions de al MSH/PUG, 1981.
32 'Rapport de M. Pingaud, consul de France à São Paulo, à M. de Robien', AMAE, Service des oeuvres, 1932–40, 'Brésil', vol. 443.
33 Based on discussions with Antonio Candido Mello e Souza, São Paulo, 8 August 2011. Antonio Candido is one of the last living witnesses who experienced the founding of the USP at first hand. He had been a student of Jean Maugüe and his wife had had Claude Lévi-Strauss as a professor.
34 Maugüe, *Les Dents agacées*, pp. 91–92.
35 Didier Eribon, *Conversations with Claude Lévi-Strauss*, Chicago, The University of Chicago Press, 1991, p. 20.
36 See Jean-Paul Lefèvre, 'Les missions universitaires françaises au Brésil dans les années 1930', *Vingtième Siècle: Revue d'histoire*, 38, 1993, pp. 24–33; and also Guy Martinère, *Aspects de la coopération franco-brésilienne*, Grenoble, PUG, 1982.
37 Maugüe, *Les Dents agacées*, p. 94.
38 Interview with Antonio Candido Mello e Souza, 8 August 2011.
39 The speech is mentioned in H. Suppo, 'La Politique culturelle française au Brésil entre les années 1920–1950', note 545. Pierre Monbeig, for his part, gave a lecture on Japanese immigration to Brazil. The theme of the crisis of

progress was already well-trodden ground; it was the title of a book by Georges Friedmann written in 1934 and published in 1936 by the prestigious French publishing house Gallimard.

40 See Christophe Charle, 'Ambassadeurs ou chercheurs?' in *La République des universitaires, 1870–1940*, Paris, Seuil, 1984, ch. 8.

41 Lévi-Strauss, *Saudades de São Paolo*, p. 10.

42 Claude Lévi-Strauss, Pierre Monbeig, and Jean Maugüe received a monthly salary of 2,600 francs, while Braudel and Hourcade, who were slightly older, earned 3,500 francs per month. Their salaries were paid half in francs and half in milreis, which elicited protests when the exchange rate resulted in a reduction in their income, AMAE, Service des oeuvres, 1932–40, 'Brésil', vol. 443, Université de São Paulo.

43 Eribon, *Conversations*, p. 19.

44 *TT*, p. 21.

45 *TT*, p. 99.

46 Eribon, *Conversations*, p. 20.

47 *TT*, p. 59.

48 *TT*.

49 This paragraph is based on the study by Johan Heilbron, 'Les métamorphoses du durkheimisme, 1920–1940', *Revue française de sociologie*, 26, pp. 203–237, and the summary given in F. Héran's piece in the same journal, p. 397.

50 See the dedication in SA, vol. 1: 'May an inconstant disciple dedicate this book which appears in 1958, the year of Emile Durkheim's centenary, to the memory of the founder of *Année Sociologique*.'

51 Letter from Claude Lévi-Strauss to Marcel Mauss, 10 November 1935, CLS Archives, NAF 28150, box 181.

52 Quoted by Suppo, 'La Politique culturelle française au Brésil'.

53 Text preserved in its entirety at the AMAE, Service des oeuvres, 1932–40, 'Brésil', vol. 443.

54 Letter from Georges Dumas to Jean Marx, 1 December 1936, AMAE, Service des oeuvres, 1932–40, 'Brésil', vol. 443, Université de São Paulo.

55 This quarrel was the subject of two reports sent by Paul Arbousse-Bastide to Jean Marx: one undated, 'Note sur le cas de M. Lévi-Strauss et Mme Lévi-Strauss', and the other dated 30 July 1936, AMAE, Service des oeuvres, 1932–40, 'Brésil', vol. 443, Université de São Paulo.

56 Eribon, *Conversations*, p. 23.

57 Maugüe, *Les Dents agacées*, p. 97.

58 Interview with Antonio Candido Mello e Souza, São Paulo, 5 August 2011.

59 *TT*, p. 102.

60 Maugüe, *Les Dents agacées*, p. 102.

61 *TT*, p. 59.

62 The course was organized as follows: 'Domestic sociology (marriage, the incest prohibition, parenthood, polygamy, clan organization, matriarchy); economic sociology (primitive forms of society, primitive communism); political sociology (primitive forms of government and law); sociology of religion (totemism); and the comparative study of social phenomena'.

63 See the seminal articles by Fernanda Peixoto and her students: Fernanda Peixoto, 'Lévi-Strauss à São Paulo: la ville et le terrain', in *Lévi-Strauss*, Paris, L'Herne, 2004, p. 74; and Fernanda Peixoto and Luisa Valentini, 'Lévi-Strauss à São Paulo: l'Université, le département de culture et la Société d'ethnographie et de folklore', *Europe*, 1005–1006, January–February 2013, pp. 71–81.

64 Peixoto, 'Lévi-Strauss à São Paulo: la ville et le terrain', p. 79.

65 Lévi-Strauss, *Saudades de São Paolo*, p. 14.
66 Letter from Claude Lévi-Strauss to Célestin Bouglé, 20 November 1935, National Archives, 61AJ93.
67 Décio de Almeida Prado, cited in Fernanda Peixoto and Luisa Valentini, 'Lévi-Strauss à São Paulo: l'Université, le département de culture et la Société d'ethnographie et de folklore', p. 75.
68 Egon Schaden, cited in Fernanda Peixoto, 'Lévi-Strauss à São Paulo: la ville et le terrain', p. 78.
69 Claude Lévi-Strauss, 'Em prol de um Instituto de Antropologia Física e Cultural', cited in Fernanda Peixoto, 'Lévi-Strauss à São Paulo: la ville et le terrain', p. 79.
70 Lévi-Strauss, *Saudades de São Paolo*, p. 18.
71 Lévi-Strauss, *Saudades de São Paolo*, p. 19.
72 Pierre Monbeig, *Pionniers et planteurs de l'État de São Paolo*, Paris, Armand Colin, 1952, p. 12.
73 *TT*, p. 47.
74 Heliana Angotti Salgueiro, 'Monbeig, un géographe sur le "vif"', *Pages Paysages*, 9, 2002, p. 47.
75 *TT*, p. 124.
76 *TT*, p. 122.
77 See Hervé Théry, 'Claude Lévi-Strauss, Pierre Monbeig et Roger Brunet', *EchoGéo*, 7, 2008, published online 24 November 2008, at http://echogeo.revues.org/9503.
78 Lévi-Strauss, *Saudades de São Paolo*, p. 46.
79 I am grateful to Jean-Louis Tissier for having, once again, guided me down the craggy paths of the history and epistemology of geography.
80 Maugüe, *Les Dents agacées*, p. 118.
81 Maugüe, *Les Dents agacées*, p. 119.
82 Maugüe, *Les Dents agacées*, p. 121.
83 *TT*, p. 154.
84 *TT*, p. 160.

Chapter 7   In the Heart of Brazil

1 Didier Eribon, *Conversations with Claude Lévi-Strauss*, Chicago, The University of Chicago Press, 1991, p. 21.
2 Antonio Candido Mello de Souza, interview with the author, São Paulo, 5 August 2011.
3 F. Peixoto and L. Valentini, 'Lévi-Strauss à São Paulo: l'Université, le département de culture et la Société d'ethnographie et de folklore', *Europe*, 1005–1006, January–February 2013, p. 76.
4 Recall Claude Lévi-Strauss's phrase in Eribon, *Conversations*, p. 18: 'The people of São Paulo saw themselves as the working arm of a nation slumbering in colonial torpor.'
5 Oswald de Andrade's text was translated into English in 1991, *Latin American Literary Review*, 19/38, July–December 1991), pp. 38–47.
6 Patrick Wilcken, *Claude Lévi-Strauss: The Poet in the Laboratory*, London, Bloomsbury, 2010, p. 54.
7 See Maria Lucia Pallares-Burke, *Gilberto Freyre, um Vitoriano nos tropicos*, São Paulo, Editora UNESP, 2005, and the review of this book by Afranio Garcia in *Annales HSS*, March–April 2006, 2, pp. 476–479.

8 Garcia, 'Review', pp. 476–477.

9 For example, the municipal library is named after him.

10 See Sergio Micelli, *Les Intellectuels et le pouvoir au Brésil*, Paris, Éditions de al MSH/PUG, 1981, p. 33ff.

11 Claude Lévi-Strauss, *Saudades de São Paolo*, Instituto Moreira Salles, Companhia das Letras, 2009, pp. 10–11.

12 Testimonial by Françoise Héritier, interview with the author, 18 April 2012.

13 Filmed interview with Manuela Carneiro da Cunha, 1985, screened at the Laboratório de Imagem e Som em Antropologia (LISA), USP. This is what he had to say about Mário de Andrade: 'He was an extraordinarily lively and intense person, who could mobilize prodigious energies around him.'

14 Cited by Fernanda Peixoto, 'Lévi-Strauss à São Paulo: la ville et le terrain', in *Lévi-Strauss*, Paris, L'Herne, 2004, p. 80.

15 The book was most likely *Música a, doce música*, published in 1933. Claude Lévi-Strauss, letter to Mário de Andrade, 25 October 1936, Mário de Andrade Archive, IEB Archive, USP. This letter was one of four published in *Les Temps modernes*, August–September–October 2004, 628, p. 259.

16 Letter from Dina Lévi-Strauss to Jean Marx, 10 December 1936, AMAE, Service des oeuvres, 1932–40, Brazil.

17 Mongolian spots are dark spots of variable size which appear at birth on the back or the buttocks of newborns. It is widespread among dark-skinned children, especially in Asia, hence its name.

18 Dina Lévi-Strauss, *agrégée* from the University of Paris, *Instruçoes praticas para pesquisas de Antropologia física e cultural*, São Paulo, Coleçao do Departamento municipal de Cultura, 1936.

19 'We were able to take anthropometric measurements of male Indians only, for the females remained coy and reserved. Impossible to obtain measurements of skeletons and bones of either the Caduveo or the Bororo of Rio Vermelho. [. . .] Blood categorization has also been impossible to carry out for the Indians are opposed to it, and they were also reluctant to let us photograph them for fear of death or enchantment.' Comments gathered by the Brazilian press upon the return of the Lévi-Strausses, cited in Luis Donisete Benzi Grupioni, 'Claude Lévi-Strauss parmi les Amérindiens: deux expéditions ethnographiques dans l'intérieur du Brésil', in *Brésil indien. Les Arts des Amérindiens du Brésil*, Paris, RMN, 2005, pp. 315–316.

20 *Diário da Noite*, 4 November 1936, CLS Archives, NAF 28150, box 232, 'Presse brésilienne, 1935–37'.

21 Letter from Claude Lévi-Strauss to Mário de Andrade, 29 April 1937, Mário de Andrade Archives, IEB Archives, USP.

22 Author of a master's thesis under the supervision of Fernanda Peixoto, 'Um laboratório de antropologia: o encontro entre Mário de Andrade, Dina Dreyfus e Claude Lévi-Strauss (1935–38)', USP, 2010, São Paulo, Alameda, 2013.

23 'Contributions pour l'étude de l'organisation sociale des Indiens Bororo', *Journal de la Société des américanistes*, 28(2), 1936, pp. 269–304.

24 *Revista do Arquivo municipal*, 3(27), pp. 8–79.

25 *Festa do Divino Espirito Santo: Mogy das Cruzes, 30 mai 1936*, filmed by Dina Lévi-Strauss (alone), *Estado do São Paulo*. Film archived at the São Paulo Department of Culture.

26 Mario Wagner, quoted in Wilcken, *Claude Lévi-Strauss*, p. 55; original source not indicated.

27 See Benzi Grupioni, 'Claude Lévi-Strauss parmi les Amérindiens', pp. 316ff.

28 Letter from Claude Lévi-Strauss to Marcel Mauss, 10 November 1935, CLS Archives, NAF 28150, box 181, 'Correspondance'.
29 Letter from Claude Lévi-Strauss to Marcel Mauss, 10 November 1935.
30 Benzi Grupioni, 'Claude Lévi-Strauss parmi les Amérindiens', p. 315.
31 Letter from Marcel Mauss to Claude Lévi-Strauss, 20 February 1936, CLS Archives, NAF 28150, box 181.
32 Letter from Marcel Mauss to Claude Lévi-Strauss, 20 February 1936.
33 CLS Archives, NAF 28150, box 11, 'Documents', 'Récit de voyage São Paulo-Porto-Esperança par Dina Lévi-Strauss', 11p.
34 *TT*, p. 162.
35 *TT*.
36 *TT*, p. 167.
37 *TT*, p. 177.
38 Jenipapo is the fruit of a tropical tree whose name means 'staining fruit'.
39 *Aldeia de Nalike*, Serra Bodoquena, Estado de Mato Grosso, December 1935–January 1936 (one of the two films is held in the library of the São Paulo Department of Culture). See Emmanuel Leclercq, 'Quelques fragments de vie primitive: Claude Lévi-Strauss, cinéaste au Brésil', *Les Temps modernes*, August–September 2004, 628, pp. 329–332.
40 Interview with Manuela Carneiro da Cunha, filmed in 1985; a copy of the film is held at the Laboratório de Imagem e Som em Antropologia (LISA), USP.
41 Letter from Claude Lévi-Strauss to Mário de Andrade, 15 January 1936, Mário de Andrade Archives, IEB Archives, USP.
42 Interview with Manuela Carneiro da Cunha, 1985.
43 *TT*, p. 214.
44 *À propos de Tristes Tropiques*, Jean-Pierre Beaurenaut, Jorge Bodansky and Patrick Menget, 1991, Arte, 46 minutes.
45 *Claude Lévi-Strauss par lui-même*, interviewed by Jean-Claude Bringuier, Pierre Dumayet, Jean-José Marchand, Bernard Pivot and Michel Treguer, 2008, Arte, 1 h 33.
46 *TT*, p. 215.
47 *TT*, p. 219.
48 *Dança do Marid'do*, Kejara, February 1936, Cinemathèque, São Paulo Department of Culture.
49 *TT*, p. 217. A Bororo man of about thirty-five years of age who had been educated by the Salesian Fathers and had learned basic Portuguese.
50 *TT*, p. 221.
51 *TT*, p. 245.
52 Claude Lévi-Strauss has said that he had 'the feeling that [he had] always been a structuralist, even as a child'. In *À propos de Tristes Tropiques*.
53 Claude Lévi-Strauss, 'Preface', in Luis Donisete Benzi Grupioni, *Brésil indien. Les Arts des Amérindiens du Brésil*, p. 17.
54 *Conselho de Fiscalizaçao das Expediçoes artisticas e scientificas n° Brasil*, whose archive is held at the Museum of Astronomy and Related Sciences (MAST) in Rio de Janeiro.
55 Benzi Grupioni, 'Claude Lévi-Strauss parmi les Amérindiens', p. 318.
56 See Benoît de l'Estoile, *Le Goût des autres: De l'exposition coloniale aux arts premiers*, Paris, Flammarion, 2007.
57 Letter from Claude Lévi-Strauss to Heloisa Alberto Torres, 5 November 1936: 'But – and this is between you and me – I don't think that what I have brought back from the Bororo would be of any interest to you. You have a

thousand times more and a thousand times better.' 'Don't imagine you will find a Kaduveo ceramic of the same calibre as the two specimens at the National Museum.' I thank Heloisa Domingues, a curator at MAST, for granting me access to the correspondence between Claude Lévi-Strauss and Heloisa Alberto Torres. See the next chapter.

58 *TT*, p. 30.
59 Eribon, *Conversations*, p. 21.
60 See Jean Jamin, 'Objets trouvés des paradis perdus: à propos de la mission Dakar-Djibouti', in *Collection Passions*, Musée d'Ethnologie de Neuchâtel, 1982.
61 *TT*, p. 158.
62 *TT.*
63 Letter from Célestin Bouglé to Claude Lévi-Strauss, 4 January 1937, Archives Nationales, 61 AJ 93. I am grateful to Thomas Hirsch for providing access to this correspondence.
64 Letter from Claude Lévi-Strauss to Marcel Mauss, 14 March 1936.
65 Year 1936, 28(28/2), pp. 269–304.
66 Letter from L. Lévy-Bruhl to Claude Lévi-Strauss, 24 April 1937, CLS Archives, NAF 28150, box 195, 'Correspondance reçue'.
67 Letter from Curt Nimuendaju, 11 November 1936, quoted in Elena Welper, *Curt Unkel Nimuendaju: Um Capitulo Alemao na Tradiçao Etnografica Brasileira*, Dissertaçao de Mestrado, Rio de Janeiro, Programa de Pos-Graduação em Antropologia Social, Museu Nacional, UFRJ. I am grateful to Elena Monteiro Welper for giving me access to this correspondence and to Luisa Valentini for translating these letters from the Portuguese.
68 Letter from Curt Nimuendaju, 11 November 1936.

Chapter 8 Massimo Lévi with the Nambikwara

1 *TT*, p. 249.
2 Eduardo Viveiros de Castro, 'Desencontros', preface to the Brazilian edition of *Longe do Brasil*, Editora Unesp, 2011.
3 Letter from Claude Lévi-Strauss to Marcel Mauss, 25 September 1937, CLS Archives, NAF 28150, box 181.
4 Roger Bastide, interview with Irene Cardoso, cited in Luis Donizete Benzi Grupioni, *Coleções e Expedições Vigiadas: Os Etnólogos nº Conselho de Fiscalização das Expedições Artísticas e Científicas nº Brasil*, São Paulo, Editora Hucitec/Anpocs, 1998, p. 139.
5 Roger Bastide, interview with Irene Cardoso.
6 Letter to Marcel Mauss, 25 September 1937, CLS Archives, NAF 28150, box 181.
7 *TT*, p. 252.
8 *TT*, p. 249.
9 See Vincent Debaene, '"Un quartier de Paris aussi inconnu que l'Amazone": Surréalisme et récit ethnographique', *Les Temps modernes*, 628, August–September–October 2004, p. 135.
10 AMAE, AM, 1918–1940, DG, vol. 206, 'Note pour M. de Bressy', quoted in H. Suppo, 'La Politique culturelle française au Brésil entre les années 1920–1950', Ph.D. dissertation, note 585.
11 *TT*, p. 253.
12 *TT*, p. 250.
13 *TT.*

14 *TT.*
15 *TT*, p. 251.
16 See Vincent Debaene, 'Notice', in *TT*, p. 1685.
17 On Rondon and the SPI, see Antonio Carlos de Souza Lima, *Um grande cerco de paz: Poder tutelar, indianidade e formação do Estado n° Brasil*, Petrópolis, Vozes, 1995; and Benoît de l'Estoile's review of that book in *Revue de synthèse*, 3–4, July–December 2000, pp. 489–492; see also Patrick Wilcken, *Claude Lévi-Strauss: The Poet in the Laboratory*, London, Bloomsbury, 2010, pp. 77–79.
18 Letter dated 6 April 1937, Lévi-Strauss file, Conselho de Fiscalzaçao das Expediçoes artisticas e scientificas file, n. Brasil, MAST. See also Luis Donisete Benzi Grupioni, 'Claude Lévi-Strauss parmi les Amérindiens: Deux expéditions ethnographiques dans l'intérieur du Brésil', in *Brésil indien. Les Arts des Amérindiens du Brésil*, Paris, RMN, 2005, pp. 327–329. The author details the exact chronology and intricacies of the bureaucratic battle that unfolded.
19 All letters quoted in this paragraph come from this same archive.
20 This entire paragraph is based on the suggestions of Heloisa Domingues, director of the MAST Archives, and Mariza Corrêa, author of *Antropologas e Antropologia*, Belo Horizonte, Editora da UFMG, 2003; 'Lettres d'une femme rangée', *Cahiers du Brésil contemporain*, 47–48, 2002, pp. 181–197; and the e-book, Mariza Corrêa and Januara Mello (eds.), *Querida Heloisa/Dear Heloisa: Cartas de campo para Heloisa Alberto Torres*, Núcleo de Estudos de Gênero (PAGU), Unicamp, 2008. I thank them both for their availability and generosity.
21 Mariza Corrêa, introduction to *Querida Heloisa*, an electronic platform that collects the letters exchanged between Heloisa Alberto Torres and anthropologists working in the field in Brazil.
22 Antonio Carlos de Souza Lima, 'L'indigénisme au Brésil: migration et réappropriations d'un savoir administratif', *Revue de synthèse*, 3–4, July–December 2000, pp. 381–410.
23 Letter to Heloisa Alberto Torres, 12 February 1938, MAST Archives, Lévi-Strauss file.
24 Letter to Heloisa Alberto Torres, 12 February 1938. French translation in Benzi Grupioni, 'Claude Lévi-Strauss parmi les Amérindiens', p. 328.
25 Letter to Mário de Andrade, undated, Mário de Andrade Archives, IEB, USP.
26 Benzi Grupioni, 'Claude Lévi-Strauss parmi les Amérindiens', p. 328.
27 Letter to Heloisa Alberto Torres, 10 April 1937, copy of a letter from the Heloisa Alberto Torres Archives.
28 'Mission *Tristes Tropiques*', *Libération*, 1 September 1988. Claude Lévi-Strauss, in an interview by Mathieu Lindon, explains: 'We had a very difficult relationship in the field. He was a "fiscal inspector" who represented the Brazilian authorities. But he was terrified, crushed under the weight of his responsibilities. He constantly tried to slow things down, to prevent me from doing what I wanted to do. And we had to remain all the while comrades, because we were living rough together.'
29 CLS Archives, NAF 28150, box 126, 'Carnet de notes de Dina, São Paulo, mai 1938, Utiarity, juillet 1938'. All quotes come from these notebooks.
30 A critique that Clifford Geertz makes in 'The world in a text: how to read *Tristes Tropiques*?', in *Works and Lives: The Anthropologist as Author*, Stanford, Stanford University Press, 1988. As Vincent Debaene points out in 'Notice', p. 1686, Geertz faults Lévi-Strauss for obscuring the general conditions of anthropological practice and thus presenting a 'heroic version' of it.

31 The mysterious story of his death by suicide recently inspired a novel by a Brazilian writer, Bernardo de Carvalho, *Nine Nights*, Vintage, 2008.

32 Questionnaire quoted in Luiz de Castro Faria, *Another Look: A Diary of the Serra do Norte Expedition, 2001*, Rio de Janeiro, Ouro Sobre Azul, 2001, p. 50.

33 CLS Archives, NAF 28150, box 126, 'Carnet de notes de Dina, São Paulo, mai 1938, Utiarity, juillet 1938'.

34 CLS Archives, NAF 28150, box 126, 'Carnet de notes de Dina, São Paulo, mai 1938'.

35 CLS Archives, NAF 28150, box 126, 'Carnet de notes de Dina, São Paulo, mai 1938'.

36 CLS Archives, NAF 28150, box 126, 'Carnet de notes de Dina, São Paulo, mai 1938'.

37 CLS Archives, NAF 28150, box 126, 'Carnet de notes de Dina, São Paulo, mai 1938'.

38 *TT*, p. 266.

39 *TT*, p. 267.

40 Letter to Mário de Andrade, 17 June 1938, Mário de Andrade Archives, IEB, USP.

41 CLS Archives, NAF 28150, box 126, 'Carnet de notes de Dina, São Paulo, mai 1938'.

42 *TT*, p. 271.

43 Letter to Mário de Andrade, 17 June 1938, Mário de Andrade Archives, IEB, USP.

44 'Rapport du Docteur Vellard sur la mission de Mato Grosso', 2 April 1939, submitted to Jean Marx, AMAE, SO, Brazil, 1932–1940, vol. 440, 56 p.

45 Letter to Marcel Mauss, Utiarity, 7 July 1938, CLS Archives, NAF 28150, box 181.

46 *TT*, p. 274.

47 Claude Lévi-Strauss, filmed interview with Manuela da Cunha, 1985, Laboratório de Imagem e Som em Antropologia (LISA), USP.

48 *Auprès de l'Amazonie: Le parcours de Claude Lévi-Strauss*, documentary film by Marcelo Fortaleza Flores, 2008, 52 min.

49 *TT*, p. 331.

50 *TT*, p. 43.

51 *TT*, pp. 332–3.

52 *TT*, p. 293.

53 Claude Lévi-Strauss's notebooks from the Brazil expedition are collected in boxes 120 to 125 of his personal archives, NAF 28150. The following quotations are taken from them.

54 See Debaene, 'Notice', p. 1687.

55 Benoît de l'Estoile, *Le Goût des autres: de l'exposition coloniale aux arts premiers*, Paris, Flammarion, 2007, p. 170. On Castro Faria's photographs, see also Michel Perrin, 'Regards croisés', *L'Homme*, 165, January–March 2003, accessible online, at http://lhomme.revues.org/index15782.html.

56 *TT*, p. 376.

57 *TT*, p. 376.

58 The text of which is available in 'En marge de *Tristes Tropiques*', Pléiade, pp. 1632–1651.

59 *TT*, p. 291.

60 Seventy-five Nambikwara, seventeen families and thirteen shelters. The episode is narrated in chapter 28 of *Tristes Tropiques*, 'A writing lesson'; this chapter on

the birth of writing and its political function was to inspire Jacques Derrida's famous critique in *Of Grammatology.*

61 *TT*, p. 299.
62 *TT*, p. 286.
63 Michel Leiris, *Phantom Africa*, Chicago, The University of Chicago Press, 2017. See also Georges Devereux, *De l'Angoisse à la méthode dans les sciences du comportement*, Paris, Flammarion, 1980.
64 CLS Archives, NAF 28150, box 125, 'Carnet (sans couverture) broché, fin de l'expédition', 1 page, 3 expedition notebooks, 'Brésil'.
65 'Rapport du Docteur Vellard sur la mission de Mato Grosso', p. 28.
66 'Rapport du Docteur Vellard sur la mission de Mato Grosso', p. 28.
67 A fermented corn-based drink prepared by the Indians.
68 *TT*, p. 360. Photographs of the protagonists are available in Claude Lévi-Strauss, *Saudades de São Paolo*, Instituto Moreira Salles, Companhia das Letras, 2009, pp. 193–197.
69 Wilcken, *Claude Lévi-Strauss*, p. 105.
70 Castro Faria, *Another Look*, p. 185: 'He doggedly persists in the same attitude that he has had throughout, keeping to himself. And since our leader seriously lacks authority and energy, I don't know how we're going to get out of this.'
71 Castro Faria, *Another Look*, p. 192.
72 *TT*, p. 364.
73 *TT*, p. 364.
74 Lindon, 'Mission *Tristes Tropiques*'.
75 Lindon, 'Mission *Tristes Tropiques*'.
76 Filmed interview by Anne-Marie Pessis for *História da antropologia nº Brasil*, University of Campinas, 1988: 'I had no vocation. I was purely and simply accompanying my husband. But then, I could not remain aloof. It was so strange, so new. I did what I could.'
77 Alain Badiou, email dated 9 February 2012.
78 Castro Faria, *Another Look*, p. 4: 'A expedição da Serra Norte foi um fracasso total.'
79 Vassili Rivron, 'Un point de vue indigène? Archives de l'expédition Lévi-Strauss', *L'Homme*, 165, 2003, p. 306.
80 See the correspondence between Lévi-Strauss and Nimuendaju, edited by Elena Monteiro Welper in *Curt Unkel Nimuendaju*.
81 Marcela Coelho de Souza and Carlos Fausto, 'Reconquistando o campo perdido: o que Levi-Strauss deve aos amerindos', *Revista de Antropologia*, 47(1), São Paulo, 2004. I am grateful to Carlos Fausto for providing me with an unpublished French version of this article.
82 '*L'Express* va plus loin avec Claude Lévi-Strauss', *L'Express*, 15–21 March 1971.
83 Eduardo Viveiros de Castro, 'Les rendez-vous manqués', preface to the Brazilian edition of *Loin du Brésil, Longo do Brasil*, Editora Unesp, 2011, p. 86.
84 Claude Lévi-Strauss, 'Le coucher de soleil: Entretien avec Boris Wiseman', *Les Temps modernes*, 628, August–September–October 2004, p. 6.
85 Lévi-Strauss, 'Le coucher de soleil', p. 6.
86 Filmed interview with Manuela da Cunha, 1985.
87 Lévi-Strauss, 'Le coucher de soleil', p. 5: 'Is it necessary to carry out fieldwork at least once to become an anthropologist?' 'Absolutely'. 'Why is that?' 'To get better at using other people's work.'

88 Anne-Christine Taylor, 'Don Quichotte en Amérique: Claude Lévi-Strauss et l'anthropologie américaniste', in M. Izard (ed.), *Claude Lévi-Strauss*, Paris, L'Herne, 'Cahiers de l'Herne', 2004, p. 82.

89 *TT*, p. 372: 'But the rapidly approaching end of my journey was being brought home to me in the first place by this ascent through layers of time.'

90 For this entire passage, again, the source is Benzi Grupioni, 'Claude Lévi-Strauss parmi les Amérindiens', pp. 330–332.

91 Letter to Heloisa Alberto Torres, 14 January 1939.

92 Lévi-Strauss file, CFE. T. 2. 054, archives of the Conselho de Fiscalização das Expedições artisticas e scientificas n° Brasil, MAST.

93 'Registro general da coleção etnografica da expediçao a Serra do Norte', Lévi-Strauss file, CFE. T. 2. 054, archives of the Conselho de Fiscalização das Expedições artísticas e scientificas n· Brasil, MAST: Utiarity, Indiens Parecis; Juruena, Nambikwara, Campos Novos, Nambikwara; Campos Novos, Nambikwara, northern group; Vilhena, Nambikwara-Tangnani; Vilhena, Nambikwara-Cabane; Vilhena, Nambikwara-Kabisi; Tres Buritis-Barao de Melgaçao-Nambikwara; Rio Pimenta Bueno-Kabisiana; Rio Machado, Tupi; Rio Machado, Urumi.

94 The preceding quotes are taken from the correspondence between Dina Lévi-Strauss and Mário de Andrade, Mário de Andrade Archives, IEBB, USP.

95 Speech delivered by Claude Lévi-Strauss on 17 June 1963 in honour of Métraux, who had recently died.

96 Alfred Métraux, *Itinéraires 1. Carnets de notes et journaux de voyage*, Paris, Payot, 1978, pp. 42–43.

Chapter 9   Crisis (1939–1941)

1 In a letter to Mário de Andrade (dated 4 March 1939), Lévi-Strauss let him know that he would be passing through Rio on 8 March and invited him to lunch on board, very much hoping that he would be able to come: 'I have so much to tell you.' But they missed each other and were never to meet again, since Mário died in 1945; Mário de Andrade Archives, IEB, USP.

2 An expression used by Lévi-Strauss to describe the character of Paul Thalamas in his draft of a novel entitled *Tristes Tropiques*, a few pages of which have been published in the 'Bibliothèque de la Pléiade' edition, p. 1629.

3 Didier Eribon, *Conversations with Claude Lévi-Strauss*, Chicago, The University of Chicago Press, 1991, p. 24.

4 To borrow an expression he applied to himself as a student, see Eribon, *Conversations*, p. 10.

5 Letter from Claude Lévi-Strauss to Marcel Mauss, 11 August 1939, Valleraugue, CLS Archives, NAF 28150, box 181.

6 According to Wikipedia, the word 'creosote' comes from the German word *Kreosot*, which stems from two Greek words: *kreas*, 'flesh' or 'meat' and *sôzein*, 'to save' or 'to preserve'. Creosote is thus that which preserves flesh, the flesh of paper and the flesh of the past.

7 'Claude Lévi-Strauss regarde son passé: Être juif à la veille de la guerre', *Le Figaro*, 22–23 July 1989: 'How did you envision the war and the threat of a Hitlerian world?' 'I didn't ask myself questions. I was just back from an expedition. [. . .] I was incredibly busy with, on the one hand, the cataloguing of the collections at the Musée de l'Homme, and on the other, moving back to Paris.'

And in addition, it was during that month that my first wife and I separated. So . . . I was elsewhere.'

8 'Claude Lévi-Strauss regarde son passé'.

9 Alfred Métraux, *Itinéraires 1. Carnets de notes et journaux de voyage*, Paris, Payot, 1978, p. 43: 'For Lévi-Strauss, German anti-Semitism is due to the jealousy felt by the German middle-classes towards the Jews who have managed to thrive during the period of inflation.'

10 These two men, future founders and martyrs of the Musée de l'Homme Network, were Russian Jews, naturalized in 1936, and hired by Rivet at around that time. Boris Vildé spent two years in Germany from 1930 to 1932, witnessing the rise of Nazism. See Julien Blanc, *Au Commencement de la Résistance: Du côté du Musée de l'Homme, 1940–1941*, Paris, Seuil, 2010, p. 77.

11 'Claude Lévi-Strauss regarde son passé'.

12 Vincent Debaene, *Far Afield: French Anthropology between Sciences and Literature*, Chicago, The University of Chicago Press, 2014.

13 'En marge de *Tristes Tropiques*', *Pléiade*, p. 1628.

14 On this point, see Claude Lévi-Strauss, 'Le coucher de soleil: entretien avec Boris Wiseman', *Les Temps modernes*, 628, August–September–October 2004, p. 9.

15 Lévi-Strauss, 'Le coucher de soleil', p. 9.

16 Letter from Dina to Claude Lévi-Strauss, dated Monday, CLS Archives, NAF 28150, box 187.

17 Interview of the author with Monique Lévi-Strauss, 24 September 2011.

18 Patrick Wilcken, *Claude Lévi-Strauss: The Poet in the Laboratory*, London, Bloomsbury, 2010, p. 113. Lévi-Strauss was interviewed by the author in 2007.

19 'Claude Lévi-Strauss regarde son passé: être juif à la veille de la guerre'.

20 Julien Gracq, *Manuscrits de guerre*, Paris, José Corti, 2011.

21 André Breton, *Anthologie de l'humour noir*. The first edition, published by Le Sagittaire in 1940, was immediately banned by the new Vichy government.

22 Eribon, *Conversations*, p. 25. Claude Lévi-Strauss was 'liaison officer W for the 2nd batallion, 164th RIF, postal sector 193'.

23 Letter of 23 May 1940. The batallion in question was the famous Black Watch infantry battalion of the Scottish Royal Regiment.

24 Eribon, *Conversations*, p. 25.

25 'Claude Lévi-Strauss regarde son passé: être juif à la veille de la guerre'.

26 'La leçon du pissenlit', *Le Monde*, 26 May 1973, Gilles Lapouge reports on what Lévi-Strauss confided to Bernard Pingaud.

27 'La leçon du pissenlit'.

28 Eribon, *Conversations*, p. 25.

29 Gracq, *Manuscrits de guerre*, p. 66.

30 Letter from liaison officer Claude Lévi-Strauss, CIP, postal sector 14014, 2 June 1940, CLS Archives, NAF 28150, box 181.

31 'Claude Lévi-Strauss regarde son passé: être juif à la veille de la guerre'.

32 Gracq, *Manuscrits de guerre*, pp. 126–127.

33 Only eighty members of parliament, most but not all on the Left, refused to vote the full powers for Marshal Pétain.

34 Marc Bloch, *Strange Defeat: A Statement of Evidence Written in 1940*, New York, W.W. Norton, 1999, p. 37.

35 Eribon, *Conversations*, p. 26. See also the letter sent to Marcel Mauss from Montpellier, on 22 July 1940: 'A long and complicated journey has landed me, with part of my unit, in Montpellier. My address here is: Pavillon Colonial, Cité Universitaire. While waiting to be demobilized, and to ward off the utter

boredom, I have found no other solution than to serve as a *baccalauréat* examiner!' He also mentions that his wife Dina is staying with mutual friends in the Gard region.

36 André Chamson was his former colleague at the National Assembly and a Protestant writer linked to the Front populaire.

37 Claude Lévi-Strauss, 'Autoportrait', remarks collected by Catherine Clément and Dominique-Antoine Grisoni, *Magazine littéraire*, 223, October 1985, p. 20.

38 Eribon, *Conversations*, p. 27.

39 Eribon, *Conversations*, p. 26.

40 'Claude Lévi-Strauss regarde son passé: être juif à la veille de la guerre'.

41 A text that was written during the war and published posthumously more than sixty years later: Hélène Berr, *Journal of Hélène Berr*, New York, Weinstein Books, 2009.

42 Eribon, *Conversations*, p. 99. For a critical reading of his 'indebtedness' to Granet, which was acknowledged late in Lévi-Strauss's career, see 'Lévi-Strauss, lecteur de Granet ou la dette refoulée', chapter 9, in François Héran, *Figures de la parenté*, Paris, PUF, 2009.

43 See Claude Singer, *Vichy: l'Université et les Juifs*, Paris, Les Belles Lettres, 1992, p. 145.

44 Lévi-Strauss, 'Autoportrait', p. 20.

45 'Claude Lévi-Strauss regarde son passé: être juif à la veille de la guerre'.

46 *TT*, p. 23.

47 See Emmanuel Loyer, *Paris à New York: Intellectuels et artistes français en exil, 1940–1947*, Paris, Grasset, 2005, pp. 34–37.

48 Eribon, *Conversations*, p. 27.

49 The quotes that follow are excerpted from letters contained in the file on Claude Lévi-Strauss, Rockefeller Archives Center (Tarrytown), R.G.1.1, entry 200, box 52, folders 609–610. I would like to express here again my thanks to both Pierre-Yves Saunier and the Foundation's archivists. For more details on the selection process described here, see Loyer, *Paris à New York*, ch. 1.

50 CLS Archives, NAF 28150, box 196, letter of 12 May 1937: 'When I think of your remarkable article on the Bororo, two English words always come to mind: "refreshing" and "stimulating". Your study is "refreshing" in that it is a change from the sterile harping that South-American anthropology has become in the hands of poor amateurs. "Stimulating" because it will inaugurate, I hope, a new era in the way studies are carried out.'

51 Eribon, *Conversations*, p. 24.

52 Conversely, Lévi-Strauss was to later enable Devereux to cross the Atlantic in the other direction and in other circumstances, by supporting his application to the EPHE (VIth section), an institution at which Devereux was to teach from 1963.

53 Letter from Miles L. Hanley, University of Wisconsin at Madison, to John Marshall, 24 September 1940, RFA, R.G.1.1, entry 200, box 46, folder 530.

54 *TT*, p. 24.

55 *TT*, p. 24.

56 See Laurent Jeanpierre, 'Varian Fry et le sauvetage des réfugiés aux États-Unis', in J.-M. Guillon (ed.), *Varian Fry, du refuge … à l'exil*, 2 vols., Arles, Actes Sud, 2000.

57 *TT*, p. 24.

58 *TT*, p. 24.

59 *TT*, p. 25.

60 *TT*, p. 25.

61 *TT*, p. 28.
62 This note was published, together with Breton's reply, as 'A commentary on the relation between works of art and documents, written and delivered to André Breton on board the *Capitaine Paul Lemerle* in March 1941', in *LLR*, pp. 143–151.
63 *TT*, p. 15.
64 André Breton, 'Troubled Waters', *Martinique: Snake Charmer*, Austin, University of Texas Press, 2008, p. 68.
65 See Eric Jennings, *Vichy in the Tropics: Pétain's National Revolution in Madagascar, Guadeloupe, and Indochina, 1940–1944*, Stanford, Stanford University Press, 2004.
66 Breton, 'Troubled Waters'.
67 Breton, 'Troubled Waters'.
68 *TT*, p. 27.
69 *TT*, p. 27.
70 *TT*, p. 29.
71 *TT*, p. 33.
72 Letter from Dina Lévi-Strauss to Mário de Andrade, 13 June 1941, Mário de Andrade Archives, IEBB, USP, São Paulo.
73 Letter from Dina Lévi-Strauss to Mário de Andrade, 13 June 1941.
74 Letter from Claude Lévi-Strauss to Marcel Mauss, 8 May 1940, 'Agent de liaison W à la zone 2ᵉ bataillon, 164ᵉ RIF, secteur postal 193', CLS Archives, NAF 28150, box 181.
75 Letter from Claude Lévi-Strauss to Paul Rivet, 21 July 1941, Lévi-Strauss-Rivet correspondence, Paul Rivet Archives, 2 AP1C, Muséum national d'Histoire naturelle.
76 Letter from Dina Lévi-Strauss to Marcel Mauss (s.d.), Archives nationales, 2 AP 4 2 B2. This letter was transmitted to me by Thomas Hirsch, whom I wish to thank.
77 Letter from Dina Lévi-Strauss to Mário de Andrade, 13 June 1941, Mário de Andrade Archives, IEBB, USP, São Paulo.
78 Claude and Dina were not to meet again until the 1980s – upon the death of Emma Lévi-Strauss, Claude's mother, to whom Dina had paid regular visits throughout – at which point they resumed contact, sending each other books.

Chapter 10   A Frenchman in New York City: Exile and Intellectual Invention (1941–1944)

1 Claude Lévi-Strauss, 'New York in 1941', *TVFA*, p. 267.
2 Patrick Waldberg, 'Au fil du souvenir', in *Échanges et communications: mélanges offerts à Claude Lévi-Strauss à l'occasion de son 60e anniversaire*, texts collected by Jean Pouillon and Pierre Maranda, La Haye, Mouton, 1970, p. 581.
3 As a matter of fact, he continued to do so, since the statute of October 1940 still allowed for part of the dismissed professor's salary – based on his career seniority – to be distributed to family members, wives, children or parents. This is how Lévi-Strauss's parents survived the war years, equipped with fake identity papers and taking shelter in their house in the Cévennes and later at René Courtin's house, in the Drôme region.
4 See Waldberg, 'Au fil du souvenir'. Over the years of exile, many a couple was made and unmade within that same small world, with their share of tragedies: Matta seduced the wife of the young Armenian-American artist

Archile Gorky; David Hare, the publisher of VVV, married Breton's partner Jacqueline Lamba, etc. Lévi-Strauss told his father about his 'Renoir' woman, and his new girlfriends regularly appeared in the sentimental chronicle of his exile. See Patrick and Isabelle Waldberg, *Un Amour acéphale*, Paris, La Différence, 1992, pp. 184 ff.

5 See Vincent Debaene, *Far Afield: French Anthropology between Sciences and Literature*, Chicago, The University of Chicago Press, 2014; Laurent Jeanpierre, 'Des hommes entre plusieurs mondes, Étude sur une situation d'exil: des intellectuels français réfugiés aux États-Unis pendant la deuxième guerre mondiale', EHESS doctoral dissertation, 2005; and Emmanuel Loyer, *Paris à New York: Intellectuels et artistes français en exil, 1940–1947*, Paris, Grasset, 2005.

6 See the work done and inspired by Bruno Latour in recent decades, whose anthropological approach has sought to redefine one of the main activities of Western modernity: science. See especially Bruno Latour and Steve Woolgar, *Laboratory Life: The Social Construction of Scientific Facts,* Beverly Hills, Sage Publications, 1979; and, most recently, *An Inquiry into Modes of Existence: An Anthropology of the Moderns*, Cambridge, Harvard University Press, 2013.

7 Letter of 30 May 1941, including in the collection *'Chers tous deux'*.

8 Aline Caro-Delvaille was Emma Lévi-Strauss's elder sister. She was married to the artist Caro-Delvaille, whom she followed to the United States at the end of the First World War. When her husband died in 1928, she remained there, making a modest living through editing, translation and journalism; she was, however, in contact with various figures whom she called upon to put together the necessary funds for her nephew to come in 1941.

9 See Henriette Nizan, *Libres Mémoires*, Paris, Robert Laffont, 1989.

10 These letters form the core of *'Chers tous deux'* and are all dated. The dates are therefore authoritative. The quotes that follow are all excerpted from this correspondence.

11 In Lévi-Strauss's own phrase when, fifty years later, he reread the letters and wrote a short text about them, which is reprinted in *'Chers tous deux'*.

12 Theodor W. Adorno, *Minima Moralia: Reflections on a Damaged Life*, London, Verso, 2005. The book comprises a series of short texts he wrote while in exile in New York, between 1944 and 1947. The 'damage' in question did not relate only to the condition of exile, but rather the latter is seen as homologous to a form of modern alienation.

13 Letter of 14 July 1941, in *'Chers tous deux'*.

14 Letter of 30 May 1941, in *'Chers tous deux'*.

15 Lévi-Strauss, 'New York in 1941', pp. 259–260.

16 Letter of 13 August 1941, in *'Chers tous deux'*.

17 Letter of 8 June 1941, in *'Chers tous deux'*.

18 Letter of 8 June 1941, in *'Chers tous deux'*.

19 Letter of 13 August 1941, in *'Chers tous deux'*.

20 Letter of 15 June 1941, in *'Chers tous deux'*.

21 Letter of 5 August 1941, in *'Chers tous deux'*.

22 Vincent Debaene, 'Comme Alice de l'autre côté du miroir . . . Claude Lévi-Strauss à New York', in *Land of Refuge, Land of Exile*, The Florence Gould Lectures, vol. 11, winter 2009–2010, p. 59.

23 See Philippe Roger, *L'Ennemi américain: Généalogie de l'anti-américanisme français*, Paris, Seuil, 2002.

24 Gustave Cohen, *Lettres aux Américains*, Ottawa, Éditions de l'Arbre, 1943, p. 36.

25 Denis de Rougemont, *Journal d'une époque, 1926–1946*, Paris, Gallimard, 1968, p. 451.
26 Letter of 30 May 1941, in *'Chers tous deux'*.
27 *TT*, p. 79.
28 Letter of 14 July 1941, in *'Chers tous deux'*.
29 Letter of 16 October 1941, in which he describes Masson as a 'kind of modern monk absorbed in his graphico-metaphysical research', ibid.
30 On his shelves were the original volumes in green and gold binding of the Annual Reports of the Bureau of American Ethnology, which he considered as sacred and was to hold on to his entire life.
31 Letter of 22 June 1941, in *'Chers tous deux'*.
32 Letter of 20 July 1941, in *'Chers tous deux'*.
33 Claudine Herrmann, 'Claude Lévi-Strauss à New York', in Émilie Joulia, *Claude Lévi-Strauss: L'Homme derrière l'œuvre*, Paris, JC Lattès, 2008, p. 20.
34 Letter of 7 July 1941, in *'Chers tous deux'*.
35 Letter of 13 August 1941, in *'Chers tous deux'*.
36 Letter of 9 December 1941, in *'Chers tous deux'*.
37 *The Mathematical Theory of Communication* (1949). Shannon demonstrated in this work that any message, whatever its content or medium (visual, aural, etc.), can be reduced to a series of 0s and 1s. His work on telecommunications was clearly at the origins of computing and digital systems.
38 Eribon, *Conversations*, p. 29.
39 Letter of 5 August 1941, in *'Chers tous deux'*.
40 Letter of 5 August 1941, in *'Chers tous deux'*.
41 Claude Lévi-Strauss, 'Autoportrait', remarks collected by Catherine Clément and Dominique-Antoine Grisoni, *Magazine littéraire*, 223, October 1985, p. 21.
42 Letter of 4 October 1941, in *'Chers tous deux'*.
43 On this distinction between 'rupture migration' and 'support migration', see Paul-André Rosental, 'Maintien/Rupture: un nouveau couple pour l'analyse des migrations', *Annales, ESC*, July–September 1990, pp. 1403–1431.
44 Victor Hugo: 'It appears that exiles are, unbeknownst to themselves, near to some sun, since they ripen quickly.' In *Oeuvres complètes*, Paris, Laffont, 1989, p. 273.
45 Letter of 26 October 1941, in *'Chers tous deux'*.
46 Letter of 26 October 1941, in *'Chers tous deux'*.
47 Letter of 22 June 1941, in *'Chers tous deux'*.
48 Letter of 22 June 1941, in *'Chers tous deux'*.
49 Letter of 22 June 1941, in *'Chers tous deux'*.
50 Letter of 22 June 1941, in *'Chers tous deux'*.
51 Letter of 22 June 1941, in *'Chers tous deux'*.
52 Letter of 17 September 1941, in *'Chers tous deux'*.
53 Letter of 5 August 1941, in *'Chers tous deux'*.
54 A pun on 'cotte de maille', the French term for 'coat of mail'. It was Claude Lévi-Strauss who coined the nickname, to escape censorship.
55 He was referring to André Labarthe, member of the first Free France who was at odds with the London-based movement and went to New York to form a left-wing opposition to de Gaulle.
56 Letter of 26 September 1941, in *'Chers tous deux'*.
57 Laurent Jeanpierre, 'Les structures d'une pensée d'exilé: la formation du structuralisme de Claude Lévi-Strauss', *French Politics, Culture and Society*, 28(1), spring 2010, p. 63.

58 Lévi-Strauss, 'New York in 1941', p. 261.
59 Jeanpierre, 'Les structures d'une pensée d'exilé', p. 65.
60 Letter of 12 June 1941, in *'Chers tous deux'*.
61 Letter of 20 August 1941, in *'Chers tous deux'*.
62 Robert Lebel, 'Paris–New York et retour avec Marcel Duchamp, Dada et le surréalisme', in *Paris–New York*, Paris, Centre Georges Pompidou, 1977, p. 69.
63 Letter of 16 October 1941, in *'Chers tous deux'*.
64 Letter of 10 October 1941, in *'Chers tous deux'*.
65 Waldberg, 'Au fil du souvenir', p. 583. For the surrealist notion of *'point suprême'*, see Breton's 'Second Manifesto of Surrealism'.
66 Denis Bertholet, *Claude Lévi-Strauss*, Paris, Fayard, 2003, p. 144.
67 Lévi-Strauss, 'Autoportrait', pp. 21–2.
68 Waldberg, 'Au fil du souvenir', p. 582.
69 Philippe Sollers, 'La nécessaire alliance des intellectuels et des écrivains', *Le Monde*, 10 February 2000.
70 Eribon, *Conversations*, p. 35.
71 Eribon, *Conversations*, p. 35.
72 Article published under the title 'Le dédoublement de la représentation dans les arts de l'Asie et de l'Amérique' in the journal of the École libre des hautes études, *Renaissance*, vols. 2 and 3, 1944–45, and republished in *SA*, vol. 1, as 'Split Representation in the Art of Asia and America', pp. 269–294.
73 *SA*, p. 273.
74 *SA*, p. 285.
75 'The art of the northwest coast at the American Museum of Natural History', in *La Gazette des Beaux-Arts*, July 1943, p. 175.
76 Lévi-Strauss, 'New York in 1941', p. 261.
77 Lévi-Strauss, 'New York in 1941', p. 261.
78 Patrick Waldberg, for his part, located an equivalent of New York's hustle and bustle and population diversity in the pages in which Flaubert describes Hamilcar's army in *Salambô*; see 'Au fil du souvenir', p. 581.
79 To quote Walter Benjamin's description of Siegfried Kracauer in his review of the latter's *The Salaried Masses*. See 'An outsider attracts attention', published as an appendix to the English-language edition, *The Salaried Masses: Duty and Distraction in Weimar Germany*, New York, Verso, 1998, p. 114. The German word he uses is *Lumpensammler*.
80 Herrmann, 'Claude Lévi-Strauss à New York', p. 24.
81 Waldberg, 'Au fil du souvenir', p. 584. The octopus reference comes from a line in the poetic novel by the Comte de Lautreamont called *The Songs of Maldoror*, which was a major inspiration for the surrealists.
82 Debaene, 'Comme Alice de l'autre côté du miroir', p. 60.
83 In an interview in *Cahiers du cinéma* in June 1964, Lévi-Strauss explained: 'All my assessments of American films are inevitably influenced by the fact that I spent several years in America, living there very intensely, and anything that reminds me of that period has a powerful attraction for me.'
84 *TT*, p. 444.
85 De Gaulle identified the permanence of French thought as one of two anchors – the other being the 'sword blade' – that France could hold on to in the midst of debacle. It is as such that he hailed the École libre des hautes études, in *Discours et messages*, Paris, Plon, 1970, p. 335.
86 P. and I. Waldberg, *Un amour acéphale*, p. 184.
87 Letter from Claude Lévi-Strauss to Henri Focillon, 2 March 1942, École libre des hautes études Archives, New School for Social Research, New York.

88 The 'Good Neighbor Policy', implemented by the first FDR administration, was intended to mark a break with the Monroe Doctrine (1823), which legitimated US intervention in Latin America.

89 Claude Lévi-Strauss, 'Ce que l'Amérique latine attend de nous', *Pour la victoire*, 4 July 1943. See also 'Les Français et le panaméricanisme', *Pour la victoire*, 24 January 1942. The anthropologist begins his article with an anecdote that is revealing about the degree to which France had penetrated Latin American culture. In 1937, in a remote hamlet in the state of Goyaz, two Frenchmen came across an old man who, upon finding out they were French, exclaimed in perfect French: 'Ah, dear sirs, France, Anatole, Anatole!' The writer Anatole France was the subject of that distant homage.

90 CLS Archives, NAF 28150, box 213, 'École libre des hautes études'.

91 Telegram from Jacques Maritain to General de Gaulle, 20 March 1943, Archives nationales, 382 AP55.

92 Eribon, *Conversations*, p. 41.

93 Claude Lévi-Strauss, 'The Lessons of Linguistics', *TVFA*, p. 138. Originally published as the preface to Roman Jakobson's *Six Leçons sur le son et le sens*, Paris, Les éditions de minuit, 1976.

94 Claude Lévi-Strauss, 'Claude Lévi-Strauss: histoire d'une amitié', *Le Monde,* 16 October 1971.

95 Lévi-Strauss, 'Claude Lévi-Strauss: histoire d'une amitié'.

96 Patrick Wilcken, *Claude Lévi-Strauss: The Poet in the Laboratory*, London, Bloomsbury, 2010, p. 137.

97 Lévi-Strauss, 'Claude Lévi-Strauss, histoire d'une amitié'.

98 François Dosse, *History of Structuralism 1: The Rising Sign, 1945–1966*, Minneapolis, University of Minnesota Press, 1997, p. 16: 'Lévi-Strauss innovated in the true sense of the word here, by importing the linguistic model into anthropology, which had been linked in France until then with the natural sciences.'

99 Claude Lévi-Strauss, 'Ce que je suis', *Le Nouvel Observateur*, 28 June 1980, quoted in Bertholet, *Claude Lévi-Strauss*, p. 123.

100 Debaene, 'Comme Alice de l'autre côté du miroir', p. 53.

101 Eribon, *Conversations*, p. 45.

102 See Loyer, *Paris à New York*.

103 Quotations are from the eight-page memorandum, typed and unsigned, and addressed to Jacques Maritain, found in the Jacques Maritain Archives, box 17, Jacques Maritain Center, Notre Dame University. A letter sent by Maritain to Lévi-Strauss, dated 23 July 1942, in which passages of the text were cited, made it possible to identify its author.

104 Claude Lévi-Strauss, 'Compte rendu de Julien Benda, *La Grande Épreuve des démocraties: Essai sur les principes démocratiques, leur nature, leur histoire, leur valeur philosophique*', New York, Éditions de la maison française, 1942, *Renaissance*, vol. 1, October–December 1943, booklet 4, pp. 324–328. Julien Benda spent the entire war in hiding in Carcassonne, and thus managed to escape anti-Semitic persecution.

105 Lévi-Strauss, 'Compte rendu de Julien Benda'.

106 CLS Archives, NAF 28150, box 210, 'Activités politiques', '23rd Meeting of the Peace Aims Group, Council on Foreign Relations, 8 February 1943', account written by Dwight E. Dee [classified as confidential].

107 See Jeanpierre, 'Les structures d'une pensée d'exilé'. See also Vincent Debaene, 'À propos de "La politique étrangère d'une société primitive"', *Ethnies*, 33–4, winter 2009, pp. 132–138.

108 Claude Lévi-Strauss, 'The social and psychological aspect of chieftainship in a primitive tribe: the Nambikwara of northwestern Mato Grosso', *Transactions of the New York Academy of Science*, 7(1), October 1944, p. 30.

109 Lévi-Strauss, 'The social and psychological aspect of chieftainship in a primitive tribe'.

110 Claude Lévi-Strauss, 'Guerre et commerce chez les Indiens de l'Amérique du Sud', *Renaissance*, 1(1–2), 1943, p. 124.

111 Jeanpierre, 'Les structures d'une pensée d'exilé', p. 66.

112 See Wiktor Stoczkowski, *Anthropologies rédemptrices: Le monde selon Lévi-Strauss*, Paris, Hermann, 2008, pp. 70ff; *TT*, pp. 132–140.

113 See Abdelmalek Sayad, *La Double Absence: Des illusions de l'émigré aux souffrances de l'immigré*, Paris, Seuil, 1999.

114 Waldberg, 'Au fil du souvenir', p. 581: 'Distraught, we still were a bit stunned, sick, reeling from the shock of exodus, the armistice, the generalized catastrophe and the countless individual tragedies to which it had given rise. All the anxiety and panic of the year 1940, the worry for those we had left behind, the nostalgia for lost illusions, could be read on our faces. We each had our litany of grief.'

115 Eribon, *Conversations*, p. 45.

116 Denis de Rougemont, 'Journal d'un retour', January 1946, *Journal d'une époque*, p. 581.

117 See Loyer, 'New York–Paris (New York): Retours d'exil', in *Paris à New York*, pp. 339–368.

118 Letter from Claude Lévi-Strauss to Roger F. Evans, 29 May 1945, Rockefeller Foundation Archives, series 200, box 52, folder 610.

119 Letter from Claude Lévi-Strauss to Roger F. Evans, 29 May 1945: 'I am certain that the generosity of the Foundation will not have been in vain, that it has served to create a sound basis for permanent and fruitful cultural cooperation between France and the United States. And I am sure that all those who have been fortunate enough to receive the aid of the Rockefeller Foundation have pledged themselves to devote all their efforts to the cause of Franco-American cultural cooperation.'

Chapter 11   Structuralism: The American Years

1 See François Héran, *Figures de la parenté*, Paris, PUF, 2009, for a critical reassessment of this debt, which, according to the author, was 'suppressed' by Lévi-Strauss, especially with regard to the work of Marcel Granet. See Chapter 10, 'Lévi-Strauss, lecteur de Granet ou la dette refoulée'.

2 Expression used by Monique Lévi-Strauss to describe especially Henri Laugier in an interview with the author, 19 June 2012.

3 On this point, see Vincent Debaene, 'À propos de "La politique étrangère d'une société primitive"', *Ethnies*, 33–4, winter 2009, pp. 132–138.

4 His parents' false papers, preserved in their son's personal archives, attest to this change of identity. Their alias kept the initials of their real name, which was often the case, evincing a desire to preserve some continuity of identity for their new underground existence, which required a complete rupture with their previous life.

5 René Courtin, a former colleague in Brazil whom Lévi-Strauss saw again in Montpellier in 1940, was among the professors who refused to swear allegiance to the Vichy regime. He was removed from his position, joined the Resistance,

and became part of the Insurrectional Government of Paris (20 August 1944). After the liberation, he became one of the founders of the newspaper *Le Monde*.

6 This quote (dated 2 October 1944) and those that follow are all taken from a series of letters written by Claude Lévi-Strauss between 2 October 1944 and 12 August 1947, addressed to his parents. This family correspondence has been kept at Monique Lévi-Strauss's home.

7 At that time, Mauss was still in Paris, his mind almost entirely gone. 'Épilogue: les années de guerre et d'après-guerre', in Marcel Fournier, *Marcel Mauss*, Paris, Fayard, 1994.

8 Letter of 2 October 1944, CLS Archives, NAF 28150, box 181, 'Correspondance'. The following quotes are all excerpted from this same letter.

9 Didier Eribon, *Conversations with Claude Lévi-Strauss*, Chicago, The University of Chicago Press, 1991, p. 46.

10 See Chantal Morelle and Pierre Jakob, *Henri Laugier: un esprit sans frontière*, Brussels, Bruylant, LGDJ, 1997.

11 De Gaulle, *Discours et messages*, Paris, Plon, 1970, p. 335: 'When the time comes, far from the tumult in which we are now plunged, for historians to assess the tragic events that have nearly tossed France into the abyss, they will note that the resistance, the hope of the nation, was held fast on the slippery slope by two anchors that will never give way: one being the sword blade, the other French thought.' Later in the speech, he saluted the 'Institut des hautes études in New York, a magnificent French achievement created at the very moment when the storm of despair was at its height.'

12 Letter of 13 November 1944, addressed to John Marshall, Rockefeller Foundation Archives (Tarrytown), entry 200, box 52, folders 609–610.

13 CLS Archives, NAF 28150, boxes 213–214, 'Rapport sur l'avenir de l'École libre des hautes études' (n.d.).

14 Eribon, *Conversations*, p. 46.

15 Eribon, *Conversations*, p. 46.

16 Eribon, *Conversations*, p. 46.

17 He was also the father of Delphine Seyrig, whom Lévi-Strauss knew as a young girl. See Eribon, *Conversations*, p. 47.

18 Claude Lévi-Strauss wrote of Seyrig in a letter to his parents, which he entrusted to the latter, dated 15 November 1944: 'I am fond of him and hold him very dear.' The photo was published in *L'Illustration* and inserted in the letter.

19 Letter to his parents, 24 January 1945, CLS Archives, NAF 28150 (179).

20 Letter of 3 December 1945 addressed to his parents.

21 Information provided by Laurent Lévi-Strauss, whom I would like to thank here. Sylvie Dreyfus-Asséo, the daughter of Pierre Dreyfus, confirmed that 'everyone in the [Dreyfus] family thought it was a bad idea'; the family looked unfavourably on this union within the family microcosm, since Rose-Marie belonged to the Ullmo family that was related to the Dreyfuses, and Claude Lévi-Strauss was almost considered as a member of the family due to his brotherly bond with Pierre. Every time he returned to Paris during his time abroad, he generally stayed with Pierre Dreyfus, and it was the latter's address – on rue de la Faisanderie – that he always gave as his contact address. Sylvie Dreyfus-Asséo, interview with the author, 6 October 2011.

22 Letter to his parents, dated 24 January 1945.

23 CLS Archives, NAF 28150, box 212, 'Spoliations allemandes et indemnités de restitution'. The agreement between the international Jewish organizations and

the Federal Republic of Germany led to the French Law of 19 July 1957, which provided for the financial compensation of victims of a programme of spoliation carried out after 1942 known as Action M. On this, see Jean-Marc Dreyfus and Sarah Gensburger, *Des Camps dans Paris: Austerlitz, Levitan, Bassano, juillet 1943–août 1944*, Paris, Fayard, 2003.

24 Letter to his parents, 15 November 1944.

25 Patrick Wilcken, *Claude Lévi-Strauss: The Poet in the Laboratory*, London, Bloomsbury, 2010, p. 136.

26 Eribon, *Conversations*, pp. 43–44.

27 Eribon, *Conversations*, p. 39.

28 To name but a few of his articles published in American journals: 'Social and psychological aspects of chieftainship', *Transactions of the New York Academy of Science*, 7, 1944, pp. 16–32; 'Reciprocity and hierarchy', *American Anthropologist*, 46, 1944; 'L'analyse structurale en linguistique et en anthropologie', *Word: Journal of the Linguistic Circle of New York*, 1(2), August 1945, pp. 1–21.

29 Eribon, *Conversations*, p. 36.

30 Some of Alfred Métraux's diaries have been published under the title *Itinéraires 1: Carnets de notes et journaux de voyage*, Paris, Payot, 1978.

31 Eribon, *Conversations*, p. 36.

32 Eribon, *Conversations*, p. 36.

33 'Changes in the bodily form of descendants of immigrants', *American Anthropologist*, 14(3), July–September 1912. The study covered 17,821 descendants of immigrants.

34 Wilcken, *Claude Lévi-Strauss*, p. 133.

35 Eribon, *Conversations*, p. 37.

36 Eribon, *Conversations*, pp. 37–38.

37 See letter to Paul Rivet, 4 January 1943, Correspondence Lévi-Strauss/Rivet, Paul Rivet Archives, 2AP1C, Bibliothèque Centrale du Muséum national d'Histoire naturelle. Claude Lévi-Strauss informed Mauss that Boas's children would be most receptive to an offer from the Musée de l'Homme to acquire their father's Americanist library, since he had been close friends with Paul Rivet. To that end, Claude Lévi-Strauss launched a fundraising campaign ($8,000), with the help of Laugier, and found a first potential donor in Georges Wildenstein, director of the *Gazette des beaux-arts*. But the deal never came to fruition.

38 Héran, 'Avant-propos', in *Figures de la parenté*, p. 13.

39 Letter to Paul Rivet, 10 February 1943, Correspondance Lévi-Strauss/Rivet, Paul Rivet Archives, 2AP1C, Bibliothèque centrale du Muséum national d'Histoire naturelle. The quotations that follow are all from the same correspondence.

40 Letter from Claude Lévi-Strauss to Paul Rivet, 6 December 1943.

41 See the article by G. Lanteri-Laura, 'Histoire et structure dans la connaissance de l'homme', *Annales ESC*, 4, 22nd year, 1967, pp. 792–828.

42 'Remarques sur l'évolution phonologique du russe comparée a celle des autres langues slaves', presentation at the International Congress of Linguists in Nijmegen in 1928, in *Travaux du circle linguistique de Prague*, Prague, 1929.

43 Claude Lévi-Strauss was later to say: 'I think it is worth noting that several anthropologists independently turned towards the concept of structure during the war years, when circumstances condemned some of us to a certain degree of isolation. Their simultaneous recognition of structure demonstrated how indispensable the concept is in solving problems that our predecessors found

632 Notes to pp. 248–52

insoluble', *SA*, vol. 2, p. 359. He was referring, notably, to the work of the Yale-based American anthropologist George Murdock, author of *Social Structure*, published in 1949, the same year as *The Elementary Structures of Kinship*.

44 Claude Lévi-Strauss, 'Structural analysis in linguistics and in anthropology', in *SA*, vol. 1, p. 34.

45 For this entire paragraph, see the illuminating book by Frédéric Keck modestly entitled, *Claude Lévi-Strauss: Une introduction*, Paris, Presses Pocket, 2005, pp. 70ff.

46 'A truly scientific analysis must be real, simplifying, and explanatory', *SA*, vol. 2, p. 43.

47 Alfred Métraux, *Itinéraires 1: Carnets de notes et journaux de voyage*, Paris, Payot, 1978, p. 171: 13 March 1947.

48 Letter from Lévi-Strauss to Paul Rivet, 16 December 1943.

49 Expressions used in a draft preface to *Structures élémentaires de la parenté* that Claude Lévi-Strauss sent to Rivet in a letter dated 9 March 1947. They were part of an attempt to define the future of sociology (in the broadest sense).

50 See Carole Reynaud-Paligot's books: *La République raciale: Paradigme racial et idéologie républicaine*, Paris, PUF, 2006; and *Races, racisme et antiracisme dans la France des années 1930*, Paris, PUF, 2007.

51 Christine Laurière, *Paul Rivet: Le savant et la politique*, Paris, Éditions scientifiques du Muséum national d'Histoire naturelle, 'Archives', 2008, p. 511.

52 CLS Archives, NAF 28150, boxes 213–214, 'École libre des hautes études'.

53 See Emmanuel Loyer, *Paris à New York: Intellectuels et artistes français en exil, 1940–1947*, Paris, Grasset, 2005, especially chapter 7, 'Les exigences du jour', focusing on the study of the political literature of exile.

54 See André Breton and André Masson, *Martinique charmeuse de serpents*, Paris, Le Sagittaire, 1948.

55 Jacques Derrida, *Writing and Difference*, Chicago, The University of Chicago Press, 1978, p. 6.

56 Yvonne Oddon and Agnès Humbert were also arrested but ultimately spared, along with Germaine Tillion. They were sent to concentration camps and all three survived.

57 Paul Rivet 'concealed' the underground activities of some of the members of his museum staff while not taking direct part in them. He was a public figure under surveillance and, in any case, little cut out for the clandestine life. Investigated, then threatened, he left France in February 1941 with a heavy heart, leaving the museum and his collaborators to their own devices. One year later, the first arrests were made. On this episode, see Laurière, *Paul Rivet*; Julien Blanc, *Au commencement de la Résistance: Du côté du Musée de l'Homme, 1940–1941*, Paris, Seuil, 2010; and Anne Hogenhuis, *Des savants dans la Résistance: Boris Vildé et le réseau du Musée de l'Homme*, Paris, CNRS Éditions, 2009.

58 All were executed at Mont Valérien on 23 February 1942.

59 Letter to Paul Rivet, 17 August 1942.

60 Derrida, *Writing and Difference*, p. 282.

61 Structuralism does not aim to reduce empirical diversity to a small number of common cultural forms, as is sometimes said. Distinct in this respect from formalism, it highlights, according to Frédéric Keck (*Claude Lévi-Strauss: Une introduction*, p. 41), 'the invariants in a field of differences, i.e. the laws that govern the distribution of these differences'. As Claude Lévi-Strauss would later explain, the specific object of structural anthropology, as in linguistics, is 'discontinuities': not only what each society is but how it is connected to others even while differing from them. See 'Postscript to Chapter XV', *SA*, vol. 1, p. 328.

62 Eribon, *Conversations*, p. 47: 'Just before the war, the French government had acquired a splendid mansion on Fifth Avenue built for an American banker in the style of a Roman palace. The mayor of New York, who was strongly anti-Vichy, had prevented the representatives of the Vichy government from occupying it. When de Gaulle came to power, the mayor finally gave permission to move in.' The mayor in question was Fiorello La Guardia.

63 Letter to his parents, 8 September 1945, CLS Archives, NAF 28150 (179).

64 Photograph published in *L'Illustration* that was cut out and inserted in a letter of 23 September 1945.

65 Letter of 3 December 1945.

66 Letter of 24 February 1946.

67 Letter of 3 December 1945.

68 Letter of 24 March 1946.

69 Letter of 17 April 1946.

70 Letter of 30 May 1946.

71 Letter of 14 November 1945.

72 Letter of 30 May 1946.

73 Letter of 3 December 1945.

74 Letter of 6 August 1946.

75 An article entitled 'French sociology', dedicated to Mauss, was published in the collection edited by Georges Gurvitch and Wilbert E. Moore, *Twentieth Century Sociology*, New York, The Philosophical Library, 1945, pp. 513–545. The other article he wrote at the time was an ethnography of American life for an issue of the journal *Esprit* on the United States: Claude Lévi-Strauss, 'La technique du Bonheur', *Esprit*, 127, November 1946, pp. 643–652.

76 Letter of 24 February 1946.

77 Letter of 10 March 1946.

78 Letter of 22 January 1947.

79 Letter to Paul Rivet, 9 March 1947.

80 Telegram of 17 March 1947.

81 Letter of 1 April 1947.

82 Letter of 7 May 1947.

83 Roman Jakobson, *Studies on Child Language and Aphasia*, The Hague, Mouton, 1971.

84 On 22 January 1947, he announced that he had fixed Rose-Marie's children's boat with the help of a power tool containing a number of drill attachments, which was the delight of all do-it-yourselfers.

85 The director of the New York Alliance française, Pierre Cartier, was for instance a staunch supporter of Pétain. It was for this reason that Lévi-Strauss regularly 'snubbed' events organized under his auspices, which earned him some reproach, as attested by a letter from General Bénouville to Ambassador Bonnet, in which the former points out that the cultural attaché 'saw fit to abstain from attending my conference in New York' on 30 April 1947, AMAE, 'Relations culturelles, oeuvres diverses, 1945–1970, États-Unis', box 55, 0.236.2.

86 Report by Claude Lévi-Strauss (3 p.) on the organization of conferences in the United States, 18 June 1946, AMAE, 'Relations culturelles, oeuvres diverses, 1945–1970, États-Unis', box 55.

87 France Forever was an organization founded in the United States during the war. It was organized into local chapters throughout the country, which sought to lend support to the policies of General de Gaulle. Its lobbying efforts were relatively effective in an America that had been very critical of Free France – and Roosevelt not the least. See the book by Raoul Aglion, head of the

Gaullist delegation to New York, *De Gaulle et Roosevelt: La France libre aux États-Unis*, Paris, Plon, 1984; and Julian G. Hurstfield, *America and the French Nation, 1939–1945*, Chapel Hill, University of North Carolina Press, 1986.

88　Telegram of 30 March 1946, AMAE, 'Relations culturelles, oeuvres diverses, 1945–1970, États-Unis', box 55, 0.236.2.

89　Letter of 11 April 1947, AMAE, 'Relations culturelles, oeuvres diverses, 1945–1970, États-Unis', box 57.

90　It is striking to find the very same idea resurface almost fifty years later (in 1991), resulting in the creation of the Bureau du livre français in New York, and in quite similar terms.

91　Letter of 3 June 1946, AMAE, 'Relations culturelles, oeuvres diverses, 1945–1970, États-Unis, box 58.

92　Claude Lévi-Strauss, interview with the author, 2 June 2000.

93　Dispatch from Claude Lévi-Strauss, 'Politique culturelle française aux États-Unis', 17 January 1947, AMAE, 'Relations culturelles, oeuvres diverses, 1945–1970, États-Unis', box 55, 0.236.1. Text cited in L. Jeanpierre, 'La politique culturelle française aux États-Unis de 1940 à 1947', in *Entre rayonnement et réciprocité*, Paris, Publications de la Sorbonne, 2002, p. 116.

94　Alice Conklin, *Mission to Civilize: The Republican Idea of Empire in France and West Africa, 1895–1930*, Stanford, Stanford University Press, 1997. See also her more recent book: *In the Museum of Man: Race, Anthropology and Empire in France, 1850–1950*, Cornell, Cornell University Press, 2013.

95　In the end, it was René de Messières who took over in the autumn of 1947 and remained until 1952.

96　He announced this to his parents in a letter dated 25 June 1947.

97　Eribon, *Conversations*, pp. 55–56.

Chapter 12　The Ghosts of Marcel Mauss

1　Agnès Humbert, *Résistance: Memoirs of Occupied France*, London, Bloomsbury, 2008, pp. 10–11: 'On its appointed date, a meeting of the "Folklore Society" is held. An unaccustomed throng squeezes into a small room in the École du Louvre. Among this crowd are unfamiliar faces and – God help us – ladies decked out in all their finery. The speaker is someone I have never heard of. Fulsome in his praise of the work of our museum and effusive in his pride in "the motherland", he flourished empty words and sentimental phrases. Not a word about science. [. . .] Most of the faces in the audience register approval. At the back of the room, however, I notice our great master and mentor Marcel Mauss. His Semitic features, alert and intelligent, wear an inscrutable smile, timeless like that of the Buddha, a combination of irony, composure and confidence. The smile of a great and serene intelligence that floats above all this, that knows everything, that foresees everything. For an instant our eyes meet, and in his gaze I find what I have been looking for. Reassured at last, I know that it is not I who have changed. It is not I who have taken leave of my senses: it is they who have gone mad.'

2　As he himself described *The Elementary Structures of Kinship* to his colleague Robert Lowie. Claude Lévi-Strauss, 'Preface to the Second Edition', *ESK*, p. xxviii.

3　Daniel Fabre, 'L'ethnologie française à la croisée des engagements (1940–1945)', in Jean-Yves Boursier, *Résistances et résistants*, Paris, L'Harmattan, p. 378: 'The hypothesis that underpins my approach is that an entire generation of French anthropology, in the broad sense, had put a lot of energy into denying and deflecting the ambiguity, temptations and even powerlessness that had characterized their position during the occupation. It was thus in the shadows of the untold history of the dark years that I propose to read certain choices of words, objects and methodologies that made up thirty years of the history of anthropology, especially in France.'

4 He was appointed senior lecturer in sociology at the Sorbonne in 1948, then professor in 1950. Prior to Raymond Aron's appointment in 1955 to a second chair in sociology, he ruled over the Sorbonne as a despot.

5 On this subject, see Laurent Jeanpierre, 'Une opposition structurante pour l'anthropologie structurale: Lévi-Strauss contre Gurvitch. La guerre de deux exilés français aux États-Unis', *Revue d'histoire des sciences humaines*, 11, February 2004, pp. 13–44.

6 Letter to Roman Jakobson, 19 January [probably 1945], CLS Archives, NAF 28150, box 281. The letters to Jakobson quoted in this chapter and those following come from the same archive.

7 Letter to Viktor Karady, 22 April 1968, Archives of the Laboratoire d'anthropologie sociale, F. LAS. F. S1.03.02.035. I would like to thank Marion Abelès for giving me access to these archives and Christine Laurière for so graciously guiding me through them.

8 This work was published by the Société des américainistes of the Musée de l'Homme, in 1948.

9 Didier Eribon, *Conversations with Claude Lévi-Strauss*, Chicago, The University of Chicago Press, 1991, p. 51.

10 Letter to R. Needham, 14 March 1962.

11 Letter to Roman Jakobson, 6 March 1948.

12 Letter dated 20 June 1948, found in the André-Georges Haudricourt Archives at Imec. I am grateful to Jean-François Bert for having passed this letter on to me, the second part of which recounts the defence of Pierre Métais, an anthropologist specializing on New Caledonia, who presented his work on 'marriage in primitive societies' in a radically different style from that of Lévi-Strauss. The entire letter pitches the one against the other at every turn (the cerebral and ceremonious Lévi-Strauss vs. the empirical and convivial Métais). 'Sur les soutenances de thèse de Claude Lévi-Strauss et Pierre Métais. Lettre de Mariel Jean-Brunhes Delamarre à André-Georges Haudricourt (20 June 1948)', presented by Jean-François Bert, *Revue d'histoire des sciences humaines*, 27, June 2015.

13 Letter from Émile Benveniste to Claude Lévi-Strauss, 5 June 1948, CLS Archives, NAF 28150, box 183, 'Correspondance reçue'.

14 Letter from Émile Benveniste to Claude Lévi-Strauss, 16 June 1948.

15 Eribon, *Conversations*, p. 131.

16 *ESK*, p. xxv.

17 *ESK*, p. xxvii.

18 *ESK*, p. 5.

19 *ESK*, p. 30.

20 *ESK*, p. 24.

21 Eribon, *Conversations*, p. 101. Lévi-Strauss then challenges the 'claims for the lack of sexual desire between individuals who have spent their early childhood under the same roof' and the examples frequently given in support – especially the Kibbutzim of Israel – as not pertinent.

22 Eribon, *Conversations*, p. 102.

23 Eribon, *Conversations*, p. 102.

24 'Language and Kinship', in *SA*, p. 46.

25 Meyer Fortes, 'Exchange and mart', *The Spectator*, 20 March 1969, p. 20.

26 On this subject, in addition to the book by François Héran already cited, see Yves Goudineau, 'Lévi-Strauss, la Chine de Granet, l'ombre de Durkheim: retour aux sources de l'analyse structurale de la parenté', in M. Izard (ed.), *Claude Lévi-Strauss*, Paris, L'Herne, 'Cahiers de l'Herne', 2004, pp. 151–162.

27 Francis Zimmermann, 'Les structures élémentaires', in Izard (ed.), *Claude Lévi-Strauss*, pp. 176–177.

28 *ESK*, pp. 497–498.

29 Eribon, *Conversations*, p. 105.

30 Review by Simone de Beauvoir, in *Les Temps modernes*, 49, November 1949, pp. 943–949; Georges Bataille, 'L'inceste et le passage de l'animal à l'homme', *Critique*, January 1951, pp. 43–61, republished in English as 'The enigma of incest', in *Eroticism: Death and Sensuality*, San Francisco, City Lights Books, 1986, pp. 197–220.

31 Eribon, *Conversations*, p. 53.

32 Review by Simone de Beauvoir, in *Les Temps modernes*, 49, November 1949, p. 949.

33 Frédéric Keck, 'Beauvoir, lectrice de Lévi-Strauss: les relations hommes–femmes entre existentialisme et structuralisme', *Les Temps modernes*, 647–8, January–March 2008, p. 243.

34 Letter from the PUF literary director, M. Angoulvent, to Claude Lévi-Strauss, 4 November 1958. All information about dealings with publishers come from the CLS Archives, CLS, NAF 28150, box 222.

35 In the meantime, the work of a Dutch scholar from the University of Leyden, excited by his reading of *Elementary Structures*, provided indirect access in English: J.P.B. de Josselin de Jong, *Levi-Strauss's Theory on Kinship and Marriage*, 1952. Claude Lévi-Strauss thanked him warmly for it in a letter dated 12 May 1953, CLS Archives, NAF 28150, box 193: 'I was profoundly moved and touched to receive the study you have so generously devoted to my work and to find the generous judgement you passed on it. In publishing your work, you have first done me an immense service, of a practical kind – for your faithful and penetrating analysis will provide Anglo-American readers with access to my theses, which they would not generally bother to seek out in such a thick book written in a difficult French. But above all, as you yourself suggest in your conclusion, the attention you have so kindly paid me is precious encouragement that gives me consolation in the face of the indifference I have encountered (especially in France). [. . .] In truth, looking back at it five years later (the manuscript was completed in early 1947), my book appears to me as a kind of monstrosity. There are mitigating circumstances: it was written in the United States, first in isolated exile, without any contact with colleagues, and then after I had joined the diplomatic service, which is another form of isolation from the scientific world. These abnormal conditions account to a certain extent for the errors and lacunas (my ignorance, at the time I was writing it, of Van Wouden's book being one of the most egregious . . .).'

36 CLS Archives, NAF 28150, box 220, 'Prizes and distinctions'.

37 Letter from Émile Benveniste to Claude Lévi-Strauss, 6 August 1949.

38 Claude Lefort, 'L'échange et la lutte des hommes', *Les Temps modernes*, 64, 1951, republished in *Les Formes de l'histoire*, Paris, Gallimard, 1978, pp. 15–29.

39 Claude Lévi-Strauss, 'Social structure', in *SA*, p. 279.

40 Emmanuel Terray, quoted in François Dosse, *History of Structuralism I: The Rising Sign, 1945–1966*, Minneapolis, University of Minnesota Press, 1997, p. 19.

41 Robert F. Murphy, 'Society where only cross-cousins wed', *Saturday Review*, 17 May 1969, p. 52.

42 Letter to Roman Jakobson, 19 January [1945] (undated), CLS Archives, NAF 28150, box 193.

43 Letter from Claude Lévi-Strauss to Roman Jakobson, 27 November 1944.

44 Letter from Claude Lévi-Strauss to Roman Jakobson, 27 November 1944.

45 See Christine Laurière, *Paul Rivet: Le savant et la politique*, Paris, Éditions scientifiques du Muséum national d'Histoire naturelle, 'Archives', 2008, pp. 359ff.

46 Indeed, Paul Rivet's successors, Henri Vallois and Robert Gessain, were both trained as medical doctors.

47 Letter to Roman Jakobson, 29 December 1947.

48 Letter of 23 March 1949.

49 Fabre, 'L'ethnologie française à la croisée des engagements (1940–1945)'.

50 Earlier, Vallois had been defeated by Rivet in the 1928 election for the chair in anthropology at the museum. Laurière, *Paul Rivet*, pp. 367–368.

51 Vallois and Rivet had hated each other for twenty years. No sooner did Vallois become director of the Musée de l'Homme than he began a relentless campaign to force Rivet out of his handsome official apartment. The latter managed to draw on his political connections to keep it until his death in 1958.

52 He was officially assistant director of the Musée de l'Homme from 25 March 1949 to 1 January 1951. Official bio-bibliographical documents, CLS Archives, NAF 28150, box 221.

53 Denis Bertholet, *Claude Lévi-Strauss*, Paris, Fayard, 2003, p. 189.

54 André Leroi-Gourhan, *Les Racines du monde: Entretiens avec Claude-Henri Rocquet*, Paris, Belfond, 1982, p. 109. Quoted by Bertholet, *Claude Lévi-Strauss*, p. 189.

55 Eribon, *Conversations*, p. 49.

56 Eribon, *Conversations*, p. 49.

57 Eribon, *Conversations*, p. 49.

58 Letter of 30 October 1949. When Lévi-Strauss paid his visits, he was 'told that [his] application would almost certainly be successful'. I am grateful to Thomas Hirsch for pointing out this series of letters deposited in the Henri Piéron Archives, Bibliothèque Henri-Piéron, University of Paris V, box 14.

59 Eribon, *Conversations*, pp. 49–50.

60 Eribon, *Conversations*, p. 50.

61 Letter to Roman Jakobson, 27 January 1950.

62 The paragraph that follows is based on research in the archives of the Collège de France, AP IV, 1949–50 assemblées. I am grateful to Paul-André Rosental for his remarks and ideas on the subject.

63 Edmond Faral recapped these events in opening the session of the assembly of 26 November 1950, which was to decide the precise title of the chair (and implicitly also choose the candidate, as is the custom at the Collège de France).

64 Paul-André Rosental and Isabelle Couzon, 'Le Paris dangereux de Louis Chevalier: histoire sociale et expertise publique au milieu du XXe siècle', in Bernard Lepetit and Christian Topalov (eds.), *La Ville des sciences sociales*, Paris, Belin, 2001, p. 195.

65 Rosental and Couzon ('Le Paris dangereux de Louis Chevalier') point out that Louis Chevalier unsuccessfully attempted to become a member of the

Fondation Carrel in 1942. The 'biological basis' of his model of the history of populations allied him to that moment in the development of demographic knowledge.

66 Letter from André Siegfried to Edmond Faral, 2 March 1950. The preceding quotations all come from the folder 'Assemblée des professeurs' of 26 November 1950. Rosental and Couzon ('Le Paris dangereux de Louis Chevalier', p. 198) note that André Siegfried was a 'true mentor' to Louis Chevalier.

67 Letter from Jean Pommier to Henri Laugier, 27 November 1950, who forwarded it with his own comments to Lévi-Strauss, CLS Archives, NAF 28150, box 199.

68 Eribon, *Conversations*, p. 50: Edmond Faral 'had coldly warned me that I would never enter the Collège!'

69 Letter to Henri Piéron, 30 November 1950.

70 Letter to Roman Jakobson, 27 January 1950.

71 Eribon, *Conversations*, p. 34.

72 See the now classic book by Brigitte Mazon, *Aux Origines de l'EHESS: Le rôle du mécénat américain*, Paris, Éditions du Cerf, 1988, as well as the work of Giuliana Gemelli, especially *Fernand Braudel*, Paris, Odile Jacob, 1995.

73 'Program and Policy, National Security, 1947–1957', RG 3900, Rockefeller Foundation Archives, quoted in Mazon, *Aux Origines de l'EHESS*, p. 126.

74 Quoted in Mazon, *Aux Origines de l'EHESS*, p. 95.

75 Originally published in French with the title 'Le dédoublement de la representation des arts de l'Asie et de l'Amérique', in *Renaissance*, a quarterly journal published by the École libre des hautes études of New York, vols. 2 and 3, 1944–5, pp. 168–186; republished in *SA*, pp. 245–268.

76 Listed in the catalogue as part of a general course called 'Civilisations primitives', 'Affiches de la VIe Section EPHE', EHESS Archives.

77 See James Clifford, *Person and Myth: Maurice Leenhardt in the Melanesian World*, Berkeley, University of California Press, 1982; and, more recently, Michel Naepels and Christine Salomon (eds.), *Terrains et destins de Maurice Leenhardt*, Paris, Éditions de l'École des hautes études en sciences sociales, 2007. The latter work provides a critical and historical contextualization that tempers Clifford's assessments and places Leenhardt within the colonial science of his time.

78 It was for this reason that Michel Leiris attended his lectures. Contribution by Michel Naepels to the seminar held by Daniel Fabre, Christine Laurière and André Marty at the EHESS, 'Les ethnologues et le fait colonial', 28 March 2013.

79 Benoît de l'Estoile, 'Une politique de l'âme: ethnologie et humanisme colonial', in Naepels and Salomon (eds.), *Terrains et destins de Maurice Leenhardt*, p. 47.

80 Letter from A.-G. Haudricourt, in Pascal Dibie, *Les Pieds sur terre*, Paris, Métaillé, 1987, p. 112; also quoted in Bertholet, *Claude Lévi-Strauss*, p. 193.

81 Letter to Roman Jakobson, 15 March 1951.

82 Letter to Fernand Braudel, 20 June 1949, CLS Archives, NAF 28150, box 181.

83 For example, the Rockefeller Foundation, Lévi-Strauss announced to Braudel, was going to give $1,000 for a socio-demographic study of the city of Vienna.

84 Eribon, *Conversations*, p. 121.

85 'History and Anthropology', 1949, republished in *SA*, p. 18.

86 'History and Anthropology', pp. 23–24.

87 Eribon, *Conversations*, pp. 121–122.

88 See the article by Thomas Hirsch, 'Un "Flammarion" pour l'anthropologie? Lévy-Bruhl, le terrain, l'ethnologie', *Genèses*, 90, January 2013. This article, based on his abundant correspondence, gives the full measure of Lévy-Bruhl's 'renown' as the 'big boss' of the French social sciences, who singularly combined scientific and institutional legitimacy with a strong political and social influence (due to his close ties with the socialist and radical-socialist milieus). Hirsch's article thus prompts us to wonder about the ultimate theoretical and historical oblivion into which this central figure fell after 1945. It is quite clear that the two texts by Lévi-Strauss discussed here contributed to the general process of erasing Lévy-Bruhl and substituting Mauss in his stead.

89 'Few teachings have remained as esoteric and, at the same time, exercised such a profound influence as those of Marcel Mauss.' This statement opens Lévi-Strauss's introduction to the collection *Sociologie et anthropologie* by M. Mauss.

90 Jean-François Bert, *Dans l'atelier de Marcel Mauss*, Paris, Éditions du CNRS, 2012, pp. 197–198. Another element promoting this restructuring was the publication in 1947 of the *Manuel d'ethnographie*, a transcription by Denise Paulme of Mauss's lectures dedicated to recommendations for prospective fieldwork – which he never practised himself.

91 Lévi-Strauss's contribution is in the second volume of *Twentieth Century Sociology*, edited by Georges Gurvitch and Wilbert E. Moore, and devoted to 'social studies in various countries', while the first volume focuses on the 'major questions in sociology'. Both volumes were first published in English.

92 Claude Lévi-Strauss, 'French sociology', in Georges Gurvitch (ed.), *Twentieth Century Sociology*, New York, The Philosophical Library, 1945, pp. 507–508.

93 Lévi-Strauss, 'French sociology', p. 518. In his introduction to the collection of Mauss's selected articles, he writes: 'Mauss still thinks it possible to develop a sociological theory of symbolism, whereas it is obvious that what is needed is a symbolic origin of society.' *Introduction to the Work of Marcel Mauss*, London, Routledge, 1987, p. 21.

94 Lévi-Strauss, 'French sociology', p. 519.

95 Lévi-Strauss, 'French sociology', p. 526.

96 Lévi-Strauss, 'French sociology', p. 527.

97 Lévi-Strauss, 'French sociology', p. 527.

98 Lévi-Strauss, 'French sociology', p. 527.

99 Lévi-Strauss, 'French sociology', p. 536. 'It would be useless to philosophize about general sociology when everything needs to be taken cognizance of, then known, and finally understood.' Extract from the article by Mauss, 'Fragment d'un plan de sociologie générale et descriptive', appearing in *Annales sociologiques*, pamphlet 1, 1934.

100 Lévi-Strauss, 'French sociology', p. 536: 'The philosophical ancestry of French sociology has played some tricks on it in the past; it may well prove, in the end, to be its bet asset.' This assessment serves as the article's concluding sentence.

101 Eribon, *Conversations*, p. 70.

102 Marcel Mauss, *Sociologie et anthropologie*, Paris, PUF, 1950. Lévi-Strauss's introduction has been published separately: see Lévi-Strauss, *Introduction to the Work of Marcel Mauss*.

103 One of the first research centres in the social sciences, in the modern sense, created within the CNRS in 1946. See Francis Farrugia, *La Reconstruction de la sociologie française (1945–1965)*, Paris, L'Harmattan, 2000.

104 Viktor Karady, 'Présentation de l'édition', in Marcel Mauss, *Oeuvres complètes*, Paris, Les Éditions de Minuit, 1970.

105 The disappearance of sociology of religion and the central place given to mechanisms of exchange and to the principle of reciprocity as foundational of society would appear to prove him right. See Karady, 'Présentation de l'édition', pp. 3–5.

106 Florence Weber, who is currently in charge of the new (and still more complete) edition at PUF of the boundless oeuvre of Marcel Mauss, agreed. Email exchanges with the author, 23 February 2013.

107 Letter from Claude Lévi-Strauss to Viktor Karady, 22 April 1968, FLAS, F.S1.03.02.035. In his *Introduction to the Work of Marcel Mauss*, p. 2, Claude Lévi-Strauss mentions 'practical considerations' that presided over the selection of the articles collected, a selection that he describes as 'random' immediately afterwards.

108 Patrice Maniglier, 'De Mauss à Claude Lévi-Strauss, 50 ans après: pour une ontologie maori', in E. Bimbenet and E. de Saint-Aubert (eds.), *Archives de philosophie*, LXIX(1), spring 2006, p. 37.

109 Lévi-Strauss, *Introduction to the Work of Marcel Mauss*, p. 1.

110 Lévi-Strauss, *Introduction to the Work of Marcel Mauss*, p. 38.

111 Lévi-Strauss, *Introduction to the Work of Marcel Mauss*, p. 38.

112 Lévi-Strauss, *Introduction to the Work of Marcel Mauss*, p. 41.

113 Camille Tarot has shown that Mauss had not read Ferdinand de Saussure, who was never cited, and it was through contact with the Indo-Europeanist Antoine Meillet that he grasped the importance of the linguistic dimension in the analysis of social facts. See *De Durkheim à Mauss, l'invention du symbolique: Sociologie et science des religions*, Paris, La Découverte, 1999.

114 Lévi-Strauss, *Introduction to the Work of Marcel Mauss*, p. 45.

115 Lévi-Strauss, *Introduction to the Work of Marcel Mauss*, p. 45.

116 Letter to Roman Jakobson, 27 March 1950.

117 Lévi-Strauss, *Introduction to the Work of Marcel Mauss*, p. 59.

118 'The universe signified long before people began to know what it signified', Lévi-Strauss, *Introduction to the Work of Marcel Mauss*, p. 61.

119 'What I would like to call (retrieving the archaic meaning of a term whose applicability to the present instance is obvious) an *anthropology*, that is, a system of interpretation accounting for the aspects of all modes of behaviour simultaneously, physical, physiological, psychical and sociological'. Lévi-Strauss, *Introduction to the Work of Marcel Mauss*, p. 26.

120 Lévi-Strauss, *Introduction to the Work of Marcel Mauss*, p. 66. Quotation from Mauss, *Sociology and Psychology*, London, Routledge, 1979, p. 32.

121 Lévi-Strauss, *Introduction to the Work of Marcel Mauss*, p. 65.

122 See chapter 5 above.

123 See Patrick Wilcken, 'On the shaman's couch', in *Claude Lévi-Strauss: The Poet in the Laboratory*, London, Bloomsbury, 2010. In a subsequent interview with Gilles Lapouge in *Le Figaro littéraire* (2 June 1962, p. 3), Lévi-Strauss acknowledged that anthropology and psychoanalysis were two disciplines in which, after an investigation, an enigma had to be resolved, involving the translation of one code into another. 'However, I completely reject the theory of psychoanalysis that seeks to make intellectual problems into affective ones. I am convinced, for my part, that reason can only be explained by reason.'

124 'History and Anthropology', in *SA*.

125 Quesalid was, more precisely, Boas's primary native informant, trained by the anthropologist. According to Vincent Debaene, Lévi-Strauss was accused

of having left out this piece of information in order to 'primitivize' this character.

126 'The Sorcerer and His Magic', in *SA*, p. 169: 'The magical situation is a consensus phenomenon.'

127 Article first published in *La Revue de l'histoire des religions*, CXXXV(1), 1949, pp. 5–27, and republished in *SA*, pp. 186–205.

128 Lévi-Strauss, *Introduction to the Work of Marcel Mauss*, p. 58.

129 Lévi-Strauss, *Introduction to the Work of Marcel Mauss*, pp. 35–36.

130 Lévi-Strauss, *Introduction to the Work of Marcel Mauss*, p. 36.

131 Lévi-Strauss, *Introduction to the Work of Marcel Mauss*, p. 65.

132 Eribon, *Conversations*, p. 73.

133 Élisabeth Roudinesco, *Jacques Lacan: An Outline of a Life and a History of a System of Thought*, New York, Columbia University Press, 1997, p. 212.

134 We have the response Lévi-Strauss gave in answer to Didier Éribon's question about what he thought of Lacan's work: 'I would have to understand it. And I always had the impression that to his fervent admirers, "understand" means something other than it does to me. It would have taken me five or six lectures. Merleau-Ponty and I used to talk about it and concluded that we didn't have the time.' Eribon, *Conversations*, pp. 73–74.

135 Information found in the 'Vente-Collection' folder, 21 June 1951, and in the catalogue that it contains. CLS Archives, NAF 28150, box 215.

136 Interview with Monique Lévi-Strauss, 4 March 2011. This is how Claude Lévi-Strauss allegedly described this painful moment in his life, to the woman who was then still only his assistant at the Musée de l'Homme.

137 Eribon, *Conversations*, p. 50.

138 Letter to Fernand Braudel, 9 June 1951.

Chapter 13 Manhood

1 *RH*, p. 19.

2 *Le Magazine littéraire*, 233, October 1985, p. 23.

3 André Breton, *Arcane 17*, in *Oeuvres complètes*, vol. III, Gallimard, Pléiade, 1999, p. 71: 'I have always believed in these forms of succour: it has always seemed to me that extreme anxiety in the way we endure an emotional ordeal, rejecting anything that might distract us from it, however slightly, refusing to engage in any kind of effort to limit its damage, was inherently likely to trigger this succour, and I think, what's more, that I have confirmed this experience many times. Whether they be ordeals from which we seem highly unlikely to ever recover, or ordeals of a lesser kind, I deem that the best course of action is to face them directly and *let oneself go.*'

4 Roger Caillois, 'Illusions à rebours', *Nouvelle Revue française*, December 1954, p. 1011.

5 Gilles Lapouge, *Dictionnaire amoureux du Brésil*, Paris, Plon, 2011, p. 413.

6 The paragraph that follows is based on information provided to me by Monique Lévi-Strauss over the course of several interviews in the autumn of 2011.

7 Monique Lévi-Strauss, *Une Enfance dans la gueule du loup*, Paris, Seuil, 2014.

8 Monique Lévi-Strauss, *Une Enfance dans la gueule du loup*.

9 See the book written about her by her daughter, Paule du Bouchet, *Emportée*, Paris, Actes Sud, 2011.

10 Interview with Carmen Bernand, 7 February 2013.

11 Interview with Monique Lévi-Strauss, 15 September 2010.

12 Interview with Monique Lévi-Strauss, 29 March 2011.

13 Didier Eribon, *Conversations with Claude Lévi-Strauss*, Chicago, The University of Chicago Press, 1991, p. 57.

14 Interview with Françoise Héritier, 15 April 2012.

15 Michel Tournier, 'Claude Lévi-Strauss, mon maître', *Le Figaro littéraire*, 1410, 26 May 1973.

16 Interview with Monique Lévi-Strauss, 29 March 2011.

17 Interview with Françoise Héritier, 15 April 2012.

18 Interview with Françoise Héritier, 15 April 2012.

19 Eribon, *Conversations*, p. 54.

20 See Claude Lévi-Strauss, 'Preface', in *AM*, p. 6.

21 Lévi-Strauss, 'Preface', p. 7.

22 Lévi-Strauss, 'Preface', p. 199.

23 Lévi-Strauss, 'Preface', p. 203.

24 Lévi-Strauss, 'Preface', p. 200.

25 Lévi-Strauss, 'Preface', p. 200.

26 Letter to Georges Balandier, 2 March (n.d.) [1950], CLS Archives, NAF 28150, box 181, 'Correspondence'.

27 Claude Lévi-Strauss, 'Le Père Noël supplicié', *Les Temps modernes*, 77, March 1952, republished as part of a collection of articles originally appearing in *La Repubblica* from 1989 to 2000, 'Santa Claus burned as a heretic', in *WAAC*, New York, Columbia University Press, 2016, pp. 2–19.

28 Lévi-Strauss, 'Santa Claus burned as a heretic', p. 18.

29 Claude Lévi-Strauss, 'Do dual organizations exist?' in *SA*, p. 162: 'Anthropology found its Galileo in Rivers, its Newton in Mauss. We can only hope that in the world of men, often as indifferent as the infinite universe whose silence terrified Pascal, the rare so-called dual organizations still functioning may find their Einstein before they – less enduring than the planets – disintegrate.'

30 'Linguistics and anthropology', in *SA*, p. 70.

31 'Linguistics and anthropology', in *SA*, p. 70. Patrick Wilcken, *Claude Lévi-Strauss: The Poet in the Laboratory*, London, Bloomsbury, 2010, p. 186.

32 For example, how to articulate two independent observations of the following kind: the Iroquois give great importance to women through a strong maternal right; at the linguistic level, there is no way to conceive of the feminine gender and dichotomy as the norm, as if it were necessary to take from one side to give to the other.

33 *SA*, pp. 79–80.

34 'Social structure' [1953], in *SA*, p. 315.

35 Eribon, *Conversations*, p. 122. There may have been a misunderstanding: the American anthropologists might have been under the impression that the term 'trash' here was meant to describe not the objects of the discipline but the populations themselves.

36 'The term "social structure" has nothing to do with empirical reality but with models which are built up after it. This should help one to clarify the difference between two concepts which are so close to each other that they have often been confused, namely those of social structure and social relations. It will be enough to state at this time that social relations consist of the raw materials out of which the models making up the social structure are built.' See 'Social Structure', in *SA*, p. 279.

37 Wilcken, *Claude Lévi-Strauss*, p. 188.

38 Letter to Roman Jakobson, 11 June 1951.

39 Letter to Roman Jakobson, 9 January 1952.

40 *International Social Science Bulletin*, 6(4), 1954.

41 Lévi-Strauss was not, however, unanimously appreciated within American anthropology. He was the subject of strong critiques, like the one published in *American Anthropologist* by two young linguists whom he did not know, which attacked the argument of his earlier article 'Language and the analysis of social laws', published in the same journal (53(2), April–June 1951). Annoyed and even aggrieved, he asked Jakobson for an explanation, thinking that there must be some 'background' of which he was unaware. See the letter of 13 March 1952.

42 Letter to Claude Lévi-Strauss dated 27 January 1950.

43 Letter from Talcott Parsons, 12 November 1953: 'We are highly cognizant of the great distinction and originality of your contribution to the field and the breadth and catholicity of your interests.' CLS Archives, NAF 28150, box 231, 'Voyages à l'étranger'.

44 Letter to Roman Jakobson, 10 May 1953.

45 His father's condition required care and so also added to his financial burden. His parents were not covered by French public health insurance and his father's hospitalization in 1952 put him in very serious financial difficulties.

46 Letter from Clyde Kluckhohn, 24 November 1953, CLS Archives, NAF 28150, box 231, 'Voyages à l'étranger'.

47 Wiktor Stoczkowski, *Anthropologies rédemptrices: Le monde selon Lévi-Strauss*, Paris, Hermann, 2008, p. 192: 'The founding ideology of UNESCO converged at several points with some of Lévi-Strauss's long-held convictions.'

48 Claude Lévi-Strauss presented a moving portrait of Lucien Bernot in the preface he wrote for the republication of the study by Bernot and René Blancart, *Nouville: Un village français*, Paris, Éditions des archives contemporaines, 1995, p. 3: 'Bernot had just received his baccalauréat and a certificate in Chinese from the Oriental Languages Institute. Over the course of our conversations, I was captivated by his rather original background and experiences. In addition to the Chinese language, these ran from the collection of indigenous French wine grape varieties (thought to have disappeared with the phylloxera epidemic), surviving specimens of which he and his father had found along railway embankments, to ancient printing techniques and the most esoteric rules of typography.' Bernot later published a thesis on Southeast Asia: *Les Paysans arakanais du Pakistan oriental*, La Haye-Paris, Mouton, 1967.

49 These studies have been 'revisited' a number of times over the last few years. See, for example, Bernard Paillard, Jean-François Simon and Laurent Le Gall (eds.), *En France rurale: Les enquêtes interdisciplinaires depuis les années 1960*, Paris, Presses universitaires de Rennes, 2010.

50 Claude Lévi-Strauss, 'Pour la réédition de Nouville', preface to *Nouville: Un village français*, p. 2.

51 Stoczkowski, *Anthropologies rédemptrices*, p. 225.

52 Letter to Fernand Braudel, 7 July 1953, CLS Archives, NAF 28150, box 181.

53 Eribon, *Conversations*, p. 60.

54 Stoczkowski, *Anthropologies rédemptrices*, p. 225.

55 Stoczkowski, *Anthropologies rédemptrices*, p. 214.

56 Paul-André Rosental, 'Géo-politique et État-Providence: le système-monde des migrations internationales dans l'entre-deux-guerres', *Annales, HSS*, 61(1), 2006, pp. 99–134.

57 In these paragraphs, I follow the analysis of Wiktor Stockzkowski in his chapter devoted to this issue: 'Portrait de Lévi-Strauss en démographe', in *Anthropologies rédemptrices.*

58 Stoczkowski, *Anthropologies rédemptrices*, p. 229.

59 Stoczkowski, *Anthropologies rédemptrices*, p. 227ff.

60 Stoczkowski, *Anthropologies rédemptrices*, p. 227ff.

61 Stoczkowski, *Anthropologies rédemptrices*, p. 222. His report was published in a seven-page version: 'The social sciences in Pakistan', *International Social Science Bulletin*, 3, 1951, pp. 885–892.

62 These three Rhodia-brand notebooks are preserved in Claude Lévi-Strauss's personal archives, NAF 28150, box 128. The quotations that follow are extracts from these notebooks, which were generally not dated.

63 'Carnet 1: Karachi'.

64 Vincent Debaene, 'Notice', in the French Pléiade edition of *Tristes Tropiques*, p. 1688.

65 This fieldwork gave rise to two articles: 'Kinship systems of three Chittagong Hill Tribes (Pakistan)', *Southern Journal of Anthropology*, 8, 1952, pp. 40–51; and 'Le syncrétisme religieux d'un village mogh du territoire de Chittagong', *Revue de l'histoire des religions*, 141(2), 1952, pp. 202–237.

66 Debaene, 'Notice', p. 1688.

67 *TT*, p. 129: 'Once, during my first teaching post in the Landes region, I had visited poultry yards specially adapted for the cramming of geese. [. . .] In this Indian setting, the situation was the same, apart from two differences: instead of geese, it was men and women I was looking at, and instead of being fattened up, they were, if anything, being slimmed down.'

68 *TT*, p. 128: 'Nowhere, perhaps, except in concentration camps, have human beings been so completely identified with butcher's meat.'

69 The two quotations are taken from 'Carnet 1'.

70 Debaene, 'Notice', p. 1690.

71 'Carnet 1'.

72 'Carnet 1'.

73 Stoczkowski, *Anthropologies rédemptrices*, p. 199. Interview with the author, 3 December 2004.

74 He was remunerated to the tune of several hundred dollars, which represented a considerable sum in 1951 for a Lévi-Strauss suffering from money problems. Stockzkowski, *Anthropologies rédemptrices*, p. 35.

75 For example, the French edition – *Race et histoire*, published by Gallimard – sold 16,323 copies over the period from 1 January to 31 December 1990. CLS Archives, NAF 28150, box 222, 'Contrats d'édition'.

76 Preamble to the UNESCO Constitution: 'Since wars begin in the minds of men, it is in the minds of men that the defences of peace must be constructed.'

77 'A Statement by experts on race problems', *International Social Science Bulletin*, 2(3), 1950, pp. 391–394. For the difficult genesis of this text, see Stoczkowski, *Anthropologies rédemptrices*, pp. 26–28, as well as Chloé Maurel, *Histoire de l'Unesco: Les trente premières années*, Paris, L'Harmattan, 2010, pp. 228ff.

78 Stoczkowski, *Anthropologies rédemptrices*, p. 30.

79 *RH*, p. 7.

80 *RH*, p. 21.

81 *RH*, p. 22.

82 *RH*, p. 46.

83 *RH*, p. 48.

84 *RH.*
85 Stoczkowski, *Anthropologies rédemptrices*, p. 210.
86 Letter to Roman Jakobson, 9 January 1952. This was a reference to John von Neumann, the Hungarian-American mathematician and physicist whose work dealt with group theory and quantum physics. His research had considerable implications for the development of computers. Of the wide range of fields Neumann touched upon, there were two that were of particular interest to Lévi-Strauss: game theory and the mathematical formalization of models of economic behaviour.
87 *RH*, p. 45.
88 Michel Panoff, *Les Frères ennemis: Roger Caillois et Claude Lévi-Strauss*, Paris, Payot, 1993.
89 Eribon, *Conversations*, p. 85.
90 A card from Henri Laugier to Claude Lévi-Strauss [1955] assuring him of his support in the dispute with Callois and informing him that Mrs Myrdal, the director of the department of social sciences at UNESCO, was perturbed by the entire affair. CLS Archives, NAF 28150, box 195.
91 In choosing this title, Lévi-Strauss wanted to establish a relationship between Caillois's argument and the tradition of Cynicism, characterized by a certain Athenian intellectual demagoguery.
92 Claude Lévi-Strauss regretted writing this text (the republication of which he never allowed), as he often confided to his wife. His regret was for allowing polemical rhetoric to become the foundation of intellectual debate, which in no way excluded engaging in scientific controversies. Interview with Monique Lévi-Strauss, 4 March 2012.
93 'Diogène couché', *Les Temps modernes*, 110, March 1955, p. 1187.
94 'Diogène couché', p. 1202.
95 'Diogène couché', p. 1214.
96 'Diogène couché', p. 1217. On the figure of Lazarus, see Vincent Debaene, 'Portrait de l'ethnologue en Lazare', in M. Izard (ed.), *Claude Lévi-Strauss*, Paris, L'Herne, 'Cahiers de l'Herne', 2004, pp. 89–96.
97 'Diogène couché', p. 1188.
98 'Diogène couché', p. 1219.
99 'We wish only that the progress of his self-analysis brings him quickly to a confrontation with his past – let us not pick a fight with him or demand anything of him, other than that he let us work in peace. And may he go elsewhere in search of his imagos'. 'Diogène couché', p. 1220.
100 'Diogène couché', p. 1216: Lévi-Strauss quoted Sartre affirming that 'the sociology of primitives [. . .] studies [. . .] meaningful totalities'. *Les Temps modernes*, 84–85, October–November 1952, p. 729.
101 Wilcken, *Claude Lévi-Strauss*, p. 192.
102 See Christophe Charle, *Discordance des temps: Une brève histoire de la modernité*, Paris, Armand Colin, 2011.
103 See Luc Boltanski, Élisabeth Claverie, Nicolas Offenstadt and Stéphane Van Damme, *Affaires, scandales et grandes causes: De Socrate à Pinochet*, Paris, Stock, 2007.
104 See chapter 10 above.
105 Aimé Césaire, *Discourse on Colonialism*, New York, Monthly Review Press, 2000, p. 73.
106 Alfred Métraux, letter to Pierre Verger, in *Le Pied à l'étrier: Correspondance*, Paris, Jean-Michel Place, 1994, p. 210, quoted in Wilcken, *Claude Lévi-Strauss*, p. 192.

107 Letter from Claude Lévi-Strauss to Dolorès Vanetti, 22 June 1955, CLS Archives, NAF 28150, box 182, 'Correspondance avec Dolorès Vanetti'.
108 Métraux, *Le Pied à l'étrier*, p. 295.

Chapter 14   The Confessions of Claude Lévi-Strauss

1 The expression is Pierre Nora's, in the preface he wrote to the new French edition of *Tristes Tropiques*, Paris, France-Loisirs, 1990, p. 15. It was this very same word that Claude Lanzmann chose when recalling, fifty years after the fact, the first time he read the book: 'I remember the bombshell of the first sentence of *Tristes Tropiques*': 'Envoi', *Les Temps modernes*, 628, August–September–October 2004, p. 1.
2 See the classic work of fragmentary autobiography by Fernando Pessoa, *The Book of Disquiet*, London, Penguin, 2002.
3 Nora, 'Préface', p. 12.
4 Pierre Mac Orlan, *La Vénus internationale*, 1923, in *Oeuvres complètes*, Paris-Genève, Gallimard, p. 398; quoted in Patrick Wilcken, *Claude Lévi-Strauss: The Poet in the Laboratory*, London, Bloomsbury, 2010, p. 194.
5 See Pierre Singaravelou (ed.), *L'Empire des géographes: Géographie, exploration et colonisation*, Paris, Belin, 2008.
6 For this entire paragraph, see Sylvain Venayre, *La Gloire de l'aventure: Genèse d'une mystique moderne, 1850–1940*, Paris, Aubier, 2002; and *Panorama du voyage, 1780–1920*, Paris, Les Belles Lettres, 2012.
7 Claude Lévi-Strauss, 'Le droit au voyage', *L'Express*, 21 September 1956.
8 The formulation is Jean Malaurie's, quoted in Vincent Debaene, *Far Afield: French Anthropology between Sciences and Literature*, Chicago, The University of Chicago Press, 2014, p. 288.
9 See chapter 12 above.
10 Account by Monique Lévi-Strauss, 29 March 2011. Lévi-Strauss would pay tribute to the role played by Malaurie in the inscription he wrote in the latter's signed copy of *Tristes Tropiques*: 'To Jean Malaurie, to whom I am much obliged for having obliged me to write this book', *Pour Jean Malaurie: 102 témoignages en hommage à 40 ans d'études arctiques*, Paris, Plon, 1990, p. 793.
11 Wilcken, *Claude Lévi-Strauss*, p. 196.
12 Contract signed with Plon (publisher) on 14 May 1954: 8% royalties for the first 10,000 copies sold; then 10% for the next 10,000; and 13% from the 21,000th. CLS Archives, NAF 28150, box 223.
13 Didier Eribon, *Conversations with Claude Lévi-Strauss*, Chicago, The University of Chicago Press, 1991, p. 58.
14 Eribon, *Conversations*, p. 58.
15 Eribon, *Conversations*, p. 60.
16 Eribon, *Conversations*, p. 58.
17 Claude Lévi-Strauss, interview with Jean-José Marchand, *Arts*, 28 December 1955, quoted in François Dosse, *History of Structuralism I: The Rising Sign, 1945–1966*, Minneapolis, University of Minnesota Press, 1997, p. 130.
18 Claude Lévi-Strauss, 'Le coucher de soleil: entretien avec Boris Wiseman', *Les Temps modernes*, 628, August–September–October 2004, p. 3.
19 The draft text of this play was transcribed by Vincent Debaene. See 'En marge de *Tristes Tropiques*', in the French Pléiade edition of *Tristes Tropiques*, pp. 1632–1650.
20 See chapter 9 above.

21 Claude Lévi-Strauss, 'Autoportrait', remarks collected by Catherine Clément and Dominique-Antoine Grisoni, *Magazine littéraire*, 223, October 1985, p. 24.

22 Lévi-Strauss, 'Autoportrait', p. 24.

23 The precise expression used by Alfred Métraux and quoted by Claude Lévi-Strauss in Eribon, *Conversations*, p. 60: 'I had unleashed my pen, as Métraux liked to say.'

24 Eribon, *Conversations*, p. 59: 'In your eyes was it a kind of synthesis of what you had done?' 'Of what I had done up to that point, yes. Also, of everything I believed and dreamed about.'

25 *TT*, p. 96.

26 Correspondence with Dolorès Vanetti, CLS Archives, NAF 28150, box 182.

27 They got married that same year, as soon as the divorce from Rose-Marie Ullmo was pronounced, on 6 April 1954.

28 Vincent Debaene, 'Notice', in the French Pléiade edition of *Tristes Tropiques*, p. 1695.

29 Interview with Monique Lévi-Strauss.

30 CLS Archives, NAF 28150, box 128, 'Carnet 1'. See *TT*, p. 131.

31 CLS Archives, NAF 28150, box 49, 'Documents préparatoires à *Tristes Tropiques*'.

32 'At home with the civilized Indians' who had achieved a kind of synthesis between wilderness and civilization, having preserved ancient civilizations while in touch with the modern world from which they borrowed. The passage is edited into chapter 17, 'Parana', *TT*, p. 155.

33 Debaene, 'Notice', p. 1695, quoting an expression of Lévi-Strauss's in his 'personal glossary', from an interview with Dominique-Antoine Grisoni, 'Lévi-Strauss en 33 mots', *Le Magazine littéraire*, 223, October 1985, p. 26.

34 *TT*, p. 96.

35 *TT*, pp. 43–44.

36 D.-A. Grisoni, 'Sur Jean de Léry: entretien avec Claude Lévi-Strauss', preface to Jean de Léry, *Histoire d'un voyage faict en terre du Brésil*, Paris, Le Livre de poche, 1994, p. 7.

37 See, for this entire paragraph, Debaene, '*Tristes Tropiques*: The Search for Correspondence and the Logic of the Sensible', in *Far Afield*, pp. 199–224.

38 Michel Leiris, 'À travers *Tristes Tropiques*', *Les Cahiers de la République*, 2, July 1956.

39 Leiris, 'À travers *Tristes Tropiques*'.

40 Leiris, 'À travers *Tristes Tropiques*'.

41 Debaene, *Far Afield*, p. 74.

42 Debaene, *Far Afield*, p. 102.

43 Debaene, *Far Afield*, p. 207. Debaene points out that this conclusion once again shows the affinity between *Tristes Tropiques* and the Proustian *Search*.

44 *TT*, p. 380.

45 Lévi-Strauss, 'Le coucher de soleil', p. 10.

46 Bronislaw Malinowski, *A Diary in the Strict Sense of the Word*, New York, Harcourt, Brace & World, 1967.

47 Eduardo Viveiros de Castro and Marc Kirsch, 'Claude Lévi-Strauss vu par Eduardo Viveiros de Castro', *Lettre du Collège de France*, 2, 2008.

48 *Works and Lives: The Anthropologist as Author*, Stanford, Stanford University Press, 1988, pp. 25–48.

49 Philippe Descola, *The Spears of Twilight: Life and Death in the Amazon Jungle*, New York, New Press, 1996.

50 *TT*, p. 378.
51 Debaene, *Far Afield*, p. 210.
52 Debaene, *Far Afield*, pp. 212ff.
53 Vincent Debaene, 'Portrait de l'ethnologue en Lazare', in M. Izard (ed.), *Claude Lévi-Strauss*, Paris, L'Herne, 'Cahiers de l'Herne', 2004, p. 90, draws parallels between the character in Lévi-Strauss's play and Sartre: 'Cinna, in the end, is just another Roquentin.'
54 See Frédéric Keck, 'L'aventure de l'ordinaire chez Sartre et Lévi-Strauss: *La Nausée* et *Tristes Tropiques*, une lecture croisée', *Les Temps modernes*, 632, July–October 2005, pp. 633–634.
55 'The place of anthropology in the social sciences and problems raised in teaching it', [1954], in *SA*, p. 378.
56 Claude Lévi-Strauss, interview with Boutang and Chevallay, 'Claude Lévi-Strauss par lui-même', cited in Wilcken, *Claude Lévi-Strauss*, p. 202.
57 Claude Lévi-Strauss, 'Jean-Jacques Rousseau, Founder of the sciences of man', in *SA*, vol. 2, p. 35.
58 Jean-Jacques Rousseau, *The Reveries of the Solitary Walker*, Cambridge, Hackett, 1992, p. 1.
59 See chapter 12 above.
60 Lévi-Strauss spoke of the 'subversive force' of Rousseau's thought, of his 'solitary and wounded existence', as 'the levers with which to shake ethics, law and society'. Lévi-Strauss took the opportunity to dispel a few misunderstandings concerning the state of nature in Rousseau. Claude Lévi-Strauss, 'Jean-Jacques Rousseau, founder of the sciences of man', in *SA*, vol. 2, p. 40. See chapter 18 below.
61 Lévi-Strauss, 'Jean-Jacques Rousseau', p. 43.
62 'Des Indiens et leur ethnographe', *Les Temps modernes*, 116, August 1955, pp. 1–50.
63 Lanzmann, in 'Envoi', p. 1, spoke of the 'dazzlement' of Sartre and Simone de Beauvoir, 'and, in truth, of us all'.
64 *TT*, p. 58: 'As for the intellectual movement which was to reach its peak in existentialism, it seemed to me to be anything but a legitimate form of reflection, because of its overindulgent attitude towards the illusions of subjectivity. The raising of personal preoccupations to the dignity of philosophical problems is far too likely to lead to a sort of shop-girl metaphysics, which may be pardonable as a didactic method but is extremely dangerous if it allows people to play fast-and-loose with the mission incumbent on philosophy until science becomes strong enough to replace it: that is, to understand being in relationship to itself and not in relationship to myself.'
65 For this entire paragraph, see Debaene, 'Notice', pp. 1715ff, and *Far Afield*, pp. 199ff.
66 'Social anatomy', *Times Literary Supplement*, 22 February 1957.
67 Letter to Dolorès Vanetti, 28 November 1955, CLS Archives, NAF 28150, box 182.
68 Interview with Monique Lévi-Strauss. *The Elementary Structures of Kinship* had sold 800 copies in five years.
69 Maurice Blanchot, 'L'homme au point zero', *La Nouvelle Revue française*, 40, April 1956.
70 Debaene, 'Portrait de l'ethnologue en Lazare', p. 93.
71 On this specific mode of registering history in film, in this case not direct footage of the camps (although this was also available) but of the 'foreclosed' images that cinema offers, in its own grammar, as 'cinematographic forms of

history', see Antoine de Baecque, *Camera Historica: The Century in Cinema*, New York, Columbia University Press, 2012.

72 Raymond Aron, 'L'ethnologue entre les primitifs et la civilisation', *Le Figaro littéraire*, 24 December 1955.

73 *TT*, p. 413.

74 *TT*, p. 414.

75 *TT*, pp. 149–150.

76 Georges Balandier, 'Grandeurs et servitudes de l'ethnologue', *Cahiers du Sud*, 337, 1956.

77 *TT*, p. 393.

78 *TT*, p. 393.

79 Letter to Jean Malaurie, 29 March 1955, CLS Archives, NAF 28150, box 196, quoted in Debaene, 'Notice', pp. 1697–1698.

80 *Le Canard enchaîné*, 31 October 1956.

81 Debaene, *Far Afield*, p. 262.

82 See, in addition to Debaene, *Far Afield*, whose subtitle is 'French anthropology between science and literature', Wolf Lepenies, *Between Literature and Science: The Rise of Sociology*, New York, Cambridge University Press, 1988.

83 François-Régis Bastide, 'Les aventures d'un nouveau Chateaubriand. Adieu sauvages! Adieu voyages!', *Demain*, 27 December 1955. Meschacebe was one of the Amerindian names for the Mississippi River.

84 Nora, 'Préface', p. 13. Note that Plon had also published Charles de Gaulle's *Memoirs* . . .

85 Jean Marcenac, 'Vers une ethnographie sans larme?' *Lettres françaises*, 16 February 1956.

86 Gaëtan Picon, '*Tristes Tropiques* ou la conscience malheureuse', in *L'Usage de la lecture*, vol. II, Paris, Mercure de France, 1956.

87 Georges Bataille, 'Un livre humain, un grand livre', *Critique*, 105, February 1956.

88 Debaene, *Far Afield*, p. 266.

89 Jean-Claude Carrière, 'Compte rendu de *Tristes Tropiques*', *La Table ronde*, January 1956.

90 Debaene, *Far Afield*, p. 269.

91 *NM*, p. 641.

92 Don C. Talayesva, ed. Leo W. Simmons, *Sun Chief: The Autobiography of a Hopi Indian*, New Haven, Yale University Press, 2013 [1942]. The French edition was published by Plon in the 'Terre humaine' series in 1956, with a preface by Lévi-Strauss. One of the series' greatest successes came later from one of these 'native informants': Pierre Jakez Helias, *Le Cheval d'orgueil* (1975), an insider's account (first written in the Breton language, and then translated into French by the author) of a society whose authentic character is pitched against that of scholars who had studied the village of Plozévet over a period of several years. See André Burguière, *Bretons de Plozévet*, Paris, Flammarion, 1975.

93 Sonia Orwell, 'The literary scene in Paris', CLS Archives, NAF 28150, box 234, 'Dossier de presse de *Tristes Tropiques*'.

94 CLS Archives, NAF 28150, box 234, 'Dossier de presse de *Tristes Tropiques*'. In the end, Roger Ikor received the prize for his novel *Les Eaux mêlées* in 1955. And in 1956, it went to Romain Gary for *Les Racines du ciel*, whose theme and inspiration, if not its prose, strongly recalled several Lévi-Straussian leitmotivs: the outcry against the desecration of nature, the greatness of the natural

and animal worlds, the critique of human omnipotence and the promotion of a reconstructed humanism.

95 See Lévi-Strauss's account of this episode in Eribon, *Conversations*, p. 34.
96 Quote taken from the document sent together with the reproductions and questionnaire, included in the correspondence with Breton, CLS Archives, NAF 28150, box 185. The other Breton quotes come from the same source.
97 Eribon, *Conversations*, p. 34.
98 Letter dated 23 August 1955.
99 Eribon, *Conversations*, p. 34.
100 Letter from Claude Lévi-Strauss to André Breton, Valleraugue, 6 July 1957, André Breton Archives, Bibliothèque Jacques-Doucet.
101 Nora, 'Préface', p. 13.
102 'The structural study of myth', *Journal of American Folklore*, 78(270), October–December 1955.
103 'The structural study of myth', p. 436.
104 'The structural study of myth', p. 422.
105 Denis Bertholet, *Claude Lévi-Strauss*, Paris, Fayard, 2003.
106 Pierre Maranda (ed.), *The Double Twist: From Ethnography to Morphodynamics*, Toronto, University of Toronto Press, 2001; see also Lucien Scubla, *Lire Lévi-Strauss*, Paris, Odile Jacob, 1998, as well as the work of the mathematicians Jean Petitot ('Approche morphodynamique de la formule canonique du mythe', *L'Homme*, 1998, pp. 106–107) and Jack Morava ('Une interprétation mathématique de la formule canonique de Claude Lévi-Strauss', appendix to the article by Lucien Scubla, 'Structure, transformation et morphogénèse ou le structuralisme illustré par Pascal et Poussin', in M. Izard (ed.), *Claude Lévi-Strauss*, Paris, L'Herne, 'Cahiers de l'Herne', 2004, pp. 197–198). Finally, see Maurice Godelier, *Lévi-Strauss*, Paris, Seuil, 2013, pp. 411–436.
107 See chapter 13 above.
108 *SA*, p. 213.
109 See Debaene, 'Préface', p. 32ff.
110 See Wilcken, *Claude Lévi-Strauss*, p. 218.
111 Roman Jakobson, *Language in Literature*, Cambridge, Belknap Press, 1987, pp. 3–4.
112 Georges Charbonnier, *Entretiens avec Claude Lévi-Strauss* [1961], Paris, Les Belles Lettres, 2010, p. 84.
113 According to another interesting interpretation, albeit a bit skewed, if Lévi-Strauss did not like modern art – which displayed and manipulated the relationship between signifier and signified, in an explicit reflexivity – it was because this art rendered structuralism 'redundant', by exhibiting – by making into its very material – certain intellectual operations that characterized structuralism. This idea has been developed by D. Smith, 'Le structuralisme au miroir: Lévi-Strauss et le modernisme', *Le Temps modernes*, 628, 2004–3, pp. 116–117. However, structuralism is not fundamentally about manipulating the signifier/signified relationship, but rather about making comparisons that refuse the separation of form and content.
114 Clifford Geertz, *Works and Lives: The Anthropologist as Author*, Stanford, Stanford University Press, 1988, p. 39.
115 Debaene, 'Préface', p. 33.
116 This expression is borrowed from Paul-André Rosental, who used it to describe a work by Louis Chevalier, *Classes dangereuses et classes laborieuses*, 1958.
117 Geertz, *Works and Lives*, p. 25ff.

118 See Debaene, *Far Afield*, p. 222: Lévi-Strauss did 'not deny the difference between art and science, but instead refused to think of it as a radical break'.

119 Walter Benjamin, *Correspondence of Walter Benjamin 1910–1940*, Chicago, University of Chicago Press, 1994, p. 488.

120 CLS Archives, NAF 28150, box 234, 'Dossier de presse *Tristes Tropiques*'.

121 CLS Archives, NAF 28150, box 234, 'Dossier de presse *Tristes Tropiques*'; *Combat*, 25 May 1956.

122 Claude Lévi-Strauss, *A World on the Wane*, London, Hutchinson, 1961. Subsequent English translations kept the French title of *Tristes Tropiques*.

123 Cited in Nora, 'Préface', p. 16.

124 Letter from Émile Benveniste, 20 December 1955.

125 Beatrix Beck, 'Claude Lévi-Strauss', *La Revue de Paris*, June 1956, p. 14. Quoted in Bertholet, *Claude Lévi-Strauss*, p. 220.

Chapter 15   Structuralist Crystallization (1958–1962)

1 Quoted in *SM*, 1966, p. 130.

2 Claude Imbert, 'Un moment épistémologique', in Philippe Descola (ed.), *Claude Lévi-Strauss, un parcours dans le siècle*, Paris, Odile Jacob, 2012, p. 226.

3 Claude Lévi-Strauss, 'Surtout ne pas confondre "pensée sauvage" et "pensée des sauvages"', interview with Gilles Lapouge, *Le Figaro littéraire*, 2 June 1962, p. 3.

4 Letter to Fernand Braudel, 26 October 1958, CLS Archives, NAF 28150, box 181, 'Correspondance'.

5 Letter to Fernand Braudel, 3 November 1958.

6 Letter from Maurice Merleau-Ponty to Claude Lévi-Strauss, 26 May 1955, CLS Archives, NAF 28150, box 196, 'Correspondance reçue'.

7 Claude Lévi-Strauss, 'De quelques rencontres', *L'Arc*, 46, 1971, p. 43.

8 See chapter 12 above.

9 Lévi-Strauss, 'De quelques rencontres', p. 43.

10 The term used by Claude Lévi-Strauss to describe the role played by anthropologists in relation to philosophy, in the eyes of Merleau-Ponty. 'De quelques rencontres', p. 45.

11 François Dosse, 'The phenomenological bridge', in *History of Structuralism*, vol. I: *The Rising Sign, 1945–1966*, Minneapolis, University of Minnesota Press, 1997, pp. 37–42.

12 Report available in *La Lettre du Collège de France*, 2, 2008, pp. 49–53. The argument is taken up and expanded in one of the most famous chapters of his final book: 'From Mauss to Claude Lévi-Strauss', in *Signs*, Evanston, Northwestern University Press, 1964, pp. 114–125. The final sentence of the chapter reads: 'These are the marks of a great intellectual endeavour.'

13 Merleau-Ponty, 'De Mauss à Claude Lévi-Strauss', p. 115.

14 Merleau-Ponty, 'De Mauss à Claude Lévi-Strauss', pp. 117–118.

15 Merleau-Ponty, 'De Mauss à Claude Lévi-Strauss', pp. 120, 122.

16 Report read at the faculty assembly, 30 November 1958, CLS Archives, NAF 28150, box 216, 'Collège de France'.

17 Letter from Claude Lévi-Strauss to Roman Jakobson, 26 December 1958, CLS Archives, NAF 28150, box 181.

18 Lévi-Strauss was eternally grateful to him for this. Indeed, despite the critiques he received from the Musée de l'Homme, of which he became director, Guiart

652   Notes to pp. 350–2

was never spoken ill of by Lévi-Strauss, however much the latter may have thought otherwise. Interview with Monique Lévi-Strauss, 28 November 2013.

19 Letter from Louis Chevalier, 5 November 1958, CLS Archives, NAF 28150, box 186, 'Correspondance reçue'.

20 Letter from Roger Dion, 19 February 1959, CLS Archives, NAF 28150, box 187, 'Correspondance reçue'.

21 Report by Merleau-Ponty to the faculty assembly, 15 March 1959, CLS Archives, NAF 28150, box 216, 'Collège de France'.

22 'Assemblée générale du 15 mars 1959': 36 votes for Lévi-Strauss, 1 for Jean Guiart, and 7 blank or marked with a cross. At that same assembly, physicist Louis Leprince-Ringuet was elected to the nuclear physics chair by a narrow margin of 24 out of 44 votes, with 20 votes for his competitor Hans Halban. Collège de France Archives.

23 Letter to Fernand Braudel, 1 February 1959: 'The unceasing friendship you have shown me over these years of "purgatory" must not cause me to forget that you are also one of my judges.'

24 Jean Jamin, 'L'anthropologie et ses acteurs', in Les Enjeux philosophiques des années 50, Paris, Editions du Centre Pompidou, 1993, pp. 112–113; see also M. Bloch, 'Une anthropologie fondamentale', in Descola (ed.), Claude Lévi-Strauss, pp. 247–263.

25 Pierre Bourdieu, Sketch for a Self-Analysis, Chicago, The University of Chicago Press, 2008, p. 40; the italics are mine.

26 The text of the inaugural lecture opens the second volume of Structural Anthropology, 'The scope of anthropology', pp. 3–32.

27 The anthropologist temporarily conceded defeat to historians: 'Neglecting the historical dimension on the pretext that there are insufficient means of evaluating it, except approximately, results in our being satisfied with an impoverished sociology in which phenomena are set loose from their context.' Lévi-Strauss remarks humorously that 'this declaration in favour of history may come as a surprise', SA, vol. 2, pp. 13, 14.

28 SA, vol. 2, p. 28.

29 Michael Leiris, Phantom Africa, London, Seagull Books, 2017: 'It is through subjectivity (brought to its height) that one reaches objectivity.'

30 SA, vol. 2, p. 15.

31 SA, vol. 2, p. 15.

32 SA, vol. 2, p. 7.

33 SA, vol. 2, p. 32.

34 Siegfried Kracauer, The Last Things Before the Last, Princeton, M. Wiener, 1995. The book was first published in the US in 1969 (by Oxford University Press), three years after the death of its author.

35 See Daniel Fabre, 'D'une ethnologie romantique', in Daniel Fabre and Jean-Marie Privat (eds.), Savoirs romantiques: Une naissance de l'ethnologie, Nancy, Presses universitaires de Nancy, 2010.

36 In the metaphorical sense in which François Hartog uses the expression in Croire en l'histoire, Paris, Flammarion, 2013, to characterize historians who built bridges [the French word for bridge being pont] between past and present, which Lévi-Strauss also did, between the past and present of his discipline.

37 As we have mentioned, Merleau-Ponty was exactly the same age as Lévi-Strauss, even though he was too vain to admit it: 'More than once, I caught him gazing at me as if in a mirror, which he refused to admit, not without reason, reflected an image comparable to his own, or even that it heralded

what it might someday be. Our common birthdate appeared to him as a falsity.' Lévi-Strauss, 'De quelques rencontres', p. 44.

38 *SA*, vol. 2, p. 5.
39 Denis Bertholet, *Claude Lévi-Strauss*, Paris, Fayard, 2003, p. 248: 'The new professor put his adolescent rebellions behind him.'
40 *SA*, vol. 2, p. 5. Lévi-Strauss also produced a short essay, 'What anthropology owes to Durkheim' (published in *SA*, vol. 2), which was added to the other tributes through the influence of Dean Georges Davy, his former doctoral supervisor.
41 See chapter 12 above.
42 Georges Gurvitch, 'Le concept de structure sociale', *Cahiers internationaux de sociologie*, 19, 1955.
43 Response written in 1956 and included at the last minute in *SA* as 'Postscript to chapter XV', p. 324.
44 'Postscript to chapter XV', p. 326.
45 'Postscript to chapter XV', p. 328.
46 See Didier Eribon, *Conversations with Claude Lévi-Strauss*, Chicago, The University of Chicago Press, 1991, pp. 69–70; and Dosse, *History of Structuralism*, vol. 1, pp. 229–231.
47 Pierre Bourdieu, *Homo Academicus*, Stanford, Stanford University Press, 1984, pp. 105ff.
48 Eribon, *Conversations*, p. 61.
49 *SA*, vol. 2, p. 328.
50 Eribon, *Conversations*, p. 68: 'I had been thinking about it for some time, and before writing *Tristes Tropiques* I took the book, or rather the idea for the book, to Gallimard. I talked to Brice Parain, who told me my ideas hadn't matured.'
51 In the mid-1960s, Pierre Nora, now in charge of the human sciences at Gallimard, approached Claude Lévi-Strauss: 'When I joined Gallimard, I went to see him to win him over. He told me: "I will do anything for you personally, but nothing for Gallimard".' François Dosse, *Pierre Nora: Homo historicus*, Paris, Perrin, 2011, p. 179.
52 Dosse, *Pierre Nora*, p. 179.
53 Maxime Rodinson, 'Racisme et civilisation', *Nouvelle Critique*, 66, June 1955; 'Ethnographie et relativisme', *Nouvelle Critique*, 69, November 1955.
54 'What is more, Rodinson attacks me in the name of Marxism, whereas my conception is infinitely closer to Marx's position than his': *SA*, vol. 2, p. 369. Lévi-Strauss pointed out on that occasion that the distinction he made in *Race and History* between static history, fluctuating history and cumulative history rested on several of Marx's texts, which he cited.
55 Jean-François Revel, *Pourquoi des philosophes?* Paris, Julliard, 1957.
56 *SA*, vol. 2, pp. 340–341.
57 Letter from Roman Jakobson, 10 July 1958, CLS Archives, NAF 28150, box 181, 'Correspondance'.
58 CLS Archives, NAF 28150, box 189.
59 Letter from Claude Lévi-Strauss, 3 August 1957.
60 Dosse, *History of Structuralism*, vol. 1, pp. 173ff.
61 Roger Bastide (ed.), *Sens et usage du terme de structure* (1959), Paris, Mouton, 1962.
62 *Entretiens sur la notion de genèse et de structure*, Cerisy Conference, July–August 1959, Paris, Mouton, 1965.
63 Eribon, *Conversations*, p. 71.

64 *RC*, p. 9.
65 *RC*, p. 9.
66 Eribon, *Conversations*, p. 75.
67 Frédéric Keck, in Claude Levi-Strauss, *Oeuvres*, 'Bibliothèque de la Pléiade', Paris, Gallimard, 2008, p. 1778. Keck has pointed out that the twin publication of a short critical work with PUF followed by a more ambitious one had already become somewhat established practice: for example, Jean-Paul Sartre, with *L'Imagination* [*The Imagination*] (PUF, 1936) followed by *L'Imaginaire* [*The Imaginary*] (Gallimard, 1940), and Merleau-Ponty, who published *Les Structures du comportement* [*The Structures of Behaviour*] in 1942 with PUF and *La Phénoménologie de la perception* [*The Phenomenology of Perception*] in 1945 with Gallimard.
68 Letter from Dumézil to Claude Lévi-Strauss, 21 March 1961, CLS Archives, NAF 28150, box 188.
69 Letter from Dumézil to Claude Lévi-Strauss, 21 March 1961.
70 Baldwin Spencer and F.J. Gillen, *The Northern Tribes of Central Australia*, London, 1904. Pastor Elkin's book was the other source on the totemic rituals of Australian Aborigines: Adolphus Peter Elkin, *The Australian Aborigines*, Sydney, Angus & Robertson, 1938.
71 Claude Lévi-Strauss, *Totemism*, New York, Beacon Press, p. 1.
72 Claude Lévi-Strauss, interview with Gilles Lapouge, *Le Figaro littéraire*, 2 June 1962.
73 See Keck, in Lévi-Strauss, *Oeuvres*, pp. 1780–1781.
74 Lévi-Strauss, *Totemism*, p. 98.
75 Lévi-Strauss, *Totemism*, p. 99.
76 Letter from Dumézil to Claude Lévi-Strauss, 28 January 1962, CLS Archives, NAF 28150, box 188, 'Correspondance reçue'.
77 *SM*, p. 9.
78 *SM*, p. 22.
79 *SM*, pp. 23ff.
80 *SM*, pp. 21–22. Mythical thought, like bricolage, builds structured sets, 'not directly with other structured sets but by using the remains and debris of events: in French "des bribes et des morceaux", or odds and ends in English, fossilized evidence of the history of an individual or society'. Here again, anthropology is a science of residue.
81 Eribon, *Conversations*, p. 110.
82 See chapter 2 above.
83 See André Mary, 'In memoriam Lévi-Strauss (1908–2009)', *Archives de sciences sociales des religions*, October–December 2009: http://assr.revues.org/index21483.html.
84 Keck, in Lévi-Strauss, *Oeuvres*, p. 1788: 'The notion of transformation, which plays a central role in *The Savage Mind*, was discovered while he was observing the morphological plates of the mathematician and biologist D'Arcy Thompson illustrating the formal homology between distinct natural species.'
85 *SA*, vol. 2, p. 18.
86 *SM*, p. 36. Lévi-Strauss himself said that 'this logic works rather like a kaleidoscope, an instrument which also contains bits and pieces by means of which structural patterns are realized'.
87 *SM*, p. 268.
88 Keck, in Lévi-Strauss, *Oeuvres*, p. 1782.
89 Interview with Gilles Lapouge, *Le Figaro littéraire*, 2 June 1962.

90 Keck, in Lévi-Strauss, *Oeuvres*, p. 1789: for they highlight a continuity between the animal and the human kingdoms (through physiognomic deformation) that Western society on the whole rejects.
91 Dosse, *History of Structuralism*, vol. 1, p. 235.
92 Eribon, *Conversations*, p. 110.
93 See, for example, Simon Schaffer and Steven Shapin, *Leviathan and the Air-pump: Hobbes, Boyle and the Experimental Life*, Princeton, Princeton University Press, 1985; and, more recently, Lorraine Daston and Peter Galison, *Objectivity*, New York, Zone Books, 2007.
94 Letter from Pierre Auger to Claude Lévi-Strauss, 14 August 1962, CLS Archives, NAF 28150, box 183.
95 The book was listed by the newspaper *France-Soir* as one of the ten most important books of the year, alongside rather literary titles: *What I Believe* by François Mauriac, *The Garden* by Yves Berger, *Explosion in a Cathedral* by Alejo Carpentier, *Vents et poussières* by Henri Michaux, *The Afternoon of Mr. Andesmas* by Marguerite Duras, and *La Fosse de Babel* by Raymond Abellio.
96 Claude Roy, 'Un grand livre civilisé: *La Pensée sauvage*', *Libération*, 19 June 1962.
97 J. Lacroix, '*La Pensée sauvage*', *Le Monde*, 17 November 1962.
98 Lacroix, '*La Pensée sauvage*'.
99 Lacroix, '*La Pensée sauvage*'.
100 Lacroix, '*La Pensée sauvage*'.
101 See Dosse, *History of Structuralism*, vol. 1, ch. 25.
102 Bernard Pingaud, *L'Arc*, 1966, quoted in Dosse, *History of Structuralism*, vol. 1, p. 326.
103 Letter from Luc de Heusch to Claude Lévi-Strauss, 7 January 1977, CLS Archives, NAF 28150, box 187.
104 Letter from Catherine Backès-Clément to Claude Lévi-Strauss, 3 February 1972, NAF 28150, box 186, 'Correspondance reçue'.
105 Catherine Clément wrote a pioneering book on the anthropologist's work, *Lévi-Strauss ou la structure et le malheur*, Paris, Seghers, 1970. In the various media outlets to which she contributed, from *Matin* to *Magazine littéraire* among others, she wrote on Lévi-Strauss, his books, his travels (to Japan), and published long interviews and selected iconography. She recounted how, as a young philosophy student in 1962, she had already read Lévi-Strauss and used it on her oral exam, to the astonishment of the members of her jury who were still unfamiliar with the anthropologist's work. Her self-confidence won them over: 'I discussed *The Savage Mind*, the brand new Lévi-Strauss. Georges Canghuilhem, the president of the jury, was not the kind of man who let on what he thought. He grumbled his thanks to me, his eyes sparkling with excitement under his big black brows.' Verdict: Catherine Backès (her name at the time) was ranked 'cacique', i.e., top of the class. In September, Lévi-Strauss, who had got wind of the event, enquired about the bold young candidate and asked to meet her. See Catherine Clément, *Mémoire*, Paris, Stock, 2009, p. 70.
106 Marc Augé, *L'Anthropologue et le monde global*, Paris, Armand Colin, 2013, pp. 12–13.
107 Letter from Régis Debray to Claude Lévi-Strauss, 25 December 1969, CLS Archives, NAF 28150, box 187, 'Correspondance reçue'.
108 François Furet, 'French intellectuals: from Marxism to structuralism', [1967] in *In the Workshop of History*, Chicago, University of Chicago Press, 1984, pp. 27–39; Raymond Aron, *The Opium of the Intellectuals*, New York, Doubleday, 1957.

109 Pierre Nora develops the same idea in his discussion of the effects of the 'structuralist charm' ('Préface', in *Tristes Tropiques*).
110 Furet, 'French intellectuals', p. 31.
111 Furet, 'French intellectuals', p. 31.
112 Michel Foucault, quoted in Dosse, *History of Structuralism*, vol. 1, p. 354.
113 Furet, 'French intellectuals', p. 35.
114 Furet, 'French intellectuals', p. 35.
115 Furet, 'French intellectuals', p. 37.
116 Furet, 'French intellectuals', p. 39.
117 See Bruno Karsenti's wonderful article recalling this incandescent and somewhat forgotten figure, 'L'expérience structurale', *Gradhiva*, 2, 2005, pp. 89–107. A revised version was published as 'Expérience structurale et dépassement du marxisme', in *D'une philosophie à l'autre: Les sciences sociales et la politique des modernes*, Paris, Gallimard, 2013.
118 This was the goal of his book, *Marxisme et structuralisme*, Paris, Payot, 1965.
119 In his personal copy of the *Critique of Dialectical Reason*, p. 8, Lévi-Strauss wrote: 'What appears to me as a verification he holds to be a demonstration. The discovery of the dialectic, i.e. that analytical reason must also give an account of dialectical reason – an extension of its programme, a transformation of its axiom. But not dialectical reason of itself and of analytical reason. The real subject of the book is: under what conditions does the myth of the French Revolution become possible?'
120 *SM*, p. xii: 'Over and above our inevitable divergences I hope that Sartre will recognize above all that a discussion to which so much care has been given constitutes on behalf of all of us an homage of admiration and respect.'
121 Letter from Claude Lévi-Strauss to Roman Jakobson, 27 June 1962, CLS Archives, NAF 28150, box 281, 'Correspondance reçue'.
122 Keck, in Lévi-Strauss, *Oeuvres*, p. 1791.
123 *SM*, p. 249.
124 *SM*, p. 254.
125 Frédéric Worms, *La Philosophie en France au XXe siècle: Moments*, Paris, Gallimard, 2009, p. 472.
126 *SM*, p. 247.
127 Keck, in Lévi-Strauss, *Oeuvres*, p. 1843.
128 *SM*, p. 252.
129 With the exception of a few remarks in a 1966 issue of *L'Arc* (no. 30) devoted to Sartre. See Dosse, *History of Structuralism*, vol. 1, p. 327: Sartre analysed the rise of the human sciences and the success of structuralism as the ideological adaptation of a technocratic society imported from the United States, which found its political illustration in Gaullism.
130 P. Verstraeten, 'Claude Lévi-Strauss ou la tentation du néant', *Les Temps modernes*, 206, July 1963.
131 P. Secrétan, 'De *La Nausée* de Sartre à *La Pensée sauvage* de Claude Lévi-Strauss', *La Tribune de Genève*, 14 January 1964.
132 '*La Pensée sauvage* et le structuralisme', *Esprit*, 322, November 1963.
133 '*La Pensée sauvage* et le structuralisme'.
134 '*La Pensée sauvage* et le structuralisme'.
135 '*La Pensée sauvage* et le structuralisme'.
136 Paul Ricœur, 'Structure and hermeneutics', in *The Conflict of Interpretations*, Evanston, Northwestern University Press, 1974, p. 30.
137 A roundtable discussion about Claude Lévi-Strauss, 'Réponse à quelques questions', *Esprit*, 322, November 1963, p. 634.

138 'Réponse à quelques questions', p. 653.
139 'Réponse à quelques questions', p. 630.
140 Walter Benjamin, *One Way Street*, Cambridge, Belknap, 2016.
141 *RC*, 1969, p. 9.
142 'Lévi-Strauss dans le XVIIIe siècle', *Cahiers pour l'analyse*, 4, September–October 1966, published by the Cercle d'épistémologie of the École normale supérieure. In addition to Jacques-Alain Miller, the editorial board consisted of Jean-Claude Milner, Jacques Bouveresse, Alain Grosrichard, François Regnault, Michel Tort and Alain Badiou. It was in this issue that Jacques Derrida's article 'Nature, culture, writing: the violence of the letter from Lévi-Strauss to Rousseau' was published, to be republished in *Of Grammatology*, to which we will turn later.
143 'Lévi-Strauss dans le XVIIIe siècle', pp. 89–90.
144 Lucien Scubla, 'Structure, transformation et morphogénèse ou le structuralisme illustré par Pascal et Poussin', in M. Izard (ed.), *Claude Lévi-Strauss*, Paris, L'Herne, 'Cahiers de l'Herne', 2004, p. 189.
145 Dina Dreyfus, 'De la pensée pré-logique à la pensée hyper-logique', *Mercure de France*, February 1963, pp. 309–322.
146 Dina Dreyfus, 'De la pensée pré-logique à la pensée hyper-logique', p. 316.
147 Dina Dreyfus, 'De la pensée pré-logique à la pensée hyper-logique'.
148 Dina Dreyfus, 'De la pensée pré-logique à la pensée hyper-logique', p. 318.
149 Letter from Claude Lévi-Strauss to Roman Jakobson, 10 July 1961, CLS Archives, NAF 28150, box 181.
150 Letter from Claude Lévi-Strauss to Fernand Braudel, 17 July 1961, CLS Archives, NAF 28150, box 181. The dealings with Sartre were probably handled by Jean Pouillon.
151 In fact, a philosophy of knowledge chair was created in 1962, and held until 1990 by Jules Vuillemin, while Martial Guéroult's chair, which was also left vacant in 1962, was changed into a chair in the history of philosophical thought for Jean Hyppolite, who held it from 1963 to 1968. This was the chair that Foucault took over in 1970, under the label 'history of systems of thought'.
152 Frédéric Keck narrates, based on archival material, the saga of the translation into English of *The Savage Mind*: see Keck, in Lévi-Strauss, *Oeuvres*, pp. 1798ff. I am only repeating a few episodes here.
153 Julian Pitt-Rivers, 'The savage mind', *Man*, 3(2), June 1968, p. 300.
154 Keck, in Lévi-Strauss, *Oeuvres*, p. 1799.
155 CLS Archives, NAF 28150, box 235, '*The American Scholar*'.
156 Marshall Sahlins, 'On the Delphic writings of Claude Lévi-Strauss', *The Scientific American*, June 1966, p. 131.
157 Susan Sontag, 'A hero of our time', *The New York Review of Books*, 28 November 1963.
158 Sontag, 'A hero of our time'.
159 Sontag, 'A hero of our time'.
160 G. Steiner (handwritten signature), 'Orpheus with his myths', *Times Literary Supplement*, 29 April 1965.
161 Michel Foucault, *The Order of Things*, New York, Random House, 1970, p. 208.
162 *SA*, vol. 1, epigraph, p. v: 'May an inconstant disciple dedicate this book which appears in 1958, the year of Émile Durkheim's centenary, to the memory of the founder of *Année Sociologique*: that famed workshop where modern

anthropology fashioned part of its tools and which we have abandoned, not so much out of disloyalty as out of the sad conviction that the task would prove too much for us.'

Chapter 16   The Manufacture of Science

1 In so doing, we are following the example of B. Latour and S. Woolgar in *Laboratory Life: The Construction of Scientific Facts*, where they called, almost forty years ago already, for the repatriation of analyses from an anthropological perspective, emphasizing the relevance of this kind of approach not only for outside our society, but for its very core, and especially its scientific core.

2 See Jean Boutier, Jean-Claude Passeron and Jacques Revel (eds.), *Qu'est-ce qu'une discipline?*, Paris, Éditions de l'EHESS, 2006.

3 Claude Lévi-Strauss, 'The place of anthropology in the social sciences and the problems raised in teaching it', in *SA*, p. 348.

4 'Introduction', in Passeron and Revel (eds.), *Qu'est-ce qu'une discipline?*, p. 8.

5 See G. Lenclud, 'L'anthropologie et sa discipline', in Passeron and Revel (eds.), *Qu'est-ce qu'une discipline?*

6 First published in a UNESCO volume entitled *The University Teaching of the Social Sciences*, Paris, UNESCO, 1954. Reprinted in *SA*, pp. 346–381. He wrote another similar article, also published by UNESCO: 'Panorama de l'ethnologie, 1950–1952', *Diogène*, 2, 1953, pp. 96–123.

7 *SA*, p. 347.

8 *SA*, p. 355.

9 *SA*, p. 328.

10 Claude Tardits, 'Un grand parcours', *L'Homme*, 143, July–September 1997, p. 50.

11 Jean Jamin, 'L'anthropologie et ses acteurs', in *Les Enjeux philosophiques des années 50*, Paris, Editions du Centre Pompidou, 1993, p. 104.

12 *SA*, p. 350.

13 *SA*, p. 351.

14 *SA*, p. 384.

15 Letter from Rivet to Claude Lévi-Strauss, 5 May 1957, CLS Archives, NAF 28150, box 200, 'Correspondance reçue'. Throughout his institutional career, Rivet had been assisted by his two sisters, known among anthropologists as the 'Rivet Misses'. It was as such that he referred to the one who was still alive. See Marianne Lemaire, 'La chambre à soi de l'ethnologue: Une écriture féminine en anthropologie dans l'entre-deux-guerres', *L'Homme*, 200, 2011, pp. 83–112.

16 The teaching faculty of the Institut d'ethnologie in 1960: Collège de France (Claude Lévi-Strauss, Georges Dumézil, Émile Benveniste, Jacques Berque, Pierre Gourou); Sorbonne faculty of letters (André Leroi-Gourhan, Roger Bastide); EPHE IVth Section, linguistics; Vth Section, religious studies (Claude Tardits, Africa) and VIth Section, economic and social sciences (Claudie Marcel-Dubois, ethnomusicology; Germaine Dieterlen, Georges Balandier, Éric de Dampierre, Denise Paulme, Africa; Georges Condominas, Vietnam; Louis Dumont, India; Jean Guiart, Oceania; Germaine Tillion, Maghreb; Maxime Rodinson, Middle-East; Henri Lehmann, pre-Columbian civilizations).

17 Letter from Claude Lévi-Strauss addressed to the Rector of the Paris Academy, 21 April 1961, LAS Archives, FLAS, B.S5, 'Correspondance avec l'Institut d'ethnologie'.

18 Letter from Claude Lévi-Strauss to Stéphane Hessel, 30 October 1961, LAS Archives, FLAS, B.S5, 'Correspondance avec l'Institut d'ethnologie'.

19 For this paragraph, I have relied on A. Drouard, 'Réflexions sur une chronologie: le développement des sciences sociales en France de 1945 à la fin des années soixante', *La Revue française de sociologie*, 23(1), 1982, pp. 55–85; see also Alain Chatriot and Vincent Duclerc (eds.), *Le Gouvernement de la recherche: Histoire d'un engagement politique de Pierre Mendès France au général de Gaulle (1953–1969)*, Paris, La Découverte, 2006.

20 André Burguière, 'Du siècle des Lumières à la Ve République: la longue histoire des enquêtes collectives', in B. Paillard, J.-F. Simon and L. Le Gall (eds.), *En France rurale: Les enquêtes interdisciplinaires depuis les années 1960*, Rennes, Presses universitaires de Bretagne, 2010, pp. 21–38.

21 Claude Lévi-Strauss, interview with Gilles Lapouge, *Le Figaro littéraire*, 2 June 1962.

22 A contract was concluded between the DGRST, the Collège de France and the LAS. A research project in social anthropology, with the unit record analysis of genealogical material (carried out by M. Izard), was commissioned for 62,248 new francs, quite a tidy sum in comparison with the laboratory's early budgets.

23 See Françoise Zonabend, 'Minot: du terrain aux textes', in Paillard, Simon and Le Gall (eds.), *En France rurale*, pp. 301–313.

24 Lucien Bernot and René Blancart, *Nouville: Un village français*, Paris, Éditions des archives contemporaines, 1995.

25 Zonabend, 'Minot', p. 302.

26 Zonabend, 'Minot', p. 307.

27 Marie-Claude Pingaud, *Paysans de Bourgogne: Les gens de Minot*, Paris, Flammarion, 1978; Yvonne Verdier, *Façons de dire, façons de faire: La laveuse, la couturière, la cuisinière*, Paris, Gallimard, 1979; Françoise Zonabend, *La Mémoire longue: Temps et histoires au village*, Paris, PUF, 1980; T. Jolas, M.-C. Pingaud, Y. Verdier, F. Zonabend, *Une campagne voisine: Minot un village bourguignon*, Paris, Éditions de la MSH, 1990.

28 Françoise Zonabend gives an account of this difficult experience in *Une campagne voisine*, pp. 312–313.

29 Claude Lévi-Strauss, 'Scientific criteria in the social and human disciplines', *International Social Science Journal*, 16(4), 1964, p. 537.

30 Lévi-Strauss, 'Scientific criteria in the social and human disciplines', p. 539.

31 Lévi-Strauss, 'Scientific criteria in the social and human disciplines', pp. 549–550.

32 See the elegant little book conceived and edited by Françoise Zonabend for the fiftieth anniversary of the LAS in 2011, *Le Laboratoire d'anthropologie sociale: 50 ans d'histoire, 1960–2010*, Paris, Collège de France, December 2010.

33 On the initiative of George P. Murdoch, this powerful database had been maintained since 1937 by an independent organization in New Haven, Connecticut, associated with Yale University. See Isac Chiva, 'Une communauté de solitaires: le Laboratoire d'anthropologie sociale', in M. Izard (ed.), *Claude Lévi-Strauss*, Paris, L'Herne, 'Cahiers de l'Herne', 2004, p. 66.

34 The VIth Section of the EPHE and the Maison des Sciences de l'Homme also participated in the funding for the *Files*.

660 Notes to pp. 385–90

35 Claude Lévi-Strauss, 'Rapport du 29 mars 1962', LAS Archives, FLAS, BS2.01.
36 Lévi-Strauss, 'Rapport du 29 mars 1962'.
37 Letter from Pierre Bourdieu, 7 March 1966, BS1. 01, Correspondence with EPHE, 1961–71, LAS Archives.
38 Chiva, 'Une communauté de solitaires', p. 61.
39 Émile Guimet, the industrialist with a passion for oriental art and civilization, and founder of the Musée Guimet, never actually lived in the mansion, which was acquired by the ministry of education in 1955. See Zonabend (ed.), *Le Laboratoire d'anthropologie sociale*, p. 6, note 9.
40 Didier Eribon, *Conversations with Claude Lévi-Strauss*, Chicago, The University of Chicago Press, 1991, p. 63.
41 Lévi-Strauss, 'Rapport du 29 mars 1962'.
42 Letter from Isac Chiva to Clemens Heller, 27 February 1964, LAS Archives, FLAS, BS1.01.
43 The information contained in this paragraph comes from Chiva's own testimony, recorded in interviews with Christian Braunberger, 'L'ethnologie en héritage', a DVD contained in the LAS records. See also the issue of *Les Temps modernes* devoted to Romania and anti-Semitism, 2003.
44 Chiva, 'Une communauté de solitaires'.
45 Nicole Lapierre, 'Lévi-Strauss: le regard rapproché d'Isac Chiva', Médiapart website, 5 November 2009, and 'Déplacements', in *Pensons ailleurs*, Paris, Stock, 2004, pp. 67–69.
46 Letter from Claude Lévi-Strauss to Isac Chiva (undated) [25 Sunday 1976]. The letters from Lévi-Strauss to Chiva were given to me by Monique Lévi-Strauss who had copies of the correspondence. I am grateful to her for this as well.
47 Letter from Claude Lévi-Strauss to Isac Chiva, 2 January 2003.
48 Claude Lévi-Strauss, 'L'homme de L'Homme', *L'Homme*, 143, July–September 1997, pp. 13–15. His first book was entitled *Temps et Roman*, Paris, Gallimard, 1946, dealing with writers such as Balzac, Stendhal, Dostoyevsky, Proust, Joyce, Kafka, Dos Passos, Faulkner and Hemingway.
49 Gilbert Rouget, 'Porteur de valise et voyageur sans bagage', *L'Homme*, 143, July–September 1997, p. 37. Like Rouget, Pouillon was friends with Robillot. As for Perec, according to Rouget the African episode in *The Void* was entirely based on Pouillon.
50 The philosopher Francis Jeanson was the leader of this group of left-wing militants who aided the Algerian National Liberation Front in its armed struggle against French colonial rule. The network was dismantled in February and the trial began on 5 September 1960.
51 Jean Jamin, interview with the author, 6 July 2011. The last attempt at getting the two 'sides' to engage in dialogue was in an issue of *L'Arc*, 26: 'Sartre et Lévi-Strauss: Analyse/Dialectique d'une relation dialectique/analytique', pp. 55–60.
52 Luc de Heusch, 'Pour Jean Pouillon', *L'Homme*, 143, July–September 1997, p. 57.
53 Lévi-Strauss, 'L'homme de L'Homme', pp. 13–15.
54 Michel Izard, 'Comme en passant', *L'Homme*, 143, July–September 1997, p. 35.
55 Françoise Héritier, 'Éclat et facettes', *L'Homme*, 143, July–September 1997, p. 20.
56 Tardits, 'Un grand parcours', p. 47.

57 Jean Pouillon, 'Le plaisir de ne pas comprendre', *Le Cru et le Su*, Paris, Seuil, 1993; quoted in Izard, 'Comme en passant', p. 36.

58 Chiva confessed to having written a false certificate to the veterinary services of the ministry of agriculture to help Lévi-Strauss realize one of his fantasies: to own a pair of African parrots. Their importation into France was illegal, due to psittacosis . . . See Lapierre, 'Lévi-Strauss: le regard rapproché d'Isac Chiva'.

59 Report of 29 March 1962, LAS Archives, FLAS, BS2.01, 'Correspondance concernant le Collège de France'.

60 Report of the Faculty Assembly, 28 March 1963, LAS Archives, FLAS, BS2.01.

61 Étienne Wolff Report, 13 June 1966, LAS Archives, FLAS, BS2.01.

62 Étienne Wolff Report, 13 June 1966.

63 Eribon, *Conversations*, p. 76.

64 Eribon, *Conversations*, p. 111.

65 LAS Archives, FLAS, BS4.02, 1966–70, 'Correspondance avec le CNRS'.

66 Chiva, 'Une communauté de solitaires', pp. 63–64.

67 See Ludovic Tournès, *Sciences de l'homme et politique: Les fondations philanthropiques américaines en France au XXe siècle*, Paris, Classiques Garnier, 2011.

68 Interview with Monique Lévi-Strauss, 5 October 2012.

69 See the correspondence with the Wenner-Gren Foundation, in the LAS Archives, FLAS, F.S.4.07.

70 Chiva, 'Une communauté de solitaires', p. 63.

71 Françoise Zonabend, interview with the author, 14 March 2012.

72 Letter from Claude Lévi-Strauss to Pierre Clastres, 1 December 1965, LAS Archives, FLAS, D.01, 'Dossier chercheurs'. All correspondence with Pierre Clastres quoted here comes from the same file.

73 Letter from Claude Lévi-Strauss to P. Clastres, 18 April 1966.

74 *SA*, p. 373.

75 *SA*, p. 373.

76 *SA*, p. 374.

77 Letter to Clemens Heller, 8 February 1963, LAS Archives, FLAS, BS1.01, 'Correspondance avec l'EPHE'.

78 LAS activity report (1965–66) written by Claude Lévi-Strauss, FLAS, B52.01.03, 1966.

79 Letter from Claude Lévi-Strauss to Isac Chiva (undated) [18 August].

80 Letter from Pierre Clastres to Claude Lévi-Strauss, 6 October 1963.

81 Letter from Claude Lévi-Strauss to Pierre Clastres, 13 December 1965.

82 Letter from Claude Lévi-Strauss to Isac Chiva (undated) [summer 1968].

83 Jean Monod, interview with the author, 26 February 2013.

84 Jean Monod, interview with the author, 26 February 2013.

85 Jean Monod, interview with the author, 26 February 2013. A controversy broke out in the US in which Napoleon Chagnon was accused of wrongdoing in Yanomami country from 1964 to 1993. The accusation, levelled by Patrick Tierney in *Darkness in Eldorado* (2000), has been largely refuted by the American anthropological community, which has nonetheless recognized certain excesses. On this affair, see Robert Borofsky, *Yanomami: The Fierce Controversy and What We Can Learn About It*, Oakland, CA, University of California Press, 2005.

86 Marion Abelès, interview with the author, 15 January 2013.

87 Nicole Belmont, interview with the author, 5 February 2013.

88 Carmen Bernand, interview with the author, 11 January 2013.
89 Arlette Frigout, 'Mission chez les Indiens Hopi d'Arizona', *L'Homme*, 5(1), 1965, pp. 113–118.
90 Monique Lévi-Strauss, interview with the author, 9 March 2013.
91 Lévi-Strauss wrote to her on 18 June 1962, after she had left for Arizona: 'Bear in mind that the first weeks of fieldwork are horrible, but things always work themselves out in the end.'
92 Nicole Belmont, interview with the author, 5 February 2013. For her doctoral work, Nicole Belmont collected material on a large set of beliefs, rituals and narratives on the theme of birth, especially uncommon births in which a child is born with a piece of the 'caul', or amniotic membrane, covering their head or body. She thus gave birth to an anthropology of childbirth.
93 Isac Chiva bragged about it: 'The LAS boasts the most beautiful female stock of all French human sciences laboratories'; Nicole Belmont, interview with the author, 5 February 2013.
94 Marion Abelès, interview with the author, 15 January 2013.
95 Nicole Belmont, interview with the author, 5 February 2013.
96 Letter from Claude Lévi-Strauss to Isac Chiva (undated) [23 June].
97 Françoise Héritier, interview with the author, April 2011.
98 Marion Abelès, interview with the author, 15 January 2013.
99 Bronislaw Malinowski, *A Diary in the Strict Sense of the Term*, New York, Harcourt, Brace & World, 1967.
100 See the book on her written by her daughter Paule du Bouchet, *Emportée*.
101 Françoise Zonabend, interview with the author, 14 March 2012.
102 See Marc Joly, *Devenir Norbert Elias: Histoire croisée d'un processus de reconnaissance scientifique, la réception française*, Paris, Fayard, 2012, p. 226.
103 Nicole Belmont, interview with the author, 5 February 2013.
104 Philippe Descola, in Zonabend (ed.), *Le Laboratoire d'anthropologie sociale*, p. 13.
105 Letter from Claude Lévi-Strauss to the anthropology department, Museu Paraense Emilio Goeldi, Belém, 7 January 1965, LAS Archives, FLAS, F.S5.01.01.003.
106 Anne-Christine Taylor, 'Don Quichotte en Amérique: Claude Lévi-Strauss et l'anthropologie américaniste', in M. Izard (ed.), *Claude Lévi-Strauss*, Paris, L'Herne, 'Cahiers de l'Herne', 2004, p. 83.
107 Letter from Claude Lévi-Strauss to the director general of the CNRS, 7 April 1961.
108 Letter from Claude Lévi-Strauss to Francis Perrin, 26 January 1967, LAS Archives, FLAS, BS2.01.05., 1968–69, 'Correspondance avec le Collège de France'.
109 Zonabend (ed.), *Le Laboratoire d'anthropologie sociale*, p. 37.
110 In *The Savage Mind*, p. 89, Lévi-Strauss gave free expression to one of his technophilic reveries: 'The greater our knowledge, the more obscure the overall scheme. The dimensions multiply, and the growth of axes of reference beyond a certain point paralyses intuitive methods: it becomes impossible to visualize a system when its representation requires a continuum of more than three or four dimensions. But the day may come when all the available documentation on Australian tribes is transferred to punch cards and with the help of a computer their entire techno-economic, social and religious structures can be shown to be like a vast group of transformations.'
111 Interview with Matthieu Lévi-Strauss, 24 September 2014.
112 Email from Françoise Héritier to the author, 23 November 2013.

113 Michel Perrin, 'En souvenir de Claude Lévi-Strauss', *La Revue lacanienne*, November 2010, pp. 113–120: 'He practised at all times what he called "the right distance", and tacitly imposed it on everyone around him.'

114 Françoise Héritier, interview with the author.

115 Interview with Françoise Héritier, *Raisons politiques*, 20, November 2005, p. 121.

116 Interview with Françoise Héritier, *Raisons politiques*, 20, November 2005, p. 121.

117 Letter from Claude Lévi-Strauss to Eliseo Veron, 14 December 1967, LAS Archives, FLAS, BSO2.O12.

118 Jean Monod, *Les Barjots: Essai d'ethnologie des bandes de jeunes*, Paris, Julliard, 1968.

119 Claude Lévi-Strauss, Jean Guiart's doctoral defence, held on 7 March 1964, 'Notes à l'occasion de lectures ou soutenances de thèses ou de mémoires', CLS Archives, NAF 28150, box 217. He continued: 'In one of the societies on which you are the undisputed expert – I mean that of the New Hebrides – the passage of each grandee from one rank to the next, within a rigid status hierarchy of about fifteen levels, is celebrated by his new colleagues through the erection, in front of his hut, of sculpted and painted fern trees, whose rich ornaments represent the various ranks in the hierarchy. When proceeding up the academic ladder, we reverse the order of obligation. It is the candidate's duty to leave at the door of his new peers, not a fern alas, but a tome whose prestige value is the greater as it approaches the shape of a cube, and as the typographic characters covering its pages are reduced in size. There can be no doubt that, according to these criteria, you have earned the rank of Khamat which, as you have taught us, reigns supreme in Malekula.'

120 Maurice Godelier, interview with the author, 21 November 2013.

121 Françoise Zonabend, interview with the author, 14 March 2012.

122 Françoise Zonabend, interview with the author, 14 March 2012.

123 Françoise Zonabend, interview with the author, 14 March 2012.

124 Pierre Bourdieu, *Sketch for a Self-Analysis*, Chicago, The University of Chicago Press, 2008, p. 34.

125 Letter to Henri Agresti, 18 November 1968, LAS Archives, FLAS, CS1, 'Séminaire de Claude Lévi-Strauss à l'EPHE'. Those enrolled in the seminar in 1969/70 were: Nicole Belmont, Carmen Bernand, Xochitl Camblor-Landa, Manuela Carneiro da Cunha, France-Marie Casevitz-Renard, Urszula Chodowiec, Hélène Clastres, Pierre Clastres, Catherine Clément, Robert Creswell, Geneviève Debrégeas-Laurenie, Hans Dietschy, Jacqueline Duvernay, Arlette Frigout, Jürg Gasche, Ellen Goyder, Roberte Hamayon, Marie-Élisabeth Handman, Tina Jolas, Michel Jouin, Ward Keeler, Georges Kutukdjan, François Lartigue, Jean-Paul Latouche, Elli Maranda, Pierre Maranda, José Merquior, Roberto Miguelez, Aurore Monod, Alejandro Ortiz-Rescanière, Marie-Claude Pingaud, Jean Pouillon, Ines Reichel-Dolmatoff, Florence Rohen y Galvez, Marshall Sahlins, Bernard Saladin d'Anglure, Maria Dolores Sanchez, Yvan Simonis, Pierre Smith, Valerio Valeri, Yvonne Verdier, Jacqueline Weller, and Françoise Zonabend. LAS Archives, FLAS, BS1.01.03, 'Correspondance avec l'EPHE'.

126 For example, the 1966 list of speakers and their subjects reads as follows: Robert Jaulin (Bari Indians of Colombia), Anne Chapman (Lenca and Jicaque Indians of Central America), Nicole Belmont (pregnancy and birthing rituals), Jacqueline Bollens (Tacana Indians), Michel Izard (Mossi people of Volta), Daniel de Coppet (Are of the Solomon Islands), Jean Cuisenier and

André Miquel from the Centre de sociologie européenne (kinship systems in Arabia and Turkey), Arlette Frigout (Hopi Indians), Françoise Izard-Héritier (Samo people of Volta), Ariane Deluz (Dan of Côte d'Ivoire), Peter Warshall (the social life of baboons and macaques), Hugo Zemp (African music), Jean Monod (delinquent youth) and Carmen Munoz (Ayoreo of Bolivia).

127 Dan Sperber presented the thesis defended in a book he had already published in 1968: *Le Structuralisme en anthropologie*, Paris, Seuil, 1968. He became a critic of structuralism in the 1970s, with *Rethinking Structuralism* (1975) and *On Anthropological Knowledge* (1985).

128 The seminar's programme and the presentation of sessions come from the archive of the Laboratoire d'anthropologie sociale, Collège de France, FLAS, CS1, 1965–71, 'Le séminaire de Claude Lévi-Strauss'.

129 A few glimpses of Lévi-Strauss's seminar can be caught in the (fiction) film by Yannick Bellon, *Quelque part quelqu'un* (1972), as well as in the television show 'L'invité du dimanche' that aired on 20 June 1971.

130 Perrin, 'En souvenir de Claude Lévi-Strauss', p. 2.

131 Françoise Zonabend, interview with the author, 14 March 2012.

132 Françoise Zonabend, interview with the author, 14 March 2012.

133 Michel Perrin, interview with the author.

134 Élisabeth Roudinesco, *Jacques Lacan: An Outline of a Life and a History of a System of Thought*, New York, Columbia University Press, 1997, p. 260.

135 Roland Barthes, 'Au séminaire', in *Oeuvres complètes*, vol. IV, 1972–76, Paris, Seuil, pp. 502–511; text originally published in *L'Arc*, 1974.

136 Nicole Belmont, interview with the author.

137 André Burguière, *The Annales School: An Intellectual History*, Ithaca, NY, Cornell University Press, 2006, p. 186.

138 Burguière, *The Annales School*, p. 186.

139 For this entire paragraph, see Burguière, *The Annales School*, pp. 226ff, and François Dosse, *History of Structuralism I: The Rising Sign, 1945–1966*, Minneapolis, University of Minnesota Press, 1997, p. 184.

140 Burguière, *The Annales School*, p. 143.

141 André Burguière, Christiane Klapisch-Zuber, Martine Segalen, Françoise Zonabend (eds.), *A History of the Family*, 2 vols, Cambridge, MA, Belknap, 1996.

142 *SM*, p. 262.

143 Marc Joly, in *Devenir Norbert Elias*, p. 289, points out that Elias was perceived as a precursor of this development, and celebrated as such in the press. The societies of the past, such as the European curial society of the seventeenth and eighteenth centuries for example, appeared as exotic as the Nambikwara.

144 Letter from Evans-Pritchard to Claude Lévi-Strauss (undated) [1964], CLS Archives, NAF 28150, box 189, 'Correspondance reçue'.

145 Edmund Leach, 'Claude Lévi-Strauss anthropologist and philosopher', *New Left Review*, 34, 1965, p. 20. And yet he devoted an entire book to him in 1970, entitled *Lévi-Strauss* (Viking Press). Translated into six languages, this book proved a powerful vehicle for the circulation of Lévi-Straussian structural anthropology in the international academic sphere.

146 Letter from Edmund Leach to Claude Lévi-Strauss, 20 March 1961, CLS Archives, NAF 28150, box 194, 'Correspondance reçue'.

147 The lucky laureate of the Viking Fund Medal receives, in addition to universal professional recognition, a few thousand dollars. The money was spent rebuilding a 500-metre-long stone wall on the property that Monique and Claude Lévi-Strauss had just acquired in Lignerolles. See next chapter.

148 Marshall Sahlins, 'On the Delphic writings of Claude Lévi-Strauss', *The Scientific American*, June 1966, p. 131.
149 See Maurice Bloch, 'Réflexions sur la réception de deux ouvrages de Claude Lévi-Strauss', Paris, Collège de France, 2008, pp. 16–20 ; regarding the context for his American reception, see also M.E. Harkin, 'Lévi-Strauss en Amérique: "L'indigénisation" du structuralisme', in M. Izard (ed.), *Claude Lévi-Strauss*, Paris, L'Herne, 'Cahiers de l'Herne', 2004, vol. 82, pp. 396–405.
150 Yet he later wrote to Didier Eribon, upon reading the latter's interviews with Claude Lévi-Strauss, *Conversations with Claude Lévi-Strauss*: 'Your book brings the reader into contact with his personal and intellectual temperament and reminded me of the charm and provocation that we used to find so exhilarating, good old Sir Edmund Leach and myself, so many years ago', 12 January 1989, CLS Archives, NAF 28150, box 197, 'Correspondance reçue'.
151 See Maurice Godelier, *Lévi-Strauss*, Paris, Seuil, 2013, ch. 4.
152 Claude Lévi-Strauss, 'Preface to the Second edition', *ESK*, p. xxxiii.
153 He sometimes demonstrated greater pessimism regarding the exchange of ideas in the academic sphere: 'The exchange of ideas, even of a polemical kind, would no doubt be more fertile if those who initiated them bothered to find out what the author they would like to rebut had in fact written on the subject', letter to Dr McKinley (undated) [1981], LAS Archives, FLAS, FS4.06.02.035.
154 Yet it must be said that the French university continued to actively resist the rise of both anthropology and structuralism. Lévi-Strauss's growing renown was a considerable annoyance to the Sorbonne mandarins. This was precisely why, in the autumn of 1963, Claude Lévi-Strauss was turned away from their bastion, the Académie des sciences morales et politiques, to which some had urged him to apply. He would hold on to the memory of this final slight. In 1987, he explained to Maurice Le Lannou, vice-president of the Académie, why he refused to take part in one of their sessions: 'Without boring you with a detailed narrative of bygone events (which would nonetheless be useful for understanding my state of mind) I consider that a quarter century ago, the Académie des sciences morales et politiques treated me rather shabbily. Later, when I was elected to the Académie française, it invited me to give a speech. I graciously agreed, if only to show there were no hard feelings. But once this unilateral gesture was made, I cannot be expected to periodically repeat it . . .': letter of 22 March 1987, CLS Archives, NAF 28150, box 195, 'Correspondance reçue'.
155 Françoise Zonabend, interview with the author, 26 December 2013. While no one specialized in the anthropology of Jewish culture, many LAS researchers were indeed of Jewish heritage. But, as we have seen regarding Lévi-Strauss himself, this should be seen in the context of the strong presence of Jews in the social sciences more generally. It was thus not specific to the LAS.
156 See the group photographs, and especially the photomontage made by Frédéric Jude in 1988, which added a surrealist touch to the group photo tradition.
157 'Aujourd'hui, Claude Lévi-Strauss', with the participation of LAS members, 1:32, INA Archives. It features Lévi-Strauss, together with Maurice Godelier, Michel Izard, Jean Pouillon, Claude Tardits, and Françoise Zonabend, as well as additional footage featuring Pierre Clastres and Françoise Héritier at the seminar, and Jacques Lizot on fieldwork.

Chapter 17   The Scholarly Life

1 *Critique*, 781–782, June 2012, p. 576.
2 *Critique*, 781–782, June 2012, p. 581: 'In the long afterlife of posterity, a work is a finished product offered up to others. But for its author, it was first and foremost a reality in the making through daily labour. This reality I propose to call the work-labour.'
3 *RC*, p. 4.
4 See the project coordinated by Christian Jacob, *Les Lieux de savoir*, Paris, Albin Michel, 2007, republished in 2011, especially vol. I, *Espaces et communautés*, Sophie Houdart, 'Un monde à soi ou les espaces privés de la pensée', pp. 363–370.
5 Claude Lévi-Strauss, 'Il y a en moi un peintre et un bricoleur qui se relaient', *Le Monde*, 21 June 1974.
6 The 'Maison ronde', as it was nicknamed for its circular shape, whose first stone was laid in 1958, was inaugurated in 1963.
7 Monique Lévi-Strauss, interview with the author, 7 February 2012.
8 Matthieu Lévi-Strauss, interview with the author, 24 September 2012.
9 Victor Hugo: 'It was a quirk of hers from earliest childhood– / Each morning, in my room she would appear; / I waited for her like the hope of sunlight; / She came, she said: 'Good morning, Father dear', / Took up my pen, opened my books, sat down on / My bed, disturbed my paperwork, and played; / Then suddenly went out like a bird vanishing.' *Selected Poems of Victor Hugo*, trans. E.H. and A.M. Blackmore, Chicago, The University of Chicago Press, 2001, p. 197.
10 Christopher S. Celenza, 'Le studiolo à la Renaissance', in Jacob (ed.), *Les Lieux de savoir*, vol. I, p. 371.
11 Lévi-Strauss tried to quit smoking to no avail; he could not write without his daily dose of nicotine. He would regularly resupply at the Civette tobacconist, in the Palais Royal. Interview with Monique Lévi-Strauss, 31 March 2012.
12 Letter from Claude Lévi-Strauss to Dolorès Vanetti, 23 December 1964, 'Correspondance avec D. Vanetti', CLS Archives, NAF 28150, box 182.
13 Didier Eribon, *Conversations with Claude Lévi-Strauss*, Chicago, The University of Chicago Press, 1991, p. 179.
14 These index files take up almost thirty boxes in the CLS Archives, NAF 28150, from box 135 to box 164: linguistic files, preparatory work for his various books and lectures at Collège de France, one file on Japan.
15 Claude Lévi-Strauss, 'Il y a en moi . . .'.
16 See William Marx, *Vie du lettré*, Paris, Les Éditions de Minuit, 2009.
17 Eribon, *Conversations*, p. 112: 'In my office I have as a souvenir an old globe of the heavens [. . .] Astronomers no longer use the instrument, but it has been of great help to me in locating the constellations mentioned in the myths. The scientific knowledge of one or two centuries ago was sufficient for my purposes!'
18 Julien Gracq, 'Julien Gracq, un homme à distance', *Le Monde*, 5 February 2002. I am grateful to Jean-Louis Tissier for graciously sharing this quote with me.
19 Letter from Claude Lévi-Strauss to Roman Jakobson, 7 March 1960, CLS Archives, NAF 28150, box 181, 'Correspondance reçue'.
20 See the summary chart drawn by Maurice Godelier in *Lévi-Strauss*, Paris, Seuil, 2013, p. 340. In 1964/65, his lectures were dedicated to a 'draft of an American bestiary', which was not directly related to the writing of *Mythologiques*.
21 He indeed had some difficulty providing required course outlines, explaining that the course – that of 1962/63 – 'marked the beginning of a long-term

undertaking, which will continue over the next year', report of 24 May 1962, LAS Archives, FLAS, BS2.01, 'Correspondance concernant le Collège de France'.

22 Patrick Wilcken, *Claude Lévi-Strauss: The Poet in the Laboratory*, London, Bloomsbury, 2010, p. 184.

23 C. Bernand, interview with the author, 7 February 2013; P. Descola used the same expression, quoted in Wilcken, *Claude Lévi-Strauss*, p. 184.

24 In a documentary devoted to him, Lévi-Strauss confesses his embarrassment to Jean-Claude Bringuier who had come to interview him, in exemplary terms: 'I find it difficult to address an interlocutor, for an interlocutor is someone', 'Une approche de Claude Lévi-Strauss', 1974, DVD 2, 'Le siècle de Claude Lévi-Strauss', by J.-C. Bringuier and M. Fortaleza Flores, Éditions Montparnasse.

25 Letter from Claude Lévi-Strauss to Isac Chiva [Lignerolles, 28 September].

26 Monique Lévi-Strauss, interview with the author, 28 October 2011.

27 Letter from Claude Lévi-Strauss to Dolorès Vanetti, 1 September 1955: 'No crayfish, no mushrooms, heaps of fruit and until the past few days, still more people fishing, families and picnickers milling about in our river as if in a sewer [. . .] It is time to leave the Cévennes and after visiting thirty-five properties in Burgundy, we shall look at yet another that I have just heard about which is on the way home.'

28 Letter from Robert Delavignette to Claude Lévi-Strauss, 18 November 1964, CLS Archives, NAF 28150, box 187, 'Correspondance reçue'.

29 Jérôme Garcin, 'Claude Lévi-Strauss à Lignerolles', in *Littérature vagabonde: Portraits 1985–1995*, Paris, Flammarion, 1995, p. 37.

30 Garcin, 'Claude Lévi-Strauss à Lignerolles'.

31 See chapter 5 above.

32 This was how Dina Dreyfus was referred to in the family, to distinguish her from another Dinah (Cahen), a friend of Lévi-Strauss's parents.

33 F.-N. Lorey and L. Duret, *Flore de la Côte-d'Or*, 2 vols., 1831; Gustave Lapérouse, *Histoire de Châtillon*, 1837; *Les Maisons fortes en Bourgogne du Nord*, two typed manuscripts by Pierre Maubeuge on the geology of the eastern side of the Paris Basin, etc.

34 Letter from Claude Lévi-Strauss to Isac Chiva, 29 July 1979.

35 Letter from Claude Lévi-Strauss to Isac Chiva, 29 July 1979.

36 Letter from Claude Lévi-Strauss to Fernand Braudel, 21 March 1967, CLS Archives, NAF 28150, box 181.

37 Claude Lévi-Strauss to Isac Chiva, on 7 August: 'I read through and revised the English translation of *The Origin of Table Manners*'.

38 Lévi-Strauss to Isac Chiva, on 7 August.

39 Letter from Claude Lévi-Strauss to Isac Chiva, 22 August 1966.

40 Letter from Claude Lévi-Strauss to Isac Chiva, 23 March 1958.

41 Monique Lévi-Strauss, interview with the author, 28 October 2011.

42 See Carlo Ginzburg, 'Clues: roots of an evidential paradigm', in *Clues, Myths and the Historical Method*, Baltimore, MD, Johns Hopkins University Press, 1989.

43 *TT*, p. 340.

44 *TT*, pp. 340–341.

45 Claude Lévi-Strauss, 'Paul Nizan, Aden Arabie', *L'Étudiant socialiste*, 8, May 1931. See chapter 3 above.

46 The information provided here comes from various interviews with Monique Lévi-Strauss and Matthieu Lévi-Strauss, conducted on 24 September 2013.

47 Monique Lévi-Strauss, interview with the author, 7 February 2012.

48 Monique Lévi-Strauss, interview with the author, 7 February 2012.
49 Monique Lévi-Strauss, interview with the author, 7 February 2012.
50 Monique Lévi-Strauss, interview with the author, 7 February 2012.
51 Letter from Roman Jakobson to Claude Lévi-Strauss, 4 December 1974: reaction to synesthetic data collected much earlier.
52 Collinot, 'Entre vie et œuvre scientifique: le chaînon manquant', p. 583.
53 Letter from Claude Lévi-Strauss to Professor Harry Levin, 19 June 1972, LAS Archives, FLAS, FS404.
54 Letter from Claude Lévi-Strauss to Professor Harry Levin, 19 June 1972.
55 Letter of 8 February 1966, LAS Archives, FLAS, D.09.02, 'Relations avec les étudiants'.
56 Letter of 2 February 1967, LAS Archives, FLAS, D.09.02, 'Relations avec les étudiants'.
57 Letter from Claude Lévi-Strauss to Yvan Mouchel, 5 March 1968, LAS Archives, FLAS, D.09.02, 'Relations avec les étudiants'.
58 Monique Lévi-Strauss, interview with the author, 31 March 2012.
59 Matthieu Lévi-Strauss, interview with the author, 24 September 2013.
60 Monique Lévi-Strauss, interview with the author, 31 March 2012.
61 *SA*, p. 68. The italics are mine.
62 Letter from Louis Dumont to Claude Lévi-Strauss, 15 December 1962, CLS Archives, NAF 28150, box 188, 'Correspondance reçue'.
63 Letter from Louis Dumont to Claude Lévi-Strauss, 20 December 1962, CLS Archives, NAF 28150, box 188, 'Correspondance reçue'.
64 Letter from Georges Balandier to Claude Lévi-Strauss, 5 January 1966, CLS Archives, NAF 28150, box 184, 'Correspondance reçue'. The book to which Balandier refers is *Daily Life in the Kingdom of the Kongo from the Sixteenth to the Eighteenth Century*, London, Allen & Unwin, 1968, originally published by Hachette in 1965.
65 Letter from Georges Devereux to Claude Lévi-Strauss, 3 March 1980, CLS Archives, NAF 28150, box 186, 'Correspondance reçue'.
66 Eribon, *Conversations*, p. 95.
67 Letter from Marcel Mauss to Henri Hubert (undated), quoted in Jean-François Bert, *Dans l'atelier de Marcel Mauss*, Paris, Éditions du CNRS, 2012, pp. 147–148.
68 Eribon, *Conversations*, p. 90.
69 Claude Lévi-Strauss, 'Autoportrait', remarks collected by Catherine Clément and Dominique-Antoine Grisoni, *Magazine littéraire*, 223, October 1985, p. 24.
70 Eribon, *Conversations*, p. 133.
71 *RC*, p. 7.
72 Letter to Lita Binne Fejos, 12 March 1968, LAS Archives, FLAS, FS4.07.01, 'Correspondance avec la Wenner-Gren Foundation'.
73 Eribon, *Conversations*, p. 93.
74 Letter from Claude Lévi-Strauss to Raymond Aron, 7 June 1971, Raymond Aron Archives, NAF 28060, box 207, Manuscripts Department, BNF.
75 Eribon, *Conversations*, p. 90.
76 *RC*, p. 12.
77 Eribon, *Conversations*, p. 90.
78 Eribon, *Conversations*, p. 95.
79 Letter from Claude Lévi-Strauss to Miss Coleman, 17 February 1965, LAS Archives, FLAS, FS404.
80 Eribon, *Conversations*, p. 95.

81 Eribon, *Conversations*, p. 133.
82 See two classic texts of the 1960s: Roland Barthes's 1968 article, 'The Death of the Author'; and Michel Foucault's talk, 'What is an Author?', given in February 1969 at the Collège de France.
83 The difficulty of translating the title to the four-volume series led to the initial English version, against Lévi-Strauss's wishes, of: 'Introduction to a Science of Mythology'. Lévi-Strauss considered this 'science' to be too much in its infancy to claim the name. Subsequent English editions used the original French *Mythologiques*.
84 *NM*, p. 640: 'The great anonymous voice whose utterance comes from the beginning of time and the depths of the mind.' The final sentence of *The Jealous Potter* (p. 206) reads: 'With an authority that cannot be denied, [mythic thought] arises from the depths of time, setting before us a magnifying mirror that reflects, in the massive form of concrete images, certain mechanisms by which the exercise of thought is ruled'.
85 Eribon, *Conversations*, p. 139.
86 Eribon, *Conversations*, p. 139.
87 *SM*, p. 263.
88 Eribon, *Conversations*, p. 140.
89 Eribon, *Conversations*, p. 141.
90 *RC*, p. 18.
91 *NM*, p. 639.
92 Eribon, *Conversations*, p. 127.
93 Eribon, *Conversations*, p. 128.
94 Eribon, *Conversations*, p. 128.
95 Godelier, *Lévi-Strauss*, pp. 348–349.
96 Today, that passage is considered to have taken place between 30,000 and 2,500 BCE.
97 Eribon, *Conversations*, p. 135.
98 *RC*, p. 4: 'If my inquiry proceeds in the way I hope, it will develop not along a linear axis but in a spiral.'
99 *SoL*, 1996, p. 189.
100 *NM*, p. 562.
101 Letter from Claude Lévi-Strauss to Bernard Fontana, 11 December 1963, CLS Archives, NAF 28150, box 190.
102 Letter from Jacques Berlioz to Claude Lévi-Strauss, 13 February 1963, CLS Archives, NAF 28150, box 184, 'Correspondance reçue'.
103 Letters from Pierre Maranda to Claude Lévi-Strauss, CLS Archives, NAF 28150, box 196, 'Correspondance reçue'.
104 Letter from Jean-Claude Pecker to Claude Lévi-Strauss, 31 January 1966, CLS Archives, NAF 28150, box 198, 'Correspondance reçue'.
105 *RC*, p. 23.
106 *RC*, p. 286.
107 *RC*, p. 28.
108 *LLR*, p. 117.
109 See Jean Jamin, 'Leiris, Lévi-Strauss et l'opéra', *Critique*, 620–621, January–February 1999, pp. 26–41.
110 *RC*, p. 23.
111 *RC*, pp. 15–16.
112 *NM*, p. 652: 'It was necessary, then, for myth as such to die for its form to escape from it, like a soul leaving a body, and to seek a means of reincarnation in music.'

113 See the friendly yet critical book by Jean-Jacques Nattiez, *Lévi-Strauss musicien: Essai sur la tentation homologique*, Arles, Actes Sud, 2008.

114 Claude Lévi-Strauss, 'Listening to Rameau', in *LLR*, pp. 39–62.

115 *RC*, p. 18.

116 Jean-Pierre Vernant, quoted in Godelier, *Lévi-Strauss*, p. 510.

117 Gildas Salmon, *Les Structures de l'esprit: Lévi-Strauss et les mythes*, Paris, PUF, 2013.

118 Salmon, *Les Structures de l'esprit*, p. 29.

119 Gildas Salmon undertook just such a 'critique of philological critique' in the second chapter of his *Structures de l'esprit*.

120 Salmon, *Les Structures de l'esprit*, p. 4.

121 Eribon, *Conversations*, p. 131.

122 *SoL*, p. 188.

123 Eribon, *Conversations*, p. 129.

124 Letter from Émile Benveniste to Claude Lévi-Strauss, 26 November 1964, CLS Archives, NAF 28150, box 184, 'Correspondance reçue'.

125 Jean Lacroix, '*Le Cru et le Cuit*', *Le Monde*, 2 January 1965.

126 Lacroix, '*Le Cru et le Cuit*'.

127 Lacroix, '*Le Cru et le Cuit*'.

128 Lacroix, '*Le Cru et le Cuit*'.

129 Lacroix, '*Le Cru et le Cuit*'.

130 Claude Mauriac, 'Lévi-Strauss et la science des mythes', *Le Figaro*, 14 October 1964. Excerpt from *RC*, p. 13.

131 *Combat*, 18 November 1964.

132 Thérèse de Saint-Phalle, 'Claude Lévi-Strauss écoute la mystérieuse musique des mythes', *Le Figaro littéraire*, 17–23 September 1964.

133 de Saint-Phalle, 'Claude Lévi-Strauss écoute la mystérieuse musique des mythes'.

134 de Saint-Phalle, 'Claude Lévi-Strauss écoute la mystérieuse musique des mythes'.

135 Jean-François Revel, 'Le miel et le tabac', *L'Express*, 13–19 February 1967.

136 Jean Lacroix, 'Le miel et le tabac', *Le Monde*, 4 March 1967.

137 See Frédérique Matonti, *Intellectuels communistes: Une sociologie de l'obéissance politique. La Nouvelle critique (1967–1980)*, Paris, La Découverte, 2005.

138 In September 1965, Aragon published an article that ran over three pages with the spectacular headline: 'Qu'est-ce que l'art, Jean-Luc Godard?'

139 Interview of Raymond Bellour with Claude Lévi-Strauss, *Les Lettres françaises*, 12–18 January 1967.

140 Interview of Raymond Bellour with Claude Lévi-Strauss, *Les Lettres françaises*, 12–18 January 1967.

141 Interview of Raymond Bellour with Claude Lévi-Strauss, *Les Lettres françaises*, 12–18 January 1967.

142 Interview of Raymond Bellour with Claude Lévi-Strauss, *Les Lettres françaises*, 12–18 January 1967.

143 Interview by Guy Dumur, *Le Nouvel Observateur*, 25–31 January 1967.

144 Interview by Guy Dumur, *Le Nouvel Observateur*, 25–31 January 1967.

145 Interview by Guy Dumur, *Le Nouvel Observateur*, 25–31 January 1967.

146 The third volume was translated and published in 1978 as *The Origin of Table Manners*, New York, Harper and Row; and the fourth, *The Naked Man*, also translated by John and Doreen Weightman, was published by Jonathan Cape ten years after its French publication in 1981.

147 Jean Pouillon, 'Une leçon de maintien', *La Quinzaine littéraire*, 55, August 1968. Pouillon's article was coupled with a review by Catherine Backès-Clément of a book on structuralism by Yvan Simonis (*Lévi-Strauss ou la Passion de l'inceste*, Paris, Aubier, 1968). For the Tolstoy epigraph, see *OTM*, p. 197, and for Rousseau *OTM*, p. 325.
148 Michel Izard, 'À l'écoute des mythes', *Le Nouvel Observateur*, 366.
149 The sombre tone of the 'Finale' was inspired – as Claude Lévi-Strauss later confided to Didier Éribon, expressing surprise that nobody had picked up on it – by the conclusion of Gobineau's *An Essay on the Inequality of the Human Races*. See Eribon, *Conversations*, p. 160.
150 *NM*, p. 625.
151 *NM*, p. 630.
152 Wilcken, *Claude Lévi-Strauss*, p. 276.
153 Letter from Claude Lévi-Strauss to Octavio Paz, 21 May 1967, CLS Archives, NAF 28150, box 198.
154 For example, in a letter to R. Bastide, dated 4 April, CLS Archives, NAF 28150, box 181: 'If the project must make sense (which I sometimes doubt), it is more than likely that I will not be able to make sense of it myself.'
155 All these objections are taken up in the 'Finale', *NM*, pp. 630–638.
156 *NM*, p. 640.
157 *NM*, p. 640.
158 *NM*, p. 640.
159 *NM*, p. 640.
160 *Le Figaro*, 24 September 1971.
161 *NM*, p. 639.
162 See Godelier, *Lévi-Strauss*, p. 436ff.
163 *NM*, p. 675.
164 See Godelier, *Lévi-Strauss*, p. 453.
165 See F. Lapointe and Claire C. Lapointe, *Claude Lévi-Strauss and his Critics: An International Bibliography of Criticism (1950–1976)*, New York, Garland, 1977.
166 Eribon, *Conversations*, p. 69.
167 According to Antoine Lilti, in *Figures publiques: L'Invention de la célébrité, 1750–1850* (Paris, Fayard, 2013), the 'history of celebrity is rooted in the eighteenth century, with the development of a critical public space, of which celebrity was to become the inseparable dark side. Jean-Jacques Rousseau is quite representative: he heralded both the manifestations of contemporary celebrity and its nefarious effects, as well as the accompanying laments.'
168 See Nathalie Heinich, *De la visibilité: Excellence et singularité en régime médiatique*, Paris, Gallimard, 2012, pp. 164ff. See also R. Debray, *Le Pouvoir intellectuel en France*, Paris, Ramsay, 1979. I am grateful to Mathilde Majorel for her research work in the Larousse Archives.
169 21 January 1968, 'Un certain regard' broadcast, 'Un essai de Michel Tréguier', Claude Lévi-Strauss interviewed by Michel Tréguier, 65 minutes, aired at 10:30 p.m., INA Archives. Monique, his wife, wrote to a friend at the end of the 1968 broadcast: 'This is a Godard moment!'
170 15 April 1959, 'Lecture pour tous', Pierre Dumayet in discussion with Claude Lévi-Strauss, together with Max-Pol Fouchet, INA Archives.
171 14 October 1964, 'Lectures pour tous', INA Archives.
172 Letter from Claude Lévi-Strauss to Roman Jakobson, 23 January 1968, CLS Archives, NAF 28150, box 181.
173 Letter to B. Hustedt, 26 September 1968, LAS Archives, FLAS, FS4.03.05.050.

174 Letter from Claude Lévi-Strauss to *Playboy*'s book review editor, 13 October 1969, LAS Archives, FLAS, FS4.03.05.050.
175 François Dosse, *History of Structuralism I: The Rising Sign, 1945–1966*, Minneapolis, University of Minnesota Press, 1997, p. 317.
176 Dosse, *History of Structuralism*, vol. I, p. 317.
177 Letter from Claude Lévi-Strauss to Thierry de Clermont-Tonnerre, 3 July 1964, CLS Archives, NAF 28150, box 222.
178 Claude Lévi-Strauss expressed himself thus on Radio-Canada. Quoted in Nattiez, *Lévi-Strauss musicien*, p. 28.
179 J.-M. Benoist, *The Structural Revolution*, London, Palgrave, 1978.
180 Raymond Boudon, *À quoi sert la notion de structure? Essai sur la signification de la notion de structure dans les sciences humaines*, Paris, Gallimard, 1968.
181 Letter to J. Mercier, 23 February 1968, LAS Archives, FLAS, FS1.03.02.
182 Eribon, *Conversations*, p. 72.
183 Letter from Georges Dumézil to Claude Lévi-Strauss, 19 November 1969: 'I do not need to tell you how far I am from Foucault, philosophically and politically. But if I am still alive, I will support him. The question for me when voting, regarding many candidates, has always been the same: to judge candidates not on the basis of their opinions, or even their methods, but to measure stature, to observe powers. This one is boiling over.' CLS Archives, NAF 28150, box 188, 'Correspondance reçue'.
184 Regarding Althusser, he admitted in a letter thanking Raymond Aron for sending him *D'une sainte famille à l'autre*: 'I must confess that prior to *D'une sainte famille à l'autre*, I had not read a single line by Althusser [. . .] Thanks to you, I now feel much better informed about that author, and justified in my instinctive sense that had caused me to turn away from him.' Raymond Aron Archives, NAF 28060, box 207, Département des Manuscrits, BNF.
185 Claude Lévi-Strauss, 'Structure and form: reflections on a work by Vladimir Propp', *SA*, vol. 2, p. 132.
186 Lévi-Strauss, 'Structure and form', p. 131.
187 On the relationship between Barthes and Lévi-Strauss, see Marie Gil, *Roland Barthes: Au lieu de la vie*, Paris, Flammarion, 2012, pp. 237ff; and Tiphaine Samoyault, *Roland Barthes*, Paris, Seuil, 2015, pp. 353–362.
188 Text published in *Paragone*, April 1965, pp. 125–128.
189 See Gil, *Roland Barthes*, pp. 285–293. Christophe Prochasson offers an analysis of this controversy in 'Roland Barthes contre Raymond Picard: un prélude à mai '68', in 'Comment on se dispute: figures de la controverse', *Mil neuf cents*, 25, January 2007. T. Samoyault, in Gil, *Roland Barthes*, pp. 358–359, quotes a severe letter, dated 18 March 1966, that Lévi-Strauss wrote to Barthes upon receiving *Criticism and Truth*, Barthes's response to Picard: 'To be honest, I am not at all sure that we are in agreement. First of all, in defending the *nouvelle critique*, in general, you seem to cover many things that in my view are not warranted. Then, you exhibit an eclecticism that manifests in an excessive complacency towards subjectivity, affectivity and, let's go ahead and use the word, in a certain mysticism vis-à-vis literature.'
190 See Dosse, *History of Structuralism*, vol. I, p. 211.
191 Eribon, *Conversations*, p. 73.
192 Gil, *Roland Barthes*, pp. 343–344. Text quoted in R. Bellour and C. Clément (eds.), *Textes de et sur Claude Lévi-Strauss*, Paris, Gallimard, 1979: 'Lignerolle, 31 March 1970. My Dear Friend, Your dazzling *S/Z*, which I am finishing reading in the country, has inspired me to write a brief folly which, to return the compliment, I am sharing with you here. In French, the word *sarrasin*

refers to a dark-skinned Arab people [Saracen], both fierce and destructive (you might say: castrating). It so happens, that from the very title onward, this male signified is coupled with a female signifier, "Sarrasine". This female signifier is in fact connected to a male signified, Ernest Jean Sarrasine, which is itself applied to a female signifier, "Zambinella", in turn connected to a male signified, introduced to the reader in the form of an old man who is connected to a female signifier: "young lady", which is not a signified, for the narrative is careful to de-individualize her and incarnate her successively into three distinct characters, to whom the old man is tied: a stranger, then Madame de Rochefide, and finally Marianina.

'The solution economy, together with the text's matrilineal emphasis, suggests that Zambinella must be Mme de Lanty's mother's brother. The "Mme de Lanty's brother" position is empty; but, on the other hand, there is a "Mme de Lanty's husband" whose value, negative in every respect, is but a compensation for the missing (positive) brother. I shall return to this. It is remarkable that the same three-storey structure is evoked in reference to Sarrasine, who has a father, and a father's father, and with whom Bouchardon plays a symmetrical and inverse role to that of M. de Lanty with his wife's children.

'Turning now to names: Marianina pertains to a "third storey", as a diminutive of Mariana, itself a diminutive of Maria. Zambinella is also a diminutive, as would also be Sarrasin*(a)* compared to *Marianina* and Zambi*nella*. Only one name excludes derivatives: Philippo, which thus stands in sharp opposition to Marianina in both the *(1st storey/3rd storey)* and (*male/female*) relations, through their contrasting flexional endings (*o/a*).

'The revelation regarding castration excludes alliance: Zambinella will not become Sarrasine's mistress, nor will Mme de Rochefide become that of the narrator. Mme de Lanty is only married "per orders" and her husband is only the inverse of the absent brother. It is thus to be expected that Marianina will not find a partner to marry. She is in the position of spouse to the old man Zambinella (a remark by Mme de Rochefide (138) that is astounding in every respect, since she should have considered any situation prior to this one, unless she is *telling* us something here that had to be pointed out). It is indeed Philippo who is the male in the 1st-generation position and who, in the 3rd, thus represents the old man (via Endymion and Antinoüs, but the latter had become an old man which is indicated (75–76) by his short and skinny legs that looked like bones, the second, an adolescent, has (22) a slender shape). I thus conclude that Philippo and Marianina, whose names represent the maximal compatible distance from the system, will thus necessarily become an incestuous couple [*Nota bene*: Whose mother's marriage to someone who is nothing else but a non-brother already provided the negative image. Mme de Lanty is the opposite of her daughter (20–21) and she has a husband and no brother; thus, the daughter who has a brother will, as a result, not have a husband. The Philippo-Marianina couple will achieve a positive synthesis of the antithetical attributes of Zambinella: Philippo is male, an adolescent "version" of the old man who, as he was castrated, had the soprano's voice that characterized (20) Marianina as a female: incest between direct relations being a castration in reverse]. Sincerely, CLS.'

193 Eribon, *Conversations*, p. 73.
194 R. Barthes, 'Réponses' (1971), in *Oeuvres complètes*, vol. III, p. 1032: 'I then ardently believed in the possibility of my integrating into a semiological science: I passed through a dream (euphoric) of scientificity (of which *The Fashion System* and *Elements of Semiology* are the residue). It was of little

importance to write books; I had time. Moreover, [. . .] I wrote many articles, which maintained my writing (the desire for writing); what followed, at least until now, revealed that my "truth" was in the second postulation, not in the first, even though I often felt the urge to claim it, insofar as I was a "semiologist", sometimes licensed, sometimes contested.'

195 Patrice Maniglier, 'La vie comme effet', preface to Juan Pablo Luchelli, *Lacan avec et sans Lévi-Strauss*, Nantes, C. Defaut éditions, 2013, p. 11.

196 Letter from Claude Lévi-Strauss, 29 January 1968, LAS Archives, FLAS, D.09.02.

197 Letter from Georges Dumézil to Claude Lévi-Strauss, 24 June 1974, CLS Archives, NAF 28150, box 188.

198 Letter from Georges Dumézil to Claude Lévi-Strauss, 29 October 1968, CLS Archives, NAF 28150, box 188.

199 *NM*, p. 693.

200 John Hess, 'The mythical Lévi-Strauss', *New York Times Review of Books*, 20 February 1972.

201 Interview with Raymond Bellour, *Le Monde*, 5 November 1971.

202 Catherine Backès-Clément, *Claude Lévi-Strauss ou la Structure et le malheur*, Paris, Seghers, 1970, p. 212.

203 Jean Pouillon and Pierre Maranda (eds.), *Échanges et communications: Mélanges offerts à Claude Lévi-Strauss à l'occasion de son soixantième anniversaire*, La Haye, Mouton, 1970.

204 There is a surviving videotape, 1970, that Monique Lévi-Strauss kindly shared with me, for which I am grateful.

205 *NM*, p. 656: 'We can guess that the phenomenon has an analogy with laughter, in the sense that in both cases a certain type of structure external to the subject, in the one instance a pattern of words or actions, in the other of sounds, sets in motion a psycho-physiological mechanism, the springs of which have been tensed in advance; but what does this mechanism correspond to, and what is happening exactly when we weep or laugh with joy?'

206 *NM*, p. 657.

207 *NM*, p. 657.

Chapter 18   The Politics of Discretion

1 In *Oeuvres complètes*, Gallimard, Pléiade, vol. II, 1995, p. 210.

2 Preface to *Soleil Hopi: L'autobiographie d'un Indien Hopi by Don. C. Talayesva*, texts collected by Leo W. Simmons, Paris, Terre humaine, 1959, p. 9.

3 Élisabeth Roudinesco, *Jacques Lacan: An Outline of a Life and a History of a System of Thought*, New York, Columbia University Press, 1997, p. 202.

4 See Bruno Karsenty, *D'une philosophie à l'autre: Les sciences sociales et la politique des modernes*, Paris, Gallimard, 2013.

5 M. Bloch, 'Une anthropologie fondamentale', in Philippe Descola (ed.), *Claude Lévi-Strauss, un parcours dans le siècle*, Paris, Odile Jacob, 2012, p. 250.

6 Pierre Zaoui, *La Discrétion: Ou l'art de disparaître*, Paris, Autrement, 2013.

7 Didier Eribon, *Conversations with Claude Lévi-Strauss*, Chicago, The University of Chicago Press, 1991, p. 92.

8 Eribon, *Conversations*, pp. 157–158.

9 Eribon, *Conversations*, p. 159.

10 See Christophe Charle, *Birth of the Intellectuals (1880–1900)*, Cambridge, Polity, 2015; Pascal Ory and Jean-François Sirinelli, *Les Intellectuels français de*

l'affaire Dreyfus à nos jours, Paris, Armand Colin, 1986; Jean-François Sirinelli, *Intellectuels et passions françaises: Manifestes et pétitions au xxe siècle*, Paris, Fayard, 1990.

11 Jean-François Bert, *Dans l'atelier de Marcel Mauss*, Paris, Éditions du CNRS, 2012, p. 48.

12 Eribon, *Conversations*, p. 81.

13 Eribon, *Conversations*, p. 158.

14 Eribon, *Conversations*, p. 158.

15 Claude Lévi-Strauss, 'Le problème ultime des sciences de l'homme consistera un jour à ramener la pensée à la vie', *Le Magazine littéraire*, 58, November 1971, p. 26.

16 Karsenty, *D'une philosophie à l'autre*, p. 20.

17 Letter from M. Leiris to Claude Lévi-Strauss, 21 August 1967, CLS Archives, NAF 28150, box 195, 'Correspondance reçue'.

18 Letter from Claude Lévi-Strauss to X, 23 March 1953, Bénichou Archives, Jacques-Doucet Library. I am grateful to Grégory Cingal for bringing this letter to my attention.

19 The petitioners solemnly vowed to 'take all action they considered, in good conscience, to be right, in any domain to which they had access, to bring an end to a war in North Africa that is a threat to the Republic as well as a crime against humanity'. The petition called for an end to repression, immediate negotiations, the repeal of the state of emergency in Algeria, the demobilization of conscripts, and an end to racial discrimination, in both overseas territories and metropolitan France. *L'Express* emphasized the ecumenical profile of the signatories and the entire piece echoed François Mauriac's editorial of the same day.

20 Letter from Claude Lévi-Strauss to Jacques Soustelle, 21 November 1955, CLS Archives, NAF 28150, box 202.

21 Claude Lévi-Strauss, 'Le droit au voyage', *L'Express*, 21 September 1956.

22 Jean Jamin, 'L'anthropologie et ses acteurs', in *Les Enjeux philosophiques des années 50*, Paris, Editions du Centre Pompidou, 1993, p. 109ff.

23 See chapter 13 above.

24 See Christine Laurière, *Paul Rivet: Le savant et la politique*, Paris, Éditions scientifiques du Muséum national d'Histoire naturelle, 'Archives', 2008.

25 Michel Leiris, 'L'ethnographe devant le colonialisme', *Les Temps modernes*, 58, 1950, pp. 357–374.

26 Eribon, *Conversations*, p. 153.

27 See Bill Ashcroft, Gareth Griffiths and Helen Tiffin, *The Post-Colonial Studies Reader*, London, Routledge, 1995. For the French context, see Marie-Claude Smouts (ed.), *La Situation postcoloniale: Les Post-Colonial Studies dans le débat français*, Paris, Presses de Sciences Po, 2007, preface by Georges Balandier.

28 Claude Lévi-Strauss, 'Cultural discontinuity and economic and social development', originally published as his contribution to a round table entitled 'Les prémisses sociales de l'industrialisation', September 1961. Republished in *SA*, vol. 2, p. 315.

29 See the classic work by Eric Williams, *Capitalism & Slavery*, London, The University of North Carolina Press, 1994 [1944].

30 See Sanjay Subramanyam, *From the Tagus to the Ganges: Explorations in Connected History*, Oxford, Oxford University Press, 2004.

31 Raymond Aron, *Memoirs: Fifty Years of Political Reflection* [1983], Teaneck, NJ, Holmes & Meier, 1990, p. 335.

32 Pierre Birnbaum, *Geography of Hope: Exile, the Enlightenment and Disassimilation*, Palo Alto, Stanford University Press, 2008, pp. 181–185.

33 Letter from Claude Lévi-Strauss to Raymond Aron, 9 April 1968, Raymond Aron Archives, NAF 28060, box 207, Manuscripts Department, BNF.
34 See Dominique Schnapper, *Jewish Identities in France: An Analysis of Contemporary French Jewry*, Chicago, The University of Chicago Press, 1983.
35 Claude Lévi-Strauss, 'Ce que je suis', *Le Nouvel Observateur*, 5 July 1980.
36 Eribon, *Conversations*, p. 156.
37 Eribon, *Conversations*, p. 157.
38 Eribon, *Conversations*, p. 157.
39 Letter from Claude Lévi-Strauss, 10 April 1968, Raymond Aron Archives, NAF 28060, box 207, Manuscripts Department, BNF.
40 Such as Élisabeth Roudinesco, who claims to have taken part in the 1968 protests as a structuralist. Interview with the author.
41 Eribon, *Conversations*, p. 80.
42 See Michel de Certeau, *The Capture of Speech and Other Political Writings*, Minneapolis, University of Minnesota Press, [1968] 1997.
43 See Roland Barthes, 'L'écriture de l'événement', *Communications*, November 1968. English translation published as 'Writing the event', in *The Rustle of Language*, Berkeley, University of California Press, 1989.
44 Eribon, *Conversations*, p. 80.
45 Jean-Marc Coudray, Claude Lefort and Edgar Morin, *Mai 68: la brèche. Premières réflexions sur les événements*, Paris, Fayard, 1968.
46 'French anthropologist at onset of 70's deplores twentieth century', *New York Times*, 31 December 1969.
47 'French anthropologist at onset of 70s deplores twentieth century'.
48 Eribon, *Conversations*, p. 160.
49 Eribon, *Conversations*, p. 160.
50 Eribon, *Conversations*, p. 80.
51 Letter from Claude Lévi-Strauss, 1 October 1968, CLS Archives, NAF 28150, box 216, 'Collège de France'.
52 Letter from Claude Lévi-Strauss, 1 October 1968.
53 Letter from Claude Lévi-Strauss, 1 October 1968.
54 Letter from Claude Lévi-Strauss to Raymond Aron, NAF 28060, box 207, Manuscripts Department, BNF.
55 'Compte rendu de réunion du Commissariat général du Plan d'équipement et de la productivité', May 1963, CLS Archives, NAF 28150, box 214.
56 'Compte rendu de réunion du Commissariat général du Plan d'équipement et de la productivité'.
57 'Compte rendu de réunion du Commissariat général du Plan d'équipement et de la productivité'.
58 'Compte rendu de réunion du Commissariat général du Plan d'équipement et de la productivité'.
59 Karsenty, *D'une philosophie à l'autre*, p. 25.
60 'Urban civilization and mental health'. Response to a questionnaire from the Institut de la Vie, published in *SA*, vol. 2, pp. 283–286. Subsequent quotations are from this text.
61 See Emmanuelle Loyer, 'Les maisons de la culture entre sanctuarisation culturelle et messianisme politique', in Philippe Artières and Michelle Zancarini-Fournel, *68: Une histoire collective, 1962–1981*, Paris, La Découverte, 2015, pp. 144–151.
62 Frédérique Matonti, 'La politisation du structuralisme: Une crise dans la théorie', *Raisons politiques*, 18, May 2005, pp. 49–71.

63 See François Furet, 'French intellectuals: from Marxism to structuralism', [1967] in *In the Workshop of History*, Chicago, The University of Chicago Press, 1984.

64 In the review of a book by Paul Rivet who, according to Lévi-Strauss, stood as a 'living symbol that all science is political', quoted in Laurent Jeanpierre, 'Une opposition structurante pour l'anthropologie structurale: Lévi-Strauss contre Gurvitch. La guerre de deux exilés français aux États-Unis', *Revue d'histoire des sciences humaines*, 11, February 2004, pp. 13–44.

65 Letter from Claude Lévi-Strauss to Denis Kambouchner, 12 January 2006, reprinted in Boris Wiseman (ed.), *The Cambridge Companion to Lévi-Strauss*, Cambridge, Cambridge University Press, 2009, p. 37. The letter was written in response to a contribution by Denis Kambouchner to the *Cambridge Companion* entitled 'Lévi-Strauss and the question of humanism'. The letter continues as follows: 'I have, through trial and error, searched for these conditions in very diverse directions – hence my apparent contradictions – only to realize that they destroyed one another and that this critique (in the Kantian sense) of humanism gradually emptied it of its substance.' His thoughts on the matter had evolved significantly 'between 1952, when [he] believed it was possible to play according to the rules set by UNESCO, and 1971, when [he] decided that the best way to help this organisation was to confront it with its own contradictions'.

66 Claude Lévi-Strauss, 'The three humanisms' [1956], in *SA*, vol. 2, p. 272.

67 Lévi-Strauss, 'The three humanisms'. The weekly *Demain* was published from 1955 to 1957.

68 *SA*, vol. 2, pp. 40–41. Subsequent quotes are also taken from this text.

69 Emmanuel Terray, 'La vision du monde de Claude Lévi-Strauss', *L'Homme*, 193, January–March 2010, p. 32.

70 Wiktor Stoczkowski, *Anthropologies rédemptrices: Le monde selon Lévi-Strauss*, Paris, Hermann, 2008, p. 270.

71 *OTM*, pp. 507–508.

72 Zaoui, *La Discrétion*, p. 50.

73 Claude Lévi-Strauss, 'Apropos of a retrospective', 1966, in *SA*, vol. 2, p. 280.

74 Patrice Maniglier, 'L'humanisme interminable de Claude Lévi-Strauss', *Les Temps modernes*, 609, June–July–August 2000, p. 231.

75 Maniglier, 'L'humanisme interminable de Claude Lévi-Strauss', p. 233.

76 *RC*, p. 6: 'This book on myths is itself a kind of myth'.

77 Maniglier, 'L'humanisme interminable de Claude Lévi-Strauss', p. 237.

78 *RC*, p. 5.

79 *SM*, p. 255.

80 Claude Lévi-Strauss, '*L'Express* va plus loin avec Claude Lévi-Strauss', *L'Express*, 15–21 March 1971.

81 Letter from Claude Lévi-Strauss to Raymond Aron, 25 December 1955.

Chapter 19   Immortal

1 Quoted by Claude Lévi-Strauss in his Académie française induction speech, 27 June 1974.

2 *WoM*, p. 7.

3 Éric Schwimmer, 'Claude Lévi-Strauss et le lièvre canadien', in M. Izard (ed.), *Claude Lévi-Strauss*, Paris, L'Herne, 'Cahiers de l'Herne', 2004, p. 203.

4 See film by Yannick Bellon.

5 Dan Sperber, *Le Structuralisme en anthropologie*, Paris, Seuil, 1973, p. 9.
6 Daniel Bell, 'Lévi-Strauss and the return to rationalism', *New York Times Review of Books*, 14 March 1976.
7 Pierre Clastres, 'The highpoint of the cruise', published in English in *Archeology of Violence*, New York, Semiotext(e), 1994, pp. 37–43.
8 Olivier Mannoni, '"Terrains" de mission?' *Les Temps modernes*, 299–300, June–July 1971, p. 2352.
9 R. Stavenhagen, 'Comment décoloniser les sciences sociales appliquées', *Les Temps modernes*, 299–300, June–July 1971, p. 2362.
10 Jean Monod, 'Oraison funèbre pour une vieille dame', *Les Temps modernes*, 299–300, June–July 1971, pp. 2393–2400.
11 Monod, 'Oraison funèbre pour une vieille dame', p. 2393.
12 Jean Monod, interview with the author, 26 February 2013.
13 Letter from Claude Lévi-Strauss to Robert Jaulin, 2 January 1974, CLS Archives, NAF 28150, box 192.
14 Didier Eribon, *Conversations with Claude Lévi-Strauss*, Chicago, The University of Chicago Press, 1991, p. 154.
15 Yves Cohen, *Le Siècle des chefs: Une histoire transnationale du commandement et de l'autorité*, Paris, Amsterdam, 2013, p. 13.
16 A field that Lévi-Strauss had, however, tackled during his New York years, as evidenced by several articles, parts of which found their way into *Tristes Tropiques*.
17 Pierre Clastres, *Society Against the State: Essays in Political Anthropology*, New York, Zone Books, 1989.
18 See chapter 15 above.
19 Jean-Paul Sartre, 'Sartre répond', *L'Arc*, 30, 1966.
20 Quoted in Christian Delacampagne, 'Du Collège à l'Académie', *Le Monde*, 25 October 1973.
21 Interview of Georges Balandier by George Steinmetz and Gisèle Sapiro, 'Tout parcours scientifique comporte des moments autobiographiques', *Actes de la Recherche en sciences sociales*, 185, p. 48.
22 'La situation coloniale: approche théorique', *Cahiers internationaux de sociologie*, 11, 1951, pp. 44–79.
23 Emmanuel Terray, 'Anthropologie et marxisme, années 1950–70', *L'Afrique, miroir du contemporain*, conference organized by the Institut interdisciplinaire d'anthropologie du contemporain, EHESS, Paris, 19 June 2007 [oai :hal. archives-ouvertes.fr :halshs-00207614].
24 Claude Lévi-Strauss, Maurice Godelier and Marc Augé, 'Anthropology, history, ideology', *Critique of Anthropology*, 2(6), February 1976, p. 48.
25 Lévi-Strauss, Godelier and Augé, 'Anthropology, history, ideology', p. 47.
26 Lévi-Strauss, Godelier and Augé, 'Anthropology, history, ideology', p. 47.
27 Lévi-Strauss, Godelier and Augé, 'Anthropology, history, ideology', p. 47. The emphasis is mine.
28 Lévi-Strauss, Godelier and Augé, 'Anthropology, history, ideology', p. 51.
29 Lévi-Strauss, Godelier and Augé, 'Anthropology, history, ideology', p. 47.
30 Published in English as the appendix to *The Logic of Practice*, London, Polity, 1990, pp. 271–283.
31 Pierre Bourdieu, 'Preface', in *The Logic of Practice*, p. 9.
32 Bourdieu, *The Logic of Practice*, p. 4.
33 The Lévi-Strauss archive contains ten letters from the 1980s; almost all were letters of thanks to Lévi-Strauss upon receiving (and reading) books he had sent. The tone, always modest in the expression of sentiments, was one of 'affectionate admiration'. CLS Archives, NAF 28150, box 184.

34 Bourdieu, *The Logic of Practice*, p. 4.
35 François Dosse, *History of Structuralism*, vol. 2: *The Sign Sets, 1967–Present*, Minneapolis, University of Minnesota Press, 1997, ch. 6, 'Durkheim gets a second wind: Pierre Bourdieu', pp. 66–75; and 'A middle path: the habitus', pp. 301–311.
36 Pierre Bourdieu, television programme hosted by Didier Éribon and Philippe Collin, *Océaniques*, 'Réflexions faites', aired 11:53 p.m., INA Archives.
37 Bourdieu, *Océaniques*.
38 Dosse, *History of Structuralism*, vol. 2, pp. 306ff.
39 Pierre Bourdieu, *In Other Words*, Stanford, Stanford University Press, 1990, p. 9.
40 Bourdieu, *In Other Words*, p. 13.
41 Bourdieu, *In Other Words*, p. 13.
42 See Frédéric Keck, 'La logique de la pratique est-elle une pensée sauvage? À partir de Bourdieu, relire Lévi-Strauss', paper written for Pierre Macherey's seminar, University of Lille III, 'La philosophie au sens large', 8 November 2000.
43 Keck, 'La logique de la pratique est-elle une pensée sauvage?'.
44 Bourdieu, *The Logic of Practice*, p. 11: 'I never thought of moving, as is commonly done nowadays, from critical analysis of the social and technical conditions of the objectification and definition of the limits of validity of the products obtained in these conditions, to a "radical" critique of all objectification and thereby of science itself. If it is to be more than the projection of personal feelings, social science necessarily presupposes the stage of objectification, and once again the necessary breakthrough is achieved with the aid of the tools provided by structuralist objectification.'
45 Bourdieu, *The Logic of Practice*, p. 3. See Pierre Bourdieu, *Algerian Sketches*, London, Polity, 2013; see also Daniel Fabre, 'Pierre Bourdieu et la guerre d'Algérie', in Christine Laurière, Daniel Fabre and André Mary (eds.), *Les Ethnologues en situation coloniale*, Paris, Éditions du CNRS, 2015.
46 Claude Lévi-Strauss, *SA*, vol. 2, p. 26.
47 Claude Lévi-Strauss, 'Histoire et ethnologie', Marc Bloch lecture, delivered 6 June 1983, *Annales, ESC*, 6, 1983, p. 1230: 'This critique, which is seemingly everywhere, is inspired by a fashionable spontaneism and subjectivism. Must we give up the search for organizing principles in the life of the human sciences, resign ourselves to an immense chaos of creative acts bursting forth at the scale of the individual, and ensuring the fecundity of a permanent disorder?' He concluded: 'Let us not fall prey to the naive notion, so common nowadays, which consists in believing that the search for an order and the exaltation of the creative powers of the individual are mutually exclusive enterprises. Quite the contrary, the analysis of strategies and individual choices opens up vast areas of research for our disciplines, into which they have until now not dared to venture.'
48 See Dosse, *History of Structuralism*, vol. 2, chs. 2 and 3, 'Derrida or ultrastructuralism' and 'Derridean historicization and its erasure'; see also Frédéric Keck, 'Jacques Derrida: Structuralisme et déconstruction', in *Claude Lévi-Strauss: Une introduction*, Paris, Presses Pocket, 2005, pp. 214–227.
49 Jacques Derrida, 'Structure, sign and play in the discourse of the human sciences', in *Writing and Difference*, Chicago, The University of Chicago Press, 1978, p. 280.
50 Frédéric Worms, *La Philosophie en France au XXe siècle: Moments*, Paris, Gallimard, 2009, p. 484.

51 Jacques Derrida, *Of Grammatology*, Baltimore, MD, Johns Hopkins University Press, 1976, pp. 118–140.

52 Keck, *Claude Lévi-Strauss*, p. 215.

53 Derrida, *Of Grammatology*, p. xc.

54 Keck, *Claude Lévi-Strauss*, p. 214: 'The question of writing became a major issue in anthropology after Derrida's reading of Lévi-Strauss, and in large part because of it.' See Jack Goody, *The Domestication of the Savage Mind*, Cambridge, Cambridge University Press, 1977; and James Clifford and George Marcus (eds.), *Writing Culture: The Poetics and Politics of Ethnography*, Berkeley, University of California Press, 1986.

55 We should keep in mind that the object of social anthropology, according to Lévi-Strauss, was precisely the study of differentials, the only means of accessing the structure.

56 See François Cusset, *French Theory: How Foucault, Deleuze, & Co. Transformed the Intellectual Life of the United States*, Minneapolis, University of Minnesota Press, 2008; and Vincent Debaene, 'Claude Lévi-Strauss aujourd'hui', *Europe*, 9/1005–1006, January–February 2013.

57 Delacampagne, 'Du Collège à l'Académie'.

58 Delacampagne, 'Du Collège à l'Académie'.

59 Jean-Paul Enthoven, 'Les rêveries d'un ethnologue solitaire', *Le Nouvel Observateur*, 10 December 1973.

60 Enthoven, 'Les rêveries d'un ethnologue solitaire'.

61 Enthoven, 'Les rêveries d'un ethnologue solitaire'.

62 See chapter 18 above.

63 The somewhat preposterously old-fashioned and ornate uniforms of the *académiciens* are green. The members are, also rather quaintly, known as the 'immortals'.

64 In his 'Réponse au discours de réception d'Alain Peyrefitte', Claude Lévi-Strauss compared himself to Peyrefitte who, precocious in every way, always suspected he would one day have a place in such company. 'By contrast, the idea that I might belong to it had never crossed my mind.'

65 'L'horreur de la compétition: entretien avec Claude Lévi-Strauss', *Le Figaro*, 25 May 1973.

66 Letter from Maurice Druon, 7 March 1973, CLS Archives, NAF 28150, box 187.

67 Maurice Druon, Speech to the National Assembly, 23 May 1973.

68 'L'horreur de la compétition.'

69 'L'horreur de la compétition.'

70 'L'horreur de la compétition.'

71 'L'horreur de la compétition.'

72 A witticism, likely apocryphal, summed up the complexity of Lévi-Strauss's relationships with the Académie. He was said to have exclaimed: 'They thought they were electing a Jew; they got two.' Daniel Fabre, interview with the author, 12 March 2012.

73 Eribon, *Conversations*, p. 83.

74 Letter from Michel Leiris, 18 March 1974, CLS Archives, NAF 28150, box 195.

75 Letter from Jean Daniel to Claude Lévi-Strauss (undated), CLS Archives, NAF 28150, box 186.

76 Letter from Catherine Clément, 5 June 1973, CLS Archives, to which Lévi-Strauss replied: 'So what, there are no academicians in the USSR?'

77 Interview with Monique Lévi-Strauss, 28 November 2011.

78 Claude Lévi-Strauss, 'Autoportrait', remarks collected by Catherine Clément and Dominique-Antoine Grisoni, *Magazine littéraire*, 223, October 1985, p. 24.
79 'Discours de réception de Claude Lévi-Strauss', Claude Lévi-Strauss's speech on joining the Académie française, 27 June 1974: 'And yet, gentlemen, would not any anthropologist be drawn to an institution such as yours, endowed with all the characteristics of historical accretion, without which no society could survive or develop, deprived as it would be of a skeletal frame.'
80 'Discours de M. Claude Lévi-Strauss', in *Discours de réception de M. Fernand Braudel et réponse de M. Maurice Druon*, Paris, Arthaud, 1986, p. 99: 'In the national tradition and the eyes of the world, the Académie remains imbued with these symbols. As in your theoretical work, it is thus to the call of the *longue durée* that you have responded.'
81 'Discours de réception de Claude Lévi-Strauss.'
82 Lévi-Strauss, 'Autoportrait', p. 24: 'Since I do not have a sense of personal identity, for me, the only way of developing one is through external markers.'
83 'Discours de réception de Claude Lévi-Strauss.'
84 'Discours de réception de Claude Lévi-Strauss.'
85 'Discours de réception de Claude Lévi-Strauss.'
86 'Discours de réception de Claude Lévi-Strauss.'
87 'Discours de réception de Claude Lévi-Strauss.'
88 *Smithsonian*, 20(10), January 1990, p. 145.
89 This is what Julien Gracq, another potential member of the Académie, wrote about the institution in 1967: 'The Académie française serves no purpose. Its dictionary is not authoritative, its grammar has never been completed. On the other hand, it does not really bother anyone. Why take issue with this dear old thing, one of the most folkloric and British of curiosities we still have? These men of much or little knowledge, who gird themselves with swords and beat drums, there is no reason to object to them – all it takes is simply to remain outside it. One can find the changing of the guard at Buckingham Palace amusing and not want to join the Horse Guards.' *Oeuvres complètes*, Gallimard, Pléiade, vol. II, 1995, p. 184.
90 *Le Canard enchaîné*, 30 May 1973.
91 Letter from Claude Lévi-Strauss to Isac Chiva, 19 July 1973.
92 See chapter 13 above.
93 Eribon, *Conversations*, p. 85.
94 Letter from Claude Lévi-Strauss to Roger Caillois (undated) [May 1974], CLS Archives, NAF 28150, box 186.
95 Bernard Rosenblum, leather artisan, made the sheath for his sword according to a sketch by Lévi-Strauss.
96 'Le siècle de Claude Lévi-Strauss', DVD.
97 'Le siècle de Claude Lévi-Strauss', DVD.
98 Lévi-Strauss, 'Autoportrait', p. 24: 'And if in my reception speech, I started with a lengthy comparison between the Académie and initiation rituals – for which Aron gently chided me, saying this kind of presentation was entirely expected and I should have been quicker about it – it was because I was addressing my students and colleagues, not the members of the Académie. I was explaining to them . . .'
99 'Discours de réception de Claude Lévi-Strauss'.
100 Gisèle Sapiro, *La Guerre des écrivains, 1940–1953*, Paris, Fayard, 1999, ch. 4.
101 Ernest Renan, 'What is a nation?' (1882). This is the final sentence of Renan's text.

102 Since the 1980s, the preferred ethnonym for this tribe is *Kwakwaka' wakw.* However, we follow Lévi-Strauss who uses the old nomenclature throughout.

103 Claude Lévi-Strauss, 'Reflections on Northwest Coast ethnology', in Marie Mauzé, Michael Harkin and Sergei Kan (eds.), *Coming to Shore: Northwest Coast Ethnology, Traditions and Visions*, Lincoln, University of Nebraska Press, 2004, p. 1.

104 For this entire paragraph, see the very thorough articles by Marie Mauzé, 'Parcours de Claude Lévi-Strauss sur la côte du Nord-Ouest', in Philippe Descola (ed.), *Claude Lévi-Strauss, un parcours dans le siècle*, Paris, Odile Jacob, 2012, pp. 33–60; and 'Esthétique et structure: la rencontre de l'art de la côte nord-ouest du Pacifique dans l'Oeuvre de Claude Lévi-Strauss', *Europe*, 91(1005–1006), January–February 2013, pp. 196–209.

105 Mauzé, 'Parcours de Claude Lévi-Strauss sur la côte du Nord-Ouest', p. 46, n. 34.

106 *WoM*, p. 3.

107 *WoM*, p. 5.

108 Marie Mauzé, interview with the author, 7 May 2014.

109 Film entitled *Behind the Mask*, 1974.

110 Schwimmer, 'Claude Lévi-Strauss et le lièvre canadien', p. 203. The purpose of the visits in 1973 and 1974 had been, in Lévi-Strauss's words, 'to locate, for his own personal edification, the mythical itineraries that he had analysed and discussed in the *Mythologiques*'.

111 Letter from Claude Lévi-Strauss to Isac Chiva, 4 August 1974.

112 'Walking through the rain forest with Lévi-Strauss', *The Vancouver Sun*, 16 July 1974.

113 *WoM*, p. 10.

114 M. Mauzé, 'Esthétique et structure', p. 36.

115 Catherine Clément, 'Adieu voyages! Adieu sauvages!' *Le Figaro*, 13 January 1990.

116 Claude Lévi-Strauss, *Des symboles et leurs doubles*, Paris, Plon, 1989, p. 259.

117 Bill Holm, *Northern Coast Indian Art: An Analysis of Form*, Seattle, University of Washington Press, 1965.

118 Marie Mauzé, 'Bill Reid: 1920–1998', *L'Homme*, 151, 1999, p. 7.

119 Claude Lévi-Strauss, 'Bill Reid', in *Bill Reid: A Retrospective Exhibition*, Vancouver, The Vancouver Art Gallery, 1974, pp. 255–256.

120 Frédéric Keck, in Claude Levi-Strauss, *Oeuvres*, 'Bibliothèque de la Pléiade', Paris, Gallimard, 2008, p. 1854.

121 Eduardo Viveiros de Castro, 'Claude Lévi-Strauss vu par Eduardo Viveiros de Castro', *La Lettre du Collège de France*, 2 (special issue), 2008, pp. 34–35.

122 Keck, in Lévi-Strauss, *Oeuvres*, pp. 1854–1855.

123 See Agnès Callu, *Gaëtan Picon, 1915–1976. Esthétique et culture*, Paris, Honoré Champion, 2011.

124 Claude Lévi-Strauss, interview with Marie Mauzé, 30 April 2014. Quoted by Marie Mauzé, in Lévi-Strauss, *Oeuvres*, p. 1858.

125 *WoM*, p. 144.

126 Jean-Marie Benoît, 'Claude Lévi-Strauss entre deux masques', *Le Figaro littéraire*, 22 November 1975.

127 Quoted by Mauzé, in Lévi-Strauss, *Oeuvres*, p. 1864.

128 Quoted by Mauzé, in Lévi-Strauss, *Oeuvres*, p. 1863.

129 Letter from Michel Leiris to Claude Lévi-Strauss, 13 November 1975, CLS Archives, NAF 28150, box 195.

130 The book was reviewed by Dominique Fernandez in *L'Express*, by Claude Bonnefoy in *Les Nouvelles littéraires*, by Pierre Daix in *Le Quotidien de Paris*, by Roger-Pol Droit in *Le Monde*, by Max-Pol Fouchet in *Le Point*, and by Jean-Marie Benoît in *Le Figaro littéraire*. To these must be added several long interviews, such as the one Lévi-Strauss gave to Maurice Olender in 1976, which aired on francophone Belgian radio, about *The Way of the Masks* and the question of aesthetics in his anthropology ('Le sensible et l'intelligible', interview with Maurice Olender, Maurice Olender Archives, Imec, published in *La Règle du jeu*, 44, 2010).
131 José Pierre, *La Quinzaine littéraire*, 224, 1–15 January 1976.
132 Georges Charbonnier, *Entretiens avec Claude Lévi-Strauss*, Paris, Les Belles Lettres, 2010.
133 Pierre Daix, 'Art indien et structuralisme', *Le Quotidien de Paris*, 16 December 1975.
134 Daix, 'Art indien et structuralisme'.
135 *WoM*, p. 148.
136 See Philippe Urfalino, *L'Invention de la politique culturelle*, Paris, La Documentation française, 1996.
137 François Hartog, 'Le regard éloigné: Lévi-Strauss et l'histoire', in M. Izard (ed.), *Claude Lévi-Strauss*, Paris, L'Herne, 'Cahiers de l'Herne', 2004, pp. 282–288.
138 See Marie Mauzé, 'When the Northwest Coast haunts French anthropology', in Mauzé, Harkin and Kan (eds.), *Coming to Shore*, pp. 63–65.
139 Claude Lévi-Strauss, 'The social organization of the Kwakiutl', in *WoM*, p. 174.
140 Claude Lévi-Strauss, 'The concept of "house" (1976–7)', in *AM*, p. 152.
141 Lévi-Strauss, 'The concept of "house"', p. 152.
142 Maurice Godelier, 'Le concept de maison', in *Lévi-Strauss*, Paris, Seuil, 2013, pp. 197–225.
143 Lévi-Strauss, 'The concept of "house"', p. 152.
144 'La notion de maison: entretien entre Claude Lévi-Strauss et Pierre Lamaison', *Terrain*, 9, October 1987.
145 Hartog, 'Le regard éloigné', p. 286.
146 Claude Lévi-Strauss, 'On Africa (1981–2)', in *AM*, p. 194.
147 Lévi-Strauss, 'On Africa (1981–2)', p. 194.
148 'Réflexions faites', 31 October 1988, *Océaniques* broadcast, prepared by D. Éribon and P. Colin, INA Archives. The other participants were the anthropologist Luc de Heutsch, the sociologist Pierre Bourdieu and the philosopher André Comte-Sponville.
149 A distinction Claude Lévi-Strauss developed in his 1949 article, 'History and anthropology', published in *SA*, pp. 18–25.
150 André Burguière, 'Histoire et structure', *Annales*, 3–4, June–July 1971, p. 1.
151 Hartog, 'Le regard éloigné', p. 286.
152 Burguière, 'Histoire et structure', p. 7.
153 Richard Marin, 'La nouvelle histoire et Lévi-Strauss', *Caravelle: Cahiers du monde hispanique et luso-brésilien*, 96, June 2011, pp. 165–178.
154 Claude Lévi-Strauss to Georges Duby, 29 March 1981, Georges Duby Archives, Imec.
155 Claude Lévi-Strauss to Georges Duby, 29 March 1981.
156 Claude Lévi-Strauss, 'Discours de remise d'épée à Fernand Braudel', 19 March 1985, 'Discours de M. Claude Lévi-Strauss', *Discours de réception de M. Fernand Braudel à l'Académie française et Réponse de M. Druon*, p. 96.

157 Lévi-Strauss, 'Discours de remise d'épée à Fernand Braudel', p. 94.
158 Lévi-Strauss, 'Discours de remise d'épée à Fernand Braudel', p. 97.
159 Lévi-Strauss, 'Discours de remise d'épée à Fernand Braudel', pp. 97–98.
160 Lévi-Strauss, 'Discours de remise d'épée à Fernand Braudel', p. 93.
161 Claude Lévi-Strauss, 'Histoire et ethnologie', Marc Bloch lecture, p. 1231.
162 Pierre Nora, letter of 17 May 1983, CLS Archives, NAF 28150, box 197.
163 Marc Fumaroli, 'La coupole', in Pierre Nora (ed.), *Realms of Memory: The Construction of the French Past*, vol. 2, *Traditions*, New York, Columbia University Press, 1998; Pierre Nora, interview with the author, 9 October 2014; Claude Lévi-Strauss, 'À propos de la République et de la Nation', *Le Figaro*, 1986: 'My experience of reading *Realms of Memory* was one of amazement. The method which consists in taking massive blocks of our historical representations and mythologies and dissecting them to show how they came into existence, and the various ways they have been used over time, is, to my mind, a brand new and original way of writing history.'
164 *WoM*, p. 185.
165 See Delphine Naudier, 'L'irrésistible élection de Marguerite Yourcenar à l'Académie française', *Cahiers du genre*, 36, January 2004.
166 For example, the opposed camp included the progressive intellectual André Chamson, a writer linked to the Front populaire, and the far right Pierre Gaxotte – a fact that did not go unnoticed by the newspapers.
167 Quoted in D. Peras, '1980: Yourcenar à l'Académie', *Lire*, 1 November 2005.
168 Marguerite Yourcenar responded most elegantly to her detractors in her acceptance speech, taking up their own arguments: 'I have too much respect for tradition, where it is still alive, potent and, if I may say so, prickly, not to understand those who resist the changes they are encouraged to accept by what we call the spirit of the times which, I admit, is often just a fad of the moment.' Speech delivered at the Académie française on 22 January 1981.
169 See her book, *L'Exercice de la parenté*, Paris, Gallimard, 1981.
170 By 2015, out of forty-four chairs, only five full professors were women, more or less the same ratio as in the Académie française . . .
171 Claude Lévi-Strauss, 'Rapport pour la création d'une chaire d'études africanistes au Collège de France', 29 November 1981 (typed manuscript), CLS Archives, NAF 28150, box 216.
172 Françoise Héritier, interview with the author, 18 April 2012.

Chapter 20   Metamorphoses

1 Didier Eribon, *Conversations with Claude Lévi-Strauss*, Chicago, The University of Chicago Press, 1991, p. 126. Quotation from Mme de Staël's 1807 novel *Corinne*.
2 *Lire*, 68, April 1981.
3 *The View from Afar* (1983), *Anthropology and Myth: Lectures, 1951–1982* (1984), *The Jealous Potter* (1986), *Conversations with Claude Lévi-Strauss* (1988), *Des symboles et leurs doubles* (1989), and *The Story of Lynx* (1991).
4 Pierre Bourdieu, *Homo Academicus*, Paris, Les Éditions de Minuit, 1984, pp. 25ff.
5 *Lire*, 68, April 1981. The question they were asked was the following: 'Who are the three living francophone intellectuals whose work you consider to have had the most profound influence on the course of ideas, literature, art, science, etc.?'

6 Pierre Nora, 'Que peuvent les intellectuels?' *Le Débat*, 1, pp. 3–19.
7 See Jean-François Lyotard, *Tombeau de l'intellectuel et autres papiers*, Paris, Galilée, 1984.
8 Nora, 'Que peuvent les intellectuels?' p. 7.
9 Françoise Giroud, 'Bloc-notes', *L'Express*, 10 May 1984.
10 All in all, more than twenty interviews were published, both in the daily – *Le Matin de Paris*, *Le Quotidien de Paris*, *Le Figaro*, *Libération*, *La Croix* – and the weekly press – *Le Nouvel Observateur*, *Le Point*, *L'Express*, *L'Événement du jeudi* – as well as in monthlies – *Le Magazine littéraire*, *Arche*, *La Quinzaine littéraire*.
11 Letter from Pierre Nora to Claude Lévi-Strauss, May 1984, CLS Archives, NAF 28150, box 197, 'Correspondance reçue'.
12 Gilles Martin-Chauffier, 'Claude Lévi-Strauss: depuis Diderot aucun intellectuel n'a fait si bien rire', *Paris-Match*, November 1985.
13 Martin-Chauffier, 'Claude Lévi-Strauss'.
14 'Claude Lévi-Strauss, le dernier géant de la pensée française', interview by Pierre Blois, *Le Figaro*, 26 July 1993.
15 Martin-Chauffier, 'Claude Lévi-Strauss'.
16 'Lévi-Strauss: "Des ratés? Nous le sommes tous plus ou moins".'
17 Philippe Simmonot, 'Un anarchiste de droite: *L'Express* va plus loin avec Claude Lévi-Strauss', *L'Express*, 17–23 October 1986, pp. 109–110.
18 Simmonot, 'Un anarchiste de droite', p. 124.
19 Simmonot, 'Un anarchiste de droite', p. 120.
20 Giroud, 'Bloc-notes'.
21 See François Cusset, *La Décennie: Le Grand Cauchemar des années 1980*, Paris, La Découverte, 2006.
22 The book co-edited by R. Bellour and C. Clément, *Textes de et sur Claude Lévi-Strauss*, Paris, Gallimard, 1979.
23 'L'idéologie marxiste, communiste et totalitaire n'est qu'une ruse de l'histoire', interview of Claude Lévi-Strauss by Jean-Marie Benoît, *Le Monde*, 21–22 July 1979.
24 Antoine Compagnon, *Les Antimodernes: De Joseph de Maistre à Roland Barthes*, Paris, Gallimard, 2005, p. 7. I am borrowing the expression 'a modern at large' from Compagnon, who uses it as the title of his introduction.
25 Compagnon, *Les Antimodernes.*
26 Charles Baudelaire, *Lettre à Manet*, 11 May 1865, quoted in Compagnon, *Les Antimodernes*, p. 8.
27 Claude Lévi-Strauss, *La Revue des Deux Mondes*, June 1984.
28 See Georges Friedmann, *La Crise du progrès: Esquisse d'une histoire des idées (1895–1935)*, Paris, Gallimard, 1936. For a recent study, see Thomas Hirsch, 'Le temps social: conceptions sociologiques du temps et représentations de l'histoire dans les sciences de l'homme en France, 1901–1945', EHESS doctoral thesis, supervised by François Hartog, 2014.
29 Claude Lévi-Strauss, *Lire*, October 1986.
30 'L'idéologie marxiste, communiste et totalitaire n'est qu'une ruse de l'histoire', interview of Claude Lévi-Strauss by Jean-Marie Benoît.
31 'L'idéologie marxiste, communiste et totalitaire n'est qu'une ruse de l'histoire', interview of Claude Lévi-Strauss by Jean-Marie Benoît.
32 Christophe Charle, 'Conclusion provisoire: la modernité dure longtemps', in *Discordance des temps: Une brève histoire de la modernité*, Paris, Armand Colin, 2011, p. 387.
33 Walter Benjamin, *The Arcades Project*, Cambridge, MA, Harvard University Press, 1999, p. 392: 'How [the past] marks itself as a higher actuality is

determined by the image as which and in which it is comprehended. And this dialectical penetration and actualization of former contexts puts the truth of all present action to the test. Or rather, it serves to ignite the explosive materials that are latent in what has been.'

34 Jacques Meunier, 'Une œuvre désormais incontournable: les réussites et les patiences de Claude Lévi-Strauss', *Le Monde*, 27 May 1983.

35 Patrick Fougeyrollas, *L'Humanité*, November 1983. On the same page, Danièle Bleitrach was similarly dismissive: 'Tropics are no longer what they used to be. The chess player has fossilized.'

36 Eribon, *Conversations*, p. 148.

37 *TVFA*, p. xiii.

38 *TVFA*, p. xiii.

39 *TVFA*, p. xiv.

40 Catherine Clément, 'La bonne distance', *Le Magazine littéraire*, July–August 1983.

41 Clément, 'La bonne distance'.

42 Emmanuel Terray, interview with the author, 15 April 2014.

43 'Pourquoi faudrait-il que tout le monde aime tout le monde?', interview of Claude Lévi-Strauss by Jean-Pierre Salgas, *Jeune Afrique*, 1171, June 1983.

44 'Pourquoi faudrait-il que tout le monde aime tout le monde?', interview of Claude Lévi-Strauss by Jean-Pierre Salgas.

45 Emmanuel Terray, interview with the author, 15 April 2014.

46 Clément, 'La bonne distance'.

47 Claude Lévi-Strauss, 'A belated word about the creative child', in *TVFA*, p. 278.

48 Lévi-Strauss, 'A belated word about the creative child', p. 274.

49 Claude Lévi-Strauss, 'A meditative painter', in *TVFA*, pp. 243–244.

50 Lévi-Strauss, 'A meditative painter', p. 278.

51 Patrice Maniglier, 'La condition symbolique', *Philosophie*, 98, February 2008, p. 49.

52 Claude Lévi-Strauss, 'Reflections on liberty', in *TVFA*, pp. 282–283.

53 Claude Lévi-Strauss, letter to the Brazilian secretary of the interior, 17 February 1982 [original in English]: 'As a scholar who over forty years ago has known the Nambikwara and shared their life, I feel allowed to express a deep concern over their fate and I respectfully urge Brazilian authorities to abide by their decision as published in the Diario Official of 2 December 1981, pp. 22, 807–22.' Claude Lévi-Strauss was alerted to the crisis by a letter from the anthropologist David Price, with whom he was in touch. CLS Archives, NAF 28150, box 199, 'Correspondance reçue'.

54 F. S1.05.02.025, March 1976, LAS Archives.

55 *Le Monde*, 4 April 1986: 'Première intervention de M. Léotard. Les plans-reliefs doivent rester à Paris.'

56 F. S1.06.01.021, LAS Archives.

57 Letter from Pierre Bourdieu to Claude Lévi-Strauss (undated) [1988], sent upon receiving a copy of Eribon's *Conversations*, CLS Archives, NAF 28150, box 184.

58 Pierre Lepape, *Télérama*, 8–14 October 1983.

59 Letter from Pierre Maranda to Claude Lévi-Strauss, 17 October 1982, CLS Archives, NAF 28150, box 196, 'Correspondance reçue'.

60 Claude Lévi-Strauss, letter to Isac Chiva (undated).

61 Eribon, *Conversations*, p. 77.

62 Photographs of the office and its view from on high – taken by Jean Jamin on 4 November 2009, a few days after Claude Lévi-Strauss's death, offering an archive of a space and a viewpoint – were published in 'Fenêtre sur *Files*', *L'Homme*, 193, 2010, pp. 9–16.

63 Françoise Héritier, interview with the author, 18 April 2012.

64 Françoise Héritier, interview with the author, 18 April 2012.

65 See Olivier Nora, 'La visite au grand écrivain', *Lieux de mémoire*, vol. 3, *La Nation*, Paris, Gallimard, 1986, pp. 567–583.

66 Laurent defended his thesis, 'La vigne et la société à Corcelles-les-Arts. Une étude des mécanismes des changements économiques et sociaux dans les campagnes françaises', at the University of Paris X-Nanterre in 1973, under the supervision of Henri Mendras.

67 Inès de La Fressange, letter to Claude Lévi-Strauss, 7 May 1984, CLS Archives, NAF 28150, box 194, 'Correspondance reçue'.

68 Claude Lévi-Strauss, letter to Inès de La Fressange (undated). Letter provided by Inès de La Fressange, to whom I am grateful.

69 Louis-Bernard Robitaille, *Le Salon des immortels: Une académie très française*, Paris, Denoël, 2002.

70 CLS Archives, NAF 28150, box 218, 'Académie française'.

71 Alain Rey, 'Préface', in Robitaille, *Le Salon des immortels*, p. 9.

72 Alain Decaux, quoted in Robitaille, *Le Salon des immortels*, p. 176.

73 'Témoignages sur l'académicien: propos recueillis par Alain Beuve-Méry', *Le Monde*, 5 November 2009.

74 Alain Peyrefitte, letter to Claude Lévi-Strauss, CLS Archives, NAF 28150, box 198, 'Correspondance reçue'.

75 'Témoignages sur l'académicien'. Florence Delay, elected in 2000: 'I hardly knew him. But I still remember a plenary session of the dictionary on the letter "R". I had only recently been elected. It was about the word "rancid". The definition submitted by the dictionary committee was entirely negative. This did not suit Claude Lévi-Strauss. He abandoned his reserve and declared that for fully one half of the world, rancid was an exquisite taste. This definition was thus wrong and expressed a strictly Europe-centric view.'

76 Bertrand Poirot-Delpech, letter to Claude Lévi-Strauss, 16 July 1991.

77 *Journal officiel*, 3 March 1984.

78 The typed manuscript of the declaration is preserved in Claude Lévi-Strauss's archives, CLS Archives, NAF 28150, box 218, 'Académie française'. Eribon, *Conversations*, p. 86.

79 Eribon, *Conversations*, p. 86.

80 Declaration of the Académie française delivered in session, 14 June 1984, CLS Archives, NAF 28150, box 218, 'Académie française'.

81 Georges Dumézil, *Le Nouvel Observateur*, 7–13 September 1983.

82 Historian Hélène Carrère d'Encausse, elected to the Académie in 1990, has been its permanent secretary since 1999.

83 Robitaille, *Le Salon des immortels*, p. 261.

84 Maurice Druon, letter to Claude Lévi-Strauss, 11 September 1984, CLS Archives, NAF 28150, box 187, 'Correspondance reçue'.

85 Monique Lévi-Strauss, interview with the author, 28 October 2011.

86 Claude Lévi-Strauss, letter to Dolorès Vanetti, 16 June 1989.

87 Claude Lévi-Strauss, letter to Dolorès Vanetti, 16 June 1989.

88 Monique Lévi-Strauss, *Cachemires: L'Art et l'histoire des châles en France au XIXe siècle*, Paris, Adam Biro, 1987, republished by La Martinière, 2012.

89 The series Monique Lévi-Strauss directed at Adam Biro is called 'Textures'.

90 Claude Lévi-Strauss, letter to Dolorès Vanetti, 4 January 1982, CLS Archives, NAF 28150, box 182.

91 Several exhibitions were held at the Musée de la Mode et du Costume in Paris in 1982, then at the Musée Historique des Tissus in Lyon in 1983. Each time, Monique Lévi-Strauss served as curator and then supervised the writing and publishing of a catalogue.

92 Claude Lévi-Strauss, letter to Dolorès Vanetti, 16 June 1989.

93 *Caractères*, 14 October 1991, television programme hosted by Bernard Rapp, Antenne 2, aired at midnight.

94 Claude Lévi-Strauss, letter to Jacques Chancel, 16 October 1991, CLS Archives, NAF 28150, box 186.

95 Monique Lévi-Strauss, interview with the author.

96 CLS Archives, NAF 28150, box 183.

97 Hence the title of a *Télérama* article on the book of interviews and the *Océaniques* television programme that aired at the same time, 26 October 1988: 'Le structuralisme se porte légèrement délavé' ['Structuralism is best worn slightly washed-out'].

98 See Daniel Fabre, 'D'Isaac Strauss à Claude Lévi-Strauss', in Philippe Descola (ed.), *Claude Lévi-Strauss, un parcours dans le siècle*, Paris, Odile Jacob, 2012, pp. 287–288, and chapter 19 above.

99 Eribon, *Conversations*, p. 94.

100 Eribon, *Conversations*, p. 93.

101 *TOFM*, 2013.

102 Michaël Ferrier, 'Les écrivains du corail. Ou d'une nouvelle arborescence – possible et souhaitable – dans la réception de la culture japonaise', paper delivered at the conference 'Paris–Tokyo–Paris: the reception of Japanese culture in France since 1945', held at the Maison franco-japonaise in Tokyo, on 6–7 September 2013. See also, by the same author, *La Tentation de la France, La tentation du Japon: Regards croisés*, Arles, Picquier, 2003; and 'Lévi-Strauss et le Japon: regarder, écouter, lire, fragments d'un corps amoureux', paper delivered at the International Forum of Anthropologists held in Tokyo, 16–18 May 2013.

103 Aude Lancelin, 'Lévi-Strauss au Japon', *Le Nouvel Observateur*, 24–30 March 2011, p. 136.

104 Documents relating to the Japan trips are collected in the CLS Archives, NAF 28150, box 231. Lévi-Strauss included many papers documenting his trips, as well as, so to speak, 'gustative' and 'olfactory' information: dinner invitations and menus were systematically preserved. Information concerning the material organization and content of his visits to Japan comes from these archives, except when otherwise indicated.

105 'I do not qualify in the least as an expert on Japanese culture and society and I fear to be pitifully unequal to the task', [written in English] Claude Lévi-Strauss, letter to Keizo Saji, president of the Suntory Foundation, 9 September 1979.

106 Claude Lévi-Strauss, letter to Keizo Saji, 9 September 1979.

107 Emmanuel Lozerand, 'La dilution du sujet japonais chez les intellectuels français au tournant des années 1970', paper delivered at the conference 'Paris–Tokyo–Paris'.

108 Watanabe Yasu, interview with the author, 16 October 2013.

109 Claude Lévi-Strauss, 'The hidden face of the moon', in *TOFM*, pp. 45–46.

110 To take part in the 'Japan Speaks' conference.

111 Lévi-Strauss gave three talks in 1984, as part of the Ishizaka Lectures, which were subsequently published under the title *Anthropology Confronts the Problems of the Modern World*: the first part considers 'The end of the West's cultural supremacy'; the second explores all together 'Three great contemporary problems: sexuality, economic development, and mythic thought'; and the third is attentive to 'What we can learn from Japanese civilization'.

112 Claude Lévi-Strauss, 'An unknown Tokyo', in *TOFM*, p. 132.

113 The fifth trip, organized in March 1988, mostly focused on Kyoto and its environs.

114 The notion relates to two important periods in Japanese history that Lévi-Strauss often drew upon. The first is the Meiji period (from 1868), i.e., Japan's entry into the industrial age through an imperial restauration and not, as in France, through a revolution that led to the destruction of ancient traditions. At a time when the historiography on the French Revolution, with the approach of its bicentennial, was particularly active and divided, the anthropologist offered a very singular perspective on the revolutionary period, which he viewed as a historical catastrophe, emphasizing its radical break from the past and taking revolutionary ambitions too much at face value – in sharp contrast with the historians, who insisted on the weight of tradition and the persistence of the old society within the new. In any case, for Lévi-Strauss, in this respect, Japan had played the modernity card differently, upholding its traditions and habits and customs. The second period is the Tokugawa period of the early seventeenth century, which marked the moment when Japan, in a historic decision without equivalent elsewhere, closed itself off to the rest of the world – and remained so for nearly three centuries, until the Meiji Restoration.

115 *TOFM*, p. 46.

116 *TOFM*, pp. 147–148.

117 Claude Lévi-Strauss, 'An unknown Tokyo', *TOFM*, p. 135.

118 *TOFM*, p. 18.

119 Claude Lévi-Strauss, 'Interview with Junzo Kawada', in *TOFM*, p. 144.

120 M. Ferrier, 'Les écrivains du corail'.

121 Claude Lévi-Strauss, 'Sengai: the art of accommodating oneself to the world', in *TOFM*, p. 106.

122 Elena Janvier has cleverly compiled a list of them in a small book entitled *Au Japon: Ceux qui s'aiment ne disent pas je t'aime*, Paris, Arléa, 2011.

123 Eribon, *Conversations*, p. 88.

124 Claude Lévi-Strauss, 'Herodotus in the China Sea', in *TOFM*, p. 86.

125 Claude Lévi-Strauss, 'The white hare of Inaba', in *TOFM*, p. 71.

126 Lévi-Strauss, 'The white hare of Inaba', p. 72.

127 Junzo Kawada's speech at the book launch for *The Other Face of the Moon*, a debate organized by Maurice Olender at the Maison de l'Amérique latine in Paris, on 17 May 2011.

128 Junzo Kawada's speech at the book launch for *The Other Face of the Moon*.

129 Claude Lévi-Strauss, 'The place of Japanese culture in the world', in *TOFM*, p. 26.

130 Lévi-Strauss, 'The place of Japanese culture in the world', p. 28.

131 *JP*, p. 197.

132 See Maurice Pinguet, 'Le texte Japon (Barthes et le Japon)', in Michaël Ferrier (ed.), *Le Texte-Japon: Introuvables et inédits*, Paris, Seuil, 2009.

133 Lévi-Strauss, 'Sengai: The art of accommodating oneself to the world', p. 93.

134 Françoise Héritier, 'Trois leçons japonaises', *Europe*, 1005–1006, January–February 2013, p. 67.
135 Héritier, 'Trois leçons japonaises', p. 116.
136 Lévi-Strauss, 'The place of Japanese culture in the world', p. 8.
137 See Eribon, *Conversations*, p. 156, and chapter 18 above.
138 See Lévi-Strauss, 'The place of Japanese culture in the world', p. 8.
139 Claude Lévi-Strauss, 'Exode sur *Exode*', *L'Homme*, 106–107, April–September 1988, p. 21.
140 Lévi-Strauss, 'Exode sur *Exode*', pp. 14–15.
141 Fabre, 'D'Isaac Strauss à Claude Lévi-Strauss', p. 290.
142 Alain Erlande-Brandenburg, 'Les collections d'objets de culte juif du musée de Cluny', in *Catalogue raisonné de la collection juive du musée de Cluny*, Paris, Réunion des musées nationaux, 1981.
143 Fabre, 'D'Isaac Strauss à Claude Lévi-Strauss', p. 292.
144 Ambroise Thomas (1811–1896) was a composer renowned for his operas, whom Isaac Strauss probably met at the Paris Conservatoire.
145 Claude Lévi-Strauss, 'Avant-propos', in *Catalogue raisonné de la collection juive du musée de Cluny*, p. 7.
146 Lévi-Strauss, 'Avant-propos', pp. 7–8.
147 Lévi-Strauss, 'Avant-propos', p. 8.
148 Eduardo Viveiros de Castro, 'Rendez-vous manqués', *Europe*, 1005–1006, January–February 2013.
149 Manuela Carneiro da Cunha, quoted in Mathieu Lindon, 'Mission *Tristes Tropiques*', *Libération*, 1 September 1988.
150 Manuela Carneiro da Cunha, interview with the author, August 2011.
151 Viveiros de Castro, 'Rendez-vous manqués', p. 88.
152 Viveiros de Castro, 'Rendez-vous manqués', p. 89.
153 Frédéric Keck, in Claude Lévi-Strauss, *Oeuvres*, 'Bibliothèque de la Pléiade', Paris, Gallimard, 2008, p. 1848.
154 *SoL*, 1995, p. xvii.
155 *SoL*, p. xvii.
156 Interview with Didier Éribon, 'Freud chez les Jivaro', *Le Nouvel Observateur*, 27 September–3 October 1985.
157 *AM*, pp. 109–111.
158 For this paragraph, see the discussion by Marie Mauzé, 'Notice', in Lévi-Strauss, *Oeuvres*, pp. 1866–1873.
159 *JP*, p. 57.
160 See in particular the articles already cited by Jean Petitot, Lucien Scubia and Pierre Maranda, as well as the article by Mauro W. Barbosa de Almeida, 'La formule canonique du mythe', in Ruben C. de Queiros and F. Renarde Nobre, *Lévi-Strauss*, Leituras Brasileiras, Belo Horizonte, editora da Universidade Federal de Minas Gerais, 2008, pp. 147–182.
161 *JP*, p. 123.
162 Letter from Pierre Nora to Claude Lévi-Strauss, 8 October 1985, CLS Archives, NAF 28150, box 197, 'Correspondance reçue'. Quoted in Mauzé, 'Notice', p. 1872.
163 *JP*, p. 185.
164 *JP*, p. 189.
165 *JP*, p. 190.
166 *JP*, p. 190.
167 *JP*, p. 186.
168 *JP*, p. 203.

169 Jacques Meunier, 'Un divertissement de Claude Lévi-Strauss', *Le Monde*, 11 October 1985.

170 Interview with Éribon, 'Freud chez les Jivaro'.

171 Robert Maggiori, 'Claude Lévi-Strauss, la potière, les jaloux et l'oiseau triste', *Libération*, 17 October 1985.

172 Maggiori, 'Claude Lévi-Strauss, la potière, les jaloux et l'oiseau triste'.

173 Maggiori, 'Claude Lévi-Strauss, la potière, les jaloux et l'oiseau triste'.

174 Quoted in Mauzé, 'Notice', p. 1872.

175 Jean Bazin, 'L'enjeu des mythes', *Le Matin*, 8 October 1985.

176 Wendy Doniger O'Flaherty, 'Shrinks and shrunken heads', *The New York Times*, 22 May 1988.

177 Pierre Enckel, 'Loué soit Lévi-Strauss', *L'Événement du jeudi*, 10–16 October 1985.

178 Mauzé, 'Notice', p. 1875.

179 The author himself placed his book, like the previous one, 'halfway between fairy tale and mystery novel', *SoL*, p. xv.

180 This also carries over into many of the narrative details. Indeed, in Amerindian thought, even breasts cannot be identical: in some Brazilian myths, one of the twins was so eager to suckle that he deformed his mother's breast.

181 Mauzé, 'Notice', p. 1875.

182 'Split representation in the art of Asia and America', in *SA*, pp. 245–268.

183 *SoL*, p. 220.

184 See François Hartog, *Anciens, modernes, sauvages*, Paris, Galaade, 2005.

185 In this respect, his interpretation differed from that of Marcel Conche, the distinguished Montaigne scholar, as their correspondence shows. CLS Archives, NAF 28150, box 186.

186 *SoL*, p. 215.

187 *SoL*, p. 215.

188 Montaigne, quoted by Claude Lévi-Strauss, in *SoL*, p. 215.

189 See Keck, in Lévi-Strauss, *Oeuvres*, pp. 1877–1878.

190 'Un entretien avec Claude Lévi-Strauss', interview with Roger Pol Droit, *Le Monde*, 8 October 1991.

191 'Un entretien avec Claude Lévi-Strauss', interview with Roger Pol Droit.

192 *SoL*, p. 217: 'The wise person finds intellectual and moral hygiene in the lucid management of this schizophrenia.'

193 *SoL*, p. 216.

194 See the correspondence between Wiktor Stoczkowski and Claude Lévi-Strauss, CLS Archives, NAF 28150, box 202. Lévi-Strauss resolutely opts for 'wisdom' and rejects the concept of 'salvation', whose Christian connotation is too strong for his own intimate philosophy.

195 *SoL*, p. 217.

196 Didier Éribon, 'Plaidoyer pour le nouveau monde', *Le Nouvel Observateur*, 5–11 September 1991.

197 François Dosse, *History of Structuralism*, vol. 2: *The Sign Sets, 1967–Present*, Minneapolis, University of Minnesota Press, 1997.

198 Roger-Pol Droit, 'Apologie de Claude Lévi-Strauss', *Le Monde des livres*, 6 September 1991.

199 Droit, 'Apologie de Claude Lévi-Strauss'.

200 Droit, 'Apologie de Claude Lévi-Strauss'.

201 Droit, 'Apologie de Claude Lévi-Strauss'.

202 Marc Augé, 'Lévi-Strauss ou la volonté de comprendre', *Le Monde des livres*, 6 September 1991.

203 *Famille chrétienne*, 11 October 1991.
204 Claude Lévi-Strauss, 'Le prix à payer du monothéisme: l'intolérance, l'impérialisme, la vérité unique', *Le Figaro littéraire*, 16 September 1991.
205 Bruno Raccouchot, 'Le miroir des primitifs', *Valeurs actuelles*, 12 November 1991.
206 Alain Finkielkraut, 'Les angoisses d'un anthropologue', *Le Figaro littéraire*, 20 September 1988.
207 Finkielkraut, 'Les angoisses d'un anthropologue'.
208 Just as *Des Symboles et leurs doubles*, Paris, Plon, 1989, a collection of several of the anthropologist's major works, from *Tristes Tropiques* to *The Jealous Potter*, was coming out. His contributions on art formed a noticeable and important part of this collection.
209 On that occasion, Jacques Chirac hosted them all at the Paris city hall.
210 The journey was covered in *Folha do S. Paulo*, 22 October 1989. The regional press also offered regular updates: 'Des Indiens en pirogue sur la Seine', *Le Havre libre*, 28 September 1989; 'Des Indiens Haida sur la Seine. Un homage à Lévi-Strauss', *Le Courrier de Saône-et-Loire*, 3 October 1989. *Libération* dispatched a reporter, Selim Nessib, who wrote 'Les Haidas entrent en Seine', *Libération*, 2 October 1989.
211 Preface to Juan Pablo Luchelli, *Lacan avec et sans Lévi-Strauss*, Nantes, C. Defaut éditions, 2013, p. 15.
212 Philippe Lançon, 'Dis papa, c'est quoi le structuralisme?' *L'Événement du jeudi*, 5–11 September 1991.
213 Keck says much the same in his commentary in Lévi-Strauss, *Oeuvres*, p. 1856: 'Lévi-Strauss returned to his times. [. . .] And it is probably not the least of the many paradoxes of these "minor mythologiques" that just as Lévi-Strauss was expected to have wandered the furthest away from his contemporaries, returning from the world of myths like Lazarus from the dead, he was in fact the most of his times. Hence the success of these books with a public that saw in them far more than the last fragments of 1960s structuralism.'

Chapter 21   Claude Lévi-Strauss, Our Contemporary

1 *SoL*, p. 217.
2 Claude Lévi-Strauss, letter to Olivier Orban, 20 September 2005, CLS Archives, NAF 28150, box 222, 'Édition'.
3 Claude Lévi-Strauss, *Anthropology Confronts the Problems of the Modern World*, Cambridge, MA, Harvard University Press, 2013; *We Are All Cannibals: And Other Essays*, New York, Columbia University Press, 2016.
4 'Le sensible et l'intelligible', an interview with Maurice Olender that aired on Belgium radio in January 1976, and was published in *La Règle du jeu*, 44, October 2010.
5 Martin Rueff, 'Notice', in Claude Lévi-Strauss, *Oeuvres*, 'Bibliothèque de la Pléiade', Paris, Gallimard, 2008, p. 1930.
6 See chapter 2 above.
7 'The cult of objects (of which I am a member from childhood) restores a form of animism in modern society', quoted in André Mary, 'In memoriam Lévi-Strauss (1908–2009)', *Archives de sciences sociales des religions*, October–December 2009: http://assr.revues.org/index21483.html, p. 11.
8 Poussin would make wax models of the characters he represented in his paintings. See *LLR*, pp. 3–38.

9 'Lévi-Strauss chercheur d'art', interview with Didier Éribon, *Le Nouvel Observateur*, 29 April–5 May 1993.

10 For this entire paragraph, see CLS Archives, NAF 28150, box 194, 'Correspondance reçue', letters exchanged with René Leibowitz.

11 The similarities with Jean Clair's views appear for instance in his 1983 book, *Considérations sur l'état des beaux-arts*, Paris, Gallimard, as well as in other of his polemical positions on the status of art, the artistic policies of museums and public policy. See also, in this same register and more recently, *L'Hiver de la culture*, Paris, Flammarion, 2011.

12 See M. Hénaff, *Claude Lévi-Strauss: le passeur de sens*, Paris, Perrin, 2008, ch. 3, 'La pensée de l'œuvre d'art: la question du sens et la crise de la figuration'. See also chapter 14 above.

13 Claude Lévi-Strauss, 'Apropos of a retrospective', *Arts*, 60, 16–22 November 1966, republished in *SA*, vol. 2, p. 277. The text is based on an interview with André Parinaud on the occasion of the opening of the exhibition 'Homage to Picasso' at the Grand Palais and Petit Palais in Paris, November 1966–February 1967.

14 In *LLR*, p. 45, Claude Lévi-Strauss quotes art historian Edgar Wind, who resorted to the same viral metaphor: 'When such large displays of incompatible artists are received with equal interest and appreciation, it is clear that those who visit these exhibitions have a strong immunity to them. Art is so well-received because it has lost its sting [for] a public whose ever-increasing appetite for art is matched by a progressive atrophy of their receptive organs.'

15 Claude Lévi-Strauss, 'Le métier perdu', *Le Débat*, 13, May–June 1981, pp. 5–9.

16 Lévi-Strauss, 'Le métier perdu', p. 9.

17 Lévi-Strauss, 'Le métier perdu', p. 6.

18 Lévi-Strauss, 'Le métier perdu', p. 6.

19 Lévi-Strauss, 'Le métier perdu', p. 8.

20 'La peinture au XIXe siècle et nous', *Le Débat*, 13, May–June 1981, p. 4.

21 Pierre Soulages, 'Le prétendu métier perdu', *Le Débat*, 14, July–August 1981, pp. 77–82.

22 The text was an excerpt of Jean Paulhan's *L'Art informel*, in *Oeuvres complètes*, Paris, Gallimard, vol. 5, pp. 244–245.

23 *Le Débat*, 15, September–October 1981.

24 Pierre Daix, 'Sur la peinture moderne', *Le Débat*, 14, July–August 1981, p. 87: 'The idea of the decline of art since it abandoned the rules of the Renaissance is not new. For the past fifty years, it has been put to good use by the legislators of socialist realism, for whom, after Courbet, it was all degenerate "bourgeois art".'

25 Letter from Claude Lévi-Strauss to Anita Albus, 9 January 1979, correspondence held at Monique Lévi-Strauss's home.

26 Letter from Claude Lévi-Strauss to Anita Albus, 9 January 1979.

27 Letter from Claude Lévi-Strauss to Anita Albus, 5 November 1978.

28 Letter from Claude Lévi-Strauss to Anita Albus, 5 November 1978.

29 Letter from Claude Lévi-Strauss to Anita Albus, 5 November 1978.

30 Anita Albus, interview with the author, 4 February 2011.

31 Letter of 9 January 1979.

32 Text republished in *TVFA*, pp. 248–257.

33 Text republished in *TVFA*, p. 252.

34 Text republished in *TVFA*, p. 257.

35 Indeed, he fought tooth and nail for her, as is made clear in this letter of 26 October 1980 to Barbara Müller, who had just sent him a catalogue of modern artists showing at her gallery – an occasion to cross swords and reaffirm with particular vehemence (due to his impatience for the arrogance of contemporary art) his convictions in this regard: 'The point is not at all, as you seem to believe, to defend an "easy" form of art. In the end, my experience as an anthropologist has constantly confronted me with art forms that were most remote from our own, and it has been my role to try to understand them and make their beauty clear to others. Emerging from childhood, I was a passionate admirer of the Cubists – who were at the time deemed "difficult". Later, I became connected with the Surrealists; I was friends with Marcel Duchamp, André Masson and Max Ernst, all artists who were also considered difficult in their day . . . This long familiarity with the so-called avant-garde in the art of the interwar period allows me, as many other people in France, and especially artists of the younger generation, to see that the avant-garde dimension of the works illustrated in your catalogues is completely obsolete. You disdainfully place Anita Arbus among the "artisans" and not the "artists". But it is precisely this distinction that must be abolished. The old masters of the late Middle Ages and early Renaissance considered themselves to be artisans – hence their greatness. It is only once we have learned to paint again by returning to their school that it will be legitimate to start looking for new modes of expression.' CLS Archives, NAF 28150, box 196.
36 Text written for the 'Murs et Fibres' exhibition by Sheila Hicks at Galérie Suzy Langlois in Paris, 1969.
37 Rueff, 'Notice', p. 1917.
38 Expression used by Claude Lévi-Strauss in his interview with Didier Éribon, *Le Nouvel Observateur*, 29 April–5 May 1993.
39 John Jackson, 'Le jardin secret de Lévi-Strauss', *Le Journal de Genève*, 14 August 1993.
40 Pierre Mayol, *Esprit*, February 1994.
41 Xavier Lacavalerie, 'La ballade d'un explorateur', *Télérama*, 14 July 1993.
42 Éribon, 'Lévi-Strauss chercheur d'art', p. 106.
43 The first emanated from the young Lévi-Strauss: 'A commentary on the relations between works of art and documents, written and delivered to André Breton on board the *Capitaine Paul-Lemerle* in March 1941'; the other is 'The Response of André Breton'. The two together comprise chapter 20 of *LLR*, pp. 143–151.
44 Antoine de Gaudemar, 'Son musée', *Libération*, special issue, March 1994.
45 *LLR*, p. 185.
46 *LLR*, p. 185.
47 *LLR*, pp. 84–85.
48 Paul Guy de Chabanon (1730–1792), a French writer and musicologist who had fallen into oblivion and to whose rediscovery Lévi-Strauss contributed.
49 Rueff, 'Notice', p. 1918.
50 Rueff, 'Notice', p. 1919.
51 Rueff, 'Notice', p. 1932.
52 *LLR*, p. 45.
53 Patrice Bollon, 'Entretien avec Claude Lévi-Strauss', *Paris-Match*, 20 May 1993.
54 'We do not condemn to death (or not to a physical death, perhaps an economic or social death) artists whom we deem devoid of talent because they do not take us beyond ourselves. [. . .] Formerly one spoke of the '"divine" Raphael,

and in its aesthetic vocabulary, the English language contains the expression "out of this world",' *LLR*, p. 182.

55 A sizeable bibliography already exists on the subject, i.e., both on the Musée du Quai Branly and on the issues and changes of which it was a symptom: Sally Price, *Paris Primitive: Jacques Chirac's Museum on the Quai Branly*, Chicago, The University of Chicago Press, 2006; Benoît de l'Estoile, *Le Goût des autres: De l'exposition coloniale aux arts premiers*, Paris, Flammarion, 2007; Bruno Latour (ed.), *Le Dialogue des cultures: Actes des Rencontres inaugurales du Quai Branly (21 June 2006)*, Paris, Actes Sud, 2007; 'Le moment du Quai Branly', *Le Débat*, 147 (special issue), November–December 2007; Herman Lebovics, 'The Musée du Quai Branly: Art? Artefact? Spectacle!' *French Politics, Culture and Society*, 24(3), winter 2006, pp. 96–110.

56 Including Louis Dumont, who expressed his views in *Le Monde* on 25 October 1996, in 'Non au musée des Arts premiers': 'The most famous of anthropologists, and honorary president of the committee, approves of the project, and judging from the passage of his letter that was published in *Le Monde*, he is doing away once and for all with anthropology, both as regards the exhibition and conservation of objects as well as research and public relations more generally.' This position was shared by the ethnomusicologist Gilbert Rouget, a friend of Lévi-Strauss's, whom the latter failed to win over to his side.

57 Philippe Descola, 'Passages de témoins', *Le Débat*, 147, November–December 2007, p. 137.

58 As director of the Musée de l'Homme Bernard Dupaigne himself recognized in 'Un musée qui n'existe pas. Le musée de l'Homme (1880–200?)', *Tribune libre: Revue des musées et collections publiques de France*, 218, March 1998, p. 3.

59 The Musée de l'Homme was financed through 5.5 million francs from its own budget and 500,000 in subsidies (from the ministry of education), with 350,000 visitors in 1985 and 175,000 in 1995.

60 CLS Archives, NAF 28150, box 219.

61 Letter (confidential) from Claude Lévi-Strauss to Germain Viatte, 2 October 1997.

62 Handwritten note, CLS Archives, NAF 28150, box 197, 'Arts premiers'.

63 Jean Jamin, interview with the author, 6 July 2011.

64 Descola, 'Passages de témoins', p. 138.

65 Descola, 'Passages de témoins', p. 144.

66 Claude Lévi-Strauss, interview with Véronique Mortaigne, *Le Monde*, 22 February 2005.

67 See chapter 1 above and Daniel Fabre, 'D'Isaac Strauss à Claude Lévi-Strauss', in Philippe Descola (ed.), *Claude Lévi-Strauss, un parcours dans le siècle*, Paris, Odile Jacob, 2012.

68 The British Empire and Commonwealth Museum in Bristol, for instance, acknowledged its colonial heritage in its name, according to de l'Estoile in *Le Goût des autres*, p. 398.

69 See Carmen Bernand, 'Aimer Branly?' in 'Le moment du Quai Branly', pp. 165–168.

70 Or else very simply to reclaim lost traditions, as Philippe Descola points out in *La Composition des mondes: Entretiens avec Pierre Charbonnier*, Paris, Flammarion, 2014, p. 333: The Spanish-speaking young Achuars (Jivaro group) read the Spanish translation of his dissertation, 'La nature domestique' [*Antropologia de la naturaleza*, Lima, Peru, IFEA, Lluvia Editores, 2003], to recover some of the skills and knowledge that were then used in the guided tours they gave at a touristic resort from which they received royalties.

Strikingly, Descola uses the same expression as Lévi-Strauss: 'It is thus a rather paradoxical twist, but one which reflects a very widespread process of knowledge circulation between anthropologists and the peoples they have described.'

71 See *We Are All Cannibals and Other Essays*. In fact, among the articles published in 2013, three were already familiar to French readers, since they had appeared in 2004 in the 'Cahier de l'Herne' issue on Lévi-Strauss: 'We are all cannibals' (1993), 'The return of the maternal uncle' (1997) and 'Mythic thought and scientific thought' (1993).

72 *Anthropology Confronts the Problems of the Modern World*, Cambridge, MA, Harvard University Press, 2011.

73 Maurice Godelier, *Lévi-Strauss*, Paris, Seuil, 2013, p. 26.

74 'The return of the maternal uncle', in *WAAC*, p. 122.

75 'The return of the maternal uncle', p. 125.

76 See also Françoise Héritier, 'La cuisse de Jupiter. Réflexions sur les nouveaux modes de procréation', *L'Homme*, 94, April–June 1985, pp. 5–22.

77 'Social problems: ritual female excision and medically assisted reproduction', in *WAAC*, p. 38.

78 'Social problems', p. 42.

79 'Social problems', p. 42.

80 Letter from Claude Lévi-Strauss to Éric Fassin, published in Cristina Ferreira, Daniel Borillo, Éric Fassin and Marcella Iacub (eds.), *Au-delà du Pacs: L'Expertise familiale à l'épreuve de l'homosexualité*, Paris, PUF, 1999, p. 110.

81 E. Fassin, 'La voix de l'expertise et les silences de la science dans le débat démocratique', in Ferreira, Borillo, Fassin and Iacub (eds.), *Au-delà du Pacs*, p. 96.

82 Irène Théry, *Le Contrat d'union sociale en question: Rapport pour la Fondation Saint-Simon*, October 1997.

83 Article published in *La Croix*, November 1998, in which Françoise Héritier, among others, sided against Pacs. Héritier also signed the petition 'Ne laissons pas la critique du Pacs à la droite!' ['Let's not leave the critique of Pacs to the right!'], *Le Monde*, 27 January 1999. For the role of anthropology, among other social sciences, in the debate around the family in France, see Camille Robcis, *The Law of Kinship: Anthropology, Psychoanalysis and the Family in France*, Ithaca, Cornell University Press, 2013.

84 The expression is Éric Fassin's, in 'La voix de l'expertise et les silences de la science dans le débat démocratique'.

85 Claude Lévi-Strauss, 'We are all cannibals', in *WAAC*, p. 86.

86 Bruno Latour, *We Have Never Been Modern*, Cambridge, MA, Harvard University Press, 1993.

87 'A lesson in wisdom from mad cows', in *WAAC*, p. 114. Article originally published in *La Repubblica*, 24 November 1996.

88 'We are all cannibals', p. 88. Article originally published in *La Repubblica*, 10 October 1993.

89 'We are all cannibals', p. 88.

90 'We are all cannibals', p. 88.

91 *WAAC*, p. 114.

92 Monique Lévi-Strauss, interview with the author, 26 October 2014.

93 *WAAC*, p. 118.

94 'Social problems: ritual female excision and medically assisted reproduction', in *WAAC*, p. 43.

95 The Australian couple only took his healthy twin sister. The entire national and international press covered the case. See 'L'Australie s'émeut du sort d'un enfant trisomique laissé à sa mère porteuse', *Le Monde*, 3 August 2014.
96 Claude Lévi-Strauss, 'Three great contemporary problems: sexuality, economic development, and mythic thought', in *ACPMW*, p. 48.
97 *WAAC*, p. 44.
98 *WAAC*, p. 44.
99 *ACPMW*, p. 55.
100 *WAAC*, p. 45.
101 *WAAC*, p. 46.
102 *WAAC*, p. 47.
103 Jeanne Favret-Saada, 'La pensée Lévi-Strauss', *Journal des anthropologues*, 82–83, 2000.
104 'The Family', *TVFA*, pp. 39–62. The original text was written in English for Harry L. Shapiro (ed.), *Man, Culture and Society*, New York, Oxford University Press, 1956, pp. 261–285.
105 *TVFA*, p. 44.
106 *ACPMW*, p. 65ff.
107 *WAAC*, p. 36.
108 Jared Diamond, *The World Until Yesterday: What We Can Learn from Traditional Societies*, New York, Viking, 2012.
109 *ACPMW*, p. 61.
110 *ACPMW*, p. 78.
111 Patrice Maniglier, 'La condition symbolique', *Philosophie*, 98, February 2008, p. 38.
112 Patrice Maniglier (ed.), *Le Moment philosophique des années 1960 en France*, Paris, PUF, 2011.
113 This is the focus of Maniglier's article, 'La condition symbolique'.
114 Maniglier, 'La condition symbolique', p. 48.
115 *NM*, p. 694, quoted in Maniglier, 'La condition symbolique', p. 48.
116 See chapter 20 above.
117 Maniglier, 'La condition symbolique', p. 50.
118 Maniglier, 'La condition symbolique', p. 50.
119 Montaigne, *The Complete Essays*, Stanford, Stanford University Press, 1958, book 1, ch. 20.
120 Monique Lévi-Strauss has recently said on a radio programme that her husband was reluctant. Convinced he had to do it, she pushed him: 'No captions, no dinner!' I am recounting this episode for the sake of the anecdote, as well as to show what historians sometimes resort to as sources . . .
121 Matthieu Lévi-Strauss, interview with the author, 9 March 2015.
122 An English edition, entitled *Saudades Do Brasil: A Photographic Memoir*, was published by the University of Washington Press in 1995.
123 Emmanuel Desveaux, *Au-delà du structuralisme. Six méditations sur Claude Lévi-Strauss*, Brussels, Éditions Complexe, 2008, p. 63.
124 Desveaux, *Au-delà du structuralisme*, p. 70.
125 Desveaux, *Au-delà du structuralisme*, p. 70.
126 Claude Lévi-Strauss, 'L'ethnologue devant les identités nationales', speech delivered at the Catalunya Prize award ceremony, 13 May 2005, CLS Archives, NAF 28150, box 220.
127 Letter from Claude Lévi-Strauss to Isac Chiva, 31 December 1999.
128 Monique Lévi-Strauss, interview with the author, 26 November 2014.
129 Letter to Isac Chiva, 2 January 1997.

130 Letter to Umberto Eco, 10 October 1996, CLS Archives, NAF 28150, box 189. Eco had asked Lévi-Strauss to accept an honorary doctorate from the University of Bologna.

131 Lévi-Strauss had turned down several offers of a presidential visit since he had not received the request from the president himself, but had only been contacted by advisers. In the end, Nicolas Sarkozy personally notified him of his visit. He was briefly received, but not without having the entire neighbourhood cordoned off. Interview with Monique Lévi-Strauss, 26 November 2014.

132 'Claude Lévi-Strauss', *Critique*, 620–621, January–February 1999.

133 Text published in *Le Monde des livres*, 29 January 1999, based on the recollections of Roger-Pol Droit, who had attended the ceremony. Indeed, as the journalist explained, 'there were no cameras or microphones. Nobody recorded these words.'

134 Jean Jamin, 'Fenêtre sur *Files*', *L'Homme*, 193, 2010, p. 9. 'I am surviving myself', he confessed to his secretary, Eva Kempinski.

135 Matthieu Lévi-Strauss, 9 March 2015: 'He had told me he hoped it would rain and that we would wear rubber boots (i.e., that it would be as informal as possible . . .). He had been so bored at all the funerals he had had to attend that he did not want to impose that on anyone. This was his argument.'

136 *TT*, p. 414.

137 Georges Duby, *William Marshal: The Flower of Chivalry*, New York, Pantheon Books, 1986, ch. 1.

138 Front page of *Libération*, 4 November 2009.

139 *Le Figaro* editorial, 4 November 2009.

140 Fernand Braudel, *The Mediterranean and the Mediterranean World in the Age of Philip II*, Berkeley, University of California Press, 1995, vol. 2, pp. 1234–1235: 'In this account of events on the Mediterranean stage, we have not mentioned in its proper place one piece of news which quickly travelled to every corner of the world: the death of Philip II of Spain, which occurred on 13th September, 1598 at the Escorial, at the end of a long reign that to his adversaries had seemed interminable. Is this a serious omission?'

141 Mary, 'In Memoriam Lévi-Strauss (1908–2009)', p. 9.

142 Letter from Claude Lévi-Strauss to Isac Chiva '10 July' [probably 2006].

143 *SM*, p. 238. I am grateful to Yann Potin for pointing out this passage.

144 *SM*, p. 242.

145 Yann Potin, 'L'historien en "ses" archives', in Christophe Granger (ed.), *À quoi pensent les historiens? Faire de l'histoire au XXIe siècle*, Paris, Autrement, 2013, pp. 101–117.

146 Letter from Antoine Gallimard to Claude Lévi-Strauss, 22 September 2004, CLS Archives, NAF 28150, box 191, 'Correspondance reçue'.

147 Claude Lévi-Strauss, *Race et histoire* and *Race et culture*, Paris, Albin Michel/UNESCO, 2001.

148 See Marie Mauzé, 'Le moment Lévi-Strauss de la Pléiade', *La Lettre du Collège de France*, November 2008; 'Non fiction, actualité des idées', 'Une grande œuvre pour comprendre le millénaire qui s'ouvre à la lumière des millénaires qui le precèdent', interview with Vincent Debaene and Frédéric Keck, remarks collected by E. Loyer and J.-C. Monod, 5 and 12 May 2008.

149 Eduardo Viveiros de Castro, 'Notes critiques', *Gradhiva*, 8, 2008, p. 131.

150 See Vincent Debaene, 'Claude Lévi-Strauss aujourd'hui', *Europe*, 1005–1006, January–February 2013, pp. 11–36; Boris Wiseman (ed.), *The Cambridge Companion to Lévi-Strauss*, Cambridge, Cambridge University Press, 2009.

151 Bernard Mezzadri, 'Claude Lévi-Strauss a encore son mot à dire', *Europe*, 1005–1006, January–February 2013, p. 3.
152 With a conference held on 28 November 2008 at the Collège de France, whose proceedings were published a few years later: Descola (ed.), *Claude Lévi-Strauss*.
153 Mezzadri, 'Claude Lévi-Strauss a encore son mot à dire', p. 3.
154 Emmanuel Desveaux, 'Claude Lévi-Strauss, œuvres', *L'Homme*, 190, 2009, p. 200.
155 Desveaux, 'Claude Lévi-Strauss, œuvres'.
156 Viveiros de Castro, 'Notes critiques', p. 130.
157 Viveiros de Castro, 'Notes critiques', p. 130.
158 Viveiros de Castro, 'Notes critiques', p. 130.
159 Roland Barthes, 'Plaisir aux classiques', in Claude Lévi-Strauss, *Oeuvres*, 'Bibliothèque de la Pléiade', Paris, Gallimard, 2008, pp. 59–61; quoted by Vincent Debaene in his preface in which he develops at length the use of the notion of a classic to describe Lévi-Strauss in particular, pp. 32–38.
160 Barthes, 'Plaisir aux classiques'. Debaene speaks of an 'availability indifferent to history', in his 'Preface', in Lévi-Strauss, *Oeuvres*, p. 33.
161 I have borrowed the phrase 'the Lévi-Strauss to come' from Klaus Hamberger, who speaks of a 'philosophy to come' in 'La pensée objective', in M. Izard (ed.), *Claude Lévi-Strauss*, Paris, L'Herne, 'Cahiers de l'Herne', 2004, pp. 339–346.
162 Debaene, 'Claude Lévi-Strauss aujourd'hui', p. 20.
163 Debaene, 'Claude Lévi-Strauss aujourd'hui', p. 15.
164 Lévi-Strauss, 'Postface', 'Question de parenté', *L'Homme*, 154–155, April–September 2000, p. 717.
165 Claude Lévi-Strauss, 'Retours en arrière', *Les Temps modernes*, March–April 1998, pp. 66–77.
166 Claude Lévi-Strauss, 'Quell intenso profumo di donna', *La Repubblica*, 3 November 1995, republished in English in *WAAC*, p. 109.
167 Claude Lévi-Strauss, 'Apologue des amibes', in *En substances: Textes pour Françoise Héritier*, Paris, Fayard, 2000, pp. 493–496.
168 Alban Bensa sought instead a 'low conceptualization' for the human sciences. He offers an account of the critical distance he took from structural anthropology in *Après Lévi-Strauss, pour une anthropologie à taille humaine. Entretiens avec Bertrand Richard*, Paris, Textuel, 2010.
169 As in the case, for example, of Michel Naepels, in his programmatic works *Conjurer la guerre. Violence et pouvoir à Houaïkou*, Paris, Éditions de l'EHESS, 2013; and *Ethnographie, pragmatique, histoire*, Paris, Publications de la Sorbonne, 2011.
170 Bruno Karsenty, *D'une philosophie à l'autre: Les sciences sociales et la politique des modernes*, Paris, Gallimard, 2013, p. 16.
171 'Anthropologie structurale et philosophie: Lévi-Strauss', *Archives de philosophie*, LXVI, January 2003.
172 'Claude Lévi-Strauss: une anthropologie "bonne à penser"', *Esprit*, 301, January 2004.
173 'Claude Lévi-Strauss: langage, signes, symbolisme, nature', *Philosophie*, 98, February 2008.
174 Letter from Marcel Hénaff to Claude Lévi-Strauss, 24 August 2003, CLS Archives, NAF 28150, box 192, 'Correspondance reçue'.
175 Patrice Maniglier, interview with the author, 17 December 2014.
176 See Maniglier, 'L'humanisme interminable de Claude Lévi-Strauss', *Les Temps modernes*, 609, June–July–August 2000, and 'De Mauss à Claude

Lévi-Strauss, 50 ans après: pour une ontologie maori', in E. Bimbenet and E. de Saint-Aubert (eds.), *Archives de philosophie*, LXIX(1), spring 2006.

177 Michaël Foessel, 'Du symbolique au sensible: remarques en marge du débat Lévi-Strauss/Ricœur', and 'Claude Lévi-Strauss, une anthropologie "bonne à penser"', *Esprit*, January 2004, p. 204.

178 Jocelyn Benoist, 'Structures, causes et raisons: sur le pouvoir causal de la structure', *Archives de philosophie*, LXVI, January 2003, p. 86.

179 Claude Lévi-Strauss, 'Lévi-Strauss en 33 mots', remarks collected by Dominique-Antoine Grisoni, *Le Magazine littéraire*, 233, October 1985.

180 Claude Lévi-Strauss, 'Le regard du philosophe', *Le Magazine littéraire*, October 1985, p. 59.

181 Lévi-Strauss, 'Le regard du philosophe', p. 59.

182 Lévi-Strauss, 'Postface', 'Question de parenté'.

183 Viveiros de Castro, 'Notes critiques', p. 130.

184 Philippe Descola and Anne-Christine Taylor, 'Introduction', in 'La remontée de l'Amazone', *L'Homme*, 22(126–128), 1993, pp. 13–24.

185 Lévi-Strauss, 'Un autre regard', *L'Homme*, 22(126–128), 1993, p. 7.

186 See Eduardo Viveiros de Castro, *Cannibal Metaphysics: For a Post-Structural Anthropology*, Minneapolis, Univocal, 2014; Manuela Carneiro da Cunha (with Mauro Almeida), *A Enciclopedia da Floresta: o Alto Jurua. Praticas e Conhecimentos das Populaçoes*, São Paulo, Companhia das Letras, 2002.

187 Philippe Descola, *Beyond Nature and Culture*, with a foreword by Marshall Sahlins, Chicago, The University of Chicago Press, 2013. See also Philippe Descola, *La Composition des mondes: Entretiens avec Pierre Charbonnier*, Paris, Flammarion, 2014; and, finally, 'Sur Lévi-Strauss, le structuralisme et l'anthropologie de la nature', interview with Marcel Hénaff, *Philosophie*, 2008, pp. 8–36.

188 Lévi-Strauss was of course aware of these works, about which he was delighted, as he told Didier Éribon in an interview, 'Visite à Lévi-Strauss', *Le Nouvel Observateur*, 10–16 October 2002: 'This is where a classical form of anthropology seems to have persisted, albeit with very significant novelties, but it also represents a theoretical reflection on a grand scale.'

189 See Anne-Christine Taylor, 'Don Quichotte en Amérique: Claude Lévi-Strauss et l'anthropologie américaniste', in M. Izard (ed.), *Claude Lévi-Strauss*, Paris, L'Herne, 'Cahiers de l'Herne', 2004.

190 Claude Lévi-Strauss, 'Réponses à quelques questions', *Esprit*, November 1963, pp. 631–632.

191 Viveiros de Castro, *Cannibal Metaphysics*, p. 93.

192 Debaene, 'Claude Lévi-Strauss aujourd'hui', p. 29.

193 Viveiros de Castro, 'Notes critiques', p. 131.

194 Anne-Christine Taylor, interview with the author, 2 May 2014.

195 See Jan Kott, *Shakespeare Our Contemporary* [1962], New York, W.W. Norton, 1974.

196 Georgio Agamben, 'What is the contemporary?' in *What Is an Apparatus, and Other Essays*, Stanford, Stanford University Press, 2009.

197 Agamben, 'What is the contemporary?', p. 45.

198 Agamben, 'What is the contemporary?', p. 50.

199 See Michel Lussault, *L'Avènement du monde: Essai sur l'habitation humaine de la terre*, Paris, Seuil, 2014.

200 See Giambattista Vico, *New Science: Principles of the New Science Concerning the Common Nature of Nations* [1744], New York, London, Penguin Books,

1999; and Alain Pons, *Vie et mort des nations: Lecture de la Science nouvelle de Giambattista Vico*, Paris, Gallimard, 2015.
201 When it came to knowledge, Lévi-Strauss became more and more convinced of this. In a letter to Isac Chiva on 2 October 1997, he wrote: 'If we took the trouble to deepen our knowledge of our great predecessors, we would no longer write much. For all we do is rediscover what they have said before.'
202 Claude Lévi-Strauss, 'UNESCO at 60', *Diogenes*, 215, August 2007, p. 9.
203 Eribon, *Conversations*, p. 125.

Works by Lévi-Strauss

'Chers tous deux.' Lettres à ses parents, 1931–1942, Paris, Seuil, 2015.

Anthropology and Myth: Lectures 1951–1982, Oxford, Blackwell, 1987.

Anthropology Confronts the Problems of the Modern World, Cambridge, MA, Belknap Press, 2013.

Conversations with Lévi-Strauss, ed. Didier Éribon, Chicago, The University of Chicago Press, 1991.

Des Symboles et leurs doubles, Paris, Plon, 1989.

Entretiens avec Claude Lévi-Strauss, with Georges Charbonnier, Paris, Plon, 2010 [1961].

Introduction to the Work of Marcel Mauss, London, Routledge, 1987.

Look, Listen, Read, New York, Basic Books, 1997.

Mythologiques 1: The Raw and the Cooked, Chicago, The University of Chicago Press, 1983 [1969].

Mythologiques 2: From Honey to Ashes, Chicago, The University of Chicago Press, 1973.

Mythologiques 3: The Origin of Table Manners, Chicago, The University of Chicago Press, 1978.

Mythologiques 4: The Naked Man, Chicago, The University of Chicago Press, 1981.

Oeuvres, 'Bibliotèque de la Pléiade', Paris, Gallimard, 2008.

Race and History, Paris, UNESCO, 1952.

Saudades do Brasil, Paris, Plon, 2009 [1994].

Story of Lynx, Chicago, The University of Chicago Press, 1995.

Structural Anthropology, vol. 1, New York, Basic Books, 1974.

Structural Anthropology, vol. 2, Chicago, The University of Chicago Press, 1976.

The Elementary Structures of Kinship, Boston, Beacon, 1969.

The Jealous Potter, Chicago, The University of Chicago Press, 1988.

The Other Face of the Moon, Cambridge, MA, Belknap Press, 2013.

The Savage Mind, Chicago, The University of Chicago Press, 1966.

The View from Afar, New York, Basic Books, 1985.

Totemism, Boston, Beacon Press, 1963.

Tristes Tropiques, New York, Atheneum, 1974.

Way of the Masks, Seattle, University of Washington Press, 1982.

We Are All Cannibals, New York, Columbia University Press, 2013.

Archives Consulted

The two principal archives consulted are indicated in the notes using the following abbreviations:

CLS Archives: Claude Lévi-Strauss Archives, NAF 28150, Département des Manuscrits, Bibliothèque National de France.

FLAS: Laboratory of Social Anthropology Archives, Collège de France.

Other archives:

In Brazil

Arquivo Conselho de Fiscalização das Expedições artísticas e cientificas no Brasil, Museu de Astronomia e Ciências (MAST), Ministério de Ciências e da Tecnologia, Rio de Janeiro.

Laboratório de Imagem e Som em Antropologia, LISA, Universidade de São Paulo, São Paulo.

Arquivo Mário de Andrade, Instituo de Estudos Brasileiros, Universidade de São Paulo, São Paulo.

Casa Heloisa Alberto Torres, Itaboraí, Rio de Janeiro.

In the United States

Rockefeller Foundation Archives, 'Intellectual Refugees', individual files, 1940–45, R.G.1.1., series 200.

New School for Social Research Archives, New York.

Jacques Maritain Papers, Jacques Maritain Center, Notre Dame University, South Bend, Indiana.

Varian Fry Papers, Butler Library Rare Books and Manuscripts, Columbia University, New York.

In France

Archives de l'Institut national de l'audiovisuel (Fonds Télévisuel), Paris.

Archives diplomatiques du ministère des affaires étrangères (AMAE), Relations culturelles, 1945–70, Service des Oeuvres françaises à l'étranger (US).

Archives du Collège de France, AP IV, comptes rendus d'assemblées de professeurs, 1949–50.

Bibliothèque scientifique de Claude Lévi-Strauss, Musée du Quai Branly, Paris.

Fonds André-Breton, Bibliothèque Jacques-Doucet, Paris.

Fonds Raymond-Aron, NAF 28 143, Département des manuscrits, Bibliothèque nationale de France.

Fonds Maurice-Deixonne, archives de l'Office universitaire de recherche socialiste, Paris.

Fonds Paul-Rivet, Bibliothèque centrale du muséum d'Histoire naturelle, Paris.

Fonds Henri-Piéron, Bibliothèque Henri-Piéron, Université Paris V-Descartes.

Abbreviations of Works by Lévi-Strauss

AM	*Anthropology and Myth: Lectures 1951–1982*, Oxford, Blackwell, 1987.
ACPMW	*Anthropology Confronts the Problems of the Modern World*, Cambridge, Belknap Press, 2013.
LLR	*Look, Listen, Read*, New York, Basic Books, 1997.
RC	*Mythologiques 1: The Raw and the Cooked*, Chicago, The University of Chicago Press [1969] 1983.
HA	*Mythologiques 2: From Honey to Ashes*, Chicago, The University of Chicago Press, 1973.
OTM	*Mythologiques 3: The Origin of Table Manners*, Chicago, The University of Chicago Press, 1978.
NM	*Mythologiques 4: The Naked Man*, Chicago, The University of Chicago Press, 1981.
RH	*Race and History*, Paris, UNESCO, 1952.
SoL	*Story of Lynx*, Chicago, The University of Chicago Press, 1995.
SA	*Structural Anthropology*, 2 vols., New York, Basic Books, 1974, 1976.
ESK	*The Elementary Structures of Kinship*, Boston, Beacon, 1969.
JP	*The Jealous Potter*, Chicago, The University of Chicago Press, 1988.
TOFM	*The Other Face of the Moon*, Cambridge, MA, Belknap Press, 2013.
SM	*The Savage Mind*, Chicago, The University of Chicago Press, 1966.
TVFA	*The View from Afar*, New York, Basic Books, 1985.
TT	*Tristes Tropiques*, New York, Atheneum, 1974.
WoM	*Way of the Masks*, Seattle, University of Washington Press, 1982.
WAAC	*We Are All Cannibals*, New York, Columbia University Press, 2013.

Illustration Credits

Illustrations in text

p. 154   The 'Picadia': a trail in the *sertão*: © BNF.
p. 155   The *sertão* in the dry season (Mato Grosso): © BNF.
p. 160   The port of Corumbá: setting off for Cuiabá by steamship on Rio Paraguay: © BNF.
p. 161   Cuiabá: 'capital' of Mato Grosso. Departure of the 'Serra do Norte' expedition (June 1938): © BNF.
p. 175   Drawing by Claude Lévi-Strauss after Emydio's accident: © BNF.
p. 199   The ship *Capitaine Paul Lemerle*: © All rights reserved.
pp. 208–9 The false Luce-Saunier identity papers: © BNF.
p. 220   The VVV review: Max Ernst © ADAGP, Paris, 2015.
p. 221   Cover of a book by André Breton with photomontage by Marcel Duchamp: © Succession Marcel Duchamp/ADAGP, Paris 2015; photo © Bridgeman Images.
p. 225   Brochure for the École libre des hautes études (ELHE): © BNF.
p. 247   The structuralist afterthought: © BNF.
p. 279   Poster for the Loubat Lectures: © BNF.
p. 292   Cover of the Drouot catalogue for the sale of 21 June 1951, 'Collection Claude Lévi-Strauss. Objets de haute curiosité': © Commissaire priseur: Maître Rheims.
p. 325   First page of the manuscript from *Tristes Tropiques*: © BNF.
p. 326   Claude Lévi-Strauss's typewriter: © BNF.
p. 333   The original cover of *Tristes Tropiques*: © Plon, 1955.
p. 389   Cover of the first issue of *L'Homme*: © All rights reserved.
p. 411   The Claude Lévi-Strauss seminar and the convivial gathering after Lévi-Strauss's final lecture at the Collège de France in 1982: © BNF/Jean-Pierre Martin/Collège de France.
p. 451   'The structuralist banquet', caricature by Maurice Henry, published in *La Quinzaine littéraire*, 1 June 1967: Maurice Henry Archives/IMEC © ADAGP, Paris, 2015.
p. 507   Cover of *The Way of the Masks*, republished by Plon in 1979: © Plon, 1979.
p. 540   'Japan Speaks, 1980': © BNF.
p. 547   Claude Lévi-Strauss with Shimon Peres in Jerusalem: © BNF/*Mishkenot Sha'ananim Newsletter*/Asher Weill.
p. 561   Google homepage: © Google Inc.
p. 562   Preliminary sketch by Claude Lévi-Strauss of the set for *L'Heure espagnole*: © BNF.
p. 584   Claude Lévi-Strauss's Leica camera: © BNF.

Plate section credits

I.   Childhood
      All images © BNF, except Claude Lévi-Strauss riding his mechanical horse: Monique Lévi-Strauss Collection; Photo Astrid di Crollalanza © Flammarion.

II.   The young man
          Oil on canvas, by Raymond Lévi-Strauss depicting his son Claude
          in 1913: Monique Lévi-Strauss Collection; Photo Astrid di
          Crollalanza © Flammarion.
          Portrait of Claude Lévi-Strauss as a young man: © BNF.
          The house at Camcabra: © BNF.
          Oil on canvas, by Raymond Lévi-Strauss depicting his wife Emma:
          Monique Lévi-Strauss Collection; Photo Astrid di Crollalanza
          © Flammarion.
          Photograph of the 158th Infantry Unit in December 1931: Monique
          Lévi-Strauss Collection.

III.   The Brazilian years (1935–39)
          All images © BNF, except photograph taken in the garden of
          the National Museum of Rio de Janeiro: © Luiz de Castro Faria
          Archive, MAST/MCFI, Rio de Janeiro, Brazil.

IV.   Two riders in the forest
          First foray outside Sao Paulo: © BNF.

V.   In the heart of the tropics
          All images: © BNF.

VI.   First expedition: the Caduveo and Bororo (December 1935–
          January 1936)
          All images: © BNF.
          Second expedition: the Nambikwara (June 1938–January 1939)
          All images: © BNF.

VII.   The ethnographer at work
          All images: © Luiz de Castro Faria Archive. Document © BNF,
          except the extracts from Lévi-Strauss's expedition notebooks:
          © BNF.

VIII.   Bohemian life in New York City (1941–44)
          Dinner at the restaurant *Au bal Tabarin* © Jean-Jacques Lebel
          Archives.
          The surrealist group: © Anonymous photograph. Association
          Atelier André Breton.
          Claude Lévi-Strauss's New York apartment: © BNF.

IX.   Lévi-Strauss, cultural attaché in New York (1945–47)
          Claude Lévi-Strauss in conversation: © American Institute of
          France. Document © BNF.
          Rose-Marie Ullmo and Laurent Jacquemin Lévi-Strauss:
          © Laurent Lévi-Strauss Collection.
          Claude Lévi-Strauss in a light-coloured suit: © Blackstone Studios
          NYC. Document © BNF.

X.   Masks
       Dzonokwa (Kwakiutl) mask (left): Photo: Rebecca Pasch © UBC
       Museum of Anthropology.
       Dzonokwa (Kwakiutl) mask (right): © Milwaukee Public
       Museum.
       Swaihwe (Salish) mask (bottom): Photo: Jessica Bushey © UBC
       Museum of Anthropology.
       Swaihwe (Cowichan) mask (opposite): © Werner Forman Archive/
       Bridgeman Images.

XI.   Collège de France
       The eminent professors of the Collège de France: © Tourte et
       Petitin. Document © BNF.
       Claude Lévi-Strauss in conversation with Jean Malaurie: Document
       © BNF.
       Collège de France professors in 1976–77: © Tourte et Petitin.
       Document © BNF.
       Roman Jakobson giving a lecture at the Collège de France in 1972:
       © Keystone / Gamma-Rapho.
       Lévi-Strauss seated at his desk in a houndstooth suit: © René
       Saint-Paul/rue des Archives.
       Lévi-Strauss's final lecture at the Collège de France: © Jean-Pierre
       Martin/Collège de France.

XII.   The Laboratory of Social Anthropology
       'Anthropology of the family or the future of entropy': © Frédéric
       Jude.
       Claude Lévi-Strauss, in his last office at the Collège de France
       © Sophie Bassouls/Sygma/Corbis
       Claude Lévi-Strauss in the Files: Document © BnF
       The anthropologist crowned by the motto of the École
       Polytechnique: © Sophie Bassouls/Sygma/Corbis.
       Claude Lévi-Strauss in his office at the Collège de France in 1970:
       © Keystone/Gamma-Rapho
       Lévi-Strauss surrounded by LAS members: © Keystone/
       Gamma-Rapho.

XIII. The Académicien
       The Académicien and his medals: © Micheline Pelletier/Sygma/
       Corbis.
       Lévi-Strauss leaving the Institute with his wife: © Michel Petit.
       Document © BNF.
       Claude Lévi-Strauss flanked by his wife and mother: © Michel
       Petit. Document © BNF.
       Session at the Académie Française: © BNF.
       Claude Lévi-Strauss's new tribe: © BNF.

XIV. United States, Canada, Japan
All images: © BNF, except Claude Lévi-Strauss at the Smithsonian Institute: © Smithsonian Institute. Document © BNF.

XV. Parental iconography
Monique Lévi-Strauss and Matthieu: Monique Lévi-Strauss Collection.
Monique Roman, in Saint-Tropez: Monique Lévi-Strauss Collection: © BNF.
Laurent Lévi-Strauss: © BNF.
Claude Lévi-Strauss at his desk: © Eva de Muschietti.
A through line spanning several generations at Lignerolles: Monique Lévi-Strauss Collection.
The Lignerolles baskets: Monique Lévi-Strauss Collection.
As a gentleman farmer in Lignerolles: Monique Lévi-Strauss Collection.

XVI. Effigies
Claude Lévi-Strauss in the country: © BNF.
Claude Lévi-Strauss in the 1950s: © BNF.
The anthropologist in his office: © André Grassart. Document © BNF.
Claude Lévi-Strauss's grave: © Matthieu Lévi-Strauss.
An animated Claude Lévi-Strauss: © BNF.
Painting by Anita Albus.

XVII. Lévi-Strauss the Amerindian
Claude Lévi-Strauss, in ceremonial cape, on the Rio Seine: Monique Lévi-Strauss Collection.
Claude Lévi-Strauss wearing an embroidered bead jacket: © BNF.

Index

Inspection Council on Artistic and
Scientific Expeditions in Brazil
144–5
Institut d'ethnologie, University of
Paris 379–80, 658n16
Institut français d'archéologie du
Proche-Orient (Beirut) 240
Institut français d'études supérieures
(Buenos Aires) 226
International Congress of Folklore 135
International Labour Organization
(ILO) 63, 309
International Social Science Bulletin
(journal) 306
International Social Science Council
(ISSC) 308–9, 465, 486
Inuits 245, 322, 395, 531
Ionesco, Eugène 494
Isabella of Spain, Queen 24
Ishizaka lectures 540, 574, 689n111
Islam 310
Israel 465–7, 518, 545, 549
Israël, Loeb *see* Strauss, Léon
Israel Museum, Jerusalem 546
ISSC *see* International Social Science
Council
Ithier, Georges 252
Izard, Georges 494
Izard, Michel 300, 343, 382, 386, 390,
398, 445, 446, 516, 590,
663n125

Jacobs, Melville 663n125
Jacobson, Claire 357
Jakobson, Roman
Albert Bayet linked to 265
arrives in New York 197
coauthors a book with Lévi-Strauss
452
coauthors a paper on structuralism
248
comment on being on television 449
Faral's hostility towards 278
friendship and correspondence with
Lévi-Strauss 9, 206, 224, 227–9,
273, 274, 276, 278, 282, 289,
293, 298, 305, 306, 315, 348,
349, 368–9
inspired by Shannon 213
invited to present his researches at
Lévi-Strauss's seminars 300
Lévi-Strauss's obituary of 9
musings on *Structural Anthropology*
356
structuralist theories 472–3

urges Lévi-Strauss to join him at
Harvard 305
visits Boas at Grantwood 245
wishes to create a 'dream team' at
Harvard 306
wishes to return to Europe 272
Fundamentals of Language 454
*Mathematical Trends in Social
Sciences* 305
*Poetry of Grammar and Grammar of
Poetry* 452
Jamin, Jean 571, 572
Janet, Pierre 97
Janson-de-Sailly, Lycée 48
Japan, Japanese 6, 111, 113, 306, 384,
435, 474, 510, 514, 517, 518,
537–45, 688n104, 689n114
Japan Productivity Centre 540
Jaulin, Robert 386, 395, 399, 401, 404,
405, 483, 483–5, 663n125
The Sara Death 483
*White Peace: An Introduction to
Ethnocide* 483, 484
Jaurès, Jean 53, 64
Jean de Léry 102–3, 107, 129, 168, 177,
182, 327–8, 518
Le Voyage faict en la terre du Brésil
102, 328
Jeanneney, Jean-Noël 588
Jeanpierre, Laurent 234
Jeanson, Francis 660n50
Jews 15, 16, 412
Alsatian 19–20, 25, 28, 241
and circumcision 546
and conscription 74
culture and heritage 665n155
during WWI 39–41
during WWII 193, 200, 234, 386,
461–2
German and Russian exiles in Paris
185
hitches in Franco-Judaism 29–31
Israel and French Jews (1967) 465–7
and Lévi-Strauss's 'narrative of
origins' 545–6, 548–9
name changes 18–19
postwar settling of scores 274–5
Jicaque Indians 663n125
Jivaro people 329, 552–3, 554
Johns Hopkins University 491
Johnson, Alvin 194, 197, 198
Jolas, Betsy 297
Jolas, Eugene 297
Jolas, Maria 297
Jolas, Tina 297, 382, 385, 399, 663n125

Sénechal, René 252
Sengai Gibon (zen artist) 544
Serge, Victor 200
Serra de Parecis (or Serra do Norte) 165
Serra Norte expedition / 'Serra do Norte Mission' 150–78
Serra Tombador 165
Serres, Michel 177
Sertão, Brazil 4
Service des oeuvres françaises à l'étranger (SOFE) 115, 239
Service for the Protection of Indians (SPI) 129, 155–6, 157, 158, 159
Seyrig, Henri 229, 230, 236, 240, 253, 257–8, 298, 630n18
SFIO (French section of Workers' International) 3, 53, 61, 64, 67, 71, 90, 232
Shannon, Claude E. 213
Shoah 523
Siegfried, André 276, 277
Silz, René 139, 157
Simiand, François 119
Simmons, Leo 7
Simon, Pierre Henri 494
Simonis, Yvan 663n125
Six-Day War (Arab–Israeli War, 1967) 465–7
Skira (Swiss publishing house) 505
Smith, Pierre 663n125
Smithsonian Institute 215, 375
Bureau of Ethnology 197
Social Research (journal) 244
socialism 67–70, 81, 474
Socialist Party 232
socialist realism 69–70
Socialist Students Group (GES) 60, 67
Societé des américanistes 135
Sontag, Susan 375
Sophocles, *Oedipus* 553
The Sopranos (TV series, 1999–2007) 456
Sorbonne 57, 58, 211, 264, 272, 274, 287, 300, 347–8, 353, 357, 468, 513, 527, 635n4, 665n154
Sorokin, Pitrim 226
SOS Racisme (French NGO) 521
Soulages, Pierre, 'The So-Called Lost Craft' 565
Soustelle, Jacques 86, 89, 202, 229, 264, 273, 274, 387, 463, 533, 609n45
Mexique: Terre indienne 609n45
South America 2, 196

South-East Asia 268
Souza Lima, Antonio Carlos de 156
Souza-Dantas, Luis de 194
Spencer, Charles, 9th earl 28
Spengler, Oswald 317
Sperber, Dan 406
Spinoza, Baruch 58, 582
Spitz, René 228
Staden, Hans 182
Stalin, Joseph 629n119
Stavenhagen, Rodolfo 484
Steiner, George 375
Sternhell, Zeev 62–3
Steward, Julian H. 197, 304
The Handbook of South American Indians 197, 215, 244
Stockhausen, Karlheinz 341
Stoczkowski, Wiktor 62, 67, 308, 309, 312–13, 474
Strasbourg 20, 29, 73
Stirn Barracks 73–4
Strauss, Amélie (1831–1909) 33
Strauss, Caroline (Judith) Hirschmann (1757–1847) 19
Strauss family (from Vienna) 23, 34
Strauss, Henriette Lévi (1809–1875) 24, 33
Strauss, Isaac (1806–1888) 15, 16, 18, 19, 20, 29, 518
appointed conductor of court balls 21, 22
as art collector 31–3, 546, 548–9, 573
caricatures of 21, 22
committed to Freemasonry 23
description of 21
musical aptitude 20
wealth and legacy 22–4
well-known composer and arranger 21–2
Strauss, Léon (formerly Israël Loeb) (1754–1844) 18, 20
Strauss, Lucie (1852–1928) 33
Strauss, Maurice (1801–) 18
Strauss, Sophie (1833–1906) 33, 34
Strauss-Rothschild collection, Paris 31
Stravinsky, Igor 50, 101, 255, 342, 562
Les Noces 49, 604n64
structural anthropology 236–7, 246–52, 269, 294, 349, 352, 355–7, 408–9, 431, 439, 453–4, 475–6, 481–2, 486–8, 491, 492–3, 494, 500, 511–14, 516, 568, 570, 582, 590, 594–5
structural linguistics 291–2